Ref 920
Encyclopedia of world
biography. Supplement

P9-DYP-272

$142.00

ENCYCLOPEDIA OF WORLD BIOGRAPHY
SUPPLEMENT

26

ENCYCLOPEDIA OF WORLD BIOGRAPHY

SUPPLEMENT

A / Z **26**

THOMSON

GALE

Detroit • New York • San Francisco • New Haven, Conn. • Waterville, Maine • London • Munich

Encyclopedia of World Biography Supplement, Volume 26

Project Editor
Tracie Ratiner

Editorial Support Services
Andrea Lopeman

Rights and Acquisitions Management
Emma Hull, Jackie Jones, Sue Rudolph

Imaging and Multimedia
Leitha Etheridge-Sims, Lezlie Light,
Mike Logusz

Manufacturing
Drew Kalasky

LIBRARY OF CONGRESS CATALOGING-IN-PUBLICATION DATA

ISBN 1-4144-0097-7
ISSN 1099-7326

This title is also available as an e-book.
ISBN 1-4144-1041-7

Printed in the United States of America

10 9 8 7 6 5 4 3 2 1

CONTENTS

INTRODUCTION

The study of biography has always held an important, if not explicitly stated, place in school curricula. The absence in schools of a class specifically devoted to studying the lives of the giants of human history belies the focus most courses have always had on people. From ancient times to the present, the world has been shaped by the decisions, philosophies, inventions, discoveries, artistic creations, medical breakthroughs, and written works of its myriad personalities. Librarians, teachers, and students alike recognize that our lives are immensely enriched when we learn about those individuals who have made their mark on the world we live in today.

Encyclopedia of World Biography Supplement, Volume 26, provides biographical information on 175 individuals not covered in the 17-volume second edition of *Encyclopedia of World Biography* (*EWB*) and its supplements, Volumes 18, 19, 20, 21, 22, 23, 24, and 25. Like other volumes in the *EWB* series, this supplement represents a unique, comprehensive source for biographical information on those people who, for their contributions to human culture and society, have reputations that stand the test of time. Each original article ends with a bibliographic section. There is also an index to names and subjects, which cumulates all persons appearing as main entries in the *EWB* second edition, the Volume 18, 19, 20, 21, 22, 23, 24, and 25 supplements, and this supplement—more than 8,000 people!

Articles. Arranged alphabetically following the letter-by-letter convention (spaces and hyphens have been ignored), articles begin with the full name of the person profiled in large, bold type. Next is a boldfaced, descriptive paragraph that includes birth and death years in parentheses. It provides a capsule identification and a statement of the person's significance. The essay that follows is approximately 2,000 words in length and offers a substantial treatment of the person's life. Some of the essays proceed chronologically while others confine biographical data to a paragraph or two and move on to a consideration and evaluation of the subject's work. Where very few biographical facts are known, the article is necessarily devoted to an analysis of the subject's contribution.

Following the essay is a bibliographic section arranged by source type. Citations include books, periodicals, and online Internet addresses for World Wide Web pages, where current information can be found.

Portraits accompany many of the articles and provide either an authentic likeness, contemporaneous with the subject, or a later representation of artistic merit. For artists, occasionally self-portraits have been included. Of the ancient figures, there are depictions from coins, engravings, and sculptures; of the moderns, there are many portrait photographs.

Index. The *EWB Supplement* index is a useful key to the encyclopedia. Persons, places, battles, treaties, institutions, buildings, inventions, books, works of art, ideas, philosophies, styles, movements—all are indexed for quick reference just as in a general encyclopedia. The index entry for a person includes a brief identification with birth and death dates *and* is cumulative so that any person for whom an article was written who appears in the second edition of *EWB* (volumes 1-16) and its supplements (volumes 18-26) can be located. The subject terms within the index, however, apply only to volume 26. Every index reference includes the title of the article to which the reader is being directed as well as the volume and page numbers.

Because *EWB Supplement,* Volume 26, is an encyclopedia of biography, its index differs in important ways from the indexes to other encyclopedias. Basically, this is an index of people, and that fact has several interesting consequences. First, the information to which the index refers the reader on a particular topic is always about people associated with that topic. Thus the entry "Quantum theory (physics)" lists articles on people associated with quantum theory. Each article may discuss a person's contribution to quantum theory, but no single article or group of articles is intended to provide a comprehensive treatment of quantum theory as such. Second, the index is rich in classified entries. All persons who are subjects of articles in the encyclopedia, for example, are listed in one or more classifications in the index—abolitionists, astronomers, engineers, philosophers, zoologists, etc.

The index, together with the biographical articles, make *EWB Supplement* an enduring and valuable source for biographical information. As school course work changes to reflect advances in technology and fur-

ther revelations about the universe, the life stories of the people who have risen above the ordinary and earned a place in the annals of human history will continue to fascinate students of all ages.

We Welcome Your Suggestions. Mail your comments and suggestions for enhancing and improving the *Encyclopedia of World Biography Supplement* to:

The Editors
Encyclopedia of World Biography Supplement
Thomson Gale
27500 Drake Road
Farmington Hills, MI 48331-3535
Phone: (800) 347-4253

ADVISORY BOARD

ACKNOWLEDGMENTS

Photographs and illustrations appearing in the *Encyclopedia of World Biography Supplement*, Volume 26, have been used with the permission of the following sources:

AP/WIDE WORLD PHOTOS: Jane Alexander, Anne Bancroft, David Beckham, Hugo Chavez, Alice Coachman, Alan Dershowitz, Henry Chee Dodge, Rainer Werner Fassbinder, Mildred Gillars, Peggy Guggenheim, E. Y. Harburg, Ada Louise Huxtable, Al Jarreau, Janis Joplin, Sam Lacy, Larisa Latynina, Dan Marino, Liza Minnelli, Carmen Miranda, Federico Mompou, Alfonso Ortiz, Pope Benedict XVI, Shania Twain, Dominique de Villepin, Wim Wenders, Reggie White.

CORBIS: Walter Hubert Annenberg, Francis Arinze, Jean Batten, Carla Bley, Margaret Burbidge, Hoagland Howard Carmichael, Violet Bonham Carter, Marguerite Duras, Sian Edwards, Mohamed ElBaradei, Dorothy Fields, Herbert von Karajan, Fritz Kreisler, Maxine Kumin, Libertad Lamarque, Geraldine Laybourne, David Letterman, Jenny Lind, Dean Martin, Ismail Merchant, Charles Mingus, Meredith Monk, Agnes Nestor, Astor Piazzolla, Georges (Herge) Remi, Oliver Wolf Sacks, Buffy Sainte-Marie, Clara Josephine Schumann, Artie Shaw, George Szell, Vesta Tilley, Lois Weber, Mary Wollstonecraft, Maud Younger, Fred Zinnemann.

GETTY IMAGES: Diane Abbott, Larry Adler, Cleveland Amory, Sir Frederick William Ashton, Isobel Baillie, Cecile Chaminade, Maurice Chevalier, John Clare, Ibrahim Ferrer, Patrick Flores, Michel Fokine, Marvin Gaye, Lorraine Heggessey, Fletcher Henderson, Odon von Horvath, Judith Jamison, Peter Jennings, Georgeanna Jones, Boris Karloff, Eartha Kitt, Jerzy Kosinski, R. D. Laing, Wanda Landowska, Ernest Lehman, Karl May, Robert Moog, Jack Paar, Pope Urban VIII, Omara Portuondo, Fritz Reiner, John Glover Roberts, Jr., Belle Starr, Luther Vandross, Robert Wise.

THE KOBAL COLLECTION: Cantinflas, Dusan Makavejev.

LANDOV: Marcel Albert Carne, John Conyers, Tom Delay, Marita Koch, Anna Magnani, Carl Orff, Pope Nicholas V, Pablo de Sarasate, Lydia Pavlovna Skoblikova, Renata Tebaldi.

THE LIBRARY OF CONGRESS: Charlotte Friend.

MARY EVANS PICTURE LIBRARY: Isaac Watts.

McCARTHY, NOBU: Nobu McCarthy.

NATIONAL ARCHIVES AND RECORDS ADMINISTRATION: Rain-in-the-face.

The following people, appearing in volumes 1-25 of the *Encyclopedia of World Biography,* have died since the publication of the second edition and its supplements. Each entry lists the volume where the full biography can be found.

AZCONA HOYO, JOSÉ (born 1927), president of Honduras, died of a heart attack in Tegucigalpa, Honduras, on October 24, 2005 (Vol. 1).

BONDI, HERMANN (born 1919), English mathematician and cosmologist, died in Cambridge, England, on September 10, 2005 (Vol. 18).

BUTLER, OCTAVIA E. (born 1947), African American novelist and essayist, died near Seattle, Washington, on February 24, 2006 (Vol. 3).

CALDWELL, SARAH (born 1924), long-time artistic director, conductor and founder of the Opera Company of Boston, died of heart failure in Portland, Maine, on March 23, 2006 (Vol. 3).

CHAMBERLAIN, OWEN (born 1920), American physicist, died of complications from Parkinson's disease in Berkley, California, on February 28, 2006 (Vol. 25).

DELORIA, VINE, JR. (born 1933), Native American author, poet and activist, died of complications from an aortic aneurysm in Denver, Colorado, on November 13, 2005 (Vol. 4).

DIAMOND, DAVID (born 1915), American composer and teacher, died of congestive heart failure in Rochester, New York, on June 13, 2005 (Vol. 4).

DRUCKER, PETER (born 1909), American author and business consultant, died of natural causes in Claremont, California, on November 11, 2005 (Vol. 21).

FAHD IBN ABDUL AZIZ AL-SAUD (Born 1920), son of the founder of modern Saudi Arabia and king, died in Saudi Arabia, on August 1, 2005 (Vol. 5).

FOOTE, SHELBY (born 1916), American author, died in Memphis, Tennessee, on June 27, 2005 (Vol. 18).

FOWLES, JOHN (born 1926), English novelist, died in Lyme Regis, England, on November 5, 2005 (Vol. 6).

FREED, JAMES INGO (born 1930), American architect, died of complications from Parkinson's disease in New York, New York, on December 15, 2005 (Vol. 6).

FRIEDAN, BETTY (NAOMI) (born 1921), women's rights activist and author, died of congestive heart failure in Washington, D.C., on February 4, 2006 (Vol. 6).

GORMAN, R. C. (born 1931), Native American artist, died of pneumonia in Albuquerque, New Mexico, on November 3, 2005 (Vol. 23).

HEATH, EDWARD RICHARD GEORGE (born1916), prime minister of Great Britain, died in Salisbury, England, on July 17, 2005 (Vol. 7).

HOWELLS, WILLIAM WHITE (born 1908), American anthropologist, died in Kittery Point, Maine, on December 20, 2005 (Vol. 7).

JABER AL-SABAH, JABER AL-AHMAD (born 1926), emir of Kuwait, died on January 15, 2006 (Vol. 8).

JOHNSON, JOHN HAROLD (born 1918), founder of the Johnson Publishing Company, died in Chicago, Illinois, on August 8, 2005 (Vol. 8).

KILBY, JACK ST. CLAIR (born 1923), American electrical engineer and inventor, died of cancer in Dallas, Texas, on June 20, 2005 (Vol. 25).

KING, CORETTA SCOTT (born 1929), American advocate of civil rights, nonviolence and international peace, died in Rosarito Beach, Mexico, on January 30, 2006 (Vol. 9).

MCCARTHY, EUGENE JOSEPH (born 1916), American statesman, died of complications from Parkinson's disease in Washington, D.C., on December 10, 2005 (Vol. 10).

MIKAN, GEORGE (born 1924), American basketball player, died of diabetes and kidney disease in Scottsdale, Arizona, on June 1, 2005 (Vol. 21).

MILOSEVIC, SLOBODAN (born 1941), president of Serbia, died of a heart attack in the Hague, the Netherlands, on March 11, 2006 (Vol. 11).

MOTLEY, CONSTANCE BAKER (born 1921), African American judge and attorney, died of congestive heart failure in New York, on September 28, 2005 (Vol. 18).

OBOTE, APOLO MILTON (born 1925), Ugandan politician, died of kidney failure in Johannesburg, South Africa, on October 10, 2005 (Vol. 11).

PA CHIN (Le Fei-kan; born 1904), Chinese novelist, died of cancer in Shanghai, China, on October 17, 2005 (Vol. 12).

PARKS, GORDON (born 1912), American photographer, composer and filmmaker died in Manhattan, New York, on March 7, 2006 (Vol. 19).

PARKS, ROSA (born 1913), American civil rights leader, died in Detroit, Michigan, on October 24, 2005 (Vol. 12).

PROXMIRE, WILLIAM (born 1915), Democratic senator for Wisconsin, died from Alzheimer's disease in Sykesville, Maryland, on December 15, 2005 (Vol. 12).

PRYOR, RICHARD (born 1940), American entertainer, died of a heart attack in Los Angeles, California, on December 10, 2005 (Vol. 19).

RAU, JOHANNES (born 1931), German Social Democrat politician, died in Berlin, Germany, on January 27, 2006 (Vol. 13).

REHNQUIST, WILLIAM HUBBS (born 1924), U.S. Supreme Court chief justice, died of thyroid cancer in Arlington, Virginia, on September 3, 2005 (Vol. 13).

ROCHBERG, GEORGE (born 1918), American composer, died from complications following surgery in Bryn Mawr, Pennsylvania, on May 29, 2005 (Vol. 13).

SAUNDERS, CICELY (born 1918), English doctor and social worker, died in London, England, on July 14, 2005 (Vol. 25).

SCHÖNHUBER, FRANZ XAVER (born 1923), German right-wing political leader, died on November 27, 2005 (Vol. 14).

SIMON, CLAUDE HENRI EUGENE (born 1913), French author, died in Paris, France, on July 6, 2005 (Vol. 25).

SIN, JAIME L. (born 1928), Filipino cardinal of the Roman Catholic Church, died of multiple organ failure in Manila, Philippines, on June 21, 2005 (Vol. 14).

STRAWSON, SIR PETER FREDRICK (born 1919), English philosopher, died on February 13, 2006 (Vol. 14).

TUCKER, C. DELORES (born 1927), African American civil rights activist, died in Philadelphia, Pennsylvania, on October 12, 2005 (Vol. 18).

WESTMORELAND, WILLIAM CHILDS (born 1914), Commander of all American forces in the Vietnam War (1964-1968) and chief of staff of the U.S. Army, died in Charleston, South Carolina, on July 18, 2005 (Vol. 16).

WIESENTHAL, SIMON (born 1908), Ukrainian Jew who tracked down Nazi war criminals, died in Vienna, Austria, on September 20, 2005 (Vol. 16).

WILSON, AUGUST (born 1945) African American playwright, died of liver cancer in Seattle, Washington, on October 2, 2005 (Vol. 16).

YARD, MARY ALEXANDER (born 1912), American feminist, political organizer and social activist, died in Pittsburgh, Pennsylvania, on September 21, 2005 (Vol. 16).

A

Diane Abbott

Diane Abbott (born 1953) became the first black female elected to British Parliament in 1987, representing the Labour Party in the Hackney North and Stoke Newington districts. Abbott, the daughter of Jamaican immigrants, remains strongly identified with the political left. In 2005, she was among 13 black members of the 659–member British House of Commons. Abbott, a former press aide, is still a frequent broadcaster and public speaker at universities, and on radio and television.

Attended Cambridge University

Abbott was born in London; her mother was a nurse, her father a welder. She attended Harrow County Grammar School and obtained her master's degree in history from Newnham College at the University of Cambridge. After college, Abbott worked for the government as a home office civil servant. She also worked for the National Council for Civil Liberties before entering journalism.

After doing considerable freelance work, she became a reporter for TV–AM, an early-morning station that aired in Great Britain through much of the 1980s, and the TV production company Thames Television. In addition, she was a public–relations consultant for public sector clients, including the Greater London Council and the left–oriented Lambeth Council. As a member of the Westminster City Council in the early 1980s, she was one of the few black female members.

Breakthrough Election in 1987

In 1987, Abbott was among a record number of non–whites running for British Parliament and political office elsewhere in Europe, reflecting the changing demographics of the continent. Though the presidential candidacy of the Reverend Jesse Jackson during that decade reflected the increasing role of minorities in U.S. politics, some observers said blacks had more of an uphill climb in Britain. "American blacks, their British counterparts repeatedly remind, have had nearly four centuries of coexistence with white society, compares [with] four decades here," Karen DeYoung wrote in the *Washington Post* in 1988.

"We're just at the beginning of the process," Abbott told DeYoung, shortly after her election. "It took slavery, reconstruction, the Harlem renaissance, the [National Association for the Advancement of Colored People], all of that to build a Martin Luther King. And it took more than 20 years to bring a Jesse Jackson." Dolly Kiffen, director of Broadwater Farm's Youth Association, told DeYoung, "You have blacks there, they're black Americans. Here in Britain, black people haven't got any identity. They like to call us by different names. Like 'ethnic minorities.' I hate that term."

Jackson visited London in 1985, after rioting had broken out at Broadwater Farm, among other places, and, according to DeYoung, urged British blacks to "fight for your share of everything that's available, vertically and horizontally . . . in the labor movement, in the government, in property ownership." Sons and daughters of Caribbean ownership, DeYoung wrote, "have grown up in a homogeneous white society that never planned for their existence and has shown little willingness to make a place for them." They were raised in such districts as Brixton and Tottenham in London, Toxteth in Liverpool and Handsworth in Birmingham.

The first generation of immigrants were reluctant to confront the largely white British establishment. In Britain, the generic term "blacks" often applied to Asians, African, Caribbean, and Middle Eastern immigrants, and their children. Whites, meanwhile, felt "swamped" by nonwhite immigrants, Conservative Party leader and future Prime Minister Margaret Thatcher said in a 1978 interview, according to DeYoung. "My generation know[s] we're here, and know[s] we're not going anywhere," Abbott said in DeYoung's article. "We don't have that awe."

Labour Struggled with Race

Abbott joined Bernie Grant, Keith Vaz, and Paul Boateng as minority Members of Parliament in 1987. Considered rebellious at times, she has called herself a Marxist, and the *Guardian* newspaper in 2005 described her as "an icon of the left." The four faced several uphill battles after joining Parliament, David S. Broder wrote in the *Washington Post* two years after their election.

Calling their struggle a "triple handicap," Broder wrote: "They lack experience and seniority. They are on the left of a party whose leadership is tugging it toward the center. And they are a handful of blacks in an institution which had been all-white since an Asian Communist was defeated after seven years' service in 1931. They express varying degrees of frustration and have chosen widely different tactics for advancing their goals and careers, causing some open divisions among them. But all of them know they cannot expect many reinforcements."

Abbott, who collaborated with Grant in forming the black caucus and over the years remained committed to black factions within the Labour Party, charged in Broder's article that "the Labour Party hasn't come to terms with race. They're like some of the leaders of the [U.S.] Democratic Party who think they can take black support for granted and win by appealing to the white middle class. Well, it didn't work in the United States and it won't work here."

Outspoken Critic of Educational Inequity

While in Parliament, Abbott served on several committees that addressed social and international concerns. In addition, she was elected to the Labour Party's national executive panel. She also served on the House of Commons Treasury Select Committee, which addressed business and financial affairs, through much of the 1990s. Abbott traveled to Washington, New York, Frankfurt, and other financial hubs, frequently meeting with bankers, financial regulators, and senior politicians. In addition, Abbott has served on the Foreign Affairs Select Committee, and has traveled to several European countries, as well as China, Hong Kong, Uganda, and Kenya. In the early 2000s, Abbott established a special committee investigating gun-related crimes. "I urge the government to move away from excessively ideological approach to the so-called magic of the private sector and to adopt a more pragmatic approach," she said, as quoted in a profile in the *Guardian.*

Abbott has said that British public education has shortchanged black children. "Something is going seriously wrong between the age of five and the age of sixteen," Abbott was quoted as saying in the *Economist,* a British newspaper. "Black children do not perform nearly as well as other ethnic minority groups, nor as well as they should," the newspaper editorialized. "But the explanations—and, hence, the solutions—have less to do with bad attitudes among teachers and pupils and more to do with the old difficulties of poverty and place."

Abbott, though, drew harsh criticism when it was revealed that she would send her 12-year-old son to the exclusive, private City of London School rather than through London's public school system. Abbott had railed against such parents in the past. Author Adam Swift, in a 1996 commentary in the *New Statesman,* called Abbott a hypocrite. "It's hard not to think she's doing exactly what she criticized [Prime Minister] Tony Blair and [leading Labour politician] Harriet Harman for doing: opting out of local schools to get something better for her child. And neither Blair nor Harman—of whom Abbott said 'she made the Labour Party look as if we do one thing and say another'—chose private schools for their children."

Swift, a professor at the University of Oxford's Balliol College, also wrote: "Yet if she had simply condemned private education, without criticizing others' choices, she might have been cleared of hypocrisy. It can be quite consistent to think that there should be no private schools, yet send your own child to one." He added: "Hypocrisy is about whether you practice what you preach. If you preach that parents should never use their money to buy their children out of the state system, and then you go ahead and do exactly that, you are a hypocrite."

Still, Swift praised Abbott for addressing the problems of educational inequity. "Unlike many who go private, she at least has taken seriously matters of the public good, has done what she can do to persuade her fellow citizens to endorse a more equitable educational system, and to improve state schools in a way that might make them adequate for all children. I'd like to see all parents of privately schooled children champion the cause of social justice with her vigor. I hope Abbott does not think she must now mute her demands for a fair educational system in which all the children get to go to decent schools."

Abbott communicated with her constituents, among other ways, through her weekly column in the *Hackney Gazette*. A 1996 column in which she complained that the arrival of Finnish nurses jeopardized employment opportunities for black women elicited a rebuke from the *New Statesman's* Darcus Howe, who otherwise has generally supported her work. "It is worse than careless for Diane Abbott to have made such remarks," Howe said. "It smacks of right-wing reaction and is anti-labor. But for me these charges are mitigated by my belief that she is facing demons of doubt about her future in the new Labour Party." Howe went on to praise Abbott for her column and her often-unappreciated work in Parliament.

"Class of '87" Left Legacy

Abbott, who married in 1991 and divorced two years later, was nearing the end of her second decade in the House of Commons as the mid-2000s beckoned. Abbott and other British minority politicians realized their appeal must be broad-based. "You don't get elected in Britain on black votes alone," Abbott said in 2005, according to the *Washington Post's* Keith B. Richburg. Unlike the United States, where all African-Americans from the House of Representatives are Democrats and nearly all come from heavily black districts, members of Parliament are elected from a party slate, meaning seats are divided commensurate with a nationwide vote total. "Though still influential, she has become sidelined," the *Guardian* wrote.

Abbott has spoken at Ivy League universities in the United States, including Harvard. She also makes frequent radio and TV appearances. She has hosted a call-in show for LBC Radio, presented a program on the treasury for BBC Radio 4 and appeared regularly on the BBC1 late-night political talk show with fellow Members of Parliament Andrew Neil and Michael Portillo.

Remained Highly Visible Member of Parliament

"She has remained one of the most well-known MPs [members of Parliament] among the general public, with her outspoken views ensuring she is never far from sight," the British Broadcasting Corporation wrote on its Web site, BBC News. Abbott strongly opposes converting to a singular currency—the United Kingdom still uses the pound, not the euro—and she is the only MP among the "Class of 1987," the four black persons elected to Parliament that year.

"Now only Abbott is left to hold the fort," Howe wrote in the *New Statesman*. Abbott and others, Richburg wrote, "are chipping away at one of the most durable color barriers in a fast-changing Europe, the doors to legislative chambers."

Periodicals

Economist, March 12, 2005.
New Statesman, December 6, 1996; November 3, 2003; March 21, 2005.
Washington Post, June 10, 1987; June 24, 1988; July 4, 1989; April 24, 2005.

Online

BBC News, Diane Abbott profile, http://news.bbc.co.uk/1/hi/uk_politics/2085582.stm (December 12, 2005).
Diane Abbott Official Web Site, Abbott biography, http://www.dianeabbott.org.uk/index.php?page=Biography (December 12, 2005).
Guardian Unlimited, Diane Abbott profile, http://politics.guardian.co.uk/person/0,9290,-4,00.html (January 3, 2006). □

Edith Abbott

Edith Abbott (1876-1957) American social reformer, author, and educator, dedicated her life to improving the social welfare of workers, immigrants, children, and women. In 1920, she was integral to founding of the first graduate-level program in social work at the University of Chicago; she became Dean of the School of Social Service Administration in 1924, holding that position until 1942. Because of her contributions to the research of practice of social work, Abbott is considered one of the most important historical figures in the field.

Early Life and Education

Abbott, the daughter of lawyer and former lieutenant-governor of Nebraska Othman Ali Abbott and early advocate for women's suffrage Elizabeth Maletta Griffin Abbott, was born on September 26, 1876 in Grand Island, Nebraska. Grand Island was a railroad town with fewer than 1,000 inhabitants at the time of Abbott's birth, but her family—which included younger sister Grace, with whom she was close throughout her life—was reasonably well-off. Abbott's mother instilled progressive values in her daughters from a young age, teaching young Edith Abbott about the importance of social reform and rights for women. Abbott attended Brownell Hall, a boarding school in Omaha, but was unable to attend college after graduation due to the recent economic downturn. Instead, she returned to Grand Island where she became a high school teacher.

Abbott continued her studies, however, despite her initial inability to attend college. At first, she took correspondence courses and attended summer sessions, but was eventually able to study at the University of Nebraska in the state's capital, Lincoln, receiving her undergraduate degree in 1901. The following year, she attended a summer session at the University of Chicago where she attracted the attention of faculty members, particularly economist Thorstein Veblen; they granted her a fellowship, enabling her to begin work on her doctorate at the institution in 1903. She graduated with honors in 1905, having written an economics dissertation on unskilled wage labor from 1850-1900. This piece was published in June 1906 by the *Journal of Political Economy,* a scholarly publication that would print many articles by Abbott throughout her life.

Women in Industry and Hull House

After completing her graduate work, Abbott moved for a short time to Boston, where she worked as the secretary for the Women's Trade Union League. She then spent several months researching the history of and problems faced by women in wage-based industrial employment for the Carnegie Institution; this research led to a series of articles published beginning in 1906 in the *Journal of Political Economy.* These articles formed the foundation for what would become her best-known book, *Women in Industry: A Study in American Economic History,* published in 1910. The year 1906 brought Abbott another professional coup: winning a Carnegie fellowship for post-doctoral study and a scholarship from the Association of Collegiate Alumnae, she traveled to London to attend the renowned London School of Economics. There, she studied under economists and social reformers Beatrice and Sidney Webb, who convinced Abbott of the importance of reform over charity in the aid of those stricken by poverty.

When Abbott returned to the United States, she taught briefly at Wellesley College outside Boston before returning to Chicago she joined her sister Grace as a staff member at Jane Addams' Hull House. Hull House, a settlement house in a poor Chicago immigrant neighborhood, offered educational and social lectures and programs for the neighborhood's families; residents were social reformers dedicated to the idea of what the Hull House Association's website calls "neighbors helping neighbors." At Hull House, Abbott became the assistant director of research under Sophonisba P. Breckinridge, another Progressive reformer who was the research director of the Chicago School of Civics and Philanthropy and who had been Abbott's mentor earlier in her career. Working with Breckinridge and with her sister Grace Abbott, Edith Abbott became particularly concerned with the problems of immigrant women workers, ultimately lobbying for legislation for the ten-hour work day as well as promoting the admission of women to labor unions. She also worked to secure better housing for individual workers.

In the 1910s, Abbott supported the cause of women's suffrage. National voting rights had not yet been granted to women—the Nineteenth Amendment, striking down voting restrictions based on sex, was not ratified until 1920— although women had limited rights in Illinois. Because

women voted using distinctive ballots and election results were split down by sex, Abbott was able to perform statistical research on the differences between men's and women's voting patterns. She found that women were more likely to vote for progressive, reformer candidates and less likely to follow party lines; this research added to the growing body of work calling for equal votes for American women.

Edith Abbott and Sophonisba Breckenridge

Breckenridge and Abbott sought to professionalize social work, which up to this time had been strictly under the provenance of charity efforts; often, reformers or wealthy people with the best intentions undertook charity work that was slapdash, poorly planned or simply ineffective. Working together, the two published studies on some of the problems faced by poor children, such as child labor, juvenile delinquency, and education. Addressing the problems of poor workers, including poor housing standards and the industrial environment, particularly that faced by women, Breckenridge and Abbott also published in scholarly journals such as the *Journal of Political Economy* and the *American Sociological Review.* The two produced longer works as well, including *The Delinquent Child and the Home,* published in 1912, and *Truancy and Non-Attendance in the Chicago Schools,* published in 1917.

Some of these works contain vivid images of the everyday lives and difficulties of Chicago's working class; in "Women in Industry: The Chicago Stockyards," published in the *Journal of Political Economy* in October 1911, Abbott and Breckinridge wrote that "within the yards there are ugly sights which are a nuisance equally with the smoke and the smells . . . a most hideous load of crimson heads [from dead animals], for example, may not infrequently be seen traveling from the south to the north end of the yards, without any attempt at concealment." Throughout her life, Abbott was appalled at such conditions and strove to better them.

Dean and Educator

In 1920, Breckenridge and Abbott helped the fiscally-ailing Chicago School of Civics and Philanthropy find a new home with the University of Chicago. There, it was renamed the School of Social Service Administration and immediately offered the first graduate-level program in the field of social work. Abbott, who believed deeply in the importance of a university-taught, graduate education as a key to professionalizing social work, became the Dean of the School in 1924; she was first female dean of any United States graduate school. She developed a program of study based on the paired studies of social, historical and legal issues relevant to the practice of social work and of field casework. In 1927, Abbott, with the assistance of Breckenridge, founded the scholarly journal *Social Service Review.* The publication, still administered by the University of Chicago, states that it "is committed to examining social welfare policy and practice and evaluating its effects"—a mission little, if at all, changed from the time of its conception.

However, Abbott's role as Dean did not stop her from continuing her reform work. From her time at Hull House,

Abbott had a special concern for the welfare of immigrants; by the 1920s, much of the general American public sentiment was anti-immigrant and in 1924, Congress passed a law setting immigration quotas. Despite this negative environment, Abbott strove for legislation protecting the rights of recent immigrants. In 1929, President Herbert Hoover appointed Abbott to the newly-formed National Commission on Law Observation and Enforcement, popularly called the Wickersham Commission. Although most of the Commission's findings centered on the crimes caused by Prohibition, Abbott examined the role of immigrants in crime, arguing that the foreign-born population of the United States in fact committed fewer crimes than the native residents.

Abbott remained at the forefront of social and governmental welfare programs in the 1930s. When New Deal programs to alleviate some of the poverty caused by the Great Depression appeared, Abbott supported their creation but expressed concern over the number of poorly-trained social service workers; when the head of the Federal Emergency Relief Administration proposed a scholarship program to train federal social workers, Abbott's school reaped the benefits of increased enrollment and added notoriety. In 1934 and 1935, Abbott, along with her sister Grace Abbott, contributed to the nascent Social Security Act legislation; although not all of the Abbott sisters' suggestions survived legislative approval, both Abbotts were pleased that the federal government was committing itself to supporting workers. The following year, Edith Abbott was recognized for her lifelong contributions by being elected the president of the National Conference on Social Work.

Last Years and Legacy

Personal tragedy struck Edith Abbott when her sister, Grace Abbott, died as the result of multiple myeloma—a relatively rare form of blood cancer—in 1939. The sisters had been close throughout their lives, living together for several years at Hull House and tied through professional interests; Grace Abbott had been active in the reform of child labor. Her death devastated her sister; always abrupt and uncomfortable outside of work situations, Abbott became, according to Lela B. Costin in *Two Sisters for Social Justice*, "more brusque, sometimes suspicious and quarrelsome. In the view of some . . . she had lost the ability to communicate meaningfully with many students and faculty." Abbott began a slow withdraw from public life. She published her final book, *Public Assistance*, in 1941 and resigned as Dean of the School of Social Service Administration in 1942. Over the next several years, she dedicated her time to teaching and to editing the *Social Service Review*.

Following the death of Breckenridge in 1948, Abbott returned to live at Hull House. Her last professional success came in 1951, when she received the Survey Award at the National Conference of Social Work; surprising most of the audience, she used her acceptance speech to call for further social reform at the national level. Later in life, when glaucoma and age made it impossible for her to live alone, she returned to Grand Island, Nebraska. Her family home had

been converted to apartments and Edith and two brothers each had their own. There, she lived out the last years of her life. On July 28, 1957, Abbott died in Grand Island from pneumonia. She was 80 years old.

Remembered today primarily for her role as the founder of modern social work education and innovator in social work research and study, Abbott was also a prolific writer. Her over one hundred articles and books cover many aspects of social welfare and history, from women and children in industry to immigration issues to the dangers of and solutions to poverty. Abbott relied heavily on factual, statistical evidence to support her claims and make recommendations for improvement. As reformer, Abbott was tireless, devoting nearly three-quarters of her life to the struggle for social welfare.

Books

Costin, Lela B., *Two Sisters for Social Justice: A Biography of Grace and Edith Abbott,* University of Illinois, 1983.

Periodicals

Journal of Political Economy, October 1911.

Online

"Gale Literary Databases: Edith Abbott," http://www.galenet.galegroup.com (January 5, 2006).
"Grand Island History," http://grand-island.com/Home/History/history_home.htm (January 5, 2006).
Luft, Margaret, "Jane Addams Hull House," http://www.hullhouse.org/about.asp (January 5, 2006).
Nutter, Kathleen Banks, "American National Biography Online: Edith Abbott," http://www.anb.org (January 5, 2006).
"Social Service Review: Description," http://www.journals.uchicago.edu/SSR/brief.html (January 5, 2006).
"SSA Tour: Edith Abbott," http://www.ssa.uchicago.edu/aboutssa/history/tour1d.shtml (January 5, 2006). □

Larry Adler

On the short list of musicians who have played the harmonica at a virtuoso level, Larry Adler (1914-2001) ranks at or near the top. His musical skills were matched by an outsized personality that delighted interviewers, attracted some of the top musicians of the 20th century as collaborators over his seven-decade career, and awakened memories of the classic era of Broadway entertainment in which Adler's career got its start.

Adler brought a level of respectability to the harmonica, often regarded as primarily an instrument played by enthusiastic amateurs. He preferred the term "mouth organ" to "harmonica," and he crossed into the realm of classical music, playing with symphony orchestras and commissioning works from prestigious composers. His playing was lyrical, often melancholy. Yet the public

also prized Adler for his fund of stories about the rich, famous, and beautiful. He numbered physicist Albert Einstein and composer Sergei Rachmaninoff among his friends, and, an enthusiastic tennis player, he once participated in a doubles match with comedian Charlie Chaplin, actress Greta Garbo, and surrealist artist Salvador Dali. He and Chaplin won.

Family Changed Name to Advance Alphabetically

Lawrence Cecil Adler was born in Baltimore, Maryland, on February 10, 1914. His parents were Russian Jewish immigrants (and fluent Yiddish speakers) who had changed the family name from Zelakovitch because they were tired of waiting at the end of long alphabetically organized lines in offices. Though they had faced discrimination in Russia, they told their son not to play with any of the African-American children in the neighborhood. Adler showed his stubborn streak for perhaps the first time by trying to make as many black friends as he could find, and he often spoke out in favor of civil rights later in his life.

Adler seemed to show musical talent, becoming a cantor in the local synagogue by the time he was ten. His parents signed him up for piano lessons and were even talked into buying a piano on an installment plan. The owner of the music store where they made the purchase threw in a harmonica as part of the deal, and Adler took to that instrument enthusiastically. When he enrolled in classes at Baltimore's Peabody Conservatory of Music, how-

ever, it was with the intention of studying piano. His lessons there came to an end after one semester (according to London, England's *Guardian* newspaper) when a teacher at a recital offended him by asking "What are we going to play, little man?" Adler substituted "Yes, We Have No Bananas" for the Grieg waltz he had planned, and he was thrown out of the program. Undaunted, Adler entered a *Baltimore Sun* harmonica contest and won, playing a minuet by Beethoven instead of the simple folk tunes the other contestants offered.

Not long after that, at the age of fourteen, Adler left Baltimore for New York with seven dollars in his pocket. Playing on the streets and auditioning wherever he could, he was turned down by a group called Borrah Minevitch and His Harmonica Rascals but was befriended by singer Rudy Vallee, who steered him toward work playing on the soundtracks of Mickey Mouse cartoons. That led to a nationwide tour playing the harmonica at intermission in movie houses, and then to opening-act slots for the likes of Eddie Cantor, Jack Benny, and Fred Astaire—top entertainers who straddled the divide between live musical shows and the growing world of cinema.

The teenage Adler was spotted by a British promoter and invited to try his luck across the Atlantic. Before he left, he managed to improvise a performance of George Gershwin's *Rhapsody in Blue* on the harmonica, with Gershwin himself accompanying on piano, although he had never tried to play the highly virtuosic piece before. Adler became an instant hit in England, spending several years there in the mid-1930s as the featured attraction in a musical revue called "Tune Inn." Larry Adler fan clubs were formed all over Britain, and his popularity there would stand him in good stead later on. At the time, however, Adler decided to return to the United States and reactivate his Broadway and Hollywood connections. He had no trouble landing parts in such films as *The Singing Marine* (starring Dick Powell), *The Big Broadcast of 1937* and *St. Martin's Lane* (1938). Gangster Al Capone was another Adler friend.

Claimed Affair with Ingrid Bergman

At that time, Adler did not know how to read music. He did learn the skill, however, around the early 1940s, saying that he had been inspired to do so by either French composer Darius Milhaud or Swedish actress Ingrid Bergman (depending on the interview). Adler entertained U.S. troops on USO tours during World War II, and at one appearance in Augsburg, Germany, he was quoted as saying in the *San Diego Union-Tribune,* that Bergman entered the room, complimented him on his playing, and asked him if he was going to notate the tune. "No, I can't, and I don't need to," Adler recalled saying, to which Bergman retorted, "You're very smug, aren't you? You're ignorant, and you're proud of your ignorance." According to Adler, he and Bergman embarked on a two-year affair although each was already married; Adler and his first wife, British model Eileen Walser, had three children before divorcing; his second marriage, to British journalist Sally Cline, produced another daughter.

After the war, Adler's increasing musical sophistication began to show. He once filled in for Miles Davis at New

York's famous Village Vanguard jazz club when the trumpeter failed to show up for a gig, and he appeared with the New York Philharmonic Orchestra. But his efforts on behalf of the troops during the war were not enough to save him from the anti-Communist frenzy that overtook the U.S. in the late 1940s and early 1950s. Adler found that jobs were drying up as left-leaning performers such as himself and Paul Draper, a dancer with whom he often worked, were blacklisted by Hollywood studios that tried to avoid running afoul of crusading Republican Senator Joseph McCarthy of Wisconsin and his campaign to root out the Communist influences he perceived as having infiltrated U.S. politics and culture.

When a Connecticut woman wrote a letter to a newspaper accusing Adler and Draper of Communist sympathies in 1948, Adler and Draper sued. The case dragged out for three years, draining the resources of the pair, and it ended in a hung jury in September of 1951. Shortly after that, Adler departed for Britain. Though he would sometimes return to the U.S. to perform after McCarthy was discredited and the anti-Communist hysteria died down, he lived in Britain for the rest of his life.

Building on the name he had made for himself in the 1930s, Adler succeeded in adapting his performing repertoire to the greater frequency with which classical music was heard in Britain. Some of Europe's best-known composers expanded the tiny classical harmonica repertoire with new compositions for Adler, including the Romance for Mouth Organ, Piano, and Strings by Ralph Vaughan Williams and concertos by Malcolm Arnold an Darius Milhaud. Composer William Walton (as quoted in the *Guardian*) even said that "the only two young musical geniuses in the world are [violinist] Yehudi Menuhin and Larry Adler." Adler composed the score for the 1953 film *Genevieve*, which garnered an Academy Award nomination even though Adler's name was stripped from American prints of the film. He composed scores for several more British films, including *The Hellions* (1961) and *King and Country* (1963). In 1963 he premiered "Lullaby Time," a George Gershwin work given to him by the composer's brother Ira.

Wrote Restaurant Reviews

The positive side of Adler's exile in England was that he fit easily into British life. He learned to play cricket, and when he tried to explain the rules of that arcane British sport to Einstein, the great physicist said (according to an Adler recollection quoted by a letter writer in London's *Independent*), "You know, Larry, I used to think time was relative, but suddenly I'm not so sure." Adler branched out beyond music, writing a book called *Jokes and How to Tell Them* and contributing articles to the *Spectator* and *New Statesman* periodicals. He served as restaurant reviewer for a magazine called *Harpers & Queen*. Quick with a one-liner, he told the same *Independent* letter writer, when she asked whether he had been christened Larry, "Honey, they've done some terrible things to Jews over the years, but christening wasn't one of them."

Adler had played "The Battle Hymn of the Republic" on the balcony of Adolf Hitler's abandoned headquarters as American troops overran Berlin at the end of World War II, and he became a supporter of the young nation of Israel, performing there during the Six-Day War of 1967 and the Yom Kippur War of 1973. Harboring little bitterness toward the U.S., he frequently returned there to perform, and he and Paul Draper staged a reunion at New York's Carnegie Hall in 1975. He never renounced his American citizenship, but he deplored the country's new rightward drift during the later decades of the century. "I come from a generation that revered Franklin Delano Roosevelt, and I admired Harry Truman" (with whom he had once performed "The Missouri Waltz"), Adler was quoted as saying in the *San Diego Union-Tribune*. "But look who they had later on—Nixon and Reagan. Wow. This does not encourage respect." Though he had lived the high life in California in the 1930s, his life in Britain, in a small apartment in London's Hampstead district, was more modest.

Adler's performing career slowed in his old age but never came totally to a halt. He issued several albums that mixed classical music and pop standards, and he wrote a book of memoirs called *It Ain't Necessarily So*. In 1994, to mark his 80th birthday, he joined with a host of pop stars—Sting, Elton John, Elvis Costello, Kate Bush, Jon Bon Jovi, and Meat Loaf among them—to record a new album, *The Glory of Gershwin*. Becoming acquainted with rock musicians prompted one of Adler's rare self-deprecatory sentiments. "I knew their names but not their work," he was quoted as saying in the *Union-Tribune*. "That is not the kind of music I usually listen to. I realized there's more to this music than I thought. I don't like admitting I was prejudiced." The album made its debut at No. 2 on British pop charts, making Adler the oldest person to ascend to top chart levels in Britain. In 1997 he recorded a new film score, one for a compendium of silent-film chase scenes called *The Great Chase*.

Surviving cancer and two strokes, Adler returned to the studio to record with other rock stars. In his 87th year, he cut a duet with Cerys Matthews, a Welsh rock star. "I'm surprised not only I'm still playing, but that I'm improving as I get older," the irrepressible Adler told Simon Hattenstone of the *Guardian* in April of 2001. A bout with pneumonia that summer, however, ended his life in a London hospital on August 6, 2001. "Resist the pressure to conform," he advised young people, as quoted in his *New York Times* obituary. "Better be a lonely individualist than a contented conformist."

Books

Adler, Larry, *It Ain't Necessarily So,* Collins, 1984.

Periodicals

Daily Telegraph (London, England), August 8, 2001.
Guardian (London, England), April 12, 2001; August 8, 2001.
Independent (London, England), October 22, 2001.
New York Times, August 8, 2001.
San Diego Union-Tribune, August 12, 2001.
Variety, August 13, 2001. □

Renata Adler

American writer Renata Adler (born 1938) began her career at the venerable *New Yorker* in 1962, and kept a berth there for nearly 40 years. She also spent time as the chief movie critic for the *New York Times,* worked on the impeachment inquiry of former U.S. President Richard M. Nixon, and wrote several books. Along the way, she acquired a reputation for sharp insight and a fearless style. And nowhere did those professional hallmarks culminate in more controversy than with Adler's 1999 book, *Gone: The Last Days of the New Yorker,* a critique of the current state of the publication that had given her her start. But the firestorm caused by the book did not mellow Adler one bit.

Birth and Education

Adler was born on October 19, 1938, in Milan, Italy. Her parents were German Jews who had left Frankfurt in 1933 to escape the Nazi regime of Adolf Hitler. A year after Adler's birth, the family, which included her two older brothers, immigrated to the United States. They settled first in New York and then in Danbury, Connecticut, where Adler was primarily reared. Her father had been a lawyer in Germany and studied law in his adopted country, but it is unclear how he supported his family in Connecticut. Arthur Lubow of the *New York Times* reported that Adler's mother's family, the Strausses, had made a fortune in the wool business in Germany and eventually set her father up with his own wool factory in Danbury. Adler, however, has vehemently denied this. She told Dennis Loy Johnson of *Salon* that her father "never had anything to do with wool in his life," and added, "No. There is no wool in our family at all." A puzzling bit of contentiousness over such a small point, to be sure, but the level of acrimony between Adler and Lubow's newspaper had reached such a pitch by 2000 (the year of both the above interviews) that the "wool argument" may have been beside the point entirely.

Whatever business her father may have been engaged in, it was sufficiently prosperous to send Adler off to boarding school when she was just seven. While not a pleasant memory for Adler, her parents reportedly justified the decision by their goal of Americanizing the young girl. Paradoxically, they also required that only German be spoken at home. Despite such familial idiosyncrasies, however, Adler did well enough in her studies to progress to Bryn Mawr, where she earned a B.A. degree in 1959. Next, it was off to the Sorbonne (Paris) to earn a D.E.S. degree in 1961, and then to Harvard University for her M.A. degree in 1962. After Harvard, Adler began her career at what many would consider the pinnacle by signing on with the *New Yorker.*

Accolades and Controversy

Adler was hired to write for the *New Yorker* by its legendary editor William Shawn in 1962. Mentored by her boss and excellent at her job, she settled in with the magazine for the long haul. Her notable reporting included covering Selma, Alabama, when civil rights strife was rampant, and she was one of the first female journalists to report from Vietnam. Despite such achievements, though, Adler's distinctive voice became best known outside her primary place of business.

Adler's first big plunge into tumult occurred when she took a position as the chief film critic for the *New York Times* in 1968. The sedate "Gray Lady" of newspapers was stunned and invigorated by Adler's incisive, no-nonsense style, as she calmly and caustically reviewed movies exactly as she saw fit. Unimpressed by a film's pedigree, Adler was just as apt to skewer a big budget production that she found lacking as that of an independent effort, much to Hollywood's dismay. Indeed, she once so incensed executives at Universal Artists that the studio took out a full-page ad in the paper calling for her head. Far from chastising Adler for generating such turmoil, her editor, Arthur Gelb, applauded it, and her successor in the job, Vincent Canby, credited her with changing the face of movie criticism itself. "She looked at movies so cleanly and with such a fresh eye," Canby told Lubow. "She cleared the air for me and everyone who came afterward." Nonetheless, Adler left the position after just over a year and headed back to the *New Yorker.*

In 1969 Adler's first book, *Toward a Radical Middle: Fourteen Pieces of Reporting and Criticism,* was published. She followed that up the next year with a reflection on her time at the *New York Times,* called *A Year in the Dark: Journal of a Film Critic.* The year 1972 saw her moonlighting as a professor of theater and film at Hunter College of the City University of New York, and in 1973 she received a John Simon Guggenheim Award. The Watergate scandal of the Nixon years broke in 1973, and Adler was hired to write for Peter Rodino, the committee chairman of the House Judiciary Committee. That experience prompted her to study law, and she went on to earn a degree from the Yale University Law School.

Adler's debut novel, *Speedboat,* was published in 1976 and won the Hemingway Prize for Best First Novel. But in 1980 the fat was in the fire once again when she acidly assessed a collection of movie reviews written by *New Yorker* colleague Pauline Kael. Adler's critique appeared in the *New York Review of Books,* and included what would soon be an infamous summing up of Kael's work: "jarringly, piece by piece, line by line, and without interruption, worthless." (As quoted by Nan Goldberg of the Newark *Star-Ledger.*) Adler's review was a matter of opinion, of course, but her scathing words were hugely controversial, especially at the *New Yorker.* But it was neither the first, nor the last, time Adler would create such a stir.

Respite

Adler continued to work for the *New Yorker,* although perhaps a bit less, after the Kael incident. She also kept busy writing for such publications as the *New Republic, Atlantic*

Monthly, Harper's, and *Vanity Fair.* In 1983 her second novel, *Pitch Dark,* was published, and *Reckless Disregard: Westmoreland v. CBS et al.; Sharon v. Time* followed in 1986. The latter was an exploration of the libel suits of General William C. Westmoreland and Ariel Sharon against CBS and *Time,* respectively, and while it generally received stellar reviews, its sympathy for the plaintiffs did little to revive Adler's flagging popularity among journalists. Indeed, she pointed to the book in 2001 as the impetus behind her ensuing battles with the established press. "The press got really cross with me," she told James Reginato of *W,* "and they don't forget."

Adler continued blithely on her way for quite some time. She adopted a son in 1986, was elected to the American Academy of Arts and Letters in 1987, wrote *Politics and Media: Essays* (1988), and contributed to numerous publications on an ongoing basis. Her image and lifestyle remained a source of fascination for many, as her arresting face was a frequent subject for famed photographer Richard Avedon, and she maintained an active and broad social calendar that included some of New York's most elite names. But Adler was to become the center of a maelstrom yet again in 2000.

Adler vs. The Press

Adler's most venomous tempest began with the 2000 publication of Adler's book *Gone: The Last Days of the New Yorker,* in which she expressed her views on what she saw as the complete decline of the magazine with which she had been so long affiliated. A kind of obituary for the publication, the book pulled no punches when it came to attributing blame. But what Adler saw as an honest assessment of the state of the *New Yorker,* others saw as a mean-spirited betrayal of her colleagues. And although the book was generally well-received in the rest of the United States, the New York press generally vilified both it and its author. The situation escalated a month later, when the late Watergate Judge John Sirica's son, a reporter for New York's *Newsday,* took issue with a one-sentence characterization of his father as corrupt and incompetent. The resulting melee was a merry chase, and the *New York Times* was largely at the helm.

Briefly put, the *New York Times* began by printing four unfavorable articles about the book, some written by *New Yorker* personnel, shortly after its release. After Sirica's son drew attention to the previously unnoticed offending sentence by demanding a retraction or proof, the newspaper took up his cause with no fewer than four more negative pieces within the space of one week in April of 2000. The charge was that Adler had made her claims with no evidence to back them up. Adler's view was that she would offer such validation in her own time, and alleged that the newspaper was using its might and credibility to tarnish her reputation. Accusations of ethics violations flew back and forth. Adler did publish her case against Sirica, along with her views on the *New York Times,* in the August 2000 issue of *Harper's.* The newspaper was not mollified, and the feud played on.

In 2001 Adler published a new collection of essays called *Canaries in the Mineshaft: Essays on Politics and Media.* The book included such well-known efforts as *Decoding*

the *Starr Report* and her famous criticism of Kael, as well as the 2000 article from *Harper's.* That piece took direct aim at the journalistic practices of the *New York Times* and those of the press in general. She viewed journalism as having become too bureaucratic, lazy, and smug and the scrutiny could hardly have further endeared her to her journalistic colleagues, but Adler remained unbowed and resolute.

Adler released *Irreparable Harm: The U.S. Supreme Court and the Decision That Made George W. Bush President* in 2004, in which she examined the 2000 U.S. presidential election. Still deemed a heretic by many, the book at least shifted her relentless gaze from the press (and from her) for the time being. But it was unlikely that this was the author's motivation. Instead, it was more likely that Adler's fierce curiosity and intelligence had simply alighted on another subject. As her editor, Michael Denneny, told Reginato in 2001, "Renata is one of the last totally freestanding intellectuals, like Hannah Arendt and Mary McCarthy. She represents nobody but herself." Love her or hate her, it was difficult to argue with that.

Periodicals

Austin American-Statesman, February 20, 2000.
New York Observer, January 17, 2000.
New York Times, April 3, 2000; July 17, 2000.
New York Times Magazine, January 16, 2000.
Star-Ledger (Newark, NJ), October 21, 2001.
W, December 2001.

Online

"Birnbaum v. Renata Adler," *Morning News,* September 16, 2004, http://www.themorningnews.org/archives/personalities/birnbaum_v_renata_adler.php (January 7, 2006).
"Fellows Whose Last Names Begin with A," John Simon Guggenheim Memorial Foundation, http://www.gf.org/afellow.html (January 3, 2006).
"Interview with the Heretic," *Salon,* August 21, 2000, http://www.salon.com/books/int/2000/08/21/adler/print.html (January 3, 2006).
"Irreparable Harm: The U.S. Supreme Court and the Decision That Made George W. Bush President," Amazon, http://www.amazon.com/gp/product/097960950/102-1912689-8153747?v=glance&n;=283155 (January 7, 2006).
"Renata Adler," Boston University, http://www.bu.edu/uni/faculty/bios/adler.html (January 3, 2006).
"Renata Adler," NNDB, http://www.nndb.com/people/799/000048655/ (January 3, 2006).
"Renata Adler," *Reports and Writers,* http://www.reportingcivilrights.org/authors/bio.jsp?authorId=86 (January 3, 2006). □

Jane Alexander

An American actress with a rarely equaled reputation for high-quality work, Jane Alexander (born 1939) has worked with equal success in the fields of film, theater, and television. She has not hesitated to take on roles with controversial content; her range as a performer is wide.

I n the 1990s, Alexander spent four stormy years as the chair of the National Endowment for the Arts (NEA), the chief arts funding agency operated by the United States government. As federal arts funding became a political football during the politically polarized administration of President Bill Clinton, Alexander struggled to uphold the ideal of the arts as a broadly beneficial force in society. After leaving the agency, Alexander returned to acting, and although she suffered along with other middle-aged actresses from a general lack of substantial film parts for women, she still found a strong demand for her talents.

Granddaughter of Buffalo Bill's Physician

Born Jane Quigley in Boston, Massachusetts on October 28, 1939, Alexander grew up in a fairly affluent household. Her father, Thomas Quigley, was a noted sports physician and surgeon whose own father had been the personal physician to the famed prairie scout and Wild West show promoter William "Buffalo Bill" Cody. Alexander grew up going to symphony and dance concerts and traveling on her own by subway to Boston's splendid art museums. She loved the arts in general from a young age, but her acting career did not begin until her years at Sarah Lawrence College. There, she auditioned for and won a part in *The Plough and the Stars,* a play by Irish writer Sean O'Casey. Alexander immersed herself in the role, and for the rest of her career she would be noted for enthusiastic research into the lives, real or imagined, of the characters she played. Her investigations began with books and would

sometimes extend to visiting places where a character may have spent time.

Upset by a friend's sudden death during her sophomore year, she left Sarah Lawrence and went to study theater at the University of Edinburgh in Scotland in 1959 and 1960. She married actor and director Robert Alexander in 1962, and their son Jason went on to become a director. Robert and Jane Alexander divorced in 1969. Her second husband, director Edwin Sherin, met Alexander when she auditioned for a play and impressed him with her total commitment to the role. They would marry in 1975, occasionally working together as director and lead actress.

Alexander's professional career began at the Charles Playhouse in Boston in 1964. The following year she moved on to the Arena Stage company in Washington, D.C. and had 15 parts in plays there between 1965 and 1968. Her career at Arena Stage culminated in her creation of the role of Eleanor in Howard Sackler's *The Great White Hope,* playing the mistress of troubled black heavyweight boxer Jack Jefferson—based on the real-life figure of Jack Johnson and played by actor James Earl Jones. The play was a major success and moved in 1969 to Broadway in New York, where Alexander's performance earned her a Tony award.

The portrayal of an interracial romance on stage, at a time when such subject matter was still rare, brought Alexander her first taste of controversy; she received hate mail that included occasional death threats. Ignoring the attacks, she continued to perform. *The Great White Hope* was filmed in 1971, once again with Alexander in the role of Eleanor, and she was nominated for an Academy Award for her performance.

Portrayed Eleanor Roosevelt

For the next several years, Alexander worked consistently in theater, films, and television. She appeared in the hit Broadway play *Six Rms Riv Vu* in 1972 and 1973, and took one of her few Shakespearean roles in *Hamlet* in 1975—despite her lifelong identification with high-quality material, Alexander was more oriented toward contemporary plays and films rather than toward theatrical classics. After small parts in *The New Centurions* (1972) and several other films, Alexander returned to the spotlight in 1976 with the starring role of Eleanor Roosevelt in the made-for-television film *Eleanor and Franklin* and its sequel, *Eleanor and Franklin: The White House Years,* the following year. She also won another Academy Award nomination for her appearance in the political drama *All the President's Men.*

In 1979 Alexander landed the high-profile supporting role of Margaret in *Kramer vs. Kramer,* playing a friend to both parties in a bitter divorce struggle. The 1980 made-for-television film *Playing for Time,* in which Alexander played one of a group of female concentration-camp prisoners who stave off death by forming an orchestra and playing music for camp commanders, was another feather in Alexander's cap critically. Many of the films that made Alexander a familiar face appeared on television, and *Testament* (1983), a tale that manifested the nuclear-war jitters of the 1980s, started out in the television medium.

In *Testament,* Alexander played the mother in a California family trying to survive in the aftermath of a nuclear attack. Some critics condemned the film as melodramatic, but it brought the dangers of the Cold War between the U.S. and the Soviet Union home to viewers in an immediate way, and Alexander gained praise for her performance as the film became a national topic of conversation and was rushed into theatrical release. Alexander showed her versatility with a complete about-face in her next role, playing the title role of Old West diarist Calamity Jane in a television film of 1984.

With new clout in the industry, Alexander could act on a desire to branch out from high-minded roles. "I get offered a lot of films that have a noble woman pursuing a noble cause, or something like that," she explained to David Sterritt of the *Christian Science Monitor.* Alexander served as both star and executive producer for *Square Dance* (1987), a family drama set in Texas that took Alexander to country-music dance clubs as she carried out her trademark research for the role. In 1989 Alexander went beyond her usual reserved image when she played flamboyant gossip columnist Hedda Hopper in the television film *Malice in Wonderland,* and she had an uncredited role in the acclaimed Civil War drama *Glory,* as the mother of Colonel Robert G. Shaw (played by Matthew Broderick), the commander of an all-black Union regiment.

Named to Head NEA

The early 1990s saw Alexander appearing on Broadway in the Wendy Wasserstein play *The Sisters Rosenzweig,* never giving a thought to entering the world of government service or politics. But a staffer for Rhode Island U.S. Senator Claiborne Pell called Alexander out of the blue and asked whether she would be interested in being considered for the chairmanship of the NEA. The agency had endured several years of controversy over what some saw as obscene art it had funded, and many conservatives in the U.S. Congress were angling for the NEA's elimination, or, at the very least, a reduction in funding. The widely respected Alexander, seen as a consensus choice who could heal wounds within the agency, soon made the short list and then was nominated by President Clinton.

Alexander, for her part, warmed to her new opportunity. As reported by *The Boston Globe* she told a Senate committee during her confirmation hearings that "the life I have led in theater, in the world of art, has given me so much personally—particularly from Endowment-supported work—that I wish at this time to give something back." Confirmed overwhelmingly in late 1992, Alexander pledged to maintain the agency's independence from political interference. "We have to," she told *Interview.* "We're upholding a democratic principle here. This is the federal government, and federal agencies do not discriminate. What we do is look for high standards of excellence in the arts."

Alexander took steps to broaden the NEA's base, traveling widely to visit community-based arts groups that benefited from the agency's increased emphasis on disbursing funds beyond the traditional culture centers of the north-eastern U.S. Over her first two years as chairman she visited all 50 states, emphasizing the important role the arts could play in local communities and economies. Live, nonprofit arts events were especially critical in an increasingly technology-dominated society, Alexander argued, telling an Economic Club of Detroit audience (according to *Vital Speeches of the Day*) that such events "will begin to seem like some of the few authentic experiences we have, and they will be places where we appreciate the artist's skill—be it music or painting or theater—and the excitement of discovering new talent."

But Congressional Republicans, who ascended to majority status in the House of Representatives after the 1994 elections, continued to threaten the NEA's existence, leaving Alexander in a defensive posture most of the time. Washington's political environment was unfamiliar for Alexander, who had spent her whole life in arts-oriented settings. The people she worked with in Washington, she complained to Marilyn Stasio of *American Theatre,* were "a whole new breed. They are not well educated. They are hostile and suspicious of the arts, and it was tough for me to persuade them otherwise." President Clinton, preoccupied with other issues, met with Alexander only after she tried for two years to get an appointment. Few controversies over the funding of specific projects flared while Alexander was chairman, but a combination of new proposals to curb the agency's independence and a desire to return to acting— she had been inducted into the Theatre Hall of Fame in 1995—led her to resign as NEA chairman in 1997. By that time NEA funding had been cut by almost half.

Chronicled Experiences in Book

Alexander wrote about her NEA tenure in the book *Command Performance: an Actress in the Theater of Politics,* recounting her clashes with congressional conservatives. Steven C. Munson of *Policy Review* in his negative review of the book blamed many of the problems on what it saw as Alexander's own high-handedness, observing that "the point . . . that Alexander seems incapable of grasping . . . is that who's running an agency in Washington, and how he or she approaches that task, can actually make a difference, for good or ill. While the NEA . . . was spared extinction, it is by no means clear that its survival was because of, rather than despite, Jane Alexander." *Art in America's* Robert Atkins viewed the book through a different lens, calling it "essentially a bildungsroman, a coming-of-age story in which an idealistic agency head loses her innocence in the snakepit of corruption and ambition that is Washington."

"After being away from theatre for all that time, I was pretty overwhelmed by how deeply moved I was to be back on stage," Alexander told Stasio. She threw herself back into her work, returning to the cinema screen for the first time in ten years with a small role in 1999's *The Cider House Rules* and taking on various theater projects in New York and Washington. A 2003 production of Henrik Ibsen's *Ghosts* at Washington's Shakespeare Theatre seemed to refer back to her NEA experiences; it was staged with sexually explicit paintings on the set, standing in for the controversial books her character liked to read in the play as originally written. In 2005 she performed in the one-woman play *What of the Night* and made a triumphant return to television, starring in *Warm Springs* and returning to her long fascination with the family of President Franklin Delano Roosevelt. Her portrayal of Sara Delano Roosevelt, the president's mother, brought her an Emmy award and another flower in a long garland of honors that recognized her craft.

Books

Alexander, Jane, *Command Performance: An Actress in the Theater of Politics*, Public Affairs, 2000.
Newsmakers 1994 issue 4, Gale, 1994.

Periodicals

American Theatre, September 1998; July 2000; July-August 2003.
Art in America, July 2001.
Boston Globe, September 25, 1992.
Christian Science Monitor, March 13, 1987.
Dance Magazine, December 1997.
Interview, July 1994.
New York Times, March 6, 1984.
Policy Review, December 2000.
Variety, April 11, 2005.
Vital Speeches of the Day, January 15, 1996.
Washington Post, November 25, 1978.

Online

"Jane Alexander," Internet Movie Database, http://www.imdb.com (December 4, 2005). □

Al-Kashi

Al-Kashi (1380-1429) was a renowned mathematician and astronomer in early fifteenth-century Persia and Central Asia. An Iranian from a humble background, he was entirely self-taught, and was one of the leading scholars at the newly created University of Samarkand in what is present-day Uzbekistan. In 1424 Al-Kashi published a treatise on circumference, in which he calculated *pi,* the ratio of a circle's circumference to its diameter, to nine decimal places. Nearly two hundred years would pass before another mathematician surpassed this achievement.

There are various spellings given for Al-Kashi's full name, but the standard English transliteration seems to be Ghiyath al-Din Jamshid Mas'ud al-Kashi. He was born in 1380 in Kashan, a desert town in Iran located near the Central Iranian Range. Kashan is a noted oasis on the road to Qom, the Shiite holy city in Iran, and archaeological discoveries cite Al-Kashi's birthplace as one the oldest inhabited places on Earth. During his childhood, however, Kashan and the surrounding area were subject to periodic raids by the conqueror Tamerlane, an Uzbek of Mongol heritage and a Muslim. Some ten years before Al-Kashi's birth, Tamerlane founded his empire, which was a restoration of a previous Mongol kingdom, at the city of Samarkand, one of the oldest inhabited urban centers in the world.

With Peace, Economic Prosperity

Tamerlane began conquering territory to the west and south, and his move into Persia in 1383 began a period of difficulty for families like Al-Kashi's. The people lived in poverty for a number of years, and were forced to move frequently due to military raids. During this time Al-Kashi taught himself mathematics and astronomy, though the possible written sources he may have used are unknown. When the emperor Tamerlane died in 1405, his fourth son, Shah Rokh, ascended to the throne of the eastern portion of the Timurid empire, which encompassed Persia and Transoxania. This ushered in a more stable period, and one in which the economic climate vastly improved. Shah Rokh and his wife, a Persian princess named Gauhar Shad, were also enthusiastic supporters of the arts and sciences, and this period became a time of intellectual accomplishment and fervor in the region that gave scholars like Al-Kashi fertile soil in which to flourish.

By the time Al-Kashi reached adulthood, the Arabic world had produced a number of great mathematicians over the past millennia. The ancient Greeks formulated many of the algebraic and geometry theories still in use in modern times, but further scholarship died out with the rise of Christianity in Europe and the Mediterranean area during the early medieval period—mathematics and astronomy were closely tied to one another, and studying the heavens was viewed as the devil's work. But Islamic centers of learning flourished during this period, and several notable men made important discoveries in mathematics in Cairo, Baghdad, and the cities of Moorish Spain.

In 1406, the year Al-Kashi turned 26, he wrote about a lunar eclipse he had observed. By this time he was already writing his first book, which he finished in Kashan in March of 1407. It was titled *Sullam al-sama* (The Stairway of Heaven, on Resolution of Difficulties Met by Predecessors in the Determination of Distances and Sizes). In 1409 Shah Rokh's oldest son, Ulugh Beg (1393-1449), became ruler of the Transoxania portion of the Timurid empire. Ulugh Beg was a noted mathematician and astronomer, and at Samarkand he began to lay the foundations for what would become this part of the world's most esteemed university.

Courted Ulugh Beg's Favor

When Al-Kashi finished his *Mukhtasar dar 'ilm-i hay'at* (Compendium of the Science of Astronomy) in 1411, he dedicated it to Iskander, a Timurid ruler in Iran. This was a common practice, because scholars relied on royal patronage in order to carry out their work and earn a living through it. Iskander was murdered in 1414, the same year that Al-Kashi completed *Khaqani Zij.* This title reflected a new patron in Ulugh Beg, who was also known as *Khaqani,* or "Supreme Ruler"; *zij* was the Persian term for astronomical tables.

Al-Kashi's astronomical tables were based on an earlier work done by another Persian, Nasir al-Tusi. These were used to calculate the coordinates in the heavens, helped astronomers measure distances, and predicted the motion of the sun, moon, and planets, as well as longitudinal and latitudinal parallaxes. The Islamic world was profoundly interested in such navigational aids because of the *qibla*, the direction that a Muslim needed to face for prayer. Since 624 CE, devout Muslims who followed the five pillars of their religion had been instructed to face the Saudi Arabian city of Mecca, Islam's holy city, five times daily when they prayed. Many Muslims were traders, or traveled on other business, and used a complex measuring device called an astrolabe to find the direction of Mecca so that they could fulfill their religious obligation without error.

Al-Kashi did not yet have a formal patron, but it is known that he spent time in Herat, an ancient city in western Afghanistan that dated back to 500 BCE and was a renowned center for the production of bronze artifacts. In 1416 he completed two new works, *Risala dar sharh-i alat-i rasd* (Treatise on the Explanation of Observational Instruments) and *Nuzha al-hadaiq fi kayfiyya san'a al-ala al-musamma bi tabaq al-manatiq* (The Garden Excursion, on the Method of Construction of the Instrument Called Plate of Heavens). The latter work contains a description of his invention for a device to predict the positions of the planets.

Ulugh Beg invited Al-Kashi to teach at the University of Samarkand. He became its leading astronomer, and later in the century was described by a historian as the second Ptolemy, referring to the second-century Greek astronomer who lived and worked in Alexandria, Egypt, when it was the greatest center of scientific scholarship. Ptolemy preserved what had been known about the stars since the first Greek astronomers, named some 48 constellations in the night sky, and devised navigational tables that were used by mariners well into the 1600s.

Rose to Prominence

Al-Kashi wrote about his life in Samarkand in letters back to his father, and these provide contemporary scholars an unusual glimpse into this time and place. He wrote of the observatory that Ulugh Beg had built at Samarkand in 1424. Known as Gurkhani Zij, it featured an immense astrolabe with a precision-cut arc made of marble that was 63 yards long.

That same year Al-Kashi finished his most famous work, the *Risala al-muhitiyya* (Treatise on the Circumference). In it he calculated *pi,* the ratio of a circle's circumference to its diameter, to nine decimal places. The last reliable *pi* figure dated from nearly 900 years earlier, and had been ascertained by Chinese astronomers of the fifth century, but it was only to six decimal places. It would be nearly two hundred years before another mathematician found a more accurate calculation for *pi,* and that was the German-born mathematician Ludolph van Ceulen (1540-1610), who calculated it to 20 decimal places. Van Ceulen lived in the Dutch cities of Delft and Leiden for many years, and his most famous work, *Van den Circkel* (On the Circle), was published in 1596.

In 1427 Al-Kashi wrote another important text, *Miftah al-Hisab* (The Key to Arithmetic). This was intended to serve as a textbook for scholars at Samarkand, providing basic and advanced math for astronomy, but it was also designed for use by students of architecture, land surveying, accounting, and commerce. It was notable for its inclusion of decimal fractions. These had been worked out a few centuries earlier by mathematicians of the school of al-Karaji (Abu Bakr ibn Muhammad ibn al-Husayn Al-Karaji, 953–1029).

Calculated *Muqarna* Surface

One of the more impressive sections of *The Key to Arithmetic* was Al-Kashi's formula for measuring a complex shape called a *muqarna*. The muqarna was a standard form used by Arabic-world architects to hide edges and joints in mosques, palaces, and other large public buildings. It was a three-dimensional polygon or wedge form combined into honeycomb patterns. Al-Kashi's muqarna measurement had a practical application, for craftspeople were not paid by the hour in this era. "Payment per cubit was common in Ottoman architectural practice," noted a University of Heidelberg scholar, Yvonne Dold-Samplonius, in the *Nexus Network Journal,* "where a team of architects and surveyors had to make cost estimates of projected buildings and supply preliminary drawings for various options. In addition to facilitating estimates of wages and building materials before construction, Al-Kashi's formulas may also have been used in appraising the price of a building after its completion."

Al-Kashi's last work was *Risala al-watar wa'l-jaib* (The Treatise on the Chord and Sine), but it was unfinished at the time of his death in 1429. It was completed by Qadi Zada al-Rumi, another renowned mathematician at Samarkand, and includes sine calculations and a discussion of cubic equations. After Al-Kashi's death, Ulugh Beg praised him as "a remarkable scientist, one of the most famous in the world, who had a perfect command of the science of the ancients, who contributed to its development, and who could solve the most difficult problems," according to a biography that appeared on the website of the School of Mathematics and Statistics of the University of St. Andrews in Scotland. Contemporary scholars, however, believe that Al-Kashi was murdered on orders from Ulugh Beg.

The buildings of Ulugh Beg's university in Samarkand survive as part of the Registan, the old commercial center of the city. The observatory, Gurkhani Zij, was lost for a number of centuries, but its ruins were unearthed in 1908.

Books

Science and Its Times, Vol. 2: *700–1450,* Gale Group, 2001.

Online

"Calculation of Arches and Domes in 15th Century Samarkand," *Nexus Network Journal,* http://www.nexusjournal.com/conferences/N2000-DoldSamplonius.html (January 12, 2006).

"Ghiyath al-Din Jamshid Mas'ud al-Kashi," School of Mathematics and Statistics, University of St. Andrews in Scotland, http://www-groups.dcs.st-and.ac.uk/~history/Mathematicians/Al-Kashi.html (January 2, 2006). □

Cleveland Amory

Cleveland Amory (1917-1998) was an author, humorist, social critic, and leading animal advocate renowned for his three best–selling books based on his cherished white cat, Polar Bear. He followed his 1987 work, *The Cat Who Came for Christmas* with *The Cat and the Curmudgeon,* and *The Best Cat Ever.* Amory also founded the animal–rights group Fund for Animals. "If animals had a say in who should speak for them, someone like Cleveland Amory might well be a popular choice. Especially among cats," the British newspaper *Economist* wrote in 1998, after Amory died of an abdominal aneurysm at 81.

Raised as a Boston Brahmin

Amory was born on September 2, 1917, in Nahant, Massachusetts, along Boston's North Shore. Family and friends called him Clippie or Clip. Amory enjoyed playing chess, which he considered social, not competitive. His father was a textile manufacturer descended from generations of wealthy merchants. His parents, Robert and Leonore Cobb Amory, were connected with Boston Brahmin high society. "His affluent and well–connected upbringing left him with a self–assured demeanor and independent spirit," Joe Monzigo wrote in the *Los Angeles Times.*

Amory attended Milton Academy and Harvard College, and as a senior, was president, or editor, of the *Harvard Crimson* campus newspaper his senior year. "If you have ever been editor of the *Harvard Crimson*. . .there is very little, in afterlife, for you," he once said, according to Monzigo. After graduating in 1939, Amory reported variously for such newspapers as the *Nashua Telegraph* in New Hampshire, the *Arizona Star* in Tucson, and was briefly the managing editor of the *Prescott Evening Courier,* also in Arizona. He then moved back east to become an editor of the *Saturday Evening Post* and youngest person to hold that title.

World War II intervened, and Amory served in Army intelligence from 1941 to 1943. For about 15 years after that, he wrote books that satirized upper–class people. Amory over the years decried what he felt was a moral decline in Boston society. "Proper Bostonians never talk about money," he once groused, according to the *Economist.* His early books included *The Proper Bostonians* and *Home Town* in 1947 and 1950, respectively. In the latter, he took aim at the book publishing business. *The Last Resorts* (1952) examined vacation getaways of the well–to-do, and *Who Killed Society?* explored the rise and decline of the affluent.

Amory, meanwhile, remained a journalist, giving social commentary on NBC–TV's "Today" show from 1952 to

1963; he was also a critic for *TV Guide* from 1963 to 1976. His *Saturday Review* column ran for 20 years, through 1972, and was a senior contributing editor for *Parade* magazine from 1980 until his death. In addition, he presented a daily radio essay, "Curmudgeon at Large."

Bullfight Triggered Animal Love

Amory's passion for animals had its roots in a bullfight he was assigned to cover in Arizona. He "was so sickened . . . that when the animal's ears were cut off as a trophy, he picked up a cushion and threw it at the matador," *People Weekly* wrote. Amory joined many animal–rights groups. "His angle was to always fight against any kind of cruelty," Marian Probst, his assistant for 37 years, told *People Weekly.* "He was the kind of guy who always swam upstream."

The writer turned animal–rights activist enjoyed his reputation as a curmudgeon, or contrarian. "A commanding presence, tall (six–foot–four), usually rumpled and with hair that looked as though it had been styled with an eggbeater, he explained that Boston was a fertile breeding ground for curmudgeons," Enid Nemy wrote in the *New York Times.* According to Nemy, he once told the *Oregonian* of Portland, Oregon, that he became one because "it suddenly dawned on me one day, when I was reading in the paper about a woman wrestler, that being a curmudgeon, that a curmudgeon was the last thing in the world that a man can be that a woman cannot be. Women can be irritating—after all, they are women—but they cannot be curmudgeons.''

In 1967, Amory founded the Fund for Animals, a New York–based organization and served as its president without pay. It sought to curb wildlife exploitation and domestic–animal abuse. ''He often said that if everyone thought about what it would be like to be in an animal's place, there might be more compassion in the world,'' Nemy wrote.

The fund had 81,000 members when Amory died in 1998. One of its most publicized actions involved the protest against the clubbing of baby harp seals in the Magdalene Islands, in Canada's Gulf of St. Lawrence. Fund workers converted a trawler to an icebreaker and cut through ice for five days. They painted the seals with a red organic dye when they reached them, rendering their coats worthless while not harming the animals. The clubbing of seals stopped in 1983.

Amory engineered the fund's 1979 purchase of Black Beauty Ranch in Murchison, Texas, about 90 miles southeast of Dallas. The nearly 1,200–acre ranch harbors abused and unwanted domestic and exotic animals from circuses and zoos. They include, mounted police and racetrack horses, cats, dogs, ostriches, iguanas, and llamas. In addition, the organization, using a Berlin-style airlift, rescued about 575 burros from Grand Canyon National Park officials, who had planned to eliminate them on grounds that they were destroying the flora. Amory even debated the virtues of animals with a Roman Catholic priest, who had insisted that animals had no souls. ''I told the good Father that if he and I were going in the future to some wonderful Elysian Field and the animals were not going to go anywhere, that was all the more reason to give them a little better shake in the one life they did have,'' Amory told the priest, according to Nemy.

Rescue of Cat Spawned Trilogy

Amory rescued a cat on Christmas Eve 1978, and thus began a series of books, based on the relationship with his find, which he named Polar Bear. It began with *The Cat Who Came for Christmas,* a 1988 work in which he chronicles how he rescued the white stray in New York and preserved it in the face of a strident woman who wanted the feline as a holiday gift for her daughter. *The Cat and the Curmudgeon* and *The Best Cat Ever* followed in 1990 and 1993, respectively. *The Cat and the Curmudgeon* sold 1.5 million copies alone; the sequels were both best–sellers. *The Best Cat Ever* was published one year after Polar Bear's death. The *Economist* editorialized: ''A book he wrote about a cat called Polar Bear that turned up on his doorstep on Christmas Eve, hungry and bedraggled, wrung the hearts of millions of Americans.''

All three expanded on the nuances between owner and cat. ''Sternly I told him that he might as well understand now and for once and for all something else. That bachelors have a reputation for being—and I emphasized this strongly—Very Set In Their Ways,'' Amory wrote in *The Cat Who Came for Christmas.* ''This time the answer, together with the tail rat-tat, came instantly. So, he was replying,

with exactly the same emphasis, Are Cats. The conflict was begun—and the issue joined.''

In his final chapter of *The Cat and the Curmudgeon,* Amory cited the bond between him and Polar Bear. ''The bald truth is that, frankly, it would take two curmudgeons working together even to begin to cope with all these things. And doing this in tandem has over the years brought us even closer together. I also believe that in these last years I have detected unmistakable signs that in certain ways Polar Bear has made a real effort to emulate me.''

He ended *The Best Cat Ever* with a eulogy to his departed pet: ''Certainly in just knowing Polar Bear, let alone being owned by him, I feel I owed him more than I could ever repay, let alone say. To me he was, and always will be, as I said at the beginning of this book, the best cat ever. I called him that, as I also said, in the special moments we had together, and I will always think of him as that.''

Critic David Greanville wrote in *The Animals' Agenda:* ''Trying to match his 1987 best–seller *The Cat Who Came for Christmas* must have surely proven a daunting challenge even for as robust an ego as Amory's. . . . Well, we needn't have worried. Amory, easily this nation's top raconteur and most underrated social commentator, is also a master of the satirical narrative. But with a twist. And that is that Amory's humor never stoops to meanness or bitterness. . . . Instead, gentleman that he is, he usually prefers to direct the barbs at himself.''

Advocacy Group Widened Scope

Through the 1980s and 1990s, Amory's Fund for Animals took aim at hunters. Using the courts, it halted a special hunting season on wolves in Minnesota and curbed black–bear hunting for one year in California, prompting Amory to say, according to the *Los Angeles Times,* ''This is [a] victory for the 98.5% of Californians who don't hunt and a victory for 100% of the bears.'' It also convinced Montana officials to prohibit the hunting of bison that meandered outside the confines of Yellowstone National Park. The group also fought against cockfighting, bear wrestling, and other forms of hunting contests. In 1985, Amory was able to convince Secretary of Defense Caspar Weinberger, with whom he attended Harvard, to let him save thousands of goats that military personnel were shooting on the Navy–owned San Clemente Island off San Diego County in California. Celebrities such as actresses Mary Tyler Moore and Angie Dickinson joined Amory in taking on the fur industry. Amory appeared in television commercials that said ''real people wear fake fur.''

Amory's last book, *Ranch of Dreams,* about Black Beauty Ranch, was published about nine months before he died. He worked a full day before dying in his sleep of the aneurysm that night. ''He liked to step back and cause people to think about what they were doing,'' animal activist and longtime friend Wayne Pacelle told the *Los Angeles Times.* ''But he did it with humor instead of moral outrage.''

The author was buried at Black Beauty, next to Polar Bear, whose tombstone reads: '' 'Til we meet again.'' Amory was survived by his sister, Leonore Sawyers; a stepdaughter, Gaea Leinhardt; and a step–granddaughter. ''He was a great writer too," Sawyers told *People Weekly*. "But animals were always his greatest concern." Leinhardt added in the same article: "He had a grumpy, crusty side, but it was a crust easily pierced."

Books

Cleveland Amory's Compleat Cat, Black, Dog & Leventhal (New York, NY), 1995.

Periodicals

Animals' Agenda, December, 1990.
Economist (US), October 24, 1998.
Los Angeles Times, October 16, 1998.
New York Times, October 16, 1998.
People Weekly, November 2, 1998.

Online

Biography Resource Center, Cleveland Amory biography, http://galenet.galegroup.com/servlet/BioRC (December 16, 2005). □

Walter H. Annenberg

Walter H. Annenberg (1908-2002), through canny anticipation of new trends in the publishing world, became one of the richest individuals in the United States. In his later years he became equally notable for giving away vast amounts of his money to educational programs, cultural institutions, and political campaigns.

Annenberg's life was not untouched by controversy. As publisher of the *Philadelphia Inquirer* newspaper in the 1950s and 1960s, he used the paper to settle personal scores and to advance his own financial agenda. Eager to be respected by society's upper crust, he did not always get his wish; a stint as U.S. ambassador to Great Britain began disastrously in 1969. But Annenberg's relationship with his British hosts improved as he opened his checkbook to fund worthwhile projects in that country, and by the time of his death, his unparalleled generosity had earned him admiration from virtually all quarters.

Born into Immigrant Family

Walter Hubert Annenberg was born into a family of German Jewish immigrants on March 13, 1908, in Milwaukee, Wisconsin. His father, Moses Annenberg, had arrived in the United States without money or even shoes, but had gotten a job at the *Chicago American* newspaper and worked his way up through the organization run by publisher William Randolph Hearst. The elder Annenberg had some extralegal enterprises on the side, including a telegraph service that transmitted horse race results to bookmakers, and the adolescent Walter was once sent out to deliver an unmarked package containing $400,000 in cash. He attended Peddie School, near Trenton, New Jersey,

which was one of the few prep schools open to Jews at the time. His business acumen showed up as he managed the school's senior prom financially and left it in the black.

Enrolling at the University of Pennsylvania's Wharton School of Business, Annenberg found himself more interested in the booming stock market than in classes; his father had given him a present of $10,000 after a winning evening at the poker table, and between 1927 and 1929 he turned it into a $2 million fortune. Annenberg dropped out of the University of Pennsylvania and joined his father's newspaper circulation business as assistant bookkeeper. The truncation of his academic career did not stop Annenberg from endowing a new school of communications at Penn in 1962. In the late 1920s he lived the high life and flirted with numerous women, including talented dancer Ginger Rogers, but married Canadian-born Veronica Dunkelman. The pair had two children, Wallis and Roger; Annenberg's son suffered from mental illness and committed suicide in 1962.

The stock market crash of 1929 turned Annenberg's $2 million into a $400,000 debt, which his father paid off. Annenberg applied himself to the family business, which was growing rapidly with the acquisition of the *Daily Racing Form* newspaper and, in 1936, the *Philadelphia Inquirer*. Both father and son were staunch Republicans who opposed the New Deal social programs of President Franklin D. Roosevelt, and the senior Annenberg used the *Inquirer* as a platform for his conservative philosophies. That, some said, drew the ire of federal tax investigators. Both Moses and Walter Annenberg, who by 1939 had become vice president of his father's Triangle Publications, were charged with tax evasion in 1940.

Moses Annenberg pleaded guilty as part of a deal with prosecutors that would keep his son out of prison. He was sentenced to three years in prison but released after two when he was diagnosed with a brain tumor. Walter Annenberg, the only son among what has been variously reported as eight, nine, or ten siblings, took over the family business. After his father's death in 1942, Walter Annenberg would always display prominently in his various offices a plaque bearing a prayer that read (according to the *Inquirer*), ''Cause my works on Earth to reflect honor on my father's memory.'' Like his father, Walter Annenberg would sometimes be criticized for using his journalistic properties to attack political opponents and other enemies; at one point the Philadelphia 76ers basketball team ran afoul of Annenberg, and the *Inquirer* was forbidden to even print the name of the popular NBA franchise.

Founded *Seventeen* Magazine

It was not long before Walter Annenberg emerged in his own right as an acute judge of trends. Noticing the growing buying power of young female consumers, he realized that this market segment was underserved by the publishing industry and in 1944 founded *Seventeen* magazine, naming his sister Enid Haupt as editor. *Seventeen* became one of American publishing's great success stories from the beginning, with huge ad sales in the first issue and sales that soon topped one million copies per issue. Annenberg continued to expand his empire with the purchase of radio and television stations in the northeastern United States.

His second stroke of genius in sensing the market for a new publication came in 1952, when he purchased a series of local television magazines and formed the magazine *TV Guide,* with national editorial content and local television schedules for large markets. *TV Guide* became the bible of the ''boob tube.'' by the mid-1970s it was selling between 15 and 20 million copies a week—one of every five magazines sold in the United States, according to one estimate. Numerical estimates of Annenberg's wealth are fluid. His profits from *TV Guide* alone were estimated at $500,000 to $1 million a week, and *Forbes* magazine eventually ranked him as one of the 100 richest individuals in the world. In Rancho Mirage, California, he built an estate called Sunnylands that had a 2,000-square-foot master bedroom for Annenberg and his second wife, Lee, and an 18-hole golf course with private greenskeepers. On the walls hung Annenberg's growing collection of masterworks of Impressionist painting. His first foray into art philanthropy came in 1962, when First Lady Jacqueline Kennedy was engaged in redecorating the White House; Annenberg contributed the so-called Thumb Portrait of Benjamin Franklin to the White House collection. The bowling alley in the White House was also paid for by Annenberg.

In 1969 Annenberg sold the *Inquirer* and the *Philadelphia Daily News* for $55 million, accepting an appointment from President Richard Nixon as ambassador to Britain. Some questioned Annenberg's fitness for the plum post; he had no diplomatic experience, and suggestions surfaced in the press that he had bought the job with campaign contributions. It was true that Annenberg and Nixon were friends, but his political contributions to Nixon began only with the ill-fated re-election campaign of 1972. Annenberg was also close to other conservative politicians and helped bankroll Ronald Reagan's ascent through the Republican party ranks to the presidency in 1980.

Annenberg's tenure as ambassador to Britain got off to a rocky start when he mangled the English language in response to a question from Queen Elizabeth II about how he was settling in; Annenberg replied (according to Grace Glueck of the *New York Times*), ''We're in the embassy residence, subject, of course, to some of the discomfiture as a result of a need for, uh, elements of refurbishment and rehabilitation.'' The merriment that followed in British newspapers was unfair to a degree; Annenberg had been born with a slight speech impediment and was never comfortable in public speaking situations. He eventually won over his British hosts with contributions to the National Gallery art museum and by overseeing what even British style mavens conceded was a well-done restoration of Winfield House, the American embassy residence. He was given an honorary knighthood by the queen in 1976, who visited Annenberg's California estate while on a trip to the United States in 1984.

Founded Educational Institute

By that time Annenberg had begun to amass the impressive track record of philanthropy that made admirers out of even those who had tangled with him in the past. The Annenberg School of Communications at the University of Pennsylvania was followed by one at the University of Southern California, and in 1976 he created the Annenberg Institute in Philadelphia, with a 180,000-volume library devoted to the origins of Western culture in the ancient Middle East. Occasionally Annenberg's largesse resulted in controversy; New York's city government resisted and finally killed an Annenberg-financed expansion of the Metropolitan Museum of Art that would have encroached on Central Park. The controversy did not stop Annenberg from naming the Metropolitan, after intense jockeying among several museums, as the recipient of his remarkable art collection after his death.

In 1988 Annenberg sold Triangle Publications to Australian-born media magnate Rupert Murdoch for $3 billion; financially astute well into old age, he negotiated a price that even Murdoch admitted was too high. (Annenberg continued to report to work daily at his office until 1999, when he was 91 years old.) After the sale, his gift-giving accelerated. According to the *Inquirer,* he often answered interviewers who asked after his well-being with ''Grateful. Grateful that I'm still around and I'm comfortable and I'm able to help people.'' On a single day in 1993 he disbursed gifts of $365 million to Harvard University, the University of Pennsylvania, the University of Southern California, and Peddie, his prep school. Two of his largest individual gifts went to the Corporation for Public Broadcasting ($60 million in 1991) to support student math and science programming, and to the United Negro College Fund

($50 million in 1990), at the time the largest gift ever given to any historically black educational institution. A strong supporter of civil rights, Annenberg cut his support for conservative Philadelphia mayor Frank Rizzo after Rizzo made racially-based campaign appeals.

It was not only educational institutions that benefited from Annenberg's largesse. A $2 million Annenberg gift endowed a new Pennsylvania Hospital institute devoted to hip replacement surgery, and named it after physician Richard H. Rothman, who had performed such surgery on Annenberg himself. In 2001 he gave the Philadelphia Museum of Art $20 million, its largest gift ever, and a total of $29 million went to the Philadelphia Orchestra, much of it to renovate the aging Academy of Music building. With Annenberg funds the Philadelphia Zoo acquired a new baby elephant. He continued to support British causes long after his return to the United States, giving five million pounds to the National Gallery in 1988 and six million pounds to the British Museum the following year.

After Annenberg's death at his Wynnewood, Pennsylvania, estate on October 1, 2002, University of Pennsylvania president Judith Rodin told the Philadelphia *Inquirer* that he "embodied the belief that those fortunate enough to acquire great wealth are obligated to use it for the good of society." Annenberg loved Impressionist art, he had told the *Inquirer,* because many of the artists who painted the works "were ridiculed, scorned, abused, denounced, and very few of them lived to see the tremendous respect they subsequently enjoyed." Annenberg himself endured his fair share of denunciation, but he emerged in the end with respect from all.

Books

Cooney, John, *The Annenbergs: The Salvaging of a Tainted Dynasty,* Simon & Schuster, 1982.

Ogden, Christopher, *Legacy: A Biography of Moses and Walter Annenberg,* Little, Brown, 1999.

Periodicals

Daily Telegraph (London, England), October 2, 2002.

Economist, October 12, 2002.

Forbes, October 21, 1991; January 17, 1994.

Irish Times, October 5, 2002.

New York Times, October 2, 2002.

Philadelphia Inquirer, October 2, 2002; October 5, 2002.

Online

"Walter Annenberg," Museum of Broadcast Communications, http://www.museum.tv/archives/etv/A/htmlA/annenbergwa/annenbergwa.htm (February 13, 2006). □

Arete of Cyrene

Arete of Cyrene (c. 400 BC–c. 340 BC) lived in North Africa around the year 400 B.C. She was an educated woman and philosopher. Many women studied philosophy during this period, but Arete was one of the only ancient women to have an actual career in philosophy. She spent 33 years of her life teaching natural and moral philosophy at the academies and various schools of Attica. She also wrote over 40 books. Her pupils numbered somewhere near 110 philosophers by the time of her death.

Raised In a World of Power

A rete was born the daughter of Aristippus, who was the head of the Cyrenaic school in Cyrene. Cyrene was located in what is now part of northeastern Libya, situated in the fertile and Jabbal el-Akhdar (Green Mountain) area, where water was plentiful, and therefore crops were abundant. At the time that Arete lived it was part of the great Greek Empire. There were five Greek cities in the area, and Cyrene was the oldest and most important of them all. Arete's city was named after the Greek myth. Cyrene was a nymph, the daughter of Hypsesus, who was king of the Lapiths, and Chlidanope, a Naiad. Apparently, Apollo found Cyrene wrestling alone with a lion and fell in love with her; he carried her off to Mt. Pelion in that part of Libya (Thessaly) where in later times he founded a city and named it after her and made her its queen. In actuality, the city of Cyrene was founded in approximately 631 BC by a group of people from the island of Thera, located in the Aegean Sea. Their leader was Battus, and he became the first king, founding the dynasty of the Battiads, whose members ruled until around 440 B.C. Under the Battiad dynasty's rule, the city flourished economically and expanded, establishing the cities of Apollonia (Marsa Susah), Barce (al-Marj) and Euhesperides, or Berenice (Banghazi). Cyrene eventually became one of the vast intellectual centers of the classical world, and included some of the best of all academic pursuits, including a medical school and such scholars as the geographer Eratosthenes, the philosopher Aristippus, founder of the Cyrenaics, and, of course, his daughter Arete.

The world that Arete lived in was much different than the world of the early twenty-first century. The Cyrene's principal export was the medicinal herb silphium, which was shown on most of their coins, and was a great contributor to their economy until it was harvested to its extinction. Silphium was found everywhere and Arete herself must have been familiar with it and probably used it for whatever ailed her. Silphium is a plant that remains extinct today. Although there are other forms of it, and other plants named the same, the plant that Arete would have known has been wiped from the planet. The plant was extremely valuable in ancient times because of its many uses. It was used as a food source, seasoning for food, and most notably as a medication. They made perfumes from the flowers, and used the stalks for the food. It was the juice and root which were used to make the various medicines. The medicines derived from the silphium were many, and they were used for a wide scope of problems, including helping with coughing, sore throats, fever, indigestion, fluid retention, seizures, as well as general aches and pains. Even the sap of the plant was supposed to remove warts and other undesirable growths. More miraculously, silphium was believed to cure such widespread issues as leprosy, baldness, poison, and was commonly used to cleanse afterbirth from the womb. Popular potions were also made from silphium to prevent birth, things that were used widely at the time. The birth control was taken as a tea made from the leaves, or as a very small globule of the sap mixed with some wine. The ancient Greeks thought the plant was a gift from Apollo, which fit nicely in with the myth of Cyrene. It was such a great source of wealth for the Cyrenes because silphium was impossible to cultivate or transplant, it was because of this that the plant eventually became extinct in the first century AD.

Followed Father's Cyrenaic School of Philosophy

Since Arete was born into a city of power, wealth, and erudite academia, she came by her career honestly. Being educated was natural for someone in her position, and her father certainly pushed her to gain as much education as she could. Aristippus, Arete's father, was a friend and student of Socrates himself. He was one of the men who wandered around Athens with Socrates as that great philosopher asked the people questions to point out their ignorance. The two were so close that Aristippus was present at Socrates' death. After his training, Aristippus returned to Cyrene and founded the Cyrenaic school of philosophy. This school would have a profound impact on Arete's life and future career.

Cyrenaics, as they were called, believed that ethics—moral values about what is right and wrong—was the principal part of philosophy. Cyrenaics were deeply interested in anything that was good for the family, as well as the larger society as a whole. The only measure they had for morality was pleasure, as it was pleasure that they believed to be the point and goal of life. They proposed that people should never defer a pleasure at hand in hopes of a future one, but should grab, enjoy, and appreciate the pleasures that came to them. Arete grew up alongside her father who was rather scandalous in his pursuit of his philosophical ideals. According to the Internet Encyclopedia of Philosophy Web Site, "[Aristippus] was willing to break the social conventions of his day and engage in behavior that was considered undignified or shocking for the sake of obtaining pleasurable experiences. . . . For instance, when Aristippus was upbraided for sleeping with a courtesan, he asked whether there was any difference between taking a house in which many people have lived in before or none, or between sailing on a ship in which many people have sailed and none. When it was answered that there is no important difference, he replied that it likewise makes no difference whether the woman you sleep with has been with many people or none." He was also one of the few philosophers who accepted money for philosophical instruction, which is something that Arete continued as she became an instructor.

Hedonism As a Philosophy

The Cyrenaic School in which Arete was raised was one of the first schools to have a basis in hedonism, although their idea of hedonism was not based on an acquisi-

tion of possessions or in selfishly pursuing pleasure at the cost of all else. They saw the balance between pleasure and pain as necessary, as there could obviously never be pleasure without pain, and pain with a knowledge of pleasure. They saw pleasure and pain as opposites in several ways, not just that one was good and the other bad. Mainly they saw the difference between the two as a temperamental one: pleasure was seen as a mild and peaceful movement while pain was a fierce one. And although pleasure was seen as life's goal, the Cyrenaics believed that people must not become preoccupied with it, or else they would lose it. In a rather Buddhist way, then, the Cyrenaics believed in separating the soul from a desire to gain pleasure as the best means to one day obtaining it. The greatest good was aloofness from desire, and an appreciation for pleasure when it appeared.

Made Name For Herself in Philosophical World

Arete studied under her father and became famous throughout the ancient world in her own right. Women were not allowed to attend public forums at the time that Arete lived, but the Plato school still welcomed women into its ranks and she attended as many private meetings as possible, and was very active in all philosophical dealings, helping to spread the ideals of the Cyrenaic School as widely as she could. She became so prominent in the philosophical world that she took over the Cyrene school after her father died. She was especially suitable for the position because her father had raised her to be prudent and practical and to detest excess of any kind, and she was a stringent follower of the ethics she had been taught. She was a good exempla of the principles of the Cyrenaic school, and therefore was an appropriate follower to lead the school. She was also raised to be an egalitarian. According to the Mount Saint Mary College website, she has been quoted as having said, "I dream of a world where there are neither masters nor slave." She sought to spread equality of sex, race, and man throughout the ancient world, and lived that way, promoting her ideas to 100s of pupils, until her death.

Arete of Cyrene is known to have published many documents, but most of them have been lost over time. It is known, however, that she was considered to be a star among the women philosophers of her age. One reason for this knowledge is that upon her death her tomb was inscribed with an epitaph that stated that she was the splendor of Greece and that she possessed the beauty of Helen, the virtue of Thirma, the soul of Socrates, and the tongue of Homer. That was quite a lot of praise for the philosopher.

Online

"Arete," Ancient Greece, http://idcs0100.lib.iup.edu/ancgreece/arete.htm (January 6, 2006).

"Arete of Cyrene," Ancient Women Philosophers, http://faculty.msmc.edu/lindeman/arete1.html (January 6, 2006).

"Arete of Cyrene," Fact Bites, http://www.factbites.com/topics/Arete/of/Cyrene (January 6, 2006).

"Arete of Cyrene," Women Philosophers of Ancient Times, http://www.geocities.com/Athens/Forum/9974/old.html (January 6, 2006).

"Women Scientists of Antiquity," Wesleyan University, http://www.wesleyan.edu/synthesis/Synthesis/Women.html (January 6, 2006). □

Francis Arinze

The highest-ranking African in the hierarchy of the Catholic Church, Nigerian-born Cardinal Francis Arinze (born 1932) has inspired speculation that he might one day become the first non-European pope in modern times.

Arinze is known as a conservative on many issues. His positions on matters of Catholic doctrine have been marked by an uncompromising defense of tradition, especially in connection with the hot-button social issues of homosexuality, priestly celibacy, and abortion. Yet he saw enough of war to emerge as a committed pacifist, and, coming from a country split down the middle between Christianity and Islam, he became an important advocate for interfaith dialogue and for the idea that communication and cooperation among representatives of different faiths might help to defuse religious extremism. Many of Arinze's ideas closely resembled those of the pope who brought him to Rome and nurtured his career: John Paul II.

Raised in Traditional Belief System

In addition to his status as an unusually high-ranking African, Arinze was also notable as a convert to Catholicism who ascended to the church's inner circle. Born in Eziowelle in southeast Nigeria's Onitsha state, Arinze was the son of a farmer, Joseph Nwankwu, and his wife Bernadette Ekwoanya. A member of the Ibo ethnic group, he was raised in the traditional Ibo belief system with its pantheon of gods who take a direct interest in human affairs. Arinze never cut his ties with the culture of his homeland; African masks hung on the walls of his Vatican apartment, and he embraced the characteristically African forms of worship that made their way into services as Catholicism expanded across the continent.

It was a school run by Irish missionaries in his home village that set Arinze on the road to conversion. "The school served in many ways," Arinze told an interviewer quoted in the *Irish Times*. "It made the children literate, and literacy opened many doors—political, cultural, economic, and religious." Arinze was baptized when he was nine, and he decided that he wanted to follow in the footsteps of the local parish priest. His father objected, telling him (according to Arinze's recollections quoted in the *Irish Times*), "You will not become a priest because if you become a priest, you are not going to marry—number one, and you won't have children. And number two, you'll be hearing all the bad things people do in your two ears, and that's not good."

Nevertheless, Arinze succeeded in winning his father's support and that of others in his village—something that was necessary, he later pointed out, if he was going to proceed.

He attended Catholic schools in Nigeria and entered the Bigard Memorial Seminary in Enugu when he was 13. He received a degree there in 1955, was ordained as a priest three years later after sailing from Nigeria to Liverpool, England, crossing the English channel, taking a train to Rome, and catching a bus to Vatican City as he dragged his luggage along. He went on for postgraduate studies at Urbania University in Rome, writing an anthropologically oriented Ph.D. dissertation on the role of sacrifice in Ibo religion.

Arinze taught logic at the Bigard Seminary for a year and then returned to England, earning a teaching degree in 1964 at the London Institute of Education. With his well-rounded education, wide experience of the Catholic world, and linguistic expertise—he speaks English, Italian, French, German, and Ibo fluently and understands Spanish and Latin—he was named a bishop in 1965 and became archbishop of Onitsha in 1967 at age 34. He was the youngest bishop, and then the youngest metropolitan archbishop, in the entire world. He also attended the Vatican II conference on Catholic reform in Rome.

Lived Through Civil War

The next several years shaped a fundamental part of Arinze's outlook. As a destructive civil war, with both religious and ethnic components, tore Nigeria apart between 1967 and 1970, he emerged as a leading figure in peacemaking and reconciliation efforts. Moving from place to place, he was often forced to take shelter when bombs began to fall in the area. "He concluded that war makes problems more acute, it doesn't solve them," Vatican-watcher Gerard O'Connell told the *Irish Times*.

After the war, Arinze became known as a young church leader to watch. His rapid rise was partly due to his success in bringing new converts to Catholicism in a country with strong Islamic and local religious traditions. Nigerians flocked to his services, and the percentage of Christians in the Onitsha archdiocese grew from roughly 20 percent to 65 percent over the nearly two decades of Arinze's leadership. In the 1970s, Arinze also made friends with another rising Catholic leader: Karol Wojtyla, later known as Pope John Paul II. In 1979 he was chosen as president of the Nigerian Council of Bishops.

Despite his rising influence, Arinze had a humble image and enforced discipline among the priests under his responsibility, forbidding them specifically from driving fancy cars. When John Paul II visited Nigeria early in his papacy, he was impressed by the growth of the church under Arinze's leadership. Conscious of the dearth of Catholics in leadership positions with origins among the fast-growing Third World legions of church members, the pope invited Arinze to come to the Vatican as president of the Pontifical Council for Inter-Religious Dialogue—the chief Catholic office responsible for relations with other faiths—in 1984. The following year, John Paul II elevated Arinze to the rank of Cardinal.

Part of Arinze's outreach to the faithful over the years was a prolific body of writing. Ibadan University Press published his dissertation on Ibo religion in Nigeria in 1970, but many of his books were simple tracts aimed at ordinary Catholics. Some of them were published by Optimal Computer Solutions in Nsukka, Nigeria. Arinze's books include *The Christian and Politics* (1982), *Answering God's Call* (1983), *Africans and Christianity* (1990), *Work and Pray for Perfection* (1990), and *Christian-Muslim Relations in the Twenty First Century* (1998), published by the Center for Muslim-Christian Understanding at Georgetown University in Washington.

Organized Interfaith Prayer for Peace

The last-named title grew out of Arinze's responsibilities as the Vatican's liaison to representatives of other faiths. In 1986 he was given the job of organizing a meeting in Assisi, Italy, of 150 leaders from 15 major faiths. The goal of the meeting was to pray for world peace. Arinze took criticism among some Catholics who felt that the group prayer had elevated prayers of other religions to a level equal to those of Catholicism. Arinze wrote letters to Hindu, Muslim, and Buddhist leaders on the occasion of major religious holidays. While Arinze, according to *The Christian Century*, rejected what he called the "relativistic" idea that "all religions are equal," he believed that Catholics should not impose their faith on others.

Arinze sought common ground with Muslim groups by promoting jointly run social projects. He argued that Christians could learn from members of other faiths. "God can speak to us through other believers," he told Erminia Santangelo in an *Our Sunday Visitor* interview. "From sincere Muslims, Christians can learn, for example, the cour-

age of sincere prayer. They pray five times a day, and no matter where they are—be it the railway station or the airport—they will do it. Whereas many Christians are ashamed of making the Sign of the Cross in a restaurant or pulling out a rosary on a train."

Well-liked not only by John Paul II but also by his chief doctrinal enforcer Cardinal Joseph Ratzinger, who eventually succeeded John Paul II as pope, Arinze was first designated as *papabile,* Italian for "suitable for consideration as pope," in 1992. As John Paul's health began to decline after he was diagnosed with Parkinson's Disease in the 1990s, speculation began to swirl around Arinze increasingly often. He would not be the first African pope in the history of Catholicism—St. Gelasius I, who reigned from 492 to 496, was a black African, and other early popes, whose personal histories are sketchy, may also have come from Africa—but he would be the first African pope in modern times and only the second from outside Italy (John Paul II being the first).

Arinze discouraged such speculation and at times became mildly annoyed by it, rhetorically asking William R. Macklin of the Knight-Ridder/Tribune News Service, "Why do people appoint themselves the doctor of the pope?" John Paul II lived and remained globally active for more than a decade after Arinze was first mentioned as his potential successor, but Arinze's profile had been permanently raised. He began to speak out around the world on issues not directly connected with his Vatican post, and on these issues, Catholic conservatives liked what they heard.

Backed John Paul II's Positions

On controversial social issues, Arinze steadfastly backed the conservative positions of his mentor, John Paul II. At times, he was even more outspoken than John Paul as he spoke out against what he called (in a Georgetown University speech quoted in the *National Catholic Reporter*) "an anti-life mentality as seen in contraception, abortion, infanticide, and euthanasia." The family, Arinze contended, was "under siege. . . . It is scorned and banalized by pornography, desecrated by fornication and adultery, mocked by homosexuality, sabotaged by irregular unions, and cut in two by divorce." Liberal Catholics at Georgetown walked out on the speech, but other Catholics found Arinze an inspiration. African-American Catholic Joseph Butler, after hearing Arinze speak in New York, told Cloe Cabrera of the *Tampa Tribune* that "He said everything I longed to hear. I felt rejuvenated. I felt a sense of belonging. It was exciting."

In 2004, Arinze inserted himself into the contentious U.S. presidential campaign of that year, telling a Vatican audience (according to the *Boston Herald*) that "unambiguously pro-abortion" Catholic politicians were "not fit" to receive communion. The comments were widely seen as a slap at pro-choice Democratic candidate John Kerry, although Arinze's statement did not compel any church official to take an particular action, and Arinze himself said that it was the province of American bishops to determine the issue. He likewise said that wearers of the Rainbow Sash, a mark of support for homosexual rights, should not receive communion. Although Arinze was a hard-liner in many respects, his personal charisma won him friends across ideological divides. "He is a popular fellow," an unidentified female diplomat told Roy Carroll of the London *Guardian* newspaper. "He makes you laugh, he doesn't stand on ceremony, he answers his own phone, and he's comfortable with women."

Arinze's task of promoting dialogue between Christianity and Islam took on new urgency in the early 2000s, especially after the terrorist attacks upon the United States of September 11, 2001. He continued to speak out on interfaith issues, but John Paul II, who in his last years elevated many of his closest associates to new positions, named Arinze as the Vatican's head of the Congregation for Divine Worship and the Sacraments in 2002. A fresh round of Arinze speculation arose after John Paul II's death on April 2, 2005. As it turned out, the College of Cardinals selected Germany's Joseph Ratzinger, who had made comments favorable to Arinze's own prospects, as the new pope. The African cardinal, many of whose books had been republished in new editions, still ranked as one of the 20th century's most important religious figures, and as a possible future pope.

Books

Arinze, Francis, *Religions for Peace: A Call for Solidarity to the Religions of the World,* Doubleday, 2002.

Periodicals

Boston Herald, April 24, 2004.
Christian Century, December 12, 2001.
Guardian (London, England), October 3, 2003.
Irish Times (Dublin, Ireland), March 19, 2004.
Knight Ridder/Tribune News Service, November 17, 1994; August 11, 1999.
National Catholic Reporter, June 6, 2003.
Newsweek, April 16, 2001.
Tampa Tribune, April 19, 2005.
Winston-Salem Journal (North Carolina), April 17, 2005.

Online

"In Dialogue with a World of Believers," *Our Sunday Visitor,* http://www.catholic.net (December 6, 2005).
"Nigerian Could Be Choice for Continuing JPII's Papacy Style," Catholic News Service, http://www.catholicnews.com/jpii/cardinals/0501842.htm (December 6, 2005). □

Frederick Ashton

The choreographer most responsible for the growth of ballet in modern-day England, Sir Frederick Ashton (1904-1988) was one of the most important twentieth-century inheritors of the classical ballet tradition, developed in France and nurtured in the late nineteenth century above all in Russia.

Much loved by dance audiences, Ashton created more than 110 ballets over his long career. Though forbidding in the level of technique they

demanded from dancers, they had a direct appeal often marked by lyrical beauty and even humor. "Romantic, passionate, and funny, Frederick Ashton's choreography captures the best and worst of what it means to be human . . ." observed *Dance Magazine* writer David Vaughan. "It's a sweet, sane world as Ashton sees it. Skaters may slip and fall, but they get up. The golden age may be lost, but the joys of a country farm remain undiminished. Even a doomed courtesan's heartbreak has its own glamour. While symmetry and form have a place, they don't undermine Ashton's essential warmth and gallantry."

Raised in South America

Born in Guayaquil, Ecuador on September 17, 1904, the man who become a central figure in English cultural life spent most of his childhood in South America. His father was a low-level diplomatic official. Finally the family settled in Lima, Peru, where Ashton grew up speaking mostly Spanish; when he attended schools in England as a teenager, his classmates teased him because he spoke with a Spanish accent. He became transfixed by dance when he saw a performance by the famed Russian ballerina Anna Pavlova in Lima in 1917.

Dance was not considered a proper occupation for young men among middle-class British families of the time, and Ashton's family refused to give him the lessons he asked for. It is probable that they also identified his homosexual orientation and tried to stamp it out. But Ashton continued to pursue his interest in dance after being sent to England.

He saw the Ballets russes (Russian Ballet) led by impresario Serge Diaghilev, the leading progressive dance company of the 1910s, and in 1921 he saw the American modern dance pioneer Isadora Duncan. Finally Ashton's brother Charlie paid for a few dance lessons, and in 1922 Ashton used money saved from his job as a translator at an import-export firm to begin studies with one of Diaghilev's lead male dancers and choreographers, Léonide Massine.

Taking up the art in his late teens, Ashton was extremely atypical in the dance world; most dancers begin their training as small children. Ashton's late start may actually have contributed to his success as a classical ballet choreographer in an age when modern dance was on the rise; the standard steps of ballet, which seemed exhausted of possibilities to creative young dancers who had studied them for years, instead represented to Ashton the exciting fulfillment of a lifelong dream. Ashton dreamed of becoming a dancer himself, but another teacher, Marie Rambert, encouraged him to develop his talent at choreography instead. By 1926 Ashton had contributed a ballet called *A Tragedy of Fashion* to an English musical revue, *Riverside Nights.*

Spending part of 1928 and 1929 in Paris, Ashton finished off his choreographic training with leading classical choreographer Bronislava Nijinska. Stung by Rambert's comment (quoted by Jack Anderson of the *New York Times*) that he was "bone lazy," he created over 30 works between 1929 and 1934, many of them for Rambert's Ballet Club company. *Les Rendezvous,* an early success, depicted lovers who meet in a park. Like his contemporary George Balanchine (also born in 1904), Ashton flirted with the idea of moving to the United States; he visited in 1934 and did choreography for the modern opera *Four Saints in Three Acts,* composed by Virgil Thomson to a text by Gertrude Stein. Ashton recruited African-American dancers from Harlem nightclubs to execute his innovative choreography.

Based Ballet on Ice Skating

Balanchine went on to become a giant of American ballet, but Ashton returned to England in 1935 to take a position as resident choreographer at the Vic-Wells Ballet, later renamed Sadler's Wells Ballet and, in 1956, the Royal Ballet. This new post gave Ashton the chance to create full-scale ballets; most of his works up to that point had been for smaller companies. He remained with the company for the rest of his career, becoming its artistic director in 1963. Ashton maintained a high level of productivity through the 1930s, often inspired by a young Vic-Wells ballerina named Margot Fonteyn, later regarded as one of the great classical dancers of the middle twentieth century. One of his most characteristic works from this period was *Les patineurs* (The Skaters, 1937), to music by Giacomo Meyerbeer. Though it had no real plot, the work was instantly accessible even to audiences with little knowledge of ballet; it depicted the various personality types—lovers enjoying the winter scenery, show-offs, fearful novices—that one might encounter on an average ice rink. Ashton also created choreography for musicals and revues in the 1930s, sometimes working with American-born tap dancer Buddy Bradley.

Another comic Ashton ballet of the late 1930s was *A Wedding Bouquet,* which depicted a series of mishaps that beset a small-town wedding in France; a drunk guest has to be carried out, and the final dance of the bride and groom is a parody of the *pas de deux* of classical ballet. Ashton put the experience of the audience in first place as he planned his dances. "I had a terror of boring people," Anderson quoted him as saying. "And I wasn't concerned with being profound. The 20's and 30's were a very frivolous period and I wasn't trying to correct this; I just went with it."

Though Ashton's choreography was becoming increasingly popular, his works were sometimes criticized as lacking in seriousness. That changed, however, after the outbreak of World War II; his *Dante Sonata* was a turbulent work with a tragic spirit. Ashton served in Britain's Royal Air Force from 1941 to 1946 and returned after his discharge with *Symphonic Variations,* an abstract work that is considered one of his most important ballets. Believing that English ballet had become too literary in its orientation, he created a pure dance work. The work had its gestation in the midst of Ashton's wartime experiences. "Fred said that if he ever got through this 'bloody war,' he would make a ballet to the César Franck score [Symphonic Variations]," dance producer Wendy Ellis Soames told Allan Ulrich of *Dance Magazine.* "He envisioned angelic bodies moving through space."

Many of Ashton's ballets were large-scale productions that fit fully into the graceful Russian-French tradition in which he had been trained. Another 1946 ballet, *Cinderella,* used the composition of that title by Russian composer Sergei Prokofiev and exemplified the fairy-tale atmosphere that has endeared ballet to generations of audiences. Yet Ashton's dance language was flexible, and he responded enthusiastically to contemporary music. His *Scènes de ballet* of 1948 was based on a dry, rhythmically intricate composition by the modernist Russian-French-American composer Igor Stravinsky. According to Joan Acocella of *The New Yorker,* Ashton said he was attracted to Stravinsky's music because of its "cold, distant, uncompromising beauty."

By the 1950s, Ashton was generally considered one of the world's premier choreographers. He augmented his busy London schedule with visits to other countries, creating works for the New York City Ballet (*Illuminations,* 1950), the Royal Danish Ballet in Copenhagen (*Romeo and Juliet,* 1955), and La Scala opera house in Milan, Italy (*La valse,* 1958). Fonteyn remained one of his most frequent collaborators, and the depth of the pair's creative partnership was one of the hallmarks of postwar ballet.

Created Ingenious Realization of Elgar Work

Ashton was knighted in 1962 by Queen Elizabeth II. As artistic director of what was now the Royal Ballet between 1963 and 1970, he did not let his executive duties interfere with his creativity. In fact, the 1960s were a peak period for Ashton in terms of ballets that became ensconced in the repertories of dance companies around the world. He returned to the comic vein of his earlier works in *La fille mal gardée* (The Girl Running Wild, 1960), which was presented in the U.S. by both the American Ballet Theatre and the Joffrey Ballet. In 1968 he took on the difficult task of creating a ballet based on Edward Elgar's *Enigma Variations,* an orchestral work consisting of a series of subtle instrumental portraits of some of the composer's friends.

"In that ballet," wrote Anderson in the *New York Times,* "he evoked not only the loneliness of genius but Elgar's friends and family and the mood of England at the turn of the century as well, and evoked them with such simple details as the eating of an apple and the arrival of a telegram." Many of Ashton's ballets of the 1960s remained in the Royal Ballet repertory and that of the Joffrey Ballet in the U.S., renowned for its large collection of notated Ashton dances. Ashton retired from the Royal Ballet in 1970 and received the Dance Magazine Award that year.

Part of the reason for Ashton's professional longevity was his personal popularity in British high society. Never a public homosexual, he nonetheless made no secret of his orientation among his acquaintances. He had a sense of humor in person to match the one he displayed on the dance stage, and among those who enjoyed it was Queen Elizabeth II, whom he once taught to dance the tango. Ashton could mimic various well-known British personalities including the queen, who, it is said, retaliated with an Ashton imitation of her own when she heard about his routine. After his retirement, Ashton created the ballet *Rhapsody* for the queen's 80th birthday celebrations in 1980.

Ashton remained busy in his later years, choreographing more than 15 new ballets in addition to *Rhapsody* between 1971 and 1985. His *Etude* was featured in *The Turning Point,* a successful ballet film released in 1977. Retiring to a country home near the town of Eye in England's Suffolk region, he often returned to London to supervise revivals of his earlier works. He died at his country home on the night of August 18, 1988; some sources give his death date as August 19.

Ashton's ballets fell into a temporary decline in the years after his death, but as the hundredth anniversary of his birth approached, dance critics raised an alarm about the prospect that his works might be forgotten (dance can be written down in notation, but the process of reconstructing them is much more complicated than it is for music). Clive Barnes wrote in *Dance Magazine* that the Royal Ballet "has in practice done very poorly" by Ashton, and opined that "the lasting value of Ashton's ballets will stand the test of time if they are not sabotaged by the cruelties of history." The Ashton centenary year of 2004 brought a host of new performances of his works, as well as testimonials from the many dancers who had learned their craft as they struggled to master his graceful and appealing works.

Books

International Dictionary of Ballet, St. James, 1993.
Vaughan, David, *Frederick Ashton and His Ballets,* A. and C. Black, 1977.

Periodicals

Dance Magazine, August 1994; December 2003; July 2004.
Guardian (London, England), august 20, 1988.
New York Times, August 20, 1988.
New Yorker, August 2, 2004.
Washington Post, August 20, 1988.

Online

"Ashton, Sir Frederick," GLBTQ, An Encyclopedia of Gay, Lesbian, Bisexual, Transgender & Queer Culture, http://www .glbtq.com/arts/ashton_f.html (December 8, 2005).
"Sir Frederick Ashton," American Ballet Theatre, http://www.abt .org/education/archive/choreographers/ashton_s.html (December 8, 2005). □

B

Mariama Bâ

Senegalese novelist Mariama Bâ (1929-1981) was catapulted to international prominence with the publication of her first novel, *Un si longue lettre,* which appeared in 1980 when the author was 51 years old. At the time, the novel was a rarity in that it had been written by an African woman, and it was especially noteworthy because of Bâ's origins in the predominantly Islamic country of Senegal.

Viewed from a wider perspective, Bâ was a writer who made valuable explorations of the terrain where African traditional cultures met influences brought by European colonialism. As a so-called "postcolonial" writer with a feminist orientation, Bâ gained wide attention from Western critics and students of literature, and the influence of her work increased following her death. Bâ wrote only two novels, but they stand as vivid portraits of the difficult situations faced by women in African societies, and they remain relevant beyond a purely Senegalese context.

Descended from Civil Servants

Mariama Bâ was born in 1929 in Dakar, the capital city of Senegal, on Africa's Atlantic coast. Senegal at the time was a department of French West Africa; it had been under French control for several centuries, and the area in which Dakar now stands was a major port for the shipment of slaves to the Western hemisphere. Bâ's family had been well placed in French colonial circles for several generations; her father's father, named Sarakholé, worked as an

interpreter for French officials in the colonial city of Saint-Louis and then came to Dakar. Bâ's father was also employed by the colonial government; he was a treasury teller in the French West African government. As the French set up independent Senegalese institutions prior to pulling out of the country, he became the first Senegalese minister of health in 1956.

Bâ's mother died when Bâ was very young, and she was raised mostly by her maternal grandparents. Her upbringing was in many ways a traditional one. She grew up surrounded by the members of a large extended family, with cousins, aunts, uncles, and the spouses of all of these living at various times in the family compound overlooking the Atlantic Ocean. The generosity of Bâ's grandfather meant that the blind and the handicapped often took refuge in Bâ's yard, and Bâ's house was one of a group that surrounded a neighborhood mosque. One aspect of her traditional family life was that Bâ's grandparents did not believe that, as a girl, she should receive a formal education. Bâ's father, however, continued to take an interest in her welfare and became her advocate. He taught her to read, gave her books and asked her to recite in French, and took her with him when he worked for a time in the neighboring country of Dahomey (now Benin). He had the power to see to it that Bâ received the best education available in Senegal at the time. She was enrolled in a French-language school in Dakar to study with a woman named Berthe Maubert, after whom the school was later named.

At the same time, Bâ had to do the work expected of a young Senegalese woman. "The fact that I went to school didn't dispense me from the domestic duties little girls had to do," she told the *African Book Publishing Record (ABPR)*. "I had my turn at cooking and washing up. I learned to do my own laundry and to wield the pestle because, it was feared, 'you never know what the future might bring!' " She also studied the Koran with one of Dakar's leading Islamic clerics. Even with these conflicting demands, Bâ managed to notch the highest score in all of West Africa in a competition that won her admission to a top French language teacher-training school, the Ecole Normale de Rufisque. Since her father was out of town, it was left to Bâ's schoolmistress Berthe Maubert to take her side against the wishes of her family, who, she told the *ABPR*, "had had enough of 'all this coming and going on the road to nowhere.' "

At this new school, Bâ encountered another helpful teacher, a Mrs. Germaine Le Goff, who "taught me about myself, taught me to know myself," Bâ told the *APBR*. At the time, much French language education in Africa was devoted to training students to assimilate into European ways, but, Bâ said, "She preached for planting roots into the land and maintaining its value. . . . A fervent patriot herself, she developed our love for Africa and made available to us the means to seek enrichment. I cherish the memory of rich communions with her. . . . Her discourse outlined the new Africa." Bâ began to write. She credited, in addition to her teachers, the moral strength of her grandmother as an influence on her writing, and as a writer she would combine mastery of the European forms of the novel and the essay with a moral fortitude that had roots in her traditional belief system.

Taught High School

Bâ wrote a book about the colonial educational system and a widely discussed nationalist essay while she was still in school. She received her teaching certificate in 1947 and worked as a teacher, starting at a medical high school in Dakar, for 12 years. Bâ married Senegalese politician Obeye Diop, and the two had nine children. Life became difficult for Bâ after she and Diop divorced and she had to raise her large family alone. She began to suffer from health problems that would plague her for the rest of her life, and she had to resign from her teaching job. Later she became a regional school inspector and worked as a secretary.

Bâ's experiences provided her with raw material for two novels, which she wrote at the very end of her life. The international feminist movement added another layer to her writer's consciousness. As her children grew, Bâ joined international women's organizations that were forming African chapters, and she began to write op-ed columns for African newspapers and to lecture on such subjects as education. One of her central concerns was the institution of polygamy, which often left married women with few legal rights. Well ahead of other feminist activists, she also took on the issue of female genital mutilation, a subject that gained in prominence only toward the end of the twentieth century.

Bâ worked for some time on her first novel, *Une si longue lettre* (So Long a Letter). After it was issued in late 1979 by the Editions Nouvelles Africaines publishing house in Dakar, it quickly gained acclaim from African and French critics. Bâ wrote in French, and translations of the book into English, Dutch, German, Japanese, Russian, and Swedish soon appeared. *Une si longue lettre* won the inaugural

Noma Award for Publishing in Africa, a prize funded by a Japanese publisher. As the title indicated, the book was written in the form of a long letter—a medium that allowed Bâ to bridge the gap between African forms of spoken storytelling and the traditional structure of a novel. The central figure in the novel is Ramatoulaye, a woman whose husband, Moudou Fall, has died of a heart attack. She reflects in her letter on her own life, that of the letter's recipient, and those of other women in her circle.

Addressed Polygamy Issue

Ramatoulaye's story includes elements of Bâ's own. She is a teacher, she has 12 children, and she has combined European-style education with a traditional life. The letter recounts a crisis in Ramatoulaye's life that develops after her husband takes a second wife, a 17-year-old friend of one of his daughters. At the young woman's insistence, Ramatoulaye's husband deserts his first family. Ramatoulaye decides to stay married, but she introduces the reader to another woman, Aissatou, who has chosen the difficult path of divorce in the same situation and has begun working for the Senegalese embassy in the United States. Aissatou is the addressee of Ramatoulaye's long letter, and her situation is somewhat different from her friend's; she has married for love, but her husband has been forced by family pressures to take a second wife.

Bâ's novel also focuses on several polygamous male characters and their various motivations. *Une si longue lettre* is a keen portrait of a society in transition, several strands of which comes together at Moudou Fall's funeral. Ramatoulaye's letter recounts the funeral's aftermath, as well as the events leading up to her husband's departure and his death. One of his brothers, according to tradition, offers to make her part of his own contingent of wives, but Ramatoulaye feels that his intention is to take control of her money and property and to bring another wage-earning wife into the family, and she refuses his proposal. Ramatoulaye's own daughter, representing another stage in the development of African women's consciousness, enters the novel at the end.

Reaction to *Une si longue lettre* was not uniformly positive; some Islamic critics charged that Bâ had unfairly implied that Islam as a religion endorsed polygamy. Nevertheless, Bâ's second novel, *Un chant éclarate* (A Scarlet Song), was quickly readied for publication by Les Nouvelles Editions Africaines. *Un chant éclarate* deals with the theme of interracial marriage and again touches on polygamy and the deeper distortions of African tradition that have resulted from European colonialism. At the novel's center is a white French woman, Mireille, the daughter of a French diplomat serving in Dakar. Mireille falls in love with and marries a black Senegalese student, Ousmane, while both are studying at a university in Dakar. Her family cuts off ties with her as a result of her decision. Ousmane takes a second wife, a traditional Senegalese woman, and Mireille begins to suffer symptoms of mental illness; she finally kills the couple's only child.

In poor health for many years, Bâ died in 1981, before *Un chant éclarate* could be published. She did not live to enjoy the rewards of her own growing reputation. Her two novels were seen as representative of the growing social consciousness of African women, and Bâ became the focus of numerous studies in American and European journals. By the late 1990s *Un si longue lettre,* especially, frequently showed up around the world in college and university curricula in the fields of literature, women's studies, black studies, and the French language.

Books

Azodo, Ada Uzoamaka, *Emerging Perspectives on Mariama Bâ: Postcolonialism, Feminism, Postmodernism,* Africa World, 2003.
Contemporary Black Biography, vol. 30, Gale, 2002.
Kempen, Laura Charlotte, *Mariama Bâ, Rigoberto Menchú, and Postcolonial Feminism,* Peter Lang, 2002.
Literature of Developing Nations for Students, vol. 2, Gale, 2000.
Parekh, Pushpa Naidu, and Siga Fatima Jagne, *Postcolonial African Writers,* Greenwood, 1998.

Periodicals

African Book Publishing Record, 1980, issue 3.
Manchester Guardian Weekly, August 22, 1982.

Online

Contemporary Authors Online, Gale, 2006. Reproduced in *Biography Resource Center,* Thomson Gale, 2006, http://www.galenet.galegrou.com/servlet/BioRC (February 13, 2006).
''Mariama Bâ (1929-1981),'' Books and Writers, http://www.kirjasto.sci.fi/mba.htm (February 13, 2006).
''Mariama Bâ (1929-1981), Senegal,'' http://www.web.uflib./ufl.edu/cm/africana/ba.htm (February 13, 2006). □

Isobel Baillie

One of Britain's foremost sopranos between the two world wars, Dame Isobel Baillie (1895-1983) was particularly associated with the oratorio. She herself estimated that she had performed the most famous of all oratorios, Handel's *Messiah,* more than 1,000 times.

The oratorio, a dramatic but unstaged classical vocal work, usually on a religious theme and featuring a chorus as well as individual soloists, was found in most European musical cultures, but the English had a special affection for it. At the large choral festivals that did much to define English musical life, Baillie was a consistent presence for many years. Her voice inspired the adjective ''silvery,'' and British musicologist Richard Capell, writing in the 1954 edition of *Grove's Dictionary of Music and Musicians,* summed up the feelings of a generation this way: ''The character of Isobel Baillie's singing and her fine technique will be indicated if it is said that her performance of Brahms's Requiem has hardly been matched in her time. The trying tessitura [vocal range] of 'Ye who now sorrow'

becomes apparently negligible, and the term 'angelic' has sometimes been applied to suggest the effect, not so much personal as brightly and serenely spiritual, made here by her soaring and equable tones.'' Isobel Baillie, in other words, made beautiful singing sound easy.

Sold Piano Rolls

Red-haired and fair-skinned as a young woman, Baillie was born in Hawick, Roxburghshire, Scotland, near the English border, on March 9, 1895. Her original first name was Isabella, and she used the name Bella Baillie early in her career but changed it to Isobel at the suggestion of conductor Hamilton Harty, who felt that Bella Baillie sounded too much like the name of a music-hall performer. Baillie's father was a baker who was industrious but not an especially good manager, and her family moved from place to place in an attempt to improve its generally meager fortunes. When Baillie was five they landed in Newcastle-upon-Tyne, England, and soon after that they moved to the large industrial city of Manchester, which boasted a flourishing musical life.

Things got even harder after Baillie's father died suddenly, but she won a scholarship to the High School in Dover Street. Singing nonstop around the house from earliest childhood, she now had the chance to perform in school pageants. The teenaged Baillie got a job at a music shop, selling piano rolls and walking to work, three miles each way. Her first paid job was in a Manchester church, where she received seven shillings and spent it on bacon for her family. A teacher named T.H. Bramwell who had recognized her talent persuaded her mother to let her take voice lessons, arranging them with a Madam Jean Sadler-Fogg. She sang the soprano part in Handel's *Messiah* for the first time when she was 15 and began to find more profitable singing jobs in local churches.

Taking a job as a clerk at Manchester's city hall, Baillie met her husband, entertainer Harry Wrigley, when she was 16. Their lengthy courtship lasted through Wrigley's deployment in France during World War I and his near-amputation after suffering a case of trench foot. They married in 1918 and had a daughter, Nancy; Wrigley returned to the front after recovering and suffered severe shrapnel wounds. He became essentially a house-husband for the rest of his life, and one day Baillie, as the main family breadwinner, totaled up her freelance singing earnings and found that they exceeded her clerk's salary. She resolved to devote herself to singing full-time.

Baillie's breakthrough into the mainstream of English musical life came about after she wrote a letter in 1920 to Hamilton Harty, the conductor of Manchester's Hallé Orchestra—one of the top orchestras in Britain outside of London. Harty, it turned out, had already heard her sing and been impressed by her voice. He assigned her to sing a difficult wordless vocal part in a new work, *The Venetian Convent,* by Italian composer Alfredo Casella. Although Baillie was convinced that she had sung poorly, and her husband concurred, Harty and the critics in the next morning's papers praised Baillie's voice, and her career was launched. Harty served as Baillie's mentor and patron. He engaged her frequently to sing for the Hallé Orchestra, suggested that she change her name, warned her against taking on roles, such as those in the operas of Richard Wagner, that were too large for her voice, and convinced her to go to Italy, leaving her daughter in her mother's care, for voice lessons with the renowned teacher Gugliemo Somma. Living in a room in what she later learned was a red-light district and fending off unwanted male advances, Baillie mastered Italian and deepened her talent.

Performed at Hollywood Bowl

Baillie made her London debut in 1923 after impressing conductor Sir Henry Wood with her performance in an unpaid touring concert that she agreed to sing as a kind of audition. She was hired to sing that season at six Promenade Concerts, the "Proms" that are central features of the annual classical music season in London. Singing light operatic arias and sacred selections, Baillie was by now a familiar face in British classical music circles. She was booked for busy seasons through the late 1920s, appearing in London and with symphony orchestras in such places as Birmingham and Liverpool in addition to Manchester. Baillie bought a cottage complete with pond, ducks, and orchard, in the English countryside, and in 1933 she took a more extended vacation to visit her brother in Hawaii. Inspired by a lifelong love of movies that led her to go to the cinema two or three times a week in between performances, she decided to stop off in California, and, given a letter of introduction by her mentors Harty and

Wood, she became the first British singer to appear at the Hollywood Bowl. Baillie wrote in her autobiography, *Never Sing Louder Than Lovely,* that she "saw many of the legendary screen idols in action and even met some of them in off-screen moments: Cary Grant, for example, badly in need of a shave and concentrating on the demolition of a hamburger and beer."

Baillie was always primarily a concert singer, although she sometimes appeared in operas such as Christoph Willibald von Gluck's *Orphée,* which she performed at the Covent Garden opera house in 1937, and Charles Gounod's *Faust.* As she advanced to middle age, she became more and more identified with oratorios and other large choral works, both British and imported. She made the premiere recording of Ralph Vaughan Williams's *Serenade to Music* and sang such weighty pieces as Sir Edward Elgar's *The Kingdom.* Baillie felt at home in these pieces. On one occasion when she sang Franz Joseph Haydn's oratorio *The Creation* under the baton of conductor Sir Thomas Beecham, she wrote in *Never Sing Louder Than Lovely,* "my enthusiasm for the genre in general and *The Creation* in particular was perhaps revealed a little too earnestly, for after we had rehearsed "On mighty pens" he turned to me, beamed, and said, 'You like singing that, don't you?' I, of course, agreed." Baillie sang with the most celebrated conductors of the golden age of English orchestral music: Beecham, Sir Adrian Boult, and Malcolm Sargent. Even the famously tough Italian conductor Arturo Toscanini was quieted by her vocal charms, seizing Baillie's hands and complimenting her with a "bene, bene:" when he came to England to conduct the Johannes Brahms *German Requiem* that Richard Capell later wrote about in such glowing terms.

Frequently heard on the BBC radio network, Baillie made a large number of 78 rpm recordings between the late 1920s and the middle 1940s. Some were collected on a CD entitled *The Unforgettable Isobel Baillie,* released in the early 2000s on the Dutton label. Reviewer Robert Levine of the Classics Today website heard "an exquisite technique, a manner of singing as natural as speech, an ease in fioriture [flowery vocal passages] devoid of aspirates, divine pianissimos, absolute control at all dynamic levels, a real trill, precise but unfussy diction, and an interest in the text that is to be admired. . . . Perhaps it will strike some as precious; for the most part such wonderful singing should simply be appreciated."

Baillie sang oratorios such as Felix Mendelssohn's *Elijah* over much of her career, making 18 appearances at England's annual Three Choirs Festival. It was *Messiah* with which she was identified above all. She sang the work with the Hallé Orchestra in the early 1920s, the first time a performance of *Messiah* was broadcast on the radio, and she performed the work with the Hallé Orchestra for 26 years in a row. She also performed the work 33 times with the Royal Choral Society at London's Royal Albert Hall, appeared at a massive Handel festival organized by Sir Henry Wood in 1939, and sang it, she wrote in *Never Sing Louder Than Lovely,* "in practically every corner of the British Isles, from London, Belfast, Cardiff, and Glasgow, to Truro, Carlisle, and Aberdeen."

Sang for Arms Builders

As World War II broke out, Baillie decided to honor bookings she had made in New Zealand, to which she traveled by way of the U.S. Her ship was hit by a German shell on the way across the Atlantic. On the return trip, an American asked her where she was going, and when she answered that she was going home to England he questioned whether there would be any England left. An aggrieved Baillie bet him ten dollars that her country would survive, and soon after she landed she sent the American a letter. He never paid, but an American woman in an audience to which she told the story made good on the debt. Baillie kept performing throughout the war, despite rationing and extreme difficulty in traveling. At one point she was taken to a secret bunker inside a mountain to sing for a group of munitions workers.

Baillie never abused her voice, and her career was an unusually long one. She made appearances all over the world, including Kenya and Korea, in the 1950s. When her concert bookings finally began to wind down in the late 1950s, she found herself in demand as a teacher and gave lessons at the Royal College of Music in London (1955-57 and 1961-64), at Cornell University in Ithaca, New York (1960-61) and at the Manchester School of Music (from 1970 onward). As a teacher, Baillie stressed the importance of natural voice production. "Singing is a natural process, and the more naturally the sound is made the more beautiful a sound will emerge," she wrote in a list of rules in her autobiography. The last item on the list was "Always *listen to the sound you make and never sing louder than lovely.*"

Baillie continued to live in Manchester, giving lectures and working on her autobiography. Having been made a Commander of the Order of the British Empire in 1951, she was elevated to the rank of Dame Commander of the Order of the British Empire in 1978. She died in Manchester on September 24, 1983, at the age of 88.

Books

Baillie, Isobel, *Never Sing Louder Than Lovely,* Hutchinson, 1982.
Blom, Eric, ed., *Grove's Dictionary of Music and Musicians,* 5th ed., St. Martin's, 1954.

Online

"Isobel Baillie (Soprano)," http://www.bach-cantatas.com/Bio/Baillie-Isobel.htm (January 11, 2006).
Review of *The Unforgettable Isobel Baillie,* Classics Today, http://www.classicstoday.com/review.asp?ReviewNum=5672 (January 11, 2006). □

Louis Wayne Ballard

Louis W. Ballard (born 1931) is the most prominent Native American at work in the tradition of classical music. A noted music educator as well, he has been a pioneer in creating a place for the Native American musical heritage in the music curricula studied by children of various backgrounds.

Ballard's music has been performed at major concert halls in America and around the world, including Carnegie Hall and Lincoln Center in New York, The John F. Kennedy Performing Arts Center in Washington, D.C., and venues in Argentina, Austria, England, China, the Czech Republic, France, Germany, Hungary, Italy, Russia, and Spain. He has written music in genres ranging from chamber works to symphonies, with special emphasis on vocal music and ballet. The author of three books about Native American music, he was at once a champion of Native American traditions and a believer in the possibility of blending them with the classical music of Europe and the United States. "I was living in two worlds," Ballard told Lynn Franey of the *Kansas City Star,* recalling a music school assignment in which he arranged an Indian round dance in the style of a European composer. "The world of my culture and the world of Western music."

Grew Up on Reservation

Ballard was exposed to both worlds early in his life. He was born in the Native American town of Devil's Promenade, near Quapaw, Oklahoma, on July 8, 1931. Ballard's background was Quapaw and French on his mother's side and Cherokee and Scottish on his father's, and both Cherokee and Quapaw chiefs were among his ancestors. He was raised in the ways of the Quapaw culture, learning to sing and lead dances in the tribal tradition by the time he was 12. He was given a Quapaw name, Honganózhe, meaning "Stands with Eagles." The European-American side of Ballard's early music education came through his mother Leona, who played the piano and composed music for children. Ballard's grandmother encouraged him to take up the piano himself, and he had some lessons at a local mission.

Ballard learned to read music, and soon he was writing down original ideas of his own in musical notation. Becoming a composer was an almost unheard-of option for a young Native American at the time, however, and it took him quite a few years of studying at various institutions before he could align his education with his musical ambitions. In the early 1950s he attended Bacone College, a missionary institution affiliated with the American Baptist Church, and Northeast Oklahoma Agricultural and Mechanical College. Ballard financed his own education with a series of part-time jobs that included janitor, waiter, dishwasher, and ambulance driver. After taking classes at the University of Oklahoma he completed a music degree at the University of Tulsa in 1954 and then spent two years as director of vocal and instrumental music for the Negaloney (Oklahoma) Public Schools. In 1956 he became director of vocal music at Webster High School in Tulsa, remaining there until 1958. From 1959 to 1962 Ballard gave private music lessons while working toward his master's degree at the University of Tulsa.

Various American composers, including Edward MacDowell and Arthur Farwell, had tried to incorporate traditional Native American music into classical forms, but

Ballard's principal inspiration came instead from a Hungarian composer, Béla Bartók, whom Ballard may have encountered at Tulsa through a Hungarian-born teacher, Bela Rozsa. Bartók was an ethnomusicological researcher who recorded traditional melodies of Eastern European folk cultures and incorporated them into his own music, and Ballard set out to do the same thing with the music he had known when he was growing up.

Composed School Anthem

Even before he received his master's degree at Tulsa in 1962, Ballard was writing music with a distinctive Native American consciousness. He was present around the time of the founding of the Institute of American Indian Arts (IAIA) Museum in Santa Fe, a pioneering institution in developing contemporary expressions of Native American culture. As recorded on the Indian Country website, "You came around and were making a song of the cottonwoods," Zuni Pueblo artist Tsabetsaye told Ballard as the two recalled the institution's early days. Ballard's song became the IAIA's anthem, and from 1962 to 1970 he served first as the school's director of music and then as director of performing arts.

In the 1960s, Ballard continued his musical education, taking composition lessons with a group of internationally known composers that included French-born Darius Milhaud and the Italian Mario Castelnuovo-Tedesco, earning a doctorate in music at the College of Santa Fe in 1973. It was during this period that Ballard's music began to be widely performed outside the Native American world. Two of his first major pieces were ballets; *Koshare,* based on Hopi legends, was performed in Spain in the early 1960s, inaugurating a long record of international interest in Ballard's works, and *Jijogweh, the Witch-Water Gull* was completed in 1962.

Ballard's reputation grew with such works as *Why the Duck Has a Short Tail,* for narrator and symphony orchestra, based on a Navajo story (and performed by the Phoenix Symphony Orchestra in 1969). Another ballet, *The Four Moons,* was used in celebrations of the 60th anniversary of the state of Oklahoma. Ballard's woodwind quintet *Ritmo Indio* won a major compositional honor, the Marion Nevins MacDowell Award, and the octet *Desert Trilogy,* which had its premiere in Lubbock, Texas, in 1971, did even better, earning the composer a nomination for the Pulitzer Prize in music, perhaps the composition world's top honor. Nearly all of Ballard's music had Native American musical content or subject matter. Even the vocal cantata *Portrait of Will Rogers* could be classified according to those criteria, for the famed Oklahoma humorist sometimes remarked that his ancestors didn't come over on the Mayflower, but met the boat. Ballard's widely performed *Music for the Earth and Sky* mixed Native American and standard orchestral percussion. Some of the top symphony orchestras in the U.S., including the Philadelphia Orchestra, the Los Angeles Philharmonic, and the St. Paul Chamber Orchestra, performed his works in concert.

One of Ballard's most ambitious and important pieces was *Incident at Wounded Knee,* whose full title was *Incident at Wounded Knee for chamber orchestra, drama-* tizing the rebellion of the Sioux Indians at the locality known as Wounded Knee in South Dakota. Ballard received the commission for the work in 1973 as a Federal Bureau of Investigation agents began a controversial occupation of the Pine Ridge reservation. The work was in four movements, with different sections inspired by Native American concepts of procession, prayer, blood, war, and ritual. Premiered in Warsaw, Poland, *Incident at Wounded Knee* continued to gain performances by American orchestras, including one at Carnegie Hall in 1999.

Became BIA Music Curriculum Director

Married twice, Ballard had three children. He continued to compose new music into the 1990s, including the opera *Moontide* (1994), which had its premiere in Germany. Many of his choral and vocal works incorporated texts in Native American languages. In 1970, however, Ballard embarked on a new phase of his professional career, becoming Director of Music Curriculum Programs for the Bureau of Indian Affairs at the U.S. Department of the Interior. It was a challenging post, for the BIA was regarded with mistrust by many Native Americans as a result of decades of attempts to stamp out indigenous cultural expression in the Indian community. Ballard largely remade music education in Native American schools, introducing both traditional and modern Indian materials and encouraging the teaching of Indian instruments in an attempt to familiarize students with the musical systems of various tribes. Ballard modestly credited innovative supervisors with his freedom to incorporate Native American cultures into the formerly hostile BIA environment, but he is widely regarded as a pioneer in the use of ethnic materials in music education. Ballard made his home in Santa Fe, New Mexico, with his second wife, Ruth, a concert pianist.

Ballard's work at the BIA fed into his work on a music-educational publication, *Native American Indian Songs.* Published in 2004, it included two compact discs containing 28 songs from various Native American cultures, photographs, text translations, cultural background, and an accompany guidebook for music teachers with instructions on how to teach the songs to students. "This guidebook means a lot to me, and to Americans everywhere, including Native Americans," Ballard said in a 2004 press release. "This is America's cultural heritage. I want the tradition of our songs and our music to live on, and the best way to do that is to teach all teachers how to teach them. Simple as that." Ballard wrote two other books, *My Music Reaches the Sky* (1973) and *Music of North American Indians* (1975), as well as numerous articles.

Ballard expanded on his aims in a statement, reproduced on the website of his New Southwest Music Publishing company, that he called the Ballard Credo: "It is not enough to acknowledge that Native American Indian music is merely different from other music. What is needed in America is an awakening and reorienting of our total spiritual and cultural perspectives to embrace, understand, and learn from the Aboriginal American what motivates his musical and artistic impulses." Ballard put these ideas into practice whenever he could, even leading a group of Indian dancers and musicians in an all-Indian halftime show at a National Football League game in Washington, D.C.

Numerous forms of recognition came Ballard's way in the 1990s and 2000s. In 1991 he participated in the Meet the Composer program underwritten by the Lila Wallace Reader's Digest Foundation. He was the first American composer to be honored with a program devoted entirely to his music at the Beethovenhalle concert hall in Bonn, Germany, and he notched another first when he became the only classical composer to attain membership in the Oklahoma Music Hall of Fame. The culmination of a series of honors he received from Native American cultural organizations was a Lifetime Music Achievement Award from the organization First Americans in the Arts. In 2000, Ballard served as distinguished visiting professor of music at William Jewell College in Liberty, Missouri, where he also received an honorary doctorate in 2001. "He is a rare man," local Indian center director Justin Orr told the *Kansas City Star*'s Lynn Franey. "He has managed to capture the essence of Indian life and translate it into an artistic form, which takes great discipline." The comment might serve as a summary of a unique compositional career.

Books

Notable Native Americans, Gale, 1995.

Periodicals

Kansas City Star, April 20, 2001.
PR Newswire, October 6, 2004.

Online

"Biography," New Southwest Music Publishing Company, http://www.nswmp.com/bio.html (January 4, 2006).
"Louis W. Ballard: Composer fuses world with Native sound," Indian Country Today, http://www.indiancountry.com/content.cfm?id = 1094135642 (January 4, 2006). □

Anne Bancroft

American actress Anne Bancroft (1931-2005) had an extraordinary career that spanned over five decades, garnered one Oscar, two Tonys, and two Emmy Awards, and earned the respect of millions. Her roster of memorable characters ranged from the heroic Annie Sullivan to the predatory Mrs. Robinson to the larger-than-life Golda Meir. No mater what the role, Bancroft made it her own.

Bronx Born

Bancroft was born Anna Maria Louisa Italiano on September 17, 1931, in the Bronx borough of New York City, to Italian immigrant parents. Her mother, Mildred, was a telephone operator and her father, Michael, a pattern maker. The urge to perform was apparent in her

even as a toddler. Tom Vallance of the London *Independent* quoted Bancroft as saying, "When I was two, I could sing 'Under a Blanket of Blue.' I was so willing, so wanting, nobody had to coax me." But encouragement, especially from her mother, she did get. Even the Great Depression and her father's unemployment in the late 1930s did not stop the family from finding a way to provide the aspiring entertainer with tap dancing lessons.

At Christopher Columbus High School, Bancroft acted in student productions and briefly considered a career as a laboratory assistant. Her mother, however, championed the young girl's dreams and insisted that she enroll at the American Academy of Dramatic Arts. Bancroft studied a year there, and began to perform on radio and television, at first as Anne Italiano, and then as Anne Marno. She supplemented her income by working as a salesgirl and as an English teacher to noted Peruvian singer Yma Sumac. Early television credits included *The Torrents of Spring* and *The Goldbergs*. Then in 1952, Anne Bancroft was born.

Hollywood—Take One

In one of those quirks of fate that often become the stuff of legend, Bancroft helped a fellow actor by reading in his screen test for 20th Century Fox, but it was Bancroft, not her friend, who was offered a contract with the studio. So Bancroft headed west. Once in Hollywood, she was given a list of possible screen names from which to choose. The London *Observer*'s Philip French quoted her simple explanation for her choice as, "Bancroft was the only one with any dignity." That dignity was not immediately transferred to Bancroft's career, however, as the next five years and 15 movies proved largely unsuited to her talents. *Time*'s Richard Corliss described this period: "She was groomed as a standard babe when Hollywood signed her at 20. It was like fitting a firestorm for a corset."

Bancroft made her film debut with her new name in 1952's *Don't Bother To Knock*. Starring Marilyn Monroe and Richard Widmark, the movie gave Monroe her first big dramatic role and featured Bancroft as a cabaret singer, but hardly made Bancroft a household name. Other films of that time included *The Kid from Left Field* (1953), *Gorilla at Large* (1954), and *Demetrius and the Gladiators* (1954). After her contract with Fox lapsed, Bancroft remained in California for a time as an independent artist, appearing in such movies as *New York Confidential* (1955), *The Last Frontier* (1955), *Walk the Proud Land* (1956), and *Nightfall* (1957). But neither did these later efforts bring Bancroft any particular notice.

Disillusioned by her stalled career and a failed marriage to building contractor Martin May, Bancroft decided to regroup. Brian Baxter of the *Guardian* quoted her recollections: "Life was a shambles. I was terribly immature. I was going steadily downhill in terms of self-respect and dignity." So Bancroft made the sensible choice of so many before her and thousands yet to come—she went home.

Two Tonys and an Oscar

After returning to New York in 1957, Bancroft lived at home and put her life back in order. She studied with a vocal coach, went into therapy, and appeared in such television anthologies as *Playhouse 90* and the *Lux Video Theater*. At least as important, she began to take acting classes with famed Viennese actor/director Herbert Berghof, whose eminent HB Studio should not be confused with the Actors' Studio, although both are located in New York City. In Bancroft's obituary in the *Independent*, Vallance quoted her recollections of those classes: "It was the beginning of a whole new approach to acting, a deeper, more fulfilling, and more thinking approach. I learned to think a little, to set certain tasks for myself. My work became much more exciting." Her career became much more exciting as well.

In January of 1958 Bancroft made her Broadway debut in William Gibson's *Two for the Seesaw*. The two-person play featured her as a bohemian girl from the Bronx who has an affair with a married businessman (Henry Fonda). It was an unmitigated success, with such glowing reviews as that of John McLain's of the *N.Y. Journal America*, as quoted by Les Spindle in *Back Stage West*: "Bancroft threatens at times to take the entire theatre under her arm and go home. She can swear outlandishly without being at all vulgar; in the next sentence, she can break your heart." The plaudits were topped off with Bancroft's winning a Tony Award for best featured actress in 1958, and her lagging career was jump-started.

The following year, another William Gibson play cemented Bancroft's reputation. She was cast as Helen Keller's extraordinary teacher, Annie Sullivan, in *The Miracle Worker*, with Patty Duke as Keller. Duke recalled the mo-

ment in the production when Bancroft's character announced to Keller's parents that she had finally broken through to their daughter. She told Spindle, "The sound that she had in her voice [at that moment] transported every creature in the theatre to the place where you find lost souls." Critics and audiences agreed, and Bancroft was awarded another Tony Award, this time for Best Actress, in 1960. The triumph was rendered even more delicious when Gibson and director Arthur Penn insisted that she reprise the role on film, against Hollywood's wishes. That performance earned Bancroft an Academy Award for Best Actress in 1963. The formerly frustrated actress had both conquered Broadway and returned to Hollywood as a star.

An Extraordinary Career

As a newly-respectful Hollywood beckoned, Bancroft appeared determined to tackle it on her own terms. Independence, intelligence, and a fair amount of non-conformity with the star system seemed to dictate her subsequent career choices. This relative autonomy was likely partially fueled by her marriage to actor/director Mel Brooks in 1964. Many found the match an odd one—he was the fast-talking funny man from Brooklyn and she was the cool beauty with more than a dash of class. But the partnership endured over forty years, and the marriage produced one child, a son, Maximilian. Director Robert Allen Ackerman described the pair's relationship to Gregg Kilday of the *Hollywood Reporter* as "one of the great show business love stories of all time. They were madly in love with each other, the most inseparable, devoted, loving couple I have ever known. He could make her laugh so hard—she thought he was the funniest man, and she was as funny as he was. She could keep up with him, and he never stopped feeling how beautiful and talented she was." Such a strong relationship, along with having with a solid career of her own, was bound to give Bancroft a sense of security and keep her priorities in line.

Bancroft's Hollywood career was a rich and varied one that yielded four more Academy Award nominations, although no more wins. Beginning with her Oscar-nominated performance in 1964's *The Pumpkin Eater*, and moving on to 1965's *The Slender Thread* and 1966's *Seven Women*, her initial outing as a movie star had her specializing in women who were victimized by men in one way or another. Thus, it must have been refreshing to read the script for what was to become, for good or ill, Bancroft's most famous role: that of the coolly predatory Mrs. Robinson in Mike Nichols's *The Graduate* in 1967. The character of a bored, middle-class housewife who seduces a young man (Dustin Hoffman) interested in her daughter was summarily turned down by other actresses as too insulting. Bancroft, however, only six years older than her co-star, sunk her teeth into the part and put an indelible stamp on the role that helped turn the film into a cultural phenomenon. But the huge success, which nabbed Bancroft another Oscar nomination, was something of a mixed blessing, in that its star never entirely escaped the character's clutches. Unlike Annie Sullivan, for instance, Mrs. Robinson and Anne Bancroft were forever one.

Whatever her possible misgivings about her most remembered role, Bancroft was too good an actress to rest.

She took a comic turn as Edna Edison in Neil Simon's *The Prisoner of Second Avenue* in 1975, received another Oscar nod for the role of Emma Jacklin in 1977's *The Turning Point,* and appeared with her husband in 1983's *To Be or Not to Be.* The year 1984 saw her in *Garbo Talks,* 1985, in her fourth Oscar-nominated performance in *Agnes of God,* and 1986, she starred in *'Night, Mother.* Her many other feature films included *84 Charing Cross Road* (1987), *Torch Song Trilogy* (1988), *Honeymoon in Vegas* (1992), *Home for the Holidays* (1995), *G.I. Jane* (1997), *Great Expectations* (1998), and *Heartbreakers* (2001).

Nor did Bancroft neglect the stage or television. She returned to Broadway in *Mother Courage and Her Children* (1963), *The Devils* (1965), *The Little Foxes* (1967), *A Cry of Players* (1968), the Tony-nominated *Golda* (1977), and *Duet for One* (1981). Among television work that included the Emmy-nominated *Broadway Bound* (1992), *Mrs. Cage* (1992), and *Haven* (2001), Bancroft also appeared in the *Oldest Living Confederate Widow Tells All* (1994) and *The Roman Spring of Mrs. Stone* (2003). She did receive two Emmy Awards, in addition to her Oscar and two Tonys, one for 1970's *Annie: The Woman in the Life of a Man,* and the other for 1999's *Deep in My Heart.* It was a rare feat to win top accolades across performance mediums as she did, but Bancroft had long since proven herself an uncommon actress.

Falling Star

By 2005 Bancroft's remarkable career had spanned over 50 years. But failing health brought her run to an untimely end. On June 6, 2005, Bancroft died in New York City at the age of 73. Two nights later, the lights on Broadway theater marquees were all dimmed in her honor. Friends and fans all over the world mourned the passing of this indomitable spirit and superior talent.

Duke told Mark Harris of *Entertainment Weekly,* "She taught me . . . the ethics and discipline of the theater. And she also had one of the best senses of humor in the world." Nichols characterized her for Les Spindle in *Back Stage West*: "Her combination of brains, humor, frankness, and sense were unlike any other artist. Her beauty was constantly shifting with her roles, and, because she was a consummate actress, she changed radically for every part." Yet, producer David Geffen may have described Bancroft most succinctly when he told *People,* "She was the consummate everything. Actress, comedienne, beauty, mother and wife. She made it all look easy."

Periodicals

American Theatre, September 2005.
Back Stage West, June 23, 2005.
Daily Telegraph (London, England), June 9, 2005.
Entertainment Weekly, June 17, 2005.
Guardian (London, England), June 9, 2005.
Hollywood Reporter, June 8, 2005.
Independent (London, England), June 9, 2005.
New York Times, June 8, 2005.
Observer (London, England), June 12, 2005.
People, June 20, 2005.
Star-Ledger (Newark, NJ), June 8, 2005.
Time, June 20, 2005.
Variety, June 13, 2005.

Online

"Actress Anne Bancroft Dead at 73; Tony-Winner Was Helen Keller's Hope in *Miracle Worker,*" *Playbill,* June 7, 2005, http://www.playbill.com/news/article/print/93413.html (January 14, 2006).
"Actress Anne Bancroft Dies," CNN, June 7, 2005, http://www.cnn.com/2005/SHOWBIZ/Movies/06/07/bancroft.obit (January 14, 2006).
"Anne Bancroft," IBDB, http://www.ibdb.com/person.asp?id=66812 (January 14, 2006).
"Anne Bancroft," IMDb, http://www.imdb.com/name/nm0000843/ (January 14, 2006).
"HB Studio Alumni," http://www.hbstudio.org/hbmenu.html (January 22, 2006). □

Jean Batten

The daring solo flights of New Zealand's Jean Gardner Batten (1909-1982) were widely chronicled in the world's newspapers and newsreels during the 1930s. She set several aviation records for long-distance travel between Britain and Australasia, a trip of more than 14,000 miles that took her over three-fifths of the Earth's entire circumference. Along with Amelia Earhart (1897-1937), who disappeared forever during one such flight, Batten was one of the era's celebrity aviatrixes whose exploits captured the public imagination.

Batten was born on September 15, 1909, in Rotorua, a spa town on the North Island of New Zealand. Her father Fred was a dentist, while Batten's mother Ellen had an independent, feminist streak that was passed on to the family's only daughter. When Batten was four, the family moved to Auckland, New Zealand's largest city, where she attended private schools. Her parents' marriage was a troubled one, riven by financial worries and Fred's adultery, and they divorced in 1920, the year she turned eleven. Batten stayed with Ellen, while her brothers lived with their father. Eventually the two sides of the family would cease all contact with one another.

Determined to Fly

Batten's mother encouraged her daughter's talents and ambitions, and there was talk of her pursuing a career as a concert pianist. But in 1928, Fred took his attractive, spirited daughter along to an evening outing in Auckland where the featured speaker was the aviator Charles Kingsford-Smith (1897-1935). "Smithy," as he was known, was one of Australia's most celebrated heroes of the era, and had achieved several firsts in Australasian aviation in its early years. He was also the first pilot to fly from Australia to the United States by way of the challenging eastward route.

Batten charmed Smithy when she was introduced to him after dinner, and told him that she, too, was going to become a pilot. Smithy gave her two pieces of advice: don't fly at night, and don't attempt to break any male flier's records. Both of these cautions, she later joked, she willfully ignored. Her father was adamantly opposed to her ambition, with one reason being that flying was quite dangerous at the time. Engine failure and other technical issues often led to fatal crashes, and it was also considered a rather unsuitable pursuit for a young woman from a middle-class family. Batten's mother, not surprisingly, took the contrary view and encouraged her daughter's aspirations. In 1930, the two women moved to London, England, where Batten's brother John had found some minor success as a film actor.

Batten signed up for flying lessons at the London Aero Club. She often asserted her goal to fellow club members, almost all of whom were men: she planned to become the first person to fly between England and New Zealand. In December of 1931, she qualified for her private pilot's license, and within a year had received a commercial license as well. To round out her education in aviation, she took courses in plane mechanics and maintenance, and impressed the men of the Club with her willingness to get her hands dirty in the grittier side work that flying entailed.

Bought a Prince's Former Plane

Batten needed her own plane in order to fulfill her dream, however. She sold her prized piano to raise some funds, and managed to secure the rest thanks to the devotion

of one of her growing legion of male admirers. A scion of a wealthy textile-merchant family helped her obtain a Gipsy Moth biplane that had changed hands several times after its original owner, the Prince of Wales, first flew it a decade earlier. The Gipsy Moth was a lightweight, open-air plane that could seat two. Built by the de Havilland Aircraft Company in Hertfordshire, England, it was one of the more affordable and reliable planes of the era, and was used in a number of record-setting flights.

Batten first set out to best the record of Amy Johnson (1903-1941), a college-educated London secretary who had taken up flying as a hobby. In May of 1930, Johnson had become the first woman to fly from England to Australia, and completed her 10,500-mile trip in 20 days, with several stops for refueling and rest along the way. Such trips were both arduous and long; navigation instruments at the time were primitive, and the top cruising speed of the Gipsy Moth-which Johnson also flew-was just 80 miles an hour.

In April of 1933, Batten departed England and made her way across Europe. After flying through sandstorms, however, she was forced to come down in the Balochistan region of southwest Pakistan. The landing damaged her propeller, but "good-tempered Baluch villagers brought her by camel to Bela," the *Times* of London reported on April 15. The overseas correspondent further noted the aviatrix, as women pilots were called in this era, then hitched an overnight ride in a truck to get across the Hubb Mountains to Karachi, where she planned to pick up a new propeller and find a pilot who would fly her back to her plane.

Just how dangerous such flights were at the time, before pilots used the two-way radio communication that became standard in aviation after World War II, was illustrated in the same London *Times* article. Its correspondent mentioned a Captain Lancaster, of whom "no news has been received." The story noted that Lancaster, flying from England to Cape Town, South Africa, was last seen taking off near a Sahara Desert oasis en route to Niger. His wrecked plane, and mummified remains, were not discovered until 1962.

Set New Women's Record

Batten's second attempt was also cut short by technical troubles. After inexplicably running out of fuel, she was forced to make an emergency landing near Rome, which once again damaged her plane and quashed her hope of beating Amy Johnson's record. Though these exploits had been unsuccessful, they did serve to make Batten famous for trying. A year after her first try, Batten left England on May 8, 1934, and made her final landing in Darwin, a city at the northern tip of Australia, on May 23. Clocking in a time of 14 days and 22 hours, she beat Johnson's flight by a stunning four and a half days.

Greeted by crowds in Darwin, Batten returned to her native New Zealand by boat, and was honored there, too. She made a six-week tour of the country, speaking about her feat to rapt audiences, before flying back to England. She still planned, however, to make the England-New Zealand flight, which was a longer distance to cover and added more than 3,700 extra miles to the flight plan. She managed to buy another British-built plane, a Percival Gull that had actual brakes for landing as well as a second fuel tank, with the income she earned from speaking engagements. Endorsement deals also provided some extra cash, including a contract to appear in advertising for Castrol motor oil. Blessed with model-like good looks, Batten often packed evening dresses in her small carry-on for the formal receptions held in her honor, and when photojournalists rushed to greet her plane on its much-anticipated landings, she emerged from what had undoubtedly been a grueling voyage wearing makeup and a glamorous white suit.

Batten planned to test her new plane's long-distance capability with a jaunt from West Africa to Brazil. She hoped to break the England-to-Brazil record set by a Scottish aviator, Jim Mollison, of 85 hours and 20 minutes back in 1933. Batten left England, and on November 11, 1935, flew from France to Casablanca, Morocco, inadvertently setting a new speed record for that route of under ten hours. She then headed south to Senegal, her African departure point, and encountered terrible weather as she crossed the Equator, which disoriented her and made her instruments difficult to read. For a time, she later said, she believed she had veered off course, but when the skies cleared she saw cargo ships, and knew she had stayed on course. She landed safely in Port Natal, Brazil, with a time of 61 hours and 15 minutes for the 5,000-mile flight, and beat Mollison's record by a full day.

Made Treacherous Crossing

Batten's fame throughout England was immense, and she was often romantically linked with a number of prominent gentlemen. Newspapers of the era dubbed her the ''Garbo of the Skies'' for her glamour and apparent nerves of steel. Those would be put to use once again when she finally departed for her historic England-to-Auckland flight on October 5, 1936. She landed six days later in Sydney, Australia, and was greeted by huge crowds once again.

The final leg of Batten's journey, however, would be its most perilous: the thousand-plus miles over the Tasman Sea. This body of water separated Australia and New Zealand, and had wrecked many a ship, for its proximity to Antarctica and other geographic features meant strong currents and often-violent weather. A newspaper editorial writer asserted that Batten was foolish to try it, for if something were to go amiss, it would be a costly effort to rescue her. In response, she issued a tersely worded statement. ''If I go down in the sea no one must fly out and look for me,'' she asserted, according to the Web site New Zealand Edge. ''I have chosen to make this flight, and I am confident I can make it, but I have no wish to imperil the lives of others or cause trouble or expense to my country.''

Batten took off in the early morning hours of October 16, 1936, and landed safely in Auckland ten and a half hours later. Predictably, she encountered bad weather over the Tasman Sea, but had not only managed to beat the previous record on the route, set by a male aviator two years earlier, but also became the first woman ever to fly it. When she landed at Auckland, a traffic jam stretched some 13 miles as scores of New Zealanders flocked to greet her. Her feat also included a new record set for an England-to-New Zealand flight, a distance of more than 14,200 miles.

Her Final Flight

Feted across New Zealand, Batten was honored by her native land's indigenous Maori community, who named her *Hine-o-te-Rangi,* or Daughter of the Skies, in a tribal ceremony. She spent several months there, and flew back to England in October of 1937, breaking the solo record from Australia to England by clocking in a time of five days and 18 hours. The London *Times* account of her arrival in England—once again, by enthusiastic crowds that rushed at her—also reported that a male pilot, a one Mr. Broadbent, was already trying to beat her England-to-Australia record, but had been forced to land in the Iraqi desert. There, the correspondent noted, Broadbent borrowed a donkey from the locals and rode four miles to find gasoline.

That flight would be Batten's last attempt to set an aviation record. During World War II, she helped raise funds and recruitment numbers for the Royal Air Force (RAF), but was not asked to serve as a ferry pilot for the RAF's Air Transport Auxiliary, which was the only opportunity for qualified women pilots to fly in the war effort. Her rival, Amy Johnson, was one of those ferry pilots, but died in 1941 when her plane crashed and she drowned in a Thames estuary.

Batten's end is perhaps even more tragic. She became a recluse in her later years, especially after the 1965 death of her mother, with whom she had lived in Jamaica, then in Tenerife, one of the seven Canary Islands in the Atlantic. Batten eventually settled in another Spanish-owned island territory, Majorca, where a dog bit her in 1982. The wound became infected, went untreated, and killed her. The once-celebrated aviatrix was buried in a pauper's grave on the island. Friends who corresponded with her began to worry when they had not heard from her in some time, and a cursory inquiry was launched but soon dropped. Finally, a documentary filmmaker and writer, Ian Mackersey, went to Majorca in search of her, and discovered that she had died five years earlier.

Batten's Percival Gull plane is preserved at Auckland Airport, where the international terminal is named in her honor.

Periodicals

Aviation History, January 2000.

Times (London, England), April 15, 1933; May 24, 1934; December 24, 1935; December 30, 1935; July 25, 1936; October 17, 1936; October 25, 1937; July 11, 1938; September 29, 1987.

Online

''Hine-o-te-Rangi: Daughter of the Skies,'' New Zealand Edge, http://www.nzedge.com/heroes/batten.html (February 19, 2006). □

David Beckham

British soccer player David Beckham (born 1975) emerged as one of the game's standouts in the late 1990s, winning fans both inside and outside the game with his spectacular play and with charisma that attracted enormous amounts of publicity.

On the field, Beckham was a star among others of equal brightness, a crowd-pleasing player with a dramatic style marked by a talent for scoring goals with long kicks that might, to the consternation of defenders, either scream forward at blinding speed or veer off in freakish curves. Off the field, Beckham was an international celebrity that few other athletes—and indeed few others in any field of endeavor—could match for the ability to command sheer public fascination. With a flair for fashion and a pop-star wife, Beckham bounced back from career disappointments and emerged more successful than ever. In the United States, the one place where household-name status eluded him, his reputation was helped along by the success of "Bend It Like Beckham," a gentle British film comedy that dealt with his career only indirectly.

Born to Soccer Fans

David Robert Joseph Beckham grew up in modest circumstances, and his transition to member of the jet set involved a period of adjustment. He was born in the Leytonstone area of London's East End on May 2, 1975 to David (known as "Ted") Beckham, a gas appliance installer, and his wife Sandra, a hair stylist. Both parents, and Ted Beckham's father as well, were passionate soccer fans, although father and grandfather disagreed over the relative merits of the rival Manchester United and Arsenal clubs. The family was pleased to encourage young David Beckham when he began to show unusual talent with a soccer ball, and he became a child star with the Ridgeway Rovers youth team when he was eight. Beckham's parents exhorted him to practice hard, and he had a natural work ethic that never flagged even during rough spots in his professional career. He tried out various sports in school, including rugby and distance racing, but soccer always came first. "I had no other career choices," he told *Sports Illustrated for Kids.* "The buzz I get from playing football [soccer] remains the same as it was when I was a kid growing up in the East End of London."

Beckham's grandfather came to the rescue as the family struggled to scrape together $230 so that the 11-year-old Beckham could attend a soccer camp run by former Manchester United star Bobby Charlton. Though he was too small for most of England's youth leagues, his abilities were obvious, and he won a national soccer skills tournament organized by Charlton, an event similar to Punt, Pass & Kick in the U.S. Manchester United scouts kept an eye on the standout youngster, grooming Beckham with summer training programs in between jobs he took—including one cleaning up drink containers at a dog track—to supplement the family income. When he was 14, Beckham signed a statement of intention to join the Manchester United organization, and in 1991 he joined the team's official training program.

Though he was only 16, and Manchester was several hours away from London, Beckham adapted confidently to life in the world of big-time sports. He led Manchester United's junior team to a Football Association (FA) championship, a nationwide crown, in 1992. Moving up to the "Man U" first team, a step below its top Premier League squad, the following year, he officially turned professional. Beckham was loaned to the lower-level Preston North End team in 1994 and 1995—a demotion that might have bitterly disappointed many players, but one that Beckham saw as an opportunity to gain large amounts of playing time, build toughness, and work on weak points in his game. Manchester's decision and Beckham's determination paid off, and he took the field for Manchester United in a scoreless game against Leeds on April 2, 1995.

Thought to be looking at a rebuilding year, Manchester United was energized by the presence of its new talent in the 1995-96 season. Beckham scored seven goals in 33 Premier League games, and the team won both the FA Cup and the Premier League title. A prime example of Beckham's ability to make headlines came at the beginning of the next season in a match against the Wimbledon team: he noticed that the opposing team's goalie had paused several steps away from the net and let fly a 60-yard curving kick from the other end of field. He scored, and television commentators began to talk about him more often. He was voted

Young Player of the Year for the 1996-97 season as Manchester United won its second league title in a row.

Dated Posh Spice

Off the field, things were likewise going well for Beckham. In the spring of 1997 he began dating Victoria Adams, better known as Posh Spice. She was one of the Spice Girls, a pop group then at the height of its fame among British female teens, and tabloid newspapers went wild with breathless news of the latest doings of "Posh and Becks." The attraction was instant and mutual if reports at the time are to be believed. When she was shown Beckham's picture, Adams said in a *Sun* interview quoted by Joanna Blonska and Alex Tresniowski of *People*, "I had no idea who he was, but I remember thinking one word: gorgeous." Beckham noticed Adams in a Spice Girls video on television. "That's the girl for me, and I'm going to get her," he told a teammate (as quoted by *People*'s Michelle Tauber). "She's my idea of perfection."

Whether naturally or by calculation, Beckham maximized the exposure that came from the romance. On an Asian vacation with Adams, he was photographed in a sarong, and from then on he showed a knack for grabbing newspaper space with a new look. He signed the first of numerous endorsement deals, a seven-year, multimillion-dollar pact with the Adidas athletic-shoe firm. Threats from a stalker worried Beckham, but he dealt well with the rising pressures of top-level fame. Beckham and Adams stayed in touch by phone as each trotted the globe, and Adams seemed to be genuinely supportive of her sports-star boyfriend as he suffered through his first brush with fan disillusionment.

The occasion was the 1998 World Cup, in the run-up to which Beckham had played well but had been accused by coach Glenn Hoddle of not focusing on the tournament. After he was benched in two matches against Colombia's team, his temper flared in a second-round match against Britain's archrival Argentina, a nation with which Britain had gone to war in the Falkland Islands not long before. Given a red card penalty and sent out of the game following a kicking foul against Argentine player Diego Simeone, who had smashed into Beckham's back, Beckham left the British team short-manned. Britain lost the game on a penalty kick and was eliminated from the tournament, with the blame, as he himself admitted, resting mostly at Beckham's feet. One particularly merciless tabloid newspaper termed him an idiot in its headline.

Though he endured boos at the beginning of the 1998-99 season, he persevered and worked his way back into fans' favor with hard work on the field. Voted the team's most valuable player that year, he was a key contributor to Manchester United's triple Premier League, FA Cup, and European Cup championships. News of Victoria's pregnancy had brightened Beckham's mood, and their son Brooklyn was born on March 4, 1999. They were married on July 4, 1999, in an $800,000 ceremony held at an Irish castle and featuring a wedding cake topped with sculptures of an almost-nude bride-and-groom pair. They moved into a $4 million estate in England's Hertfordshire region that was dubbed Beckingham Palace; it had its own recording studio,

and the walls of one of its bathrooms were covered entirely with pictures of Audrey Hepburn, Victoria Beckham's favorite actress.

Avenged Argentina Disaster

For the next several years, Beckham went through cycles of public adulation and disillusionment. He shaved off all his hair, then wore it in cornrows, and he anticipated the "metrosexual" look by wearing nail polish at times. On the field he had hot streaks and was becoming more and more consistently recognized as one of the best players in the world. In 2000 he was edged out by boxer Lennox Lewis for the title of BBC Sports Personality of the Year, but he won the award in 2001. In June of 2002 Beckham demanded and received a payment of $32,000 a week from Manchester for his image rights, over and above his salary as a player, which was already enough to make him the best-compensated player in the world. Despite a series of injuries that attracted get-well wishes from Britons from Prime Minister Tony Blair on down, he delivered on the field; in a 2002 World Cup match against Argentina, Beckham avenged the 1998 fiasco by netting a penalty kick after shrugging off a conciliatory handshake from a player who had earlier goaded him into losing his temper.

Beckham's second son, Romeo, was born in September of 2002 (a third son, Cruz, was born February 20, 2005). In 2003 Queen Elizabeth II bestowed upon Beckham the title of Officer of the Order of the British Empire. He continued his involvement in British sports, playing for British national teams and working behind the scenes to promote London's ultimately successful bid for the 2012 Summer Olympics. In June of 2003, however, after clashes with Manchester United coach Alex Ferguson, Beckham signed with a team in Spain. The Real Madrid (Royal Madrid) club was something of a dream team, stocked with international superstars such as France's Zinedine Zidane and the single-named Brazilian striker Ronaldo. Beckham, entering his prime playing years, was trying to take his game to yet a higher level.

The four-year contract netted Beckham an estimated $41 million. Real Madrid shirts with Beckham's name sold out in one day, and his move to Spain topped international headlines. Despite all the hoopla, Spanish fans were cool to Beckham as Real Madrid floundered in 2003 and 2004. His claim that he had no time to learn Spanish, and Victoria's allegation that Madrid smelled like garlic, did not help his image. But Beckham's work ethic once again carried the day; after he agreed to play in the unfamiliar and highly physical position of defensive midfielder, things improved.

Beckham's personal life suffered in the crucible of superstardom. The Beckham family had a scare when an intruder wielding a gasoline can climbed the wall of their English estate while Beckham was at a team practice in Spain; the intruder was stopped by guards. Allegations of extramarital affairs, most notably by his former personal assistant Rebecca Loos, dogged Beckham and drove tabloids into high gear. But the marriage endured, and Beckham became even more of a true British icon when an unusual video portrait of him was installed at London's venerable National Portrait Gallery.

Slated as captain of Britain's World Cup team in 2006, Beckham continued to play for Real Madrid and had few mountains left to climb on the soccer field. One major challenge facing him in the mid-2000s was to extend his popularity in the comparatively soccer-deprived United States. He was aided in that quest by the makers of the 2003 British film ''Bend It Like Beckham,'' which depicted an Indo-British girl who hopes, against her family's wishes to become a soccer player. Beckham was shown only once, walking through an airport. But the film, an unexpected hit in America, introduced his name and his fame to Britain's former colonies, and Beckham began to snare American endorsement deals. His knack for putting himself in the middle of fashion tastemaking was undiminished, and he began to form friendships with hip-hop mogul P. Diddy and R&B star Usher. With several years of playing still ahead of him, David Beckham seemed well on the way to becoming an athlete like very few others—Michael Jordan and Muhammad Ali were named as comparisons—whose names were instantly known all over the world.

Books

Beckham, David, with Tom Watt, *Beckham: Both Feet on the Ground,* HarperCollins, 2003.

Periodicals

Economist (U.S. ed.), September 17, 2005.
People, May 4, 1998, p. 71; June 9, 2003.
Sports Illustrated for Kids, March 1, 2005.
Time International, May 10, 2004.
Vanity Fair, July 2004.

Online

''Beckham Joins Real Madrid,'' BBC Sports, http://news.bbc.co .uk/sport2/hi/football/1998868.stm (November 4, 2005).
''David Beckham,'' JockBio.com, http://www.jockbio.com/Bios/ Beckham/Beckham_bio.html (November 4, 2005).
''David Beckham,'' Real Madrid soccer club, http://www .realmadrid.com (November 4, 2005). □

Heinrich Ignaz Franz von Biber

Composer Heinrich Ignaz Franz von Biber (1644-1704) wrote some of the most imaginative music of the Baroque era in Germany. His music increased sharply in popularity between the late 1980s and the early 2000s. A highly talented violinist himself, he wrote difficult music that continues to challenge violinists today, and his music for other instruments was equally original.

Living and working in Austria and in German-speaking Bohemia (now part of the Czech Republic) in the late 1600s, Biber (pronounced BEE-ber) employed un-usual and arcane violin techniques such as scordatura (retuning the violin's strings) to produce sounds from the instrument that no other composer has called for, before or since. Working his way up from modest origins—a composer during this period was often considered no more than a servant of a powerful family or ecclesiastical authority—Biber gained renown as deputy music director and later music director to the Archbishop of Salzburg, Maximilian Gandolph von Khuenburg. In later years he redirected his compositional efforts from violin music to the more sumptuous genres of opera and choral music, but many of his later works have unfortunately been lost.

Skipped Out on Instrument-Buying Trip

Biber was born around August 12, 1644 in Wartenberg, Bohemia, a German-speaking region near what is now the Czech city of Liberec. He may have taken music lessons with a local organist and received a basic education in a Jesuit school. Little is known of his background and early life. His birthplace was part of an estate owned by the brother of the powerful Bishop of Olmütz, and after he did a brief stint as a musician in the employ of a prince in Graz, Austria, a violinist friend, the Czech-born performer Pavel Vejvanovsky, arranged a job for Biber in the bishop's musical retinue. Even in his early 20s, Biber was a compelling violin performer who gained friends and influence around Bohemia, and he soon decided he was destined for bigger things. When the bishop sent him on a trip in 1670 to purchase new violins for his orchestra, Biber quietly left town. He made his way to Salzburg in western Austria, a city rich in church music where Mozart later was born and began his career, and his talents quickly won him a place in the archbishop's orchestra.

The Bishop of Olmütz was not pleased by this turn of events, and Biber later tried to atone for his insult by composing new music and sending it to the bishop. Nevertheless, Biber's decision proved a smart one. When he was hired, his official status was equivalent to that of the archbishop's servants who carried firewood. But the fortunes of a composer in the 1600s and 1700s often depended on the attitude toward music of the powerful church official or aristocratic family for whom the composer worked, and Archbishop Khuenberg was a lover of music—specifically of the violin and the other relatively new members of the stringed-instrument family that were undergoing rapid technical development and attracting a new breed of virtuoso performers.

Biber was one of those performers, and he was part of a tradition of German and Austrian violinist-composers that included Johann Paul von Westhoff and Johann Heinrich Schmelzer. These figures did not have the international fame of Italy's Arcangelo Corelli, who laid down technical and compositional foundations for violin music that in many cases have persisted to the present time. The Germanic tradition, however, led directly to the awe-inspiring solo violin works of Johann Sebastian Bach, and Biber gained admirers as far afield as England. A hundred years later, the English essayist and music historian Charles Burney would write (according to Alex Ross of the *New*

York Times) that "of the violin players of the last century, Biber seems to have been the best, and his solos are the most difficult and most fanciful of any music I have seen of the same period."

A presumably early work by Biber, the *Sonata representativa*, shows the composer's imagination at its most vivid. Programmatic music, or music that depicts non-musical beings, scenes, or stories, was common in the Baroque era (1600-1750), but Biber here took it to a new extreme in a sonata in which the violin is made to imitate a whole menagerie of animals including the nightingale, cuckoo, frog, hen, quail, rooster, frog, and cat. Various unusual violin techniques, including the sounding of harmonics on the instrument's strings, are pressed into service in Biber's little animal portraits.

Performed for Holy Roman Emperor

The Catholic Church in Austria during this period was both an ecclesiastical and a civil authority, for much of Austria was part of the Holy Roman Empire, the lands directly under the rule of the church in Rome. Biber wrote both sacred and secular music for the archbishop, and his work quickly found favor. He composed new music for large ceremonial events, and in 1672 he felt secure enough to marry Maria Weiss, a member of one of Salzburg's prominent merchant families. Biber and his wife had eleven children, four of whom survived to adulthood; three of those became musicians. In 1677 Biber was chosen to travel to Luxembourg to perform for the Holy Roman Emperor Leopold I. The emperor rewarded Biber's performance with a gold chain.

We do not know exactly what music Biber performed on this occasion, but it is clear that he had developed a completely distinctive voice as a composer to go with his fearsome violin skills. His music had a spiritual, inward quality that modern listeners often experience as moody and dramatic, and he heightened his music's emotional effects with groundbreaking technical wizardry. It was probably just before he departed for Luxembourg that Biber completed one of his most famous compositions, the group of so-called Mystery or Rosary sonatas for violin and continuo (basically a simple harmonic accompaniment). This set of 15 sonatas, rounded out in their original manuscript by an extremely difficult Passacaglia (a composition utilizing a repeating sequence of bass notes), had its roots in Biber's membership in a religious society in Salzburg devoted to the Catholic Rosary.

Each of the 15 sonatas is associated (and accompanied in the manuscript by an appropriate engraving) with one of the Mysteries of the Rosary, representing a stage in the story of Jesus Christ's immaculate conception, life, and death. Other Baroque composers such as Antonio Vivaldi used violin music to draw vivid pictures in sound, but Biber instead takes a subtler approach. Beginning with the four strings of the violin tuned to their normal pitches of G, D, A, and E, he specifies that different tunings be used as the set proceeds. This technique is known as scordatura. The sound of the violin changes as new tunings are used, and the instrument becomes capable of new combinations of tones. At the dramatic center of the work, the sonata representing

Christ's crucifixion, Biber directs that the violin be played with two of its strings crossed, probably symbolizing Christ's cross itself or the meeting of heavenly and earthly realms.

Needless to say, this procedure entails fiendish difficulties for the violinist who aims to perform the work and must learn new fingerings for each tuning. Modern violinists often use a set of pre-tuned violins, but some contend that the work's essence is best brought out if a single instrument is put through Biber's changes. English violinist Andrew Manze, as quoted on the All Music Guide website, notes that "as it is pulled into different tunings, the violin undergoes experiences, some pleasant (as in the *Visitation* and *Coronation*), some traumatic (the *Agony* and *Crowning with Thorns*), for example." Biber's other works for stringed instruments, such as the Sonatas for Violin Solo (published in 1681), the *Fidicinium Sacro-Profanum* (1683), and the *Harmonia artificiosa-ariosa* for two stringed instruments and continuo, also make use of the scordatura procedure and pose similar technical and interpretive challenges.

Biber's music for orchestra was no less original than his compositions for solo violin or violin with accompaniment. Much of it was programmatic. His *Battalia* (The Battle) was a remarkable depiction, not just of a military conflict but of its aftermath, with cannon fire, the groans of wounded men, and the off-key singing of drunken soldiers after the fight—all represented on the instruments of a small orchestra, with no voices involved. The dissonant quality of the drunken-singing section is regarded by some music writers as being hundreds of years ahead of its time. The work may have been written for a Carnival celebration in 1683. Biber's delightful Sonata for Six Instruments subtitled "The Farmers on Their Way to Church" likewise makes human beings—a group of farmers singing a chorale as they walk into town on a Sunday morning—come alive within a purely instrumental context.

In 1679 Biber was appointed deputy Kapellmeister (music director) at the archbishop's court, and in 1684 he was elevated to Kapellmeister and made director of the archdiocesan choir school. After performing twice more for Emperor Leopold and asking for a formal enhancement of his status, he was made a knight in 1690 and allowed to add the noble "von" to his name. His salary was a generous 60 gulden a month, plus room, board, and wine. The musician who had once been equal in status to the archbishop's firewood carriers now received free firewood as well.

Responsible for training the archbishop's top choral singers, Biber had large choirs at his own disposal. Later in life he turned his attention to the more formal genres of choral and vocal music. His choral compositions were performed in Salzburg's magnificent cathedral, and he exploited the complex architecture of that structure by writing what are known as polychoral pieces—works for several choirs. Most impressive among them was the *Missa Salisburgensis* (Salzburg Mass) of 1682, written for the 1,100th anniversary of the establishment of the post of Archbishop of Salzburg. This enormous work had 53 vocal parts, grouped into five separate choirs, each accompanied by its own orchestra, with two separate instrumental ensembles of trumpets and tympani.

Toward the end of his life Biber wrote operas and school dramas—smaller vocal works with dialogue intended for students at Salzburg's Benedictine University. Most of these works have been lost, and only one opera, *Chi la dura la vince* (Victory Comes to Those Who Persist, 1687), has survived. Music historians consider it less significant than Biber's instrumental or choral works. Biber died in Salzburg on May 3, 1704.

Biber's music and performances were remembered through the 1700s, but after that he was almost completely forgotten. His music was published in academic editions, and he was known to historians of the violin, but public performances of his works were rare. As interest in music of the Baroque era began to grow in the late 20th century, however, Biber was rediscovered. Numerous recordings of the Mystery Sonatas appeared, each with a slightly different twist. Performers also began to unearth new wonders among the approximately 60 works by Biber that have survived. Baroque music, as heard in the works of composers such as Bach, Handel, and Vivaldi, had once been thought of as regular, clearly structured, almost mathematical at times. The music of Biber, however, revealed a very different profile on the other side of the coin.

Books

"Heinrich Ignaz von Biber," *The New Grove Dictionary of Music and Musicians,* 2nd ed., Macmillan UK, 2001.

Periodicals

American Record Guide, September-October 1996; July-August 1999.
New York Times, October 8, 1995.
Notes, June 2003.
Plain Dealer (Cleveland, OH), November 20, 2002.

Online

"Heinrich Biber," All Music Guide, http://www.allmusic.com (November 7, 2005). □

Carla Bley

One of the true freethinkers in the jazz tradition, composer, bandleader, and pianist Carla Bley (born 1938) has gained a moderate-sized but stalwart body of fans on both sides of the Atlantic Ocean since the beginnings of her career in the mid-1960s.

"Great jazz musicians thrive by upsetting expectations, and Carla Bley is no exception," noted Minneapolis *Star Tribune* writer Chris Waddington. Bley has made her reputation primarily as a composer in a field dominated by instrumentalists. She has drawn on influences ranging from European classical music to tango, and in a jazz era marked by seriousness and modernist ambition, her music has offered elements of humor, satire, and whimsical collage. Largely

self-taught and only indirectly a product of the type of long apprenticeship modern jazz musicians tend to serve, Bley had a distinctive style that remained strongly recognizable even to casual listeners over her long career. Though she claimed to dislike the process of improvising, she made a living by touring and issuing live recordings in which her improvisations figured prominently.

Grew Up with Little Supervision

Bley was born Carla Borg In Oakland, California on May 11, 1938. Her parents were fundamentalist Christians who had met at Chicago's Moody Bible Institute. Bley grew up playing the piano and singing in a church choir, but her mother died when she was young, and her father did not maintain her strict upbringing. "I was allowed to stay out all night when I was five years old and he just let me do whatever I wanted," Bley told Richard Wolfson of the *Financial Times.* "I often didn't go to school; I'd just leave in the morning and go to the zoo." She taped a performance of Erik Satie's extremely offbeat French dance score *Parade* off the radio, and her tape recorder broke after the music ended. So for a long time that was the only recording she owned.

When she was 12, the formerly religious Bley became an atheist. She had a part-time job as an accompanist to a dance class, but her real passion over the next few years became not music but roller skating, and she notched a seventh-place finish in a statewide competition. She quit school when she was 15 and got a job in a music store. After a few years of working there and playing occasional music gigs, Bley headed for New York City when she was 19. She got jobs as a cigarette girl in several of the city's top jazz clubs, including Birdland and Basin Street. It was at that point that her real musical education began.

Sometimes Bley ignored customers' requests when she was particularly entranced by a solo coming from the stage, but the experience was crucial. On any given night, top talents of the bebop era might be holding forth where Bley was working. Her later music was marked by innovative fusions and collages, but the freedom of bebop improvisation lay at the foundation of her style. "When I started being interested in jazz, the musicians I adored were the black heroes of bebop," she told Duncan Heining of London's *Independent* newspaper. "When I started out checking European roots, that was quite late in my career, in the Sixties or Seventies. In the beginning, I just loved the beboppers. They were the only ones I knew."

Another benefit from that stint working in New York clubs was her marriage to Canadian-born jazz pianist Paul Bley, who suggested that she write original material for his band. The two spent several years in Los Angeles but returned to New York in the early 1960s. Bley worked as a movie theater usher but then returned to the jazz world, taking a job as a coat check girl at the Jazz Gallery. By that time she had amassed a body of original compositions that interested musicians other than her husband. Trumpeter Art Farmer and clarinetist-saxophonist Jimmy Giuffre were among the top jazz performers who recorded Bley's pieces. She performed on piano at the Phase Two coffee house in the Greenwich Village neighborhood, and the cream of the city's jazz talent might stop by to join her.

Co-founded Orchestra

Bley and trumpeter Michael Mantler joined several other musicians, including rising saxophonist Archie Shepp, to form the Jazz Composers' Guild Orchestra in 1964. The aim of the group was to provide a forum for new jazz compositions. The group went through several name changes and achieved only modest success on its own, but it proved to be a turning point for Bley in several ways. For one thing, Mantler became her second husband; they two had a daughter, Karen, who went on to become a jazz musician.

For another, the experience confirmed for Bley the importance of operating on her own, with creative control. In the mid-1960s, jazz had a moderate presence on major record labels, and many musicians aimed toward the national and international distribution and marketing that superstars such as John Coltrane enjoyed. But Bley—partly because her music often enjoyed more popularity in Europe than in the U.S.—has mostly issued her music through enterprises of her own. Well in advance of the spate of artists who marketed their own music in the 1990s, she and Mantler formed the Watt Works label in 1973.

Bley's Jazz Composers' Orchestra Association (JCOA), as the Guild Orchestra became known, succeeded in widening the circle of musicians who were familiar with her compositions, and she enjoyed some high-profile recordings in the late 1960s. Vibraphonist Gary Burton recorded Bley's composition cycle *A Genuine Tong Funeral* with his quartet

in 1967, and the record's success made jazz listeners aware of Bley as a name. Bassist and composer Charlie Haden used both Bley's piano and arranging talents on his politically oriented *Liberation Music Orchestra* LP of 1969, a widely known release around the counterculture of the day.

After working on it for at least five years, Bley finished a large-scale vocal-theatrical work, the surrealistic *Escalator Over the Hill,* in 1972. Set to texts by poet Paul Haines and originally inspired by the Beatles' *Sgt. Pepper's Lonely Hearts Club Band,* the work was issued by the JCOA on record but was not performed live until the late 1990s in Europe. *Escalator Over the Hill* featured contributions from 54 musicians, ranging from pop vocalist Linda Ronstadt to Indian-influenced guitarist John McLaughlin, and drew on an enormous variety of jazz, pop, rock, classical, and historical European styles. Many observers later regarded it as Bley's masterpiece.

Launched Own Ten-Piece Band

The ambitious *Escalator Over the Hill* got the attention of major arts grant making organizations, and Bley received fellowships from the Guggenheim Foundation and the National Endowment for the Arts in the early 1970s. She used the proceeds to put in place the foundations of an independent career, founding and touring with a ten-piece band that performed her own music and beginning to issue recordings on Watt Works and on the ECM label. She composed a second vocal work to texts by Haines, *Tropic Appetites.*

The late 1970s and early 1980s saw Bley touring frequently in Europe and Japan, where she remained better known than in the United States. "I mean I'm not happy about it, but that's just the truth," Bley told Heining. "I don't work a lot in the States. I don't teach at a school. I don't live in the city, go to parties or anything." She reunited with Haden and the Liberation Music Orchestra for *The Ballad of the Fallen* in 1982.

The highly eclectic nature of Bley's style concealed the fact that in one way it was quite traditional within the tradition of jazz composition: like Duke Ellington, whose music she paradoxically disliked, she was expert at handling the capabilities and individual instruments and instrumentalists. Bley wrote tight arrangements for the six horns in her ten-piece band—a rare talent, and rarer still among musicians with little formal training. Characteristically, Bley downplayed her talent, telling Wolfson that "It doesn't seem hard; I never went to school to learn it [arranging]. I just know what the horns sound like and I have a little book which says how high and how low they can play, and that's about it." She did allow that she paid close attention to her band, telling Waddington that "I like to write for people I know—I think I know what makes these guys sound good and what makes them grow."

Bley maintained her adventuresome spirit in the 1980s and 1990s, branching off constantly in new directions. In 1985 she edged closer to pop music with *Night-Glo* an album featuring former Gary Burton bassist Steve Swallow; she and Swallow became romantically involved, moved in together, and remained personal and creative partners into the new millennium. She wrote a set of original pieces for classical pianist Ursula Oppens called *Romantic Notions* in

1988. Despite an initial aversion to the big-band format, Bley broadened her arranging and composition into that arena and enjoyed one of her stronger-selling releases with *The Very Big Carla Bley Band* in 1990. Typically eclectic, the album ranged from polka and march music to salsa in a 15-minute piece called "United States."

Played in Duo with Swallow

At the same time, Bley began to focus the spotlight on her own piano (and sometimes organ) playing. Often performing with Swallow, she displayed a quirky, often minimal style that had some parallels with that of bebop-era innovator Thelonious Monk. Often minimizing her piano skills (". . . it sounds like a two-year-old-child," she told Wolfson), she nevertheless agreed with observers who felt her lack of formal training actually worked to her advantage. "I'm sure it leads to a certain originality, because you don't know what the correct thing to do is," she told Wolfson. "They always say that if you can play it you will play it, so in a way it's good to have a handicap."

With her long blonde hair and matchstick-thin figure, Bley seemed to change little in appearance as she approached senior citizen status, but she never repeated herself musically. In the early 2000s she toured with a quartet called the Lost Chords. Her 2003 big-band album *Looking for America* seemed to comment on the surge of patriotism that engulfed the U.S. after its invasion of Iraq; Thom Jurek of the All Music Guide praised Bley for what he called "the most bluesed-out version of 'Old MacDonald Had a Farm' in the history of American popular music," noting that "Stan Kenton would have been proud of this arrangement with its funky rhythmic structure, interwoven solos, and bassline harmonic architecture that expands as the tune goes." As of 2005 Bley was at work on a large-scale piece dealing with the career of disabled actor Christopher Reeve.

Books

Contemporary Musicians, volume 8, Gale, 1992.

Periodicals

Financial Times, November 16, 2004.
Independent (London, England), November 16, 1999.
Star Tribune (Minneapolis), June 28, 2003.

Online

"Carla Bley," All Music Guide, http://www.allmusic.com (December 8, 2005).
"Carla Bley Biography," http://www.wattxtrawatt.com.biocarla .htm (December 8, 2005). □

Helen Violet Asquith Bonham Carter

English political figure Helen Violet Bonham Carter (1887-1969), the Baroness Asquith of Yarnbury, supported the British Liberal Party philosophies em-

braced by her large and politically connected family. A good friend of Winston Churchill, she produced a well-known biography of the famed Prime Minister. Throughout her career and public life, she was a renowned orator and was very active in British political and cultural affairs.

Lady Helen Violet Bonham Carter, the future Baroness Asquith of Yarnbury, was born as Helen Violet Asquith on April 15, 1887, in Hampstead, London in England, into a large, influential family heavily involved in the British political system. Her father was Herbert Henry Asquith, who later became the first Earl of Oxford and Asquith. More importantly, from 1908 to 1916, he served as Prime Minister of Great Britain. Her mother was Helen Kesall Asquith (nee Melland).

Carter was the only daughter and fourth child in a family of five children. Her brothers included Raymond, Herbert, Arthur, and Cyril. Though her brothers received formal schooling, Carter obtained her early education privately at home from governesses. When she was older, she received formal education in Dresden, Germany and Paris, France. Her studies focused on languages.

Mother Died During Family Holiday

In 1891, when Carter was only four years old, her mother died of typhoid fever while the family was on holiday in Scotland.

Three years later, in 1894, Herbert Henry Asquith married his second wife, Emma Alice Margaret (Margo) Tennant. After the marriage, Carter's family moved to a residence at 20 Cavendish Square, which was a wedding present from Emma Tennant's father, Sir Charles Tennant, who was a prominent member of Britain's Liberal Party, as well as a noted manufacturer and patron of the arts. Asquith's second marriage produced two more children, Anthony and Elizabeth. Anthony Asquith grew up to become a film director whose credits include well-known British films such as *The Winslow Boy* (1948), *The Browning Version* (1951), and the highly regarded adaptation of Oscar Wilde's *The Importance of Being Earnest* (1952).

According to author Colin Clifford, whose book *The Asquiths* detailed the extended family's political and financial fortunes, Carter's stepmother felt "distinctly antipathetic" toward her stepchildren. "She never appreciated the traumatic effect, especially on the two younger children, of the loss of their mother; nor did she understand how intimidating her own powerful personality could be," wrote Clifford. "All she could see was the contrast between the anarchic personalities of herself and her siblings and what appeared to her to be the overly serious Asquith children."

Clifford also indicated that Carter experienced a complex family life because her father's two marriages brought into the household so many children of different ages and personalities. Moreover, both parents avidly pursued separate and distinct interests. Stepmother Margot enjoyed horses, hunting and expensive clothes, while father Herbert was absorbed by his political career. In addition, ongoing tension existed between Carter and her stepmother. To handle the pressure, Herbert Asquith reportedly sought solace in the company of younger women.

Became Involved in Father's Career

Still, Carter would ever remain her father's staunchest supporter. During Asquith's career, Carter actively campaigned for him, in the process developing her own oratorical skills, which were deemed considerable. After his death, she carried on the family's Liberal tradition and became known as the voice of "Asquithian Liberalism."

Around the time Carter was born, Herbert Asquith was a rising politician who would ascend fast and far. In the same year that his first wife gave birth to their only daughter, he had just become a member of the House of Commons. In 1892, he became Home Secretary in Prime Minister William Gladstone's fourth and final administration. In 1905, he became Chancellor of the Exchequer. Only three years later, in 1908, he became Britain's Prime Minister.

As a child, Carter suffered from poor health, so she was away from home when her father assumed the all-important role of Prime Minister. However, Carter would develop a keen interest in politics and, because of her father's career, she witnessed up close the rise and fall of the Liberal Party. Even at a young age, she demonstrated a strong intellectual grasp of the political arena, and she liked to discuss politics with her father. Like Asquith, Carter was a staunch liberal.

Marriage Followed Aborted Engagement

In 1909, Carter became engaged to Archie Gordon. The proposal was not destined to find its fulfillment in marriage, however, as it essentially amounted to nothing more than deathbed gesture. Gordon was one of Carter's closest friends. In 1909, he suffered extremely serious injuries in an automobile accident. In Winchester Hospital, knowing that he was going to die from his injuries, he asked Carter to marry him, and she and Gordon became engaged. Gordon passed away before they could actually be married and, in 1910, Carter raised money and helped establish the Archie Gordon Club, an organization for deprived boys in the depressed Hoxton area of East London. Her partner in the founding was Maurice Bonham-Carter, her father's principal private secretary.

On November 30, 1915, Carter, who usually went by her middle name of Violet, married Bonham-Carter, who would later become Sir Maurice. Their marriage produced four children, two girls and two boys: Helen Laura Cressida Bonham-Carter, Laura Miranda Bonham-Carter, Mark Raymond Bonham-Carter, Baron Bonham-Carter, and Raymond Henry Bonham-Carter.

Even while raising a family, Carter continued actively supporting her father. She campaigned for him in the Paisley by-election of 1920, when he returned to Parliament after losing his East Fife seat in 1918. Afterward, however, she was forced to endure her father's declining political status. After Asquith regained his seat at Paisley, he lost it four years later in the 1924 General Election. The loss accompanied Britain's Conservative Party's rise in power over the once dominant Liberal Party. Asquith then entered the House of Lords as Earl of Oxford and Asquith, but he suffered one last humiliation in 1925 when Oxford University rejected him as its Chancellor. Instead, the university chose Lord Cave, a Tory. Asquith died of a stroke in 1928.

Through the years, Asquith had developed a strong relationship with his only daughter. She adored him and he, in turn, came to depend on her, especially when his political career was on the decline. When her father's political stock fell, Carter staunchly defended his reputation. She would not easily suffer any criticism of Asquith, no matter how slight. Family friend Sir Winston Churchill called Carter her father's "champion redoubtable."

Friend of Churchill

Carter first met Churchill when she was eighteen years old. The future Prime Minister would become the other main political figure in Carter's life besides her father. Carter sometimes disagreed with Churchill, but she also strongly supported him when the cause was right. For instance, Carter, a fervent anti-Nazi, was a strong advocate of Churchill's anti-appeasement campaign. The two would remain close friends throughout their lives.

Later in her life, she wrote a book about Churchill entitled *Churchill as I Knew Him* (which was also published under the title "Winston Churchill: An Intimate Portrait"). It was the only book Carter ever authored, and it was published in 1965, the year that Churchill died. Originally,

Carter intended to publish a multi-volume work about Churchill. But she only completed the one volume, which detailed her relationship and experiences with Churchill.

Long and Accomplished Career

Carter had a wide range of interests, and she was very active and highly visible in Great Britain's political and cultural affairs until 1964. She gained recognition as a highly effective orator, and her first reported speech came in 1909, when she was only twenty-two years old. Throughout her life, she championed Liberalism, the only political philosophy that she felt exemplified morality. Appropriately, she served as President of the Women's Liberal Federation between 1923 and 1925 and held the office a second time, from 1939 to 1945.

Her long career became filled with numerous appointments and titles. From 1936 to 1939, she was Liberal vice-president of Churchill's Focus in Defense of Freedom and Peace. An ardent advocate for the League of Nations, she became a member of that body until 1941, the year she was appointed a governor of the British Broadcasting Corporation (BBC). Reportedly, she took a great deal of pleasure in her role with the BBC, but she resigned in 1945 to run for political office, contesting the Wells Division of Somersetshire as Liberal candidate. Her campaign was unsuccessful and Carter, who by this time was publicly known as Lady Violet Bonham Carter, was reappointed to the BBC after she was defeated. The only other time she sought political office came in 1951, running for the Colne Valley in Yorkshire. Again, she lost.

In 1945, she became the first woman president of the Liberal Party Organization, holding the office until 1947. She served as vice president from 1947 to 1965. After World War II, she embraced the European Ideal and, in 1947, she became vice-chairman of the United Europe Movement. Also, from 1947 to 1949, she was a member of the Royal Commission on the Press.

In 1949, she became a delegate to Commonwealth Relations Conference in Canada. In 1953, she was invested as a Dame Commander of the Order of the British Empire.

Entered House of Lords

On December 21, 1964, at the age of seventy-seven, she was awarded a life peerage and entered the House of Lords as Baroness Asquith of Yarnbury. After Churchill died on January 24, 1965, Carter gave her maiden speech in the House of Lords the following day. In part, her speech was a eulogy for her lifelong friend.

Throughout her life, she made frequent public-speaking appearances on a variety of subjects. In 1963 she became the first woman to give the Romanes lecture at Oxford, speaking on "the impact of personality on politics," a subject she knew a great deal about. In 1967 she was the first woman to speak at a Royal Academy dinner. She also made regular radio and television appearances, most often as a panel member on the radio program *The Brain Trust.* Perhaps her most significant television appearance came in 1967, when she did an interview with Kenneth Harris on the *As I Remember* program.

Died in London

Carter passed away in London, England on February 19, 1969. She was eighty-one years old. She was preceded in death by her husband Maurice, who died in 1960.

Following her death, two volumes of her letters and diaries were published. These included *Lantern Slides, The Diaries and Letters of Violet Bonham Carter 1904-14,* published in 1995, and *Champion Redoubtable, The Diaries and Letters of Violet Bonham Carter 1914-45,* published in 1998.

Carter herself wrote numerous articles in magazines as well as letters to newspapers that addressed national and international subjects. She also wrote radio and television scripts. In addition, as a result of her involvement with the BBC, she became a frequent broadcaster on both radio and television.

Other distinctions in her long and accomplished career included serving as a governor of the Old Vic from 1945 to 1969. In 1955, she became a trustee of the Glyndbourne Arts Trust, a post she held until 1969. She was also president of Royal Institute of International Affairs from 1964 to 1969. She continued attending the House as an active member until her death in 1969.

During her lifetime, she was fortunate to see the continuation of her family's Liberal traditions. Her daughter Laura married Jo Grimond, who later became the leader of the Liberal Party, and her son Mark, running as a Liberal, won Torrington, Devon at a by-election in 1958.

Online

"Helen Bonham Carter," *Bodleian Library-University of Oxford,* http://www.bodley.ox.ac.uk/dept/scwmss/wmss/online/modern/bonham-carter/bonham-carter.html (December 30, 2005).

"(Helen) Violet (Asquith) Bonham Carter," *Contemporary Authors Online,* Gale, 2006. Reproduced in Biography Resource Center. http://galenet.galegroup.com/ (December 30, 2005)

"Herbert Henry Asquith," *Direct.gov.uk,*, http://www.number10.gov.uk/output/Page140.asp (December 30, 2005)

Clifford, Colin. "The Asquiths," *Cercles,* http://www.cercles.com/review/r17/clifford.htm (December 30, 2005)

"Violet Bonham Carter," *Liberal Democrat History Group,* http://www.liberalhistory.org.uk/record.jsp?type=page&ID;=122&liberalbiographies;=liberalbiographies (December 30, 2005) □

Brahmagupta

Brahmagupta (c. 598-c. 670) was one of the most significant mathematicians of ancient India. He introduced extremely influential concepts to basic mathematics, including the use of zero in mathematical calculations and the use of mathematics and algebra in describing and predicting astronomical events.

nfluenced by the spread of Greek mathematical ideas eastward during the imperial expansion of the ancient Roman empire, Brahmagupta's ideas in turn had an impact on later European developments; they were translated into Arabic from his own Sanskrit language, and thus took their place among the foundation stones of Western mathematics. Brahmagupta's writings contain mathematical and astronomical concepts that are taken for granted today, but they were concepts that he pioneered or refined from ideas he inherited. His estimates of the length of the year were strikingly accurate for their time. Although it is difficult to pinpoint a single inventor of the concept of zero, Brahmagupta is a reasonable candidate for that title. A writer of his own time, Bhaksara II, called him *Ganita Chakra Chudamani,* which means "the gem in the circle of mathematicians."

Headed Ancient Indian Observatory

Brahmagupta was born in c. 598, perhaps in the astronomically significant ancient Indian city of Ujjain—a place near the tropic of cancer that occupies a place in Indian history somewhat comparable to that of Greenwich in England. It was a central reckoning point for ideas of time and space, and it became a major astronomical and mathematical center. The first of his two surviving treatises, according to internal evidence, was written in Bhillamala, now the city of Bhinmal in Rajasthan state. Brahmagupta's first treatise, the *Brahmasphutasiddhanta* (meaning "The Correctly Established Doctrine of Brahma" but often translated as *The Opening of the Universe*), was written in 1628, when he was about 30 years old. His second, the *Khandakhadyaka* (whose title means something like "Edible Bite"), is less well known; it expands on the work of an earlier astronomer, Aryabhata, whose chief contribution was the idea of beginning each day at midnight. It was written in 665, near the end of Brahmagupta's life.

Little else is known of the life of this mathematician and astronomer who flourished 1,400 years ago, other than that he was a devout Hindu who took care not to antagonize his own religious leaders, attacking an idea advanced by thinkers in the competing Jain religion (correctly, as it turned out) that the earth rotated on a central axis. He based his conclusion on the faulty premise that large buildings would fall down if this were true. Brahmagupta did, however, reject ancient Hindu ideas that the earth was flat or bowl-shaped; like ancient Greek thinkers, including Aristotle, he realized that it was a sphere.

Brahmagupta is known mostly through his writings, which cover mathematical and astronomical topics and significantly combine the two. Brahmagupta's descriptions of the motions of the stars and planets were based on mathematical calculations to a degree that earlier astronomers had not achieved. As a result, some of his estimates of celestial cycles remained among the most accurate available for several centuries. He was able, for example, to reliably predict the rising and setting of the planets and trace their trajectories across the sky. While the ancient Greeks and even the Babylonians had dealt superstition a major blow by predicting eclipses, Brahmagupta refined their computa-

tional methods and helped to spread an understanding of these phenomena throughout societies where eclipses were still regarded as divine signs.

Brahmagupta's first manuscript, the *Brahmasphutasiddhanta,* was a revision of an older astronomy book, the *Brahmasiddanta* (Doctrine of Brahma). It opened with three chapters on the position and motions of the planets and stars, and on the cycle of daylight and night. Two chapters dealt with lunar and solar eclipses, respectively, and one with the heliacal risings and settings of stars, planets, and moon—the seasonal reappearances (and disappearances) of these celestial bodies as they pass the horizon line before (or, during heliacal setting, after) being hidden by the sun. Brahmagupta goes on to discuss phases of the moon, planetary conjunctions (what appear to be close approaches of planets in the sky), and conjunctions between planets and stars. One chapter in the middle of the book is devoted to a discussion of previous astronomical treatises. At the end of the book he devotes chapters to instruments and units of measure.

Estimated Length of Year

Brahmagupta's first manuscript calculated the length of the solar year at 365 days, 6 hours, 5 minutes, and 19 seconds, among the most accurate of early reckonings and remarkably close to the actual value of 365 days, 5 hours, 48 minutes, and about 45 seconds. In the *Khandakhadyaka* Brahmagupta revised his conclusion and went a small distance in the wrong direction, proposing a length of 365 days, 6 hours, 12 minutes, and 36 seconds. It is thought, however, that he relied on the work of Aryabhata in arriving at this figure. All were remarkable estimates in an era that had no telescopes or scientific instruments in the modern sense.

After his discussion of astronomy, Brahmagupta then turned to mathematics, discussing what would now be called arithmetic and algebra—his terms were *pati-ganita,* or mathematics of procedures, and *bija-ganita,* or mathematics of equations. These ideas laid the foundation for much of the later development of mathematics in India. Some of Brahmagupta's discussions will sound familiar to the modern student of mathematics. His directions for the multiplication of large numbers involve multiplying one number by each digit of the other in a manner close to what students are taught today, although the numbers are written out in a different configuration. A curious feature of Brahmagupta's treatise is that it is largely written in verse, and his preferred multiplication method, according to the mathematics history website maintained by St. Andrews University in Scotland, is given the name *gomutrika* by Brahmagupta, meaning "like the trajectory of a cow's urine."

Brahmagupta also introduced new methods for solving quadratic equations that would be recognizable to modern students of mathematics. He illustrates such procedures with story problems such as the following (quoted on the St. Andrews University site), which could essentially have come from any modern algebra textbook: "Five hundred drammas were loaned at an unknown rate of interest. The interest on the money for four months was loaned to another at the same rate of interest and amounted in ten months to 78 drammas. Give the rate of interest." Brahmagupta devised formulas for calculating the area (and the lengths of the diagonals) of a cyclic quadrilateral, a four-sided figure whose vertices are points on a circle. His method is still known as Brahmagupta's theorem. Brahmagupta investigated various higher functions of algebra and geometry, in each case building on and refining the mathematical heritage of the ancient world.

Perhaps Brahmagupta's most important innovations, however, pertained to his treatment of the number zero. Several different discoveries converged to form the concept of zero. The circular symbol for the number and the idea of representing orders of magnitude in a number through the use of places arose at different times and places in advance of Brahmagupta's work. Brahmagupta, however, was the first to propose rules for the behavior of zero in common arithmetical equations, relating zero to positive and negative numbers (which he called fortunes and debts). He correctly stated that multiplying any number by zero yields a result of zero, but erred, as did many other ancient mathematicians, in attempting to define division by zero. Nevertheless, Brahmagupta is sometimes referred to as the "Father of Zero."

Brahmagupta's *Khandakhadyaka* refers to a date in the year 665 and is thought to have been written at that time, when Brahmagupta was about 67—an extremely old man by the standards of the time. He died sometime soon after that, perhaps in 670. A line of Indian mathematicians and astronomers working at the Ujjain observatory revered Brahmagupta and extended his ideas over the next decades and centuries.

The real impact of Brahmagupta's discoveries was felt in the Islamic world, where King Khalif Abbasid al-Mansoor (712-775) invited the Ujjain scholar Kanka to lecture on Brahmagupta's applications of mathematics to astronomy. The king ordered Brahmagupta's writings translated into Arabic in 771, and they had a major impact on subsequent writers in the Arab world, including al-Khwarizmi, the "father of algebra." The mathematical thought of medieval and early modern Europe was influenced by Arabic models that had been in existence for centuries. Distant from modern mathematics in time and place, Brahmagupta nevertheless exerted a definite influence on mathematics as the discipline is known today.

Books

Boyer, Carl B., *A History of Mathematics,* Wiley, 1968.
Datta, B., and A.N. Singh, *History of Hindu Mathematics, Part I,* Motilal Banarsi, Das, 1935.
Gillispie, Charles Coulston, *Encyclopedia of Scientific Biography,* Council of Learned Societies, 1970.
Science and Its Times, vol. 1, Gale, 2001.
World of Mathematics, 2 vols., Gale, 2001.

Online

"Brahmagupta (598-668)," Department of Mathematics, Simon Fraser University (British Columbia, Canada), http://www.math.sfu.ca/histmath/India/7thCenturyAD/Brahmagupta.html (February 17, 2006).
"Brahmagupta (ca. 598-ca. 665)," Wolfram Research, http://www.scienceworld.wolfram.com/biography/Brahmagupta.html (February 17, 2006).
"Brahmagupta," School of Mathematics and Statistics, St. Andrews University, http://www-groups.dcs.st-and.ac.uk/~history/Mathematicians/Brahmagupta.html (February 17, 2006).
"Brahmagupta," Vidyapatha, http://www.vidyapatha.com/scientists/brahmagupta.php (February 17, 2006). □

Fredrika Bremer

Swedish novelist Fredrika Bremer (1801-1865) is known in the United States primarily for the written observations she made during her American travels in the late 1840s and early 1850s, many of them dealing with the lives of African-American slaves. In her own time, however, Bremer's novels were known all over Europe and the United States, appearing in translated versions almost as fast as they were published in Swedish.

As a writer, Bremer was a pioneer advocate for women's rights. Her novels were built around female characters who were more independent than any others in Swedish literature up to that point, and who suffered the effects of a repressive, completely male-dominated society. Bremer's novel *Hertha* (1856) dramatized the need for legal rights for women, and it was credited with providing the impetus for reforms improving the status of women that were implemented in Sweden in the years following the book's publication. In many ways, Bremer was a full counterpart to the women writers in larger European countries who worked to develop the new political and cultural consciousness that led to a broader demands for women's rights.

Intentionally Malnourished Despite Wealth

Bremer was born on August 17, 1801, in Åbo, Finland, which was ruled by Sweden at the time. In 1804 her banker father moved to the Swedish capital of Stockholm; they also had a castle called Årsta in the Swedish countryside and spent their summers there. Bremer's strict Lutheran upbringing was restrictive even by the standards of the nineteenth-century European upper classes, which generally kept young women cloistered and subjected them to strict regimes of social indoctrination. Her mother, believing that a dancer-like build represented an ideal of femininity, severely limited the amount of food Bremer and her four sisters could eat, and she probably suffered from what would now be called clinical malnutrition. The Bremer sisters, only one of whom ever married, were essentially kept housebound for most of their youth, forbidden even to take short walks. However, Bremer did receive, from tutors and governesses, a solid education that included the classics of Swedish and German literature, philosophy, and religious and ethical thought.

When Bremer was in her late teens, she undertook a Grand Tour—a tradition among privileged European families according to which a young person on the verge of adulthood would visit the great capitals of the Continent, visiting art collections, hearing concerts and studying music, and generally rounding out his or her cultural education while seeing something of the wider world. Bremer was still kept under very tight rein. When the family's carriage became stuck in the mud, she was not allowed to get out, no matter how long the predicament might last. But Bremer's Grand Tour was nevertheless a profound formative experience in many ways. Her diaries began to show a sharp feminist consciousness, and after visiting a Swedish university library she wrote sarcastically to a friend that if she had dared to actually open a book, a professor would have materialized to remind her that there were no cookbooks in the collection. "All my youth was strange—I had a constant feeling of being able to go mad suddenly and instantly," she wrote in another letter quoted on the Official Gateway to Sweden website.

And for the first time, Bremer saw how the other half lived. In her book *Life in the Old World* (as translated by Sarah Death on the website of the Årstasällskapet for Fredrika Bremer Studies), she recalled what she saw from her carriage as it rolled through Paris. "Beauty and ugliness, luxury and misery were overtly displayed alongside each other," she wrote. "Splendid processions of people riding and in carriages thronged the boulevards; the crowd of spectators extended into the side alleys, where wretched creatures exposed open wounds and maimed limbs, women lay on the ground covered in black cloth, surrounded by pale, semi-naked children. The young gentlemen of the boulevard stepped right over them."

Bremer returned to Stockholm, hardly ready to marry and enter the whirl of high society. Instead she had a strong desire to learn more about the world and to change it. She made the acquaintance of a radical young Lutheran minister, Per Johan Böklin, who suggested philosophical books for her to read, and with whom she corresponded voluminously. In the 1820s she began to do charitable work teaching children and taking care of the old and the sick. And, partly in order to fund an expansion of this enterprise, she began to write novels, issuing a series of them under the collective title *Sketches of Everyday Life*. The first one, *Axel and Anna* (English translations of all of Bremer's novels appeared in London in the 1840s and 1850s), was published in 1828, and she produced them steadily until 1848. One of the most widely read was *The H Family* of 1831, later retranslated as *The Colonel's Family*. They were stories of domestic life, written primarily for women and drawn from Bremer's own experiences and those of her contemporaries. Although they did not have the overtly feminist themes of Bremer's later writing, they featured women as central characters, and they displayed humor and an insight into women's feelings that had to that point been unknown in Swedish literature.

Continued to Live with Parents

Beginning around 1840, Bremer's writing started to become internationally famous. European audiences snapped up new translations of her novels, and she was well enough known even in the United States that long lines of autograph seekers greeted her when she arrived in that country in 1849. Yet ironically this success did little to change Bremer's living situation. As a woman, she had no control whatsoever over her own financial or legal affairs. For the first part of her writing career, she remained in her mother's home (her father died in 1830). At one point she asked for a room of her own where she could write and study, even in the attic, but her mother turned the request down.

Bremer made a declaration of independence of sorts when Böklin proposed marriage to her; she refused the proposal and did not see the minister for several years, although they continued to write to each other. It is possible that her decision was the result of a conviction that, at the time, a woman would find it impossible to combine domestic life with a full commitment to writing. Bremer was twice (in 1831 and 1843) awarded the Gold Medal by the Swedish Academy, and her writing had begun to deepen. Her 1842 novel *A Diary* was the first book in the history of Swedish literature to be written by a woman about a single woman. On its second page, the main character describes herself this way (as translated by Sarah Death): "Independent in fortune and position in life, I am now able to taste freedom after many long years of captivity, a freedom to follow, at the age of 30, nothing but my own inclination." In the first half of the nineteenth century, those were revolutionary words. *Brothers and Sisters* (1848) deserted the world of Stockholm high society for a depiction of a utopian experiment founded along the lines dreamed of by philanthropic societies. Bremer's progressive spirit remained animated by her Christian beliefs, and she once remarked that Christ was the originator of true liberalism.

One major step Bremer took as a result of her new independence was to begin to travel. She made two lengthy international trips; the first, to the United States and Cuba, has been more closely examined, but the second was also remarkable. Bremer arrived in New York in 1849, knowing no one but known by many. She stayed in the United States for two years, traveling all over the country. Bremer's motivation in visiting America was that she wanted to glimpse humanity's future; she saw it as a country of people who hoped to build a new world, and she was fascinated by idealistic religious groups such as the Quakers.

Bremer immersed herself in American life. Carrying a sketchbook, she went west to spend time among Native Americans. She visited Washington and sat in the gallery as the struggles over slavery that led to the Civil War were waged in Congress, and she cultivated close contacts in the intellectual centers of New York and Boston, visiting writers such as the philosopher Ralph Waldo Emerson. She visited prisons and went to the rough Five Points neighborhood in Manhattan for a first-hand look at the American underclass. Bremer's observations were published in several volumes in 1853 and 1854 under the title *Homes of the New World*. Again, the book found an international readership and was translated into English immediately.

Made Close Observations of Slave Culture

The most unusual sections of the book dealt with the institution of slavery, which Bremer considered a severe failing of America's otherwise free society. Bremer visited plantations and wrote down slave narratives, music, and folkways. When she went still farther south to Cuba, she proved an acute observer of the presence of African cultural traits in the lives of black Cubans, traits that were more hidden under the institution of American slavery. Bremer's writings about slaves constitute one of the largest bodies of detailed observations that have come down to us about slave life.

On the way back to Sweden, Bremer stopped in England to visit the Great Exhibition of 1851 and its fabulous Crystal Palace, the first World's Fair. Back in Sweden, she plunged into the nation's political life to a degree she had avoided up to that point. In 1854, during the Crimean War, she wrote a newspaper column urging Christian women's organizations worldwide to join in an anti-war alliance. Her proposal was criticized by conservative writers, including the editorial board of the *Times* of London that published her article in England.

Criticism intensified after Bremer published *Hertha, or The Story of a Soul,* a novel whose title character was a mouthpiece for Bremer's views on women's rights. As Bremer predicted, the novel stirred strong controversy, partly as a result of a scene in which its heroine applies bandages to the knee of her fiancé—such close physical contact between unmarried people was considered taboo. The main thrust of the novel was to promote the majority—the conferring of full civil rights—to women at the age of 25 in Sweden. Bremer was backed by liberal elements in Swedish society, and her book was credited with spurring passage of a law in 1858 that revoked many of the privileges of the Swedish patriarchy.

By that time, Bremer was already in the middle of another odyssey. She traveled through Switzerland to Italy, where she met the pope, and then through Greece to the Middle East, where she delved into the region's long history, traveling at times on horseback, at the age of about 60. The several Swedish-language travel narratives that resulted were later collected under the English title *Life in the Old World.* Bremer returned to fiction writing upon her return to Sweden, but her final novel, and her satisfaction at witnessing the evolution of democracy in Sweden, were cut short by her death at Årsta on December 31, 1865. One measure of her lasting influence was the large number of women's peace groups that continued to flourish throughout the twentieth century and beyond.

Books

Rappaport, Helen, *Encyclopedia of Women Social Reformers,* ABC-CLIO, 2001.
Stendhal, Brita K, *The Education of a Self-Made Woman: Fredrika Bremer, 1801-1865,* Edwin Mellen Press, 1994.

Online

"Fredrika Bremer: A Contemporary from the Last Century," Sweden.se: The Official Gateway to Sweden, http://www.sweden.se (January 13, 2006).

Translated passages from *Bremer: En biografi* (Swedish-language biography of Bremer), Årstasällskapet för Fredrika Bremer-studier, http://www.fredrikabremer.net/burman.htm (January 13, 2006). □

E. Margaret Burbidge

E. Margaret Burbidge (born 1919) appeared on the science scene quite early on, and made controversial, but important, discoveries ever since. She became recognized for the production of the first accurate estimate of the masses of galaxies, for her work with quasars, and for work she did concerning the metal contents of stars. She was also part of the committee that planned and outfitted the Hubble Space Telescope.

Early Interest in Science

Burbidge was born Eleanor Margaret Peachey in Davenport, England on August 12, 1919. She was born to Stanley John Peachey, a lecturer in chemistry at the Manchester School of Technology, and Marjorie Stott, a chemistry student there. The family relocated to London when Burbidge was almost two years old where her father set up a laboratory after he acquired some patents in the field of rubber chemistry. In this setting Burbidge was allowed and encouraged to develop her interest in science. She eventually attended the University of London where she took First Class Honors for her bachelor's degree in Science in 1939. She continued on at the University for her graduate education at the University's Observatory. Even though World War II was waging at the time, one of the Observatory's smaller telescopes was left intact and assembled and Burbidge spent the evenings doing her studies in the darkened city. Many of the Observatory's leaders were called to work for the military, and so Burbidge was appointed general caretaker, and she took her responsibilities very seriously, taking very special care of the observatory and its telescopes. She even went so far as to repair damage done to the observatory's dome during an air raid. She eventually received her Ph.D. in 1943, having done her studies on the physics of hot stars. When the war was over, Burbidge left the University while reconstruction was taking place throughout the city.

Burbidge returned to the University to continue her studies in 1947 once peace was established and London had been cleaned up. She met Geoffrey Burbidge, a fellow graduate student, at that time. They were married in April of 1948. The couple eventually had one daughter.

Burbidge took on the role of assistant director and acting director of the Observatory in the late 1940s. Then in 1951 the Yerkes Observatory of Harvard University offered Burbidge a fellowship to come study with them. She and her husband, who himself had been offered an Agassiz

fellowship, moved to Cambridge to continue their separate studies there. They enjoyed America, but unfortunately had to leave and return to England when their fellowships were over in 1953.

Work with Hoyle and Fowler

In 1954 Burbidge took a job with the University of Chicago's observatory in Texas while her husband took a position at Cambridge University. It was in 1954 while Geoffrey was working at Cambridge University that the couple teamed up with the English astronomer Fred Hoyle and the American physicist William A. Fowler to study the make–up of stars. Burbidge was always drawn to the notion, which Hoyle introduced, that matter was created successively at different times in the Universe's life, rather than by one single event such as the Big Bang, so she was very excited to be working with the well–known astronomer. The four scientists started by continuing the research into the astronomical spectroscopy and evaluation of the surface layers of stars that Burbidge had done for her PhD. Through their studies they discovered that stars start out by burning lighter gases, starting with turning hydrogen into helium, but as they grow and age they build more and more complex metals, partly building on the metals left behind by previous stars. They found the only recently discovered and named element technetium in the spectral lines of the stars called red giants. Red giants are stars that are old and dying. When stars like the Sun die they grow cold and then expand until their outer skins create huge, red stars. Technetium is a complex, unstable element that could not possibly have

been part of the star when it was new—this led the four scientists to the idea that the red giants must have produced this element rather recently in its life. The Burbidges, along with Hoyle and Fowler used this fact to show that stars, which start out made entirely of hydrogen, fuse these hydrogen elements together to make helium. They then fuse the helium elements together to form carbon, then nitrogen, then oxygen, and so on down the periodic table, making more and more complex elements as they go. By studying supernovae they discovered that the heavier elements, including iodine, platinum, gold, and uranium could be produced in those supernovae whose explosions—that occur when the stars are dying, which is when the stars explode outward till they are enormous and then collapse in on themselves—produce enough energy to make the heavier elements. When these supernovae explode, a large part of the old stars material is blown out into outer space to be absorbed by other stars. They also noted that the heavier elements like carbon, nitrogen, and oxygen, which are known to be found in all the living organisms on Earth, are also found inside ancient stars that have been dead for a long time. They concluded, therefore, that planets like Earth and all its inhabitants are actually composed of material from dead stars.

Both Burbidge and her husband obtained positions with the University of Chicago in 1957, although they continued their collaboration with Hoyle and Fowler. In fact, in 1957 the four published a paper on their discoveries about the composition and structure of stars that turned out to be one of the most important discoveries in modern astronomy. No one had proven before that stars were actually each a factory that produced all the elements of the universe. It was an amazing discovery that helped redirect the study of the universe and the humans' place in it. Those in the field referred to the paper simply as B2FH, with the B2 referring to the Burbidges, the F to Fowler and the H, obviously, to Hoyle.

Studied Rotation of Galaxies and Quasars

While they were doing this, the Burbidges also, in the 1950s and 1960s, together studied the rotation of galaxies. They were especially concerned with the internal dynamics and masses of those galaxies. Burbidge obtained the spectra of several spiral galaxies. She used these to measure the velocities of the ionized gas clouds in their nuclei and disks. They noted that galaxies rotated on an axis and that they managed to stay together in shapes like the Milky Way's spiral shape, and not fall apart because of centrifugal force. That is the same force that keeps water in a bucket when you spin it around in circles very quickly: the gravity keeps the water in the bucket, and the same force keeps galaxies together as they spin. They discovered that to find out a galaxy's actual weight and how the mass is distributed within it, you had to measure the rotational speed.

The Burbidges moved to San Diego, California in 1962 where Burbidge took a job at the University of California at San Diego. She became a full professor in 1964 and took over control of the University's Center for Astrophysics and Space Sciences from 1979 to 1988. Geoffrey took the position of professor of physics there. In the 1960s Burbidge turned her focus to quasars. Quasars are objects in space that have always been thought to be the farthest objects in space away from Earth, farther than the stars and other galaxies. Quasars have been demonstrated to emit vast amounts of radiation, even though they are very small, but no one knew what they were. Some of Burbidge's early discoveries were so exciting and intriguing that they led to her husband turning his focus to quasars as well, and the two worked together once again. Burbidge primarily studied the red shift of the quasars, which measures the speed at which an object is moving away from the Earth. The quasars had such a large red shift, compared to relatively closer objects like stars and galaxies that at first the Burbidges, along with scientists before them, deduced that the quasars must be at the very edge of the galaxy—the farthest things observable from Earth. And the farther an object is from Earth, the longer it takes for its light to reach Earth. Therefore, the light from the quasars that the Burbidges were seeing must have been in existence an amazingly long time ago. It was like finding dinosaur bones on Earth—the quasars were like ancient fossils, telling a story of the galaxy far different than anything closer and newer did. This large red shift of quasars has always been one of the things that scientists based their Big Bang Theory on. If everything in the universe started from one place and then there was an explosion throwing all sorts of matter into space, then the objects that were the farthest out, thrown first, would be moving at the fastest rate, just like the quasars were.

Questioned the Big Bang Theory

In order to be seen from such a distance, the Burbidges deduced that the quasars must have an enormous amount of energy, although they appeared to be quite small. This was a discrepancy that was difficult to explain, and something which bothered the Burbidges so much that they continued their studies. The quasars, oddly enough, also appeared to be grouped with nearby galaxies. After much research the Burbidges decided that the quasars, although they appeared to be a great distance away, must really be closer and have been pushed out of nearby galaxies. This was a very controversial deduction because it meant that the red shift could not be relied upon to determine how far something was away from the Earth, or for how fast the Universe was expanding. Burbidge's research with her husband eventually led to the pair challenging the truthfulness of the Big Bang Theory, which had been based on this red shift and seemingly increasing expansion of the Universe. The Burbidges published a book with their discoveries in 1967. It was called *Quasi–Stellar Objects.* It was and still is a very controversial study.

In 1972 Burbidge returned for a very short while to Britain where she became the first female director of the Royal Greenwich Observatory, but she quickly returned to San Diego as she preferred observing at a telescope rather than sitting behind a desk. For years after her return to the United States, Burbidge continued her observational research programs at the Lick Observatory of the University of California, working with students, fellows, and colleagues from around the world. Along with these others, she continued her research into the red shifts of quasars, the absorption

lines in those quasars, and the distribution of quasars in the universe, all questions that pushed the boundaries of astronomical research and questioned old, accepted theories.

When it was proposed that there should be a telescope in space that would be able to see further than anything else on Earth could, Burbidge was very interested. She became part of the committee that designed and set up the telescope, which despite initial problems after launch has been quite successful in penetrating deeper into space than anyone on Earth has ever seen before. Over the many years of her research, Burbidge garnered many awards, including the Helen Warner Prize, which she was given with her husband by the American Astronomical Society in 1959, an organization that Burbidge herself became president of from 1976 to 1978; the Bruce Medal, given by the Astronomical Society Pacific in 1982; the National Medal of Science, given in 1984; the Russell Prize, given in 1984; and the Albert Einstein World Award of Science Medal, given in 1988. She was also elected to the National Academy of Sciences in 1978. In 1990 Burbidge became a professor emeritus.

Books

Notable Scientists: From 1900 to the Present, Gale Group, 2001.
Scientists: Their Lives and Works, Vols. 1–7, 2004.

Periodicals

Smithsonian November 2005.

Online

"Burbidge, E. Margaret," International Center for Scientific Research, http://www.cirs.net/investigadores/Astronomy/Burbidge.htm (January 6, 2006). □

Rahul Dev Burman

The wildly eclectic scores of Indian composer Rahul Dev (R.D.) Burman (1939-1994) did much to define the internationally popular "Bollywood" sound of Indian film music, which became internationally popular as electronic dance producers with Indian roots began to draw on Burman's music as raw material.

T he music from Burman's more than 300 scores furnished an inexhaustible trove of samples for dance recordings and remix specialists. Some of Burman's compositions, sung by top Indian movie stars in films filled music, became hits. At the center of Burman's achievement, however, were his film scores themselves. No musical genre anywhere in the world could be ruled out for potential incorporation into Burman's kaleidoscopic scores, which featured flavors from Indian classical and regional traditions, jazz, rock, swing, circus music, Mexican mariachi, and Brazilian bossa nova, among other styles. Burman also numbered the leading contemporary classical string quartet in the United States, the Kronos Quartet, among his admirers.

Started on Harmonica

The son of pioneering Indian film composer and singer Sachin Dev Burman, Burman was born in Calcutta (now Kolkata) on June 27, 1939. For most of his life he was commonly referred to by the nickname Pancham, which he acquired as a baby, according to one story, when Indian singer Ashok Kumar heard him babble the syllable ''Pa'' repeatedly. ''Pa'' was the name of a note in the Indian scale system, meaning ''fifth'' in Sanskrit and comparable to ''sol'' in the Western solfèe scale. Burman built on this promising musical beginning. He was raised mostly by a grandmother in Calcutta while his father spent time in the film industry center of Bombay (now Mumbai), and he knew India's urban poverty. At one point Burman's family and another family shared a one-room house. But he learned the harmonica well enough to perform at a school assembly, and his father, in attendance, realized that his son had musical talent. The next morning, Burman's father asked him how long he had been practicing. ''I replied that I'd been having a go for the past eight months and wanted to be a better music director than he,'' Burman recalled in a *Filmfare* interview reproduced on the Pancham Online website. ''My answer must have surprised him.''

From that point on, S.D. Burman took a greater interest in his son's musical education. At first, Burman was given a grounding in the basics of India's complex classical music system. His father groomed him as a composer and encouraged him to learn different instruments so that he would become familiar with their capabilities. Beginning in his pre-teen years and starting on the tabla drum, he then studied the sarod, a difficult Indian stringed instrument, with Ali Akbar Khan and Ashish Khan, two of India's greatest classical musicians. Burman went on to write some scores in traditional classical styles, and he included elements of classical instrumentation in many others. He also began writing songs in the manner of those heard in India's growing film industry, which became the largest in the world.

Burman's father wanted to take him from Calcutta to Bombay to train him in film composition, but his grandmother resisted the idea because she believed the environment of the film industry would have a corrupting influence on Burman, who had already begun to take a rebellious attitude toward his studies. Once, Burman's father asked his son whether he had done any composing, and Burman responded by playing 15 songs he had recently written. A year later, watching a film called *Funtoosh*, Burman heard a familiar-sounding song in the score his father had composed. ''I blurted out aloud—'My God, that's my tune,' '' he told *Filmfare*. ''I wrote and accused my father of flicking my tune and he admitted he had.'' The song, entitled ''Ae meri topi palat ke aa,'' went on to become a big hit, strengthening Burman's determination to become a composer.

Burman finally began working in films as an assistant to his father, earning his first credit on the 1955 film *Pyaasa*. He played several instruments on that film's soundtrack, and his father began schooling him in the finer points of film composition and assigning him to work with different singers and directors. More and more actual composition work was handed off to Burman, who was often credited as assistant music director on films scored by his father in the late 1950s, and the two developed a spirit of friendly competition that honed Burman's skills. Burman was signed as music director for a 1959 film called *Raaz,* but the film was shelved before shooting could be completed. His first official credit as music director was *Chhote Nawab* (1961).

Quoted Chubby Checker Song

Burman worked as assistant music director on several more of his father's films in the early 1960s and began to add non-Indian influences to his musical makeup. He accompanied jazz musician friends to recording sessions and developed a strong appreciation for the form, believing that a knowledge of jazz and its improvisation techniques were essential for an Indian film music director. The international Twist dance craze also marked the beginning of a strong Western pop influence. Burman featured a tune very much like that of American vocalist Chubby Checker's ''Let's Twist Again'' in the 1965 film *Bhoot Bungla*. By that time Burman was consistently working as a music director rather than as an assistant to his father.

The many and varied borrowings of non-Indian music that were characteristic of Burman's scores occasionally led to charges that he had simply copied Western hits, perhaps illegally. Burman disputed the allegation, telling *Filmfare* that ''If I like a particular line I take it but after that I improvise. I only borrowed eight bars from Abba's ''Mamma Mia.'' He pointed to the fact that he had not encountered significant copyright problems: ''If you copy in toto you may have trouble. Again, there are common phrases in music . . . and two people using the same may just be a coincidence.'' The list of Burman songs modeled on Western hits is a long one, and Burman enthusiasts have compiled his borrowings on websites.

Burman's breakthrough film was *Tesri Manzil* (1965), for which he landed the position of music director after director Vijay Anand arranged a session with producer Nasir Hussain at which Burman could demonstrate some of his tunes. Actor and matinee idol Shammi Kapoor, listening in, is said to have ''screamed 'Yahoo' in sheer appreciation'' (according to the Down Melody Lane website), and Hussain signed Burman to a six-film contract. Burman's ''Aaja Aaja'' soon became one of Indian cinema's famous seduction songs, and his career ascended rapidly. At the height of the Brazilian bossa nova craze in 1966, he introduced the style into his score for *Pati Patni,* and he continued to adapt other international popular styles as fast as his ear could soak them up. He was equally adept, however, in using purely Indian traditions, including Indian classical and folk genres. Burman often based his original music on tunes he heard while dreaming.

In 1970, Burman scored fewer than ten films and this qualified as a rest break for the composer. He hit a lifetime peak in 1972 with a staggering 19 scores, but his output in several other years was slightly lower. Burman occasionally was heard as a singer on his own soundtracks, usually overdubbing on-screen actors. He scored a solo hit with ''Mehbooba Mehbooba'' from the 1975 film *Sholay,* but more often he was heard in duets with another vocalist,

Asha Bhosle. Burman had married a woman named Rita in 1960. They divorced in 1971, and Burman and Bhosle added a personal relationship to their professional one, marrying in 1980. Bhosle's became the voice most prominently associated with Burman's music. Thanks to his prolific musical output, she became by some accounts the most recorded singer in human history, with more than 13,000 recorded songs.

Used Bottles as Instruments

Between 1980 and 1985 Burman's output of scores never dropped below ten per year. He kept up with new developments in pop electronics coming from the West, but he also had a knack for matching sound to situation using very low-tech means; he used soda bottles as instruments, and on "Mehbooba Mehbooba" he played on a Listerine bottle. When the Kronos Quartet gathered Burman material for its 2005 album *You've Stolen My Heart,* they tried to replicate the varied instrumental sounds of Burman's soundtracks but were understandably unable to identify the Listerine bottle without help. "When I think of Burman as an orchestrator, he belongs in the same sentence as a Stravinsky or a Debussy," Kronos Quartet violinist David Harrington told Ernesto Lechner of the *Chicago Tribune.* Burman won Indian *Filmfare* awards in 1982 (for *Sanam Teri Kasam*) and 1983 (for *Masoom*).

Burman's popularity finally was dented somewhat by new styles in the late 1980s, and demand for his services, although not his productivity, dropped off. After a 1988 heart attack, he claimed to have composed 2,000 new tunes in his head while recuperating. He remained active in the early 1990s, composing music for several little-known films and bouncing back with one widely acclaimed masterpiece, the film *1942: A Love Story* (1993). The movie won Burman's third *Filmfare* award, but sadly was not released until after his death on January 4, 1994. He had composed music for 331 films: 292 were in Hindi, 31 in Bengali, three in Telugu, two each in Tamil and Oriya, and one in Marathi. One film, a 1980 Indo-Russian co-production of *Ali Baba and the 40 Thieves,* contained Russian-language songs. Burman also released five albums unconnected with films and wrote non-cinematic songs for other artists, mostly in the Bengali language. Indian-American director Mira Nair included Burman's "Chura liya hai" in her 2000 film *Monsoon Wedding,* an affectionate tribute to Indian cinema.

The continuing presence of Burman's creations in the language of Indian music was ensured when a generation of dance music creators who had grown up with his music began to use it for samples and remixes in new dance-oriented recordings. As Indian fusions gained popularity in England and even in the United States, Burman's name became better known. Kronos Quartet violinist Harrington began to investigate Burman's career when he realized that it was Burman who had composed his favorite Bollywood scores, and the result was the 2005 album *You've Stolen My Heart,* which brought the septuagenarian Asha Bhosle out of retirement to perform on the album. That collection of 12 Burman songs promised to provide a new springboard for the appreciation of the man whom many considered Indian film music's greatest composer.

Periodicals

Chicago Tribune, September 25, 2005.
Denver Post, October 16, 2003.

Online

"Biography," http://www.panchamonline.com (February 13, 2006).
"R.D. Burman," http://www.downmelodylane.com/pancham.html (February 13, 2006).
"R.D. Burman: 'My God, That's My Tune,'" http://www.panchamonline.com (February 13, 2006).
"Rahul Dev Burman," Internet Movie Database, http://www.imdb.com/name/nm0005983 (February 13, 2006). □

C

Cantinflas

Cantinflas (1911-1993) was one of Mexico's most beloved cinematic figures, a masterful comedian who cast himself as the resourceful voice of the common people. With a stream of his trademark nonsense talk, he could neutralize the powerful or work around the most absurd forms of bureaucracy.

That nonsense talk was so well known that by the end of his life Spanish dictionaries listed a new verb, cantinflear, meaning to talk a lot without really saying anything. Cantinflas released some 45 films over his long career, gaining some recognition among English-speaking audiences when he appeared in the 1956 crowd-pleaser *Around the World in 80 Days.* Often considered a Mexican counterpart to silent-film comedian Charlie Chaplin—an impression reinforced when Chaplin, according to the *Houston Chronicle,* called him "the greatest comedian alive"—Cantinflas actually blended verbal comedy in a way that recalled various figures of early English-language cinema without resembling any of them closely.

Performed on Streets

The youngest of eight surviving children in his family, Cantinflas (cahn-TEEN-flas) was born Mario Moreno Reyes August 12, 1911, in Mexico City. His father, a post office worker, hoped for professional success for his son and enrolled him in good schools. But Cantinflas preferred to watch the Mexican capital's numerous street performers and, as soon as he was old enough, to try to imitate their tricks and acrobatic feats. Although he did not grow up in extreme poverty, he soon gained sympathy for those who

did. Cantinflas was sent to a government agricultural school when he was 15, but he dropped out to join a *carpa*—the Mexican version of the American tent show.

For a while, Cantinflas was a jack-of-all trades after dropping out of school. He acquired his unusual stage name, which had no real meaning in Spanish, very early on. Several stories have circulated as to its origin, but he seems to have derived it from "En la cantina, tu inflas" (In a bar, you drink), a line that amused him when it was hurled his way by a drunken heckler one night in a bar. He was looking for a stage name, anyhow, for he still hoped to hide his performing career from his parents. Cantinflas was active as both a boxer and a bullfighter, activities that demanded quick thinking.

In the bull ring, Cantinflas was a *torero bufo,* a comic matador so popular that pawnshops had to be closed to stop poor fans from putting their possessions in hock so they could see him perform. Later, in films (including *Around the World in 80 Days*) he performed versions of his bullfighting routine, in which he would walk into the ring, head buried in a newspaper, and remain motionless until the charging bull was inches away. Cantinflas was a ham in the boxing ring as well, and on stage in the tent shows he was popular as a dancer.

None of these appearances required him to speak much, however, and one night when he filled in for a sick friend as a tent show's emcee he was seized with stage fright. As he tried to deliver his lines, he began to talk nervously and rapidly, saying the first thing that came into his mind just so that he could keep going. The audience, thinking that the rapid-fire patter was part of his routine, started to laugh, and Cantinflas kept on dishing up more of it. As he refined his unexpectedly successful act, the central part of his performing personality was born. His nonsense

speech was a mixture of double-talk, mangled high-class mannerisms, malapropism, and pantomime, at which he always excelled—one of his specialties was a full-scale game of pool, with no table, balls, or cue stick. In a country with a small hereditary aristocracy and a growing urban underclass, Cantinflas used his nonsense speech to twit upper-class ways.

Joined Follies Bergère

Cantinflas climbed his way up the theatrical ladder and in 1935 joined the cast of the Follies Bergère variety show in Mexico City. He made his first film appearance the following year in *No te engañes, corazón* (Don't Kid Yourself, Sweetheart), but the film had little success. In 1937 he married Valentina Ivanova Zubareff, the daughter of a Russian-born tent show owner. The two stayed together until Valentina's death in 1966 and raised a son, Mario. Valentina urged Cantinflas to keep trying to crack the growing world of cinema, and he appeared in several more films. In the late 1930s he made a series of comic short subjects in which he was featured in a short story but that were essentially commercials for various products, shown along with newsreels between film presentations. The director of these films signed Cantinflas to make two full-length features, *Ahí está el detalle* (Here's the Point, 1940) and *Ni sangre ni arena* (Neither Blood Nor Sand, 1941). These films had Mexicans lining up in the street and outgrossed the top imported comedy of 1941, Chaplin's *The Great Dictator;* it was apparently *Ni sangre ni arena* that inspired Chaplin to put Cantinflas's talents above his own.

Cantinflas and two partners formed their own production company, Posa Films, and between 1941 and the mid-1950s he regularly released one or more films every year. His persona was that of the *pelado* (the word means "one who is broke"), the down-and-out but resourceful son of the Mexico City streets. Like Chaplin, Cantinflas had a trademark moustache (his was pencil-thin), and he sometimes wore a hat made of newspaper. He could gain unlimited comic mileage out of the old vaudeville technique of wearing a pair of pants held up by a length of string, always threatening to fall down. Combining physical and verbal comedy, he was, in the words of Octavio Roca of the *San Francisco Chronicle,* "all the Marx Brothers rolled into one."

Another way in which Cantinflas resembled the great comedians of American cinema was that he mastered the trick of playing different characters in each new film but still keeping a consistent personality that came through to the audience. "Cantinflas had a pact with his audience," wrote *Houston Chronicle* reporter Fernando Dovalina. "Even though Cantinflas never stepped out of his character while he was on, the whole act was done with a knowing, subtle, and unseen nod to the common people. He was one of them. The adults could laugh at the witticisms-with-a-wink, and the children could laugh at the farce." Such films as *El circo* (The Circus, 1942), *Un día con el diablo* (One Day with the Devil, 1945), *El mago* (The Magician, 1948), and *Abajo el telóon* (Bring Down the Curtain, 1954) were consistent hits. By 1951 Cantinflas was so popular that a mural of Mexican heroes by artist Diego Rivera depicted him in its center panel.

Dovalina saw Cantinflas's films as a child in south Texas in the 1940s, and they became very popular in Mexican-American neighborhoods north of the border. Cantinflas's verbal routines, however, were impossible to translate into English, and he remained unknown among English-speaking audiences. Cantinflas frequently traveled to the United States, however, and he later acquired homes in the Los Angeles and Houston areas. Cantinflas made powerful American friends, including then Congressman Lyndon Johnson of Texas. In 1966, when Cantinflas's wife was suffering from cancer, the by-then-President Johnson sent a jet to bring her to the U.S. for treatment.

Appeared as Valet

There was obviously potential profit to be made if Cantinflas's popularity could be expanded into the English-speaking world, but the comedian's grasp of English was shaky, and the right opportunity never came along. Finally, in 1956, Cantinflas was cast, over the initial objections of director Michael Todd, in the adventure romance *Around the World in 80 Days.* Cantinflas played the role of Passepartout, a valet to well-heeled traveler Phineas Fogg (David Niven). Passepartout was intended to be of French origin, but Cantinflas convinced Todd that a change in nationality would work, and, moreover, would give him the chance to trot out one of his comic bullfighting routines. His intuition was vindicated when *Around the World in 80 Days* became an international hit and earned Cantinflas a Golden Globe award for best actor in a musical or comedy.

Meanwhile, Cantinflas suffered no slowdown in his Spanish-language career, *Sube y baja* (Up and Down, 1958), in which he played an elevator attendant, achieved some international distribution. An attempt to use Cantinflas in a starring English role was unsuccessful, however; *Pepe*, which starred the comedian as a ranch hand who takes off for Hollywood to try to find a prize horse who has been sold to an alcoholic film director, was a big-budget flop despite the presence of a roster of stars (Bing Crosby, Shirley Jones, Jack Lemmon, Janet Leigh, Jimmy Durante, and many others). Cantinflas returned to the Mexican market, now sometimes working in Hollywood. He released new films consistently through the 1960s, ending his career with *Patrullero 777* (Patrolman 777, 1977) and *El barrendero* (The Street Cleaner, 1981). He made one more appearance in the Mexican television film *México . . . estamos contigo* (Mexico, We Are With You) in 1985.

By that time Cantinflas, who had invested his money cannily and sheltered some of it in offshore locations to avoid Mexican taxes, was a wealthy man. Part of his mystique among Mexicans grew from his generosity in plowing money back into neighborhoods like the one in which he had grown up. His annual charitable donations were once estimated at $175,000. At one point he single-handedly supported 250 families in the Mexico City neighborhood of Granjas, and he built and sold off dozens of low-cost housing units.

In his later years Cantinflas lived off and on in Houston. He carried on a relationship there with an American woman, Joyce Jett, and largely stayed out of the limelight. He remained a folk hero in Mexico, however, and appeared on television in that country with Mexican president Carlos Salinas de Gortari over the 1992 holiday season. After a lung cancer diagnosis, he died in Mexico City on April 20, 1993. Salinas, according to Mike Reid of the London *Guardian*, called him "a Mexican legend," and his funeral service, initially planned to be restricted to family and close friends, was crowded with thousands of Mexicans great and small.

Cantinflas's reputation continued to grow after his death. Several Spanish-language books chronicled the comedian's career, and an English-language academic study, *Cantinflas and the Chaos of Mexican Modernity,* sought to relate his film comedy to the tremendous social changes that had overtaken Mexico during his career. A biographical, bilingual play, *Cantinflas!,* was presented in San Francisco and Houston, and it seemed that, despite the continuing language barrier, one of the great comic figures in the popular culture of the 20th century was becoming better known outside Latin America.

Books

Contemporary Hispanic Biography, vol. 4, Gale, 2003.

Pilcher, Jeffrey M., *Cantinflas and the Chaos of Mexican Modernity,* Scholastic Resources, 2001.

Stavans, Ilan, *The Riddle of Cantinflas: Essays on Hispanic Popular Culture,* University of New Mexico Press, 1998.

Periodicals

Guardian (London, England), April 23, 1993.

Houston Chronicle, April 23, 1993; September 21, 1993.

Independent (London, England), April 24, 1993.

Los Angeles Times, April 11, 2001.

New York Times, April 22, 1993.

San Francisco Chronicle, September 17, 2002.

Times (London, England), April 22, 1993.

Variety, April 22, 1993.

Online

"Cantinflas," All Movie Guide, http://www.allmovie.com (January 22, 2006). □

Cao Yu

Chinese playwright Cao Yu (1910–1996) was an innovator of the *huaju* or "spoken play" genre, even referred to by many as "the Shakespeare of China." His 1933 play *The Thunderstorm* marked the height of Chinese Modern Drama and remains one of the most celebrated plays of any period.

Early Life

Cao Yu was a professional pseudonym for Wan Jiabao, born on September 24, 1910 in Qianjiang Country in the Hubei Province of China. He was raised in Tianjin (Tientsin) where his father worked as a bureaucrat, serving as secretary to President Li Yuanhong at one time. Cao Yu's mother died when he was still just a child, but he remembered attending traditional Chinese theatre productions with her at the early age of three. He also learned early that he had a gift for expressing himself through writing, and even recalled composing sentimental poetry as a child—a tendency that would blossom into a finely–honed aesthetic talent in his later literary career.

Education

Cao Yu attended Nankai Middle School in Tianjin from 1922 to 1928. While enrolled there, he eagerly joined Nankai Middle School's New Theatre Troupe—an exceptionally innovative and well-established Western-style theatre program in northern China. The troupe flourished under the tutelage of well-known dramatist, Zhang Pengchun. Cao Yu, a young teen, proved to be a natural at acting—particularly when forced to play female roles—and he used the experience as an opportunity to absorb the spirit and minutiae of the theatrical environment. Performing as an actor helped Cao Yu develop an acute perception of the larger picture as a playwright—allowing him to write for and relate to the actors he later directed in his own productions. After finishing at the Middle School, Cao Yu was enrolled at Nankai University in Tianjin from 1928 to 1930 with the intention of studying political economy. The draw of the arts was strong, however, and he soon transferred to the western literature program at Qinghua (sometimes spelled "Tsinghua") University in Beijing and studied there from 1930 to 1933. The years Cao Yu spent at Qinghua proved to be very influential for his development as a writer. The young author read works by playwrights like Aeschylus, Shakespeare, Henrik Ibsen, George Bernard Shaw and Eugene O'Neill—all of whom used drama at one time or another to challenge social corruption. Cao Yu admired this dynamic, and developed it to serve as a platform in his own early writing. From 1935 to 1940 Cao Yu taught at the National Academy of Dramatic Art in Nanjing, and spent some time serving as Dean of that institution. He also spent a short time in 1940 teaching English to students of the Women's Normal College in Hubei Province. Before graduating from Qinghua, however, Cao Yu unknowingly launched his career as a playwright when he wrote and staged *The Thunderstorm*.

Life as a Playwright

While still a student at Qinghua University, Cao Yu wrote and published his first significant play at the age of 24, titled *The Thunderstorm* (*Leiyu,* 1933). The work was described by critics from the *Welcome to China* website as "a full–length modern drama [that] features the complicated relationships among the members and servants of a large well–off family and [their] disintegration as a result of the morbidity and corruption in old China." This landmark drama was adapted for film twice and was even performed as a ballet in 1983 by the Shanghai Ballet Troupe. The next play in what would turn out to be Cao Yu's dramatic trilogy was "Sunrise" (*Richu,* 1934)—a tale of vice and opulence among the rich portrayed in stark contrast to the misery of the poor in old China. This play, too, was adapted for film as well as performed as a musical by the Musical Center of China. Cao Yu's daughter, Wan Fang, wrote the scripts for both the film, and the musical staging. The final play in Cao Yu's trilogy was "Wilderness" (*Yuanye,* 1935)—described by Eric Pace's *New York Times* 1996 obituary as a story about "an unjustly imprisoned peasant who escapes to get revenge on a family of rich, corrupt landowners". *New York Times* critic Ben Brantley, who saw "Wilderness" staged at the Manhattan's Playhouse 46 by the Pan Asian Repertory in English in 1994 described Cao Yu's third drama as "a fascinating example of a transitional society's theater in search of a new form." Other popular plays written by Cao Yu included "Metamorphosis" (*Shuibian,* 1940), "Peking Man" (*Beijing Ren,* 1940) and a 1941 dramatic adaptation of Ba Jin's novel, "The Family" (*Jia*). While all of what Cao Yu produced was well–accepted by critics and audiences alike, none of his later works ever prompted the intense response and lofty praise that *The Thunderstorm* enjoyed.

The *huaju* genre—sometimes translated "word drama" or "spoken play" and referred to as Modern Chinese Drama—differed from the musically vocal traditional Chinese dramas in which the players sang operatically. Cao Yu was particularly adept at crafting and directing vivid, resonant female characters, and he displayed a gift for dialogue that was described in the *McGraw–Hill Encyclopedia of World Drama* as "snappy, minutely detailed [and] 'psychological' . . ." The adoption and adaptation of the spoken Western format did not lead to mimicry as far as Cao Yu was concerned. One literary source from the *Renditions* website of Chinese culture expressed that

"Although heavily influenced by Western theatre, [Cao Yu's] plays are thoroughly Chinese in manner and material." Although Cao Yu was not the only playwright dedicated to presenting and exploring the cultural and social changes that had taken place during and after the country's transformation from "Old China" to "New China", he was certainly the most prominent, and his efforts did not go unnoticed. In 1936, *The Thunderstorm* won the Dagong Bao Literary Prize, and Cao Yu enjoyed his pick of political titles and positions.

Beyond the Stage

In 1937 Cao Yu co-founded the Dramatic Society of China, and he spent 1939 as an instructor at the Sichuan National Dramatic School. He married Zheng Xiu in 1939, and they had two daughters, but were divorced in 1951. While Cao Yu was adept at disseminating social questions via the stage, he also found other ways to reach people, which included using the power of academics to provide people with a view inside Chinese society. In 1946 he was invited, along with peer Lao She, to take part in a lecture tour of the United States, educating academic audiences about Chinese drama. He welcomed the opportunity, and spoke eloquently about the infusion of Western character into Eastern culture. In March of 1949 he served as a Chinese delegate at the World Peace Council Session held in Prague, and two years later he married his second wife, Deng Yisheng, and had two more daughters before she died in 1980. Cao Yu, alongside his colleagues Jiao Juyin, Ouyang Shanzun and Zhao Qiyang founded the Beijing People's Art Theatre in 1952 and in May of 1956, Cao Yu was appointed as its director.

In July of 1956, Cao Yu officially joined the Chinese Communist Party in response to a movement to enlist founding thinkers. He had, in his life and career, been appointed to numerous political positions, until China's Cultural Revolution. In December of 1966, Cao Yu was labeled a counterrevolutionary and—like so many other Chinese intellectuals—accused of bourgeois thinking. Accused of dissident behavior due to the ways in which his plays challenged audiences to think and question social inequalities and injustices, he joined the ranks of other artists and academics that were seen as both dangerous and arrogant. The Revolution sought to restore a sense of practical humility to the intellectual population, and in compliance with this Cao Yu was taken from his home in the middle of the night and sent to a "re–education" camp in the countryside. He and his peers spent the prescribed amount of time performing manual labor and cultivating the required level of social meekness. The *Cambridge Guide to Theatre* describes how Cao Yu was "rehabilitated" and eventually reintroduced as a "father figure of the modern theatre."

Cao Yu spent the time in the countryside and the rest of the Revolution "creatively inactive", and returned with a propaganda piece titled "Bright Skies"—sometimes translated "Clear, Bright Day"—(*Minglangde tian,* 1956), which was performed at the Beijing People's Art Theatre and touched on more modern issues such as the medical community and germ warfare. William Dolby of the *McGraw–Hill Encyclopedia of World Drama's* noted how "In his earlier plays Cao was concerned with conflicts within family and society between the traditional and new aspirations and ethics . . . something of the style remains in his more recent plays (1984), which often assert, however, a vigorous ideological mood.'' Approximately ten years later, in January of 1975, Cao Yu made his first public appearance since his denunciation, and was woven back into the culture. He was offered and accepted many more political appointments throughout the remainder of his life and was the recipient of numerous awards, including the French Légion d'Honneur awarded in 1987. His second wife had died during the Cultural Revolution, and he married a third time (Li Yuru) at the end of his life. Critics agreed that the work he produced post–Cultural Revolution was somewhat tainted by transparent propagandistic agendas, but that Cao Yu remained a master of his craft.

End Scene

Cao Yu died on December 13, 1996 in Beijing, China. He was 86 years old when he passed, and had been hospitalized for eight years prior to his death. While this gifted author is no longer generating new works, his plays continue to move audiences all over the world and have been translated into multiple languages including Japanese, Russian and English. Awards have been endowed in Cao Yu's name, such as the Cao Yu Drama Literature Awards held in Xi'an—the capital of the Shaanxi Province in northwestern China—in November of 2000. His dramatic trilogy (*Thunderstorm, Sunrise* and *Wilderness*) is considered by critics to be the culmination of Chinese drama's growth, and his prowess is made all the more significant by the fact that playwrights were constantly facing the challenge of attracting audiences in a time of increasing media saturation—fighting for attention with pop music, television programs and variety game shows.

Another tribute created in Cao Yu's memory was Wang Mei's 2002 landmark modern dance drama, ''Thunder and Rain.'' Editor and journalist Richard Lee of *www.china taiwan.org* explained that although ''modern dance [in China] is often considered an 'insider's art' because of its complex expression and lack of mass popularity . . . one woman with a fighting spirit has pushed this peripheral art to the forefront of China's artistic scene. Wang Mei, a professor of choreography at Beijing's Dance Academy, is considered one of China's premier modern dance choreographers. 'Thunder and Rain', her signature work, is recognized as China's first modern dance drama . . . adapted from the late literary giant Cao Yu's trademark play 'Thunderstorm', Wang Mei's 'Thunder and Rain' [was a] huge success [and] marked a watershed in Chinese modern dance.'' Cao Yu was truly a man of many talents, with capabilities as an actor, a director, a screenwriter and a playwright. While the Chinese Modern Drama genre saw its peak with Cao Yu's early works, the combative spirit of his accomplishments has cast a significant shadow on the face of modern theatre.

Books

The Cambridge Biographical Encyclopedia: Second Edition, edited by David Crystal, Cambridge University Press, 1998.
The Cambridge Guide to Theatre, edited by Martin Banham, Cambridge University Press, 1995.
Chambers Biographical Dictionary, edited by Melanie Parry, Chambers Harrap Publishers, Ltd., 1997.
Dolby, William, *International Dictionary of Theatre: Playwrights*, edited by Mark Hawkins-Dady, St. James Press, 1994.
Dolby, William, *McGraw-Hill Encyclopedia of World Drama*, edited by Stanley Hochman, McGraw-Hill, Inc., 1984.
The International Who's Who 1993-94: Fifty-Seventh Edition, Europa Publications, Ltd., 1993.
The Oxford Encyclopedia of Theatre and Performance: Vol. 1 A-L, edited by Dennis Kennedy, Oxford University Press, 2003.
The Far East and Australasia 1980-81, Europa Publications, Ltd., 1980.
Who's Who in the People's Republic of China: Second Edition, edited by Wolfgang Bartke, Institute of Asian Affairs, 1987.

Periodicals

New York Times, December 16, 1996.

Online

''Cao Yu,'' *Beijing People's Art Theatre*, http://www.bjry.com/english/founder.jsp (January 5, 2006).
''Cao Yu,'' *Encyclopedia Britannica Online*, http://www.britannica.com/eb/article-9104151 (January 5, 2006).
''Cao Yu,'' *Hubei*, http://www.cnhubei.com/200502/ca677340.htm (January 5, 2006).
''Cao Yu,'' *Renditions*, http://www.renditions.org/renditions/authors/caoyu.html (January 5, 2006).
''Cao Yu and His Trilogy,'' *China Culture Information Net*, http://english.ccnt.com.cn/?catog=drama&fil;=040301&ads=service_001 (January 5, 2006).
''Cao Yu Drama Literature Awards Announced in Xi'an,'' *People's Daily*, http://english.people.com.cn/english/200011/05/eng20001105_54397.html (January 5, 2006).
''Choreographer: Wang Mei,'' *Taiwan, China*, http://www.chinataiwan.org/web/webportal/W5180042/Uadmin/A5589184.html (January 9, 2006).
''Modern Chinese Drama,'' *Welcome to China*, http://www.wku.edu/~yuanh/China/drama.htm (January 5, 2006). □

Hoagy Carmichael

A giant among composers of American popular music, Hoagy Carmichael (1899-1981) wrote ''Stardust,'' the song that has according to many reckonings been recorded more often than any other in the history of music. Several other songs—''Georgia on My Mind'' and the infectious ''Heart and Soul''— have been hardly less popular, reaching nearly universal familiarity among listeners born decades after they were written. Likewise successful as an actor and as a musical performer, he did much to establish the image of the songwriter in the American mind.

Carmichael's songs are often described as nostalgic in tone; many of them unfold in a landscape of American small towns and countryside scenes and draw some of their emotional power from the attachment Americans have held for the country's agrarian past.

Country singers including Willie Nelson and Crystal Gayle have shown an affinity for his material. Yet in another way Carmichael was the most modern, the hippest, of his songwriting contemporaries, even though he grew up in Indiana and did not share the urban background that has nurtured the bulk of the popular tradition in his time and in our own. More than almost any other white songwriter of his age (George Gershwin being one of the exceptions), Carmichael understood jazz and incorporated it successfully into his musical language. This insight did not await the investigations of musical historians; jazz musicians, both black and white, took to Carmichael's music from the beginning, and they were the first to identify the incredible potential contained in the wandering melody of "Stardust."

Family Faced Money Problems

Carmichael was born in Bloomington, Indiana on November 22, 1899. His father was an electrician and general laborer who found work only intermittently and often moved the family around as he searched for employment. They traveled as far as Montana at one point, always returning to Indiana. The experience of poverty shaped Carmichael's personality—he had a lifelong skinflint side, even after becoming wildly successful—and gave him an ambitious streak. One positive side to the family's shaky financial straits was that Carmichael's mother, a talented ragtime pianist, took jobs entertaining partygoers at Indiana University fraternities in Bloomington; Carmichael grew up hearing music and sometimes dozed on two pushed-together chairs as his mother played. Sometimes the family lived in

racially integrated Bloomington neighborhoods, and Carmichael was exposed to the sounds of African-American gospel music.

Though he assumed he would go into a professional career, there were forces pushing Carmichael toward the arts as well. The family knew the nationally prominent Indiana poet James Whitcomb Riley. And when they moved to Indianapolis in 1916, the teenaged Carmichael found himself in a large city that was an important popular-music crossroads. He took piano lessons from an African-American barber and ragtime pianist named Reginald DuValle, and aside from some childhood studies with his mother that was the only structured musical training he ever received. That set him apart from other songwriters, the vast majority of whom had classical training of some sort. Soon Carmichael had dropped out of high school and was playing piano in Indianapolis nightspots high and low, paying the bills by driving a cement truck and working in a slaughterhouse during the day. DuValle's son recalled (according to a *New York Review of Books* article reproduced on the Official Hoagy Carmichael website maintained by his family) that "In our neighborhood we seldom had any white people. So he kind of stood out, if you know what I mean."

Carmichael's mother Lida warned him (as has often been reported, for example by Daniel Okrent in *Forbes*) that "Music is fun, Hoagland, but it don't buy you cornpone." His financial ambitions reasserted themselves, and he returned to Bloomington to finish high school. Getting wind of the new jazz music of the day, however, he booked a Louisville Band led by a musician named Louie Jordan (not the later singer of "Ain't Nobody Here But Us Chickens") to play a party. Jazz hit Carmichael full force. As quoted on the Hoagy Carmichael website maintained by his family, he recalled that hearing this band "exploded in me almost more music than I could consume." Enrolling at Indiana University, Carmichael took law classes but also formed a jazz band called the Carmichael Syringe Orchestra and Carmichael's Collegians.

A second strong shot of jazz influence came when Carmichael heard a performance by Iowa-born cornetist Leon "Bix" Beiderbecke, often regarded as the first great white jazz musician. Booked by Carmichael for a series of ten fraternity dances, Beiderbecke befriended Carmichael and suggested that he try his hand at songwriting. Carmichael complied with a pair of songs, "Free Wheeling" and "Washboard Blues" (the latter a depiction of an African-American washerwoman), that, thanks to Beiderbecke, began to spread around the Midwestern jazz world. Carmichael bought a cornet and began to play it so obsessively that his friends eventually hid the instrument. He recalled (according to *Washington Post* writer Martin Weil) that "Bix showed me that jazz could be musical and beautiful as well as hot."

Heard Own Song Performed in Store

Carmichael received his bachelor's degree in 1925 and his law degree the following year. He moved to West Palm Beach, Florida, hoping to cash in on the Florida land boom. Those plans quickly changed when one day he heard a jazz band called Red Nichols & His Five Pennies playing "Washboard Blues" in a local store. He returned north to Indiana and started writing music seriously, making a series of recordings for the Gennett label in Richmond, Indiana, in 1927. Among them was an instrumental called "Star Dust"—originally spelled with two words. The African-American jazz band McKinney's Cotton Pickers performed "Star Dust" and recorded it in 1928, but both their version and Carmichael's own were up-tempo renditions that seemed to smother the melody's delicate filigree. In 1929 he headed for New York City to try to make it in the music business.

Still working days for a stockbroker, he circulated among jazz clubs at night and met Louis Armstrong, whom he had heard and admired in Chicago earlier in the decade, as well as several future swing titans: clarinetist Benny Goodman and bandleader brothers Tommy and Jimmy Dorsey. The young lyricist Johnny Mercer became one of his favorite collaborators. Things picked up when he sold "Star Dust" to the Mills Music Company. The song went nowhere when it was issued as a sheet-music instrumental in early 1929, and even a poetic set of lyrics added by songwriter Mitchell Parrish did little to help. Jazz bands continued to be attracted to "Stardust," however, and the Isham Jones Orchestra tried out a slower tempo on a 1930 recording. A flood of other recordings followed, and Bing Crosby had a hit with his vocal version in 1931. Within a few years "Stardust"—a lost-love song about love songs—had achieved the status of standard that it still holds today. Carmichael (as quoted on his family's website) recalled feeling a "queer sensation that this melody was bigger than me" the first time he heard a recording of the song. "Maybe I hadn't written it at all. . . . I wanted to shout back at it, 'maybe I didn't write you, but I found you.' "

Carmichael was hitting his peak creatively and turned out numerous hits in the early 1930s, many of them sharing the relaxed but jazzy groove of "Stardust." "Rockin' Chair," released in 1930, harked back to the African-American spiritual cadences of Carmichael's youth (he wrote the lyrics himself) in its depiction—quite unusual for a popular song—of an old woman "chained to my rockin' chair" and awaiting her Judgment Day. Carmichael recorded "Georgia on My Mind" in 1930 and published it the following year. The lyrics were by Carmichael's Indiana classmate Stuart Gorrell.

Beiderbecke's death at age 28 from alcohol-related complications hit Carmichael hard emotionally, and his music, whether for that reason or simply because of larger changes in the language of popular song, gradually became less jazzy. In 1936, the year he married Indianan Ruth Meinardi, Carmichael headed for Hollywood. The pair had two sons, Hoagy Bix and Randy, before divorcing in 1955. Carmichael, often working with lyricist Frank Loesser, had lost none of his melodic gift; his late 1930s hits included "Small Fry," "Two Sleepy People" and, in 1938, "Heart and Soul," a tune so simple that children and other musical novices quickly learn to pick it out on the piano, yet so ingeniously structured as to be instantly memorable for a lifetime. The latter two hits were among the comparatively small number of love songs in Carmichael's oeuvre.

Became Familiar Film Presence

Carmichael's career in the movies began in 1937 with a bit part in *Topper.* He performed his own material in many films, playing a nightclub pianist in the 1942 hit *To Have and Have Not,* starring Humphrey Bogart and Lauren Bacall. Carmichael's biographer Richard Sudhalter has credited him with fostering the growth of the singer-songwriter profession in American music; certainly he was in the minority among songwriters of his time in becoming well known for his own renditions of his songs. The year 1942 brought Carmichael another major song hit with "Skylark," written to a lyric by Johnny Mercer. He sang his own "Ole Buttermilk Sky" in the 1945 *Canyon Passage,* helping that song along to standard status as well.

As vocalists came to the fore after World War II, a spate of new recordings of Carmichael's songs appeared; during the year 1946, Carmichael songs held three of the top four places on the national Hit Parade ranking at one point. Carmichael continued to write new material, and in 1951 "In the Cool, Cool, Cool of the Evening," with Mercer once again as lyricist, won an Academy Award for Best Song. He appeared in various films including the Beiderbecke biography *Young Man with a Horn,* hosted a television show called *The Saturday Night Review,* and even had a non-musical role in the late 1950s in the Western television series *Laramie.*

With the coming of rock and roll, Carmichael's string of hits seemed to be at an end. In the 1960s he wrote two classical orchestral works, *Johnny Appleseed* and *Brown County in Autumn,* but they gained little attention. Yet his songbook became ever more securely ensconced in the American musical mind. If "Stardust" became a trifle less pervasive (at least until Willie Nelson's hit recording of 1978), "Georgia on My Mind" gained new life through Ray Charles's recording in 1960, on the album *The Genius Hits the Road.* It became one of the songs most identified with the great rhythm-and-blues legend.

An enthusiastic golfer and coin collector, Carmichael lived the high life in California in his old age. He married actress Wanda McKay in 1977. Carmichael lived long enough to attend ceremonies for several major awards bestowed upon his body of work; in 1972 he received an honorary doctorate from his alma mater, the University of Indiana, which established an archive of Carmichael materials in 1986. After suffering a heart attack, he died in Rancho Mirage, California, on December 27, 1981. The awards rolled on, and a Hoagy Carmichael U.S. postage stamp was issued in 1997. Jazz chanteuse Norah Jones's recording of Carmichael's "The Nearness of You" in 2002 testified to the continuing vitality of his work in the new millennium.

Books

Sudhalter, Richard, *Stardust Melody: The Life and Music of Hoagy Carmichael,* Oxford, 2002.

Periodicals

Detroit Free Press, April 5, 2002.
Fortune, March 29, 1999.

New York Review of Books, September 26, 2002.
New York Times, December 28, 1981.
San Francisco Chronicle, May 2, 2002.
Sunday Telegraph (London, England), April 14, 2002.
Washington Post, March 31, 2002.

Online

John Edward Hasse, "Brief Biography," The Hoagy Carmichael Collection (University of Indiana), http://www.dlib.indiana.edu/collections/hoagy/research/bio/index.html (December 10, 2005).
"A Short Biography by William L. Wheatley," The Official Hoagy Carmichael Website, http://www.hoagy.com/bio_short.html (December 10, 2005).
"Hoagland 'Hoagy' Carmichael," Red Hot Jazz, http://www.redhotjazz.com/hoagy.html (December 10, 2005). □

Marcel Carné

French film director Marcel Carné (1906-1996) is regarded as one of Europe's great filmmakers. Though he had a long career, his reputation rests on the six films he made from 1937 to 1945. One of the films in that period, *Les Enfants du paradis* (1945), is regarded by critics and film historians as one of the greatest movies ever made. In his best works, he collaborated with popular French poet and screenwriter Jacques Prévert.

Carné was born on August 18, 1906, in Paris, France. He was the son of Paul and Maria (Recouet) Carné. He was educated at the Education Ecole d'Apprentissage du Meuble in France, and worked as an apprentice cabinet maker and an insurance clerk in the mid-1920s. In the late 1920s, he broke into film. In 1928, he worked as an assistant to cameraman Georges Périnal on *Les Nouveaux Messieurs,* for director Jacques Feyder, who would influence both Carné and the direction of French Cinema. The following year, Carné made his first film, a short documentary entitled *Nogent, Eldorado du dimanche.* He also made a number of publicity shorts, but his documentary so impressed Rene Clair that, in 1930, the great French director hired Carné as his assistant director on *Sous les toits de Paris* (Under the Roofs of Paris).

In the 1930s, Carné again worked with Feyder, serving as his assistant director on *Pension Mimosas* (1934) and *La Kermesse heroique* (Carnival in Flanders, 1935). During this period, Carné also worked as a film critic, sometimes publishing his articles under the pseudonym Albert Cranche. He was editor-in-chief of *Hebdo-Film* and wrote for *Cinemagazine, Cinemonde,* and *Film Sonore.*

Began Collaboration with Jacque Prévert

In 1936, with the help of Feyder and his actress wife, Francoise Rosay, Carné secured his first feature-length film assignment, directing *Jenny.* Though this first feature film has been described as a "routine melodrama," Carné would soon establish himself as one of the leading directors in France. Moreover, his works would be praised throughout Europe as well as the world.

The script for *Jenny* was written by Jacques Prévert, and the collaboration initiated an ongoing, fruitful professional relationship that helped develop Carné's reputation. Prévert, a poet, would write the scripts for most of Carné's greatest films. In his poetry, Prévert, who was associated with the Surrealist movement in France, blended humor, sentimentality, fatalism and social satire. This style, described as poetic realism, was popular in the years leading up to the German occupation of France and World War II, and it informed many of his screenplays.

Carné's best work resulted from his collaborations with Prévert and included *Quai des brumes* (Port of Shadows, 1938), *Le Jour se lève* (Daybreak, 1939), *Les Enfants du paradis* (Children of Paradise, 1945) and *Les Portes de la nuit* (Gate of the Night, 1946).

Bringing the attitudes of poetic realism into cinema, these films were both lyrical and pessimistic, contrasting or combining dismal reality with an intuited metaphysical realm, and self-determinism with cruel fate. They were characterized by Carné's richly detailed recreations of gritty social environments.

Their collaborative film works would dominate the French film industry for ten years. But the professional relationship did not survive long after World War II, and the team ended their working relationship in 1947.

Established as a Major Director

Carné's second feature film, *Drôle de drame* (Bizarre, Bizarre), a crime/comedy/fantasy released in 1937, was a great improvement over *Jenny*, due in large part to Prévert's contribution. The film itself has been described as peculiar, and it initially confused French audiences. It reflected Prévert's taste for the absurd and the surreal. The story is set in England in the early 1900s, and the filmmakers took aim at the bourgeoisie. Today, its blend of "screwball comedy" elements and dark humor seem ahead of its time.

The film also marked the start of ongoing collaborations with set designer Alexandre Trauner and composer Joseph Kosma. Previously, Carné and the Hungarian-born Trauner worked together on Feyder's *La Kermesse heroique.*

As much as an improvement that Carné's second feature represented, it was *Quai des brumes* (1938) and *Le Jour se lève* (1939), two more collaborations with Prévert, that truly established Carné as a major European director. The two films were imbued with the romantic fatalism that typified poetic realism and that would characterize this era of French cinema. In the films, lovers find fleeting happiness in a violent and bleak world.

Le Jour se lève especially epitomized poetic realism, as it focused on working-class people and had a fatalistic, tragic plot. Released in France in December 1939, during the occupation, just before the start of World War II, the film was banned by French authorities because of its defeatism.

Displaying the essence of poetic realism, the film was moody and atmospheric, involving characters locked into circumstances beyond their control. Careful attention was paid to elements such as lighting, detailed sets and music. Composer Kosma set Prévert's poem "Les Feuilles mortes" to music, and the distinct melody formed the basis of a popular song that became known in the United States as "Autumn Leaves." The melody befitted a film whose overwhelming effect is best described as haunting.

The film features a unique and elaborate flashback plot structure that would influence later films. The story involves "Francois," a decent man driven to commit murder for love. At the outset of the film he is hiding out from police in his apartment. During the siege, he recalls the circumstances that led him to kill another man. Everything is revealed in a series of flashbacks, which tell the story of how Francois fell in love with Francoise, a young flower vendor under the spell of the evil Valentin, a dog trainer who performs at a music hall.

The film had a pungent atmosphere developed, in large part, from Carné's characteristic careful attention to detail. Carné and set designer Trauner created an apartment set as a single unit without movable walls. In addition, Carné, seeking realistic effect, insisted that real bullets be used for the scenes when the police fire upon Francois' apartment.

In this film, as in his best works, Carné was greatly influenced by Feyder, who developed a style of French filmmaking that exhibited a strong visual flair, with realism created in the artificial environment of a studio. The style also involved elaborate scripts, intelligent dialogue and actors that could display "star" presence. As a result of the unique plot structure and the well-written dialogue, Hollywood took notice and remade the film in 1947 as *The Long Night,* directed by Anatole Litvak and starring Henry Fonda, Barbara Bel Geddes and Vincent Price as a sinister magician.

German Occupation Coincided with Career Peak

In between *Quai des brumes* and *Le Jour se lève,* Carné released *Hotel du Nord* (1938), with a script written by Jean Aurenche instead of Prévert. Still, it was a fatalistic romantic melodrama, like the other two films.

Though their previous films were banned during the Occupation, Carné and Prévert were allowed to continue working together. In addition, Carné continued working with Trauner and Kosma, but the collaborations had to be conducted in secret, as the set designer and the composer were both Jewish. However, Carné was limited in what he could depict on film. Contemporary events were off limits under the German occupation, and films reflecting the pessimistic poetic realism were forbidden, so Carné and Prévert turned to historical subject matter. This resulted in a new visual style. Instead of working in the gray shades of urban, working-class despair, Carné turned to the more ornate and theatrical look of the period-film spectacle. Made in 1942, *Les Visiteurs du soir* (The Devil's Envoys), a costume romance-drama, was an allegory about love and death set in medieval times. Though the film was successful at the time, it has aged badly.

Carné's next film, *Les Enfants du paradis,* released in 1945, was his masterpiece. An ambitious work, it is considered one of the greatest films ever made. Filmed during the war, but not released until after the liberation of France, the movie runs for over three hours and it included two parts, each a full-length feature. It contains both intimate scenes between actors as well as large crowd scenes, and Carné handled both with the skill of a master. Containing elements of farce and tragedy, *Les Enfants du paradis* is a love story set in the theater society of nineteenth century Paris. More specifically, it is a fictionalized depiction of the life of French mime Jean-Gaspard Deburau. Set in 1840, the plot concerns four men, including Deburau, who are in love with the same mysterious woman. However, only Deburau harbors honorable intentions. "Carné would be a world-ranking director with this film alone," wrote film critic and historian Parker Tyler in 1962 in his book *Classics of the Foreign Film.*

Post-War Career Decline

When World War II ended, and *Les Enfants du paradis* was released, Carné was still a young man—he was only in his late thirties—and his future seemed bright. However, his first post-war film, *Les Portes de la nuit,* which returned to the pre-war concerns of poetic realism, was an expensive failure, despite a script by Prévert.

The previously successful collaborators next began work on *La Fleur de l'âge,* but the film was abandoned soon after production started. It turned out to be the last time that Carné and Prévert worked together. Carné's career would continue, lasting until the 1970s, but his films never reached the levels of his earlier efforts.

In 1953, he filmed *Thérèse Raquin,* an adaptation of the Emile Zola novel. The film was a popular success, but critics were less enthusiastic than the public. His next four films, *L'Air de Paris* (1954), *Le Pays d'òu je viens* (1956), *Les Tricheurs* (The Cheaters, 1958), and *Terrain vague,* had nowhere near the impact of his earlier work.

By this time, Carné's career had fallen victim to changing film fashions. His brand of studio-anchored film had been replaced by the "new wave" cinema, advanced by young directors such as Francois Truffaut and Jean Luc Godard. The works of these new directors took filmmaking outside of the studio and into the streets. Their films were low-budget productions made on location and featuring relatively unknown or non-professional actors. This combined to create a greater sense of reality. Further, the films possessed a spontaneous and improvisational feel that made older, studio-bound films feel artificial and passé. The emergence of this new style provoked Carné to comment, "The new wave assassinated me. But then it assassinated the cinema, too." However, his condemnation was far too harsh, as the "new wave" brought new life into the cinema.

Further, the new breed of filmmakers did not end Carné's career. Rather, he persevered. In 1962, he made *Du mouron pour les petits oiseaux.* This was followed by *Trois Chambres à Manhattan* (1965), *Les Jeunes Loups* (1967), *Les Assassins de l'order* (1971), and *La Merveilleuse Visite* (1974).

In 1976, he made what turned out to be his last film, a documentary called *La Bible,* which was released both theatrically and to television.

Honored for Career in Film

In 1984, he received a career tribute from the French film industry, which dedicated that year's Cannes Film Festival to him in honor of his 75th birthday. In 1992, Carné attempted to make one more film, an adaptation of Guy de Maupassant's novel *Mouche.* However, Carné became ill during early production stages, and financing for the film was withdrawn.

Carné died on October 31, 1996, at age 90 in Clamart, near Paris, in France. In the 1990s, in a poll that included 600 French film critics and film professionals, *Les Enfants du paradis* was voted the "Best French Film of the Century."

Books

International Dictionary of Films and Filmmakers, Volume 2: Directors, fourth edition. St. James Press, 2000.
Tyler, Parker, *Classics of the Foreign Film,* Citadel Press, 1968.

Periodicals

Economist, November 16, 1996.

Online

"Biography for Marcel Carné," *Turner Classic Movies,* http://tcmdb .com/participant/participant.jsp?scarlettParticipantId = 29168 &afiParticipantId; = 0 (December 29, 2005).

"Marcel Carné," *Encyclopedia Britannica Online,* http://www .britannica.com/eb/article-9020400?query = new %2Bgerman%2Bcinema&ct = (December 28, 2005). □

Cécile Chaminade

French composer Cécile Louise Stéphanie Chaminade (1857-1944) enjoyed considerable success between about 1880 and 1910, touring as a pianist and performing her own works. In the United States she was so popular that a national group of musical clubs was named after her, and in England her Prélude for organ was played at Queen Victoria's funeral in 1901.

I n the years after World War I, Chaminade's music was mostly forgotten. There may be several reasons for its neglect, but a bias against the works of women composers certainly played a role. Even at the height of her career, Chaminade faced an insoluble dilemma when she aimed her work at male critics: if she focused on lighter genres such as small piano pieces and songs, which were mostly the province of female musicians, her work was thought to be trivial, but if she attempted to work in larger forms, she was criticized for her lack of feminity.

Talent Spotted by Bizet

Chaminade was born in Paris on August 8, 1857 (earlier sources list 1861 as her birth year). Her father was a prosperous insurance office manager for the Parisian branch of a London firm. The family moved to the village of Le Vésinet, west of Paris, when Chaminade was young, in the process acquiring the famed operatic composer Georges Bizet as a neighbor. Chaminade began playing the piano, composing keyboard music and pieces for her local Catholic church when she was very young, and Bizet was reputed to have praised her talent when he visited the family in 1869. Around the same time, she may have played for and impressed the aging Franz Liszt, the undisputed king among piano virtuosi of the nineteenth century.

The beginnings of Chaminade's musical education came from her mother, who played the piano and sang. Even beyond what musical celebrities may have said about her talent, it was clear that she possessed special gifts, and she was taken to meet a professor at the Paris Conservatory named Le Couppey. The teacher urged her to enroll immediately in music theory classes at the Conservatory in Paris, but Chaminade's father, Hippolyte, forbade her to enter the school, believing that it would be improper for a young woman of the upper middle class. A compromise was reached: Chaminade could take private lessons with Conservatory faculty.

In 1875 Chaminade got her first inkling of how the French musical establishment could crush those whom it did not choose to favor: she attended the premiere of Bizet's opera *Carmen,* which is now considered among the greatest

house. Important musical personalities in attendance praised the opera and discussed mounting it during a season of the Opéra-Comique company, but it was never given a full performance.

Chaminade's music continued to gain momentum throughout the 1880s; the Suite for orchestra was performed as far afield as Brussels, and a ballet, *Callirhoë,* was given to great fanfare in Marseilles in 1888. The ballet was performed numerous times, and one section, the *Scarf Dance,* arranged for keyboard, became one of Chaminade's most popular piano pieces. Chaminade mostly failed, however, to crack the top levels of Parisian concert life; her music was performed mainly in smaller cities.

Two important events in the late 1880s conspired to push Chaminade's career in a new direction. The first was the death of her father in 1887. Chaminade's family had fallen on comparatively hard times and had sold their large house in Paris, moving permanently to Le Vésinet. Chaminade, who lived at home until her mother's death, had no ready source of income. But the problem was partly solved with the premiere in Belgium of Chaminade's *Concertstück* (Concert Piece) for piano and orchestra in 1888—it became one of her few large-scale Parisian successes when she repeated the performance in that city the following year. The work became one of Chaminade's most successful; it was soon performed around Europe and even in Chicago, often independent of any appearance by Chaminade. More significant from a financial point of view was that Chaminade's execution of the difficult work propelled her into the top rank of concert attractions. For the next 20 years it was Chaminade the pianist, and tangentially Chaminade the composer, who was in demand.

Chaminade toured steadily around Europe in the 1890s, finding special success in England. She first appeared there in 1892, and gave concerts at St. James Hall and other venues at least once in most years over the next two decades. After her first flush of success she was hardly a critical favorite; one journalist in 1897 disparagingly compared her new works to new fashions coming off the boat from Paris. But audiences, from the Queen on down, loved her. Queen Victoria invited her to perform at Windsor Castle, and the frequency with which she was invited to perform in London testifies to her continuing popularity. Chaminade turned out new music—songs and short piano pieces—to capitalize on the market for her music that these performances created.

Chaminade Clubs Formed

These pieces also found a strong audience in the United States, where Chaminade Clubs—named for Chaminade but devoted to musical events of various kinds—began to spring up around 1900. By 1904 Chaminade estimated that there were 200 separate chapters. The clubs were mostly composed of female musical amateurs. Club members in Brooklyn, New York, made an anagram out of Chaminade's name (quoted in Marcia J. Citron's *Cécile Chaminade: A Bio-Bibliography*) to describe their aims: "C—Concentrated & Concerted Effort; H—Harmony of Spirit & Work; A—Artistic Ideals; M—Musical

of all operas but which was savaged by Parisian critics at the time. The disheartened and ailing Bizet died a few months later. Chaminade was one of those who realized the work's value at the time, and she later wrote an essay condemning the way its composer had been treated.

In 1877 Chaminade performed at the Salle Pleyel concert hall in Paris, and one of her pieces, an Etude (or Study), was published and well reviewed. She followed with a larger concert at Le Couppey's house on April 25, 1878, consisting entirely of her own music. The concert was a success, and Chaminade began to write music for larger ensembles in addition to piano music. She wrote two trios for piano, violin, and cello, and in April of 1881 her Suite for orchestra, a four-movement symphony-like work, was performed on a program mounted by France's National Music Society. Reviews were mixed, but Chaminade's relative youth was noted in prophecies that she might have a bright future as a composer.

Wrote Opera

In the early 1880s, Chaminade's career as a performer picked up; she often appeared in concerts of her own music and as part of chamber music groupings (chamber music is music for a group of a few instruments). She also still had ambitions to write music in larger forms and completed an opera, *La Sévillane* (The Woman from Seville) in 1882. Chaminade, mindful of what had happened to Bizet, proceeded slowly with the project, mounting a performance, accompanied by herself on the piano, at her parents'

Merit Maintained; I—Inspiration; N—Notes (every kind except Promissory); A—Ardor & Aspiration; D—Devotion to Duty; E—Earnest Endeavor." New clubs were established at least through the 1930s.

In 1901 Chaminade married Louis-Mathieu Carbonel, a Marseilles music publisher. Carbonel was 20 years older than Chaminade, and the two agreed to live apart and not to have sexual relations. It was by all appearances a marriage of convenience, but Chaminade spent several years caring for Carbonel after he fell ill with a lung disease during one of her concert tours in 1903. Her career lost precious momentum between that year and the time of Carbonel's death in 1907. In the fall of 1908, though she disliked the idea of making the transatlantic journey, she accepted a lucrative offer to visit the United States and gave concerts in 12 cities. Most were sellouts, and Chaminade's opening recital at Carnegie Hall grossed a near-record $5,000.

By that time, Chaminade's music had begun to seem somewhat old-fashioned. Her lyrical, melodic piano pieces looked back to the short piano works of Frédéric Chopin, with occasional influences from the more dramatic Franz Liszt, but critical attention had shifted to the harmonically daring, impressionistic works of Claude Debussy, which Chaminade herself disliked. Chaminade's popularity, and her musical output, declined somewhat in the 1910s. Aggressive and sometimes explicitly male-centered ideologies of modernism had little use for pleasant music like Chaminade's; her commercial success worked against her, and often her music was characterized as domestic, as intended for the drawing room or salon. Feminist scholars later pointed out the ways in which such characterizations were designed to suppress women's creativity.

Chaminade received some rare recognition in her home country in 1913, when she became the first female composer inducted into the Legion of Honor. The outbreak of World War I put a stop to her creative activity. Living in a villa near Toulon that had been purchased by her husband, Chaminade worked as a nurse for French soldiers in a recovery facility near her home. After the war ended, she resumed performing and made some piano rolls for the Aeolian Company in London. Her health declined in the 1920s and 1930s, and in 1938 her left foot had to be amputated. Living by then in Monte Carlo and being cared for by relatives, she was heartened by the reception of birthday greetings around the world as a result of a campaign organized by the American music magazine *The Etude*. She died in Monte Carlo on April 13, 1944.

A few of Chaminade's pieces—the *Scarf Dance,* the *Concertstück,* and the Concertino for flute and orchestra—remained in the classical repertory, but for a time she was almost completely forgotten. Near the end of the twentieth century, investigations into the music of women composers revived some of her popularity. In her book *Gender and the Musical Canon,* which investigated the more general reasons for the absence of works by women among the most frequently performed classical works, Marcia J. Citron suggested that one movement of Chaminade's Piano Sonata of 1895 may have been organized in such a way as to subvert the common characterization of themes in a sonata move-

ment as "masculine" and "feminine." Many other works by Chaminade, however, awaited rediscovery by performers and music writers. These included the choral symphony *Les amazones* (The Amazons) of 1888—one of just a few large Chaminade works with specifically gender-based content. More generally, the broader phenomenon of Chaminade's popularity, including the Chaminade clubs, invited further investigation.

Books

Citron, Marcia J., *Cécile Chaminade: A Bio-Bibliography,* Greenwood, 1988.
———, *Gender and the Musical Canon,* Cambridge University Press, 1993.

Online

"Cécile Chaminade," *All Music Guide,* http://www.allmusic .com (January 19, 2006).
"Cécile Chaminade," Classical Composers Database, http://www.classical-composers.org (January 19, 2006). □

Hugo Chávez

Venezuelan leader Hugo Chávez (born 1954) has seized an important role on the world political stage with his stance of confrontation toward the United States and his ambitious program of social reforms.

Even more so than other Latin American countries, oil-rich Venezuela has historically been a country sharply divided between rich and poor. Chávez has faced vigorous opposition from the country's traditional elites, spending two years in prison after a 1992 coup attempt, surviving a coup launched against him in 2002, and beating back a recall attempt in 2004. He was popular, even venerated, among poor Venezuelans, for he took steps in the first years of his rule to distribute more of the country's burgeoning oil income among its poorer citizens. Yet Venezuelans were deeply split over the merits of Chávez's reign, and international observers pointed to a growing atmosphere of repression and a concentration of power in Chávez's hands. After meeting Chávez, Colombian novelist Gabriel García Márquez said, according to the London *Independent*: "I was overwhelmed by the feeling that I had just been with two opposing men. One to whom the caprices of fate had given an opportunity to save his country. The other an illusionist, who could pass into the history books as just another despot."

Became Star on Diamond

Chávez was born in Venezuela's Western grasslands region, near the town of Sabaneta in the state of Barinas, on July 28, 1954. Both his parents were schoolteachers, but that was hardly a lucrative profession in the Venezuelan backcountry; his father had only a sixth-grade education himself, and the family was poor as well as dark-skinned, in a country with strong racial divisions and an almost

exclusively white-skinned elite. Chávez was sent to live with his father's mother in Sabaneta and helped raise extra money for the family by selling homemade candies produced by his grandmother. The young Chávez possessed an ability that set him apart from the crowd in Venezuela: he was an excellent baseball (and softball) player in a baseball-crazy country. He played on a national baseball team called the Criollitos de Venezuela in 1969 and continued to excel at the sport as an adult, playing for teams connected with military or educational institutions.

With a desire to make something of himself, Chávez thought about trying to become a major league baseball player. He also thought vaguely about entering politics. After attending the inauguration of Venezuela's president when he was 19, he wrote in his diary (as quoted by Alma Guillermoprieto in the *New York Review of Books*) that he "imagined myself walking there with the weight of the country on my own shoulders." But a political career was not a feasible option, and Chávez joined the military. He studied engineering at Venezuela's national military academy, and though he was never a top-notch student he focused on his work and graduated eighth in his class in 1975. Chávez was immediately popular with his fellow soldiers, and he rose through the military's officer ranks. He was elevated to colonel, heading an elite unit of paratroopers.

Along the way he noticed that the Venezuelan military, like many of the country's other institutions, was riddled with corruption. Chávez spent his spare time reading about

his country's history, and he flirted with the Marxist ideas that had made inroads in Nicaragua and other Latin American countries, often nurtured by progressive religious figures. But his real heroes were the nationalist military leaders who had thrown off Spanish rule in the nineteenth century—above all Simón Bolivar, the father of Venezuelan independence and a figure of mythical dimensions, sometimes known as the George Washington of South America. With his natural charisma, Chávez drew other soldiers to his ideas. Starting with small cells, he built a network of supporters within the Venezuelan military. It was called MBR 200, the Bolivarian Revolutionary Movement.

A defining event in Chávez's military career came in 1989, after falling oil prices had devastated the Venezuelan economy and led President Carlos Andrés Pérez to institute a series of austerity measures. Riots erupted in the capital city of Caracas after an announcement that bus fares would be increased, and the army was sent into the streets to quell the protests. Chávez was part of the group deployed, and he was angered by orders to shoot at Venezuelan citizens who he felt had legitimate grievances. The experience was a primary motivation for the military coup he organized against the Pérez government three years later.

Radio Announcement became Popular Slogan

The 1992 Chávez coup was quickly put down, but his co-conspirators launched attacks on government installations around the country. In hopes of preventing further bloodshed, the government allowed Chávez a 45-second television address so that he could tell others to lay down their arms. It was a mistake on the government's part, for Chávez made the most of the time he had available, announcing to his fellow Venezuelans that his movement had for now—"por ahora"—been unsuccessful in achieving its goal. Within a few days, "por ahora" graffiti appeared around Caracas, and Chávez had emerged as the standard-bearer for Venezuela's masses of hillside slum dwellers.

Chávez was jailed but was given the comparatively mild charge of rebellion and spent only two years in prison, despite the fact that his associates mounted a second coup attempt nine months after the first. After he was pardoned by president Rafael Caldera and given an honorable discharge from the military, Chávez launched a bid to win power by peaceful means. He and a group of leftist politicians formed a new party called the Fifth Republic Movement, which fielded Chávez as its presidential candidate. On December 6, 1998, he was elected to the Venezuelan presidency, his first political office, with 56 percent of the vote.

Chávez moved quickly on both political and public relations fronts to consolidate his power. He pushed through a new constitution that replaced Venezuela's American-style bicameral legislature with a single National Assembly, and provided for a six-year presidential term that could be extended by re-election. In 2000 Chávez scheduled a special election that would install him for the new six-year term. Running on an anti-corruption platform, he was elected with 60 percent of the vote, Venezuela's largest mandate in several decades.

Like Cuban leader Fidel Castro, with whom he cultivated closer ties, Chávez had the habit of giving lengthy speeches to his people, speeches that combined policy statements and general pep talks. Sprinkled with quotations from Jesus Christ and Simón Bolivar, Chávez's addresses took the form of a television program, *Alo, Presidente*. Chávez might touch on any topic from baseball to nutrition to the United States, which Chávez blamed for the problems of South America's poor. As the United States sought to expand hemispheric commerce through free-trade agreements, Chávez emerged as a major opponent of globalization and a general thorn in the side of the new U.S. administration of President George W. Bush.

Opponents Staged Coup

Chávez was also despised by Venezuela's upper classes, partly out of prejudice against his modest origins and partly over substantive policy disagreements. After Chávez fired the managers of Venezuela's national oil company in 2002, a group of business executives with supporters in the Venezuela army and in large labor unions launched a coup against the Chávez government on April 12. Groups of anti- and pro-Chávez demonstrators clashed in front of the presidential palace, and Chávez was taken away by the coup plotters. When the insurgents announced that they were dissolving the constitution, however, the tide turned in Chávez's favor; a palace guard contingent that had remained loyal to him joined with a large crowd of demonstrators, and the coup collapsed after 50 hours. The United States, which had hailed the change of government, was forced to backtrack, and Chávez blamed Americans—accurately, according to many foreign press reports—for aiding the insurrection.

Chávez's opponents did not give up. In 2004 they gathered signatures for a recall election that, if successful, would have removed him from power. The recall went forward after judicial wrangling over the legitimacy of some of the signatures. But by this time the United States had invaded Iraq and oil prices were headed skyward. Average household income in Venezuela rose 30 percent in 2004, and Chávez began to spend lavishly on new schools and public works projects. The success of Chávez's antipoverty initiatives has been a matter of debate, but loans for small businesses and rural cooperatives, a centerpiece of Chávez's economic strategy, were abundant. Top religious leaders such as Venezuelan Cardinal Ignacio Velasco had backed the coup against Chávez and opposed him, but Chavez had support among the religious rank-and-file, and he often accused Catholic church leaders of not following Christ's path. Chávez handily beat back the August 15 recall with just under 60 percent of the vote.

Victory emboldened Chávez in various ways. Dissent within the Venezuelan armed forces was now dealt with harshly, and the 3.2 million Venezuelans who had signed recall petitions found themselves discriminated against. Chávez missed no opportunity to criticize the United States. He brought charges against an election-monitoring group, Sumate, that he claimed was a front for U.S. operatives, and he expelled U.S. missionaries after charging them with spying. Chávez claimed that Venezuelan spies had uncovered U.S. plans to invade the country, and he stockpiled arms in anticipation of such an eventuality. In 2005, a U.S. religious evangelist played into Chávez's hands by publicly advocating Chávez's assassination.

Chávez skillfully made use of such events, gaining supporters at home as well as in the United States, where he offered aid in the wake of Hurricane Katrina in 2005 and directed Venezuela's state oil company, which did business in the United States under the Citgo name, to provide low-cost heating oil to residents of U.S. cities. Visiting the United States in 2005, Chávez greeted supporters in the New York borough of the Bronx and met for an interview with *Newsweek*, telling the magazine that "the media is trying to make the American people see me as an enemy." Questioned about his assertion that the United States was a terrorist state, Chávez told the magazine, "What I said is that this U.S. administration—the current [George W. Bush] government—is a terrorist administration, not all U.S. governments."

Despite clashes between Venezuela and the United States (Chávez also engaged in war of words with Mexican president Vicente Fox), Venezuela continued to supply between 8 and 15 percent of U.S. energy needs, and U.S. oil purchases financed the social programs that cemented Chávez's hold on power. Chávez-style populism seemed to be spreading in South America as Bolivians elected a socialist, Evo Morales, to the presidency. New tensions flared in early 2006 when Chávez expelled a U.S. naval attaché from Venezuela, charging him with spying. But Chávez seemed likely to win a second term in his re-election bid that year.

Books

Contemporary Hispanic Biography, vol. 1, Gale, 2002.
Gott, Richard, and Georges Bartoli, *Hugo Chávez: The Bolivarian Revolution in Venezuela*, Verso, 2005.

Periodicals

Christian Science Monitor, May 20, 2005; February 6, 2006.
Independent (London, England), March 20, 2004.
New Statesman, October 10, 2005.
Newsweek, October 3, 2005; December 19, 2005.
New York Review of Books, October 6, 2005; October 20, 2005.
Smithsonian, January 2006.
Sojourners, May 2004.

Online

"Profile: Hugo Chavez," BBC News, http://www.news.bbc.co.uk/2/hi/americas/3517106.stm (February 11, 2006). □

Maurice Chevalier

Over a performing career that spanned seven decades, singer and actor Maurice Chevalier (1888-1972) became one of the most familiar figures in the entertainment world. With his trademark straw hat and a cheerful romantic image, he was as popular in the United States as in his native France.

Baby Jesus." For the rest of his life, even with all his success as an actor and as a recording artist, the medium that brought out Chevalier's best was the one-man nightclub show, mixing music, humor, and skits with hand gestures and pantomime.

By the time he was 17, Chevalier was a well-known figure among those who frequented Paris nightspots, and he had performed as far afield as Marseilles in southeastern France. "Records and radio and movies did not exist at that time," Chevalier was quoted as saying by Alden Whitman of the *New York Times*. "It took years of traveling and playing to a few hundred people a night to build a reputation."

Found Love During Rug Routine

Unlike most of his contemporaries, Chevalier had begun paying his dues in early adolescence, and he was ready when a big break came his way in 1909: while performing at the Folies-Bergère music hall in Paris, he was assigned to partner Mistinguett, the leading female music-hall performer of the day. Their routine began with the pair rolled up together in a rug; as it unrolled, it deposited them on stage, and they began to sing and dance. The routine made Chevalier's name with the Paris public, and the rug encounter touched off the first of his well-publicized romances; after Chevalier won a street fight with Mistinguett's aggrieved ex-boyfriend, the two were romantically involved for several years and even moved in together, although they never married.

The romance lasted through Chevalier's brutal experiences in World War I; he was drafted, suffered a punctured lung after being hit with a piece of shrapnel that passed through his backpack, and spent more than two years as a German prisoner of war. The only positive aspect of this ordeal was that he talked a fellow prisoner into teaching him English. After he was released, Chevalier was awarded the Croix de Guerre, a military honor roughly equivalent to the U.S. Purple Heart. Chevalier launched a solo career after the war and the relationship with Mistinguett cooled, although the two continued to perform together occasionally. He adopted his trademark straw hat after seeing a man on a London street wearing a tuxedo and straw hat that he liked.

Chevalier had appeared in films as early as 1914, and his acting career picked up during the golden age of silent film even though the art form could not accommodate his singing as yet. In 1922 and 1923 he had starring roles in the French films *Gonzague, Le mauvais garçon* (The Bad Boy), and *Par habitude* (By Habit). Later in the 1920s, Chevalier suffered from what would now be called major depression. Twice he attempted to commit suicide, and he completely lost confidence in his performing ability. A year in a Swiss rehab facility did him no good, but finally a doctor forced him to perform for a small group of Swiss villagers and things began to turn around. In 1927, for the first and only time in his life, Chevalier married; his relationship with dancer Yvonne Vallée was stormy, and they divorced in 1935. Gradually, Chevalier rebuilt his rapport with crowds, although he froze up completely during his first American film audition.

Born in Paris on September 12, 1888, Chevalier grew up in poverty. His alcoholic father, Victor, deserted the family when Maurice was eight, and his mother scraped together a living for herself and her three children as a lacemaker. When she got sick and was unable to work for a short period, Chevalier was placed in a government-run group foster home. Chevalier and his two older brothers were very close to their mother and gave her the nickname of La Louque—a word that had no meaning beyond its use as a term of endearment. Her real name was Josephine.

Fall Ended Acrobatic Career

Chevalier was determined to escape this hard life, and he saw the performing arts as a way out. At first he auditioned at a circus as an acrobat, but after he was injured in a fall his mother tried to steer him toward safer work. He became an engraver's apprentice, he tried carpentry, and he worked in a tack factory. He was fired from each of these jobs. He was fixed, however, in his desire to become a performer, even after he was laughed off the stage when he performed at an amateur-night event at a Paris café. Josephine Chevalier changed her tune and began to tell her son she was sure he would become a star.

So Chevalier kept at it and soon did well enough, at least, to earn free coffee when he sang in a café. Chevalier's theatrical instincts began to show when he began singing comic songs and added to his café performances some comedy routines that poked fun at his own youth. Café owners picked up on the joke and began to bill him as "the

Parodied by Marx Brothers

His next attempt went much better, and 1929's *The Love Parade,* directed by Ernst Lubitsch and co-starring Jeannette MacDonald, kicked off a series of American film hits for Chevalier, whose ability to combine singing, romantic interest, and comedy was tailor-made for the new "talkies." Chevalier garnered a pair of Academy Award nominations for Best Actor in 1930, one for *The Love Parade* and the other for *Innocents of Paris.* He sang his hit song "Paris" in both films. Other mostly French-themed movies followed, with the debonair Chevalier as romantic lead: *The Big Pond* (1930), *The Playboy of Paris* (1930), and *Love Me Tonight* (1932) all helped make Chevalier an American screen idol. He co-starred with Claudette Colbert in *The Smiling Lieutenant* (1931) and with Norma Shearer in *The Merry Widow* (1934). Chevalier was well known enough that the Marx Brothers could parody his singing of "If a Nightingale Could Sing Like You" in their 1934 farce "Monkey Business," confident that their nationwide audience would get the joke.

Never a top-notch singer, Chevalier succeeded on the strength of his ability to read and play to an audience. Among the performers he admired was vocalist Al Jolson, who was noted for powerful personal charisma in his live shows. Chevalier had some of the same ability to forge a bond with audiences, and, unlike Jolson for the most part, he was able to carry that ability over to the big screen. According to Alden Whitman in *The New York Times,* he attributed his success partly to his modest vocal skills. "Thank God, it was my good luck not to have any voice," he said. "If I had, I would have tried to be a singer who sings ballads in a voice like a velvet fog, but since I am barely able to half-talk and half-sing a song, it made me look for something to make me different from a hundred other crooners who are neither good nor bad."

Chevalier cut his own American film career short after a dispute with producer Irving Thalberg in 1936 over whether he or MacDonald should receive top billing in their next film. His popularity at home as a stage performer continued unabated, although he made no more films in France until that late 1940s and in the U.S. until the 1950s. Hitting his peak years as a cabaret performer, Chevalier found his life and career disrupted by World War II.

His situation was a dangerous one, for he was living with a Jewish woman, a young actress named Nita Raya. Chevalier kept a low profile after German troops overran France in the early stages of the war, and the two hid out at a house in the Free French zone, under Nazi government. At one point, Chevalier agreed to perform for a group of French prisoners held by the Germans. He was attacked as a Nazi collaborator, and the *Washington Post* editorialized that "evidently he was one of those artists who are at all times prepared to sing for their supper without bothering too much about the respectability of the host." Chevalier contended that he had performed in order to facilitate a prisoner exchange, and the controversy simmered down when General Dwight D. Eisenhower backed Chevalier's version of events. Chevalier later told Eisenhower's wife Mamie that the future president had saved his life—French resistance fighters were known to have gunned down suspected Nazi sympathizers.

Signed Anti-Nuclear Letter

Appearing with sympathetic friends such as songwriter Noel Coward, Chevalier worked his way back into public favor. He appeared in the French film *Le silence est d'or* (Silence Is Golden, released in the U.S. as *Man About Town*) in 1947 and gave a one-man show in New York that year. In 1951 he was set to return to Hollywood to resume his American film career, but the country was in the grip of anti-Communist hysteria, and Chevalier was denied entry because he had signed the Stockholm Appeal, a letter urging governments to renounce the use of nuclear weapons. He was finally allowed to enter the U.S. in 1954 and made several more concert tours.

Chevalier returned to American films in 1957 with a role in the Gary Cooper-Audrey Hepburn romantic farce *Love in the Afternoon,* for which he received a Golden Globe award nomination. The culmination of Chevalier's second career was the lavish film musical *Gigi* (1958), set in Paris and starring the young Leslie Caron but featuring Chevalier as an aging playboy. He was once again nominated for the Golden Globe best actor award, and he received a special Academy Award that year for career accomplishments.

Though he had spoken English for many years, Chevalier still had an imperfect command of the language. Some said that he carefully maintained the imperfections in his English diction, and indeed they became part of his image, heightening the charm of the witticisms that often dropped from his lips. When he turned 78 and was asked how it felt to have reached that age, his often-quoted reply was that he felt wonderful, considering the alternative.

Chevalier remained active into old age, staying in shape by doing calisthenics and playing golf, and he enjoyed adulation during several rounds of farewell tours. He appeared in films through the 1960s, including *Fanny* (1961), *In Search of the Castaways* (1962), *I'd Rather Be Rich* (1964), and *Monkeys, Go Home!* (1966), and he had a role in the animated feature *The Aristocats* in 1970. Shortly before his death he recorded the theme song for the French version of that film. Chevalier died in Paris on New Year's Day of 1972, at age 83.

Books

Chevalier, Maurice, *I Remember It Well,* Macmillan, 1970.
———, *The Man in the Straw Hat,* Crowell, 1949.
———, *With Love,* Little, Brown, 1960.

Periodicals

New York Times, January 2, 1972.
Washington Post, January 2, 1972.

Online

"Maurice Chevalier," All Movie Guide, http://www.allmovie .com (November 5, 2005). □

John Clare

John Clare (1793-1864), dubbed the Peasant Poet of Northamptonshire when he created a sensation in early 1820s London, was a noted poet of the Romantic era, often concerned with the natural world he came to know well while living on a small English farm.

Long ranked among the minor English poets, Clare experienced a critical and even a popular resurgence beginning in the 1990s. This resurgence had roots both in Clare's work and in his biography. Clare, who grew up in a household with a father who could barely read and a mother who was illiterate, was a powerful user of the English language but one who was never comfortable with its grammatical conventions. In a modern society increasingly comfortable with spoken poetry rather than words on a printed page, Clare's work seemed newly significant. Public fascination likewise resulted from the fact that Clare was institutionalized in an asylum in later years. The precise nature of his illness is elusive, and his madness seems at least to have begun with his realization that he was at fundamental odds with the artistic culture in which he worked, and that life, as a result, was beginning to twist its way around him.

Had Hard, Rustic Upbringing

Clare was born on July 13, 1793, in Helpston (or Helpstone, as it was sometimes spelled at the time), a village in the English region of Northamptonshire. His father Parker Clare was a farm worker and, Clare wrote in an autobiographical sketch quoted in *John Clare in Context,* ''one of fate's chance-lings who drop into the world without the honor of matrimony.'' Two of Clare's three siblings, including a twin sister, died in infancy, and Clare grew up in grinding rural poverty. He was working in the fields with his father by age 10. Clare's mother, despite her own illiterate state, was a believer in education, and Clare went to school with local tutors for about three months of the year—scanty by modern standards or by those of a noble youth in his own time, but enough to open a new world that was unknown to his peers. His early reading exercises consisted of working his way through the family Bible and prayer books.

When Clare was 13 he got a job as a potboy—a server of ''pots'' of liquor in a local tavern. For much of his life he would be a heavy drinker, with debatable results for his overall health. In his teens Clare did hard labor, much of it connected with enclosure—the fencing and hedging of common pasture land that over several centuries transformed the English countryside into something less free and more restricted by property rights. Clare dug ditches and cut hedges, and scholars believe that the enclosure process had a subtle but definite effect on his later poetry. While he was working, however, he was also composing poems in his head. Clare liked poetry from the start, and an uncle gave him a book of poems by John Pomfret when he was 11. Two

years later he acquired a copy of a long and well-known nature poem cycle, James Thomson's *The Seasons* of 1730. The poem, he said (as quoted on the John Clare Page website), made his heart ''twitter with joy.'' He dove over a wall at a local estate, Burghley House, and hid in a forested area so that he could read it undisturbed, and on his way home he composed his first poem, ''The Morning Walk.''

Clare worked as a gardener at Burghley house beginning around 1807, dodging his supervisors as he read and wrote poetry on the sly. He also wrote poetry on Sundays, skipping church to practice what he called the religion of the fields. Clare tried out his poems on his parents, at first claiming that they had been written by someone else but gradually gaining confidence. Clare's material circumstances did not improve during this period. He spent several years in the Northamptonshire Militia and worked as a lime-burner, a filthy, dangerous job involving the incineration of limestone to produce a variety of useful agricultural and industrial chemicals. Clare fell in love twice, once with a farm girl named Mary Joyce, and then, in 1820, with Martha ''Patty'' Turner, who became his wife.

By that time, Clare had accumulated a collection of poems and spread his literary wings. In the town of Stamford he met a bookstore owner named Edward Drury and a local editor, Octavius Gilchrist. Drury sent him to London to meet a publisher cousin, John Taylor, who had issued some of John Keats's poetry. In 1820, Taylor published Clare's *Poems Descriptive of Rural Life and Scenery*. On the title page of the book he was billed as a Northamptonshire

Peasant. The billing was an astute one, for the modern fascination middle-class audiences have for "roots" cultures is traceable to the early 19th century. With the Scottish dialect poems of Robert Burns and the Irish songs of Thomas Moore in the air, prospects looked bright for a talented young writer from rural England.

Found Admirers in London

Poems Descriptive of Rural Life and Scenery sold more than 3,000 copies in its first year, an astounding total for an unknown poet, and it was soon reprinted three times. Clare traveled to London and for the first time he encountered famous creative artists. He met the painter Edward Rippingille, and on subsequent trips the poet John Keats, the critic William Hazlitt, and the opium-eating essayist Thomas De Quincey, among others. Clare acquired several noble patrons who would later stick with him through difficult times. He quickly followed up his first book with *The Village Minstrel and Other Poems,* published in 1821. It was well received but did not become the sensation of the moment as his first book had.

Through the 1820s, Clare worked energetically on a variety of projects, most of which were never published. They are notable for their variety and their sheer quantity; Clare's lifetime output, even as he spent half his adult life in institutions, ran to thousands of pages. Much of what is known of his early life comes from his autobiographical *Sketches in the Life of John Clare,* which he began in 1821 but which remained unfinished. Clare also started a book called *A Natural History of Helpstone* and wrote a long satirical poem, *The Parish,* which cast a critical eye on small-town life. He began collecting the songs of ballad singers in the Helpston area, making him one of the very first close observers of what would now be known as folk music. Clare was also interested in the music of the gypsy or Romany people who moved through the area.

Indeed, Clare's father was a reasonably good tavern singer, and Clare felt close to musicians who passed down their songs by ear rather than writing them down. He often referred to traditional ballads or even adapted their words in his poetry. And his notebooks reveal a creative process more oriented toward his own thoughts than toward the model of the printed page. He rarely used punctuation, paid little attention to spelling, and used verbal patterns drawn from the local Northamptonshire dialect. Since so much of Clare's work was never published, modern editors have wrestled with the question of whether to standardize his writing when readying it for inclusion in new collections.

One Clare book that was published was *The Shepherd's Calendar; with Village Stories and Other Poems,* in 1827. That book, a sort of country calendar with poems, sold only 400 copies, which spelled financial trouble for Clare since he and his wife by that time had seven children. Clare became moody, wrangled with his publisher, and sometimes went on drinking binges. In 1828, frustrated by his prospects, he returned to farming.

Settled in Cottage

A cottage and a small plot of land on an estate in nearby Northborough, provided in 1832 by one of Clare's aristocratic admirers, gave him a temporary fresh start. Clare threw himself into writing a new set of poems, to be called *The Midsummer Cushion,* which he hoped would be judged on its merits rather than as the freakish product of an uneducated farmer. Soon, however, Clare's difficulties returned. His new farm was undercapitalized, and expenditures kept pace with or exceeded income. Orders for Clare's new book lagged, and it was finally published in 1835, after what Hugh Haughton and Adam Phillips in *John Clare in Context* called "mutually soul-destroying negotiations" with John Taylor, as *The Rural Muse,* in a heavily cut form.

Clare complained of writer's block and memory loss, and friends who visited him were disturbed to find him muttering incoherently. In 1837 Taylor led an intervention in which Clare was taken to the High Beech Asylum, a progressive institution that bore little resemblance to the hellholes to which the mentally ill were usually consigned. Clare had free run of the grounds and surrounding woods, and was able to write. Other signs, however, were less encouraging: he began to develop multiple personalities, sometimes saying that he was the poet Lord Byron or a boxer named Jack Randall. He began to describe Mary Joyce as his first wife, although the two had never been married.

Modern observers have disagreed as to the precise nature of Clare's illness; speculation about schizophrenia gave way to those involving more contemporary maladies. Some argued that Clare was not mentally ill at all. They found support in the fact that even Clare's most deranged communications seemed to make a kind of symbolic sense; Clare's illusion of being a boxer might have been intended as a way of saying he felt at odds with the world. It is also significant that Clare's poetry, although he wrote less while institutionalized, showed no decline in creativity. One of his most often anthologized poems, "I Am," dated from 1841, the last year of his first term in the asylum. "I am: yet what I am none cares or knows," Clare wrote. "My friends forsake me like a memory lost; I am the self-consumer of my woes."

In the summer of that year, Clare escaped from the asylum and walked the approximately one hundred miles to Northborough, recording his experiences in a manuscript titled *Journey Out of Essex.* He spent about five months with his family and was then taken to the Northamptonshire General Lunatic Asylum, where he spent the rest of his life. Clare wrote nearly 1,000 pages of poetry between 1861 and his death on May 20, 1864, and some of it filtered out to literary magazines and was published. Clare complained bitterly about his incarceration, and one often-quoted visitor (as for example by Haughton and Phillips) recorded that he said "they have cut off my head, and picked out all the letters of the alphabet—all the vowels and consonants—and brought them out through my ears; and then they want me to write poetry! I can't do it." Before his death, however, he wrote another famous poem, the quizzical "To John Clare."

Clare's poetry exerted an increasing fascination as the 20th century went on, especially as society in general began to wrestle with the nature of mental illness. Poet Theodore Roethke, who himself wrestled with mental demons, admired Clare, as did radio host and poetry anthology editor Garrison Keillor. Indeed, suggested Jeredith Merrin in *The Southern Review*, "the American audience may be especially primed now to enjoy Clare's poetry," which was subjective, rather undisciplined, and sometimes very sexy ("Lay by thy woollen vest. / Drape no cloak o'er thy breast: / Where my hand oft hath pressed / Pin nothing there: / Where my head droops to rest, / leave its bed bare," Clare wrote in one poem quoted by Merrin). Most important of all, Merrin argued, was the semi-oral nature of Clare's poetry in a time when spoken poetry, thanks to hip-hop music and poetry slams, was on the rise. Whatever the reason, Clare was the focus of numerous new editions and scholarly studies from the 1980s onward.

Books

Bate, Jonathan, *John Clare: A Biography,* Picador, 2003.
Haughton, Hugh, et al., ed., *John Clare in Context,* Cambridge, 1994.

Periodicals

Contemporary Review, October 1997.
Southern Review, Autumn 2004.

Online

Contemporary Authors Online. Gale, 2006. Reproduced in *Biography Resource Center.* Farmington Hills, MI: Thomson Gale. 2006. http://galenet.galegroup.com.servlet/BioRC (January 23, 2006).
John Clare Page, http://www.johnclare.info (January 23, 2006).

□

Alice Coachman

American athlete Alice Coachman (born 1923) became the first African American woman to win an Olympic gold medal when she competed in track and field events in the 1948 Olympic Games. As such, Coachman became a pioneer in women's sports and has served as a role model for black, female athletes. She established numerous records during her peak competitive years through the late 1930s and 1940s, and she remained active in sports as a coach following her retirement from competition.

On the way to becoming one of the top female track and field athletes of all time, Coachman had to hurdle several substantial obstacles. Not only did she compete against herself, other athletes and already established records, Coachman successfully overcame significant societal barriers.

Even though her race and gender prevented her from utilizing sports training facilities, and her parents opposed her athletic aspirations, Coachman possessed an unquenchable spirit. Resourceful and ambitious, she improvised her own training regimen and equipment, and she navigated a sure path through organized athletics. At the peak of her career, she was the nation's predominant female high jumper. She was at the top of her game in high school, college and Olympic sports, and led the way for other female athletes, in particular future African-American female competitors. In a 1995 article published in *The New York Times,* William C. Rhoden wrote, "Her victory set the stage for the rise and dominance of black female Olympic champions from the United States: Wilma Rudolph, Wyomia Tyus, Evelyn Ashford, Florence Griffith Joyner and Jackie Joyner-Kersee."

Early Life

Coachman was born on November 9, 1923, in Albany, Georgia, when segregation prevailed in the Southern United States. The daughter of Fred Coachman and Evelyn (Jackson) Coachman, she was the fifth and middle child in a family of ten children.

Coachman's father worked as a plasterer, but the large family was poor, and Coachman had to work at picking crops such as cotton to help make ends meet.

Coachman's early interest gravitated toward the performing arts, and she expressed an ambition to be an entertainer, much like her personal favorites, child star Shirley Temple and jazz saxophonist Coleman Hawkins.

Developed Childhood Interest in Sports

Her true talents would flourish in the area of competitive sports, however. A bundle of childhood energy and a display of an inherent athleticism, Coachman accompanied her great-great-grandmother on walks in the rural Georgia landscape, where she liked to skip, run and jump as hard, fast and high as she could. Later, when she watched a boys' track meet, and realized her favorite activities had been organized as a highly coordinated event, she knew she wanted to pit her abilities against others. She was particularly intrigued by the high jump competition and, afterward, she tested herself on makeshift high-jump crossbars that she created out of any readily available material including ropes, strings, rags and sticks. Her crude and improvisational training regimen led to the development of her trademark, unconventional jumping style that blended a traditional western roll with a head-on approach.

Coachman's parents were less than pleased with her athletic interests, and her father would even beat her whenever he caught her running or playing at her other favorite athletic endeavor, basketball. They simply wanted her to grow up and behave like a lady. Fred Coachman's harsh brand of discipline, however, instilled in his children a toughness and determination. Ironically, by teaching his offspring to be strong, he bolstered Coachman's competitive urge. She continued practicing behind his back, pursuing a somewhat undefined goal of athletic success.

Despite her enthusiasm, at this point in her life, Coachman could not graduate to the more conventional equipment available at public training facilities, due to existing segregation policies. Undaunted, she increased her strength and endurance by running on hard, dirty country roads—a practice she had to perform barefoot, as she couldn't afford athletic shoes.

Encouraged by Educators

Coachman's athletic ambitions became somewhat more concrete when she received crucial support from two important sources: Cora Bailey, her fifth-grade teacher at Monroe Street Elementary School, and her aunt, Carrie Spry. Spry defended Coachman's interest in sports and, more importantly, Bailey encouraged Coachman to continue developing her athletic abilities. She suggested that Coachman join a track team. Soon, Coachman was jumping higher than girls her own age, so she started competing against boys, besting them, too.

Competed in Academic Athletics

Coachman entered Madison High School in 1938 and joined the track team, competing for coach Harry E. Lash, who recognized and nurtured her raw talents. Her strong performances soon attracted the attention of recruiters from the Tuskegee Institute in Tuskegee, Alabama, a preparatory high school and college for African-American students. She was offered a scholarship and, in 1939, Coachman left Madison and entered Tuskegee, which had a strong women's track program. She trained under women's track and field coach Christine Evans Petty as well as the school's famous head coach Cleveland Abbott, a future member of the National Track and Field Hall of Fame. Before the start of her first school year, the sixteen-year-old Coachman participated in the well-known Tuskegee Relays. Competing barefoot, Coachman broke national high school and collegiate high jump records.

In 1943, the year of her high school graduation, Coachman won the Amateur Athletic Union (AAU) Nationals in the high jump and the 50-yard dash events. After high school, she attended the Institute's college, where she earned a trade degree in dressmaking in 1946. Along the way, she won four national track and field championships (in the 50-meter dash, 100-meter dash, 400-meter relay, and high jump). In addition, she was named to five All-American track and field teams and was the only African American on each of those teams. She also played basketball while in college. An outstanding player in that sport, too, Coachman earned All-American status as a guard and helped lead her team to three straight Southern Intercollegiate Athletic Conference women's basketball championships.

For a ten-year period Coachman was the dominant AAU female high-jump competitor. From 1938 to 1948, she won ten-straight AAU outdoor high jump titles, a record that still exists today. She was indoor champion in 1941, 1945, and 1946. Had there been indoor competition from 1938 through 1940 and from 1942 through 1944, she no doubt would have won even more championships.

Entered Olympic Competition

It would seem only natural that an amateur athlete as talented and accomplished as Coachman would graduate to Olympic competition. However, in 1940 and 1944, during her prime competitive years, the Olympic Games were cancelled because of World War II.

Finally, she got her chance in 1948. Although Coachman was not considering Olympic participation, and her peak years had come earlier in the decade, United States Olympic officials invited her to try out for the track and field team. Coachman enthusiastically obliged. At the trials held at Brown University in Rhode Island, she easily qualified when she obliterated the American high jump record by an inch and a half with a five-foot four-inch jump, despite suffering from back spasms. Her record lasted until 1960.

The 1948 Olympics were held in London, and when Coachman boarded the ship with teammates to sail to England, she had never been outside of the United States. At the end of the trans-Atlantic journey, she was greeted by many British fans and was surprised to learn that she was a well-known athlete. At the time, track and field was a very popular sport outside of the United States, and Coachman was a "star."

During the Olympic competition, still suffering from a bad back, Coachman made history when she became the first black woman to win an Olympic gold medal. (She was also the only American woman to win a medal at the 1948 Games.) On August 7, 1948, and before 83,000 spectators,

Coachman achieved a winning mark of 5-feet, 6 1/8 inches, setting a record that endured for eight years. Even though her back spasms almost forced her out of the competition, Coachman made her record-setting jump on her first attempt in the competition finals.

During the course of the competition, Coachman defeated her biggest challenger, British high jumper Dorothy Tyler. England's King George VI personally presented Coachman with her gold medal, a gesture which impressed the young athlete more than winning the medal itself. In a 1996 interview with *Essence* magazine, she said, "I had won so many national and international medals that I really didn't feel anything, to tell the truth. The exciting thing was that the King of England awarded my medal."

Became a National Figure

Coachman returned to the United States a national hero, a status that gained her an audience with President Harry S. Truman. She also met with former First Lady Eleanor Roosevelt. Right after her ship arrived back home in New York City, renowned bandleader Count Basie held a party for Coachman.

In her hometown of Albany, city officials held an Alice Coachman Day and organized a parade that stretched for 175 miles. Coachman waved to the crowds who cheered her on every step of the journey. Later, in Albany, a street and school were named in her honor (Alice Avenue and Coachman Elementary School).

However, her welcome-home ceremony, held at the Albany Municipal Auditorium, only underscored the racial attitudes then existing in the South. Audiences were segregated, and Coachman was not even allowed to speak in the event held in her honor. Coachman received many flowers and gifts from white individuals, but these were given anonymously, because people were afraid of reactions from other whites.

The following year, Coachman retired from competition, despite the fact that she was only twenty-six years old. But she felt she had accomplished all that she set out to achieve. In addition to her Olympic gold medal, she amassed 31 national track titles. Moreover, Coachman understood that her accomplishments had made her an important figure for other black athletes as well as women. In an interview with *The New York Times,* she observed, "I made a difference among the blacks, being one of the leaders. If I had gone to the Games and failed, there wouldn't be anyone to follow in my footsteps. It encouraged the rest of the women to work harder and fight harder."

Became an Educator

After she retired, she continued her formal education and earned a bachelor's degree in home economics from Albany State College in Georgia in 1949. She settled in Tuskegee, Alabama and married N. F. Davis (they later divorced and Coachman remarried, to Frank Davis). They had two children, Richmond and Evelyn, who both followed their mother's footsteps into athletics.

Coachman remained involved in academics and athletics, becoming an elementary and high school physical education teacher and a coach for women's track and basketball teams in several cities in Georgia. She also taught and coached at South Carolina State College and Albany State University. In addition, she worked with the Job Corps as a recreation supervisor.

In 1952, she signed a product endorsement deal with the Coca-Cola Company, becoming the first black female athlete to benefit from such an arrangement. In an ensuing advertising campaign, she was featured on national billboards.

In 1994, she established the Alice Coachman Track and Field Foundation, a nonprofit organization that not only assists young athletes and but helps retired Olympians adjust to post-competition life.

In 1996, during the Olympic Games, which were held in her home state of Atlanta, Georgia, Coachman was honored as one of the 100 greatest athletes in Olympic history. As a prelude to the international event, in 1995, Coachman, along with other famous female Olympians Anita DeFrantz, Joan Benoit Samuelson, and Aileen Riggin Soule, appeared at an exhibit entitled "The Olympic Woman," which was sponsored by the Avon company to observe 100 years of female Olympic Game achievements.

In addition to those honors, in 1975, Coachman was inducted into the National Track and Field Hall of Fame. In all, she gained membership in eight halls of fame, several of which included the Albany Sports Hall of Fame, the Georgia Sports Hall of Fame, the Black Athletes Hall of Fame, and the International Women's Sports Hall of Fame.

Books

Contemporary Black Biography, Volume 18. Gale Research, 1998.
Contemporary Heroes and Heroines, Book IV, Gale Group, 2000.
Notable Sports Figures, Gale, 2004.

Online

"Alice Coachman," *National Women's History Project,* http://www.nwhp.org/tlp/biographies/coachman/coachman_bio.html (December 30, 2005).
"Alice Coachman, *New Georgia Encyclopedia,* http://www.georgiaencyclopedia.org/nge/Article.jsp?path=/SportsRecreation/IndividualandTeamSports/Track&id;=h-731 (December 28, 2005).
"Alice Coachman," *SIAC.com,* http://www.thesiac.com/main.php?page=person&&item;=alicecoachman (December 30, 2005).
"Alice Coachman," *United States Olympic Committee,* http://www.usoc.org/36370_37506.htm (December 30, 2005). □

Camilla Collett

Camilla Collett (1813-1895) broke new ground in Norwegian literature with the publication of her first

novel in 1854. *The District Governor's Daughters* is considered the first feminist tract from a Norwegian writer, as well as Norwegian literature's first piece of modern fiction, for its use of psychological themes to relate a tale of romance thwarted by social convention.

Collett's novel has been described as "a demand for the emotional and intellectual liberation of women" by scholars Irene Engelstad and Janneken Øverland, discussing its place in the literary history of the Scandinavian nation. They further noted that it was "regarded as a breakthrough for the cause of sexual equality in Norway."

Schooled in Denmark

Collett was born into a prominent, politically connected family that included a brother, Henrik Wergeland, who would later enjoy immense literary acclaim. Their mother, Alethe Dorothea Thaulow Wergeland, came from a long line of government officials, and had an artistic temperament she passed on to both children. Collett was born on January 23, 1813, in Kristiansand, on the southern coast of Norway, but she would be linked to the town of Eidsvoll, outside Oslo, for a number of reasons. Her family settled there in 1817, when her father became the Lutheran pastor of Eidsvoll, but Nikolai Wergeland had already taken part in Norway's constitutional assembly in Eidsvoll some three years earlier. Collett's father was a well known pastor and leader in the independence movement, and at that 1814 political gathering, Norway formally declared its independence from Sweden and Denmark, the two neighboring powers that had dominated it for centuries.

Collett's father was a progressive man, who supported the idea of a formal education for Camilla as well as her brother Henrik, who was five years her senior. She was sent to the Herrnhut Institute at Christiansfeld, in present-day Denmark. By the time she was 17 years old, Henrik had emerged as a celebrated new literary name in Norway, which was in the midst of a cultural awakening spurred by nationalist fervor. Like his father, Henrik had also studied for the ministry, but by the late 1820s had become the leader of a new romantic nationalist movement in Norway. His poetry and drama celebrated Norwegian culture at a time when the fashion among many of the more established writers and literary critics was to maintain and even strengthen artistic ties with Sweden, Denmark, and the rest of Europe. Because of this culture war, Wergeland's work was usually subject to scathing criticism by Norway's literary establishment. One of his harshest critics was Johan Sebastian Welhaven (1807–1873).

For a period of time in the early 1830s, Wergeland and Welhaven carried on a vigorous debate in newspapers and magazines, with attacks, counter-attacks, and input from others, including Pastor Wergeland. Welhaven was also the son of a pastor, but unlike Collett's brother, he was of a more conservative mind. It was Welhaven who supported the idea of bringing Norwegian culture into step with movements and styles elsewhere in Europe.

Became Enamored of Family Foe

One of this feud's more fascinating aspects, however, was the fact that the Wergeland-Welhaven quarrel–which historians of Norwegian literature have generally termed a defining event in the formation of a national cultural identity–was conducted around the same time that Camilla Collett was romantically involved with Welhaven. Her personal recollections of this time were revealed in *Optegnelser fra Ungdomsaarene,* which was written when she was in her early twenties but published posthumously. It began as a journal of this period of time, but she made many revisions and added footnotes to it over the course of her life. "The book, though cast in the form of a private diary, reads throughout like a novel," noted a 1927 review by G. M. Gathorne-Hardy in the *Times Literary Supplement,* but the critic also faulted it for sentimentality. Her tale, Gathorne-Hardy continued, "particularly in its earlier stages, falls constantly into bathos and occasionally reads like a parody of the style by which it was inspired."

Collett's recollections are mainly of her contact with Welhaven, whom she occasionally refers to as "Saint Sebastian," and there is only some discussion of the literary feud. She does write at one point that she erased part of her brother's manuscript when she found a diatribe against Welhaven on the page, which angered Henrik. Over time, the ardor between Collett and Welhaven cooled, and each married another. She revisited her journal over the years, and the attention she gave to it seems to suggest that the romance was a pivotal event in her life, though she later wondered if she was merely a pawn in the literary feud. *Optegnelser fra Ungdomsaarene* included letters from Welhaven expressing his love, and in one footnote, she wondered, "Did he carry on this lengthy game with cold-blooded calculation? Was it his insatiable hatred for my family which drove him ingeniously to strike them in their most vulnerable point, in me?"

In 1834 Collett left Norway for France. She spent the next three years there and in Germany, studying literature. In 1841 she wed Jonas Peter Collett, who was nearly 70 years old at the time. He had also taken part in the Eidsvoll event, and had served a number of years as a high-ranking government minister by then. In 1845 her brother Henrik died of tuberculosis, and Jonas died in 1851, leaving her a widow with two young sons. After that, she left Norway and settled in Copenhagen, Denmark, and produced her most famous literary accomplishment, *The District Governor's Daughters.*

Published First Novel

In its original Norwegian title, *Amtmandens døttre* appeared anonymously in 1854-55. The story is set 20 years earlier, in Eidsvoll, and relates the tale of Sofie Ramm, who falls in love with Georg Kold, the young man her family has taken in to serve as a tutor to her younger brother. But matches based on romantic love were rare at the time in Norway, and middle class or even nominally landed families generally arranged their offsprings' marriages. The unions were carefully considered in order to provide the maximum advantage to the social or economic status of the family. "Collett never forgave society for its complicity in smothering women's capacity for love, which she regarded as the supreme feminine instinct," wrote Sherrill Harbison in a review of *The District Governor's Daughters* for *Scandinavian Studies.* "Conventional marriage, her novel warns, was a trap designed by society to deaden the aches of love sacrificed; 'in a word, they suffocated woman's entire faith in great happiness and gave her small pleasures as compensation.'"

In the novel, both Sofie and Georg are believers in the idea of a marriage based on love, not one that merely furthers the family interests. But a misunderstanding ends their contact, Sofie predictably marries another man, "and begins her descent to cheerless drudge," noted a contributor to *Publishers Weekly* in a review of the English-language edition, which did not appear until 1992. The same critic also called Collett's novel "a portrait of the rigid Scandinavian society of the period," and mentioned her later influence on the bleak works of Henrik Ibsen, Norway's most famous playwright and considered the founder of the modern drama form.

Collett's novel was doubly notable because there were few authors of merit writing in the Norwegian language during the early 1850s. Most literature lovers read English or French novels in translation, with the works of Charles Dickens and Victor Hugo among the top sellers. Though *The District Governor's Daughters* met with a somewhat lukewarm critical reception, "it had a great influence on later Norwegian writing," wrote Harald Beyer in *A History of Norwegian Literature.* Beyer cited one work by Ibsen that appeared less than a decade later as a particularly obvious descendant. *Love's Comedy,* dating from 1862, is Ibsen's critical look at bourgeois marriages, and its characters mention what they view as an absence of love in arranged matches.

Realized Novel was Her Polemic

The District Governor's Daughters was also the first piece of Norwegian fiction to examine the lives of women. At the time when it appeared, women in Norway had very few legal rights. Unmarried women, for example, could not enter into financial transactions regarding property they had inherited without the approval of a male relative, and married women had no rights whatsoever, and were subject entirely to their husband's authority until an 1888 law ended this. Though Collett's novel did not address specific reforms, "instead she demanded a change of attitude," wrote Beyer, "an understanding of the woman's heart. Into this cause she flung all her glowing passion, writing with bitterness and sympathy and an amazing boldness. She spoke of her novel as a 'shriek,' and many felt it to be just that."

Collett's novel was translated into other European languages after its original publication, but did not appear in English until the early 1990s. In the review of this translation for *Scandinavian Studies,* Harbison discussed its place in

nineteenth-century women's fiction in general. "Stylistically it bridges romanticism and realism," the critic asserted, "sharing features with . . . Jane Austen's comedies of manners, and Charlotte Brontë's headstrong heroines colliding with Victorian ethics of female self-sacrifice." Beyer asserted that Collett's "example helped to encourage other women to enter the literary arena, most of them minor though interesting figures. Not until Amalie Skram did one arrive who could equal or surpass the writing of Camilla Collett."

Collett spent the remainder of her years living in various European capitals, including Stockholm, Berlin, and Paris, and devoted her subsequent literary energies to nonfiction and political essays. She returned to Norway around 1885. In 1893 she was feted on the occasion of her 80th birthday, and no less than Ibsen himself was her official escort to the party. She died on March 6, 1895, at the age of 82. Other works of merit from her pen include *I de lange Nætter* (In the Long Nights), a memoir of her childhood and early years that appeared in the early 1860s, and two collections of essays, *Fra de Stummes Leir* (From the Camp of the Mute) and *Mod Strømmen* (Against the Mainstream). In 1977 she became the first woman whose image appeared on a Norwegian banknote.

Books

Beyer, Harald, *A History of Norwegian Literature,* Translated and edited by Einar Haugen. New York University Press/The American-Scandinavian Foundation, 1956.

Periodicals

Publishers Weekly, July 20, 1992.
Scandinavian Studies, Summer 1993.
Times (London, England), March 15, 1895.
Times Literary Supplement (London, England), June 9, 1927.

Online

"Norwegian Women Writers," http://www.reisenett.no/norway/facts/culture_science/norwegian_woman_writers.html (January 12, 2006). □

John Conyers

Among the longest-serving members of the United States Congress, John Conyers (born 1929) has remained a most productive lawmaker in terms of legislation introduced and passed.

He was one of just a few members of the House of Representatives whose career stretched back to the civil rights era of the 1960s, and many of the key political advances of those years either bore his name as sponsor or cosponsor. Conyers had a curious spirit that led him into areas beyond civil rights, however, and he worked over his long career on issues ranging from alcohol warning labels to the intellectual property rights of musicians in a

on—was the path breaking saxophonist John Coltrane. Conyers kept an acoustic bass in one corner of his Washington office as a congressional representative, and in the 1970s he even hosted a jazz program on Washington radio station WPFW.

The 1943 Detroit race riots, in which blacks were pulled off streetcars and attacked by white mobs, began to awaken Conyers' political consciousness, but music and school came first for a long time. Conyers breezed through high school, often skipping classes to play pool but still graduating in 1954. There was no money for college, so he relied on his father's influence to get a job as a spot-welder at a Lincoln auto plant. He became the director of his United Auto Workers local unit. Hungry for further education, he took night classes covering levels of chemistry and physics he had not reached in high school. He went on to take more night classes connected with Detroit's Wayne State University and finally enrolled there on a union-backed scholarship in the late 1940s, taking courses in civil engineering.

As the U.S. moved toward war in Korea, Conyers enlisted in the U.S. Army in 1950. Spending part of his officer training program at Fort Belleville in Virginia, he went to Washington to watch Congress in action and, according to Jessica Lee of *USA Today,* thought to himself, "I could do that!" Reaching the rank of second lieutenant in the Army Corps of Engineers, Conyers was sent to Korea and saw combat, winning several military honors.

Started in Politics as Precinct Delegate

Veterans' benefits allowed Conyers to continue his education after his army discharge, and he returned to Wayne State in 1954, switching from engineering to pre-law. He joined Detroit's Young Democratic Club and ran for the post of precinct convention delegate, inaugurating his winning political ways with a narrow victory over a rival. He graduated from Wayne State in 1957 and finished a law degree at the same school the following year, passing the bar exam and co-founding the law firm of Conyers, Bell, and Townsend soon after that.

An accident of geography helped rekindle Conyers' political ambitions: his law office was in the same building as that of veteran Michigan U.S. Representative John Dingell, who as of 2005 was the only lawmaker with more seniority than Conyers. The arrangement was beneficial from a business standpoint, as people involved in landlord-tenant disputes filtered into Conyers' office. Conyers took the chance to broaden his circle of political contacts, working in Dingell's office from 1959 to 1961 and snaring a political appointment from Michigan governor John Swainson as a state workmen's compensation referee. In 1963 Conyers served on the National Lawyers Committee for Civil Rights Under Law, a group spearheaded by President John F. Kennedy. He was active as a lawyer in the civil rights movement in the southern states and often represented clients in voter registration cases.

The Michigan government post lasted from 1961 until 1964, at which time Conyers resigned and declared his candidacy for a northside Detroit U.S. House seat. He

changing technological world. As American politics swung to the right with the election of President George W. Bush, in 2000, Conyers continued to raise his voice in support of liberal causes and of his urban constituency.

Father Was Union Activist

A lifelong resident of Detroit, Michigan, Conyers was born on May 16, 1929. His father was a Georgia-born laborer who dropped out of high school and came to Detroit to work at a Chrysler auto plant; when he realized that black auto painters were being paid less than their white counterparts, he made a personal protest to company president Walter P. Chrysler. The elder Conyers' union organizing activities cost him jobs, but he eventually rose to a high position within the United Auto Workers union. John Conyers Jr. was his oldest son; another son, Nathan, went on to open one of Detroit's and the country's first African-American-owned auto dealerships.

The younger Conyers grew up in culturally rich Northwest Detroit, and the passion of his high school years was music. Receiving a letter for playing trumpet in his high school band, he also studied bass, piano, tenor saxophone, and trombone. Several jazz musicians who became national stars were part of Conyers' circle of friends in high school. "Sonny Stitt and Milt Jackson were there," he told Hollie I. West of the *Washington Post.* "I went to Northwestern High School with Betty Carter. And Tommy Flanagan and Kenny Burrell and I were at Wayne State University together." His favorite performer—and another friend later defeated future Michigan Secretary of State Richard Austin by 44 votes in the Democratic primary but was never seriously challenged again in a House election, even though the boundaries of his district were changed several times and extended into Detroit's predominantly white suburbs. He was elected to represent Michigan's First Congressional District; later redistricting renumbered it as the 14th.

It did not take Conyers long to make his mark legislatively. He signed on as a cosponsor of the landmark Voting Rights Act of 1965, and he backed the liberal social legislation, including the establishment of the Medicare program, championed by President Lyndon Johnson. In 1967, Conyers took the lead in resisting a bill backed by southern conservatives that would have delayed legislative redistricting according to the principle of one person, one vote. After the assassination of the Rev. Martin Luther King Jr. in 1968, Conyers introduced a bill that would designate King's birthday as a national holiday. In 1983, he saw the measure become law.

Made Nixon "Enemies" List

In 1969 Conyers became a founding member of the Congressional Black Caucus and was for many years its senior figure. A member of the House Judiciary Committee since his first year in Congress, he participated in the impeachment proceedings against President Richard Nixon in the wake of the Watergate scandal in 1974. He had earned the 13th spot on Nixon's notorious "enemies list" of political opponents, with a notation that read (according to USA Today's Jessica Lee), "Coming on fast. Emerging as a leading black anti-Nixon spokesman. Has known weakness for white females." Conyers' durable marriage to the former Monica Esters, who was African-American, produced two children, John III and Carl Edward.

Identified with social and racial justice issues for the bulk of his career, Conyers has also become involved with various other kinds of legislation. He introduced and worked to bring forward a bill requiring health warning labels on the packaging of alcoholic beverages; the bill became law in 1988. Conyers was one of the first lawmakers to urge a systematic study of the differing treatment blacks and whites received at the hands of police, and the U.S. Department of Justice launched a major national investigation of the issue partly in response to his concerns. Conyers introduced or worked on major legislation dealing with hate crimes, voter registration, and violence against women. On a lighter note, he sponsored legislation that designated a National Tap Dancing Day. "When you ask people about my legislative agenda, it's all over the place," he told Lee. Conyers continued to rack up huge majorities in his congressional races but lost in two runs for mayor of Detroit. In the 1980s he was a prominent opponent of President Ronald Reagan's Strategic Defense space-based weapons initiative, commonly known as Star Wars.

In 1998 Conyers participated in his second impeachment proceeding as the House Judiciary Committee took up charges that President Bill Clinton had lied about his involvement with intern Monica Lewinsky. Though he often wrangled with prosecutor Kenneth Starr, Conyers maintained cordial relationships with Republican House members despite the bitterly partisan atmosphere. Conyers, the senior Democrat on the committee, was the de facto leader of Clinton's defense in the House against impeachment charges.

In 2000 Conyers lent his voice to a growing effort by some African-American leaders to raise the issue of reparations that could be paid or otherwise given to African Americans as compensation for the forced expropriation of their labor during the era of slavery and beyond. In an Ebony essay laying out the case for reparations, Conyers stressed that the movement was "not coming forward in an accusatory tone toward any citizens or their ancestors," but that "we simply think that Congress should take a look at the lingering effects of slavery so that we may get a deeper appreciation of them and reach some consensus about what the solutions may be. The issue of reparations is not something beyond our understanding," Conyers wrote. "It's a pretty fundamental issue if you look at it. I'm saying it's time we did."

Gained Watchdog Reputation

Although he occasionally ran into trouble with House investigators himself—his House checking account was frequently overdrawn, and allegations surfaced in 2003 that some of his staffers had engaged in prohibited political activities—Conyers had a reputation for keeping a close eye on the activities of his Republican adversaries. That tendency came to the fore with the U.S. invasion of Iraq in March of 2003, the authorization for which Conyers voted against. Conyers questioned the stated rationale for the war and added his name as plaintiff to a lawsuit contending the war was unconstitutional because it had not been declared by Congress.

In 2005 he gathered 500,000 signatures on an online petition asking President George W. Bush to address the so-called Downing Street memo, a British government document that appeared to suggest that the Bush administration had settled on war with Iraq regardless of the outcome of diplomatic initiatives. "If these disclosures are true," Conyers said at a House committee meeting (as quoted by Nicole Saunders of Essence), "then brave Americans and innocent Iraqis would have lost their lives for a lie."

In 2005 Conyers and Representative Stephanie Tubbs Jones introduced the Voting Opportunity and Technology Enhancement and Rights (VOTER) Act, designed to address voting problems that plagued both the 2002 and 2004 elections, and in the eyes of many observers had an unfair impact on African Americans who were attempting to vote. Conyers also worked on measures to help the impoverished Caribbean nation of Haiti and supported a variety of measures designed to insure that musicians could maintain copyright to their works. Clearly the dean of African-American politicians had lost none of his energy as he reached senior citizen status.

Books

Bruner, Richard, Black Politicians, McKay, 1971.
Smith, Jessie Carney, ed., Notable Black American Men, Gale, 1998.

Periodicals

Billboard, April 7, 2001.
Ebony, August 2000.
Essence, September 2005.
USA Today, December 18, 1998.
Washington Post, April 13, 1977.

Online

"John Conyers," DAAHP (The Detroit African-American History Project), http://www.daahp.wayne.edu/biographiesDisplay .asp?id=75 (December 12, 2005).
"John Conyers Jr.'s Biography," Congressman John Conyers Jr. webpage, http://www.house.gov/conyers (December 12, 2005). □

Mihaly Csikszentmihalyi

Psychologist and educator Mihaly Csikszentmihalyi (born 1934) has gained wide recognition and even best-selling author status for his investigations into the nature of happiness and creativity. He is best known for the concept of "flow"—the state of "being completely involved in an activity for its own sake," he told John Geirland of *Wired.* "The ego falls away. Time flies. Every action, movement, and thought follows inevitably from the previous one, like playing jazz. Your whole being is involved, and you're using your skills to the utmost."

Psychology as a discipline is more often concerned with human dysfunction than with situations or activities that result in deep satisfaction. When Csikszentmihalyi published *Flow: The Psychology of Optimal Experience* in 1990, readers found in it a set of blueprints for the pursuit of happiness. The book affected world leaders (United States President Bill Clinton and British Prime Minister Tony Blair both numbered among Csikszentmihalyi's admirers), business management theorists, a leading National Football League figure (Dallas Cowboys coach Jimmy Johnson used *Flow* in preparing for the 1993 Super Bowl), and others, on down to ordinary readers who had occasionally lost themselves in challenging tasks and wondered why they found the experience so enjoyable. Csikszentmihalyi was a research psychologist, not a self-help writer, and his books were based on academic methodologies. In the 1990s and 2000s, though, they were read far beyond the academic discipline of psychology.

Played Chess as Escape

Mihaly Csikszentmihalyi (pronounced me-HIGH chick-sent-me-HIGH-ee) was born in Fiume, Italy (now Rijeka, Croatia), on September 29, 1934. His family was Hungarian, and his father Alfred, a member of the Hungarian diplomatic corps, had been posted to Italy. Csikszentmihalyi grew up in Fiume, Florence, and Rome, speaking Hungarian, Italian, and German fluently. World War II disrupted Csikszentmihalyi's life completely. Though still a child, he was held for a time in an Italian prison camp. He fared better than many people he knew, however. By 1944, he told Dava Sobel of *Omni,* "Many relatives and friends in Budapest had been killed. One of my brothers died in combat, and another had been taken prisoner by the Russians and sent to a forced labor camp in Siberia. I discovered chess was a miraculous way of entering into a different world where all those things didn't matter. For hours I'd just focus within a reality that had clear rules and goals. If you knew what to do, you could survive there."

Csikszentmihalyi's father was named Hungarian ambassador to Italy after the war, but was fired after Communists took over the Hungarian government in 1948. The family decided to stay in Rome as refugees, opening a restaurant there. After finishing school, Csikszentmihalyi worked as a travel agent and news photographer. He did paintings on the side and began to realize how addictive creative work could be. Traveling in Switzerland when he was about 16, he heard a lecture by the early psychoanalyst Carl Jung about the mass delusion that had seized the European mind and resulted in the destruction of the war. "That struck me," he told Sobel, "because as a child in the war I'd seen something drastically wrong with how adults—the grown-ups I trusted—organized their thinking. I was trying to find a better system to order my life. Jung seemed to be trying to cope with some of the more positive aspects of human experience."

Fascinated by psychology, Csikszentmihalyi began reading Jung's books and those of Sigmund Freud. He decided to study psychology at the university level, but he found that few European universities offered courses in the still-young discipline. Learning that psychology was better entrenched in American universities, Csikszentmihalyi applied to the prestigious University of Chicago. His interest in the idea of happiness as something humans could make for themselves was deepened when he met Hungarians who had spent time in the gulag prison system in the Soviet Union. Why, he wondered, did some of them seem serene rather than psychologically destroyed?

Csikszentmihalyi was accepted at Chicago, but several obstacles remained in his path. He spoke little English, but he partially remedied that situation by studying "Pogo" comic books owned by U.S. armed forces members he met. A bigger problem was the loss of his parents' life savings to a scam artist they had employed at their restaurant in Rome. Csikszentmihalyi landed in Chicago in 1956 with a total of $1.25 in his pocket.

Worked as Hotel Auditor

Csikszentmihalyi solved the immediate financial crisis by getting a job as a night auditor at a downtown Chicago hotel. He was discouraged at first by the curriculum at Chicago, which focused on issues of conditioning by means of techniques such as rat experiments rather than on the studies of human psychology that had attracted him to the field. There were precedents in the U.S. for what Csikszentmihalyi was trying to accomplish, however—the writings of psychologist Abraham Maslow on self-actualization focused on optimum life paths.

Csikszentmihalyi did well enough in his coursework, in his fourth language, that he was given a scholarship at the beginning of his junior year. As he got to know the faculty at Chicago better, he met one who was interested in the phenomenon of creativity and agreed to serve as his advisor. Csikszentmihalyi graduated from the University of Chicago in 1959 and was accepted into the psychology Ph.D. program there. He married writer Isabella Selega in 1960, and the couple raised two sons.

After receiving his Ph.D. in 1965, Csikszentmihalyi was hired at Lake Forest College in suburban Chicago as an instructor. He was elevated to assistant professor (in 1967) and associate professor (in 1968), serving as chair of the sociology and anthropology department from 1967 to 1969. In 1968 he became a U.S. citizen. The following year he returned to Chicago as an associate professor, and became professor of human development in 1980 and remained there until 2000. Chicago offered Csikszentmihalyi the chance to pursue the large-scale, survey-based, multi-year projects that would be necessary to the development of his ideas.

Csikszentmihalyi, who has written over 120 articles and book chapters on a variety of subjects, came to his formulation of the idea of "flow" from a variety of different approaches, contributing to studies of creativity and focusing at first on young people in his own research. One key to human satisfaction, he realized, was that it was never passive, and was never simply the result of a set of external conditions. Csikszentmihalyi had moved from the hell of Europe during World War II to the wealthiest country in the world, materially speaking, but he found that young people were especially disaffected and alienated. Csikszentmihalyi's first book was *Beyond Boredom and Anxiety*, published in 1975. One of his best-known works prior to the publication of *Flow* was *Being Adolescent: Conflict and Growth in the Teenage Years* (1985), which he co-authored with Reed Larson. That work relied on a unique research method: Csikszentmihalyi gave beepers to 75 high school students and had teams of graduate students contact them at random points during the day and ask them about their feelings at that moment. The high schoolers were unhappy most of the time, unsurprisingly, but Csikszentmihalyi observed patterns in their lives and found that they turned around when they directed their energies toward challenging tasks. He continued to write about adolescence throughout his career, coining the term "autotelic" for an activity that is done for its own sake, and arguing that teenagers who engaged in such activities benefited from avoiding passive experiences such as television viewing.

Csikszentmihalyi first used the term "flow" in a 1988 collection of essays, *Optimal Experience: Studies of Flow in Consciousness*, that he co-edited with his wife, Isabella. He was occasionally conflicted about the use of the term because of its potential association with the passive "go with the flow" ethos espoused by adherents of some forms of New Age spirituality, but "flow" seemed to capture the suspension of time that people experienced when

engrossed in a task that stretched their abilities. *Flow: The Psychology of Optimal Experience* was published by the nonacademic Harper house in 1990, during a period in which few high-profile academics addressed general audiences. Even so, Csikszentmihalyi had no ambitions to become famous and was surprised when the book, which was based partly on observations of artists, appeared on bestseller lists. By late 1991 it had sold more than 300,000 copies.

Presented Eight Characteristics of Flow

Some critics took Csikszentmihalyi to task for what they saw as a simplistic quality in his reasoning. "It's just tautology," British psychologist Oliver James told Maurice Chittenden of the *Times* of London, England. "If people are very absorbed in something it stands to reason that they are going to be happier—a drug addict would be absorbed with pursuing cocaine." Csikszentmihalyi, however, developed the idea of "flow" in detail that went beyond simple characterizations of enjoyment or job satisfaction. "Flow" was not just a feeling of well-being, but had eight separate components. First, it is the result of a challenging task. Second, the person experiencing "flow" becomes part of the task rather than standing outside it. "Flow" is involved with the pursuit of definite goals (third) and depends on immediate feedback (fourth). It requires a high level of concentration (fifth). Sixth, it gives the user a sense of control without a striving for control, something Csikszentmihalyi called the paradox of control. Seventh, a sense of self disappears. And finally, the sense of time is altered. Various parts of this scheme had shown up in other classifications of psychological states, but Csikszentmihalyi's combination of them was unique. "Flow" was not the same as fun, or as joy. It did not depend, as did Maslow's idea of self-actualization, on the meeting of a basic need for security, and indeed it sometimes arose in highly negative situations.

Csikszentmihalyi extended the idea of "flow" in several more books: *Creativity: Flow and the Psychology of Discovery and Invention* (1996, based on interviews with more than 90 creative figures from all over the world), *Finding Flow: The Psychology of Engagement with Everyday Life* (1997), and *Flow in Sports* (2000, written with Susan A. Jackson). An enthusiastic mountain climber, he often used that activity as an example of the sort of structured, demanding task that could produce the "flow" experience. Csikszentmihalyi took one criticism to heart, however: "flow" as he first formulated it could apply to socially undesirable tasks as well as desirable ones. A bank robber executing a complex heist might well experience "flow" in Csikszentmihalyi's terms. Csikszentmihalyi tried to join the idea of "flow" with that of evolutionary progress in his book *The Evolving Self: A Psychology for the Third Millennium* (1993). "Flow" resulted not just from surmounting complexity, he argued, but, as he put it to Sobel, from the realization of "future-oriented goals." "Individual enjoyment seems an evolutionary potential in humans, responsible in large part for technical and social advances," he told Sobel.

New York Times writer Richard Flaste called Csikszentmihalyi "a man obsessed by happiness," and in a society likewise obsessed, Csikszentmihalyi became known as something of a guru. Followers held meeting devoted to "flow" theory, in Europe as well as the U.S., and government officials wondered how to translate the idea of "flow" into public policy.

Csikszentmihalyi's greatest appeal, perhaps, was to the business community, which tried to apply his ideas toward the goal of maximizing employee productivity. In 2000, Csikszentmihalyi left Chicago for the position of professor of psychology and management and director of the Quality of Life Research Center at the Peter F. Drucker and Masatoshi Ito Graduate School of Management in Claremont, California. A 2002 *Scientific American* article he co-authored with Robert Kubey argued that habitual television watching bore scientifically demonstrable resemblances to physical addition; the article received wide publicity. Csikszentmihalyi made his own contribution to the discussion of business applications of "flow" in his 2003 book *Good Business:*

Leadership, Flow, and the Making of Meaning, and, past retirement age, he remained a vital voice in the modern dialogue over how to make a well-lived life.

Periodicals

Independent (London, England), October 30, 1991.
New York Times, October 8, 1989; March 18, 1990.
Omni, January 1995.
Psychology Today, January-February 1994; July 1999.
Sunday Times (London, England), December 21, 1997.
USA Today, April 21, 2003.
Washington Times, July 14, 1996.
Wired, September 1996.
Western Mail (Cardiff, Wales, England), January 26, 2002.

Online

"The Man Who Found the Flow," Shambhala Sun Online, http://www.shambhalasun.com/Archives/Features/1998/Sep98/Flow.htm (January 13, 2006).
"Mihaly Csikszentmihalyi: Flow Theory," Brain Channels, http://www.brainchannels.com/thinker/mihaly.html (January 13, 2006). □

D

George Bernard Dantzig

American statistician George Bernard Dantzig (1914-2005) affected the world enormously with the mathematical discovery of the simplex method. Devised by Dantzig in the late 1940s, this mathematical formula, or algorithm, is used by industry—and governments—to identify the best possible solutions to problems with many variables. The simplex method is useable in calculations that involve resource allocation, worker scheduling, and production planning. Airlines use the algorithm to coordinate routes for commercial flights and governments use it to schedule refuse collection. In addition, the simplex method is embedded on most computers through spreadsheet programs.

Dantzig also worked as an applied mathematics and statistics professor, producing more than 50 doctoral students, many of whom became leaders in their fields. "He was brilliant, very gentle, and not at all arrogant, and quite approachable," former student and Stanford University mathematician Richard Cottle told the *San Francisco Chronicle's* Steve Rubenstein. "Some famous scientists can be pretty wrapped up in themselves, but he wasn't that way."

Born into Immigrant Family

Dantzig was born to Tobias and Anja Dantzig on November 8, 1914, in Portland, Oregon. Dantzig's parents wanted him to become a writer so they named him after George Bernard Shaw. His younger brother, Henry, was named after the famed French mathematician Henri Poincaré. During Dantzig's early childhood, the family strained to make ends meet as his Russian–born father struggled to establish himself in the United States. Tobias Dantzig fled his native land after he was caught distributing anti–Tsarist propaganda. He reached Paris, where he studied mathematics at the Sorbonne under Poincaré. While there, he met Anja Ourisson, and after they married, the couple moved to the United States, settling in Oregon in 1910.

The future looked bleak, however, because Tobias Dantzig believed his thick, Russian accent would relegate him to a life as a laborer. Initially, he worked as a painter, lumberjack, and road builder, barely earning enough to support his family. Eventually, Tobias Dantzig was able to continue his studies and around 1917 earned a doctorate in mathematics from Indiana University. Over the next several years, Tobias Dantzig held positions at Johns Hopkins University and the University of Maryland. Likewise, Anja Dantzig continued her education, earning a master's degree in French. She became a linguist at the Library of Congress in Washington, D.C.

Struggled with Math as Child

By the time Dantzig was a teenager, the family was living in Washington, D.C., and Dantzig attended Powell Junior High School and Central High School, though he initially earned poor grades in math. At one point he was flunking algebra. Dantzig's mathematician father, however, kept after him, handing him countless problems to solve. Eventually, Dantzig developed a love for geometry and his math grades improved, as did his analytical ability.

As a teenager, Dantzig aided his father with his hallmark book on mathematics, titled, *Number, The Language*

81

of Science, published in 1930. The younger Dantzig prepared figures for the book. Writing in *OR/MS Today,* Saul I. Gass, a former doctoral student of the younger Dantzig, said Albert Einstein called the book ''beyond doubt the most interesting book on the evolution of mathematics which has ever fallen into my hands.''

In 1936, Dantzig earned a mathematics and physics degree from the University of Maryland and that summer he married Anne Shmuner. Dantzig earned his a master's degree in mathematics at the University of Michigan in 1938. Dantzig decided not to pursue a doctorate at this time after realizing he lacked a passion for applied mathematics. Dantzig spent the next two years working at the U.S. Bureau of Labor Statistics. There, he studied the work of mathematical statistician Jerzy Neyman and realized statistics could be used in everyday life. This prospect excited Dantzig and he soon enrolled in a doctoral program at the University of California, Berkeley, to study statistics under Neyman.

During that first year, Dantzig proved a rising star. The discovery of his abilities, however, was somewhat accidental. One day, Dantzig slipped in late for Neyman's statistics class and spied two problems scribbled on the chalkboard. Naturally, Dantzig assumed the problems were homework, though he found them quite challenging. The problems, in fact, were not homework, but were two unconfirmed theorems. Dantzig eventually solved the problems.

''A few days later I apologised to Neyman for taking so long to do the homework—the problems seemed to be a little harder than usual,'' he recalled in a 1986 interview with the *Journal of Mathematical Programming,* according to the *Daily Telegraph.* Dantzig could usually solve the homework problems in a few hours, but worked on these for several days. ''About six weeks later, one Sunday morning about eight o'clock, Anne and I were awakened by someone banging on our front door. It was Neyman. He rushed in with papers in hand, all excited: 'I've just written an introduction to one of your papers. Read it so I can send it out right away for publication.' '' Dantzig's ideas for solving the problems became the basis for his dissertation. This Dantzig anecdote is said to have inspired a scene in the 1997 motion picture *Good Will Hunting.* In the film, a math prodigy and janitor named Will Hunting solves a blackboard problem that had stumped veteran mathematicians.

Civilian Servant During War

World War II, however, interrupted Dantzig's studies. In 1941 he took a job with the U.S. Army Air Force in Washington, D.C., joining the Combat Analysis Branch of Statistical Control. Dantzig collected data on sorties flown, bombs dropped and aircraft lost, then used this information to help officials decide about aircraft procurement and troop training. He earned the Exceptional Civilian Service Medal from the U.S. War Department.

After Dantzig returned to UC–Berkeley in 1946 and completed his doctorate work, the university offered him a position. His wife told him to turn it down because she did not believe the pay offered them enough to live on, now that they had a child. Instead, Dantzig returned to work at the Pentagon, becoming the chief mathematician to the comp-

troller of the U.S. Air Force. While at the Pentagon, Dantzig developed his simplex method.

One of Dantzig's tasks at the Pentagon was to help the military effectively and efficiently deploy forces and equipment—such as pilots and aircraft—as well as schedule training and provide logistical support for all these activities. Figuring out how to coordinate all these activities involved thousands of conditions and variables, from getting the supplies to coordinating the necessary people. In effect, the task involved coming up with a time–staged distribution schedule for training and supply activities. At the time, Dantzig could write his problems in a mathematical equation but lacked a computational method to solve them.

The mathematical method Dantzig devised for solving these types of problems became known as the simplex method and the type of problem it solved was called linear programming. Dantzig is thus known as the father of linear programming. Dantzig's linear programming module had many applications and grew into a field called operations research. Linear programming has countless applications; it can be used to figure out how to price products, schedule shipments and workers, and control supply chains, as well as evaluate policy alternatives. Shipping companies such as United Parcel Service of America and Federal Express use it to determine how many planes they need and where to place their delivery trucks.

In 1952, Dantzig left the Pentagon and became a research mathematician at the Rand Corporation. Here, he continued his work with linear programming, generally for practical applications—sometimes for use in the military or in industry. In 1960 he returned to UC–Berkeley, joining the industrial engineering department. He also established its Operations Research Center and became its director. Dantzig proved a hands–on mentor and thesis adviser who always had time for his students. In 1966, Dantzig began teaching at Stanford University and helped countless doctoral students. He became a professor emeritus in 1985, but continued his teaching and research until 1998.

Revered in Math World

Dantzig was also involved in many organizations. He was chairman of the Mathematical Programming Society from 1973–74 and was senior editor of the *Mathematical Programming* journal. He was elected to the National Academy of Science in 1971 and to the American Academy of Arts and Sciences in 1975, as well as the National Academy of Engineering in 1985. He enjoyed painting and woodworking and was also a movie fanatic. Dantzig was writing a science fiction novel when he died.

Dantzig wrote two books over the course of his life. The first, *Linear Programming and Extensions,* published in 1963, was a culmination of his work at Rand and the Pentagon. It remains the authoritative text on the subject. The book includes his research and computations on the mathematical theory, and how he has applied them to industrial problems. He co–wrote *Compact City: A Plan for a Liveable Urban Environment,* 1973, with Thomas L. Saaty. The book discusses the feasibility of building a city that uses all resources, including time and space, more wisely. The book studies whether facilities could be used around the clock.

Colleagues and former students remember Dantzig as a well–rounded thinker who was concerned not only with mathematical challenges but also with solving political, economic and household problems. Writing in *OR/MS Today*, former Dantzig student Mukund Thapa, who traveled from India to study at Stanford under Dantzig, said "the best times in my life were interactions with George." Thapa said Dantzig treated everyone as an old friend. Thapa recalled that Dantzig once worried that he was bothering the renters below him so he cut open some tennis balls and placed them on the legs of the tables and chairs in his dining room so as not to disturb the downstairs neighbors.

Dantzig died at his home in Palo Alto, California, on May 13, 2005. His family said he succumbed to complications from diabetes and heart disease. He was survived by his wife of more than 65 years, Anne Dantzig, as well as two sons, David and Paul Dantzig, and a daughter, Jessica Klass.

Periodicals

Daily Telegraph (London), May 27, 2005.
Mathematical Programming, January 2006.
New York Times, May 23, 2005.
OR/MS Today (Operations Research/Management Sciences Today), August 2005.
San Francisco Chronicle, May 16, 2005.

Online

"George Dantzig," University of St. Andrews, Scotland, School of Mathematics and Statistics, http://www-history.mcs.st-andrews.ac.uk/Mathematicians/Dantzig_George.html (December 30, 2005). □

Tom DeLay

One of the most powerful political figures in America in the early 2000s, Tom DeLay (born 1947) rose through the ranks in the United States House of Representatives to become the leader of the majority Republican party. He seemed a strong candidate to attain the still more powerful position of Speaker of the House until he was indicted on charges involving violations of Texas campaign finance law in 2005.

DeLay was motivated to enter the political arena by a strong dislike of government regulation that he developed as a small business owner in Texas in the 1970s. He was also a strong social conservative, aligned with political initiatives supported by evangelical Christian figures. As important as these two aspects of his political personality seem, however, they are dwarfed by DeLay's sheer mastery of the machinery of politics, particularly fundraising. Expanding his own influence, DeLay assembled a vast money-raising machine that he used to help other Re-

publicans as the party took control of Congress during the presidency of George W. Bush. "Tom has solid-gold status," former Representative Bill Paxon told Julie Mason and Karen Masterson of the *Houston Chronicle.* "He has spent the last 25 years networking with the business community, the Republican partisan community, and conservative interest groups. He has performed again and again and again. There is not a month that goes by that his imprint (on policy) is not clear and distinguished."

Spent Part of Childhood in Venezuela

A native of Laredo, Texas, on the U.S.-Mexican border, DeLay was born on April 8, 1947. His strongly religious parents were members of the Baptist church, but his oil-worker father, Charlie Ray DeLay, was a violent alcohol abuser who often consumed a quart of Scotch whiskey in the course of a single evening. "My father was a wildcatter straight out of the movie 'Giant,' " DeLay said in an interview quoted by Chuck Lindell in the *Atlanta Journal-Constitution.* "He was a boisterous, domineering alcoholic." Charlie Ray DeLay was also a fluent Spanish speaker, and an oil field supervisor job led him to move the family to Venezuela when DeLay was nine. Venezuelan cowboys showed the youngster how to crack a bullwhip, a skill DeLay retained years later when he became U.S. House Republican whip and kept an actual bullwhip in his office.

DeLay's experiences growing up in Latin America also had more serious effects. Several times the family was caught in the crossfire as leftist rebels fought against

Venezuelan government troops, and the young DeLay saw local villagers gunned down. According to his official House website, "DeLay points to this early exposure to political violence as the source of his lifelong 'passion for freedom.' " The adult DeLay became a lifelong enemy of left-wing regimes around the world.

Back in the U.S., the family settled in the suburbs of Corpus Christi, Texas. DeLay played lineman for the football team at Corpus Christi's Calallen High School, from which he graduated in 1965. There, he met his future wife, cheerleader and athlete Christine Furrh. The pair married in the late 1960s and had a daughter, Danielle, born in 1972. Planning a career as a doctor, DeLay enrolled at Baylor University, a Baptist school in Waco, Texas. But he ran afoul of school authorities after several alcohol-related incidents and a vandalism incident at Baylor's sports archrival Texas A&M. DeLay was not welcomed back to Baylor after finishing his sophomore year, and he transferred to the University of Houston.

Majoring in biology and nurturing a student draft deferment and a lucky draft lottery draw though the years of peak U.S. troop strength in Vietnam, DeLay graduated in 1970. For three years he worked as a chemist for a pesticide manufacturer, mixing the ingredients for rat poison among other products. By 1973 he had enough money to purchase a small exterminator business in the Houston area. He did not like the company's name, Albo, but decided to keep it after market research showed that its similarity to the name of a leading dog food brand might help further the firm's name recognition.

Angered by Outlawing of Fire Ant Poison

DeLay's company flourished. Settling in the newly upscale Houston suburb of Sugar Land, he benefited from the need for extermination services in Houston's burgeoning housing developments, many of them built on landfilled swamps. But the pest control business also brought DeLay face to face with an unusual degree of government regulation, in the form of the federal Environmental Protection Agency (EPA). DeLay rebelled against business taxes and against the paperwork necessary to gain approval for the use of pest control compounds. Several times he was hit with Internal Revenue Service liens in disputes over payroll taxes. DeLay's anger grew with a decision by the state of Texas to license exterminators. Becoming involved in local Republican politics, DeLay ran for and won an open Texas State House seat in 1978, running on a platform favoring business deregulation and becoming the first Republican elected from his district since the Reconstruction era. Continuing to fight what he considered unreasonable government rules, he was outraged by a new EPA regulation outlawing Mirex, one of the few pesticides effective against the Texas scourge of fire ants. According to Lindell, DeLay called the EPA "the Gestapo of government."

In the late 1970s, DeLay shared an Austin apartment with several other state representatives, some of them Democrats. The apartment was a party spot dubbed Hot Tub Heaven. "He was one of the most fun, humorous guys I hung around with . . ., former Texas Representative John

Sharp told Mason and Masterson. Reflecting on DeLay's later highly partisan stance, Sharp said, "I just think either Washington is a really bad place, or somebody really pissed this guy off."(DeLay rejoined that he did not think he had changed, and that "I don't see myself as mean-spirited. I'm just passionate.") In 1984, after deciding to run for the U.S. House, DeLay shaved off his moustache on the advice of political image researchers.

Few observers of Texas politics picked DeLay as a future leader. But after winning his House race, once again becoming the first Republican elected from his district, DeLay grew as a politician. At least two forces were at work. One was his arrival in Washington during the long ascendancy of conservative thought during the presidency of Ronald Reagan; DeLay had enjoyed campaign support from national Republican figures. Another factor, perhaps even more important, was a new dedication to evangelical Christianity, inspired by a videotape made by Focus on the Family founder James Dobson. DeLay gave up alcohol and, later on, tobacco use. He grew closer to his wife and daughter Dani, who worked in his political organization when she grew to adulthood, but, according to a *Vanity Fair* profile by Sam Tanenhaus, he grew apart from his mother and siblings. DeLay's father died in 1988, and DeLay has said that he learned little from his father other than the value of hard work. DeLay became involved with child welfare issues, and he and his wife opened their Sugar Land estate to three foster children. Later, in the midst of bitter partisan struggles in Washington, DeLay would work with Democratic New York Senator Hillary Clinton on child welfare legislation. He often used his skills as an auctioneer to raise money for charities in his district.

Criticized Bush Tax Measure

DeLay's identification with the right wing of the Republican party became complete in 1990 when he criticized a group of new taxes agreed upon by Congress and President George H.W. Bush as the federal deficit ballooned. DeLay had a knack for campaign-style moves that gained attention at the national level, passing out Red Tape Awards for what he regarded as particularly overbearing examples of federal regulation, and once spraying Raid insecticide in the halls of the U.S. Capitol building as layers of bureaucrats filling out forms struggled to obtain the proper materials to combat a cockroach infestation. At a less public level, DeLay became known as one of the Republican party's most reliable workers in the trenches at election time. In 1994 he had a consultant identify Republicans in close races nationwide and pinpointed those races with extensive fundraising efforts. The Republicans took control of the House in the 1994 elections, and newly elected Republican House members, not all of them sharing DeLay's staunch conservative philosophy, reacted with gratitude, electing DeLay majority whip—the member responsible for enforcing party discipline in the House. DeLay assumed his new position on what he called (according to Mason and Masterson) "the first day of the rest of the revolution."

Although during this time he tried unsuccessfully to restrict the power of the EPA that he had fought earlier in his career, he was effective in mobilizing Republicans to frustrate the legislative initiatives of Democratic President Bill Clinton, and his influence grew. He acquired the nickname "the Hammer" for his hard-edged attitude and iron party rule. In 1996 DeLay overreached and failed after trying to engineer the removal of an archrival, House speaker Newt Gingrich. DeLay was a major mover behind the impeachment of Clinton in the aftermath of his sexual involvement with White House intern Monica Lewinsky in 1998. Soon Gingrich—struggling with ethics problems and weakened after Clinton's 1996 reelection and Democratic gains in 1998—resigned, and DeLay emerged as a Republican kingmaker. He engineered the selection of Robert L. Livingston as the next House Speaker, and then, after Livingston was ensnared in a sex scandal, the choice of another close associate, Representative Dennis Hastert of Illinois.

By the time Republicans retook the White House in 2000, DeLay was considered the party's real leader in the House. His fundraising efforts on behalf of fellow Republicans were only magnified during the 2000 and 2002 elections, and he played key roles in shepherding President Bush's agenda, including the Congressionally authorized war in Iraq, through Congress. Staunchly opposed to environmental regulation, he formed a bulwark against any consideration of American participation in international programs to reduce the emission of "greenhouse" gases generally thought to contribute to global warming. Republican control was solidified with takeover of the Senate in 2002, and DeLay was elevated to the post of House Majority Leader by the new Congress the following year.

DeLay now embarked on a new challenge: the Texas congressional delegation, to DeLay's dismay, remained solidly Democratic, and he mounted a two-pronged attack designed to change that state of affairs. First, his lieutenants in the Texas legislature, despite a well-publicized walkout by Democratic lawmakers, successfully implemented an unorthodox off-year redistricting plan designed to improve the chances of Republican candidates, although the U.S. Supreme Court, in December of 2005, agreed to hear a challenge to the plan's legality. And second, DeLay mounted one of his trademark fundraising drives in advance of the 2004 election.

That effort succeeded, as the Republicans once again picked up House seats in 2004. But it also led ultimately to DeLay's indictment and resignation as majority leader in 2005. DeLay had long specialized in rolling up corporate donations to Republicans in Washington. Texas law prohibited direct corporate contributions to political campaigns, but Texas grand jury indictments on September 28 and October 3, 2005, alleged that DeLay had improperly funneled corporate monies through his political action committee, Texans for a Republican Majority (TRMPAC) and then through an account at the Republican National Committee. DeLay denied that the funds returned to the Texas races had originally come from Texas corporations, and he maintained that the indictments constituted a partisan vendetta on the part of prosecutor Ronnie Earle, a Democrat from more liberal Austin, Texas. Earle, however, had a long record of prosecuting Democrats as well as

Republicans. Under indictment, DeLay was forced to resign his leadership post.

One of the two indictments, on a conspiracy charge, was thrown out by a judge in December of 2005, but the other, describing alleged money laundering, was allowed to stand. DeLay's future was unclear as of the end of 2005. Moderate Republicans in the House, many of whom had always disliked DeLay, had begun to criticize him, and rivals were angling for his leadership post. A host of other ethical issues, some involving controversial lobbyist and DeLay associate Jack Abramoff, loomed as legal threats. But DeLay had amassed an enormous network of friends over more than a quarter century as a masterful and ideologically committed politician, and no one was counting him out.

Books

Dubose, Lou, and Jan Reid, *The Hammer, Tom DeLay: God, Money, and the Rise of Republican Congress,* Public Affairs, 2004.

Periodicals

Atlanta Journal-Constitution, April 10, 2005.
Houston Chronicle, June 22, 2003; December 9, 2005.
New Republic, February 19, 1996.
Time, March 21, 2005.
U.S. News & World Report, October 10, 2005.
Vanity Fair, July 2004.

Online

"About Tom," Official Tom DeLay House Website, http://www.tomdelay.house.gov/Biography (December 13, 2005). ☐

Alan M. Dershowitz

American criminal defense lawyer and Harvard law professor Alan M. Dershowitz (born 1938) came to prominence through his vigorous representation of such high-profile clients as Claus von Bulow and O.J. Simpson. An emphatic proponent of civil liberties, he was also a prolific writer and frequent guest on radio and television programs. While some have found his choice of clients and knack for publicity offensive, Dershowitz has remained firm in his view that he is fighting the good fight.

Brooklyn to Harvard

Dershowitz was born on September 1, 1938, in Brooklyn, New York. He was the first baby in his family to be delivered outside the home, and his father was a wholesaler of blue jeans. As a child Dershowitz was happy and outgoing, but scarcely anyone's idea of a scholar. Boston colleague Harvey Silverglate explained to Pope Brock of *People,* "Alan was not slated to be a great success when he was a kid. He was a disciplinary problem.

In some ways I suppose he still is. He almost didn't go to college.'' According to Michael Neill of *People*, Dershowitz's principal at Yeshiva University High School was not overly impressed with the young man's potential, either, telling him in a counseling session, ''You have a good mouth on you, but no head. So you gotta do something that you need a good mouth for but no brains. Become a lawyer.'' It took a while, but Dershowitz followed the advice to unexpected levels.

A turning point came when Dershowitz was accepted into Brooklyn College, where his rambunctious spirit was not just tolerated, but encouraged. He engaged in convivial and spirited arguments with everyone from the college president, anti-Communist Harry Gideonse, to conservative professor Eugene Scalia (father of eventual U.S. Supreme Court Justice Antonin Scalia), and thrived while doing so. Dershowitz credited the college with having allowed him to come into his own. According to Marek Fuchs of the *New York Times,* Dershowitz felt that ''his acceptance letter from Brooklyn College [was] the most important document of his life.'' (Not incidentally, he repaid the debt many years later by donating all his papers to his alma mater.) He graduated in 1959.

Dershowitz took his new-found resolve and ambition to Yale Law School, where he was editor of the *Yale Law Journal* and graduated first in his class in 1962. Before his graduation, however, he was given a sharp reminder of ugliness in the world when anti-Semitism closed Wall Street's doors to the promising young law student looking

for a summer job. Luckily it was a minor setback. After receiving his law degree, Dershowitz clerked for Supreme Court Justice Arthur Goldberg before hiring on as an assistant professor of law at Harvard Law School in 1964. He became a full professor there three years later at the age of 28, making him the youngest such in the school's history. But Dershowitz did not simply rest on his Harvard laurels.

Criminal Defense

During his long tenure at Harvard, Dershowitz taught such courses as criminal law, constitutional litigation, human rights, civil liberties and violence, the Bible and justice, and neurobiology and the law. By all accounts, he was a very popular teacher and he steadfastly maintained that it was what he liked to do most. Nonetheless, it was Dershowitz's part-time practice as an appellate litigator that made him famous.

An avid advocate of civil liberties, Dershowitz soon became noted for a parade of what many considered unsavory, or even odious, clients. Although he defended indigent people as well as high profile clients, it was naturally the latter for which he became known. The list included porn star Harry Reems, boxer Mike Tyson, ''Queen of Mean'' Leona Helmsley, evangelist Jim Bakker, and deposed Philippine leader Ferdinand Marcos. Perhaps the first of such clients to put Dershowitz squarely in the spotlight was socialite Claus von Bulow, who was convicted of trying to kill his wife in 1982. Thanks to Dershowitz's appellate work, the conviction was overturned in 1984 and von Bulow was found not guilty in his second trial. The case became a media circus, and Dershowitz drew fire by publishing a book about it, *Reversal of Fortune: Inside the von Bulow Case,* while a civil suit was still pending against the defendant. The attorney strongly denied any wrongdoing, the book was made into a successful movie in 1990, and Dershowitz became as well known as his client.

A commentary on Dershowitz's notable cases would hardly be complete without mention of the O.J. Simpson case in the mid-1990s. As a member of the defense team that prevailed in the murder trial of the ex-football great, Dershowitz became not just famous, but infamous. The trial was undoubtedly the most highly-publicized of its time, and it was televised, giving the public front row seats for the entire spectacle. Dershowitz was often vilified after the acquittal, but he ardently believed that the case's very unpopularity was what made his taking it important. ''I knew I would get criticism, including from my mother,'' he told Byron York of the *National Review.* ''But I'm proud of my work in that case, particularly because it was so unpopular. I see that as being absolutely consistent with being a Harvard professor. That's precisely the kind of case that a Harvard Law professor should be in.'' Indeed, Dershowitz clearly considered the controversy that was inherent in taking such cases to be a badge of honor. As he later told Fuchs, ''A criminal defense attorney has to be as proud of his enemies as of his friends.'' But it is important to note that Dershowitz was not criticized for simply defending such unpalatable clients; apparently his real ''crime'' was in winning for them.

Media Darling

As Dershowitz's courtroom successes increased his stature as an attorney, his writing and media appearances broadened his audience and made him a household name. He was a prolific contributor to myriad magazines, journals, and newspapers, including the *Wall Street Journal, Los Angeles Times,* and *New York Times.* As of 2006, he had written over 20 books (primarily non-fiction), including *Chutzpah* (1991), *The Advocate's Devil* (1994), *The Abuse Excuse: And Other Cop-outs, Sob Stories, and Evasions of Responsibility* (1994), *The Genesis of Justice: Ten Stories of Biblical Injustice That Led to the Ten Commandments and Modern Law* (2000), and *America On Trial: Inside the Legal Battles That Transformed Our Nation* (2004). He had a gift for putting arcane legal concepts into readily accessible language. As he told Sarah F. Gold of *Publishers Weekly,* "My theory is, if I can't explain to the general public a complicated legal problem, it's my fault. . . . This is democracy. If they can't explain it, they're hiding something from you."

This talent for plain speaking also made Dershowitz a favorite on television and radio programs, from the *McNeil-Lehrer News Hour* to *Today* to *Nightline,* to the *Oprah Winfrey Show* and *Larry King Live.* Besides radio and television, he was profiled in major publications, and had his own talk radio program. Unsurprisingly, the ongoing publicity was also a lightning rod for criticism. Accusations of self-aggrandizement and a runaway ego were common. Dershowitz, however, maintained his high profile was misleading and that defending his well-known clients actually took up only a small portion of his time. The time it did consume, he believed, was worth it in order to reach the proverbial "person on the street." "We have to build a much deeper commitment to civil liberties," he told Brock. "I don't think it's enough to persuade five [Supreme Court] Justices. I have to persuade Joe Sixpack." And, to his credit, Dershowitz never denied that he enjoyed it. He told York, "I can't deny that it's fun. . . . But the TV stuff is very much an extra. If I spend, say, two hours a week on television, and 50 hours a week doing my work quietly, it's the two hours that people see."

Civil Libertarian

Even if one believed Dershowitz was merely an arrogant publicity hound with an agenda, it was hard to dispute that his agenda included an abiding devotion to the First Amendment, civil liberties, and the law in general. His 1979 Guggenheim Fellowship for his work in human rights, 1993 appointment as Harvard's Felix Frankfurter Professor of Law, 1996 Freedom of Speech Award from the National Association of Radio Show Talk Hosts, and many other accolades spoke to those commitments, as did such books as *Supreme Injustice: How the High Court Hijacked Election 2000* (2001) and *Shouting Fire: Civil Liberties in a Turbulent Age* (2002). He could certainly be abrasive and aggressive, but many saw those qualities as testaments to his convictions about civil liberties. Silverglate told Brock, "Alan is stubbornly principled. He's opposed to any form of tyranny. People like that manage to alienate everybody at some point."

Dershowitz told Chris Lamb of *Editor & Publisher* that he was "criticized by people of all political persuasions, including conservatives for defending liberal causes and liberals for defending conservative causes." And that, in his view, was the way it was supposed to be. He was, after all, an advocate. "The system of justice is only as good as it is toward the worst person," he explained to Brock. "Once it begins to compromise there, the slippery slope begins. So because I want that system to be there for you and me, I want it to be there for everyone. Even for, say, a Josef Mengele [a Nazi war criminal]." It is hard to imagine how Dershowitz could have put it more understandably and pointedly than that.

Periodicals

Boston Globe, July 9, 2005.
Editor & Publisher, September 10, 1994.
Long Island Business News, February 16, 2001.
National Review, February 5, 2001.
New York Times, June 22, 2005.
People, October 3, 1988; July 30, 1990.
Publishers Weekly, June 18, 2001.

Online

"Alan Dershowitz," NNDB, http://www.nndb.com/people/013/ 000023941/ (January 4, 2006).
"Alan Dershowitz, Felix Frankfurter Professor of Law, Harvard Law School, Attorney at Law, Author," Harvard Law School, http://www.law.harvard.edu/faculty/dershowitz/biography .html (January 4, 2006).
"Alan M. Dershowitz," Harvard Law School, http://www.law .harvard.edu/faculty/directory/facdir.php?id=12 (January 4, 2006).
"Alan M. Dershowitz," IMDb, http://www.imdb.com/name/ nm0220641/ (January 4, 2006).
"Dershowitz, Alan," New York Public Library, http://www .catnyp.nypl.org (January 8, 2006). □

Abby Morton Diaz

American author and activist Abby Morton Diaz (1821-1904) drew young children into a deeper love of literature with her 1870 publication *William Henry's Letters to his Grandmother,* and strove to help further liberate womankind with the power of her words, as well as with the force of her actions.

Early Life

Diaz was born Abigail Morton—the only child of Patty (Weston) and Ichabod Morton—on November 22, 1821, in Plymouth, Massachusetts. Ichabod Morton—a shipbuilder born and raised in Plymouth—was a direct relative of pilgrim George Morton, who wrote an account of the sea voyage and subsequent settling of Plymouth titled *Mourt's Relation.* He was, himself, an active social reformer, and he passed this ambitious temperament on to his daughter. Harriet Townsend's 1916 edition of *Reminiscences of Famous Women* recalled the author's recollections of Diaz. She began, "One who has ever come under the spell of the quaint personality of Mrs. Abby Morton Diaz will never forget her. . . . I am moved to record my impressions of a woman whose word by tongue or pen was a source of moral uplift always worthwhile." Diaz's mother died not long after she was born, and her father re–married and fathered five sons.

Townsend described how "Abby grew up in an atmosphere of reform; . . . to take as her watch–word the old Greek saying, 'It is not life to live for one's self alone, let us help one another.'" She became socially active early, acting as a member of the "Fragment Society"—organized by a paternal aunt to help distribute donated clothing to the poor—at the tender age of four, and later serving as the Secretary for the Juvenile Anti–Slavery Society before she had reached the age of twelve. The *American National Biography's* Lucy M. Freibert recorded that, according to Diaz's own recollections, in order to pay the weekly 25 cent Society membership dues, the conscientious young girl knit and sold garters and chose to forego having butter with her meals. This thread of self–sacrifice not only ran throughout her character, giving it a simple strength, but she also wove it into her future work and writing.

Education

Diaz attended the Plymouth high school for girls—started by her father and his peers within the community—and excelled both academically and socially. In 1843, Diaz moved with her family to Brook Farm—a utopian commune formed by George and Sophia Ripley in Roxbury, Massachusetts in 1841. She and two of her brothers attended the school there until their father found the Farm's financial situation to be too precarious for his liking. He and the rest of the family left, but Diaz chose to stay behind and serve as a teacher in the Farm's Infant School. On October 6, 1845 she married Manuel A. Diaz—a Cuban student from Havana who, in time, taught Spanish at the school—and they had three boys: Robert, Manuel and Charles, who died at the age of two. She remained at the Farm, teaching in the Infant School until 1847 when the utopian community was dissolved. The Diaz marriage went sour, and Diaz moved back into her parents' home to raise her boys on her own.

Freibert pointed out that, in her attempt to combine "thinker and doer in one person", Diaz threw herself whole–heartedly into multiple enterprises with the intention of maintaining a stable home life for her sons. She took over their education herself and while trying to make ends meet, she conducted a singing school, served the community as a nurse, and taught dancing in Plymouth. Eager to do her part during the Civil War, Diaz distributed Army sewing jobs to women. Freibert noted that Diaz quickly realized that these experienced, competent women were "grossly underpaid" and that "this observation motivated her later advocacy for working women." In May of 1861 Diaz's literary life took off when a story that she had submitted—"Pink and Blue: how I won my Wife"—was published in

Atlantic Monthly. She was awarded a check of forty dollars for its publication, and promptly decided to focus on writing as a career.

Career as an Author

Diaz's determination and ingenuity paid off, and she enjoyed an acclaimed and prolific literary career. Over time, her stories and essays appeared in publications such as *Youth's Companion, Cottage Hearth, St. Nicholas, Our Young Folks, Hearth and Home, Arena* and *Wide Awake.* Diaz was best known as an author of encouragingly didactic children's stories. Her tales were imbued with a keen sense of humor and a genuine appreciation for the innocence of the child's mind. She believed in teaching from the heart as well as from the head, and she always claimed that it made more sense to "right form" rather than "reform" a child.

Her most beloved work was *William Henry's Letters to his Grandmother* (1870), which followed the trials and tribulations of a young boy's life at a boarding school. The protagonist, a roguish redhead, is sent away from his grandmother's home to prevent her from spoiling him. Children of all ages paid rapt attention as William Henry's adventures unfolded in the book's epistolary format. Two sequels followed this, in part, *William Henry and His Friends* (1871) and *Lucy Maria* (1874). Jane Benardete of *American Women Writers* (1979) noted that the latter was "loosely autobiographical, [concerning] a girl who took up 'school–keeping with too much self confidence' and soon concluded that it is a 'very solemn thing' to give 'even one life its first direction.' Lucy Maria wants to do 'heart–teaching,' rather than head–teaching . . . [and] like [Morton Diaz] at Brook Farm, [Lucy] takes her students into the woods to interest them in 'flowers, trees, insects—all natural objects.'" Diaz also wrote respected essays for adults covering domestic topics. The *Feminist Companion to Literature in English* (1990) quoted Diaz as stating that housework was "woman–killing"—a problem she addressed in her 1875 essay, *A Domestic Problem* when she stated that men "should share household tasks, so that they may appreciate the difficulty of women's work." Benardete pointed out that many of Diaz's stories were "set in small towns that have little social life. Isolated and repressive, they are half–way stations between the old–fashioned village and the modern city." As an author, Diaz was sensitive to this transitional quality that marked her time, and it was a tribute to her skill that her characters managed to bridge the resulting gaps in their social settings.

Became Suffragist

Townsend noted that it was Diaz's "supremest joy to awaken women to a sense of their own vital needs and to make them realize their power to help each other. . . . The key note of her life work was the thought that the elevation of women means the elevation of the race . . . that 'applied Christianity' means equalization of opportunities, not equal distribution of goods or acquirements, but equal chances for the elevation of all human kind." To this end, in 1877, Diaz helped set up the Women's Educational and Industrial Union of Boston—an organization dedicated to providing legal recourse for women who had been economically victimized by their employers. She was a staunch supporter of lightening the housewife's load so that women had the time, energy and means to better themselves culturally, rationally and spiritually. While she did not personally desire the right to vote beyond the social issues that directly affected her, Diaz was very vocal about a woman's right to vote as she chose.

Diaz was as active outside her written musings as she was within their pages. She served as active vice–president of the Women's Educational and Industrial Union of Boston from 1892 to 1902, and kept the title until her death in 1904. Benardete explains that Diaz intended the Union to be a " 'sisterhood' allying urban women of means with country girls seeking work in the city." Eager to support the women's movement outside the boundaries of her immediate geographical area, she traveled extensively in the 1880s and 1890s helping other women to establish their own local unions in New York, Washington, D.C., Rhode Island, New Hampshire and Minnesota. She stopped in at feminist clubs to speak at their functions and meetings, urging women to take the steps necessary to gain their own "freedom" and making the argument that the next step to follow the abolition of slavery should be the emancipation of women from domestic drudgery.

Spiritual Pioneer

Although Diaz was raised and remained Unitarian until her death, she was the epitome of open–minded tolerance. She was a fervent adherent of "New Thought"—an intellectual, spiritual and philosophical movement that tried to develop new understandings of old theologies in the interest of addressing social and physical ills that were not being healed by traditional faith–based religions. She experimented with metaphysical healing, and her admiration for what *Notable American Women* called "the Emersonian injunction to find morality in external nature and the inner voice of conscience" lead her to the firm belief that although youth takes place in an innate state of goodness, as a child grows they must be instructed in how to turn to Nature to help them maintain this innocent state. Diaz was an activist in this arena as well, and guest lectured at a gathering of the Free Religious Association. She displayed a keen interest in the infusion of spirituality and science, and was among the first of the 19th century activists to oppose vivisection as cruel and unnecessary experimentation.

The Final Chapter

Diaz died of pneumonia on April 1, 1904 at the age of 82 at her home in Belmont, Massachusetts. She had moved to Belmont in 1880 to raise three of her grandchildren who needed a home. Diaz's work entertained both the common, and the influential. United States President Theodore Roosevelt in his 1913 autobiography described *William Henry's Letters to his Grandmother* as "one of the favorite books of his boyhood: 'first–class, good healthy stories, interesting in the first place, and in the next place teaching manliness, decency, and good conduct.' " Her dedication to usefulness not only informed her fiction, it also guided her, time and again, into supervisory positions within her community. Freibert recorded that Diaz "held leadership roles in organizations such as the Boston Woman's Christian Temperance Union and the Women's Exchange, the Massachusetts Women's Suffrage Association, the Belmont Suffrage League, and the Belmont Educational League." Described in biographies as "versatile", "resourceful", "energetic", "lively", "bustling" and "cheerful", Townsend assures that Diaz "never seemed old, and to the last week of he life continued her service to humanity. Courageous and happy, she approached the heavenly life eager to begin her mission there."

Books

Benardete, Jane, *American Women Writers,* edited by Lina Mainiero, Frederick Ungar Publishing Co., 1979.
———, *Notable American Women 1607-1950,* edited by Edward T. James, The Belknap Press of Harvard University Press, 1971.
Dictionary of American Biography, edited by Allen Johnson and Dumas Malone, Charles Scribner's Sons, 1958.
The Feminist Companion to Literature in English, edited by Virginia Blain, Patricia Clements and Isobel Grundy, Yale University Press, 1990.
Freibert, Lucy M., *American National Biography,* edited by John A. Garraty and Mark C. Carnes, Oxford University Press, 1999.
Index to Women of the World from Ancient to Modern Times: A Supplement, edited by Norma Olin Ireland, The Scarecrow Press, Inc., 1988.
The National Cyclopaedia of American Biography, James T. White and Co., 1901.
The Oxford Companion to Children's Literature, edited by Humphrey Carpenter and Mari Prichard, Oxford University Press, 1984.
Tumber, Catherine, *Handbook of American Women's History: Second Edition,* edited by Angela M. Howard and Frances M. Kavenik, Sage Publications, Inc., 2000.
The Twentieth Century Biographical Dictionary of Notable Americans, edited by Rossiter Johnson, The Biographical Society, 1904.

Online

"Abby Morton Diaz," *About: Women's History,* http://womens history.about.com/library/bio/blbio_abby_morton_diaz.htm (January 5, 2006).
Townsend, Harriet, "Days With Abby Morton Diaz," *About: Women's History,* http://womenshistory.about.com/library/etext/bl_townsend_diaz.htm (January 5, 2006). □

Henry Chee Dodge

Native American Henry Chee Dodge (c.1857-1947) was one of the most famous and revered Navajo tribal leaders. Developing bilingual skills early in his life, Dodge served as a translator and interpreter, providing a bridge between the United States Army and the Navajos. Later he served many years as the Navajo head chief. He was also the first chairman of the Navajo Tribal Council, an organization that he helped establish.

Dodge was born at Fort Defiance in what is now Arizona. In his early life, he endured poverty, starvation and the subjugation of his people by the U.S. Army. From those circumstances, he grew up to become a prosperous businessman and landowner. But, more importantly, he became a respected tribal leader and an advocate for the improvement of the lives of the Navajo people.

It is not clear exactly when Dodge was born, and there has been disagreement about just who his parents were. However, in recent years, facts have been pieced together that begin to offer a more definitive account. Some historians dated Dodge's birth at 1860 and reported that his father was Juan Anea (also known as Anaya, Cocinas or Cosonisas, and Gohsinahsu). Anea was a Mexican silversmith who worked for Captain Henry L. Dodge, a Navajo Indian agent at Fort Defiance, where Henry Chee Dodge was born. Supposedly, Anea had named his son after Captain Dodge, whom he greatly respected.

On these points, there are questions as to whether Anea was truly Chee Dodge's father, but it does appear true that the future Navajo leader was born at Fort Defiance. The fort had been established as a military base from which the U.S. Army could patrol the Navajo territory in what is now New Mexico and Arizona. (The fort was later used as an internment camp and then became a governing agency for the tribe.)

In 1888, in a sworn affidavit, Henry Chee Dodge himself stated that he was born at the fort. But even he was uncertain of his own birth year, as he wrote that he was "about" thirty years old. He also said that he was the son of a white army officer and a Navajo woman. His mother was most likely Bisnayanchi, who was a Navajo-Jemez Pueblo woman from the Ma'iideshgizhnii (Coyote Pass) clan. The army officer was the aforementioned Henry L. Dodge, and it appears most likely that he was indeed Henry Chee Dodge's father. Historian David M. Brugge, in an essay titled "Henry Chee Dodge: From the Long Walk to Self Determination," reported that, in 1875, Augustus C. Dodge, who was Henry L. Dodge's brother, revealed that he had an eighteen-year-old nephew, the son of a Navajo woman and his brother, who lived at Fort Defiance.

Henry L. Dodge and the Navajos

Historian and author Marc Simmons, Ph.D., in an article published in *The New Mexican* helped shed more light on the story. Simmons indicated that Henry L. Dodge, who was killed by Apaches in 1856, was "an interesting and well-known character on the Southwestern frontier."

Henry Dodge was a native Missourian who fought in the Black Hawk Indian War when he was twenty-two years old. After he left the army, he later turned up in New Mexico, in early 1846. Simmons reported that Henry Dodge was appointed treasurer of the new American government formed in Santa Fe, and then the army made him agent for the Quartermaster Department at the outpost of Cebolleta in the mountains west of Albuquerque, close to Navajo country. The appointment had a profound effect on his life. "Henry L. Dodge," wrote Simmons, "found his true love— the Navajo people."

Henry Dodge learned the Navajo language and became an agent for the tribe in 1853. In that position, he was determined to make sure the people were treated fairly. In turn, the Navajos liked and respected Dodge and called him Bi'ee lichii (red shirt), because of his favored piece of apparel. Dodge also married a Navajo woman.

In November 1856, after Coyotero Apaches attacked Zuni Pueblo, Henry Dodge joined army soldiers in their pursuit. When he left the group to go deer hunting, the Apaches killed him. A few months later, Henry Dodge's wife gave birth to a boy who became known as Henry Chee Dodge. This would place his birth at 1857, and not 1860. His name was a combination of his Navajo name, Kiilchii' (which meant red), and his father's name.

Other accounts of Henry Chee Dodge's parentage are variations of a basic narrative containing similar elements (e.g., Navajo mother, father who was murdered). For instance, in one account, which indicated that Dodge was the son of a Bisnayanchi and Anea, the Mexican silversmith reportedly was killed while trying to recover stolen Navajo horses. But, beyond the accounts of Henry Chee Dodge's origins, all narratives seem to agree on the basic facts regarding his early life.

Chee Dodge Lost and Found

After Henry L. Dodge was killed, Bisnayanchi took her infant son with her when she rejoined her people, the Coyote Pass Clan. Simmons reports that Henry Chee Dodge lived in the Navajo world until he was seven or eight, unaware of his true parentage.

In 1864, the Navajos' world was ripped apart by the U.S. Army invasions, which were launched in response to Navajo raids that took place around Fort Defiance. Navajos who were not killed or captured split off into small groups that tried to stay one step ahead of the marauding soldiers.

Dodge and his mother were part of one such group. Their fugitive existence entailed hardships and starvation. One day, Bisnayanchi told her son that she was going to set out across the desert to look for food, and she left Dodge with relatives. She never returned.

Dodge was passed from family to family, until one day he got separated from his people and wandered alone in the wilderness for several days. Fortunately, at the point when Dodge neared starvation, he was found by an old man and his eight-year-old granddaughter. They were part of the "Long Walk" to Fort Sumner, where Navajos were being sent by the U.S. Army. After the U.S. Army had subdued the Navajos in the 1864 campaign, Colonel Kit Carson and a group of officers forcibly marched the surviving Navajos to the Bosque Redondo Reservation at Fort Sumner, which was essentially a concentration camp. The forced "walk" stretched several hundred miles, from what is now northeast Arizona to northwest New Mexico. At the end of the march, the Navajos—that is, those that survived the grueling ordeal—were incarcerated.

Educated at Fort Defiance

Dodge accompanied the old man and his granddaughter to the reservation, where he lived with them for four years. In 1868, Dodge returned to Fort Defiance with other Navajos. He met an aunt and lived with her. The woman, one of his mother's sisters, had married an Anglo trader named Perry H. Williams, who subsequently taught Dodge the English language and gave him a clerking job at his trading post. In that position, Dodge used his bilingual skills as a translator. He also learned Spanish.

Dodge also lived with an Indian Agent named W. F. M. Arny, who allowed the young boy to attend the Fort Defiance Indian School, where he learned to read and write. In addition, Dodge found work with a freight company, as well as with renowned ethnographer Washington Matthews at Fort Wingate. Later, because of his considerable language and translation skills, Dodge helped Matthews write two books about the Navajos, *Navajo Legends* (1897) and *The Night Chant* (1901).

In the late 1870s, Arny hired Dodge to be the official Agency interpreter. By this time, Dodge developed a deep understanding of Navajo culture and, with language skills coupled with a keen sense of diplomacy, he often helped settle territorial disputes that arose between Navajos and encroaching settlers.

In 1883, Dodge was appointed chief of the Navajo police force, which had been established to help keep peace on the reservation. Again, his language skills proved useful, as he assisted as an interpreter in police investiga-

tions. He also managed to bring a calming, bilingual voice into potentially violent situations.

The following year, Commissioner of Indian Affairs Dennis M. Riordan appointed Dodge chief of the police force and, in 1885, Riordan made him head chief of the Navajo tribe at Fort Defiance. Also in 1885, Dodge, accompanied by a delegation of Navajo leaders, went to Washington, D.C., to meet with President Chester A. Arthur.

Bought Land and Went into Business

All of his various job positions, from clerking to serving a chief, enabled Dodge to save a substantial amount of money. In 1890, he bought a sheep ranch near Crystal, New Mexico, where he built a large home and started a successful trading post.

Settled and established in business, Dodge married his first wife, Asdzaa' Tsi'naajinii. Reportedly, he later divorced her because her gambling habit threatened his financial security. According to some historical accounts, Dodge then married a woman named Nanabah and her younger sister. At that time, polygamy was both an accepted and expected practice in the Navajo culture. Coincidentally, Nanabah was a daughter of the girl who, with her grandfather, had found Dodge when he was a child.

In the meantime, his business continued growing and his ranch thrived. Nanabah proved to be as successful in business as her husband. She eventually amassed great wealth through real estate and cattle. As their separate business interests kept the husband and wife apart, Dodge married another woman, named K'eehabah. In all, Dodge would have eight wives and six children (Tom, Ben, Antoinette, Annie, Veronica and Josephine). He proved to be a caring father but a strong disciplinarian, and he made sure that his children were well educated.

Became a Navajo Leader

In the last decade of the nineteenth century and the first decade of the twentieth, Dodge spent much of his time tending his ranch and business, but he also continued working as an interpreter at Fort Defiance, helping agents resolve disputes. He also encouraged Navajos to become involved in issues related to mineral development and land rights as well as with federal programs. Further, he encouraged Navajo parents to send their children to the school at Fort Defiance.

In the early part of the twentieth century, Dodge grew in stature as a Navajo leader, and his guidance helped steer the tribe toward modernization. From 1864, the time of the U.S. Army attacks that sent the Navajos scattering, up until 1923, the tribe had no central leadership or tribal government. They lived as dispersed extended families, bound only by marriage ties and a shared language and culture. Dodge started bringing the people back together, at least in an organizational sense, when he helped form the first Navajo Tribal Council in 1923.

The council grew out of a Navajo business council that Dodge formed in 1922 with Dugal Chee Bekiss and Charley Mitchell to handle requests for oil exploration leases near the Fort Defiance reservation. The Navajo Tribal Council held its first meeting on July 7, 1923. Dodge was elected its first chairman four days later. He held the position until 1928. The council represented all nine of the existing Navajo districts and included 12 delegates and 12 alternate members.

At the time of council's formation, the U.S. Government did not invest it with many substantial powers; still, the council managed to conduct a great part of Navajo business with the government and big business, as those entities sought to exploit the rich mineral and oil reserves on Navajo land. As leader of the council, Dodge did everything in his power to protect the rights of the Navajo people.

Moreover, with Dodge as its leader, the council itself steadily gained power. In one significant development, it earned the right to determine how oil lease royalties would be spent. In 1927, Dodge advocated before the government that the Navajos should receive 100 percent of the royalties from oil found under the reservation. This led to the creation of the Indian Oil Act of 1927, which directed that those states where oil was found were entitled to 37.5 percent of the royalties. Those states could only spend those funds on projects that benefited the Native American population, however. Further, the states had to first consult with the indigenous population before moving forward with any proposed projects.

Fought for Sheep Rancher's Rights

Dodge stepped down as the council's leader in 1928 because he wanted to spend more time at home, tending his sheep ranch and trading post. However, he remained active in Navajo politics throughout the next decade. One issue in particular involved his own business interests, as it had to do with sheep.

In 1934, John Collier, the commissioner of the Bureau of Indian Affairs, was alerted to a problem of overgrazing on the Navajo reservation. Overgrazing been a problem before, because of the erosion it caused. In 1933, the Bureau had suggested that the Navajo reduce the number of sheep grazing on the reservation as a way of reducing the problem. But in 1934, Collier ordered the Navajo to reduce their livestock by more than half. Obviously, this upset the Navajo ranchers, and many of them became defiant.

The government had the upper hand, however, because of the Indian Reorganization Act of 1934. Overall the Act represented an advance for the Navajos, as it provided them with more authority. At the same time, it allowed the government to limit the amount of livestock that could be raised on Indian reservations. Mustering his best diplomatic and negotiating skills, Dodge pleaded with Collier, citing the needs and feelings of the Navajo people; Collier remained unmoved. The government did offer to buy ewes for about one-dollar-a-head, and many Navajo ranchers agreed to reduce their herds. Other ranchers kept their most productive stock.

By 1936, hundreds of healthy sheep were being sacrificed to stock reduction, leading Dodge to accuse Collier of creating hunger and sickness among the Navajo people.

Dodge even took his cause into a congressional hearing, without success.

Collier later admitted the sheep reduction was a bad idea, but by that time, the damage had been done. Dodge himself lost three-quarters of his own herd. Some Navajos put up a violent resistance, and they were either killed or imprisoned.

Later Years

In 1942, Dodge was re-elected as chairman of the Navajo Tribal Council. By this time he was in his eighties. He spent his last active years informing the U.S government about the ongoing problems encountered by the Navajos and suggesting solutions.

In 1946, Dodge was elected vice-chairman of the Navajo Tribal Council, but he was unable to assume office. He contracted pneumonia and died on January 7, 1947, in Ganado, Arizona.

He was buried in the cemetery at Fort Defiance. He had become a well-known, well-respected and even well-loved figure during his life and hundreds of people, from various ethnic and cultural backgrounds, attended his funeral.

His legacy lived on. Several of his children followed their father's footsteps into leadership positions in the Navajo political system. In 1963, his daughter, Annie Dodge Wauneka, was awarded the Presidential Medal of Freedom.

Throughout his life, Dodge placed great importance on education for children. Appropriately, in 1989, a school, the Chee Dodge Elementary School, located in Yahtahey, New Mexico, was named in his honor.

Books

Contemporary Heroes and Heroines, Book IV., Gale Group, 2000.
Dictionary of American Biography, Supplement 4: 1946-1950, American Council of Learned Societies, 1974.
Notable Native Americans, Gale Research, 1995.

Periodicals

New Mexican, October 29, 2005.

Online

''About Chee Dodge,'' *Chee Dodge Elementary School,* http://www.cheedodge.org/matriarch/MultiPiecePage.asp_Q_PageID_E_130_A_PageName_E_aboutushistory (January 6, 2006).
''Henry Chee Dodge 1857-1947,'' *Southwest Indian Relief Council,* http://www.swirc.org/bio_henrycheedodge.cfm?ep=9&ec=11 (January 5, 2006). □

Marguerite Duras

Marguerite Duras (1914-1996) was one of France's most famous writers of the twentieth century. Her talents ranged across fiction, film, playwriting, and

journalism, and all through her long career, just the mention of her name could be counted on to start a spirited discussion in a Parisian café or in an American or English college literature or women's studies department. A compulsive worker, Duras wrote 34 novels and a wide variety of shorter works, returning to writing even after a stroke robbed her of the use of her dominant hand.

Duras revealed her own tumultuous experiences in many of her writings, but she used fiction to disguise, dig into the underlying motivations behind, or elaborate upon actual events. She wove the clues of her own life into her writings, but her public utterances contradicted one another and tied biographers in knots. Key episodes in her early life are subjects of dispute, and Duras' own outspokenness and intensity made it hard to know when to take her statements at face value. Yet the dance of veils choreographed by Duras' fiction and public image was all part of her appeal. Duras was a daring innovator, using fiction to view the events of her life through a constantly changing set of lenses.

Spoke Fluent Vietnamese

Duras retold the events of her early life over and over again in her books. She was born Marguerite Donnadieu on April 4, 1914, in Gia Dinh, near Saigon (now Ho Chi Minh City) in the French colony of Indochina, now the country of Vietnam. As a young woman she learned to speak Vietnamese fluently, and, except for two years she spent at a family home near the town of Duras in southwestern France, she grew up in southeast Asia. Her father, a math teacher, died when she was four.

After Henri Donnadieu's death, Duras' mother Marie tried to put the family on a solid financial footing by buying a rice plantation on the coastline of what is now Cambodia. She was swindled, however, by corrupt officials in the French colonial government, and she found that the land she had acquired was so often swamped by seawater that it was unsuitable for farming. Repeated unsuccessful attempts to build a seawall further drained the family's savings. Duras attended high school in Saigon, but finances had declined to a point where she found herself poorer than many of her Asian classmates.

Encouraged by her mother, Duras embarked on a romantic and sexual liaison with a wealthy Asian man. One of Duras' many biographers, Laure Adler, working from an unpublished Duras diary, has asserted that Duras was essentially sold into prostitution by her mother in order to finance the drug habit of her brother Pierre, but this characterization of events has been strongly disputed by her son, Jean Mascolo. Both the affair and the family battle with the encroaching ocean would recur as motifs in Duras' writing.

That writing career would take more than a decade to get underway. Duras moved alone to France in 1932 and was admitted to the Sorbonne, a prestigious university in Paris. She studied law, political science, and mathematics there, and after she received her degree in 1935 she took a job with the Ministry of Colonies, working for the same bureaucracy that had cheated her mother out of the family inheritance. As with so many other aspects of her life, controversy has attended Duras' work during this period; using the name Marie Donnadieu, she penned a propaganda volume that laid out justifications for France's colonial adventures in Asia. It may be, however, that she was acting as a ghostwriter for a higher official. In 1939 Duras married a writer, Robert Antelme. The couple's first child was stillborn in 1942.

Became Involved with French Resistance

Duras' actions during World War II are likewise uncertain. Adler's biography claims that she worked for the Nazi puppet government in Vichy, France as a de facto censor, controlling the distribution of paper in occupied France. This claim, too, has been disputed by Mascolo. It is clear, however, that World War II turned Duras' life upside down, causing her to reevaluate her earlier life and present situation. She struck out in new directions both politically and artistically. By 1943, Duras was working for the French anti-Nazi resistance, and her first novel, *Les impudents* (The Impudent Ones) was published that year.

The head of her resistance cell was a man she knew as Morland who later became better known as François Mitterand, president of France for 14 years beginning in 1981. Duras herself narrowly escaped arrest by the Nazis, but her husband and sister-in-law were seized and sent to concentration camps. She claimed to have once saved Mitterand's life, and German rule fell apart toward the war's end with the advance of American troops, Mitterand returned the favor, finding Antelme near death in the Dachau camp and rescuing him.

Meanwhile, Duras' literary career had begun to rise from the ashes of war. *Les impudents* dealt with a fictionalized version of her family's part-time hometown of Duras, and she soon adopted the town's name as her own. Her second novel, *La vie tranquille* (The Tranquil Life, 1944), was also set in Duras, and the two novels both featured a negative mother figure whom Duras would revisit in various ways in many later writings. *La vie tranquille* attracted the attention of writer Raymond Queneau, who shepherded the book toward publication at the prestigious Gallimard house in Paris.

After the war, Duras joined the Communist party but resigned her membership in 1950 upon finding Communist doctrine too restrictive. She helped nurse Antelme back to health but also began an affair with writer Dionys Mascolo. For a time the three lived as a *ménage à trois,* and Mascolo became the father of Duras' only son, Jean Mascolo. Duras scored a critical breakthrough in 1950 with the publication of her novel *Un barrage contre le Pacifique* (translated as *The Sea Wall*), which was drawn on her family's experiences in Indochina.

Wrote Prescient Essay

Duras wrote voluminously in the 1950s, venturing into journalism as well as fiction. As her reputation grew, she became one of France's most familiar public intellectuals, quick with a sharp opinion even if she might sometimes contradict herself. "I think the future belongs to women," Duras said in an interview quoted in *Women Filmmakers and Their Films.* "Men have been completely dethroned. Their rhetoric is stale, used up. We must move on to the rhetoric of women, one that is anchored in the organism, in the body." Yet she also once said, according to the *Scotsman,* that "I am in favor of total submission to men. This is how I've got everything I wanted."

Some of Duras' early novels were sprawling, detailed narratives influenced in part by the expansive style of American writer Ernest Hemingway, but gradually she came under the influence of modernist trends. She won praise for the 1955 novel *Le square* and for 1958's *Moderato cantabile,* both composed nearly entirely of dialogue that seems to circulate around the edges of unspoken events. In 1959, leading French film director Alain Resnais asked Duras to write a screenplay for him. Although Duras had done little dramatic writing, *Hiroshima, mon amour* became one of the most celebrated films of all time. The story of a love affair between a French actress and a Japanese architect in Tokyo during World War II, the film juxtaposed a world of private feelings with the overwhelming tragedy of war.

Duras went on to make numerous short films of her own in the 1960s and 1970s, often working on a shoestring budget and using her own Paris apartment as a set. Although she was less well known as a director than other prominent French experimentalists of the day, her work attracted the attention of young film industry figures such as actor Gérard Depardieu, who played a truck driver in the film *Le camion* (The Truck). The film consisted of a single one-hour-and-twenty-minute conversation between a truck driver and a female hitchhiker, played by Duras herself. Her 1975 film *India Song* was a more elaborate production that won the grand prize of France's Cinema Academy.

The author of a number of plays between 1960 and the late 1980s, Duras continued to write novels at a steady pace. Many of them dealt with themes of love and passion. Her greatest success came at age 70 with *L'amant* (The Lover, 1984), which won France's top literary honor, the Goncourt Prize. In 1992 the novel was filmed by director Jean-Jacques Annaud; the film, at first condemned but later embraced by Duras, became internationally successful.

Returned to Scenes from Youth

L'amant succeeded in tying together many of the themes and techniques Duras had explored over her long career. Minimalistically told like many of her later novels, the novel took Duras' youthful affair with her Asian lover for its subject matter. Viewed in one way, it was part of an effort at self-revelation that Duras made as she looked back on her life; biographies of Duras had begun to appear, and she revealed more and more of her secrets to literary scholars. Sometimes, however, her revelations created more mysteries than they clarified. Another autobiographical work, *La douleur* (1985, translated as *The War: A Memoir*), traced Duras' experiences during World War II. Literary scholars have debated the levels of truth versus fiction in both books.

A heavy consumer of alcohol for much of her life, Duras suffered from health problems in the 1980s and 1990s. She underwent a detox program in 1982 that only worsened her health. In 1988 she fell into a coma for five months and was not expected to live. But she recovered and resumed writing, putting her own experiences, now those associated with impending death, front and center as before. Her novel *La pluie d'été* was published in 1990, and in 1992, partly as a reaction against what she saw as errors on Annaud's film of *L'amant,* she wrote a new version of the tale, *L'amant de la chine du nord* (The Lover from Northern China). Her last book, published in English as *No More,* was a series of diary entries tersely chronicling her physical decay. She continued to write until shortly before her death on March 3, 1996, in Paris.

That event did not dent Duras' popularity as a writer; it was once estimated that more undergraduate theses in American colleges and universities had been written about Duras than about any other figure, and new studies of her work continued to appear at a rapid pace. Even the twilight of her life held fascinating for the public; the 2003 film *Cet amour-là* dealt with her affair with the young philosophy student and obsessive fan, Yann Lemmée (renamed Yann Andrea by Duras), which began in 1980 and lasted until Duras' death. "I did not deprive my heart of anything," she wrote in a fable that was read (according to the *Guardian*) at her funeral. "But the sun rises, and sets, and goes back to the place where it is to rise again. I have understood that all is vanity and vanity for vanity's sake. It is food to the wind."

Books

Adler, Laure, *Marguerite Duras: A Life,* translated by Anne-Marie Glasheen, University of Chicago, 2000.

Ricouart, Janine, editor, *Marguerite Duras Lives On,* University Press of America, 1998.

Women Filmmakers & Their Films, St. James, 1998.

Periodicals

Capital Times (Madison, WI), March 8, 1996.

Financial Times, March 9, 1996.

Guardian (London, England), March 4, 1996; March 8, 1996; July 28, 1998; October 17, 1998.

Independent (London, England), March 4, 1996.

New York Observer, April 14, 2003.

New York Times, March 4, 1996.

Scotsman (Edinburgh, Scotland, U.K.), March 9, 1996.

Times (London, England), March 4, 1996.

Washington Post, March 4, 1996.

Online

''Marguerite Duras,'' Books and Writers, http://www.kirjasto.sci .fi/duras.htm (November 10, 2005).

''Marguerite Duras: The Unspeakable, She Said . . .,'' The Written Word, http://www.diplomatie.gouv.fr/label_france/ ENGLISH/LETTRES/DURAS/duras.html (November 10, 2005). □

E

Sian Edwards

British conductor Sian Edwards (born 1959) has attempted, with mixed success, to penetrate the virtually all-male ranks of major classical conductors. Her tenure as music director of the English National Opera in the mid-1990s has remained a source of controversy.

Since she stepped down from that post, Edwards's career in her native England has suffered. She has continued to maintain a busy conducting schedule in other countries, however, and her attitude toward making music is still marked by the kind of enthusiasm she displayed as she bounded onto the stage to begin her orchestral appearances. Edwards never set herself forth as a trailblazer among female conductors, nor alleged that she had been the victim of gender discrimination, although several incidents that occurred during her career would certainly have given her good cause. She was devoted above all to the chance to stand in front of an orchestra and to shape its interpretation of a piece of music.

Arranged Music for School Dance Band

Edwards was born in West Chiltington, south of London in the English county of West Sussex, on May 27, 1959. Her vivid red hair and her first name (pronounced "Shawn") were signs of her Celtic background; her father was Welsh. Edwards began playing the piano at age seven and added French horn at eleven. At her single-sex high school she and a group of other girls formed a dance band, and the musically literate Edwards was picked to arrange some of the more complicated pieces, emerging as the band's leader.

"We played these Glenn Miller-like arrangements that I wrote," she told Jesse Hamlin of the *San Francisco Chronicle.* "We put on little concerts. I conducted and loved it. Conducting sort of took over from playing. Perhaps I needed a larger canvas."

Still, when Edwards enrolled at the Royal Northern College of Music in Manchester, England, it was to study French horn, not conducting. But she kept gravitating toward conducting, leading small student ensembles in concerts when she had the chance. After receiving her music degree she headed for London and took private conducting lessons with Charles Groves and Norman Del Mar. She attended a conducting camp in the Netherlands in 1981 and marveled at the seemingly effortless style of Estonian conductor Neeme Järvi. Increasingly sure of what she wanted to do, Edwards applied to the British Council, a government agency that funded overseas graduate studies, for a stipend that would allow her to study music at the Leningrad Conservatory in the Soviet Union. She took up the Russian language and learned to speak it fluently.

It was not only the British Council she had to persuade, however, but also the Soviet bureaucracy. Discouraged about her prospects for acceptance, she began working at a McDonald's restaurant in Manchester, England. Unexpectedly, however, she was informed that she had been accepted, and that she would need to be on a plane to Leningrad the next morning. Edwards made the flight, and spent the next two years studying with the legendary Russian conducting teacher Ilya Musin. "I studied very, very hard for the first time in my life under Professor Musin, a wonderful teacher," she told Philippa Coates of Australia's *Courier-Mail* newspaper. "He was so generous, I realized it was my big chance to learn about conducting. Up until then I had done the things I wanted to, but I hadn't really found

out what you do with your hands when you're up on the podium, you know, what connection they have with the sound." Edwards felt that the structured approach to conducting in the Russian conservatory system helped her learn the art. "In Britain, the way you learn to conduct is to get your fellow students together and do it yourself," she reflected to Wilma Salisbury of the Cleveland *Plain Dealer.*

As to the difficulties of living in the totalitarian Soviet Union, "I have to say that, as a woman, I found Leningrad in the Soviet era a much less frightening place than I found central Manchester when I came back." While still studying in Leningrad, Edwards entered the inaugural Leeds Conductors' Competition in 1984. She won, and Musin named her as his most promising student. Back in England, conductor Groves invited her to tea and introduced her to an agent, and Edwards began to find guest conducting engagements with British orchestras.

Suffered from Lack of Role Models

Male conductors tend to fall into lineages, with legendary conductors inspiring their protégés down through the generations. For Edwards, that kind of role modeling was difficult to find. She admired some of the male stars in the conducting field, like American Leonard Bernstein, Germany's Herbert von Karajan, and especially the legendary Russian Yevgeny Mravinsky, whom she had seen while studying in Leningrad. But, she told Hamlin, "I could never identify with them. Because I'm a girl, I couldn't take them seriously as role models. In a way, their image—the erudite,

white-haired man with great charm and teeth of iron— perhaps held women back." One conductor Edwards did identify with was City of Birmingham Symphony Orchestra conductor Simon Rattle, a rising star during the 1980s; he was young, and Edwards sometimes felt that her youth presented more of an obstacle than her gender.

It was Rattle who gave Edwards her big break. In 1986, forced to pull out of a Scottish Opera production of Kurt Weill's *Mahagonny,* he recommended Edwards as his replacement, saying (according to Gerald Larner of the London *Guardian*), "She's a very smart lady, and if anyone is going to carry the banner for women conductors it will be her." The Scottish Opera engagement led to conducting jobs for Edwards at other English opera houses and concert halls, and she was influenced by Rattle in her frequent choice of modern material; Rattle had made a name partly by specializing in music other conductors had neglected.

Edwards's next major conducting engagement after *Mahagonny* was a 1987 Glyndebourne Opera production of Verdi's familiar *La traviata,* but for the 1989-90 season at London's Covent Garden opera house she took on a work that fit that modern-and-unusual category—British composer Sir Michael Tippett's *The Knot Garden.* When she stepped to the conductor's podium, Edwards became the first woman to conduct at Covent Garden. The experience was notable for Edwards in another way; during rehearsals she met Tippett's biographer, Ian Kemp. The two married, moved to Edwards's native Sussex, and had a son, Finn.

Edwards made her debut in the United States with an appearance conducting the prestigious St. Paul Chamber Orchestra in 1989; her Canadian debut, with the National Arts Centre Orchestra, followed two years later. Audiences responded positively to the energetic Edwards, who charged onto the stage and conducted without a baton. She made recordings with the Royal Liverpool Philharmonic Orchestra and the London Philharmonic Orchestra. Word spread fast about the young conductor who stood out from the crowd. But there were dissenters. *Detroit Free Press* critic John Guinn, reviewing an Edwards appearance in that city, argued that she "at best demonstrated a student-like competence. He noted that one of the orchestra's players was reading a book during the concert, but he did not mention the disrespect that the player showed, nor address the question of whether a male conductor would have been so treated.

Named ENO Music Director

Among the organizations following Edwards's progress was London's English National Opera (ENO), where she conducted a performance of Sergei Prokofiev's *The Gambler* in 1990. The ENO, which performed foreign-language operas in English translation, was a less formal outfit than its neighbor Covent Garden, and Edwards seemed to display a fresh, contemporary approach. She emerged as a strong, if still inexperienced, candidate for music director. She had conducted opera, but had never run an organization or tried to hammer out a musical vision and steer it through the musical and political shoals of a large classical music institution.

Edwards was named as the new music director of the ENO at the end of 1991, and took over for the 1993 season.

Martin Kettle of the *Guardian* called her rapid promotion "a make-or-break gamble on all sides," for the company was a troubled one, with shifting management personnel and falling audiences. Initial reviews of Edwards's conducting in her first production as music director, leading performances of Tchaikovsky's *The Queen of Spades,* were mixed, with several critics praising Edwards's contribution even while expressing reservations about the production as a whole.

The pattern continued with the company's fall showpiece, a production of the perennial Giacomo Puccini crowd favorite *La bohème.* The staging of the opera, with its four acts run together into one and the setting modernized to the 1950s, was savaged, and Edwards essentially went down with the ship. "Just occasionally, Sian Edwards promises to pull everything together, to make the evening at least equal to the sum of its parts," wrote Andrew Clements in the *Guardian.* "But she conducts in fits and starts, responding well to Puccini's textures and colors, much less convincingly to the opera's singing lines, and never managing to achieve a decent balance between stage and pit." Players reportedly complained of indecisive conducting in rehearsals for a later production, and reports began to surface of disagreements between Edwards and general director Dennis Marks.

In 1994 Edwards conducted fewer performances, and the following year she decided, as she told Charles Huckabee of the *Philadelphia Inquirer,* that "it seemed better to call it a day" and resigned. After two years, she had not really had a chance to put her stamp on the organization. Critics looking back at the situation disagreed over whether Edwards had been treated fairly. Norman Lebrecht wrote in the London *Evening Standard* that "Sian Edwards was thrown to the wolves by unsupportive bosses at English National Opera," while Rupert Christiansen referred in London's *Daily Telegraph* to a "disastrous decline in standards while Sian Edwards was at the helm."

Edwards rose above the negative situation, conducting an English Chamber Orchestra concert two nights after her resignation, winning good reviews, and showing equanimity in the face of adversity. A few months later, the *Washington Post* praised her "buoyant, cheerful, athletic eagerness." For several years, Edwards was rarely heard as a conductor in Britain, but she continued to appear with American orchestras, and in 1999 she led an orchestra at an outdoor festival in Sydney, Australia, before an audience of 135,000 concertgoers. Edwards also conducted opera performances in Copenhagen, Denmark, Aspen, Colorado, Helsinki, Finland, and Paris, France, where she led the world premiere of *Clara,* an opera by Hans Gefors. In 2005 she returned to the podium in England, leading the City of Birmingham Symphony Orchestra in a performance of Gustav Holst's *The Planets* that, wrote Richard Morrison in the London *Times,* "deftly delineated details that are obscured in 99 performances out of 100." Looking back on her rapid, perhaps too-rapid, ascent, Edwards told the *Guardian* that "it all happened so fast that I didn't have a chance to plan things. Since then I've been consolidating: I needed to develop myself as a musician and a person. Conducting careers don't work neatly, and don't have an obvious full stop. I'm hoping that I'll keep going gracefully, chugging along."

Books

Sadie, Stanley, ed., *The New Grove Dictionary of Music and Musicians,* 2nd ed., Macmillan, 2001.

Periodicals

Akron Beacon-Journal, May 16, 1993.
Courier-Mail (Australia), July 11, 1990.
Daily Telegraph (London, England), January 15, 1999; May 11, 2005.
Detroit Free Press, October 18, 1992.
Evening Standard (London, England), July 27, 2005.
Guardian (London, England), December 6, 1991; April 6, 1993; September 17, 1993; July 22, 1994; November 8, 1995; February 24, 1996; January 12, 2006.
Independent (London, England), April 28, 1993; September 19, 1993.
Jerusalem Post, March 21, 1995.
Ottawa Citizen, December 4, 1991.
Philadelphia Inquirer, March 14, 1997; March 15, 1997.
Plain Dealer (Cleveland, OH), May 20, 1993.
San Francisco Chronicle, April 26, 1990; April 28, 1990.
Scotsman, February 21, 1994.
Star Tribune (Minneapolis, MN), November 30, 1989.
Times (London, England), January 21, 2005.
Washington Post, January 20, 1996.

Online

"Sian Edwards," http://www.bach-cantatas.com/Bio/Edwards-Sian.htm (February 23, 2006). □

Mohamed ElBaradei

Mohamed ElBaradei (born 1942), Director General of the International Atomic Energy Agency (IAEA), was awarded the Nobel Peace Prize in 2005. Later that year he was appointed to a third term as IAEA director.

A lifelong diplomat and one of just a few individuals from the Arab world active at the top levels of the world of international relations, ElBaradei was active in trying to resolve conflicts at several of the world's major flashpoints, all of them involving new nuclear threats. The IAEA, an intergovernmental organization affiliated with the United Nations (UN), conducts inspections and negotiates with governments in an attempt to stop the spread of nuclear weaponry and to insure that nuclear materials are used exclusively for peaceful purposes. ElBaradei's activities brought him into conflict with the United States in the twin trouble spots of Iraq and Iran, but the Nobel Prize and his subsequent reappointment signaled a strong vote of confidence from the international community.

Won Squash Tournament

ElBaradei (the name is generally spelled without a hyphen in Western lettering but appears as El-Baradei on the website of the Egypt State Information Service) was born into a professional family in Cairo, Egypt, on June 17, 1942.

His father, Mostafa ElBaradei, was a lawyer who once became president of Egypt's national bar association. ElBaradei's mother, Aida Hegazi, recalled (according to America's Intelligence Wire) that her son was a standout from an early age. "I hope he has a bright future," his kindergarten teacher told Hegazi. "I can tell he is brilliant." As a boy he loved athletics, excelling at squash and winning a national tournament in that sport. But as time went on, he decided that he wanted to take after his father, and enrolled in law school at the University of Cairo.

ElBaradei received his law degree in 1962, and two years after that, at the age of 22, he joined the Egyptian Ministry of Foreign Affairs. "His early diplomatic training is apparent in everything he does—from the relaxed but careful way he talks to journalists, to his dealings with countries' nuclear programs," noted a BBC News profile. Twice he was sent abroad to Egypt's United Nations missions, once to Geneva, Switzerland, and once to New York City, New York. There he enrolled at New York University (NYU) and earned a doctoral degree in international law in 1974. As part of Egypt's UN delegation he had responsibility for political, legal, and arms control issues. He also became a lifelong fan of the New York Knickerbockers' professional basketball team.

Becoming a special assistant to Egypt's Foreign Minister, ElBaradei was part of the delegation that traveled to the U.S. presidential retreat of Camp David in 1978 and concluded a groundbreaking set of peace accords with Israel. A youthful star of the international diplomatic corps, he took a

job in 1980 with the United Nations as a senior fellow, directing the program in international law at the UN Institute for Training and Research. This post took ElBaradei back to New York City, where he served from 1981 through 1987 as an adjunct professor of international law at NYU.

Familiar with a wide range of legal and diplomatic issues, ElBaradei joined the IAEA as a legal adviser in 1984. He held several policy posts within the organization, rising to assistant director-general for external relations in 1993. The IAEA is based in Vienna, Austria, and ElBaradei made his home there with his wife, Aida Elkachef, and the couple's son, Mostafa, and daughter, Laila. Mostafa became a television director, Laila a lawyer; both live in London. Aida Elkachef worked as an early childhood educator. "I find a lot in common in the way I manage things and the way Aida manages three-year-olds," ElBaradei observed to Jennifer Cunningham of the Glasgow, Scotland, *Herald.* "We humans are the same when we are three years old and when we are 50."

Named IAEA Director-General

In 1997 ElBaradei succeeded Hans Blix of the Netherlands as director-general of the IAEA. He was backed for the post neither by Blix nor by the Egyptian government, but it was due partly to the influence of the United States (ironically, in view of the conflicts that were to come) that ElBaradei won the support of a majority of the member governments on the IAEA board. At the time, his background seemed to have an ideal mix of Western education and familiarity with the Third World. "ElBaradei is exactly the kind of person you would want in the role—someone from a developing country who has a Western intellect but a Third World sensitivity," former U.S. IAEA ambassador John Ritch told Tom Hundley of the Knight-Ridder/Tribune News Service. The IAEA board appointed ElBaradei to a second term in 2001.

Up to this point, ElBaradei's name was little known except among those who followed arms control efforts, but the terrorist attacks of September 11, 2001, led to a period of international tension concerning the possibility that terrorists or rogue states might acquire nuclear weaponry. In his 2002 State of the Union address, U.S. President George W. Bush charged that Iraq, Iran, and North Korea constituted an "axis of evil" that sponsored terrorism at the state level, and that all three of those states had historically been involved in attempts to manufacture an atomic bomb. Lurking in the background was renegade Pakistani scientist A.Q. Khan, who gave technical assistance to a variety of nuclear aspirants. Suddenly ElBaradei's name was in the headlines, and his work was closely scrutinized.

The immediate area of concern was Iraq, where the Persian Gulf War (1991) had uncovered a clandestine nuclear program proceeding under the direction of Iraqi dictator Saddam Hussein. That program, ElBaradei reported, had been largely dismantled after the war, but U.S. diplomats, led by Secretary of State Colin Powell, claimed that it had been restarted on several fronts. A team of United Nations inspectors, led by Blix and including ElBaradei, went to Iraq to search for banned weapons, but found none. The United States went ahead with its case for war, despite ElBaradei's March 7, 2003, announcement before the United Nations

Security Council that a piece of evidence central to the U.S. argument, a letter pertaining to the alleged purchase of uranium by Iraq from the African country of Niger, had been shown to be a forgery.

A small coalition of countries led by the United States and Great Britain invaded Iraq on March 20, 2003, and U.S. officials were reportedly angered by ElBaradei's challenges to their claims about Iraq's nuclear program. Iraq, however, was not the only state on ElBaradei's nuclear proliferation agenda. North Korea expelled IAEA inspectors and remained, in ElBaradei's view, a serious threat. "My gut feeling is that they have a [nuclear] capability," he told *Newsweek*. "They probably have enough plutonium to make a few bombs. That makes [North Korea] the most dangerous proliferation situation . . . a country that is completely beleaguered, isolated, has nothing to lose and a weapons capability." Talks involving North Korea, South Korea, China, Russia, Japan, and the United States led to preliminary agreement by North Korea to give up its nuclear weapons program in 2005, but North Korea remained a nuclear danger point.

Favored European Approach in Iran

In Iran, where a dissident group revealed the existence of a nuclear weapons program unknown to the IAEA, ElBaradei was pressed by the United States to take a hard line by referring the matter immediately to the U.N. Security Council. ElBaradei agreed (as quoted in *Newsweek*) that "Iran's policy of concealment over a number of years [has] created a confidence deficit," but he favored a European Union-backed strategy of negotiation. "You will never solve your problem until you sit around the dinner table and put your grievances on the table and find out how to move forward," he told the *Chicago Tribune*. "Some people equate that with being soft—that if you do not pound on the table and if you do not scream, then you are being soft. I think this is a total misconception." ElBaradei's approach contributed to an agreement by Iran in November of 2004 to temporarily halt its nuclear program, but the issue flared again in 2005.

In October of 2005 ElBaradei was named the winner of the 2005 Nobel Peace Prize. The award was seen by some as a rebuke to the United States for its largely unilateral approach to the Iraq situation, but Nobel committee chairman Ole Danbolt Mjoes said (according to the *Tribune*) that the selection was "not a kick in the legs to any country." ElBaradei agreed. "I don't see it as a critique of the U.S.," he was quoted as saying in the *Seattle Times*. "We had disagreement before the Iraq war, honest disagreement. We could have been wrong; they could have been right." ElBaradei said (as quoted in the *Tribune*) that the award "recognizes the role of multilateralism in resolving all the challenges we face today," and that it would "strengthen my resolve and that of my colleagues to speak truth to power." As an international black market in nuclear arms components grew, ElBaradei argued, multinational cooperation became more and more important, and he criticized existing nuclear powers, including the United States, for their lack of progress in arms control. ElBaradei was Egypt's fourth Nobel Prize winner, following president Anwar Sadat, novelist Naguib Mahfouz, and chemist Ahmed Zewail. The selection of ElBaradei followed a pattern: figures devoted to the control of nuclear arms had been chosen for Nobel awards on several anniversaries of the U.S. atomic bombing of Hiroshima and Nagasaki, Japan, in 1945.

The United States, led by hardline U.N. ambassador John Bolton and Secretary of State Condoleezza Rice, attempted to derail ElBaradei's bid for a third term as IAEA director-general, proposing Australian foreign minister Alexander Downer instead. But the American delegation got nowhere with other countries represented on the IAEA board, and had to retreat after evidence surfaced that U.S. intelligence services had tapped ElBaradei's office phone. ElBaradei was unanimously approved for a third term in October of 2005, and he said that he considered his disagreements with the United States to be closed questions. The Bush White House offered congratulations on his reappointment.

Even after receiving the Nobel Prize, ElBaradei continued to receive criticism from some observers on both ends of the political spectrum. Conservative *National Review* commentator Jay Nordlinger derided ElBaradei as "the classic international-organization man"; he quoted writer Joshua Muravchik's contention that "for 'rogue' regimes, the IAEA has presented few barriers." From a different perspective came critiques by several Arab commentators described in Egypt's Al-Ahram Weekly Online, who argued "that the IAEA chief would have never received the prize had it not been for his determined avoidance of any criticism of Israel's policy of nuclear ambiguity"—though Israel is generally believed to possess nuclear weapons, it has never officially confirmed them. As the Iranian situation heated up again at the end of 2005, with the country's Islamist president Mahmoud Ahmadinejad's announcements that the country would move toward restarting its uranium enrichment program, ElBaradei's third term promised to be a busy one. He has often stated that his greatest fear is that nuclear weapons may fall into the hands of terrorists.

Periodicals

America's Intelligence Wire, October 7, 2005.
Chicago Tribune, October 7, 2005.
Herald (Glasgow, Scotland), October 8, 2005.
Knight-Ridder/Tribune News Service, February 1, 2005.
National Review, November 7, 2005.
Newsweek, February 9, 2004; July 11, 2005.
New York Times, October 8, 2005.
Seattle Times, October 8, 2005.
U.S. News & World Report, October 17, 2005.

Online

"Atoms for peace," Al-Ahram Weekly Online, http://www .weekly.ahram.org/eg/2005/764/eg2.htm (January 6, 2006).
"Dr. Mohamed ElBaradei: Director General," International Atomic Energy Agency, http://www.iaea.org/Abotu/DGC/ dgbio.html (January 6, 2006).
"Mohamed El-Baradei," Egypt State Information Service, http://www.sis.gov.eg (January 6, 2006).
"Profile: Mohamed ElBaradei," BBC News, http://www.news.bbc .co.uk/2/hi/middle_east/2596447.stm (January 6, 2006). □

F

Rainer Werner Fassbinder

Despite his abbreviated career that was cut short when he died of a drug overdose at age 37, Rainer Werner Fassbinder (1946-1982) has been ranked among the most important German filmmakers of the modern era. "In the 20 years since [his death]," wrote Tony Pipolo in *Cineaste*, nothing comparable to Fassbinder's brief but galvanizing engagement with cinema has emerged in Germany."

Following on the experiments of the French New Wave in the 1960s, the filmmakers of the so-called New German Cinema, of which Fassbinder was one, cultivated darker themes, often with a lurking consciousness of the horrors Germans had perpetrated before and during World War II. Fassbinder made films about outsiders of various kinds, and his films, filled with betrayal, crime, and fringe existences, were often unpleasant to watch. Few people knew Fassbinder well, for he himself was an unpleasant drug abuser who tended to drag others down with him; two of his homosexual lovers committed suicide. Yet his films were wildly imaginative, and critics hailed many of them as masterpieces. Working with feverish rapidity, he never repeated himself. Fassbinder managed to tie many of his preoccupations together into an epic story, *Die Ehe der Maria Braun* (The Marriage of Maria Braun), which achieved financial as well as critical success internationally.

Grew Up amid Postwar Chaos

Like the early stages of *Die Ehe der Maria Braun*, Fassbinder's early life took place against a backdrop of a devastated Germany in which crowding, disorder, and substandard housing were the norm. He was born in Bad Wörishofen, near Munich, Germany, on May 31, 1946. Fassbinder's father was a doctor who treated prostitutes, and Fassbinder, though he was warned away from them, grew up with an open mind toward people who lived or worked on the streets. His mother was a translator who, among other works, created the German versions of several books by Truman Capote. Fassbinder's parents divorced when he was six, and both before and after that he was left on his own for much of the time.

These experiences, according to various statements made by Fassbinder himself, colored the emotional tone of his films black. "I was lucky, growing up in a family where close relationships didn't exist," he was quoted as saying by Vincent Canby of the *New York Times*. When I was a child, I suffered a lot from that, but today I'm kind of happy about it. It makes me freer than people are in general." American movies of the 1950s were widely available in Germany, and the young Fassbinder spent most of his time soaking up one after another. He was especially impressed by the huge melodramas of the German-Danish-American director Douglas Sirk, whose visually imaginative style was plastered over stories that revealed layers upon layers of personal deception born of the efforts people make to live in a corrupt society. Sirk's films, such as *Written on the Wind* and the racially based tearjerker *Imitation of Life,* influenced the films Fassbinder would make as an adult, and even though he was a radical outsider who would hardly have fared well in Hollywood, he always professed an admiration for American films. His own work loomed large in the minds of independent American directors oriented toward social critique, such as Todd Haynes and Gus Van Sant.

In 1964 Fassbinder took a job with Munich's *Süddeutsche Zeitung* newspaper, but his heart was in stories he wanted to tell through drama and film. In 1965 he applied to the West Berlin Film and Television Academy but failed the entrance exam. In the famously conservative German city of Munich, Fassbinder and a group of like-minded souls began to mount experimental stage productions, taking the leftist-oriented theater of German playwright Bertolt Brecht as a point of departure. Fassbinder was influenced by the radical French filmmaker Jean-Luc Godard and by the general revolutionary spirit that grew among European young people around the especially violent year of 1968. After Fassbinder's group Action-Theater was shut down by the police, he co-founded a second troupe called Anti-Theater and continued to write plays and radio plays even after beginning to devote most of his intense energy to films. Several of his Anti-theater plays were later collected in books.

Several of the actors and production artists Fassbinder met and worked with in Munich's theater scene became the nucleus of the creative talent he would draw on in his films. Fassbinder realized his homosexual orientation as a teenager and never attempted to conceal it, although he briefly married actress Ingrid Caven in 1970. Only a few of his films dealt with gay themes, and he was criticized by some in the gay community for his negative portrayals of gay characters. Others defended him, however, pointing out that nearly all of the characters in Fassbinder's films were portrayed negatively, regardless of background or sexual orientation.

Lived on Wild Side

In his personal life, Fassbinder went well beyond the party-happy dissolution often practiced by film-industry figures and creative artists in general. He often drank two quarts of cognac a day, downed a variety of pills, ate voraciously and soon became overweight, and was fond of violent sadomasochistic games. In an episode reported by his biographer Ronald Hayman, after the trio had gone for a swim in the nude, he ordered his Algerian-born male lover, El Hedi ben-Salem, to cut Caven's hair off with a kitchen knife. Her struggles left her with a throat wound, but she was luckier than ben-Salem, who eventually, like Fassbinder's second long-term male partner Armin Meyer, committed suicide. When he appeared in public, Fassbinder was surrounded by a posse of associates who discouraged approaches by outsiders.

After making several short films, Fassbinder made his real debut with *Liebe ist käter als der Tod* (Love Is Colder than Death) in 1969. The title might serve as an epigram for many of his films, which, despite their wide variety of style and subject matter, often involved betrayal as a theme or plot element. Fassbinder was soon making films that critics would later number among his best. *Katzelmacher,* a depiction of a group of unemployed proto-punks in Munich, was praised for its innovative style; Canby wrote in the *New York Times* that "the major presence in the film . . . is Fassbinder's camera, which appears to be just as lazy and cruel as any other of the characters." Fassbinder's fourth film, *Warum läuft Herr R amok?* (Why Does Herr R Run Amok?, 1969) depicted a middle-class husband and father who suddenly goes berserk and attacks his family with a blunt instrument. Several of Fassbinder's films presented negative depictions of middle-class life; in *Der Händler der vier Jahreszeiten* (The Merchant of Four Seasons, 1971), a soldier named Hans faces rejection from both his wife and his mother after returning from service abroad and drinks himself literally to death in a harrowing scene that to some foreshadowed Fassbinder's own demise.

Such storylines, however, only hint at the dizzying diversity of Fassbinder's work; he was able to pick up almost any kind of conventional cinematic narrative and bend it to his emotional outlook. His 1970 film *Whity,* starring the African-German actor and longtime Fassbinder associate Gunther Kaufmann, was set in the southern United States and drew on Western imagery in its tale of an African-American slave who kills a degenerate family that includes his master, who is also his father. Fassbinder's *Die bitteren Tränen der Petra von Kant* (The Bitter Tears of Petra von Kant, 1972), one of the best known films of the first part of his career, is set completely in a single apartment and depicts a manipulative lesbian fashion designer. The satirical *Mutter Küsters fahrt zum Himm* (Mother Küsters Goes to Heaven, 1975) was the closest Fassbinder came to comedy; it told the story of a cleaning woman who becomes famous after her husband murders his boss upon learning he is to be fired; political parties of various persuasions try to exploit her situation for their own benefit.

Fassbinder worked with incredible speed, turning out more than 40 films over his 13-year career. Many said that they varied in quality, but there was rarely agreement as to which the good ones and bad ones might be. He wrote the scenario of *Die bitteren Tränen der Petra von Kant* in the course of a 12-hour flight from Germany to Los Angeles. Often Fassbinder moved on to a new film while the current one was still being completed, and, in marked contrast to the other cinematic auteurs venerated by film students, he rarely shot more than one take of a single scene. "Rainer Werner Fassbinder made films the way he smoked—all the time, more than one at a time, sometimes without seeming to notice or care—and then tossed them away, like butts deserving to be swept up with the rest of our garbage," mused David Thomson in *The New Republic*. He took a short break from this feverish activity to return to stage plays as a director with the Theater am Turm company in Frankfurt, but returned to filmmaking after the company went under.

Traced Postwar German History

Until 1978 Fassbinder's films were mostly known only in Germany, but that year his *Die Ehe der Maria Braun* (The Marriage of Maria Braun) gained international attention. The film tells the story of a woman, Maria Braun, whose husband disappears in the late stages of World War II. As she attempts to survive, she makes a series of morally questionable choices that eventually bring her prosperity; her story parallels the *Wirtschaftswunder*, the "economic miracle" of postwar Germany as it rose from ashes to become an economic titan. Fassbinder underlines his questioning of materialist German society with an ambiguous ending in which Maria is betrayed. The film starred actress Hanna Schygulla, who appeared in many of Fassbinder's films but held herself somewhat apart from his personal excesses. *Die Ehe der Maria Braun* became a commercial success in the U.S., and film festivals and later videotapes and DVDs circulated the rest of his work among American film students and enthusiasts.

Working on larger budgets than he had been allowed as an independent enfant terrible, Fassbinder made two more films about women in postwar Germany, *Lola* (1981) and *Die Sehnsucht der Veronika Voss* (The Longing of Veronika Voss, released in English as *Veronika Voss*, 1982), and they received wide attention. He filmed the massive 1920s German novel *Berlin Alexanderplatz* (Alexander Square, Berlin) for German television, and along with fellow German directors Wim Wenders and Werner Herzog he achieved a measure of international celebrity despite his unpleasant ways. Fassbinder, however, was visibly deteriorating physically as a result of his dissolute ways. He was found dead at his Munich home on June 10, 1982, by his roommate and film editor Juliane Lorenz. Police issued a statement a week later indicating that his death was likely due to a massive ingestion of sleeping pills and cocaine. Fassbinder's reputation continued to grow, and in the 1990s and 2000s his work was the subject of several important museum retrospectives, and an enormous literature of Fassbinder studies grew in universities and film schools worldwide.

Books

Hayman, Ronald, *Fassbinder: Film Maker*, Simon & Schuster, 1985.
International Dictionary of Films and Filmmakers, Volume 2: Directors, 4th ed., St. James, 2000.

Periodicals

Advocate (The National Gay & Lesbian Newsmagazine), July 9, 2002.
Artforum International, February 1997.
Cineaste, Fall 2004.
New Republic, December 31, 1984.
New York Times, June 11, 1982; June 19, 1982; June 20, 1982; October 3, 1982.

Online

"Rainer Werner Fassbinder," All Movie Guide, http://www.allmovie.com (December 14, 2005). □

Pierre Fauchard

Pierre Fauchard (1678-1761) is often called the founder of modern dentistry. A highly respected Paris practitioner, Fauchard authored *Le chirurgien dentiste* (The Surgeon Dentist) in 1728, the first scientific book devoted exclusively to the subject. Until this point in the history of human medicine, the care of teeth and gums was a generally barbaric practice, driven by lingering medieval superstitions. "Fauchard revolutionized dentistry in part simply by promulgating all he knew," wrote James Wynbrandt in *The Excruciating History of Dentistry: Toothsome Tales and Oral Oddities from Babylon to Braces*. "Previous practitioners had done their best to conceal whatever wisdom they thought they possessed."

Fauchard came from Brittany, the peninsula of northwest France with historic ties to the British Isles. He was born in 1678, during the reign of Louis XIV, France's Sun King. At the age of 15, Fauchard enlisted in the French navy against the wishes of his parents, and served for three years at sea. It was here that he was informally trained in dentistry, as the assistant to a talented ship's surgeon, Alexander Poteleret. He returned to the Brittany area in 1696, and opened his own practice in the university town of Angers.

Worms and Dead Mice

At the time, dentistry was just emerging as a recognized medical specialty, and France was at the forefront of this development. For centuries, superstition and quack science dominated human knowledge about the care of the teeth and gums. Tooth decay was common due to poor hygiene in an era when dental care was nonexistent, and the subsequent rotting of the tooth structure eventually led to painful toothaches, which Fauchard noted in his book was an affliction "we all have." Since ancient times, most people believed that tiny worms invaded the mouth and caused teeth to rot. Toothache remedies ranged from the bizarre—early Egyptians thought that the half-body of a still-warm dead mouse was an effective treatment for pain—to the useless, and most diseased teeth eventually had to be pulled. In an era before anesthesia, this was a painful experience that, if done improperly, could lead to infection and death.

In the cities of late Renaissance Europe, local barbers extracted diseased teeth for a fee, among the other minor surgical procedures and medical treatments they provided. In the countryside towns, itinerant tooth-pullers occasionally set up shop, and gathered a crowd of potential customers through deceptive practices. But France had been making notable advances in dentistry for many years prior to the time of Fauchard's career. The surgeon Guy de Chauliac, a professor at the University of Montpelier, left an impressive text on surgical procedures behind when he died in 1368, and it discussed several diseases of the mouth. De Chauliac's work was also the first written mention of the term "dentista," as well as "dentator" and "dentateur," all of which referred to those who specialize in surgeries of the mouth. Later, a renowned French barber-surgeon of the sixteenth century, Ambrose Paré, made several advances in the treatment of gums and teeth. Other pioneers elsewhere in Europe, such as the Flemish anatomist Andreas Vesalius (1514-1564) and his Italian cohort, Bartolomeo Eustachi, left behind detailed scientific examinations of the human tooth and surrounding anatomy.

Obsessed with Cosmetic Dentistry

Louis XIV ruled France for 72 years, the longest-serving European monarch in history. The Sun King was known as an autocratic ruler, and at the immense palace complex he built at Versailles, he commanded his entire court to spend most of the year with him there, where extravagant spending was obligatory. A premium was placed on one's appearance, and the care of teeth became important. Thanks to this development, France became the leader in dentistry during the latter half of the 1600s. There were a growing number of well-trained professionals to serve the aristocratic class, and many became particularly adept at fashioning and fitting dentures for those who had lost most of their original teeth to decay. In Paris, an examining board was established in 1697 to test new entrants to the profession, and three years later the French College of Surgeons established a department for dental surgery. Only the wealthy, however, could afford such services. The rest of the citizenry relied on quack dentists, and in Paris they gathered at the Pont-Neuf bridge over the Seine every morning.

Fauchard called himself a "Chirurgien Dentiste," or surgeon dentist, in Angers. He was a talented practitioner, and was said to have been ambidextrous, or able to use both the right and left hands with the same ease. His reputation grew, and he decided to move to Paris around 1718. Within a short time he was known as one of the best dentists in the city. He used his position to rail against the Pont-Neuf charlatans who, he claimed, often hoodwinked the crowd with the help of a paid "audience member" who came forward complaining of a toothache. The quack dentists would then surreptitiously insert a tooth wrapped in a membrane containing chicken blood on the pretext of examining the sufferer, and then would wave a hand or ring a bell, and the paid performer would spit the bloody tooth out, to the awe of the crowd.

Fauchard decided that education was the best way to combat the quackery and superstition that dominated dentistry. He set out to write the definitive book on the subject, and finished *Le chirurgien dentiste* (The Surgeon Dentist) in 1725. He then asked several respected professionals to review it for accuracy, and it was published in 1728. *The Surgeon Dentist* is an immense, two-volume work that is 863 pages in length. It was the first scientific text exclusively on the subject of teeth, and was soon translated into other languages and became the standard text for the profession. "The teeth in the natural condition are the most polished and hardest of all the bones of the human body; but at the same time they are the most subject to diseases which cause acute pain, and sometimes become very dangerous," Fauchard wrote in his introduction.

Sought to End Quackery

In his book, Fauchard attempted to dispel many of the commonly held beliefs about teeth. He railed against the practitioners on the Pont-Neuf, and those who claimed that a tooth was proving to be difficult to pull because it was an "eye" tooth. People actually believed that some teeth were connected by nerves or muscles to the eye, and that pulling such a tooth would result in a loss of vision. Fauchard wrote about less ethical practitioners who were known to put acids on a tooth, which caused them to decay; when the patient returned with a complaint of a toothache, the dentist could then extract the tooth for a fee. He also warned that some practitioners charged for gold fillings that were actually tin with a layer of gold on top. Others, he noted, had no knowledge of dentistry at all. Cutlers, or knife-makers, sometimes came up with new tools, and "apparently the instruments which they make gives them an itch to try them," wrote Fauchard, and mentioned one such tradesperson he knew of in Paris. "This particular man who had seen several charlatans operate, thinking that it would be as easy to draw teeth as to make knives, has joined the ranks. . . . if he does not always take out the tooth whole he does manage to take a piece of it."

Fauchard's book described five kinds of instruments that dentists should use. The gum lancet was used to separate the tooth or root from the gum; a punch pushed the tooth inward; pincers "pinched" it out for easier removal; a lever could lift it, but Fauchard noted that this was more likely to break the tooth than extract it. The last standard tool he cited was known as the pelican, named for its hooks that pointed inward like pelican's beak, and he noted that this should be the primary method of extraction. Fauchard also suggested that instead of pulling a tooth, it would be better to scrape the diseased cavity clean and then fill it with lead or gold leaf. His text contained detailed procedures for filling and treating cavities. Removing the diseased part could be done with a primitive type of drill that he invented. His was made from catgut (actually treated cord made from the intestines of sheep or goat) which was used for violin strings; he twisted his around a cylinder, which produced a rotating motion that could dig out the diseased parts of a tooth.

Fauchard disdained the still-prevalent idea that worms caused decay, suggesting instead that sugary foods were to be avoided. He provided recipes for mixtures to treat infections of the mouth, which used items commonly available from apothecaries, such as oil of cloves and cinnamon. One of his more unusual recommendations to patients, however, was "rinsing out the mouth every morning and also evening . . . with some spoonfuls of their own urine, just after it has been passed . . . it is true that it is not very agreeable, except inasmuch as it brings distinct relief." The use of urine was not entirely unusual at the time, and had persisted in many previous cultures and eras throughout history as a medical remedy.

Professional Heirs Continued Progress

Some of the innovations that Fauchard devised were chronicled in *The Surgeon Dentist,* while others came later in his lengthy career. He devised sets of dentures that used real teeth, with springs to connect them, and wrote about crowns and bridges, which could either replace or cover parts of teeth that were missing. In his book are some of his more innovative ideas about how to fasten these to the root of the tooth with threads of silk, linen, or metal; some of these techniques were still used in modern times. He also suggested ideas for straightening crooked teeth, which would make him the founder of modern orthodontics. His book also offered guidelines for the best treatment position for patients and dentists. Oftentimes the dentist sat on the floor, with a patient's head on his lap. Fauchard recommended using a chair instead, in which a patient could recline. The dentist should be behind the patient, not in front; this helped reduce fear in the patient, he believed, and did not block the light the dentist needed to see inside the mouth.

Fauchard died on March 22, 1761, in Paris. A successor of his, Nicholas Dubois de Chemant, created a set of teeth made out of mineral paste that were then glazed in a kiln in 1788. These were the first dentures created entirely from artificial materials, and de Chemant settled in England to work on creating dentures with the famous Wedgwood porcelain factory by the early 1790s. Some reports note that he later became the first to set up a dentistry practice in New York City. France remained a leader in the profession for a century after Fauchard's death, until it was overtaken by the United States, which became home to the first professional school for dentistry in the world, the Baltimore College of Dentistry, in 1847. There are professional awards named in Fauchard's honor, as well as an international society, the Pierre Fauchard Academy, which provides scholarships, mentoring, and research fellowships.

Books

Lerner, K. Lee, and Brenda Wilmoth Lerner, Eds., *Gale Encyclopedia of Science,* 3rd ed., Gale, 2004.
Lauer, Josh, and Neil Schlager, Eds., *Science and Its Times: Understanding the Social Significance of Scientific Discovery,* Gale, 2000.

Wynbrandt, James, *The Excruciating History of Dentistry: Toothsome Tales and Oral Oddities from Babylon to Braces,* St. Martin's Press, 1998.

Periodicals

Skeptical Inquirer, May-June 1999.

Online

"Who is Pierre Fauchard? A Remembrance/ by Monsieur Jean Claude de Vaux," Pierre Fauchard Academy, http://fauchard .org/publications/remembrance.htm (January 2, 2006). □

Ibrahim Ferrer

Cuban vocalist Ibrahim Ferrer (1927-2005) was a moderate star for much of his life in his native Cuba, but he skyrocketed to international popularity in his old age after appearing on the album *Buena Vista Social Club,* a collection of performances by elderly Cuban musicians. A film that followed the album's release featured a duet between Ferrer and his female contemporary Omara Portuondo, and that duet entranced the musical world, seeming to open a portal into a vanished era of arch-romantic Latin song.

That album led to a chance for Ferrer to fulfill a lifelong ambition. He was a skillful and enthusiastic exponent of the mid-century romantic style of Cuban song known as the bolero, but bandleaders had steered him instead toward more upbeat styles as a younger man. And then, during the era of Fidel Castro's Cuba, the new dance style of salsa grew on the island and was exported around the world; Ferrer's boleros were mostly forgotten, and by the time the *Buena Vista Social Club* album was recorded he was one of the few remaining vocalists with complete mastery of the style. In the eight years between the release of *Buena Vista Social Club* and his death in 2005, Ferrer made up for lost time, touring almost nonstop and becoming something of an international phenomenon.

Birth Began During Dance

Ferrer's background was multiracial and included African, French, Spanish, and Chinese strands. His father sang, and his mother was an enthusiastic dancer. It was during a dance on February 20, 1927, in fact, that Ferrer's mother went into labor and he was born in San Luis, Cuba, in Santiago province. Ferrer was fond of saying that he had begun singing and dancing in the womb. His mother gave him the name Ibrahim because she was fascinated with the Arab world, another piece of the Latin cultural mosaic.

Both of Ferrer's parents were dead by the time he was 12, and he made a living for a while by selling fruit on the street, unloading boats at a dock, and doing light carpentry. At the end of one year, when he was in his early teens, a

cousin asked him to join a group called Jóvenes del Son—the Young Men of Son, *son* (pronounced with a long "o") being the African-inspired ancestor that had roots in eastern Cuba and was salsa's direct ancestor. Performing at a New Year's Eve party, they were paid one and a half pesos. It was a modest start, but it led to other appearances in the Santiago area at parties and festivals. Ferrer was drawn to the musical life, and he took odd jobs when he had to so that he could keep performing.

Ferrer's musical education occurred when he began to find jobs with other Santiago groups, each of them emphasizing a slightly different part of Cuba's complex musical culture. The *son* ensembles were growing into big bands, and Ferrer filled backup singer slots with several of them, sometimes taking lead vocals. Ferrer admired American crooner Nat "King" Cole as well as Cuba's classic bolero singers, but bandleaders pushed him to sing upbeat dance pieces instead. In the band Maravilla de Beltrán he initially sang tango music under bandleader Pancho Alonso. Singing lead vocals with a top Santiago big band, the Orquesta Chepin-Choven, Ferrer had a hit in 1955 with a song called "El platanar de Bartolo," but he was not credited on the record. Despite Cuban society's reputation for being essentially color-blind, Ferrer, as an Afro-Cuban, probably suffered discrimination in his early years.

With his musical prospects on the rise, Ferrer moved to Havana in 1957. he signed on as a backup vocalist with two of the top big bands of the day, the Orquesta Ritmo Oriental and the Banda Gigante, led by singer Beny Moré. The

Communist revolution in 1959 put a dent in Cuban musicians' livelihoods, for the number of American tourists crowding Havana clubs was soon greatly reduced. Ferrer refused to join the large group of Cuban musicians who fled to the United States. In later years he was a staunch supporter of the revolution. He rejoined Alonso, whose band had been renamed Los Bocucos. He was still rarely allowed to sing boleros, partly because he was so effective as a jazz-like improviser in dance music. "I was always told that my voice was only suited to dance songs," he was quoted as saying by the *Times* of London. "That disappointment marked me forever."

Encounter with History

Los Bocucos performed in Paris in 1962 and then went on to Eastern Europe and the Soviet Union. In Red Square in Moscow, for the first time, Ferrer saw snow. He met Soviet premier Nikita Khrushchev at a reception, knowing nothing of the crisis that had been developing in Cuba while he was on tour. "Imagine you've got a hedgehog in your hand. What do you do?" Khrushchev asked him. Ferrer answered that he would let go of it, and Khrushchev said, "Cuba is just the same. You can't touch it." The group was stranded in the Soviet Union as the U.S. blockaded the island. Finally returning home to Havana, Ferrer started a family with his wife, Caridad. Their large set of children has been variously numbered between six and eleven.

Ferrer continued to perform with Los Bocucos, eventually making some recordings for the state-owned Cuban record label Egrem and drawing a small but steady salary as a government-approved musician. He felt that the elimination of the wealthy American component of the group's audiences had actually had positive results. "The music got better after the revolution because we weren't playing for tourists so much," he was quoted as saying by Spencer Leigh of the *Independent*. "There was a greater identification between the musicians and the audience, which was Cuban." Still, Ferrer had to do construction work to make ends meet in the family's small apartment, which contained an old American refrigerator and some icons relating to the Afro-Cuban santería religion (a fusion of Catholicism and West African beliefs), of which Ferrer was an adherent.

Ferrer officially retired in 1991, having the bad luck to do so just as the fall of Communism in the Soviet Union led to the withdrawal of its support for Cuban economy. He was forced to work shining shoes on the streets of his Havana neighborhood, and it was in that situation that he was approached one day in 1996 by Juan de Marcos González, a Cuban musician and producer who had hatched the idea of the Buena Vista Social Club sessions together with American rock guitarist and world music enthusiast Ry Cooder.

Cooder had suggested the idea of a romantic song on the album to balance the African sounds of the other musicians, and Marcos González said that there was only one musician who could fill the bill. At first reluctant to become involved, Ferrer came to the studio and agreed to perform after experiencing an impromptu reunion with the other musicians, who were of his generation or even older—pianist Rubén González was 77, and guitarist Compay

Segundo was 89. When Ferrer and González performed a classic bolero called "Dos Gardenias (para ti)" (Two Gardenias for You), the room was entranced and the album was another step closer to becoming a huge success.

Made Solo Debut

Even Cooder could not predict just how successful the album would become at the time. "I thought, 'Ten old guys playing Cuban music. Who's going to listen to it?' " he told Leila Cobo of *Billboard*. But the *Buena Vista Social Club* album sold more than six million copies around the world and spawned a variety of spin-offs, one of which was the 72-year-old Ferrer's debut solo album, *The Buena Vista Social Club Presents Ibrahim Ferrer,* released in 1999. The album, said England's *Daily Telegraph,* "showcased Ferrer's gift for balladry, heavy with nostalgia and sentiment, redolent of cigar smoke, sawdust, and jacaranda." It revived songs from the classic era of the bolero, from the late 1940s through the early 1960s. The album sold more than one and a half million copies on its own, reaching the number two position on *Billboard* magazine's world music and Latin music charts. A duet between Ferrer and female vocalist Omara Portuondo, "Silencio," was featured in a *Buena Vista Social Club* film directed by German filmmaker Wim Wenders.

Ferrer now found a large international demand from music lovers who wanted to experience his music in live performance. "The next time I saw Ibrahim Ferrer" after recording his solo album, Cooder told Cobo, "he's walking on stage at Carnegie Hall. The reaction to the human onstage—and this is a direct line from the audience, this poor anorexic audience starved for humanity— they go crazy. It's a wonderful case of what real beauty can do to the world." Ferrer toured nearly nonstop during the last several years of his life, winning the Best New Artist honor at the Latin Grammy awards at age 73 in the year 2000. He became a widely recognizable figure thanks to a signature golf cap he always wore. A series of concerts he performed in Japan that year with Rubén González and Omara Portuondo resulted in sold-out 10,000-seat halls for ten nights in a row.

A second Cooder-produced Ferrer album, *Buenos Hermanos,* won a Grammy award (for best traditional tropical album) in 2003, but U.S. relations with Cuba had worsened under the administration of President George W. Bush, and Ferrer was denied a visa to attend the ceremony. Cooder's trip to Cuba to produce the album itself had been made possible only by a directive signed by outgoing president Bill Clinton shortly before leaving office. *Buenos Hermanos* joined Ferrer's talents with those of other Buena Vista Social Club musicians as well as those of non-Cuban performers such as Mexican-American accordionist Flaco Jimenez and the Five Blind Boys of Alabama, an African-American gospel ensemble. Ferrer also recorded a duet with English alternative rock star Damon Albarn.

Ferrer undertook a new European tour in 2005, but the ravages of emphysema—he was a lifelong smoker—had begun to catch up with him. He often expressed the idea that since he had gotten the chance to live the musical life of his dreams in his 70s, he was going to make the most of it while

he could. Asked by Garth Cartwright of the *Guardian* why he kept touring, he answered, "I love to sing, to make music. Making music is the greatest joy." Ferrer died in Havana on August 6, 2005, but his legacy was due for expansion by a wealth of material that lay unreleased at his death.

Books

Contemporary Musicians, volume 44, Gale, 2004.

Periodicals

Billboard, June 26, 1999; August 27, 2005.
Daily Telegraph (London, England), August 9, 2005.
Economist (US), August 20, 2005.
Guardian (London, England), August 9, 2005.
Independent (London, England), August 8, 2005.
New York Times, August 8, 2005.
Times (London, England), August 9, 2005. □

Dorothy Fields

Broadway musical and Hollywood film lyricist Dorothy Fields (1905-1974) wrote the words to some of the best-known standards of American song, including "I Can't Give You Anything but Love," "I'm in the Mood for Love," and "A Fine Romance." One of very few women to achieve top-level success as a writer during the classic era of Broadway song, Fields was a creative contributor to the musical *Annie Get Your Gun* and other major shows.

Fields remained active throughout a career that stretched from the vaudeville era to the age of rock, and her gift for direct, natural language appropriate to its time never faltered. She collaborated with a variety of composers, a fact that helps account for her comparative lack of renown—she was never part of a recognizable songwriting team like Rodgers and Hammerstein or Lerner and Loewe. But Fields was second to none in the economically expressed sentiments and urbane, sometimes sexy wit of her lyrics. She became the first woman inducted into the Songwriters Hall of Fame.

Delivered by Newsstand Worker

A New Yorker through and through, Fields was nevertheless born in the resort town of Allenhurst, New Jersey, where her family had gone on vacation. She was delivered by a newsstand operator who also happened to be a midwife. Fields grew up in a show business family; she was the youngest of four children of touring vaudeville performer Lew Fields, who was part of a duo called Weber and Fields, and of his wife, Rose. The year Dorothy was born he gave up performing and launched a career as a producer and impresario. At times during Dorothy's childhood the family struggled financially, but she grew up around songwriters such as Richard Rogers and Lorenz Hart. Her older brothers Joseph and Herbert broke into popular music, and she

thought about entering the music business herself after she discovered a talent for verse in English class at New York's Benjamin Franklin School for Girls, from which she graduated in 1923.

Fields's parents, however, tried to keep her away from the performing arts. She won a part as an actress in a summer theater production in Tarrytown, New York, but her father intercepted her letter of acceptance. In 1924 Fields briefly married physician Jack Wiener, but the marriage was a disaster; Fields spent her wedding night walking back and forth on the porch of the couple's honeymoon cottage. She worked for a time as a teacher and laboratory technician, submitting light poems to newspapers on the side. One of her poems was published in a column in the Sunday New York *World* newspaper. Then, while playing golf with a friend, she met songwriter and publisher's agent J. Fred Coots, who encouraged her to try her hand at writing lyrics. The songs they wrote together went nowhere, and Fields blamed herself. "The music was good, but the lyrics were terrible," she was quoted as saying by biographer Deborah Grace Winer. The problem was that she was trying to imitate Lorenz Hart, by then one of the hottest lyricists on Broadway. "I was so impressed by Larry's inner rhyming and feminine hybrid rhymes that I wasn't doing anything but trying to be like Larry, and consequently, mine weren't very good."

Coots, however, was impressed enough to recommend Fields to his employer, the publisher Jack Mills Music. Fields was commissioned by owner Jack Mills to devise a quick lyric for a song called "Our American Girl," a topical

number about pioneering female aviator Ruth Elder. Fields came through. Her song was never published, for Elder died during her attempt to fly across the Atlantic. But Fields received other assignments, netting a $50 fee for each song. She was consistent, according to Winer, and became known as "the fifty-dollar-a-night girl."

In 1927 Fields settled into a songwriting partnership with Mills staffer Jimmy McHugh. The following year, the two jumped at an opportunity to provide material for an all-black musical revue at the Cotton Club in New York's Harlem neighborhood, featuring then-unknown bandleader Duke Ellington. Fields's parents continued to resist her chosen career, telling her that ladies did not write song lyrics, but Fields (again according to Winer) retorted, "I'm not a lady, I'm your daughter," and added that she would write lyrics for the Westminster Kennel Club if asked to do so. From then on she never looked back, although she herself was a bit scandalized when Harlem singers sexed up her lyrics in live performance. She and McHugh collaborated on "I Can't Give You Anything But Love," originally included in the revue *Blackbirds of 1928*.

Moved to Hollywood

The song bombed at first but gained popularity through the Depression era with its hard-luck sentiments ("Gee, I'd love to see you lookin' swell, baby / But diamond bracelets Woolworth's doesn't sell, baby"). It was later recorded by Cliff "Ukulele Ike" Edwards, Gene Austin, Billie Holiday, and Louis Armstrong, who had a strong identification with several other Fields songs as well, and it was given a memorable performance by Cary Grant and Katharine Hepburn in the 1938 film *Bringing Up Baby*. Other hits such as "Exactly Like You" and "On the Sunny Side of the Street," both written for the *International Revue,* moved the careers of Fields and McHugh forward, and in 1930 they joined the rush to Hollywood as sound films suddenly caught on with a vengeance. The music for several early Fields hits, including "I Can't Give You Anything but Love" and "On the Sunny Side of the Street" may have been written by jazz pianist Fats Waller.

Immediately scoring a hit with "Go Home and Tell Your Mother" (from a forgettable golf romance film called *Love in the Rough*), they followed it up with "Cuban Love Song," written for a film of the same name, starring opera singer Lawrence Tibbett in 1931. For much of the 1930s, Fields divided her time between New York and Los Angeles, working in both films and live theater. She preferred the stage, which gave her the chance to hone her lyrics as a show went through out-of-town performances and previews before opening night. But some of her best-known songs were written for films, such as "I'm in the Mood for Love" and "I Feel a Song Comin' On," which first appeared in the 1935 film *Every Night at Eight*. Among the many artists who covered "I'm in the Mood for Love" was black pop heartthrob Billy Eckstine, in 1946.

Every Night at Eight marked one of Fields's last collaborations with Jimmy McHugh. In the late 1930s she worked with a variety of composers, including immigrant Austrian violinist Fritz Kreisler, who tried his hand at pop music with some songs for the 1936 film *The King Steps Out*. Perhaps

Fields's favorite collaborator, though, was the aging Broadway composer Jerome Kern, whose smooth melodies pushed Fields to a new level of lyric sophistication. Kern and Fields became lifelong friends and joined forces on the pop standard "A Fine Romance," an unusual comic ballad of sexual frustration included in the 1936 film *Swing Time.* The film also included another Fields-Kern standard, "The Way You Look Tonight," which brought Fields an Academy Award for best song.

Fields collaborated with Kern on two more films in the late 1930s. In 1939 she married businessman Eli Lahm, and the couple had two children. Fields cut back on her involvement with songwriting but kept a hand in theater, writing the "book"—the story and spoken dialogue—for three musicals with songs by Cole Porter, *Let's Face It, Something for the Boys,* and *Mexican Hayride.* She took up songwriting once again in 1945 with the musical *Up in Central Park,* with music by the veteran operetta composer Sigmund Romberg. The show, based on the career of nineteenth-century New York politician "Boss" Tweed, contained the enduring hit "Close as Pages in a Book."

Originated Idea for Berlin Musical

In 1946 Fields had the idea for a musical based on Old West sharpshooter Annie Oakley. She and Kern were hired to write the show, but Kern died before work could begin. *Annie Get Your Gun* was handed off to Irving Berlin, who, unlike most Broadway composers, wrote both words and music for his shows. Though that may have been a disappointment for Fields, she was strongly affected by Kern's sudden death and might not have been emotionally ready to switch gears and work with another songwriter. The book remained Fields's creation, and Berlin retained several of her song titles.

With four musicals, lyrics for four films, and credits in the television musical *Junior Miss* (1957), Fields was almost as busy in the 1950s as she had been two decades earlier. Her best-known show of the decade was *A Tree Grows in Brooklyn* (1951), with music by Arthur Schwartz. Two of her film soundtracks, *Mr. Imperium* and *The Farmer Takes a Wife,* were written with *Wizard of Oz* composer Harold Arlen. In 1959 the Fields musical *Redhead,* with music by Albert Hague, won the Antoinette Perry (Tony) Award for best musical of the year.

Even the advent of rock music did not slow Fields down. The 1966-67 season brought to the stage one of her most famous creations of all, the musical *Sweet Charity,* with book by Neil Simon and music by Cy Coleman. Among the standards to emerge from the show were "If They Could See Me Now" and "Big Spender," the latter a typical Fields song in its subtle, irregular verbal rhythm ("The minute you walked in the joint / I could see you were a man of distinction / A real big spender"). Fields was always admired by her fellow songwriters; if she experienced any gender discrimination it went nowhere, for her successful track record was hard to argue with. "What I like best about Dorothy Fields," *West Side Story* lyricist Stephen Sondheim was quoted as saying by Winer, "is her use of colloquialism and her effortlessness, as in 'Sunny Side of the Street,' which is

just perfect as a lyric.'" Fields was inducted into the Songwriters Hall of Fame in 1971. Another honor came the following year with Fields's inclusion in New York's Lyrics & Lyricists concert series. A live recording of the concert devoted to Fields was later issued on compact disc.

In the late 1960s Fields wrote several songs with future Michael Jackson producer Quincy Jones. But several larger projects fizzled, including a proposed musical based on the life of Eleanor Roosevelt. Fields and Cy Coleman produced one more show, *Two for the Seesaw,* in 1973. Fields died at home on March 28, 1974, after a stroke that occurred during a rehearsal for the show. Among her posthumous honors was her inclusion in a series of U.S. postage stamps devoted to songwriters, and a CD issued by the music publisher Shapiro Bernstein & Company brought together recordings of some of her best-loved songs, performed by singers including Frank Sinatra, Fred Astaire, and Peggy Lee.

Books

Winer, Deborah Grace, *On the Sunny Side of the Street: The Life and Lyrics of Dorothy Fields,* Schirmer, 1997.

Periodicals

Billboard, April 16, 2005.

Online

"Biography," http://www.dorothyfields.co.uk (February 6, 2006).
"Dorothy Fields: Biography," Songwriters Hall of Fame, http://www.songwritershalloffame.org/exhibit_bio.asp?exhibitId=65 (February 6, 2006).
"Dorothy Fields," *Broadway: The American Musical* (Public Broadcasting System), http://www.pbs.org/wnet/broadway/stars/fields_d.html (February 6, 2006).
"Dorothy Fields: On the Sunny Side of the Street," All About Jewish Theatre, http://www.jewish-theatre.com (February 6, 2006). □

Patrick Fernandez Flores

American Archbishop Patrick F. Flores (born 1929) became the first Mexican American to rise to a high rank in the Roman Catholic Church in the United States. When appointed Archbishop of the Archdiocese of San Antonio in Texas, he became the head of the largest provinces of dioceses in the country. Throughout his life and career, Flores was greatly admired and well-liked, as he supported civil rights causes, actively helped the poor, and sought to bring together people and leaders of other faiths.

In 2005, Galán Incorporated, a film production company, announced that it wanted to produce a documentary about Roman Catholic Bishop Patrick F. Flores. The chosen subject matter seemed highly appropriate for a motion picture, as Flores is a charismatic figure whose life and

legacy offer the kind of drama and inspiration that makes for a compelling narrative. Flores rose from humble beginnings to become America's first Mexican-American Catholic Bishop. In his early life, Flores was a migrant worker and cantina custodian but, after he entered the priesthood, he rose to the highest levels in the church hierarchy. Along the way, his career was filled with accomplishment, controversy and even danger.

Early Life and Career

Flores, the seventh of nine children born to Patricio and Trinidad Fernandez de Flores, was born on July 26, 1929, in Ganado, Texas. Flores attended Ganado Elementary School, Pearland Elementary School and Christian Brothers' Kirwin High School in Galveston, Texas. In 1946, when he was in the tenth grade, Flores wanted to drop out of high school when his father became ill and could not work. He was persuaded against that route, however, when a nun convinced a bishop to finance his education at the Catholic school. His education thus salvaged, Flores diligently applied himself to his studies and completed a three-year program in two years. He managed to accomplish this even while studying Latin on the side.

To earn money for his family and himself, Flores worked in a cantina, picking up empty beer cans from the floor and sweeping up cigarette stubs. The working environment coupled with his chores compelled him to want to make the whole world a cleaner and more habitable place,

and he felt the best way he could do that was by becoming a priest.

Intent on following his calling, after he graduated from Kirwan, Flores entered St. Mary's Seminary in La Porte, Texas in 1949. He later attended St. Mary's Seminary in Houston. He never wavered in his decision to become a priest. Once again displaying academic ambition, he completed eight years' of seminary education in seven. When he completed his work at the Houston seminary, he took his holy vows. He was ordained into the Catholic priesthood at St. Mary's Cathedral in Galveston on May 26, 1956, by Bishop Wendellin J. Nold.

Now known as Father Flores, he celebrated his first mass at the Guardian Angel in Pasadena, Texas. Shortly afterward, he was assigned to the Diocese of Galveston-Houston, where he served as an assistant pastor in several parishes.

Humble Activist

Concerned with the plight of the poor and oppressed, Flores began displaying activist inclinations in the early 1960s, when he directed the Christian Family Movement in the Galveston-Houston diocese and the Bishop's Committee for the Spanish Speaking, a ministry that encouraged bilingual congregations. At the end of the decade, in October 1969, Flores joined forty-seven other Hispanic priests to establish PADRES, an organization that draws attention to the problems of Hispanics in the church. In between, he received his first pastorate, at the Guardian Angel Parish in Pasadena, in 1963; in 1967, Flores became pastor of St. Joseph-St. Stephen Parish in Houston.

In May of 1970, Pope John Paul VI made Flores the auxiliary to the archbishop of San Antonio. Later that year, he became a bishop, the first Mexican American to attain that high a position in the Roman Catholic Church. Being bilingual, and coming from a poor background himself, Flores managed to develop a strong relationship with the parishioners.

Also in May of 1970, Flores was appointed chairman of the Texas State Advisory Committee to the U.S. Commission on Civil Rights, and in July he became national chaplain for the League of United Latin American Citizens.

Even in such positions of respect and power, Flores remained humble and continued directing his activities toward helping the less fortunate. In 1972, he co-founded the Mexican-American Cultural Center in San Antonio and served as its honorary chairman. He then helped form the National Foundation of Mexican American Vocations and the National Hispanic Scholarship Fund, which helped hundreds of young people to obtain a college education. The following year, he helped raise more than $20,000 for earthquake victims in Mexico, and then he joined picketers at a supermarket who were protesting the stocking of non-union lettuce and grapes.

Flores' activities did not go unnoticed. *Time* magazine named him "an emerging leader of America" in 1974. He gained more media attention in 1976 when he helped establish "Telethon Navideno" (Nativity Telethon), a broadcast event held on the first Sunday of December to raise money for indigent Latino families. Proceeds paid for emergency rental finances, utilities, and medication for single women with children, the elderly, the unemployed and the sick. By this time, Flores had spent twenty years in the priesthood. However, as humanitarian as his aims were, his activities were not without personal danger. In August of 1976, he visited Ecuador to attend a conference, but he ended up being held at gunpoint by the country's army for 28 hours with 56 other prelates.

Appointed Archbishop

In May of 1978, Flores returned to San Antonio when he was appointed the bishop of the diocese. Then, on October 13, 1979, he was named by the Pope to be the archbishop of the diocese. As the archbishop, Flores became the leader of nearly one million Catholics in the largest province of dioceses in the United States. The diocese encompassed a large territory that reached from the Texas-Mexico border and into the uplands of Texas. In addition, the appointment made Flores the highest-ranking Hispanic American in the hierarchy of the Catholic Church in the United States.

Despite that distinction, throughout his career, Flores never thought of himself as an ethnic role model. Instead, he felt his role was to administer to people of all racial, cultural and ethnic backgrounds, in particular the poor. Well-liked, influential, and inspirational, Flores was affectionately given the nickname of the "mariachi bishop," as he enjoyed bringing a celebratory quality into his ministry, which included Latino music and dance.

In his high-ranking position, Flores never became pompous or overly pious. Often, he was referred to simply as "Patrick" or "Patricio." His efforts were as tireless as they were humanitarian and often required great tolerance and even courage. His character and accomplishments were greatly appreciated and, in 1979, he was invited by President Jimmy Carter to take part in the Camp David discussions. In 1983, he was one of four bishops called upon to represent the United States Catholic Church hierarchy at that year's Synod of Bishops in Rome. During his 10-week stay, he extended an invitation to the Pope to visit San Antonio. The Pope eventually followed up on the invitation on September 13, 1987, when he was Flores' house guest in his apartment on the Catholic chancery grounds.

Also in the 1980s, Flores became a member of the Hispanic Caucus Committee (1980) and he founded Catholic Television of San Antonio, the first diocesan television station in the United States (1981). In January of 1985, he was one of three American bishops invited to visit Cuba as part of a courtesy exchange for the Episcopal Bishops Conferences. He returned to Cuba a year later, as the only U.S. Bishop invited for the week-long conference to discuss the future of the Catholic Church in Cuba.

Recognized for his Work

During the 1980s and 1990s, he received several significant honors for his work. In 1985, he received the Ellis Island Medal of Honor, during the celebration of the Statue of Liberty's 100th Birthday, and he received the Hispanic Heritage award for leadership in 1986. In October of 1989, Flores became the first San Antonian to receive the Anti-Defamation League's Ben and Julie Rogers Ecumenism Award, which is given to religious leaders for promoting clerical harmony and cooperation. In 1995, he received the Distinguished Churchman Award by the San Antonio Council of Churches and the Ford Salute to Education award. In 1999, he received the B'nai Brith International Humanitarian Award.

By the end of the 1980s, he was back on the international stage. In 1988, he was one of three U.S. bishops to meet with church and government leaders in Mexico. In the following year, he participated in a summit meeting between the Vatican and thirty-six U.S. archbishops. At the event, he was one of 10 bishops chosen to address the participants. Through July and August of 1990, he toured Romania, Bulgaria, and Hungary to prepare a report on how Americans could help support the churches and its people.

Supported Controversial Causes

In the 1990s, as all throughout his career, Flores lent his support to numerous causes, some of them controversial. In 1993, he established a support group for "Parents with Sons on Death Row" to provide parents with spiritual and financial support as well as transportation to visit their sons at the Huntsville State Penitentiary. In 1999, he became involved in a land-use lawsuit that went all the way to the Supreme Court. Flores represented the congregation of Beorne, Texas, who demanded rights to a permit from the city to enlarge a church that had been declared a historic property. In January of 1999, he raised money to help keep the San Antonio Metropolitan Ministry shelter dining room open. He even donated two months of his own salary.

Flores was also involved in a campaign against violence. When the Texas concealed handgun law went into effect in 1996, he put up red-and-white "no guns" signs, written in English and Spanish, to indicate that no weapons were permitted on church property.

In 2001, during a reinvigorated campaign to ensure that theology teachers at seven Catholic institutions in his archdiocese remained true to the faith, Flores proposed a loyalty oath that would affirm intent to teach authentic Catholic doctrine. Flores displayed his characteristic openness and tolerance, though, when he refused to expel teachers who refused to sign the oath.

Flores' open-mindedness and tolerance extended to people of all faiths and drove his desire to bring them together in a commitment to spiritual faith. This led to some rather significant inter-denominational efforts. In 1997, when famed evangelist Dr. Billy Graham brought his religious crusade to San Antonio for a four-night event at the city's Alamodome, Flores taped radio spots in English and Spanish to help promote Graham's appearance. Grateful for the support, Graham credited Flores with generating a large response from the area's Catholic Hispanics.

In 2000, during a joint Catholic-Protestant service at Trinity Lutheran Church in San Antonio, Flores and Lutheran bishop James Bennett publicly embraced, a symbolic gesture that commemorated the abolition of long-standing doctrinal condemnations that Protestants and Catholics once issued against each other during the Reformation. "When I'm with non-Catholic ministers and rabbis, I feel at home with them and they feel at home with me," Flores told reporters from the *San Antonio Express*. His various outreaches earned him praise and recognition, including several honorary doctorates.

Involved in Hostage Situation

Flores' strong skills as a spiritual counselor came into play in June of 2000, when he was at the center of a potentially deadly hostage crisis. In a situation that made national news, Flores and his secretary, Myrtle Sanchez, were taken hostage by Nelson Antonio Escolero, an unemployed, 40-year-old Spanish-speaking immigrant from El Salvador who equipped himself with a hand grenade.

Escolero had been living in the United States legally for many years but was not a citizen. He was afraid he would get deported after being charged with driving with a suspended license, and he demanded that Flores help him. After Escolero entered the chancery office, he ripped out the telephone and threatened to detonate the make-shift hand grenade. (Police later reported that the device was a "fake.")

An office employee who had escaped turned on a silent alarm that alerted police. A nine-hour standoff then ensued, involving police, SWAT teams, FBI negotiators and Escolero's wife and son. The incidence attracted 100 spectators who stood in 90-degree heat to see how the situation would play out.

During the standoff, Flores, through his calm and understanding counsel, convinced Escolero to release Sanchez. Later, Escolero agreed to release Flores. Neither Sanchez or Flores were harmed, but medical attendants at the scene took the precaution of removing the archbishop by stretcher. This was prudent, as Flores was seventy years old. He spent a night in a hospital for observation, and then was released.

Demonstrating his characteristic compassion, Flores publicly forgave Escolero and expressed his sympathy for the man's problems. Later, Flores told *America* magazine, "I forgive. In this I have no choice. If I want to be forgiven, I have to forgive."

Addressed Sexual Abuse in his Archdiocese

Throughout the late 1990s and early 2000s, the Catholic Church in the United States endured wide-scale accusations of sexual abuse committed by its priests, as well as allegations of subsequent cover-ups by high-ranking church officials. Flores' own diocese was not immune.

In particular, he faced accusations that the diocese covered up a child molestation scandal involving two of its priests, Father Xavier Ortiz-Dietz and the Reverend Federico Fernandez. In June 1998, the church had arranged a four-million dollar settlement with the families of seven boys who had been sexually abused by Ortiz-Dietz between 1987 and 1992.

In June of 2002, after a national policy was established to suspend priests known to have abused minors, Flores announced that he wanted to make the policy even stricter by asking the Vatican to defrock all such priests in his archdiocese. On February 29, 2004, Flores, who by this time had headed the Archdiocese of San Antonio for 25 years, apologized to parishioners when national figures related to priests and sexual abuse became public.

Reached Mandatory Retirement Age

By the early 2000s, Flores was nearing the mandatory retirement age, and he starting thinking of stepping down. By this time, his health was also beginning to become a concern. In March of 2001, he underwent emergency septuple bypass surgery. In July of 2004, he was treated for a bout of Meniere's disease. He was hospitalized for the condition in November of that year.

In July 2003, Flores prepared his official letter of resignation that he would later send to the pope. In December of 2003, he began making plans to step down as archbishop, as his next birthday (July 26, 2004) would bring him to the mandatory retirement age of seventy-five.

In December 2004, the Most Reverend Jose. H. Gomez, an auxiliary bishop from Denver, Colo., succeeded Flores as archbishop.

Before his retirement, some church officials reportedly proposed that Flores should be elevated to the position of cardinal. There was even some talk of his election to the papacy. Flores disregarded such suggestions with his characteristic humility.

Books

Contemporary Hispanic Biography Volume 1, Gale Group, 2002.
Dictionary of Hispanic Biography, Gale Research, 1996.

Online

"Chronology of Archbishop Patrick Flores," *My San Antonio,* http://www.mysanantonio.com/news/religion/stories/MYSA021405.flores.chronology.a97dff42.html (January 3, 2006).
"Documentary Film on First Mexican American Bishop", *Galán Inc.,* http://www.galaninc.com/site/ (January3, 2006).
"Most Rev. Patrick F. Flores Archbishop of San Antonio," *Las Misiones,,* http://www.lasmisiones.org/site/pp.asp?c=hsJSJ2OTF&b=83201 (January 3, 2006).
"Texas Archbishop Unharmed after Hostage Ordeal," *BeliefNet* http://www.beliefnet.com/story/31/story_3117_1.html (January 3, 2006). □

Michel Fokine

Sometimes known as the father of twentieth-century ballet, Russian choreographer Michel Fokine (1880-1942) revived the art of dance, bringing new

**expressiveness, dramatic impact, and unity to an art
form dominated by entrenched classical ideas.**

Fokine's work served as a bridge between the great ballets of Russian tradition and the innovative, often shocking world of modern dance. Working closely with musicians and stage designers, Fokine provided the choreography for several of Russian composer Igor Stravinsky's important early works. Later, living in the United States, Fokine did much to encourage a ballet scene that was still in its infancy. If other choreographers went on to create dance innovations of which Fokine hardly dreamed, he nevertheless paved the way for the new freedoms others exploited. In the words of *Dance* magazine writer Lynn Garafola, "Fokine's works wrested ballet into the 20th century, giving it new life and a whole new raison d'etre, even as they touched the collective heart and mind. Had Fokine never lived, it's safe to say, 20th-century ballet would have been very different."

Skills Persuaded Father to Back Career

Fokine was the 17th of 18 children, but only five survived to adulthood. He was born on May 5, 1880 (April 23 or 25 in the old-style Russian calendar), in St. Petersburg, Russia; his birth name was Mikhail Mikhailovitch Fokin, but in francophile Russia it was not unusual for an artistically ambitious young person to use a French form of his or her name. Fokine's father was a prosperous businessman, and

there was plenty of money for family trips, music lessons, and other endeavors. Fokine's mother loved the theater and passed on an appreciation of the arts to her children, several of whom embarked on creative careers. One of Fokine's older brothers, an army officer, attended dance performances and stimulated Fokine's own enthusiasm for ballet. His father, however, discouraged him from pursuing a dance career. Fokine auditioned in secret for admission to St. Petersburg's Imperial School of Ballet, one of the great institutions of the old classical style. After he came home with news that he had achieved the top score at the audition, his father gave in.

Fokine's education at the Imperial School was a broad one. He studied the piano, mandolin, and balalaika, became a painter and read classic literature, and was a noted soccer player. His ballet training was strict, emphasizing the techniques specified by classic Russian choreographers such as Marius Petipa of St. Petersburg's famed Maryinsky Ballet. A handsome, athletic dancer, Fokine was a standout student. After graduating from the Imperial School in 1898, he quickly began to find solo roles at the Maryinsky and elsewhere. In 1902 he was invited to join the school's dance faculty.

By that time, the ballets of Petipa were several decades old. Classical Russian ballet was an impressive spectacle, marked by awe-inspiring displays of technique from individual dancers, lavish sets, and huge, symmetrical choreographic patterns. Fokine grew frustrated with the inconsistencies of the ballets staged at the Maryinsky: they showcased Russia's greatest dancers, but they often failed to make sense dramatically. The choreographer, the composer, the costume designer, and the set designer might each be a top-notch talent, but all too often they worked in isolation rather than cooperating in the service of a well-told story and a unified mood.

In 1904, the radical American dancer Isadora Duncan visited Russia, and Fokine saw her perform. Fokine himself never became fully sympathetic to the wilder experiments of modern dance, and he later deplored Duncan's work specifically, but at the time the expressivity of Duncan's solo dances unleashed his own creativity. His first major ballet, *Acis and Galatea,* was choreographed for an Imperial School graduation ceremony in 1905. He married one of his students, Vera Antonova, that year; she interpreted many of her husband's dances, and the two raised a son, Vitale, who became a dancer himself.

Fokine had danced with one of Russia's top ballerinas, Anna Pavlova, in the early 1900s, and now, aware of his growing reputation, she asked him to create a new dance for her to perform. He obliged with *The Dying Swan,* based on a piece called *The Swan,* by French composer Camille Saint-Saëns, that Fokine had been playing on the mandolin at home prior to his conversation with Pavlova. The simplicity of the work and its attempt to create an evocative interpretation of a well-known orchestral piece showed Isadora Duncan's influence. Pavlova performed *The Dying Swan* all over the world, and years later, on her deathbed, she uttered her last words: "Prepare my swan costume."

Created Ballet Based on Chopin's Music

Fokine's 1907 ballet *Le Pavillon d'Armide* was his first to be staged at the Maryinsky Theatre and marked another breakthrough: he coordinated his work closely with designer Alexandre Benois to produce carefully wrought visual effects. His *Chopiniana* of the same year was a novelty; based on the music of composer Fryderyk Chopin, it may have been the first plotless ballet. Fokine revised the work in 1908 and retitled it *Les Sylphides,* under which name it became one of the most famous ballets of the twentieth century. Fokine was rapidly becoming recognized as Russia's most innovative young choreographer, and in 1909 he was selected by impresario-producer Serge Diaghilev to become ballet master for his new Ballets Russes (Russian Ballet) company, a touring ensemble that would bring the best of Russian dance to Western Europe.

The move put Fokine in the company of creative artists who were thinking along similar lines, and over the next five years he created classic after classic as the Ballets Russes thrilled audiences in Paris and London. He drew on Russian folklore in *Polvotsian Dances from Prince Igor* and *Scheherazade,* the latter based on the famed orchestral tone poem by composer Nikolay Rimsky-Korsakov. Fokine emphasized the importance of careful research into cultural traditions underlying the setting of a ballet. His vigorous choreography, using male dancers to an unprecedented degree, was matched by explosively colorful sets designed by artist Leon Bakst. Fokine found his greatest collaborator in composer Igor Stravinsky, for whose edgy scores *The Firebird* and *Petrouchka* he provided the original choreography.

Fokine's treatment of dancers by this time differed radically from the ballet he had been taught. Where traditional ballet emphasized footwork and leg motions, Fokine demanded that dancers use their entire bodies to express the ideas that a composer or writer was trying to communicate. Ballerina Tamara Karsavina, speaking to dance historian John Drummond and quoted in the *New Statesman,* said that Fokine "was like a sculptor. Sometimes [when] he wanted a pose, he wouldn't explain very much, he would show it and then come and arrange it." In a letter he wrote to the London *Times* in 1914, Fokine explained his widely quoted Five Principles of ballet: expression must be appropriate to the subject of a dance; dancers' gestures are meaningful only insofar as they relate to dramatic events; dancers must be ready to use their entire bodies; a ballet is not a vehicle for a virtuoso soloist but an integrated conception involving everyone on stage; and dance, music, and décor must work together in the service of the story.

Partially Eclipsed by Nijinsky

The revolution that Fokine helped to unleash partially overtook him as Europe lurched toward political crisis. His star dancer, Vaslav Nijinsky, ventured into new realms where Fokine himself, with one foot in classical tradition, would not go, and Nijinsky displaced Fokine as the chief choreographer of the Ballets Russes, creating dances for Stravinsky's most daring score yet, *The Rite of Spring* (1914), a piece that included pounding rhythms, irregular accents, and visceral subject matter. Fokine returned to Russia and during World War I he toured with his wife, giving dance concert performances.

In 1918 the pair left Russia, fearing for their safety due to the Bolshevik Communist takeover. After touring in Scandinavia they settled in the United States the following year. In their new home, they found themselves at the opposite end of the spectrum from their native Russia in terms of the degree to which dance was rooted in the community; ballet and ballet schools were rare outside of New York City, and opportunities for Fokine to make use of the full reach of his choreographic talents were rare. The Fokines opened a dance studio on Riverside Drive in New York and undertook more of their relatively inexpensive duo concert tours, traveling around the country. Often Fokine lent his expertise to the world of popular dance, doing choreography for musicals, revues, and even nightclub acts. He had little interest in the world of real modern dance, where America led the world in new developments; in a celebrated 1931 incident he wrangled with modern dance pioneer Martha Graham, who told him that he knew nothing about body movements. Fokine founded two short-lived ballet companies, the Fokine Ballet in 1922 and the American Ballet in 1924.

Some felt that Fokine's talents were being wasted in America; *New York Times* critic John Martin, quoted on the Yonkers History website, bemoaned Fokine's scramble to make a living and opined that "it is as if Beethoven were giving piano lessons instead of composing." Yet Fokine drew huge crowds to some of his performances; a trio of Fokine concerts at New York's Lewisohn Stadium drew a total of 48,000 people. When American ballet took off in the late 1930s under the leadership of George Balanchine, dance companies were heavily populated by dancers Fokine had trained. Fokine became a U.S. citizen in 1932.

Returned to Europe

Fokine continued to travel widely, premiering new works in South America as well as in the U.S. Between 1934 and 1936 he returned to Europe and choreographed several new works there for the Ballets Russes. In Germany he clashed with cultural officials from the new Nazi regime. Fokine and his wife returned to the U.S. in 1936 and purchased a large house in the New York suburb of Yonkers. In 1938 he choreographed a production of the Jerome Kern musical *Show Boat,* and he joined with composer and fellow Russian emigré Sergei Rachmaninoff to create a new ballet with original music, *Paganini,* the following year.

At an age when he could easily have slipped into retirement, Fokine threw himself into new work. The new Ballet Theater company, later renamed the American Ballet Theater, formed in the early 1940s and developed into the nation's most influential dance organization. Fokine created the ballet *Bluebeard* for the new company in 1941. He traveled to Mexico City for rehearsals of another new work, *Helen of Troy,* in the summer of 1942 but cut his trip short after suffering a blood clot in his left leg. His condition worsened, and he contracted pneumonia. Fokine died in New York on August 22, 1942. He was the creator of 81 ballets, and *Les Sylphides,* his most famous work, was performed as a tribute after his death by 17 different ballet companies around the world. Toward the end of the twentieth century his works were performed less frequently, but a slew of revivals in the early 2000s testified to his continuing influence.

Books

Beaumont, Cyril, *Michel Fokine & His Ballets,* C.W. Beaumont, 1935 (repr. Dance Horizons, 1981).
Bremser, Martha, ed., *International Dictionary of Ballet,* St. James, 1993.

Periodicals

Dance Magazine, October 2003; May 2005.
New Statesman, September 18, 2000.
Star-Ledger (Newark, NJ), June 20, 2005.

Online

"Michel Fokine, Father of Modern Ballet," Yonkers History, http://www.yonkershistory.org/fokine.html (November 9, 2005). ☐

Charlotte Friend

Charlotte Friend (1921-1987) was a medical researcher who made breakthrough discoveries about viruses and their roles in causing cancer. She defended her research in the face of strong initial skepticism, eventually becoming recognized as a scientist on the forefront of medical microbiology.

The mouse virus that Friend discovered in the 1950s was named the Friend Leukemia Virus (FLV), and a newly discovered leukemia cell type was also named after her. It has been estimated that in the two decades following her discovery of the FLV in the mid-1950s, one-third of all cancer researchers spent time working on her ideas. Her discoveries suggested new techniques in the fight against cancer, and they had implications for the effort to develop a vaccine against the Human Immunodeficiency Virus (HIV) that causes AIDS, and they loomed large in medical research a half-century after she made them.

Family Savings Wiped Out by Depression

The daughter of Russian immigrants, Friend was born in New York City, New York, on March 11, 1921, and grew up in Lower Manhattan. Her father Morris, a businessman, died of a heart infection when she was three. Friend's mother had hoped to become a pharmacist, but she set her career aside to raise Friend and her two siblings (one brother and one sister). Keeping food on the table took up even more of her time when the stock market crash of 1929 swept away the inheritance Morris Friend had left. For a time, the family was forced to go on home relief, a New York City welfare program.

In spite of these difficult conditions, Friend's mother insisted that her children focus on their schoolwork. Perhaps as a result of her father's illness, Friend became interested in medicine from an early age. When she was ten, she wrote a school paper called "Why I Want to Become a Bacteriologist." Even with her strong focus on science, though, she never locked herself away with her textbooks; she was as a teenager, and remained as an adult, an avid consumer of the cultural events New York had to offer in such abundance. She applied to Hunter College High School, one of New York's tuition-free magnet schools for talented students, and was admitted. She then went on to Hunter College, putting herself through school by taking night classes and working in a doctor's office during the day.

After graduating in 1943, Friend enlisted in the United States Navy. After Midshipmen training at Smith College, she was commissioned at the rank of ensign and rose to lieutenant junior grade after being assigned to a blood lab at a naval hospital in Shoemaker, California, and becoming its deputy commander. The experience convinced Friend that she had what it took to do scientific lab work. After her discharge from the Navy in 1946, she began to look for educational opportunities.

It was an auspicious time for a young woman with no financial means to be pursuing higher education, for the Servicemen's Readjustment Act of 1944, popularly known as the G.I. Bill of Rights or the G.I. Bill, provided veterans with full payment of tuition and bills for supplies. Finally making the decision to pursue a scientific career instead of going to medical school—a choice she had struggled with for some time—Friend enrolled in the Ph.D. program in microbiology at Yale University. She impressed the faculty by seeking out top scientists in New York for help on her projects, and in 1950 she was granted her degree after finishing a thesis on the effect of aspirin on the human immune system.

Observed Mouse Tumors

Her choice of subject showed an instinct for productive research avenues, for aspirin would become a hot topic in decades to come. Friend, who never married or had children, went on to a research post at New York's Sloan-Kettering Institute for Cancer Research, then a new facility on its way to becoming one of the most prestigious facilities in the cancer research world. Studying under virologist Alice Moore, Friend did research on cancer in mice. In 1952 she took on the post of associate professor in a program run jointly by Sloan-Kettering and Cornell University. Whenever she could, however, she avoided classroom teaching in favor of pure research.

The reason was simple: Friend was a paragon of pure curiosity in the laboratory. When she and another newly minted Ph.D., Cecily Canann Selby, found a Sloan-Kettering electron microscope lying unused, they were excited by the potential of the newly invented instrument and decided to use it to examine an Ehrlich ascites carcinoma, a mouse tumor frequently used in cancer studies. What they saw surprised them; the arrays of particles in the cells resembled those seen in virus-infected cells used in other research. The idea that viruses had anything to do with cancer had been raised by a few scientists, including *Journal of Experimental Medicine* editor Peyton Rous, but it was still quite novel at the time. Nevertheless, Friend set out to determine whether the mouse tumor cells might be viral in nature. In a series of experiments lasting for several years, she succeeded in infecting healthy adult mice with leukemia by injecting them with tissue taken from diseased mice—and in transmitting the disease from one mouse to another.

Friend summarized her findings in a paper presented at the 1956 meeting of the American Association for Cancer Research in Atlantic City, New Jersey. In the words of Leila Diamond from the *National Academies Press* website, "This was a time when the concept of viruses causing cancer was still viewed with extreme skepticism, and the presentation of such data by an attractive young woman not long out of graduate school was met by disbelief and derision." Friend was met by a barrage of hostile questioning that, despite Rous's plea to his colleagues to keep an open mind, seemed to overstep the bounds of civility. Friend was distressed by the paper's reception and later said that she could never have imagined the controversy that it engendered. Eventually she was able to laugh about the professionally traumatic event, saying (according to Diamond) that she and her few sympathizers had been accused of having "either holes in their heads or holes in their filters"—filtering of the diseased tissue being a key issue in determining whether a viral agent was in fact at work.

The key point was that Friend did not back down. Working with Rous, she laid out her research in a paper,

"Cell-Free Transmission in Adult Swiss Mice of a Disease Having the Character of a Leukemia" (*Journal of Experimental Medicine,* 1957). Her cause got a boost when a top medical researcher, Jacob Furth, confirmed her results. Other researchers began to expand on her ideas, and one of Friend's own subsequent papers, a 1959 investigation into the immunization of mice against the type of virus infection she had discovered, was often cited by later researchers working on an AIDS vaccine. By the early 1960s the ridicule Friend had received was turning into academic recognition, and in 1962 she received the Alfred P. Sloan Award for Cancer Research. She used the financial proceeds from that prize to travel to Australia, Israel, and France, circling the globe and realizing a lifelong dream of doing research at the Pasteur Institute in Paris.

Treated Mouse Cancer Cells with Drug

Sloan-Kettering director Cornelius Rhoads, a strong professional backer of Friend's, died in 1959, and she began to look for more congenial surroundings. In 1966 she moved from Sloan-Kettering to the Center for Experimental Cell Biology at New York's Mount Sinai School of Medicine. Her title there was professor and director of the center, but she did no teaching, and she steered the institution in the direction of the basic research she loved. "Her presence was a major factor in establishing at the fledgling medical school a balance between emphasis on clinical care and on basic scientific research," Mount Sinai dean Nathan Kase told Harold M. Schmeck Jr. of the *New York Times.*

Once again, Friend threw herself into research and began to open up new avenues of experimentation. Chemotherapy and other cancer treatments, broadly speaking, work by killing cancerous cells in the body, with the undesirable side effect that many healthy cells are killed as well, wreaking havoc with the body's immune system. Working once again with mice, Friend observed that cancer cells could, under certain conditions, be caused to develop along normal paths—to transform themselves into healthy, noncancerous cells—if they were treated with a chemical, dimethyl sulfoxide. The potential implications of this discovery were enormous, for it suggested an entirely new way of treating cancer. The discovery brought Friend a new series of honors. The cells she created were named Friend erythroleukemia cells (FELC), and she received one of the highest honors in American science, election to the National Academy of Sciences, in 1976. She was also elected president of the American Association of Cancer Research, and in 1978 she became the first woman president of the New York Academy of Sciences.

Friend was well-liked among her peers, and her apartment in lower Manhattan became known as "the Friend Hotel" because it was so generously thrown open to visitors. Friend herself rarely if ever complained about gender discrimination, but her professional support became especially important in the research lives of younger women scientists, whom she mentored and nurtured by working to insure publication and conference-presentation opportunities. Friend enjoyed traveling, and she spent a year in Rome, Italy, doing research with a friend, Italian National Research

Council Laboratory director Rita Levi-Montalcini. Friend had strong political beliefs, and even during the anti-Communist hysteria of the 1950s she spoke and wrote in favor of the rights of blacklisted colleagues—a decision that could have damaged her own career. She was a staunch supporter of the nation of Israel and a lifelong enthusiastic New Yorker. Showing the lingering effects of her early attraction to medicine, she was fond of dispensing medical advice to friends and often humorously accused herself of practicing medicine without a license.

In her later years, the amount of time Friend had to allot to dealing with federal government funding administrators distracted her somewhat from basic research. Diagnosed with lymphoma in 1981, Friend continued to work despite the debilitating effects of cancer treatment. In 1985 she became part of the first group of recipients of the Mayor's Award of Honor for Science and Technology in New York. She died in New York on January 13, 1987. In all, she wrote more than 100 papers, reviews, and book chapters. In an age when most scientific papers list several collaborative authors, the free-thinking and imaginative Charlotte Friend often worked alone, doing much to advance the study of cancer research.

Books

Notable Scientists: From 1900 to the Present, Gale, 2001.

Periodicals

New York Times, May 19, 1985; January 16, 1987.

Online

Diamond, Leila, "Charlotte Friend: March 11, 1921-January 13, 1987," National Academies Press, http://books.nap.edu/html/biomems/cfriend.html (December 23, 2005). □

Elisabeth Frink

Dame Elisabeth Frink (1930-1993), one of twentieth century Britain's foremost sculptors, is best known today for her naturalistic, powerful massive style exemplified by works featuring horses, dogs, and male figures. Her sculptures typically displayed strength and aggression, and are now found throughout the world. In addition to her work as a sculptor, Frink was a long-time art instructor at the college level and created lithographs and other works to illustrate books.

Early Life and Education

A child of an upper-middle-class British family, Frink was born November 14, 1930 in Thurlow, Suffolk, in the East Anglia region of the country. Her father was in the army, causing the family to move several times

during Frink's childhood; she attended school in Aldershot, Hampshire and also in Scotland, but commented in *Frink: A Portrait* that "the house [in Suffolk] is what I remember best." After Frink's father returned from fighting in World War II, the family traveled to Dorset, on the southern coast of England, where Frink developed an interest in drawing. When Frink went with her mother to visit her father, then stationed at Trieste, Italy, she solidified her interest in art after visiting museums in Venice.

In 1947, Frink entered the Guildford School of Art. After a brief flirtation with painting, she became a student of sculpting, the format that would dominate her artistic output for the rest of her life. Frink completed eighteen months at Guildford before continuing her education in London at the Chelsea School of Art, where she had gotten a scholarship. Upon moving into Chelsea from suburban North London after her first year of study, Frink enthusiastically entered into the bohemian lifestyle traditionally associated with art school. In 1952, Frink held her first London exhibition as part of a show with three or four other contemporary sculptors. The show was a success, with London's prestigious Tate Museum buying one of Frink's pieces. Promptly, Frink became associated in minds of art critics with a number of "new school" sculptors, despite being several years older than she was.

Career began to Rise

In mid-century Great Britain, the possibilities for artists to make their livelihood exclusively from their artwork were limited. Most earned a steady income from teaching and Frink was no exception. After her graduation from Chelsea School of Art in 1953, she took a post as an instructor at the School, where she remained until 1961. From 1954 to 1962, she also taught at St. Martin's Art College in London. However, in the early 1960s the tide in sculpture was turning to the more purely abstract as influenced by contemporary American art, while Frink's work retained a measure of the figurative. Despite being pushed out by these art world changes, Frink enjoyed teaching and considered her years as an instructor to be useful for her development as an artist.

Her duties as a teacher did not stop her from producing sculpture. In 1955, she had her first solo exhibition at St. George's Gallery, London, and by 1957 was receiving major commissions. In 1958, she joined Waddington Galleries, a business relationship which would last nearly until the end of her life. Throughout the late 1950s and early 1960s, Frink participated in numerous group exhibitions and occasional solo exhibitions, including three in the United States in 1961.

During this period of Frink's life, she met architect Michel Jammet, a Frenchman living with his family in Dublin, Ireland. The couple married in 1955, afterward living primarily in London but often visiting Ireland. Jammet and Frink had a son, Lin, in 1958; however, their marriage dissolved and they divorced in 1963. The following year, Frink remarried to native Britisher Edward Pool. In the early 1960s, commissions for massive sculptures and sculpture groups came in from public institutions and private businesses as Frink's popularity and notoriety increased. Her distinctive style, emphasizing the powerful and masculine, intrigued critics and solidified her position in the art world. From 1965 to 1967, Frink resumed teaching as a visiting lecturer at the Royal College of Art in addition to her regular work, which now including lithography and etchings.

To France and Back

In 1967, Frink and her husband, along with Lin, moved to a house they had purchased in France a few years previously; in the book *Frink: A Portrait,* Frink once commented that "it was really rather ironical that I should be living in France with my British rather than my French husband." The arrangement was comfortable, particularly since Frink's young son spoke fluent French and could attend local schools. Although she was now living on the Continent, Frink continued work apace and often exhibited in England, traveling back and forth over the English Channel as necessary and maintaining connections to her native land. This period also saw her illustrative work reach its height, with the publication of editions of *Aesop's Fables* in 1968 and of *Chaucer's Canterbury Tales* in 1972 featuring Frink's drawings. Otherwise, the family lived in France quite happily until the summer of 1970, when Frink met Hungarian count Alexander Csàzy. Almost immediately, the two began having an affair. The relationship remained secret from even Frink's closest friends until 1973, when, deciding she was deeply in love with Csàzy, she informed her shocked husband that she was leaving him for the count. By April 1973, Frink had returned to London and was living with Csàzy. The couple married in June of the following year; however, Frink's professional triumphs held par with her personal pleasures.

In 1974, Frink devoted some of her time to non-traditional sculpture projects: a racing trophy studded with diamonds as well as the Frink Medal for British zoologists. While the former project produced only one piece, the latter has continued through the years, with the award still given annually. An edition of Homer's *Odyssey* containing Frink's illustrations appeared. She also became an Associate of the Royal Academy, a group considered antiquated by most contemporary artists; however, Frink believed that her role in the Academy would allow her to promote younger artists by selecting them to show at national exhibitions. The mid and late 1970s brought several commissions, including ones for large horse sculptures, animals for the Zoological Gardens, and portrait busts. Frink's works were also exhibited both throughout Great Britain and internationally at major cities including Johannesburg, South Africa, New York City, New York, and Toronto, Canada. The late 1970s also saw Frink relocating from the London area to Dorset, in the south of England, where she would live for the rest of her life.

Active Until the Last

The 1980s held capstones for Frink's career. In 1982, a new publishing firm proposed to produce a Catalogue Rai-

sonné of all of her works to date; and the Royal Academy planned a retrospective of her life's work, a great honor. The date of the retrospective, originally to be held in 1986, was moved forward a year due to space demands at the gallery, causing Frink some headaches due to her busy commissioned work schedule. In 1985 alone, she was committed to two major projects: a set of three figures for a corporate headquarters, one of which was a nearly seven-foot tall male nude; and the other, a grouping entitled *Dorset Martyrs* to be placed in Dorchester, England. However, despite the potential for conflict, the retrospective was a success and spurred the art world to hold more exhibitions of Frink's worth, with four solo exhibitions and several group ones coming in the following year. Tirelessly, Frink continued to accept commissions and sculpt, as well as serve on advisory committees, meet with art students who had expressed an interest in her work, and pursue other public commitments.

Frink kept up this hectic pace of sculpting and exhibiting until early 1991, when an operation for cancer of the esophagus caused an enforced break. However, short weeks later Frink was again creating sculptures and preparing for solo exhibitions. In September, she underwent a second surgery. Again, Frink did not let this hold her back, proceeding with a planned trip for exhibitions to New Orleans, Louisiana, and New York City. The exhibitions were a success, but Frink's health was clearly deteriorating. Despite this, she was working on a colossal statue, Risen Christ, for the Liverpool cathedral. This sculpture would prove to be her last; just one week after its installation, Frink died as a result of her cancer on April 18, 1993, at the age of 62. Her husband had predeceased her by only a few months. In *Frink,* Stephen Gardiner, Frink's official biographer, argued that this final sculpture was appropriate: "This awesome work, beautiful, clear and commanding, a vivid mirror-image of the artist's mind and spirit, created against fearful odds, was a perfect memorial for a remarkable great individual."

Books

Gardiner, Stephen, *Frink: The Official Biography of Elisabeth Frink,* HarperCollins, 1998.
Humphries, Lund, *The Art of Elisabeth Frink,* Noyes Press, 1972.
Lucie-Smith, Edward, and Elisabeth Frink, *Frink: A Portrait,* Bloomsbury, 1994.

Periodicals

New York Times, April 20, 1993.

Online

"Dame Elisabeth Frink," http://www.sculpture,org.uk/biography/ElisabethFrink (January 1, 2006).
"Dame Elisabeth Frink," Grove Art Online, http://www.groveart.com (January 1, 2006).
"History of the Frink School of Figurative Art and Sculpture," http://www.frinkschool.org (January 2, 2006). □

G

Marvin Gaye

American singer Marvin Gaye (1939-1984) was one of popular music's most successful and innovative recording artists. He expanded the boundaries of the rhythm and blues and soul genres as he explored social and sexual themes in his music. Gaye began his career with Motown records, where he recorded a long list of records that rose to the top of the charts. Later, he blazed new trails with albums such as *What's Going On* and *Let's Get it On*. His life and career were cut short in tragic fashion when he was shot by his own father.

Gaye was born as Marvin Pentz Gay, Jr., on April 2, 1939, in Washington, D.C. Named after his father, he would later add the ''e'' on the end of his last name when he became a professional entertainer. Gaye was the second of four children of Alberta and Marvin Gay, Sr., who were devout Seventh-Day Adventists. Gaye's father was a minister.

With brother Frankie and sisters Jeanne and Zeola, Gaye grew up in a poor and segregated section of Washington. Their physically abusive father who, according to accounts, drank heavily and enforced strict religious discipline further oppressed their lives. All throughout his life, Gaye had a very troubled relationship with his father, a circumstance that would later have tragic repercussions. Gaye's mother was a contrast to her husband: a responsible woman who was regularly employed as a maid.

Gaye exhibited a talent for music very early in his life. When he was only three years old, he began singing gospel hymns in his father's church choir. At the time, Marvin Gay Sr. was a preacher in a church called the House of God.

Gaye's musical interests continued into his teenage years. At Cardozo High School he studied drums, piano, and guitar. Further displaying his versatility, he also played the organ. As a teenager, Gaye was handsome but shy, and he immersed himself in his music. He showed little interest in other studies and, in 1957, he dropped out of school to join the Air Force, hoping to learn how to fly. He soon realized, though, that he wasn't military material. The U.S. government agreed and gave him an early and honorable discharge.

Early Career

Marvin Gay Sr. wanted his son to apply his musical talents toward a religious vocation, but Gaye had other ambitions. Once back in Washington, D.C., Gaye had no interest in returning to choir music. Rather, he started singing with a rhythm and blues vocal group called the Rainbows. Other members included future recording stars Don Covay and Billy Stewart. Later, he formed his own group, the Marquees, with friends Reese Palmer, James Nolan, and Chester Simmons.

In public appearances, the Marquees mostly performed for high school audiences. However, the group attracted the attention of famed guitarist Bo Diddley, and he helped the Marquees produce a single on the Okeh label, a subsidiary of Columbia Records. Despite the commingling of talent, the 45-rpm record–''Hey Little Schoolgirl'' backed with ''Wyatt Earp''–, which Diddley produced, did not sell very well.

To help make ends meet, Gaye worked as a dishwasher, a humiliating position that he resented. Then he met Harvey Fuqua, a music promoter who recognized

Gaye's potential. At the time, Fuqua was reforming his old group, called the Moonglows, and he wanted the Marquees to be his back-up singers. In 1959, the group became known as Harvey and the Moonglows, with Fuqua singing lead vocals. They had a hit single with "Ten Commandments of Love."

As the group achieved modest success, Gaye got his first taste of life on the road as a touring performer. It proved an unpleasant, eye-opening experience, as he experienced first-hand the blatant racism prevalent in different parts of the country.

Became a Star at Motown

Fuqua soon disbanded the group and moved to Detroit, where he intended to form his own record company with the help of his girlfriend, Gwen Gordy. Gaye accompanied the pair and, in 1960, Gwen Gordy introduced him to her brother, Berry, an entrepreneur who was starting his own label, Motown-Tamla Records.

Gaye signed on with Berry Gordy and worked as a session drummer and vocalist for various Motown acts. Most significantly, he worked on the early records of a group called the Miracles (which would later become Smokey Robinson and the Miracles). Gaye worked in that capacity for about a year before he signed a contract with the company as a solo vocal artist. At this time, he added the "e" to his last name and professionally became Marvin Gaye. Later, this was seen a defiant gesture designed to get back at his father.

Also around this time, Gaye married Berry Gordy's sister, Anna. As she was thirty-seven years old, and Gaye was in his early twenties, observers felt Gaye only married her to further his developing career. Whatever Gaye's motives, the union did help launch an enduring solo vocal career. In 1961, Gaye recorded his first album, *The Soulful Moods of Marvin Gaye,* which, as the title implied, was a collection of low-key, smooth ballads with a jazz feel. Gaye recorded other albums in this vein, but they weren't successful, so he was encouraged to change his style to target the younger audiences who favored the more upbeat and popular rhythm and blues genre. Though he embarked in this direction with reluctance, his next single, "Stubborn Kind of Fellow," released in 1962, became a top-ten hit. This was followed by a string of hits that made him a star. These included "Hitch Hike," "Can I Get a Witness," and "Pride and Joy," all released in 1963. In 1964, he again made the record charts with "Try it Baby," with background vocals supplied by the Temptations, another popular Motown act; "You're a Wonderful One," with background vocals by the Supremes, who would later become Motown's top act; and "Baby Don't You Do It."

During this period, Gaye continued doing session work for Motown. A talented songwriter as well as singer, Gaye co-wrote "Dancing in the Street," which became a huge hit for Martha and the Vandellas, one of the top early Motown female groups. He also played drums on several early recordings by Stevie Wonder (who was then known as "Little" Stevie Wonder).

In late 1964, Gaye, who would prove an ever-evolving performer throughout his entire career, modified his style somewhat with "How Sweet It Is (To Be Loved By You)", which was a bit more sophisticated than typical Motown offerings. He continued in this direction with two more hit singles, "I'll Be Doggone" and "Ain't That Peculiar," both released in 1965.

Because of his shifting styles, Gaye became a somewhat enigmatic public personality, a characteristic that defied the developing Motown approach, which was heavily based on formula and carefully cultivated personas. The singles released by other major label performers, especially the Four Tops and the Supremes, exhibited a calculated and commercial same-ness of sound. Gaye, on the other hand, wasn't so easily pigeon-holed.

Teamed with Female Performers

Still, Motown tried to narrowly define Gaye's role, even though he was given latitude to experiment, an indulgence that resulted from his success. In 1965, he was allowed to record an album of Broadway show tunes. However, the company took note that the public liked him best as a rhythm and blues singer. Even more, Motown realized that Gaye was beginning to be perceived as a sex symbol. One of the few solo performers in the label's group-oriented stable of stars, Gaye developed a reputation as an attractive "ladies' man." To capitalize on this perception, the heads of Motown came up with the idea of teaming him up with its female solo artists to record romantic duets.

Gaye's first partner was Mary Wells, who became famous in 1964 with the smash hit single ''My Guy.'' Their better-known duets included ''Once Upon a Time'' and ''What's the Matter With You,'' both released in 1964. Gaye also recorded with Kim Weston, whose biggest Motown hit was a solo recording, ''Take Me in Your Arms (Rock Me a Little While), released in late 1965. But Gaye's most successful teaming came when he was paired with Tammi Terrell, a young singer who showed a great deal of promise. With Gaye, she blossomed.

The duo worked with the talented songwriting team of Nickolas Ashford and Valerie Simpson. Their first effort, ''Ain't No Mountain High Enough,'' was a big hit in the spring of 1967 and the first of nine successful singles. The best-known Gaye-Terrell duets included ''Ain't Nothing Like the Real Thing,'' ''Your Precious Love,'' and ''You're All I Need To Get By,'' all released in 1968.

But tragedy befell the partnership. In 1968, Terrell developed a brain tumor and collapsed on stage in Gaye's arms. Three years later, she died. She was only twenty-four years old. Gaye had become very close to Terrell and took her death extremely hard. It was later said that he never really got over it.

By this time, his marriage to Anna Gordy was falling apart. Also, without Terrell, Gaye no longer wanted to perform in public. Further, he began suffering depression, started using cocaine, and often seriously contemplated suicide.

Career Rejuvenated Through the ''Grapevine''

Gaye experienced personal and professional revitalization in late 1968, with the release of the single ''I Heard it Through the Grapevine.'' It became Motown's biggest selling record of all time.

Another version of the song, performed by Gladys Knight and the Pips, was released earlier in the year and achieved substantial chart success. However, the two versions were different as night and day. Knight's version was an up-tempo, very danceable recording, despite the song's bitter message. Gaye's version, with its ominous instrumental arrangement, was slower-paced, much darker and very brooding. Compared to the typical fare that came out of Motown, Gaye's ''Grapevine'' was startling.

Renowned rock critic Dave Marsh, in his book *The Heart of Rock & Roll: The 1001 Greatest Singles Ever Made,* deemed it the best single ever recorded. Describing the record's—and Gaye's—strengths, he wrote, ''Gaye plays out the singing with his characteristic amalgam of power and elegance, sophistication and instinct: now hoarse, now soaring, sometimes spitting out imprecations with frightening clarity, sometimes almost chanting in pure street slang, sometimes pleading at the edge of incoherence, twisting, shortening, and elongating syllables to capture emotions words can't define. And Gaye does this not just in a line or two or three but continuously. As a result, a record that's of absolutely stereotypical length creates a world that seems to last forever.''

Gaye followed that triumph with an album called *M.P.G.,* a deeply personal 1969 release that focused on his crumbling marriage and his increasing depression. In the summer of that year, he scored a number-one hit with ''Too Busy Thinking 'Bout My Baby.'' However, still grieving over Terrell's untimely death, Gaye spent most of the following year in seclusion.

Came Back with ''What's Going On''

Gaye wasn't idle in seclusion, however. He was working on a collection of personal songs that would comprise an album that amounted to another career triumph. The 1971 release of that album, entitled *What's Going On,* not only demonstrated Gaye's resilience; it was further evidence of his ongoing development as an artist.

Gaye wrote all of the songs in what was essentially a cohesive ''concept'' album that addressed contemporary problems such as war (the seemingly interminable Vietnam war, now carried out by the Nixon administration, had entered its ugliest phase), racism, poverty, pollution and political corruption. The work arose from Gaye's disillusionment with what was happening in the world and, especially, in the United States. In particular, Gaye had been greatly upset by the killing of four students at Kent State University in 1970 (who were protesting America's invasion of Cambodia) and he was troubled about the horrific details about the Vietnam war after his brother, Frankie, returned from a tour of duty.

The album contained three hit singles, all released in 1971 and all with socially relevant themes: ''What's Going On,'' ''Inner City Blues (Make Me Wanna Holler),'' and ''Mercy Mercy Me (the Ecology).'' Ironically, Motown did not even want to release the album. The company did not appreciate its topical content. Berry Gordy called the single, ''What's Going On,'' the worst song he ever heard. However, after the album's enormous success, Motown—ever opportunistic and focused on what would sell in the marketplace—suddenly became ''relevant,'' and much of the music subsequently emanating from the company contained a socially conscious ''message,'' albeit superficial and trendy.

The album was as personal as its scope was broad. Underscoring the complexity and sophistication of Gaye's songwriting skills, the lyrics were multi-leveled, at once addressing relationships within his family and the world at large. In lyrics he wrote for the title song, Gaye directly referred to his brother (''Brother/brother/brother/There's far too many of you dying'') and his father (''Father/father/father/We don't need to escalate/You see, war is not the answer, for only love can conquer hate''). In retrospect, the message to the ''father'' was as pointed and private as it was poignant.

Moreover, the album was not one of Motown's typical assembly line productions. Gaye's fingerprints were all over every element of the recording. He oversaw the musical arrangements, providing the work with a sound that went far beyond anything that ever came out of the Motown recording studios.

The album was not only a resounding critical success; it scored big with the record-buying public and fellow musicians. Stevie Wonder and Smokey Robinson both later commented that it was their favorite album of all time. In a special issue devoted to the five-hundred greatest albums of all time, *Rolling Stone* magazine placed it at number-six (exceeded by only the Beatles' *Sgt. Pepper's Lonely Hearts Club Band, Revolver,* and *Rubber Soul,* and the Beach Boys' *Pet Sounds* and Bob Dylan's *Highway 61 Revisited.*)

The success of *What's Goin' On* resulted in accolades. In 1971, Gaye received Billboard's Trendsetter of the Year award and Cashbox's Male Vocalist of the Year award, as well as an NAACP Image Award.

Despite his ongoing success and this sudden career peak, Gaye's personal life was spinning out of control. His drug use increased and, in 1971, he began an affair with a sixteen-year-old girl, Janis Hunter.

Nevertheless, work continued. The following year, Gaye composed the soundtrack for *Trouble Man,* a film that came out of the "blaxploitation" movie genre that was popular in the early to mid-1970s. Then Gaye shifted gears yet again for his next album, *Let's Get it On,* released in 1973. Whereas, *What's Goin' On* expressed his social consciousness, Gaye's new release was an expression of sexual politics. The title song was a number-one hit single.

In 1974, it was back to the romantic duets, as Motown teamed Gaye with Diana Ross, who had emerged as a major solo performer after she left the Supremes. Together, Gaye and Ross offered an album of sensuous songs, and their collaboration produced a hit single, "My Mistake (Was to Love You)."

Marriage Fell Apart

By 1975, Janis Hunter had one child with Gaye and was pregnant with another. Anna Gordy filed for divorce. Gaye was hit hard in the settlement and he had to file for bankruptcy. Gaye and Hunter eventually married in 1977. Their two children included a daughter, Nona, and a son, Frankie.

The divorce forced Gaye to delay work on his next album, *I Want You.* It was eventually released in 1976, garnering critical acclaim and healthy sales. Two songs from the album became hit singles: the title track and "Got to Give it Up (Pt. 1)."

However, in 1978, hoping to escape personal problems (drugs and marital woes) and trouble with the Internal Revenue Service (IRS), Gaye moved to Hawaii. The following year, he released a double album, *Hear My Dear,* which dealt with the pains experienced in his first marriage. As part of the divorce settlement, Gaye was ordered to pay all royalties from the album to his ex-wife.

In 1980, continuing pressure from the IRS compelled Gaye to flee even farther, to Europe, where he recorded his next album, *In Our Lifetimes.* When the record appeared in 1981, Gaye was aghast. Motown, he claimed, had altered the work without his consent and released an essentially unfinished album without his permission. In retribution, Gaye left the label in 1982 and signed with CBS records.

Motown must have rued the development, as Gaye's first album for CBS, *Midnight Love,* was a tremendous success. It sold two million copies and included the song "Sexual Healing," which was a hit single and earned Gaye a Grammy Award for Best R&B Vocal Performance (Male).

In 1983, Gaye made a number of rare public appearances. He performed live at that year's Grammy broadcast and performed some concert dates. In addition, even though Gaye had ended his twenty-year relationship with Motown, he appeared on the company's memorable 25th anniversary television special.

Tragedy at Home

Despite Gaye's continued success, and his enduring stature as a major musical force, all was not well. During this period, Gaye reportedly exhibited erratic personal behavior and an increased dependence on cocaine. During his brief concert tour, Gaye had to be hospitalized for physical problems arising from his drug use. In addition, he reportedly developed an acute case of depression. Those closest to the singer indicated that Gaye suffered remorse over his two failed marriages—Janice Hunter, now Janice Gaye, had filed for divorce in 1979—and that he felt powerless to control his drug use and continued to grieve over the death of Terrell.

His physical and mental problems drove him back home, which proved unfortunate. In 1983, Gaye moved in with his parents, in the Los Angeles home he had bought for them eleven years earlier. This placed him under the same roof with his difficult father and only aggravated the longstanding hostility existing between the two men. In the dysfunctional environment, Gaye experienced sudden mood changes that provoked arguments with Marvin Gay, Sr.

Finally, on April 1, 1984, Gaye and his father reportedly got into an argument about money, and things turned violent. Marvin Gay, Sr. shot his son twice, at close range, with a .38 caliber revolver. Later, he claimed that he acted in self-defense. Following the shooting, Gaye was taken to the California Hospital Medical Center, where he was pronounced dead. The next day, Gaye would have been forty-five years old.

Gaye's death, and its violent nature, stunned an adoring public who had embraced the charismatic singer through all phases of his career. More than ten thousand people attended Gaye's open-casket funeral in Los Angeles, California. Robinson and Wonder delivered heart-felt eulogies.

After Gaye's death, Columbia and Motown collaborated on the 1985 release of two albums, *Dream of a Lifetime* and *Romantically Yours,* that included unreleased material from the 1970s and the "Midnight Love" sessions. In 1997, Motown released *Vulnerable,* an album of unreleased ballads.

Beside his wives, Gaye's survivors included Marvin III, whom he adopted during his first marriage, and son Frankie and daughter Nona, from his second marriage.

Marvin Gaye was inducted into the Rock and Roll Hall of Fame in 1987. In 1992, his daughter Nona launched her own recording career on Third Stone Records.

Books

The Heart of Rock & Soul: The 1001 Greatest Singles Ever Made, Plume, 1989.
The Scribner Encyclopedia of American Lives, Volume 1: 1981-1985, Charles Scribner's Sons, 1998.

Periodicals

Ebony, June 1994.
Rolling Stone, December 11, 2003; December 9, 2004.

Online

"Marvin Gaye," *Classic Motown,* http://classic.motown.com/artist.aspx?ob=per&srs=prd&aid=1 (January 3, 2006).
"Marvin Gaye," *History of Rock,* http://www.history-of-rock.com/marvin_gaye.htm (January 3, 2006).
"Marvin Gaye," *Soulwalking,,* http://www.soulwalking.co.uk/Marvin%20Gaye.html (January 3, 2006). □

Francesco Geminiani

At the height of his career in eighteenth-century London, violinist and composer Francesco Geminiani (1687-1762) was ranked alongside the two great composers who shaped English musical life at the time; the Italian violin virtuoso Arcangelo Corelli and the German-born composer George Frideric Handel.

Geminiani's music was explosive, choppy, and difficult to play; it did not fit into the common symmetrical, repetitive patterns of the Baroque era (c. 1600-1750) in which he worked. Even so, it was well known in London and in Dublin, Ireland, where Geminiani lived for a time; two sets of concertos, published in 1732, sold well when they were published, and insured Geminiani's reputation. He later wrote accompanied sonatas for solo violin that provide modern players with considerable technical challenges, and the various instructional writings he penned toward the end of his life are valuable repositories of information about Baroque-era violin technique. Geminiani's music was mostly forgotten for a time, even as the works of other Baroque composers like Antonio Vivaldi were rediscovered. But the flowering of the historical performance movement, whose practitioners perform Baroque music on original instruments and according to the techniques of its own time, finally brought Geminiani's music alive once again.

Studied with Corelli

Geminiani was baptized in Lucca, Italy, on December 5, 1687; it is likely, when local customs are taken into account, that he was born two days earlier. Records of his life are spotty, and some events in his career have to be deduced from publications by other writers that mention him in passing. His father was a violinist employed by the city of Lucca. Geminiani himself is known to have remained in Lucca until 1704, at which time he probably moved to Rome to seek his fortune in music. He may have played in an opera orchestra in Lucca and been dismissed for missing too many performances. In contrast to most composers of his time, who found employment with noble courts or with theaters in major cities, Geminiani moved from place to place for much of his life, making a living by performing, publishing his music, and undertaking side ventures. In Rome he met some of the top musicians of the day, and he is thought to have studied with Corelli, the player and composer who did more than anyone else to give the violin the status of difficult yet lyrical solo instrument that it still enjoys today. In Geminiani's instructional *Treatise of Good Taste in the Art of Musick* (1749), he recalled detailed conversations with Corelli.

Perhaps finding Rome overpopulated with talented young violinists, Geminiani moved on to Naples in 1706 and took a post as the leader of an opera orchestra at the Fiorentini Theater. According to the English musical historian Charles Burney, who was not sympathetic to Geminiani, he was demoted from orchestra leader to a chair in the viola section because the other players could not follow his beat. Geminiani returned to Lucca and took over his father's job. After two years his salary was doubled, probably because city administrators knew that their native son was a major talent who might well move on to bigger things. Geminiani did just that, leaving for London in 1714.

There were several reasons why a young Italian musician might have chosen London. Corelli's music was already extremely popular there, and a talented violinist who could play in the Corelli style was a strong candidate for profitable employment. The prosperous city's concentration of noble families and a growing middle class ensured a vibrant concert scene, and many potential patrons had traveled to Italy when they were young, as part of a Grand Tour, a voyage through the capitals of Europe that served some of the same functions as the undergraduate semester abroad in modern times. Geminiani's intuition about London proved to be absolutely correct; within two years, he had given a performance for King George I, with Handel himself accompanying him on the harpsichord, and he published his first known compositions, a set of 12 sonatas for violin with continuo (or harmonic) accompaniment. Even though these sonatas were almost impossible for ordinary violinists to play, they were often reprinted in subsequent decades.

In the late 1710s and the 1720s, Geminiani augmented the income from these pieces by teaching the violin and by giving concerts in the houses of wealthy patrons. Even though he rarely gave public concerts, his name became well known in London musical circles. In 1725 he was named to the hiring committee when the post of organist at St. George's Church fell open, a sign that he was considered an important musical authority. Around this time, he became a founding member of two influential musical organizations, the Academy of Vocal Music (even though he himself wrote very little for voices) and the Philo-Musicae et Architecturae Societas, a group affiliated with the Masonic order. The latter group raised funds, via subscription to the eventual printed music volumes, to publish a set of six Geminiani arrangements of Corelli violin sonatas for violin and orchestra.

Turned Down Irish Post

In 1728 the Earl of Essex, one of Geminiani's well-born violin students, put forth the composer's name for the post of master and composer of state music in Ireland, a high-level post and a lucrative one in the days when governments largely controlled the printing business. Geminiani declined the position, but his reasons for doing so are not clear. One writer at the time suggested that he might have been religiously motivated; the Italian Geminiani was a Catholic, but Ireland at the time was ruled by England, and he would thus have been in the service of Anglicanism, the English state church. It seems more likely that Geminiani simply enjoyed his freelance status.

For a time, that decision seemed to work out well. Geminiani had composed and often led performances of two new sets of concerti grossi (a concerto grosso is a composition that contrasts a small group of solo instruments with a larger orchestral group), and in 1731 he organized a series of 20 concerts at a small hall called Hickford's Room. The aim was to raise money to publish the concerti grossi, and they appeared, with much attendant publicity in London newspapers, as the composer's Op. 2 and Op. 3 (classical compositions at the time were sometimes listed by opus number, or published work number) in 1732. These works are now considered Geminiani's most significant.

Then, as now, however, the music business was plagued by piracy, and unauthorized editions cut into Geminiani's profits. To make money on the side, he turned to dealing in fine art, traveling back and forth between Paris and London to acquire new paintings for sale. Geminiani's passion for visual art was genuine; he was a painter himself, and a visitor once found that he insisted on devoting their entire conversation to art rather than music. His head for business, however, was weak, and he made some unsuccessful investments. Deeply in debt, Geminiani was jailed for a short time in the early 1730s when a creditor demanded payment. He was released after the Earl of Essex interceded.

Geminiani now decided to accept the invitation of another noble patron, the Baron of Tullamore, to visit Ireland. He arrived there with little money but got back on his feet with several public concerts. Opening a combination concert hall and art gallery called Geminiani's Great Room, he shuttled between Dublin and London between 1733 and 1740 and made a reasonable living. His wheeler-dealer image did not sit well, however, with English music writers. Other star violinists presented themselves as being in touch with supernatural forces, and Geminiani seemed crass by contrast. "It is to be feared that a propensity toward chicane and cunning . . . operated a little upon Geminiani; whose musical decisions ceasing to be irrevocable in England, determined him to try his hand at buying cheap and selling

dear; imposing upon grosser ignorance with false names, and passing off copies for originals," wrote English critic Charles Burney (as quoted by Enrico Careri in his book *Francesco Geminiani*). Partly as a result of such attitudes, Geminiani's historical reputation suffered, obscuring his importance in the tradition of violin music even two centuries later.

Met Turlough O'Carolan

One famous incident in the annals of Irish traditional music involved Geminiani during his stay in Dublin. Geminiani was told of the legendary skills of Ireland's greatest traditional musician, the Irish harp player Turlough O'Carolan, and decided to test his skills. Geminiani took an Irish melody, rewrote it in such a way that the original melody was well hidden, and sent it to be performed for O'Carolan. After listening to the piece, O'Carolan said, in Gaelic, that it was an admirable piece but that it "limps and stumbles," and he in turn played a corrected version of the music that restored the original melody. This was sent from Connaught, where O'Carolan lived, back to Dublin, where Geminiani gave the opinion that O'Carolan was a musical genius.

Geminiani returned to London by 1741, performing for the royal family at the Haymarket Theatre and publishing several volumes of new music: a set of sonatas for cello and accompaniment and a new set of concerti grossi, Op. 7. Although Geminiani's Op. 3 set was by now considered a classic, these new works sold less well than he had hoped. For the last 15 years of his life, Geminiani devoted himself mostly to instructional treatises, although he did emerge to write music for a pantomime called *The Enchanted Forest* in 1754.

Beginning with *Rules for Playing in a True Taste* in 1748, Geminiani wrote six instructional books in all; one was devoted to the art of accompaniment, and another, in 1760, concerned the guitar. Other violinists had published instructional books before Geminiani, but his were at a higher level than those of any of his predecessors. They were aimed at professional violinists rather than at novices, and they included valuable details, much studied by performers today, on how to improvise details that a composer might not fully write out in musical notation, something now considered critical to the authentic performance of Baroque music. Geminiani's most important treatise was *The Art of Playing on the Violin* (1751). His instructional works, aimed at the English market, often used English, Irish, and Scottish folk songs as examples.

Geminiani continued to travel to London and Paris through the 1750s, but he eventually settled in Ireland as music master to a nobleman named Charles Coote. Living in Dublin, he gave his last concert in 1760, by which time musical fashions had changed considerably from his heyday. He died in his home on September 17, 1762.

The idea of a body of "classical" music embodying the best work of the past is of comparatively recent invention; earlier ages tended to discard the old as they discovered the new, and all but the most famous works of even Handel and Johann Sebastian Bach were mostly forgotten in the century after their deaths. The twentieth century saw an explosion of renewed interest in music of Geminiani's Baroque era, but it was not until very late in the century, when the spectacular virtuosity of Baroque violin music was fully investigated and appreciated, that Geminiani's music was rediscovered. With a free-spirited quality that seemed to match its composer's attitude toward life, it was performed more and more often in the first years of the twenty-first century by violinists with an interest in the Baroque era.

Books

Careri, Enrico, *Francesco Geminiani,* Clarendon Press, 1993.
Sadie, Stanley, ed., *The New Grove Dictionary of Music and Musicians,* 2nd ed. Macmillan, 2001.

Online

"Francesco Geminiani," Baroque Composers and Musicians, http://www.baroquemusic.org/bqxgem.html (January 22, 2006).
"Francesco Geminiani," http://www.geocities.com/connid sunday/geminiani.html (January 22, 2006). □

Mildred Elizabeth Gillars

Convicted American traitor Mildred Gillars (1900-1988) was a radio personality who became famous during World War II for her propaganda broadcasts for Radio Berlin in Germany. Nicknamed "Axis Sally" by her American soldier listeners, she was found guilty of treason in a United States court after the war and spent twelve years in prison.

Gillars was born on November 29, 1900. She was born as Mildred Elizabeth Sisk in Portland, Maine, to Mae Hewitson Sisk, a painter, and Vincent Sisk, an indifferent husband and father who didn't cherish the idea of having children.

When Gillars was seven years old, her father abandoned the small family. She then moved with her mother to Greenwich Village in New York City. When she was eleven, her name was changed to Mildred Gillars, after her mother officially divorced Vincent Sisk and married Dr. Robert Bruce Gillars, a dentist. The family eventually moved to Ohio.

Dreamed of Becoming an Actress

As a child, Gillars displayed exceptional talent as a pianist. She was capable of memorizing compositions by the time she was five years old. Her artistic mother financed her daughter's piano lessons by making silhouettes. But Gillars had other ambitions; she dreamed of becoming a famous star of the stage. Appropriately, she performed in school plays at the high school she attended in Conneaut, Ohio. After she graduated, she enrolled in Ohio Wesleyan University in Delaware, Ohio, where she studied dramatic

arts. Despite excelling in speech, language and her drama studies, she failed to graduate.

Still intent on an acting career, she returned to New York City, where she lived alone and took a series of menial jobs. She worked as a sales clerk, cashier, and waitress to finance her drama lessons. When not working, she went to auditions and was hired for small parts, which kept her hopes alive. She worked with touring stock companies and in vaudeville, but her efforts never led to anything more substantial.

Later, with financial assistance from her grandmother, she enrolled at Hunter College in New York. In 1925, while at Hunter, she met Max Otto Koischwitz, a German immigrant professor who would later have an enormous impact on her life. She had an affair with the charismatic professor until he revealed that he was married.

Moved to Europe

In 1929, she went to Europe with her mother. Although details about this part of her life are somewhat hazy, it appears that she studied music and worked in a variety of disparate jobs. Various accounts have her working as a governess, an artist model and sales girl and studying music in Paris or Germany.

Later, she returned to America, where she continued pursuing an acting career, but she returned to Europe in 1932, where she once again encountered Koischwitz, who was now handling propaganda on Radio Berlin for the emerging German Nationalist Party. In Europe, Gillars still tried to become a famous actress but, once again, her ambitions were thwarted. Koischwitz encouraged her to work with him as a broadcaster, and she was enticed by the exposure the job would provide.

Koischewitz was Radio Berlin's program director, and he would become Gillars' supervisor. Reportedly, Gillars worked as a DJ who played music and engaged in on-air anti-semitic rants. The job proved lucrative—she was one of the highest paid staff members—and it satisfied her desire for recognition. In addition, she once again became Koischwitz's lover. She would remain at the broadcasting post until Germany was defeated by Allied Forces in World War II.

Became "Midge"

With Radio Berlin, Gillars' official title was "Station Mistress of Ceremonies for the Entertainment Programs of the European Services of Reich Broadcasting," and she hosted a propaganda program called *Home Sweet Home*. She dubbed herself "Midge at the Mike," and her duty was to offer the "expatriate American community" music as well as a German perspective on world affairs. Essentially, that translated into providing listeners with news and views slanted toward the Nazi Party line, as her material was in part prepared by Josef Goebbels and other high-ranking German officials.

During World War II, for a period lasting from December 11, 1941 to May 6, 1945, her show was heard across Europe, in the Mediterranean region, and in North Africa. It was even beamed into the United States. For the most part, the program was broadcast from Berlin, but Gillars also worked from German-occupied territories including Chartres and Paris in France and Hilversum in the Netherlands.

Her broadcasts were designed to weaken the morale of U.S soldiers. She played sentimental American music intended to make them feel homesick and, more significantly, she taunted the soldiers by suggesting, in not-so-subtle fashion, that their wives and girlfriends were being unfaithful while they were overseas. She even obtained information about specific towns and people, to make her lurid suggestions more credible.

Reportedly, most of the American soldiers who listened to her show, which usually aired from 8 p.m. to 2 a.m., where unaffected by Gillars' on-air wiles, and they took to calling her "Axis Sally." Her voice was sultry and sexy and they found her to be entertaining, in a skewed sort of fashion.

Still, Gillars demonstrated a resourceful deviousness that greatly offended the stateside audience and the U.S. government. She managed to obtain the names, serial numbers and hometown information of wounded and captured U.S. soldiers, and she used this information to provoke fear and worry in the soldiers' families. With her broadcasts reaching the United States, avid listeners included members of the Federal Communications Commission (FCC) stationed in Silver Hill, Maryland. Soldiers may have been amused by "Axis Sally's" on-air antics, but the commission was not. The FCC monitored and recorded her broadcasts,

which provided prosecutors with evidence when Gillars was later transported back to the United States to stand trial for treason.

The Damning "Vision" Broadcast

During this period, Gillars even posed as a representative of the International Red Cross, visiting American prisoners of war and trying to coerce them into recording messages to their families that she could intersperse with her typical propaganda. This activity, too, would come back to haunt her during her treason trial.

But what turned out to be her most damning effort was a broadcast entitled "Vision of an Invasion." This radio drama, which depicted a failed Allied invasion, aired on May 11, 1944, several weeks before the D-Day invasion of Normandy. For the broadcast, Gillars, ever the aspiring actress, portrayed an Ohio mother who experiences a vivid dream of her son's excruciating death on a ship destroyed by Germans as it attempts to cross the English Channel. The show was specifically aimed at American troops stationed in England who would take part in the large-scale military operation. The message was that the Allied soldiers who invaded Europe would face wholesale slaughter.

The broadcast was replete with realistic and unnerving sound effects, including the cries of wounded soldiers and the sound of gunfire and explosions. The impression created was that of a massacre, and the ambitious effort would later prove Gillars' undoing in the American court.

Charged with Treason

Obviously, Gillars lost her job when the war ended. After Germany was defeated in May 1945, Gillars became an anonymous figure among the half-million Germans either leaving Berlin or seeking food and shelter from the occupying Allied forces. By December of that year, she was nearly starved and almost frozen and spent three weeks in an American hospital.

Afterward, she was placed in an internment camp, but she was granted amnesty in 1946 and moved to the French Zone in Berlin. Eventually, she was recognized and arrested by the U.S. army. She was transported to the United States and, on August 21, 1948, was jailed in Washington, D.C. She was charged with ten counts of treason— though it was eventually reduced to eight to speed up the trial—by a federal grand jury.

Placed on Trial

Gillars' trial began on January 25, 1949, in a district court in Washington, D.C., with Judge Edward M. Curran presiding.

In stating its case, the prosecution, led by John M. Kelley, Jr., alleged that Gillars had signed an oath of allegiance to Nazi Germany after she was hired by Radio Berlin. Kelly also presented witnesses who testified that Gillars had posed as a worker for the International Red Cross in order to obtain recorded messages from American soldiers that she could use in her propaganda broadcasts. Jurors also heard testimony from American soldiers who Gillars tried to coerce into taking part in her broadcasts. They also listened to tapes of Gillars' radio show.

Gillars' defense team, headed by James J. Laughlin, argued that her broadcasts, however reprehensible, did not amount to treason. "Things have come to a pretty pass if a person cannot make an anti-Semitic speech without being charged with treason," he reportedly told the court, Dale P. Harper recounted in *World War II* magazine.

Further, the defense tried to convince the jury that Gillars, in essence, was not responsible for her actions. They argued that she was easily led by Koischwitz, who exercised a strong emotional power over her. To help with this strategy, Gillars took the stand and testified that she had felt that Koischwitz was her "man of destiny." In a dramatic high-point of the trial, she broke down and cried when she learned her former lover and mentor had died. Observers called these emotional displays her greatest performance.

Found Guilty

The trial lasted six weeks and ended on March 8, 1949. The jury, made up of seven men and five women, only found her guilty of one count of treason, and that count involved the broadcast of the "Vision of Invasion" radio play.

Though it was only one count, it was enough for Judge Curran to impose a harsh sentence on Gillars. On March 26, in addition to being fined $10,000, she was sentenced to 10 to 30 years in prison, eligible for parole after 10 years. In essence, it could have been worse. Six other World War II radio broadcasters tried for treason had been sentenced to life in prison. The reason Gillars didn't receive a life sentence is that she had not written the "Vision of Invasion" script herself. Authorship was attributed to the late Koischewitz.

Following her sentencing, Gillars was taken to the Federal Women's Reformatory in Alderson, West Virginia. That same year, an appeal on her behalf was filed in the U.S. Court of Appeals for the District of Columbia. However, the court upheld the ruling that Gillars did indeed commit treason by taking part in a Nazi propaganda radio show broadcast over American radio lines. In addition, the court indicated that Gillars had no right to avoid U.S. prosecution by remaining in Germany. Treason can be committed by American citizens residing in enemy countries, the court ruled, and Gillars had committed treason by breaking her allegiance as an American national.

Released from Prison

When Gillars became eligible for parole in 1959, she waived the right to seek freedom. It was speculated that she chose to remain in prison rather than face possible public ridicule.

She was finally released on June 10, 1961, after serving 12 years of a possible 30-year sentence. Early release was, no doubt, a result of her good behavior. Nina Kinsella, a reformatory warden, described Gillars as a "cooperative prisoner" in the *Charleston Daily Mail* and that she was "helpful and had a very good attitude toward our rehabilita-

tion program." It was reported in the local press that Gillars, ever the actress, strode out of prison with a "flourish."

After serving her time, Gillars went to live in a convent in Columbus, Ohio, where she taught Roman Catholic schoolgirls. Later, she went back to Ohio Wesleyan University. She completed her bachelor's degree in speech in 1973. She died in Columbus, at the age of 87, on June 25, 1988.

Periodicals

Charleston Daily Mail, July 10, 1961.
New York Daily News, September 6, 2005.
World War II, November 1995.

Online

"Axis Sally," *B-24 Liberator Crew,* http://www.liberatorcrew .com/01_Home.htm (December 28, 2005).
"Mildred 'Axis Sally' Gillars," *findagrave.com* http://www.find agrave.com/cgi-bin/fg.cgi?page = gr&GRid = 23000&PIgrid = 23000&PIcrid = 658911&pt = Mildred + 'Axis + Sally' + Gillars&ShowCemPhotos = Y& (December 28, 2005).
"Mildred Elizabeth Gillars," *Biography Resource Center Online* http://galenet.galegroup.com/servlet/BioRC (December 28, 2005).
"Mildred Elizabeth Sisk," *Reference.com* http://www.reference .com/browse/wiki/Mildred_Elizabeth_Sisk (December 28, 2005). □

Sofia Gubaidulina

One of the most widely acclaimed composers to emerge from the Soviet Union in its final decades of existence, Sofia Gubaidulina (born 1931) forged a unique musical language marked by such diverse elements as Christian spirituality, musical symbolism, unique structures derived from fragmentation and repetition of simple material, and the use of folk instruments from the Central Asian regions where her own roots lay.

"Every composition is an enormous labor for me," Gubaidulina told Karen Campbell of the *Christian Science Monitor.* At the beginning, she said, she hears in her head "a vertical sound of colorful, moving, clashing chords, completely mixed up and jumbled. It is wonderful and beautiful, but it isn't real. My job is to turn that vertical sound into a horizontal line. Those two lines, horizontal and vertical, make a cross, and I think about that when I compose." That statement might serve as a kind of compositional credo for Gubaidulina, whose work has successfully merged spiritual influences with extremely original techniques. That combination hampered Gubaidulina's early career, when the repression of creative artists by the Soviet state was at its height, but in the eclectic 1980s and 1990s she became one of the hottest new composers on the international classical scene.

Had Mixed Islamic and Orthodox Background

Gubaidulina was born on October 24, 1931, in Chistopol, in the Tatar Autonomous Republic of the Soviet Union. She grew up in the Tatar capital of Kazan, on the Volga River. Her mother was of Russian, and Russian Orthodox, background, but her father was a Tatar, a member of an ethnic minority group with its own language and a predominantly Islamic tradition. Gubaidulina's father, a surveyor, adhered to the official atheism of the Soviet Union (and never liked Gubaidulina's religious tendencies), but his own father had been a Sunni Islamic mullah. At the height of dictator Josef Stalin's attempts to use his vast gulag to remake the whole of Soviet society, this fact put Gubaidulina's family at risk of imprisonment and death. "Our family lived in permanent stress, expecting his arrest every night," Gubaidulina told Vera Lukomsky in a *Perspectives of New Music* interview. I remember all the family shivered with fright. Actually, the whole country shivered. Though Gubaidulina had her own troubles with the Soviet state later on, she believed that her own situation was not even comparable to that of her father.

World War II brought the deaths of tens of millions of people in the Soviet Union and tremendous hardship to many more. For Gubaidulina's family the later stages of the war meant extreme hunger and poverty, and when Gubaidulina was sixteen she suffered a case of scurvy, a gruesome disease in which the body begins to break down as a result of vitamin C deficiency. But she survived, and after the war she was able to fulfill a dream she had had since childhood, enrolling at the Kazan Conservatory of Music to study piano and composition.

She impressed her teachers there well enough that she was able to move on to the Moscow Conservatory, one of the premier music-educational establishments in the Soviet Union. There she began to run into trouble almost immediately, for her style, though still developing, bore little resemblance to the Socialist Realism prescribed by the Communist Party, with its overblown choral cantatas and operas celebrating the lives of the proletariat. Gubaidulina and a group of other graduate composition students were subjected to what she called a severe critique. For her graduation exam, the famed composer Dmitri Shostakovich, who had had his own brushes with Party commissars, was the chair of her faculty committee.

Party functionaries on the committee attacked Gubaidulina's work while admitting that it was well made. She was defended by Shostakovich and eventually passed the exam, graduating in 1959. After the exam, Gubaidulina told Lukomsky, Shostakovich told her that "everybody thinks you are moving in the wrong direction. But I wish you to continue on your 'mistaken' path." The words were an inspiration to Gubaidulina, who told Lukomsky that "he supported me in my striving for freedom, my striving to be myself. It means that he defended the right of an artist to be him- or herself and go along his or her own path, even if it seemed 'false.'"

Wrote Film Scores

Hardly in good standing with the Soviet state cultural establishment, Gubaidulina supported herself by writing film scores in the 1960s—an occupation Shostakovich also pursed at various stages of his career. On the side, however, she was moving toward a yet more experimental style. She was one of a group of Soviet composers who circulated around Filipp Herschkowits, an Austrian student of Arnold Schoenberg and Anton Webern who had fled to the Soviet Union to escape fascism in the 1930s. Gubaidulina also studied with composer Vissarion Shebalin. By 1962 she had written the first of her works that later became well known in the West: the *Chaconne* for piano. Her Piano Sonata of 1965 was a major work showing the sharp contrast between large dissonant masses of sound and passages of seemingly religious calm that were to become characteristic of her work. Though composed during this time, these pieces were not recorded until 1995. In the late 1960s Gubaidulina was part of an experimental improvisation and electronic music group called Astrea.

Gubaidulina remained virtually unknown for the first part of her career, and in Russia much of her music remained difficult to obtain until around the turn of the millennium. Things began to change, though, when Gidon Kremer, a Latvian-born violinist who had moved to the West but kept in touch with Soviet developments, began to champion her work. Kremer focused on the works of composers, such as Estonia's Arvo Pärt, who cultivated simple yet rigorous styles with an aspect of spirituality, and Gubaidulina's *Offertorium,* a piece for violin and orchestra originally contemplated as part of a setting of the Mass, seemed tailor-made for his concerts. He often performed that work and others by Gubaidulina in the 1980s. Gubaidulina also made an international impression with *The Seven Words,* a work that fell into a long tradition of classical compositions that used instruments to evoke the seven last words of Jesus Christ as he was crucified. The work was written for cello, accordion, and string orchestra, with the expansion and contraction of the accordion symbolizing Christ's breathing. Musical representations of the cross were also woven into the work at various points, and its forces included a bayan, a Central Asian instrument. Other Gubaidulina works also used musical symbolism over the course of a structure that often seemed to end with some kind of state of enlightenment.

In 1985 Gubaidulina was allowed to leave the Soviet Union for the first time, traveling to Europe. She came to the United States in 1987 to attend a "Sound Celebration" performance by the Louisville (Kentucky) Symphony Orchestra, an ensemble with a long history of presenting contemporary music, and she returned the following year for *Making Music Together,* a Boston, Massachusetts, event designed to featured cooperation between American and Russian musicians and to capitalize on the new freedoms Russian creative artists enjoyed during the *glasnost* period of cultural openness promoted by Soviet president Mikhail Gorbachev. In 1990, Gubaidulina began to experiment with specifications of colored lighting in the score for her *Alleluia,* a work for chorus, boy soprano, and orchestra.

Gubaidulina's music remained better known in the West than in her homeland. After receiving a series of prizes that included the Prix de Monaco in 1987, she moved to Germany in 1992, making her home near Hamburg. Commissions from top Western orchestras and small ensembles began to flow her way, and her *String Quartet No. 4* was premiered by San Francisco's hugely popular Kronos Quartet in 1994. Gubaidulina's scores sometimes called for unorthodox instrumental techniques, a longtime hallmark of the concert-music avant-garde; in her *Dancer on a Tightrope,* also from 1994, the pianist must strike the instrument's strings with a thimble or drinking glass. She refused to be labeled as an avant-garde composer, however, arguing that composers should strive for depth rather than innovation. In 1997, Gubaidulina's *Viola Concerto* (a concerto is a work for soloist and orchestra) was showcased on a Chicago Symphony Orchestra concert with violist Yuri Bashmet.

Composed Massive Religious Work for Millennium

Well into senior citizenhood, Gubaidulina showed little sign of slowing down. For the turn of the millennium in 2000, she composed a huge work for chorus and orchestra, the *Passion and Resurrection of Jesus Christ According to St. John,* mixing texts from the Gospel of John with others from the Book of Revelations and the Book of Ezekiel. "The result," wrote *Guardian* critic Gerald McBurney, was "an apocalyptic vision in which, despite sumptuous musical resources used with almost cinematic grandeur, the words dominate. . . . However imposing and colorful the accumulating thunder of voices, orchestra, and organ, the score of Gubaidulina's Passion and Resurrection is still at heart . . . 'poor' stuff, disturbingly stripped down and made of very simple things." A 2005 work called *The Light of the End,* composed for the Boston Symphony Orchestra, "describes a journey from confusion and darkness—in the form of blurry clouds of orchestral color at the beginning—to a radiant close, dominated by the piercing brightness of the clearest bell sounds," McBurney wrote. Gubaidulina began work on another large composition, slated to be performed by the combined Philadelphia and Pittsburgh symphony orchestras in 2006.

Gubaidulina's list of prizes continued to grow, and in 2002 she shared the Polar Music Prize, awarded by the Royal Swedish Academy of Music, with South African vocalist Miriam Makeba. The two artists were picked because they had both made music under politically oppressive conditions. "In my case," Gubaidulina told Jeffrey de Hart of *Billboard,* "it was ideological oppression. Those artists who decided to be true to themselves had to face very difficult living conditions. We were able to write and paint what we wanted, but we knew that we would be poor people." Indeed, despite her $100,000 proceeds from the Polar Music Prize, Gubaidulina continued to live modestly in Germany. What mattered to her was the importance of music in contemporary society. "The whole world is threatened by spiritual passivity, an entropy of the soul, a transition from more complex energy to a simpler form . . . amorphousness," she told Karen Campbell. "What puts the

brakes on that process is the human spirit, and, in part, art, and that is a matter for serious music." Although Gubaidulina's works were quite distinct from one another, she was fairly prolific; her catalog numbered close to 100 works as of 2005.

Books

Contemporary Musicians, volume 39, Gale, 2003.
Sadie, Stanley, ed., *The New Grove Dictionary of Music and Musicians,* 2nd ed., Macmillan, 2001.

Periodicals

Billboard, June 15, 2002.
Christian Science Monitor, August 27, 1997.
Guardian (London, England), August 12, 2005.
Perspectives of New Music, Winter 1998.

Online

"Sofia Gubaidulina," All Music Guide, http://www.allmusic .com (December 20, 2005). □

Lalo Guerrero

Eduardo "Lalo" Guerrero Jr. (1916-2005) is known as the father of Chicano music. His career began in the 1930s and continued on until his death in 2005, contributing along the way to most of the new developments in Mexican-American music in the southwestern United States.

Early in his career, Guerrero composed romantic songs that became successful on both sides of the U.S.-Mexican border. He recorded big-band swing and music in tropical dance styles. During and after World War II his music played a central role in the Latino youth culture of the Los Angeles area. He recorded a series of hit Spanish-language parodies of Anglo-American hit songs, and he wrote and sang topical corrido ballads until very late in his life. And for many Latin Americans, Guerrero remains best known as a children's musician, recording with his group Las Ardillitas, the Little Squirrels. Arizona mariachi musician José Ronstadt told the *Arizona Daily Star* that Guerrero "was really an incredible man. . . . To me the most interesting phenomenon about Lalo Guerrero was that different generations knew Lalo through his different expressions of music."

Collected Bottles for Bootleggers

Born on December 24, 1916, in Tucson, Arizona, Guerrero was one of 11 surviving children in his family; many others died in infancy. "It seemed like almost every year there was another little white coffin in the living room," Guerrero wrote in his autobiography, *My Life and Music.* Guerrero almost died himself when he contracted smallpox, which left him scarred and vulnerable to taunts from neighborhood children. Guerrero's father, like many other

Mexican immigrants in Tucson, had been drawn to the United States by work available on the expanding railroad system. Guerrero was given the nickname Lalo and was also known as Eddie after he began to learn English at a Catholic school. The Barrio Viejo neighborhood of Tucson where he grew up was poor but buzzing with activity, and Guerrero earned money by selling fruit or newspapers, and by collecting empty bottles that he could sell to bootleggers for a nickel apiece during the Prohibition era.

Guerrero's mother Concepción, who enjoyed singing Mexican popular songs, taught him to play the guitar. He also received strong musical influences from American movies, trying to emulate the crooner Rudy Vallee and watching the Al Jolson movie *The Jazz Singer,* the first sound film, over and over again. He began to perform at student assemblies, and a teacher introduced him to classical music. "When it came to music, I was like a funnel," he wrote in his autobiography. "I'd take everything in. I didn't care where it came from or whether it was in English or Spanish. I liked Burl Ives's ballads and Bob Wills and His Texas Playboys. I learned American songs from the movies and Mexican songs from Mamá's records and both from the radio." He began to dream of making music a career.

With two high school friends, Guerrero formed a trio called Eddie, Manny, and Rudy, which performed in English on Tucson radio station KGAR, and another, El Trio Salaz y Guerrero, that sang in Spanish on Tucson's KVOA. In 1934 the family went to live for a while in Mexico City, accepting a U.S. government offer of a $200 payment to Mexican Americans who agreed to be repatriated. Guerrero brought with him a song he had already written; *Canción Mexicana* (Mexican Song). A piece written in praise of Mexican music, it quoted melodies from around Mexico, and it later caught on among Mexican vocalists and was recorded by stars including Lucha Reyes and Lola Beltrán. Decades later it was still well known as a kind of unofficial anthem, but Guerrero was never credited as the writer or paid proper royalties. Even so, of the hundreds of songs he composed, he later named "Canción Mexicana" as his favorite.

Mexican audiences did not take to the performances of Guerrero himself, however; they termed him "pocho," or Americanized. Guerrero returned to Tucson and formed another vocal group, Las Carlistas, that did well enough to try its luck in Los Angeles and even performed at the 1939 New York World's Fair. They backed cowboy star Gene Autry in his film *Boots and Saddles,* and Guerrero, discovered walking down a street by Vocalion records talent agent Manuel Acuña, soon made his first solo recordings.

Zuit Suit and Romantic Style

Guerrero married his first wife, Margaret Marmion, in 1939, and the couple raised two children. During World War II Guerrero worked in an aircraft factory, receiving draft deferments because of his military work and his six-month-old son. Guerrero entertained U.S. troops in nightclubs, leading bands that played swing and newly popular Cuban dance styles. During the "zoot suit" anti-Latin riots of 1942, he was chased by a group of U.S. Marines but eluded them by taking refuge in a darkened movie theater. He was

drafted in 1945, shortly before two atomic bombs were dropped on Japan and ended the war.

In Los Angeles after the war, Guerrero was signed to make more recordings by Acuña, who had moved to the new independent Imperial label. Forming bands called Lalo y Sus Cincos Lobos (Lalo and His Five Wolves) and El Trio Imperial, Guerrero at first recorded mariachi music. But he soon became aware of the hip "caló" slang that flourished among Latino young people in Los Angeles, mixing Spanish, English, and words that had not previously been part of either language. A quick learner of language and music ever since his childhood, when he watched Mexican street musicians improvise lyrics on the spot and tried to imitate them, Guerrero quickly turned out new songs designed to take advantage of the new Latino youth culture, drawing on the hard-edged boogie and rhythm-and-blues styles that preceded the emergence of rock and roll. He enjoyed hits with such songs as "Los Chucos Suaves" (Cool Cats), "Chicas Patas Boogie" (The Chicanos' Boogie), and "Marijuana Boogie," recording with his Cincos Lobos and several times with black Los Angeles musicians as well. Several of these songs were featured in the play and film *Zoot Suit* in the late 1970s, and it was only at that point that Guerrero acquired an actual zoot suit of his own.

As Anglo-American pop made a transition from swing and jazz dance styles to vocal romantic ballads, Guerrero did the same, recording "Pecadora" (The Sinner) with an orchestra for Imperial in 1948. The song became a major hit in the Latin American market, generating a packed homecoming dance with Guerrero as headliner at Wetmore's Ballroom in Tucson, and spreading his name as far afield as Texas, where he had previously been little known. Guerrero toured the Southwest nonstop over the next several years, writing new material in a romantic style. One of his songs, "Nunca Jamás" (Never Again), was originally written as a response to domestic abuse; with its lyrics sanitized, it became a Mexican pop standard that was recorded by such vocal stars as Javier Solis and José Feliciano.

Guerrero and two Anglo-American partners formed a new label, Discos Real, around 1955 in Los Angeles, and that year he spotted a group of Mexican-American youngsters on the street, trying to sing Spanish lyrics to one of the top English pop hits of the day, "The Ballad of Davy Crockett." Inspired, Guerrero composed and recorded a parody with Spanish lyrics about an immigrant named Pancho Lopez, born in Chihuahua in 1903. The song became a hit, not only in the Southwest but all over Latin America; in Mexico it even served as the basis for a film (once again with no royalties paid to Guerrero). Hollywood recording executive Al Sherman suggested that Guerrero record the song in English, promising that he could sell one million copies. "Writing a parody is harder than most people think—especially if the parody is in a different language than the original," Guerrero wrote in his autobiography. "You have to be completely bilingual and bicultural. . . . To be funny, it has to be different but recognizable." Guerrero was successful in translating his parody into English, and Sherman very nearly made good on his promise, as Guerrero's first English-language hit reached gold-record status with sales of over 500,000 copies. Threatened with a lawsuit by Walt Disney (the copyright holder of the original song), Guerrero settled for a 50-50 split of the considerable profits.

Recorded Satirical Parodies

"Pancho Lopez," which used the word "wetback," was later criticized as derogatory toward Mexican Americans, but Guerrero sometimes added a degree of social commentary to the parodies he continued to write, and record buyers snapped them up. Elvis Presley's "It's Now or Never" (itself a parody of an Italian popular song, "O Sole Mio") became the Spanish-English "No Hay Tortillas" (There Are No Tortillas, There's Only Bread); "Tacos for Two" parodied the pop standard "Cocktails for Two"; and in the 1970s Guerrero turned the country hit "Mamas, Don't Let Your Babies Grow Up to Be Cowboys" into "Mama, Don't Let Your Babies Grow Up to Be Busboys," noting that "jobs ain't easy to find, and they're harder to hold." Guerrero's most beloved parody, however, was "Pancho Claus," which imagined a Mexican cousin of Santa Claus.

That song was popular among children, and so were the recordings Guerrero made with his group Las Ardillitas, a trio (Pánfilo, Anacleto, and Demetrio) of electronically speeded-up voices that resembled those of the English-language novelty act the Chipmunks. Guerrero, in fact, was sued by the originators of the Chipmunks, but he argued that he had devised the idea independently, after his producer accidentally left a speaker on while fast-forwarding a tape. The squeaking sound reminded Guerrero of the speech of Martians in science-fiction films, and the first Ardillitas song was in fact entitled "El Marciano" (The Martian). The suit was dropped, and Guerrero, once again working with Manuel Acuña, succeeded in distributing the Ardillitas records all over Latin America. About 20 Las Ardillitas records were made in all, and some were reissued on compact disc.

Beginning in his Discos Real days, Guerrero had been an adept talent spotter, and in the 1960s he ran a successful nightclub, Lalo's, in Los Angeles. He sold the club in 1972 and moved to the Palm Springs, California, area with his second wife, Lidia. In his autobiography Guerrero called this his "so-called retirement," for he remained busy and productive as a musician. In his later years, Guerrero often used the Mexican-American corrido form, a storytelling ballad, to comment on current events. His "La Tragedia del 29 de Agosto" depicted the death of a *Los Angeles Times* reporter during a 1970 antiwar demonstration, and Guerrero wrote a corrido honoring Mexican-American farm labor activist Cesar Chavez. His song "La Mosca" was used in California's battle against the Mediterranean fruit fly in the late 1980s. In 1985 Guerrero joined the Mexican-American rock group Los Lobos on their children's album *Papa's Dream*.

Guerrero received several major awards, including a National Medal of the Arts that brought him to the White House to meet President Bill Clinton in 1995. His autobiography, *Lalo: My Life and Music,* appeared in 2002, and at its end he announced that he was not through making music

yet. He performed for school groups and other organizations until shortly before his death on March 17, 2005, in Palm Springs, California.

Books

Contemporary Musicians, vol. 55, Gale, 2006.
Guerrero, Lalo, with Sherilyn Meece Mentes, *Lalo: My Life and Music,* University of Arizona Press, 2002.

Periodicals

Arizona Daily Star, December 23, 1996; March 18, 2005; April 21, 2005.
Fresno Bee, March 29, 2003.
New York Times, March 19, 2005.
Star-Ledger (Newark, NJ), January 1, 2005.
Variety, March 28, 2005. □

Peggy Guggenheim

American art collector Peggy Guggenheim (1898-1979) was instrumental in the promotion of modern art in the twentieth century. Independently wealthy, she lived most of her life in Europe; she had a particular affection for Venice and her longtime home there is now a renowned museum for art dating from the first half of the twentieth century. Today, her name remains associated with the avant-garde, Cubist, Surrealist and Abstract Expressionist movements in art.

A Child of Wealth

Marguerite Guggenheim, known throughout her life as Peggy, was born into the massively wealthy Guggenheim family on August 26, 1898. Her father, Benjamin, was the fifth of Meyer Guggenheim's seven children and her mother, Floretta Seligman, came from a New York banking family. The Guggenheims were among the most prominent of New York's Jewish families, and the young Guggenheim had a privileged upbringing. When she was barely a teenager, however, personal tragedy struck the family when Benjamin Guggenheim died as a passenger on the Titanic; famously, he and his valet sat on the deck in formal evening wear, drinking brandy and smoking cigars while the liner sank. Foregoing college, Guggenheim first worked in support of the war effort and later at a radical bookstore, the Sunwise Turn. At the age of 21, Guggenheim came into her inheritance and shortly thereafter moved to Paris.

Marriage, Divorce, and Other Loves

In Paris, Guggenheim became fascinated with the growing Post-World War I avant-garde movement among artists and writers. One of these writers, Laurence Vail—known as the "King of Bohemia"—attracted Guggenheim's attention; quickly, the two were romantically involved and

soon married in March 1922. The marriage produced two children: son Michael, called Sindbad, in 1923 and daughter Pegeen in 1925. The family settled in the south of France where Guggenheim recollected in her memoirs that "we had a wonderful life," enjoying the picturesque rural atmosphere and the company of friends such as radical activist Emma Goldman and dancer Isadora Duncan. The "wonderful life" was however marred by frequent fighting between Guggenheim and her husband; in 1928, Guggenheim, in the throes of an affair with writer John Holms, left Vail. The two did not officially divorce for two more years and remained lifelong friends.

Guggenheim and Holms carried on an intense love affair for several years, traveling throughout Europe and finally settling in London after Holms suffered a painful wrist injury. Five months after dislocating his wrist, Holms underwent an operation to repair it; during the operation, his heart stopped and he died. After his death, Guggenheim, as she said in her memoirs entitled *Out of this Century,* "was in perpetual terror of losing [her] soul." For the rest of her days, she continued to consider Holms to be her great love. Guggenheim found some comfort with Douglas Garman, the English publisher with whom she began an affair shortly after Holms' passing. The two lived together at rural Yew Tree Cottage, where Guggenheim had a rather isolated life. This continued for three years, until 1936, when three events which foreshadowed the rest of Guggenheim's life occurred: first, French Surrealists held a wildly successful show in London, although Guggenheim declined to attend, at that time considering Surrealism over; second, Guggen-

heim spent ten delightful days vacationing alone in Venice; and lastly, she and Garman separated.

The First Gallery

After ending her relationship with Garman, Guggenheim found herself at loose ends. Looking for an occupation, she followed the suggestion of a friend and opened a London art gallery, Guggenheim Jeune, in January 1938. The gallery's first show, featuring works by eccentric French artist and poet Jean Cocteau and curated by famed Modernist Marcel Duchamp, was a success. Later shows by notable Surrealist, Cubist and other contemporary artists including Wassily Kandinsky, Henry Moore, and Max Ernst, among others, made the gallery one of the most important in the modern art movement; however, the gallery was not financially successful—Guggenheim took to buying something from each artist she exhibited so they would have at least one sale, a sympathetic move that became the genesis of her art collection—and decided to exchange her gallery for ownership of a modern art museum. However, with the onset of World War II in 1939, plans for the museum were indefinitely delayed and Guggenheim settled again in Paris.

There, often advised by Duchamp, she began actively purchasing art. Guggenheim spent the next two years building her art collection at a terrific rate before the German occupation of France finally drove her to return to the United States in 1941, accompanied by her ex-husband Laurence Vail, his current wife, painter Max Ernst, and the seven children associated with the adults. The last few weeks Guggenheim spent in France, at times, terrified her; a Jew, she was questioned by the authorities and only by repeatedly insisting that she was an American and not admitting her religion was she able to go free. Ernst and Guggenheim took up a romantic relationship around the time of their journey to America; the couple married in 1942. This marriage was, like Guggenheim's first, a particularly stormy one marked by quarrels and occasionally physical violence.

Return to New York City

Guggenheim's second gallery, Art of this Century, opened in New York City in October 1942 even as her marriage to Ernst was rapidly deteriorating. The gallery's interior was designed by architect Frederick Kiesler to present the paintings in a setting as surreal as they were; the initial exhibition, featuring Guggenheim's entire personal collection of 171 pieces, was greatly successful. At the opening night of the gallery, Guggenheim famously wore one earring by Surrealist artist Yves Tanguy and another by Abstract artist Alexander Calder to show that she supported both movements equally. More exhibitions followed, including the first American show devoted entirely to works by women artists and one dedicated to artists under the age of 35.

Art of This Century was one of the first galleries to show modern American artists alongside their European predecessors and contemporaries, lending them a credibility that may otherwise have eluded them; the gallery particularly helped Abstract Expressionists like Jackson Pollock and

Mark Rothko, both of whom held their first shows at Guggenheim's New York gallery, gain notoriety. In 1943, she commissioned a mural from Pollock which was the largest work he had executed to date; putting the piece off for several months, Pollock eventually turned out the over twenty-foot long, six-foot high painting in one long day. Upon delivering the piece to Guggenheim's home, he discovered the painting was eight inches too long and at the advice of Marcel Duchamp, simply cut the extra length from one end. Guggenheim would later donate this work to the University of Iowa. Art of This Century continued to show works by an increasingly all-American group of artists until financial losses caused its closure in 1947.

Naturally, Guggenheim's life was not entirely confined to art during the mid-1940s. Her marriage to Ernst had officially ended in divorce in 1946, the same year that marked the publishing of the first volume of her memoirs. Entitled *Out of this Century,*—a suggestion of Laurence Vail's—the book was written in 1944 and 1945 after Guggenheim was approached by a publishing house. A deeply personal work, and for the era quite scandalous, *Out of this Century* describes Guggenheim's love life in great detail. While many speculate that Guggenheim somewhat exaggerated the tales of her many lovers in her book, her thinly-veiled pseudonyms did nothing to disguise the identities of those she discussed. In his biography *Art Lover* Anton Gill commented that "those maligned would find no protection under their noms à clef, since they were so close everyone would immediately make the connection . . . if anyone failed to, the photographs included in the book left no room for doubt." Most critics attacked the book as being stylistically and morally lacking, but the memoirs sold reasonably well.

Life in Venice

The end of World War II also marked the end of the art world as it had been. The originators of the modern art movements were aging or dying; their heyday was over. The European artists who had moved to the United States during the war slowly returned to Europe. A return visit to Venice in summer 1946 convinced Guggenheim to head back to Europe as well. After her New York gallery's closure in 1947, she settled in Venice, finding a permanent home there, the Palazzo Venier dei Leoni, in 1948. That year, she also exhibited her collection in Venice, suitably shocking a populace accustomed to Renaissance art. By this time, her collection had very nearly reached its final form. Over the remaining decades of her life, Guggenheim bought only a few pieces as her interest in the changing contemporary art lessened and prices on all art rose. (Despite her personal wealth, Guggenheim was notoriously thrifty—in some cases, outright thrift turned to outright stinginess.)

Both locally and internationally known artists and writers as diverse as artist Marc Chagall, Hollywood actor Paul Newman, and American Southern author Truman Capote continued to visit Guggenheim in Venice. Sometimes feeling overwhelmed with visitors, Guggenheim became increasingly concerned for her privacy, although in the early 1950s she opened her home with its collection to the general public on three afternoons a week. "Some people," she noted in her memoirs "think that I should be included as a sight." However, Guggenheim lived remarkably quietly in Venice, dedicating herself more and more to the care of her collection, daily gondola trips through her adopted hometown, and her brood of Lhasa Apsos dogs. In 1960, she published a second and less scandalous volume of her memoirs, entitled *Confessions of an Art Collector.*

Guggenheim's collection left her palazzo for two major exhibitions in the 1960s, the first in 1965 at London's Tate Museum and the second in 1969 at New York City's Solomon R. Guggenheim Museum. At the time of the 1969 exhibition, Guggenheim agreed to donate her collection to the Solomon R. Guggenheim Foundation upon her death on the condition that the collection would remain intact in Venice and would be recognized as hers. The Foundation assumed responsibility for both the collection and for Guggenheim's palazzo.

Final Years and Legacy

In the early 1970s, Guggenheim, by then nearly 75, truly began her withdrawal from the world. Her art collecting ceased, her social circle dwindled as friends aged and died, and even the numbers of her dogs declined as she quit replacing pets that died. In 1974, her collection was shown at Paris's Louvre to great success. As the decade progressed, Guggenheim's health faded; she at last died on December 23, 1979 at the age of 86. She was cremated shortly thereafter and her ashes buried in her palazzo's garden near those of her beloved dogs. Within days, her palazzo was again opened to the public as the Peggy Guggenheim Collection, under the management of the Solomon R. Guggenheim Foundation. To this day, the collection can be seen in her former home, still complete as it was at the time of her death.

Books

Dearborn, Mary V., *Mistress of Modernism: The Life of Peggy Guggenheim,* Houghton Mifflin, 2004.
Gill, Anton, *Art Lover: A Biography of Peggy Guggenheim,* HarperCollins, 2002.
Guggenheim, Peggy, *Out of this Century: Confessions of an Art Addict,* Anchor Books, 1980.
Unger, Irwin and Debi Unger, *The Guggenheims: A Family History,* HarperCollins, 2005.

Online

"American National Biography Online: Peggy Guggenheim," http:www.anb.org (January 7, 2006).
"Peggy Guggenheim Collection: Peggy's Biography" http://www .guggenheim-venice.it/English/ (January 7, 2006). □

Alice Guy

French filmmaker Alice Guy (1873-1968) was the first woman to make a movie, as well as one of the very first directors in the history of cinema to work with a script.

Her short film from 1896, *La Fée aux choux* (The Cabbage Fairy), which was one minute in length, is thought to have been only the second piece of cinema to depict a fictional tale. Over the next 20 years, Guy made hundreds of other short films, but many of them have been lost to time. Only later in her career did she gain recognition as a film pioneer and as the first of her gender to attain success.

Guy was born on July 1, 1873, in Saint-Mandé, a section of Paris, France. Her parents were bookstore owners in Chile, but her mother had sailed back to France to give birth, and then deposited her daughter in the care of a grandmother in Switzerland and returned to Chile. For a time, Guy lived with her parents in South America, and at the age of six entered a parochial school for girls, Convent du Sacré-Coeur, in Viry, France. After another stint at a school in Ferney, she headed to Paris to learn a skill so that she could support herself.

Quickly Learned New Technology

Guy took classes in stenography, a form of shorthand writing that was a necessary job requirement for a secretary at the time. In 1895, the year she turned 22, Guy was hired as the secretary to Léon Gaumont. He was a talented mechanical engineer and was working for a camera manufacturer at the time, but was fascinated by the new form of "moving" pictures. When his employer's company ran into financial trouble, Gaumont and a few others—including Gustav Eiffel, for whom the Eiffel Tower was named—bought the company and formed a new company they called L. Gaumont et Cie. The firm began manufacturing the equipment to make motion pictures, and began making short films to promote their product.

The first notable motion picture recorder was the Kinetograph, designed by American inventor Thomas Edison, which came onto the market in 1894 and was widely copied elsewhere. In France, two brothers, Auguste and Louis Lumière, entered the field in 1895 with their cinématographe, which was both a camera and projector. They briefly pursued the commercial possibilities, making dozens of short films that were shown in arcades to the paying public. By 1897, a magician named Georges Méliès was making films with a rooftop backdrop in Montreuil, just outside of Paris. Méliès used actors who performed in front of what were essentially stage sets.

In between the first films of Lumière and Méliès, Guy made a short film, *La Fée aux choux* (The Cabbage Fairy). It is just 60 seconds long, and she appears in it dressed as a man. It came after the Lumière brothers' *L'Arroseur arrosé*, first screened in December of 1895 and believed to be the first narrative, or non-documentary film. Film historians believe Guy shot *The Cabbage Fairy* in April of 1896, and Méliès made his first film within a month or two after that. Record keeping from this earliest era of filmmaking was imprecise, and there are debates over which of the pioneers were first in the industry with various camera and editing devices that later became standard.

Became Head of Production

Gaumont liked Guy's efforts so much that he put her in charge of production at his newly created film division by 1897. For the next few years, she made dozens of very short films, most averaging just 75 feet in length. She also worked on some of the first motion pictures that featured sound. This innovation, which occurred around 1900, came thanks to the Chronophone, designed by Gaumont and his engineers. It twinned the film projector with sound from a wax cylinder recording.

Within a decade, Gaumont's company had become the number-two filmmaker in France, just after Pathé, and began to own and operate its own movie theaters. They showed Guy's first full-length feature film, *La Vie du Christ* (The Life of Christ), in 1906. It was shot in 25 scenes at great expense, including payroll for 300 extras. She also made *La Fée Printemps* (The Spring Fairy), which used some rudimentary color special effects, that same year.

Technological advances and the success of *Etablissements Gaumont,* as the company was known after 1906, allowed Guy to make longer and more elaborate feature films. She wrote her own scripts, and her cast included clowns, acrobats, and opera singers who took roles in fanciful stories she based on fairy tales, folklore, or the Bible. Though she was not the first person to make a feature film, film historians have credited her with two technical innovations, each of which came by accident—running the film in reverse, and the double exposure.

Moved to United States

In 1906 Guy was working with another prolific director at Gaumont, Louis Feuillade, on a short titled *Mireille* when she met Herbert Blaché, who headed distribution for Gaumont in Britain and Germany. They were wed the following year, and Herbert Blaché was made head of a newly created Gaumont subsidiary for distribution in U.S. theaters. The newlyweds moved to the United States, and Guy had two daughters while serving as production manager and living in the New York City area. In 1910 she and her husband, along with a third Gaumont executive, founded their own company, Solax.

Guy's first American film credit was *A Child's Sacrifice* in 1910, which was also the first film released by Solax. Their company was based in Flushing, New York, and its studio and production facility made some 325 films over the next few years. Herbert Blaché usually served as the production manager and cinematographer, while Guy was the artistic director. Titles from these years include *The Violin Maker of Nuremberg* from 1911, and *Fra Diavolo* and *Mignon,* both from 1912 and based on operas; they were shown in theaters with live orchestral accompaniment. In 1912 Guy directed *A Fool and His Money,* believed to be the first motion picture filmed with an entirely African-American cast, and later preserved at the American Film Institute archives.

Solax was so successful that Guy and her husband moved to a massive new studio in which they had invested $100,000–an enormous sum at the time–in Fort Lee, New

Jersey. This was rapidly becoming the film capital of America, and nearly all the major studios making pictures in the pre-World War I era were based in or around the city, before the possibility of year-round outdoor shooting lured them to Southern California's warmer climate. A company called Metro Pictures was launched in 1916 as a distributor of Solax films, but one of its founders, Louis B. Mayer, launched his own production company, which became Metro-Goldwyn-Mayer, or MGM, one of the major entertainment industry players of the twentieth century.

Guy was well-known in the industry during this era, and an article about her accomplishments appeared in the March 1912 issue of *Photoplay*. She wrote an article titled, "Woman's Place in Photoplay Production" for *The Moving Picture World* in its edition of July 11, 1914. She also taught some of the first courses in filmmaking at Columbia University in 1917.

Studio Went Under

Guy continued to make films, including *Her Great Adventure*, released in 1918. Its plot concerns a Broadway hopeful who becomes an overnight sensation, dates a movie star, and finally reunites with the humble chorus boy who was her first love. But after World War I, there were many changes in the film industry in the United States, and a period of consolidation began. Some suffered financial setbacks, and Solax was one of them. Guy and her husband were forced to rent their Fort Lee property to others, then finally sell it.

The 1920 film *Tarnished Reputations* would be the last film that Guy ever directed. By this time she and her husband were working under contract to other studios, including Pathé, where *Tarnished Reputations* originated. The story revolves around a naïve young woman from the countryside, whose portrait is painted by an artist passing through; she falls in love with him, the townspeople gossip about their relationship, and when the painting sells and makes the artist famous, she never hears from him again. She follows him to the city, is mistaken for a prostitute and arrested on a morals charge, and ends up in a reformatory for teenaged girls. Eventually she meets a writer, who casts her in his play, and in the end she is reunited with the artist.

Guy's own personal story was almost as melodramatic. By 1922 she and Blaché had divorced, and she suddenly found it impossible to find work as a director on her own. She went back to France with her daughters, and hoped to renew her contacts there. She was unable to bring with her any prints of her numerous films, however, and little had survived of her Gaumont years. Therefore she had no proof

that she had ever done her own film work, and failed to win any jobs. In 1927 she returned to the United States. She spent hours in the Library of Congress in Washington, D.C., searching for prints of her work in its film depository, but most seemed to have been lost save for six early one-reelers.

Pioneer Across Several Genres

Guy remained an unknown pioneer in filmmaking until 1955, when she was honored with France's Legion of Honor medal as the world's first woman filmmaker. She had resettled in the country of her birth by then, but returned to the United States one final time at the age of 91, in 1964, to be near her daughter. Four years later, she died in Mahwah, New Jersey. A volume of her memoirs, *Autobiographie d'une pionnière du cinéma 1873-1968,* was published in 1976, and ten years later in English translation by her daughter Simone Blaché as *The Memoirs of Alice Guy-Blaché.* Later film historians succeeded where she did not, and managed to rescue about 110 of the films she directed. Some of these were featured in a 1995 documentary *The Lost Garden: The Life and Cinema of Alice Guy.*

A 2002 biography by Alison McMahan, *Alice Guy-Blaché: Lost Visionary of the Cinema,* settled some of the questions about Guy-Blaché's early work. Though she was not the first person to make a feature film, for instance, she was the first filmmaker ever to use the close-up shot, a technique that had long been attributed to D.W. Griffith. McMahan's book also discussed Guy's role in the history of gay cinema. As noted, she sometimes appeared in men's clothing in her own films, which were some of the earliest representations of cross-dressing on film. One of her Solax films, *Algie the Miner* from 1912, relates the story of an effeminate young man who must prove his masculinity by heading West. This film is usually cited as the first portrayal of homosexuality in American film.

Books

International Dictionary of Films and Filmmakers, Volume 2: *Directors,* 4th edition, St. James Press, 2000.
McMahan, Alison, *Alice Guy-Blaché: Lost Visionary of the Cinema,* New York: Continuum, 2002.

Periodicals

Cineaste, Winter 2003.
New York Times, August 6, 1978.

Online

"Who's Who of Victorian Cinema," British Film Institute, http://www.victorian-cinema.net/guy.htm (January 18, 2006). □

Prince Hall

The founder of the first black lodge within the Masonic Order, Prince Hall (c.1735-1807) was a leading black citizen of Boston during the Revolutionary War era. A skilled orator, he pointed to the inherent hypocrisy of a war being waged in the name of freedom by a people that practiced the enslavement of others.

Hall supported the Revolution and may well have fought against the British. He emerged as a leader of Boston's African-American community in the years after the war. Using his position as Worshipful Master or Grandmaster of Boston's African Lodge No. 459 as a bully pulpit, he organized efforts to improve education for black Bostonians, to begin a back-to-Africa colonization movement, and to resist Northern participation in the slave trade. In the words of his Masonic biographer Charles H. Wesley, "His drive for freedom had a dual thrust. One directed against the dominating rule of a foreign power in the American colonies, and the other against the bondage of blacks."

Organized Masonic Fraternity

Records of the first third of Hall's life are sparse. The slave trade in Massachusetts was heavy during the first half of the eighteenth century, and Hall's speeches on behalf of African Americans sometimes referred to Africa as a native land, so he may have been born in Africa, but no records have surfaced to support either this idea or another early account stating that he was Barbadian by birth. The best

guess as to Hall's birthdate comes from records and newspaper accounts of his death in late 1807 that gave his age as 72, and thus probably places his birth in 1735. The first documentary evidence of his existence comes in the late 1740s in a list of slaves owned by William Hall of Boston, a leather-dresser or leather craftsman. It was probably from his master that Hall took his last name.

In 1756 Hall fathered a son, Primus, who likewise was involved with the Revolution and became an influential black Bostonian. The mother was a servant named Delia who worked in a nearby household. Hall joined a Congregational church in 1762 and married another slave, Sarah Ritchie (or Ritchery, the spelling on her gravestone), the following year. After her death, Hall was married four more times: to Flora Gibbs in 1770, Affee Moody in 1783, Nabby Ayrauly in 1798, and Zilpha (or Sylvia) Johnson in 1804. He learned the leather trade from his master and was given his freedom, in the form of a certificate of manumission, by William Hall in 1770. By Gibbs he had another son, Prince Africanus.

Soon after marrying Gibbs, Hall acquired a small house with a workshop and opened a leather goods store called The Golden Fleece. He also worked as a caterer. Hall's store later became a meeting place for the Masonic fraternity he organized. What drew Hall to Masonry in the first place is not known for certain, but fraternal organizations of various kinds served important community functions among free blacks at various stages in American history. Hall noticed that British soldiers in Boston had set up satellite chapters of Masonic lodges in their home countries, and he may have concluded that joining the Masons represented a path toward integration into the mainstream of American society. He may also have been motivated by the summary rejection of antislavery petitions by the colony's government in 1773 and 1774. In 1775, just before the outbreak of war in Lexington and Concord, Hall was one of a group of 14 free blacks who became members of a Masonic lodge set up by British troops stationed in Boston, perhaps an offshoot of the Irish Lodge No. 441 in the city of Dublin. The date was said to be March 6, 1775.

The membership seemed to confer only partial rights within the Masonic organization, however. When the British garrison withdrew just days later, the sergeant who had headed the British group gave Hall and his companions permission to meet as a lodge and to march in public and funeral processions. But the group was not officially chartered and could not confer membership or degrees on other Masons. With Hall as master and leader, the black Masons formed the African Lodge No. 1 on July 3, 1775; it was the first black order of Free and Accepted Masons anywhere in the world.

Made Drum Heads for Military

The question of Hall's actual participation in fighting against the British remains to be settled. Several histories of the large African-American presence in the American army (according to some estimates, one in every seven soldiers was black) state that he took up arms, but the name Prince Hall was a fairly common one. What can be documented is that Hall provided Revolutionary troops with leather drumheads, according to a 1777 bill of sale.

It was at around this time that Hall began to lead his fellow black Bostonians in trying to persuade the young nation to live up to its ideas of liberty and equality for all. He was one of four signers at the head of a 1777 petition demanding the abolition of slavery in Massachusetts. The petition's aim, in its own words (as quoted by Sidney Kaplan in *The Black Presence in the Era of the American Revolution*), was that the "inhabitanc of these Stats" would, if slavery were abolished, no longer be "chargeable with the inconsistancey of acting themselves the part which they condemn and oppose in others." The Massachusetts legislature sent a bill introduced by sympathetic white lawmakers along to the national Congress of the Confederation, but the petition was not acted upon; slavery in Massachusetts would not be abolished until 1783, when it was ended by a state judicial decision.

Hall continued to operate his successful leather shop and to seek official recognition for his small Masonic lodge, its numbers further decimated as blacks joined the American army and were dispersed along the battlefront. In 1782 he penned a retort to a newspaper article that disparagingly referred to the lodge as "St. Blacks" and made light of its Feast of St. John observances. In 1784 Hall (as quoted by Kaplan) wrote to Masons in England that "this Lodge hath been founded almost eight years and we have had only a Permit to Walk on St. John's Day and to Bury our Dead in manner and form . . . we hope [you] will not deny us nor treat us Beneath the rest of our fellowmen, although Poor yet Sincere Brethren of the Craft." The lodge's official charter was granted, but three years passed before it was issued and brought to America. What had been known as African Lodge No. 1 was now African Lodge No. 459.

Hall by that time was a Boston property owner, taxpayer, and voter, and the change solidified his status as a community leader. As a revolt among dispossessed farmers and war veterans broke out in western Massachusetts under the name Shays's Rebellion, Hall and other blacks faced the problem of which side to support—and of whether their support would be welcomed. Hall wrote in November of 1786 to Massachusetts governor James Bowdoin offering to raise black volunteers for the effort to put down the rebellion. The offer was turned down by a state government afraid of what an armed black militia might do.

Proposed African Colony

Disillusioned by this turn of events, Hall threw his support behind a still-tiny back-to-Africa movement. In time, the idea of African colonization would gain support and result in the establishment of the nation of Liberia, but Hall brought together 12 members of his lodge to sign a petition dated January 4, 1787, that was presented to the Massachusetts House, years ahead of even the earliest actual return voyages to Africa by African Americans or African Canadians. The importance of Hall's petition lies less in its effect—it went nowhere—than for what it reveals about the deferral of African-American dreams that followed the American Revolution. Hall's petition (quoted and reproduced by Kaplan) referred to "very disagreeable and disadvantageous circumstances; most of which must attend us, so long as we and our children live in America."

With the failure of this initiative, Hall turned his attention to improving the living conditions of black Bostonians. In 1787 and again in 1796, he led drives to provide free state schooling for black Massachusetts children, which, he argued, they were entitled to inasmuch as black tax payments supported white schools. Finally, in 1800 he offered his own home for use as a school; two students from Harvard University agreed to serve as instructors.

Hall began to discuss the evils of slavery in general, and he developed into a powerful orator. In a 1797 Feast of St. John address to the African Lodge in West Cambridge (quoted by Kaplan), he spoke of the abuse black Bostonians endured on holidays at the hands of "a mob or horde of shameless, low-lived, envious, spiteful persons" who in groups of "twenty or thirty cowards fall upon one man" or tear the clothes off old women. But he looked to the slave revolt that had occurred in Haiti as a sign of hope: if liberty had begun "to dawn in some of the West-Indian islands, then, sure enough, God would act for justice in New England too, and let Boston and the World know, that He hath no respect of persons; and that that bulwark of envy, pride, scorn, and contempt, which is so visible to be seen in some . . . shall fall, to rise no more."

The idea of black Masonry began to spread, especially as Hall's lodge received chilly treatment from white Masonic groups. New lodges, often bearing Hall's name, were chartered in other cities, beginning in 1797 in Providence, Rhode Island. A black Masonic lodge in Philadelphia played a key role in the evolution of independent black institutions in that city. Hall remained active until his death in Boston on April 4, 1807; his final interment the following year was attended by a large crowd of African Americans. The branch of Freemasonry he founded continued to exert a strong influence in black communities. The list of famous Prince Hall Masons in the twentieth century was a long one, and included educator Booker T. Washington, writer W.E.B. DuBois, Supreme Court Justice Thurgood Marshall, author Alex Haley, bandleaders William "Count" Basie, Lionel Hampton, and Edward Kennedy "Duke" Ellington, boxer Sugar Ray Robinson, publisher John H. Johnson, and Los Angeles mayor Tom Bradley, among many others.

Books

Kaplan, Sidney, *The Black Presence in the Era of the American Revolution, 1770-1800,* New York Graphic Society, 1973.
Smith, Jessie Carney, ed., *Notable Black American Men,* Gale, 1998.
Wesley, Charles H., *Prince Hall: Life and Legacy,* United Supreme Council Southern Jurisdiction, Prince Hall Affiliation, 1977.

Online

"Prince Hall Freemasonry," http://www.freemasonry.org/phylaxis/prince_hall.htm (February 13, 2006).
"Who Is Prince Hall?" http://www.mindspring.com/~johnsonx/whoisph.htm (February 13, 2006). □

Shoji Hamada

Japanese potter Shoji Hamada (1894-1978) is one of the most celebrated ceramists of the modern era. A forerunner in the Japanese folk art movement, Hamada embodied a principled respect for handmade wares in a period of ever–increasing textile industrialization.

Early Life

Shoji Hamada was born on December 9, 1894 in Kawasaki (Kanagawa prefecture), Japan. Not much has been recorded regarding his father, Kyuzo Hamada, and his mother, Ai. Hamada found himself drawn to the arts at an early age. When he was eight, he accompanied an older relative to classes at the Tokyo School of Fine Art and watched the students and their work closely. He also tagged along when the same relative went on painting expeditions. At sixteen he was submitting woodcuts to periodicals for publishing and being awarded frequent prizes for his work in art class at the school he attended. The Pucker Gallery (Boston, Massachusetts)'s online biography of Hamada revealed that he was "first interested in painting, but discarded it in favor of pottery, figuring, 'Even a bad pot has some use, but with a bad painting, there is nothing you can do with it except throw it away.'" This utilitarian mindset became an integral part of Hamada's personal character, and clearly informed the temperament of his work, which was praised for its practical elegance.

Education

In 1913, Hamada attended the Tokyo Industrial College (sometimes referred to as Tokyo Advanced Technical College, and now called the Tokyo Institute of Technology) and enrolled in their ceramics program. While studying there he met influential potter and friend, Kanjiro Kawai. A year before, in 1912, he had been to the Ginza district of Tokyo to view the pottery exhibitions in the galleries there, and come upon pieces and etchings by renowned British potter Bernard Leach. He found Leach's work captivating, and identified with the Western potter's straightforward, skillful designs. Hamada graduated from Tokyo Industrial College in 1916, and he and his colleague, Kawai Kanjiro, both went to work at Kyoto's Ceramic Testing Institute (sometimes referred to as the Municipal Ceramic Laboratory). Hamada finally met Leach in 1919 during a one-man exhibition that Leach put on in Tokyo. The two potters quickly bonded, finding that they shared similar styles, and Hamada was asked to accompany Leach to Abiko to meet and work with other major potters. This excursion sparked a lifetime of mutual friendship and admiration between the two artists that bridged the distance between their respective cultures.

World Wise Craftsman

Leach invited Hamada to England in 1920 to assist in the formation of the St. Ives kilns for the Leach Pottery Studio in Cornwall. While there they also did trial work with lead-glazed slipware. Hamada's experience and expertise were welcomed and praised, and the Leach Pottery remains active—boasting a much-visited museum featuring both Leach and Hamada's work. One of Hamada's main contributions to the St. Ives project was his oversight of the building of a traditional Japanese *noborigama* or "climbing" kiln—the first of its kind in the West. While in England, Hamada had his first one-man exhibition at London's Paterson Gallery in 1923 and returned to England periodically, presenting shows at Paterson in 1929, and again in 1931. Hamada spent four years in England with Leach, and then returned to his native country and was welcomed into an Okinawan potting community. In 1924 he married Kazue Kimura and had six children; four sons and two daughters. His first one-man exhibition in Japan was displayed in 1925.

Hamada eventually became heavily involved in the Japanese folk art, *mingei,* movement and quickly established himself as a leader. The term *mingei* (literally "folk art" or "art of the people") was coined by Soetsu Yanagi—author of *The Unknown Craftsman.* Scholars explain that it was Yanagi's opinion—and Hamada whole-heartedly agreed—that the "anonymous individuals in village cultures [craftsmen] . . . were not consciously trying to make 'art', but interestingly, much of [their]work is now considered art." Whereas, "the contemporary artist/potter was too caught up in the desire to produce art, and the cult of celebrity." The philosophy suggests that the desire to produce art "would have to be abandoned in order for real art to be produced" and one would have to "[work] with one's hands, naturally and unselfconsciously, using local materials and traditional techniques to produce meaningful work for one's fellow human beings." Hamada traveled all over Japan, China and Korea looking for unique folk art pieces and perfecting and improving his own potting and firing methods.

In 1931, Hamada settled among a group of rural artisans in Mashiko (Tochigi prefecture) and established a modest but successful business there. The *Kodansha Encyclopedia of Japan* (1983) explained that Mashiko had been "a pottery center since the latter part of the Edo period (1600-1868)" and Hamada did not initially receive a warm welcome. He was viewed as an outsider, and none of the local artisans would accept him as an apprentice at first because they distrusted his urban education. Eventually, a compassionate local potter took Hamada under his wing. Hamada became so popular and well known that Mashiko became synonymous with his name. Regardless of his celebrity, however, he remained both a humble artist and a diligent worker—relatively unspoiled by his fame.

Despite Hamada's advanced technical training, he chose to specialize in thrown, molded and hand-modeled pieces using the local clay and readily available organic materials such as salt and cinder for his glazes. The *Chambers Biographical Dictionary* defines Hamada's work as being "primarily in stoneware using ash or iron glazes producing utilitarian wares in strong, simple shapes brushed with abstract design." The Pucker Gallery's biography confirmed Hamada's distinctive gift, saying "His works were not merely copies of the styles he studied, but were unique products of his own creative energy." In 1936, Hamada and colleagues Soetsu Yanagi and Kanjiro Kawai founded the Japanese Folkcraft Museum.

In his 1960 memoir, *A Potter in Japan,* Leach describes the two years he spent with Hamada and other ceramists (1952-1954) developing his skills and sharing cultures. The book is dedicated, in part, to Hamada and praises the potter's efforts to uphold and expand the values and expressions of the folkcraft movement, which focused on infusing the new with the old so that Japan's cultural traditions would not degrade. Leach's memoir provided an intimate description of the Hamada potting compound in Mashiko. "He has built up his establishment from a humble start; it consists of several acres on a slope coming down through bamboos, cryptomerias, garden land and trees to the edge of the paddies. Everyone seems to share a spirit of content and mutuality, there is no Western excitability . . . Hamada works alone in the main house . . . [sitting] cross–legged on [a low platform into which the wheel is sunk] . . . The freedom and ease with which he does this is a marvel. But the more one watches, the more one realizes that it is the result of a balance in Hamada himself. Clear and quiet conceptual thought proceeding spontaneously into equally clarified, articulated actions."

From 1952 and into 1953 Hamada visited Europe and the United States as part of a culture tour, inspiring other celebrated potters. Leach recalled the trip, "from the East to the West coast of America, teaching, lecturing, and demonstrating." The tour began with the International Conference of Potters and Weavers—its events held at Dartington Hall in Devon, England in August of 1952. The goal of the conference was the spirited exchange of thoughts and ideas regarding the participants' artistry, and it lasted ten days with a host of over one hundred delegates from more than twenty countries—with Hamada and Yanagi representing Japan. Everyone present had much to learn from Hamada and Yanagi, as Leach explained in his 1960 memoir: "The Japanese Craft Movement . . . is the most vigorous, widespread and unified in the world today. With about 2,000 active and supporting members, one central and three provincial museums, some thirty groups of craftsmen and about half that number of craft shops, with an unusual[ly large] turnover . . . it has more impact upon society than any other movement of which I know."

During the tour, Hamada was quiet and unassuming to the point that people thought he did not speak English. It was his choice to serve the purpose of the tour by doing demonstration after demonstration, silently spinning tangible examples of the principles of the folk art movement that people could see and touch. Leach—in his memoir—praised Hamada's mastery of the "deeper aspect of Oriental thought . . . concerned with Thusness, Nakedness, or Emptiness, a condition of being called in Japanese 'Mu', a quality to be found in all good art . . .," and he wasn't alone in his admiration. Hamada was the recipient of frequent accolades and awards. In 1955 Hamada was designated a Living National Treasure (also referred to as Holder of Intangible Cultural Property) by the Japanese government. In 1962, Hamada was appointed director of Japan's Folk Art Museum, succeeding his friend and peer, Soetsu Yanagi, and in 1968 he was awarded the Order of Culture (Bunka-sho).

A Potter Remembered

Shoji Hamada died in 1978 in Mashiko, Japan, but the scope of his influence included multiple continents. The Pucker Gallery's biography stated that "Because he spoke English and traveled widely, Hamada's influence on potters around the world is incalculable." As a craftsman, he worked tirelessly to maintain Japanese artistic and cultural integrity while, at the same time, never failing to express his own personal and unique perceptions of aesthetic beauty. In his lifetime he was an honored member of such organizations as the Japanese Folkcraft Society, the Society of Japanese Painters (Kokuga Kai), and the Council for the Protection of Cultural Properties of Japan. He was awarded numerous accolades, including the Japanese Medal of Honour with Purple Ribbon in 1964, an honorary doctorate in Fine Arts from Michigan State University in 1967, the Okinawa Times Prize in 1968, and an honorary citizenship to Mashiko in 1969. Both his studio in Mashiko—which has been renovated into a museum—and the still active Leach Pottery in Cornwall draw a steady stream of admirers. As Leach expressed in his memoir, "Wherever industry penetrates, the products of the primary tool of man, the human hand, diminish and decline. . . . The only compensation, and it is quite inadequate to replace the wide array of beauty in the common things of life previously provided by hand by the people themselves, is to be found amongst a mere handful of conscious artist-craftsmen. . . ." Of that handful, Shoji Hamada stands out as a figure of exceptional purpose and talent, and is remembered the world over for his ability to balance innovations, and traditional techniques.

Books

The Cambridge Biographical Encyclopedia, edited by David Crystal, Cambridge University Press, 1998.
Chambers Biographical Dictionary, edited by Melanie Parry, Chambers Harrap Publishers, Ltd., 1997.
The International Who's Who: Fortieth Edition 1976-77, Europa Publications Ltd., 1976.
Japan Encyclopedia, edited by Louis Frederic, Belknap Press of Harvard University Press, 2002.
Kodansha Encyclopedia of Japan, Kodansha, 1983.
Leach, Bernard, *A Potter in Japan 1952-1954,* Faber and Faber, 1960.
The Penguin Dictionary of Decorative Arts, edited by John Fleming and Hugh Honour, Viking/The Penguin Group, 1989.

Online

"Hamada Shoji Museum," *Akari,* http://www.city.yokosuka .kanagawa.jp/speed/mypage/m-imajo/akari/akarimuseum/ folder2/hamadashoji-e.html (January 5, 2006).
"History of World Ceramics," *Glendale Community College,* http://netra.glendale.cc.ca.us/ceramics/hamadastone warevase.html (January 5, 2006).
"Shoji Hamada," *Pottery Studio,* http://www.studiopottery.com/ potters/hamadashoji.html (January 5, 2006).
"Shoji Hamada," *Pucker Gallery,* http://www.puckergallery .com/hamada.html (January 5, 2006).
"Shoji Hamada," *The Leach Pottery,* http://www.leachpottery .com/English/hamada.htm (January 5, 2006). □

E. Y. Harburg

Popular song lyricist E.Y. "Yip" Harburg (1896-1981) was quoted as saying by Clyde Haberman of the *New York Times* that "songs are the pulse of a nation's heart, a fever chart of its health."

Harburg wrote the words to at least two familiar songs that reflected and embodied aspects of the American national outlook: "Over the Rainbow," from the musical film *The Wizard of Oz,* was a timeless expression of yearning, while "Brother, Can You Spare a Dime?" was a hard-luck story of the Great Depression that shaped so many American lives.

There was much more to Harburg than just those two songs, however. During the era of classic Broadway song, Harburg was a frequent collaborator with the top tunesmiths in the business, *Wizard of Oz* composer Harold Arlen above all. Harburg wrote lyrics for musicals whose stories he had developed from scratch, including several, such as *Finian's Rainbow,* that reflected his progressive political convictions. Harburg wrote romantic songs, comic songs, and serious songs in proportions roughly equivalent to those found in the productions of other songwriters. What defined his work above all was a sensitivity to the craft of the lyricist, often the forgotten partner in songwriting collaborations. "The magic in song only happens when the words give destination and meaning to the music, and the music gives meaning to the words," Harburg told his son Ernie (as quoted by Edward Guthmann of the *San Francisco Chronicle.* "Together as a song they go places you've never been before."

Raised on Lower East Side

The youngest of four surviving children (out of ten born), Edgar Yipsel Harburg was born Irwin Hochberg in New York, New York, on April 8, 1896. His parents were Yiddish-speaking, Orthodox Jews who immigrated from Russia, and he grew up in the poor, crowded, and culturally vibrant Lower East Side neighborhood that spawned a host of other creative careers. Harburg came to his familiar name in stages. An unusually active child, he was called Yipsel, a Yiddish word for squirrel, or Yip for short. He made the nickname into a middle name when he married Alice Richmond in 1923, changing his name to Edgar Yipsel Harburg. Harburg liked the musical stage from the beginning. His parents, worried that he would have to perform on Jewish holy days, steered him away from acting, but his father sometimes took him to the theater when the two were supposed to be going to a synagogue.

In high school Harburg made friends with Ira Gershwin, a lyricist with talents equal to his own and later a mentor, for Gershwin, in tandem with his brother George, entered the music business long before Harburg did. After the death of his older brother Max from cancer at age 28, Harburg renounced his Jewish faith and became an agnostic. (A little Harburg poem reproduced in the biography *Who Put the Rainbow in The Wizard of Oz* reads, "Poems are made by fools like me / But only God can make a tree / And only God who makes the tree / Also makes the fools like me / But only fools like me, you see / Can make a God who makes a tree.").

Harburg loved to go to plays and musicals, in both English and Yiddish. He also admired and studied the works of two of the great comic stage writers of past generations, especially W.S. Gilbert of the Gilbert & Sullivan light-opera duo and playwright George Bernard Shaw. Moving on to the City College of New York, Harburg remained friends with Gershwin, and the two contributed a humorous column to a college newspaper, signing it "Yip and Gersh." Harburg graduated from City College in 1917 and took a job with the Swift meatpacking company in the South American nation of Uruguay. The job was considered related to the national war effort and thus helped him avoid being drafted.

Many of Harburg's classmates took off to visit Europe in the 1920s, but Harburg, who felt a sense of satisfaction at supporting his still very poor parents, went into the electrical appliance business with a friend, Harry Lifton. The partnership prospered, and Harburg estimated that the two were worth a quarter of a million dollars at the peak of the economic boom. Married and with two children, Harburg continued to work in business through the 1920s, sometimes contributing light verse to newspapers on the side. He and his wife divorced in 1929, and he lost most of his money in the stock market crash of that year.

Welcomed Crash

The Depression feared by so many was welcomed by Harburg, for it gave him the chance to devote all his time to writing songs. "I was relieved when the Crash came," he told writer Studs Terkel in an interview quoted in *Who Put the Rainbow in The Wizard of Oz.* "I was released. Being in business was something I detested. When I found that I could sell a song or a poem, I became me, I became alive. . . . When I lost my possessions, I found my creativity." Even before the crash, Harburg had renewed a contact with Ira Gershwin, who by that time was one of the best-known lyricists in the United States. Gershwin introduced Harburg to composer Jay Gorney, who had abandoned a career as a lawyer to try songwriting, and in the summer of 1929 they had contributed songs to a revue called *Earl Carroll's Sketchbook.*

Harburg worked with 31 different composers between 1929 and 1934, and for the rest of his life, in contrast to other lyricists who worked only in songwriting teams, he collaborated freely with almost any composer who came his way. His biggest successes at the beginning, however, came with Gorney, and none was bigger than "Brother, Can You Spare a Dime?" The song, written in 1932 when the Depression was at its worst, was part of a revue called *Americana* that had an unusual level of social commentary for the Broadway stage of its day. Harburg started out to write a love song, but the lyric went through various drafts as it evolved first into a sharp satirical attack on the monied Rockefeller family and finally into the portrait of a ruined

worker ("Once I built a tower / To the sun / Brick and rivet and lime / Once I built a tower / Now it's done / Brother, can you spare a dime?") that it finally became.

That same year, Harburg also teamed up with the high-born composer Vernon Duke on the revue *Walk a Little Faster,* which contained the standard "April in Paris." (The two disliked and avoided each other but still managed to write several enduring songs.) It was also in 1932 that Harburg first collaborated with Harold Arlen. They contributed a little-known song called "Satan's Li'l Lamb" to *Americana,* but their second song, inserted into the play *The Great Magoo,* was another standard—"It's Only a Paper Moon." Harburg and Arlen went on to write 109 more songs; among Harburg's roughly 375 song credits, Arlen's name appears far more often than that of any other composer.

Their most famous collaboration was undoubtedly "Over the Rainbow." Harburg had experienced great success through the 1930s, working with various composers on songs premiered by great musical performers like Bert Lahr and Ray Bolger. In 1937, for the first time, he originated the idea for a show, writing book and lyrics together (the music was Arlen's) for the politically oriented revue *Hooray for What?* Harburg and Arlen were brought together for *The Wizard of Oz* by producer Arthur Freed.

Shaped Conception of Film

Harburg wrote all the lyrics for the songs in *The Wizard of Oz,* and the film reflected his creative input in many ways. As the screenplay took shape, it was Harburg who suggested the seamless integration between songs and story that gives *The Wizard of Oz* much of its appeal; the technique was rare in musicals at the time. The dialogue between Aunt Em and Dorothy that precedes "Over the Rainbow" in the film was written by Harburg, and the rainbow image, which did not appear anywhere in the book *The Wizard of Oz,* was entirely his creation. It dovetailed splendidly with the film's then-novel use of color. Harburg also demonstrated a sexy streak in his songwriting that year with "Lydia the Tattooed Lady" ("She has eyes that folks adore so / And a torso even more so"), written for film comedian Groucho Marx.

Writing musicals through World War II, Harburg returned to Hollywood with *Cabin in the Sky* (1943), a musical with an all-black cast that included a young Lena Horne. *Cabin in the Sky* featured another Harburg-Arlen standard, "Happiness Is a Thing Called Joe." Moving between Hollywood and New York for several years, Harburg wrote lyrics for *Bloomer Girl* (1944) an innovative musical, set just before the Civil War, that addressed issues of race and gender equality. As far as his personal life during this time, he married Edelaine Roden in 1943.

The issue of race came to the fore in Harburg's greatest musical of the postwar years, *Finian's Rainbow* (1946). The show arose in Harburg's mind as a result of his anger at segregationist legislation introduced in the U.S. Senate by Mississippi lawmakers Theodore Bilbo and John Rankin. "The only way I could assuage my outrage against their bigotry was to have one of them turn black and live under his own [Jim Crow] laws and see how he felt about it,'' Harburg said in a speech quoted in *Who Put the Rainbow in The Wizard of Oz?* The show, with music by Burton Lane (Arlen turned it down on the grounds that it was too political), verged on a Marxist theme but was loaded with great Irish-flavored melodies like ''How Are Things in Glocca Morra?,'' giving Harburg another major hit.

Although he was never a member of the Communist Party, Harburg was blacklisted in Hollywood beginning in 1950 along with a host of other progressive artists. The blacklist affected Broadway less severely, however, and Harburg continued to work in New York. Among his hits of the 1950s was *Jamaica* (with music by Arlen), a Lena Horne vehicle that ran for 550 performances. Harburg had another success with *The Happiest Girl in the World* (1961), in which he set words to preexisting melodies by French operetta composer Jacques Offenbach.

In his old age, Harburg published two volumes of light verse. He continued to write songs, premiering a new one, ''Time, You Old Gypsy Man,'' at a concert held at New York's 92nd Street YMCA in 1980. The following year he had a heart attack while driving alone in Los Angeles; his car swerved into the path of traffic, and he was killed. Although lyricists have received comparatively little recognition in comparison with composers in studies of popular song, Harburg's reputation was secure and his work is certain to endure.

Books

Furia, Philip, *The Poets of Tin Pan Alley,* Oxford, 1990.

Meyerson, Harold, and Ernie Harburg, *Who Put the Rainbow in The Wizard of Oz?,* University of Michigan Press, 1993.

Scribner Encyclopedia of American Lives, Volume 1: 1981-1985, Scribner's, 1998.

Periodicals

Daily News (Los Angeles), January 28, 1999.

New York Times, March 7, 1981; January 13, 1993; May 3, 2005.

San Francisco Chronicle, November 17, 2004.

Washington Post, March 7, 1981; November 16, 1993. □

Alison Hargreaves

British mountaineer Alison Hargreaves (1962-1995) was hailed as one of the finest climbers in the world. In 1993 she was the first person to climb by herself, and in one season, the six north faces of the Alps. Two years later she made history again as the first woman, and only the second person ever, to reach the summit of Mount Everest without porters, climbing partners, or supplementary oxygen. Then, tragedy trumped triumph in August of 1995, when Hargreaves's conquering of Pakistan's fearsome K2 ended in her death during the descent from the summit.

Rocks and Rebellion

Hargreaves was born on February 17, 1962, and grew up the middle child of three in Derbyshire, England. Her mother was a teacher and her father a scientific officer, and both were mathematicians and avid hill walkers. From the time she was six, Hargreaves joined her family walking the hills of England and Scotland, and her fearlessness was soon evident. ''When she was about 9 years old, we went climbing on Ben Nevis, the highest mountain in Britain,'' her father recalled to David Ellis of *People.* ''Suddenly, she dashed ahead of us, and we got quite worried. We found her sitting quite happily about 500 feet higher up.''

Hargreaves's fascination with climbing was cemented when she was introduced to rock climbing at the age of 13. In an interview conducted by fellow climber Matt Comeskey at her K2 expedition's base camp in 1995, and quoted by Julie Smyth of the London *Sunday Times,* Hargreaves recounted those school days in Derbyshire. ''Hilary Boardman was a teacher there. Everyone at that school did a morning's rock climbing. I had really looked forward to that first morning for weeks, and it was brilliant. I could channel my aggression, but still use mental agility to get myself up. That was the first rock climb.'' By the time she was 14, the diminutive (she was only 5'2'') climber was seeking out rock faces all over Britain. And although Hargreaves took the appropriate tests in high school to follow her parents' and sister's paths to Oxford University, mathematics never really stood a chance. ''It took over,'' she told Peter Gillman of London's *Sunday Times.* ''I desperately wanted to go climbing all the time.''

Part of Hargreaves's ambition and decision was undoubtedly fueled by her relationship with amateur climber Jim Ballard. She met him while working in his climbing shop when she was 16, and although he was nearly twice her age, the two eventually fell in love. She left home to live with him at age 18, to the great disappointment of her parents, and the couple married in 1988. Unfortunately, the less-than-warm relations between husband and parents did not improve with time.

Training and Housekeeping

Having officially abandoned her academic pursuits and set up housekeeping with Ballard, Hargreaves was free to pursue her passion at will. The pair ran an outdoor equipment shop, while Hargreaves trained and climbed in her spare time. By the age of 21, she was cultivating an extraordinary stamina by running over the surrounding hillsides for two hours at a stretch. Next up were the Alps, and she then traveled to the Himalayas for the first time in 1986. The year 1988 saw her back at the Alps, where she successfully scaled the formidable north face of Switzerland's Eiger while nearly six months' pregnant with her first child, Tom. When that became widely known after Hargreaves had later achieved celebrity, some criticized her for climbing while pregnant. Her response, as quoted by Joan McFadden of the

London *Daily Telegraph,* was both unarguable and succinct. "I was pregnant, not sick," she said.

Motherhood did change Hargreaves's workload, as she took a four-year hiatus to raise Tom and his younger sister, Kate. She kept herself otherwise occupied as chairman of the local children's playgroup during that lull, and maintained her physical condition with an early morning running regimen. But as with so many other parents, Hargreaves's career drive and ambition soon called once again.

At the Top

Mountaineering is a difficult pursuit for many reasons, but one of the most banal of these can be the most trying: money. Without independent wealth of their own, climbers must rely on sponsorships to provide for such expenses as travel and gear. And, naturally, such funding does not appear unless the climber has proved his or her mettle. Hargreaves's early career had been a financial drain on her family, and this came to a head in 1993 when, again finding no sponsor for her work, the couple sold their home, pulled up stakes, and moved to Switzerland. The family traveled and lived in an old Land Rover, so that Hargreaves could continue to climb. Their sacrifice appeared to pay off that year when she became the first person ever to scale the six north faces of the Alps—the Eiger, Matterhorn, Dru, Badile, Grandes Jorasses, and Cima Grande mountains—alone and in one season. It was a marvelous feat that did attract some sponsorship attention, and it accelerated Hargreaves's reputation in mountaineering circles. But a resulting book, *A Hard Day's Summer,* had disappointing sales. Despite having made history, Hargreaves had not yet reached the level of financial success that would assure her, and her family's, future.

The allure of the legendary Mount Everest became inescapable for both personal and financial reasons, and Hargreaves made her first attempt on it in 1994. Determined as she was, she aptly displayed her pragmatism by abandoning the ascent just 1,500 feet from the summit because of the threat of frostbite. Smyth quoted Hargreaves's comments on turning back: "My finger-ends had gone numb and I'd lost all feeling in my toes. It was obvious that if I kept going I'd lose my fingers and toes, so I turned around and came down. I was feeling great, but I wasn't prepared to lose any digits over it." Still, the disappointment was palpable, and Hargreaves resolved to try again.

On May 13, 1995, Hargreaves finally achieved acclaim by becoming the first woman, and only the second human being in history, to reach the 29,028-foot summit of Mount Everest without supplemental oxygen or companionship of any kind. Understandably jubilant about her unprecedented success, her first message was to her children: "I am on top of the world and I love you dearly," as quoted from the London *Times.* The sponsorship offers finally poured in, and Hargreaves came home a national heroine.

Finest of Mountaineers

Flushed with her singular success, Hargreaves quickly began making plans for the next venture. By conquering the world's remaining two highest mountains—K2 and Kangchenjunga—her thirst for adventure might be temporarily slaked and her family's security would be all but certain. She decided to attempt K2 first, and leave Kangchenjunga until the following spring in order to spend more time with her children. Toward that end, and just two weeks after returning home from what most would call the victory of a lifetime, Hargreaves set out for K2.

With a summit of approximately 28,250 feet, Pakistan's K2 is the second-highest mountain in the world. It has also acquired the dubious reputation of being the most wickedly daunting to climb. Known as the "Savage Mountain," its wildly unpredictable weather and fierce winds have routinely vanquished those who deigned to try and master its heights. As opposed to the hundreds of successful ascents of Mount Everest, there had only been 113 confirmed successes for K2, and of those, a startling 37 climbers did not survive.

Hargreaves arrived at K2's base camp in June of 1995 and promptly sent off a drawing of the mountain to her children, along with loving wishes for an enjoyable summer. Then the frustrations began. She missed good weather for the climb, after deciding to split with her intended climbing partner and join an American team. The stormy weather kept the new group at base camp for weeks; a situation that must have been particularly aggravating to Hargreaves as her original partner had taken advantage of the earlier good conditions to summit on July 17. Finally she ascended to Camp Four, from which the pinnacle was a tantalizing 12 hours away. Then, on a clear and sunny August 13, she soared into the history books once again.

What happened on that date, three months to the day after Hargreaves's historical capture of Everest, remains unclear in its entirety. What is certain is that the indefatigable British woman did indeed reach the summit of the storied K2 and enter the record books as the first woman to climb the world's two highest peaks without supplemental oxygen. What is equally beyond doubt is that a horrific storm prevented her, along with her five fellow-mountaineers, from safely descending. All were lost in K2's fury.

Aftermath

Hargreaves's death reverberated around the world, and much of the press soon lost sight of her incredible accomplishments in favor of exploring rumors about her home life and her fitness as a mother. Once cheered as a woman to be exalted, arguments about the state of her marriage and devotion to her children became paramount. None of this was helped by the ongoing friction between her husband and her parents, as they jockeyed to gain legal possession of her diaries and memoirs. Nonetheless, Hargreaves's achievements could not be denied and time did march on.

By 2006 Hargreaves's children were both teenagers. Her son had begun following in his mother's formidable footsteps by demonstrating both an interest in, and aptitude for, climbing. Her daughter also enjoyed the sport, but had her eye on a career as an actress. Speculation and fascination about their mother's life continued, and was renewed with the publication of such books as 2000's *Regions of the Heart: The Triumph and Tragedy of Alison*

Hargreaves and 2005's *Savage Summit: The True Stories of the First Five Women Who Climbed K2, the World's Most Feared Mountain.* But perhaps the best way of understanding what drove a woman of Hargreaves's talent and determination is through her own words. Shortly after his wife's death, Ballard told Ellis, "I can hear her repeating her favorite saying, 'One day as a tiger is better than a thousand as a sheep.' That sums up Alison perfectly." And, undoubtedly, the summation of the daughter Hargreaves had left behind was equally telling. "My mother did whatever she wanted to do," Kate told McFadden. "And I'm glad she did." A fitting eulogy for an extraordinary woman.

Periodicals

Daily Record (Glasgow, Scotland), May 13, 2005.
Daily Telegraph (London, England), October 1, 2005.
People, September 4, 1995.
Publishers Weekly, May 29, 2000.
Sports Illustrated, August 28, 1995.
Sunday Times (London, England), August 20, 1995; September 3, 1995; June 7, 1998; June 14, 1998.
Times (London, England), August 21, 1995.

Online

"The Last Ascent of Alison Hargreaves," *Outside,* November 1995, http://www.xs4all.nl/~rmvl/en/alison.html (January 2, 2006).
"Regions of the Heart," Penguin Group (New Zealand), http://www.penguin.co.nz/nf/Book/PrinterFriendly/0,,0140286748_,00.html?sym=SYN (January 2, 2006).
"Savage Summit," Curled Up, http://www.curledup.com/savagesu.htm (January 2, 2006). □

Gwen Harwood

Though Gwen Harwood (1920-1995) began to publish her poetry relatively late in life, in her late thirties, she became a favorite of both readers and critics around Australia and beyond. "By the end of her life," wrote Alison Hoddinott in *The Australian,* "Gwen Harwood was arguably the finest and most highly acclaimed poet writing in Australia."

Harwood belonged to no school or trend, and her poetry is difficult to classify as a whole. She wrote about her rural upbringing and about the natural environment on the island of Tasmania, where she lived as an adult. Yet the quizzical Austrian language philosopher Ludwig Wittgenstein also influenced her as a writer, and her poems occasionally refer to him or embody his ideas. Involved with music throughout her life, she often wrote about it in her poems. And no list of the qualities of Harwood's writing would be complete without a reference to her sense of humor. Hilariously sharp letters she wrote as a young woman were later published and enjoyed by the Australian public, and her poems abound with jokes, puns, and, in one famous case, an obscene acrostic.

Grew Up on Citrus Farm

Born Gwendoline Nessie Foster in Taringa, Queensland, Australia on June 8, 1920, Harwood spent her early childhood near Mitchelton, then a rural area but now part of greater Brisbane. Her family, as she later sketched them in her letters, was slightly eccentric; her father, a salesman and war veteran, had a dachshund to whom he fed tea in the morning. Citrus trees and vegetable gardens surrounded their small cottage, and they kept a small population of livestock. The family moved to Auchenflower, closer to Brisbane, when she was seven. Harwood was sad about leaving her rural paradise when she started school, and she was never enthusiastic about the classroom. She graduated from the Brisbane Girls Grammar School in 1937 and said, according to Hoddinott, that as a student she was "undistinguished in everything except music and poetry."

It was in the former field that Harwood first thought about making a career. Having taken piano lessons from an early age, she dreamed of a career as a concert pianist. At one point she auditioned for the great pianist Arthur Rubinstein when he was visiting Brisbane. The performance did not go well for Harwood. "Once she played / for Rubinstein, who yawned," she later wrote in a poem (according to the *Dictionary of Literary Biography*). Harwood switched to music education, taking courses with Australian musicologist Robert Dalley-Scarlett. She was awarded a music education certificate with honors in 1939 and took a job as organist at Brisbane's All Saints' Church.

Attracted to an assistant clergyman there, she gave him free piano lessons as a way of getting to spend more time around him. But the romance fizzled, and a disillusioned Harwood entered an Anglican convent in 1941. That course of action did not last, either, and she took a job at the War Damage Commission, a veterans' insurance agency.

It was during this period that Harwood struck up a correspondence with Tony Riddell, a friend who was serving in the Australian navy. Harwood's voice as a writer flowered in these letters, and they were later collected and published in a collection called *Blessed City,* her name for Brisbane. It was named book of the year by the Australian newspaper *The Age.* She explained to Riddell that she drew on one of three alternate personalities when she had to attend a wedding; the Young Genius, the Soulful Maiden, or the Embittered and Disillusioned Musician. Any one of the three might help herself to snacks set out for those at the head table. The bureaucrats at the War Damage Commission came in for rough treatment at Harwood's hands. She teased her supervisor by talking to herself in German because he "has that strange habit, that public servants acquire after long years, of reading his mail over to himself in a mumbling voice, with slight inflections at the paragraphs," she wrote to Riddell (as quoted in *The Australian*). "This makes me laugh so much that he looks up, and because he doesn't know what I'm laughing at, he gets frantically annoyed and then goes on reading and mumbling with suppressed rage. Today he asked me why I didn't behave in a normal manner, and I replied, 'Little Gwendoline was never quite like other girls.'"

Moved to Tasmania

One of her poems, "The Rite of Spring," was published in the literary journal *Meanjin,* in 1944. But by that time Riddell had introduced her to a navy friend, Bill Harwood, and the two were married in September of 1945. Harwood's husband was an aspiring professor of linguistics, and when he was offered a job at the University of Tasmania, the couple moved to Hobart, Tasmania. At first Harwood missed the mild climate of mainland Australia (Tasmania is a large island off Australia's southeastern coast), but she came to love her new home and remained in Tasmania for the rest of her life.

Harwood knew little of linguistics or philosophy before meeting her husband, but the *Tractatus Logico-Philosophicus* of Ludwig Wittgenstein made a deep impression on her when she happened to pick it up and leaf through it. A dense work, the *Tractatus* is filled with aphorisms and philosophical conundrums that fascinated Harwood. "When I came to the end I felt like someone who'd come upon a new religion, . . . she wrote (according to the *Dictionary of Literary Biography*). "When I read in Wittgenstein, 'Not how the world is, is the mystical, but that it is' I took my first step towards being a poet." Quotations from Wittgenstein showed up in Harwood's poetry, and she wrote poems about other philosophers and philosophical issues as well.

It would be several years, however, before Harwood could put her poetic ideas down on paper. She and her husband raised four children, and she had a fifth that was stillborn. Harwood shared childcare duties with a friend who was likewise creatively inclined. Although she called motherhood a "beautiful tyrannic kingdom" in one poem, she rarely wrote about her husband or her family. Feminist scholars later debated the degree to which childbearing had interrupted Harwood's career as a writer.

By the late 1950s, working on poems in her head late at night and early in the morning, Harwood was ready to seek out publication opportunities. Two poems, "Death of a Painter" and "Daybreak," appeared in *Meanjin* in 1956, and by 1960 her work was appearing regularly in that journal and in another, *The Bulletin*. She began to win prizes, but they did not dampen her high spirits. After a disagreement with the editor of *The Bulletin,* she sent in two poems that were published in the magazine. The staff realized too late that the first letters of each line of one poem constituted a kiss-off to the magazine itself, while the other poem formed an obscene acrostic aimed at editors in general.

Wrote Under Pseudonyms

In the early 1960s Harwood published poems under her own name but also used several pseudonyms: Francis Geyer, Walter Lehmann (under whose name the nasty acrostics originally appeared), and Miriam Stone. Scholars again debated Harwood's motivations, suggesting that she adopted the mostly male pseudonyms in order to get around editorial prejudice against women poets. Harwood's own testimony on the matter varied; at first she claimed that the move was merely an example of her often-noted trickster qualities, but she later said that she had used the pseudonym device simply because she had written a large number of

what she considered worthwhile poems and wanted to see as many of them in print as possible.

Philosophy was far from the only subject treated in Harwood's work, and she was often described as many-voiced. She wrote about Tasmania and about the rural atmosphere of her own childhood, often presenting versions of herself as a mischievous or troublesome child. One poem, "Barn Owl," recounts what happened when she took her father's gun to shoot an owl: she wounded but did not kill it, and it hopped toward her. "I saw / those eyes that did not see / mirror my cruelty / while the wrecked thing that could / not bear the light nor hide / hobbled in its own blood," she wrote. After her father comes in and tells her to fire the gun again to put the owl out of its misery, "I leaned my head upon / my father's arm, and wept / owl blind in early sun / for what I had begun." She wrote poems about close friends, about art, about poetry in German (a language she spoke well). After being treated for breast cancer in 1985, she wrote about the experience in a book called *Bone Scan* (1988).

Another frequent topic of Harwood's poems was music, and she remained closely involved with classical music for her entire life. From the 1960s until the end of her life she wrote texts for vocal compositions, often working with composer Larry Sitsky. One of their first projects was an opera based on Edgar Allan Poe's *The Fall of the House of Usher.* In 1993 they completed the opera *The Golem,* and it was performed at the Australian Opera in Sydney.

Despite her growing success in the 1960s and 1970s, Harwood still worked mostly in isolation. In the 1960s and early 1970s she had to contribute to the family income by working as a medical secretary. But the publication of her *Selected Poems* in 1977, with 30 new poems written especially for the book, finally brought her to a higher level of prestige. She began to show up on, and then to lead, panels at literary conferences, and a series of poetry prizes began to come her way. In 1989 she was made an Officer of the Order of Australia. She gained attention in England but was little known in the United States.

Late in life, Harwood answered a *Contemporary Authors* questionnaire about her outside interests with "building a yacht, breeding geese and other poultry." Diagnosed with cancer once again, she lasted for months longer than doctors expected; "she was ready to die but she was damn sure she wasn't going to do it any earlier than she had to," poet Norman Talbot told Christopher Dore of *The Weekend Australian.* "She was a great hero, that lady." She lived to see the publication and positive reception of her last book, *The Present Tense.* Harwood died on December 5, 1995, but before she did, she asked that her ashes be scattered over the Brisbane River.

Books

Dictionary of Literary Biography, Volume 289: Australian Writers, 1950-1975, Gale, 2004.

Hoddinott, Alison, *Gwen Harwood: The Real and Imagined World,* Angus & Robertson, 1974.

Trigg, Stephanie, *Gwen Harwood,* Oxford University Press Australia, 1994.

Periodicals

Australian, December 12, 1995; December 14, 1995.
Herald Sun (Melbourne, Australia), December 14, 1995.
Weekend Australian, December 9, 1995. □

Lorraine Heggessey

When she became the controller of the BBC1 television channel in 2000, Lorraine Heggessey (born 1956) became the first woman to hold that executive position at the flagship television station of the venerable British Broadcasting Corporation. She remained in that position until 2005, when she resigned to become chief executive of TalkbackThames, one of Britain's leading independent production studios.

Heggessey's tenure at the BBC was controversial. Some credited her with revitalization of programming that even in the opinions of older viewers had become staid, and BBC1 viewership rose sharply under her administration. On the other hand, it was often charged that Heggessey had dumbed down BBC1's programming—a charge she vigorously contested. Well educated but not a product of the English university programs that stocked many of the country's top management ranks, she sometimes quoted a maxim of media theorist Marshall McLuhan in support of her programming philosophy: "Anybody who thinks education and entertainment are two separate things doesn't understand either."

Produced Family Newspaper

Heggessey was born on November 16, 1956. When she was young, she told Lennox Morrison of *Scotland on Sunday,* she was "a pretty conscientious girl; I always did my homework." Her media career began with a newspaper she produced at the age of eight, chronicling the goings-on in her family household. Her parents were the only customers. Heggessey attended Durham University and graduated with an honors degree in English. She hoped to join the BBC after graduating but was turned down when she first applied. Instead, in 1978, she got a job as a junior reporter with the *Acton Gazette* newspaper. One of her first assignments was to follow trash collectors as they made their daily rounds. She was accepted by the BBC the following year as a news trainee.

She rose through the ranks at the BBC, cutting her teeth at positions in the network's prestigious hard-news divisions. After two years as a news subeditor in 1981 and 1982, she was promoted to assistant producer and then producer (in 1983) in the Current Affairs department, with responsibility for the *60 Minutes* and *Panorama* news programs. Though the Soviet Union was mostly closed to Western media at the time, Heggessey sneaked in by posing as a tourist and put together a *Panorama* story. In 1986 she left the BBC for a producer position at Thames TV, a predeces-

sor to the company she joined in 2005. From there she moved to an independent network, Channel 4, where she was a deputy editor on a program called *Hard News* and a producer for another news program, *As It Happens.* She also worked briefly for a news program on the independent ITV network and was arrested by troops in Zaire as she tried to film a story about the growing threat of AIDS.

It was during this period that Heggessey first made waves on British television. She produced a feature that dealt with the treatment of British union leader Arthur Scargill by an aggressive investigative reporter, Roger Cook, but Cook refused to be interviewed. Turning the tables on the stocky reporter, the five-feet-tall Heggessey pursued him down a street, peppering him with questions. As she captured the chase with a rolling camera, she hit Cook with a demand to "answer the question. . ." (according to the *Daily Mail*). The fast-moving world of independent television news gave Heggessey a thick skin and a demeanor often described as feisty or fearless.

When she returned to the BBC in 1991, she broadened her work beyond news. She created and edited a viewer-feedback show called *Biteback,* and she served as series producer for a show about organized crime, *The Underworld.* Married to Dutch-born musician and composer Ron de Jong—who worked at home and usually kept an eye on the couple's two daughters as the demands of Heggessey's career grew—she was caring for her one-month-old baby daughter when the chance came to interview "Mad Frankie" Fraser, one of Britain's most notorious gangsters. "She woke up and wanted feeding and I thought, 'What am I going to do?'" Heggessey recalled to Charlie Catchpole of the *Mirror* tabloid. "I decided not to ask Frankie's permission because it might embarrass him. So I just got on with it in front of him. He wasn't the least bit fazed." The interview made both Fraser and Heggessey better known, and Heggessey moved up to the level of executive producer for various programs in 1994.

Resuscitated Eccentric Figure's Career

One of those programs was *Animal Hospital,* a traveling animal-welfare show that won National Television Awards for Most Popular Factual Entertainment Show in 1995, 1996, 1997, 1999, and 2000. Heggessey went a long way toward insuring the show's success when she chose as its host Rolf Harris, an eccentric, Australian born musical figure who had first come to prominence as the vocalist who sang the international hit "Tie Me Kangaroo Down, Sport" in the 1960s and had more recently issued a bizarre cover version of Led Zeppelin's "Stairway to Heaven." Heggessey asked an assistant for a list of celebrities who had contributed to animal-welfare charities. When she came to Harris's name on a list of donors to the Cats Protection League, she told Catchpole, "I said, 'That's it!' and everybody looked at me as if I was mad." But Heggessey's judgment was vindicated as Harris's career took off in renewed full flower.

Heggessey helmed a science show, *The Human Body,* in 1996 and 1997, and during this period she was once again wooed by independent television organizations. Part of what persuaded her to stay at the BBC was the offer of a job as head of the network's children's programming, an attractive post inasmuch as her daughters had reached the ages of four and eight. Heggessey made headlines during this period when she personally went on the air to explain to youthful viewers why a popular host had been fired after being charged with cocaine use. Heggessey remained head of children's programs at the BBC until 1999, and in 1999 and 2000 she rounded out her resumé further as joint director of the network's Factual and Learning division and as director of programs for the BBC Productions unit.

With a wide range of experience and a demonstrated capacity for toughness, Heggessey was a logical choice when the position of BBC1 controller—the channel's chief operating officer—came open in 2000. Her hiring was announced in September of that year, and she became the first woman to hold the position. BBC Director of Television Mark Thompson praised her to the *Birmingham Post* as "a program maker through and through, [with] a great knack of recognizing the original idea and making it work." Heggessey for her part said that she had always wanted the job.

It came with serious challenges, however. Once the unchallenged leader of the international broadcast world, the government-owned BBC—funded through license fees levied on everyone in Britain who watched television—had suffered under competition from privately run broadcasters. Ratings were on the decline, and the BBC had been bested in audience measurements by the privately owned ITV (Independent Television) for several years in a row. The BBC had acquired the affectionate but hardly hip nickname of

"Auntie," and even senior citizens polled in surveys opined that the network's programming was old-fashioned. Some in Britain even talked of privatizing the legendary broadcaster.

Took Steps to Raise Ratings

Heggessey, with a team of four immediate subordinates, now had full responsibility for all of BBC1's programming. After making obligatory remarks about high-quality programming, Heggessey stated her aims as controller in no uncertain terms. "My job will clearly be to arrest the ratings decline, if not reverse it," she told Matt Wells of the *Guardian.* She was aided by a decision to move the BBC's evening news program from nine to ten o'clock, a decision made before she was hired but that she executed smoothly. Her first move was to drop a popular symbol of the network, a red and yellow balloon that had cost 500,000 pounds. "The balloon to me feels very slow," Heggessey told Thomas Quinn of the *Mirror.* "It goes across this majestic landscape but doesn't feel in touch with viewers."

She also quickly made program changes. Some of them, such as a move of the *Survivor*-style quiz-show *The Weakest Link* to prime time, alarmed traditionalists who felt that she was taking the network in a down-market direction. *Panorama,* which had once been one of Heggessey's prize responsibilities, was moved to a late-night slot. But Heggessey's programming was not, as one critique had it, entirely made up of makeover and do-it-yourself shows. Several new high-quality dramas were introduced and competed successfully against reality-television programs on independent networks. Heggessey created a show called *The Nation's Favorite Proms,* a viewer-friendly introduction to Britain's famed Proms classical music concerts. And she turned once again to Rolf Harris, selecting him to host an art program, *Rolf on Art.*

The results were quick and dramatic: by early 2002 the BBC was topping archrival ITV in peak-time viewership. Lists of the most powerful women in British entertainment routinely began to feature Heggessey's name, and the crucial under-35 demographic, never the BBC's strong suit, began to break in the network's favor. Heggessey could point to a variety of new nonfiction shows, including history series on the Greek city of Pompeii and Rome's Coliseum, and a science show that dealt with the history of the number one. Heggessey told Tom Leonard of the *Daily Telegraph* that she felt that BBC's job was to "serve all the viewers some of the time," and she seemed to be making headway toward that goal. As for the reality shows—Heggessey created a show called *Fame Academy* to compete with ITV's *Pop Idol,* comparable to *American Idol* in the United States—she told Leonard that "Very few people want to watch one kind of programming—they want a variety."

By 2004, Heggessey was speculating that she might become BBC1's longest-serving controller in history. She had several new successes under her belt, including the consumer-advocacy show *Watchdog* and *Strictly Come Dancing,* a unique ballroom-dancing program that paired celebrities with amateur dancers. Well-received arts programs had blunted some of the criticism that she had moved too far in a populist direction, and although the BBC's government overlords spoke of reviews evaluating BBC1's adherence to the network's overall goals, Heggessey had strong support from her immediate supervisor and seemed unlikely to encounter any level of criticism beyond what she had experienced before. Her appetite for pugnacity showed in a dust-up between the BBC and media tycoon Rupert Murdoch, whom she termed a capitalist imperialist who worked against everything the BBC stood for.

So it was something of a surprise when she departed for TalkbackThames in 2005. A hefty increase in salary was one motivation. "Obviously it's good to get to a stage where you feel you can capitalize on your experience and you can start to make a bit of money," she told Raymond Snoddy of the *Independent.* "But money is not my main motivating factor. Happiness in my job and whether the job challenges and stimulates me is the main thing." The new job made her head of a company of her own, albeit one owned by a German multinational corporation, and it put her in a position to deliver programming to the BBC as well as its rivals. Budget cuts at the BBC also seemed to herald an era of austerity. In any event, Heggessey's status as one of the most powerful figures in British entertainment seemed likely to continue for some time to come.

Periodicals

Birmingham Post (England), September 15, 2000.
Daily Mail (London, England), March 31, 2003.
Daily Telegraph, September 26, 2003.
Evening Standard (London, England), February 14, 2005.
Express on Sunday, December 23, 2001.
Financial Times, October 2, 2001.
Guardian (London, England), September 15, 2000, p. 9; April 16, 2001; March 22, 2004; February 14, 2005.
Independent (London, England), July 27, 2004; September 19, 2005.
Mirror (London, England), October 23, 2000; January 24, 2001; January 2, 2002.
Scotland on Sunday, August 26, 2001.
Televisual, October 12, 2005.
Variety, September 18, 2000; February 15, 2005. □

Fletcher Henderson

Fletcher Henderson (1897-1952) was a key figure in the development of the ensemble jazz style known as swing. As a bandleader and composer himself, and as an arranger for the Benny Goodman Band in that group's golden years just before World War II, he nurtured both the sound of swing and the players who made the music.

Henderson did not grow up playing jazz or improvised music of any kind, and as a musician himself, he was no more than adequate. Historians have differed as to his significance in jazz history. Some argue that the swing genre sprang practically full-blown from his arranger's pen, while other better-known musicians reaped the benefits of his discoveries. Other writers contend that Hen-

derson happened to be at the center of a vital musical scene in New York City just as the new music was taking shape, and that other musicians deserve equal credit for swing's artistic accomplishments and growth in popularity. Henderson's biographer Jeffrey Magee takes a middle ground, writing in *The Uncrowned King of Swing: Fletcher Henderson and Big Band Jazz* that "to get at what Henderson did, it might be best to describe him as a musical catalyst, facilitator, collaborator, organizer, transmitter, medium, channel, funnel, and 'synergizer,' if such a word existed."

Studied Classical Music

Henderson was born in Cuthbert, Georgia, on December 18, 1897. His father was an educator, and both his parents played the piano. Henderson enjoyed an unusually good education for an African American in the South at the height of segregation. His father mortgaged the family home to the hilt to finance his son's education. Henderson attended Howard Normal School, a black prep school in Atlanta, and then majored in chemistry at Atlanta University, graduating in 1920. He began taking classical piano lessons at age six. His parents steered him clear of ragtime piano and the other African-American musical traditions of the rural South, but he developed sharp musical instincts and a good ear that allowed him to learn new musical traditions quickly. In the Atlanta University chapel he served as the school organist.

With ideas of studying chemistry at Columbia University, Henderson moved to New York in 1920. Higher education, in the sciences as elsewhere, was still highly segregated, and he ended up working as an assistant in a chemistry lab. Music actually offered him greater opportunities. Rooming with a pianist, he filled in for his roommate on a riverboat job and was noticed and hired for further work by Fred "Deacon" Johnson, an influential booker who had worked with the Clef Club orchestra, the leading black ensemble of the pre-jazz years. Soon Henderson had a full-time job as a song plugger—a salesman who promoted songs to artists—with the Pace & Handy music publishing firm, recently formed by legendary blues arranger W.C. Handy and Atlanta University alumnus Harry Pace.

In 1921 Henderson moved on with Pace to the new black-oriented Black Swan record label. The classically trained Henderson turned out written musical arrangements quickly for use in the Black Swan studios, and Henderson was picked to lead the backing group for Black Swan artist Ethel Waters on her national tour. It was on that tour that Henderson began to grasp the energy of blues, jazz, and popular African-American rhythms. "On that tour Fletcher wouldn't give me what I call the 'damn-it-to-hell bass,' that chump-chump stuff that real jazz needs," Waters recalled (as quoted by Magee). She gave Henderson some piano rolls by the Harlem "stride" pianist James P. Johnson. "To prove to me he could do it, Fletch began to practice," Waters said. "He got to be so perfect, listening to James P. Johnson play on the player piano, that he could press down the keys as the roll played, never missing a note. Naturally he began to be identified with that kind of music, which isn't his kind at all."

Back in New York, Henderson began to show up on records as accompanist to an increasingly wide variety of singers. The piano or small-band accompaniments heard on the mid-1920s recordings of jazz-influenced "classic blues" singers such as Bessie Smith and Gertrude "Ma" Rainey are often Henderson's. His name became better known among musicians, and by 1923 he had joined with an eight-piece band of his own, performing at New York's Club Alabam. The college-educated Henderson was picked as leader because it was thought that he projected the personable image the group would need in order to crack the New York high society market. Henderson proved to be an astute judge of emerging talent. His 1923 band included future saxophone superstar Coleman Hawkins, then 19 years old, and another saxophonist with arranging talents, Don Redman. By the following year, when Henderson settled in for a long residence at New York's Roseland Ballroom, his band had expanded to ten and then to sixteen musicians, and had taken on a trumpeter recently arrived from New Orleans—Louis Armstrong.

Added Jazz Elements to Dance Styles

Henderson experienced success partly because he identified an unfilled niche: a top-notch African-American dance band that could read music and compete on equal terms with white ballroom orchestras like that of Paul Whiteman was bound to make a splash among both black and white audiences. For downtown appearances, trumpeter Howard Scott recalled (as quoted by Magee), that Henderson "was a very strict leader. Every night you had to

. . . stand inspection. He'd look at your hair, your face, see if you shaved, your shoes, see if they're shined. You had to be perfect to suit him." In Harlem, musicians sought to emulate Henderson by learning to read music. The big bands of the swing era, which depended partly on musical notation, would soon be stocked with players who had either worked directly with Henderson or been inspired by him indirectly.

But Henderson did not simply imitate the sound of white bands. Armstrong, who remained with Henderson for 14 months, and the other young jazz players Henderson hired, pushed the sound of the band toward the freer, more energetic type of jazz that was flowering as Americans became more and more aware of the non-notated ensemble improvisations coming out of New Orleans and traveling northward toward the Midwest. Armstrong and Henderson both characterized their relationship as a mutually beneficial exchange. Don Redman began writing arrangements that balanced the talents of individual improvisers with varied large-band textures, and Henderson's band began to gain popularity beyond New York. He took over some of the arranging chores in 1927 after Redman departed to form his own group, and the music he made during this period features the textures that became characteristic of swing in general: interaction between brass and reed sections, a smooth surface with plenty of dance-floor energy coming from drummers, and solo interludes that provided a space for the artistry of talented individual players.

Saxophonist Benny Carter, another important entertainer who emerged from the Henderson band, also wrote arrangements for the band, creating effective showcases for his own playing. The innovative arrangements of the Henderson band were closely followed by other musicians. One who credited Henderson as a direct influence was bandleader Edward Kennedy "Duke" Ellington, who raised the Hendersonian art of showcasing distinctive individual players to a level of perfection. White clarinetist and bandleader Benny Goodman was another Henderson admirer who began purchasing Henderson's arrangements and compositions. That helped Henderson and his big band stay afloat financially when Henderson suffered injuries in an auto accident in 1928. But Goodman's appropriation of Henderson's material also disguised Henderson's contribution to jazz at a key point in its history—the emergence of swing onto a national stage. One of the Benny Goodman band's most-played pieces, "King Porter Stomp," was based heavily on a Henderson arrangement. But the Great Depression severely curtailed the activities of recording companies, and the musical activities of Henderson himself during the Depression years are poorly documented. Even so, Henderson pieces like "The Stampede" and "Rocky Mountain Blues" became well-known jazz standards.

Henderson led a band at the Harlem club Connie's Inn in the early 1930s and continued to record sporadically. His popularity dropped somewhat with the emergence of newer swing bands led by Ellington, Count Basie, the Dorsey Brothers, and other musicians. His business skills were inferior to his musical ones, and jazz historian John Lincoln Collier (as quoted in *American Heritage*) noted that Henderson had "an almost pathological lack of self-assertiveness."

Henderson's group disbanded when he ran out of money to pay them after a Detroit engagement in 1934. He had not lost his eye for talent, however; a new group he formed for a 1936 residency at Chicago's Grand Terrace ballroom included future trumpet star Roy Eldridge. Henderson's role with the Goodman band expanded as the band rose to the top of the charts, thanks to appearances on the *Camel Caravan* radio program sponsored by the R.J. Reynolds tobacco firm. Henderson took a full-time job as staff arranger with the bandleader in 1939, dissolving his own group and sometimes playing piano in the newly integrated Goodman band.

Toured in Battle of Sexes Act

Goodman's recordings made between 1935 and 1940 came to be seen as emblematic of swing at its height, and Henderson was a key unseen presence behind their creation. Henderson's work for Goodman brought financial rewards, but he soon gravitated back to the bandstand himself. During World War II he formed a band that took on the International Sweethearts of Rhythm, an all female Jazz-band, in a touring "Swing Battle of the Sexes." After the war he continued to work with a diminished Goodman band and came full circle by touring as accompanist once again for Ethel Waters. Always quick to catch on to new trends, Henderson adapted to the decline of swing by forming a sextet that appeared at New York's Café Society club. In the late 1940s he was slowed by a variety of health problems.

Henderson suffered a series of strokes beginning in 1950, and became partly paralyzed. He died in New York City on December 28, 1952. The specific talents of the swing giants who came after him eclipsed his pioneering contributions, and Henderson's name was forgotten for a time. Reissued LPs helped revive his musical reputation, as did the historical studies of jazz that were undertaken in the late twentieth century; enthusiasts and jazz scholars traced the careers of jazz musicians in the 1920s and 1930s, and they noticed how many jazz career paths intersected with Henderson's.

Whatever his specific role, it is indisputable that the bands Henderson led in the 1920s and 1930s were on the forefront of new developments in jazz. Henderson drew on his unusual musical background to facilitate the incorporation of improvisational jazz styles from New Orleans and other areas of the country into the musical life of New York, and into a dance band tradition that relied on arrangements written out in musical notation. The new music that developed under Henderson's leadership struck a balance between improvisation and compositional planning—a balance that continues to shape jazz today.

Books

Bushell, Garvin, as told to Mark Tucker, *Jazz from the Beginning,* University of Michigan Press, 1990.
Contemporary Black Biography, vol. 34, Gale, 2002.
Magee, Jeffrey, *The Uncrowned King of Swing: Fletcher Henderson and Big Band Jazz,* Oxford, 2005.
Porter, Lewis, and Michael Ullman, *Jazz from Its Origins to the Present,* Prentice Hall, 1993.
Schuller, Gunther, *The Swing Era,* Oxford, 1989.

Periodicals

American Heritage, November 1994.

Online

"Fletcher Henderson," *All Music Guide,* http://www.allmusic .com (February 8, 2006).
"Fletcher Henderson," *Jazz: A Film by Ken Burns,* http://www .pbs.org/jazz/biography/artist_id_henderson_fletcher.html (February 13, 2006).
"Fletcher Henderson (1897-1952)," Harlem 1900-1940: the Schomburg Center for Research in Black Culture, http://www .si.umich.edu/CHICO/Harlem/text/fhenderson.html (February 13, 2006).
"James Fletcher Henderson," Red Hot Jazz, http://www .redhotjazz.com (February 13, 2006). □

Fanny Mendelssohn Hensel

Composer Fanny Hensel (1805-1847) lived for much of her life in the shadow of her more famous brother, Felix Mendelssohn. Most of her works were known only to her family and her immediate circle of acquaintances, but renewed interest in the music of women composers led to the rediscovery of her works and convinced many researchers and musicians that her talent was unique.

Hensel's musical career suffered because the middle-class German family in which she grew up held the typical belief that women should devote themselves to domesticity and child-rearing, pursuing creative work as a strictly limited hobby if at all. It was her brother Felix who steered her away from publishing her music, which would have led to wider renown; her husband, painter Wilhelm Hensel, encouraged her work, and she began to publish some of her more than 500 compositions shortly before her sudden death at age 41. Although he worked to squash her career, Felix Mendelssohn was well aware of his sister's talent and often consulted her on musical matters.

Was Granddaughter of Jewish Philosopher

The Mendelssohn family were well-off citizens of Hamburg, Germany, where Hensel was born, Fanny Mendelssohn-Bartholdy, on November 14, 1805. They moved to Berlin in 1809. Hensel was the oldest of four children; Felix Mendelssohn was four years younger, and the two were close from early childhood onward. Their grandfather, Moses Mendelssohn, was a well-known philosopher who tried to establish a basis for friendly coexistence between Jewish and Christian Germans. By the generation of Fanny and Felix Mendelssohn his project had begun to progress: Jews found more opportunities in Germany and became more integrated into German culture. But opportunity and integration often carried a price; both Hensel and Felix Mendelssohn converted to Lutheranism.

Most of their musical education was shared between the two. Hensel was taught to play the piano by her mother Lea, and she went on to take piano lessons from top performers in Berlin and Paris. She became a top-flight pianist, and unlike most other piano works by amateur composers of the nineteenth century, hers are generally difficult to play. Both Hensel and Felix Mendelssohn studied musical composition with Carl F. Zelter, a song composer well known for his settings of the classic poetry of Johann Wolfgang von Goethe. Zelter also introduced both Mendelssohn siblings to the century-old music of Johann Sebastian Bach, today considered some of the greatest ever written but largely forgotten at the time. Felix Mendelssohn went on to lead a revival of Bach's music in Germany, and it made a strong impression on Hensel as well. By the time she was 13 she could play all of Bach's *Well-Tempered Clavier,* a collection of 48 piano pieces covering all 24 major and minor keys twice through, from memory. Her first composition, written when she was 14, was a song celebrating her father's birthday.

In 1820 she enrolled at a music school, the Berlin Sing-Akademie. She wrote numerous lieder (German-language songs) and piano pieces during this period. Often she wrote short, evocative, highly melodic piano pieces called Songs without Words; Felix Mendelssohn often cultivated the genre, but it is unclear which sibling originated it. Just as her career was beginning to flower, her family threw roadblocks in her way. Her father discouraged her from composing, and Felix Mendelssohn, by now an internationally known composer, refused to help her find a publisher for her works.

His reasons for this discouragement have been much discussed by historians. Certainly, in devaluing the creative powers of women, he was very much a product of his time. Yet he may also have been acting out of sheer competitiveness. Several of Hensel's songs were published under Felix Mendelssohn's name between 1822 and about 1830; one of them, "Italien" (Italy), became widely known, and Felix Mendelssohn, during an audience with England's Queen Victoria later in his life, had to admit the fraud when the queen requested the song and proclaimed it her favorite.

Founded Salon

Fanny Mendelssohn married Wilhelm Hensel, court painter to the King of Prussia, in 1829; a pencil portrait of her that he drew that year reveals a woman who strongly resembled her famous brother physically. The marriage finally gave Hensel an outlet for her music, even if it was not an international platform: her husband backed her efforts to compose, and soon she founded a salon—a regular (often weekly) gathering for individuals interested in the arts and intellectual trends. In this she followed two of her great-aunts who had been enthusiastic salon participants. The Hensel home became one of Berlin's most important intellectual gathering places. Hensel was able to write music for her own salon and perform it there, and she soon began to develop the musical ideas she had formed during her training.

Piano music and songs remained at the center of Hensel's output, but now she began to attempt larger works: an orchestral Overture in C major in 1830, for example, and a 35-minute *Oratorio on Scenes from the Bible* (an oratorio is a dramatic but unstaged work for chorus, soloists, and orchestra, often on a religious theme) the following year. That work remained unheard between whatever initial performance it may have had and the year 1982, when it was rediscovered. Like many of the choral works of Felix Mendelssohn, Hensel's oratorio was steeped in the music of J.S. Bach. *San Francisco Chronicle* critic Joshua Kosman opined that "it's hard to know where to fault this masterly work, or how to explain its neglect as anything but simple sexism." Kosman pointed to such passages as the chorus "Wir leiden um unsrer Sünden willen" (We suffer for our sins), in which Hensel "builds a splendid fugue [a difficult passage in which voices enter at different times with the same melodic material] on a strangely gnarled, disjointed theme." She also wrote chamber music—music for small instrumental ensembles—including a String Quartet in G minor that took after similar works by her brother. She also wrote a considerable amount of music for women's chorus.

Whatever tensions may have existed in their relationship, Hensel and Felix Mendelssohn continued to work together closely when it came to music. She is thought to have played a role in the composition of some of his major works, including the oratorio *Paulus* (St. Paul, 1837), and in general he played through his music to get her opinion and suggestions before notating it in finished form. Felix Mendelssohn married that year, and his marriage seemed to free Hensel from some of her career restrictions. In 1838, Hensel made an appearance as a pianist, performing Felix Mendelssohn's Piano Concerto No. 1.

Traveled to Italy

Between 1839 and 1845 Hensel and her family (she had one son and may have suffered a miscarriage) made two trips to Italy. The voyages were musically rich ones for Hensel, who made the acquaintance of the young French composer Charles Gounod and influenced his music. In 1841 she composed the piano work "Das Jahr" (The Year) as a memoir of the first journey; it consisted of twelve short pieces, one for each month of the year, plus a final chorale (a harmonization of a German Lutheran melody). "This is an outgoing cycle: even the ruminative, bittersweet Serenades, June and July, grow into densely textured virtuoso works, and most of the pieces have more of [Robert] Schumann's audaciousness than Felix Mendelssohn's delicacy . . .," noted *New York Times* reviewer Allan Kozinn after hearing the work in 1996. Indeed, not all of Hensel's music resembled Felix Mendelssohn's; she also drew on the meatier innovations of younger innovators of the day such as Schumann and Franz Liszt.

Late in her life, Hensel decided to publish some of her music regardless of what her family thought. A long statement on this decision in one of her letters, reproduced on the website of the music publisher W.W. Norton, testifies to her lack of confidence about her decision: "I hope I shall not disgrace you all, for I am no femme libre [liberated woman]," she wrote. About 25 publications of her music, mostly of songs and piano pieces, appeared in all, some of them after her sudden death from a stroke in Berlin on May 14, 1847, while she was leading a rehearsal of Felix Mendelssohn's choral *Erste Walpurgisnacht* cantata. Felix Mendelssohn was strongly affected by her death, and died himself six months later.

For well over a century, Hensel's music was almost completely forgotten. Her manuscripts remained in the possession of her family, and in 1965 they became part of an archive of Felix Mendelssohn materials held at the West Berlin State Library (now the Berlin State Library) in Germany. As feminism began to make inroads in academic musical circles, scholars unearthed records of Hensel's career. But the archive's director, Rudolf Elvers, pooh-poohed the interest of what he called (according to Christopher Swan of the *Christian Science Monitor*) "all these piano-playing girls who are just in love with Fanny," and he dragged his feet in making Hensel's music available. Musicians who asked to see the manuscripts were told to wait while priorities were sorted out.

The situation began to change in the 1990s, and recordings of Hensel's music appeared. A four-disc set devoted to Hensel was issued by Germany's CPO label, and the Thorofon label issued three volumes of her vocal and keyboard music. Printed editions of selections from her body of work were published, but most of her manuscripts remained locked up in the Berlin State Library or held in private collections. As of the early 2000s, most of her music was still inaccessible to performers.

Critical opinion was divided, sometimes but not always along gender lines, about those Hensel pieces that had been placed before the musical public. "You feel like you're listening to a major composer, the workings of an authentic creative soul," Pulitzer Prize-winning composer Stephen Albert told Christopher Swan in reference to Hensel's Piano Trio of 1846. "I'll tell you, she's certainly more adventurous than her brother. She's plenty talented. . . . There's a clarity of thought, a real inevitability to her music. . . . This last movement is very Brahms-like. Only it was written when Brahms was around 14 years old." Composer Gunther Schuller told Swan that "she was extremely prolific, but on a very high, consistent level. The kind of thing where you say, 'Why don't we know this music better?' "

Edward Rothstein of the *New York Times* dissented, calling Hensel's short piano pieces "works of some charm but uncompelling character" and asserting that "the lieder were also relatively banal, with a few moments of surprising modulation." Some writers took the position that Hensel was a composer with raw talent to equal her brother's, but that she had never been allowed to develop it fully. A full evaluation of Hensel's creative contributions awaited deeper research into her life and works. The year 2005 saw the modern premiere of an Italian-language concert aria by Hensel, "Io d'amor, oh Dio, mi moro" (I die, O Lord, of love). Perhaps in future years Hensel's remaining and as of yet unreleased body of work will be discovered and enjoyed.

Books

Citron, Marcia J., *The New Grove Dictionary of Music and Musicians,* 2nd ed., Macmillan, 2001.
Citron, Marcia J., ed., *The Letters of Fanny Hensel to Felix Mendelssohn,* Pendragon, 1987.
Tillard, Françoise, *Fanny Hensel,* trans. Camille Naish, Amadeus, 1996.

Periodicals

American Record Guide, March-April 1998; July-August 1999; May 2000.
Christian Science Monitor, March 27, 1986.
New York Times, September 29, 1991; March 23, 1996.
Observer (London, England), May 1, 2005.
San Francisco Chronicle, February 5, 1990.

Online

"Fanny Mendelssohn Hensel," W.W. Norton publisher, http://www.wwnorton.com/classical/composers/hensel.htm (November 10, 2005). □

Hergé

Georges Remi (1907-1983), known as Hergé, was the creator of Tintin, one of the most popular comic book characters in the entire history of the genre. He drew Tintin from 1929 until just before his death.

Even in the United States, where the comics were less popular than in Europe, the Tintin comics influenced a generation of artists with the precise drawing technique that Hergé used, called the "ligne claire" or clear line. But the Tintin character, a young, tow-headed reporter, became a beloved figure for a variety of reasons that extended beyond Hergé's artwork. The Tintin books were action-packed, humorous, and filled out with memorable minor characters—the cursing but never profane Captain Haddock, two ineffectual detectives named Thompson and Thomson, a rather addled Professor Calculus, and, last but not least, Tintin's faithful dog Snowy. Tintin's popularity survived controversy and generational change, and Remi's hometown of Brussels now boasts a Tintin statue as well as a Tintin subway station mural that Hergé himself designed.

Reversed Initials to Form Pen Name

Remi was born in Etterbeek, Belgium, a Brussels suburb, on May 5, 1907. He never used his real name professionally, forming the pen name Hergé by reversing his initials and spelling them out phonetically in French (air-ZHAY). His strict Catholic household was not an especially happy one. Hergé's mother suffered from mental problems and died when he was young. He attended school under German occupation for several years, sometimes drawing cartoons showing a little figure fighting the invaders. A bright spot in Hergé's life was his membership in the Boy Scouts, an organization that helped shape his basic outlook. The character of Tintin, indeed, had many Scout-like qualities. Hergé took

almost no formal drawing lessons, giving up on the few art classes he did take at the Catholic St. Boniface high school, but did well in his other studies. Hergé was a habitual sketch artist from very early in his childhood, and he never stopped trying to improve his drawing skills.

After he finished school at 18, Hergé found a job with the circulation department at a conservative, Catholic-oriented daily newspaper, *Le Vingtième Siècle* (The 20th Century). On the side, he devised and drew a comic strip called *The Adventures of Totor* for Belgium's national boy scout magazine. Hergé spent a year in the Belgian military in 1926 and 1927, continued to work on the Totor strip, and found expanded responsibilities as an engraver and cartoonist waiting for him at *Le Vingtième Siècle* after his discharge. When the paper added a weekly youth magazine in 1928, Hergé experimented with a strip called *The Adventures of Flup, Nenesse, Poussette, and Cochonnet.*

The following year, however, he returned to his round-faced boy scout character, making him a reporter, sending him to a country conservative Belgians despised, and naming him Tintin. The first Tintin sequence, *Tintin in the Land of the Soviets,* had a staunchly anticommunist theme. Hergé had studied American comics such as ''Krazy Kat,'' and his strips were filled with action and satire of a sort European comics readers had rarely encountered. *Tintin in the Land of the Soviets* became so successful that promotional events arranged in connection with it, such as a ''homecoming'' staged at a railway station for an actor playing Tintin, drew huge crowds.

Hergé's second Tintin book, *Tintin in the Congo,* appeared in 1931 and was later criticized for its racist stereotyping of Africans. But *Tintin in America* (1932) drew negative reactions from a different direction; Hergé was sympathetic to the plight of African Americans and Native Americans (whose culture he researched, beginning a career-long habit), and an American publisher demanded that he excise positive black characters from the strip so as to avoid losing Southern readers. Political controversies continued to swirl around Hergé for most of his life. ''For years the left has said I'm right and the right has said I'm left,'' Hergé said in a Belgian interview quoted in the *New Statesman.* ''I don't like to contradict either.'' Certainly part of the energy of the early Tintin comics came from their engagement with current events; it was later that *Tintin* evolved into a pure adventure narrative. Hergé's 1936 book *The Blue Lotus* took a critical stance toward Japan's invasion of China, prompting heated protests from Japanese diplomats.

Inspired by Chinese Art Student

Both the ideas and the techniques in *The Blue Lotus,* which represented a creative breakthrough for Hergé, were stimulated by a Chinese art student name Chang Chong-Jen whom he had met in 1932. The student inspired Hergé to devote himself wholeheartedly to cartooning as an art as well as introducing him to Chinese culture. Hergé also married Germaine Kleckens that year, and he continued to issue successful new strips, most of them politically oriented. The 1938 *Anschluss* expansion of German authority into Austria showed up in *King Ottokar's Scepter.* Individual Tintin strips continued to appear in *Le Vingtième Siècle* and were then issued in book form by the publisher Casterman. With each successive volume, his precise clear line drawing technique became more apparent.

When German troops overran Belgium in the early days of World War II, Hergé suffered through a second occupation of his homeland. The war had several long-lasting effects on Hergé's art. Nazi authorities declared the political content of Hergé's strips off-limits, and as a result the Tintin stories began to take on their characteristic atmosphere of exotic adventure, free from social themes. *The Crab with the Golden Claws* (1941), set among counterfeiters in Morocco, was a typical example. It was during this period that Hergé introduced several of the Tintin strip's best-loved eccentric characters, including the hard-drinking but amiable Captain Haddock and his non-profane oaths such as ''billions of blistering barnacles.'' (The Tintin strips were enormously popular in England; the characters, except for Tintin, all had their own English names, and nearly all the Tintin books were issued in English translations.) Owing to paper shortages, the size of the Tintin strips was reduced; Hergé responded by honing his drawing technique to yet a finer edge. By the war's end, each frame of a Tintin strip contained enough detail that a viewer might peruse it several times without finding all the elements it contained.

The most significant outcome of the war years for Hergé grew from the fact that he published his work in the Nazi-controlled newspaper *Le Soir.* Hergé argued that he had merely obeyed the instructions of Belgium's King Leopold; that citizens of the country should go about their work normally. He refused offers to do illustration work for a Belgian fascist group, but after the Germans were defeated he was accused of being a Nazi collaborator. He was arrested several times, was briefly imprisoned, and was not allowed to work for almost two years.

Hergé's reputation was rehabilitated when a leader of the Belgian anti-Nazi resistance, the publisher Raynmond Leblanc, offered to back a new magazine, called simply *Tintin.* Hergé had to work at breakneck speed to meet Leblanc's deadlines, but he was soon back in the good graces of the Belgian people and of Western Europeans in general. The series of Tintin books resumed, with adventure remaining as a chief plot element, and by 1955 there were 18 of them, with sales totaling over one million copies annually. Hergé hired assistants to help with the crush of work and established the Studio Hergé in 1950.

Predicted Space Flight

Despite the nonpolitical nature of his later works, Hergé never gave up on his desire to do careful research on the settings he depicted. That research was on impressive display in Hergé's 1953 Tintin adventure *Destination Moon*—Tintin's space suit resembled those eventually worn by American astronaut Neil Armstrong and his crewmates when they set foot on the moon 16 years later, and he accurately depicted the moon's desolate landscape. Other details in the book rang true because of Hergé's extensive reading on lunar exploration; he even sent strips to top European space experts and asked them to check for inaccuracies. Hergé's guess that the eventual lunar launch would be nuclear-powered turned out to be incorrect, but at the time his story was in line with the research of top rocketry experts like the German-American Wernher von Braun. Hergé also became interested in abstract art, and close observers of Tintin strips can find small duplicates of famous abstract paintings hanging on the walls of rooms.

Outwardly oriented though it was, Hergé's work also drew on his own troubled inner life. His marital life was unhappy, and he and his wife Germaine separated in 1960. By that time he had already begun an affair with a young illustrator in his studio, Fanny Vlamynck, whom he later married. The affair caused the Catholic Hergé strong feelings of guilt, and he began to have nightmares in which he was trapped in a featureless white landscape. A psychoanalyst suggested that the fields of white might represent a sense of lost purity, but Hergé decided to confront his feelings in his art, sending Tintin to a snowy mountain landscape in 1960's *Tintin in Tibet.* That book reintroduced a character based on Chang Chong-Jen, who had first appeared in *The Blue Lotus,* and Hergé and his friend were finally reunited in 1981, for the first time in 44 years. Chang had survived the Cultural Revolution in China and become the director of the Academy of Fine Arts in Shanghai.

Hergé finally divorced his first wife in 1973 and married Fanny two years later, but he was increasingly troubled by depression. Whereas he had long stuck to his goal of producing one Tintin book a year, his pace slowed in the

1960s and 1970s to two or three per decade. One Tintin book, *Tintin et L'Alph-Art,* was left unfinished at his death, and it was generally agreed that the creation of Tintin was so closely bound up with Hergé's own personality that no one else should attempt to complete it. Tintin traveled and received various prestigious awards including Belgium's Order of the Crown, Officer Grade, in 1979. That year, which marked a half-century of existence of Tintin, Hergé received a Mickey statuette from the Walt Disney Company. His popularity in the United States had never reached the level of adulation he enjoyed in Europe (and around the world as far afield as Indonesia, in numerous translations), but his American admirers included director Steven Spielberg, who made plans to direct an American Tintin film.

Hergé was diagnosed with leukemia in 1980 and died on March 3, 1983, in Brussels. Funeral observances across Europe resembled those accorded a head of state, and in Belgium, among other honors, the significance of Hergé's art led to the opening of a major comics museum, the Centre Belge de la Bande Dessinée or Belgian Comic Strip Center. By 2004, "known now in some 60 different languages," as writer Michael Farr observed in *History Today,* "Tintin can lay a safe claim to being Belgium's best-known international figure."

Books

Authors and Artists for Young Adults, Vol. 55, Gale, 2004.

Periodicals

Daily Telegraph (London, England), November 23, 2002.
History Today, March 2004.
Mail on Sunday (London, England), April 4, 2004.
New Scientist, April 3, 2004.
New Statesman, January 26, 2004.
Time International, January 18, 1999.
Times (London, England), June 16, 1986.

Online

"Hergé (Georges Remi)," Lambiek Comiclopedia, http://www
.lambiek.net/artists/h/herge.htm (January 12, 2006).
"Hergé: Creator of Tintin," Tintinologist.org, http://www
.tintinologist.org/guides/herge/ (January 12, 2006). □

Rosella Hightower

Native American dancer Rosella Hightower (born 1920) was an internationally renowned ballerina from the 1940s through the 1960s.

Dancing with such companies as the Ballet Russe de Monte Carlo, the Grand Ballet du Marquis de Cuevas, and the American Ballet Theatre, and with other luminaries such as Rudolf Nureyev, her strength and lyricism delighted critics and audiences alike. In addition to a stellar career as a dancer, Hightower was noted for founding a distinguished dance academy in the South of France and being the first American to direct the famed Paris Opera Ballet.

Childhood

Hightower was born on January 30, 1920, in Ardmore, Oklahoma, to Choctaw Native American parents. When she was still in infancy, the family moved to Kansas City, Missouri, where Hightower was reared. It was during the time of Prohibition, dance crazes such as the Charleston, and little tolerance or acceptance of Native American culture or rituals.

Hightower's early years were an unusual combination of hardscrabble existence and highbrow ambition. On the one hand, she worked the fields with her family, as was expected. Lili Cockerville Livingston, author of *Native American Ballerinas*, told Lyndy Franklin of *Dance Spirit*, "When (Hightower) brought in her first bag of cotton that she picked, she earned her place in the family. She was always a tomboy." On the other hand, she developed an interest in ballet at a very young age—an interest that must have been at least partly encouraged by her parents.

Referring to Hightower and four other famous Native American dancers that hailed from Oklahoma (Maria and Marjorie Tallchief, Moscelyne Larkin, and Yvonne Chouteau), Livingston told Franklin, "They were exposed to the old dance companies that were touring the Midwest in the 1930s and they saw something magical. They were bitten by the bug." But surely that bug could have come nowhere near Hightower in her youth without her parent's approval—else, how could a youngster have witnessed the performances? Similarly, it is unlikely that Hightower could have studied with ballet teacher Dorothy Perkins in Kansas City without parental support. Study she did, and the die was cast.

Early Professional Years

In 1938 famous ballet master Leonid Massine's Ballet Russe de Monte Carlo was performing in St. Louis, Missouri. The then-18-year-old Hightower tracked him down after a performance and convinced him to allow her to audition. Her powers of persuasion must have been formidable, as the master reportedly missed his train to accommodate the aspiring ballerina's request. And against the odds a second time, he was sufficiently impressed with her talent to ask her to join his troupe in southern France. Years later, Hightower recalled that time to Karyn Bauer of *Dance*. "I didn't even know where Monte Carlo was. But I got there, on a boat. It [took] two weeks!"

Hightower made her debut with Massine's company in *Seventh Symphony* in 1938. She continued to dance under him until 1941, learning the troupe's repertoire while performing on tour at American military bases during World War II. Among her other early roles with the company were parts in *Swan Lake* (1940) and in *Carnaval* (1941). Hightower would return to work with the ensemble as a soloist after it became the Original Ballet Russe, but 1941 saw her back in New York to make her mark with the Ballet Theatre (later the famed American Ballet Theatre).

Hightower's technical gifts and effortless lyricism on the stage came into the spotlight when she performed as a soloist with the Ballet Theatre under Lucia Chase. She debuted as Carlotta Grisi in *Pas de quatre* in 1941, and subse-

quently performed such roles as the Lover-in-Experience in *Pillar of Fire* (1942), Calliope in George Balanchine's *Apollo* (1943), the White Witch in *Fair at Sorochinsk* (1943), Odette in *Swan Lake* (1944), and the title role in *Giselle* (1944). It was Hightower's rendition of *Giselle* that brought her first major praise, and secured her a place as a ranking ballerina. But she was destined to soar to still greater heights.

Prima Ballerina

Hightower joined the Original Ballet Russe in 1946, and went on to tour North and South America. Her notable ballets, now as principal dancer, for that company included the *Don Quixote* Pas de deux in 1946, the classic *Black Swan* Pas de deux (from *Swan Lake*) in 1946, and Jerome Robbins's *Pas de trois* in 1947. In 1947 she became principal dancer and then prima ballerina with the Marquis de Cuevas's Grand Ballet de Monte Carlo (later the Grand Ballet du Marquis de Cuevas). It was with this company that Hightower had her longest affiliation as a dancer (until 1962), and that brought her unequivocal international acclaim.

Other than taking time out to marry Jean Robier in 1952 and have a child three years later, Hightower concentrated on her art. As de Cuevas's favorite dancer, she toured Europe, Asia, and South America with his company for 15 years. She began with *Brahms Variations* in 1947, and moved through a repertoire that included *Concerto Barocco* (1948), *Persephone* (1950), *Le Prisonnier du Caucase* (1951), *Scherzo* (1952), *La Sylphide* (1953), *Corrida* (1957), *Gaite Parisienne* (1958), and *The Sleeping Beauty* (1960). Hightower was hailed as one of the finest dancers of her generation, and once received a remarkable 15-minute standing ovation for a performance with the troupe. She also began to attract notice as a choreographer with the production of such concert works as *Salome* and *Scaramouche*. In 1962, however, the Grand Ballet du Marquis de Cuevas disbanded. And while an immensely successful chapter of Hightower's life had certainly ended, she wasted little time resting on her many laurels.

Educated the Provinces

After the dissolution of the Grand Ballet du Marquis de Cuevas, Hightower founded a dance school in Cannes, France, in 1962. Originally called Le Centre de Danse Classique and eventually known as l'Ecole Superieure de Danse, one of its prime designs was to raise the quality of dance by expanding its center outward from the major cities. Hightower told Bauer, "It was a challenge to open a school in Cannes at the time, because dance was London, New York, or Paris; it wasn't Cannes!" With an eye toward exposing both students and audiences to a variety of styles, the school's curriculum included ballet, jazz, and contemporary dance, and students were encouraged to become adept at all three. Monet Robier, Hightower's daughter and an instructor at the school, explained the philosophy to Caitlin Sims of *Dance* in this way: "The good thing about the school is that when students are trained early in different styles, it is similar to being raised speaking two languages. Without even thinking, you can speak both languages."

By promoting such variety and quality in the provinces, Hightower believed she could help raise the level of dance in general. Also toward that end, she was a firm proponent of regional dance companies, directing the Nouveau Ballet Opera de Marseille from 1969 to 1972 and the Ballet de Nancy from 1975 to 1978. Yet, even these other significant pursuits were not the sum total of Hightower's career.

Beyond de Cuevas

Hightower continued to perform after 1962, often sharing the stage with such fellow stars as Sonia Arova, Erik Bruhn, and Rudolf Nureyev. She appeared on television and in films, and was the principal dancer for the Theatre of the Champs–Elysees in 1965. Ballets she danced with that company included *La Robe de plumes* and *Profile de silence.* In 1967 Hightower returned to Oklahoma to take the stage in the world premier of *The Four Moons,* a production honoring the state's 60th year of statehood and featuring three of the other acclaimed Oklahoman ballerinas. Even long after she officially hung up her shoes in 1977, Hightower appeared as the lead in *Harold and Maude* in 1991, at age 71.

After her retirement, Hightower concentrated on directing, teaching, and choreography. Those efforts included the staging of *The Sleeping Beauty* for the Stuttgart Ballet in 1977 and assistance in the staging of film director Franco Zeffirelli's updated version of *Swan Lake* at La Scala in Milan (1985). But undoubtedly the most noteworthy of Hightower's post-dancing pursuits was her turn as the first American director of the Paris Opera Ballet. During her tenure there from 1981 to 1983, the former prima ballerina took pains to shake up the venerable institution's status quo. Always a champion of the dance, Hightower attempted to build a company that had room for the nurturing and development of all its performers, not merely its principals. Many of her innovations were controversial, including the initiation of a programming system in which the troupe was divided into three groups: one to perform at the opera house, one to tour, and a third to perform modern works. Another was her staging of *Hommage au ballet,* which featured a rare on-stage appearance of the entire company at one time. The performance was designed to drive home the idea of a unified ballet company. Describing the Paris Opera Ballet as the "company of the decade" in 1989, John Percival of the London *Times* wrote, "The company's ascendancy began with the arrival of Rosella Hightower as director. . . . Her opening (program) was a manifesto and a survey of the company's history and achievements. . . . Hightower's skill lay in choosing established successes from elsewhere which (sic) would show off the dancers and develop their flair." In short, she was a dancer's director.

Hightower's long and impressive career was filled with variety, determination, and talent. The French government recognized her contributions with some of its highest honors. Among those were the Grand Prix des critiques de danse in 1949, the Medaille Universitaire de la danse in 1967, the Chevalier de la Legion d'Honneur in 1975, the Officier de la Legion d'Honneur in 1988, the Grand Prix

national de danse in 1990, and the Officier de l'Ordre National du merite. Nor did her birth state forget her, as she was honored with the Oklahoma Cultural Treasure Award in 1997.

In December of 2001 the then-81-year-old Hightower passed on the directorship of her beloved l'Ecole Superieure de Danse to her hand-picked successor, Monique Loudieres. The move coincided with the school's 40th year in operation and its relocation to spacious new quarters in a former hotel on the outskirts of Mas de Campane in 2002. It was hard to imagine the renowned institution without its founder, but Hightower appeared to be content with her decision. Nonetheless, as Robier told Sims in 1996, "She is really the spirit of the school." Even without its physical manifestation, that spirit was bound to endure.

Books

American Decades, Gale Research, 1998.
International Dictionary of Ballet, 2 vols., St. James Press, 1993.
Notable Native Americans, Gale Research, 1995.

Periodicals

Dance, January 1996; February 1998; December 2001.
Times (London, England), December 28, 1989.

Online

"Dancing Out of the Dust Bowl," *Dance Spirit,* November 2001, http://www.dancespirit.com/backissues/nov01/onyourtoes .shtml (January 14, 2006).
"Oklahoma Cultural Treasure Award," Oklahoma Arts Council, http://www.arts.ok.gov/resources/cultreas.html (January 14, 2006).
"Rosella Hightower," The Ballerina Gallery, http://www .ballerinagallery.com/hightower.htm (January 14, 2006). □

Maurice Ralph Hilleman

Over six decades, American microbiologist Maurice Ralph Hilleman (1919-2005) unlocked the secrets of immunology and went on to develop about 40 vaccines. Among his credits are vaccines for measles, mumps, hepatitis A and B, chickenpox, meningitis, and pneumonia, all of which are routinely recommended for youngsters. Each year, Hilleman's vaccines save millions of people worldwide from death, deafness, blindness, and other permanent disabilities.

Raised on Western Frontier

Hilleman was born August 30, 1919, in Miles City, Montana, a rough–and–tumble frontier town bursting with cowboys, gamblers and barkeepers. He was the eighth child born to Robert and Edith (Matson) Hilleman. His mother, however, did not survive his birth; neither did a twin sister. Robert Hilleman, overwhelmed by the prospect of raising such a large family alone, sent the children off to live on a nearby relative's farm.

The hardships of growing up on a farm on the brittle outskirts of the rugged frontier marked Hilleman for life, yet shaped him into a gritty, stop–at–nothing scientist. The farm also served as his first laboratory, providing Hilleman with early lessons on biology and disease, life and death. He raised chickens, tended cattle, harvested hay and grew vegetables. Hilleman also helped with the family's side business—manufacturing horseradish and brooms, which were sold in town. "Life on a farm in an economically underdeveloped area of the western frontier during the Great Depression was not easy," Hilleman recalled in an article he wrote for *Immunological Reviews*. "But, it was of immense value in providing hands–on experience in the worlds of biology and mechanics, and in creating sobriety and an intensive work ethic that has proved highly useful."

In addition, Hilleman turned to textbooks to learn more about science. Around eighth grade, Hilleman discovered Charles Darwin's book *On the Origin of Species,* in which Darwin described his theory of evolution by natural selection. Hilleman read the book one Sunday at the family's ultraconservative Lutheran church and the minister, who believed in creationism, admonished him. The minister tried to confiscate the book but Hilleman told him it was public property because it belonged to the library and he would notify authorities if the minister tried to take it. Hilleman also listened to a radio station from distant Bismarck, North Dakota, which broadcast a Sunday afternoon show called *Meet the Scientists,* which originated at the University of Chicago.

Escaped to College

In 1937, Hilleman graduated from Custer County High School and took a retail job at the local J.C. Penney. For a poor farm boy, college seemed out of the question. A short time later, however, an elder brother returned home on break from ministerial school and told the family they needed to find a way to send the brainy Hilleman to college. Luckily, Hilleman was offered a scholarship to Montana State University. He promptly quit his job and moved to Bozeman, graduating with a bachelor's degree in 1941. Hilleman went on to study at the University of Chicago, receiving a doctorate in microbiology and virology in 1944 after writing an award–winning dissertation on the venereal disease chlamydia.

Hilleman then took a job in New Brunswick, New Jersey, with the pharmaceutical company E.R. Squibb & Sons. Though he could have stayed in academics, Hilleman chose industry, believing scientists to serve society. "Science has to produce something useful," Hilleman once told the *Philadelphia Inquirer*. "That's the payback to society for support of the enterprise." Within a year of joining the company, Hilleman developed a vaccine for Japanese encephalitis, which was infecting and killing U.S. soldiers stationed in the Pacific during World War II.

In 1948, Hilleman began working for the Walter Reed Army Institute of Research in Washington, D.C. There, he conducted research on respiratory viruses. Hilleman en-

tered the field at an exciting time—the capabilities of the electron microscope had recently improved, enabling biologists to directly study small organisms, such as viruses, for the first time. Hilleman discovered that the flu virus underwent some small mutations every year. The changes, called a "drift," were so small that people who had been infected with a previous version of the strain were still naturally immune to the new virus. But Hilleman also discovered that every so often, the flu virus underwent a major genetic change, rendering it so different from previous ones that people had no immunity. This was labeled a "shift."

Prepared U.S. for Flu Pandemic

In April of 1957, Hilleman read in the *New York Times* about a flu outbreak in Hong Kong that had affected 250,000 people. At once he realized the flu virus had probably undergone that major shift. Hilleman believed a similar shift had occurred in 1918, launching the Spanish flu pandemic that killed 20 million people worldwide, including roughly 600,000 U.S. citizens. Looking back at the 1918 death-rate data, Hilleman predicted the new virus would cause more than a million U.S. deaths once it hit the continent.

To check his theory, Hilleman ordered the military to get throat swabs from the Hong Kong victims. After receiving the samples, Hilleman and his colleagues worked 14–hour days for more than a week to isolate what Hilleman believed was a new strain of flu. Next, the team analyzed blood samples taken from people worldwide and found that no one had antibodies to this form of the flu. This proved Hilleman's hypothesis—it was a new strain, which meant it could kill millions. Hilleman knew the flu would eventually spread to the United States so he sent vaccine manufacturers samples of the new strain. The labs made it ready for use by growing it in fertilized chicken eggs, thus weakening it and making it ready for human inoculation. One company, Merck & Company, went through 150,000 eggs per day.

When the flu did hit the United States the following fall, 40 million doses of the vaccine were ready and distributed, saving probably hundreds of thousands of lives. The U.S. death toll still hit 69,000. Fifty years later, public–health agencies creating the annual flu vaccine still use Hilleman's discoveries concerning virus mutations. While preparing for the pandemic, Hilleman left Walter Reed and joined Merck on New Year's Eve in 1957 to run its viral research program. Merck had offices and labs in West Point, Pennsylvania, and Whitehouse Station, New Jersey.

Developed Mumps, Other Vaccines

In the 1960s, Hilleman developed the mumps vaccine, thanks in large part to his daughter's infection. In 1963, five–year–old Jeryl Lynn woke her father in the middle of the night, whining about a sore throat. Seeing her swollen glands, Hilleman realized it was the mumps, a disease caused by a virus that grows in the salivary glands. At the time mumps was common, infecting about 200,000 U.S. children a year. Of those, about half developed a mild form of meningitis, an infection of the brain. Sometimes, the meningitis caused permanent deafness or death.

Hilleman saw opportunity in his daughter's suffering. Though it was the middle of the night, he drove to his Merck lab to pick up some swabs. He then swabbed his daughter's throat and preserved the virus in some beef broth in the freezer. Hilleman had been eager to collect the virus because he was leaving on a trip to South America the following day and knew the virus would be gone by the time he returned.

Later, Hilleman isolated the mumps virus from the swabs. Next, he took chicken embryo cells and grew the virus in it to produce what is called an attenuated form of the virus. An attenuated virus is weak enough that it will not cause the disease, but strong enough to force the body into using its natural defenses to trigger immunity. Making the mumps vaccine took several years; it was not available until 1967. Hilleman's other daughter, Kirsten, participated in the trials.

Hilleman also developed vaccines for measles, rubella, chickenpox, bacterial meningitis, flu, and hepatitis B. In developed countries, his vaccines have virtually wiped out many of these once–common childhood maladies. Of the fourteen vaccinations routinely recommended for youngsters, Hilleman developed eight. "Over his career he certainly contributed more vaccines than anyone, and probably more than anyone will ever contribute," Merck colleague Roy Vagelos told the *Lancet's* Ivan Oransky. "I don't know how many people will have been spared a disease because of the vaccines he developed, but it's a lot."

Another breakthrough came in 1971 when Merck released Hilleman's new MMR vaccine, a one–shot injection that protects children from measles, mumps, and rubella. Another crowning achievement was Hilleman's development of a vaccine for hepatitis B, a debilitating blood–borne virus. Because one complication of hepatitis B is hepatoma, a liver cancer, his vaccine was hailed as the first to prevent a human cancer. It hit the market in 1981.

Besides developing vaccines to eradicate human diseases, Hilleman also developed vaccines for the poultry industry. In 1971, Hilleman introduced a vaccine for Marek's disease, a virus that causes lymphoma in chickens, at one time causing millions of dollars in losses each year. In addition, Hilleman is credited with co–discovering numerous viruses, including the hepatitis A virus and the rhinoviruses that cause colds.

Left Mark on Medical World

Though Hilleman retired from Merck in 1984, he continued office hours and consulted with national and international public health organizations until his death. He continued working, believing vaccines for malaria, tuberculosis and AIDS were necessary.

According to colleagues, Hilleman was an enigma of sorts. The six–foot–one–inch scientist was known to punctuate his sentences with country–boy obscenities. Hilleman also made peers nervous because, unlike many scientists, he insisted in watching over all stages of a project, managing basic research, clinical research, and even development and production. After vaccine trials, Hilleman frequently popped into the manufacturing facility to ensure quality control. "I ran into conflict with just about everybody," Hilleman told *Nature Journal's* Alan Dove. Asked if anyone else could have had as successful a career, he said no. "It takes somebody who's a bastard," Hilleman conceded. "I don't think there are basically any people at all left who would have the dedication."

Hilleman died of cancer at a Philadelphia hospital on April 11, 2005. His first wife, Thelma Mason, preceded him in death in 1962. He was survived by two daughters, as well as his second wife, Lorraine Witmer, whom he married in 1963. Though Hilleman remained loyal to his work, his second wife said he always made it home for family dinner each night, even if it meant driving back to the lab later on.

Because of Hilleman's achievements, human life expectancy has grown by leaps and bounds. Speaking to the *Philadelphia Inquirer's* Susan FitzGerald shortly after Hilleman's death, Paul A. Offit, chief of infectious diseases at Children's Hospital of Philadelphia, said: "It's safe to say his vaccines save in the order of eight million lives a year. I think it can be said without hyperbole that he was a scientist who saved more lives than any other modern scientist."

Periodicals

Economist, April 23, 2005.
Immunological Reviews, August 1999.
Independent (London), April 20, 2005.
New York Times, April 12, 2005.
Philadelphia Inquirer, April 12, 2005.

Online

"The Man Who Saved Your Life," New Jersey Association for Biomedical Research, http://www.njabr.org/njsor/science_superstars/maurice_hilleman/printer/ (December 31, 2005).
"Maurice Hilleman," *Nature Medicine,* http://www.nature.com/nm/journal/v11/n4s/full/nm1223.html (December 31, 2005).
"Maurice R. Hilleman," *The Lancet,* http://www.thelancet.com (December 31, 2005). □

Ishiro Honda

Japanese filmmaker Ishiro Honda (1911-1993) directed 44 films and served as assistant director on several more, including some of the classics of modern Japanese cinema. But he is known above all for one film: *Godzilla,* the 1954 release that became the king of all monster movies.

*G*odzilla was an international smash and even spawned an entire Japanese film genre, *kaiju-eiga,* or monster films. Honda became a celebrity in Japan for *Godzilla* and a host of sequels he directed, each of them, in the opinions of many critics, more ridiculous than the last. Yet despite the popularity of the original *Godzilla,* Americans knew the film only in a drastically altered version until a restored version was released in the United States in 2004. That restoration clearly revealed Honda's intention to make an anti-nuclear statement with *Godzilla,* an aspect mostly lost when the film was re-cut for McCarthy-era American audiences. It became clear that the strange power of the *Godzilla* films, despite their often second-class production values, resided in a subtext of violence and war, phenomena with which Honda had been quite familiar in his own life.

Watched Film Industry Grow

Honda (whose first name was often misspelled "Inoshiro") in Western publications, was born in Yamagata Prefecture, Japan, on May 7, 1911. His father was a Buddhist priest. The young Honda loved to go to see silent films, at first because he was fascinated by the *benshi,* the live narrators who were distinctive to silent film in Japan. As he grew older, however, he began to think in career terms about his love of movies. "I watched movie theaters being built and regular theaters being turned into movie theaters, and eventually I realized there could be a pretty well-paying future for me in the business," he said in a *Tokyo Journal* interview quoted on the Godzilla Shrine website. "It all came together. I enjoyed telling stories and could find work in an industry that was financially successful and artistic to boot."

At first, Honda enrolled at Nihon (or Nippon) University as an art student, but he soon signed up for a film apprenticeship program run by PCL (Photography Chemistry Laboratory), a studio that was an ancestor of the Japanese postwar moviemaking giant Toho. Honda did well in the program and was working as a cameraman by 1933, before he graduated. He made two key contacts and friendships at PCL. One, Kajiro Yamamoto, was a director and film teacher who inspired a number of younger Japanese filmmakers. Honda rose in the PCL hierarchy and remained with the company as it was absorbed into Toho. He worked as an assistant director for Yamamoto in the late 1930s and early 1940s on such films as *Uma* (Horses, 1941). The other important acquaintance Honda met at PCL was Akira Kurosawa, considered one of the greatest directors in Japanese history. Honda and Kurosawa met in 1937.

By that time, Honda had been drafted into the Japanese army and sent to China to participate in Japan's invasion of that country. He served three tours of duty as an infantryman, returning to Tokyo in between tours to resume his film career. On one of these trips, he met his wife Kimi, a Toho script assistant who would play an active role in his career, often discussing his films with him as they were made. They raised a son and daughter. Honda kept a close watch on new developments in Japanese film, and he was impressed by the special effects in a 1942 Japanese war film called *The War at Sea from Hawaii to Malaya.* The following year, he worked for the first time with the earlier film's special effects coordinator, Eiji Tsuburaya, as the two assisted Yamamoto on *Kato's Flying Action Forces.* They did not get along at first, as Tsuburaya criticized the way Honda had staged a shot of some model fighter planes. But it was the beginning of a famous partnership.

While serving in the military in China, Honda often had a fear of being ambushed by a large crowd, and that image showed up as a motif in many of his films. In 1945 his fears were realized as he was seized and held as a prisoner of war for more than a year. He heard about the dropping of two atomic bombs on Japan from his prison cell. Released after Japan's surrender, he returned home and worked for a variety of studios.

Assisted Kurosawa on *Stray Dog*

In 1949 Honda was reunited with Kurosawa and signed on as assistant director for Kurosawa's *Stray Dog,* a police drama starring frequent Kurosawa collaborator Toshiro Mifune. "I had Honda do mainly second-unit shooting," Kurosawa recalled in his book *Something Like an Autobiography* (as quoted in the *Independent*). "Every day I told him what I wanted and he would go out into the ruins of postwar Tokyo to film it. There are few men as honest and reliable as Honda. He faithfully brought back exactly the footage I requested, so almost everything he shot was used in the final cut of the film. I'm often told that I captured the atmosphere of postwar Japan very well in *Stray Dog,* and if so I owe a great deal of that success to Honda." Honda also made two documentaries around 1950.

Successful work like this led to Honda's being given the chance, by the Toho studio, to step behind the cameras himself for a major studio release. His first feature film, 1951's *Blue Pearl,* was about female pearl divers. He became the first Japanese director to film underwater, and the unusual movie was well received. Among the five films Honda made over the next two years was *The Man Who Came to Port* (1952), which likewise had an exotic environment: set among Japanese whalers, it involved a sequence set at the South Pole. Eiji Tsuburaya, with whom Honda was now collaborating, did not film on location but simulated the Antarctic environment by using rear-screen projection. Honda and Tsuburaya reunited for the war film *Eagle of the Pacific* (1953), and they worked together again on the romantic war story *Farewell, Rabaul* the following year.

Honda's participation in *Godzilla,* known in Japan as *Gojiro,* came about almost by accident; he had been slated to direct another film called *Sanshiro the Priest,* but plans for that film fell through and he was moved to *Godzilla,* the idea for which had been hatched by Tsuburaya. The movie features an unstoppable dinosaur that had languished in hibernation since the era of the dinosaurs' extinction but is awakened and mysteriously strengthened by a hydrogen bomb test explosion. Godzilla is first seen attacking a small fishing boat—a scene with strong resonances for Japanese audiences who had just recently heard about the illnesses of Japanese fishermen who had found themselves too close to the American H-bomb tests at Bikini Atoll in the Pacific.

More generally, Godzilla was seen as a symbol of the atomic bomb. Honda himself, as quoted by Brent Staples of the *New York Times,* said that he conceived of the fire-breathing dinosaur as a way of "making radiation visible," and he hoped to make an explicitly anti-nuclear statement. "Believe it or not, we naively hoped that the end of Godzilla was going to coincide with the end of nuclear testing," he was quoted as saying by Staples. The famous scenes of Godzilla rampaging through Tokyo are primitive by modern special-effects standards, but they made a strong impact in a country that had experienced total devastation just nine years earlier. The film became a huge hit, and analytical articles in mainstream publications discussed the film for decades afterward in Japan.

Drew on Wartime Experiences

Honda was in many ways the ideal choice to direct *Godzilla*. In making the film he drew not on Japan's rich tradition of fantasy but on the plain, unsentimental style of military dramas, and on his own impressions of World War II. "Most of the visual images I got were from my war experience," he was quoted as saying on the Godzilla Shrine website. "After the war, all of Japan, as well as Tokyo, was left in ashes. . . . If Godzilla had been a big ancient dinosaur or some other animal, he would have been killed by just one cannonball. But if he were equal to an atomic bomb, we wouldn't know what to do. So, I took the characteristics of an atomic bomb and applied them to Godzilla."

Until the re-release of the original in 2004, *Godzilla* was seen only in a distorted form in the U.S., with an entire new character, a reporter played by Raymond Burr, added in and most of the references to the nuclear menace excised. Nevertheless, enough of the compelling quality of the film remained to make *Godzilla* a reference point in American popular culture. The film's sequels were dubbed into English as quickly as Honda could make them and were staples of American movie theaters and then late-night television for decades.

The high point of the monster craze Honda created came in the 1960s. He introduced another memorable monster with Mothra in 1961, pitting monsters against each other in *King Kong vs. Godzilla* (1962), *Mothra vs. Godzilla* (1964), and *Godzilla vs. Monster Zero* (1965). Later Godzilla films were straight monster movies, lacking the nuclear commentary. Occasionally Honda rebelled against filling the Godzilla-director slot for Toho, making the romantic comedy *Come Marry Me* in 1966. He refused to direct Godzilla films when he did not like the scripts, taking a break from filmmaking completely in the 1970s. "I'm not sure if the success of the Godzilla movies was a good thing or not," Kimi Honda was quoted as saying on the Godzilla Shrine website. "They were so popular that Mr. Honda became trapped. He had to work on them." Honda was a favorite among Japanese film-industry people, some of whom wished he could be given the chance to work on more artistic projects.

Honda got that chance to a degree in 1980 after several years of working in television (directing episodes of such series as *Return of Ultraman*) and returning to the Godzilla series in 1975 with *Terror of MechaGodzilla*, a film centered on a robot Godzilla double. He reunited with his old friend Kurosawa, becoming assistant director on some of the Japanese master's most acclaimed films; *Kagemusha* (1980), *Ran* (1985), *Dreams* (1990), *Rhapsody in August*, (1991), and *Madadayo* (1992). He directed a segment of *Dreams*, a set of eight short stories; Honda's section was a fantasy sequence in which a man meets figures from Japan's military past in a tunnel. It was perhaps as close as Honda came

to returning to his wartime experiences as a filmmaker. He died of respiratory failure in Tokyo on February 28, 1993, and was honored at a memorial service crowded with hundreds of his cinematic associates and capped by a eulogy from Kurosawa. Despite his ambivalent attitude toward his most famous creation in later life, he considered *Godzilla* his greatest film, and as the monster's second half-century of existence began it was still his most familiar creation. The Godzilla Series rolled on with the release of *Godzilla: Final Wars* in 2004.

Periodicals

Daily Yomoiuri (Japan), March 2, 1993.
Guardian (London, England), March 5, 1993.
Independent (London, England), March 3, 1993.
New York Times, May 1, 2005, section 4.
Times (London, England), March 12, 1993.

Online

"Ishiro Honda," Godzilla Shrine, http://wwww.gojira.20m.com ./ishiro_honda.htm (January 5, 2006).
"Ishiro Honda," Internet Movie Database, http://www.imdb .com/name/nm0393094/bio (January 5, 2006).
"Ishiro Honda," Kaiju Headquarters, http://www.kaijuhq.org/ directors.html (January 5, 2006). □

Ödön von Horváth

Hungarian writer Ödön von Horváth (1901-1938) captured in his novels and plays the degradation of language and the bitterness of lower-middle-class life that preceded the emergence of Nazism. Well known in German-speaking countries, he is regarded as a writer who saw fascism coming and grasped the underlying social trends that produced it.

A few of Horváth's works deal directly with the early fascist era; two of the novels he wrote at the end of his short life were widely translated and read as the clouds of world war gathered. His 17 plays, however, are seen only occasionally outside of the German linguistic sphere, for they are uniquely difficult to translate. This difficulty stems from the most characteristic feature of Horváth's work—his fascination with, and frequently satirical attitude toward, the speech patterns of common people. That was a trait Horváth shared with another German-language dramatist of his time, Bertolt Brecht, although in other respects the works of the two are very different. In Germany today Horváth and Brecht are regarded as the two greatest dramatists of the era between the world wars.

Had Multilingual Upbringing

Horváth was born on December 9, 1901, in the city of Fiume, on the Adriatic Sea at the southern extremity of what was then the Austro-Hungarian Empire and is now Rijeka, Croatia. Horváth's father was an Austro-Hungarian

and in Paris. He moved to Berlin, the freewheeling German capital and the center of German intellectual life, in 1924.

Horváth made friends among German creative figures such as Carl Zuckmayer, who encouraged his attempts to write. For several years he worked for a nonprofit group, the German League for Human Rights. This stint gave him raw materials for his creative works, as did his habit of spending time on the fringes of society—he liked to sit and write in cafés frequented by circus performers, for example. Horváth's first major play, *Die Bergbahn* (The Mountain Railroad), was begun in 1927 and premiered in 1929. It was based on real-life labor strife that broke out after several workers died while building a cable-car system in the Bavarian mountains.

His next play, *Zur schönen Aussicht* (The Pleasant View Hotel), featured a group of shady characters hiding out in a cheap hotel. From this point on, Horváth would set his works mostly among petit-bourgeois or lower-middle-class people whom he treated satirically but not unsympathetically. His female characters, especially, were depicted as being forced to select from among bad choices in a corrupt society. Horváth's plays drew on the tradition of the *Volksstück* or folk play—a genre with a long German-language history featuring scenes of small town life. Horváth, however, turned the genre inside out in order to show what he saw as the negative influences of mass culture. His plays were often funny, and Krishna Winston, writing in the *Massachusetts Review,* likened them to the 1970s television series *All in the Family.* The malapropisms and bigotry of *All in the Family*'s Archie Bunker could have come out of the mouth of a character in one of Horváth's plays, but, like the writers of *All in the Family,* Horváth did not condemn his characters but rather the society in which they lived. His characters spoke in what Horváth called *Bildungsjargon*—an "educated jargon" filled with mass-media clichés and, increasingly, extreme nationalism.

Sharpened Satire as Political Situation Deteriorated

Horváth wrote a novel called *Der ewige Spiesser* (The Eternal Philistine) in 1930, tracing the adventures of a rather crass car dealer and a journalist as they travel around Europe. He hit his stride as a dramatist in the early 1930s, just as Germany, having suffered through defeat in World War I and then through waves of crippling inflation and economic depression, was becoming polarized between leftist and fascist extremes. Sometimes Horváth's plays reflected political realities directly. His 1931 play *Italienische Nacht* (Italian Night) was a farce with dark undertones, depicting a clash between leftist and rightist social clubs in a Bavarian village. A fascist critic later took note of Horváth's stance of ridicule toward the Nazi party and warned that he was in for a surprise, but the play was a hit and won Horváth a major theatrical honor, the Kleist Prize.

More and more often, politics lurked under the surface in Horváth's writing. His 1931 play *Geschichte aus dem Wiener Wald,* with its title parodying that of a famous Johann Strauss waltz, eviscerated the sentimental myth of Old Vienna with its unflattering portrayals of the city's

diplomat, and his mother was of Czech background. Speaking mostly German at home, Horváth became fluent or near-fluent in a large number of languages: German, Hungarian, Serbo-Croatian, Czech, Yiddish, French, and Latin. His family moved frequently from place to place; his father was sent to Munich, Germany, in 1909, but Horváth went to an Episcopal church school in Budapest until 1913. He spent three years in school in Munich, often arguing with a religiously oriented teacher, and his academic career worsened when he was sent to school in Pressburg (now Bratislava, Slovakia) and was almost expelled after writing a satirical essay that pilloried his professors. Adding to the instability of his life was the upheaval of World War I; he was quoted as saying in a *Dictionary of Literary Biography* essay that "my life begins with the declaration of war. . . . The World War darkened our youth, and we hardly have any childhood memories."

Horváth passed high school exams in Vienna after the war. His parents had bought a house in the mountain resort town of Murnau, and he enrolled at the University of Munich in 1920. Theater classes interested him, but he was a mostly indifferent student, throwing himself into side projects such as a pantomime play a student composer asked him to write. Five hundred copies of the play, titled *Das Buch der Tänze* (The Book of Dances), were printed, but Horváth later bought them all up and destroyed them. He also wrote satirical short stories for the magazine *Simplizissimus.* In 1922 he dropped out of school without finishing and spent time at his parents' house in Murnau, modern-day citizens; it, too, was a hit in Berlin, and Horváth emerged as one of Germany's best-known playwrights. His 1932 play *Kasimir und Karoline* brought his adult home town of Munich in for similar treatment; set entirely during the city's famous Oktoberfest, it is centered on a dysfunctional couple that breaks up amid the festivities.

Horváth wrote one more play in the *Volksstück* vein; *Glaube Liebe Hoffnung* (Faith, Hope, and Charity) was slated to be performed in Berlin in late 1932 and dealt with a woman who tries to sell her body to medical researchers. But as Adolf Hitler seized power in the first months of 1933, Horváth's situation quickly changed. His plays were banned in Germany and he was harassed by German police. The fact that he was a Hungarian national bought him some time, and he emigrated to Salzburg, Austria, and then made his way to Vienna, where some of his plays were produced in small underground theaters. While there he married a German Jewish singer, Maria Elsner. They divorced in 1934, and it is thought that the marriage had been undertaken in order to help Elsner gain Hungarian citizenship and evade German persecution.

At the beginning of the Nazi era, Horváth, along with other German writers, hoped that Hitler's government would not last. Horváth returned to Germany, wrote some uncontroversial movie scripts, and kept a close watch on developments. After police ransacked the Horváth family home in Murnau, however, he left Germany for good, settling in Vienna. He continued to write and to try to stage his plays in German-speaking areas of Austria and Czechoslovakia. Two of his plays of the mid-1930s, *Figaro lässt sich scheiden* (Figaro Gets a Divorce) and *Don Juan kommt aus dem Krieg,* transplanted characters from Mozart's operas into chaotic modern situations. Horváth's plays of the 1930s remained mostly unpublished until much later; cut off from German audiences, he was marginalized in the theatrical world.

Wrote Anti-Nazi Novel

Partly as a result, Horváth turned to writing fiction once again. In a six-month burst at the end of 1937 he wrote two novels, *Jugend ohne Gott* (Youth Without God) and *Ein Kind unserer Zeit* (A Child of Our Time). *Jugend ohne Gott* appeared in English, French, Dutch, Spanish, and Chinese. One English translation had the title *The Age of the Fish,* taken from a scrap of dialogue in the novel in which a minor character says, "Cold times are coming—the age of the fish. In these times, the human soul will become immovable, like the face of a fish." The novel's central figure is a schoolteacher who hears Nazi slogans coming out of the mouths of his students, and becomes embroiled in a murder committed at a paramilitary training camp. One of the first writings that dealt with the experiences of ordinary people under fascism, the novel gained a wide readership in the West; its importation into Germany was banned, even though Horváth did not refer specifically anywhere in the book to the German state.

The link between fascism and the power of the mass media was a major theme in *Jugend ohne Gott,* as the teacher observes the way in which radio and newspapers

shape the thinking of his students. The same theme echoes through *Ein Kind unserer Zeit,* the "child" of whose title is a soldier whose thinking is deformed by repetitive Nazi ideas. Winston referred to the continued relevance of Horváth's writing, noting that "thanks to television, our expression and our thoughts are increasingly dominated by advertising catch phrases, news clichés, technical jargon, political slogans, sports terminology, and other elements of prefabricated speech."

As German troops overran Austria in March of 1938, Horváth was forced to flee once again. He stayed briefly with a friend in Czechoslovakia and then made his way to Amsterdam in the Netherlands by way of Hungary, Italy, Switzerland, France, and Belgium. Plans were discussed for an American film version of *Jugend ohne Gott,* and Horváth spoke of moving to neutral Switzerland to work on a new book. Horváth visited a fortune-teller in Amsterdam, and she is said to have told him that in Paris, at the end of May, he would experience the greatest adventure of his life. Horváth avoided leaving his Paris hotel room for several days in late May, but when he went out on June 1, 1938, he was caught in a freak thunderstorm and killed by a falling tree branch.

Horváth's works were mostly forgotten for two decades after his death. When a younger generation of writers began to investigate the roots of German fascism, however, his work was rediscovered and the mix of anti-fascism and Christian humanist elements in his later works, which stood in contrast to the socialism of Brecht, was appreciated anew. *Jugend ohne Gott* was often assigned to German students, and even in translation, Horváth's work found new admirers. *Kasimir und Karoline* was staged in a new production in New York in 2005.

Books

Dictionary of Literary Biography, Volume 85: Austrian Fiction Writers After 1914, Gale, 1989.
Dictionary of Literary Biography, Volume 124: Twentieth-Century German Dramatists, 1919-1992, Gale, 1992.
Four Plays by Ödön von Horváth, introduction by Martin Esslin, PAJ, 1986.
Huish, Ian, *Horváth: A Study,* Heinemann, 1980.
International Dictionary of Theatre, Volume 2: Playwrights, St. James, 1993.

Periodicals

Massachusetts Review, Spring 1978.

Online

"Ödön von Horváth," Schlossmuseum Murnau, http://www .schlossmuseum-murnau.de/Rundgang7.htm (February 21, 2006). □

Ada Louise Huxtable

Ada Louise Huxtable (born 1921), chief architecture critic of the *New York Times* from 1963 to 1982, has been a consistent and sharp-edged advocate for high

always loved cities; I've always been concerned about them. I like buildings and think of them as the cultural and historical roots of a city." For much of her youth, Huxtable lived in an apartment building on posh Central Park West. The seeds of her future interest in historical preservation were sown, perhaps, when she had to move out of an East Side building because it was slated to be torn down.

Attending Hunter College (now part of the City University of New York), Huxtable majored in art and architecture history and she graduated *magna cum laude* in 1941. She went on for graduate study in those fields at the Institute of Fine Arts, a division of New York University. Working as a furniture display assistant and salesperson at Bloomingdale's department store during the Museum of Modern Art's Organic Design furniture competition, she got a taste of cutting-edge design. In 1942 she married industrial designer L. Garth Huxtable. The two often worked together; Garth Huxtable brought a sense of nuts-and-bolts reality to his wife's otherwise quite ideological columns, and Huxtable opened up contacts that helped make her husband well known in his field. Under severe time pressure the pair created a set of 140 tableware items for the restaurant in New York's famed Seagram's building, a landmark structure designed by Mies van der Rohe and Philip Johnson.

Huxtable continued to study at the Institute of Fine Arts, but her coursework tailed off after she found a job in her field as assistant curator of architecture and design at New York's Museum of Modern Art in 1946. "I never set myself a course or an ambition or a career," she told F. Paul Driscoll of *Opera News.* "One thing sort of led to another." She wrote exhibition display texts, helped to set up exhibitions, including one in her field of Italian design, and worked on scholarly articles. In 1950 Huxtable received a Fulbright fellowship and left the Museum of Modern Art to go to Italy for further design and architecture studies. Her fellowship was renewed in 1952, and she remained in Italy for another two years.

Back in New York City, Huxtable wrote freelance articles about architecture for both academic and general interest publications. She worked on a book about Pier Luigi Nervi, an Italian architect and engineer, finishing it with the help of a prestigious Guggenheim fellowship in 1958. The book was well reviewed when it appeared in 1960, but Huxtable was becoming disenchanted with the limited reach of scholarly writing. "It's nonsense just to write scholarly papers for other scholars," she said in a *House Beautiful* interview quoted in *Contemporary Authors.* When she was writing for a newspaper audience, she said, "I'm not selling pretty or ugly buildings. I'm dealing with the environment."

Pioneered Newspaper Architecture Criticism

Some newspapers, including the *New York Times,* included writing about architecture in the early 1960s, but it appeared on an irregular basis and was generally relegated to the advertising-heavy real estate section. In 1962 the *Times* was in need of an architecture writer because part-time contributor Aline Loucheim had married top architect Eero Saarinen, and thus was thought to have a conflict of

standards in architecture and urban design. Her books and her often-collected newspaper columns reflect a passionate concern with the urban environment of her native New York, a keen eye for history as manifested in buildings, and a strong belief in historic preservation at a time when the concept was still fairly new.

Huxtable's pen had an acid tip. Some real estate developers, she admitted to Marilyn Hoffman of the *Christian Science Monitor,* considered her to be "public enemy No. 1," and others "would be glad to have my head on a platter." Even Huxtable's admirers conceded that she sometimes had a too-opinionated streak and yet her detractors conceded that she was ardently devoted to the cause of good design. Something of an intellectual in action, Huxtable had an impressive record of saving landmark buildings from demolition, and lovers of New York City's classic streetscapes have much to thank her for.

Home Demolished

Huxtable was born Ada Louise Landman on March 14, 1921, in New York City, and has remained a lifelong resident there. Her father, Michael Louis Landman, was a doctor. It appeared that, from a very young age, Huxtable knew what career path she would eventually take. She recalled to Hoffman, "I seemed to have a sense of urbanization and of building from the time I began to have reactions at all. I have interest. Loucheim recommended Huxtable to Sunday *Times* editor Lester Markel. When Huxtable joined the *Times* staff in 1963, she became the first full-time architecture writer in American newspaper journalism. In the words of Carole Rifkind, writing in *Metropolis,* Huxtable "virtually created architectural journalism in America."

Huxtable believed that she filled a need. "People are better informed about art" than about architecture, she reflected to Driscoll. "They are capable of understanding art in a way that they do not understand architecture. People will look at a building and say, 'What's good about that?' Well, what's 'good' starts with purpose and structure, with expressiveness, with how creative the architect is in taking the bones of a building and turning it into a concept of some originality, or something exquisitely proportioned." Huxtable, who wrote her columns in longhand, required some time to get used to the fast pace of a daily newspaper, but once she hit her stride, her polemical columns often were placed on the front page.

A typical Huxtable column, quoted in *Newsweek,* bemoaned the cookie-cutter suburban developments that were springing up along New York's edges. "The promise of . . . a new, improved suburbia in the greater metropolitan area, the dreams of beauty and better living are mired in mud," Huxtable wrote. New "ugly and expensive" developments on Staten Island "could not be better calculated to destroy the countryside if . . . planned by enemy action." Huxtable's take-no-prisoners style garnered her a host of awards in the late 1960s, including a Front Page award from the Newspaper Women's Club of New York in 1965 and a medal for architectural criticism from the American Institute of Architects in 1969. By no means a curmudgeon, Huxtable also praised monuments of modern architecture by the likes of I.M. Pei and Robert Venturi. She was at her most effective when advocating for the preservation of historic structures, during an era when historic-district zoning was still far in the future. Her campaign to save the original 1903 Pennsylvania Station train terminal was unsuccessful (although a part of the building was incorporated into the new design), but she was credited with prodding the city government to implement new preservation statutes.

In 1973 Huxtable moved from the third floor of the *Times* offices to the tenth and joined the paper's editorial board, becoming only the second woman named to that body. A testimonial dinner held in her honor featured speeches even from some of the architects she had severely criticized. *Times* editor John B. Oakes, quoted in the *New Yorker,* gave attendees a glimpse of Huxtable's self-assured personality, describing her as "unpredictable, perhaps; uncontrollable, certainly; unerring in her aim; undeviating in her standards; unshaken in her principles; undaunted in her courage; and, I might add, unflinching in her attack on the editor who dares to tamper with her copy. You think this frail little wisp of a woman needs protection? Try to cut a line from a Huxtable editorial and, as one of her former colleagues once observed, you'll find she needs protection like Attila the Hun."

Received MacArthur "Genius" Grant

Huxtable's best columns of the 1960s were collected into a book called *Will They Ever Finish Bruckner Boulevard?* in 1970, and she retained her loyal following through three more essay collections, *Kicked a Building Lately?* (1976), *Architecture, Anyone?* (1986), and *Goodbye History, Hello Hamburger* (also 1986). Despite her tendency toward sharp critique she could also be optimistic; *Kicked a Building Lately?* recounted some of the successes of the historic preservation movement. She deplored, however, the ways in which a city could milk a historic district for maximum profit, which had the effect of "canning" it (as she was quoted as saying in *Metropolis*)—sealing it off from the surrounding landscape. Her *Times* columns were as avidly read as ever. In 1981, however, Huxtable received a major award that changed the course of her career: the MacArthur Foundation fellowship (popularly known as a "genius grant") was a no-strings-attached $200,000 cash award (later increased to $500,000) designed to allow creative individuals to pursue their ideas unfettered by financial concerns. Huxtable left the *Times* in 1982 and began writing full-time.

Huxtable's 1984 book *The Tall Building Artistically Reconsidered: The Search for a Skyscraper Style* was both a history of the skyscraper and an appreciation of its numerous practitioners of the 1950s and 1960s. Huxtable admired the spare glass boxes of such architects as Holland's Mies van der Rohe, and she disparaged the more playful postmodern style that followed it. In her 1997 book *The Unreal America: Architecture and Illusion,* Huxtable trained her rhetorical fire directly on postmodernism in a broad-based commentary, examining large projects such as colonial Williamsburg and Disneyland, and arguing that architects and designers were leading Americans to prefer illusion over reality.

The profusion of neo-traditional housing developments such as the Disney Corporation's model town of Celebration, Florida, came in for a healthy dose of Huxtable scorn. In her attack on postmodernism, however, Huxtable was swimming against the intellectual tides of the 1990s, for modernism had rapidly fallen out of favor. *The Unreal America* attracted some negative reviews, including one in the *New York Times* itself and another in *Architecture,* in which Diane Ghirardo opined that "Huxtable's quintessentially elitist perspective recognizes no possible alternative: Elitist culture is the best; everything else is but a pale reflection." Other critics continued to praise Huxtable, however, and she did express admiration for some contemporary architects, including Frank Gehry.

As the century turned, Huxtable was as active as ever. She served on the jury for the annual Pritzker Architecture Prize. An opera fan, she was a familiar figure at cultural events in New York City. In 1997 she began to write newspaper architecture columns once again, this time for the *Wall Street Journal,* and in 2004 she published *Frank Lloyd Wright,* a biographical study of the iconoclastic American architect, a commentary on his work, and an attempt to link his unusual life story with his career. Living in an apartment on Park Avenue in Manhattan, Huxtable roosted atop the world of American architecture writing.

Periodicals

Architecture, May 1997.
Booklist, November 1, 2004.
Christian Science Monitor, April 9, 1969.
Newsweek, August 23, 1965.
New Yorker, December 17, 1973.
Opera News, July 1999.
Smithsonian, June 1987.

Online

"Faking It," *Metropolis,* http://www.metropolismag.com/html/
    content_0198/ja98hux.htm (January 21, 2006).
"L. Garth Huxtable: Design Work in the 1950s," http://www
    .public.coe.edu/~rroeder/huxtable/1950s.htm (January 21,
    2006). □

Flo Hyman

Flo Hyman (1954-1986), acknowledged as the best female volleyball player of her time, was the U.S. face of the sport as it evolved from recreational to highly competitive. "Hyman was known for her awe-inspiring spiking abilities, her equally strong defensive skills, and her personal integrity and charisma," Nancy Foley wrote in *Sports Illustrated for Women.* Hyman helped lead the United States to a silver medal in the 1984 Summer Olympic Games; less than two years later, while playing professionally in Japan, Hyman collapsed and died at age 31 of the congenital heart disorder Marfan syndrome.

Raised in Inglewood, California

Hyman, who was born on July 29, 1954, grew up in the Los Angeles suburb of Inglewood, California, and graduated from Morningside High School. Her father, George W., was a railroad janitor and her mother, Warrene, owned a café. She played basketball and ran track and field for Morningside High but did not play competitive volleyball until reaching her full height—six-foot-five. She did, however, play in volleyball tournaments at the beach with her older sister.

University of Houston coach Ruth Nelson was impressed with Hyman's play on a club team, and awarded her the first female athletic scholarship at the school; Hyman, having overcome adolescent doubts about her height, became a three-time All-American volleyball player for the Cougars while majoring in mathematics and physical education.

She left college to join the fledgling—and struggling—national team in Colorado. It fared poorly in the 1964 and 1968 Summer Olympic Games, failed to qualify for the

Games in 1972 and 1976 and even operated for three months of 1975 without a coach until Polish-born Arie Selinger took over and stabilized the program after succeeding similarly in Israel. Hyman, hesitant at first about Selinger's style of aggressive play, ultimately embraced it. "We refused to disband," Hyman recalled. "As long as we stuck together, we were the national team." Selinger realized Hyman's leadership value. "If Flo plays well, the team follows," Selinger said, according to *HickokSports.com.*

Hyman helped steer U.S. volleyball to a fifth-place finish at the 1978 world championships after Selinger moved the team to the U.S. Olympic Training Center in Colorado Springs, Colorado. The United States qualified for the 1980 Olympics and was even considered a favorite to capture a gold medal, but Hyman and her teammates did not compete as President Jimmy Carter ordered a boycott of the Summer Games in Moscow over the Soviet Union's invasion of Afghanistan in December of 1979. The United States was one of 62 nations to do so.

Generated Worldwide Respect

In a run-up to the 1984 Summer Games in Los Angeles, Hyman excelled for the Americans in the 1980 and 1982 World Volleyball Championships. In between, she earned the best hitter, or spiker, award at the 1981 World Cup in Tokyo, Japan, which essentially ranked her among the world's six best volleyballers. "I had to learn to be honest with myself," Hyman said, according to Foley. "I had to recognize my pain threshold. When I hit the floor, I have to realize it's not as if I broke a bone. Pushing yourself over the barrier is a habit. I know I can do it and try something else crazy. If you want to win the war, you've got to pay the price."

Bob Beeten, the longtime director of the U.S. Olympic Sports Medicine and Research Center, told *Sports Illustrated* at the time that the volleyball players were among the strongest female athletes he had ever tested. "Fitter even than the track and field women, with the exception of the distance runners," Beeten said, as quoted by Jerry Crowe in the *Los Angeles Times.* Hyman drew respect from opponents, media, and other observers worldwide. "As that team became successful and one of the dominant teams in the world, she was the best player on the team. And she was the most recognized," former United States Volleyball Association Clifford McPeak told Crowe. "She was kind at heart, yet incredibly competitive on the court." Robert McG. Thomas, Jr., wrote in the *New York Times,* "Miss Hyman's spike shot was likened to a Julius Erving slam dunk, and her spin serve was compared to a Fernando Valenzuela screwball."

Silver Medal and Civil Rights

Hyman finally got her chance to compete in the Olympics in 1984, in her hometown. By then, corporate sponsorship and spectator interest was on the rise. She was the oldest female athlete at age 29, and called herself the "old lady" of the team, but impressed many with her power. She had earned the nickname "Clutchman" and could serve at speeds up to 100 miles per hour. "The audience would hold its breath when she rose for a spike," Joan Ackerman-

Blount wrote in *Sports Illustrated.* The United States defeated West Germany, Brazil, and China in Pool B competition, then toppled Peru in a semifinal match. China, however, defeated the Americans in a rematch for the gold medal, taking three of four sets. Still, the silver represented the first medal for U.S. women's volleyball. "The family was up in the stands, crying," Hyman's sister told George Vecsey in the *New York Times.* "But Florie came by and waved. You could see her smile. She was happy. She had reached her goal. She had played for a gold medal. I thought to myself, if she is happy, why am I crying?"

After the Olympics, Hyman joined civil rights leader Coretta Scott King, Democratic vice–presidential candidate Geraldine Ferraro and astronaut Sally Ride in lobbying for the Civil Rights Restoration Act and women's sports causes during the presidential election year. Hyman and Cheryl Miller, a basketball standout at the University of Southern California and later a broadcaster, testified on Capitol Hill in Washington on behalf of strengthening Title IX, the breakthrough 1972 legislation that prohibited sex discrimination by athletic programs in universities that receive federal funding. "Flo Hyman typifies the new generation of women athletes who emerged in the 1970s and 1980s," said an entry in African American National Biography.

Died During Match in Japan

With professional opportunities limited in the United States, Hyman moved to Japan, where corporate sponsors underwrote teams. She emerged as a star for Daiei, backed by the supermarket chain by that name. In two years, Daiei rose from third division to first division.

She had intended to return to the United States after 1986, but never got the chance. On January 24, 1986, after the third set of a match in Matsue City, about 380 miles northwest of Tokyo, Hyman collapsed on the bench and died at Matsue Red Cross Hospital of heart failure. She had "no measurable pulse" when she arrived, according to the *Los Angeles Times,* and despite placing Hyman on a respirator and giving her an external massage, emergency personnel could not revive her. Rita Crockett, Hyman's teammate for Daiei as well as the Olympic team, finished the match, unaware of Hyman's grave condition. "It was the third set, and Flo had just come off the court," said Marty Kuehnert, broadcaster, sports marketer and Hyman friend who was living in Tokyo. "She was sitting in the middle of the bench, cheering for her team, and she just keeled over," Kuehnert said of Hyman, according to the *Los Angeles Times.* "Flo had fainted in the past. Rita was told that Flo had just fainted, so she thought it was OK to continue to finish the match." According to Kuehnert, a team manager summoned Crockett off the bus. "Rita asked, 'Is Flo OK?' and the manager just started crying and shook his head no," Kuehnert said. Crockett told Selinger's wife, Aia, that Hyman had been playing well and nothing had seemed wrong on the court. "There wasn't anything strange about her health before the match," team director Yasuhiro Doi told the Associated Press, according to the *Los Angeles Times.* "She didn't have any health problems."

"Gone too soon. It's a story we've heard all too much in the general world and the sports world," Tony McLean wrote for the website *BlackAthlete.com.* "At the time of her death, Flo Hyman was arguably the best volleyball player in the world."

Awareness of Marfan Syndrome

Doctors attributed the death to Marfan syndrome, which caused an aortic rupture. In Hyman's case, it went undetected. According to the National Marfan Association website, others afflicted with the hereditary disease include former U.S. President Abraham Lincoln; Tony Award–winning playwright Jonathan Larson; actor Vincent Schiavelli; and former French President Charles de Gaulle. Despite Hyman's healthy appearance, the excessive stress of competitive sports had damaged her aorta. Hyman's brother, one of seven siblings she left, underwent treatment and survived, thanks to early detection.

Her death brought attention to a disease that was little known in the mid–1980s. About 20 years later, however, advocates still cited a need to promote awareness. According to Cheryl Wittenauer of the Associated Press, about 50,000 Americans had Marfan syndrome in 2005, and an additional 200,000 have related connective–tissue disorders. "Persons with Marfan syndrome typically are tall, thin, and lanky with long, thin fingers and toes," Wittenauer wrote. According to cardiologist Alan Braverman, director of the Marfan Syndrome Clinic in St. Louis, many victims have a curved spine or abnormal chest wall and a long, narrow face with deep eyes. "We want to diagnose and enhance awareness that a lifesaving treatment is available," Braverman said in Wittenauer's article.

Award Recognizes Hyman Legacy

The Women's Sports Foundation in 1987 established the annual Flo Hyman Award, which it announced on National Girls and Women in Sports Day "to a female athlete who captures Hyman's dignity, spirit and commitment to excellence," the foundation said on its website. Recipients have included Martina Navratilova, Chris Evert, and Monica Seles (tennis), Jackie Joyner–Kersee and Evelyn Ashford (track and field), Bonnie Blair and Kristi Yamaguchi (ice skating) and Lisa Leslie (basketball). "Hyman's inspirational life and untimely death spurred a women's sports movement in the United States to create new opportunities for women and girls in athletics, all in Hyman's name," the foundation said in a profile of Hyman on its web site. In that profile, Crockett said: "There has been nobody even to compare to her. Even to this day I've never seen anyone better," and Arie Selinger called her "The Goddess of Volleyball."

"To be true to one's self is the ultimate test in life," the foundation quoted Hyman as saying. "To have the courage and sensitivity to follow your hidden dreams and stand tall against the odds that are bound to fall in your path. Life is too short and precious to be dealt with in any other fashion. This thought I hold dear to my heart, and I always try to be true to myself and others that I encounter along the way."

"You can attribute the growth of volleyball in this country to a lot of things, but you've got to have stars.

You've got to have models at the top. And people all over this country know who Flo Hyman is and grow up wanting to be like her," McPeak told the *Los Angeles Times.* "She meant a lot to the sport of volleyball, not only in the United States, but all over the world. She was a real force in the growth of the sport in this country."

Periodicals

Associated Press Newswires, August 3, 2005.
Los Angeles Times, January 25, 1986.
New York Times, January 25, 1986.

Online

African American National Biography, Flo Hyman profile, http://www.fas.harvard.edu/~aanb/SHTML/sampleEntries .shtml#Sample05 (December 26, 2005).

Biography Resource Center, Flo Hyman profile, http://galenet .galegroup.com (December 16, 2005).
"Flora (Flo) Hyman, Volleyball," *Sports Illustrated for Women,* http://sportsillustrated.cnn.com/siforwomen/top_100/69/ (November 22, 2005).
HickokSports.com, Flo Hyman profile, http://www.hickoksports .com/biograph/hymanflo.shtml (November 22, 2005).
"Inspiration and Courage: A Look at the Life of Flo Hyman," Women's Sports Foundation Web site, http://www .womenssportsfoundation.org/cgi-bin/iowa/athletes/article .html?record=70 (December 26, 2005).
National Marfan Foundation Web site, http://www.marfan.org/ nmf/index.jsp (December 26, 2005).
"Volleyball Pioneer Flo Hyman," Black Athlete.com, March 17, 2004, http://www.blackathlete.com/Volleyball/index.shtml (November 22, 2005). □

Elsie Inglis

British physician Elsie Maude Inglis (1864-1917) was one of the first British female doctors. During World War I, she helped establish hospitals, staffed entirely by women, throughout Europe that cared for wounded soldiers. She was also an active suffragist who advocated for women's political freedom.

Inglis, the future British female physician and women's rights advocate, was born at Naini Tal hill station in India on August 18, 1824. Her father, John Inglis, was employed in the Indian civil service, serving as the commissioner of Rohilcund District. Her mother, Harriet Thompson, was the daughter of an Indian civilian.

Inglis reportedly had a happy childhood and enjoyed traveling and camping throughout the Indian countryside. She enjoyed a very strong relationship with her father, who would help guide her during her subsequent medical education and early career. Even though Inglis, who spent her childhood in both India and the United Kingdom, was raised in the male-dominated Victorian society, in which women were limited to roles of wives and mothers, her father believed that a daughter's education was just as important as a son's. Thus, Inglis was able to pursue her early ambition to enter the medical profession.

In 1878, when Inglis was fourteen years old, her father retired from his civil service job, and the Inglis family returned to its former home country of Scotland, settling in Edinburgh. In 1882, John Inglis sent his daughter to Paris for a year of schooling. Shortly after she returned from France, Inglis lost her mother to scarlet fever. She then assumed the household responsibilities and provided her father with companionship and comfort during his final years.

Improved Women's Health Care

Inglis began her medical studies at the Edinburgh School of Medicine for Women, a revolutionary institution established by Doctor Sophie Jex Blake. Then, in 1891, Inglis took a positive step toward furthering her career when she entered the Glasgow Royal Infirmary, studying under Sir William McEwen. The facility was better equipped than the Edinburgh school to provide clinical education for its medical students, and Inglis passed her examinations for triple qualification (as a doctor, surgeon and educator). The following year, in London, England, she became a house surgeon and teacher at the New Hospital for Women, appointed by the facility's founder, Elizabeth Garrett Anderson.

While practicing in London, Inglis became greatly concerned about the existing poor standard of care and lack of specialization for the care of female patients. Intent on improving medical care for women, she helped establish a maternity hospital and midwifery resource center for destitute women in Edinburgh. Originally called the Edinburgh Hospital and Dispensary for Women and Children, the facility, which was staffed entirely by women, eventually became the Elsie Inglis Memorial Hospital, and Inglis often waived fees for medical services and even paid for patients' continuing treatment.

Advocated Women's Rights

During this period, Inglis, an advocate of women's political freedom, became actively involved in the suffrage movement, which sought to provide women the right to vote in local and national elections. She joined the National

Union of Women's Suffrage Societies in 1906 and helped set up the Scottish Women's Suffrage Federation. She founded the Federation in part to help advance the improvement of women's medical care. As part of her suffrage activities, she organized meetings throughout Scotland, gave lectures and essentially made herself available wherever help for the cause was needed.

After her father died, a loss which left a gaping hole in her life, Inglis filled the void with her medical work and her suffrage activities.

In November of 1899, the Edinburgh maternity hospital moved to Bruntsfield Lodge. That same year, the Medical Women's Club, which was then headed by Inglis, opened the George Square Nursing Home, a seven-bed hospital. In 1904 the Home was renamed the Hospice, and its expressed goal was to provide assistance to destitute women in Edinburgh during their pregnancies. In 1910, the Hospice merged with the Brunstfield Hospital. The move seemed a logical one, as the two facilities already shared staff in a cooperative arrangement: Bruntsfield performed medical, surgical and gynecological work, while the Hospice performed obstetrics and infant work. Both facilities benefited from the involvement of Scotland's best-known and highly skilled female medical professionals, and both sought to provide medical care for women, as well as practical experience to aspiring female doctors.

Established Medical Units in World War I

As much as Inglis contributed to women's care and health care in general, however, it was her medical efforts related to World War I that gained her the greatest notoriety. When the war broke out in Europe in August of 1914, Inglis wanted to create medical units, staffed by women, to treat wounded soldiers on the war's Western Front. The British government essentially rejected her idea. At the start of the war, most people thought the conflict would be short-lived and that victory celebrations would be held before the end of a year.

However, the French government was much more prescient and receptive. In 1914, Inglis, working with her Scottish Women's Suffrage Federation, went to France and, within three months after the start of the war, she helped set up the Abbaye de Royaumont hospital, housed at the thirteenth-century Royaumont Abbey. The medical facility included nearly 200 beds. Her team included renowned female medical professionals such as Evelina Haverfield, Ishobel Ross and Cicely Hamilton. The circumstances and conditions, however, were appalling. In 1917, a second French hospital was established at Villers Cotterets.

Eventually, Inglis would set up fourteen medical units. These included organized women's medical units in Serbia, Salonika, Romania, Malta, Corsica, and Russia. At first, Inglis remained at home in the British Isles, where she oversaw all hospital operations. Later, she served in Serbia, where she tried to improve hygiene.

She had to take command of the Serbian unit herself when its acting head came down with diphtheria. The hospital was situated at Kraguievatz, and it was established to fight typhus, a pernicious disease that was widespread in Serbia in 1915. Inglis arrived at Kraguievatz in May of that year and found that the unit had taken on 250 more beds than the original 300 it was designed to handle. The typhus epidemic had dictated the increased capacity.

Conditions in Serbia were reportedly horrifying. Patient wards were overcrowded, with little space existing between the straw beds. Two patients were assigned to each bed, placed head to feet to save space. Sanitation was negligible, and patients were fed a poor diet. Patients close to death would arrive at the hospital in filthy wagons. Sometimes the sick had to be turned away. Inglis had to battle with Serbian officials to prevent overcrowding. Still, after putting up a strong fight, she often set up makeshift accommodations outside the hospital, to care for even more patients. Despite the conditions, Inglis' efforts were successful in helping to reduce typhus and other epidemics.

Captured by German Army

In the summer of 1915, during a major Austrian offensive, Inglis was captured but, eventually, with the help of American diplomats, British authorities were able to negotiated for the release of Inglis and her medical staff.

Her capture came about when Serbia was besieged by German and Austrian troops. Inglis was compelled to evacuate Kraguievatz, where she was then stationed, and she and the members of her unit made their way to Krushevatz, taking with them as much equipment as they could carry. When Sir Ralph Paget, the British Red Cross commissioner at the time, went to Krushevatz to make arrangements for the evacuation of her hospital, Inglis refused to budge, and defiantly told him that she would not leave.

When the Germans finally arrived, she was taken prisoner. For several months, she was allowed to continue her work. Then she was sent to Vienna and Zurich. Finally, she returned home. For a few months, she conducted her work from the two committee bases in London and Edinburgh.

Became Ill in Russia

Afterward, Inglis gained permission to raise funds for a hospital unit and transport section, to be staffed by eighty women, in Russia. In 1916, Inglis began working there, working long hours and under horrendous health conditions. In Russia, she witnessed even more of the horrors of war. Following a Russian retreat, all semblance of civilization seemed to have broken down. The countryside was overrun with soldiers who had been separated from their regiments, and crowds of refugees filled the streets, fleeing in panic.

Russian officials greatly appreciated the work performed by Inglis and her staff, and they tried to make Inglis as comfortable as was humanly possible. However, Inglis still endured profound hardships, which were beginning to take a physical toll. As each day passed, she appeared to lose strength.

Not surprisingly, she became ill and was forced to return to England, where she died on November 26, 1917, only one day after her arrival in Newcastle-Upon-Tyne.

It was reported that when she was traveling home, despite her poor health, she planned the organization of yet another hospital unit. In addition, during this journey home, and despite excruciating pain and her bedridden condition, she continued overseeing hospital operations.

The night before the transport arrived at Newcastle, Inglis' health took a turn for the worse. Still, she insisted on getting to her feet the following morning, so that she could say goodbye to her Serbian staff. When she left the boat, she was described as "a splendid and dignified figure, dressed in her worn uniform coat, and wearing her faded service ribbons, her face ashen and drawn with pain," according to her biography on the *Electric Scotland* website.

By the time she reached her hotel, she was in a state of complete exhaustion. She was treated by local doctors, who were unable to save her from the complications that arose from an infection.

Honored After Death

After Inglis died, her body lay in state at St. Giles in Edinburgh. She was buried in Dean Cemetery, in Edinburgh. At her burial, the flags of Great Britain and Serbia were placed on her coffin, and the lilies of France were placed around her body. Historic Scottish banners were placed over her head. Serbian officers lowered her coffin into her grave.

After her death, Winston Churchill wrote that Inglis and her nurses "would shine forever in history." Also, as recorded by the *Welcome to Scotland* website, Arthur Balfour, Foreign Secretary for Britain at the time of her death, and a fellow Scot, commented that Inglis was "a wonderful compound of enthusiasm, strength of purpose and kindliness. In the history of this World War, alike by what she did and by the heroism, driving power and the simplicity by which she did it, Elsie Inglis has earned an everlasting place of honour."

After her death, Inglis was recognized as someone who demonstrated a great deal of compassion, yet at times could be a demanding stickler, one who was quick to anger. She could be a fearsome figure for both patients and her staff.

Ironically enough, Inglis, a fierce advocate of women's political rights, never was able to cast a vote in an election. Shortly before her death, women over the age of 30 were finally granted the right to vote, but Inglis wouldn't live long enough to participate.

Online

"Elsie Inglis," *Welcome to Scotland*, http://www.fife.50megs.com/elsie-inglis.htm (December 22, 2005).

"Elsie Maud Inglis," *Electric Scotland*, http://www.electricscotland.com/history/women/wh53.htm (December 22, 2005).

"Famous Scots-Elsie Inglis (1864-1917), *rampantscotland.com*, http://www.rampantscotland.com/famous/blfaminglis.htm (December 22, 2005).

"Notable Individuals of the Great War," *The Western Front Association*, http://www.westernfront.co.uk/thegreatwar/articles/individuals/notableindividualsitl.htm (December 22, 2005).

"Who's Who: Elsie Inglis," *firstworldwar.com*, http://www.firstworldwar.com/bio/inglis.htm (December 22, 2005). □

J

Aletta Jacobs

Aletta Jacobs (1854-1929) notched a long list of firsts: she was the first female university student in the Netherlands, the first female doctor, and the operator of perhaps the first birth control clinic in the world. On a personal level, she was one of the first women to keep her maiden name after marrying. She campaigned for women's rights, and she was part of an international group of early feminist leaders who opposed war in general and were outraged by the grinding carnage of World War I.

Jacobs faced resistance nearly every step of the way, from examiners who tried to block her from entering medical school to fellow doctors who attacked her promotion of birth control. Yet Jacobs bore these controversies with a matter-of-fact determination. She did not set out to be a pioneer, only to follow in the footsteps of her physician father, and throughout her career she insisted only on being treated equally with her fellow students and practitioners.

Teased Because of Tomboy Qualities

The eighth of eleven children born to progressive Jewish parents, Jacobs was born in the medium-sized Dutch city of Sappemeer on February 9, 1854. She loved to climb trees, jump ditches, play tennis, row and swim, all traditionally non-feminine activities that attracted unfavorable attention from townspeople, who called her a tomboy. But the Jacobs family valued education and sacrificed so that all 12 children could receive schooling. According to Jacobs's autobiography *Memories*, her father often gave them the

sentence "The cultivation of knowledge for the sake of the common good is the highest of all pursuits" as a writing exercise. From the start, Jacobs wanted to become a doctor like her father. Her parents tried to steer her toward more feminine pursuits, apprenticing her to a dressmaker and sending her to a finishing school. The latter experiment ended after two weeks when Jacobs failed to master the curtsy and refused to practice looking down when a man looked at her on the street.

Finally it was decided that Jacobs should study to become a pharmacist's assistant, although that was a field that so far had been open to very few women. Through a combination of home schooling and work with the female assistant of her brother Sam, who had started a pharmacy in the city of Arnhem (but refused to help her with her studies), Jacobs managed to acquire the necessary background. She did well in her pharmacy school entrance exam in Amsterdam in 1870, and her examiners encouraged her to study to become an actual pharmacist rather than an assistant.

Jacobs, however, had bigger plans. Against the wishes of even her supportive father, she wrote to the reform-minded prime minister of the Netherlands, Johan Rudolf Thorbecke, asking that she be allowed to attend medical classes at the University of Groningen. He wrote back, asking her father whether she was really ready for such a move, but Thorbecke finally signed a letter giving his permission just before his death. In 1871, Jacobs became the first woman to enter a Dutch university.

Despite having to contend with hostility from her brother Johan, who refused to speak to her for 18 months, from other students (such as one at the University of Leiden who wrote to Groningen students urging them to make her life miserable), and sometimes from faculty members, Jacobs made steady progress toward her degree. She had backers on the faculty who agreed to her requests that she not be excused from anatomy lectures or any other subject considered too sensitive for a woman, and though she was haunted by the portions of the curriculum that involved dissection, she persisted. (She was unable, however, to dissect live frogs.) Jacobs's biggest problem was her poor health; she suffered repeated bouts of malaria, and when they were augmented by a case of tuberculosis at one point, she tried to commit suicide. Her father intercepted her in the act.

Received Medical Degree

At her three-week final exams in Utrecht in 1878, Jacobs faced hostile treatment from two of her four examiners but was defended by the other two. She received her medical degree on April 2 of that year, wrote a doctoral thesis on brain diseases, and was awarded a doctorate in medicine on March 8, 1879. Jacobs took over her father's practice temporarily after he suffered a stroke and her confidence was boosted when she saw how people obeyed her orders in a crisis situation as she treated a man who had fallen off a cart while drunk and been dragged on the ground. Late in 1879 she opened her own practice in Amsterdam, ignoring the advice of male doctors that she confine herself to gynecology or midwifery, or that she charge less than they did. "You should count yourself lucky that I stick to the rules instead of exploiting my exalted position as the first Dutch woman doctor to charge more than other practitioners," she retorted to one critic (according to her *Memories*).

Jacobs caused a sensation in Amsterdam with her disregard of social norms. As a student she single-handedly spread a fashion for ice skating among Amsterdam women, among whom the sport had hitherto been considered improper. She walked from house to house to visit her patients, an unheard-of act for a single woman, and when she was groped by a male pedestrian, a policeman to whom she complained told her that if she stayed indoors, she would avoid problems. Nevertheless, Jacobs's renown grew, and she made the acquaintance of writers, political figures, and early women's rights activists, both in the Netherlands and in England, where she traveled shortly after receiving her doctorate.

As a student Jacobs had worked with prostitutes at Amsterdam's main hospital, and she continued to devote her talents to helping poor women in Amsterdam after she established her own practice. Inspired by conversations with Dutch trade unionist B.H. Heldt and with the wives of other union leaders, she began giving early childhood health classes to young women and opened a free clinic for the destitute, which she maintained for 14 years. She campaigned against prostitution and in favor of better working conditions for Dutch women working in retail shops.

Jacobs's most far-reaching and controversial innovation, however, was her introduction of large-scale birth control into the Netherlands. At the time, the modern type of diaphragm had only recently been invented; Jacobs read about it in a German medical journal in 1882 and wrote to the article's author. After testing the device, called a Mensinga pessary, on willing volunteers, Jacobs announced that she could provide safe and effective contraception to women wishing to avoid pregnancy.

Attacked by Medical Establishment

This announcement brought the full wrath of Holland's medical establishment down upon Jacobs's head, and she was attacked for everything from promoting adultery to threatening the country's economic future. Rumors flew about Jacobs's personal life, and her experiences, Jacobs wrote in her *Memories*, "thoroughly undermined my trust in other people." But Jacobs did not lose her determination and edge during this difficult period. "It was an age steeped in hypocrisy!" she wrote. "I am particularly thinking of those clergymen who would denounce contraception from the pulpit and then pack their wives off to my office. I also remember women who were only too pleased to use the means I prescribed for them yet never lost a chance to condemn me at every tea party and sewing circle."

Support from grateful patients helped keep Jacobs's spirits up. One supporter she had during this period was Carel Victor Gerritsen. The two had become acquainted when Gerritsen sent Jacobs a long letter of congratulations after she passed her medical exams, but they did not meet face to face until two years later, in 1880, when the politician sent a note asking whether he could stop by the home Jacobs shared with her sister. He found Jacobs doing needlework, and in response to his expression of surprise that she would have such a domestic hobby, she asked whether he thought she spent her entire life with her nose stuck in a book. The two became friends and embarked on a wide-ranging exchange of letters.

Jacobs and Gerritsen (in her writing she often referred to him simply by his last name) contemplated living together but decided that the disapproval such a move would cause would be too strong. They did take vacations together through the 1880s, and they finally decided to marry in 1892. Jacobs was incensed by the vow of obedience she had to give during the marriage ceremony, and she later campaigned for its removal. "For, in fact, even in the most conservative families, no one honestly expects 'obedience' of a wife," she wrote in her *Memories*. "Since many people consider their wedding to be the most important day of their lives, why should they be forced to take a vow that they have no intention of keeping?" Jacobs and Gerritsen had one son, who died due to a midwife's error when he was only one day old. The couple traveled widely, but their vacations were certainly not ordinary. On one such trip, they got stuck in a British coal mine due to a shaft malfunction, and viewed the experience as a taste of what miners experienced on a regular basis.

Many of Jacobs's activities in the later years of her life revolved around the issue of women's suffrage. She had tried to register to vote as early as 1883, finding that there was no specific legal barrier to her doing so, but Dutch lawmakers responded by writing a males-only requirement into the country's voter registration laws. Jacobs became president of the Dutch Association for Woman Suffrage in 1903 and retired from her practice the following year, 25 years after she had begun it. After Gerritsen's death in 1905 she devoted much of her energy to the suffrage cause, and she lived to see Dutch women receive the right to vote in 1919.

Some of Jacobs's pro-suffrage work was carried out together with the American feminist Carrie Chapman Catt, whom Jacobs met on a visit to New York for a conference in 1904. The two traveled around much of the Eastern hemisphere together in 1911 and 1912, giving lectures in favor of women's rights and meeting with local leaders. They traveled to South Africa, up Africa's east coast, through the Middle East, and to the Philippines, China, and Japan, with Jacobs returning through Russia and Catt going on to Hawaii and the United States to complete a circumnavigation of the globe. In 1910 Jacobs translated *Women and Economics,* a feminist classic by Charlotte Perkins Gilman, into Dutch.

Jacobs helped found the Women's International League for Peace and Freedom during World War I; the group became one of the most durable anti-war bodies of the twentieth century, and actively continues into the twenty-first. In her old age she moved to The Hague, eventually living with a family there. She died in Baarn, the Netherlands, on August 10, 1929. A statue of Jacobs stands in an Amsterdam street, and she is well remembered in her country. After the publication of her *Memories* by the Feminist Press in 1996, her pioneering role became better known in English-speaking countries as well.

Books

Jacobs, Aletta. *Memories: My Life as an International Leader in Health, Suffrage, and Peace.* Edited by Harriet Fineberg, translated by Annie Wright. Feminist Press, 1996.
Notable Women Scientists. Gale Group, 2000.

Periodicals

Guardian (London, England), February 7, 1994.

Online

"Aletta Jacobs (1854-1929)," Rijksuniversiteit Groningen, http://www.rug.nl/alumni/bekendeAfgestudeerden/verleden/Jacobs (December 24, 2005).
"Aletta Jacobs (1854-1929)," Sunshine for Women, http://www.pinn.net/~sunshine/whm2001/jacobs6.html (December 24, 2005).
Aletta Jacobs Online, http://www.alettajacobs.org/english/index.html (December 24, 2005). □

Judith Jamison

Tall, powerful, and charismatic, Judith Jamison (born 1944) was a featured dancer with the Alvin Ailey American Dance Theatre (AAADT) from the late 1960s through the 1980s. She took over as artistic director of the company following Ailey's death in 1989 and has become generally recognized as one of the most important figures in modern American dance.

One of Ailey's most famous dance pieces, "Cry," was created with Jamison in mind. That dance evoked the condition of African-American

women, and Jamison and Ailey formed something of a creative partnership for many years as she realized his choreographic visions. Yet Jamison was also a versatile dancer who was open to numerous influences, and after Ailey's death she was instrumental in maintaining the variety and universality of appeal that were the AAADT's trademarks.

Attended Famed Black Church

Born May 10, 1944, in Philadelphia, Pennsylvania, Jamison grew up, she told *Newsweek,* in "a household of people who sang and played the piano. So I came from a disciplined house. You don't arrive to places late, you are polite, you do unto others as you would have them do to you." Her mother was a teacher, her father a sheet-metal worker and part-time musician who supported his daughter's passion for dance because he thought it might help her work off the energy that built up as a result of her generally hyperactive nature. Jamison started dance lessons at age six at the Judimar School of Dance in Philadelphia. She also took piano lessons from her father and played the violin well enough to join a local orchestra in her teens. One other influence was the Mother Bethel African Methodist Episcopal (AME) Church, where Jamison remained a frequent attendee even after she rose to the top of the dance world. Founded by breakaway Methodist preacher Richard Allen in 1787, Mother Bethel was a historic institution rich in African-American culture and history.

Jamison got the attention of teachers and had top-flight teachers from the start, winning a place in a class taught by top choreographer Anthony Tudor when she was ten. As a young woman Jamison immersed herself in the arts, going to museums and attending operas and plays, but dance was her greatest passion. African-American dancers were still rare at the time, but the walls of Jamison's bedroom were festooned with pictures of ballerinas and modern dancers of all backgrounds. She sought out a broad variety of dance training that would benefit her later on, focusing on classical ballet but also studying tap dancing, Afro-Caribbean and jazz dance, modern dance, and acrobatics. She appeared in the role of Myrtha in the French ballet *Giselle* when she was 15.

Graduating from high school two years later, Jamison was at first seduced by the lure of professional objectives. She enrolled at Fisk University in Tennessee, intending to study psychology, but she lasted only three semesters. Returning home, she enrolled at the Philadelphia Dance Academy (now part of the University of the Arts).

Taking a wide variety of courses that included one in the highly complex system of dance notation, Jamison once again got noticed. When Agnes de Mille, a highly popular choreographer who was the niece of film impresario Cecil B. DeMille, taught a master class at the school, she was impressed by Jamison's dancing and invited her to take a role in a new ballet to be staged at New York's Lincoln Center. That did not immediately launch Jamison's career; she worked as an amusement-park ride operator at the 1964 New York World's Fair before getting her next big break. That came when she auditioned for a dance part in a television special starring actor Harry Belafonte. The audition did not go well. "I was never very good at picking up that one-two-three showgirl stuff," Jamison recalled to Octavio Roca of the *San Francisco Chronicle*. But Ailey, who was looking on, saw in Jamison a dancer who could realize his powerful choreographic visions of African-American life.

Traveled to Africa

Almost immediately, Jamison began to tour with Ailey's company, traveling in 1966 to Europe and then to the World Festival of Negro Arts in Dakar, Senegal. The experience was an eye-opener for Jamison. "Everybody was there—from [poet] Langston Hughes to [choreographer] Katherine Dunham to [bandleader] Duke Ellington to [Senegalese] President Senghor," she told Suki John of *Dance Magazine*. "There were dance companies from all over the diaspora." Jamison danced with the Harkness Ballet while the still struggling AAADT took a break from performing, but she signed on for good when it got a new lease on life in 1967. Before long, Jamison was taking starring roles with the company. She modestly attributed that to her height; at five feet, ten inches tall, with what she described to Judith Mackrell of England's *Guardian* newspaper as "an inseam that went on forever," she stood out from a sea of petite dancers and was a natural for solo roles. But there was more to it than that.

Ailey's famous dances, such as the Ellington-inspired *Pas de Duke, Blues Suite,* and *Revelation* (which Jamison began learning the day she joined the AAADT), came alive anew when Jamison danced them. In *Pas de Duke,* Jamison often appeared in a duet with ballet star Mikhail Baryshnikov. *Revelation,* drawing on the religious life of his family in rural Texas during his childhood, was Ailey's most famous piece, and Jamison brought a power and spirituality to the work that made her an audience favorite. In 1969, Jamison joined the AAADT as it became the first American dance company in decades to tour the Soviet Union and was greeted with enormous ovations there.

The creative relationship between Jamison and Ailey reached a new level with *Cry* (1971), a solo piece the choreographer created for Jamison. "That dance—15 minutes of movement—embodied 400 years of Black women's pain, passion, and perseverance, and elevated Judith Jamison to the ranks of modern ballet superstardom," noted Asha Bandele of *Essence. Cry* became Jamison's trademark, but after she took the reins at the AAADT she encouraged younger dancers to bring their own interpretations to the work rather than trying to duplicate her style.

In 1972 Jamison won the Dance Magazine Award, a prestigious annual prize, and she was named by President Richard Nixon as an advisor to the National Council on the Arts. She married fellow Ailey dancer Miguel Godreau that year, but the marriage ended in divorce. The 1970s were a growth period for American dance, and Jamison constantly traveled, gave interviews, and was featured in new productions. Ailey was unusually open to featuring the work of choreographers other than himself, and Jamison appeared in dances by Talley Beatty and other rising creative figures.

Starred in *Sophisticated Ladies*

In 1980, Jamison decided to strike out on her own. Taking a starring role in the Broadway musical *Sophisticated Ladies,* she performed as a soloist with other ballet companies and also returned to the Ailey troupe. With Ailey's support, she began to develop her own skills as a choreographer. Two of her works, 1984's *Divining* and 1988's *Tease,* were performed by Ailey's organization, and other companies as far afield as Caracas, Venezuela, and Brussels, Belgium, also mounted productions of her works. In 1988 she founded a dance company of her own, the Judith Jamison Project.

Her plans took a sharp turn, however, when Ailey revealed to her, in the midst of the hustle and bustle of a tour, that he was seriously ill. "We were in St. Louis when Alvin decided to tell me that he wasn't well, and that he wanted me to take over the company," Jamison recalled to Joy Duckett Cain of *Essence.* "He's asking me, and I'm going, 'Oh, yes, sure,' without batting an eye—and without thinking of just how tremendous the responsibility was." Jamison was at Ailey's bedside when he became a casualty of the AIDS epidemic in December of 1989.

The shift from dancer and choreographer to artistic director was challenging for Jamison—and not because it was hard for her to give up dancing. Looking at videotapes of her performances, she realized that she had been near the end of her performing career. Learning the art of administration, however, was a new stage in Jamison's career as she brought in dancers from her own troupe to replace some Ailey stalwarts. Jamison faced pressures from advisers who wanted her to take the company in new directions or, conversely, maintain its repertory unchanged as a shrine to Ailey's career. She carefully steered a middle course.

One aspect of Ailey's legacy that Jamison maintained was its diversity and its aspiration toward universal appeal. Assistant director Masazumi Chaya was of Japanese background, and as the company's repertory grew under Jamison, dancers attempted works with a variety of subject matter. "I've had angry letters from people who felt that all our dancers should be Black," Jamison told Bandele. "But the company is the Alvin Ailey American Dance Theater. And while we're here to celebrate the Black experience, we're not here to be exclusionary about who can do that with us. Being inclusive is part of our African tradition."

Troupe Appeared in American Express Commercial

Indeed, Jamison sometimes gave the AAADT a populist orientation. American young people who were unable to name any other dance company became familiar with the AAADT after an American Express commercial featuring the company was broadcast on television during the Academy Awards ceremony. "To get young people to a live concert, we first must go where they are the most: in front of computers and televisions," Jamison pointed out to Suki John of *Dance Magazine*. Under Jamison's astute financial leadership, the company prospered. She presided over an entire Manhattan building that was home to two Ailey companies, 200 classes a week, and numerous other projects and workshops.

By the early 2000s, Judith Jamison was an icon of American dance. Among her long list of awards was a Kennedy Center Honor in 1999, where she received a prize that Ailey himself had been awarded earlier, and where she shared a stage with another idol, singer Stevie Wonder. President George W. Bush awarded National Medals of the Arts to her and to the Alvin Ailey Dance Foundation in 2001, marking the first time the medal had gone to a dance organization. She continued to nurture young dancers and to exert positive force on the American arts scene. Jamison, who often said that if she had not become a dancer her second choice of career would have been airline pilot, surveyed the various sectors of the Ailey empire and remarked to John that "I'm a pilot at heart, and this is a great ship to be piloting."

Books

Jamison, Judith, with Howard Kaplan, *Dancing Spirit: An Autobiography*, Doubleday, 1993.
Smith, Jessie Carney, ed., *Notable Black American Women, Book 1* Gale, 1992.

Periodicals

Daily News (Los Angeles), March 13, 2001.
Daily Telegraph (London, England), June 8, 2002.
Dance Magazine, December 1999.
Essence, June 1998; August 2003.
Guardian (London, England), September 6, 2001.
Newsweek, October 24, 2005.
Philadelphia Inquirer, May 10, 2004.
San Francisco Chronicle, February 10, 2002. □

Al Jarreau

American singer Al Jarreau (born 1940) built his long career on a distinctive sound that encompassed many musical styles. The five-time Grammy winner was one of the very few artists ever to receive best vocalist awards in the three genres of jazz, pop, and rhythm and blues. And in 2005, 30 years after the release of his first recording, Jarreau was far from contemplating retirement.

Education First

Jarreau was born on March 12, 1940, in Milwaukee, Wisconsin. His father was a minister, and Jarreau and his brothers began singing in the church as youngsters. As he recalled to Mike Osegueda of the *Fresno Bee*, "The real truth is that the singing was first and was a love since I've been conscious. I've always done it. I can't remember a time when I didn't." Despite this early certainty about his passion, however, Jarreau had many interests and sufficient practicality to explore other avenues as well.

As a student at Milwaukee's Lincoln High School, Jarreau was a star athlete and earned respectable grades. Intent upon expanding his world view, he started undergraduate studies at Wisconsin's Ripon College in 1958. He became a productive member of the college community there, involving himself in such pursuits as basketball, student council, and service as the freshman class president. Nor did he neglect music, as he was a member of a four-person jazz vocal ensemble called The Indigos. The group performed at local venues around the state until Jarreau graduated with a degree in psychology in 1962.

Singing remained a sideline for Jarreau as he headed to the University of Iowa to earn a master's degree in vocational rehabilitation. He then moved to San Francisco, California, to work as a rehabilitation counselor. It was not long, however, before Jarreau's first love began to rise to the forefront of his aspirations.

Five-Time Grammy Winner

In San Francisco, Jarreau met another celebrity-in-the-making, George Duke, and began performing with his trio. As the group played small jazz clubs in the Bay Area, Jarreau became convinced that music would become not just an avocation, but his career. Toward that end, he moved to Los Angeles and started working the club circuit there. He cut his teeth at such noted venues as Dino's and the Bitter End West before expanding his efforts to the East Coast of the United States, where he gained national exposure on network television via such household names of the time as Johnny Carson, Merv Griffin, and David Frost. He also provided musical interludes for such up-and-coming comics as John Belushi, Bette Midler, and Jimmie Walker at the famed comedy club—The Improv— in New York City,

New York. It took a while before the record companies noticed Jarreau, but it did not take forever.

In 1975 Jarreau's faith in following his dream was rewarded with a recording contract with Warner Brothers Records. The resulting debut album, *We Got By,* which garnered a German Grammy for best new international soloist, launched a career that spanned decades and earned the artist worldwide fame.

Jarreau went on to release many highly acclaimed recordings, including the Grammy-winning *Look to the Rainbow* (1977), *All Fly Home* (1978), *Breakin' Away* (1981) and *Heaven and Earth* (1992). *Breakin' Away* earned him two Grammys, one for best male pop vocal performance and one for best male jazz vocal performance; and his fifth Grammy (best male rhythm and blues performance, for *Heaven and Earth*) completed the triumvirate by placing Jarreau in the rarefied position of winning Grammys in three categories: jazz, pop, and rhythm and blues.

Jarreau also racked up Grammy nominations for 1980's *This Time,* 1987's *Moonlighting* (the theme song for the hit television series of the same name), and 1988's *Heart's Horizon.* Later recordings included *Tenderness* (1994) and his first compilation album, *Best of Al Jarreau* (1996). Along the way the singer found time to branch out into acting, with a stint on Broadway in *Grease!* and guest appearances on such television programs as *New York Undercover* and *Touched By An Angel.*

For all his success and accolades, however, Jarreau remained frustrated that his distinctive singing style never received the radio play and record sales of a pop star. His technique combined the qualities of jazz great Jon Hendricks with the cool interpretations of the legendary Nat King Cole, without neglecting the clarity of a Frank Sinatra or scatting worthy of the matchless Ella Fitzgerald. Jarreau's singular style created a new sound altogether and it was, undoubtedly, the very versatility of his voice that caused him to be labeled a jazz vocalist. But that did not lessen the sting. "I'm not as bitter as I am disappointed," he told Cathalena E. Burch of the *Arizona Daily Star.* "My name gets mentioned alongside Lionel Richie and Stevie Wonder and Al Green. These guys have had really big records. I've never sold a million records in an outing. . . . I'd like to really have some chart success." Still, Jarreau was not a man to waste time questioning a career that did, after all, include awards that other musicians only rarely achieve. Being downhearted was simply not his way and, besides, there was work to be done.

Strong Later Career

After nearly 25 years with Warner, Jarreau was reunited with his old friend and producer Tommy LiPuma when he signed on with GRP Records at the close of the twentieth century. GRP was a division of the Verve Music Group, of which LiPuma was chairman, and Jarreau seemed delighted to be working again with the man who had produced his 1970s recordings *Glow* and *Look to the Rainbow.* He told John Soeder of the Cleveland *Plain Dealer,* "When Tommy and I get together to work, we kind of fulfill in our own little way the dreams of the music muses by continuing a relationship that began years ago." The new collaboration resulted in *Tomorrow Today* (2000), *All I Got* (2002), and a greatly-anticipated foray back into jazz standards, *Accentuate the Positive* (2004). Despite being commercially thwarted by being pigeonholed as a jazz vocalist for so long, Jarreau maintained that *Accentuate the Positive* was the first true jazz recording he had ever made. "It's really the first jazz record I've ever done," he told Dan Ouellette of *Billboard.* "Everything else that came before was pop and R&B. If people called the early stuff jazz, that's fine. . . . My audience has been asking for a full-on, straight-ahead jazz album. So, it's for them as well as myself. This is a thanks to the kind of music that made me the person I am today." Recorded live in a sound studio, the recording was unique in both content and sound. There were no string arrangements, no background vocals, and no overdubs. And the material included Jarreau's singular take on such standards as Johnny Mercer's *Accentuate the Positive* and Duke Ellington's *I'm Beginning to See the Light,* as well as new lyrics and spins on such tunes as Eddie Harris's *Cold Duck Time* (re-named *Cold Duck)* and Dizzy Gillespie's *Groovin' High.* He described the effort to Zan Stewart of the Newark *Star-Ledger:* "This is not what Betty Carter or Jon Hendricks or Carmen (McRae) would do. It's Jarreau's step into that arena."

The new century also saw fresh recognition for Jarreau, as more awards were added to an already burgeoning roster that included (in addition to his five Grammys) an honorary doctorate in performing arts (1988) and a Distinguished Alumni Award (1982) from Ripon College. The later additions included a star on the Hollywood Walk of Fame in March of 2001, and the Ford Freedom Award Scholar honor in July of 2005. Jay Albert, managing director of Cleveland's 26th annual Tri-C JazzFest, was apparently not understating the case when he described Jarreau to Soeder as a "perennial favorite."

Clearly, Jarreau's entry into his 60s (including major back surgery in 2002) did little to slow his pace or limit his musical contributions. As he told Soeder, "However late this is in my life, the old dog has gotta learn a few new tricks. I hate being boring to people." He was mindful of his debt to a variety of musical genres, telling *Jet,* "There's such great music to make in this world, and I've been exposed to a lot of it. I've absorbed it all into my system and I think that accounts for the diversity." The versatile singer continued to tour and record with spirit and facility, and succeeded in retaining both a continuing love of his art and a positive outlook. He described the latter to Ouellette: "Music is the fountain of youth. The creative process rejuvenates me. I live to experience that vitality." At least as much to the point were Jarreau's words to Ed Condran of the *Virginian Pilot.* "I feel like I'm just starting the second half of my career. I hope I'm fortunate enough to be doing this well into my 70s and 80s. . . . I know this isn't the case for everybody at my age or even younger, but I still get so turned on by the craft. The great thing about this business is making the music. I've never gotten caught up with the trappings. You can't get caught up in the limousines and the chicks. The most important thing is the music." Thirty years in the business, and Jarreau's commitment to the music was still knocking them out.

Periodicals

Arizona Daily Star, February 15, 2002.
Billboard, October 26, 2002; August 21, 2004.
Fresno Bee, November 29, 2002.
Houston Chronicle, March 12, 2005.
Jet, March 26, 2001; September 16, 2002; July 4, 2005.
Milwaukee Journal Sentinel, December 11, 1999; December 11, 1999.
Plain Dealer (Cleveland), April 15, 2005.
Post-Standard (Syracuse, NY), June 21, 2002.
Star-Ledger (Newark, NJ), August 20, 2004.
Virginian Pilot, August 13, 2001.

Online

"About Al," Al Jarreau, http://www.aljarreau.com/about/official bio/ (January 15, 2006).
"Al Jarreau," NNDB, http://www.nndb.com/people/173/0000 24101/ (January 15, 2006).
"Alwin 'Al' Jarreau," Ripon College Archives, http://www.ripon .edu/library/archives/reference/jarreau.html (January 15, 2006).
"Discography," Al Jarreau, http://www.aljarreau.com/ discography/ (January 15, 2006). □

Peter Jennings

The urbane face of ABC television's *World News Tonight* for over 25 years, Peter Jennings (1938- 2005) embodied the highest standards of American television news journalism.

Never an avuncular father figure like longtime CBS anchor Walter Cronkite, Jennings nevertheless earned viewers' trust through a combination of hard work, authoritative expertise on world affairs, and a certain charisma born of unflappable composure. Though cooped up behind an anchor desk during the best-known phases of his career, Jennings was a foreign correspondent at heart. Viewers expected him to report from the scene at important world events, microphone in hand and dressed in a trademark trench coat, and when he failed to show up in south Asia after the disastrous tsunami of 2004, they correctly guessed that something was wrong.

Hosted Program at Age Nine

The man who became one of the best-known television personalities in the United States came from Canada and took American citizenship only two years before his death. His skeptical outsider's viewpoint on American politics and culture became part of his appeal; in the words of newscaster Robert MacNeil, he had an "ironic distance" that meshed perfectly with his international sense of savoir faire. Jennings was born in Toronto, Ontario, Canada on July 29, 1938. Broadcast journalism was in his blood; his father Charles Jennings was a pioneer newscaster on the then-new Canadian Broadcasting Corporation network. Peter Jennings often called his father his hero. Thanks to his father's influence, Jennings made his broadcast debut at age nine, with a children's radio show called "Peter's Program."

Jennings's father tried to steer him away from a career in journalism, however, and in school he floundered. When he was 11 he stole a pack of cigarettes from his grandmother and introduced his sister as well as himself to an unyielding addiction. Spending more time on comic books than on classes, he dropped out of school in the tenth grade and worked for several years as a bank teller. As a result, he has often been cited in lists of people who have risen to the tops of their professions without benefit of a college or even a high school degree. Yet Jennings was far from uneducated; he soon began to read voraciously and to soak up information on almost any subject he encountered. "I have never spent a day in my adult life where I didn't learn something," he said in an interview quoted in *People*. "And if there is a born-again quality to me, that is it."

Jennings also minimized the impact of his lack of formal education by starting at the bottom of his chosen field and steadily working himself up. He became a reporter and disc jockey at a small radio station in Brockville, Ontario when he was 17, and he soon gained national notice with his on-the-scene reporting of a train crash. A series of career moves followed, each of them occurring when news executives spotted him as a rising young talent and recruited him as an asset for a new organization. In 1961 he was hired by a television station that became part of the launch of Canada's first privately owned television network, CTV. At first his duties involved a music-and-dance show modeled on "American Bandstand," but when CTV launched its own national news broadcast in 1963, Jennings was named co-anchor.

From the start, he showed a propensity to go to the story rather than having correspondents bring it to his desk. He traveled to New York to cover the Democratic Party's national convention there in 1964, and ABC news executive Elmer Lower was impressed by his smooth manner and James Bond-like confidence. ABC at the time was an upstart competitor to the better-known NBC and CBS, and Jennings was picked in 1965 to anchor a 15-minute evening news broadcast.

Teased by Cronkite

Jennings was only 26, and his competition was formidable: the legendary Walter Cronkite at CBS and the duo of Chet Huntley and David Brinkley at NBC. Once, when Jennings appeared on a panel with these three veterans, Huntley remarked that his only show-business practice he permitted on NBC's news broadcast was to have a makeup artist paint out the bags under his eyes. "Yeah, Jennings steps in and has them painted on," quipped Cronkite (according to Jamie Malanowski of *Entertainment Weekly*). ABC's evening news program failed to take off in the ratings, partly because at the time the network did not have the news-gathering resources to match those of its better-established competitors. Jennings stepped down as anchor in 1968.

He took the failure to heart and decided that he needed a wider range of experience in the news business. Requesting and receiving a posting to the Middle East, he became ABC's only correspondent covering hot spots in Asia, Africa,

and the Arab world. Jennings immersed himself in the history and politics of the countries he covered, developing the beginnings of a wide general expertise that later enabled him to comment comfortably on almost any topic in spontaneous on-air situations. In 1969 he opened an ABC news bureau in Beirut, Lebanon—the first full-time American television news office in the Middle East. He and a sound engineer were briefly imprisoned by Lebanese authorities as tensions with Israel flared. Jennings traveled tirelessly by plane around the Third World, often wearing a trench coat that had belonged to his father.

The world got a good idea of Jennings's cool in a crisis when he reported from the 1972 Olympics in Munich, Germany on the Black September terrorist attack on Israel's contingent of athletes in the Olympic Village. Jennings hid out in a bathroom as police moved other correspondents out of the area, then set up a post on a balcony with a view overlooking the dormitories where the athletes were being held hostage. His reporting was widely praised in the aftermath of the tragedy, and his days as a young and pretty face in the news business were over.

In 1974 Jennings received a Peabody Award for a profile of Egyptian president Anwar Sadat. Another profile he did during this period proved prophetic of future events; he gained an interview with Iran's militant Ayatollah Khomeini, then in exile in Paris, and elicited a frank statement that Khomeini planned to overthrow the Shah of Iran. Jennings moved to London that year, and then, in 1975, back to the U.S. to become anchor of ABC's *A.M. America*, a forerunner of the network's long-running *Good Morning America*. As always, he was restless in the anchor's chair, and by 1977 he was back in London.

Became Part of Three-Anchor Format

The following year, ABC found a meeting point between Jennings' globetrotting ways and its own desire to elevate the person widely perceived as the network's most accomplished journalist to an anchor position. Jennings, working from London, became one of three anchors of ABC's new *World News Tonight,* reporting on world events while Frank Reynolds delivered Washington news and Max Robinson explored domestic "heartland" issues from ABC's Chicago affiliate. Jennings's footprint showed in the greater airtime *World News Tonight* devoted to international stories as compared with evening news programs on CBS and NBC. The triple-anchor arrangement lasted until Reynolds's death from cancer in 1983; Robinson, who also died later in the 1980s, left the network, and Jennings became the sole anchor of *World News Tonight.*

By that time Jennings had the semblance of a more regular lifestyle. He had two children, Elizabeth and Christopher, by his third wife, Kati Marton. Once described by ABC newsman and *Nightline* host Ted Koppel (according to Malanowski) as "catnip to women," Jennings was married four times. His first wife was Canadian; his second, Annie Malouf, was a Lebanese photographer he met during his years in Beirut. He and Marton remained friends after he married television producer Kayce Freed, his fourth wife. Early in his career, noted Charles Glass of England's

Independent newspaper, Jennings carried the nickname "Stanley Stunning." On the set, however, the perfectionist Jennings had a different moniker: his boss Roone Arledge, reported *People*'s Mike Lipton, called him "Prickly Pete."

Even at the start of his second solo anchor slot, Jennings seemed a senior presence on American news airwaves. His speech was peppered with Canadianisms like his pronunciation of "schedule" with an initial "sh" sound, giving him a faintly exotic air. He presided over a group of ABC reporters like Sam Donaldson who often took an adversarial stance toward the administration in power in Washington, and his own erudition showed through in interviews and in fast-moving breaking news situations. Barbara Walters, as quoted by Harold Jackson of England's *Guardian* newspaper, said that Jennings "sometimes . . . drove me crazy because he knew so many details." He once ended a newscast with a novelty story about a small Welsh town, delivering a letter-perfect pronunciation of its name—Llanfairpwllgwyngyllgogerychwymd-robwllllantysiliogogogoch—with a twinkle in his eye. By 1986, "World News Tonight" had topped its competitors in audience, and it would not relinquish that position for many years.

In 1989 Jennings, who had seen the construction of the Berlin Wall, reported live as it was torn down by jubilant German crowds. He followed the collapse of Communism closely and broadcast a widely seen interview with Russian president Mikhail Gorbachev in 1991.

Volunteered Time to Charity

Jennings became a familiar figure among New Yorkers, from society's upper crust to street people, for whom he served up meals as a volunteer for the Coalition for the Homeless. He often rode the bus and conversed with passengers rather than take the limousine he had at his disposal. Jennings came to think of New York as home. "What always pleased me, as a New Yorker," he was quoted as saying by Rebecca Dana in the *New York Observer*, "is that so many came to find that New York was different from what they anticipated. It was softer, more generous, and more grateful to other people."

Jennings reported from the scene as apartheid fell in South Africa, as India and Pakistan came to the brink of nuclear war, as civil war flared in the former Yugoslavia, and as the 2000 U.S. presidential election turned into a marathon standoff. Perhaps his toughest assignment of all came when his adopted city came under attack by airborne terrorists on the morning of September 11, 2001. Jennings was on the air for 60 hours over the next several days, taking only short sleep breaks.

The stress of covering that earthshaking event led Jennings to resume smoking; he had essentially kicked the habit some years earlier, but staffers occasionally glimpsed him slipping into an unoccupied room to sneak a cigarette. Late in 2004 he began to sound hoarse, and, complaining of fatigue, he uncharacteristically declined to travel to Southeast Asia to report on damage from the December 26 tsunami. Still, he was shocked when he was diagnosed with lung cancer. He announced his condition to viewers on April 5, 2005, planning to take a leave of absence and return

to the airwaves, but his condition steadily worsened. After his death in New York on August 7, 2005, New Yorkers taped bouquets of roses to bus-station advertisements that bore his photograph.

Books

Goldberg, Robert, and Gerald Jay, *Anchors: Brokaw, Jennings, Rather and the Evening News*, Birch Lane Press, 1990.

Periodicals

Broadcasting & Cable, August 15, 2005.
Entertainment Weekly, August 19, 2005.
Guardian (London, England), August 9, 2005.
Independent (London, England), August 9, 2005.
New York Observer, August 15, 2005.
Newsweek, August 22, 2005.
People, August 22, 2005.
Plain Dealer (Cleveland, OH), August 9, 2005. □

Francisco Jiménez de Cisneros

Francisco Jiménez de Cisneros (1436-1517) was born into a noble Castilian family, but chose to turn his back on all the riches of his birth and instead became a Franciscan friar. He retained his acquaintances in society, and because of them was offered the position of confessor to Queen Isabella, a position he held until the day she died. He retained his own hermetic approach to life while gaining more and stronger influence over Spanish politics, culminating in his elevation to the Cardinal of Toledo. In a fit of religious fervor Cisneros instituted a religious reformation across his country. He also was responsible for the printing of the *Complutensian Polyglot*, which was a consolidation of the Latin, Greek, Hebrew, and Aramaic texts of the Bible.

Destined for the Church

Jiménez de Cisneros was born in 1436 into a low noble family in Torrelaguna in Castile. He was destined for the church early in life, and so his education was inclined towards that end; he was interested in politics and law, and attracted by the ways in which he could use them to further his religious policies. He began his education at the hands of an uncle before he was sent to attend the Alcala de Henares school. From there he went on to attend the University of Salamanca, where he graduated around 1460 with a bachelor's degree in Law. Upon graduation he traveled to Rome to take on the role of consistorial advocate, which meant that he essentially worked for the assembly of cardinals. While there he came to the notice of Pope Sixtus V, who was impressed by the young cleric.

The Pope bestowed upon Jiménez a letter that gave him possession of the first vacant benefice (a church position that offered a way to make a living), which turned out to be Uzeda. Archbishop Carillo refused to accept the letter, however, preferring to give the benefice to one of his own followers, and when Jiménez argued, he was jailed. He was free to leave prison at any time if he would give up all rights to the position, but Cisneros refused. He stayed in prison for six years until Carillo gave in and gave the benefice to him. Jiménez, in turn, exchanged the benefice immediately for a chaplaincy at Siguenza, under Cardinal Mendoza the bishop of Siguenza. Mendoza then gave him the position of vicar-general of his diocese.

Chucked In Prominence for Life of Franciscan

In his positions, Jiménez gained much acclaim for his work, and by the early 1480s Jiménez was a prosperous and successful clergyman on his way to high rank in the church, but he seemed to have changed his mind about his life's direction. Instead of a highly paid and admired position, Jiménez chose to enter the poor Franciscan Order, which at the time was the leading religious reform movement, proposing a return to stricter and more orthodox Christianity. He began a life of retreat at the friary of San Juan de los Reyes, which had recently been founded by King Ferdinand and Queen Isabella at Toledo. Although he led a life of solitude, he maintained contacts with Cardinal Mendoza and the court. He built a hut in the woods near the friary of Our Lady of Castanar and lived there at times, away from the rest of the world. This was not to last for very long, however.

Served as Confessor for Queen Isabella

Because of his worldly contacts, when Queen Isabella, who was a devout Catholic, was looking for a personal confessor in 1492, a comrade suggested Jiménez for the position. He agreed to take on the post as long as he was able to keep to his religious life and only go to court when called for. Isabella quickly agreed and the two developed a strong and longstanding relationship that would last the rest of her life. As Jiménez's relationship with Isabella strengthened, so his power throughout the Kingdom rose. Isabella came to depend on Jiménez not only as her confessor, but also for his council about affairs of state. He became so invaluable to her, in fact, that she brought him to Barcelona in 1493 when she and her husband King Ferdinand moved there. He was moved in order to oversee the reforms in Catalan monastic life, as well as to continue his job as royal confessor. Isabella admired him so much that in 1494 she appointed him to the position of Minister provincial of the Catalan order for Spain.

Jiménez's old friend, Cardinal Mendoza, died in 1495, and Isabella secretly obtained a papal bull naming Jiménez to Mendoza's Archdiocese of Toledo, the richest and most powerful position in Spain. The Archdiocese came also with the office of chancellor of Castile, quite a different life, it would seem, from the one that Jiménez wanted and was

pursuing. Even with all of his obligations, however, Jiménez maintained a simple life. For a cardinal, Jiménez was very austere and simple, so much so that not long after his ascension to his cardinalship he received a missive from Rome berating him for his lack of circumstance. He was told that he should change his way of life to more suitably reflect the grandeur of his rank. Jiménez, however, despite the admonishment, continued to maintain only the outward appearance of richness, using it to hide his personal asceticism.

Initiated Crusade For Religious Reform

Jiménez managed to keep to his ascetic lifestyle so well that at court he impressed people with his way of life as well as his sense of purpose and mission. He was so austere, in fact, that he did not just accept the usual lack of luxuries, but increased them immensely. Just a few of the things he added to his religious rights were the fact that he insisted on sleeping on the bare ground, wearing a hair shirt, and doubling his fasts, and generally denied himself any luxuries at all, and all done with a fervor. And he kept the Spartan–like lifestyle up for his entire life, no matter how high his rank reached.

Jiménez, in his position of Cardinal, instantly started a vigorous program of clerical reform. He managed to obtain a papal bull in 1495 that gave him the necessary permission to visit and help the regular clergy of his archdiocese to put through the reforms the Jiménez found were essential for the health of the Spanish church. In 1499 another papal bull entrusted him with visiting and reforming the mendicants throughout Spain. Mendicants were an order of friars that were not allowed to own property, and so work and beg for a living. Jiménez was constantly on the lookout for any situation within the church that might need his attention. He epitomized, at this time, the crusading fervor of Spain during the 1500s. When Isabella decided to expel Jews from Spain in 1492, it was seen as Jiménez who helped her make the decision. He was also seen as very intolerant of the Granadine Moors who had recently been conquered by the Spanish. It was Jiménez who wanted to strengthen those church movers who were interested in firmly following the laws of the church against their counterparts, those who believed in accumulating wealth. He also took steps to ensure that nunneries were suitably funded and were attached to the reformed congregations of their particular orders, rather than the more radical ones. His acts were very influential on a generation of reformers, but unfortunately for Jiménez, the mercilessness with which he carried out his reforms often aggravated people and created resentment in the ranks, ensuring that the changes were slow and would be of short duration. Because of this, Jiménez's work remained largely unfinished until after the Council of Trent, which took place from 1545 to 1563. The Council was a strong reform movement that Jiménez would have approved of, but he was long gone when it occurred.

Crucial in Ascendancy of the Throne

These delays caused Jiménez to be incredibly impatient at the slow progress, so to deal with the issues, Jiménez started a forced conversion of the Muslim population. This coercion goaded even larger rebellions in the kingdom of Granada and foreshadowed the horrible death of Spanish Islam over the subsequent century. To Jiménez this forced expulsion of non-Christians was a return to the early church's fervor and he wished to spread the reformation even further. He next extended what became known as the Isabelline Reconquista to Africa, where he sent troops on crusading campaigns to the Barbary Coast. In 1509 the crusaders managed to conquer Oran, which was Jiménez's goal.

In the meantime there were a few problems back at home. Isabella died in 1504, and then her heir, Philip of Austria, died in 1506. These events triggered a severe crisis about who would reign over Spain. King Ferdinand the Catholic was made to give up his title of King of Castile when his wife, Isabella, died. When her heir died too, Ferdinand was established as regent until Charles of Ghent, the next person in line to rule, was old enough to rule. Jiménez, dealing with his crusades and other religious reforms, was also forced to deal with the mess of who would rule Spain. It was he who managed to bring about this agreement, doing so against opposition from the Castilian nobility. For his help, Ferdinand saw to it that Jiménez was made the inquisitor general in 1507. The two men remained in collaboration until Ferdinand died in January of 1516. At that time Jiménez took on the role of regent on Charles's behalf. This created even more unrest and the country remained seriously fractured until Charles made it to Spain in September of 1517; Jiménez was more than equal to the challenge, however, of keeping all the disquieted peoples at bay and any bloodshed from occurring. He did this by establishing a permanent militia of around thirty thousand men to crush any serious rebellions. Charles was from the Flemish court and had to transfer power over Spain to his court; it has been thought that the successful transition would not have occurred if it had not been for Jiménez's statesmanship. Jiménez was on the way to meet with young King Charles when he died at Roa on November 8, 1517.

Set Up University of Alcala de Henares

Even after all the political and religious reforms that Jiménez managed to bring about in his lifetime, he was mostly remembered for his role later in life as Renaissance patron and founder. In 1499 he started his construction on the University of Alcala de Henares, which opened in 1508. One of the greatest things the University did, under Jiménez's orders, was called the *Complutensian Polyglot*, which was a consolidation of the Latin, Greek, Hebrew, and Aramaic texts of the Bible. It was published between 1513 and 1517 and was comprised of six volumes. He was also responsible for the publication of the works of Vincent Ferrer, Catherine of Siena, Angela da Foligno, and Girolamo Savonarola, to name a few, all great spiritual leaders in the church.

Books

Encyclopedia of the Renaissance, 6 volumes, Charles Scribner's Sons, 2000.
Merriam-Webster's Biographical Dictionary, Merriam-Webster Incorporated, 1995.

Online

"Francisco Jimenez de Cisneros," NNDB, http://www.nndb .com/people/675/000094393/ (January 6, 2006).
"Francisco Ximenez de Cisneros," New Advent, http://www .newadvent.org/cathen/15729b.htm (January 6, 2006).
"The Iberian Peninsula," Bartleby, http://www.bartleby.com/67/ 601.html (January 6, 2006).
"Jimenez de Cisneros, Francisco, Cardenal," Brittanica Online, http://www.britannica.com/eb/article/9043646 (January 6, 2006). □

Georgeanna Jones

Georgeanna Seegar Jones (1912-2005) was a pioneering reproductive endocrinologist (someone who studies glands). Along with her husband, Jones did the first in-vitro fertilization in the United States. From that day she and her husband became known for helping thousands of women who could not otherwise become pregnant to carry their offspring to term and birth them.

Childhood Inspired Desire to Become Doctor

Jones was born on July 6, 1912 in Baltimore, Maryland, to J. King B.E. Seegar, an obstetrician who just happened to have delivered the man Jones would eventually marry: Howard W. Jones, Jr. When Jones was five years old, she broke a bone that got infected and caused her a lot of pain and problems. The experience was so hard on young Jones that it led her to think of medicine as a career, as she dreamed of helping those who were in pain, maybe even lessening or eradicating the worst of it.

To that end, Jones graduated from the Girls Latin High School in 1928, after which she attended Goucher College where she obtained a bachelor's degree in Chemistry. From there, in 1932, Jones started at Johns Hopkins University School of Medicine in Baltimore. She threw herself wholeheartedly into her studies and managed to graduate with her M.D. in 1936. She went on to postgraduate study, which she also completed at Johns Hopkins University. After graduation she applied for a fellowship from the National Institute of Health, which she happily received. The fellowship allowed Jones to continue her research until 1939 when Jones took a position with Johns Hopkins Medical School.

Discovered Location of Chorionic Gonadotropin

While she was at Johns Hopkins, Jones held such positions as director of the school's laboratory of reproductive physiology and gynecologist in charge of the hospital's gynecological endocrine clinic. This position made her one of the first reproductive endocrinologists on a medical school faculty in the United States. She kept both positions

until her retirement in 1978. She eventually made full professor of gynecology and obstetrics. During her early work at Johns Hopkins, Jones discovered that the pregnancy hormone, chorionic gonadotropin, was located in the placenta, not the pituitary gland as had previously been thought. That single discovery led to the invention of the home pregnancy test, which has helped people around the globe plan their reproductive lives.

While working at Johns Hopkins, Jones married Howard Jones in 1940. It proved to be a good marriage for many reasons, not least of which was that the Joneses collaborated on their future gynecological studies and discovered many important things together, leading both of them onto the world stage of gynecological medicine. They eventually had two sons Howard Wilbur Jones III (who would become an obstetrician and gynecologist), and Lawrence Massey, and a daughter, Georgeanna Jones Klingensmith (who would become a pediatrician). During their collaborative years, Jones, along with her husband, was responsible for much of the respect that the gynecological part of Johns Hopkins hospital received.

Described the Luteal Phase Deficiency

In 1949, Jones conducted research into infertility, especially luteal phase deficiency, which she described as a cause of infertility and pregnancy loss. These problems, she studied, were caused by the inadequate secretory transformation of the endometrium (the membrane that lines the uterus), resulting from deficient production of progesterone,

the female hormone which is secreted by the corpus luteum. Corpus luteum, which has to do with the luteal phase, is a yellow progesterone-secreting mass of cells that forms from an ovarian follicle after the release of a mature egg. Without it there can be no pregnancy. Finding and then describing the process of the luteal phase and the problems that occur during it had never been accomplished before. Jones's work helped with a more thorough understanding of reproduction and infertility. Jones held a belief that the more that was known about the causes of infertility, the better the chance was that it could be fixed. "She was a real leader in the field as far as endocrine aspects were concerned," *The Lancet* quoted Alan DeCherney as having said. DeCherney was a professor of obstetrics and gynecology at the David Geffen School of Medicine at the University of California, Los Angeles, and was also the editor of the publication *Fertility and Sterility*.

While she was engaged in her research with the causes of infertility and the processes involved in becoming pregnant, Jones was also involved with other things like teaching and writing. Her skill and success at research led others to seek out her advice and answers when they had questions about medical fertility issues. Along with her husband, Jones, seen as an authority on the subject, edited *The Obstetrical and Gynecological Survey* for 30 years. Jones also authored more than 300 peer-reviewed articles and more than 20 chapters that were included in various medical books.

With these and other issues to occupy her attention, Jones's life was very busy. She always found time to watch carefully over the educational and personal needs of her trainees, however, as she took her role as a teacher very seriously. She was even known to visit her trainees' houses when they were sick, bringing them groceries and other necessities that they could not get for themselves. *The Lancet* quoted Zev Rosenwaks, director of Cornell University Medical Center's Center for Reproductive Medicine and Infertility in New York, as having said of Jones, "She had everything. She was a great teacher, a superb clinician, and an excellent academician—the true triple threat. In other aspects of life, she was not only endowed with fortune that she had a wonderful family, but she was also exceedingly aware of the world around her and she cared deeply about it." Jones also became the first female president of the American Fertility School in 1970. (It is now called the American Society for Reproductive Medicine.) She was the type of clinician who not only scientifically cared for her patients, but did personally as well.

Jones retired from her official positions in the late 1970s. Her retirement was full of work rather than rest, though, and it was her work after her official retirement that garnered Jones most of her praise. After her retirement in 1978, Jones and her husband were recruited by the Eastern Virginia Medical School to teach for a few years. The Medical School wanted to make use of such respected doctors to enhance their own school's programs. It was certainly a success. At the Eastern Virginia Medical School Jones and her husband worked together again. In the late 1970s it was announced that a physician in Britain had produced the first test-tube baby, and the couple, full of the vigor of competition and dedication, put all their plans for a quiet and peaceful life on hold. They were determined to first copy the process that British doctors had used, and then to better it.

First In-Vitro Fertilization in the United States

The Joneses started by creating the first in-vitro fertilization clinic in the United States at the school they were teaching at: Eastern Virginia Medical School. They worked night and day to bring about their miracle, and all the hard work paid off. In 1981, just three years later, the couple managed to create the first ever test-tube baby in the United States, which was born after in-vitro fertilization. The method used by the Joneses involved ovulation induction with gonadotropins, which is what made the their program so successful. Gonadotropins are a hormone that stimulates the growth and activity of the gonads, which is an organ that produces gametes, the reproductive cells such as a fertile egg or sperm.

The first child was born on December 28, 1981 at Sentara Norfolk General Hospital. The five pound, 12 ounce baby was named Elizabeth Jordan Carr, born to Judith Carr, a 28-year-old Massachusetts schoolteacher. The team, headed by the Joneses, successfully joined Carr's husband's sperm in a laboratory dish with a ripe egg cell the doctors had removed from her own ovaries. According to the *Washington Post*, "They transplanted the growing clump of new cells into Carr's womb to let gestation take its normal course. The process also involved the use of fertility-inducing hormones by Dr. Jones, who was an expert on hyperstimulation of the ovaries. The hormones made the mother ovulate at a fixed time. 'All of this sounds so simple,' a member of the Jones team told *The Washington Post* on the day of the baby's birth, 'but there's a lot of stress in it all. And it works because a lot of people have worked a lot of long hours to make it go.' " Jones was almost as ecstatic as the Carrs were, who had tried to have a child several times without success. If it had not been for the Joneses and their team, the Carrs might have never been able to have a child.

The success of the experiment raised the profile of the school and doctors from around the world came to the school to train under the Joneses. Jones, especially, was looked up to as a strong and loyal person. She had a devoted following of past students who were loyal to her too. That loyalty even stretched to many of those children who were born at the clinic. Every year many of those children gathered at the Jones' school every Mother's Day for some time after. The Jones Institute of Reproductive Medicine at the school was named in the couple's honor. The Institute then set up the Georgeanna Seegar Jones Research Fund to make certain that research in the field of women's infertility would continue.

Chosen to Advise Pope John Paul II

As a show of the respect given to her, Jones was also, along with her husband, involved with international delegations to discuss the issues involved in reproduction and other medical gynecological issues. For instance, Jones and her husband were the only American gynecologists invited to the Vatican to take part in a panel advising Pope John Paul II on medical and ethical issues involving assisted reproduction. The Pope wanted as much information as possible about the process to decide whether or not assistance with reproduction was against the laws of the Catholic Church.

Jones died from heart failure on March 26, 2005, in Norfolk, Virginia; after having been afflicted by Alzheimer's disease. Jones's amazing contributions to the field of gynecological research earned her a myriad of honors and awards. These included the Rubin Award, in 1966; the Barren Foundation Award, in 1971; Virginia Woman of the Year, in 1982; Medical College of Pennsylvania's Woman Scientist of the Year, in 1982; Woman Scientist of the Year, from the Medical College of Pennsylvania, in 1985; election to the Society of Hopkins Scholars, in 1986; Distinguished Service Award Medal, by the Cosmopolitan Club of Norfolk, in 1988; and the Johns Hopkins Distinguished Alumnus Award, in 1997. She also received many honorary degrees from such institutions as Amherst College and Old Dominion University. Jones contributed much to the field of women's fertility, and she will long be remembered for it.

Periodicals

The Lancet, April 23, 2005.
Washington Post, March 28, 2005.

Online

"Georgeanna Jones," *Biography Resource Center Online*, Gale 2005 (January 6, 2006).
"Georgeanna Seegar Jones Research Fund," Jones Institute, http://www.jonesinstitute.org/research_fund.html (January 6, 2006). □

Janis Joplin

Janis Joplin (1943-1970) was one of the most popular and influential female singers to emerge from the West Coast "counterculture" that thrived in the mid- to late-1960s. Her compelling stage and recording persona effectively transcended any regional boundaries. Her trademark raucous performing presence, combined with the raw emotion conveyed in her bluesy singing style and her unconventional but trend-setting and highly personal taste in fashion, captivated a national audience who sensed both her toughness and vulnerability and, in turn, embraced her without condition. Joplin, who was given to emotional excess and susceptible to unhealthy indulgence, passed away at the height of her fame.

Joplin, the future blues and rock song stylist, voiced her first full-throated, attention-demanding shriek on January 19, 1943. The first child of Seth and Dorothy Joplin, she was raised in Port Arthur, Texas, a small oil-industry town located on the Gulf Coast, fifteen miles from Louisiana.

At the time, Port Arthur was a conventional middle-class community, where many residents worked for oil companies. Her family enjoyed middle-income comforts. Her father was a canning factory worker (and later a Texaco employee) and her mother was a registrar at Port Arthur College, a business school.

In retrospect, its easy to see how such an environment would prove stifling to someone of Joplin's sensitivities and sensibilities, but her early life gave little indication of the unconventional, hard-living, hard-working performer she'd later become. She got along well with her parents and younger siblings, Michael and Laura. Joplin did demonstrate artistic interests as a child, and her parents encouraged these inclinations. Still, her life pretty much conformed to Port Arthur standards. She earned good grades, regularly attended church and displayed her artwork at the local library. But things started to change when she began high school.

Troubled Adolescence

As it is with many young students, high school proved a painful period for Joplin. Afflicted with severe acne and a weight problem, she suffered the humiliations of peer-group torment and rejection. Understandably, Joplin was greatly hurt and, at first, she responded by becoming somewhat of a loner. However, she soon adapted more extroverted responses to her ostracization: she began wearing wild clothes, affected vulgar language and, in general, cultivated a reputation as a rebel.

Further, her artistic interests took a bohemian turn, and she started listening to folk and blues records—not exactly the kind of music appreciated by fellow Port Arthur teenagers during the late 1950s. Her favorite artists were Odetta, Leadbelly and Bessie Smith. Joplin sung along to the artists' recordings, developing what would later become her signature vocal style.

A typical non-conformist, Joplin rejected traditional roles and expected behavior, and fell in with a group of like-minded, rebellious peers. While rejecting social norms of her community, she embraced causes such as equal rights and identified strongly with what was then termed the "beatnik" culture. Her interests included poetry and music, particularly jazz and blues. As is often the case with individuals who march to the cadences of a different drummer, however, Joplin often was overwhelmed by a sense of alienation and she suffered bouts of depression—feelings that she'd battle throughout her relatively short life.

The Runaway

After Janis graduated from high school in May, 1960, she enrolled at Lamar College in Beaumont, Texas. She lasted two semesters before she turned her face to the wind and answered the call of the open road. When she was only seventeen years old, she left home—or, as some more specifically define it, she "ran away"—at first working in country and western clubs in various Texas towns and cities. Eventually, she made her way to southern California. Though it was only the early 1960s, Joplin essentially adopted the "hippie" lifestyle, dropping in and out of colleges, working at odd jobs, and even living in a commune.

During her meanderings and wanderings, Joplin made friends with a man named Chet Helms, who later would have an enormous impact on her career direction. In January 1963, Helms talked Joplin into going with him to San Francisco.

During this period in her life, she sang in coffee houses in the North Beach area, and she also began experimenting with various drugs, and developed a fondness for alcohol. Experimentation led to an addiction to amphetamine, which, most likely was partially driven by poor self image fostered by what she felt was an ongoing weight problem.

Returned Home to Recover

By 1965, her lifestyle had taken its toll, and Joplin returned to Port Arthur. Reportedly, she only weighed 88 pounds. Back home, Joplin worked on restoring her physical and emotional health. She stayed sober, ate well, and toned down her appearance. She even stopped singing for a short while, as she felt it reinforced an excessive lifestyle.

With weight regained, and feeling emotionally stronger, she enrolled at the University of Texas in Austin, where she studied art. At first, she felt at home. In college, where she mixed in with a diverse population of students, she found kindred spirits among the academic bohemians who shared her artistic interests and social experiences. She became involved in the local folk scene, and she continued her dalliance with drugs and alcohol, developing a reputation as an enthusiastic drinker who could keep up with the boys. This helped to differentiate her from fellow students and underscored her sense of alienation.

Soon, she was subjected to the same kind of hurts she experienced in high school, only this time there was a far more cruel edge. The torments reached a height when fraternity members sought to have her recognized as the "ugliest man on campus," a highly visible campaign carried out in the college newspaper.

Music provided a solace, and Joplin sang and played autoharp with the Waller Creek Boys, a trio from Austin. While performing with the Wallers, Joplin began to truly develop the harsh but alluring vocal style that gained her fame. The small lineup included R. Powell St. John, who wrote songs for a rock and roll band called the 13th Floor Elevators, a Texas group whose primitive garage-band style engendered a cult following through the years. In the spring of 1966, the group asked Joplin to become a member, and she seriously considered the offer. But she was diverted from this course when Helms got back in touch with her, encouraging her to return to San Francisco. There was a band called Big Brother and the Holding Company, he told her, and they needed a female singer.

Joined Big Brother and the Holding Company

Actually, Helms was the manager for the group. Since Joplin had last seen him, Helms had become a major player in the burgeoning San Francisco music scene. He was part of an urban hippie commune called the Family Dog, and he owned the Avalon Ballroom, a popular entertainment venue that hosted rock concerts and "psychedelic dances."

In June 1966, following Helm's advice, Joplin returned to San Francisco. By this time, the city had become a counter-cultural Mecca. The beatnik/bohemian scene of the late 1950s and early 1960s had evolved into the so-called "hippie scene." In this trend-setting hub, "flower children" promoted "love, peace and understanding" while flaunting alternative lifestyle choices and a spiritual awakening fueled by the drug LSD, and music had become a central preoccupation.

First as a band calling itself the Warlocks, the Grateful Dead were at the vanguard of what would soon be termed the "San Francisco sound," and they were followed by other bands poised for stardom including Country Joe and the Fish, Jefferson Airplane and Quicksilver Messenger Service. With the addition of Janis Joplin, Big Brother and the Holding Company would soon join that West Coast pantheon.

Before Joplin, Big Brother developed a strong following as the house band at Helm's Avalon Ballroom. Like other local bands, the group's performances often ventured off into extended instrumental improvisations that the media would tag as "psychedelic music." Personnel included guitarist and vocalist Sam Andrew, guitarist James Gurley, bassist Peter Albin and drummer David Getz.

Joplin agreed to join the band, and she immediately felt at home, both in the city and with her new professional situation. Even though she had no experience working with a rock band, her vocal style proved a highly appropriate complement to Big Brother's loose and loud style. After its debut on June 10, 1966, at the Avalon, the new-version Big Brother became an immediate hit on a local level.

Afterward, the band hit the road and pretty much worked continuously. Only two months later, after performing at a club in Chicago, Joplin and her band mates were asked to sign a recording contract with Mainstream Records, a small, independent company. Gratified and encouraged, the group immediately went into the studio, putting together its first album. However, the deal turned out to be a fiasco. Andrew told *Rolling Stone* that it was a "disaster."

"We were naïve kids," Andrew recalled. "The club was burning us and here was this cat saying come on down to the recording studio tomorrow, sign up and let's go to the lawyer and make sure it's all cool. . . ."

But it wasn't "cool." The sessions were rushed and under-financed, and Mainstream delayed the album's release for almost a year. In addition, the company, and the lawyer, was out to exploit the band rather than nurture the relationship. "We asked [the lawyer] for $1,000, and he said no," Andrew recalled in *Rolling Stone* in 1970. "We said 500? He said no. Well, can we have plane fare home? He said not one penny . . . we got back and it was a good time in San Francisco, small gigs. . . ."

Stole the Spotlight at Monterey

Big Brother kept performing throughout California, providing itself with the exposure that translated into an ever-increasing and adoring audience. Their hard work and growing reputation earned them an invitation to perform at what would turn out to be a historic event: the Monterey International Pop Festival of 1967.

This seminal event in rock music history, which predated later music festivals such as Woodstock (where Joplin also appeared), was organized by music executive Lou Adler and musician John Phillips (founder of the Mamas and the Papas). It was designed as sort of an alternative to the popular and ongoing Monterey Jazz Festival, as a means to spotlight rock music, which was just beginning to be perceived as a major cultural force.

The festival, held in Monterey, California on June 16-18, 1967, at the beginning of what became known as the "Summer of Love," included the some of the best known names in the pop and rock music scene such as the Mamas and The Papas, the Association, The Who, the Byrds, Paul Butterfield Blues Band, Scott McKenzie, Canned Heat, Buffalo Springfield, Johnny Rivers, Electric Flag (with legendary guitarist Michael Bloomfield), Eric Burdon and the Animals, and Simon and Garfunkel. The up-and-coming San Francisco bands featured included Jefferson Airplane, Country Joe and The Fish, The Grateful Dead, the Steve Miller Band, Quicksilver Messenger Service and Moby Grape. Moreover, reflecting the increasing diversity of popular music styles, the eclectic lineup also included Lou Rawls, Otis Redding, Booker T. and The MGs with The Mar-Keys, Hugh Masakela, Laura Nyro, and Indian sitarist Ravi Shankar.

Despite the strong lineup, the festival proved to be the breakout occasion for what would become two major entities in rock music. Rising far above the rest of the big-name talent were the Jimi Hendrix Experience and Big Brother and The Holding Company. Indeed, today, along with Otis Redding, the names most closely associated with the Monterey festival are Jimi Hendrix and Janis Joplin.

Originally, Big Brother was slated for only one appearance, during the festival's afternoon show. However, Joplin's performance so electrified the audience that festival organizers quickly made a spot for the group in the evening show. Joplin's star-making performance was recorded for posterity by filmmaker D. A. Pennebaker (who previously made the Bob Dylan documentary *Don't Look Back,* and it appears in his film of the festival called *Monterey Pop.*

Response to Joplin and the group was so great, and word-of-mouth enthusiasm spread so fast and far, that Mainstream records felt commercially compelled to release the group's album. On initial release, the album was a moderate national hit, and today it is considered an essential classic by rock album connoisseurs.

More importantly, though, Big Brother and the Holding Company—and especially Janis Joplin—had caught the attention of the major record labels. Famed music business manager Albert Grossman, whose clients included Dylan, signed the band to a management deal and secured Big Brother a recording contract with Columbia Records.

Recorded "Cheap Thrills"

By late 1967 and early 1968, Big Brother had developed into a major performing act across the country. In the winter of 1968, the group toured the East Coast for the first time and, on February 18, they made their first-ever New York City appearance, garnering rave reviews in the area's influential alternative press.

The rest of the country was now getting an up-close look at Joplin's unique presence and style, and she became their "Janis." In performance, characteristically footstomping her way across a stage, Joplin was a swirl of colors and physical movement. With psychedelic stage lights highlighting her tossed and wild red hair, feather boas flowing about her flailing arms and writhing body, streaming sweat glistening on her face like copious tears as she belted the blues, swigging openly and unapologetically from the bottles of Southern Comfort that accompanied her both onstage and off—Joplin was harnessed lighting unleashed inside a concert hall. She was at once uncontrolled, physically dirty, foulmouthed, yet endearing and inspirational, not to mention sensual and sexy. Audiences had never seen anything like her before, and they were easily seduced.

In the March and April of 1968 the group was hard at work on its second album, at that point tentatively titled *Dope, Sex, and Cheap Thrills.* When the record was released in August, the provocative title was shortened to just *Cheap Thrills,* and the band's live billing was now "Janis Joplin with Big Brother and the Holding Company," which indicated the shifting status within the band. Joplin's stature was outdistancing the rest of the members'. People even began referring to the group as Janis and the band.

During the late summer and early fall, the album's single "Piece of My Heart" became a huge radio hit. The album itself reached the top of the Billboard chart on October 12, 1968, and proved the artistic equal of other major albums released in the very same period. *Cheap Thrills* held its own against late-summer/fall releases that included The Beatles' *White Album,* The Band's *Music From Big Pink,* Jimi Hendrix's *Electric Ladyland* and Cream's *Wheels of Fire.*

Big Brother Breakup

With success came the usual pressures that would sink many a rock and roll band: ego conflicts, hurt feelings and the increased drug and alcohol use that often accompanied increased income. Joplin, with her fragile emotional state, was particularly susceptible to the entrapments of stardom. She reportedly used liquor and heroin to help ease the pain of a loneliness that never seemed to go away, even before an audience of adoring fans.

Eventually, and predictably, the band broke up. Big Brother, with Joplin, made its final appearances together in December 1968, even as *Cheap Thrills* remained at the top of the charts and national audiences were just getting to know the group. The drink and the drugs began affecting both the performing and personal relationships. More significantly, however, the personal dynamics within the band were similar to those within a relationship or marriage that nears its end when one partner achieves greater success than the other. There was a widening gulf between Joplin and the rest of Big Brother. Albin recalled for *Rolling Stone* what is was like: "The kind of performance she would put out would be a different trip than the band's. I'd say it was a star trip, where she related to the audience like she was the only one on the stage, and not relating to us at all."

But to many observers, it did not appear that Joplin was on a ego trip. Rather, she simply outgrew the group. Big Brother was considered a good band that became a great band with Janis Joplin. The prevailing opinion became that the band was sloppy and informal, and Joplin was way out of its class.

Joplin's Kozmic Blues

Soon, Joplin and Andrew formed a new band, one with a horn section that would add a necessary element to Joplin's vocal style and song choices. The band became known as Janis Joplin and Her Kozmic Blues Band, and she took it on the road for her one and only European tour. Throughout 1969, the band played with Joplin in her appearances at major rock festivals including the Newport '69 Pop Festival, the Atlanta Pop Festival, and Woodstock.

In October 1969, Joplin released the album *I Got Dem Ol' Kozmic Blues Again, Mama!,* which earned gold-record status. But the band only remained together for about a year.

Going Full-tilt Toward Tragedy

In 1970, on April 4, Janis performed with Big Brother and the Holding Company for a reunion concert in San Francisco, but she was in the process of forming a new band that would be called the Full Tilt Boogie Band. The new lineup went into the studio to record Joplin's last album called *Pearl*, the singer's nickname adopted by her closest friends. At this point, everything seemed to be going well for Joplin. The new band demonstrated more professionalism, and Joplin herself had appeared to quit using drugs. In addition, with the new band, she felt she finally landed on a sound that best reflected her vocal style.

She was never able to completely free herself from the lure of drugs, though, or her continuing affection for alcohol, and this resulted in her sudden death from an accidental overdose in a Hollywood motel in October 1970.

According to reports, Joplin's body was found in the Landmark Hotel on October 4, 1970. Apparently, the death followed a night of drinking and drug use. The condition of her body and her state of dress generated a great deal of speculation. She was found wearing only underwear, and her body was wedged between the bed and night stand. There were fresh needle marks in her arm, her lip and nose were bloodied, and $4.50 in bills and change were clenched in one fist.

Much was also made of that fact that Joplin had created a will shortly before she died. But signing a will is typically a legal move that someone decides to make when things are going well—and, indeed, things were going well for Joplin. She appeared on the verge of greater success, she had found a set of musicians who seemed in sync with her artistic ambitions, she had bought a house, and, reportedly, she was in a healthy and loving relationship.

But the actual circumstances of her death were more sordid than sensational. The scenario that was eventually pieced together from evidence indicated that Joplin, who was staying in the motel while recording the *Pearl* album, had indulged in alcohol and heroin, then went out to get change for cigarettes. She arrived back in her room around one o'clock in the morning, and partially undressed she suddenly lurched forward, in a drug-and-alcohol-induced spasm, striking her face on the nightstand.

Joplin's body was found hours after she died, making it a sad and lonely death, all the more perplexing because of the affection she easily attracted both from her listening audience, fellow professionals, family and close friends. She was just 27 years old. She was cremated and her ashes were scattered off the California coast.

The *Pearl* album was released posthumously several months later, becoming one of the best-selling albums of 1971. It held the number-one spot on the Billboard charts for nine weeks. The single released from the album, "Me and Bobby McGee," also reached number one. But more than that song, or the equally popular "Mercedes Benz," the highpoint of the essentially unfinished album was "Cry Baby," Joplin's stunning interpretation of the soul song originally performed by Garnett Mims and the Enchanters in 1963. It provided an appropriate coda, both to a professional career waiting to realize its full potential and to a sad life of a much beloved performer.

Books

Graham, B., R. Greenfield, *Bill Graham Presents: My Life Inside of Rock and Out,* Doubleday, 1992.
Contemporary Musicians, Volume 3, Gale Research 1990.
Stokes, G.; K. Tucker, E. Ward, *Rock of Ages: The Rolling Stone History of Rock and Roll,* Rolling Stone Press, 1986.

Periodicals

Rolling Stone, October 29, 1970; November 12, 1970.
Washington Post, May 5, 1998.

Online

"Janis Joplin Biography," *Official Janis,* http://www.officialjanis.com/bio.html (December 30, 2005). ☐

K

Kabir

Kabir (c. 1440-c. 1518), thought to be active in India during the first half of the fifteenth century, was a religious mystic who spoke in poetic sayings that were passed down to his followers. It is difficult to say much more about his life with any certainty, for his life is perhaps more encrusted with legend than that of any other religious figure.

Kabir was probably not literate. The sparse information about his life and work that has come down from his own time has been embellished by oral tradition and manipulated by religious groups with their own agenda, to a point where it is impossible to establish even such basic facts as the places and dates of Kabir's birth and death. Yet Kabir has exerted a strong hold on religious and literary imaginations in both India and the West. He certainly existed, and has an establiished body of followers in India who explicitly proclaim devotion to his ideals, and he is admired for his nonsectarian mysticism and the intensity of his poetic language. Features common to many accounts of his life are thought to be accurate aspects of his biography. If Kabir posed insuperable challenges to biographers, he nevertheless continued to be a substantial spiritual presence in modern life.

Rejected All Organized Religions

Accounts of Kabir's life, in both India and the West, offer conflicting information regarding his birth. Indian admirers of Kabir list long life among his remarkable feats. Some have claimed that he lived as long as 300 years, and

the lifespan of 120 years is still commonly given, with a birth year of 1398 and a death year of 1518. He spent much of his life in the city of Benares, and the book that introduced Kabir to the West placed his birth there in 1440, with the common date of 1518 given for his death. Many other towns in northern India have been proposed as his birthplace, with Magahar named perhaps more often than any other.

It is somewhat clearer that Kabir was born into the Islamic faith, for Kabir or al-Kabir, meaning the Great One, is a common name in the Islamic world and is one of the 99 names of God given in the Quran. In spite of what appears to have been his steadfast rejection of organized religion in all its forms, both Hindus and Muslims have tried to claim Kabir as one of their own. One common legend holds that Kabir was the child of the widow of a Brahmin, a member of the priestly caste of Hindu India, and that he was given to a Muslim weaver's family to raise. Sources and legends concur that Kabir practiced the weaver's trade, and this may be regarded as one of the few solid facts in his biography.

A story often told about Kabir's early life, and generally ascribed to his own words, sheds some light on his religious orientation. The story concerns Kabir's initiation into the life of a religious mystic. Despite his Muslim background, Kabir hoped to become a disciple of the Hindu mystic Ramananda. Realizing that his chances were slim, he hid on some steps leading down to the Ganges river, steps that Ramananda generally used in the morning while making his way to the river to bathe. The Hindu ascetic accidentally stepped on Kabir, and called out "Ram! Ram!"—roughly, "My Lord! My Lord!" Kabir went on to claim that this mantra spoken by Ramananda initiated him into discipleship of the Hindu mystic. Ramananda's Hindu attendants as well as local Muslim observers were outraged, but

Kabir continued to claim discipleship with the Ramananda, and the great saint was impressed with his persistence. Kabir's own poems mention Ramananda as his guru, and the direct, devotional language of the two mystics has many common aspects. Ramananda was at one time thought to have died in the first half of the fifteenth century, but it is now believed that he was born around 1400 and died around 1470. If Kabir was indeed a young religious seeker when he met Ramananda, the date of 1440 emerges as potentially close to his birth date.

Manual Labor Influenced Poetry

It is generally agreed that Kabir was a weaver, and that he never went to school or learned to read and write. This background of manual labor had a strong impact on Kabir's poetry, which uses common imagery of family and natural phenomena to communicate sometimes very subtle riddles and conundrums to point the way to the nature of the divine. Scholars have disagreed, however, as to how vigorously Kabir pursued his trade after he embarked on a life of mysticism. Evelyn Underhill, in the introduction to Bengali poet Rabindranath Tagore's well-known English translation of Kabir's poems, opined that "Like Paul the tentmaker, [German mystic Jacob] Boehme the cobbler, [English preacher John] Bunyan the tinker, [and German religious writer] Gerhard Tersteegen, he knew how to combine vision and industry; the work of his hands helped rather than hindered the impassioned meditation of his heart." Other writers, however, have pointed to words ascribed to Kabir in which he appears to recount arguments with his wife, or his mother, over the problems a religious sage experienced in supporting a family. Kabir was married at least once, and had one or more children.

The most striking features of Kabir's poetry are its ecstatic feeling and its rejection of both Hinduism and Islam in favor of a direct relationship with the divine. Kabir's poetry is best known in the West in Tagore's translation, published in 1915; all quotations in this essay are taken from that translation. The authenticity of the 100 "Songs of Kabir" contained in that volume has been questioned, but there is no such thing as an authentic body of Kabir's words. "I have had my Seat on the Self-Poised one," Kabir said. "I have drunk of the Cup of the Ineffable. / I have found the Key of the Mystery. / I have reached the Root of Union. / Traveling by no track, I have come to the Sorrowless Land: very easily has the mercy of the great Lord come upon me. . . . There the whole sky is filled with sound, and there that music is made without fingers and without strings; / There the game of pleasure and pain does not cease. / Kabir says 'If you merge your life in the Ocean of Life, you will find your life in the Supreme Land of Bliss.'" Kabir used many kinds of imagery to convey ideas of religious ecstasy, but very common among them are images of music (especially "unstruck" or unsounded music) and marital love. He was apparently a musician himself and probably sang his poems rather than speaking them.

Like other great mystics, Kabir pointed to the inward life of the mind as the source of contact with the divine. "Do not go to the garden of flowers!" he said, in Tagore's transla-

tion. "O Friend! go not there; / In your body is the garden of flowers. / Take your seat on the thousand petals of the lotus, and there gaze on the Infinite Beauty." Kabir's thoughts on consciousness could express metaphysical subtlety: "Between the poles of the conscious and the unconscious, there has the mind made a swing: / Thereon hang all beings and all worlds, and that swing never ceases its sway. . . . All swing! The sky and the earth and the air and the water; and the Lord himself taking form: / And the sight of this has made Kabir a servant." For the most part, though, his language was simple and directed toward common people; ordinary Indians responded to his words and formed a Hindu sect devoted to his writing. A count of members of these "Kabir-panthis" in 1900 found about one million of them.

Experienced Religious Persecution

In his own time, however, Kabir seemed to have antagonized religious authorities and to have been persecuted for his beliefs. It is easy to see why; Kabir had no use for religious observances and sometimes ridiculed specifically denominational religious teachers. "O servant, where dost thou seek Me?," he has the divinity ask in one of the best-known poems in the Tagore translation. "Lo! I am beside thee. / I am neither in temple nor in mosque; I am neither in Kaaba nor in Kailash: / Neither am I in rites and ceremonies, nor in Yoga and renunciation. / If thou art a true seeker, thou shalt at once see me; thou shalt meet me in a moment of time." Kabir believed that the divine could be found everywhere, in common substances, and his thought had some aspects in common with the modern doctrine of pantheism. He rejected both Hindu worship of idols and the Islamic sacred text. "The images are all lifeless; they cannot speak: / I know, for I have cried aloud to them. / The Purana and the Koran are mere words: / lifting up the curtain, I have seen."

Late in life, Kabir was apparently charged by the Indian emperor Sikandar Lodi with claiming that he had divine powers. He was forced to leave Benares and wandered from place to place around northern India. In poems thought to date from the end of his life, he lamented that his fingers could no longer make the music to accompany his songs of praise. Venerated soon after his death, which perhaps occurred in 1518, Kabir eventually became the object of a kind of adoration he would probably have discouraged while he was alive. Of the dozens of legends that surround his life and death, an especially poetic one concerns his burial: Hindus and Muslims wrangled over his dead body, with the Hindus wanting to cremate it according to custom, while Muslims argued that he should be buried. In the midst of the argument, Kabir appeared in the air and told the disputants to pull back the cloth that covered him. They did so, and found a pile of flower petals. The petals were divided, with the Muslims burying their half and the Hindus burning theirs.

Some of the esteem in which Kabir is held in India today results from the belief that he succeeded in merging Islamic and Hindu streams of thought. He has influenced Hinduism and also the Islamic mystical tradition of Sufism, and some have found links between Kabir's songs and traditions of Christian mysticism. The Tagore translation of Kabir's poems was followed by other renderings of his work in English, and some of his works have been set anew to music. Kabir enriched the modern Hindi language with many expressions and turns of phrase, and in 1952 a Kabir image (although none is known to have been made while he was alive) appeared on an Indian nine-rupee postage stamp.

Books

Hedayetullah, Muhammad, *Kabir: The Apostle of Hindu-Muslim Unity,* Motilal Banarsidass (India), 1977.
Tagore, Rabindranath, trans., *Songs of Kabir,* Macmillan, 1915.
Varman, Ram Kumar, *Kabir: Biography and Philosophy,* Prints India, 1977.
Vaudeville, Charlotte, *Kabir,* Oxford, 1974.

Online

''Biography of Kabir,'' http://www.poetseers.org/the_poetseers/kabir (February 13, 2006).
''Kabir: The Mystic Poet,'' http://www.boloji.com/kabir/index.html (February 13, 2006). □

Herbert von Karajan

Over 30 years as its conductor, Herbert von Karajan (1908-1989) molded the Berlin Philharmonic Orchestra into perhaps the finest of the world's large classical music ensembles. He was a superstar among conductors—his thick, steel-gray hair and authoritative manner was instantly recognizable around the musical world.

Von Karajan had the kind of powerful personality that stirred disagreement—even beyond the controversy generated by his allegiance to German Fascism early in his career. Critics and audiences marveled at the flawless sheen he could elicit from the Berlin Philharmonic and the other ensembles he conducted, but some found his interpretations almost too polished, lacking in soul and drama. Von Karajan was an autocrat on the podium, and his fabled perfectionism resulted in exhilarating orchestral sound but did not encourage fresh thinking. He lived a jet-set lifestyle, seeking and often receiving publicity, and he had a taste for adventure. Some called him egotistical or ruthless, and musicians cracked jokes in which God aspires to reach von Karajan's level. Yet, whatever divergent opinions music lovers might hold, few would disagree that von Karajan loomed large in the musical imagination of the twentieth century.

Studied Piano from Young Age

The son of Salzburg's chief medical officer, von Karajan grew up in that musically rich Austrian city, the hometown of Mozart. He started piano lessons at age three, gave a recital at eight, and generally benefited from his family's support. Von Karajan embarked on piano studies at the Salzburg Mozarteum but temporarily switched to an engineering program at the University of Vienna. When he was 20, he heard an opera performance by the legendary Italian conductor Arturo Toscanini, an artist whose single-mindedness and drive von Karajan himself would seek to emulate. ''From the first bar it was as if I had been struck a blow,'' Von Karajan later wrote (as quoted by Martin Kettle in London's *Guardian* newspaper). ''I was completely disconcerted by the perfection which had been achieved.''

Soon von Karajan was taking conducting lessons with Franz Schalk and leading a student ensemble. In March of 1929 he made his public debut as a conductor, leading a performance of Mozart's opera *The Marriage of Figaro* in Ulm, Germany. He remained on the staff of the Ulm opera house for five years but often returned to Salzburg to conduct orchestral performances there and to appear at the city's annual festival. Word spread about his talents, and critics began to prophesy a great future for the young conductor; one early newspaper review referred to him as *Das wunder Karajan.*

After Adolf Hitler rose to power in Germany, von Karajan flirted with fascism as early as 1933. When he was offered a job as music director at the municipal opera house in the German city of Aachen in 1934 or 1935, he agreed to join Germany's National Socialist (Nazi) party as a condition of employment. Details of von Karajan's involvement with the Nazis emerged slowly over the years, troubling many observers, and he never explicitly apologized for his support of Hitler's regime. The general consensus among historians, however, was that von Karajan had little interest in politics and joined the party because that seemed to be a good professional move at the time.

Indeed, von Karajan ran into trouble with the fascist overlords of German culture during the Nazi period. At first, with his striking good looks and fearsome energy, he created a sensation in German musical circles. In the late 1930s he was the toast of musical Berlin thanks to highly successful stints conducting *The Marriage of Figaro* and the gigantic Wagner opera *Tristan and Isolde* at the Berlin State Opera, where he became music director in 1938. He feuded with the other leading German conductor of the time, Wilhelm Furtwängler, who never joined the Nazis but maintained strong control over musical life in Germany. Hitler's deputy, Hermann Goering, admired von Karajan's work, but Hitler himself disliked it. That was a strong sign of trouble for von Karajan, who remained at work in Berlin during the first part of the war, but eventually fled to Italy with his second wife, Anna Maria. She was one-quarter Jewish, which further complicated the couple's status under the German government's system of racial classification.

Underwent American De-Nazification Procedure

After the war, von Karajan returned to Austria and submitted himself to questioning by an American de-Nazification tribunal. At first he was prohibited from performing, but was cleared to conduct a concert by the Vienna Philharmonic Orchestra in 1946. In the audience was Walter Legge, a top producer and executive with England's EMI record company. Amazed by von Karajan's energy, Legge smoothed the way for von Karajan to record with the Gesellschaft der Musikfreunde, a Vienna music society orchestra, and later to conduct the Philharmonia Orchestra in London. Even at this stage the ambitious von Karajan drove a hard bargain; a series of recordings Legge made with von Karajan conducting the Philharmonia took months of negotiation.

In 1947, finally given an unconditional green light by officials of the American occupation, von Karajan began to conduct frequently and resumed much of his former star status. The following year he was hired as conductor at La Scala, the Milan, Italy opera house that stood at the center of Italian operatic tradition. It was a measure of von Karajan's versatility that over much of his career he was considered among the world's top conductors of Italian opera, something uncommon among composers trained in the German-Austrian tradition. Despite his authoritarian streak he was a talented handler of singers with equally strong personalities; African-American soprano Leontyne Price, according to John Rockwell of the *New York Times*, called von Karajan "one of the kindest men I ever met."

In Germany and Austria, too, von Karajan's mystique grew. Partly because, aside from Furtwängler, he had few competitors at his level in the German-speaking world; many of Germany's top musicians had been Jewish and had fled, if they could, to the United States and other countries. The expansion of classical music as recordings migrated from three-minute 78 rpm discs to LPs, which were much

better suited to compositions that might be an hour or more in length, also played a role in his growing success. Von Karajan toured widely with the Philharmonia and Vienna Philharmonic orchestras. To relieve the pressure associated with his growing renown, he took up yoga; he later practiced Zen Buddhism.

Finally, in 1955, von Karajan had his chance. Furtwängler, the conductor of the Berlin Philharmonic, died before the orchestra, Germany's most prominent, could undertake an American tour—its first since the war, and a potent symbol of Germany's full restoration to membership in the international cultural community. Von Karajan offered himself as the ideal replacement. The claim was justifiable, but von Karajan, with characteristic calculation, also insisted that he be named the orchestra's conductor for life. The orchestra's administration agreed, and the protests and pickets that met von Karajan in the U.S. were soon silenced by his dynamic presence on the podium.

Made More Than 800 Recordings

Von Karajan's appointment as the Berlin Philharmonic's conductor inaugurated a long reign at the top of the classical music world. The classics were at the top of their postwar popularity, and conductor-stars such as Leonard Bernstein flourished in both the U.S. and Europe. None could rival von Karajan, however, in terms of a reputation for absolute mastery over an orchestra. Signed to West Germany's premier classical label, Deutsche Grammophon, von Karajan recorded Beethoven's cycle of nine symphonies on three separate occasions. He amassed a total of over 800 recordings over his long career. The Berlin Philharmonic was his "instrument," but he was in demand as a guest conductor. An often-told anecdote related how von Karajan got into a taxi at an airport and, when the driver asked him where he wanted to go, he replied that it didn't matter; people wanted him everywhere.

Named the artistic director of the Vienna State Opera in 1956, von Karajan became as famous in opera houses as he was in orchestral concert halls. He conducted Wagner's massive four-opera *Ring* cycle at the Bayreuth theater in southeastern Germany, where it had been premiered a century before. Von Karajan also assumed the directorship of the Salzburg Festival in his hometown, revitalizing an event that had come to seem a rather lifeless shrine to Wolfgang Amadeus Mozart and his music. Where other German conductors tended to restrict themselves mostly to the classic Austro-German strand of classical music running from Haydn and Mozart through Beethoven and Brahms, von Karajan ranged farther afield, winning special acclaim for his interpretations of the orchestrally lush symphonies of Finnish composer Jean Sibelius. He continued to appear frequently in Italy and to conduct the music of Verdi, Puccini, and other Italian operatic composers.

Von Karajan on the podium was an unforgettable figure for those who saw him in concert, and even more so for the players who worked under him. Philharmonia orchestra flutist Gareth Morris (as quoted by Terry Teachout in *Commentary*) recalled von Karajan's conducting of Ravel's *Bolero* this way: "With the eyes closed and the hands barely chest high, von Karajan gave us the beat with a single finger, and even that barely moved. . . . With each slight lift of the hands the tension became even greater. By the end of the piece, the hands were above his head. And that power of that final climax was absolutely colossal.'' Von Karajan generally conducted with his eyes closed, as if to say that the music existed in an abstract world beyond the conductor and musicians. Indeed, controlling though he may have been, his interpretations did not draw attention to themselves in a radical way; he aimed instead to erase the boundary between music and listener.

French fashion model Eliette Mouret became von Karajan's third wife, and he lived the high life in his spare time, maintaining houses in the Austrian Alps, in the Swiss resort of St. Moritz, and in the glamorous French town of St. Tropez. Von Karajan learned to fly his own plane, at first a two-seater and finally a Lear jet that he shared with an Austrian airline. He was a mountain climbing enthusiast, and he could often be found on Europe's ski slopes. Von Karajan drew photographers and gossip journalists with outlandish statements; he once, for instance, said that he was considering having himself cryogenically frozen so that he could later be thawed and re-record pieces from the standard classical repertory.

The ego revealed by such statements grated on some observers during the last phases of von Karajan's career, and some of the bloom came off his reputation in the late 1970s and 1980s. Reviewers sometimes charged that he was repeating himself as he performed and recorded the same works again and again, and even the musicians of the Berlin Philharmonic began to resist his authority; when he tried to add a young protegée, clarinetist Sabine Meyer, to the orchestra, the (all-male) group of musicians, which traditionally held the prerogative to make personnel decisions, rebelled, and von Karajan was forced to give in. Von Karajan did, however, succeed in making an international star of another protegée, violinist Anne-Sophie Mutter, whose playing had the same steely quality of perfection that von Karajan cultivated as a conductor. In increasingly poor health after a stroke and several other serious medical crises, von Karajan resigned as conductor of the Berlin Philharmonic in April of 1989. Though he continued to work, he lived only three more months and died at his home in the Austrian Alps on July 16, 1989. Some called him the last great conductor in the German-speaking world's great tradition.

Books

Osborne, Richard, *Herbert von Karajan: A Life in Music,* Chatto & Windus, 1998.
Vaughan, Roger, *Herbert von Karajan,* Norton, 1986.

Periodicals

Billboard, August 7, 1999.
Commentary, May 2000.
Guardian (London, England), July 17, 1989.
National Review, August 18, 1989.
New York Times, July 17, 1989.
Washington Post, July 17, 1989. □

Boris Karloff

British actor Boris Karloff (1887-1969) created a cinematic icon when he played the role of the monster in the 1931 film *Frankenstein*.

The ghoulish makeup he wore and the lurching walk he adopted in the film have become conventions, even cliches, of horror films. And beyond the individual techniques Karloff used when playing the role of the monster, he created a feeling of sympathy for the character, a technique that has since become a more general trait of successful horror films, whose monsters often gain intensity by fascinating audiences as well as repelling them. Karloff became a star with *Frankenstein,* which he made when he was already well into middle age. His life up to that point had been colorful, and attracted a host of biographers in spite of his reticence about his personal affairs. After *Frankenstein,* Karloff made many other films, some of them quite significant. He enjoyed a successful run as a stage actor and became a familiar figure on radio and then television. It was *Frankenstein,* however, that put his name in lights and led to his being billed, at the height of his fame, simply as ''Karloff.'' That name recognition was something only a few other movie stars have achieved.

Groomed for Government Career

The youngest of nine children, Karloff was born William Henry Pratt on November 23, 1887, in Camberwell, a suburb of London, England. His father, Edward Pratt, had worked for much of his life in India, as a salt tax administrator for the British colonial government. The elder Pratt married three times; his third wife, Eliza, was Karloff's mother. Her family had lived in India as well, and some have speculated, as a way of explaining Karloff's unusually dark complexion, that she may have been partly of Indian ancestry. Edward Pratt left the family when Karloff was a year old, and he was raised largely by his stepsister Emma. Several of his older brothers entered the British civil service, and some of them followed their father's example and took posts in India. It was assumed that young Karloff would do the same.

Karloff's interests at school ran more to sports and music than to studying, however. His stage debut came in 1896 in a school play, a version of *Cinderella.* He loved to play and watch cricket, an enthusiasm he held for his entire life. Moving on from Enfield Grammar School to Merchant Taylor's School and the Uppingham School in London, Karloff kept on top of his studies and won admission to King's College at the University of London in 1907.

There he took courses that would lead to a place in Britain's diplomatic corps, but he spent more time attending plays in London. He dreamed of a theatrical career himself, but his family ridiculed the idea. In 1909 Karloff found himself frustrated with university studies. He was receiving poor grades and was supremely restless. Deciding to leave Britain, he flipped a coin to decide whether he would go to Canada or Australia. Canada won, and after coming ashore

of the border; Karloff entered the United States for the first time via North Dakota in October of 1913, and traveled through the upper Midwest. He left and rejoined the St. Clair group as he found work with other theatrical stock companies, and eked out a living while traveling around the country. When World War I broke out, Karloff volunteered to join the British army but was rejected because of a heart murmur. The St. Clair Players sputtered to a halt for good in 1917, but by that time they had reached Los Angeles, California, landing Karloff at the doorstep of the growing film industry.

Touring with several theater companies in southern California, Karloff began appearing as an extra in films. His first film credit may have been for *His Majesty, the American,* starring Douglas Fairbanks, in 1919; he appeared in several dozen films during the silent era, and his memory of the very earliest ones was hazy. By the early 1920s he was finding consistent film work, often playing Native Americans, Mexicans, or Asian characters as a result of his exotic looks—at the time, Hollywood films were virtually an all-white preserve. Even after several years of working in the lower levels of the industry, Karloff saw few prospects of a breakthrough, and took a job in 1923 unloading giant putty casks from a building materials truck. He had married musician Montana Laurena Williams in 1920, after a first marriage, to actress Olive de Wilton, ended in divorce sometime after 1912. Karloff married dancer Helene Vivian Soulee in 1924, Los Angeles librarian Dorothy Stine in 1930, and English-born Evelyn Hope Helmore in 1946.

After meeting with silent film horror star Lon Chaney Sr. in the late 1920s, Karloff received some much-needed encouragement. Chaney (as quoted by Nollen) told him that "the secret of success in Hollywood lies in being different from anyone else. Find something no one else can or will do—and they'll begin to take notice of you. Hollywood is full of competent actors. What the screen needs is individuality!" Karloff took the advice to heart, stepping into negative roles that took advantage of his gaunt, rather unnerving appearance. His career took a step up with a role in *Scarface* under director Howard Hawks in 1931, and later that year he was sitting in a Universal Studios lunchroom when English-born director James Whale, in the process of casting *Frankenstein,* noticed him and envisioned him in the role of the monster.

Karloff got the part after Bela Lugosi turned it down to pursue another project, and he became a major star almost overnight. The film was a tremendous box office success, touched off a vogue for horror films that lasted through much of the 1930s, and was soon hailed as a classic. Three-quarters of a century later the film still held up well, largely thanks to the strongly human qualities of Karloff's performance. "There are more moments of quiet power (most of them involving the strikingly effective Boris Karloff as the monster who simply wants to be loved) than you'll find in a fistful of big-budget horror films," noted Dan Jardine in the *All Movie Guide.* Karloff wore several pounds of makeup and donned heavy asphalt shoes that gave the monster his characteristic gait.

in Montreal in May of 1909, Karloff soon found himself rounding up horses in a field at 4:30 in the morning, having been hired as a farmhand. Karloff soon made his way to western Canada, moving from Banff, Alberta, to Vancouver, British Columbia, paying his way with such jobs as race-track digger, streetcar track builder, and coal shoveler.

A place on a survey crew with the British Columbia Electric Company brought both a salary raise and an improvement in working conditions for Karloff, but he still nurtured hopes of becoming an actor. Hearing of a job with a troupe called the Jean Russell Players, he took a train to Kamloops, British Columbia, to audition. He devised the stage name Boris Karloff, claiming that Karloff was a name from his mother's family background, and he was quoted as saying in Scott Allen Nollen's book *Boris Karloff* that he pulled the name Boris "from out of the cold, Canadian air." Karloff claimed to have had experience on stage in England, and was hired. The troupe's managers quickly saw through the ruse and cut his salary in half, but Karloff barnstormed around Canada with the troupe for two years, until a Saskatchewan tornado brought the Jean Russell Players to an abrupt end.

Entered United States

Karloff signed on with another troupe, the St. Clair Players. This job was hardly more lucrative; Karloff recalled having to cook his breakfast by frying an egg on an electric iron propped upside down between a Gideon Bible and a bedpost. But the St. Clair Players did operate on both sides

Made Over $3,000 a Week

Karloff signed a contract with Universal Studios that gave him a salary of $750 a week in 1932. After several more hits, including *The Mask of Fu Manchu* (1932) and *The Black Cat* (1934, with Lugosi), his weekly salary had risen to $3,750. He earned his keep, making nine films during 1932 alone. His films varied in quality, but his elegant variations on the persona he had established with *Frankenstein* made them consistently compelling. Karloff and his wife Dorothy moved out of what they described as a shack in Laurel Canyon into a series of increasingly elegant lodgings, culminating in a mansion in the Coldwater Canyon area, where Karloff could indulge his passion for gardening. He also amassed a collection of unusual pets that included a tortoise, a parrot, egg-laying chickens, a cow named Elsie, a four-hundred-pound pig, and several dogs, two of which were named Angus Dei and Silly Bitch. Even as he personally experienced tremendous success, Karloff emerged as an advocate for the welfare of actors who labored in the trenches, as he had for so long. In 1933 he became a co-founder of the Screen Actors Guild union.

Often bemused by the Frankenstein phenomenon, Karloff also had a certain affection for the monster and was reluctant to make sequels that would degrade the impact of the original film. He made one, *Bride of Frankenstein,* in 1935, and another, *Son of Frankenstein,* in 1938, in the year his only child, a daughter Sara, was born. In 1940 he returned to the stage, starring in the original Broadway production of the comic horror play *Arsenic and Old Lace,* and going on tour with the company as it toured 66 cities during World War II. During the war years Karloff also edited two best-selling collections of horror and suspense stories, *Tales of Terror* and *And the Darkness Falls.*

Karloff made numerous films after the war, but he became increasingly known for his work on radio and television. He hosted the radio program *Starring Boris Karloff* beginning in 1949, and the show successfully made the transition to television in the early 1950s. Two 1950 projects, the radio show *Boris Karloff's Treasure Chest* and the Broadway show *Peter Pan,* demonstrated Karloff's appeal to children and opened up a successful career avenue for him in his later years. Karloff and his wife Evelyn moved to New York in 1951, eventually taking up residence in the Dakota apartment building.

Continuing to find joy and energy in performing, as he had since his youth, Karloff remained busy as an actor until his last days. Broadening his repertoire well beyond horror, he appeared on Broadway in *The Lark* in 1955 and was nominated for an Antoinette Perry (Tony) Award. Beginning the following year and continuing until 1968, Karloff recorded a daily radio program, *Tales from the Reader's Digest.* In 1962 he earned a Grammy nomination in the children's recordings category for his LP *Rudyard Kipling's Other Just So Stories: The Cat Who Walked by Himself,* and in 1966 Karloff narrated an animated television special, *How the Grinch Stole Christmas.* A broadcast of the program became an annual tradition, and Karloff became almost as familiar to baby-boomers for that role as he was for *Frankenstein.*

Karloff never took American citizenship. He lived with his wife in London during his last years, returning to the United States to work on projects in concentrated bursts. Among the most interesting products of his later years was the 1967 film *Targets,* directed by Peter Bogdanovich and starring Karloff as an aging horror film star who wants to retire because he finds the real world more horrifying than anything in the movies. Karloff continued to work on new films despite poor health; his last film was *Chamber of Fear* (1968), made in Mexico. He died in a hospital in Midhurst, Sussex, England, on February 2, 1969.

Books

Buehrer, Beverly Bare, *Boris Karloff: A Bio-Bibliography,* Greenwood, 1993.
International Dictionary of Films and Filmmakers, Vol. 3: Actors and Actresses, 4th ed., St James, 2000.
Jensen, Paul M., *Boris Karloff and His Films,* Barnes, 1974.
Nollen, Scott Allen, *Boris Karloff,* McFarland, 1991.
Underwood, Peter, *Karloff: The Life of Boris Karloff,* Drake, 1972.

Periodicals

New York Times, February 3, 2006.

Online

"Frankenstein," *All Movie Guide,* http://www.allmovie.com (February 19, 2006). □

Eartha Kitt

An actress, cabaret performer, and All-American success story, Eartha Kitt (born 1927) has entertained audiences around the world over the course of a career that has lasted more than 60 years and shown few signs of slowing down.

Kitt is perhaps best known for a stint as Catwoman in the 1960s television series *Batman,* but her career has gone through many different stages, both before and after that TV appearance. In the years after World War II she became a nightclub-singing star in France. She appeared in plays and films, and she notched several hit recordings in the 1950s, singing in various languages. After a much-publicized attack on the Vietnam War, delivered in person at the White House in 1968, Kitt returned to Europe, for she found doors closed to her in the American entertainment industry. But her career was revived in the 1980s, and, well past an age when most performers would have been long since retired, she kept her exotic yet by then familiar face in the spotlight with high-profile theatrical experiences and near-constant touring.

Faced Extraordinarily Difficult Childhood

For much of her life, Kitt did not know for certain where or when she had been born, but research by students at Benedict College in the 1990s unearthed a birth certificate

from St. Matthews, South Carolina, dated January 17, 1927. Her name was Eartha Mae Kitt-Fields. Kitt's father, whom she never knew, was white, and her part-Cherokee mother, struggling to survive at the height of the Depression, moved from place to place, doing chores and odd jobs wherever she could. Finally Kitt's mother met a man who asked her marry him, but he rejected Kitt because of her mixed-race background. Her mother's response was to leave her in the care of a local family, who abused her physically. The abuse was matched by kids in the area, who tied her to a tree and threw rocks at her. "I was told I was an ugly duckling, a yellow gal, even lower than the 'N' word," Kitt recalled to Leslie Gray Streeter of the *Palm Beach Post.* "I was not accepted by anybody on either side."

When she was about ten, Kitt was called to New York City by a woman she was told was her mother's sister. She heard that her mother had died, but, she told Karen S. Schneider of *People,* "I didn't even cry." It was in New York's Pennsylvania that she saw electric lights and indoor plumbing for the first time. Things did not immediately improve for Kitt; her aunt mostly ignored her, and Harlem school kids were as harsh as those in South Carolina had been. But teachers began to respond to Kitt, who always did well in school—she had a passion for reading and later enjoyed contemplating the works of philosophers such as Plato and Nietzsche. One gave her a ticket to see the play *Cyrano de Bergerac,* and she walked through Central Park afterward, wishing that she could have a career in which she enjoyed the adulation that the show's star, Jose Ferrer, had received. Another steered her in the direction of New York's

High School for the Performing Arts, the incubator of numerous show-business careers. "But what really opened me up was a beautiful Black woman who was a member of my Harlem church," Kitt recalled to Pamela Johnson of *Essence.* "One day she put her hand on my shoulder—it felt so spiritual. Then she said I was born with the hand of God on my shoulder. It gave me a spark inside, a fire that started burning in me."

Hoping to get away from her aunt, Kitt ran away from home several times. She got a job sewing clothes in a Harlem sweatshop and succeeded in living on her own and in eluding juvenile law enforcement officers. She was inspired to act on her performing ambitions after she saw the Katherine Dunham Dance Company—the first African-American troupe to gain a major reputation in the world of ballet—in a movie. After a lifetime of bad luck, Kitt received a break when one of the company's dancers stopped her on a Harlem street to ask for directions; Kitt parlayed that chance encounter into an audition and won a place in Dunham's troupe for a salary of ten dollars a week.

To the 16-year-old Kitt, it was a fortune. Her life began a dizzying upward spiral as the well-regarded company traveled around the Americas and Europe after the war. Dunham picked her for solos, and the athletic, exotic-looking Kitt found herself the object of attention from well-heeled men. The company toured France and England in 1947, and Kitt received rave reviews. "They didn't call me a beautiful woman," she told Schneider. "It was 'the beautiful creature.'" Kitt decided to capitalize on her growing fame; she resigned from the Dunham company in 1949 or 1950 and was booked into an upscale Paris nightclub.

Cast by Orson Welles

Kitt quickly became the talk of the town. She had picked up bits of foreign languages while living in Harlem, and she had no trouble mastering French. Her voice was not conventionally beautiful, but it had an odd timbre that probably worked to her advantage, for it complemented her exotic looks. Some observers compared her with Josephine Baker, an earlier American performer who had found success in Paris. Among the throngs that showed up to catch her act was legendary film director Orson Welles, who was in the process of casting a production of Christopher Marlowe's play *Doctor Faustus.* He tabbed Kitt to play the role of Helen of Troy. Welles also starred in the play, and he got carried away when he reached the lines "Helen, is this the face that launched a thousand ships? Helen, make me a mortal with a kiss": "Crunch, right into my bottom lip," she told Charles Osgood of CBS News. "The blood is seeping down my chin, and [Welles] has a hold of me so I can't get away. . . . And when I ran into him afterwards, and asked, why did you bite me? He said, 'I got excited.'" If Kitt was confused by such events, they also filled an emotional need. "Orson Welles called me the most exciting woman in the world," she told Ed Condran of New Jersey's Bergen County *Record.* "It was so nice to be accepted."

Returning to the United States. in 1952, Kitt won a part in the Broadway revue *New Faces.* She signed a recording contract with the RCA label, and by the mid-1950s she was well on her way to replicating her French success. Two songs she had added to her act in Paris, "C'est si bon" and the Turkish-language "Usku dara," became hits in the United States once more, and "I Want to Be Evil" furthered her sex-kitten image. She was one of just a few black vocalists to receive regular radio airplay outside of the urban rhythm-and-blues format prior to the rock and roll era. Kitt made two films in France, but mostly she stuck to the stage in the United States, for serious roles for black actors were rare. "I couldn't compromise on playing quote unquote nigger parts," she told *Ebony's* Richette Haywood. "We're here to carve a path for others, and if you don't take challenges you are not going to make it better for those people who are going to come behind you." In 1958 she had a major success on Broadway in *Shinbone Alley,* and she did appear in a film that year; costarring opposite actor Sammy Davis Jr. in the African-American family drama *Anna Lucasta* and becoming romantically involved with Davis.

Attention from gossip magazines may have helped Kitt's career by raising her profile, but her romantic life was not happy. In addition to Davis she dated Charles Revson, the founder of the Revlon cosmetics line, and Arthur Loew Jr., a member of the family that owned the Loews chain of movie theaters. The latter romance was perhaps the closest Kitt came to a mutually rewarding relationship, but any talk of marriage was scotched by Loew's family, which disapproved of the interracial pair. Finally, in 1960, Kitt married Bill McDonald. The couple had a daughter, Kitt, but soon divorced amid Kitt's allegations that her husband, who installed himself as her accountant, had handled her financial affairs dishonestly.

In the 1960s, Kitt rose to national entertainment prominence. She appeared in Bill Cosby's early television series *I Spy* and on *Mission: Impossible,* and she cracked the talk/variety show that defined the middle-American mainstream, *The Ed Sullivan Show.* Her biggest success was a stint as Catwoman on *Batman,* a role that was played by a series of actresses. Although Kitt was only involved with the show for a short time in 1967, she was identified with the part for decades afterward. The only weak spot in Kitt's popularity, ironically, was among African-Americans, some of whom perceived her as a product of the white-dominated entertainment industry.

Shut Out After War Critique

A major African-American leader came to Kitt's defense, however, as she was enveloped by controversy in 1968. Invited to a White House luncheon by Lady Bird Johnson, wife of President Lyndon Johnson, Kitt thought about the women she had met while giving dance workshops in the Watts neighborhood of Los Angeles; they told her that it was primarily poor people who were being sent to fight in Vietnam, while well-off college students avoided the war through student deferments. Kitt in turn told the assembled dignitaries at the White House that the Vietnam War was to blame for growing civil unrest in the U.S. "You send the best of this country off to be shot and maimed. No wonder the kids rebel and take pot," she was quoted as saying by Schneider. During the firestorm of criticism that

followed, the Reverend Martin Luther King called her and said she should be recommended for the Nobel Peace Prize. The antiwar student counterculture of the day also came to Kitt's defense, and "Eartha Kitt for President" buttons were seen on college campuses.

Signed contracts for performances quickly evaporated, however, and Kitt was not even allowed to appear on *Hollywood Squares,* a well-known haven for careers on the way down. She was effectively blacklisted in the United States and did not work there again until 1978. Kitt was investigated by the Central Intelligence Agency (which once issued a report calling her a sadistic nymphomaniac) and suffered losses of friends and money. But she was unrepentant. "This country has given all Americans IOUs: freedom of speech, freedom from oppression, freedom from hunger, etc.," she told Haywood. "Then I tell the truth, and I get my face slapped. . . . If you don't want my honest opinion, then don't ask me the question." Kitt kept her career going with performances in Europe, and, having faced criticism from conservatives in the United States, she took more from liberals when she appeared in apartheid-era South Africa in 1974. She was unrepentant about that, too, pointing to the humanitarian projects she had funded with proceeds from the show.

In 1978 Kitt was rehabilitated in the U.S. with an appearance in the Broadway musical *Timbuktu,* and President Jimmy Carter invited her to sing at the White House. Though she was at an age when most performers slow down, she climbed back to popularity. A disco recording, "Where Is My Man?" (1983), added a homosexual contingent to her fan base, and she began to find stage and film roles. Cameos in *Ernest: Scared Stupid* (1991) and in Eddie Murphy's *Boomerang* (1992) kept her camp-sexy image before the public, and she stayed in shape with an exercise-and-raw-juice regime that allowed her to pull off her act convincingly. In 1996 she appeared in the one-woman show *Lady Day,* a biographical treatment of the life of jazz singer Billie Holiday. Major stage successes came with appearances as the Wicked Witch in *The Wizard of Oz* in 1998, and as the Fairy Godmother in *Cinderella* (2001). She supplied the voice of the sorceress Yzma in the film *The Emperor's New Groove,* and in 2005 she was still going strong, touring and taking over for the late cabaret singer Bobby Short with a recurring engagement at the Hotel Carlyle in New York City. Eartha Kitt seemed indestructible—and indeed she had to have been, considering some of the trials she had faced.

Books

Kitt, Eartha, *Confessions of a Sex Kitten,* Barricade Books, 1991.
Kitt, Eartha, with Tonya Bolden, *Rejuvenate! (It's Never Too Late),* S. & S. Audio, 2001.

Periodicals

Book, November -December 2001.
Ebony, October 1993.
Essence, January 1993; July 2003.
Palm Beach Post, November 21, 2005.
People, July 21, 1997; October 25, 1999.
Record (Bergen County, NJ), May 27, 2005.
Variety, April 6, 1998.

Online

"Eartha Kitt: Orphan Turned Star," CBS News, http://www
.cbsnews.com/stories/2005/08/28/Sunday/main798791
.shtml (December 20, 2005). □

Marita Koch

German sprinter Marita Koch (born 1957) was, in the words of track coach Miroslav Kvac, "the most remarkable woman sprinter of our time," (as quoted on the website of the International Amateur Athletic Federation, or IAAF). The degree to which she dominated her competition in short distance races during her peak years in the late 1970s and early 1980s has rarely been matched, in track and field or in any other sport. Some have called her the greatest female athlete of all time.

Before her retirement in 1987, due to injuries, Koch broke world records 31 times. At one point, she had notched the six fastest times ever run by a woman in the 400 meters, as well as eight of the ten fastest times in the 200 meters. One of her individual records, her blistering pace of 47.60 seconds in the 400-meter race at the 1985 World Cup in Canberra, Australia, still stands and is the second-oldest record in any sport in Olympic competition. No runner has even approached that record. Koch also held records at distances down to 50 meters. She lost 400-meter races only twice during her peak years. Only one set of jewels was missing from her racing crown, but it was politics, not competition on the track, that kept them from her. At the peak of her career, she was unable to compete in the 1984 Olympic Games in Los Angeles, California, due to a boycott of the games on the part of the Soviet Union and its Communist satellites. After Communism fell, in 1989, investigations into steroid use in the national athletic programs of the former East Germany implicated Koch, but she maintained her innocence. □

Competed Against Boys

Koch was born in the East German city of Wismar on February 18, 1957. Her athletic talent was apparent from the beginning; while still a very small child, she took on older boys in races and won. Koch lived in Wismar, East Germany, until passing her high school graduation exams, and then moved on to the University of Rostock, where she planned to study medicine. But a naval engineer and part-time athletic trainer named Wolfgang Meier had other plans for Koch. He had noticed her talent even when she was a student in Wismar, and he followed her to Rostock with the sole intention of directing her training program.

It did not take him long to get results. Koch's best times at 400 meters dropped from 60.3 seconds when she was 15 to 51.60 seconds at 18 and to 50.19 seconds the following year. Her name first began to show up in championship rolls

at the European Junior Championships in Athens, Greece, in 1975, where she won a gold medal as part of a relay team and a silver medal at 400 meters. A muscle tear kept Koch on the sidelines at the 1976 Olympics in Montreal, and in the 1977 World Cup she was a silver medalist behind Irena Szewinska of Poland. That was the last time Koch would lose at 400 meters until 1981.

The year 1978 marked the beginning of Koch's run at the top of world track-and-field rankings. She set her first world record in Poland on May 22, 1978, running 200 meters in 20.06 seconds, and in July of that year, in Leipzig, East Germany, she shaved a full tenth of a second off the 400-meter world record with a time of 49.19 seconds. Koch had competition at the 50-meter, 100-meter, and 200-meter distances from East German teammate Marlies Gohr and from Evelyn Ashford of the United States, who emerged as a sentimental favorite to edge out Koch at 200 meters in the 1979 World Cup. Koch regarded 400 meters as her specialty, however; as powerful as she was in the shorter races, she took them on, she once said, partly in order to check her progress in what would be different stages of a 400-meter race. Her explosive start was one of her strengths, developed partly through intensive work in shorter sprints. In 1979 she lowered her 400-meter world record twice in one week, to 48.89 and then 48.60 seconds.

The world beyond track and field began to know Koch's name when she won two gold medals (at 400 meters and in the 4x400 meter relay) at the Montreal Olympics in 1980. The races revealed to television audiences a powerful but graceful runner. Mexican sprinter Maritza Laguardia told the Mexico City newspaper *El Norte* that Koch had "a tremendous physical build—one meter and 78 centimeters tall, more or less, and all muscle." Viewers did not get to know Koch on a personal level, however; press and public access to Koch and other East German athletes was severely curtailed by East German officials fearful of athlete defections. Compounding the situation was Koch's natural shyness; even after German reunification, she gave few interviews.

Earned Triple Golds at One Event

Koch suffered one of her rare losses in the 400 meters against arch-rival Jarmila Kratochvilova of Czechoslovakia in 1981, but she soon resumed her winning ways. She lowered her 400-meter world record once again to 48.15 seconds at the 1982 European Championships, where she also took a relay gold. Koch won three gold medals at the 1983 World Track and Field Championships in Helsinki, Finland, in the 200-meter, 4x100-meter relay, and 4x400 relay events. That made her the most successful athlete in the meet's inaugural year. She lost the 400-meter world record to an inspired Kratochvilova, who broke the 48-second barrier. But Koch seemed a star in the making in advance of the 1984 Summer Olympics in Los Angeles, California. Even American coach Pat Connolly conceded to Bill Shirley of the *Los Angeles Times,* "Marita is the best woman runner we've ever had," and marveled that "there is a fluidity about Marita that is pleasing to watch."

But Koch's star status was not to be—the United States had boycotted the 1980 Moscow Olympics in protest of the Soviet Union's invasion of Afghanistan the previous year, and the Soviet Union retaliated by leading most Communist countries in a boycott of the Los Angeles games. Koch and the other members of the East German Olympic team, groomed since childhood, were disappointed with the boycott and had no choice but to accept the situation. Koch, in her late twenties, was at the peak of her career.

The following year, Koch seemed determined to make up for lost opportunities. At the World Cup games in Canberra, she took gold medals at 200 meters and in the 4x400-meter relay, but it was her record-setting time of 47.60 seconds at 400 meters that made headlines around the world. Koch told the *Times* of London, "I have never felt more relaxed at the 300-meter mark that I did today. I couldn't see the clock at the end, but I could tell from the crowd noises that I must be running at world-record pace." After shaving nearly four-tenths of a second off Kratochvilova's existing record—a striking margin in the world of sprints, where margins of a few hundredths of a second are the rule—Koch, according to the *Times,* "re-emphasized her claim to be considered the finest woman athlete of the past decade, if not in the history of the sport."

That single sprint seemed to drain Koch's energy. She told the *Times,* "All I can think about now is going home and having a holiday." Koch entered her name into the lists of preliminary competitors for the 1988 Olympics in Seoul, Korea. Suffering from Achilles tendon problems, however, she found her competitive drive waning. She officially retired in 1987. "It was getting harder and harder to motivate

myself anyway," she told Philip Hersh of the *Chicago Tribune.* "I would go to the track and all these 14- and 15- and 16-year-olds would be out there and I would think, 'What am I doing here?'" Her last event was the 1986 Grand Prix in Rome, where she won the 400-meter race.

Opened Sporting Goods Store

Koch was engaged to her coach Wolfgang Meier at the time, and the two soon married. They had a daughter, Ulrike, in 1989. Initially, Koch planned to resume her studies in pediatric medicine, but the dissolution of East German Communism as the border with the West was opened on November 9, 1989, turned Koch's life upside down. "It was a different business life and personal life," she told Hersh. "No one was telling you what to do. There used to be one insurance company; now there were hundreds. It was very difficult not knowing where to go or what to do." The twin demands of medical school and motherhood also proved burdensome.

Koch and Meier decided to open a sporting goods store in Rostock. The business was successful and later expanded to a second store. She told the German television network ZDF that the business was not making them rich, but that it did provide a good living. Consistent with her reserved nature, Koch hung nothing on the walls of the shop that gave even a hint of her famous athletic career. "This way," she told ZDF, "people don't come in to marvel at the Olympic or World Championship gold medals. They're planning to buy something."

Only one thing threatened to disturb Koch's low profile: the growing controversy over the use of performance-enhancing drugs in sports generally and in Olympic competition specifically. Rumors of drug treatment had dogged the phenomenally successful East German state athletic programs through the 1980s, and in 1992 a British Broadcasting Corporation television documentary featured a West German scientist who claimed to have cracked the codes contained in East German records and identified Koch as one of the athletes who had been treated with steroids.

The controversy resurfaced in 1995, as French Olympic champion Marie-Jo Perec of France—another Wolfgang Meier protegee—pointed to a slowing of sprinters' race times as new drug controls were implemented in the late 1980s. Perec pointed to Koch's own record as one that was suspect, but Koch, in conversation with Hersh in 2000, retorted, "Now that you are training with my husband, you will learn how I worked" to reach her level of accomplishment. In 2005 newly declassified German secret police files also seemed to raise the possibility that Koch had been given drugs. She continued to deny the charges categorically, telling Simon Turnbull of London's *Independent on Sunday* that "at the World Championships in Helsinki in 1983 I had to go to dope testing three times, and always I was clean. The same applies to my career overall. I was a mature and responsible athlete." Indeed, Koch looked back fondly on her remarkable athletic career. "It was a wonderful time," she recalled to ZDF. "Sports have given me a lot, even when the victories cost a lot of hard work. I would do it all again exactly the same way."

Books

Uglow, Jennifer S., ed., *The Continuum Dictionary of Women's Biography,* Continuum, 1989.

Periodicals

Boston Globe, December 13, 1991.
Chicago Tribune, September 14, 2000.
El Norte (Mexico City), August 15, 2002.
Guardian (London, England), June 8, 1992.
Independent on Sunday, October 23, 2005.
Los Angeles Times, June 24, 1983.
New York Times, February 3, 1987.
Sports Illustrated, February 16, 1987.
Times (London, England), February 4, 1987; October 7, 2000.
Washington Post, August 25, 1979.

Online

"Marita Koch," International Amateur Athletic Federation, http://www2.iaaf.org/athletes/legends/Koch.html (February 18, 2006).
"Meier-Koch, Marita: Porträt," http://www.mdr.de/riverboat/ 963231 (February 18, 2006).
"Unsere Besten: Sportler des Jahrhunderts," Zweite Deutsche Fernsehen (ZDF), http://www.zdf.de/ZDFde/inhalt/28/ 0,1872,2147836,00.html (February 18, 2006). □

Jerzy Kosinski

Polish-American writer Jerzy Kosinski (1933-1991) authored three of the most widely read novels of the 1960s and 1970s: *The Painted Bird, Steps,* and *Being There,* the last of which also became a hit film.

Kosinski spent much of his childhood amid the chaos of World War II, when making up a convincing story about one's actions and one's identity could literally mean the difference between life and death. He was a skilled storyteller, not only in his books but also when it came to his own life, and after his career hit its peak many of the established facts of his biography were called into question. He was charged with plagiarism and relying on editors to produce the actual texts of his books. Kosinski defended himself vigorously against these accusations, and he was backed up by major journalistic and literary figures who concluded that the author's biographical facts extended far back into his tangled past. Kosinski wove a tangled web with his life and work, and the controversies that surrounded him were still present 15 years after his death, by suicide, in 1991. The reputations of his major novels were little touched, however; remaining widely available in inexpensive editions and discovered by new generations of readers.

Family Eluded Nazism

The web of stories surrounding Kosinski began with his name; after he had been in America for many years it was revealed that he was born Jerzy Nikodem Lewinkopf, in

Łódź, Poland, on June 14, 1933. His parents, Moses and Elzbieta Lewinkopf, were Jewish professionals; Moses Lewinkopf was a translator and a scholar of classical literature, and Elzbieta was a concert pianist who had attended the Moscow Conservatory in Russia. They found themselves in grave danger when German troops overran Poland in 1939, and they made the decision to try to pass as Gentile, moving to a small town in eastern Poland and telling their six-year-old son to deny he was Jewish if asked. Moses Lewinkopf changed his name to Mieczyslaw Kosinski, and his son went for a time by the name of Jurek Kosinski.

What Kosinski experienced as a child amid the most horrible depths of World War II and the Holocaust may never be known. He drew on his experiences during this period, however, in *The Painted Bird,* a gruesome novel in which a young boy wanders through a nightmarish European landscape, experiencing torture at the hands of strangers and witnessing act after act of extreme cruelty. At one point the boy loses the power of speech after being thrown into a pit of manure. The boy is called the Gypsy, but his ethnic identity is left hazy. Kosinski intimated early in his American career that the novel was based on fact, and it was often described as semi-autobiographical. He later retreated to the position that the stories in the book were realistic, given established accounts of the horrors perpetrated on ethnic minorities in Eastern Europe.

Asked by the London *Guardian* shortly before his death whether he had experienced the events described in the book, Kosinski replied, "I don't want to say, even to myself.

That ambiguity is what fiction is all about. What is not ambiguous is that the novel is about childhood traumatized by war. My elementary reactions were formed by the war.'' It appears probable, however, that Kosinski did not undergo a long separation from his parents, unlike the protagonist of *The Painted Bird,* and that the Lewinkopf family's psychologically perilous ruse was successful; unlike most of their Jewish compatriots, they survived the war.

Indeed, they prospered in the late 1940s as Kosinski's father embraced the ascendant Polish Communist Party. Kosinski attended the University of Łódź, studying political science and going on for a master's degree in history. His research covered both the Soviet Union and the United States, and he published a Party-approved text, in Polish, on American sociology, becoming a professor and Ph.D. candidate at the Polish Academy of Arts and Science in Warsaw. Both parents and son began to chafe against the restrictions of totalitarianism, however. Kosinski's parents tried without success to emigrate to Israel, and Kosinski, possibly using forged recommendation letters (this was another chapter in the life story he created as he went along), managed to get permission to leave Poland in 1957 for an academic exchange with the United States. Poland, like other Communist countries, briefly became more receptive to Western influences in the mid-1950s but soon clamped down once again.

Published Studies of Soviet Life

Kosinski arrived in the United States with few resources, but he received a Ford Foundation grant to enroll in the sociology graduate program at Columbia University in New York. While he was there he wrote two books about life in the Soviet Union, *The Future Is Ours, Comrade* (1960) and *No Third Path* (1962), publishing them under the pseudonym of Joseph Novak and later giving conflicting explanations as to why he did so. The books depicted life under Communism in a negative light, and allegations, never corroborated, later suggested that they were financed by the U.S. Central Intelligence Agency (CIA). They did attract the attention of a widowed steel-industry heiress, Mary Hayward Weir, whom Kosinski married in 1962. They divorced in 1966, and she died in 1968 of what was described at the time as a brain tumor but may have instead been suicide or complications from alcoholism.

By that time, Kosinski had published *The Painted Bird* and became a literary celebrity. A perfectionist to the extreme, Kosinski went through 15 drafts of the novel before agreeing to its publication. The book, dedicated to Weir, was one of the first to try to encompass the full impact of the Holocaust, and critics hailed it as a probable classic. *The Painted Bird* won France's Best Foreign Book award in 1966, and in the U.S. Kosinski had his pick of prestigious honors and university fellowships for several years. He spent 1967 as a Guggenheim Fellow, teaching English at Wesleyan University and readying his second work of fiction, *Steps,* for publication in 1968. More experimental than *The Painted Bird, Steps* consisted of a sequence of extremely short chapters, many of them erotic in nature and some of them violent. The plot shuttled back and forth

between the childhood and adulthood of a graduate student who once again seemed to be modeled on Kosinski himself.

Steps won the National Book Award in 1969, and in the 1969-70 academic year Kosinski was named a Senior Fellow at the Council for the Humanities at Princeton University. He taught at the Yale University drama school from 1970 through 1973. In a bizarre episode, Kosinski planned to visit the home of actress Sharon Tate on the night she and a group of others were murdered by serial killer Charles Manson; he was saved because he was delayed due to lost airline luggage. In 1971, Kosinski's third novel, *Being There,* was published. Unlike his first two novels, this one had no clear autobiographical component. Its central figure was a developmentally disabled gardener named Chance, who through a series of satirical misunderstandings—he speaks in simple sentences seemingly freighted with symbolic meaning—is taken to be a social and political sage named Chauncey Gardiner and, thanks to the power of the mass media, comes to national prominence. As the power of television grew in the last decades of the twentieth century, the novel seemed more and more relevant. In the 1970s, Kosinski served two terms as president of PEN, an international organization devoted to safeguarding the rights of authors in repressive societies. He often appeared on television's *Tonight* show, which made his purported life story familiar to millions of American viewers.

Kosinski wrote four more novels over the course of the 1970s, *The Devil Tree* (1973), *Cockpit* (1975), *Blind Date* (1977), and *Passion Play* (1979). These books once again drew on Kosinski's own experiences; he was a cockfighting fan, and like the central character in *Passion Play* he was an enthusiastic player of the unusual sport of polo. These novels were less well received by an audience of critics than his first three had been. The strong sexual elements in many of his books were also drawn from life; he visited swingers' clubs and engaged in a variety of sexual affairs despite his longtime attachment to German aristocrat Katherina von Frauenhofer. The two married four years before Kosinski's death. A wealthy man by this time, Kosinski hobnobbed with New York's jet-setters and maintained a part-time residence in Switzerland. In 1979, Kosinski adapted *Being There* for a film starring British comedian Peter Sellers as Chance; his screenplay won several awards. In 1981 he appeared as Russian revolutionary figure Gregory Zinoviev in actor Warren Beatty's film *Reds.*

Attacked in *Village Voice* Article

Kosinski's world came crashing down in 1982 when New York's weekly *Village Voice* published an article entitled ''Tainted Words,'' alleging that he had written *The Painted Bird* in Polish and had it translated by editors, on whom he relied heavily in many of his other writings. The article also raised the issue of Kosinski's CIA affiliation and alleged that *Being There* had been largely plagiarized from a Polish novel of the 1920s, *The Career of Nikodem Dyzmy,* by Tadeusz Dolega-Mostowicz. Kosinski vigorously denied the charges in full, and he was supported by colleagues and by a 6,000-word article in the *New York Times* that traced some of the charges to a campaign of character assassinations carried out by Polish communists angered by Kosinski's defection and by the negative portrayal of Poland in *The Painted Bird*. Until the late 1980s *The Painted Bird* was never published in Poland.

Kosinski was distressed by the controversy and attempted to incorporate it into a massive new novel, *The Hermit of 69th Street* (1988). The novel's protagonist was named Kosky—Kosinski without the sin, he often said. He was further depressed by the poor critical reception of the novel and by mounting health problems; he suffered from a heart condition in his later years. The fall of Communism in Poland, where he was finally acclaimed, stimulated him to revisit his homeland and to participate in the founding of an American-owned bank there. But on May 3, 1991, despondent over a prolonged period of writer's block, he committed suicide in his New York apartment by putting a plastic bag over his head.

The truth of the *Voice* charges remained a matter of debate. A detailed and generally sympathetic biography of Kosinski by writer James Park Sloan lent credence to the picture of Kosinski as heavily reliant on editorial assistants and pointed to strong correspondences between *Being There* and *The Career of Nikodem Dyzmy*. An *Atlantic Monthly* reviewer wrote in 1997, however, that "the plagiarism charge, unless actual copying of the victim's text is found, can be dismissed as absurd. Creators have presumably been borrowing from their predecessors ever since the first yarn spinner sat by a cave fire explaining how the mammoth got away." A 2001 play, *More Lies About Jerzy*, was based on the whole controversy. As with many of the details of the life of one of the twentieth century's most talented yarn spinners and most troubled individuals, the truth of the matter remained for historians and literary scholars to sort out.

Books

Sloan, James Park, *Jerzy Kosinski: A Biography*, Dutton, 1996.

Periodicals

Atlantic Monthly, April 1997.
Guardian (London, England), May 25, 1991.
Houston Chronicle, March 10, 1996.
Jerusalem Post, May 5, 1991.
New York Observer, February 5, 2001.
New York Times, November 7, 1982; May 4, 1991.
San Francisco Chronicle, March 24, 1996.
Times (London, England), May 6, 1991.
Village Voice, June 22, 1982.
Washington Post, May 4, 1991.

Online

Contemporary Authors Online, Gale, 2006. Reproduced in *Biography Resource Center.* Farmington Hills, Mich. Thomson Gale. 2006. http://www.galenet.galegroup.com/servlet/BioRC (January 2, 2006). □

Fritz Kreisler

Austrian-born violinist Fritz Kreisler (1875-1962) was one of the most famous classical musicians in the world during the first decade of the twentieth century. His rhythmic vigor and his heavy use of vibrato have influenced violinists down to the present day, and his original compositions—some of them originally passed off as works by composers of the distant past—remain staples of the violin repertoire.

Kreisler led a long and colorful life, the substance of which he embellished still further through a consistent habit of exaggeration and storytelling. He served two stints in the Austrian army and was drafted for a third. A natural talent, he rarely studied or practiced the violin after the age of twelve. Kreisler was also something of a link between the nineteenth and twentieth centuries in music. He knew the Austrian composer Johannes Brahms personally, and his music was suffused with the mood of old Vienna. Yet he was touched by the modern era of music in many ways; he made numerous records, played concerts on radio, and tailored his violin compositions to the attention spans of popular audiences; his three-minute works were the hits of their day, instrumental counterparts to the best-selling vocal recordings of Italian tenor Enrico Caruso. For many lovers of classical music, Fritz Kreisler seemed to sum up the whole tradition of the violin.

First Instrument Made from Cigar Box

Kreisler was born in Vienna, Austria on February 2, 1875. Kreisler's father Salomon was of Jewish background, a fact that Kreisler tried to downplay later in life, but that may have undergirded his staunch resistance to German fascism. Kreisler's father and other relatives often indulged in a leisure-time activity that was very common among Viennese middle-class families: they enjoyed performing music in small groups at home. One occasional visitor to their evenings of music was a young violinist and student of human nature named Sigmund Freud, who later became the founder of psychiatry. Young Fritz looked on as a string quartet was played, following along on a violin made from a cigar box. One time, when he was four, he was handed a child-sized violin and proceeded to amaze the group by playing the Austrian national anthem straight through in perfect time and pitch.

Admitted to the Vienna Conservatory at seven, he became the school's youngest student ever. His mother had lied about his age in order to help him win admission, but soon it was clear that his talents did not need help from any deception. The boy studied harmony and composition with Anton Bruckner, one of Austria's greatest composers of the day, and he taught himself to play the piano. Kreisler made his concert debut in 1884 and was then sent off to the Paris Conservatory in France for a still-higher level of musical finishing. His mother was too ill to accompany him, so he went alone. In 1887, at 12, he was awarded the Conservatory's Premier Premier Prix (First First Prize) over four adult students. The Conservatory had no more to teach him, and at that time his musical education was over.

Such a feat was all the more astonishing in view of Kreisler's lifelong aversion to practicing. He often claimed that playing the violin was something that happened more in the brain than in the hands, and indeed he seemed to have an uncanny ability to absorb musical lessons when he heard a performance by one of the few violinists who was above his own level. He soaked up concerts by the world-famous musicians who came to perform in Vienna, and in an interview quoted by Amy Biancolli in *Fritz Kreisler: Love's Sorrow, Love's Joy* he said, "I really believe that hearing [German violinist Joseph] Joachim and [Russian pianist Anton] Rubinstein play was a greater event in my life and did more for me than five years of study!" Kreisler realized, however, that he was a special case, and later in life he emphasized the importance of practice.

It is possible that Kreisler's casual attitude toward music actually delayed the flowering of his career by several years. He was signed to tour the United States with pianist Moriz Rosenthal in 1888-1889 and was thrilled with his first view of the New York City skyline. Reviewers, however, were mixed in their evaluations—they were impressed by his technical skills but he plainly did not yet have the interpretive magic he would later acquire, and the tour, while generally successful, did not bring Kreisler the renown he had imagined. When he returned to Vienna, he dropped out

of music for several years, finishing his high school education at the Piaristen Gymnasium, a Catholic institution, and then enrolling in medical school at the University of Vienna. His parents, not wanting to rush him into a musical career, supported his decision. "In those youthful days," Kreisler was quoted as saying by Biancolli, "I had some very weird thoughts about my future career. I envisaged myself operating on a patient in the morning, playing chess in the afternoon, giving a concert in the evening, and (in anticipation of a glorious military career) winning a battle at midnight." Indeed, still short of his medical degree, Kreisler enlisted in the Austrian army in 1894. He edged back into music as he and his commanding officer sometimes played music recitals for other officers.

Rebuilt Technique Above Tavern

After he finished his term of service in 1896, Kreisler recommitted himself to the violin. He rented a room in a tavern-inn and began to rebuild his technique systematically, more or less hiding out for eight weeks but emerging at times to play for the tavern's patrons. Kreisler began writing music during this period and produced, among other small compositions, two new cadenzas—a quasi-improvised passage played by the violinist at the end of a movement of work for violin and orchestra—for Beethoven's violin concerto. When Kreisler returned to the concert stage, he did not have the novelty of being a child star any longer, but his playing had gained depth. His 1898 debut with the Vienna Philharmonic was hailed by Eduard Hanslick, the city's top music critic, and he created a real sensation with his Berlin Philharmonic debut the following year.

In 1902 Kreisler married Harriet Lies Woerz, a divorced American tobacco heiress; he had met her the previous year on the *Prince Bismarck* ocean liner while returning from an American tour and proposed before the ship had even docked. Her wealthy family opposed the match, but the strong-willed Harriet went through with the wedding anyhow. It was possibly to please her that Kreisler avoided talking about his Jewish background, which was well known to other musicians. Kreisler's career steadily gained momentum, and in the years before World War I broke out he often performed more than 250 concerts a year. Russian pianist Sergei Rachmaninoff, who sometimes performed with Kreisler, said that it was because he played so many concerts that he did not need to practice.

One of the top concert draws in the world, Kreisler nevertheless enlisted once again in the Austrian army when the war began. He spent most of 1914 in the military and was sent to the Russian front for four weeks. He claimed that thanks to his musical ear he could distinguish the sounds of the different armies' shells as they whizzed past. Discharged in November of 1914 after a wound whose severity is a matter of historical dispute, Kreisler wrote a small book, *Four Weeks in the Trenches,* about his experiences. The book gained attention in the United States, and Kreisler continued to give successful concerts there for most of the war. When the U.S. entered the war on the side of England and France in 1917, however, Americans with backgrounds in German-speaking countries faced discrimination, and Kreisler was forced to cancel a major concert tour. He was soon welcomed back to the U.S. after the war, but did not perform in France for six years. In the 1920s, Kreisler and his wife lived mostly in Berlin.

In the midst of his growing career before the war, Kreisler found himself short of the kind of convincing but little-known material that would keep his concerts fresh. He composed music of his own but was not convinced that he had the stature to introduce a great deal of original music in his concerts. So he began to write music that was vaguely in the style of almost-forgotten composers from the distant past—France's François Couperin, Germany's Karl Ditters von Dittersdorf, and others—and to claim that he had unearthed the music in libraries and monasteries. Older music was little known at the time, and the reverse-plagiarized music became a favorite component of Kreisler's concerts. Kreisler finally revealed the hoax in 1935 when he was jokingly asked by *New York Times* music critic Olin Downs whether he had actually written the older pieces and answered the question truthfully.

Fakes Caused Controversy

Kreisler's admission touched off an uproar, with some critics attacking his deception while others praised the artfulness of his counterfeits (there were 17 of them) and contended that the audience's enjoyment of the music was the most important thing. Kreisler explained his original reasons for writing the pieces and argued that, unlike in the case of a counterfeit painting, no one had been harmed by his forgeries. Kreisler weathered the controversy; his popularity in the late 1930s was undiminished. Heard today, the counterfeits sound very little like Couperin or Dittersdorf and a great deal like Kreisler's other music. For his entire life, Kreisler was a teller of tall tales that were sometimes accepted as fact; he once claimed, for example, to have been held at gunpoint by a cowboy in Butte, Montana, who wanted to hear a specific violin work by Johann Sebastian Bach.

By the 1930s, the music Kreisler composed under his own name was familiar to most concertgoers, and several pieces remain staples of classical concert life today. Kreisler composed some large, virtuosic pieces (and several little-known operettas), and various shorter works that were flavored by ethnic or national traditions. His best-known compositions, however, were short, sentimental pieces that showcased his awe-inspiring vibrato and were ideally suited to the length of the 78 rpm records Kreisler made in abundance after being signed to an exclusive contract by the Victor label in 1910. Such Kreisler works as the *Caprice viennois* (Viennese Caprice), *Schön Rosmarin* (Beautiful Rosemary), and most of all the pair of works called *Liebesfreud* and *Liebesleid* (Love's Joy and Love's Sorrow) could be played either by violin and orchestra or violin and piano, and they closed out many a concert in which a violinist was featured.

Kreisler refused to perform in Germany after the Nazi party took control of the government in 1933, and he left the country for good after being threatened, despite his ad-

vanced age, with being drafted into the military when the *Anschluss* of 1938 put Austria under Germany's control. He briefly took French citizenship but by the following year he was back in the United States. In 1941, Kreisler was hit by a delivery truck on a New York street and spent several weeks in a coma. But he recovered and resumed giving concerts in 1942. He became a U.S. citizen in 1943 and continued to perform through the war years, appearing on the *Bell Telephone Hour* radio show from 1944 through 1950. His last concert appearance was at Carnegie Hall in 1947. Kreisler and his wife spent much of their energy during his last years on charitable enterprises, including several aimed at indigent musicians. He died in New York on January 29, 1962, at the age of 86.

Books

American Decades, Gale, 1998.
Biancolli, Amy, *Fritz Kreisler: Love's Sorrow, Love's Joy,* Amadeus, 1998.

Periodicals

Economist, December 7, 1991.

Online

''Fritz Kreisler,'' Legendary Violinists, http://www.thirteen.org/publicarts/violin/kreisler.html (January 29, 2006).
''Fritz Kreisler,'' Museum of Hoaxes, http://www.museumofhoaxes.com/kreisler.html (January 29, 2006).
Kreisler, Fritz, *Four Weeks in the Trenches,* http://www.lib.byu./edu/~rdh/wwi/memoir/Kreisler/Kreisler/htm (January 29, 2006). □

Maxine Winokur Kumin

American writer and poet Maxine Kumin (born 1925) has published numerous books of poetry, including the Pulitzer Prize–winning volume *Up Country: Poems of New England.* Highly decorated for her literary works, she has also written several children's books, a short story collection and a handful of novels, among others. She has served as a Library of Congress consultant on poetry and is the former poet laureate of New Hampshire.

Early Life and Influenced by Anne Sexton

The youngest of four children, Kumin was born Maxine Winokur on June 6, 1925, to Jewish parents in Philadelphia, Pennsylvania's Germantown neighborhood. As a child, she attended Catholic schools; as a young adult, she traveled to Boston, Massachusetts, for her higher education. There, she completed her Bachelor's degree at Harvard's Radcliffe College in 1946. That same year marked her marriage, in June, to Victor Kumin, an engineering consultant with whom she would later have two

daughters and one son. In 1948, Kumin received a Master's degree also from Radcliffe; during her years at the college, she studied with notable literary scholars including the prolific literary critic Harry Levin.

After completing her M.A., Kumin taught English at colleges in the Boston area, notably Tufts University from 1958-1961 and again from 1965-1968. From 1961 to 1963, she was a Bunting Fellow at Radcliffe's Bunting Institute. Throughout her career, Kumin would teach and lecture at universities around the United States, from large, prestigious institutions such as Columbia and Princeton to small, regional learning centers like Davis and Elkins in West Virginia. In recent years, Kumin has limited her teaching engagements to universities in warmer climates such as Louisiana and California, finding that her body is no longer able to handle the harsh northern winters well.

At a poetry workshop taught by John Holmes at the Boston Center for Adult Education in 1957, Kumin met and befriended two other poets of what is called the "confessional" of writing: Anne Sexton and Sylvia Plath. The works of these poets were particularly noted for their intensely personal reflection on their own psychological states and problems. Sexton, who had taken up poetry writing in the mid-1950s following her second nervous breakdown, had become immediately successful and was a major influence on Kumin's work. The two women were close friends and collaborators until the time of Sexton's death in 1974, writing four children's books together: 1963's *Eggs of Things,* 1964's *More Eggs of Things,* 1971's

Joey and the Birthday Present, and 1975's *The Wizard's Tears.*

Kumin's relationship with Sexton was a remarkably close one. Critics often mention the two writers in the same breath; speaking years after Sexton's suicide, Kumin admitted in her book *Inside the Halo and Beyond: The Anatomy of a Recovery* that "we were very, very important to each other. That I have not been able to reproduce, that kind of intimacy: the word, the line, the phrase, the shape, the close reading." Much of Kumin's early poetry was read and commented on by Sexton; Kumin recollected that the two would physically move poems around her living room floor, deciding what order to place her poems in for projected books. Although later in life, Kumin found other writers and poets with whom to discuss her work, she never recaptured that working and personal relationship she had developed with Sexton.

Moved to New Hampshire

In 1976, Kumin and her family relocated from Boston to rural New Hampshire, a setting that would inspire much of her later poetry. The Kumins had purchased the 200-acre former dairy farm, which they named PoBiz—short for Poetry Business—in 1963 and had used it for family weekend and vacation trips before permanently moving there. In *New Letters,* Kumin was quoted as saying "everything that happens [on the farm] is related to my poetry. . . . It is my life. It's just that simple." Kumin's husband commuted back into Boston for his job for a short period of time before the couple settled full-time at PoBiz.

Poetic Works

Kumin published her first collection of poetry, *Halfway,* in 1961. Influenced by the confessional style of poetry, it was followed in 1965 by *The Privilege* and in 1970 by *The Nightmare Factory,* both of which explore her Jewish identity and family. These kinds of personal reflections are typical of the confessional school of poetry, leading to Kumin's grouping with her contemporaries Sexton and Plath. However, much of Kumin's work focuses on what *Women's Writing in the United States* called "the rhythms of life in rural New England," comparable to the poems of more traditional writers like Robert Frost. This interest in New England drove Kumin's third book of poetry, 1973's *Up Country: Poems of New England,* inspired by life on the Kumin family's New Hampshire farm. This volume won Kumin the 1973 Pulitzer Prize Award for Poetry.

Over the decades, Kumin has steadily produced poetry. The 1970s saw Kumin publish two more volumes of poetry: *House, Bridge, Fountain, Gate* in 1975 and *The Retrieval System* in 1978. In 1982, she released *Our Ground Time Here Will be Brief: New and Selected Poems* and in 1989, *The Long Approach. The Retrieval System* and *Our Ground Time Here Will be Brief* have been noted for their musings on life and death, particularly Sexton's 1974 suicide. Beginning in the 1980s, Kumin began to address contemporary social issues in her poetry. After *Nurture* in 1992, Kumin wrote her most prestigious volume since *Up Country. Looking for Luck,* published in 1993, garnered Kumin a

National Book Critics Circle Award nomination as well as the Outstanding Work of Poetry for 1993 award from the New Hampshire Writers and Publishers Project and, in 1994, The Poets' Prize. This collection was followed by 1996's *Connecting the Dots: Poems* and 1997's compilation, *Selected Poems, 1960-1990*. In 2001, Kumin returned to her roots with poems on her nearly fifty-year marriage to Victor Kumin and her deep affinity—what *Library Journal* called "a kind of covenant between the poet and her environment"—for her New England surroundings in *The Long Marriage*. Many of Kumin's previously rare poems were published together in 2003's *Bringing Together: Uncollected Early Poems, 1958-1988*.

Writing on Kumin's poetry, Meg Schoerke commented in *Women's Writing in the United States* that "throughout her career as a poet, Kumin has struck a balance between her sense of life's transience and her fascination with the dense physical presence of the world around her. At its worst, this latter impulse causes her to weigh her poetry down with catalogs of material details and an overabundance of similes; such poems seem to be merely exercises in record keeping. But at its best, her poetry offers details whose blend of quirkiness and exactness beautifully ground her meditations on endurance in the face of loss."

Other Works

Kumin's extensive written output has not been limited to poetry. Quoted in the *Washington Post* in 1980, Kumin said "I like writing prose. It keeps you honest: those simple, declarative sentences. It's good discipline after the ellipses of poetry." Her explorations into prose have primarily included children's books, but also novels for adults and essays on a variety on topics. These books include novels *Through Dooms of Love,* also published as *A Daughter and Her Loves,* released in 1965; *The Passions of Uxport* published in 1968; *The Abduction,* published in 1971; *The Designated Heir,* published in 1974; and mystery novel *Quit Monks or Die!,* published in 1999. This last piece mirrored Kumin's lifelong love of animals and her interest in social concerns; in *Contemporary Authors Online, Quit Monks or Die!* was described as "an unusual tale centering around the disappearance of a pair of monkeys at a testing lab and a murder of the lab director." The uncommon plot drew critical acclaim, reflecting Kumin's standing as not only a respected poet but also an accomplished novelist.

In addition to Kumin's novels, she has written collections of essays and short stories. Her short story collection *Why Can't We Live Together Like Civilized Human Beings?,* published in 1982, discussed the interpersonal relationships between men and women, another recurring theme in Kumin's work. Two collections of purely essays appeared in the 1980s, first *To Make a Prairie: Essays on Poets, Poetry, and Country Living* in 1980 and later, *In Deep* in 1987. One mixed work of essays and stories, *Women, Animals, and Vegetables: Essays and Stories* was published in 1994. Kumin is also an accomplished children's book author. In addition to the four children's book she wrote with Anne Sexton, Kumin published numerous works for children in the 1960s and 1970s.

Career Achievements

In addition to the 1973 Pulitzer Prize for Poetry, Kumin has received many poetry awards. These include the 1972 Eunice Tiejens Memorial Prize; the 1978 Radcliffe College Alumnae Recognition Award; the American Academy and Institute of Arts and Letters award, 1980, for excellence in literature; the 1986 Levison award; the 1994 Poets' Prize; and in 1999, the prestigious Ruth Lily Poetry Prize. In 2005, Harvard University awarded Kumin the 11th annual Harvard Arts Medal.

In 1976, Centre College awarded Kumin an honorary Doctor of Hebrew Letters degree, the first in a series she would receive over the ensuing twenty years. Other institutions honoring Kumin include the University of New Hampshire and Keene State College. Another professional honor came in 1980, when she was made the poetry consultant to the Library of Congress in Washington, DC; she served from 1981-1982 and was only the fifth woman to hold the position. During her tenure at the Library of Congress, Kumin split her time between her New Hampshire home and Washington. In 1989, New Hampshire made Kumin their Poet Laureate, a position she held until 1994.

Kumin in Recent Years

In 1998, the 73-year-old Kumin was injured when a horse she was training for a marathon carriage competition was spooked. Thrown to the ground, Kumin avoided being trampled by the animal but was crushed under the 350-pound carriage; the accident left her with fractured vertebrae, broken ribs, a punctured lung, a damaged kidney and liver, internal bleeding, loss of neurological function and temporary numbness. Although she suffered from extensive injuries—enough to kill most people within minutes—Kumin remarkably recovered enough to again ride horses and lead a normal life. In 2000, she published a memoir of her accident and recovery process titled *Inside the Halo and Beyond: the Anatomy of a Recovery.* Stephanie Schorow, reviewing the book for the *Boston Herald,* noted that "the memoir eschews platitudes, gratitude and misplaced grace. Kumin will have none of the pious and the pat . . . What she does celebrate is the resilience of the human spirit."

Despite her injuries and advanced age, Kumin continued to teach, write and publish; she has been reported to be at work on a sixth novel and to still write poetry at her typewriter. In 2000, Anne Roiphe wrote in the *New York Times* that Kumin "is a woman with a certain spiritual wholeness, as if her mind, unlike so many of her readers', had not been fractured with resentments, failures of humankind. Her respect for life in all its forms, animal, vegetable and mineral, is both gracious and soothing." This respect continued to inform her poetry and prose, and made Kumin as well-respected today as she was early in her career—a career that survived the author's personal injuries as well as Kumin herself had.

Books

Kumin, Maxine, *Inside the Halo and Beyond: The Anatomy of a Recovery,* W.W. Norton, 2000.

Periodicals

Boston Herald, May 18, 2000; April 16, 2005.
New Letters, Vol. 66, Issue 3, 2000.
Times-Picayune, November 8, 2000.
Washington Post, May 6, 1980.

Online

''Gale Literary Databases: Maxine (Winokur) Kumin,''
http://www.galenet.galegroup.com (January 1, 2006).
''On Maxine Kumin's Life and Career,'' http://www.english.uiuc
.edu/maps/poets/g_l/kumin/life.htm, includes excerpt from
Women's Writing in the United States, Oxford University
Press, 1995. □

L

Sam Lacy

Sam Lacy (1903-2003) became a pioneering sports-writer for the *Afro-American* newspaper in Baltimore and was one of the most important early forces in the integration of Major League Baseball.

The sportswriter inherited his pioneering spirit from his grandfather, Henry Erskine Lacy, who was the first black detective on the Washington, D.C., police force. Perhaps the most amazing thing about Lacy's story is not that he covered all the giants of the twentieth-century sporting world—Joe Louis, Jesse Owens, Jackie Robinson, Sugar Ray Robinson, and Muhammed Ali, to name a few—but that he continued to cover sports well into his nineties. He left home for the office at the *Afro-American* at three o'clock in the morning. to do three weekly columns and supervise the layout of the paper. When he became too old to drive after suffering a stroke in 1999, his son brought him to work. When his fingers became too riddled with arthritis to type, he wrote out his column longhand, continuing until shortly before his death in May, 2003. Lacy's story began with his selling peanuts to the Jim Crow section of old Griffith Stadium in Washington, D.C., and it continued until he reached a place of honor in the writers' wing at baseball's ultimate shrine, the Hall of Fame in Cooperstown, New York.

Lacy was born on October 23, 1903, in Mystic, Connecticut, to Samuel Erskine Lacy, a researcher in a Washington, D.C. law firm, and Rose Lacy, a full-blooded Native American from the Shinnecock tribe. Lacy's family moved to Washington, D.C., early in his life. Lacy's father taught his son to love baseball, and Lacy began to hang around the stadium. The young fan would do errands for the players

such as buying cigarettes and picking up their laundry. By the time Lacy was nine years old, he was shagging balls in the outfield before games at batting practice and eventually worked at the stadium selling popcorn and peanuts in the stands. He also caddied for Englishman "Long Jim" Barnes, the winning golfer at the 1921 U.S. Open, which earned Lacy the sum of $200. His tip was so enormous that the young man had a difficult time making his mother believe he had earned the princely sum by carrying around a golf bag for four days.

Advocated for Desegregation in Sports

Lacy attended Armstrong High School in Washington, D.C. and played football, baseball and basketball. After he graduated from high school, he was good enough to play baseball in the local semipro leagues but decided he needed to further his education. He attended Howard University and earned a degree in education with the intention of becoming a coach. Little did he know that his part-time job would turn out to be his career and his crusade.

While attending school in the 1920s Lacy worked part-time at the local African-American paper, the *Washington Tribune,* earning a nickel for every inch of copy he wrote. After graduation he joined the paper full-time and soon moved into the sports department, where he began a lifelong crusade for fairness in the world of sports. The first big story Lacy wrote involved a black football player at Syracuse University; to allow the player to continue on the team, the university claimed that he was not black but a Hindu with Indian ancestry. Lacy wrote a story in 1937 proving that the player was not Indian, but born in Washington, D.C., to African-American parents. When the University of Maryland found out about the black player, it refused to play the game with Syracuse unless Wilmeth Sidat-Singh

was removed from the team. The player was taken off the team and Syracuse lost, but the reaction against both universities was so strong that Sidat-Singh played against Maryland the following year.

Lacy then turned his attention to the game of baseball. He met with Clark Griffith, the owner of the Washington Senators, then the local major-league team that eventually became the Minnesota Twins. Lacy suggested that Griffith's last-place team could be turned around by an infusion of new talent from the Negro Leagues: Satchel Paige, Cool Papa Bell, and Josh Gibson were suggested to the owner. Lacy told Sam Donnellon of the *Philadelphia Daily News* about his first meeting with a major-league owner: "I used that old cliché about Washington being first in war, first in peace, and last in the American League, and that he could remedy that. But he told me that the climate wasn't right. He pointed out there were a lot of Southern ballplayers in the league, that there would be constant confrontations, and, moreover, that it would break up the Negro Leagues. He saw the Negro Leagues as a source of revenue."

But a cause was born: Lacy became one of the earliest and most outspoken voices for desegregation in baseball. In 1940 Lacy moved to Chicago to join the *Chicago Defender,* a black paper with a national readership. On numerous occasions he sought a meeting with baseball commissioner Kenesaw Mountain Landis to talk about the integration of Major League Baseball, but Lacy never received a reply. After three years of wrangling and agitating, Lacy finally was given a place on the agenda at the 1943 baseball meetings

in Cleveland to discuss the issue. At the last minute the paper decided to send noted athlete and actor Paul Robeson to make the case for the black baseball player, a decision on the part of the paper that Lacy took very personally. He told D.L. Cummings of *The New York Daily News* about his reaction to the snub: "That made me furious. All this work I had done on this, for them to send Paul Robeson, who had known Communistic leanings, I questioned the good sense of it all. I knew when the owners saw this guy who admitted to being Communist-oriented, they would simply say, 'OK, we heard you and don't call us, we'll call you.'"

Lacy immediately moved to the *Afro-American* in Baltimore and continued to press the race issue. He wrote to the owners and suggested an integration committee be formed. Lacy was named to just such a committee with Branch Rickey of the National League's Brooklyn Dodgers and Larry MacPhail of the New York Yankees. The group tried to meet, but MacPhail never attended any of the meetings, so Rickey told Lacy that he was going to be integrating baseball on his own. In April of 1945 Major League Baseball got a new commissioner who was not opposed to integration, and six months later the league got its first black ball player when Rickey signed Jackie Robinson to a contract for Brooklyn's Triple A team in Montreal.

Covered a Pioneer

The *Afro-American* allowed Lacy to cover Robinson exclusively for the next three years. The black press was unanimously in support of Robinson, and all agreed he was the man to take the first giant step in integrating Major League Baseball. Robinson had attended UCLA, a racially mixed college, competed against white players, had served with honor in the military, and was engaged to be married. Lacy traveled with Robinson from Montreal, where Robinson played Triple A ball, to the deep south for spring training, and even to Cuba for winter baseball. Lacy witnessed all the trials that Robinson experienced and told Kevin Merida of the *Washington Post* that it was difficult for Robinson to keep all of his pain and frustration to himself: "There were a lot of things that were bothering him. He was taking so much abuse that he said to me that he didn't know whether or not he was going to be able to go through with this because it was just becoming so intolerable, that they were throwing everything at him."

Lacy endured many of the same indignities as Robinson, eating with him in separate facilities and staying at the same segregated rooming houses. Once they woke up in the middle of the night to find a cross burning in front of the rooming house where Robinson and other black journalists were staying. Lacy faced discrimination in the press box also. Lacy had to report on some Dodger games from the dugout because he was not allowed to sit with the other reporters. In New Orleans he was forced to go up on the roof of the press box, but there he was joined by some white writers from New York. As late as 1952 Lacy was denied entry into Yankee Stadium to cover the World Series, though he had been a member of the Baseball Writers of America since 1948 as the organization's first African-American member. But Lacy never dramatized his own situation; he kept the focus on the athletes. He told Merida, "It would have been a selfish thing for me to be concerned about myself and how I was treated."

After his victory in desegregating Major League Baseball, Lacy continued to press for fairness in sports. He saw that black ballplayers were having a major impact on their team's records and also on their team's bottom lines. He campaigned to increase their salaries and to have the "separate but equal" accommodations eliminated. Lacy first brought up the issue of blacks and whites staying in different hotels with the New York Giants (before the team moved to San Francisco). He told the story to *Sports Illustrated*'s Ron Fimrite: "I pointed out to Chub Feeney (then the team's general manager) that he had guys like Willie Mays and Monte Irvin and Hank Thompson holed up in some little hotel while the rest of the players, people who might never even wear a major-league uniform, were staying at the famous Palace. Chub just looked at me and said, 'Sam, you're right.' He got on the phone to (owner) Horace Stoneham, and that was the end of that."

A Legend was Born

After twenty years in the business Lacy earned recognition as one of the best sports journalists in the profession. He received numerous offers to move on to bigger and more widely read publications—*Sports Illustrated* came calling as early as 1950—but he stayed at the *Afro-American*. He told Bill Kirtz of *The Quill* why he stayed put in Baltimore: "No other paper in the country would have given me the kind of license. I've made my own decisions. I cover everything that want to. I sacrificed a few dollars, true, but I lived a comfortable life. I get paid enough to be satisfied. I don't expect to die rich." Lacy continued to work nearly until his death at the age of 99, always striving to achieve a greater sense of fairness in the sporting world. He fought the major networks for their refusal to hire black broadcasters; he chastised major corporations for their failure to sponsor more black golfers; he fought for the inclusion of players from the old Negro Leagues into baseball's Hall of Fame in Cooperstown; and he took the National Football League to task for hesitating to hire black head coaches. In addition to his crusading, Lacy helped edit the paper and covered six different Olympic Games and some of the biggest prizefights of the twentieth century.

In 1997, on the fiftieth anniversary of Robinson's integration of Major League Baseball, everyone suddenly wanted to speak to Lacy. He was given an honorary doctorate at Loyola University, was honored by the Smithsonian Institute with a lecture series, and then the following year won the Associated Press's Red Smith Award and the Baseball Hall of Fame's J.G. Taylor Spink Award for sports writing. In 1998 Lacy achieved the ultimate reward for a baseball writer. He was inducted into the writers' wing of baseball's shrine. Though Lacy was awestruck that he was even considered for induction into the Hall of Fame, others recognized the important role he played in the history of baseball and racial desegregation in the United States. Jackie Robinson's widow, Rachel, told Cummings of *The New York Daily News* about Lacy's contribution: "We had

a great deal of respect for Sam and the other black journalists. They were really crusaders. They really paved the way for the integration of baseball because they were so persistent in their criticism of the owners. They never gave up and I don't think their efforts have ever been properly recognized or appreciated for the role they played behind the scenes." Upon his death on May 8, 2003, broadcasting great Bob Wolff told *Editor & Publisher* that Lacy was "a monument in the business."

Periodicals

Editor & Publisher, May 19, 2003.
New York Daily News, February 7, 1997.
Philadelphia Daily News, April 9, 1997.
Quill, January-February, 1999.
Sporting News May 26, 2003.
Sports Illustrated, October 29, 1990.
Washington Post, June 11, 1997. □

R. D. Laing

Psychotherapist R. D. Laing (1927-1989) became a counterculture hero in the 1960s for his renegade ideas about treating the profoundly mentally ill.

One of his most daring theories was that the root causes of some mental illnesses, including schizophrenia, might not be biological in origin, but were rather the result of environmental factors, particularly those that could exist within the sufferer's immediate family. Though he achieved fame in the era before a new generation of pharmaceutical remedies were developed for use in the field of mental illness, depression and associated disorders, Laing had long argued that his profession was deeply misguided. According to a 1971 *Times Literary Supplement* review of one of his books, Laing claimed that "a psychiatrist who professes to be a healer of souls but who keeps people asleep, treats them for waking up, and drugs them to sleep again, helps to drive them crazy."

Laing's own background seemed to be a textbook case for dysfunctional interpersonal relationships. He was born on October 7, 1927, in Glasgow, Scotland, the only child in a middle-class home, but his mother Amelia claimed that she was still a virgin when he was born, and both parents insisted they had not had sexual relations for some time prior to his conception. He was a lonely child, and his parents neither socialized with neighbors nor let him play with other children. Amelia once allegedly burnt her son's favorite wooden horse because he was so attached to it, but from his father he did inherit a deep appreciation for music and literature.

Appalled by Conventional Psychiatry

Laing read voraciously as a teenager, excelled in Greek and Latin as well as track, and was drawn to psychiatry after reading French playwright Antonin Artaud, who had a history of psychiatric hospital stays. He decided to enter

medical school at the University of Glasgow, and after receiving his degree in 1951 went on to serve two years in a medical corps unit of the British army. He continued his professional training in psychiatry in Glasgow, and took his first job as a staff psychiatrist at the Glasgow Royal Mental Hospital in 1955. The standard treatments of the era included electroconvulsive therapy, or shock treatment, which Laing considered not just barbaric but useless, as well as surgical procedures such as the lobotomy. Another common procedure was the insulin-induced coma, and all of these, Laing felt, served to isolate mentally ill persons from society, not heal them. One experience that was particularly saddening to him was the first New Year's Eve he spent at work, when the patients joined with the staff in singing ''Auld Lang Syne,'' the classic musical farewell to the old year. The patients smiled, laughed, and participated in the revelry as if they were not ''different'' from the staff. ''If any drug had this effect, for a few hours, even minutes,'' he wrote many years later in his autobiography, ''it would be world famous.''

Laing also saw early in his career that his fellow doctors seemed to distance themselves emotionally from their disturbed patients, and came to consider this a deeply flawed professional approach. He was able to put some of his daring ideas into practice when he convinced colleagues at the Gartnaval Hospital outside Glasgow to set up a ''rumpus room'' for some of the patients in a ward where 60 women were housed. The women, all deeply disturbed, were not allowed any personal possessions whatsoever, and had little personal autonomy. Laing took 12 of them and let them spend a day in a much cozier setting, a room with rugs,

books, and magazines, and where they were allowed to choose their own clothes and even have their hair styled. The women's communication skills improved markedly, and many were even discharged from the hospital, though they were all eventually readmitted over the next year.

Published Groundbreaking Book

Laing moved to London in 1956, taking a post at the Tavistock Clinic there. He began putting his revolutionary theories on paper, and the first of his books, *The Divided Self: A Study of Sanity and Madness,* was published in 1960. In it, he argued that schizophrenia was merely an adaptive reaction to what he termed the loss of self. There were two types of families, he explained: serial and nexial. Serial types allow each member a greater sense of individuality, in which members consider themselves a family unit though their primary actions, and activities are not dependent on one another. The other kind, nexial, is characterized by relationships that are much more interdependent. In this second kind of family, Laing wrote, the weaker or more insecure members may begin to internalize personality traits of stronger members. This leads to the fragmented or split personality that is the hallmark of schizophrenia.

The idea that madness could be the result of an individual's inability to conform to the expectations of others had already been theorized a few years earlier by Gregory Bateson, and was known as the double-bind theory, but Laing would receive much more media attention for this, thanks in part to his controversial statements. According to a *Times Literary Supplement* article by Aubrey Lewis, in *The Divided Self* Laing admitted to ''a certain personal difficulty I have in being a psychiatrist . . . Except in the case of chronic schizophrenics[,] I have difficulty in actually discovering the signs of psychosis in the person I am myself interviewing.''

Laing won a study grant to carry out extensive research on family relations at Tavistock in the early 1960s, and also took a post as director of the Langham Clinic for Psychotherapy around this same time. The family relations study involved extensive interviews with relatives of those who suffered from schizophrenia, and similar interviews with so-called ''normal'' families. Meeting with the control group, he once said, ''was a more gruelling experience than speaking with the families of schizophrenics. They were just so dead and stifling and, at the same time, it was very hard to describe what the deadening was. So it was difficult to say what the difference between the two was, except that in the normal family nobody cracked up,'' he wrote, according to a Harriet Stewart article in the *Guardian*.

Laing also challenged another standard wisdom of the psychiatric profession, which asserted that the gibberish speech of the psychotic patient was irrelevant to their treatment. He argued instead that such disoriented speech might be a legitimate articulation of their problems, and could be analyzed, in much the same way that non-structured Symbolist poetry was parsed by scholars. In a third contentious theory, Laing argued that psychotic episodes could be viewed as part of the mental health journey, rather than setbacks on it. Disturbances, rather than being disruptive, might instead be seen as a type of shamanic journey to find one's true inner self.

Opened Kingsley Hall

Laing began to emerge as the leading figure in what was known as the anti-psychiatry movement, though he was not technically a committed adherent. He did, however, raise many objections to the standard treatments of the time, and argued for a more humane approach. In 1964 he founded the Philadelphia Association, a charity that ran hostels offering schizophrenics a more compassionate course of therapy. Several other leading professional names were also involved in this project, and the most famous of the treatment facilities was at Kingsley Hall in London's East End. Here, staff attempted to erase the lines between themselves and their patients, and to become a model for an alternative mental asylum of the future. As a result, the staff sometimes behaved oddly, illicit drug use was rampant, and raucous parties upset the neighbors. Counterculture celebrities, including members of the Beatles, often stopped by to witness the mischief.

Laing realized that the Kingsley Hall experiment was not working out as well as he had hoped. "My dictum was *no transgressive behaviour*," he once said, according to Theodor Itten, an Austrian professional who became one of Laing's many protégés and delivered a symposium on the Philadelphia Association work in 2005. "Just because you are out of your mind doesn't mean you can take a hammer and bash someone's skull in. . . . However, my attitude in that respect wasn't shared by other people who were actually there. This was the area of doing [your] own thing, you know, if someone needs to smash a door backwards and forwards for several hours every night and keep everyone in earshot awake, well that's their thing. I couldn't negotiate with what I thought was a complete loss of common sense."

Kingsley Hall and its founder's theories were often mocked by the more mainstream members of the psychiatric profession. One of the reasons Laing's detractors refused to take him seriously was his lack of standard scientific evidence that his practices worked better than the standard treatments. He countered with the argument that most in his profession were still working to isolate the mentally ill from the rest of society. In his 1967 book, *The Politics of Experience/The Bird of Paradise*, which also emerged as a classic text of the counterculture and the left, he theorized that perhaps it was society that was truly ill, not the mentally ill person. Although Laing's ideas and revolutionary treatments stirred great controversy in the profession, many of his more sympathetic ideas eventually found their way into the care and treatment of the mentally ill. Psychiatric nurses, who in Laing's college days were prohibited from speaking to severely ill patients lest they bring on a psychotic episode, found that greater interaction with their patients seemed to indeed have therapeutic benefits, and also made their jobs more rewarding.

Arrested for Drug Possession

Laing's fame grew as the decade progressed. He made lecture tours of the United States, and was featured in a

Canadian Broadcasting Corporation documentary series. Along the way he became acquainted with other heroes of the hippie era, such as Timothy Leary, best known for his support of the acid trip, or LSD experience. Back in London, local authorities finally shut down Kingsley Hall in 1970 in response to complaints from neighbors, but other Philadelphia Association hostels continued to operate in the London area for a few more years. Laing busied himself with other projects, including "rebirthing" seminars in which participants emerged from special bags sewn from gnu skins, and he also began writing poetry. He practiced privately for a number of years, and wrote more books, including volumes of poetry and extractions from extensive interviews with children.

Laing was arrested in 1977 for possession of hallucinogenic drugs, and admitted a few years later that he had been a heavy drinker at one point in his life. His autobiography, *Wisdom, Madness, and Folly: The Making of a Psychiatrist*, was published in 1985. According to Alfie Kohn's review of the book for *Psychology Today*, Laing wrote that he was "still more frightened by the fearless power in the eyes of my fellow psychiatrists than by the powerless fear in the eyes of my patients." He died of a heart attack on August 23, 1989, while playing tennis in the French Riviera resort town of St. Tropez.

Periodicals

Guardian (London, England), July 26, 1996.
Independent (London, England), May 13, 1997.
Independent Sunday (London, England), August 4, 1996.
Psychology Today, December 1985.
Sunday Times (London, England), August 4, 1996.
Times (London, England), May 14, 1977; December 11, 1981; August 24, 1989; August 16, 1994.
Times Literary Supplement (London, England), May 18, 1962; July 2, 1964; December 31, 1971; October 11, 1985.

Online

"All the Lonely People Where Do They All Come From?" Society of Laingian Studies, http://www.laingsociety.org/colloquia/thercommuns/allthelonelypeople.htm (January 4, 2006). □

René Lalique

French glassware and jewelry designer René Lalique (1860-1945) is recognized as one of the late nineteenth and early twentieth centuries' finest creators of Art Deco and Art Nouveau decorative items. Lalique's glassware was both stylistically and technologically innovative, leading to great success for the designer both in personal and architectural glass products. Today, Lalique is particularly remembered for his decorative glass, such as vases and bowls; the Lalique Company continues to produce art glass and jewelry to this day.

orn April 6, 1860, in Ay, a small village in the Marne region of France, Lalique came from humble beginnings to become one of the world's most renowned glassmakers. When Lalique was still a toddler, his family relocated to his businessman father's hometown in suburban Paris. However, they often returned to Ay on summer holidays, allowing Lalique to retain a close connection to his birthplace. From an early age, Lalique demonstrated a marked interest and ability in art. In 1872, Lalique enrolled in the Turgot collège, where he studied drawing under Jean-Marie Lequien. Lalique proved his early aptitude for art by winning a first prize in drawing while at the collège. He then continued his art studies at the Paris School for the Decorative Arts while also studying jewelry making.

In 1876, Lalique's father died and Lalique took regular employment as a jewelry-making apprentice under Louis Aucoc, one of Paris's premier jewelers, while attending evening courses at the Paris School for the Decorative Arts. This apprenticeship provided Lalique with an unparalleled opportunity to learn essential crafting skills hands-on, as well as offering an introduction to the kinds of raw materials used in jewelry design. After two years with Aucoc, Lalique moved to London, where he studied at Sydenham College, initially built as an art school in the famed Crystal Palace, a huge iron-and-glass building designed to house the Great Exhibition of the Works of Industry of All Nations in 1851. Although Lalique's reasons for going to England at this time are not obvious, Nicholas M. Dawes speculates in his book *Lalique Glass* that Lalique may have been "drawn to England by the blossoming arts and crafts movement, whose ideals and concepts were refreshingly distinct from those of fashionable Paris society and clearly more sympathetic to his own." Indeed, during the period of Lalique's studies in England, the first stirrings of his individual, naturalistic style became apparent.

First Professional Successes

Returning to Paris in 1880, Lalique worked both as a jewelry designer for a relative, M. Vuilleret, and, over the next few years, as an independent contract artist. He also studied sculpture and modeling under Lequien at the Ecole Bernard Palissy, completing his formal art training. Quickly, Lalique built up his contract clientele, designing jewelry for such major houses as Cartier and Boucheron. By 1885, Lalique was ready to strike out on his own, opening a small atelier which commenced work the following year. Here, he could produce his own unique style of jewelry stemming from the Art Nouveau style, still in its formative stages. Lalique particularly became known for his use of semi-precious gems, enamels, ivory, and other hard stones.

Lalique's success grew quickly and by 1887, he needed more space. He rented another atelier and ran both workshops until 1890, when he combined operations in one, larger location, with room for thirty workers. Working with two father-and-son sculptors, Lalique designed the decorations for the atelier's walls and ceilings; he would later marry Augustine Alice Ledru, the daughter and sister of these two sculptors. During his tenure in this workshop, Lalique truly came into his own as a designer. He made

pieces for such luminaries as actress Sarah Bernhardt; Tony L. Mortimer noted in *Lalique* that Bernhardt's patronage "proved a valuable commercial asset which immediately gained him an international reputation." Lalique also began his first forays into glass work, either incorporating bits of glass into his jewelry designs or making such small pieces of glassware as perfume vials. On a personal note, in 1892 Lalique's first child, daughter Suzanne, was born.

The 1890s continued to hold triumphs for Lalique. By 1894, Lalique's pieces were sold in Siegfried Bing's La Maison de l'Art Nouveau, the shop which would lend its name to the Art Nouveau movement. In 1897, he exhibited some ivory-and-horn combs at Paris' Salon and was dubbed the "inventor of modern jewelry" by Emile Gallé. That same year, Lalique participated in the International Exposition at Brussels, Belgium, where he was awarded the Grand Prize. To cap off the year, he was made a Knight of the Legion of Honor.

In 1898, Lalique established a workshop devoted to glassware. Although Lalique's period of experimentation with items made completely of glass was short-lived, he continued to use the material in conjunction with other metals. Lalique began working with bronze, perhaps encouraged by his wife's family. By the turn of the century, Lalique had begun creating large panel and bas-relief glass pieces, often framed in bronze. Intrigued by recently developed processes allowing glass to be cast into any form using a hollow mold, Dawes noted that "Lalique recognized the commercial potential in the malleable properties of [this kind of] glass and developed his own glass body, termed demi-cristal, with the same properties."

In 1900, Lalique exhibited with great success at the World's Fair at Paris. After this, Lalique turned more and more to the creation of glassware, finding many of his nature-inspired designs to be copied by rival jewelry makers. Lalique also celebrated the birth of his second child, son Marc, in September 1900 and was promoted to Officer of the Legion of Honor. In 1902, the Lalique family moved to a large house which Lalique had specially built, designing the striking front doors himself with a pine branch and pinecone motif.

Shifted to Glassware

Continuing to exhibit in major art shows both in France and throughout Europe, Lalique opened a store in 1905 on Paris' famed Place Vendôme offering both jewelry and glass. The boutique's location near perfumer François Coty's shop led to a providential partnership around 1908, with Lalique initially designing labels and later glass bottles for Coty's perfumes. This was the first time perfumes were packaged in distinctive, rather than traditionally classical, bottles; Lalique's designs for Coty were so evocative of the fragrance that he went on to design bottles for many major perfumers of the era. Lalique did not have the production capabilities necessary for the large amount of bottles Coty required for his mass market perfumes, so the earliest bottles were designed by Lalique but produced by Legras and Company; in 1909, Lalique opened his own glassworks just outside of Paris, allowing him to use his preferred demi-cristal type of glass, better showing Lalique's distinctive style. However, the year also held sorrow for Lalique: his wife, Augustine Alice Lalique-Ledru, died.

In 1911, Lalique turned definitively away from jewelry and to glassware following his exposition at the first show of the Salon de la Société Nationale des Beaux-Arts devoted exclusively to works in glass. The following year, he designed architectural features including doors, windows, and interior fittings for an upscale French residence and for the Coty Building on New York City's Fifth Avenue. With the outbreak of World War I in 1914, Lalique's production output changed from purely decorative items to include practical ones: laboratory glass for hospitals and pharmacies. After the war, however, Lalique found such a high demand for his products that in 1921 he built a large glassworks, Verrerie d'Alsace René Lalique et Cie, at Wingen sur Moder, in the east of France. (This factory remains in use by the Lalique Company today.)

Internationally Esteemed

In 1925, Lalique exhibited a number of decorative glass pieces in the emerging Art Deco style at the Exposition des Arts Décoratifs in Paris. This style, less naturalistic than the Art Nouveau style, became highly popular after the 1925 Exposition and Lalique successfully blended his existing style into the new Art Deco technique. This decade saw Lalique's glassware become available throughout France and indeed the world, with stores in the United States, England and Argentina among other countries offering Lalique pieces to the public. Lalique became particularly well-known for his mass produced frosted glass vases, first produced in 1926. His glassworks primarily turned out these small, relatively inexpensive pieces, although occasionally Lalique designed large pieces, including interior fittings and decorations for luxury French ocean liners; church windows throughout France; and a dining car of the world-famous Venice Simplon Orient Express, a luxury train running across Europe.

Throughout the late 1920s and early 1930s, Lalique also made his mark as a designer of the car mascot. The forerunner of modern hood ornaments, the car mascot was a small decorative item, often mounted on a car's radiator cap—at that time conveniently fitted with a screw-top metal attachment—or bolted over the engine casing. Lalique first designed a mascot for French car manufacturer Citroën in 1925; over the next several years, he created twenty-seven different mascots for car companies including Bentley and Rolls-Royce. The mascots could also serve as paperweights and had typically Lalique nature-related designs, often stylized animals such as grasshoppers, peacocks, eagles, or frogs. After car companies began designing their own logos to serve as mascots, Lalique marketed the pieces' other function, selling them as paperweights or bookends.

Lalique continued this course into the 1930s, primarily making small glass pieces but occasionally venturing into large, commissioned works, most notably with the design of fountains installed on Paris's Champs-Elysées, American department stores fixtures, and a Tokyo palace. Still producing a small amount of jewelry, in 1931 Lalique designed the popular cabochon ring. In 1935, Lalique opened a shop on the Rue Royale, in Paris, where the company still operates their offices and flagship store.

World War II and Lalique's Legacy

Although Lalique's products remained immensely popular, the company suspended operations in 1939 when its factory in Wingen sur Moder was occupied by an invading German force. The area remained under German control and the glassworks remained closed until the end of the war in 1945. Unfortunately, René Lalique did not live to see his factory re-open after the war; he died on May 9, 1945, at the age of 85, after a productive and successful life in creative jewelry and glass design. However, the death of Lalique did not mean the end of his company. In late 1945, Lalique's son Marc re-opened the Wingen sur Moder factory, designing new pieces and using a new, brighter form of glass. Marc Lalique's daughter, Marie-Claude Lalique, came to work with her father in 1956 and became the head of the glassworks in 1977 upon her father's death. Today, the Lalique Company continues to produce highly respected decorative glass and jewelry, with outlets throughout the world; Lalique's original, turn-of-the-century pieces can be found in such internationally-known museums as the Metropolitan Museum of Art in New York City, New York, the Musée d'Orsay in Paris, France, and the Victoria and Albert Museum in London, England.

Books

Bayer, Patricia and Mark Waller, *The Art of René Lalique,* Quintet, 1988.
Dawes, Nicholas M., *Lalique Glass,* Crown Publishers, 1986.
McDonald, Jesse, *Lalique,* Brompton Books, 1995.
Mortimer, Tony L., *Lalique,* Chartwell Books, 1989.

Online

"René Lalique, 1860-1945," http://www.cristallalique.fr/v1/biographie_en.htm (December 29, 2005). □

Libertad Lamarque

During the late 1930s and early '40s, Buenos Aires, Argentina, developed into the Hollywood of Latin America and during this time, Argentina's own Libertad Lamarque (1908-2000) became its biggest and brightest star. Over seven decades, Lamarque's face was rarely absent from television or movie screens. She starred in 65 films and countless Latin American telenovelas and recorded more than 800 songs, including many memorable tangos.

Born a Natural Showgirl

The youngest of ten children, Lamarque was born November 24, 1908, in Rosario, Santa Fe, Argentina. Her French-Uruguayan father, Gaudincio Lamarque,

was jealous and suspicious of the actors whose company Lamarque kept. Their marriage was over in a flash, yet it took them a dozen years to separate because Argentina, at the time, had laws forbidding divorce.

Along the way, Lamarque signed a deal with the RCA Victor label, agreeing to make one record per month for a fee of 150 pesos each. Lamarque soon became the preeminent tango singer of her time and helped popularize the seductive, passionate and romantic song and dance style that the Buenos Aires working-class poor had developed in the mid-nineteenth century. In the late 1920s Lamarque, alongside three guitarists, toured Argentina and Paraguay, sharing her soprano voice. Most of her albums included a fusion of intense tangos, Mexican rancheros and boleros. Her most popular album, released in 1991, was *Nadie se va del todo* (Nobody Does it Better), which went platinum. Once Lamarque began recording, she was relentless in churning out songs. In 1976, RCA recognized her with a special award commemorating 50 uninterrupted years of recording.

Made Film Debut

Despite her schedule, Lamarque found ample time for acting. In 1929, Lamarque made her screen debut in *Adiós Argentina* (Goodbye, Argentina), which was shot in one day. Although *Adiós Argentina* was a silent film with no speaking parts, it was the first Argentine-produced film with a soundtrack. The actors recorded their songs on Vitaphone, a sound-film process that allowed the playing of phonograph soundtracks in sync with the film. Lamarque sang the title song, a tango. Her second film, *Tango,* came out in 1933 and featured the most popular tango singers and orchestras of the day.

By the mid-1930s, Lamarque received only starring roles in the blockbuster Argentine films of the day. Lamarque came of age during what has been called the "Golden Era" of Latin America cinema, the 1930s and '40s. Previously, Hollywood had tried to dub English films into Spanish for Latin American filmgoers, but it never really caught on. As one U.S. film distributor told Alfred A. Frantz of the *New York Times* in 1940: "The average moviegoer in South America knows just as well as the average moviegoer in the United States that Greta Garbo does not speak Spanish. Therefore, dubbed films did not ring true and the South American public turned thumbs down on even the best of them."

Lamarque came into her own as Buenos Aires developed into the Hollywood of the Latin American cinema. Lamarque understood the nuances of film acting and realized it went beyond singing and dancing mechanics. Lamarque used the lighting and cameras as tools. Most of the films Lamarque made during this time were musical comedies and dramas, including *Adúdame a vivir* (Help Me to Live) in 1936; *Besos Brujos* (Bewitching Kisses) in 1937; *La Ley que olvidaron* (The Law They Forgot) and *Madreselva* (Honeysuckle), both in 1938; and *Puerta Cerrada* (Closed Door) in 1939.

In 1939, *Madreselva* (Honeysuckle) made it to the Spanish theater in New York. One *New York Times* movie reviewer said that "one can easily understand why Libertad

made a living as a scrap dealer, though in his youth he had been a contortionist. Lamarque's Spanish immigrant mother, Josefa Bouza, was a seamstress. When Lamarque was born, her anarchist father was in prison for political dissent, so he suggested naming the baby girl "Libertad," which is Spanish for liberty.

Lamarque took to singing and dancing at a young age and often amused relatives with her theatrical renditions of traditional folk songs. Her uncles threw flowers and coins at her feet. Lamarque once said according to the *Independent*'s Austin Mutti–Mewse, "I soon discovered that I adored performing, especially to an audience."

Alongside her brothers and sisters, Lamarque got plenty of opportunities to perform in her father's touring theater troupe. Their father wrote the plays, often political in nature, and their mother sewed the costumes. Lamarque quickly stood out among the family members and by age 12 she was acting professionally. In the early to mid-1920s, the family relocated to Buenos Aires, where Lamarque sang in the local theaters and nightclubs. She also performed tangos in variety shows in the Calle Corrientes theater district.

Signed to Record Label

Around this time Lamarque became acquainted with music producer Emilio Romero and the two laid down an album of tangos. Working together on the album sparked a romance and they were married by 1928. Soon, Lamarque had a daughter, Mirtha Romero Lamarque. As Lamarque's popularity grew, so did her work hours. In addition, Romero

Lamarque has become so popular among Ibero–American cinema patrons." The reviewer added that Lamarque "possesses an undefinable attraction all her own." The musical dramas Lamarque starred in generally portrayed her as a longsuffering woman who finds solace in the tango amid a life filled with cheating men, unrequited love and double-crossing female friends.

Forced out of Argentine Cinema

Lamarque's success continued without incident until 1944 when she locked horns with another actress, Eva Duarte, during the filming of *La Cabalgata del circo* (The Circus Parade). The two clashed over the script and their costumes. According to rumor, Duarte showed up one day wearing one of Lamarque's dresses and an infuriated Lamarque slapped Duarte across the face. Another version says Lamarque slapped Duarte for loafing around.

Soon, Duarte married Colonel Juan Domingo Perón and later adopted the name "Evita." When Perón took power in 1946, Duarte became Argentina's all-powerful first lady and promptly banned Lamarque's voice from the radio airwaves. In addition, she coerced filmmakers into dropping Lamarque from their films. Lamarque, however, did not give up her career so easily. She moved with her second husband, Alfredo Malerba, to Mexico and continued acting. In her memoirs, Lamarque denied ever slapping Duarte, though she acknowledged their animosity.

Some political insiders have suggested the clash was over Colonel Perón's affections. Though Perón was displaced from power in the mid-1950s, it was not until after 1960 that Lamarque returned to visit Argentina. She was welcomed with open arms. Fans filled the airport with signs proclaiming "Welcome Back" and "Long Live Libertad."

Nicknamed "Sweetheart of the Americas"

The films Lamarque made in Mexico became box-office smashes and she was soon counted as a national treasure in her adopted homeland. Standout films from this period include *Gran Casino* (Grand Casino) in 1947, and *Escuela de música* (Music School) in 1955. As an actress, Lamarque fussed over her scripts and at times changed the ending to keep her character alive and well. Lamarque made more than 40 films in Mexico and recorded 180 songs. At the height of her career, the volume of fan mail she received rivaled that of her Hollywood counterparts. In fact, Lamarque had to hire a staff to tend to the mail. In 1947 she was invited to perform at New York City's famed Carnegie Hall.

Lamarque's fame extended well beyond Mexico and Argentina and she found a following in many Latin American countries, including Chile, Puerto Rico, Cuba, Venezuela, the Dominican Republic, Guatemala, El Salvador and Honduras. "Strangely, even with a strong Argentine accent that never quite went away, she became the darling of Mexican cinema," Latin American film expert Carl Mora told the *New York Times'* Simon Romero. "Her magnetic presence made for quite a life trajectory." Lamarque was given the nickname "Sweetheart of the Americas," (Latin America).

Hollywood tried to lure her to the U.S. screen. Paramount and MGM offered contracts, but she refused. Speaking to the *Independent*'s Mutti–Mewse, Lamarque discussed her decision, "I was scared. Some Latin–American actresses like Lupita Tovar and Mona Maris had already found success in Hollywood, making a living making Spanish versions of American box–office hits. ... I couldn't speak a word of English and didn't want to be taken advantage of. I have no regrets."

Performed Up Until Death

Lamarque later was a guest on television talk shows. She also starred in Spanish telenovelas and thanks to this work remained popular in Latin American countries until her death. During the 1980s, Lamarque appeared in *Soledad* (Solitude) and in 1998 joined the telenovela *La Usurpador* (The Usurper). Both were produced in Mexico. She also starred in the Venezuelan soap opera *Esmeralda* and Argentina's *Armada*.

When Lamarque was 80, she told the *Miami Herald*'s Juan Carlos Coto she had no intention of retiring just because the calendar said she was getting old. "I am not mummified. I am a lively person who enjoys her work and is healthy. What matters is that I can appear on a stage or television and that I keep being a figure that attracts attention, the applause and the love of the people. That's why I keep working." Even after she hit 90, Lamarque was still going strong. She was on the set filming an episode of the popular telenovela *Carita de Ángel* (Angel Face) two weeks before she died. In this show, Lamarque played a nun in charge of a boarding school.

In her later years, Lamarque divided her time between Mexico and Coral Gables, Florida, where she lived with a housekeeper and eight cats. She died of pneumonia at 92 on December 12, 2000, at a Mexico City hospital. Survived by her daughter, Lamarque's body was cremated and her ashes were spread in the sea.

Books

Clark, Walter Aaron, ed., *From Tejano to Tango: Latin American Popular Music*, Routledge, 2002.

Periodicals

Guardian (London), January 26, 2001.
Independent (London), December 19, 2000.
Miami Herald, February 4, 1989; December 13, 2000.
New York Times, August 19, 1939; August 11, 1940; December 25, 2000. □

Wanda Landowska

Perhaps more than any other single individual, keyboard performer Wanda Landowska (1879-1959) was responsible for the revival of the harpsichord— the instrument that was the piano's most important ancestor.

Important composers of the Baroque era (c.1600-1750), such as Johann Sebastian Bach, George Frederic Handel and François Couperin, wrote solo keyboard works, and keyboard parts in larger works, with the harpsichord in mind. Today, performances of Baroque music on "period" or historically appropriate instruments are at least as common as those using modern ones. Modern harpsichord performers owe Landowska a tremendous debt, for she single-handedly researched the instrument's construction, commissioned new examples from builders, investigated performance styles, wrote polemical articles promoting the use of the harpsichord, and, most importantly, repopularized the instrument by performing on it over a five-decade concert career. Her influence extended even beyond her chosen instrument; essayist Allan Evans, in an essay appearing on the website of the Arbiter Records label, asserted that "one of the many debts of gratitude we owe to Wanda Landowska is for her having viewed music as a continuum rather than a progressing art ever perfecting itself." She helped lead classical music audiences to realize that music of the past is often best appreciated on its own terms.

Family Converted to Catholicism

Born in Warsaw, Poland, on July 5, 1879, Landowska was the daughter of attorney Marian Landowski and linguist Eva Lautenberg. Her mother produced the first translations of American author Mark Twain's novels into Polish. Landowska's background was Jewish, but her family had converted to the Catholic faith. A child prodigy, Landowska gave her first piano recital at age four. Her parents signed

her up for lessons with two high-level teachers at the Warsaw Conservatory (named Klenczynski and Michalowski) who were exponents of the style of Polish-born nineteenth-century composer and pianist Fryderyk Chopin. But even as a young woman she liked the music of earlier eras when she heard it, which was rarely—although Johann Sebastian Bach (1685-1750) is now considered among the greatest composers in history, his music was mostly forgotten in the late 1800s. She also heard and reacted strongly to the harpsichord music of French composer Jean-Philippe Rameau when played on the piano. Her teachers realized that she had talent and unusual instincts, and they let her pursue her interests to some degree.

A small growth on one hand temporarily sidelined Landowska's keyboard career but had the effect of broadening her musical horizons—her mother sent her to study composition with Heinrich Urban in Berlin, Germany, after she graduated from the Warsaw Conservatory in 1896, and she began to find her place within the international musical community. Landowska remained for just a few years in Berlin, but while she was there she met fellow Pole Henry Lew, a folklorist and writer, who supported her in her musical ambitions. They moved to Paris, France, in 1900 and got married there. Lew supported Landowska's growing interest in the harpsichord, and that interest was stimulated still further when she began to cultivate contacts at Paris's Schola Cantorum and became acquainted with the group of top music scholars who were active there. These included composer Vincent d'Indy and the great organist and Bach specialist Albert Schweitzer. She heard more Baroque-era music, by French composers François Couperin and Jean-Philippe Rameau.

Landowska's next move was to launch intensive research into harpsichord design. Most of the models she had to work with were in museums, for it had been a century since harpsichords had been made in appreciable numbers. Complicating Landowska's task was the fact that harpsichords differed in major ways from one another; unlike the nineteenth-century piano market, which was dominated by a few major manufacturers, harpsichords were made by individual builders and might be large or small, with anywhere from one to four sets of strings, one or two keyboards, and a variety of technical specifications. The few performers who had tried to play existing harpsichords in public concerts had been met with indifference or ridicule from audiences who found the instrument's sound anemic or worse—its strings are plucked rather than hammered like those of a piano when a key is struck, and it is not capable of gradations between loud and soft dynamics (the word "pianoforte," the piano's original name, means "soft-loud" in Italian).

In 1903 Landowska devoted a segment of a piano recital to a performance on a small harpsichord built by the Pleyel piano firm, and as her body of research grew she began to work with the firm's engineers on a larger instrument. She also began to prepare the ground for the harpsichord revolution with her writings; the influential article "Sur l'interpretation des oeuvres de clavecin de J.S. Bach," (On the Interpretation of the Harpsichord Works of J.S.

Bach), appeared in 1905, and in 1909 she and Lew coauthored a book, *La musique ancienne* (Early Music). Some of Landowska's writings were combative as she strove to counter the widespread perception that the harpsichord was of purely antiquarian interest. In 1912 Landowska introduced a new two-keyboard Pleyel harpsichord at the Breslau Bach Festival in Germany, and her renown began to grow.

Arrested During War

One mark of Landowska's new influence was that she was hired in 1913 to teach harpsichord at the Hochschule für Musik in Berlin, among Germany's top university music programs. Having come from France, she and her husband were arrested after World War I broke out in 1914 and spent much of the war as paroled civil prisoners—they were not criminally charged, but most of their possessions were confiscated. After the end of the war, Landowska participated in a performance of Bach's *St. Matthew Passion,* playing the continuo part (a chordal accompaniment) on the harpsichord for the first time in decades, and perhaps since Bach's death. In 1919 Lew became an early auto-accident fatality, and Landowska left Germany, giving a series of recitals in Switzerland and Spain and then returning to Paris to take a teaching post at the Ecole Normale de Musique.

In Paris in the 1920s, Landowska often attended and performed at a salon—an intellectual-social gathering—that was later reported to have had a lesbian orientation. The nature of her marriage to Lew has been variously described, but he was clearly supportive of her musical endeavors. Landowska had numerous private students in Paris, and one of them, Denise Restout, later became her editor, general assistant, and life companion.

In the 1920s and 1930s Landowska reached the peak of her fame. Several major composers wrote new harpsichord compositions for her, including Francis Poulenc, who was quoted by Evans as saying that "the way in which she has resuscitated and re-created the harpsichord is a sort of miracle." Landowska toured the United States for the first time in 1923, sailing from Europe with four harpsichords and making 78 rpm recordings for the Victor label.

The crowning achievement of Landowska's life in France was the construction of her own three-story house in the Paris suburb of St.-Leu. Finished in 1925, it included a garden and a small detached concert hall that became a routine stop for Parisians and visitors interested in new musical developments. Younger keyboard players interested in the harpsichord flocked to Landowska's studio, and her own concerts were packed. In 1933 she performed Bach's massive *Goldberg Variations* on the harpsichord for the first time in the twentieth century.

Fled Nazis

As German soldiers approached Paris in the summer of 1940, Landowska, due to her Jewish background, found herself in grave danger. She and Restout fled south, hitchhiking out of the city—Restout bribed a passing driver, and they slipped out of Paris at four o'clock in the morning, taking only a few cases of books and manuscripts with them. The house in St.-Leu, with its collection of antique instruments and its large library, was ransacked by the Nazis. Landowska and Restout were refugees in the south of France for about a year and a half, staying with friends and watching their funds dwindle as they moved from place to place. Finally they made their way to the Portuguese coast and sailed for the U.S.

Landowska and Restout were admitted to New York through Ellis Island, where they had to wait among transported Japanese-American internees despite a sheaf of recommendation letters gathered from American acquaintances. Of their $1,300 in remaining money they had to post $1,000 as a bond.

But things improved when Landowska was able to return to performing. Her first U.S. concert was an impromptu recital she gave on a piano she found pushed against a wall on Ellis Island, but by February of 1942 she was performing at the Town Hall auditorium and basking in rave reviews from Virgil Thomson and other leading American critics of the day. Word of Landowska's innovations in Baroque music performance had reached the U.S., and even jazz bandleader Artie Shaw had experimented with the unique tone color of the harpsichord on occasion. The Victor label, now called RCA Victor, released more Landowska recordings, and by 1947 she was able to afford to move to a country home near Lakeville, Connecticut. Another resident of the area was French mystery novelist Georges Simenon.

Perhaps the greatest of Landowska's American recordings was a complete rendering of Bach's *Well-Tempered Clavier,* a set of 48 short but intricate harpsichord pieces intended to demonstrate the complete set of musical keys made possible by the tempered tuning system that had just recently been introduced in Bach's time. In 1975, the recording was added to the National Academy of Recording Arts and Sciences hall of fame. Later recordings of that work and others went beyond Landowska's in sheer authenticity; heard today, her performances seem more concerned with the spirit of a piece of music than with its exact notated score, and she sometimes added ornaments that would later be regarded as questionable. Her big Pleyel harpsichord was likewise superseded by later research, and, noted Richard Dyer of the *Boston Globe* in his review of the video *Landowska: Uncommon Visionary,* "the finger-lifting technique and distorted hand positions required to play it go against most of what is known about healthy muscular uses of the hand . . . and it is not surprising to hear her last record producer, RCA's John Pfeifer, remark that the sessions for her late recordings of Bach's *Well-Tempered Clavier* proved very difficult."

Dyer nevertheless asserted that earlier Landowska recordings heard in the video had "an authority, rhythmic spring, virtuoso elan, and emotional immediacy that has not been surpassed by any of her successors." Landowska was interviewed for an installment of the NBC television series *Wisdom* in 1953, and she continued to write and perform, never giving up the piano entirely, until her death in Lakeville, on August 16, 1959. Her home was preserved as the Landowska Center; her recordings continued to form cornerstones of many a classical music library; and her influence was magnified into the plethora of harpsichord recordings that had appeared by the twentieth century's end and continued undiminished into the twenty-first.

Books

Gelatt, Roland, *Music Makers,* Knopf, 1953.
Restout, Denise, ed., *Landowska on Music,* Stein and Day, 1964.
Sadie, Stanley, ed., *The New Grove Dictionary of Music and Musicians,* 2nd ed., Macmillan, 2001.

Periodicals

Boston Globe, January 23, 1998.

Online

"Landowska, Wanda," GLBTQ, An Encyclopedia of Gay, Lesbian, Bisexual, Transgender & Queer Culture, http://www.glbtq.com/arts/landowska_w.html (December 22, 2005).
"Wanda (Aleksandra) Landowska," Arbiter Records, http://www.arbiterrecords.com/musicresourcecenter/landowska.html (December 22, 2005). □

Susanne K. Langer

One of the most widely read philosophers of the twentieth century, Susanne K. Langer (1895-1985) was also a pioneer in the field and one of the few modern thinkers who devised a rigorous, systematic, philosophical theory that accounted for artistic expression and tried to relate it to other activities of the human mind.

In the terminology of philosophy, Langer was an aesthetician—a specialist in the branch of philosophy dealing with beauty, art, and the human perception of these subjects. She was often considered a maverick, for these considerations had played only a minor role in philosophy for many decades before she began to write. Even within the field of aesthetics, Langer was unusual; she had little interest in the concept of beauty. Instead, she believed that art and music were fundamental forms of human activity, related to and equal in significance to spoken language although different in their basic structures. Langer's book *Philosophy in a New Key* (1942) was for many years one of the most frequently assigned philosophy books in liberal arts college courses.

Talked for 40 Minutes on Frogs

The daughter of a German-immigrant lawyer, Langer was born Susanne Knauth on December 20, 1895, in New York, New York. Her mother never learned to speak English well, and Langer herself grew up speaking German and always spoke English with a slight accent. As a small child she suffered a severe case of cocaine poisoning due to a prescription error, but she recovered. Langer grew up with two sisters and two brothers in a household that valued serious study and music. At first the young Susanne was most fascinated by natural phenomena, and she loved to

wander on hiking trails when the family made trips out of New York. Her relatives called her the Forest Witch. Someone gave her a book about frogs, and she was asked to give a little talk about the amphibians to her family. They got an idea of her powers of concentration when she delivered a well-organized 40-minute lecture, never referring to any notes.

Langer was schooled partly at home, owing to her initially limited English skills. Later she attended the private Veltin School in New York. She read voraciously, and was interested in difficult works of philosophy from the start. "In my early teens, I read *Little Women* and [German philosopher Immanuel] Kant's *Critique of Pure Reason* simultaneously," she told Winthrop Sargent of *The New Yorker.* As a young woman, Langer was for the most part an independent learner. She wrote a play called *Walpurgisnacht* that was performed in a woodland grove by a group of her family members.

Langer's father did not believe that his daughters should go to college, but she was encouraged by her mother and entered Radcliffe College. At that point, she took a more systematic approach to her studies. She liked her philosophy courses, especially logic, and she benefited from having top American philosophers, including Harvard's Alfred North Whitehead, as professors. The precision of Langer's mind was demonstrated anew when she asked Whitehead for his opinion of a German children's song she had learned years before; the song referred to Sleeping Beauty and Snow White, and said that "each has at her side/the handsomest prince." (The tale was told in a 1960 *New Yorker* profile of Langer.) Were there two princes, Langer wanted to know, or just one, sitting between the two fairy tale characters? Whitehead agreed with her that there was just one prince.

Before she graduated from Radcliffe in 1920, she met Harvard graduate student William Langer. The two fell in love, married in 1921, and went to Vienna, Austria, together for a year. The couple had two sons. "It is questionable whether two deeply preoccupied parents can create the ideal environment for a family of children," Langer told Sargent. But she remained close to her sons in old age. After William Langer got a job teaching at Harvard, the family moved back to Cambridge, Massachusetts. Susanne Langer earned Master's (1924) and Ph.D. (1926) degrees at Radcliffe, and the school hired her as a philosophy tutor the following year.

Wrote Children's Book

Langer's first published book was not a work of philosophy at all. In 1923 she wrote a children's book, *The Cruise of the Little Dipper and Other Fairy Tales.* The drawings were done by Helen Sewell, who went on to become a leading children's book illustrator. The book was reprinted in 1963 but remains a rare artifact of Langer's early career. A children's book might seem tangential to Langer's main interests, but some felt, given the important role myth would play in her system of philosophy, that the book showed her coming to grips with the ideas that fascinated her. Langer's next two books were textbooks: *The Practice of Philosophy* appeared in 1930, and *An Introduction to Symbolic Logic,* published in 1937, continued to be used in college courses and was reissued in 1953. These books, again, were more than detours in Langer's path toward original thought; they looked toward contemporary issues in philosophy and gave full weight to meaning and symbol in the human mental makeup.

Langer was influenced by German philosopher Ernst Cassirer, who came to the United States after the Nazis rose to power. Cassirer's belief that religion, science, art, and myth were different but coequal branches of human thought had a fundamental impact on the ideas Langer expressed in *Philosophy in a New Key,* which for many years was one of the best-selling titles in the catalog of Harvard University Press. The book eventually sold more than a half million copies. "I believe that in this physical, space-time world of our experience there are things which do not fit the grammatical scheme of expression," Langer wrote. "But they are not necessarily blind, inconceivable, mystical affairs; they are simply matters which require to be conceived through some symbolistic schema other than discursive language." With their children grown, and with that book having established Langer's reputation, Langer and her husband divorced in 1942.

Any quick summary of *Philosophy in a New Key* would distort more than it clarifies, but it can be said that the idea of the "symbol" was central to the book. For Langer, the making of symbols or representations was what distinguished humans from other animals. Symbols, Langer argued, might be "discursive," and the primary example of a set of discursive symbols was language, which in previous philosophies of meaning had nearly always held a central place. Langer, however, pointed out that language could embody a phenomenon only in sequential expressions, not in simultaneous ones.

Certain phenomena were being discussed at the time, due to the work of Sigmund Freud—for example, dreams and feelings–and they were notoriously resistant to expression in language. Humans, Langer reasoned, dealt with these phenomena through the use of "presentational" symbols such as music, art, and myth-making, as ways of bringing meaning to a realm that language philosopher Ludwig Wittgenstein had called "unspeakable."

Langer's philosophy was not simple, but she had a lucid prose style, influenced by that of British philosopher Bertrand Russell, that yielded its secrets to concentrated reading. Her ideas were novel and her mode of expression unique, but her attempt to come to grips with seemingly irrational aspects of human mental activity had many parallels in the ideas of other key modern thinkers. In rejecting the absolute primacy of discursive scientific reasoning, Sargent pointed out, "Mrs. Langer finds herself in the company of some modern psychologists, notably the disciples of C.G. Jung, but she is a far more lucid and coherent thinker than Jung and, unlike him, she abhors the easy, irrational path of mysticism." *Philosophy in a New Key* began to find a readership among undergraduate philosophy and liberal arts students interested in the nature of creative expression, and Langer's fame grew. She was hired as a lecturer in philoso-

phy at Columbia University in New York in 1945, remaining there until 1950.

Lived in Rural Locations

Langer expanded on the ideas of *Philosophy in a New Key* in two more books, *Feeling and Form: A Theory of Art* (1953) and *Problems of Art* (1957). In *Feeling and Form* she drew distinctions between the ways the arts shaped the basic materials of feeling. Each art form focused on a different aspect of human experience: music was concerned with time, for instance, art and sculpture with space, and dance with what Langer called virtual power. *Problems of Art* collected some of Langer's public lectures and featured accessible observations on common topics of discussion related to the arts and creativity. Langer refined the common notion that a work of art expresses the feelings of the artist, arguing that the artist expresses "not his own actual feeling, but what he knows about human feeling." She added (as quoted in the *New York Times*) that "once he is in possession of a rich symbolism, that knowledge may actually exceed his entire personal experience." In 1954 Langer got a job teaching at Connecticut College. She moved out of New York and bought a farmhouse in Old Lyme, Connecticut.

Living alone and filling index cards with ideas, Langer devoted herself more and more to writing. She sought still greater solitude by buying a small rural retreat in Ulster County, New York, which had no electricity and which offered her unlimited opportunities to indulge her girlhood passion for walking in the woods. Langer collected animals like lizards and frogs, which she kept as pets and gave erudite literary names. She disliked any kind of background music or extraneous noise, but she continued to enjoy performing (on cello and piano) and hearing classical music. She told Sargent that she concentrated on music so intensely that listening to a half hour of music took as much effort for her as ten hours of writing philosophy—which she did in longhand.

Langer retired from Connecticut College in 1962 and devoted the rest of her life to writing full time; supported at first by a grant from a foundation, the Edgar J. Kaufmann Charitable Trust. She remained in high demand as a guest lecturer at various academic institutions, and though she enjoyed her simple, rural lifestyle, she was not averse to marathon car trips to reach these destinations. Sometimes, almost as a break, she contributed articles to general-interest magazines, but it was the life of the mind that absorbed her the most. "I'm really happy," she told Sargent, "as long as I have a theory." Langer was awarded honorary degrees from Columbia and several other schools in the 1960s.

Having a theory kept Susanne Langer going for a long time. The last years of her life were devoted to the completion of a massive study of the human mind that attempted to incorporate feeling into a grand scheme of human thought. The study, entitled *Mind: An Essay on Human Feeling,* appeared in three volumes, in 1967, 1973, and 1982; it ranged across many academic disciplines in a manner that was new to the discipline of philosophy. Langer kept writing almost until her death at age 89, on July 17, 1985, stopping only when she was nearly completely blind.

Periodicals

New York Times, July 19, 1985.
New Yorker, December 3, 1960.

Online

Contemporary Authors Online. Gale, 2005. Reproduced in *Biography Resource Center.* Farmington Hills, Mich.: Thomson Gale, 2005.
"Susanne K. Langer," Books and Writers, http://www.kirjasto.sci .fi/langer.htm (December 21, 2005). □

Ruth Laredo

A pathbreaker among female performers, pianist Ruth Laredo (1937-2005) was a powerful player who ranked among the top American classical musicians of her generation.

L aredo's career was noteworthy for reasons other than her gender. She tackled and mastered some of the most extremely difficult pieces in the entire piano repertory, those by the Russian composers Sergei Rachmaninoff and Alexander Scriabin, releasing pioneering, complete recordings of their piano works. Although few classical pianists were comfortable playing jazz, Laredo performed enthusiastically with jazz legends, and, in contrast to most other classical musicians, Laredo often talked about the music she played. A thinker and investigator as well as a thrilling virtuosa, Ruth Laredo was an innovative presence in classical music over a career that lasted more than 40 years. She was often called "America's First Lady of the Piano."

Played "God Bless America" at Two

Born Ruth Meckler on November 20, 1937, in Detroit, Michigan, Laredo showed early signs of becoming a child prodigy. When she was two years old, she played "God Bless America," without any instruction, on the family piano. Her mother Miriam started giving her lessons and took her to see Vladimir Horowitz, a legendary concert pianist, when she was eight. Horowitz, she recalled (as quoted by Matt Schudel of the *Washington Post*) "sat a mere five feet away from my Buster Brown shoes. . . . The world stood on its head when I heard this man play." From that day on, Laredo was determined to become a concert pianist.

Another noteworthy feature of that Horowitz concert was that he played the music of Scriabin, an unorthodox composer of early twentieth-century Russia, who had a strong interest in synaesthesia (cross-sensory perceptions, such as seeing colors when one hears music). His music was rarely heard in the United States at the time. From then on, Laredo developed a strong interest in Russian music. She took piano lessons from a Russian immigrant, Mischa

Kotler, who gave her faint praise, and she began giving recitals at the Music Club of Metropolitan Detroit.

Enrolling at the Curtis Institute in Philadelphia, Pennsylvania, Laredo studied piano with Rudolf Serkin, a Bohemian-born pianist whose tastes and skills ran to the Beethoven-Schubert-Brahms line of Central European composers. The atmosphere was high-minded. "The word 'career' was never mentioned," Laredo recalled to Bernard Holland of the *New York Times.* At first, he took a dim view of her passion for the music of Rachmaninoff, a Russian virtuoso who had fled Communism and spent the last part of his life in the U.S. In the summer, she went to the Marlboro Festival in Vermont for further studies with cellist Pablo Casals. She graduated in 1960 and married Bolivian-born violinist Jaime Laredo. The marriage broke up in the mid-1970s but produced a daughter, Jennifer Laredo, who was raised by Ruth Laredo during the years that marked the apex of her career.

In 1962 Laredo made her debut at an orchestral concert, performing with the American Symphony Orchestra under flamboyant conductor Leopold Stokowski at New York's Carnegie Hall. In the early years of her career, Laredo devoted herself mostly to appearing as an accompanist to her husband. She was still young, and appearances by female pianists were still comparatively rare. "Every time we did interviews in those early days," Laredo's manager James Murtha told Daniel J. Wakin of the *New York Times,* she was asked how does it feel to be a woman pianist. She wanted to be a pianist, period."

Explored Scriabin Sonatas

In 1967 Laredo made a well-received album of piano music by French composer Maurice Ravel, also renowned for music full of pianistic challenges. But it was a series of recordings of Scriabin's ten piano sonatas for the Connoisseur label that, Laredo said (according to the *Daily Telegraph*), "put me on the map." At the time, few recordings of Scriabin's music were available, and Laredo's sparked a new wave of interest in the composer. *New York Times* critic Holland wrote of the Scriabin set that "Ms. Laredo's sensuous, beautifully controlled playing caught its mad and slightly evil quality." Laredo's Scriabin LPs were reissued on the Nonesuch label and remained in print decades later. Laredo was fascinated by the evolution in Scriabin's musical personality over time; beginning with a conventional musical language derived from Chopin and other well-loved nineteenth-century piano composers, he evolved into a highly personal style filled with mystical allusions, some of them concerned with dark, occult themes. She was untroubled by those, telling Holland that "I don't know what words like 'good' or 'ennobling' mean in terms of music, but I know what beautiful means, and Scriabin is very beautiful."

Next, on a series of seven LPs made for the major Columbia label between 1973 and 1979, Laredo turned to her other major Russian interest, Rachmaninoff. Her teacher Rudolf Serkin, despite his earlier discouragement, now urged her on: "I went to Rudy and asked, 'Do you think I can do it?' " she told Holland. " 'You must do it,' was the answer he gave me." Her lack of confidence was natural, for Rachmaninoff's music was perhaps the toughest in the mainstream classical repertory. Well over six feet tall, he had large hands, and he wrote much of his music for his own use as a touring concert pianist. His works posed major challenges for the five-foot Laredo, who had to undergo hand massages after practicing some of Rachmaninoff's more fiendish scores. "I had to learn the many, many Rachmaninoff pieces that no one plays, and I found out why no one does," she told Holland. "It's because they're so hard." The Rachmaninoff album set won a best keyboard artist award from *Record World* magazine and brought Laredo one of her three Grammy award nominations.

In the 1970s and early 1980s, however, Laredo reaped the rewards of her Rachmaninoff boot camp. The plum spots on American concert seasons began to come her way; she made her debut with the New York Philharmonic Orchestra in 1974, and gave a solo recital at Carnegie Hall in 1981. That year, she also edited a series of printed scores of Rachmaninoff's piano music. Other high-profile appearances included concerto performances with orchestras in Boston, Philadelphia, and Detroit. She played at the Library of Congress in Washington and made an appearance at the White House.

Despite her star status, Laredo continued to enjoy performing chamber music—music for small ensembles—with other musicians. She frequently appeared in concert with the Tokyo String Quartet and several other top quartets, performing piano quartets (piano plus three stringed instruments) and piano quintets (piano plus string quartet). An intense artist, Laredo sometimes had a reputation for being difficult to get along with, although others disputed this characterization.

Began to Offer Concerts with Commentary

Laredo moved slightly out of the spotlight in the late 1980s and 1990s, but she continued to perform extensively. She also succeeded in broadening her activities beyond conventional classical concerts, and in the process she found an outlet for her desire to express her thoughts about music. Beginning in 1988 or 1989, she performed a series called Concerts with Commentary at New York's Metropolitan Museum of Art, playing piano works from various eras of the classical tradition and also discussing them verbally. The concerts were out of the norm in the classical scene, where an age-old idea that music speaks for itself created a tradition in which performers tend to enter, play, and leave the stage silently. But many of the concerts sold out, and they continued until May 6, 2005, three weeks before Laredo's death. Laredo also wrote a column for *Piano Today* magazine and filed reports as a special correspondent for the "Morning Edition" news program on National Public Radio (NPR).

She also wrote a combination autobiography and guide for aspiring classical performers, *The Ruth Laredo Becoming a Musician Book*. A familiar figure on New York City stages in the 1990s, Laredo sometimes showed up in fashion magazine spreads thanks to the simple but distinctive designer gowns in which she performed. But she also traveled to small towns and college auditoriums to perform; she believed that being a classical musician brought both joys and challenges associated with carrying on a long artistic tradition, and she was always an eloquent spokesperson for that tradition.

On September 13, 2001, Laredo faced the unenviable task of performing the first concert at New York's Lincoln Center since the terrorist attacks of September 11 of that year. The concert had been slated to honor Laredo on the 25th anniversary of her New York recital debut at Alice Tully Hall, but the concert, in the words of Anne Midgette of the *New York Times*, turned into "an effort to raise a voice against the towering silence." "It was important for me to play," Laredo told the audience before the concert (according to Midgette). "Great music gives us spiritual sustenance and gives us hope. It is in that spirit that I play tonight." She concluded the program with Maurice Ravel's *La valse* (The Waltz), a work of the World War I era in which a reminiscence of the golden age of the waltz filters through a musical landscape filled with violence and gloom.

Toward the end of her life, Laredo turned to jazz, an enterprise in which she once again had few forerunners in the classical sphere. She often appeared with jazz revivalist pianist Dick Hyman and NPR "Piano Jazz" host Marian McPartland, trading licks with them on the same keyboard at times. Laredo also enjoyed pop music and could be seen jogging around Manhattan's Upper West Side, where she lived, listening to the music of rock group Genesis. In the year 2000, Laredo was seen performing a classical concert in the Woody Allen film *Small Time Crooks*.

In addition to her landmark Rachmaninoff and Scriabin sets, Laredo made about 30 other albums, most of which remained in print at the time of her death. Some, such as a duo recording she made with pianist James Tocco of the two-piano version of Igor Stravinsky's ballet *Le sacre du printemps* (The Rite of Spring), gained wide attention. Laredo was considered a Romantic pianist in the vein of the great virtuosos whose works she played; pianistic fireworks balanced by carefully textured quieter passages remained the primary attractions of her performances. But her recordings covered music of various eras and places; she performed French and Spanish music enthusiastically, looked back to Beethoven and the earlier Romantics, and recorded piano music by the American melodist Samuel Barber.

Few people knew that Laredo was suffering from ovarian cancer for the last several years of her life; she continued to perform and make recordings almost without interruption. In 2004 she visited the Minneapolis-St. Paul area in Minnesota to serve as a judge in a two-week piano competition. "We had no idea she was ill," competition director Alexander Braginsky told Michael Anthony of the Minneapolis *Star Tribune*. "She was so feisty and opinionated, a powerful personality." The First Lady of American Piano died at her New York apartment on May 25, 2005.

Books

Laredo, Ruth, *The Ruth Laredo Becoming a Musician Book*, European American Music Corp., 1992.

Periodicals

Daily Telegraph (London, England), June 10, 2005.
Independent (London, England), June 1, 2005.
Fresno Bee, March 18, 2001.
Keyboard, September 1, 2005.
New York Times, January 16, 1981; September 20, 1987; September 15, 2001; May 27, 2005.
Roanoke Times, October 2, 2003.
Star Ledger (Newark, New Jersey), May 28, 2005.
Star Tribune (Minneapolis, Minnesota), June 12, 2005.
Washington Post, May 28, 2005.

Online

"Discography," Ruth Laredo Official Website, http://www.ruthlaredo.com (December 18, 2005). □

Larisa Latynina

Russian gymnast Larisa Latynina (born 1934) won a stunning eighteen Olympic medals between 1956 and 1964. Her medal tally stands as a record high for any athlete in the history of the Games, and she was also the first female Olympian to win nine gold medals. Her crowd-pleasing gymnastic displays began an era of Russian domination in the sport, and Latynina was the first in a series of talented women gymnasts to gain world attention outside the Soviet Communist bloc.

Latynina epitomized the ideal Soviet athlete, in an era when an authoritarian state socialism dominated that part of the world and tightly regimented the lives of its citizens. She came from humble beginnings, her talents were recognized early and cultivated with the help of generous state funding for sports, and when she began winning, she deflected praise from her individual achievement by speaking of the pride she felt for her country as its Olympic representative. But Latynina would later express disillusionment about the way political propaganda had tainted her career.

Classic Soviet Tale

The future Olympian was born Larissa Semyonovna Dirii on December 27, 1934, in Kherson, Ukraine, when that country was part of the Union of Soviet Socialist Republics (U.S.S.R.). At the time of her birth, Ukrainians had been forcibly resisting the collectivization of their individual farms under Soviet leader Josef Stalin for the past few years, and Moscow's retaliatory policies had led to widespread famine across the once-fertile Ukraine.

World War II brought even greater hardships. With the country at war against Nazi Germany, the average Soviet citizen endured enormous hardships and food and fuel shortages. Latynina had lost both of her parents by the time the war ended in 1945. She turned 11 years old that year, and around this same time she began taking ballet classes.

She aspired to become a dancer, but standard ballet training at the time involved occasional gymnastic exercises with hoops and balls, and Latynina proved so talented at this that her teachers redirected her toward the sport.

By the age of 16, Latynina had won the national schools gymnastics championship. She graduated from high school in 1953, and a year later took part in the 1954 World Gymnastics Championships in Rome, Italy, where she placed fourteenth. She also began courses at the Physical Training College in Kiev, the Ukrainian capital. She married a fellow student there, Ivan Latynin, and began competing as Larisa Latynina. Her next major event came with the 1956 Summer Olympic Games, held that year in Melbourne, Australia. Soviet athletes were a relatively new element in the Games, having participated only since the 1952 Olympics after a 40-year absence from the games.

Won First Olympic Gold

In Melbourne, Latynina was part of a team of Russian women gymnasts who swept the competition that year. It marked the beginning of the Soviet women's domination of the sport for the next 40 years. She took six medals, four of them gold. Her first-place finishes came in the individual all-around competition and on the vault, and she tied for another gold medal in the floor exercise with Ágnes Keleti of Hungary. She also won a silver medal for the uneven bars, a bronze for the team drill with portable apparatus—a segment that was later discontinued—and another gold for team competition. These victories helped the Soviets advance past the

United States in the all-important medal count by a large margin, 98-74. Both countries viewed the Olympics as a showcase for the merits of their respective ideologies—for the Soviets, the collective spirit as an expression of national solidarity, and for the Americans, the triumph of individualism. At the 1956 Summer Games, held during the height of Cold War tensions between the two nations, the Melbourne medal tally was a decisive Soviet propaganda victory, and marked the first time the U.S.S.R. had beaten the United States in the Olympic numbers game.

It was also an era when Soviet gymnasts began to dominate the sport, and were commended for displaying grace as well as the requisite athleticism. Latynina was the first gymnast to achieve celebrity status on an international level thanks to her Olympic performance in 1956. Many years later, she was interviewed for *Red Files,* a PBS documentary film series that utilized recently declassified documents of the Soviet Communist era. Latynina was featured in the *Soviet Sports Wars* segment of the series. She recalled that after her Melbourne win, she enthusiastically participated in the propaganda campaign. "I was a very big patriot," she said. "My gymnastics was not only mine–it belonged to my Soviet motherland and all the people."

Latynina's winning streak continued at an impressive pace. She won every event in the European Gymnastics Championships in 1957, and a year later won every event except the vault. She also won in competition in 1958 while five months pregnant, and had not let the competition physicians know of her condition, because she would have been forced to withdraw. Her daughter Tanya was born in December of 1958, and Latynina was forced to sit out the 1959 European Championships. At the 1960 Summer Olympics in Rome, she returned triumphantly, winning another six medals. This time, three were gold—for all-around, floor exercise, and in team competition—followed by two silver for the balance beam and uneven bars, and a bronze for vault. She was one of the undisputed stars of those Games, along with American boxer Cassius Clay (later Muhammad Ali) and Wilma Rudolph, the U.S. sprinter. Again, the Soviets dominated these Games, winning 103 medals overall versus a U.S. tally of just 71.

Expressed Gratitude, Not Pride

Latynina was honored at home with some of the U.S.S.R.'s most prestigious civilian awards, including the Order of Lenin and the Soviet Badge of Honor. Each granted her special perks, such as a better apartment and chance to purchase hard-to-obtain consumer products. Expected to voice enthusiastic support for her country in return, she fulfilled her obligation without hesitation. In a 1964 interview with Alexandr Maryamov for *Soviet Life,* an English-language magazine produced in the Soviet Union to showcase life in the U.S.S.R., she expressed proper enthusiasm for her sport, and respect for those who had helped her succeed in it. Maryamov asked her which of her awards was her favorite, and she replied that it was "the small gold medal I was awarded in 1953 for graduating from school with honors. It was at school that I first took up gymnastics and, with the fine guiding hand of our school coach Mikhail

Sotnichenko, came to like it. That was when I won my USSR Master of Sports badge. When I got back home to Kherson from the Melbourne Olympics, I presented one of the medals I had won there to my first coach."

Latynina continued to train diligently, and her winning streak remained an impressive one. At the 1961 European Championships she won first place in two events, and finished second in two others, a feat she repeated the following year at the 1962 World Championships. She was one of only four women ever to win four consecutive World Championship titles, along with two other Russian women, Lyudmila Turishcheva and Svetlana Khorkina, and the American gymnast Shannon Miller. The 1964 Tokyo Olympics would be Latynina's final one as a competitor, however, for she was nearly 30 years old and past the usual age for women gymnasts.

Latynina was still in peak competition form, however, and in Tokyo won gold medals in the floor exercise and team competition, silver medals for individual all-around and vault, and a pair of bronze for the balance beam and uneven bars. Her performance in the floor exercise event was recalled some twenty years later by a British sports journalist Rex Bellamy in the *Times* of London. Bellamy was actually writing about the Wimbledon tennis championships of 1984, and of the grace on the court of a relative unknown, Carina Karlsson. Watching her, Bellamy asserted, "Takes me back . . . to the Tokyo Olympics, when the floor exercises of a Russian gymnast called Larisa Latynina so beautifully exemplified youth, beauty and joy that when she had finished, we simply stood up and cried."

Retired from Competition

At the 1965 European Championships, Latynina won four silver medals and a bronze. A year later, at the 1966 World Championships, she finished in eleventh place, and officially retired from competition. She had already moved over to the second segment of her career, coaching a new generation of elite Russian gymnasts, and became the Soviet national team coach in 1966. Her position as the top Soviet women's gymnast was taken over by her protégé, Natasha Kuchinskaya. At the 1968 Summer Olympics in Mexico City, Kuchinskaya was the gold-medal-winning star gymnast, but back at home, Latynina recalled in the *Soviet Sports Wars* documentary, Kuchinskaya began to balk at the rules. "She began to disappear, to miss trainings. She'd complain: 'I don't want to do this, or I don't want to do that.' Well, for us it seemed like her fame had gone to her head."

Kuchinskaya was supplanted by another Russian woman to emerge as the sport's newest darling: the petite Olga Korbut, a crowd favorite at the 1972 Munich Summer Games and an overnight media sensation. Korbut dominated the European and World competitions, but Latynina voiced some rare public criticism of her student in late 1973 in *Komsomolskaya Pravda,* the national newspaper for the Communist Party's youth organization. At the time, few statements from public officials ever made it into the Soviet press unless they had been officially sanctioned at some level. In that article, Latynina claimed that the other top Soviet woman gymnast, Lyudmila Turishcheva, was actually the leader in Russian women's gymnastics. The Russian-language article was recapped by the *Times* of London, and quoted Latynina as saying that Korbut's star status "was fully deserved but popularity is not leadership. The right to leadership is won not by appraisals of the fans." She also asserted that Turishcheva, who had recently won the European Championships after Korbut had an injury, "has held that right for a long time."

A more candid explanation of the official Soviet displeasure with Korbut-mania was offered by Latynina in the *Soviet Sports Wars* interview a quarter-century later. "Korbut was more popular in America than in the Soviet Union," Latynina said. "She was, well, how should I say it: she didn't behave properly–always demanding attention. She was a primadonna. That's not how we were raised." But Korbut's fame would be fleeting, for at the 1976 Montreal Olympics she was ousted from her slot by Nadia Comaneci of Romania. This seemed to signal the end of Latynina's career coaching Olympic-caliber gymnasts. "The sports committee acted like I'd committed some deadly sin because we'd lost," Latynina recalled in *Soviet Sports Wars* about the 1976 Games. "They said I was outdated, obsolete. I was so insulted. I said, well, if I am outdated, then I won't waste your time. So I gave them my resignation, and walked out."

After 1977, Latynina served as a coach for an elite Moscow team and was the director of gymnastics for the 1980 Summer Games in Moscow. Twice divorced, she married another athlete, Yuri Israilevich Feldman, with whom she lived in Kolyanino, near Moscow. Still revered as one of the Soviet era's greatest athletes, Latynina expressed mixed feelings about her participation in the Cold War sports showdowns. Her summation of her career was chosen to end the *Soviet Sports Wars* documentary. Its final shot featured Latynina and her words. "I believed in our system," she admitted. "I believed and believed and believed. Now, sadly, I don't anymore. I realize it was all cheap propaganda. We athletes used to call out to our people: go forward. Now, all my work and all my beliefs have left me with nothing. Absolutely nothing."

Books

Notable Sports Figures, 4 vols. Gale, 2004.

Periodicals

Soviet Life, September 1964.
Times (London, England), October 22, 1964; November 7, 1969; December 7, 1973; July 3, 1984.

Online

Red Files: Soviet Sports Wars, PBS.org, http://www.pbs.org/redfiles/sports/ (January 19, 2006). □

Geraldine Laybourne

American business executive Geraldine Laybourne (born 1947) has been a groundbreaking pioneer in

the field of cable television programming. She helped turn the children's network Nickelodeon into one of the most powerful in television, and in 2002 she launched Oxygen, a new cable network geared exclusively toward women.

As undeniably one of the most powerful women in American broadcasting, Laybourne defied convention in rising to her current position as chairman and CEO of Oxygen Media, a 24-hour cable television and media conglomerate geared toward women. In fact, along with business partners such as media moguls Oprah Winfrey and Microsoft magnate Paul Allen, Laybourne can rightly be considered, in the multi-billion dollar world of American broadcasting, as among the most influential and groundbreaking executives regardless of gender. As a woman who has seen women's expectation levels rise from "the kitchen" to "the boardroom" in her lifetime, the 59-year-old grandmother has compromised neither her femininity nor her sense of humor while following her groundbreaking career path.

Having entered the cable industry in its early days, Laybourne has been honored for her many contributions to the industry, including being named as one of the 25 most influential people in America by Time magazine in 1996. She has received many of television's most prestigious awards, including the Annenberg Public Policy Center award for Distinguished Lifetime Contribution to Children and Television, the New York Women in Communications Matrix Award for Broadcasting, and the Creative Coalition's Spotlight Award. In 1995 she was inducted into the Broadcasting and Cable Hall of Fame.

Family First, Then a Career

Unlike many businesswomen of today, who have considerably more career options, Laybourne was born in 1947, in a time before women were encouraged to work outside of the home, much less as heads of major corporations. What makes her success even more remarkable is the fact that she did marry, raise two children, and then switched careers (she had been a teacher) before embarking on a business career in her early thirties. Born in Plainfield, New Jersey, Laybourne had no shortage of strong, business-minded women around her while she was growing up. Her grandmother founded a seed potato company in North Dakota, and her mother was a strong community activist. "My grandmother was tough as nails," Laybourne told a Colorado Women's Chamber of Commerce audience, as quoted on WomenOf.com, "but people thought it was great working for her. And my mother was one of the most gifted people I knew. She made sure her daughters knew how important it was to make a difference, and to be economically independent."

After receiving a bachelor's degree in art history from Vassar College in 1969 and a master's degree in education from the University of Pennsylvania in 1971, Laybourne worked for a brief period as a teacher while raising her two children (her husband is veteran television producer and animator Kit Laybourne). In 1973 she began working as an independent producer developing children's television. After two pilots failed to sell, Laybourne began working on projects with a new cable company geared toward children, called Nickelodeon. In 1980 she joined Nickelodeon as a program manager, using her own two children as springboards for ideas. "I'd make my kids watch endless hours of TV from Canada and Czechoslovakia, then call to ask them for the names of the shows," Laybourne told *Multichannel News.* "They were very influential in the development of Nick."

Seeking to separate Nickeldoeon from more conventional programming, such as the more strictly educational fare from PBS and the mindless cartoons from the other networks, Laybourne helped establish Nickelodeon's creative, edgy style on such programs as *Double Dare* and *Ren & Stimpy.* Children enjoyed the way that Nickeldoeon programs were fun without insulting their intelligence, and ratings grew steadily. By 1989 Laybourne was president of Nickelodeon, and the network to this day has remained one of the most powerful in television, present in 66 million homes, with spinoff marketing, movies, and more. Much of that success has been due to Laybourne's creative drive in the network's early days. "Nothing daunted Gerry," former colleague Anne Sweeney told *Multichannel News.* "She was a force of nature, and you could just feel the momentum." Laybourne stayed with Nickelodeon until 1995, and from 1993 to 1995 she served as vice chairman of the network's parent company, MTV Networks. From 1996 to

1998 Laybourne served a brief term as president of Disney ABC Cable Networks, but by this time her creative bent was formulating a plan for her most ambitious project yet.

A New Network for Women

After leaving Disney in 1998, Laybourne received a call from her friend, television producer Marcy Carsey, part of the Carsey-Tom Werner-Caryn Mandabach team that had produced such hits as *The Cosby Show, Roseanne* and *Third Rock from the Sun.* Carsey promised that if Laybourne started a new network for and about women, then she, Werner, and Mandabach would develop the programming. Laybourne named her new venture Oxygen. "It came from a sense that everybody needed more breathing room." Laybourn explained in *Newsweek.* "It felt like a good rallying cry."

Next order of business: find a backer with the star power and financial muscle to get a fledgling network off the ground. Laybourne had to look no further than the first person on her list—Oprah Winfrey. It turned out that Winfrey was already somewhat familiar with Laybourne's work, having read an inspirational article about the executive in the *New York Times.* The growing team then traded part ownership rights to America Online in exchange for three of its top women's online websites, for it was Laybourne's vision to support the television network with a vibrant convergent internet strategy. Eventually Oxygen Media grew to 13 internet sites. An equally ambitious plan called for a budget of $450 million to produce many hours of original programming.

Broke Traditional Management Rules

Working out of the company's New York offices, in a renovated former cookie factory, Laybourne brought to her work the same energetic, playful management style that had become industry legend from her days at Nickelodeon. She has been known, for instance, to start her days with boxing lessons at seven o'clock in the morning. At Nickelodeon she helped staff loosen up by instituting afternoon "recess." At Oxygen all new employees get a gift basket along with a wallet-sized card that carries the company's mission statement: "Releasing the energy of women to do great things." There are "idea-sheets" hanging in strategic locations on the bathroom walls, and, in accordance with her open-door policy, Laybourne's office has a conference table that any staff member can commandeer for an impromptu meeting.

While this kind of "outside the box" management may be more acceptable in 2006, it was certainly a new approach back when Laybourne was getting started. At Nickelodeon in the 1980s it was bold enough that she was running the company as a woman, much less that she was breaking the time-honored management rules of "the good old boy network." At a time when businesswomen were counseled to dress more like men in business suits, and to use sports metaphors that men might understand, Laybourne was mature and confident enough to be herself. It helped that she was a mother running a children's network, and that the cable industry was a new and lightly regarded industry. "No one wanted my job," she joked on

WomenOf.com. And in a speech to the Colorado Women's Chamber of Commerce, quoted on the WomenOf.com website, she counseled her audience on the advantages women bring to the workplace.

Laybourne, in her speech (quoted on the Women Of.com website), discussed the ability of women to understand the value of relationships and teambuilding; men want a winner and a loser, while women want a collaborative process where everyone wins. She mentioned that women have 12 percent more space in the prefrontal cortex of the brain, allowing them to hold multiple thoughts and switch from one topic to another with ease. Laybourne believes that women want a purpose greater than just making money and women are good at "coaching, listening, and empowering." In the same speech, Laybourne further defined her philosophy by pointing out where women tend to fall short in business. She spoke of women lacking decisiveness, and women being less assertive in making sure they get credit for their own accomplishments. Laybourne feels that women become discouraged—and are not quick enough to "get over it,"—when things do not go their way. She also mentions that older women in particular, perhaps because they want to be taken seriously, are sometimes too directed and not playful enough about their work.

Grew Steadily at Oxygen

Laybourne's keen programming sense and business acumen have contributed greatly to her success, and though Oxygen has experienced some ups and downs in its first five years, in 2006, she and Oxygen appeared poised to break through with another winner.

After a rocky first year that saw her scrap Oxygen's online strategy, lay off 250 staffers, and feel the heat from such big-money partners as Winfrey and Microsoft's Allen, Laybourne refocused her efforts on comedy programming. In 2002 she hired branding guru Dale Pon to create the "Oh!" marketing campaign featuring Madonna and other celebrities. Meanwhile, Laybourne continued to use her considerable experience and reputation to get Oxygen placement on prime cable operators' lineups. While progress was slow, it was steady, and ahead of Laybourne's personal goal. By 2004 the network had become profitable, with a presence in 54 million homes. "We continue to double our advertising base every year," Laybourne told *Cable World* in 2005. "We went from 8 million to 54 million homes, growing at about almost 10 million a year. And the increases in our ratings from 2002 to 2005 are up 374 percent (in prime time). . . . and we're in the vicinity of Bravo, E!, and VH1." Industry executive Michael Willner credited Laybourne's eternal optimism as crucial in producing Oxygen's rise against such difficult odds. "She accomplishes so much by the simple belief that nothing is impossible," Willner told *Cable World*. "That's the underlying reason why Oxygen succeeded without the help of mega-media ownership."

Periodicals

Cable World, February 21, 2005.
Forbes, June 7, 1993.

Multichannel News, October 11, 2004.
Newsweek, November 15, 1999.
Time, June 17, 1996.

Online

"Geraldine Laybourne: Chairman and CEO," Oxygen Network, http://www.oxygen.com/basics/founders.aspx (March 17, 2006).
"Woman of the Month: Geraldine Laybourne," WomenOf.com, http://www.womenof.com/News/wm_10_6_03.asp (March 17, 2006). □

Ernest Lehman

American screenwriter Ernest Lehman (1915-2005), though not especially known for prodigious output, wrote screenplays for some of the most famous and best-loved films produced in the mid-twentieth century. His credits include screen adaptation for major Broadway productions including *West Side Story*, *The Sound of Music*, and *Who's Afraid of Virginia Woolf?*

Throughout his career, Lehman received six Academy Award nominations and, in 2001, he received an honorary Academy Award for his career accomplishments, the first time a screenwriter was ever presented with a special award from the Academy of Motion Picture Arts and Sciences. Though he was considered a highly talented adapter of source material (e.g., plays and novels), perhaps his most highly regarded work is the original screenplay for one of director Alfred Hitchcock's best films, *North by Northwest*.

Lehman was born on December 8, 1915, in Long Island, New York, the son of Paul and Gertrude Lehman. The couple jointly owned and operated women's clothing stores. Reportedly, his family was affluent, but its finances were severely affected by the Great Depression. Lehman was raised in New York City and attended the College of the City of New York, where his educational interests included chemical engineering as well English and creative writing. When he graduated, he first earned a living as a freelance writer.

His first published work, appearing in 1939 in *Collier's* magazine, was a profile of contemporary entertainer Ted Lewis. After that, Lehman turned out stories and articles that appeared in such popular and mainstream magazines as *Esquire, Liberty, Redbook,* and *Cosmopolitan.* However, he found freelancing too stressful—it was a "very nervous way to make a living," he once remarked—so he found a steady job as a copywriter for a publicity firm that specialized in theatrical productions and celebrities. In addition, Lehman worked for a while as a publicity writer for *The Hollywood Reporter* columnist Irving Hoffman. Lehman, a resourceful and observant writer, used these early career experiences as background for later stories and screenplays (in particular

Holden with one of his more memorable roles, the film helped define Hepburn's screen persona. Lehman co-wrote the script with Wilder and Samuel A. Taylor. Adapting the script from Taylor's play *Sabrina Fair,* the writing team was nominated for an Academy Award for Original Screenplay and received a Writers Guild of America Award.

In 1956, Lehman worked with director Wise again, writing the screenplay for *Somebody Up Their Likes Me,* a "biopic" about heavyweight boxer Rocky Graziano that helped catapult Paul Newman into the ranks of major American actors. That same year, Lehman, working for Twentieth Century-Fox, adapted for the screen the popular Rodgers and Hammerstein musical *The King and I,* for which he received his second Writers Guild of America nomination.

Sweet Success for Lehman

During the decade, Lehman also worked on the Mark Robson-directed *From the Terrace,* an adaptation of John O'Hara's best-selling novel. But Lehman's greatest achievements are considered his work on *The Sweet Smell of Success* (1957) and Alfred Hitchcock's *North by Northwest* (1959). The first was based on Lehman's own experiences as a publicity copywriter and presented a powerful and grim account of the dark underside of the glamorous "show-biz" world of New York City. Featuring stark black-and-white cinematography (supplied by master cameraman James Wong Howe), directed by Alexander Mackendrick, and starring Tony Curtis and Burt Lancaster (turning in perhaps their greatest career performances), the film was unrelenting in its unpleasantness, but it was nevertheless considered a great film. Based on Lehman's previously published magazine stories, the script was co-written by famous playwright Clifford Odets, who wrote most of the searing dialogue. Ironically, the film was a box-office failure at the time.

His script for Hitchcock's *North by Northwest* (1959) arguably represents Lehman's highest career achievement. It was his first original screenplay, and it provided the foundation for one of the greatest suspense films of all time. Released by MGM, *North by Northwest* is placed by film scholars and critics among the pantheon of "masterpieces" directed by Alfred Hitchcock in the 1950s and 1960s that included *Strangers on a Train* (1951), *Rear Window* (1954), the 1956 version of *The Man Who Knew Too Much, Vertigo* (1958), *Psycho* (1960), and *The Birds* (1963). The script included such memorable set-pieces as the famous crop-dusting scene that takes place at a cornfield bus stop as well as the memorable pursuit on Mount Rushmore. The writing achievement earned Lehman another Academy Award nomination and another Writers Guild of America nomination. If Lehman had decided to never write again, his name would have remained a legend among screenwriters for his *North by Northwest* script.

Adapted Broadway Smash Hits

In the 1960s, Lehman lent his scriptwriting talents to Hollywood "blockbusters." In 1961, he wrote the screenplay adaptation of the Broadway smash hit *West Side Story.* The film, an updated Romeo and Juliet story was set in contemporary New York City and depicted urban warfare

for the 1957 film *The Sweet Smell of Success*). In 1948, he sold one of his stories to Hollywood, and it became the basis for *The Inside Story,* directed by Allan Dwan.

Moved to Hollywood

After his short story "The Comedian" appeared in *Collier's* in 1953, Paramount Studios enticed him to move to Hollywood, where he would work on the screenplay adaptation. Though the project was cancelled, Lehman found other work and soon settled in California.

After signing on with Paramount Pictures as a screenwriter, Lehman was almost immediately loaned out to Metro-Goldwyn-Mayer (MGM), where he wrote his first screenplay, for the film *Executive Suite.* Produced by John Houseman, who got his start with Orson Welles' famous Mercury Theater productions, directed by the up-and-coming Robert Wise, and adapted from a novel by Cameron Hawley, the film provided a harsh look at Wall Street. A major production with an all-star cast (it featured William Holden, Frederic March, Barbara Stanwyck, June Allyson, Shelley Winters and Walter Pidgeon), the film received good notices. Lehman would later collaborate with Wise on other enormously successful projects, including the screen adaptations of *West Side Story* and *The Sound of Music.*

Following the success of *Executive Suite,* Lehman was asked to work on Paramount's romantic comedy *Sabrina,* a Billy Wilder-directed film that starred Audrey Hepburn, William Holden and Humphrey Bogart. Though it was not considered a typical "Bogart" film, nor did it provide between street gangs, the Jets and Sharks, it also provided Lehman with another opportunity to work with Wise. In addition, this screenplay earned him a third Academy Award nomination, as well as a third Writers Guild Award. The film won ten Academy Awards, scoring an Oscar for every category in which it was nominated, except for screenwriting.

In 1963, Lehman wrote the screenplay for *The Prize*, adapted from the Irving Wallace novel, starring Paul Newman as a Nobel Prize-winning novelist who gets caught up in foreign intrigue when he travels to Stockholm to accept his award. Robson directed the film.

In 1965, Lehman wrote the screenplay for one of the most beloved films of all time: *The Sound of Music*. Again, Lehman was working with source material that came from a huge Broadway musical hit, and it marked his fourth collaboration with Wise. However, his work in this Academy Award-winning film (it was Best Picture of the year) did not earn him even a nomination. Still, Lehman earned praise for his deft reordering of the song sequence and the restructuring of the story line. Many felt that his changes made the movie even more effective than the stage production.

Produced First Film

For his next film, Lehman wrote the screen adaptation for *Who's Afraid of Virginia Woolf?*, the stage drama written by famed playwright Edward Albee. Lehman also produced the film, as he sought to have more creative control. At first, his choice for his first-ever producing effort seemed an odd one. Albee's play, though powerful, was rather unpleasant and Lehman's contemporaries did not believe the vehicle had much potential at the box office. However, Jack Warner, the head of Warner Brothers, the company that released the film, strongly supported Lehman's choice.

The results more than justified Warner's somewhat risky move. The film was one of the big box-office hits of 1966, and it received thirteen Academy Award nominations. Lehman received writing and producing nominations. The latter nomination was especially appropriate, as Lehman made all of the right choices in putting together the project. To direct the film, he selected successful stage director Mike Nichols, who was making his cinematic debut (Nichols later went on to direct *The Graduate,* one of the big film hits of the 1960s). For the lead roles of "George" and "Martha," the hard-drinking, combative married couple, Lehman cast the real-life husband-and-wife team of Richard Burton and Elizabeth Taylor, who proved letter-perfect in their portrayals. The film's vivid black-and-white photography was accomplished by talented cinematographer Haskell Wexler. In addition to his Academy Award nominations, Lehman received another Writers Guild of America Award.

Lehman closed out the decade with another combined writer-producer effort, albeit a somewhat less successful one, with the film, *Hello, Dolly!* The 1969 adaptation of the long-running Broadway production, did receive an Academy Award nomination for Best Picture, as well as six other nominations (Lehman was again nominated as a producer), however, the film was a disappointment at the box-office.

Hello, Dolly! was denigrated by film critics, even with Barbara Streisand in the starring role and famous dancer and choreographer Gene Kelly performing the directorial duties.

Moved on to Other Literary Projects

Following *Hello, Dolly!,* Lehman's film career never again reached the heights he attained in the 1950s and early 1960s; however, he always kept himself busy with a variety of projects. In 1972, Lehman directed his one and only film, *Portnoy's Complaint,* which was based on Philip Roth's best-selling and controversial novel. The film, which starred Richard Benjamin, was a total failure.

In 1976, Lehman re-teamed with Alfred Hitchcock, writing the screenplay for the suspense master's last film, *Family Plot.* Lehman adapted the script from the novel *The Rainbird Pattern* by Victor Canning. While the tongue-in-cheek film—the plot centered around a fake medium—received warm notices from critics, it did not measure up to Hitchcock's previous work.

Lehman followed that film by co-writing the script for *Black Sunday,* a thriller directed by John Frankenheimer about a terrorist plot to bomb the Super Bowl. After that, Lehman tackled literary projects outside of films. In 1977, Lehman published *The French Atlantic Affair,* a suspense novel about an attempted "shipjacking." The book was a best-seller and it became a television mini-series in 1979.

During the 1980s, he remained very active. In 1982, he published his second novel, *Farewell Performance.* Throughout the 1970s, he was a columnist for *American Film* magazine and, in 1981, a collection of his columns was released in book-form as "Screening Sickness."

From 1983 to 1985, Lehman served as president of the Writers Guild of America, West. In 1986, he wrote a screenplay for a film to be called *I Am Zorba,* but the project was never completed. In 1987, 1988, and 1990, Lehman wrote and helped coordinate the 59th, 60th, and 62nd Academy Awards shows on ABC-TV.

Lehman continued writing in the 1990s. He wrote an adaptation for Noel Coward's *Hay Fever* but it was never filmed. He also worked on an original screenplay, *Dancing in the Dark,* and an autobiography. Both remain unpublished.

Received Honorary Academy Award

In 2001, Lehman received an Honorary Award by the Board of Governors of the Academy of Motion Picture Arts and Sciences "in appreciation of a body of varied and enduring work." In announcing the award, Academy President Robert Rehme said, "Ernest Lehman has written and produced some of the most memorable films ever made. He is not only a prolific screenwriter, but an accomplished novelist, journalist and motion picture producer, whose films rank as genuine classics."

Upon receipt of the honorary award, as quoted in the *Hollywood Reporter,* Lehman told his audience, "I accept this rarest of honors on behalf of screenwriters everywhere, but especially those in the Writers Guild of America. We have suffered anonymity far too often. I appeal to all movie critics and feature writers to please always bear in mind that a film production begins and ends with a screenplay.''

As his comment suggested, Lehman championed the cause of writers throughout his career. Besides serving as president of the Writers Guild of America from 1983 to 1985, he served two terms on the Guild's board (1954-56, 1961-70), served as vice president of the screen branch (1965-67, 1980-88), and he sat on many Guild committees. In 1972, Lehman received the Guild's prestigious Screen Laurel Award.

Suffered Long Illness

During the last years of his life, Lehman suffered a prolonged illness and died of a heart attack, July 2, 2005, at the UCLA Medical Center in Los Angeles, California, at 89 years old. He was survived by his second wife, Laurie, a son from his second marriage, Jonathan, and two sons from his first marriage, Roger and Alan. His first wife, Jacqueline, died in 1994. Lehman remarried in 1997.

Books

International Dictionary of Films and Filmmakes, Volume 4: Writers and Production Artists, Fourth Edition, St. James Press, 2000.

Online

''Ernest Lehman,'' *Hollywood.com,* http://www.hollywood .com/celebs/fulldetail/id/194185 (December 20, 2005).
''Ernest Lehman voted honorary Academy Award,'' *Academy of Motion Picture Arts and Sciences,* http://www.oscars.org/ press/pressreleases/2001/01.01.25.html (December 20, 2005).
''Famed Screenwriter Ernest Lehman, 89,'' *Hollywood Reporter,* http://www.hollywoodreporter.com/thr/article_display .jsp?vnu_content_id=1000973530 (December 20, 2005).
''The Ernest Lehman Collection,'' *Harry Ransom Humanities Research Center at the University of Texas at Austin,* http://www .hrc.utexas.edu/collections/film/holdings/lehman/ (December 20, 2005). □

David Letterman

Comedian and television personality David Letterman (born 1947) has entertained American television audiences for more than two decades, first as host of NBC's *Late Night with David Letterman* from 1982 to 1993, then on CBS's *Late Show with David Letterman* from 1993 to the present.

Anyone who was alive in the United States in September of 2001, and who was old enough to remember, will likely never forget the palpable grief and pall that fell over the entire nation in the wake of the September 11 terrorist attacks in New York City and Washington, D.C. Stunned silence led to horror, confusion and, ultimately, anger and outrage, as America and the world

tried to comprehend the awful events. The tragedies were made all the more vivid as they were played out on live television, and many wondered if life would ever be the same again.

In his New York offices just uptown from the fallen World Trade Center, the comedian and late-night talk show host certainly did not think life would remain the same. ''At first, Dave said flatly, 'We'll never do a show again,' '' said Letterman's long-time producer, Rob Burnett, in *People* magazine. What Letterman was wrestling with was quite significant for entertainers and, indirectly, for the public as a whole: When would it be okay to laugh again? Almost since the inception of television, and mostly due to legends such as Jack Paar and Johnny Carson, the late night talk show had become an American institution. That hour or so of laughter and breezy conversation at the end of a long day had become a routine way for people to unwind and, through humor and satire, even gain a bit of perspective. And so, one week after the tragedy, on September 18, *The Late Show with David Letterman* aired at its usual 11:30 time slot, with no scheduled guests and nobody, not his staff nor even Letterman himself, knowing exactly what he would say.

''What we all saw was a Letterman shaken and stirred: rattled to his bones about the assault on the city his show inhabits, and moved to anger, grief, and bafflement,'' declared *People* in a cover story that week. ''He brought out Dan Rather, who shed tears and with whom Letterman tried to engage in some explanation of the cruel devastation. Later, out came a Dave-fave guest, Regis Philbin. The host fixed him with a glare and, out of left field asked, 'How did you first meet Joey Bishop?' This silly non-sequitur capped a triumphant night.''

It was a courageous step into the unknown for Letterman, and for the country. In many ways Letterman had spent the better part of two decades in show business preparing for that moment, throughout a career that had seen many ups and a few downs as well. He was only a year into recovery from serious heart bypass surgery, and the *Late Show,* though still quite popular with viewers, had been playing second fiddle in the ratings to rival Jay Leno's *Tonight Show* for several years. And yet it was Letterman—whose humor had always come with a harder edge than some preferred—who took the first big risk and suggested that humor might help in the healing.

"He was the Magellan spacecraft that we sent out," said another television talk host, Jon Stewart, according to *People.* "There's a part of me that really looked to him not just for my own emotional well-being afterward, which is a heavy burden to place on him, but for what to do as someone who's in this industry. For us, it felt like Dave had already kicked in a window and let in some fresh air."

Destined for Show Business from a Young Age

The son of H. Joseph (a florist) and Dorothy (a church secretary) Letterman, "Dave," as he is commonly referred to by fans and guests, was born into a typical middle class, Midwestern home on April 12, 1947, in Indianapolis, Indiana. Much of Letterman's quirky humor can likely be traced to his father. "He was the circus. He was the show. When he walked through a room the lamps would rattle," Letterman told *Esquire*'s Bill Zehme. The elder Letterman also had heart problems, suffering his first heart attack at age 36 and eventually dying of a massive coronary at age 57, a tragedy that stunned his adoring son. Letterman's youth was otherwise ordinary. He was reportedly a bit of a class clown who made mediocre grades, ran track, and packed groceries. From an early age he knew he wanted to work in broadcasting, especially television, and he worshipped Johnny Carson, iconic host of *The Tonight Show,* and a man who would play a big role in Letterman's future career.

In the 1960s Letterman enrolled in the communications program at Ball State University in Muncie, Indiana, and almost immediately began working part-time in local television there. After graduating in 1969 he returned to his hometown and a job as an announcer and weekend weatherman at the ABC affiliate in Indianapolis. There, he quickly began honing his trademark style by injecting his ironic sense of humor into otherwise ordinary weather forecasts (raindrops "as big as canned hams") and even children's programs (poking fun at his young guests). Eventually Letterman began writing jokes and comedy sketches, even sending scripts to producers of such television programs as *The Mary Tyler Moore Show.* At the urging of his wife, Michelle Cook (they divorced in 1977), the young comedian took his act to Los Angeles, in 1975, and began working the comedy club circuit, where he quickly became a popular draw.

Collided with Jay Leno

At about this time, Letterman first met another young comedian, Jay Leno of Massachusetts. At the time, as Letterman told Zehme, he was awed and a bit intimidated by Leno's craft. "When I first saw him, I just thought I might as well go home. Because his attitude and his style were so crystallized and so right on the money and he had such good observations. I mean, his entire life and existence seemed to be a setup, and then he would provide the perfect punch line. I thought, Jeez, that's the way it ought to be done. So I really started patterning my material after him."

But Letterman was enjoying success of his own, too, and in 1978 he received the ultimate compliment for any young comedian when he was invited to perform on *The Tonight Show.* Even better, he was invited to sit down and chat with his longtime idol, Carson, after his sketch—an honor rarely bestowed upon first-time comic performers. In fact, Carson enjoyed Letterman so much he asked him to come back and guest-host the program, first once, then twice, until eventually he became the show's unofficial guest host during the dozens of vacation days Carson would take in a year. Whispers grew louder that Letterman was the inside man to take over *The Tonight Show*—Letterman's lifelong dream—when Carson eventually retired.

Late Night Enjoyed Cult Hit Status

In the meantime NBC decided to give Letterman his own show, carving out time for him directly after Carson, in the 12:30 to 1:30 early morning slot. From its debut in February of 1982, *Late Night with David Letterman* became a cult hit with its audience, which was mostly younger and hipper than that of *The Tonight Show.* Letterman had a style unique to the genre—his humor was edgier, his interviews more unpredictable and often confrontational to the point where guests were disarmed or even angered. Letterman would purposely dress badly, mismatching colors, wearing outrageous plaid jackets and clumsy white shoes. He was as willing to poke fun at himself as at anyone else, and audiences loved it. He found humor in the ordinary, taking his cameras to the surrounding neighborhood in New York and making stars out of local business owners. One recurring stunt had Letterman dropping various things—such as watermelons or sofas—from high atop the NBC building and watching them smash on the street. And his daily Top Ten List quickly became the most quoted and talked about bit on late-night television.

Because *Late Night* aired at such a late hour, the host seemed liberated to try anything. After all, who was watching? His guests were rarely of the "A-List" type, and most were relatively unknown. Some bigger stars hesitated to come on as guests, because Letterman had quickly achieved a reputation for pushing his guests out of their comfort zone. Everybody was fair game. Other guests, such as the comedian and actor Andy Kaufman, loved to play along. Kaufman himself had a reputation for outrageousness, and he seemed to thrive in Letterman's world. *Late Night* viewers were also treated to the sight of Letterman smashing ordinary items in a huge hydraulic press, covering his body in Alka-Seltzer tablets and diving into a tub of water, or donning a suit of Velcro and catapulting himself against a Velcro wall to see if he would stick (he did).

Feuded Over *Tonight Show* Position

Another frequent guest was Jay Leno, who was such a hit with *Late Night* viewers that he eventually became the regular guest host when Letterman was out. So it was ironic when, in the early 1990s, the two became rivals in the struggle to replace the venerable Carson as host of *The Tonight Show*. After some serious backroom negotiating that saw Leno apparently first winning the job, then a last-minute offer to Letterman, the issue was finally resolved when an angry Letterman spurned NBC and accepted a lucrative offer from CBS to start a new late-night show on that network. Though never becoming truly bitter, the Letterman-Leno relationship became decidedly frosty from that time on. The two hosts have continued to go head-to-head in the ratings battle for more than a decade, with no end in sight.

Ever the professional, Letterman threw himself whole-heartedly into the *Late Show with David Letterman* on CBS. There were subtle changes. Gone were the plaid jackets in favor of conservative, double-breasted suits, and some of the wackier bits were jettisoned. But mostly it was the same Letterman, and for two years the *Late Show* was consistently trouncing Leno's *Tonight Show* in the ratings. Eventually, though, the program's Achilles heel—its base in New York—began to wear it down. In many ways the *Late Show*'s energy seemed to emanate from its New York home in the Ed Sullivan Theater, but New York was also a long flight from Los Angeles, where a majority of the big-name celebrities live. On the other hand, Leno's program aired right in Burbank, and *The Tonight Show* could easily coax virtually any star to make the short drive and tape a program. Also, Leno was becoming a star in his own right. From the mid-1990s onward, *The Tonight Show* was consistently beating Letterman for ratings.

Letterman was always known to be hyper-critical of his show and his own performance, and rarely found himself measuring up. While his show remained relatively successful, and can now be considered part of the fabric of American daily life, the years of losing in the ratings war began to wear on him. "The decline in ratings is apparently enough to drive him visibly crazy," wrote critic Tom Shales in the *Washington Post* at the time. The stress apparently began to effect his health. Letterman had always been haunted by his father's death from heart trouble and the knowledge it might be hereditary. In January of 2000 he stunned his staff one morning by announcing that he was going in for multiple heart bypass surgery.

A Chance to Reevaluate

While it was certainly dangerous and the recovery long and difficult, Letterman's surgery in retrospect was, in some ways, probably just what he and his show needed. After just six weeks of recovery, he returned to the set on February 18, 2000, brought out the entire medical team from the hospital he'd attended, and actually broke down after thanking them. When his first guest, actor Robin Williams, cracked

up his host by walking onstage with a large cooler labeled "human organs," it was apparent that the old Letterman was back. That night, wrote Zehme, Letterman seemed to have risen above many of the demons that had haunted him over the previous decade, even the feud and bitterness over *The Tonight Show*. Zehme recalled that during his opening remarks, Letterman quipped, " 'Bypass surgery—it's when doctors create new blood flow to your heart. A bypass is what happened to me when I didn't get *The Tonight Show!* It's a whole different thing.' It was a joke, yes, but it was something more. We learned that he had perspective."

It was also that night that Letterman first publicly admitted to a certain significant other in his life. Notoriously private, Letterman had kept his longtime relationship with Regina Lasko, a former *Late Night* staffer, a secret. Ever the setup man, Letterman had even more shocking news two years later when he announced that he and Lasko were expecting their first child. On September 12, 2003, Letterman brought the house down when he told his live audience, "I have an announcement to make. I'm terribly excited about this. I'm scared silly about this. I'm going to be a father." The couple's son, Harry, was born a few months later. Then 56 years old, Letterman seemed to have found a sense of balance between his personal and professional life and showed no sign of backing away from the late-night television talk show "wars." Despite the competition, it was a job he had wanted all his life, and fatherhood had seemingly given him a second wind. "I can't do this forever, and it'd be nice to have the kid take over the family business," he said in *People*.

Books

Carter, Bill, *The Late Shift: Letterman, Leno and the Network Battle for the Night*, New York: Hyperion Books, 1994.

Periodicals

Entertainment Weekly, March 15, 2002; November 2, 2002; December 22, 2002.
Esquire, May 2000.
Forbes, July 8, 2002.
People, February 11, 2002; September 29, 2003. □

Leona Marshall Libby

Leona Marshall Libby (1919-1986) was a founder of high-energy physics. She was also known as a pioneer in nuclear energy technology, and she discovered cold neutrons and researched isotope ratios. She was one of the only women who worked on the Manhattan Project, the project that created the nuclear reactor and built the first atom bomb.

Libby was born on August 9, 1919, in Le Grange, Illinois. She was born to Wreightstill Woods, a lawyer, and Mary Holderness Woods, a teacher, and was one of three girls and two boys raised on the family farm.

When the depression hit in 1929, the family was hit hard and Libby's family struggled to make ends meet.

Interested in Chemistry

Libby had developed an early interest in chemistry and commenced studies rather quickly, she did not let her family's financial straits stop her from pursuing her education. Libby won a scholarship to go to college because of the quality of some of her early work, and then while she was attending her college classes, she worked twenty hours a week to pay for the part that her scholarship did not cover. She graduated in 1938, at age nineteen, from the University of Chicago with a Bachelor of Science degree. Her counselor at the time warned Libby that women in the field of science would most likely have a difficult time of it, as there were not many women accepted in the field at that time, and that she might starve if she continued on her path. Libby, however, luckily ignored the warning, and continued to pursue her goals single-mindedly. She persisted in her studies and eventually obtained her Ph.D. from the University of Chicago in 1943.

For her Ph.D., Libby studied quantum chemistry and diatomic molecular spectroscopy with Nobel Laureate Robert Mulliken. Diatomic molecular spectroscopy is the science of working with things made up of two atoms: a diatomic molecule, emphasizing the individual responses or structures of the behavior of these two molecules while dealing with the theory and interpretation of interactions between matter and radiation. Basically, it is concerned with the types and amounts of radiation produced by the combination of two molecules.

The Manhattan Project

While studying for her Ph.D., Libby also began working with Italian physicist Enrico Fermi. Fermi was involved in working on the first nuclear reactor at the Chicago Metallurgical Laboratory in Chicago's Manhattan District, and Libby was to become the first woman to join Fermi's team of scientists. Libby was chosen to be part of the project because her dissertation studies familiarized her with the vacuum technology needed to build the boron trifluoride counters that were required for the project. These counters were used to measure neutrons into piles of graphite and uranium blocks to create a chain reaction, a necessary step in producing atomic bombs. This project took shape before World War II because Germany was growing in strength and power. The scientists working on the project felt a sense of urgency as there was an ever-mindful fear that Germany might produce the bomb before the United States did. The project later became known as the Manhattan Project, which developed the first nuclear fission reactor in the world, called CP–1, and also helped build the first atomic bomb. Libby herself was in charge of constructing the neutron detectors. She was the only woman present at the first nuclear chain reaction, which took place under the football stands at the University of Chicago on December 2, 1942.

Libby was known to describe her workings on the Manhattan Project to her family as being akin to the science involved in the famous Buck Rogers television series. She

and the other scientists were connected to a project that seemed so cutting edge at the time that it was almost from a different world. The scientists who collaborated on the Manhattan project worked so closely together that Libby came to consider them part of her family. But Libby was not only involved in her work, during leisure time, Libby could be found swimming in Lake Michigan almost daily during the summer months. She also built a true, personal friendship with Fermi, who was known to be consistent in his encouragement of young women. This was an especially important personality trait, as it was rare among the men of science to choose women to join them. For this and other reasons Libby and Fermi became fast friends.

Worked While Pregnant

While she was working on the project, Libby met her first husband, John Marshall, Jr. They married on July 3, 1943, and the couple eventually had two children. When she was pregnant with her first child she was afraid that she would be fired from the project, so she disguised it, wearing large overalls and shoving things into the pockets to camouflage her growing stomach. She worked up until just before she gave birth and returned a week later to the project to continue her work. In fact, Libby worked during both her pregnancies, something she was very proud of, because she said it proved that the nuclear technology they were all working on was not dangerous or harmful in the least. Whether or not that was true, Libby and her children suffered no ill effects from Libby's work during her pregnancies, and on the contrary Libby gained much admiration and respect from her fellow scientists for her unflagging dedication to the project.

In 1944, while World War II was still waging, Libby took the position of consulting physicist at the Hanford plutonium production reactor in Washington state. It was while she was there that America dropped the atomic bombs on Hiroshima and Nagasaki, although there is no record of what Libby might have thought about either attack made with the weapons she helped create. No one expected the atomic bombs to be possessed with such great power, and since the time that such power was realized, no atomic bomb has been dropped on such a populated area. In the meantime, Libby missed her studies and returned to the University of Chicago as a research fellow in 1946 after the war was over. In 1948 she became a research associate at the University of Chicago's Institute for Nuclear Studies where she continued to work on nuclear power, trying to perfect and improve it.

Turned to Particle Physics

In 1953 she took on the position of assistant professor of physics at the University of Chicago—a job she held for seven years. While she was teaching, she began researching fundamental particle physics, concentrating on the nucleus. Particle physics, as its name implies, is the branch of physics that deals with subatomic particles or particles that are smaller than the atom, which at one time had been thought to be the smallest material an object could be broken down to. The nucleus, then, is the positively charged dense center of an atom, the part of the cell containing DNA and RNA and which is responsible for growth and reproduction. One of Libby's great discoveries was the detection of cold neutrons. Neutrons are electrically neutral subatomic particles, having a mass much greater than that of the electron. Neutrons, along with the proton, form nearly the entire mass of the nucleus. Cold neutrons are those with a temperature well below room temperature, something that was unusual and had not yet been discovered. Libby built the first rotating neutron spectrometer from her discovery. A spectrometer is an instrument for producing and observing spectra equipped with scales for measuring wavelengths or indexes of refraction. She also at this time investigated nuclear explosions and neutron diffusion.

In 1958 Libby took a position at the Brookhaven National Laboratory in New York. She moved in 1960 to New York University where she became an associate professor, teaching atomic and nuclear physics. In 1964 she moved to Colorado where she took a position at the University of Colorado at Boulder, teaching physics. Libby also won a fellowship at Princeton University's Institute for Advanced Study, where she conducted research with the renowned physicist J. Robert Oppenheimer. From 1963 to 1970 Libby worked at the Rand Corporation in Santa Monica, California, as a physicist.

Studied Cosmology and Ancient Climates

Libby and John Marshall divorced in 1966 and not long after she met and married Willard Frank Libby, a chemist who had won the Nobel Prize in 1960. On a professional front, Libby's interests had changed a bit and she began studying cosmology, which is the study of the physical universe. She was especially excited when she discovered that tree rings could measure ancient climates. In 1970, although still living in Boulder, Libby became a visiting professor at the University of California at Los Angeles's School of Engineering, where she helped develop the department of environmental science and engineering. She left Boulder two years later to move to Los Angeles and become an adjunct professor there.

Libby's second husband died in 1980. Almost immediately she began editing his papers for publication, as they were sought after by many chemists in the field. She was interrupted from her work, however, because around this time there were many demonstrations and ponderings about the safety of nuclear energy. Indignant by the doubters, Libby became a spokesperson for nuclear energy when there were protests against its dangers. She was a staunch endorser of nuclear energy, defending its use until the day she died.

Studied Quasars Until Death

Libby, ever insatiable about finding new and challenging things to research, turned her attention again, at the beginning of the 1980s, and began researching quasars. Unfortunately, she was unable to complete her research before her death. After a long life of exciting, cutting-edge scientific study, Libby died on November 10, 1986, in Santa Monica, California. She left behind a legacy of explo-

ration and innovation, and has been seen as a role model for women who have intended to become scientists in any field of study.

Throughout her life Libby published extensively, writing many books and articles. In particular, Libby was the author of *The Uranium People,* a book that discussed the details of the events surrounding the Manhattan Project. She also co-edited several works, including *The Life Work of Nobel Laureate Willard Frank Libby,* which was the result of her editing his papers, which she managed to finish before her death. In addition, she served as an associate editor for the *Physical Review* from 1960 to 1962. She was a member of the American Physical Society, the Royal Geographical Society, and the National Science Foundation Postdoctoral Fellowship Evaluation Board. In 1992 Libby was posthumously named one of the Women Pioneers in Nuclear Science for her work on the CP–1 nuclear fission reactor.

Books

Notable American Women: A Biographical Dictionary, The Belknap Press of Harvard University, 2004.
Notable Women Scientists, Gale Group, 2000.
Scribner Encyclopedia of American Lives, Volume 2: 1986–1990, Charles Scribner's Sons, 1999. □

Jenny Lind

One of the most celebrated opera performers of the nineteenth century, Swedish-born Jenny Lind (1820-1887) dazzled European and American audiences with her radiant soprano voice and with an image that emphasized wholesomeness and purity.

During the brief American phase of her career, between September of 1850 and May of 1852, Lind toured and gave vocal recitals; yet she became something different from simply a vocal performer. Her trip to the United States was organized by the great showman Phineas T. Barnum, best remembered today for his association with the circus that bears his name, but the promoter of various kinds of public events during the middle decades of the nineteenth century. He may never have had a greater triumph than his launch of Lind's tour: tickets for her concerts were auctioned and reached astronomical prices, and Lind's image soon adorned an incredible range of consumer items. Barnum profited handsomely, and Lind became perhaps the first person who could be described using the distinctly modern term "celebrity."

Grew Up in Poverty

Johanna Maria Lind, born October 6, 1820 in Stockholm, Sweden, grew up being shuttled from house to house as the daughter of a struggling single mother. Her parents, Niklas Johan Lind and Anna Maria Radberg, finally married when she was 15, but during her girlhood her father, from

whom she inherited her musical gifts, was generally absent by reason of his considerable skills as a tavern musician. Lind lived at various times with her mother in a shelter for indigent women, with a Lutheran church organist and clerk, and with neighbors her mother met in a Stockholm apartment building. During what must have been very lonely days, she developed the habit of singing to herself or to a pet cat she had.

One day when she was nine, an attendant to a Stockholm ballet dancer heard Lind singing through a window and rushed to ask her mistress to come and listen. The dancer in turn brought Lind to the director of Sweden's Royal Opera, who reacted incredulously when he was told Lind's age, but was equally surprised when he heard her sing. Lind was enrolled in the opera's training program, and even early in her years of singing lessons she showed a natural aptitude for being on stage—even if she suffered from what would develop into lifelong stage fright. Her mother, whose life was beginning to stabilize, gave her lessons on the piano and in the French language, and those around her began to realize that Lind's talent was something special.

Lind made her formal operatic debut in a performance of Carl Maria von Weber's *Der Freischütz* (The Marksman) on March 7, 1838. Never classically attractive, lacking confidence in herself, and generally seeming shy and quiet to people she met, Lind was an entirely different person on stage. "I awoke this morning as one person and retired in the evening as another," Lind said (as quoted in a biography

by musicologist Eva Öhrström appearing on the Official Gateway to Sweden website). "I had found out what my strength consisted of."

Moving into the home of one of Stockholm's leading composers, Adolf Fredrik Lindblad and his family, Lind made new contacts in the artistic community and gained a strong core of admirers in her native country. (Lindblad became one of the many men who hoped to become romantically involved with Lind but were turned down.) After she moved to Paris in 1841, teacher Manuel Garcia told her that the way she had been taught to sing was ruining her voice. Ordered to take several months off, Lind came back stronger than before. When she returned to Stockholm and sang in the operas *La sonnambula* (The Sleepwalker) and *Norma,* she had developed a large range, a luminous vocal quality that captivated even veteran music writers, and an uncanny ability to seem to hover gently while singing quiet passages.

Conquered New Countries

Learning to speak German and eventually English (although the latter language gave her a great deal of trouble), Lind embarked on an international career. She performed in Copenhagen, Denmark, in 1843 and attracted romantic attention from writer Hans Christian Andersen there, an episode that was later turned into an opera of its own by English alternative rock star and classical composer Elvis Costello. French composer Giacomo Meyerbeer was one of her early admirers and wrote an opera (*Ein Feldlager in Schlesien,* or *A Silesian Camp*) with a role specifically designed for her. The opera had its premiere in Berlin, Germany, in December of 1844, and Lind, performing in various Italian, German, and French operas, won acclaim across Germany for much of the following year. Steering clear of the image of illicit sexuality that often attended opera singers and stage stars in the nineteenth century as it does with today's movie stars, Lind cultivated a respectable image. She often performed concerts for charity. For a time she lived in Munich, Germany, in the home of a prominent intellectual who introduced her to Felix Mendelssohn, one of the greatest composers of the era. Despite Mendelssohn's happy marriage, the two shared a romantic attraction.

In 1846 Lind was signed to perform at the Theater an der Wien in Vienna, Austria, the home of Mozart and Beethoven, and the toughest audience she had yet encountered. Showered with applause and flowers after her innovative, spiritual performance of the title role in Bellini's *Norma,* Lind charmed the tough Viennese audience as it demanded an encore, asking (according to the *International Dictionary of Opera*), "May I first have five minutes to drink some lemonade?" In addition to her wholesome image, Lind succeeded in creating the impression that she was something of a natural, a down-to-earth, ordinary individual endowed with supernatural talent. That aspect of her image would serve her well when she encountered P.T. Barnum.

In the German city of Aachen, Lind gave three concerts with Felix Mendelssohn, and the huge crowds that turned out to greet the pair's arrival gave a foretaste of the celebrity worship that was to come. That celebrity worship came to full flower when Lind made her long-delayed English debut in May of 1847, before the cream of Victorian society, and went on to sing and to enchant Queen Victoria herself. Everywhere Lind went, crowds of people pressed inward, hoping to catch a glimpse of the famous singer. Often the result was that some of them lost consciousness and had to be carried away to receive medical attention; a dangerously packed-in crowd became known as a "Jenny Lind crush," and her name was also attached to a new locomotive on the London & Brighton Railway.

What would later become known as marketing kicked into high gear. Lind's image showed up on candy wrappers, handkerchiefs, snuffboxes, small ceramic figures, and many other mass-produced objects, and songs and instrumental dances were written about her. Lind, who by this time was commanding large paychecks for her concerts, took the commotion in stride and became attached to England after an initial period of uncertainty caused by her lack of familiarity with the language. It was in England, not America, that Jenny Lind mania really had its start. But it took the fine art of American publicity to raise it to a new level.

Negotiated Own Contracts

One of P.T. Barnum's representatives enjoyed perfect timing when he approached Lind in Lübeck, Germany, in 1849. Uncomfortable with what she saw as the taint of immorality associated with opera, she was in the process of giving up operatic performances and was ready for new income-producing opportunities. Gifted with strong business sense, Lind negotiated a profitable contract with Barnum, who was forced to borrow money to meet her demand that he deposit $187,500 in a London bank as upfront money prior to her departure. Opera in the United States was in its infancy, and Lind was hardly known there, so Barnum's associates predicted that he would suffer embarrassing financial losses in mounting her expensive tour. But Barnum stuck with his plans; he was hungry for new respectability after being associated with such dubious entertainments as the dwarf Tom Thumb and an African-American woman whom he fraudulently claimed was 161 years old and had nursed George Washington.

Barnum seized on Lind's new nickname, the "Swedish Nightingale," and promoted her less as a famous European artist than as a miraculous natural talent. Detractors termed her "Barnum's Bird," but they were silenced as a crowd of 30,000 turned out to meet Lind's ship in New York Harbor on September 1, 1850. Thousands surrounded her hotel, and Barnum began to recoup his investment when a hotel owner paid him $1,000 a day for the privilege of hosting Lind. The frenzy grew as Barnum announced that tickets would be auctioned for her first New York concert; even the unflappable Lind was amazed when the bidding rose to $650 a ticket and beyond.

As Lind made triumphant appearances in New York and then toured the eastern seaboard and the cities of the West along the Mississippi River, the British Jenny Lind mania was repeated and amplified. The list of products to which her name or image was attached grew to include the Jenny Lind crib, still so called today (it is the common

wooden type of crib with vertical bars on the sides) and even Jenny Lind soup, an unlikely concoction containing rutabagas and Gruyère cheese. Barnum hawked furniture, clothes, and pianos that Lind had supposedly endorsed, and Jenny Lind polkas and quadrilles flooded music shops. Carefully tailoring her repertoire to America's democratic tastes, Lind sang popular songs such as "Home, Sweet Home" (a tune actually of English operatic origin) along with opera arias. She met President Millard Fillmore, and her photograph was taken by Mathew Brady, photography's first big star. Her earnings from her Barnum tour were estimated at $3,000,000 in her *Times* of London obituary (other estimates have been lower); Barnum made perhaps five times as much as Lind did.

Finally, after the crowds began to thin out somewhat, Lind and Barnum went their separate ways in the spring of 1851. She hired German musician Otto Goldschmidt, a former student of Mendelssohn's, as an accompanist and conductor and continued to tour, drawing healthy audiences but not stirring the frenzy that Barnum's promotional techniques could generate. The later parts of her tour brought Lind one unexpected benefit; she and Goldschmidt married on February 5, 1852. The couple returned to Europe in May and settled in Dresden, Germany. In September of 1853 Lind had a son, Walter. A daughter, Jenny, followed in 1857, and a second son, Ernst, was born in 1858.

By that time, the family had moved to Lind's beloved England. The rest of her life was fairly quiet, although Lind and Goldschmidt numbered Queen Victoria and Prince Albert among their family friends. Lind continued to perform although her best years were behind her vocally, taking solos in oratorios like Mendelssohn's *Elijah* as late as 1883. Living at first in the London suburb of Wimbledon, Lind later moved to the Malvern Hills in the rural Shropshire region. She suffered from cancer in the 1880s and died on November 2, 1887.

Books

International Dictionary of Opera, St. James, 1993.
Kyla, Elisabeth, *The Swedish Nightingale,* Holt, Rinehart and Winston, 1965.
Ware, W. Porter, et al., *P.T. Barnum Presents Jenny Lind: The American Tour of the Swedish Nightingale,* Louisiana State University Press, 1980.

Periodicals

Birmingham Post (England), December 4, 2004.
Milwaukee Journal Sentinel, March 11, 2001.
New York Times, January 23, 2000; May 28, 2000.
Star Tribune (Minneapolis, MN), April 15, 2001.
Times (London, England), November 3, 1990.

Online

Öhrström, Eva, "Famous Swedes: Jenny Lind—The Swedish Nightingale," Sweden.se, The Official Gateway to Sweden, http://www.sweden.se/templates/cs/BasicFactsheet_5789.aspx (November 27, 2005).
"The Jenny Lind Archive: The Lost Museum," Center for History and New Media, George Mason University, http://chnm.gmu.edu/lostmuseum (November 27, 2005). □

Little Milton

American blues singer and guitarist "Little" Milton Campbell (1934-2005) learned his craft as a young man growing up in the Mississippi Delta. He went on to distinguish himself with a legendary recording and performance career that lasted more than 50 years and won him a place in the Blues Hall of Fame.

Aworld-renowned musician born and bred in a region of the southern United States widely known as "the home of the blues"–the Mississippi Delta–Campbell managed to remain true to traditional blues while incorporating elements of country and soul into his music to craft a style distinctly his own. He came to be known to blues fans as simply Little Milton, and while the guitarist and singer never truly gained wide-scale crossover success on the pop charts, within the blues world he came to stand shoulder-to-shoulder with such all-time greats as B.B. King, Sonny Boy Williamson, and Bobby "Blue" Bland, among others. "Those guys elevated blues to a level where it was accepted by all people, black and white," Mississippi radio station owner Stan Branson told Mississippi's *Clarion-Ledger.* "Little Milton could write, play, perform. And he was a true professional." Little Milton died at the age of 70 on August 4, 2005, a few days after suffering a stroke at his Memphis home.

A riveting live performer who cut his chops on the road in the deep South as a teenager, Little Milton possessed a soulful voice and a spare, stinging guitar sound. Deeply loyal to his roots in the Delta blues tradition, he was also a maverick committed to his own groundbreaking musical instincts. He pushed the edges of what the blues could be throughout his career. "I am the type of artist who will not record anything that I cannot feel, or anything I can't add something to and at the same time get something out of," Little Milton told Jeff Weiner on the BluesAccess website. "I don't record nothing that I don't feel, that I don't like. I don't give a damn who writes it or who says you should do it. When I go into the studio, I am my own boss. I have advisors and friends, I listen to them and I listen to their points. But if I feel that I can't do it without putting all of me into it, then I say, 'No, we are not going to do it.' " It was a philosophy he never abandoned during a career that lasted more than 50 years. "When you hear his records," said blues promoter Roger Clarksdale in the *Clarion-Ledger,* "you notice there's nobody who did exactly what he did."

Independent Voice Stayed in the Shadows

For Little Milton, it was always about the music first and his popularity as a blues artist lingered in the shadows. His greatest hits were played the world over by blues cover bands and musicians, many of whom could not have identified the man who wrote them. Writing of one Little Milton song in particular, "The Blues is Alright," Weiner illustrated

this point: "Little Milton's proud signature tune is heartily sung by local, national, and international blues bands each night in every corner of the globe. Unofficially dubbed the 'International Blues Anthem,' most musicians *live* to write a song ingrained so deeply in the American blues fabric as is 'The Blues is Alright.' It resonates with people worldwide, even though the majority of fans who shout out the call-and-response chorus, as well as some of the local bands who play it nightly, may not realize they're covering Little Milton, one of the true consummate professionals of the blues."

A driving force behind his professionalism was Milton's unique ability to keep his focus on what was really important—his listeners and fans. "The stars are the people sitting out there in the audience," he told Weiner. "The people that go to the record stores, buy your product and pay their money to see you—those are the stars. You are just a tool to give some humor, some pleasure, some sadness, because your songs make them happy about good things that have happened. The songs will make them reminisce about some things that weren't so pleasant and give them hope that they can change."

Started Young and Never Looked Back

Little Milton was born in a modest sharecropper's home on September 7, 1934, near the Delta town of Inverness, Mississippi. One of 13 children, he was influenced by the playing of his father, local blues musician "Big" Milton Campbell. As a young man he was also heavily influenced by the gospel music he heard in the churches, by the country music that came over the radio from Memphis, and by one of his favorite programs, the Grand Ole Opry. He took to the guitar, becoming a serious student of the instrument and imitating every song from every genre he heard until he had mastered it.

Quickly coming to be known as Little Milton—both because of his father's notoriety and the fact that he was just a young teen when he began to perform—the hungry, focused musician began to play throughout the South, wherever he could, including the street corners and back alley dives that likely gave him more of an education than he sometimes bargained for. He absorbed everything he could, and soon developed a rollicking stage presence that created a sensation wherever he played, attracting the attention of local promoters and record labels.

One musician who took a particular liking to Little Milton was a young Ike Turner, who would go on to have a sterling career of his own. Turner took Little Milton under his wing, encouraged him to move north to East St. Louis, and the pair became stars on the club circuit in that legendary blues town. Little Milton told music writer Andria Lisle, as quoted in *Sing Out!,* "[Ike] and I worked 12 to 15 dates a week up there, playing three or four gigs a day on the weekend. We'd play St. Louis, Missouri, where they had a curfew. Everything would close down at 2 a.m., and we'd head across the river to the Illinois side, where it was 24/7. We worked nonstop."

Distinguished Recording Career on Several Hallowed Labels

Turner also introduced Little Milton to Sun Records executive Sam Phillips in the early 1950s, around the time Phillips was developing the early career of another unknown prospect from Mississippi named Elvis Presley. He recorded his first single, "Beggin My Baby," in Memphis with Sun Records, but failed to distinguish himself at the label. He soon moved to Bob Lyons's Bobbin Records, recording several sides there, including his first hit, "I'm a Lonely Man," in 1958. He also began to emerge as a credible businessman with an eye for talent, bringing future stars Albert King and Fontella Bass to Bobbin as their A&R man.

Now a rising star in his own right, Little Milton was signed to the Checkers label under the ownership of the famed Chicago company Chess Records. From 1962 through 1969, when the label folded after the death of founder Leonard Chess, Little Milton's career blossomed at Checkers. His hit song "We're Gonna Make It" rose to number one on the R&B charts in 1965 and became an anthem of the civil rights movement. This kicked off a successful run of Top Ten R&B singles that included "Grits Ain't Groceries," "Baby I Love You," "Who's Cheating Who?," "If Walls Could Talk," and "Feel So Bad."

From Checkers, Little Milton moved to the Memphis-based Stax Records label for another productive six years, working alongside such 1970s-era R&B heroes as Albert King, Isaac Hayes, and Booker T. and the M.G.'s. His Stax hits included "Walkin' the Back Streets and Cryin' " and "That's What Love Will Make You Do." When Stax folded, Little Milton signed briefly with Miami-based TK/Glades Records, which also closed shop. In 1983 he had his only major label release album with *Age Ain't Nothin But a Number* on MCA.

In 1984 Little Milton returned home, literally and musically, when he began a three-decade relationship with Jackson, Mississippi-based Malaco Records, a label dedicated to keeping Southern soul and blues music alive. It was at Malaco that he recorded "The Blues is Alright," as well as such other blues standards as "Little Bluebird," "Annie Mae's Café," and "Comeback Kind of Love." His hit albums *Cheatin Habit* and *Little Milton's Greatest Hits* were among 14 albums he recorded at Malaco.

Legend Continued to Grow

Among the numerous awards and honors he received throughout his career, Little Milton was given the W.C. Handy Blues Award as Entertainer of the Year in 1988. He was inducted into the Blues Hall of Fame that same year. His 1999 Malaco release, *Welcome to Little Milton,* a collection of duets featuring such artists as Lucinda Williams and Delbert McClinton, was nominated for a Grammy Award.

The album was a way for the blues great to extend his legacy, and his love for the blues, to a younger audience that troubled him in later years with its abandonment of traditional American roots music for new formats like hip-hop and rap. "People forget about their heritage," he lamented on BluesAccess.com. "I believe this is why you find so much crime, so much racial hatred and ignorance, because I don't think the kids are being taught the true values of life, of respect, of love, of commitment, of consideration and fair play for their fellow human being. They get so disgusted with the way things are and they just go out and do anything. They are in a turmoil of defiance. . . . Nobody's there to teach them."

He added, "I'm still a contributor. . . . I still love it, and I know as long as I can enjoy what I'm doing, there'll be no retiring." Always known as a breathtaking live performer, Little Milton remained a touring headline act until his final days. "The time that I'll retire is when they lay me down, fold my arms and y'all come by and say, 'That sorta look like him. Yeah, that's him!' Other than that, as long as God grants me the time on earth, I'm gonna enjoy doing what I'm doing."

Little Milton did continue to play and record. In April of 2005 he traveled to London to headline a Memphis blues festival, and the next month his album *Think of Me* was released to rave reviews. After having a stroke, Little Milton was visited in the hospital by longtime friend and producer, Greg Preston, who played Little Milton's music to him as he lay in a coma. In the Associated Press as captured by the *Clarion-Ledger,* Preston reflected on Little Milton's uncanny ability to draw great emotion from such a spare musical style. "Most guitar players, they think the more notes the better," Preston said. "Milton, B.B. (King), Albert King–their style was you make every note count. Because one note can touch an amazing amount of people. It's not how many you play or how fast you play, it's how you play that one note. That was his style."

Books

Nothing But the Blues, Edited by Lawrence Cohn, New York: Abbeville Press, 1993.
Sonnier, Austin Jr., *A Guide to the Blues,* Greenwood Press, 1990.

Periodicals

Billboard, August 20, 2005.
Clarion-Ledger (Mississippi), August 5, 2005.
Daily Variety, August 18, 2005.
Sing Out!, Winter 2005.

Online

"Biography of Little Milton," Little Milton Official Website, http://littlemilton.com (February 16, 2006).
"Open the Door and Welcome Little Milton!," BluesAccess, http://www.bluesaccess.com/no_41/milton.htm (December 10, 2005). □

M

Anna Magnani

Italian stage and screen actress Anna Magnani (1909-1973) gained international fame with her passionate performance in director Roberto Rossellini's *Open City*, the first major work of the Italian neorealist cinema movement. In the United States, Magnani was nominated twice for an Academy Award for Best Actress, winning the Oscar in 1955 for her role in *The Rose Tattoo*.

Details of Anna Magnani's early life could have provided plot elements for the grim Italian "neorealist" films that later made her an international star. She was born in Rome, Italy, on March 7, 1908, an illegitimate child who never knew her father and was deserted by her mother. Responsibility for her upbringing fell upon her maternal grandmother. The pair led a poverty-stricken existence in the harshest parts of Rome.

Magnani received her early education at a French convent school in Rome. Later, she enrolled at the Academy of Dramatic Arts, also in Rome. To earn a living and support her schooling, she sang risqué songs in cabarets and nightclubs; she also performed in vaudeville. In 1926, she joined a company of performers that toured Italy and, in 1927, Argentina.

Early Film Career

She made an inauspicious film debut in 1927, playing a bit part in the silent film *Scampolo*. But at this time, films were not her main career focus, as she also sang and acted on the stage.

Magnani returned to films in 1934, for what some consider to be a legitimate film debut, in *La cieca di Sorrento* (The Blind Women of Sorrento). In 1935, she married film director Goffredo Alessandrini. Although Alessandrini did not consider Magnani a strong film actress, he gave her a supporting role in his 1936 film *Cavalleria*. The marriage was unsuccessful, and the couple went through a long period of separation that finally ended with an annulment in 1950. They had one son, Luca.

For the next five years, Magnani's acting work—on both stage and screen—was somewhat spotty, but she gained validation as a film actress when she appeared as the second female lead in *Teresa Venerdi* (Friday Theresa or Doctor Beware), by great Italian filmmaker Vittorio De Sica, who would later direct the neo-realist masterpiece *The Bicycle Thief* (1949).

Gained Fame in *Open City*

Magnani's true cinema breakthrough came nearly eighteen years after she made her first screen appearance in 1945 when she played "Pina" in director Roberto Rossellini's *Roma, città aperta* (Open City), the seminal work that launched the Italian neo-realist film movement in the immediate post-World War II period. The film dealt with the final days of Nazi occupation of Rome. Her performance earned her international attention, largely due to her memorable, well-acted death scene, which has been described as a great moment in film history. In 1946, in the United States, she was selected by the National Board of Review as the best foreign actress of the year for her work in the film.

Soon, she would work with some of Europe's greatest directors and, in Italy, she became a star, despite her unconventional looks—by film standards—and lack of glamour. Her dark hair, dark-circled eyes, somewhat plump frame

and short stature provided her with a sensual look often described as "earthy." Because of her appearance and acting style, Magnani was often cast as working-class women or passionate widows or mothers. On screen, Magnani came across as fiery, tempestuous, loud, aggressive and at the same time vulnerable. When not exploding, she could be quiet but seething, her raw emotions evident in her countenance. She was blessed with an incredibly expressive face that enabled her to silently, yet easily, communicate characters' feelings. Her skills inspired De Sica, her former director, to call her "Italy's finest actress and one of the most interesting actresses in the world," as quoted on the theoscarsite.com, website.

Her off-screen life at times could be equally as dramatic. During this period, Magnani had a highly visible off-screen relationship with Rossellini. This lasted for several years, until Rossellini began his rather notorious affair with actress Ingrid Bergman. Earlier, in 1942, she became involved with actor Massimo Serato. Their affair produced her second—and illegitimate—son. Later, the child became a victim of polio, and Magnani devoted a great deal of her personal life to his care.

Magnani again worked with Rossellini in 1948, first in the *Il Miracolo* (The Miracle), a story segment presented in an episodic film called *L'Amore* (Love), and in *The Human Voice.* In the first, she played a pregnant outcast peasant who was seduced by a stranger and comes to believe the child she subsequently carries is Christ. American censors condemned *Il Miracolo* as blasphemous. *The Human Voice*

was based on a play by famed French artist and writer Jean Cocteau, and, in a *tour de force* performance, Magnani portrayed a desperate woman trying to save a romantic relationship on the telephone.

Became Post-War Neo-Realist Heroine

After *Open City,* Magnani provided the screen with powerful performances as typical neo-realist female characters including strong-willed prostitutes and suffering mothers. In 1947, in *L'onorevole Angelina,* she played an Italian housewife who bravely fought against black market activities that were rampant in post-war Europe. In 1951, Luchino Visconti, another great Italian director who earned his reputation in neo-realist films, moved into the realm of satire with *Bellissima,* and he cast Magnani as "Maddelena," an overly aggressive stage mother intent on getting her daughter into movies. The moment when the character realizes that the studio heads are laughing at her daughter's screen test provides cinema with one of its great poignant moments, thanks to Magnani's considerable talents.

Other works from this period included *Abbasso la miseria* (1945); *Devanti a lui tremava tutta Roma* (Before Him All Rome Trembled), *Abbasso la richezza,* and *Un uomo ritorna, Il bandito,* all in 1946; *La sconosciuto di San Marino, Assunta spina, Molti sogni per le strade,* and *Vulcano* in (1949).

In 1952, she worked with renowned French director Jean Renoir in *Le Carrosse d'or* (The Golden Coach), playing a *commedia dell'arte* actress. She also starred in *Camicie rosse,* directed by former husband Alessandrini.

Won Academy Award for *The Rose Tattoo*

With Magnani's international reputation firmly established, it was only natural that Hollywood would seek her considerable talents. Her American debut turned out to be one of her most famous movies and one of her greatest parts. She played the widow of a truck driver in the *The Rose Tattoo,* the film version of Tennessee Williams's play. Magnani was friends with the famous playwright, and Williams had written the role with Magnani in mind.

The film was directed by Daniel Mann, and Burt Lancaster co-starred with Magnani, who earned a mantle full of awards for her performance, including the New York Film Critics Circle Award for Best Actress, the British Film Academy Award for Best Foreign Actress, the Golden Globe Award for Best Actress-Drama, and the National Board of Review Award for Best Actress.

Ironically, following her triumph in *The Rose Tattoo,* the number of her film roles began to dwindle, even though she continued providing strong performances. In 1957, she was again nominated for the Academy Award for Best Actress for her work in *Wild is the Wind,* a film by George Cukor, some consider one of America's finest directors.

Worked With Brando

In 1959, Magnani became involved in a major film project that, although it resulted in immediate failure, turned out to be perhaps her most interesting American movie. Further, it combined her considerable talents with those of arguably America's greatest actor, Marlon Brando, as well one of the movie industry's best directors, Sidney Lumet, and one of the country's finest playwrights, Tennessee Williams.

By the late 1950s, Brando and Magnani were the male and female actors whose names were most closely identified with Williams's work. In 1948, Brando's stage performance as "Stanley Kowalski" in William's play *A Streetcar Named Desire* electrified Broadway audiences and propelled him toward super-stardom; and Magnani, with her performance in *The Rose Tattoo,* personified, in many peoples' minds, the typical Williams female character. Thus, a Williams-Brando-Magnani collaboration seemed highly appropriate, and it turned out to be *The Fugitive Kind,* an adaptation of *Orpheus Descending,* one of William's earlier and lesser-known plays.

Brando starred as "Valentine Xavier," a guitar-playing drifter who finds his way into a small Louisiana town, where he encounters and develops a romantic relationship with an emotionally vulnerable woman (played by Magnani) who is married to a cruel man dying of cancer.

Brando demanded and got an unheard-of million-dollar contract, but the film's producers expected a smash hit, considering all of the talent assembled for a work by Williams. At the time, Williams was hot in Hollywood. His reputation had already been well established with his plays *A Streetcar Named Desire* and *The Glass Menagerie,* and the movie version of his play, *Cat on the Hot Tin Roof,* was a current box office success. In addition, his new play, *Suddenly, Last Summer,* was doing well on Broadway, and the screen rights had already been sold.

But *The Fugitive Kind* failed to live up to expectations, and trouble began even before the filming started. Author Peter Manso reported in "Brando," his 1994 biography of the temperamental star, that Brando and Magnani's working relationship became strained during rehearsals and further deteriorated when filming began. Essentially, two massive egos collided. "Magnani, who was notorious for her stormy affairs with her leading men as well as her directors in the past, was now offended at Marlon's courtesy, which had become obsequious to the point of parody," wrote Manso. "Not surprisingly, Brando was testing her the way he tested everyone."

As for the film, the final results were odd, and both audiences and critics were turned off. "With a few scattered exceptions, the reviews were terrible," wrote Manso.

One of those exceptions was Bosley Crowther, then the influential film reviewer for *The New York Times.* He wrote: ". . . at the center of his drama, which grimly and relentlessly takes place in the sweaty and noxious climate of a backwash Louisiana town, there are two brave and enterprising people whose inevitably frustrating fate assumes, from the vibrance of their natures, the shape of tragedy. And because Marlon Brando and Anna Magnani play these two people brilliantly, 'The Fugitive Kind' has a distinction and a sensitivity that are rare today in films."

Acting Appearances Decreased

Following that film, but not as a result of its critical reception, Magnani's screen activity shrank even more. Her age was probably more responsible for her diminished activity: In 1960, she was fifty-two years old, and acting opportunities for women in that age bracket were limited; especially for a singular performer like Magnani.

During her American period, Magnani also continued working overseas with European directors. In 1956, she starred in *Suor letizia.* Two years later, she starred with Giulietta Masina, another major international actress (she appeared in Frederico Fellini's classic *La Strada* [The Street, 1954] and she later married the director), in *Nella città l'inferno* (And the Wild, Wild Woman), a drama taking place in a female prison. Magnani played a prostitute.

In 1962, she had yet another opportunity to work with a highly regarded European director, when she appeared in Pier Paolo Pasolini's *Mamma Roma.* Again, Magnani played a prostitute; it was her last film role of substance.

Later in the decade, in 1969, she appeared in the comedy *The Secret of Santa Vittoria,* directed by Stanley Kramer. Her last screen role was a cameo in Fellini's *Roma* in 1972.

In this later period of her career, she also appeared on Italian television and acted on the stage, most notably in 1965 when she starred in *La Lupa* (She-Wolf), directed by Franco Zeffirelli, and 1966 when she played the lead in playwright Jean Anouilh's *Medea,* directed by Gian Carlo Menotti.

Died of Cancer

Magnani battled pancreatic cancer late in her life, and she finally succumbed to the disease in Rome on September 26, 1973. She was 65 years old. It was reported that an enormous crowd turned out for her funeral in Italy, in a final public salute that is more typically reserved for Popes. She was laid to rest in the family mausoleum of Roberto Rossellini, who had remained her longtime friend and favorite director.

She was later honored in the United States with a star on the Hollywood Walk of Fame on Hollywood Boulevard.

In 2002, she was the subject of a "Billy Rose Tribute" at the Museum of Modern Art in New York City. The two-week career retrospective included screenings of Magnani's most important films.

Books

International Dictionary of Films and Filmmakers, Volume 3: Actors and Actresses, fourth edition, St. James Press, 2000.
Manso, Peter, *Brando: The Biography,* Hyperion, 1994.

Periodicals

The Village Voice, January 16-22, 2002.

Online

"Anna Magnani," *The Oscar Site,,* http://theoscarsite.com/whoswho3/magnani_a.htm (December 19, 2005).
"Anna Magnani Biography," *Hollywood.com,* http://www.hollywood.com/celebs/fulldetail/id/193906 (December 20, 2005).

"Spotlight on Anna Magnani," *Italiamia,* http://www.italiamia
.com/cinema_magnani.html (December 19, 2005). □

Dusan Makavejev

One of the most innovative filmmakers to emerge from Eastern Europe in the 1960s and 1970s, Dusan Makavejev (born 1932) had an anarchic streak that antagonized authorities in both the East and West. His 1971 film *WR—Mysteries of the Organism,* dealing with the career of psychiatrist Wilhelm Reich, has been a favorite of critics.

Makavejev was a native of the Communist nation of Yugoslavia and worked there for the first part of his career. His outrageous films breathe the spirit of the 1960s counterculture, and it is perhaps surprising that an artist who took the ideas of that era to their most daring extremes should have come from behind the "Iron Curtain" that divided the West and the Communist world. Yet he was an equal-opportunity satirist, taking aim at Western militarism and capitalist excess as often as he skewered Communist absolutism. Makavejev's works had sex and sexuality high on the list among their main themes; he saw sexuality as an unstoppable chaotic force that was inimical to the objectives of established regimes everywhere. Accordingly, some of his films had scenes that could be classified as pornographic, and they were banned in various countries. They seem to overflow with ideas, often containing multiple stories mixed with interviews real and staged, documentary-style footage, quotations from other films, and more. Makavejev was, in the words of *New York Times* writer Kevin Filipski, "one of the boldest, most anarchic filmmakers around, an honest purveyor of cinematic treatises that explore taboo topics in the political, social, psychological, and sexual arenas."

Saw *Snow White* in Original Run

Makavejev was born in the Yugoslav capital of Belgrade (now the capital of Serbia and Montenegro) on October 13, 1932. The man who shocked moviegoers with *WR—Mysteries of the Organism* was, ironically enough, first inspired by Walt Disney's *Snow White and the Seven Dwarfs*—the first animated feature in color. "I was five years old at the time, and this made me very proud. It made me feel this was made for me, for my generation," Makavejev told interviewer Ray Privett of Chicago's Facets Multimedia. He attended an English-language kindergarten in Belgrade, where he was also entranced by another pioneering piece of animation, *Felix the Cat.* Makavejev learned to speak several languages, and the films he would make as an adult were almost international in nature, switching among different languages through the use of subtitles.

Growing up amid the devastation of World War II, Makavejev would feature anti-militaristic themes in his films. He finished school after the war and enrolled at the University of Belgrade, from which he graduated in 1955. He majored in psychology, and the drives and compulsions hidden within the human psyche would also furnish material for his films later on as he studied with the intellectual descendants of the founders of modern psychology in Vienna, Austria. "We got Gestalt psychology, then later some Freudian stuff because we had a professor who studied in Vienna with one of Freud's pupils," he told Privett. Makavejev was influenced by the German-born Marxist philosopher Erich Fromm, who extended Freud's ideas into the political realm, positing freedom as a basic psychological state—exhilarating but terrifying enough that humans try to escape from it through authoritarianism and militaristic violence.

But the Freud disciple who influenced Makavejev to the greatest extent was the most unorthodox one, Wilhelm Reich. "I discovered Wilhelm Reich in the early '50s, and tried to read him, but I could not find anything. I didn't know he was in jail at the time," Makavejev recalled to Privett. Reich posited the existence of a physical force called orgone energy, expressed in human sexuality and emotion but also in the phenomena of the natural and celestial worlds. He and his followers were early exponents of what would later be called sexual liberation. Reich, who had emigrated to the United States, was harassed by the FBI and charged with making false medical claims for his "orgone accumulator" devices; he died in prison in 1957.

In the late 1950s, Makavejev attended the Academy for Theatre, Radio, Film, and Television in Belgrade. He had begun making films as a university student in 1953, and now he found work making documentaries and other short films for the Yugoslav state. One of them, made in 1959, was called *What Is a Workers' Council?* A stint in the Yugoslav army in 1959 and 1960 began to focus Makavejev's ideas, and he worked on scripts that explored the psychology of military organizations. His documentary career resumed after his discharge, and film scholars believe that, although his career took a drastic turn away from Communist orthodoxy in the late 1960s, he never completely renounced the Communist-realist style of filmmaking—most of his films had documentary elements or showed the influence of the propaganda classics of Soviet cinema. Makavejev married Bojana Marijan in 1964.

Took Advantage of American-Inspired Distraction

At the time, Makavejev was unable to realize his ideas within the restrictions imposed by Yugoslavia's state-run film industry, which banned nudity and even any expression of overt sexuality. In the late 1960s, however, the country did open up to some Western investment. This had cinematic ramifications: American film studios began making films in Italy to cut costs, resulting in the "spaghetti Western" phenomenon, and Italian producers such as Dino de Laurentiis began to move production to nearby Yugoslavia. The government, anxious for foreign investment, put the resources of the country's film industry at their disposal—and Makavejev stepped into the resultant suspension of the normal ways of doing things in order to make his first two films, *Man Is Not a Bird* of 1966 and *Love Affair: Or the Case of the Missing Switchboard Operator* of the following year. The films were never officially approved, but Makavejev made them under the radar of the authorities.

"I got my cinematographer and my set designer . . . and we said, why don't we start now?" Makavejev told Privett, recalling the genesis of *Love Affair*. They found three empty rooms in the basement of a studio building. "Some crew had recently left the place. We said, let's call the film 'Love Affair,' and the set designer wrote 'Love Affair Film Crew' on the door. We were there, just talking about anything." A middle-aged production manager in a shirt and tie knocked, and Makavejev feared the group had been caught. "We were all in our 20s and he was in his 40s." But the production manager, it turned out, was looking for work and signed on to Makavejev's still rather formless film. "He was a workaholic, so he found us. . . . We didn't have the heart to tell him that the production was not yet approved." The production manager reserved supplies, and shooting went on unimpeded. Officials "were too busy shooting this gigantic Hollywood movie that they either didn't realize or care what we were doing. . . . The people who did realize what we were doing loved us. We were young guys who were doing something interesting."

Man Is Not a Bird, with its comic story of a love triangle set in a Serbian copper mining town, was a relatively conventional piece of Communist filmmaking, but its frank treatment of sexuality pushed the envelope, and its mix of documentary and narrative elements were innovative. Its main character, a straitlaced engineer who has an affair with a local hairstylist but then loses her to a truck driver, was seen as a symbol of the ruling Communist order. But it was *Love Affair* that put Makavejev on the international cinema map. As the above description of its genesis indicates, it has a quality of being made up as it went along, something it would share with most of Makavejev's subsequent films. Its basic plot—a switchboard operator, Isabella, becomes involved with an Arabborn exterminator, Ahmed, who is later arrested for her murder—serves merely as the springboard for a whole collage of little stories and details, including digressions into rat control, the making of strudel, imaginary interviews with scholars including a sexologist, and footage of churches being destroyed during the October Revolution of 1917 that led to the founding of the Soviet Union.

Makavejev's next film, *Innocence Unprotected* (1968) was equally innovative; beginning with a Serbian romantic film of the 1940s, Makavejev superimposed interviews with the film's original makers, hand-tinted parts of the original black-and-white film, and added other elements in an attempt to bring out (or create anew) an anti-Nazi subtext in the film and perhaps to draw a contrast between imperialist power and local culture. Makavejev's reputation among international film observers was on the rise, and he was awarded a Ford Foundation grant in 1968—one of the few times he succeeded in tapping large-scale sources of arts funding in the West.

Released Unorthodox Reich Documentary

The shocking elements of Makavejev's *WR—Mysteries of the Organism* went a long way toward explaining the funding difficulties that would plague him for the rest of his career. The "WR" in the title referred to Wilhelm Reich, and part of the film consisted of one of Makavejev's typically freeform documentaries, tracing Reich's philosophies and his problems in the U.S., and included interviews with his surviving relatives. The film also delved into the U.S. student counterculture of the 1960s, with footage of demonstrations against the Vietnam War, and into pornography, featuring an interview with an editor of *Screw* magazine. Yet other strands were woven in; part of the film, set in Yugoslavia, is a fictional story of a female Reich admirer whose head is cut off (with a skate) by a Russian ice skater with whom she has had an affair. In the scene, her decapitated head is still capable of speech.

The sheer originality of *WR—Mysteries of the Organism* fascinated Western film critics, and the film was a staple of the university cinema series of the era. In Yugoslavia, however, it was not at all well received by the authorities. The film was never released there, and the Yugoslav regime turned up the heat on Makavejev and declared him an enemy of the state. "One day in '73 I went for a drive in my car and heard a strange sound," the director told John Petkovic of the Cleveland *Plain Dealer*. "The bolts on one of the wheels were unscrewed. I knew it was time to leave."

Relocating to Paris, Makavejev attempted to recapture the symbolic richness of *WR—Mysteries of the Organism* in *Sweet Movie* (1974), structured around a story of a beauty queen who is abused by her industrialist husband and finds renewal in a radical sex commune. *Sweet Movie,* with chocolate-drenched sex scenes barely distinguishable from those of many pornographic films, was banned in many countries and condemned by critics as over-the-top. *Montenegro* (1981), set in Sweden among a group of Balkan immigrants, fared better; it starred American actress Susan Anspach as an American-Swedish woman who becomes involved with the group. "I planned to place at the beginning of the film the following text: 'This film is dedicated to the new invisible nation of Europe, the fourth largest, of 11 million immigrants and guest workers who moved North to exploit rich and prosperous people, bringing with them filthy habits, bad manners, and the smell of garlic,'" Makavejev told *New York Times* writer Annette Insdorf.

But Makavejev was forced to range farther and farther afield in search of support from controversy-leery investors. A 1985 Australian film, *The Coca-Cola Kid,* floundered despite the presence in the lead role of Eric Roberts, brother of the famed American star Julia Roberts. Makavejev returned with the anti-Communist satires *Manifesto* (1988) and *Gorilla Bathes at Noon* (1993), but they did not find wide distribution. Makavejev made a living by teaching film courses, including one at Harvard University. In the 1990s he was frequently visible as an essayist, bemoaning the ethnic strife that resulted in the breakup of his native Yugoslavia. In London, in 1991, he agreed to camouflage two scenes in advance of a television showing of *WR—Mysteries of the Organism,* one of them showing a couple having sex at the Woodstock music festival. In 1995 he made a short documentary, *A Hole in the Soul,* that juxtaposed reminiscences of his own career with scenes of the chaos in the former Yugoslavia. He continued to live in Paris, and in the early 2000s he was reported to be at work on a new film entitled *M-99.*

Books

International Dictionary of Films and Filmmakers, Vol. 2: Directors, 4th ed., St. James, 2000.

Periodicals

Cineaste, Winter 2001.
Guardian (London, England), January 28, 1995; June 3, 1999.
Independent (London, England), April 5, 1991.
New York Times, November 8, 1981; April 29, 2001.
Plain Dealer (Cleveland, OH), May 1, 2000.

Online

"Dusan Makavejev," All Movie Guide, http://www.allmovie.com (December 20, 2005).
"Makavejev, Dusan," Facets Multimedia, http://www.facets.org (December 20, 2005). □

Dan Marino

When quarterback Dan Marino (born 1961) was still available late in the first round of the 1983 National Football League draft, the Miami Dolphins were sur-

prised and delighted. Marino set many major passing records over 17 seasons before retiring after the 1999 season, while leading the Dolphins to 10 postseason appearances and one Super Bowl. Marino, inducted into the Pro Football Hall of Fame in 2005, went on to become a broadcaster and product endorser after his retirement from professional football.

Raised in Blue-Collar Neighborhood

Marino grew up in Pittsburgh, Pennsylvania's, working-class Oakland neighborhood. His father, Dan Sr., worked the graveyard shift delivering bundles of the *Pittsburgh Post–Gazette* and threw footballs in the backyard with his son. Young Marino, who rooted for the Pittsburgh Steelers as a youth, played his early football on a street so narrow that teams had four players maximum; the end zones were telephone poles and curbs constituted the sidelines. Buses and cars often served as the linebackers he had to dodge. "If Marino didn't have anything else to do, he threw at the telephone poles," Larry Schwartz wrote for *ESPN Classic.*

He emerged as a *Parade* magazine All-American while at Central Catholic High School. Marino pitched and hit so well that the Kansas City Royals selected him in the fourth round of baseball's amateur draft, but Marino rejected the team's offer of a $35,000 signing bonus in order to play college football instead, at the University of Pittsburgh, just five blocks from his home. "Something, maybe my heart, told me to stay home and go to Pitt," he told Schwartz.

Had Ups and Downs as Panther

Halfway through his freshman season, Marino became Pittsburgh's starting quarterback and never looked back. The Panthers reeled off three straight 11-1 seasons, winning the Fiesta, Gator, and Sugar bowls. In Marino's junior season, 1981, Panthers Head Coach Jackie Sherrill turned his quarterback loose with a more wide-open offense and Marino responded with 37 touchdown passes, which led the entire National Collegiate Athletic Association, and 2,876 yards with a nearly 60 percent completion rate. He saved his best for last that year. Facing Georgia in the Sugar Bowl in New Orleans, and with the Bulldogs still having an outside shot at a national championship, Marino stared down a Georgia blitz and hit tight end John Brown with a 33-yard touchdown pass with 42 seconds remaining to give the Panthers a 24-20 victory. Moments earlier, Marino had talked Sherrill out of attempting a game-tying field goal.

Pittsburgh ended the 1981 season ranked fourth in the Associated Press poll, and the Panthers harbored national title hopes the following season with Marino back for his senior year. Marino, however, threw more interceptions than touchdowns (23 to 17) and Pittsburgh finished 9-3—disappointing compared with expectations. The last two games were especially disappointing. The regular-season finale was an embarrassing 48-14 loss at home to in-state rival Penn State, and the Panthers failed to score a touchdown in a 7-3 defeat to Southern Methodist in the Cotton Bowl. "The bottom fell out my senior year at Pittsburgh," Marino wrote in his book, *Dan Marino: My Life in Football,* excerpts of which appeared on the Pro Football Hall of Fame Web site. "It's never fun to play poorly or to be questioned. It certainly wasn't for me that senior year at Pitt. But I think it served me well to learn how to handle everything that came with the game's ups and downs. Some people call it growing another layer of skin. I just call it growing up."

Dolphins Needed a QB

Marino's mystifying senior slump befuddled many observers—and him—and dropped his value on draft day. That the player pool was stocked with promising quarterbacks—Schwartz called it the "Quarterback Class of '83,"—didn't help Marino, either. Quarterbacks John Elway, Todd Blackledge, Jim Kelly, Tony Eason, and Ken O'Brien all went ahead of Marino. Other teams that had expressed their interest took running backs and defensive tackles. Miami, meanwhile, had liked what they saw of Marino at the annual scouting combine in Indianapolis but assumed he would not be available late in the first round, when the Dolphins were scheduled to pick 27th, or next to last.

Marino received a phone call from Miami coach Don Shula. "Hey, you want to come to Miami? Because we need

a quarterback," Shula said, as Marino recalled in his book. Marino's reply: "You bet." Miami had reached the Super Bowl three months earlier, losing 27-17 to the Washington Redskins, but the Dolphins lacked the franchise quarterback they were missing since Bob Griese retired in 1980.

Still, Marino had some critics to silence. "I worked my butt off that summer in hope of making a good first impression," Marino wrote in his book. The young quarterback had a good team around him. The Dolphins had reached the Super Bowl with a standout defense and a strong offensive line that anchored a ball-control offense in the absence of a high-scoring attack. Shula, once Marino was ready, would let the Dolphins open up offensively. "Right from the start, Don Shula was the perfect coach to help develop me into [a quarterback] quickly."

Three games into the 1983 season, Marino took over from David Woodley as starting quarterback. In 1984, he blossomed into a star. He set two headline-grabbing, single-season records: most touchdown passes (48, which Peyton Manning of the Indianapolis Colts broke in 2004) and most yards completed (5,084). He impressed other coaches and media for his maturity as well. "Quite frankly, Marino just doesn't make mistakes," Paul Attner wrote in the *Sporting News* in November of 1984. "Remarkably, Marino goes about his destruction so easily, so calmly, so *naturally,* that you forget he was in college just two years ago or that he is confronting complex defenses that are employing every possible sleight–of–hand to confuse the young lad or that even an esteemed coach like Tom Landry once said it takes every five years to mature into an NFL quarterback." Hall of Fame defensive back Ronnie Lott said, as quoted on the ESPN Classic Web site: "You were basically at Dan's mercy. All the great ones see the game so quickly that when everybody else is running around like a chicken with their head cut off, they know exactly where they want to go with the ball."

Marino and the Dolphins won the American Football Conference championship in 1984, avenging a home upset loss to the Seattle Seahawks in the playoffs a year earlier. Super Bowl XIX featured Marino against another of the game's best young quarterbacks, Joe Montana of the San Francisco 49ers. Montana, already with a Super Bowl title under his belt, was the game's Most Valuable Player three years earlier. After two weeks of Montana vs. Marino headlines and sound bites, the quarterbacks and their teams met at Stanford Stadium in Palo Alto, California. Though the Dolphins led 10-7 after the first quarter, the rest of the game was all 49ers. They led 28-16 at halftime and won 38-16, and Montana had another Super Bowl MVP award. Marino, with his team playing catch-up all day, completed 29 of 50 passes for 318 yards, threw for one touchdown pass and had two interceptions. The 49ers sacked him four times.

His Commercial Value Rose

Despite the Super Bowl defeat, Marino's value as quarterback and commercial endorser soared. Soft-drink bottler Pepsi took advantage of the Montana-Marino hype and featured both in a television ad shortly after the game. "Joe, next year I'm buying," Marino said in the ad, after Montana bought him a Pepsi at a machine. Marino also endorsed

Isotoner gloves after Aris-Isotoner vice president Richard Rubin chose the quarterback over race-car driver Mario Andretti and a heart surgeon. The company's slogan was "Take care of the hands that take care of you." According to Barry Jackson of the *Miami Herald,* Rubin said Isotoner's sales increased by 500 percent over the first five years of Marino's marketing agreement, which ended in 1994 with a management turnover. "The Isotoner ads have been off the air for more than a decade, but people still ask Marino about them," Jackson wrote. "In the winter, Dan can walk down the streets of New York and get Isotoner comments," Marino's marketing manager, Ralph Stringer said in Jackson's article. "A person will say, 'I saw your commercial [very recently].' I say, 'You didn't see that commercial.' "

Marino never played in another Super Bowl, despite the Dolphins' many playoff appearances. In 1985, they hosted the AFC title game but lost at home 31-14 to a New England Patriots team that had not won in Miami since 1966. Miami also came up one victory short in 1992, falling at home 29-10 to Buffalo. Marino had talented receivers in Mark Clayton and Mark Duper, but the defense faltered over the years and there was never a running game solid enough to balance the offense. "We used to laugh when we heard every single year that the Dolphins were committed to the running game," said Kelly, the quarterback who led Buffalo to four straight AFC titles from 1990 to 1993 and is in the Hall of Fame. "They never had a running game, and we knew if it came down to it, it was going to come down to No. 13 [Marino]."

Marino, who stayed healthy in an injury-prone position for most of his career, set 25 NFL records and shared five others. Shula resigned as coach in 1995, opting for an executive position while Jimmy Johnson, who had won titles with the Dallas Cowboys and the University of Miami, took over on the sidelines. In his final season, 1999, Marino threw more interceptions (17) than touchdown passes (12) for the first time since his senior year in college. After an embarrassing 62-7 playoff loss to the Jacksonville Jaguars, Marino announced his retirement. His regular-season career statistics included 4,967 completions in 8,358 attempts for 61,361 yards and 420 touchdowns. He was named to the All-Pro first or second team eight times and all-AFC six times. Marino also played in nine Pro Bowls.

Turned Down Executive Position

The Dolphins retired Marino's number, 13, the following season. He, quarterback Bob Griese (12), and running back Larry Csonka (39) are the only players so honored by the franchise, which began play in 1966. Marino was elected to the Hall of Fame on the first ballot in 2005.

Marino has been busy as a broadcaster for CBS and HBO; in 2004, three weeks after agreeing to become the Dolphins' senior vice president of football operations, he abruptly quit. "Dan Marino made the best audible of his life," Joe Schad wrote in the *Palm Beach Post.* "He didn't realize what he had gotten himself into. He didn't realize how many hours at the office this would require." Schad saw the hiring as celebrity window dressing. "[Owner Wayne] Huizenga was the restaurant owner. [General man-

ager Rick] Spielman was the chef. [Head coach] Dave Wannstedt was the waiter. And they would let Marino make a few plate decorations. It was absurd. Marino, the greatest and most popular player in the history of the Dolphins, should not have lowered himself to that."

Marino is still in demand for endorsements. Late in 2005 Marino was endorsing Samsung Electronics, among other companies. "Even five years after retirement, Marino remains ubiquitous," Jackson wrote in the *Miami Herald.* "Marino has become one of the rare celebrity athletes whose popularity has endured long after he left the field." He is still visible in broadcast and print ads and on billboards, and has dabbled in film. "He represents quality based on the career he has established," said Ralph Stringer, who handles Marino's marketing deals. "Danny comes across as the boy from Pittsburgh. He's believable," Stringer told Jackson. "He has achieved the best, so you think he would associate with the best."

Periodicals

Palm Beach Post, February 4, 2004.

Online

"100 Greatest College Football Endings," Collegefootball news.com, http://www.collegefootballnews.com/Almanac/ Top_100_Finishes/100_Best_College_Football_Finishes_ 40_31.htm (December 19, 2005).

"Dan Marino: My Life in Football," Pro Football Hall of Fame, http://www.profootballhof.com/hof/enshrinement/release .jsp?release_id=1586 (November 22, 2005).

"Marino's Golden Arm Changed the Game," ESPN Classic http://espn.go.com/classic/biography/s/Marino_Dan.html (November 22, 2005).

"Nobody Does It Better," *Sporting News,* November 5, 1984, http://www.sportingnews.com/archives/marino/1984.html (November 22, 2005).

Pro Football Hall of Fame, Dan Marino profile, http://www .profootballhof.com/hof/member.jsp?player_id=238 (November 22, 2005).

"Thriving in the Pocket," *Miami Herald,* August 7, 2005, http://www.miami.com/mld/miamiherald/sports/columnists/ dan_le_batard/12277863.htm (December 19, 2005). □

Dean Martin

American entertainer Dean Martin (1917-1995) was known for his nonchalant style and breezy wit. Immensely popular in his time, he first became famous as the straight man of the comic duo Martin and Lewis in 1946.

M artin also recorded hit records in his distinctive baritone, starred in motion pictures, and had his own long-running television program. But any snapshot of the multi-talented Martin would be incomplete without mention of his legendary affiliation with Hollywood's Rat Pack and his ever-present, if somewhat exaggerated, cocktail personae.

Early Years

Martin was born Dino Paul Crocetti on June 7, 1917, in Steubenville, Ohio. His parents, Angela and Gaetano (a barber), had emigrated from southern Italy around the turn of the nineteenth century and the young Martin reputedly spoke only Italian until he was five years old. Steubenville was a tough town in those days, known as "Little Chicago" because of its affinity for gambling and other assorted vices, and Martin was not immune to the influences of his environment. He dropped out of high school at 16 and worked for a while as a liquor runner for bootleggers. But even this somewhat less than auspicious beginning could not hide his early tendency to perform. "He was a comedian," Martin's childhood friend Mario Camerlengo told John Soeder of the *Houston Chronicle.* "He always disturbed the class. When the teacher would say, 'Dino, you'll have to leave,' he'd hit me on the head as he shuffled out."

After his stint running booze, Martin tried his hand at amateur boxing under the name "Kid Crochet." That pursuit did not last long, as, according to Rob Parker of the London *Observer,* Martin often recalled in later years, "I won all but 11 of my 12 fights." He went on to work variously as a shoeshine boy, gas station attendant, steel mill laborer, and croupier before striking out to make his name as a singer.

Although blessed with a smooth baritone voice, Martin's early career as a singer progressed slowly. He sang with club bands around the Midwest, and made his coast-to-coast radio debut on Cleveland's WTAM (AM) in 1942, but failed to cause much of a stir at first. Bing Crosby's renowned crooning was imitated by most young singers of the day, and Martin was no exception. J.D. Reed of *People* quoted Martin as saying, "I copied Bing until I had a style of my own." In the 1940s the emulation of his idol accorded Martin sufficient success to make him a regular at New York City nightclubs and on radio, but it was a fateful pairing in nearby Atlantic City, New Jersey, that rocketed him to fame.

Martin and Lewis

In 1946 Martin was booked for a six-week engagement at Atlantic City's 500 Club. A wacky young comedian named Jerry Lewis was also working there, and kismet struck when the illness of another performer put the pair on the same bill. Martin's mildly bemused and effortlessly elegant straight man combined with the wildly frenzied antics of Lewis to become an instant hit with audiences, and formed the basis of a tremendously popular partnership that would last ten years. Indeed, half a century later comedian Alan King told Reed, "I've been around 50 years, and no one ever created the kind of pandemonium they did."

The duo's success led them to the Copacabana in New York, where they gained top billing and the then-princely salary of $5,000 a week. Two years later they conquered the West Coast at Slapsie Maxie Rosenbloom's nightclub in Beverly Hills, and a movie deal with Paramount Pictures soon followed. Martin and Lewis made sixteen films together, starting with 1949's *My Friend Irma* and ending with *Hollywood or Bust* in 1956. In between were such crowd pleasers as *At War with the Army* (1950), *The Caddy* (1953), and *Living It Up* (1954). *The Caddy* was also notable because it clearly established Martin's singing credentials, generating the top ten solo effort and Oscar-nominated hit *That's Amore.*

Despite one of the most successful partnerships in the history of show business and the resulting fortunes made by both members, Martin and Lewis had a mercurial relationship. Temperamentally disparate, the two had little in common off the screen and stage, and the ongoing volatility reportedly became wearing for Martin. In 1956 things came to a head, and the pair parted company. Few expected Martin's career to survive, but the kid from Steubenville surprised them all.

The Rat Pack

Martin's detractors were hardly shocked when Martin's first solo movie effort, *Ten Thousand Bedrooms,* was a resounding flop in 1957. They were taken aback, however, when 1958's *The Young Lions* showcased a heretofore unsuspected dramatic talent in Martin. He followed that up with a critically-acclaimed performance with John Wayne in *Rio Bravo* and another with Frank Sinatra and Shirley MacLaine in *Some Came Running.* Thus having beaten the odds and demonstrated his merit as a serious actor, Martin stood ready to reinvent himself yet again.

Martin's newest personae took shape as he aligned himself with an offshoot of a group originated by Humphrey Bogart. By the late 1950s the clan had morphed into

Sinatra's infamous "Rat Pack," and Martin was installed as second in command. The core of the Pack consisted of Sinatra, Martin, Sammy Davis Jr., Peter Lawford, and Joey Bishop; and as they performed together in movies and, most notoriously, Las Vegas, they came to epitomize an irreverent style of hip sophistication that defined the early 1960s. Amidst all that panache, no one was more urbane, laid back, or surpassingly cool than Martin. Tuxedo-clad, cigarette in one hand and cocktail in the other, Martin's latest role was that of a debonair boozer with a nonchalant wit.

The Rat Pack's slightly risqué focus on sex, liquor, and general carousing made Las Vegas their natural playground. Gambling, drinking, and womanizing were the order of the day (and night); but the group worked hard as well, and their casino nightclub act was hugely popular. While some tongues may have wagged at the level of excess, nobody doubted that Sinatra and his boys were having a great time. As Martin's old friend, actor Debbie Reynolds, told Reed, "A lot of people wished they could have a third as much fun as [the Pack] did." Martin, dubbed the "Clown Prince" of the clan, expressed his satisfaction in a typically offhand manner at a Rat Pack tour press conference by saying, according to *Newsweek*'s Karen Schoemer, "We're happy to be doing this thing. What the hell."

Top Talent Across Media

Martin's association with the Rat Pack did not hamper his solo career. He continued to record as a singer, producing his first number one hit, *Memories Are Made Of This,* in 1955. He famously repeated that achievement in 1964, when he bumped The Beatles out of the top spot with his recording of *Everybody Loves Somebody.* According to Schoemer, Martin was spurred to such a feat by frustration with his son's non-stop admiration of the British pop sensation, and reportedly said, "I'm gonna knock your little pallies off the charts." By the end of his recording career, 40 of Martin's singles had hit the charts, including seven in the top ten. He also recorded 11 gold albums.

Martin also made his mark on television. The year 1965 saw the debut of *The Dean Martin Show,* a variety program that lasted nine years on NBC. The show was such a success that Martin was able to negotiate a lucrative contract that was the largest of its time and earned him a place in the *Guinness Book of World Records* as the highest paid entertainer of his day.

Nor did Martin neglect the silver screen, although his later reviews never quite equaled those of his early work. His vehicles ranged from light comedy to westerns, including his only musical, 1960's *Bells Are Ringing, Kiss Me, Stupid* in 1964, *Rough Night in Jericho* in 1967, and *Airport* in 1970. He also made four Matt Helm films, which were send-ups of James Bond, in the 1960s. In short, Martin had proved himself a major talent across a variety of venues during the course of his career.

Fade Out and Reprise

With time, Martin began to fade slowly out of the limelight and appeared content to do so on his own terms.

His last movie was 1984's kitschy *Cannonball Run II.* In 1988 he bowed out of a Rat Pack reunion tour after only a short time on the job. Sometime before that, he had stopped making records. He also declined to take part in a 1992 retrospective on Martin and Lewis with his old comedy partner. Instead, Martin played his beloved golf and contented himself with solitary dinners at a favorite Italian restaurant in Beverly Hills.

Part of the self-imposed isolation of Martin's later years was undoubtedly a reflection of his basically solitary personality. He was never much for talking or taking things too seriously. As his son Ricci told Reed, "He joked that it wasn't the chat that bothered him, it was the chit." And director Richard Corliss of *Time* quoted Vincente Minnelli as saying, "Dean would rather die than have you believed he cared." But care he did, and that caring was widely thought to play a large part in his withdrawal.

Martin had married and divorced three times by 1976, and had fathered seven children. One of those children, Dean Paul Martin (known as Dino Jr.), was tragically killed in a plane crash during a California Air National Guard training mission in 1987, at the age of 35. That tragedy, coupled with the losses of such old friends as his assistant Mack Gray and the Rat Pack's Davis, pierced the studied nonchalance of the aging performer and almost surely contributed to his increasing reclusiveness. Martin's storied drinking, once mainly a stage prop of apple juice, escalated in earnest and he moved further into the very mystique that had made him a star. When he died on Christmas Day in 1995, Martin had long been out of the public eye.

The public remembered Martin nonetheless. As late as 2004, Capitol Records released a compilation called *Dino: The Essential Dean Martin,* which soared to number 28 on the *Billboard* 200 chart and became one of iTunes' Top Five Digital Downloads. Musician and actor Steven Van Zandt described his appeal in the liner notes for the CD, as quoted by Soeder: "Dino represented a traditional style that would prove to be timeless. . . . He was the coolest dude I'd ever seen, period." As Martin might have said, "No question about it, pally."

Periodicals

Billboard, January 6, 1996.
Broadcasting & Cable, November 8, 1999.
Entertainment Weekly, January 12, 1996.
Houston Chronicle, June 20, 2004.
Newsweek, January 8, 1996.
Observer (London, England), April 18, 2004.
People, January 8, 1996.
Plain Dealer, June 4, 2004.
Sunday Times (London, England), December 31, 1995.
Sunday Telegraph, October 31, 2004.
Time, January 8, 1996.
Times (London, England), December 27, 1995.

Online

"Dean Martin," IMDb, http://www.imdb.com/name/nm0001509/ (January 4, 2006).
"Dean Martin," NNDB, http://www.nndb.com/people/871/000023802/ (January 4, 2006). □

Karl May

Probably the best-selling German writer of all time, Karl May (1842-1912) was known around the world for his adventure novels, set in the American West and in the Middle East. He was least popular in English-speaking countries, but he remains a much-loved figure as far as Indonesia.

May's lack of renown in the United States, where many of his books were set, is not as paradoxical as it might seem. He described the world of Indians and cowboys without ever having seen any of it; indeed, he did not set foot in the U.S. until 1908, and he traveled only as far west as Niagara Falls at that time. When he visited the Arab world several years before that, he experienced disappointment that it did not much resemble the world he created in his books. May's works reflect popular attitudes in the German culture of his time, but beyond that, their success is testimony to the sheer power of imagination.

Blinded in Childhood

May (pronounced ''my'') showed imagination from a very early age, but it took many years before he learned to direct it into socially acceptable channels. The son of a weaver, he was born in central Germany, in the small town of Ernstthal near Chemnitz. The family suffered dire poverty during May's youth as the German cloth trade fell victim to competition from English factories. People in May's circle sometimes had nothing to eat but potatoes, and when he was one year old he began to suffer vision problems. He soon went completely blind, possibly a result of vitamin A deficiency. For several years May learned to interpret the world in large part through fairy tales told to him by a grandmother. May attributed his future success to his childhood blindness. ''For me there were only souls, nothing but souls,'' he was quoted as saying on the Australian Friends of Karl May website. ''And so it stayed, even after I learned to see, from my youth on until the present day. This is the difference between myself and the others. This is the key to my books.''

May's blindness was cured after his mother sought out training to become a midwife and asked the doctor who was instructing her to look at her son's eyes. He attended school for several years and was particularly entranced one day by a puppet show that came through town and performed for the families of the weavers' guild. The flip side of the imagination-centered education, which May received during his years of blindness, came when his father drilled facts and figures into him, backing up his lessons with a whip that May called Johnny the Birch. At his father's behest, May served as a drummer boy in the local militia. May was forced to memorize a 500-page geography book, an exercise that did help him learn to retain large amounts of descriptive landscape detail.

The Western tales of American writer James Fenimore Cooper were popular in German translation, and May tried

his hand at writing stories about Indians as early as 1858. The family's plan for him at this time, however, was that he would enroll in a teacher-training school in the town of Waldenburg. He received several warnings there for missing church services and was thrown out at the end of 1859, after stealing six candles to give to his still-poor family to put on their Christmas tree. After the intercession of his parish priest, he was allowed to finish classes at another school. He got a job at one school, but was fired after making a pass at the wife of his landlord. Another teaching job proved unsuccessful when May was accused of stealing a roommate's watch; though he protested his innocence, he was jailed for six weeks. The prison had a large library, and May read widely during his incarceration there.

Between 1862 and 1864 May seems to have wandered from town to town with a theater group, carrying on a relationship with a dancer for part of the time. He was imprisoned twice more, from 1865 through early 1868 and from 1870 through 1874, both times after low-grade swindles in which he impersonated a government official or other authority figure. May seemed less interested in financial gain than in respectability. When he was released from prison, he told officials that he planned to emigrate to America. He followed through with this story, eventually embellishing it with so many details that some think he came to believe it himself. But he did not leave Germany at this time; he got a job in a blacksmith's shop and set to work as a writer. Soon he had produced a historical romance, *The Rose of Ernstthal*.

Landed Editor Job

In 1875 May renewed his acquaintance with the publisher H.G. Münchmeyer and, having published *The Rose of Ernstthal*, was offered a job as an editor. The company specialized in books and magazines for Germany's newly literate lower middle classes, and May's writing hit the sweet spot for Münchmeyer. He was incredibly productive, writing stories, serialized novels, and nonfiction. Late in 1875 he introduced the figure of Winnetou, an Apache chief, for the first time in a short story. Münchmeyer, impressed, tried to build a closer professional relationship with May. His wife gave May a piano. The family rented rooms in Dresden near the newly popular author and made it known that he would be looked on favorably if he wanted to marry their daughter Minna. But May was on his way in the literary world and ignored these overtures. He left his editor job after a year and married a girl from Ernstthal, Emma Pollmer, in 1880.

Münchmeyer did not let his disappointment interfere with a chance to share in the profits from May's work, however, and the company published several of May's novels over the next decade. Some of them originally appeared in serial (or episode) form in a magazine called *Der Deutsche Hausschatz in Wort und Bild* (The German Home Treasury of Words and Images). May's first novel set in the American West was *Im fernen Westen* (In the Far West) of 1879. In the 1880s he wrote a series of enormous adventure novels (roughly 2,000-pages) that sold well and forever put an end to his need to hold a day job. The most successful of them bore the impressive title of *Das Waldröschen oder Die Verfolgung rund um die Erde: Grosser Enthüllungsroman über die Geheimnisse der menschlichen Gesellschaft* (The Little Forest Rose, or The Chase Around the World: A Great Revelatory Novel About the Secrets of Human Society).

May also began to work on two large series of novels, sometimes introducing already completed short stories where appropriate. The Fehsenfeld publishing house issued these works and bound them handsomely with illustrated covers giving a taste of the adventures contained within. For a family that might not own a large library of books, these novels were attractive household possessions. May began these two series, in 1892, under the collective title of *Gesammelte Reiseromane* (Collected Travel Novels) and added to them through the 1890s and beyond; by the time of his death the *Gesammelte Reiseromane* comprised 32 volumes, and they continued to sell well through the 20th century.

One of the two series that made up the *Gesammelte Reiseromane* consisted of novels of the American West, often featuring a German-born hero called Old Shatterhand. (The significance of the name was that the character could destroy an opponent in a fight with a single punch.) May's most successful Western novel, and the best seller among all his books, was *Winnetou, der rote Gentleman* (Winnetou, the Red Gentleman), which appeared in 1893 but was not translated into English until 1977. The novel featured a friendship between Old Shatterhand and Winnetou, a cultured Indian chief who resists the exploitation of white invaders. Unlike in American Westerns, the villains in May's books were usually white Americans; Winnetou represented a "noble savage"

figure that could undergo self-improvement by contact with European culture. In *Winnetou*, the Indian cheif refuses to disclose the location of a large gold deposit, and in a later book in the series he converts to Christianity. As for Old Shatterhand, May, at times, implied in lectures that the adventures the character experienced were actually his own. With the profits from the *Winnetou* books, May built a large rural estate that he called Villa Shatterhand. He stocked it with a large collection of Western artifacts that he showed off to visitors.

Traveled Through Islamic World

May's other major series of novels took place in the Middle East and North Africa. Like the *Winnetou* tales they featured a figure, Kara Ben Nemsi (or Karl the German) who was a potential stand-in for May himself; the novels were highly readable adventure yarns of intrigue, capture, escape, and deception. Kara Ben Nemsi had a comic sidekick, Hadschi Halef Omar. May based many of the details in these novels on what he learned from his large library of books about the Islamic world, but when the author finally traveled to some of the lands he wrote about he found the landscape had little resemblance to his imaginative constructions. May journeyed through the Middle East and went as far as Indonesia in 1900; when he returned, his outlook was altered.

Back home, May encountered problems as well. While he was traveling, his detractors launched a campaign against him in German newspapers, seizing on the some of the fantasies he promoted and pointing out that he had taken the title of Doctor without the benefit of any medical or scholarly degree. May also struggled, for much of the rest of his life, against pirated editions of his books. May's ultimately successful libel suit against the journalist Rudolf Lebius spanned several years, and his marriage broke up. His wife sided with his opponents in lawsuits and public controversies.

In 1903 May married again; his wife Klara was the widow of one of his friends. His writings in the last decade of his life represented a major shift in direction from his Western-style and Middle Eastern novels. *Ardistan und Dschinnistan* (1909) still featured Kara Ben Nemsi as hero, but depicted a fictional pair of Eastern realms, one beautiful and enlightened, the other in the grip of materialism and violence. His new books were filled with symbolism and allegory, and in lectures he began to claim that his earlier books, too, had had symbolic meanings; taken as a whole, he said, they represented the rise of humanity from primitive superstition to enlightenment. His popularity declined, but it had been so great to begin with that he found a large reservoir of readers who were willing to follow his new path.

In 1908, May visited the United States for the first and only time. He lectured to German-American groups but, perhaps mindful of his disappointments in the Middle East, he went only as far west as Buffalo and Niagara Falls. His touring lecture was entitled "Three Questions for Mankind: Who Are We? Where Do We Come From? Where Are We Going?" Around this time May began to suffer from various health problems, and doctors advised him to cancel a lecture in Vienna, Austria, entitled "Rise to the Realm of the Man of Nobility." He went anyway, and was well received by an audience that included the young Adolf Hitler (an admirer of May despite May's ardent pacifism).

May died soon after returning home to Villa Shatterhand, in Radebeul, Germany, on March 30, 1912. His novels were continually issued in new editions by an official Karl-May-Verlag (Karl May Publishing Company), and after their copyright finally expired in 1962, a host of paperback publishers reprinted the works. A century later, May's novels remained an inspiration to German children who used their imaginations and dressed up as cowboys and Indians.

Books

Dictionary of Literary Biography, Volume 129: Nineteenth-Century German Writers, 1841-1900, Gale, 1993.

Periodicals

Economist (US), May 26, 2001.
New Republic, July 14, 1986.

Online

"Karl May (1842-1912)," Books and Writers, http://www.kirjasto .sci.fi/karlmay.htm (January 24, 2006).
"Karl May—Life and Works,: Australian Friends of Karl May, http://karlmay.ziby.net (January 24, 2006).
May, Karl, *My Life and My Efforts, Volume II* (translation of *Mein Leben und Streben, Band I*), http://www.karlmay.leo.org/ kmg/sprachen/englisch/primlit/bio/lebvel/kmlae 10h.htm (January 24, 2006).
"A Short Biography of Karl May," http://www.karlmay.leo.org/ kmg/sprachen/englisch/primlit/bio/lebvel/kmlae 10h.htm (January 24, 2006). □

Nobu McCarthy

Nobu McCarthy (1934-2002) went from being one of the top models in Japan to becoming one of the most famous Asian actresses in the United States.

Whatever McCarthy put her mind to, she did with aplomb and passion, and she seemed to have a talent for attracting attention wherever she went. She arrived on the shores of the United States in the 1950s, where an agent discovered her while she was eating in a restaurant. After this encounter, her acting career took off. She started alongside Jerry Lewis in 1958's *Geisha Boy,* and then spent the next five decades playing popular and famous roles on television shows and in movies alike.

Love of Performing Developed Early On

McCarthy was born Nobu Atsumi on November 13, 1934, in Ottawa, Ontario, Canada, where her father was serving as a Japanese diplomatic attaché to Prince Tokugawa. When she was still young her family moved back to Japan and McCarthy spent most of her youth there. Her parents were Masaji, a diplomat and later fashion de-

signer, and Yuki. She was four when her parents took her to see a production of *A Midsummer Night's Dream,* and from that time forward McCarthy has said she developed a keen interest to be a performer of some sort. She affirmed her love of performing when she was still young, as she was enrolled in piano, modern dance, and voice classes by the age of six. She took to performing with a passion and it was soon discovered that she was very good at it. In fact, before she had even become a teenager McCarthy became a contract singer for King Records, performing both on the stage and for radio audiences. When she was eleven she entered the Pavlova School of Ballet in Tokyo, where she studied dance seriously for the next seven years.

Growing up in Japan was very difficult at times for young McCarthy. She grew up during and after World War II, and was picked on by her peers due to the fact that she had been born outside of Japan, and that her father could speak English. She has said that she was embarrassed over the fact that she had been born outside of Japan, and her classmates were rather merciless about it. The would call her "Mary," which was a name that was used to infer that the person being called the name was pro–Western in their thinking and belief system, something that was seen as despicable in post-War Japan. But McCarthy, rather than being kowtowed by her classmates' disparagement, was energized by it. The teasing only served to motivate the young performer, who, the more cruel her classmates became, the more determined she became to show them that she was not somebody to be taken lightly. McCarthy, in fact, has said in interviews that if there was anything that could be pointed to as an explanation for her success, it would be her peers teasing her. It acted as a catalyst that pushed her to succeed. She made a vow to herself that she would show all her tormentors one day that they were wrong about her, and that she could be a success in whatever path she chose to follow.

Became Top Japanese Fashion Model

Fortunately, besides her determination, McCarthy had very supportive parents who backed her in all she attempted to do. In fact, they encouraged her strongly to follow whatever path she felt a calling to follow, and to complete with energy and dedication whatever she started. And she did. McCarthy took her parents' words to heart as she explored the world around her to find something to do that filled her with joy. Partly because of the grace she learned as a dancer and partly because of her fierce devotion, McCarthy became Japan's leading high fashion model in the 1950s.

Her father had retired from his diplomatic career years earlier and had begun a career as a fashion designer. When McCarthy was just beginning to think about entering the industry, her father created all the clothes she modeled. McCarthy had a friend who was acquainted with a fashion editor. That friend told the editor all about McCarthy, a young, beautiful dancer who was interested in modeling and who wore clothes designed by her father, and suggested the magazine should run a story on them. The photographs and the article that the friend wrote were so impressive that the editor hired McCarthy to be a model solely for that magazine, and McCarthy's career had begun. Within a year, McCarthy had become one of Japan's leading fashion models. Even though things were financially difficult in Japan after World War II, McCarthy made enough money with her modeling that she was able to put her four brothers through school. She eventually won the title of Miss Tokyo when she entered the pageant. Things seemed primed for a lovely career and life for McCarthy in Japan.

Discovered by Talent Scout While Eating

In 1955, however, McCarthy met and married a United States Army sergeant, David McCarthy, who was stationed in Japan at that time. Her family did not want her to marry David, but McCarthy was determined, and as she had been taught to follow her dreams, so she followed them at this juncture and was wed. The couple moved to America not long after the marriage. They eventually had two children: Marlan and Serena. One day, after McCarthy had settled into life in America, she was eating at a Little Tokyo restaurant when talent scout, Fred Ishimoto, discovered her. She had turned her hand to acting while she was still living in Japan and had not really enjoyed the experience, so she did not jump at the agent's offer. Eventually, however, Ishimoto convinced her to give acting another try. Ishimoto was drawn to McCarthy because of her vibrant beauty. He felt that McCarthy would make an instant sensation in the already beauty-filled industry, and he was not wrong. McCarthy's film acting debut was in 1958's The Hunters. It was a small part, but it attracted the attention of comedian Jerry Lewis, and she was called in to try out for a larger part in his next film. The movie, Geisha Boy (1958), alongside Jerry

Lewis, was her first starring role, and it put her on the Hollywood map.

McCarthy was subsequently cast in a number of television shows and motion pictures, including a guest appearance on an episode of Perry Mason in 1959. At that time she began really studying the craft of acting so she could make herself into the best actress she could be, and her work paid off. Some of her early notable works were Wake Me When It's Over (1960), with Dick Shawn and Ernie Kovacs, and Love with the Proper Stranger (1963), alongside Steve McQueen and Natalie Wood. She very soon was acting alongside some of the United States' best actors, including Gary Cooper, Cary Grant, Fred Astaire, Sammy Davis, Jr., Marlon Brando, and Anthony Quinn, among others. The Japanese beauty queen had made just the impression on Hollywood that Ishimoto predicted, and it seemed that nothing would ever hold her back.

From Divorce to *Farewell to Manzanar*

Unfortunately, despite the numerous roles she was offered, McCarthy quickly realized that roles for Asians, especially Asian women, were limited in scope and were not exactly the plums that all actresses craved. This was one reason why she did not mourn too much when she was forced, for personal reasons, to put her acting on hold. In the late 1960s McCarthy and her husband were divorced, although she kept his name until the day she died. Dealing with the emotional repercussions of her divorce from her husband, McCarthy stopped acting. She was simply so overwhelmed and depressed that she felt incapable of doing much of anything, let alone trying to pretend to be someone else. The divorce was finalized in 1970, and by the time it was over, McCarthy was on the mend. When she finally returned to acting it was to act alongside the Los Angeles East West Players, which is the oldest Asian-American theatre in the United States. Meanwhile, in 1976, McCarthy met and married William J. Cuthbert, an attorney.

That was the same year that McCarthy co-starred in the NBC TV–movie Farewell to Manzanar. In the movie she played an old granny type character, hardly something that would seem to lend itself to an increased stardom, but it was this role, that of mother in Farewell to Manzanar, that has been considered a turning point in her career. In the movie she played a grandmother—they had to put makeup on her to age her looks. She was so good at the part, that she seemed to be typecast afterwards to always play an old granny type, even though she was still considered to be one of the most beautiful women in Hollywood. This was not something that upset her, however. After Farewell to Manzanar, McCarthy has said that she was offered more honest, human roles, rather than the stereotypical Asian ones she had been offered previously. And the actress reveled in the opportunities.

Artistic Director of Los Angeles Theatre Center

While she continued her acting career, McCarthy also taught acting at California State University in Los Angeles from 1982 to 1987. From 1991 she expanded her teaching arena to encompass other universities, including the University of California, at Los Angeles. In 1986 McCarthy took on the stage in a production of *As the Crow Flies* at the Los Angeles Theatre Center. Then in 1988 McCarthy received critical attention for her leading role in the play *The Wash*.

In 1989 she became artistic director for the Los Angeles East West Players, a position she held until 1993. She had originally turned down the position, but she eventually agreed because she decided she would like to help other Asian-American actors get their feet in the door. The group was going through problems at the time and was deteriorating, but McCarthy breathed fresh air into it. "This former starlet reinvigorated the theatre by expanding the board, increasing fundraising and opening up the institution to a more diverse multiethnic constituency. The stability she established made possible a smooth transition in 1993 to [the next] artistic director Tim Dang, one of many young talents she had mentored," according to *American Theatre*. One of the main things she did was take the small theatre group and turn it into a full-fledged training facility, including the Professional Actors' Training Program and the David Hwang Writers' Institute.

Done with her role as director in 1993, McCarthy returned full time to acting. She was very successful for a decade until April 6, 2002, when she died of an aortal aneurysm during filming in Londrina, Brazil. *American Theatre* said, "Hers was a spirit so free that, I have no doubt, it continues to flourish someplace today—still growing and taking on new challenges, looking at life with that same mischievous smile." She won, among other honors, the Los Angeles Drama–logue Award.

Books

Contemporary Theatre, Film and Television, Volume 42, Gale Group, 2002.
Notable Asian Americans, Gale Research, 1995.

Periodicals

American Theatre, September 2002.

Online

"Nobu McCarthy," Internet Movie Database, http://www.imdb .com (January 6, 2006). □

Ismail Merchant

Producer Ismail Merchant (1936-2005) and director James Ivory created magnificent films that were largely the result of Merchant's financial wizardry. "Mention Merchant Ivory, and the mind begins to wallow in visions of Edwardian elegance," noted *The Economist*. Throughout their 40-year partnership, Merchant contributed greatly to the independent filmmakers' world.

With a string of successful film adaptations of classic novels in the 1980s and 1990s, Merchant Ivory became renowned for classy, impeccably detailed productions that captured the lives of the English and American upper classes of a bygone era. They also focused on Merchant's home country of India, a place that fascinated the American Ivory as well. The partnership of Merchant and Ivory, which lasted for more than 40 years, was listed in the Guinness Book of World Records as the longest collaboration in film history. It was often Merchant's energy and his mastery of the production process that kept the partnership going.

A Multicultural Childhood

Born Ismail Noor Mohammed Abdul Rehman on December 25, 1936, in Bombay (now Mumbai) in British-occupied India, Merchant was the son of a prosperous seller of textiles. As a child he spoke both the local Gujarati language and Urdu, the Islamic variant of Hindi that his family used at home. To these languages he soon added Arabic and English, learned at St. Xavier, a Jesuit-run school in Bombay, where his parents enrolled him in search of a top-quality education. Merchant's father was a member of the Muslim League, which promoted the creation of an independent state in what would become predominantly Islamic Pakistan. Many of Merchant's own friends were Hindus, however, and even his father declined to move to Pakistan later on. The "butchery and riots" (as he was quoted as saying in England's *Daily Telegraph*) that followed the partition of India and

Pakistan in 1947 occurred when Merchant was 11 and left a lasting impact on him.

Merchant first got a taste of his own persuasive powers when he addressed a Muslim political rally, while still a student, but politics were not his main interest. Fascinated by movies, he hoped to become an actor, and he got an initial break when he met and was befriended by the single-named Indian actress Nimmi. She steered Merchant toward several modeling jobs, and for his entire life he would be known as a sharp, fashionable dresser. His film career began with roles as extras in several Indian productions.

His real genius from the start, though, lay in the area of production work. He began organizing variety shows at St. Xavier, sometimes staging them in the school's main quad-rangle as fundraisers for the institution. Merchant's family exhorted him to focus on his studies in political science and English literature, but he began to spend more and more time on theatrical productions. Soon he was in business for himself, financing theatrical shows by selling advertising space in the printed program. "I'd get two beautiful girls, and we would go round in a big car to various companies," he was quoted as saying in the *Daily Telegraph*. "Out of hundreds of doors you knocked on, maybe 20 would buy space."

These shows put money into Merchant's own pocket as well as St. Xavier's coffers, and by the time he graduated in 1958 he had saved enough money to move to New York and enroll in a master of business administration program at New York University in the United States. He soaked up film after film in the rich cinema atmosphere of New York, learning for the first time about the works of the great Bengali Indian director Satyajit Ray. To make ends meet, he worked as a messenger at the United Nations building. Already looking toward his film career, he buttonholed Indian dignitaries, who were visiting the United States, and asked them to finance his new production company. Again, he was successful in spite of his youth and his unknown status. After a stint as an account executive at an advertising agency he moved to Hollywood, confidently sending out a press release in advance of his arrival stating that a top Indian producer was coming to town. He made a short film called *The Creation of Woman*, booked it into theaters at his own expense in advance of the Academy Award deadline, and scored a nomination in the lightly contested category. He also entered the short at the Cannes Film Festival in 1961.

Co-Founded Merchant Ivory Productions

At Cannes, Merchant met a young American director, James Ivory, who was screening a documentary about India, *The Sword and the Flute*. He was impressed by Ivory's knowledge of India, and the conversation that they struck up was to be the beginning of a lifelong partnership. By 1962 they had set up a production company, Merchant Ivory Productions. The partnership was personal in addition to professional; the *Daily Telegraph* quoted him as saying that "Our lives are knitted together, and our films are knitted together." In later years the two men shared a vacation home in upstate New York and lived in different apartments in the same building in New York City.

Living in yet another apartment in that building was novelist and screenwriter Ruth Prawer Jhabvala, a woman of German background who had married an Indian man. In 1963 she had furnished the screenplay for the first Merchant Ivory release, *The Householder*, and from then on she was a key member of their creative team. Some of her screenplays were adapted from novels of her own. Part of Merchant Ivory's success was due to their having found an accomplished writer who could realize their aim of creating intelligent films set in India for Western audiences. Early Merchant Ivory films such as *Shakespeare Wallah* (1965), the story of an English theatrical troupe that slowly loses its audience as independence comes to India, gained an international viewership.

The successful launch of Merchant Ivory was not due exclusively to creative factors, however. They were able to set the company up on a firm financial footing. Merchant identified a source of unused funds—American film company profits that had been nationalized by India's left-leaning government of the 1960s and were essentially lying unused. It was the first, but by no means the last, example of creative funding to ferment in the brain of Merchant, leading *Forbes* writer Richard C. Morais to speculate that "maybe Merchant Ivory itself deserves to be nominated as the best-run film company in the word."

Merchant's film finance exploits were legendary. His formula rested on equal parts cost control and tireless hounding of potential investors. As Merchant and Ivory established their reputations, top actors willingly took pay cuts in order to participate in their high-quality productions. Large catering bills were not part of the expense picture for Merchant, who would often entertain a film's cast and crew with curry parties and eventually published several Indian cookbooks of his own. He and Ivory sometimes wrangled as Merchant held his partner to a strict production schedule, appearing on the set to recite an insistent refrain of "Shoot, Jim, Shoot." As for investors, he told Morais that "you have to bully them." An unsuccessful example came when he banged on the door of cosmetics executive Estee Lauder but was not admitted.

Influenced by *Masterpiece Theater*

The Merchant Ivory films from the first part of the duo's career continued to be set in India, and they continued to focus on India with major films such as *Autobiography of a Princess* (1975) and *Heat and Dust* (1983). Their work remained only moderately successful financially, however, until they hit on the idea of dramatizing famous English and American novels. They began thinking along these lines after noting the success of the television series *Masterpiece Theater*. Their first film of this type was a 1979 film of Henry James's novel *The Europeans*, starring Lee Remick as a young woman climbing her way through Boston's layers of high society. That was also their first film made in the U.S., and its success was once again a team effort; Ivory had a keen eye for the rituals and details of aristocratic life; Jhabvala proved an extremely effective translator of complex novels to the big screen; and Merchant found inexpensive alternatives to building large numbers of period sets, such as leaning on friends who owned country estates and persuading them to allow filming there. The result was a set of films with modest budgets (typically two or three million dollars) that looked like big-budget costume extravaganzas.

Merchant and Ivory returned with another Henry James adaptation, *The Bostonians,* in 1984, and when it grossed $8 million on costs of $2.8 million Merchant's financial profile grew higher. In advance of the 1986 Merchant Ivory film *A Room with a View,* an adaptation of a novel by E.M. Forster, Merchant forecast gross receipts of $50 million, which would give his investors a 200 percent return on their money. As it turned out, the film grossed $60 million and became an international success. It was nominated for eight Academy Awards and won three.

Several more major successes in the same vein followed, including *Mr. and Mrs. Bridge* (1990), another Forster adaptation, *Howard's End,* in 1992, and *The Remains of the Day,* from a novel by Kazuo Ishiguro about a taciturn but inwardly passionate butler (played by Anthony Hopkins). Their success bred a certain degree of backlash as some detractors (according to Tom Vallance of the *Independent*) characterized their output as "the Laura Ashley school of film-making." Merchant directed several films of his own in the 1990s, returning to Indian subjects. His 1993 film *In Custody* was made in the Urdu language, and *Cotton Mary* (1999) told the story of a domestic worker of Indian background in the 1950s. His 2001 film *The Mystic Masseur* was adapted from a book by Indo-Trinidadian-British novelist V.S. Naipaul. He also produced films by directors other than Ivory.

Merchant received the Padma Bhusan, India's equivalent of knighthood, in 2002, and became an honorary fellow of the British Academy of Film and Television Arts the following year. He and Ivory remained active as a partnership, releasing *The Golden Bowl* in 2000, and *Le divorce,* starring Glenn Close, in 2003. In 2005 they had two projects in process: *The Goddess,* a musical about Shakti, a figure in the Hindu pantheon, and *The White Countess,* which was set in China. After a grueling filming schedule there, he returned to England in poor health and died on May 25, 2005, after complications from ulcer surgery. "He had endless passion," *Howard's End* star Helena Bonham Carter told Missy Schwartz of *Entertainment Weekly,* "and made films because he believed in beauty."

Books

International Dictionary of Films and Filmmakers, Volume 4: Writers and Production Artists, 4th ed., St. James, 2000.

Periodicals

Economist (US), February 29, 1992.
Daily Mail (London, England), June 3, 2005.
Daily Telegraph (London, England), May 26, 2005.
Entertainment Weekly, June 10, 2005.
Forbes, March 23, 1987.
Guardian (London, England), June 3, 2005.
Independent (London, England), May 27, 2005.
Interview, May 2002.
New Statesman, August 15, 1997. □

Charles Mingus

American jazz musician Charles Mingus (1922-1979) is regarded by many as one of the best double bass players of the genre. He became equally well known for his prowess as a composer, and he has received ever-growing recognition since his early death in 1979 at the age of 56. Mingus's volatile, at times violent, personality, led to numerous high-profile disagreements with fellow musicians and critics and a reputation as "jazz's angry man," but also fueled a music known for its passion and spiritual depth.

Mingus was born on April 22, 1922, in Nogales, Arizona, where his father, Sgt. Charles Mingus Sr., served on a U.S. army base. Soon after the birth of his son, Sgt. Mingus received an honorable discharge from the military in order to care for his ailing wife. The family relocated to the Watts section of Los Angeles, California, where Mingus's mother, Harriet Sophia Mingus, sought medical treatment for chronic myocarditis. She died, however, on October 3, 1922. The Mingus family remained in Los Angeles, and young Charles and his sisters, Grace and Vivian, were raised by Charles Sr. and his new wife, Mamie. The emotional call-and-response spirituals performed in the neighborhood Holiness Church served as one of Mingus's earliest musical influences. Although the Mingus children were only permitted to listen to devotional music under the elder Mingus's authoritarian house rules, Mingus secretly listened to pianist/composer Duke Ellington's "East St. Louis Toddle-Oo" on the earphones of a crystal set, sparking his interest in jazz.

Self-Taught Musician

Mingus, whose sisters trained on violin and piano, started out playing the trombone. When his instructor proved less than able, Mingus taught himself the basics of the instrument by ear. He grew frustrated, however, and soon switched to the cello, earning a spot in the Los Angeles Junior Philharmonic while still in elementary school. In high school he switched again, to the double bass, and joined future jazz greats Dexter Gordon, a saxophonist, and Chico Hamilton, a drummer, in an orchestra. He began studying his new instrument privately with jazz musicians Joe Comfort and Red Callender, as well as Herman Rheinschagen, a former bassist with the New York Philharmonic. Mingus also studied composition with Lloyd Reese and turned out two compositions, "What Love" (1939) and "Half-Mast Inhibitions" (1940), that he would record 20 years later.

Mingus began playing professionally with jazz outfits in Los Angeles and San Francisco while still in high school. In 1940 he replaced his former teacher, Callender, in a band headed by Lee Young, a drummer and brother of noted saxophonist Lester Young. The following year, Mingus joined trumpeter Louis Armstrong's group, where he remained until 1943 and, under the name "Baron Mingus,"

compositions: "If Charlie Parker Were a Gunslinger There'd Be a Whole Lot of Dead Copycats."

Moved East

Mingus relocated to New York City in 1951 and began working with many of the best known jazz musicians of the day, including Parker, trumpeter Dizzy Gillespie, drummer Art Tatum, and pianist Bud Powell. He also joined Ellington's band. There, the violent temper that would come to partially define Mingus led to his being one of the few musicians Ellington ever fired; during an altercation with a bandmate, trombonist Juan Tizol, he brandished a fire ax. Tizol defended himself with a machete. Fueling Mingus's hot temper was long-simmering anger about the treatment of African Americans; Mingus once explained that the fight with Tizol was prompted by Tizol's use of a racial epithet. "Charles was a man who wanted peace and his best person was kindly and wise. But he wasn't always able to access that," observed tuba player and former Mingus bandmate Howard Johnson in a 2002 retrospective in *Down Beat*. "He was stung by racism a little harder than others. If you're black, every day on the street you encounter slights. Some people can toss them off as the behavior of racist idiots. But Charles couldn't let the slights roll off him. He accumulated them all."

Mingus's intolerance of racism and disdain for the record industry, which he strongly believed treated African-American jazz musicians unfairly, led to the 1952 formation of Debut Records, a collaboration with drummer Max Roach and Mingus's second wife, Celia. He returned to work at the post office that year as well. In 1953 Mingus began participating in the highly regarded Jazz Composers Workshop, but in 1955 he formed his own workshop with a rotating cadre of musicians. The new workshop enabled Mingus to exercise his own unique compositional style, which eschewed traditional notation and was characterized by saxophonist Yusef Lateef in Brian Priestley's *Mingus: A Critical Biography*: "For example, on one composition I had a solo and, as opposed to having chord symbols for me to improvise against, he had drawn a picture of a coffin, and that was the substance upon which I was to improvise." Mingus also often dictated lines individually to each player. Several highly regarded albums grew out of these workshops, including 1956's *Pithecanthropus Erectus*, *Blues and Roots*, *Mingus Dynasty*, and *Mingus Ah Um*, all released in 1959. The latter includes the composition "Good Bye, Pork Pie Hat," a tribute to Lester Young, who died while the album was being recorded. Mingus employed politically charged commentary with the composition "Fables of Faubus," a reference to the governor of Arkansas who called in the National Guard to fight public school integration.

While his talent was highly regarded, Mingus also became known for his bitterness and volatility. He routinely chastised musicians on stage, damaged musical equipment (including once dropping and shattering his own $2,000 bass), and launched into at least one long, legendary harangue against his audiences. "If my band is loud in spots, ugly in spots, it's also beautiful in spots, soft in spots. There are even moments of silence. But the moments of beautiful

began leading outfits of his own. In the mid-1940s he began playing with vibraphonist Lionel Hampton and began to draw attention for his impossibly fast, highly charged solos. Critics would later note, as recounted by John Rockwell in a 1979 *New York Times* obituary, that Mingus's tendency to play slightly ahead of the beat lent his playing a "frenetic rhythmic tension." Mingus dropped music to take a job with the U.S. Postal Service for a period, and then returned to music in 1950, joining vibraphonist Red Norvo's trio. This ensemble has been credited with introducing West Coast "cool jazz" to a broad audience.

While playing on the West Coast, Mingus discovered the music of saxophonist Charlie "Bird" Parker, which influenced him tremendously. "I studied Bird's creative vein with the same passion and understanding with which I'd studied the scores of my favorite classical composers, because I found a purity in his music that until then I had only found in classical music," Mingus wrote in the notes to the 1959 album *Mingus Dynasty* (as reprinted in Gene Santoro's 2000 biography *Myself When I Am Real*). "Bird was the cause of my realization that jazz improvisation, as well as jazz composition, is the equal of classical music if the performer is a creative person. Bird brought melodic development to a new point in jazz. . . . But he also brought to music a primitive, mystic supra-mind communication that I'd only heard in the late Beethoven quartets, and even more, in Stravinsky." *Mingus Dynasty* featured the Parker tribute "Gunslinging Bird," the full title of which reveals the sly humor Mingus often employed when naming his own silence are hidden by your clanking glasses and your too wonderful conversations,'' he declared from the stage of New York's Five Spot one night, as recounted by Priestley. ''You haven't been told before that you're phonies. You're here because jazz has publicity, jazz is popular, the word jazz, and you like to associate yourself with this sort of thing, but it doesn't make you a connoisseur of the art because you follow it around. You're dilettantes of style.'' Other times, Mingus made his points more subtly. Another night at the Five Spot, he simply played a phonograph on stage while the band members played cards. When passed over by taxi drivers, presumably because of his race, he was known to set up a chair in the middle of the street and begin reading the newspaper.

Mingus began one of his most significant musical collaborations in 1959, when reed player Eric Dolphy first joined his ensemble. While all of Mingus's musicians were at times subjected to their bandleader's outbursts, Mingus demonstrated a particular respect for Dolphy. When Dolphy left the band in 1964 in order to spend time in Europe, Mingus developed a composition titled, alternately, ''Farewell Eric Dolphy'' or ''So Long Eric.'' After the reed player died suddenly on June 29 of that year, Mingus named a son (with third wife, Judy) Eric Dolphy Mingus. A year earlier, Mingus had released his debut album on Impulse!, *The Black Saint and the Sinner Lady*. Always bucking tradition, Mingus had his psychoanalyst write the liner notes, telling him, according to Santoro, ''I never pay you so at least this way you can make $200.''

Overcame Obstacles

By the mid-1960s, increasingly plagued by psychological problems, Mingus was finding regular employment harder to secure. In 1966 he was forcibly evicted from his apartment for failure to pay rent. This sad event was captured by a documentary crew for the film *Mingus*. By 1970 Mingus elected to go into semi-retirement with financial assistance from his ex-wife Celia and her new husband, Saul Zaentz. Zaentz had purchased the Fantasy Record label, as well as the now-defunct Debut's back catalog. During this period, Mingus took comfort in his neighbors. ''For about three years, I thought I was finished,'' he told Nat Hentoff in a 1972 *New York Times* interview. ''In that neighborhood, they didn't know me from the man in the moon, but they took an interest in me. I'd go into a bar, sit by myself, and I'd hear someone say, 'There's something wrong with this guy. He doesn't come out of his house for four or five days at a time.' And they'd invite me to join them. I got to know what friends are.''

Mingus began to re-emerge in the late 1960s, and in 1971 he once again drew widespread attention with the publication of his autobiography, *Beneath the Underdog*. That same year, he was awarded a prestigious Guggenheim fellowship in composition. He became a part-time instructor at the State University of New York in Buffalo and was commissioned to write film scores. Choreographer Alvin Ailey debuted a work with the Joffrey Ballet featuring new arrangements of Mingus's music. Mingus released the Columbia album *Let My Children Hear Music* in 1972. In 1975,

the same year he released the albums *Changes One* and *Changes Two*, Mingus married longtime on-again, off-again partner Sue Graham Ungaro. Sadly, Mingus's second round in the spotlight was short-lived. In 1977 he was diagnosed with amyotrophic lateral sclerosis, also known as Lou Gehrig's disease. He continued to compose, dictating into a tape recorder when he could no longer work with his hands, and collaborated on a recasting of his compositions with folk singer Joni Mitchell for her album *Mingus*. He attended an all-star jazz concert at the White House in 1978, where he was honored with a standing ovation and a hug from President Jimmy Carter, which brought him to tears.

Mingus died in Cuernavaca, Mexico, where he had gone to seek alternative treatments for his illness, on January 5, 1979. In accordance with his wishes, Sue Mingus scattered his ashes in the River Ganges in India. Mingus's music lives on through two musical groups organized by Sue Mingus, Mingus Dynasty and the Mingus Big Band. Even before his untimely death, Mingus's many collaborators began reflecting on his influence. ''Mingus is not little stuff,'' observed trumpeter John Handy, a veteran of Mingus's workshops. ''He's big stuff musically. He is definitely, in the true sense, a giant and maybe even a genius. He has all the qualities.'' Mingus summed up the force behind his talent, in an open letter to Miles Davis published in *Down Beat* in 1989. ''My music is alive and it's about the living and the dead, about good and evil. It's angry, yet it's real because it *knows* it's angry.''

Books

Priestley, Brian, *Mingus: A Critical Biography*, Quartet Books Ltd., 1982.
Santoro, Gene, *Myself When I Am Real*, Oxford University Press, 2000.

Periodicals

Down Beat, December 7, 1978; September 1989; April 2002.
New York Times, January 30, 1972; January 9, 1979.

Online

''Charles Mingus,'' *Biography Resource Center Online*, Gale Group, 2006, http://galenet.galegroups.com/servlet/BioRC. □

Liza Minnelli

Liza Minnelli (born 1946), actress, singer and entertainer, came from a show business family to achieve success on her own merits. She is one of few entertainers to have won at least one Oscar, Tony, Grammy and Emmy Award. Although she is often identified with her tabloid-ready battles with drugs, alcohol, and stormy love matches, Minnelli stands as one of the most respected entertainers of the last half of the twentieth century.

A Child of Fame

Minnelli was born March 12, 1946, in Los Angeles, California, to famed actress Judy Garland and her second husband, film director Vincente Minnelli. A part of the entertainment world from birth, Minnelli made her film debut in a 1949 Garland picture, *In the Good Old Summertime.* Due to her mother's moodiness and increasing dependence on alcohol and pills, Minnelli developed a close relationship with her father, even as a toddler; when Garland and Vincente Minnelli divorced in early 1951, the custody agreement placed five-year-old Liza with each parent for part of the year. As Wendy Leigh notes in *Liza: Born a Star,* "although [Garland and Minnelli] were divorcing one another, they definitely were not divorcing Liza."

Minnelli idolized her father and was in return, by his own admission, spoiled by him "outrageously." Garland's relationship with her daughter, although loving, was not as close; she remarried in 1952, to producer Sidney Luft, and was often caught up in her own substance abuse and mental problems. As a child, Minnelli dealt with her mother's repeated suicide threats and attempts, as well as her increasing alcohol and drug problems. Vincente Minnelli's two remarriages and the birth of another Minnelli daughter caused Liza Minnelli a great deal of jealousy; however, she remained a committed "daddy's girl."

Began a Career

Adolescence brought Minnelli's first genuine forays into performing. She discovered acting during her brief attendance at New York's High School of the Performing Arts, followed by a stint working in summer stock productions. Minnelli did not graduate from high school and never completed any kind of formal education; instead, she moved to New York City in early 1963 to make her way as a stage actress. Her first show, *Best Foot Forward,* debuted on April 2, 1963. After a brief illness, Minnelli accepted a touring role with *Carnival* and several months later appeared in *The Fantastics.*

Minnelli released her first album, *Liza! Liza!,* in 1964. Later that year, she shared the stage of the London Palladium with her mother. After the show, Minnelli met a protégé of Garland's named Peter Allen; within weeks, the two were engaged. Minnelli landed the lead role in the Broadway musical *Flora, the Red Menace,* in early 1965. Although the show itself received mixed reviews, Minnelli was a great success, becoming the youngest performer to win a Tony Award for Best Actress in a Musical for her performance. After her Broadway show closed, Minnelli set out in September 1965 on a nightclub tour.

In late 1966, Minnelli traveled to Manchester, England to shoot her first film, *Charlie Bubbles.* By March 1967, she had returned to New York City where she married Peter Allen in a private ceremony. The following year brought Minnelli a starring role in Alan J. Pakula's film *The Sterile Cuckoo.* The film's 1969 release garnered Minnelli good reviews from critics and an Oscar nomination. For all the success of the year, however, Minnelli also experienced personal losses: her mother, Judy Garland, died on June 22, 1969, from an accidental overdose of barbiturates; and her marriage steadily weakened, culminating in a formal separation in April 1970.

Award-Winning Performances

In 1971, Minnelli traveled to Berlin to film the role of Sally Bowles in Bob Fosse's film-version of the musical *Cabaret.* Released in February 1972, the highly successful movie cemented Minnelli's reputation as a performer; indeed, Leigh comments that "just as Judy [Garland] had reached the pinnacle far too soon with The Wizard of Oz, so it would transpire, did Liza with *Cabaret.*" Later that year, Minnelli taped a television special called *Liza with a Z.* Both *Cabaret* and *Liza with a Z* garnered Minnelli honors; *Cabaret,* a Best Actress Academy Award as well as a Golden Globe Award; and *Liza with a Z,* an Emmy Award. However, despite professional successes, Minnelli's personal life remained tumultuous. Her divorce from Peter Allen became final in 1972. By this time, Minnelli had been publicly connected to several high-profile men, most notably Desi Arnaz, Jr., to whom she was engaged for some time, and British actor Peter Sellers.

In early 1974, Minnelli returned to Broadway with the opening of her one-women show, *Liza at the Winter Garden.* Although the show had only a three-week run, it was quite successful and won Minnelli her second Tony award. Later that year, Minnelli met Jack Haley, Jr.—the son of the actor who had played the Tin Man in *The Wizard of Oz*—while narrating part of Haley's documentary film, *That's Entertainment*. In September of that year, the two wed in Los Angeles. After their honeymoon, Minnelli resumed her hectic work schedule. Spring 1975 found her in Mexico for the filming of the comedy *Lucky Lady*. In late summer, Minnelli returned to New York City for five weeks to fill the role of Roxie Hart in the Broadway musical *Chicago*. By the end of the year, Minnelli was back in Europe, this time working with her director father on what would be his final film, *A Matter of Time*. Both *Lucky Lady* and *A Matter of Time* were critical and commercial failures.

Personal Turmoil in Public

Minnelli continued to work steadily, however. In 1976, she filmed the Martin Scorsese musical *New York, New York,* starring opposite Robert DeNiro. By the time the film was released, the press had latched onto the rumors of cocaine use on the set, helping to dampen the already lukewarm reception for the movie. Scorsese and Minnelli continued to work together despite the relative failure of *New York, New York,* with Scorsese directing Minnelli in his first-ever stage production, *The Act*. Although never a great critical success, *The Act* ran for several months in New York City (October 1977-July 1978) and won Minnelli her third and final Tony Award.

Minnelli's personal battle with illegal drugs continued, particularly as she became a regular at famed New York City disco Studio 54. Along with close friend and fashion designer Halston, Minnelli frequented the club nearly every night. During this time, Minnelli continued to perform nightly while staying out until dawn at Studio 54 or other nightclubs. This lifestyle took its toll on her health, causing Minnelli to miss increasing numbers of performances in early 1978 as well as take weeks off from the show to recuperate from a viral infection. In February 1978 Minnelli and husband Jack Haley, Jr., officially separated, although they did not divorce until December of that year.

The Act closed in July 1978 and Minnelli went back on the road; with her as stage manager went Mark Gero, the man who would become Minnelli's third husband. Her tour was immensely successful, foreshadowing a critical and commercial hit at New York City's Carnegie Hall the following September, *Liza in Concert*. In December 1979, Minnelli and Gero married; less than a week after the wedding, Minnelli suffered a miscarriage. After her recovery, she resumed working steadily, returning to television with a 1980 special, *Goldie and Liza Together,* which featured comedienne Goldie Hawn. Leigh noted that at this time Minnelli's "heart was still set on achieving cinematic success and reliving her *Cabaret* glory days." To further this goal, she accepted a role in the comedy *Arthur*. By summer 1981, another album, *Liza in Concert,* had been released to critical acclaim and *Arthur* was proving to be Minnelli's first film success in nearly a decade.

Rehabilitation and Reconciliation

Through the early 1980's, Minnelli continued to tour and perform around the world. Her hectic, party-fueled lifestyle had calmed down, although rumors regarding heavy drug use and marital infidelity continued to plague her. In 1984, she performed in the Broadway musical *The Rink,* a drama that garnered Minnelli another Tony nomination. However, Minnelli's personal life was again on the rocks. Minnelli and Gero had separated and in July 1984 she checked herself into the Betty Ford Clinic, for seven weeks, hoping to break herself of her dependency on drugs and alcohol. In early 1985, Minnelli checked into the Hazelden Clinic in Minnesota, another facility treating chemical dependencies. However, she was well enough to embark on another concert tour by summer. Also in 1985, Minnelli found time to film the television movie *A Time to Live;* this performance won her a Golden Globe Award. The following winter Minnelli returned to England for a tour, accompanied by her now-reconciled husband.

Personal tragedy struck again for Minnelli when Vincente Minnelli died on July 25, 1985. Still close to her father, Minnelli was severely shaken by his death; however, she did not return to drugs or alcohol. She spent the next several months working on her marriage and arranging tributes to her father. In early 1987, Minnelli went to Rome to film another movie with Burt Reynolds, *Rent a Cop*. That May, she opened a three-week engagement at Carnegie Hall, the longest continuous engagement by a solo performer in the Carnegie's history. The performances were captured in an album, *Liza at Carnegie Hall,* released in September.

Rent a Cop was released to disappointing reviews in January 1988; Minnelli, however, found success in the spring with a television drama called *Sam Found Out: A Triple Play*. A sequel to *Arthur* opened in summer 1988 to mixed reviews. That fall, Minnelli set out on the road with Sammy Davis, Jr., and Frank Sinatra, in what was dubbed the Rat Pack Tour. While the tour was visiting London in April 1989, Minnelli met with pop group the Pet Shop Boys and recorded a dance version of Stephen Sondheim's "Losing My Mind." This unlikely pairing made for a hit record, Minnelli's first pop success, charting on the Billboard dance charts.

Minnelli continued a steady stream of work, entertaining audiences across America, and in 1990 she received the Grammy Legend Award; completing her collection of major entertainment honors. By the end of the year, however, Minnelli's marriage had again faltered. She and Gero again separated, this time for good. In April 1991, Minnelli debuted a new show at Radio City Music Hall that was so successful that she took it on an extensive American tour. Toward the end of 1991, Minnelli premiered a new film, *Stepping Out,* which received very little attention and was shown in only a few theaters.

Returned to the Spotlight

Throughout the 1990s Minnelli continued to appear on stage and screen. Minnelli filled in for Julie Andrews in the 1997 revival of musical *Victor/Victoria,* as well as appearing in many television specials including Broadway revival *The West Side Waltz*. In 1999, Minnelli developed a one-woman Broadway tribute to her father, *Minnelli on Minnelli,* a great success. Otherwise, however, during the late 1990s, Minnelli was primarily out of the limelight battling health problems. In 1997, Minnelli had hip replacement surgery; she would undergo the surgery again in 2001. She additionally had a knee replacement and a dangerous bout with viral encephalitis in 2000.

In March 2002, Minnelli returned to the spotlight with her marriage to producer David Gest. Later that year, Gest helped orchestrate Minnelli's stage comeback and follow-up album, *Liza's Back!* However, the remarkably rocky union served as tabloid fodder and ended in separation after only 16 months. After their separation, Gest famously claimed Minnelli had beaten him, although the charges were later dropped. In 2003, Minnelli began a recurring guest role on critically acclaimed comedy series *Arrested Development,* her most public role in several years. In December 2005, Minnelli filmed an episode of the respected television show *Inside the Actor's Studio.* Nearly 60 years old—and with no signs of giving up performing—Minnelli seems assured a place in entertainment history far beyond that of being simply Judy Garland's daughter.

Books

Carrick, Peter, *Liza Minnelli,* Ulverscroft, 1993.
Leigh, Wendy, *Liza: Born a Star,* Dutton, 1993.

Online

"CNN Larry King Weekend: Interview with Liza Minnelli, April 4, 2002," http://www.transcripts.cnn.com (December 22, 2005).
"Liza Minnelli," CMG Worldwide, http://www.cmgworldwide.com/stars/Minnelli/biography.htm (December 23, 2005).
Reeder, Sheryl S., "IMDb Mini Biography for Liza Minnelli," http://www.imdb.com/name/nm0591485/bio (December 22, 2005). □

Carmen Miranda

At the peak of her career, Brazilian singer Carmen Miranda (1909-1955) was the highest paid woman in Hollywood. Known for her colorful outfits and fruit-bedecked headgear, Miranda was one of the first ambassadors of Latin American popular culture. She appeared in more than a dozen movies, often alongside the era's top stars, but was usually typecast as the exotic songstress in the plots. "Many of her compatriots never forgave her for the pastiche of mischief and malaprops that became not only Miranda's trademark Hollywood act but also synonymous with Latin America itself," Mac Margolis wrote in *Newsweek International.*

Miranda was born in Portugal in February of 1909, and christened Maria do Carmo Miranda da Cunha. Her parents, Jose and Maria, left the town of Marco de Canaveses, near Oporto, when she was

still an infant; they settled in Brazil, home to many Portuguese immigrants. They lived in central Rio de Janeiro and her father worked as a salesperson and a barber. The nickname "Carmen" dated to Miranda's childhood, when her family reportedly dubbed her that after the Georges Bizet opera by that name.

Sang for Co-Workers

Miranda was raised in a strict Roman Catholic household. Nuns schooled her at the Santa Teresinha convent academy for girls, but her education ended at age 14, when she had to take a job to help support her family. She worked in a Rio department store as a model and millinery saleswoman, and during her breaks she often performed popular Brazilian hit songs to entertain co-workers. When a guitarist overheard one of her impromptu performances, he invited her to sing with him on a local radio show. Soon Miranda was offered a nightclub singing job, but her conservative father strongly opposed the opportunity at first. Reportedly, he changed his mind when he learned of the generous offer and agreed to let her perform, provided he serve as her manager and she not be billed under her family name. Thus, she became "Carmen Miranda."

Miranda recorded a few albums with composer and violinist Josue de Barros, but these failed to catch on with Brazilian listeners. Her breakthrough came in 1930, when she made "Prá Você Gostar de Mim," a traditional Brazilian *marcha* tune by composer Joubert de Carvalho. The record was a massive hit, propelling Miranda to a string of top-sellers that turned her into one of her country's biggest stars of the 1930s. While not a particularly gifted vocalist, her style was appealing, and she was sometimes billed as "The Singer With The 'It' On Her Voice."

The movie *A voz do carnaval,* a musical comedy made in Brazil and released in 1933, marked Miranda's big-screen debut. She made several more films, in between a heavy touring schedule that took her across South America several times. She was usually backed by her own five-man band, called Banda da Luna (Band of the Moon). During one of her shows at a casino in the Rio district of Urca, well-known American theater manager Lee Shubert spotted her and offered her a role on Broadway.

Succeeded on Broadway

Miranda arrived in New York in 1939 to perform one song in *The Streets of Paris,* a musical review at the Broadhurst Theater that ran from June of 1939 until the following February. She sang it in Portuguese, and spoke very little English when she came to New York, but she was game enough to give an interview to promote the show. Her limited vocabulary became a long-running joke in that and subsequent stories in the press about her. She enthusiastically repeated a few words, including "yes," "no," "money," and "hot dog." Though her treatment in the press seemed to reinforce stereotypes about Latin Americans, Miranda's *Streets of Paris* number was a hit with audiences, and led to an engagement at the Waldorf-Astoria hotel. She also made her first film for a Hollywood studio, the musical romance *Down Argentine Way,* starring Don Ameche and Betty Grable. Miranda was cast as herself in the 1940 release, which was one of the first musicals filmed entirely on location, in both Buenos Aires and New York, due to her still appearing nightly in *The Streets of Paris.*

Miranda returned to Brazil after the Broadway show closed, but found she was viewed as a traitor. Brazilians asserted she had turned their beloved culture into a joke, and she was ridiculed in the press for selling out. Riots erupted when *Down Argentine Way* was released in Buenos Aires for its depiction of Argentine customs. Her response was the song "*Disseram Que Eu Voltei Americanizada*" (They Say I've Become Americanized), which did little to help her land new performances. Hoping to continue her career, she returned to the United States when the Hollywood powerhouse studio 20th Century Fox offered her an exclusive contract.

Miranda was promoted as the "Brazilian Bombshell" by 20th Century Fox and she began appearing in its films as a featured performer. Some were set in South America, and sometimes representatives from the film division of the Office of the Coordinator of Inter-American Affairs, a government agency that worked to promote U.S. foreign policy initiatives, offered suggestions on the script or other aspects. The interference was linked to the "Good Neighbor Policy," which had been in effect since the mid-1930s. U.S. President Franklin D. Roosevelt sought to forge better diplomatic relations with Brazil and other South American nations, and pledged to refrain from further military intervention, which had sometimes been done to protect U.S. business interests in industries such as mining or agriculture. Hollywood was asked to help out with the Good Neighbor Policy, and both Walt Disney Studios and 20th Century Fox participated. Miranda was considered the goodwill ambassador and promoter of intercontinental culture.

Inspired Fashion Trends

Miranda became a household name in the United States, thanks to her films and singing engagements. She sang in Portuguese, often accompanied by frenzied gesturing that was widely caricatured as a hallmark of the exotic Latina songstress. She had brought from Brazil her trademark look, which was known as *bahiana* in her country. The term was taken from Bahia, Brazil, home to many African-Brazilians, and was characterized by many layers of bright fabrics, often with ruffles or rick-rack, along with a turban-style hat. Miranda's look usually featured a long skirt, midriff-baring halter, lots of jewelry, and headgear topped by flowers or fruit. The elaborate banana headdress became her Hollywood trademark, and soon more subdued styles of hats embellished with fake fruit were turning up in millinery collections in department stores. The singer also received credit for starting a trend for platform shoes, which she wore because she was just five feet, three inches tall.

In 1943, Miranda appeared in an extravaganza from noted director Busby Berkeley called *The Gang's All Here.* Berkeley's musicals were known for their lavish production, and Miranda's role as Dorita featured her number "The Lady in the Tutti-Frutti Hat." An optical trick from the set behind her made the fruit-bedecked hat she was wearing appear even larger than humanly possible. By then, Miranda seemed to be locked into such roles as the exotic songstress, and her studio contract even forced her to appear at events in her trademark film costumes, which grew even more outlandish. One song she recorded, "Bananas Is My Business" seemed to pay somewhat ironic tribute to her typecasting.

Miranda became the highest-paid female performer in the United States during World War II. She sang regularly at New York's Copacabana nightclub, where her turban even became part of its logo. She led a subdued personal life, befitting her conservative Roman Catholic background, and did not marry until age 38. Her marriage to David Sebastian, a minor Hollywood producer, was said to have been problematic. Some reports hint that Sebastian was physically abusive, and conspired with the studios to check any ambitions of hers to move beyond her "Brazilian Bombshell" persona. Only once was she ever cast as the romantic lead in a movie, which came in 1947 with *Copacabana.* She played opposite comedian Groucho Marx, and had a dual role as a spicy Latina performer and blonde French cabaret singer.

Fondly Remembered

Miranda's final film appearance came in 1953 with *Scared Stiff,* which starred the comedy duo Dean Martin and Jerry Lewis. Her stage persona had deteriorated by then, with Lewis grotesquely mimicking her style in one scene in the film. By this time, she was a frequent guest on variety shows that were broadcast on a new medium, television.

Her last performance came on one early series, *The Jimmy Durante Show,* in August of 1955. After she finished her song, the show's host came out to applaud her, and Miranda appeared to come close to fainting, but Durante quickly moved to catch her. She smiled, waved, and exited the soundstage, but she died the following day at her home in Beverly Hills, California. Her death was officially reported as a heart attack, but it was later revealed that the 44-year-old star was pregnant, and died of pre-eclampsia, a pregnancy-related condition characterized by high blood pressure and kidney malfunction.

The Brazilian government sent a plane to California to retrieve Miranda's coffin, and a crowd estimated at well above half a million lined the streets of Rio de Janeiro when her funeral cortege made its way to São João Batista cemetery. For a later generation, Miranda was viewed as a contemptible example of Hispanic stereotyping in American popular culture. The subject was explored in a 1995 documentary *Carmen Miranda: Bananas is My Business,* made by Brazilian filmmaker Helena Solberg. A decade later, Miranda's posthumous reputation seemed to have undergone rehabilitation, with several events taking place in 2005 that marked the fiftieth anniversary of her death. These included a film and costume retrospective, "Carmen Miranda Forever," at Rio's Museum of Modern Art, and a serious biography written by Ruy Castro, author of several books on Brazilian culture. Brazilians "tend to forget," Castro told Margolis in *Newsweek International,* that "no Brazilian woman has ever been as popular as Carmen Miranda—in Brazil or anywhere."

Books

Dictionary of American Biography, Supplement 5: *1951-1955,* American Council of Learned Societies, 1977.
International Dictionary of Films and Filmmakers, Volume 3: *Actors and Actresses,* 4th edition, St. James Press, 2000.

Periodicals

Americas, January-February 1996.
Newsweek International, January 23, 2006.

Online

"Brazilian Bombshell," Palma Louca, http://palmalouca.com/0,,0,33,00.html (January 20, 2006). □

Frederic Mompou

The music of Catalonian-Spanish composer Frederic Mompou (1893-1987) is radically simple, spare, mystical, and utterly unclassifiable as to style—all this in a century that favored intellectual feats on the part of composers who classified themselves into schools and "isms." The work he regarded as a summation of his life's efforts was given the quizzical title *Música callada*— (music that has fallen silent).

The restraint of Mompou's music was matched by the composer's near-total refusal to engage in self-promotion. Mompou's music, mostly for piano or voice and piano, at first attracted only a small, highly devoted following. Wider audiences began to discover his works toward the end of the twentieth century, when the Minimalist movement of composers such as Steve Reich and Philip Glass heralded a new spirit of extreme simplicity in classical music, and a new emphasis on the experience of hearing musical raw materials stripped down to their basic forms. John Rockwell of the *New York Times,* in fact, wrote in Mompou's obituary that the composer was "an early Minimalist, [who] sought to achieve deep emotional effects through the sparest of musical means."

Family Background Included Bell Maker

Mompou's full name was Frederic Mompou i Dencausse. He was born on April 16, 1893, in Barcelona, Spain. Barcelona is in Spain's Catalonia region, a culturally distinctive area with its own language, Catalan (a blend of Spanish and an old southern French dialect), and a range of indigenous folk music traditions that differ from those heard elsewhere in Spain. Music critic Wilfrid Mellers suggested that Mompou was influenced by these regional traditions. He wrote in the study *Le Jardin retrouvé: The Music of Frederic Mompou,* "Even today, when we listen to or play one of the piano pieces he calls *Cançó i dansa* [Song and Dance] we should remember that they are not mere parlor pieces but recollections of activity that is also ritual." Mompou used both the Catalan (Frederic) and Spanish

(Federico) forms of his first name. His last name is generally pronounced as in French (mom-POOH), but Mompou told an interviewer that in Catalonia it would properly be pronounced mom-POH-oo, with all the vowels sounding.

Another major influence on Mompou's creation of his magically simple sound was bells. His maternal grandfather was a member of a French bell-making family that had been in the profession since the 1400s; he had come to Barcelona to set up a bell factory. Mompou himself spent time at the factory, worked there briefly, and learned to tune his ear to the subtle sounds of bells. A unique harmony in his music, known as the metallic chord, was derived from the sound of ringing bells.

Mompou was close to his parents, and they encouraged his interest in music. Friends and extended family often came to the Mompou home to sing and dance, and Mompou was given lessons after he showed talent on the piano. He attended the Conservatorio del Liceo music school in Barcelona and made rapid progress, giving his first concert at age 15. But the severely shy Mompou never really enjoyed performing. He quickly changed direction after hearing pianist Marguerite Long, with the great French composer Gabriel Fauré in attendance, play a concert of Fauré's music the following year. The concert was, he told Dorle J. Soria of *Musical America,* his first encounter "with contemporary music of my time and it gave me a great desire to compose." His first published work was a set of piano pieces called *Impresiones intimas* (Intimate Impressions), written between 1911 and 1914. "It already had his personality," Mompou's wife, Carmen, told Soria, and music historians have agreed, finding the characteristic simple, almost naive quality of Mompou's adult music already present in the early *Impresiones intimas.*

Like most of the other young Spanish composers of his day, Mompou decided to study music in Paris, where French composers had written nationalistic Spanish music before Spanish composers themselves began to do so. He arrived at the Paris Conservatory in 1911 with a letter of recommendation written by the leading Spanish composer Enrique Granados, but, typically, was too shy to show it to the admissions committee. Nevertheless, his music stood on its own merits, and he studied piano and harmony at the Conservatory for two years. Remaining in Paris until 1914, he returned home when World War I broke out and became involved in a Catalonian arts movement called Noucentisme, which rejected the confrontational spirit of the avant-garde and emphasized a return to classical values of balance.

Influenced by French Composers

Mompou had the knack of absorbing influences from various composers while writing music that was quite dissimilar to theirs. Despite his shyness he interacted with other musicians and became acquainted with the leading edge of French music of the early twentieth century. He admired the iconic composers of Paris during the years of World War I, and took something from each of them. Like Claude Debussy, he eschewed any strong sense of directional motion in music, preferring to paint musical colors on an almost static background. Like Maurice Ravel, he was fascinated by the world of childhood and the musical creativity that seemed to reside near its surface; he had a gift for melodies that seemed unassuming, but haunted listeners, who responded to his unique language. From the unconventional, ironic Erik Satie he inherited a belief that radical simplicity had its place, and he showed the same tendency to go his own way rather than follow the prevailing musical fashion. The harmonic stasis of Mompou's music was matched by an absence of strong rhythmic drive; he frequently wrote his music without bar lines separating one rhythmic unit from another.

Stimulated by the Parisian scene, Mompou returned to Paris in 1921 and remained there for 20 years. The period from World War I through about 1930 was Mompou's most productive, and he published such piano works as *Suburbis* (Suburbs, 1917), *Scènes d'enfants* (Scenes of Children, 1918), the *Cants màgics* (Magic Songs, 1919), and the first four of his *Cançós i dansas* (Songs and Dances, 1928), along with the beginnings of a small but influential group of French-language songs. His *Comptines* of 1931 were songs based on children's number rhymes. Mompou's lifetime output was slender, amounting to about 200 mostly short pieces collected into a few dozen sets. In the highly competitive and polemical Paris atmosphere, Mompou rarely gave concerts, although he liked to perform for small groups of artists and writers. He lived alone and stayed out of the headlines. Yet a select group of observers were captivated by his music. Critic Emile Vuillermoz wrote of Mompou, in a famous newspaper article quoted by Soria, that "in the Middle Ages the people would have condemned to the stake an artist gifted with such powers." The argument was an apt one, for Mompou aimed not just at simplicity but at what he called a *recommencement,* a new beginning that would put music back in touch with its aboriginal power. Mompou was a friend to the French composers Francis Poulenc and Georges Auric, but declined to join the composers' collective *Les Six* (The Six), of which they were members.

The 1930s were a melancholic period for Mompou and he stopped composing almost completely between about 1931 and 1937. He reemerged in 1937 with a piano work called *Souvenirs d'exposition* (Souvenirs of the Fair) and began working on another piece, *Variations on a theme of Chopin,* that would occupy him for many years. In 1941 Mompou fled the war in France and returned to Barcelona. While judging a piano competition there he was impressed by the performance of a young woman named Carmen Bravo, 30 years his junior. Several years later they married, each for the first time. Mompou joined with a group called the Independent Catalan Composers Movement and reconnected with his musical roots, while still maintaining contact with friends in France.

With these stimuli working in his favor, Mompou began to compose again, continuing to work until he was slowed by a stroke at age 87. In the post-World War II era, dominated by the complex serialist or 12-tone system and its harsh dissonances, Mompou was completely out of fashion—and completely unconcerned. "I am in revolt against the excessive cerebration of our age," he was quoted as saying by Soria. "Music must cease to be a laboratory product and acquire the lyrical and evocative qualities which spring from personal experience and meditation."

Wrote Vocal Works

Mompou branched out beyond piano music after World War II, writing a number of Catalonian-language songs and pairing them with texts by poet Josep Janées i Olive. These included the widely recorded *Suite compostelana* (Compostela Suite) for guitar (1962), and various works for chorus, including the *Cantar del alma* (Song of the Soul) to a text by the Spanish mystic and ascetic, St. John of the Cross (1542-1591). Mompou was fascinated by St. John of the Cross and borrowed a phrase from one of his writings for the title of the major work of his later years, *Música callada.*

The 28 pieces in *Música callada* (four albums, 1959-67), never move faster than a moderate tempo; in free rhythms, they are unassuming yet strangely powerful. This music, Mompou was quoted as saying by Isabelle Leymarie in the *UNESCO Courier,* "is heard internally. Its emotion is secret, and becomes sound only by reverberating in the coldness of our solitude." The work, completed in 1967, was premiered in 1972 by Spanish pianist Alicia de Larrocha, to whom it was dedicated. A host of recordings of the work appeared in the late 1990s and early 2000s.

Mompou wrote an oratorio—an unstaged dramatic work—called *Los improperios* (The Ungrateful Ones) in 1963; although it was his only work to feature a full symphony orchestra, it showed no lack of skill in handling that medium. The text of the work dealt with the Good Friday speech of the crucified Christ rebuking the crowd for its ingratitude, and Mompou set it in a spare style comparable to that of his piano music. Well into his ninth decade Mompou wrote more choral music and a work for cello and piano, *El pont.* Admirers of Mompou expanded the collection of his works by arranging some of his piano music into two ballets, *The House of Birds* and *Don Perlimpin.* Mompou died at age 94 on June 30, 1987, and his popularity only increased following his death.

Books

Mellers, Wilfrid, *Le Jardin Retrouvé: The Music of Frederic Mompou,* Fairfax, 1987.
Sadie, Stanley, ed., *The New Grove Dictionary of Music and Musicians,* 2nd ed., Macmillan, 2001.

Periodicals

High Fidelity/Musical America, November 1978.
New York Times, July 1, 1987.
Times (London, England), July 3, 1987.
UNESCO Courier, November 1996.

Online

"Federico Mompou," *All Music Guide,* http://www.allmusic .com (February 8, 2006).
"Federico Mompou: Biographical Notes," *ACT Music,* http://www.actmusic.com/mompou_e.htm (February 8, 2006). □

Meredith Monk

Since the 1960s, American performing artist Meredith Monk (born 1942) has earned renown as a composer, singer, dancer, choreographer, filmmaker and critic. Although trained originally as a dancer, she pioneered the multi-textured extended vocal technique and her vocal compositions and performances are known for their emphasis on sounds, syllables and invented language. Monk has received numerous prestigious awards, including a McArthur Foundation "genius" grant. In 2004, the Danspace Project and the House Foundation for the Arts honored Monk's 40-year career at St. Mark's Church in New York.

Monk was born on November 20, 1942, in Lima, Peru, to Theodore Glenn Monk and Audrey Zellman. Her mother, a pop singer who performed as Audrey Marsh and was a vocalist in radio commercials for Muriel cigars, was performing in Peru when she was born. Monk was raised in New York until age seven and then in Stamford, Connecticut. The family's musical talent covers several generations. Monk's great–grandfather was a cantor in a Moscow synagogue and her grandparents founded the Zellman Conservatory of Music in Harlem. Monk was exposed to music and dance at an early age. She began piano lessons at age three with a teacher who shunned traditional lessons and instead introduced her to such composers as Dmitry Kabalevsky, Igor Stravinsky and Bela Bartok. "Much of my early childhood was spent in radio control rooms, watching and listening to my mother sing jingles for soap operas, or ballads and swing tunes for radio variety shows," Monk recalled in a 1999 essay for the *New York Times.* "I remember hot summer nights, sitting in the corner of a huge studio while men in undershirts sweated as they played their saxes, violins and trombones, and the singers, with their backs to me, crooned the same eight bars over and over before the actual recording session."

To improve her daughter's physical coordination, which was hindered by a visual problem, Monk's mother enrolled her in Delcroze eurhythmic classes. The courses, which taught movement through music, profoundly affected Monk. "Usually, what happens is, kids learn music through movement, dancing, and catching balls in rhythm," Monk told Gus Solomons, Jr., in a 2001 interview for *Dance Magazine.* "Most people were learning music through movement, but I was learning movement through music. Movement and music are so unified for me." Monk began studying ballet at age eight and composing piano pieces while still in high school. She attended Sarah Lawrence College, near New York City, where she continued her classical dance studies and also studied modern dance with Bessie Schoenberg. Courses in music for dance with Ruth Lloyd greatly influenced her.

Paired Dance and Voice

Upon graduating from Sarah Lawrence with a degree in dance in 1964, Monk joined New York's Judson Church group, a well-known downtown avant-garde ensemble. She eventually developed a three-octave range and pioneered a vocal approach called "extended vocal technique," which incorporates overtone, throat singing, yodeling, keening, percussive sounds and micro-tonality. "[I] had a revelation around 1965 of singing—doing my own singing—that idea of exploring my own instrument: seeing all the things it could do, stretching the range, combining male and female within a voice, and so forth," Monk told Solomon. "By applying what I had come from in dance to my voice, I found I had a much more virtuosic instrument as a singer." Two of Monk's best-known pieces composed for the Judson Church ensemble, both from 1966, are "Duet with Cat's Scream and Locomotive," a collaboration with Kenneth King, and "16-Millimeter Earrings." Both are interdisciplinary pieces emphasizing communication themes. "Duet," based on the interactions between a man and a woman, employed the sounds of a roaring engine and a howling cat, while "Earrings" used props, film and a recording of Monk's own voice repeating the word "nota."

Monk founded her own company, The House, which emphasized interdisciplinary works, in 1968, and the Meredith Monk Dance Ensemble as well as a second group, Vocal Ensemble, 10 years later. During this time, she became known both for her defiance of easy categorization and her nontraditional approach to performance. "I think of myself as a verb, not a noun," Monk told the *Chicago Tribune*'s Sid Smith in 1996. "I compose. I do movement. I deliver text. And, depending on the form I'm working in, I orchestrate. Another way to put it is I make a mosaic. I lay down tiles and make an overall configuration from those strands." Monk's performances typically focused less on technical skill than on raw energy and creativity, which riled some audiences and critics. "We're purposely not doing a virtuosi kind of movement. It's more primal, not striving for that Western European tradition of line in space and geometry. It's more an axial idea of the body," she told Solomon. "When we did 'The Politics of Quiet' [1996] the first time in Copenhagen, people really hated the folk dance; they said, 'Some of these people are not dancers!' To me, the way they did the movement was so authentic! The idea of a folk dance is that everyone in the village can do it."

Rock and roll music largely influenced her approach to composition and performance, Monk said in her 1999 *New York Times* essay. "Rock-and-roll was also a strong presence for me and for many other composers at that time, reminding us to go back to the heartbeat, raw energy, blood, fearlessness, thrust," she wrote. "I was very much alone in those early experiments, trying to make my voice a conduit for the raw, essential vocal impulses that I was exploring and then shaping into pieces. Yet I was encouraged by my jazz and rock musician friends, who recognized in those first relentless songs the beginnings of an authentic musical sensibility."

Unconventional Performances

Monk also staged her pieces unusually. For example, "Juice: A Theatre Cantata," a 1969 piece, was staged in installments, beginning with a woman riding a horse down Fifth Avenue in New York, followed by 85 singers playing Jew's harps along the Guggenheim Museum's spiraling ramps and performances in front of paintings by Roy Lichtenstein. A second installment took place three weeks later in a theater on the campus of Barnard College and a third installment in Monk's loft. A 1971 piece, "Vessel: An Opera Epic," which sets the story of Joan of Arc in modern-day New York, began in Monk's loft, then took performers by bus to The Performing Garage performance space and concluded in a parking garage. Autobiographical elements entered Monk's work as well. One early piece, "Education of the Girlchild," featured Monk transforming from an old woman back into a small child. The 1976 opera "Quarry," contained childhood memories and referred to Monk's Polish and Russian Jewish ancestors.

By the late 1970s, Monk had begun to incorporate film into her work. "Ellis Island," the film sequence to the 1979 opera "Recent Ruins," which depicted archeologists of the future excavating New York, appeared on its own on the Public Broadcasting System in the United States as well as on European television. The film won a CINE Golden Eagle in 1982. Monk also created a feature-length film, *Book of Days,* in 1989, that was set in the fourteenth century, using that period in time as a metaphor for the modern world.

In 1985, Monk began practicing Shambhala meditation, which is associated with Tibetan Buddhism. The ritual has impacted both her approach to composition and her interactions with performers. In a 1998 interview with Gia Kourlas for *Dance Magazine,* Monk explained that she hoped her compositions and performances, too, were spiritual journeys. "It's a quest of trying to offer another kind of experience for people who are bombarded and who live in a world that has a lot of speed," she said. "In a sense, it's thinking of time as timelessness rather than being a mirror of the particular society that we live in. I realized that when you offer a mirror, people go home and don't have anything to work with because, in a sense, we all know what the problem is. What would happen if you showed a different kind of behavior, or if you offered a place for people to relax that part of their minds, to come out feeling a sense of revitalization and awakeness? I think, in both voice and movement, that you really can experience a depth of emotional experience. That you might want to demand more in your life."

Appreciated as an Artist

In 1991, the Houston Grand Opera commissioned a full-length piece from Monk. Employing wordless syllables in lieu of almost any text, *Atlas* centers on a small girl who grows up to become an explorer. In fairy-tale style, the girl visits farming communities, forests, a wilderness filled with icy demons, a desert and a joyful spiritual realm. The opera concludes with the explorer sitting at a table sipping a cup of coffee.

Amid a frenzied modern pace, Monk has continued to strive for a more relaxed, transformative tenor to her work. "Every piece is a journey into the unknown," she told Deirdre Mulrooney of the *Irish Times* in 2001. "I think that's really important in our world, because everybody wants to know what something is going to be before it's done. The business world people want to know how long is it going to be, what's the name of it, and what's your tech requirement two years in advance." Monk said she sees her job as resisting such demands. "What is really beautiful about making art is not giving in to that at all," she told Mulrooney. "And sometimes in that process, making it incredibly uncomfortable by allowing yourself to hang out in the unknown. And you really don't know. You have some clues and you keep following them; it's a very intuitive thing. Discovery is what, to me, makes everything worthwhile—as opposed to being a product-maker."

In response to this impetus, Monk created her 1999 touring work, "A Celebration Service." The piece served as a retrospective of sorts on Monk's long career, incorporating both old and new material, along with a range of spoken texts. Monk told the *Christian Science Monitor*'s Karen Campbell in 1999 that the piece was, in part, a reaction to the frantic pace of contemporary culture. "I had been wondering how to make a form that offers a sense of sacred space. The community, the communion experience is still very valuable. I think it's nice to offer people a space in time where they can let go of the discursive yakety-yak that's going on in the mind all the time," she said.

Monk celebrated her 40th year as a professional artist in 2004. That year, the Danspace Project and the House Foundation for the Arts staged a weekend-long anniversary festival and tribute to her work at St. Mark's Church and Monk performed a four-and-a-half hour concert at Carnegie Hall featuring several well known contemporary avant-garde artists, including DJ Spooky, John Zorn, the Bang on a Can All-Stars and Björk. Several years earlier, Kourlas explained Monk's enduring appeal, in her 1998 *Dance Magazine* article. "[S]he has carved out a unique, brilliant style of wordless singing that treats the voice as a dancing voice and movement as a singing body," Kourlas wrote. "Her voice has all the character, texture, sensuality, and color of her movement."

Periodicals

Christian Science Monitor, May 14, 1999.
Dance Magazine, July 2001.
Houston Chronicle, October 6, 1985.
Irish Times (Dublin), October 25, 2001.
New York Times, October 31, 1999.

Online

"Meredith (Jane) Monk," *Biography Resource Center Online,* Gale Group, 2005, http://galenet.galegroups.com/servlet/BioRC (December 13, 2005).
"Merdith (Jane) Monk," *Grove Music Online,* http://www.grovemusic.com (December 13, 2005). □

Robert Moog

As the inventor of the Moog synthesizer, Robert Moog (1934-2005) brought electronic sound synthesis out of university electronics laboratories and into the wider world of music. The all-pervasive presence of keyboard electronics in contemporary popular music is ultimately the result, in large part, of his pioneering efforts.

Attempts to use electronic devices to create new sounds go back to the early years of the twentieth century. Yet a synthesizer that was financially and operationally within reach of ordinary musicians was unthinkable, until the Moog synthesizer—the first commercially available, voltage-controlled, modular synthesizer—came on the market in 1964. Innovative musicians began to experiment with it almost immediately, and its commercial potential was dramatically demonstrated with the release of the million-selling *Switched-On Bach* album in 1968. The Moog and its descendant, the MiniMoog, were staples of the progressive rock movement of the 1970s. Although these Moog synthesizers were supplanted by later synthesizers that developed further along the lines Moog had originally laid down, electronic musicians of every stripe hailed Moog as a pioneer, and the sound of the original Moog became one of the first flavors of nostalgia to arise in the field of electronic music.

Inspired by Theremin

Moog (the name rhymes with "rogue") was born on May 23, 1934, a native of the Flushing neighborhood in the New York City borough of Queens. Something of a class geek, he was often tormented by schoolmates, but things improved for him as his radio-operator father cultivated his love for electronics and his mother enhanced his knowledge of music with piano lessons. Moog built radios from kits he ordered by mail, but what attracted him to the then-minuscule field of electronic music was his discovery of the theremin, an electronic instrument developed in the 1920s by Russian experimenter Leon Theremin (and later used in the Beach Boys' "Good Vibrations"). The player of a theremin moves his or her hands near a loop that generates an electromagnetic field; the body of the instrument is never touched. Moog read about the theremin in *Electronics World* magazine when he was 14, and he was fascinated enough by the magazine's simple instructions for building the instrument that he quickly came up with an improved design of his own and described it in an article that was published in *Radio and Television News*. Working with his father, he formed the R.A. Moog Company and began to sell theremin kits by mail himself.

"I didn't know what . . . I was doing," he said in an interview quoted by David Bernstein in the *New York Times.* "I was doing this thing to have a good time, then all of a sudden someone's saying to me, 'I'll take one of those and two of that.' That's how I got into business." Winning admission to the Bronx High School of Science, one of New York's premier citywide magnet high schools, Moog went on to Queens College, where he majored in physics, and then to the electrical engineering program at Columbia University. His educational career began to slow down as his business picked up; in 1961 he developed a transistorized version of the theremin, wrote another article that was used as the cover story in *Electronics World,* and sold another 1,000 theremin kits (for $49.95 each) out of his three-bedroom apartment. Another step in Moog's electronic music apprenticeship came when he designed a circuit board used in the Clavivox, an early synthesizer designed by inventor Raymond Scott.

By the time Moog enrolled in the Ph.D. program in engineering at Cornell University in Ithaca, New York, he came into contact with the Ivy League university labs that at the time were on the cutting edge of experimentation with electronic music, especially those at Columbia and Princeton universities. These labs had built synthesizers that would do much of what the Moog synthesizer would later be capable of, and the RCA Corporation had even marketed a commercial version of the instrument, but there were important differences. They were unwieldy stacks of electronic components and wires, controlled mostly by dials or computer punch cards that initiated sequences of binary code. And RCA's synthesizer cost upwards of $100,000. Attending the New York State School Music Convention in 1963, Moog met composer Herbert Deutsch, who suggested the possibilities of a simplified synthesizer design. By the middle of the following year Moog was ready with a prototype that he displayed at the Audio Engineering Society's annual convention, and the new Moog synthesizer went into production by the end of 1964.

The Moog, as it came to be known, cost around $10,000. Despite the reservations of Princeton lab director Vladimir Ussachevsky, who told Moog that his decision would result in the synthesizer being used simply as an unusual-sounding piano—as it was controlled by a piano-style keyboard—it still consisted of a large group of electronic components. Those components were now distinct, modular units that could be connected with patch cords to create a desired sound. Several of those components were new inventions. An ADSR (attack-decay-sustain-release) envelope generator allowed the player to control the sound of a note as it began and developed. The ADSR became a standard feature of synthesizer design. The final device used to control the color and texture of a tone was a filter; Moog's improved version became known as a Moog filter.

Affected Both Pop and Classical Musicians

Musicians on both sides of the classical/pop divide began to work with Moog's new invention. The Monkees may have been the first rock group to use the Moog (on their *Pisces, Aquarius, Capricorn and Jones Ltd.* album of 1967, with Paul Beaver playing the Moog). Moog worked with experimentalist John Cage, and university electronics labs became customers of Moog's growing company, to which he devoted his full attention after receiving his Ph.D. from Cornell in 1965. Another classical musician interested in the Moog was Wendy Carlos (at that time named Walter Carlos), who conceived the idea of recording an all-Moog album of famous pieces by Johann Sebastian Bach. It was an ambitious undertaking, for the Moog, unlike later synthesizers, was monophonic—it could produce only one line of music at a time. Carlos laboriously recorded and mixed Bach's complex polyphonic music line by line and released *Switched-On Bach* in 1968.

That was the first solo Moog LP, and it marked a moment of triumph for the instrument's creator. It sold more than one million copies, a record for a classical album at the time, and it led to a short-lived Moog synthesizer craze. Some of the music that followed in its wake was serious in its intent; Carlos was signed to create a Moog score for Stanley Kubrick's dark, futuristic film *A Clockwork Orange,* and the Beatles (working partly from an instrument George Harrison had installed in his home) used the Moog on several tracks on their *Abbey Road* album. In 1969 novelty ragtime pianist Dick Hyman released *Moog: The Eclectic Electrics of Dick Hyman,* and jazz musicians soon followed suit; a Sun Ra concert recorded in Paris in 1970 (and released on the album *Nuits de la Fondation Naeght*) included a 20-minute Moog solo. Technology-savvy keyboardist Herbie Hancock was another early Moog adopter. Moog complained about the disposable quality of many of the early Moog records, however. "A few still stand up," he said in a *Vintage Synthesizers* interview quoted in the London *Independent.* "But mostly they were cynical, inept, opportunistic things: throw together a group, lay down some strings and horns and vocals, leave some space for a novelty melody line from the synth. That was the scene in '69. 'Moog records.' "

The Moog moved from novelty to a permanent part of the rock musical vocabulary with Moog's next invention, the MiniMoog, which first went on sale in 1970. Much more portable than the original Moog, it could easily be used in concert, and it became a favorite of electronics-oriented progressive rock bands of the 1970s such as Pink Floyd, Yes, Tangerine Dream, and Emerson, Lake and Palmer (whose *Tarkus* LP pushed the instrument's capabilities to their limits). Yet the MiniMoog's popularity was not restricted to rock musicians. The instrument showed up on one of the most ambitious R&B hits of the era, Stevie Wonder's "Living for the City" (1973), and on other songs on the *Innervisions* album of which it was a part. And the German collective Kraftwerk, whose work helped give birth to the new techno genre, used a Moog on its early releases. Later, a MicroMoog would become the last extension of the original Moog line.

Innervisions also contained an Arp synthesizer, one of the instruments that sounded the death knell for Moog's original company. The Arp had a 40 percent share of the synthesizer market by 1975, and a host of synthesizers issued by Japanese manufacturers were developed along the lines laid down by Moog. The Moog was eclipsed partly because its creator did not have the financial expertise to steer his company through periods of slow sales. He sold off his creation in stages, first to a suburban Buffalo, New York company called muSonics and then to the Norlin Corporation in 1973. The company, known now as Moog Music, continued to operate, and the Moog experienced a temporary

resurgence in popularity when it was featured on Donna Summer's 1977 disco single "I Feel Love." Moog himself worked for the company through the 1970s but departed in 1977, as soon as his contractual obligations allowed.

Worked with MacArthur Foundation Grant Recipient

Moog had a lifelong affection for the Blue Ridge mountain range, and he moved to a home near Asheville, North Carolina, after leaving Moog Music. He founded a new company, Big Briar, taught electronic music at the University of North Carolina at Asheville, and worked on projects that interested him. These included a new refinement of the theremin he called an Ethervox and an effects module, the Moogerfooger. He worked with composer and MacArthur Foundation "genius grant" recipient John Eaton on a touch-sensitive electronic keyboard that could be played expressively, like a mechanical musical instrument. Moog served as vice president for new product research for the Kurzweil Corporation, an American synthesizer manufacturer, between 1984 and 1988. He married twice; his marriage to his first wife, Shirleigh, produced five children but ended in divorce, and he met his second wife, Ileana, while both were professors at UNC Asheville.

Various factors led to a new appreciation of Moog's legacy over the last decade of his life. In 1994 he appeared in a successful documentary about his idol, Leon Theremin. Original Moog synthesizers became collector's items and commanded premium prices from musicians anxious to exploit a sound they perceived as warm compared with later digital synthesizers. "I understand exactly why that is so," Moog commented in an interview reproduced by Jeff Miers of the *Buffalo News.* "It is so because dirty, imprecise sound is more complex, and therefore more interesting to listen to." Between 2000 and 2002 Moog prevailed in a court battle to regain rights to the Moog name, which he had lost in the 1970s; by that time a new generation of musicians and bands, including Beck, Sonic Youth, and Widespread Panic, were Moog customers. A "Moogfest" staged in New York City paid tribute to his influence, but the following year he was diagnosed with an untreatable brain tumor. He died in Asheville on August 21, 2005.

Books

Contemporary Musicians, volume 46, Gale, 2004.

Periodicals

Billboard, February 15, 1992.
Buffalo News, August 23, 2005; August 26, 2005.
Daily Telegraph (London, England), August 23, 2005.
Guardian (London, England), August 25, 2005.
Independent (London, England), August 24, 2005.
New York Times, September 29, 2004; August 23, 2005.
Remix, August 1, 2002.
U.S. News & World Report, March 3, 1997.
Variety, August 29, 2005.

Online

Official Moog Music website, http://www.moogmusic.com (December 28, 2005). □

Vinicius de Moraes

Brazilian writer Vinicius de Moraes (1913-1980) helped to create two of the icons of twentieth-century culture, the play *Orfeu da Conceição,* which became known in English as *Black Orpheus* after it was made into an internationally successful film, and the song "Garota de Ipanema," better known as "The Girl from Ipanema."

Those two works formed only a small fraction of what Moraes accomplished. He wrote poetry for specialists and popular songs for the Brazilian people. A complete list of his occupations would also include diplomat, film critic, film censor, screenwriter, singer and recording artist, advice columnist, radio host, non-practicing lawyer, and general nonconformist with a taste for good whiskey. Moraes was always seeking something new, and that tendency helped make him a great crossover artist who fused Western and African cultural ideas in *Black Orpheus* and brought subtle Brazilian music to the top of the international charts with "The Girl from Ipanema."

Named after Character in Novel

Moraes—in full, Marcus Vinicius da Cruz de Mello Moraes—was born in Rio de Janeiro, Brazil, on October 19, 1913, to well-off parents who named him after a character in the Henryk Sienkiewicz novel *Quo Vadis?,* which was set in ancient Roman times. His father liked to recite poetry at family gatherings, and his mother sang and played the guitar. Moraes wrote his first poem at seven, was sent to some of Brazil's top schools, and earned a law degree by the time he was 20, also entering Brazil's army reserve. Moraes devoted little or no time to the practice of law, however, for he was devoting his energy to artistic pursuits.

Moraes and a pair of brothers named Paulo and Haroldo Tapajós (or Tapajóz) were friends in childhood, and formed a small musical group at the Colégio Santo Inácio school. When the two brothers began to gain national fame in Brazil as teenage recording stars, Moraes continued to work with them, writing songs in popular dance genres like the foxtrot. At age 15, Moraes had his first two hits as a songwriter with a pair of compositions called "Loura ou morena" (Blonde and Brunette) and "Canç da noite" (Song of the Night). He was also fascinated by trends in modern poetry. As he was finishing his law degree he published his first book of poetry, *O caminho para a distância* (A Road into the Distance), following it up with the sophisticated *Forma e exegese* (Forms and Interpretations) in 1935. Moraes spent several years working in Brazil's film industry. In 1938 he won a scholarship to study at Oxford University in England, and also wrote several volumes of difficult poetry, some of it in a mix of Portuguese and English.

The following year Moraes married his first wife, Beatriz. He was married several times, in official and unofficial ceremonies (later in life he was an adherent of an Afro-Brazilian variant of Catholicism), and he had four daughters.

(The last, Maria, was born in 1970.) Forced to return to Brazil at the outbreak of World War II, Moraes wrote film criticism and worked as a film censor for the government. Though it was rather late in the game to be taking such a position, he penned articles condemning sound film and extolling the virtues of silent cinema. He also was heard for a time on the Portuguese-language shortwave radio service of the British Broadcasting Company. Moraes joined Brazil's diplomatic corps in 1943. At this point in his life he still shared his family's conservative political outlook and was ready to become a servant of Brazil's government and its interests. He was even sympathetic to fascism in the early stages of World War II.

Traveled Around Brazil

All that changed after Moraes met American leftist writer Waldo Frank in 1945. He was sent to provide safe passage around Brazil for Frank, who had been physically attacked by fascists in Argentina, and Moraes told Selden Rodman of *Saturday Review* that as the two traveled around the country, "I saw crime and sexual degradation and poverty for the first time. Within 30 days I was no longer a boy, no longer a citizen of the upper middle class, prepared by the priesthood to be a good rightist. I swung full circle." For the rest of his life Moraes was a defender of Brazil's sometimes troubled democracy and an advocate for social justice.

Further broadening of his horizons occurred when he was posted to Los Angeles, California, as Brazilian vice-consul in 1946. He spent three years in the United States, taking in jazz and Hollywood cinema and passing time with celebrities like director Orson Welles and actress Rita Hayworth. Moraes backed off his opposition to sound film, explaining, according to Kirsten Weinoldt of *Brazzil* magazine, that "I was and continue to be, not a cinematographic mute, as many think, just a little bit of a stutterer." He edited a film magazine, but it lasted for only two issues.

In 1950, after his father's death, Moraes returned to Brazil. He moved in with the 19-year-old sister of a friend, living in a Rio apartment with no electricity, for he had been forced to take a salary cut when not in a foreign post. Supplementing his income as a film critic for the newspaper *Ultima hora,* Moraes was forced to write an advice column as part of the job. But the environment of Rio stimulated his creative impulses. Visiting nightclubs, he heard upcoming musicians in the infectious samba genre and began writing song lyrics once again.

He also undertook a larger project. While sitting at home in Rio, he told Rodman, he heard "somewhere in the distance the Batucada drums were beating their samba rhythms. I was reading a French anthology of classical myths. Suddenly—boing!—the two ideas connected." By the next day Moraes had completed the first act of the play (his first and only one) that became *Orfeu da Conceição.* The title, he told Rodman, had the meaning that "Orpheus Jones" would have in English, but the play, a transposition of the Greek Orpheus myth to Rio's Afro-Brazilian slums, was renamed *Orfeu negro* (Black Orpheus) when it was filmed in the late 1950s. It took several years for Moraes to finish the play—while his divorce from his first wife was becoming final, he lost part of the completed manuscript and had to reconstruct it from memory.

Play Gave Birth to Bossa Nova

Orfeu da Conceição was staged at Rio's Teatro Municipal in 1956; it was the first time, aside from a Brazilian production of Eugene O'Neill's *The Emperor Jones,* that an all-black cast had performed at the theater. In the play, Orpheus is a streetcar driver, and Eurydice is a young woman from northeastern Brazil who is pursued by a jealous ex-boyfriend. She is killed, not by a snakebite as in the original myth, but by a live streetcar wire. The underworld into which Orpheus goes to try to rescue her is the city morgue. Moraes adds characteristically African images to the story at several points, and the songs, with lyrics by Moraes and music by the then-unknown Brazilian jazz musician Antonio Carlos Jobim, had a quiet sophistication that soon was given the name of bossa nova.

The film of *Orfeu da Conceição* had a screenplay by Moraes, but was directed by French filmmaker Marcel Carné. The film, a kaleidoscopic color spectacle of music and dance at Carnival time, won Cannes Film Festival and U.S. Academy Awards (the latter for best foreign film) in 1959, and became an international success. Moraes, along with many other Brazilians, was dissatisfied with the final product, believing that it treated Afro-Brazilian culture as an exotic attraction rather than capturing the essence of a serious play. The film did propel Moraes and Jobim to a new level of success as a songwriting duo, with such compositions as "Chega de saudade" (No More Blues) becoming bossa nova standards.

The pair's most famous composition came about while they were sitting at a sidewalk table at a bar near Rio's Ipanema beach, and became infatuated with a young woman they saw walking by. "Garota de Ipanema" became an international hit in 1963 when it was sung by the quiet-voiced Astrud Gilberto (wife of Brazilian star João Gilberto), and the song was given a verse of English lyrics. The music and lyrics were a perfect combination—just enough to communicate the sensuous atmosphere of Rio's beaches to American listeners. Under the title "The Girl from Ipanema," the song brought Moraes and Jobim a Grammy Award for record of the year. It was later recorded by Frank Sinatra and more than 100 other artists. The street where the bar was located was later named after Moraes. The woman who inspired the song, whose name was Helen Pinheiro, later entered a dispute with the families of Moraes and Jobim over rights to the "Girl from Ipanema" name.

Erudite, yet devoted to the art of living well, Moraes became a familiar figure in Brazil. He savored long baths and sometimes conducted interviews from his bathtub. He claimed to have sampled every brand of whiskey on the market, and often told drinking companions that beer was a waste of time. Moraes continued to write poetry, and recorded some of it on a spoken word LP, but he was best known during the last 15 years of his life as a musical performer. He formed a group called Quarteto em Cy in 1965 and had a hit with "Arrastão."

In the late 1960s Moraes antagonized Brazil's right-wing government and was finally forced out of the country's diplomatic corps for good. He continued to perform through the 1970s, however, frequently making fun of the regime; his status as one of Brazilian culture's most accomplished figures kept him out of serious trouble. Moraes made more than 20 albums, and two of them were later reissued on CD by the Circular Moves label under the titles of *Live in Buenos Aires* and *Days in Mar del Plata.* He suffered from a lung disease in the late 1970s and succumbed to it on July 9, 1970, while working on a new song in his bathtub. Brazilian writer Carlos Drummond de Andrade wrote the next day (as quoted by Ashley Brown in *World Literature Today*) that "Vinicius became the most exact figure of the poet that I have ever seen in my life. He was a poet in books, in music, and in life. Three forms of poetry." Tribute albums and biographies followed in the years after his death, and an edition of his complete poetry and prose appeared in 1998. The following year, *Orfeu da Conceição* was filmed once again by new-wave Brazilian director Carlos Diegues.

Books

Contemporary Hispanic Biography, vol. 2, Gale, 2002.

Periodicals

Brazzil, May 31, 1999.
Los Angeles Times, July 14, 1980.
New York Times, July 11, 1980; August 20, 2005.
Saturday Review, February 9, 1974.
Washington Post, April 20, 2003.
World Literature Today, Summer 1982.

Online

"Black Orpheus," Rootsworld, http://www.rootsworld.com/rw/feature/brazil-orpheus.html (February 4, 2006).
"Vinicius de Moraes," All Brazilian Music, http://www.cliquemusic.com.br (February 4, 2006). □

Mountain Wolf Woman

Winnebago autobiographer Mountain Wolf Woman (1884–1960) committed to posterity an autobiographical account—*Mountain Wolf Woman: Sister of Crashing Thunder*—that captured the complex challenge of blending traditional and contemporary cultural experiences. A full–blooded member of the Winnebago Tribe, Mountain Wolf Woman was revered by many as a woman who lived from the age of horses to the age of airplanes. Her vivid personal account lent value to the genre of female autobiographies in general, and inspired other significant Native American women to share their own stories.

ountain Wolf Woman was born in April of 1884 at her maternal grandfather's home in East Fork River, Wisconsin. She was the youngest of seven children born to Charles Blowsnake and Lucy Goodvillage. Although Mountain Wolf Woman was born a member of her father's Thunder clan, she was later given a name that included her in the Wolf clan—considered to be holy due to its wealth of healers. The sketch on Mountain Wolf Woman in Liz Sonneborn's *A to Z of Native American Women* (1998) tells of how she contracted a "mysterious illness" as an infant, and "in desperation, her mother took her to see a wise elder, known as Wolf Woman, and begged her for a cure."

According to Winnebago tradition, Mountain Wolf Woman's mother figuratively "gave" her daughter to the old woman despite the fact that the child would physically remain with her immediate family. The healer chose to give her life-force to the sick girl, believing that someone who did not live a full one hundred years could bestow future health, longevity and the strength of their personal power on someone they felt worthy of receiving such a gift. Mountain Wolf Woman was healed and added the protection of the Wolf Clan spirit to that of the Thunder Clan that she had been born into.

Drawn to Healing

From early on, Mountain Wolf Woman felt drawn to the world of medicines and the art of healing. Her maternal grandfather, Naqisaneinghinigra (Naqiwankwaxopiniga) or "Spirit Man", taught the young Mountain Wolf Woman about tribal medicine. She had two years of formal education at an Indian school in Tomah, Wisconsin, from age nine to age eleven, but was pulled out—despite liking it very much—in order to travel and work with her family. From the 1830s through the 1900s, members of the Winnebago Nation were driven out of their native Wisconsin by government interests in the state's lead mines, and relocated time and time again in other U.S. states such as Iowa, Minnesota, Mississippi, South Dakota and Nebraska—Mountain Wolf Woman's family was at odds regarding the U.S. government's offer of "resettlement". Although both parents belonged to clans that were not, by nature, tied to the Earth—her father was of the Thunder clan, and her mother a member of the Eagle clan—they disagreed regarding the U.S. government's offer of forty acres. Her father was openly critical of the buy-out, and refused to be a part of the program, but her mother chose to accept the land and oversaw the building of a log cabin on the property. Mountain Wolf Woman attended the Lutheran Mission School in Wittenberg for a short period of time as a teenager, but was taken out once again—this time to be married.

Marital Misery

Mountain Wolf Woman's early life was characteristic of the majority of Native American women at the time. In her book *Sending My Heart Back Across the Years: Tradition and Innovation in Native American Autobiography*, Hertha Dawn Wong relates that Mountain Wolf Woman's older brother, Sam Blowsnake (Crashing Thunder), awoke

from a drunken sleep to find a good Samaritan keeping the mosquitoes from biting his face. In an effort to repay this thoughtfulness, Sam promised Mountain Wolf Woman to the man. Wong explains that Mountain Wolf Woman could not protest the marriage because ". . . she could not embarrass her brother or violate the taboo that might end in suffering for him."

Mountain Wolf Woman recalled in her autobiography that her mother stated, "this matter cannot be helped. When you are older . . . you can marry whomever you yourself think that you want to marry." *Notable Native Americans* explained that marriages within the Winnebago culture were considered "economic arrangements" rather than love matches. Although Mountain Wolf Woman was bitter about the union—she refused to call her first husband by name, referring to him instead only as "that man"—she stayed with him until her brother's debt was released. They were divorced soon after her second child was born.

Mountain Wolf Woman lead a fairly transient lifestyle, moving frequently to find better jobs or living conditions. She devoted years of her remarkable life to healing people. She served as a midwife until the 1930s, when Winnebago women started to choose hospital births over home births. In the 1940s she acted as the Black River Falls mission health officer, where she recorded illnesses among her people for the county's Public Health department. Mountain Wolf Woman wed her second husband, Bad Soldier—a member of the Bear or Soldier clan—and remained happily married to him until his death in 1936. It was during the delivery of her third child that Mountain Wolf Woman tried peyote, medicinally, for the first time.

Peyote Pupil

Peyote, *Lophophora williamsii,*—a cactus plant with hallucinogenic properties native to Texas and Mexico—prompted those who ingested a "button" of it to experience intense, spiritual visions. Mountain Wolf Woman and her family were living in Nebraska when they became devout members of the Native American Church—faithfully attending Saturday peyote gatherings in their communities and participating in a variety of spiritual peyote ceremonies, including the Half–Moon and Cross Fire rituals. Mountain Wolf Woman's experiences with peyote were positively spiritual, and their integrity assured her that the peyote church was a true and legitimate extension of the Christian God. In one of her personal mystical visions while on peyote, she was transformed into an angel and communicated with Christ directly. Mountain Wolf Woman and her family were also active members of the peyote religious community in Martin, South Dakota. Whenever they moved, they always chose to settle among other "peyote eaters" due to the intolerance expressed by those outside the Church. In 1958, Mountain Wolf Woman also financed a 50th Anniversary meeting in honor of peyote's arrival in Wisconsin.

Spiritual Synthesis

Mountain Wolf Woman maintained a devout interest in the traditional spiritual practices of the Winnebago, and sang and danced in tribal ceremonies and celebrations—performing both the Scalp Dance, and the Medicine Dance. She was also a practicing Christian. Mountain Wolf Woman adopted what she found useful from all three spiritual landscapes: Winnebago traditions, Christianity and the Native American Church's peyote sacraments. Her commitment to her tribal roots went a long way towards preserving the Winnebago culture in a time of growing dissolution. She, like so many of her people, underwent a transformation as an adult when she and her people were forced into reservation life and barred from the nomadic traditions that had defined them.

Landmark Autobiographer

Ethnologist Nancy Oestreich Lurie had both a professional and personal relationship with Mountain Wolf Woman prior to their professional collaboration. Lurie is described in Helen Jaskoski's *American Indian Biographies* entry as Mountain Wolf Woman's "adopted kinswoman," and in other sources as her "adopted niece." Lurie had been immersed in Winnebago history and tradition specifically, and Native American history in general long before connecting with Mountain Wolf Woman. She had been doing fieldwork in 1944 when she met Mountain Wolf Woman's blood relative, Mitchell Redcloud, Sr., who happened to be ill at the time of their meeting. Lurie visited Redcloud repeatedly to learn about the Winnebago culture. Concerned that he would not survive an impending surgery, Redcloud adopted Lurie. She was given a Winnebago name and clan affiliation, as well as a list of relatives to call on in her efforts to understand the Winnebago culture. Redcloud wrote to Mountain Wolf Woman to inform her of Lurie's new status, and Mountain Wolf Woman accepted the ethnologist as her niece.

In 1958, Mountain Wolf Woman flew to Ann Arbor, Michigan, and spent five weeks relating the story of her life to Lurie's tape recorder. She spoke first in Winnebago, then again in English while Lurie made an audio recording. The finished autobiography was published in 1958, and *Notable Native Americans* noted that it was praised by critics and scholars alike as a significant contribution to "the literature of cultural crisis and change." Mountain Wolf Woman's grandniece, Frances Thundercloud Wentz, helped Lurie with the translations and Lurie included cultural notes for non-Winnebago readers. The autobiography covered mundane childhood activities as well as life-altering events, and is usually treated as a companion volume to anthropologist Paul Radin's biography of her brother, Crashing Thunder. Mountain Wolf Woman's brother also contributed to the "Trickster" myth cycle (1956) and material for Radin's ethnology *The Winnebago Tribe* (1923).

Because autobiographies at the time tended to focus almost exclusively on male subjects, Mountain Wolf Woman's story provided vital information that was missing from her brother's cultural account—presenting, in collaboration, a more complete perspective on Winnebago history. Sonneborn explained, "Characteristic of the role Winnebago men played in their society, [Crashing Thunder]'s story was full of adventure and bluster. In contrast, Mountain Wolf Woman's book represents in style and content the concerns of traditional Winnebago women . . . modest and often self–mocking . . . [tales] of ordinary occurrences, of small triumphs and failures, of relatives and friends."

Gretchen M. Bataille and Kathleen Mullen Sands (*American Indian Women: Telling Their Lives*) praised the autobiography for its literary merits which, they felt, made its ethnographic content uniquely accessible to readers. Mountain Wolf Woman was no stranger to the forgotten art of oral storytelling. Some of her fondest memories were of the mythic and sacred tales that her father recited for her and her siblings. Both she and her brother's histories have contributed to studies of Native American culture and are sometimes used simultaneously as study materials in academic programs. Her autobiography is considered particularly valuable because it has remained in print and serves as a fundamental text in Native American and Women's Studies courses. Mountain Wolf Woman's autobiography was released in film format in 1990 by producer Jocelyn Riley, and won a certificate of recognition from the Wisconsin Department of Public Instruction's American Indian History and Culture Program. The video uses still photography as a backdrop for segments of Mountain Wolf Woman's autobiography spoken in voice-over by Mountain Wolf Woman's granddaughter, Naomi Russell.

Not Forgotten

Mountain Wolf Woman prophesied her death, fulfilling the Winnebago belief that some elders were capable of such a feat. She died in her sleep at the age of 76 on November 9, 1960, in Black River Falls, Wisconsin, of pleurisy resulting from chronic pneumonia. Family and friends respected her eclectic collection of beliefs with a traditional Winnebago wake, a peyote meeting held in her honor and a Christian burial in the Black River Falls mission cemetery in Wisconsin.

Mountain Wolf Woman had eleven children—three of which died early—and cared for a number of her 38 grandchildren of sons and daughters who fell prey to alcoholism and transient lifestyles. *Notable Native Americans* notes that Mountain Wolf Woman was one of the first women in her tribe to own and drive a car, to travel by train, and that she took her first airplane flight at the age of 74 to work with Lurie in Ann Arbor, Michigan. Sonneborn identified Mountain Wolf Woman's greatest strength as "an ability to adapt easily to new circumstances . . . to cope with cultural change by combining the best of both old and new ways." She became a skilled negotiator between herself and other members of her tribe and government representatives—recognizing that to succeed and receive what was due to them, Native Americans had to learn how to communicate with officials and bureaucrats and insist on fair treatment. Words used to describe Mountain Wolf Woman include "autonomous," "witty," "independent," "empathic," "assertive," "intelligent," "forthright" and "fearless" and her autobiography stands as both a testament and an inspiration to Native Peoples and women of all generations.

Books

A to Z of Native American Women, edited by Liz Sonneborn, Facts on File, Inc., 1998.

Clarke, Joni Adamson, *Native American Women: A Biographical Dictionary,* Routledge, 2001.

Contemporary Authors: New Revision Series vol. 90, Gale Group, 2000.

Encyclopedia of American Women and Religion, edited by June Melby Benowitz, ABC-CLIO, Inc., 1998.

The Encyclopedia of Native American Biography, edited by Bruce E. Johansen and Donald A. Grinde, Jr., Da Capo Press, 1998.

The Encyclopedia of Native American Religions: An Introduction, edited by Arlene Hirschfelder and Paulette Molin, Facts On File, Inc., 1992.

The Feminist Companion to Literature in English: Women Writers from the Middle Ages to the Present, edited by Virginia Blain, Patricia Clements and Isobel Grundy, Yale University Press, 1990.

Jaskoski, Helen, *American Indian Biographies,* Salem Press, Inc., 1999.

Notable Native Americans, Gale Research, Inc., 1995.

Wong, Hertha Dawn, *Sending My Heart Back Across the Years: Tradition and Innovation in Native American Autobiography,* Oxford University Press, 1992.

Online

"Ho-Chunk Nation," http://www.ho-chunknation.com/heritage/culture_history_page.htm#The%20Ho-Chunk%20Nation%20-%20A%20Brief%20History (December 10, 2005).

Kidwell, Clara Sue, "Native American Women," http://college.hmco.com/history/readerscomp/women/html/wh_026500_nativeameri4.htm (December 10 2005).

"Mountain Wolf Woman," *AAA Native Arts,* http://www.aaanativearts.com/article1121.html (December 10, 2005).

"Mountain Wolf Woman," *Media Rights,* http://www.mediarights.org/film/mountain_wolf_woman (December 10, 2005).

"Mountain Wolf Woman," *Native American Rhymes,* http://nativeamericanrhymes.com/women/mountainwolf.htm (December 10, 2005).

"Mountain Wolf Woman," *WLA Literary Awards Committee,* http://www.wla.lib.wi.us/lac/notable/1999notable.htm (December 10, 2005).

"Native People," *Teacher's Guide to Native People,* http://64.233.167.104/search?q = cache:wCxoHBFwmxcJ:www.wisconsinhistory.org/publications/oss/documents/TeachersGuideNativePeople-Chapter4.pdf + mountain + wolf + woman&hl = en&start = 11 (December 10, 2005). □

N

Agnes Nestor

Agnes Nestor (1880-1948), known for her work as a union leader, spent the majority of her life actively involved in issues of human rights, especially focusing on women's rights issues. She was key in implementing the standard eight-hour work day and fought for minimum wage.

Moved from Michigan to Chicago

Nestor was born on June 24, 1880, in Grand Rapids, Michigan, to Thomas Nestor, an Irish-born immigrant who worked as a machinist and grocery store operator, before becoming involved in politics, and Anna McEwen, an orphan, originally from upstate New York, who worked as a cotton mill operator and shop girl. When Nestor was young, her father owned a grocery store, and her entire family pitched in to make the grocery store a success. While she was still young Nestor's father entered politics, becoming an alderman and city treasurer, and gave up the family's grocery store in lieu of a government office. Nestor, always interested in learning, gained much knowledge about the political world at his side, studying the issues involved in leadership. He was also a member of the Knights of Labor, as he was always interested in labor unions set up to protect the rights of workers that were otherwise exploited by their employers. The things Nestor's father taught her about unions would serve Nestor well later in life.

When the economy turned bad in the late 1890s, Nestor's father lost his political job. As he had sold his grocery store when he became a politician, he had no income and there was little opportunity for him to find one in Grand Rapids. With this in mind, Nestor's father moved to Chicago, Illinois, to find work, and the family followed him a short while later, in 1897.

Worked at the Eisendrath Glove Company

After moving to Chicago, the family members were forced to find work, and Nestor herself found a job at the Eisendrath Glove Company, stitching gloves. Nestor was skilled at her job, but there was a lot of unrest in the company, mainly because the girls were forced to pay for the power to run their machines, had to supply their own needles, and had to provide machine oil to keep their machines running. Also at the time, the Glove company workers, along with most factory workers, had to work a 60-hour workweek, something that was standard at the time. Nestor had said that she was so tired sometimes from the grueling schedule that she could barely get herself to work the next day, let alone run the machines with any assurance of correctness. Somehow, however, she managed to not only do the work, but to excel at it.

Conditions for the women at the factory were poor, despite the grumblings of the workers. The male cutters of the factory, who were also dealing with horrible work conditions, had organized a union just before Nestor started at the company, and they encouraged the women to join them, but at that time no one had dared to do so. All the women were afraid that if they joined the union they would lose their jobs and in a depression there were not that many jobs to be had. It was a terrifying prospect.

Became Leader of Rebellion

Finally, in 1898, unwilling to deal with their situation anymore, the female workers rebelled, with Nestor rising to lead them. She was a small woman, but very smart and quick–witted, and she was said to have the natural charisma that is necessary in a leader, as well as the knowledge she had gleaned from her father's years as an alderman. Her father who was a union man of long standing had taught her a lot about the principles of trade unionism, and her knowledge of the ways that unions worked would become invaluable. The women, to an extent, joined the male's union as an offshoot of their organization.

There was a great uproar at the glove company as the women picketed, and the owners of the factory ordered the girls to get back to work, threatening, as the women had feared, to fire them all and replace them with other workers, but Nestor and her fellow strikers refused to back down. The History Matters website quoted Nestor as having said, "We had taken a bold step. Almost with spontaneity we had acted in support of one another. Now we all felt tremulous, vulnerable, exposed. With no regular organization, without even a qualified spokesman, how long would such unified action last? If anyone ever needed the protection of a firm organization, I for one, at that moment felt keenly that we certainly did." Things looked like they might never work out, but after a week the woman's hopes began to rise. Due in large part to Nestor's calm and firm voice amidst the chaos of the rebelling, after ten days' time the women won

their demands and things at the factory improved for them dramatically.

Set Up Women's Trade Union League

In 1902 Nestor suggested that the women separate themselves from the male's union. She became president of the new union of women, the Women's Trade Union League, an organization that also included her fellow Eisendrath Glove Company workers. She took her position very seriously and quickly had their small union registered with the larger International Glove Workers Union in Washington, D.C. She served as a delegate to the convention of the International Union and soon after, in her fervor to help in whatever way she could to improve the lot of women workers everywhere, became its national vice-president, a position that was voluntary.

In 1906 she obtained a full-fledged paid position in the union as secretary-treasurer, a position that came at a very opportune time, as she had suffered from ill health just a short time before the job was offered to her, and had been unable to return to work at the factory. She had been wondering what she would do to support herself when the offer came through. She relished her new position, as it gave her the power to try to implement the changes and improvements in women's work conditions that she envisioned. At first, her emphasis was on the glove trade, but she soon saw a need to help women and children in all fields. In a short time Nestor looked around for an organization that could help her broaden the scope of her philanthropic works. Her sights came onto work being done by the National Women's Trade Union League, and she liked what she saw. She joined the group and became president of the Chicago branch in 1913, a position she held until 1948. She also served on the executive board of the national league. This Trade Union League allowed Nestor to meet such famous persons in female legislature as Mary McDowell, Jane Addams, and Margaret Dreier Robins. She worked alongside these women willingly to help improve female conditions across the country in many areas of life.

Established the Eight Hour Work Day

Because of her work for the National Women's Trade Union League, Nestor began spending a lot of time in Springfield, the capitol of Illinois, lobbying for a maximum-hours-law for women. Remembering her struggle with the 60-hour workweek at the Eisendrath Glove Company, Nestor was eager to help others obtain a better work-life arrangement than she had had. At first the political structure of lobbying was alien to Nestor, but she became a skilled lobbyist in short order, and eventually, in 1909, brought about the law that stated that women working in factories could only work a ten-hour day. In 1911 Nestor managed to get the law expanded to include all women workers, those working outside factories, as well as within them. It was a triumph that was long in coming and would not have been possible if Nestor had not lobbied for better conditions.

It was in 1937, though, that Nestor's triumph really came through when she managed to get the eight-hour work day passed into law—it is Nestor's work that has led to the twenty-first century standard workday, quite a feat from a woman who started out stitching gloves in a factory. In the meantime Nestor began taking part in major strikes and started organizing drives among the women of several different trades in Chicago and across the country. She was involved in the great garment workers' strikes of 1909 and 1910-1911, both of which ended in improved circumstances for the workers involved. She also became an articulate supporter of women's suffrage, fighting alongside other lobbyists to push for a woman's right to vote. After all, if a woman could work and belong to unions, both of which helped the country, they should have the right to vote for the legislature of that country. She also pushed for a minimum wage, as no such thing existed at the time, and the discrepancies amongst employers was enormous, as well as for maternity health legislation.

Women's Committee of U.S. Council of National Defense

Her successes as a lobbyist led to Nestor's appointment to the National Commission on Vocational Education. During World War I, Nestor was offered a position on the Woman's Committee of the United States Council of National Defense. As part of her responsibilities in this position, she participated in goodwill missions to England and France. Then in 1928 she decided to campaign as a Democrat for a seat in the Illinois state legislature. Her bid was unsuccessful, but it showed the amount of power she had garnered that she could get herself on the ballot in the first place. She sat on the Illinois Commission on Unemployment and Relief during the Great Depression, and was part of the board of trustees of the Chicago Century of Progress Exposition from 1933 to 1934. Nestor was given an honorary LL.D., from Loyola University in Chicago, in 1929 for all her work with labor's rights. Although she had expanded her areas for concern throughout her career, Nestor continued to be a strong, active voice in the labor movement.

Nestor's health began to deteriorate in 1946. Doctors managed to diagnose the problem as being tuberculosis, and she went through an operation for a breast abscess in October of 1948 at St. Luke's Hospital in Chicago. Her health, despite the operation, never improved, and on December 28, 1948, Nestor died of uremia. Her remains were interred at Mount Carmel Cemetery in Hillside, Cook County, Illinois.

Books

Dictionary of American Biography, Supplement 4: 1946–1950, American Council of Learned Societies, 1974.

Online

"Agnes Nestor," Spartacus Educational, http://www.spartacus .schoolnet.co.uk/USAWnestor.htm (January 6, 2006).

"Agnes Nestor," Women's History, http://womenshistory.about .com/library/bio/blbio_nestor_agnes.htm (January 6, 2006).

"Working Her Fingers to the Bone: Agnes Nestor's Story," History Matters, http://historymatters.gmu.edu/d/5728/ (January 6, 2006). □

O

Carl Orff

Known primarily for a single work, the rhythmically intense set of choral songs titled *Carmina Burana*, German composer Carl Orff (1895-1982) developed a unique conception of musical structure and performance that had many manifestations beyond that single work. One lasting product of Orff's original thinking was not a piece of music but the internationally popular system of music education called Orff Schulwerk.

The crossover success of *Carmina Burana,* especially its monumental "O Fortuna" opening chorus, has somewhat obscured the fact that Orff was, in several respects, a composer ahead of his time. *Carmina Burana* was based on a set of medieval poems, and Orff was one of the first composers to look to the distant past of European music and culture for inspiration. Orff pioneered a stripped-down musical language that anticipated the minimalist style of the last decades of the twentieth century, and he believed in merging music with other arts to create a total performance experience much like what would later become common in the music video. Orff anticipated a strong interest among classical musicians regarding non-Western drums and percussion instruments, and his works often had a ritual feel that would have been more at home in the 1960s and 1970s than in Orff's troubled homeland of Germany at mid-century. *Carmina Burana,* one of the most popular concert works of the twentieth century, also seems one of its most unusual when it is understood in relation to the rest of Orff's output.

Grew Up in Military Family

Born July 10, 1895, Orff grew up in Munich, Germany, a city he made his home for almost his entire life. His father and grandfather were both military officers. Very early in life Orff showed signs of musical ability and creativity of an unusual kind. When he was three, he wrote a poem that he planned to read at his grandfather's birthday party. But then he forgot the poem. "I could have wept," he later wrote (as quoted by Matthew Gurewitsch in the *Atlantic Monthly*), "but to cry in front of grandfather—that I did not want to do. So I grabbed his trouser legs and shook them with all my might, like a plum tree. Everybody laughed, but my grandfather did not laugh. He bent down to me and said, 'Thank you. I understand very well what you wanted to say.'" Orff sometimes liked to bang on the keys of the family piano with a mallet—annoying, perhaps, but a foretaste of what was to come.

Orff started studying the piano at age five and also took organ and cello lessons. But he was always unmotivated as a performance student, and he found creating original music much more interesting. Orff wrote and staged puppet shows for his family, devising original music for piano, violin, zither, and glockenspiel to go with them. He had a short story published in a children's magazine in 1905 and started to write a book about nature. In his spare time he enjoyed collecting insects. By the time he was a teenager, Orff was writing songs, although he had never studied harmony or composition; his mother helped him set down his first works in musical notation. He wrote the texts himself, and he learned the art of composing not from a teacher but by studying the great works of classical music on his own.

When Orff was 16, some of his music was published; many of his youthful works were songs, often in the settings of texts by famous German poets. They fell into the patterns laid down by Richard Strauss and other leading German

under the guidance of two of Germany's leading scholars, Heinrich Kaminski and Curt Sachs. His primary areas of interest were music of the sixteenth and seventeenth centuries—rare specialties at the time—and, to a lesser extent, ethnomusicology. In the latter field, he was fascinated by the array of percussion instruments from around the world that he encountered after meeting Sachs; he attended African dance performances and experimented with the drums that were used to accompany them.

In the mid-1920s Orff began to formulate a concept he called *elementare Musik,* or elemental music, which was based on the unity of the arts symbolized by the ancient Greek Muses (who gave music its English name) and involved tone, dance, poetry, image, design, and theatrical gesture. Like many other composers of the time he was influenced by the Russian-French emigré Igor Stravinsky. But while others followed the cool, balanced "neoclassic" works of Stravinsky, it was works like the composer's *Les noces* (The Wedding), a pounding, quasi-folkloric evocation of prehistoric wedding rites, that appealed to Orff. He also began adapting musical works of earlier eras for contemporary theatrical presentation, including Claudio Monteverdi's opera *Orfeo* (1607). Orff's German version, *Orpheus,* was staged in 1925 in Mannheim, Germany, under Orff's direction, using some of the instruments that had been used in the original 1607 performance. The passionately declaimed opera of Monteverdi's era was almost unknown in the 1920s, however, and Orff's production met with reactions ranging from incomprehension to ridicule.

Orff also involved himself in educational efforts. With dancer Dorothee Günther he formed the Güntherschule in Munich in 1924. This was a progressive dance and gymnastics school that had the goal of involving children in music-making as well as movement. Orff created new materials for the school, including adaptations of German folk songs (later adaptations of his method in other countries would stress the importance of using local roots music), percussion exercises, and eventually a battery of simple percussion instruments. Orff codified his materials into a large manual called the *Orff-Schulwerk* (Orff Educational Method), which was published in stages between 1932 and 1935. Orff music education caught on in other countries, including the United States; one estimate in the 1990s put the number of U.S. teachers trained in the method at five thousand.

Orff continued to stage innovative reimaginings of works from the earlier eras of classical music, and his new productions gained greater popularity than did his Monteverdi experiments. He presented a *St. Luke Passion,* thought erroneously at the time to be by Johann Sebastian Bach, in an innovative staged version in the Munich area; the original work had dramatic dialogue but would normally have been sung in concert, not staged. Orff turned it into what would now be called a multimedia production, setting the story of Christ's life among south German peasants and illustrating it with projections of centuries-old woodcuts from the area. The *Lukaspassion* caught on in Bavaria and is now staged annually in April as a traditional event.

composers of the day, but they contained hints of Orff's distinctive language. In 1912 Orff wrote a large choral work, *Also sprach Zarathustra* (Thus Spoke Zarathustra, based on a passage in a philosophical work by Friedrich Nietzsche), and an opera, *Gisei, das Opfer* (Gisei: The Sacrifice), the following year. He heard the Impressionist music of French composer Claude Debussy and began to cultivate the use of unusual combinations of instruments in his orchestration.

Another major formative experience for Orff came in 1915, when he got a job as rehearsal leader and conductor at the Munich Kammerspiele (Chamber Players) theater. At the time, plays were often presented with live musical accompaniment, much like a later film soundtrack. The experience cemented Orff's view of music as a component of a total artistic experience, and he began working on a quasi-operatic adaptation of William Shakespeare's *A Midsummer Night's Dream.* The work was not finished until 1939, but parts of Orff's basic creative outlook were forged early in his career. Drafted into the German army in 1917 at the height of World War I, Orff was unhappy despite his family background. He was wounded, suffered from stress, and was finally declared unfit for duty. Orff spent the last year of the war in theatrical jobs in the German cities of Mannheim and Darmstadt, and then returned to Munich.

Studied Music of Renaissance and Baroque Eras

The final component of Orff's mature style was added to his creative arsenal when he began studying musicology

Set Latin Love Poems

Around 1930 Orff became fascinated by love poetry in the Latin language, some of which had erotic subject matter. He wrote two sets of unaccompanied choral songs to texts by the ancient Roman poet Catullus, the *Catulli Carmina* (Songs of Catullus), in 1930 and 1931. This music prepared the way for Orff's masterpiece, the *Carmina Burana* of 1937. This work was based on medieval Latin poems contained in the so-called Benediktbeuern manuscript, housed in a Bavarian monastery. The title *Carmina Burana* (Songs of Beuren) refers to the manuscript, and though the texts were originally written by religious students, they have a strongly secular outlook, celebrating pleasures of the flesh, lamenting the bad luck that befalls human beings, and sometimes poking fun at religion. Orff brought together all the strands of his musical education, opening the work with an imposing chorus addressing Fortuna, the Roman goddess of luck, and delivering a work filled with arresting music, kinetic rhythms, and effective arrangements for both adult and children's choruses. Like the *St. Luke Passion*, it was accompanied at its premiere by slide-projected images; Orff called them *imagines magicae*, or magic images.

The work has been a resounding worldwide success ever since its premiere, and even seven decades later, lawyers for Orff's estate are kept busy fighting the unauthorized uses of the music, which is still under copyright. At the time, however, it was harshly condemned by Nazi-oriented critic Herbert Gerigk. Orff, who remained in Germany during the Nazi era while many other composers departed, has sometimes been criticized as a collaborator with fascism. He never joined the Nazi party, and his music found little official favor within Hitler's cultural apparatus. His detractors point to his 1939 music for *A Midsummer Night's Dream;* the most famous music for the play had been written by Felix Mendelssohn, a German composer of Jewish background, and Orff's work was seen as an attempt to provide a purely Aryan replacement for the Mendelssohn score.

Orff regarded *Carmina Burana* as the real beginning of his career, and ordered his publisher to destroy all his previous works (an instruction that fortunately was disregarded). After World War II he continued to explore ancient texts and their possibilities for generating a new musical and ritual language. *Carmina Burana,* another set of *Catulli Carmina* songs (1941-43), and a like-minded work called *Trionfo di Afrodite* (The Triumph of Aphrodite), were assembled by Orff into a massive three-part theatrical piece called *Trionfi* in the early 1950s. After *Carmina Burana* he wrote two theater pieces based on German fairy tales: *Der Mond* (The Moon, 1938) and *Die Kluge: Die Geschichte von dem König und der klugen Frau* (The Clever Girl: The Story of the King and the Clever Girl, 1942). The latter opera was based on the well-known folk tale of a peasant girl who marries a king after solving a series of riddles.

Most of Orff's later works—*Antigonae* (1949), *Oedipus der Tyrann* (Oedipus the King, 1958), *Prometheus desmotes* (1967), and *De temporum fine comoedia* (A Play for the End of Time, 1971)—were based on texts or topics from antiquity. They extend the language of *Carmina Burana* in interesting ways, but they are expensive to stage and are not operas in the conventional sense. They are occasionally performed, most often in Germany. Orff's major contributions remain the much-performed *Carmina Burana* and the Orff-Schulwerk system. Orff died in Munich on March 29, 1982.

Books

Contemporary Musicians, vol. 21, Gale, 1998.
Liess, Andreas, *Carl Orff,* translated by Adelheid and Herbert Parkin, Calder and Boyars, 1966.
Sadie, Stanley, ed., *The New Grove Dictionary of Music and Musicians,* 2nd ed., Macmillan, 2001.

Periodicals

Atlantic Monthly, August 1995.
Dance Magazine, September 1994.

Online

"Biography," http://www.orff.de (February 8, 2006). □

Alfonso Ortiz

Native American scholar, anthropologist and activist Alfonso Ortiz (1939-1997) was unique in the realm of academia as a Pueblo Indian whose primary field of study was his own people. This perspective was first demonstrated in his 1969 book *The Tewa World: Space, Time, Being and Becoming in a Pueblo Society*, and was highly praised by Ortiz's fellow anthropologists, although not so well received within in his own culture at the time. The noted scholar was also recognized for his tireless activism on behalf of Native Americans, in general, and contributions to society at large.

Influenced and Educated

Ortiz was born on April 30, 1939, to Sam and Lupe (Naranjo) Ortiz, in San Juan Pueblo in northern New Mexico. His father was Native American (Pueblo) and his mother was Hispanic. The Pueblos, of which Ortiz was a member, spoke Tewa, one of the three Kiowa-Tanoan languages of New Mexican Pueblos (there is also one Tewa-speaking group in Arizona). Ortiz, who was reared by his grandparents, well remembered the importance that was placed on knowing his native tongue. He recalled in the *Seattle Post-Intelligencer* that his grandmother "taught me that if I couldn't explain what I was doing in the Tewa language, it probably wasn't worth doing."

Although he grew up poor, Ortiz remembered his childhood with fondness. On the website Living Treasure of Santa Fe he recalled, "I was roused at 4 A.M. by my grandfather to go to the fields, to irrigate and transplant. During the hottest hours, the boys went swimming in the Rio Grande, then, it

was back to the fields. It was a life of hard work, discipline, activity, and lots of fun." Those early lessons in tenacity and self-control paid off when the young Ortiz decided to buck the family tradition of religious service in order to pursue an academic career. But the influence and pull of his cultural roots remained with him for years to come.

After graduating from high school in Espanola, New Mexico, Ortiz studied sociology at the University of New Mexico and was awarded his degree in 1961. That same year he was married to Margaret Davisson, with whom he eventually had three children. He briefly considered a legal career, but chose instead to pursue a master's degree in Indian education at Arizona State University. That venture was also short-lived, as Ortiz's mentor, anthropologist Edward Dozier, persuaded the young scholar to broaden his perspective by continuing his education farther from home. Ortiz did so at the University of Chicago, where he earned a master's degree in 1963 and a Ph.D. in anthropology in 1967. Thus armed with stellar credentials, he was poised to make his mark on academia.

Wrote a Book on Pueblos

Ortiz's scholarly talents had not gone unnoticed while he was still in school. His master's thesis, for instance, had earned him the Roy D. Albert Prize for Outstanding Thesis in 1964. So it was not, perhaps, surprising that his first book was born of his doctoral dissertation. That work, published in 1969 by the University of Chicago Press, was called *The Tewa World: Space, Time, Being and Becoming in a Pueblo*

Society. A pioneering exploration of the very society in which Ortiz had grown up, the book gave a unique anthropological insight into that culture's inner workings. The book was widely acclaimed in academic circles, assuring Ortiz's position as a respected scholar, but its reception among his own people was something less than welcoming.

As late as 2005, there remained debate among Tewa speakers as to whether their language should exist in written form or be preserved solely through oral tradition. And although by that time many had decided that the written word was an acceptable way to pass on their language, the discussion had not progressed that far in the late 1960s. Further, the New Mexican Pueblos had long been reticent about sharing their culture with outsiders, and Ortiz's book was seen as violating this code. Although he maintained that he had only put existing knowledge into a coherent form, as opposed to revealing any secrets, Ortiz found himself suddenly ostracized by some of his own. However, time passed, and recognition from others eventually worked its magic on the situation.

Famed Academic and Activist

Ortiz began his teaching career at Pitzer College in Claremont, California, in 1966. After a year there, he joined the faculty at Princeton University, where he stayed until 1974. During his tenure in the Ivy League, Ortiz's academic reputation increased and he became a sought-after speaker, as well as a consultant for such entities as the Xerox Corporation, the John Hay Whitney Foundation, and the Ford Foundation. He also began his long-term activism on behalf of Native Americans, aligning himself with such public service groups as the National Advisory Council of the National Indian Youth Council (member from 1972-1990) and the Association on American Indian Affairs, Inc. (AAIA; president from 1973-1988). In addition, Ortiz continued his research and writing. *Indian Voices: Proceedings of the 1st Convocation of American Indian Scholars* was published in 1970, and *New Perspectives on the Pueblos* was published in 1972. Celebrated as both a scholar and an activist, Ortiz decided to head back to his native state, where he accepted a professorship at the University of New Mexico (UNM) in 1974. He remained there for the rest of his exceptional career.

At UNM, Ortiz was a popular teacher who took special pride in mentoring young Native American students. Former colleague Joe Sando told Paul Logan of the *Albuquerque Journal,* "He was outgoing, very easy, friendly, very articulate. Many students came to UNM because of his name." Richard Erdoes, his collaborator on two books, described Ortiz to David Steinberg of the same newspaper as "a very jolly man, a wonderful friend who had a great sense of humor and was a great scholar, but who didn't put on any airs if you wanted to talk to him." Indeed, Ortiz's compelling, yet slightly whimsical, personality reminded many of the famous coyote of Pueblo folk legend—a trickster who takes pleasure in disturbing the status quo.

Ortiz was certainly not content with the world as it was and he continued his efforts on behalf of Native Americans. As president of the AAIA, Ortiz was instrumental in obtaining such benchmark accomplishments as the reclamation of the Taos Pueblo people's sacred Blue Lake, the assessment of the Alaska Native Claims Settlement Act, and Congress's passage of the Indian Child Welfare Act. Other activities included membership in the Native American Rights Fund and chairmanship of the advisory board of the D'Arcy Mc-Nickle Center for the Study of the History of the American Indian at the Newberry Library in Chicago. Indisputably, Ortiz was a tireless crusader for his people, but he did not stop there. He was equally willing to lend his time to more wide-reaching causes, from the rights of uranium miners to religious freedom.

Ortiz's scholarly work remained superior and noteworthy. He wrote more than 60 essays and articles, and edited, compiled or wrote several more books. The latter included editing two volumes of the Smithsonian Institution's *Handbook of American Indians* (1979 and 1983). His works and editing ventures also included *American Indian Myths and Legends* (1984), *North American Indian Anthropology: Essays on Society and Culture* (1994), *The Pueblo* (1994), and *American Indian Trickster Tales* (published posthumously, in 1998). In his researches, Ortiz continued to examine his culture of origin with an insight, fondness, and respect that completely set his work apart. The *Seattle Post-Intelligencer* quoted him saying as a young man, "This country has honored too long the war chiefs. There is also a tradition of peace chiefs who deserve to be memorialized and honored." Ortiz did his best to make sure that was so.

Honored and Remembered

Despite ongoing unease among some Pueblo elders, Ortiz's work by no means went unnoticed or unappreciated. In 1975 he was named a fellow of the John Simon Guggenheim Memorial Foundation. The year 1982 saw him being honored with the Indian Achievement Award from the Indian Council Fire of Chicago for his contributions to the area of Native American studies. That same year Ortiz was awarded a prestigious John D. and Catherine T. MacArthur Foundation fellowship—the so-called "genius grant."

In the 1990s Ortiz's health began to suffer, eventually forcing him to take medical leave from UNM. He had appeared to be on the mend, however, when he died unexpectedly from heart failure on January 27, 1997, at the age of 57. "The university is very much impoverished by this loss," UNM's anthropology department chair Marta Weigle told Patricia Guthrie and Ollie Reed Jr. of the *Albuquerque Tribune.* "It's hard to imagine how we'll replace him." San Juan Pueblo Governor Joe Garcia acknowledged the past to the same reporters, while recognizing Ortiz's accomplishments at the same time. "There has been some friction because of some of the things he printed," said Garcia. "But, in the Indian way, there was forgiveness. . . . This is a great loss to the Indian community. There was a lot of knowledge and wisdom in that man." Erdoes also commented on this friction and redemption to Steinberg. "There were two ceremonies, one Catholic and one traditionally Indian, at San Juan Pueblo, and after the ceremonies his soul was released. The elders came together and forgave him for having written books of the Tewa world." Ortiz's son, Nico, described his father's legacy most succinctly when he told Tom Sharpe of the

Albuquerque Journal, "At the time he went to college and got his Ph.D., there were only a handful of Native American scholars, and he was a trailblazer for them to show it could be done. I think that he'd want to be remembered as somebody who made a difference in the world—someone whose achievements left the world a better place."

Ortiz was remembered in many ways for many reasons. Among the most tangible of these was the opening of the Alfonso Ortiz Center for Intercultural Studies at UNM in October of 2000. One of the center's prime directives was to help eliminate barriers between the university and the community by providing a forum for professional anthropologists to interact with laypersons. As a longtime proponent of the demystification of academic institutions via the inclusion of informal scholars from the surrounding community, Ortiz could only have been pleased by the new center that bore his name. This center, set alongside a career of prodigious academic and societal contributions, were all a long way from Ortiz's humble beginnings in the fields. Or perhaps, after all, they were not.

Books

Notable Native Americans, Gale Research, 1995.

Periodicals

Albuquerque Journal, January 30, 1997; January 31, 1997; February 1, 1997; April 26, 1998; December 4, 1999; October 7, 2000.
Albuquerque Tribune, January 29, 1997.
Rocky Mountain News, January 31, 1997.
Seattle Post-Intelligencer, February 5, 1997.
Time, February 10, 1997.

Online

"Alfonso Ortiz," Living Treasures of Santa Fe, http://www.livingtreasures.kxx.com/bios/alfos.html (January 15, 2006).
"Alfonso Alex Ortiz," Native American Authors Project, Internet Public Library, http://www.ipl.org/div/natam/bin/browse.pl/A70 (January 15, 2006).
Contemporary Authors Online, Gale, 2006, Reproduced in *Biography Resource Center.* Farmington Hills, Mich.: Thomson Gale. 2006.
"Dr. Alfonso Ortiz," Alfonso Ortiz Center for Intercultural Studies, http://www.unm.edu/~ortizctr/dr_ortiz.html (January 15, 2006).
"Tewa Indian Pueblos," Access Genealogy, http://www.accessgenealogy.com/native/newmexico/tewaindianhist.htm (January 18, 2006).
"Tewa Language (Tano, Nambe, Pojoaque, San Ildefonso, San Juan, Santa Clara, Tesuque)," Native American Languages, http://www.native-languages.org/tewa.htm (January 18, 2006). □

Alexander Ostrovsky

Alexander Ostrovsky (1823-1886) was one of nineteenth-century Russia's most highly regarded playwrights, though his works are rarely performed in the West in the modern era.

Literary historians deem Ostrovsky the founder of Russian national drama, for he was the first to depict on the stage the ordinary merchants, government bureaucrats and other middle-class denizens of Moscow and the Volga River region. There were few acclaimed Russian playwrights before him, but when Ostrovsky began his career in the 1840s, "Russian theatre was more entertainment than art," asserted London *Sunday Times* writer John Peter. "The idea that it should present brutal comedies by an unknown young civil servant pillorying the dreadful behaviour and abysmal moral standards of those pillars of the Russian community, the merchant class, seemed inconceivable."

Born on March 31, in 1823, Ostrovsky was the son of a lawyer who held a post inside the Moscow municipal court system. His mother's family had run a bakery that made the communion bread for church services. The Ostrovskys lived in the part of Moscow known as *Zamoskvorech'e* (meaning "beyond the Moscow River"), an area that was a commercial district as well as home to many lower middle-class families. It was a neighborhood of strivers, of less educated folk who seemed to a young Ostrovsky to be wholly preoccupied with financial gain. His first plays would scathingly depict this world and its more unscrupulous characters.

Entered Exclusive Academy

Ostrovsky was the first of four children in the family, and his mother died when he was eight. At the age of 12, he entered the First Moscow Gymnasium, a prestigious academy that schooled boys from the city's more elite families.

He spent five years there, and in 1840 enrolled at Moscow University to study law. Though he did well during his first year in college, he seemed to lose interest in his studies after that. He began failing his courses, and spent a disproportionate amount of time attending performances at the Moscow Imperial Theater. This was a popular form of entertainment for university students in the era, but the future playwright went further and began socializing with the actors, stagehands, and other personnel in his spare hours.

After dropping out of Moscow University in 1843, Ostrovsky entered the civil service with the help of his father's connections. At first he worked as a copyist in court offices near Red Square and the famous debtors' prison, Iama, that was located there during this period. From his office window he could see Iama's gates, and was riveted by the daily procession of merchants, gamblers and scofflaws who went in and out of the place. Around 1845, Ostrovsky transferred to the commercial court of Moscow, which formally handled the debt and bankruptcy cases of Iama's incarcerated. Again, he was fascinated by the stories of how fortunes were made, squandered or stolen. He also still found time to frequent the theaters of Moscow, and formed an artistic *kruzhok,* or circle, with two friends. They were deeply interested in the work of English language authors in translation, including Charles Dickens and James Fenimore Cooper, but were also devoted to Slavic folk culture and customs.

Ostrovsky began writing his first plays around 1846. These early works drew upon the Zamoskvorech'e neighborhood, though his father had risen professionally and the family now owned several residential properties in a more well-to-do quarter of the city known as Nikola-Vorob'in. His early dramas featured characters drawn from the innumerable clerks and civil servant classes of Moscow. The court clerks were notoriously underpaid, and bribes were commonplace, which Ostrovsky depicted for the stage. His first finished play was originally titled *Iskovoe proshenie* (The Claim Request), and was read aloud at one of the literary salon evenings held at the home of Stepan Petrovich Shevyrev, a literature professor at Moscow University. It was well-received by those in attendance that night, and Ostrovsky published it soon afterward as *Kartina semeinogo schast'ia. Kartiny moskovskoi zhizni* (Picture of Family Happiness. Pictures of Moscow Life). When he tried to have it produced later that year, however, it was officially banned by Tsarist government censors, and would not be performed until 1855.

Condemned by Government Officials

Ostrovsky went to work on a second play, *Bankrut* (The Bankrupt), which was published in the March 1850 edition of *Moskvitianin* (The Muscovite) to great acclaim. Its plot centers around a greedy merchant, Bashov, who makes a fraudulent bankruptcy application with the help of his clerk and a crooked lawyer. The accomplices actually do abscond with Bashov's assets, and the clerk wins the hand of Bashov's daughter as well, sending the man to professional and psychological ruin. This play is also sometimes referred to as *Svoi liudi—sochtemsia!* (It's a Family Affair–We'll

Settle It Ourselves!), the title under which Ostrovsky submitted it to the censorship committee. It was rejected on the grounds that the characters were "first rate villains," according to Paul Taylor in London's *Independent*. "The dialogue is filthy," it was further judged. "The entire play is an insult to the Russian merchant class."

Bankrut caused Ostrovsky an undue amount of trouble. Not only was it banned from production, but he earned an official reprimand and was put under police surveillance. Within a year he had lost his job at the court. His literary career, however, was well underway by then, and the official reaction only secured his reputation as a maverick new playwright. Even Nikolai Gogol, Russia's most famous dramatist at the time, was present at one of the secret living-room readings of *Bankrut*, and gave his approval. Ostrovsky's next work, *Bednaia nevesta* (The Poor Bride), also troubled government censors, and so Ostrovsky finally decided to write something that they would have to accept for performance. The result was *Ne v svoi sani ne sadis!* (Keep to Your Own Sledge! or, alternately, Don't Bite Off More Than You Can Chew). Its plot centers on a young, dishonest city man who heads to the countryside to find a rich bride. He nearly dupes one into marriage, but is foiled and receives his comeuppance. The play was staged at the Bol'shoi Petrovskii Theater in January of 1853, and went on to the St. Petersburg stage, where Tsar Nicholas came to see it and even made laudatory comments about it a few days later.

Ostrovsky's next work, *Bednost' ne porok* (Poverty Is No Vice), stirred intense literary debate for its themes after a premiere at the Maly Theatre in January of 1854. Its story revolves around two brothers: Gordei is a callous, profit-minded factory owner who wants to become less Russian and more European. This puts him at odds with "his drunken, feckless brother Liubim, a positive figure who represents Russian sincerity and genuineness," noted Robert Whittaker in *Dictionary of Literary Biography*. "The play brought Russian folk customs of Christmas celebrations to the stage with singing and dancing, which reinforced the national, homey nature of its pro-Russian, patriotic message," Whittaker continued. The cultural elite in Moscow and St. Petersburg were divided over the play's merits and whether Liubim was a heroic or tragic figure, and the controversy further boosted Ostrovsky's fame.

Incorporated Folklore Elements into Dramas

Tsar Nicholas died in 1855, and theaters in Russia were closed for a six-month period of mourning. A year later, Ostrovsky became part of an expedition that explored the northern sources of the Volga River. This was an official project of the Marine Ministry, and Ostrovsky was expected to write about his experiences. The trip north would provide him with a rich literary trove of folk customs, which he put to use in his subsequent plays. Many of these works would be set along the estates of the great river, where Moscow's elite owned estates. Later in life he acquired his own property, an estate called Shchelykovo, located in the Kostroma district to the north. His father had originally owned it, and

Ostrovsky and his brother eventually bought it from their stepmother. Ostrovsky was the black sheep of the family, despite his fame. His common-law wife was probably of a peasant background—in an era when Russian peasants were technically the property of their landlords. It is only known that her name was Agaf'ia Ivanovna, and that they lived together after 1849.

Critics consider *The Storm* to be one of Ostrovsky's best plays. It was first produced under its original title, *Groza*, at Moscow's Maly Theatre in November of 1859. The work is set on a Volga estate, and features a dreadful, scheming widow and landowner, Kabanikha, who terrorizes her meek daughter-in-law, Katerina. *Groza* was a commercial triumph, and a personal one for Ostrovsky as well: he fell in love with the performer who played Katerina, Liubov' Pavlovna Kositskaia-Nikulina, and the affair lasted for a year before she moved on.

For many years Ostrovsky traveled frequently between the theater districts of Moscow and St. Petersburg, and to Shchelykovo as well. In 1862 he went abroad for the first time, visiting several countries in Europe. During this period of his career he had far fewer problems with the censors, for the new hereditary ruler, Alexander II, was a much more liberal tsar who enacted many important reforms. For a time in the mid-1860s, Ostrovsky turned to writing historical dramas, but these were difficult to stage and not considered among his best works.

Heralded for Satire

Na vsiakogo mudretsa dovol'no prostoty (Even a Wise Man Stumbles) returned him to familiar ground: the deceitful social striver. First produced at the Alexandrinsky Theatre, in St. Petersburg in 1868, it went on to a staging at the Maly Theatre where an enthusiastic opening night audience actually halted the performance midway through to call Ostrovsky out for an ovation. The play is sometimes titled *Enough Stupidity in Every Wise Man*, *The Scoundrel*, or *Diary of a Scoundrel*. Its lead character is Yegor Gloumov, who writes disdainfully about the wealthy and well-connected on the pages of his private journal, but flatters them in person; his comeuppance comes when the scathing diary is published.

Ostrovsky's common-law wife, Agaf'ia, died in early 1867. Two years later he wed Mar'ia Vasil'evna Bakhmet'eva, an actress by whom he already had three children, two of whom were born when he still lived with Agaf'ia. He was writing at least one new play a year, and scored another triumph in *Les* (The Forest) in 1871. The play was first produced at the Alexandrinsky Theatre in St. Petersburg, and remains one of Ostrovsky's most critically acclaimed works. Again, a greedy widow behaves badly: Gurmyzhskaia sells off pieces of her nephew's land inheritance, and keeps her niece in the household as a servant, refusing to let her marry her suitor. The arrival of the nephew, an actor, along with his fellow traveling colleague help to resolve the crises.

During the 1870s, Ostrovsky's plays fell somewhat out of favor in St. Petersburg, though they remained popular in Moscow. A fairy-tale play, *Snegurochka* (The Snow Maiden)

drew heavily upon Russian folklore, and the composer Peter Ilych Tchaikovsky wrote the music for its staging at Moscow's Bol'shoi Theater in 1873. *Volki i ovtsy* (Wolves and Sheep), first produced in 1875, is another well-known work from his pen. By this time he had been writing for nearly 30 years. "Tastes had changed under the influence of light opera and sentimental melodrama, however, and Ostrovsky's reviewers became increasingly disparaging," wrote Whittaker. "They accused him of repeating himself and having exhausted his talent."

Another six-month mourning period after the 1881 assassination of Alexander II shuttered Imperial Russia's theaters, and this time Ostrovsky suffered heavy financial losses as a result. His brother Mikhail, however, was a high-ranking government minister by then, and helped secure a state pension for Ostrovsky in 1884. After 1886 he served as director of repertoire for the Moscow Imperial Theaters and administrator of the Theater School. He was by then in his sixties, however, and the taxing work and travel schedule irreparably damaged his health. He died at his desk in the Shchelykovo residence on June 2, 1886. Though generally unknown outside of Russia, Ostrovsky is a respected figure in the literary heritage of his country, especially in its nationalist drama. So many of his works premiered at the Maly Theatre in Moscow that it was still referred to as "The House of Ostrovsky" a century after his death. A statue of him stands outside the landmark.

Books

Dictionary of Literary Biography, Volume 277: *Russian Literature in the Age of Realism.* Alyssa Dinega Gillespie, ed., Gale, 2003.

International Dictionary of Theatre, Volume 2: Playwrights, St. James Press, 1993.

Periodicals

Back Stage, March 9, 2001.

Independent (London, England), January 27, 1999.

New York Times, March 31, 1962.

Sunday Times (London, England), October 18, 1992. □

P

Jack Paar

American entertainer Jack Paar (1918-2004) made his name in 1940s radio before going on to become the host of *The Tonight Show* in the late 1950s. As a late-night host and later of a weekly prime-time show, he helped fuel the careers of many entertainers including Bill Cosby, Bob Newhart, and The Beatles. Incredibly popular and well-known for his comedy, Paar left television at the height of his career in the mid-1960s, returning to public view only a few times in the following decades.

Midwestern Youth and Early Radio Career

Born in Canton, Ohio, on May 1, 1918, Paar was the second son of Howard and Lillian Paar. Paar's father was a division superintendent for the New York Central Railroad, causing the family to move around the Midwestern part of the United States; most of Paar's boyhood was spent in Jackson and Detroit, Michigan. Paar's youth was not an auspicious one. Richard Severo noted in the *New York Times* that "when [Paar] was 5 years old, an older brother was killed by a car. When he was 10, his best friend died. When he was 14, he had tuberculosis." Despite this litany of misfortunes and a long-lasting childhood stammer, Paar decided he wished to work in radio broadcasting. As a teenager, he got a job at the local radio station in Jackson, announcing the station's call letters and performing other minor chores.

Paar left formal schooling at age 16 to take a job in Cleveland, Ohio, with radio station WGAR. This position became the first in an early career with radio stations throughout the Midwest in places like Indianapolis, Indiana; Youngstown, Ohio; Pittsburgh, Pennsylvania; and Buffalo, New York. As a young man, Paar married, divorced, re–married and finally divorced for the second and last time his first wife, Irene. In 1938, while a radio announcer at WGAR in Cleveland, Paar worked through Orson Welles' infamous *War of the Worlds* broadcast, which purportedly told of a Martian force invading New Jersey. Like many other Americans, Paar was taken in by the hoax—much to his later embarrassment.

Paar's radio career took a brief detour in 1942 when he was drafted into the United States Army for service in World War II. As a member of the Army's Special Services Division, responsible for entertaining the troops, Paar put on stand-up comedy shows in the South Pacific. There, joking that the attacking Japanese forces were in fact trying to bring the U.S. servicemen food, Paar discovered—in the words of *The Independent*'s Dick Vosburgh—that "the laughter, applause and cheers he quip produced made him realize that tilting against authority was his strong suit." During these early wartime years, Paar married his second wife, Miriam Wagner Paar, with whom he would later have his only child, daughter Randy. (Paar and his wife had expected to have a boy; when they instead had a girl, they changed their plans of naming the baby after Paar's grandfather by altering "Andy" to "Randy.") In the later years of the war, Paar returned to radio as an announcer and became quite popular. His fame among the servicemen led to recognition in the United States; at the end of the war, Paar found himself in demand.

Post-War Variety

Paar first signed with movie studio RKO as an actor, although his film career was short-lived. He held small roles in several films, including *Variety Time* (1948); *Easy Living* (1949); *Walk Softly Stranger* (1950); *Love Nest* (1951), an early Marilyn Monroe film; *Footlight Varieties* (1951); and *Down Among the Sheltering Palms* (1953). His undistinguished movie career paralleled a more successful stint in radio. Paar substituted for radio personality Don McNeill, whose show *The Breakfast Club* was one of the most popular on the 1940s and 1950s, and in 1947 served as a summer replacement host on Jack Benny's Sunday night show. By 1952, Paar's career seemed unlikely to live up to its early promise.

With the expiration of his RKO contract, Paar left California for New York City, where he hosted a game show, *Up to Paar,* and appeared on variety and game shows such as *What's My Line?* and *Toast of the Town.* During his early New York years, Paar also hosted CBS radio show *Bank on the Stars* and took over for host Walter Cronkite on the *CBS Morning Show* in 1954. As with his previous endeavors, however, none of these shows proved to be particularly successful.

Hosted *The Tonight Show*

Nevertheless, Paar was once again thrust into the limelight in 1957 when he accepted the job as host of *The Tonight Show.* The show's first host, Steve Allen, was a respected entertainer who had typically featured sketch comedy and musical numbers on the show. Paar turned to the format more to talk, causing television luminary Merv Griffin to note decades later in an article written by Tim Feran for *The Columbus Dispatch* that "Jack invented the talk-show format as we know it: the ability to sit down and make small talk big." On the show, Paar was joined by a number of supporting players including announcer Hugh Downs; pianist Jose Melis; French singer Genevieve; and comedians Cliff Arquette, Jonathan Winters, Dody Goodman and Peggy Cass. Paar's guests were a mix of famous entertainers such as Peter Ustinov and Judy Garland, notable politicians like Robert Kennedy and Barry Goldwater, and up-and-coming stars including Bill Cosby and Carol Burnett. When asked by young comedian Dick Cavett, then a writer for *The Tonight Show,* what his secret was to having such successful interviews, Cavett wrote in *The New York Times* that Paar replied: "Don't make it an interview, kid. Make it a conversation. Interviews have clipboards." *The Tonight Show,* bolstered by Paar's somewhat emotional, personal handling of it, grew immensely popular—so much so that the show was renamed *The Jack Paar Show* only a year after he took over hosting duties.

Paar's emotional nature colored his years with *The Tonight Show.* He publicly feuded with newspaper columnists, particularly Walter Winchell and Dorothy Kigallen, as well as fellow comedians. Dramatically, he quit *The Tonight Show* in February 1960 over their censorship of one of his jokes. The joke referenced a water closet—a British term for a toilet—and was removed by network censors who deemed it inappropriate. Feran recounts that a distraught Paar walked off the set of the show after announcing "I am leaving *The Tonight Show.* There must be a better way of making a living than this." Three weeks later, he returned with the words: "As I was saying before I was interrupted . . ." He completed the thought by responding to his own assertion that there must be a better way to make a living by saying: "Well, I looked, and there isn't."

Paar courted controversy during his tenure as *Tonight Show* host in other ways, as well. He was openly outspoken against Cuba's Batista regime and interviewed Fidel Castro on the show, despite loud public denunciation. Following the Bay of Pigs, the Kennedys—both John and Robert Kennedy having also been Paar's guests—approached Paar to serve as a go-between in some negotiations with Cuba. In 1961, he broadcast from Berlin while the Berlin Wall was being erected. Although Paar drew negative attention for these activities, his popularity did not flag. In 1962, Paar tired of the stress of a daily late-night talk show and left *The Tonight Show* to be replaced by Johnny Carson. From the relatively unsuccessful show Paar had taken over five years previously, with only two sponsors and distribution in 62 markets, he had developed a behemoth carried by 115 channels and boasting complete sponsorship.

Paar then began hosting a weekly Friday-night prime-time variety show, *The Jack Paar Program.* This show had much the same format as had *The Tonight Show* under his tenure, but did not last as long. However, *The Jack Paar Program* did have the distinction of being the first television show to introduce the Beatles to the United States; although popular memory gives that nod to Ed Sullivan's 1964 live airing of the group, Paar showed British taped recordings of the band on his show before that time, not because he enjoyed their music but because he thought they were funny. In 1965, Paar essentially retired from the public eye. He reappeared occasionally over the ensuring decades, briefly hosting an ABC late-night show in 1975 and appearing on career retrospectives in the 1980s.

Retirement and Death

Paar remained primarily out of the public eye, however. In the late 1960's, he purchased television station WMTW in Poland Springs, Maine, which he ran for several years before selling it at an immense profit. Also in the late 1960s, he produced a series of documentaries focusing on international cultures. Paar spent his remaining years traveling, spending time with his family, and dedicating himself to hobbies like electronics and gardening and by all accounts simply enjoying life in Connecticut. This public invisibility prompted James Lileks to comment in Minneapolis' *Star Tribune* shortly after Paar's death; "Jack Paar was alive? His was one of those obituaries that makes you wonder how many others whose death you've assumed are still drawing breath." At his height, Paar was watched nightly in seven million American households; by the time of his death, he was more visible through his influence of the performances of contemporary talk show hosts like David Letterman than through anything else. In addition to his radio and televisions successes, Paar was a bestselling author. Over the course of his life, he wrote four light-hearted non-fictional books based on his life, memories and travels: 1960's *I Kid You Not*—the title taken from his *Tonight Show* catchphrase; 1961's *My Saber is Bent*; 1965's *Three on a Toothbrush*; and finally 1983's *P.S. Jack Paar.*

During his brief return to late-night television in the mid-1970s, Paar agreed to film a public service health announcement. In the course of the spot's taping, he realized that he himself exhibited all the symptoms of the disease about which he was informing the viewers: diabetes. Despite his condition and his avowal in *P.S. Jack Paar* that "when you reach your sixtieth birthday, there is not a lot to look forward to except falling down in the bathtub and breaking your hip," Paar lived well past the age of 60, albeit in relative obscurity. In 2003, he suffered a mild stroke; the following year, he died on January 27 at his home in Greenwich, Connecticut, accompanied by his wife of sixty years and their daughter. He was 85.

Writing in the *New York Times* after Paar's death, comedian Dick Cavett said that Paar "was smart, sentimental, witty, irritable, loyal, insecure, infuriating, hilarious, neurotic and totally entertaining." Remembered today as the man who was if perhaps not the inventor of the talk show, then certainly the one who molded it into its present form, Jack Paar is recognized as a pioneer in both radio and television broadcasting whose enduring legacy can be seen on television screens both in the United States and around the world.

Books

Paar, Jack, *P.S. Jack Paar* Doubleday, 1983.

Periodicals

Chicago Sun–Times January 28, 2004.
Columbus Dispatch, January 28 2004.
Guardian, January 29, 2004.
Independent February 2, 2004.
New York Times, January 28, 2004; January 29, 2004.
Plain Dealer, January 28, 2004.
Star Tribune, February 1, 2004.
Washington Post, January 28 2004.

Online

"Biography of Jack Paar," http://www.imdb.com/name/nm0654967/bio (January 16, 2006).
"Jack Paar: A Life Lived on Television," http://www.jackpaar.com/Career/biography.html (January 16, 2006).
St. James Encyclopedia of Pop Culture, "Jack Paar," http://www.findarticles.com/p/articles/mi_g1epc/is_bio/ai_2419200921 (January 16, 2006). □

Arthur Caswell Parker

Arthur C. Parker (1881-1955) was among the most important Native American scholars and intellectuals of the twentieth century. Of an ethnically diverse background, he was a complex figure familiar from childhood with both Native American and European American cultures, but not always fully at home in either atmosphere.

Parker's writings on the Seneca and Iroquois cultures are still read and used today by anthropologists. Additionally, he filled the role of public intellectual several times during his career, writing books about Native American culture for general audiences and attempting to advance awareness of modern Native American identity among the general American public. Parker held leadership positions in pan-Indian institutions, and his efforts to promote trans-tribal solidarity among Indian groups, though they ran into difficulties at the time, had lasting influence. Parker's museum work, too, was influential; he was one of the first museum administrators to view the museum as a tool of cultural education, and he was an early adopter of such familiar museum elements as the diorama.

Considered Non-Indian

Born April 5, 1881, on the Seneca tribe's Cattaraugus Reservation in New York's Finger Lakes region, Parker had a complex identity from the start. He was descended on his father's side from a long line of Seneca leaders; his uncle Ely Parker was a Civil War veteran who had been part of the inner circle of General Ulysses S. Grant and later became the first Native American named United States Commissioner of Indian Affairs. Parker's father and grandfather, however, both married women of European descent; Parker's mother Geneva was a missionary and teacher of Scottish background. Since Seneca clan membership is matrilineal (reckoned through the mother's side), neither

Parker nor his father was considered a Seneca. Parker's father worked for the New York Central Railroad and continued to live, however, on a family farm on Seneca land, so Parker spent most of his childhood there. Adding to the complications of his background was the fact that though he was raised as a Christian, his family had ties to the traditional Seneca religion that had been carried forward into the modern era by the prophet Handsome Lake. And, he wrote in the introduction to *Skunny Wundy,* his book of Seneca stories, into the family home would come "many a visitor from the wilder parts of the reservation, visitors who lived back in the woods or on the hill where the long-house people dwelt, they who followed the old Indian customs and had grotesque masks and dances and who wore feathers and buckskins."

Parker's family left the reservation and moved to White Plains, New York, north of New York City, in 1892. Parker graduated from high school there in 1897, although he would return to school several times, his high school diploma represented his last completed degree. Intensely curious, and later a prolific writer who issued some 250 books and articles, he nevertheless was restless in formal educational settings and abandoned them when he felt called to turn directly to important work. Plus, wherever he went to school, he never quite fit in. "I was too far ahead for a government [Indian] school and too poor to go to college," he wrote (as quoted by his biographer Joy Porter in *To Be Indian: The Life of Iroquois-Seneca Arthur Caswell Parker*). "I worked my way through the rudiments of an education and when I was through school I realized that my education had just begun. I studied faithfully ever since, laying out a course of study for myself every year."

Briefly attending the Centenary Collegiate Institute in Hackettstown, New Jersey, Parker got his real education when he became a frequent visitor to the American Museum of Natural History in New York. Curators there, including Harvard anthropology professor Frederick W. Putnam, were impressed by Parker's serious attitude and took time to answer his questions, even when he brought in birds' eggs or random pieces of pottery he found. Parker also became acquainted with writer Harriet Maxwell Converse, a poet and journalist with an interest in Native American culture. He called her Aunt Hattie and attended a "salon"— an intellectual discussion group—at her home that included both Indian and white members.

A friend of Converse's introduced Parker to anthropologist Franz Boas, who was in the process of founding a highly influential Ph.D. program in anthropology at Columbia University in New York and urged Parker to apply. But Parker was not comfortable with Boas, partly because Boas disparaged the work of pioneer ethnographer Lewis Henry Morgan, a close friend and associate of Ely Parker. Parker chose instead to take the advice of a clergyman on the Seneca Reservation and enrolled in 1900 at Dickinson Seminary in Williamsport, Pennsylvania, planning to become a minister. He left that program after three years, however, without a degree.

Honed Writing Skills as Reporter

Parker continued to do archaeological work on the side while at Dickinson, working on digs on the nearby Cattaraugus Reservation and at the Oyster Bay Indian mounds on Long Island. The trips back to Seneca land were homecomings that deepened his interest in Indian traditions. He apprenticed himself to archaeologist Mark Harrington, to whom Putnam had recommended him. Sometimes he wrote science articles for the *New York Sun* newspaper, and his voluminous future writings, whether technical or not, were generally clear and accessible. Parker gained a reputation as a hard worker, and other archaeological assignments, on Iroquois land and elsewhere, began to come his way. On his own he began an organized plan of action to collect information about Seneca culture, and he was recognized as a rising authority on the tribe. In 1903 he was made a Seneca in a ceremony and given the name Gáwasowaneh (or Gawaso Wanneh), which meant Big Snow Snake. Other anthropologists had been similarly honored, but another ceremony, in which Parker was inducted into an Iroquois secret medicine society, was more unusual. Later in life Parker's friends in the museum world gave him yet another name, "The Chief."

Hired in 1903 as a field ethnologist by the New York State Library and Museum, Parker collected speeches, folk tales, and objects relating to Iroquois culture. The following year he married Beatrice Tahamont, a woman of Abenaki background. They had two children but later divorced. By a second wife, Anna, he had one child. After passing a state civil service exam, Parker advanced to the position of staff archaeologist with the state museum. This period of his life was productive in terms of scholarly writing; he wrote several major books on Seneca and Iroquois culture, but one of them, *The Constitution of the Five Nations* (1916), was criticized because reviewers felt he had not sufficiently investigated the origins of the documents he used. Among Parker's other books were *An Erie Indian Village and Burial Site* (1907), *Iroquois Uses of Maize and Other Food Plants* (1910), *The Code of Handsome Lake, Seneca Prophet* (1913, with drawing by Seneca artist Jesse Cornplanter), *Seneca Myths and Folktales* (1923), and *Red Jacket: Last of the Seneca,* reprinted as *Red Jacket: Seneca Chief.* As Parker advanced in the museum profession he had less and less time to spend on research, but he continued to write when he could. He remained at the New York State Museum until 1924.

Another major time commitment for Parker came when he helped found the Society for American Indians (SAI) in 1911, later advancing to the positions of secretary and president of that organization. The SAI was something of a Native American counterpart to the National Association for the Advancement of Colored People (NAACP); it was a group that worked toward the full integration of Indians into American life even as they retained and built on their identities as Indians. Parker, like many other Native Americans, felt tension between those goals, and the issue of Indian participation in World War I led to disagreements within the group. Parker believed that the integration of Native Americans into the U.S. armed forces would help their position in society in general, but others asked why Indians, who were not citizens, should fight for a country that denied them civil rights. After editing the society's *American Indian Magazine* for five years, Parker left the organization. He acted as a consultant on Indian affairs to Presidents Theodore Roosevelt, Taft, Wilson, and Coolidge, but later in life he became discouraged about the possibilities for full assimilation of Indians into American society.

Appointed Museum Director

In 1925 Parker became the director of the Rochester Museum, later renamed the Rochester Museum of Arts and Sciences. He fit the profile of a museum director: photographs and testimonies of the time reveal a dignified-looking man, with a slight Iroquois accent, who was slow to anger and had a gift for putting strangers and associates at ease in conversation. Parker's influence in the museum world went beyond Indian affairs. He said (according to the introduction to his book *Red Jacket: Seneca Chief*) that a museum was "the university of the common man," and he viewed museums as places that could educate rather than simply dazzle their visitors. Some credited Parker with originating the idea of the museum as an educational institution, and the look of the modern historical museums, with its detailed, authentic three-dimensional displays and dioramas, owes something to Parker, who sweated over the details of such displays in Rochester. He instructed museum staff to base the painted backgrounds of displays on actual scenes from Iroquois lands, and the figures who inhabited his display villages were made from life masks of living Native Americans.

The job of museum director was a demanding one as Parker shepherded the Rochester Museum through funding hazards during the Depression and World War II eras. He led the museum in acquiring a massive collection of Iroquois artifacts that remains very important, and he also worked to further the efforts of contemporary Native American craftspeople, buying their works and becoming involved with the Depression-era Works Progress Administration to make sure that Native Americans received a fair share of the art projects sponsored by the government agency during those years. In the midst of all this, Parker found time to write several more books, including *Skunny Wundy*, an enduring collection of Seneca stories for children.

Later in life Parker received various honorary degrees, including an honorary master's degree in science from the University of Rochester in 1922, and honorary doctorates from Union College (in 1940) and Keuka College in 1945. A particularly significant honor for him was his ascent to the 33rd Degree level of the Order of Masons, an organization with which he remained closely involved for much of his life. Parker retired from the Rochester Museum in 1946, continued to write, and became active in a new pan-Indian organization, the National Congress of American Indians. He died on January 1, 1955, in Naples, New York, in a home he had built overlooking what he believed to be land where his ancestors had lived.

Books

Notable Native Americans, Gale, 1995.
Parker, Arthur C., *Skunny Wundy: Seneca Indian Tales,* Syracuse University Press, 1994.
———, *Red Jacket: Seneca Chief,* University of Nebraska Press, 1998.
Porter, Joy, *To Be Indian: The Life of Iroquois-Seneca Arthur Caswell Parker,* University of Oklahoma Press, 2001.

Online

"Arthur C. Parker," Encyclopedia of the American Indian, http://college.hmco.com/history/readerscomp/naind/html/na_027800_parkerarthur.htm (January 31, 2006). □

M. Scott Peck

American psychologist and author M. Scott Peck (1936-2005) rose to national prominence when he published *The Road Less Traveled* in 1978. The book was one of the most popular self-help books of all time, selling ten million copies. With subsequent books and public appearances, Peck ascended to a position of influential and spiritual leader.

Though Peck is not responsible for establishing the literary genre, his name became synonymous with "self help" books. The unique vision he communicated in a series of books published from the late 1970s to the late 1990s was characterized by a blend of science, spirituality, psychology and philosophy. His writings struck a chord in the latter part of the twentieth century, and many readers were influenced by his work.

The future spiritual teacher was born on May 22, 1936, in New York City, New York, the second of two sons of David Warner Peck and Elizabeth (Saville) Peck. Peck's father was a prominent lawyer who later became a judge.

Religious matters and spiritual philosophies, in one way or another, found their way into Peck's life during his early years. He once described his half-Jewish father as someone trying to pass as a WASP (white Anglo-Saxon Protestant). Peck attended a Quaker day school while growing up and, fascinated by religion, he became a Zen Buddhist when he was 18 years old. (Later in his life, he flirted with Jewish and Muslim mysticism when he was in his thirties and he converted to Christianity in his forties.)

As a child, Peck had literary ambitions and dreamed of one day writing a great novel. However, his education took him in other directions. After being expelled from Middlebury College in Middlebury, Vermont, during his sophomore year—he refused to attend mandatory ROTC (Reserve Officers' Training Corps) classes—he attended Harvard University in Boston, Massachusetts. Peck later admitted that his father's connections got him into the school. At Harvard, Peck studied social relationships and he graduated magna cum laude with a bachelor's degree in 1958.

Studied Medicine

Peck also enrolled in a pre-med course at Columbia University in New York City, attending night classes while working during the day in Bellevue Hospital's psychiatric division. From there, he went to Case Western Reserve University School of Medicine in Cleveland, Ohio. His experiences at Bellevue fostered in him a negative impression of psychiatry, so he intended to become a general practitioner. He received his medical degree in 1963.

While studying at Columbia, he met the woman who would become his first wife, Lily Ho, who was from Singapore. They were married in 1959, during Peck's first year of medical school, and eventually would have three children. Both Peck's and Ho's parents strongly disapproved of the union. Peck's father disowned him for a while, but the estrangement was short-lived, and David Peck even helped pay for his son's medical school tuition.

Joined the Army

Upon graduation from Case Western, Peck joined the U.S. Army, reasoning that it was the least expensive way to continue his medical education. It also provided him with a wage sufficient to support a family.

Oddly enough, Peck joined the army as a psychiatrist. He was not exactly enthusiastic about the service—he became opposed to the Vietnam War—but he was grateful for the opportunity to observe how individuals and organizations behaved. From 1967 to 1970, he was head of psychology at the U.S. Medical Center at Okinawa. From 1970 to 1972, he served as assistant chief of psychiatry at the Surgeon General's office in Washington, D.C. He resigned with the rank of lieutenant colonel and he earned a Meritorious Service Medal with oak leaf cluster.

After leaving the army, Peck moved to New Preston, Connecticut, where he established a private psychiatric practice. He operated the practice successfully from 1972 to 1983. In 1976, he experienced a flash of literary inspiration, and he started writing a self-help book that combined psychology with spirituality.

Produced a Best-seller

Two years later he submitted the manuscript, which he titled *The Psychology of Spiritual Growth,* to Random House, who turned it down. Simon and Schuster then purchased it for $7,500 and changed the title to *The Road Less Traveled: A New Psychology of Love, Traditional Values and Spiritual Growth.*

Initially, the book enjoyed modest sales. That would change, however, thanks to word-of-mouth recommendations, as well as a rave review that appeared in *The Washington Post.* An enthusiastic reviewer, Phyllis Theroux, called it a "magnificent boat of a book." Comparing it to other spiritual self-help books, she said Peck's work "is so obviously written by a human being who, both in style and substance, leans toward the reader for the purposes of sharing something larger than himself." She later said that she wanted to write a review that "would force people to buy the book."

To help increase sales of the book, Peck copied the review and sent it to newspapers throughout the country. In its first year after publication, *The Road Less Traveled* sold 12,000 copies in hardcover and 30,000 copies in paperback. In its paperback edition, the book became a publishing phenomenon. Sales figures doubled over the next two years. By 1983, the book finally entered the all-important *New York Times* best-seller list, where it remained for 694 weeks, or more than 13 years.

Eventually the book sold more than ten million copies, and royalties made Peck a wealthy man. It was translated into 20 languages and led to successful sequels including *Further Along the Road Less Traveled* (1993) and *The Road Less Traveled and Beyond* (1997).

Opening his book with a simple, declarative statement, "Life is difficult," Peck advanced the notion that existence is full of problems that can only be effectively remedied through self-discipline. Further, it is the nature of the human condition for people to avoid problems, but this only creates even more trouble. Only through self-discipline, delayed gratification, and accepting responsibility for one's own actions, all combined with a spiritual and active love, could people transform weakness into strength and overcome life's difficulties. Moreover, the love that Peck spoke of was "real love," as opposed to "romantic love," which he felt was a lie. "Real love," on the other hand, fosters spiritual growth, he believed.

The book provided the kind of message that resonated with the public. In addition, Peck imbued his writing with a conversational and comforting style that helped readers accept what was essentially a demanding and complex remedy. Interestingly enough, Peck himself was a man with very human flaws and habits, which he readily admitted. In interviews, he described himself as a self-delusional neurotic who was fond of gin, cigarettes and marijuana. He also indicated that he had trouble with relationships, an admission made evident by his marital infidelities and his inability to relate well to his parents and his own children.

At the same time, however, he continued on an evolving spiritual path, which would take him from Eastern mysticism into Western Christianity. The road he was taking included some activities and enterprises that would seem incongruous or even odd. In 1980, when Peck was 43 years old he was baptized by a Methodist minister in an Episcopalian convent, a place he had frequently used as a retreat. In 1983, he considered running for president with the expressed purpose of being "a healer to the nation," but health concerns forced him to reconsider.

The following year, Peck and his wife helped establish The Foundation for Community Encouragement, a nonprofit educational organization designed to advance principles of community. The international foundation included 70 trained leaders who conducted workshops for the general public as well as churches, schools, government agencies, prisons, universities and businesses. Peck eventually retired from the foundation's board of directors, but he maintained his ties through an "elder" status. For his work, Peck received the 1984 Kaleidoscope Award for Peacemaking and the 1994 Temple International Peace Prize.

Became a Prolific Author

Following the success of *The Road Less Traveled,* Peck wrote a number of other books. In 1983, he published a second book, entitled *People of the Lie: The Hope for Healing Human Evil.* This followed his conversion to Christianity, and the book examined the human soul, combining psychology with religion. Peck postulated the idea that some patients come out of psychiatric treatment with their self-destructive behaviors fully intact and even more firmly ingrained. He also maintained that some people are evil, and that their treatment should include exorcism of demons. *Los Angeles Times* book critic Malcom Boyd wrote that the book "is a curious mix, linking professional expertise with personal opinion, case history with moral preachment, political liberalism with religious dogmatism. It is a stubborn, sometimes arrogant treatise. . . . Yet useful and promising creative ideas are in these controversial pages."

By this time, Peck had lost interest in his private practice and went on the lecture circuit, earning $15,000 for each appearance. In 1985, he released a third book, *What Return Can I Make? Dimensions of the Christian Experience.* As with his previous books, it was published by Simon & Schuster. The volume contained both essays and audio commentary. (In 1995, the book was re-released by Harpers under the new title, *Gifts For the Journey: Treasures of the Christian Life.*) This was followed by *The Different Drum: Community Making and Peace* in 1987.

Peck's fifth book, published by Bantam in 1990, was a work of fiction entitled *A Bed by the Window: A Novel of Mystery and Redemption.* In 1996, he published a second novel, *In Heaven as On Earth: A Vision of the Afterlife,* an allegory about the life after death involving Christian concepts of Heaven, Purgatory and Hell.

In between the works of fiction, Peck authored *The Friendly Snowflake: A Fable of Faith, Love and Family* (1992), aimed at both children and adults. Peck's son, Christopher, created the book's illustrations. That was followed the next year by *A World Waiting To Be Born: Civility Rediscovered,* a book about organizational behavior published by Bantam. Also in 1993, Peck released sequels to *The Road Less Traveled* including *Meditations from the Road* and *Further Along the Road Less Traveled: The Unending Journey toward Spiritual Growth,* a collection of edited lectures (1979-1993), both published by Simon & Schuster.

In his next book, *In Search of Stones: A Pilgrimage of Faith, Reason and Discovery,* published by Hyperion in 1995, Peck frankly wrote about his extramarital affairs. The book was his personal favorite, and it recounted a 1992 trip he took with his family to see the neolithic monuments in Great Britain. Susan Cheever, a noted author herself, and the daughter of writer John Cheever, reviewed the book for *The New York Times,* calling it "an engrossing mixture of travelogue and sermon." Peck described the book as "the closest thing to an autobiography that I will ever write."

Continued on "The Road"

In 1997, Peck completed yet another follow-up to *The Road Less Traveled,* this one titled *The Road Less Traveled and Beyond: Spiritual Growth in an Age of Anxiety.* As with the other "Road" books, this one was published by Simon & Schuster. It was a collection of lectures that addressed the importance of personal spirituality within psychological treatment. It also provided readers with Peck's concept of a four-step process of spiritual development that, he suggested, went far beyond the development obtained by religious zealots, recognized saints and the average churchgoer. The work met with mixed reviews. Reviewer Matthew Scully, writing in *American Spectator* suggested that Peck had lost the "clarity and humility" that characterized the earlier "Road" books. On the other hand, reviewer Ray Olson, writing in *Booklist* praised it, calling it a "compelling" book.

Peck addressed "topical" matters in his next book, *Denial of the Soul: Spiritual and Medical Perspectives in Euthanasia and Mortality,* published by Harmony Books in 1997. As indicated by the title, Peck wrote on the controversial subject of euthanasia from a spiritual perspective, and he took a strong stance against physician-assisted suicide. Like his previous book, it generated mix reviews.

Peck followed this with somewhat lighter matter. In *Golf and the Spirit: Lessons for the Journey,* published by Harmony Books in 1999, and featuring illustrations by Christopher Peck, he employed the sport of golf as a spiritual metaphor. Even so, reviewer Ian Dunlop, writing in the *Times Literary Supplement,* commented that Peck took himself too seriously in the work. But other readers and reviewers felt that the unique metaphor provided an accessible way to discuss complex spiritual and philosophical matters.

Suffered Illnesses Late in Life

Peck's later years were personally difficult, fraught with illness and divorce. He suffered from Parkinson's diseases and experienced an impotence that curbed his extra-marital activities. His first wife, Lily Ho, left him in 2003. After the couple was officially divorced, Peck married Kathleen Kline Yates Peck in 2004. In his final years, Peck was semi-retired. He continued to write and he also performed management consultant services.

Peck died on September 25, 2005, at his home in Warren, Connecticut, from complications arising from pancreatic and liver duct cancer. He was survived by his second wife and the three children from his first marriage, including son Christopher and daughters Belinda and Julie.

Near the end of his own road, in the introduction he wrote for the twenty-fifth anniversary edition of *The Road Less Traveled* published in 2003, Peck wrote: "The most common response I have received to 'The Road Less Traveled,' in letters from readers, has been one of gratitude for my courage, not for saying anything new, but for writing about the kind of things they had been thinking and feeling all along, but were afraid to talk about."

Although his more conventional and traditional colleagues in the mental health profession sometimes criticized the way he blended spirituality and science, Peck received distinctive honors from his profession and academia. In 1992, he was selected by the American Psychiatric Association as a distinguished psychiatrist lecturer "for his outstanding achievement in the field of psychiatry as an educator, researcher and clinician." In 1996, he received the Learning, Faith and Freedom Medal from Georgetown University.

Periodicals

The New York Times, September 28, 2005.
Washington Post, September 28, 2005.

Online

Billen, Andrew, "Gin, cigarettes, women: I'm a prophet, not a saint," *timesonline.com,* http://www.timesonline.co.uk/article/0,,8123-1606175,00.html (December 20, 2005).
Contemporary Authors Online, http://galenet.galegroup.com/servlet/BioRC (December 21, 2005).
"M. Scott Peck," *telegraph,* http://www.telegraph.co.uk/news/main.jhtml?view=DETAILS&grid=&xml=/news/2005/09/28/db2801.xml (December 21, 2005).
"M. Scott Peck Biography," *mscottpeck.com,* http://www.mscottpeck.com/html/biography.html (December 21, 2005). ☐

Astor Piazzolla

Astor Piazzolla (1921-1992) was an Argentine musician who revolutionized the tango form, infusing that passionate, somewhat melancholy dance tradition with elements of classical music and jazz. His "tango nuevo" (new tango) at first brought only angry rejection in his home country, but his energy and prolific creativity—"I promised myself I'd write a tango a day and that's what I did," he told Caleb Bach of *Americas*—finally brought his unique music to the attention of the world.

Even so, Piazzolla's death in 1992 merited only moderate notice from obituary writers outside Argentina, where he had slowly become a national icon. In his old age, Piazzolla was discovered by musical tastemakers, performing with hip groups like San Francisco's Kronos Quartet. In the decade after his death, however, his music exploded in popularity. Not easily classifiable as classical music, pop, jazz, or traditional tango, Piazzolla seemed fascinating to a generation of music fans who were used to crossing genre boundaries and hearing music that drew freely from various traditions. And there were few musicians of the 20th century who wove together diverse strands of their own experiences as skillfully as Astor Piazzolla did.

Moved with Family to New York

Born on March 11, 1921, in Mar del Plata, Argentina, Piazzolla was of Italian background. Argentines pronounce his name "Pia-SO-la." His family moved to New York in 1925, settling in the Little Italy neighborhood, and he learned to speak Spanish and English equally well. His father Vincent, a barber, however, longed to return to Argentina. He christened his motorcycle "The Spirit of Buenos Aires," and he spent $19 in a pawnshop on a bandoneón for his son. The bandoneón is a large Argentine version of the German concertina, an instrument related to the accordion. Piazzolla took lessons and learned quickly.

Numerous other influences were at work in Piazzolla's life in New York as well. He had hoped to become a boxer, giving up the dream after coming out on the losing end of matches against childhood friends Rocky Graziano and Jake La Motta. Piazzolla always felt that the sport had given him the toughness needed to survive in the world of music. "If you want to change the tango," he said in an interview quoted by Richard Williams in the London *Guardian*, "you had better learn boxing, or some other martial art." Piazzolla soaked up the jazz that was entering a golden age in New York, sneaking into clubs where Duke Ellington and other swing bandleaders created intricate musical arrangements that remained rooted in dance music yet reached new levels of subtlety. And a Hungarian-born pianist and neighbor, Bela Wilda, introduced Piazzolla to classical music.

Piazzolla immersed himself in the intellectual compositions of Johann Sebastian Bach, observing the complexities of such forms as the fugue, a sort of large-scale round in which new lines of music must enter with the same musical material already presented by the lines that have already begun. Piazzolla would later name Bach as a major influence, and he would go on to create such novel fusions as the tango fugue. His leap into the professional musical world, however, came about when he met one of Argentina's musical icons, vocalist Carlos Gardel, who was making a film in New York. Piazzolla was 13 at the time, and on the street he met an assistant of Gardel's who had lost his building key. Piazzolla volunteered to climb in through a window. The singer hired him as an interpreter and later, after discovering his musical talents, as a bandoneón player. Since he was so young, Piazzolla's family turned Gardel down when he offered Piazzolla a place in his touring band—a fortunate refusal, for Gardel was killed in a plane crash in 1935.

Piazzolla's family moved back to Argentina in 1936, and Piazzolla began playing in tango orchestras. He moved to Buenos Aires in 1938 and began writing arrangements, looking for chances to deepen his compositional skills. In 1939 he joined the greatest of the traditional tango orchestras, which was led by bandleader Anibal Troilo. Still fascinated by classical music, he knocked on the door of visiting piano virtuoso, Arthur Rubinstein. The star pianist came to the door with a plate of spaghetti and was impressed by Piazzolla's enthusiasm. Rubinstein arranged for Piazzolla to take composition lessons with Argentina's leading modernist-minded composer, Alberto Ginastera.

Wrote Classical Works

Piazzolla married Dedé Wolff in 1942, and the couple raised two children, Daniel and Diana. Under Ginastera, he began to study contemporary classical music and culture seriously. His arrangements for Troilo became so experimental that the bandleader began to censor them, and he left Troilo and formed his own group, Orquesta del 46. He told Bach that a new music was "gestating in my gut." Piazzolla wrote a series of increasingly ambitious classical works, culminating in the *Sinfonia Buenos Aires* in 1951. The work won first prize at the Sevitzky Competition in Indianapolis, Indiana, in 1953, but Argentine audiences rejected the work because it used the allegedly low-class bandoneón in a classical setting. Tango audiences were no more receptive to Piazzolla's music, and a frustrated Piazzolla accepted a grant to study classical music in France.

He sought out the top French composition teacher of the century, Nadia Boulanger. She listened to various pieces he had written, and, upon hearing one of his tangos, she said (as Piazzolla recalled to Caleb Bach), "This is Piazzolla, not that [i.e., the other music he had brought]. Throw the rest away!" Piazzolla took the advice to heart and began writing the tangos that made him famous. It was tango, but with a strong contemporary classical influence in its density and its use of dissonant harmonies; Piazzolla once called it New Tango in Tails. Piazzolla also renewed his acquaintance with American jazz in Paris, and his new music was partially written out in the classical fashion, and partly improvised. At the center of its sound was Piazzolla's own bandoneón.

Argentines were still unreceptive to the music of Piazzolla's Octeto Buenos Aires (Buenos Aires Octet); he was

refused service by an angry taxi driver, and one crazed tango traditionalist pointed a gun at him on the street. Piazzolla moved to New York in 1958, trying to find work performing in clubs or composing for films, but he had little success there. He returned to Argentina following his father's death in 1959, composing one of his most famous pieces in his father's honor, "Adiós Nonino" (Nonino was his father's nickname).

Opening a new club called Jamaica in Buenos Aires (he patterned it after the renowned New York jazz club Birdland) and paring his sound down to a jazz-like quintet consisting of bandoneón, violin, bass, piano, and electric guitar, Piazzolla and his Quinteto Tango Nuevo finally began to make headway with progressive elements of the Argentine public in the 1960s. One breakthrough came when his tango opera, *María de Buenos Aires,* was positively received after its premiere in 1968. Several instrumental excerpts from the opera, including the "Fuga y misterio" (Fugue and Mystery) became well known, and the surrealistic work, with a text by Uruguayan poet Horacio Ferrer, seemed to capture the spirit of the Argentine capital. "I am my town!" sings the opera's main character (in Spanish, as translated by the All Music Guide). "María tango, María slum, María night, María fatal passion, María of love of Buenos Aires, that's me." Individual Piazzolla tangos such as "Buenos Aires Hora Cero" (Buenos Aires Zero Hour) cemented the association between Piazzolla and the city that had at first derided his efforts.

Suffered Heart Attack

The hard-living Piazzolla, who enjoyed such pastimes as shark fishing, was divorced from his first wife in the mid-1960s and remarried twice. He expanded his group to a nonet for a series of concert recordings for Italian national radio starting in 1971, and also wrote a choral work, *El Pueblo joven,* that was premiered in Saarbrücken, Germany. Piazzolla's reputation in Europe was on the rise, but he was slowed by a massive heart attack in 1973. Undeterred from his energetic pace, he spent much of the 1970s in Europe, living in a variety of places (including Ginastera's home in Switzerland for a time) and making recordings. Many of the Piazzolla recordings that remain available date from this period; some are authorized, while others were illicit tapings made as Piazzolla kept up a busy performance schedule in concert and on radio. He kept writing new pieces, including the acclaimed "Libertango."

Piazzolla returned to live in Buenos Aires in 1984 after scoring a huge success with a concert at the Teatro Colón in Buenos Aires the previous year. His return to the Western hemisphere helped stimulate a new awareness of his work in the United States, where a revival of interest in the tango and other classic ballroom dances also led music enthusiasts to his work. The cutting-edge, boundary-crossing Kronos Quartet commissioned a new piece from Piazzolla, and he complied, enjoying substantial sales with the *Five Tango Sensations* album. He wrote a concerto for bandoneón and orchestra, performing it with the prestigious orchestra of St. Luke's. In 1987 Piazzolla and his quintet performed in one of America's largest musical venues, New

York City's Central Park. Piazzolla continued to compose new individual tangos and tango songs (the latter, often written with Ferrer, remain an underappreciated facet of his output, perhaps because of the language barrier that exists outside of Spanish-speaking countries). His music varied according to the ensemble and situation for which it was written but maintained a distinctive and instantly identifiable mixture of tango, contemporary classical music, and jazz. He composed a set of four tangos depicting Buenos Aires in different seasons, the *Verano Porteño, Invierno Porteño, Otoño Porteño,* and *Primavera Porteña* ("porteño," or "porteña," is an adjective referring to Buenos Aires), and they were often performed as a kind of tango counterpart to classical composer Antonio Vivaldi's *Four Seasons* group of violin concertos.

Piazzolla was about to launch a major tour of the U.S. and Europe in 1989 when he suffered a major stroke. He lived on for several years and was able to function after intensive physical therapy, but his more than 50-year performing career was over. Piazzolla died in Buenos Aires on July 4, 1992, but his popularity only continued its upward trend. Younger tango musicians in Argentina venerated him, and musicians of all kinds began to perform his compositions. They became staples of classical concerts after Latvian-born violinist Gidon Kremer and Chinese-born cellist Yo-Yo Ma issued highly successful recordings featuring Piazzolla works and demonstrated that it could easily survive the transfer from the bandoneón to more conventional classical instruments. Jazz musicians such as guitarist Al DiMeola also began to experiment with Piazzolla's music. His more than 1,000 compositions were beginning, as of the early twenty-first century, to assume the status of enduring classics, no matter what genre classification they may be given.

Books

Piazzolla, Astor, and Natalio Gorin, *Astor Piazzolla,* trans. Fernando Gonzalez, Timber/Amadeus, 2001.

Periodicals

Americas, September-October 1991.
Billboard, December 6, 1997.
Guardian (London, England), November 27, 2004.
New York Times, July 6, 1992.
Times (London, England), July 21, 1992.

Online

"Astor Piazzolla," All Music Guide, http://www.allmusic.com (January 10, 2006).
"Astor Piazzolla: Chronology of a Revolution," http://piazzolla.org/biography/biography-english.html (January 10, 2006). □

Elena Lucrezia Cornaro Piscopia

Elena Lucrezia Cornaro Piscopia (1646-1684) was probably the first woman in the world to receive a

Ph.D. degree; she is definitely the first woman to have been recorded doing so. She was a respected and noted philosopher and theologist, although she never received a degree in the latter because the church would not allow it. Students and scholars from around Europe would come to discuss philosophical issues with Piscopia and to learn at her side. Monuments to her honor have been placed around the world, all in dedication of her amazing intelligence and accomplishments.

Born into the Noble House of Cornaro

Piscopia was born on June 5, 1646, in Venice, Italy, into the noble Venetian House of Cornaro. The Cornaro family is most famous for commissioning over many years the creation of palaces, chapels and church art, villas, paintings, theaters, and more, assuring their place in Venetian history as most of them still stand in the twenty-first century. The Cornaro family was also well known for being able to trace its roots all the way back to the noble Roman family of Cornelii, which included such people as the famous general Scipio Africanus and numerous consuls of Rome. They were also distinguished for having turned out four Venetian Doges, a Queen of Cyprus, and nine Cardinals of the Roman Catholic Church. Cornaros were involved as fierce soldiers in leading Venice in battle against Hungary, Milan, the Ottoman Turks, and the League of Cambrai. They too were involved in expanding the empire of Venice into the Eastern Mediterranean. The husband of the queen of Cyprus—who was related to the family—gave the Piscopia castle to the Cornaros, and it became the seat of the family thereafter.

It was Piscopia's family background, then, that is most likely responsible for opening doors to education for the young scholar that most women at the time were not allowed through, although Piscopia must have shown a capacity for study very early on for her father to encourage her as he later did. Piscopia's father, Gianbattista Cornaro Piscopia, was the Procurator of San Marco, which is a term that denotes the civilian job of agent for the church, and her mother, Zaneta Giovanna Boni of Val di Sabia, was of common origins. Piscopia had two older brothers, one older sister, and one younger sister. She grew up in a rather erudite atmosphere, full of studying and learning and a knowledge of what their family's history represented.

Showed Early Aptitude for Learning

Piscopia began her studies early, being tutored by the family priest, Monsignor Gianbattista Fabris, in philosophy and theology. Other teachers, including John Valier, Doctor Bartolotti, Alexander Anderson, and Luigi Ambrosio Grandenigo, filled in the gaps in her education by teaching her grammar, dialectics, mathematics, astronomy, music, science, and languages. She excelled especially at philosophy and theology, as well as at languages; she spoke and read Latin, Greek, Hebrew, Spanish, French, Arabic, and Chaldaic. Her excellence in languages earned her the title "Oraculum Septilingue," a phrase which meant that she was a master (an oracle) at seven languages besides her own native language of Italian.

Her education also incorporated the arts, considered to be more feminine, including reading and writing music. Piscopia played the harpsichord, clavichord, harp, and violin. She was also an accomplished singer. Her father encouraged her to continue with her learning, and by the time Piscopia was 19 she was widely acknowledged to be the most learned woman in Italy. People from all over Europe, some of the best scientists, clergymen, and noblemen in the European world, came to the Palazzo Cornaro in Venice, and later to the smaller Palazzo Cornaro in Padua, to meet Piscopia. She was always being asked to participate in academic debates, something the young scholar loved to do and excelled at. She also learned the skill of debating early on, something that would stand her in good stead later on in her academic career.

Wanted to Become a Nun, But Father Refused

In addition to her academic development, Piscopia was also a very devout Catholic. When she was 11 she took a secret vow of chastity, one she took seriously and never broke. Because of her vow she never married, although, of course, coming from such a noble family and being so well known herself, she had many offers. She secretly kept to the codes and laws of the Benedictine Order of Nuns, which she wanted and had plans to enter. When she was old enough, she asked her father if she might do so. Her father, however, refused her, insisting instead that his incredibly intelligent daughter attend university, a thing that was not at all common for women at the time. He was exceptionally supportive of his daughter, but he wanted her to make the most of her God given talents, and those talents leaned towards higher education. Piscopia was disappointed at being denied to take orders as a nun, but she came around to the idea quickly and soon expanded her learning with enthusiasm.

In 1672 Piscopia's father sent her to the University of Padua to study, buying a house for her to live in near the school. While in Padua, Piscopia studied theology. She had been suffering from sickness before she matriculated at the University of Padua, but the illness seemed to disappear once she had commenced her studies. Piscopia wrote to her father from Padua a little while after she'd been at the university: "With the joy of my studies, the salubrity [healthfulness] of the air, and the diligent care of the physicians, I feel much stronger; therefore, I hope that in the future I may resume my studies and thus rescue the name of our House from extinction and oblivion." While she was attending classes, Piscopia continued meeting with people from around Europe, and especially carried on her debates with renowned scholars that she enjoyed so much. These debates became famous throughout Venice and even more widely throughout Europe. On one occasion in 1677, Piscopia held a debate in front of the entire University of Padua, a great part of the Senate of Venice, many citizens of Venice, and even those from other parts of the continent. The debate was a philosophical one, done in Greek and Latin, against Giovanni Gradenigo and Fathers F. Caro and G. Fiorello. The three were well-known and highly respected, and Piscopia held her own against the trio with much aplomb. It was thought that her performance at this debate had a lot to do with the fact that she was allowed to get her degree from the University, since the school had never granted one to a female before, and even though she was attending classes there, it had not been assumed that she would have received an actual certificate for her work.

Became First Women to Obtain a Ph.D.

Piscopia eventually earned all the necessary credits to receive her Ph.D. in Theology, the year after the famed debate took place, but she was not awarded the degree, nor was she allowed to graduate. The reason for this was that the Roman Catholic Church did not think it was proper that a woman earn a degree in theology. Up to and including the early twenty-first century the Catholic Church banned females from being ordained as priests, and although that was not what Piscopia wanted, the church felt that granting a female such a degree was close enough to being ordained to be dangerous and against their precepts. Members of the University were upset by the Church's decision, and so after it was made high members of the school assembled and decided on a solution. Rather than obtaining her Ph.D. in theology, the University allowed Piscopia to graduate with her Ph.D. in Philosophy instead.

Piscopia, at 32 years of age, became the first documented woman in the world to obtain the degree of Ph.D. According to the Lindenburg Home Page from the University of California at San Diego Web Site, "[Piscopia's] doctoral examination became legendary. Elena's brilliant answers dazzled her examiners, who determined that her vast knowledge was far beyond that necessary for the Doctorate in Philosophy, which she received on June 25, 1678." She was awarded her degree at a ceremony at the cathedral in Padua. Ceremonies of the sort were usually held in one of the University's buildings, but there were so many people who wanted to come watch the proceedings that they could not all fit into University Hall, and thus they chose a larger place to hold the ceremony. It was a remarkable feat for a woman of her time period. It was especially so when it is considered that the University of Padua, where Piscopia received her degree, did not award another Ph.D. to a woman for over 300 years.

Taught and Became a Benedictine Oblate

After graduation Piscopia finally fulfilled her desire to become a Benedictine oblate. She spent the rest of her short life ministering to the poor as well as continuing to pursue her philosophical studies with people from all over the world who continued to travel to discuss the matters with her. She also became a lecturer on theology and music. In another unprecedented move, she became an instructor at the University of Padua in mathematics in 1678. She was a member of many academies and remained highly esteemed all over Europe.

Piscopia died on July 26, 1684, of tuberculosis. She was buried very simply in the Church of Santa Giustina at Padua. In 1895 Abbess Mathilda Pynsent of the English Benedictine Nuns in Rome had Piscopia's tomb opened in order that her remains could be put into a new, more elaborate casket with a tablet inscribed to her memory placed on it. Throughout her life Piscopia wrote many essays and treatises on religious and philosophical issues, including academic discourses, translations, and devotional treatises. They were published at Parma in 1688. Unfortunately, very few of her writings have survived, and those that have are mainly poetry and letters; most of her academic works have been lost. Despite this loss, Piscopia has not been forgotten by the world. The year after her death, the University of Padua coined a medal in Piscopia's honor. Many years later in tribute to such a great intellectual, Vassar College created a stained glass window, visible in the Gothic Library, of her commencement. The University of Pittsburgh painted her portrait on the wall of its Italian classroom of the Cathedral of Learning, and the University of Padua created a statue to commemorate her doings, which stands inside the old University Building in Padua.

Books

Notable Women Scientists, Gale Group, 2000.

Online

"Dott. Elena Lucrezia Cornaro-Piscopia (D-94)," Italian Culture and History, http://www.boglewood.com/cornaro/xd94.html (January 6, 2006).

"Elena Lucrezia Piscopia Cornaro," New Advent, http://www.newadvent.org/cathen/04373b.htm (January 6, 2006).

"Elena Cornaro Piscopia," Women's History, http://womenshistory.about.com/library/bio/blbio_elena_piscopia.htm (January 6, 2006).

"Piscopia," University of California at San Diego, http://hypatia.ucsd.edu/~kl/piscopia.html (January 6, 2006). □

Pope Benedict XVI

German theologian Joseph Ratzinger (born 1927) took the name Pope Benedict XVI following the death of the immensely popular Pope John Paul II in 2005. As Prefect of the Congregation for the Doctrine of the Faith under John Paul II, he had been responsible for enforcing many of the conservative theological stances of his predecessor within the Catholic hierarchy, and his actions in the first weeks and months of his papacy were closely scrutinized by observers keen on finding clues to the direction he would take as leader of the Roman Catholic Church, the world's largest religious body.

Upon his election as pope, two distinct pictures of Benedict XVI emerged. He was seen as a strict conservative, as a staunch defender of the Christian faith generally in an increasingly secular and spiritually multivalent world, and of Catholicism as the one true church. Some theologians who had crossed doctrinal swords with Ratzinger in the past had ended up disciplined in some way, and his detractors gave him unflattering nicknames such as God's Rottweiler. Yet those who knew the new pope well described a very different individual: an erudite yet warm presence who inspired those who studied and worked with him, a lover of music and of cats, and a thinker who drew on the church's deepest traditions, cherishing intellectual give-and-take even with those whose positions he did not share.

Fascinated by Catholic Liturgy

Born on April 16, 1927, in Marktl am Inn, Germany, Ratzinger grew up in the small town of Traunstein in the southern German region of Bavaria. His father Joseph was a policeman who took a dim view of the Nazi ideology that was on the rise, and later suffered a job demotion as a result. Bavaria was the heartland of German Catholicism, and the church's complex and all-encompassing rituals moved Ratzinger. "The Church year gave the time its rhythm, and I experienced that with great gratitude and joy already as a child," Ratzinger wrote in a memoir quoted by Anthony Grafton in a *New Yorker* magazine survey of Ratzinger's writings. "It was a riveting adventure to move by degrees into the mysterious world of the liturgy, which was being enacted before us and for us there on the altar.'' Ratzinger learned Latin as a teenager and went on to master a total of eight languages, including ancient Greek and Hebrew.

Even the horrors of World War II did not shake Ratzinger's developing immersion in the life of faith. Indeed, Catholicism served him as a something of a refuge as he was forced to join the Hitler Youth organization in 1941, and was drafted into the army and assigned to guard a BMW factory where prisoners of war worked. Although he never saw combat, he later was sent out to set tank booby traps in eastern Germany. During this mission, he saw a trainload of Hungarian Jews on its way to a concentration camp. As German resistance dissolved in 1945, Ratzinger deserted his post. He was captured and briefly held as an American prisoner of war in 1945. Shortly thereafter he was released, and he made his way back to his little hometown and its comforting cycles of Catholic spirituality.

After the war he enrolled at St. Michael's Seminary in Traunstein, Germany and realized, as Munich Archbishop Michael von Faulhaber celebrated Mass in the city's great cathedral, that his beloved Catholic Church had survived the war more or less intact. He had wanted to become a priest since he was a teenager, and now his life's direction was set. Ratzinger's brother Georg and sister Maria both devoted themselves to the Church as well; Georg became the director of the internationally known Regensburg Cathedral Choir, and Maria served as Joseph Ratzinger's personal secretary. Ratzinger was ordained in 1951 and moved on for further theological and philosophical study at Ludwig-Maximilian University in Munich.

Wrote Dissertation about St. Augustine

It was Ratzinger's writings as a graduate student that first got him noticed in German theological circles. His doctoral dissertation was about St. Augustine, the North-African Christian mystic philosopher of late antiquity who did much to define a realm of Christian thought and existence that was separate from the everyday world. Asked later by an interviewer what books he would take with him if he were to be marooned on a desert island, Ratzinger named the Bible and Augustine's *Confessions*. German universities vied for his services in the 1950s and 1960s, and even after he became ensconced in the Catholic hierarchy later on he retained a fondness for intellectual discussion and sought it out whenever he could. He began teaching at Freising College in Augsburg in 1958, moved to the University of Bonn in 1959 and the University of Münster in 1963, and was recruited by one of Germany's top theologians and most renowned public intellectuals, Swiss-born Hans Küng, to teach at the University of Tübingen in 1966.

By that time, Ratzinger was a recognized expert on Catholic theology. As such, he was invited to serve at the Second Vatican Council (Vatican II) as a theological consultant to Archbishop Josef Frings of Cologne, Germany, one of the central figures of that groundbreaking reform conclave. Ratzinger as a young writer was considered a reformer like Küng, and he inquired in some of his writings as to the limits of papal power. According to his biographer John Allen, Ratzinger spoke of a ''horizontal Catholicity'' made up of

bishops and lay church members that should function as a counterpart to centralized church power in Rome. It was Ratzinger who wrote a section of Frings' speech at Vatican II that condemned the Spanish Inquisition as a scandal. Ratzinger wrote a textbook, *Introduction to Christianity*, in 1968.

In May of 1968, campuses across Europe erupted in student protests, some of them violent. Ratzinger's negative reaction to the leftist movement brought about a sharp change in his overall outlook, and he turned from a reformer into a doctrinal conservative and into a defender of faith as the word has traditionally been understood. He himself believed that his views had gradually evolved rather than dramatically shifted—''I see no break in my views as a theologian,'' he told *Time*, but he moved to the conservative new University of Regensburg in 1969. He founded a widely read journal of Catholic ideas, *Comunio*, in 1972. In 1977 he was made a Cardinal by Pope Paul VI and became Archbishop of Munich and Freising.

Oversaw Catholic Doctrine

Pope John Paul II named Ratzinger head of the Congregation for the Doctrine of the Faith in 1981—the office that had once carried out what was known as the Inquisition. In this post, he was the chief overseer of Catholic doctrine. Over the years, Ratzinger consistently reaffirmed traditional church teachings on birth control, homosexuality (which he once, according to *People*, called ''an intrinsic moral evil''), divorce, priestly celibacy, and other hot-button issues on which American Catholics increasingly challenged Rome's authority while Europeans simply shrugged as church attendance dropped. He was one of the few church figures to read the much-discussed Third Prophecy said to have been given by an apparition of the Virgin Mary to a Portuguese girl, Lucia dos Santos, in 1917, but his few comments on the matter did little to dampen speculation as to the message's contents.

He played a key role in severely limiting the reach of the activist liberation theology movement that flourished in much of Latin America in the 1970s and 1980s, believing that the movement erred in associating salvation too closely with good works. Ratzinger required one of the movement's leaders, Brazilian theologian Leonardo Boff, to stop writing and teaching. He also worked to limit the influence of his former mentor Hans Küng, who was quoted by David van Biema of *Time* as saying that a conversation with Ratzinger was like talking with the ''head of the KGB,'' the secret police of the Communist-era Soviet Union.

Ratzinger's hard work was rewarded with a steady rise into John Paul's inner circle. In 1998 he became Vice Dean of the College of Cardinals, and in 2002 Pope John Paul II approved his selection as Dean—making Ratzinger, at the very least, a figure of key importance in the selection of the next pope. After the death of the much-beloved John Paul on April 2, 2005, speculation centered on whether the College of Cardinals would opt for continuity with John Paul's conservatism or change direction in some way. Campaigning for the papacy was done only in the subtlest of ways, but the 78-year-old Ratzinger did not avail himself even of those; he made no secret of his desire to return to a life of quiet study in Germany after his 25-year-stint as doctrinal point man. Nevertheless, after a relatively brief two-day papal conclave of the College of Cardinals, Ratzinger was elected pope on the fourth ballot. He took the name Benedict XVI in honor of St. Benedict, one of the great fathers of Catholic monasticism.

Fed Stray Cats

Portraits of the new pope emerged in the press. Many of his associates described him as gentle and took issue with any attempt to characterize him as a hard-liner, asserting that he listened carefully to all sides of an issue and was open to divergent views. In answering a question, wrote the pope's friend George Weigel in *Newsweek,* Benedict "pauses, reflects—and then speaks in complete paragraphs (in his fourth language)." It emerged that Benedict XVI liked Mozart and Beethoven, played the piano himself, and fed stray cats near the Vatican, some of which would come running when he passed by. Animal-rights groups uncovered remarks in which Benedict condemned factory farms and gave the new pope high marks.

With the Catholic Church in the throes of large-scale international change, some observers suggested that the selection of the aging Ratzinger was designed to install a caretaker in advance of a larger transition that might see the election of the first non-European pope or even one from the rapidly growing archdioceses of the Third World. In his first months as pope, Benedict embarked on a series of initiatives that quickly dispelled any idea that his would be a low-key papacy.

He plunged into an Italian vote that would have ended restrictions on in-vitro fertilization, leading the ultimately successful attempt to defeat the measure. Asked in the wake of terrorist bombings of London's underground subway on July 7, 2005, whether he considered Islam a religion of peace, Benedict was noncommittal; *Time*'s van Biema quoted him as saying that "I wouldn't want to label it with big general words. Certainly there are also elements that can favor peace and other elements. We must try to find the best elements to help." In the wake of the sex-abuse scandal that plagued American Catholicism especially, Benedict, who had downplayed initial reports of the scandal and pointed out that it involved only a tiny minority of priests, issued new instructions banning active homosexuals and those with strong homosexual tendencies from the priesthood. On his first pilgrimage outside Rome, he broached the idea of a rapprochement between Catholicism and the Eastern Orthodox Church; the two branches of Christianity had diverged almost a century before.

In general, Benedict seemed to emphasize a theme sounded, in various inflections, by many other religious leaders: he called for spiritual renewal. As quoted by van Biema, he called the West "a world that is tired of its own culture . . . that has arrived at a time in which there's no more evidence of the need for God, much less Christ, and in which it seems that man alone can make himself." Though he did not have, and did not seek to possess, the star quality of John Paul II, he drew crowds comparable to those that had flocked to Rome's St. Peter's Square to catch a glimpse of his predecessor. Young Catholics meeting in Cologne, Germany, in August of 2005 at the church's World Youth Day, where John Paul had been warmly venerated, began to regard him with equal affection. Beyond his positions on specific issues, Pope Benedict XVI saw a return to faith as an answer for a world in spiritual crisis, and he began anew to work to defend and extend the faith that had yielded such rewards in his own life.

Books

Allen, John L., *Cardinal Ratzinger: The Vatican's Enforcer of the Faith,* Continuum, 2000.
———, *Pope Benedict XVI: A Biography of Joseph Ratzinger,* Continuum, 2005.

Periodicals

America, May 9, 2005.
New Yorker, July 25, 2005.
Newsweek, May 2, 2005; August 15, 2005; November 7, 2005.
People, May 2, 2005.
Time, May 2, 2005; August 8, 2005.

Online

"Benedict XVI," Official Vatican website, http://www.vatican .va/holy_father/benedict_xvi/index.htm (November 5, 2005). □

Pope Leo XII

Leader of the Roman Catholic Church from 1823 to his death in 1829, Pope Leo XII (1760-1829) ruled during a time when the traditional balance of power between the Church and the governments of Europe had shifted in the wake of the secularizing influences of the Enlightenment.

Appointed leader of the Church of Rome in 1823 at the age of 63, Leo XII was chosen for his weaknesses, not his strengths. Despite rising through the ranks of the Vatican, Leo was not prepared to navigate the political landscape of modern Europe. Charged with leadership following the death of Pius VII, Leo proved to be an unpopular pope, and the brevity of his reign did little to restore strong moral and spiritual underpinnings among an increasingly secular society.

Rose through the Ranks

Leo XII was born Annibale Sermattei della Genga, in Spoleto, Papal States, on August 22, 1760. He was of noble birth on his father's side; his mother, Maria Luisa Periberti, counted him fifth among her seven sons. As was common for younger sons in such wealthy families, della Genga was destined for a life in the Church. At age 13, he was sent to the Collegio Campana of Osimo, and at 18 followed the traditional course to the Vatican, from Rome's Collegio

Piceno to the Accademia dei Nobili Ecclesiastici. He was ordained a priest in 1783, after receiving a papal dispensation due to his youth.

Handsome and charismatic, the 23-year-old della Genga attracted the notice of Pope Pius VII, who named him his personal secretary. By the time he was in his early thirties, della Genga had gained a reputation for his diplomacy. Without angering the crowned heads of Europe, he successfully delivered the funeral oration following the death of Emperor Joseph II of Austria in 1790. He became a canon of the Vatican church, and in 1793 was made archbishop of the Mediterranean city of Tyre (now in Lebanon). After serving as papal ambassador to Lucerne, Switzerland, he was transferred to the nunciature at Cologne, Germany, in 1794.

Pleased with della Genga's diplomatic abilities, Pius VII appointed him nuncio extraordinary to Regensburg, Bavaria, in 1805, hoping to end conflicts between the German Church and the Prussian government. Although his presence angered Napoleon Bonaparte of France, who objected to the Church's continual interference in his plans to unite Europe under his imperial reign, Pius sent della Genga to Paris in 1808 to facilitate an agreement between the Holy See and Bonaparte. Napoleon was ruling Italy, on the verge of taking Prussia, and desirous of bringing the Papal States surrounding Rome under his control as well. He received della Genga coldly and the negotiations faltered. Returning to Rome after failing in his task, della Genga watched as the French emperor continued to undermine the authority of Pius VII, and temporal rule over the Papal States fell to Napoleon's appointees. After French troops occupied Rome and imprisoned Pius in his palace in January 1808, it was clear there was little della Genga could do to bring Napoleon in line.

With Pius now sequestered in Savona, Papal States, as a prisoner of the French emperor, della Genga retired to the Abbey of Monticelli, which had been granted to him for life. With little interest or training in administering to the spiritual needs of the region, he devoted himself to organizing a choir of local peasants and building tombs for his family members. In ill health and expecting to live out his remaining years at Monticelli, Genga was once more called into service after the abdication of Napoleon Bonaparte in 1814 and Pius VII's return to Rome. Appointed as papal envoy to Paris, he was charged with conveying congratulations to King Louis XVIII after his ascension to the throne of France and initiating negotiations for the return of Church lands. Dismissed by the pope's powerful secretary of state Cardinal Consalvi due to his inability to represent the interests of the Vatican during these negotiations, a humiliated della Genga returned once more to Monticelli to retire. In 1816, however, Pius VII appointed his former secretary cardinal of Santa Maria in Trastevere and bishop of Sinigaglia, but della Genga's poor health prompted him to resign the see of Sinigaglia in 1818 in favor of becoming bishop of Spoleto. In 1820 della Genga was made vicar of Rome, as well as arch-priest of the Liberian Basilica and prefect of a number of small congregations.

Became Pope by Default

On September 2, 1823, 26 days after the death of Pius VII, della Genga was named pope and took the name Leo XII. He was not the popular choice of the College of Cardinals assigned to the task of electing Pius's successor; but rather was selected by the conclave as a way to mediate factions. Politically liberal Austrian interests backed Cardinal Castiglioni and his moderate views, while an equally strong conservative faction known as the *Zelanti* backed Cardinal Severoli, who desired to restore the moral and spiritual underpinnings of the Church. After a veto of Severoli was made by the Austrian cardinal, della Genga's name was put forth as an alternative. Conservative and yet ineffective due to his advanced years and meticulous temperament, the elderly della Genga was accepted because he was not likely to live long. The more moderate Castiglioni, in fact, would be named Pope Pius VIII upon Leo's death, although Castiglioni would reign only 20 months.

Surprised by the news of his appointment, the sickly, puritanical della Genga at first declined the office, reminding the cardinals of his ill-health with the statement, "Will you elect a skeleton?" Ultimately crowned on October 5, 1821, he quickly dismissed Consalvi, not realizing that the secretary of state's expertise would have been valuable in navigating the many competing political interests of early nineteenth-century Europe. A conservative in both philosophy and temperament, Leo's first acts were designed to preserve and in many cases restore the status quo among the faithful. Unable to respond to the social changes then underway in response to such liberalizing forces as the Enlightenment, he attempted to fight the growing move toward increased social liberty by restoring archaic traditions.

Opposed to the concept of "indifferentism," a liberal viewpoint that extended equality to all forms of religion, Leo battled the growing tide of Protestantism across Germany and elsewhere and expanded the influence of the conservative Jesuits as a way to bolster weakened religious orders. Leo also balked to pressure by Ferdinand VII of Spain to keep sees unmanned in Mexico and Colombia in order to maintain Spain's hegemony in the region and weaken the rebel movements of Simon Bolivar and others. Ignoring the diminished role of the Church in the political realm, he insisted upon appointing missionary bishops to unattended posts in America, viewing it as a way to curb the influence of evangelical Protestants. Meanwhile, in Italy, secret societies such as the Carbonari and the Freemasons flourished, prompting Leo's condemnation of them in his encyclical *Quo graviora: Condemning Secret Societies*, dated March 13, 1826.

Was Medieval Ruler in a Modern Age

In addition to imposing strict moral guidance among Catholics, Leo took seriously his role as both spiritual and temporal overseer of the 3,500,000 citizens of the Papal States. These Church-owned lands immediately surrounding Rome had been wrestled from Pius VII by Napoleon and only recently returned to the Church. Believing that the region required firmer religious guidance than it had received from his predecessor, Leo determined to set things right. He quickly enacted laws forbidding women to wear tight dresses and men to play games on Sundays and feast days. Rome's bars were prevented from selling alcoholic beverages, and actors were arrested for making ad-lib comments critical of current affairs.

Leo also enforced an ordinance forbidding Jews and Christians from engaging in business with each other, and imposed other restrictions on Jews living in Rome. Freed from their ghettos during the French Revolution only decades before, Jews living in the Papal States were now ordered to return to segregated communities, which Leo had walled in. Many Jews were also told to attend weekly Christian sermons. Not surprisingly, Leo's reign as ruler of the Papal States was unpopular and marked by nonviolent though vocal uprisings. Meanwhile, beleaguered Jews fled the area, hurting the region's economy in the process.

Despite his inability to understand the changes in society, Leo did oversee some positive changes. During his reign the Vatican's Library was revived with the addition of new books, its printing presses restored to their pre-Napoleonic order, and work was continued on the ongoing restoration of St. Paul's Cathedral. He also revived several spiritual traditions, such as proclaiming a universal Jubilee in May of 1824. He commented on the revival of jubilees in the encyclicals *Quod hoc ineunte,* dated May 24, 1824, and *Charitate Christi,* dated December 25, 1825.

Due to his physical frailty, Leo could not sustain his efforts to preserve the traditions of the old Church as the early nineteenth century society changed dramatically. Continually threatened by bad health, Leo XII's reign was characterized by overall inaction. On February 5, 1829, following a meeting with secretary of state Cardinal Bernetti, Pope Leo XII once again took ill. Four days later he became unconscious and died the following morning.

Rigidly disciplined and old fashioned in his approach, Leo XII proved unable to understand or cope with the social, cultural, and philosophical changes fomenting throughout Europe and the New World during his brief reign. Unpopular in the Papal States, he left behind a papacy diminished in stature in an increasingly secularized world of new ideas, fresh viewpoints, and technological change.

Books

Duffy, Eamon, *Saints and Sinners: A History of the Popes,* Yale University Press, 1997.

Greenslade, S. L., editor, *The Cambridge History of the Bible: The West from the Reformation to the Present Day* Cambridge University Press, 1963.

Holmes, J. Derek, *The Triumph of the Holy See: A Short History of the Papacy in the Nineteenth Century,* Doubleday, 1972.

Kelly, John N. D., *Oxford Dictionary of Popes,* Oxford University Press, 1976.

Wiseman, N., *Recollections of the Last Four Popes and Their Times,* [London, England], 1855.

Online

New Advent, http://www.newadvent.org/ (February 28, 2006).

□

Pope Nicholas V

Nicholas V (1397-1455) was first of the Renaissance popes. Befitting the times, Nicholas V was a complex man whose character mixed humanism with religious fervor.

Born Tommaso Parentucelli in 1397 at Sarzana, Papal States, near Lucca, he was the son of a poor physician. Nevertheless, he was educated at the University of Bologna and was a tutor in the Strozzi household in Florence. As an impoverished priest, Parentucelli rang bells in the churches of Florence. During these years, he developed a love of antiquity and the arts that fully complemented his love of learning. While at the university he came under the patronage of Niccolò Albergata, the bishop (and later cardinal) of Bologna. After Bishop Albergata died in 1443, Parentucelli entered the service of Cardinal Candriani. Parentucelli learned much about papal diplomacy during these years.

Garnered Early Successes

In 1444 Pope Eugenius IV elevated him to Bishop of Bologna. In 1446 he and Aeneas Sylvius (later Pope Pius II) held successful negotiations on the Vatican's behalf in Germany with Frederick III. The German princes withdrew their opposition to Eugenius, which left the antipope, Felix V, out on a limb. For his work, Eugenius made Bishop Parentucelli a cardinal in December 1446. In less than three months, Eugenius died; and on March 6, 1447, Cardinal Parentucelli was elected pope. He was a compromise choice; but one of the candidates and faction leaders, Cardinal Prospero Colonna, quickly embraced his election. The Cardinal announced the decision and crowned him on March 19. As pope he took the name Nicholas V in honor of his first patron.

Outmaneuvered the Antipope

The dynamic Nicholas had early political successes, including removing mercenaries from the Papal States, renewing the allegiance of other Italian cities to the Papal States, and restoring order to Rome. The Concordat of Vienna of 1448 further sealed the Vatican's hold over Germany. By its agreement Frederick III recognized both the spiritual supremacy of the Vatican over his subjects and all Vatican appointees and *annates* (annual taxes). This repudiated the decrees of the Council of Basle.

Hostile to the papacy because of corruption and the nepotism of Pope Martin V, the Council of Basle had convened on March 7, 1431. By the end of the year, the Council was clashing with Pope Eugenius IV, who had ordered it dissolved. In 1435 the Council passed a decree abolishing annates. On January 24, 1438, the Council deposed Eugenius IV and voided his acts. They replaced him with the former duke of Savoy, Amadeus VIII, who in 1431 had taken up a life of religious contemplation. Amadeus took the name Felix V. However he enjoyed very little

support among Europe's powers, and by the irregularity of his election became an antipope.

The Council of Basle was permanently weakened by the Concordat of Vienna, and Nicholas was able to focus on Felix V. In April 1449, he persuaded Felix to resign his dubious office with the generous terms of the rank of cardinal-bishop and a pension. In addition, he was to be viewed as second only to Nicholas in the Church. Within weeks of Felix's resignation, the Council of Basle dissolved itself.

Nicholas proclaimed 1450 to be a jubilee year, which further enhanced Rome's prestige as pilgrims came to the city. He also organized several missions aimed at reform and reconciliation within the church in Germany, France, and Austria. In 1450 Pope Nicholas canonized the charismatic St. Bernardino of Siena, whose preaching style had attracted numerous followers throughout the Italian peninsula. On March 19, 1452, Nicholas crowned Frederick III Holy Roman Emperor, the last time the emperor was crowned in Rome. The papacy had reached its most prestigious level in decades.

Dealt with Setbacks

Although largely successful, Nicholas also faced numerous crises that went badly. The jubilee, for instance, was twice marred by tragedy. The summer of 1450 was a plague season that took the lives of many pilgrims in Rome and throughout the Italian peninsula. When the plague subsided, the pilgrims resumed their journeys. But on Decem-

ber 19, 1450, during the jubilee's final week, a stampede of pilgrims on the Ponte Sant' Angelo (begun by a bucking mule) caused the deaths of more than 200 people; some were trampled and others fell in the Tiber River and drowned. Nevertheless, the jubilee was a success; and the money the Vatican acquired through tributes funded Nicholas's restoration programs.

Setbacks of a political nature could not be overlooked. A plot to assassinate Nicholas was uncovered in January 1453. Later that year, after Constantinople fell to the Turks, Nicholas sought ways to aid the Greeks. On September 29, 1453 he issued a decree calling for a crusade, but his call went unheeded. Elsewhere, the Vatican played no part in the 1454 Peace of Lodi between Milan and Venice, which took place in spite of Nicholas's failed efforts at a peace conference of Italian city-states. Subsequently, Nicholas and the king of Naples and Sicily agreed to the terms of the Peace of Lodi, and the Italian League was formed. It was Nicholas's final important diplomatic act. He died on March 24, 1455 and was buried in St. Peter's Basilica.

Initiated Rebuilding Program

By far Nicholas's most enduring successes, that for which he has rightly earned the title of the first Renaissance pope, were the numerous architectural and art projects he sponsored in Rome. Although it was Eugenius IV who brought Fra Angelico to Rome, Nicholas is most associated with the early Renaissance artist and his frescoes of the lives of Sts. Stephen and Lawrence that adorn the chapel of San Lorenzo. The chapel itself was completed during Nicholas's tenure as part of his restoration program. Nicholas's rebuilding program also attracted some of the finest architects of the time, including Leo Battista Alberti. Nicholas sponsored the renovation of churches and ancient walls, the Castle of San Angelo, and a good deal of the Capitol, as well as roads and bridges. He began rebuilding St. Peter's Basilica; the construction of the Vatican Palace was also begun in his time.

Beginning in his student days, Nicholas had accumulated manuscripts and achieved a reputation as a collector even before his elevation to pope. His personal library consisted of 807 manuscripts in Latin and 353 in Greek. After his death, this collection became the foundation for the Vatican Library.

Books

Duffy, Eamon, *Saints & Sinners: A History of the Popes,* Yale University Press, 1997.

John, Eric, editor, *The Popes: A Concise Biographical History,* Hawthorn Books, Inc., 1964.

McBrien, Richard P, *Lives of the Popes: The Pontiffs from St. Peter to John Paul II,* HarperCollins, 1997.

Online

''Pope Nicholas V,'' *Catholic Encyclopedia,* http://www .newadvent.org/cathen/11058a.htm (February 28, 2006). □

Pope Urban VIII

Born to the esteemed Barberini family of Florence, which had produced many popes, Urban VIII (1568-1644) enjoyed a lengthy but controversial pontificate marred by war, nepotism, and anti-intellectualism. A complicated man, he was also a patron to artists, canonized a number of saints, and extended the papal territory. On his participation during the Thirty Years War, the Barberini pope remains a conundrum.

Educated by his Mother

Maffeo was born to the esteemed Florentine Barberini family in 1568. His father, Antonio (who died when Barberini was only three), and mother, Camilla Barbadoro, were both of the nobility. Barberini was educated by his mother, who later took him to Rome to begin his philosophical studies under his uncle Francis Barberini, "apostolical protonotary," a title denoting a member of the first college of prelates of the Roman Curia.

Continuing his formal education with the Jesuits at their leading seminary, the Collegio Romano, Barberini graduated from Pisa in 1589 with a doctorate in law. He returned to Rome, where Pope Clement VIII (1592) made him governor of Fano, then protonotary. In 1601, as nuncio to the French court, Barberini traveled to France to congratulate Henry IV on the birth of his son, the future Louis XIII. During his years of service he gained influence in the French court, and in 1606 Pope Paul V (1605-1621) named him cardinal.

Transferred in 1608 from Montorio to the See of Spoleto, Barberini completed the seminary there and built two additional ones at Spello and Visso. In 1617 Paul V appointed him legate of Bologna. In July 1623, Barberini joined fifty-four other cardinals to elect a successor to Gregory XV. Barberini garnered fifty of those votes.

Became Urban VIII

Barberini took the name Urban VIII. The coronation, however, was postponed for nearly two months as Barberini battled the fever epidemic that had struck Rome. It is said that he prayed to be left to die if his leadership would not be of benefit the Church.

On his first day in the office of pope he issued Bulls of canonization for three saints: Philip Neri, Ignatius Loyola, and Francis Xavier. During his reign he canonized Elizabeth of Portugal (1925) and Andrew Corsini (1629), and beatified eight saints. In 1625, Urban VIII codified the regulations for beatification. He restricted, for example, the depiction of haloes to images of those beatified or canonized. Urban VIII also condemned the book *Augustinus,* the posthumous work of Dutch theologian Cornelius Jansen, who believed

in predestination, which was in opposition to the Jesuits' beliefs.

The literary interests of his youth found expression in his writing of numerous hymns, Scriptural paraphrases, and revisions of the breviary. A book of Latin verse written while he was a cardinal, *Maphei Cardinalis Barberini poemata,* was published in 1637. But of all his proclamations, one in particular would have enormous historical impact.

Befriended, then Rejected Galileo

Urban VIII was initially enthusiastic about the scientific discoveries of Galileo, who dedicated his 1623 work on comets, *Il Saggiatore (The Assayer),* to his patron, friend, and pope, Urban VIII. While still a cardinal, Urban VIII had supported Galileo one evening at court as Galileo challenged Cardinal Gonzaga on a scientific question regarding floating bodies. And after ascending the throne, Urban VIII summoned Galileo to Rome, promising him that he could continue to write about Copernican theory, which put the sun rather than the Earth at the center of the universe, as long as he treated it as a mathematical hypothesis.

When Galileo published *Dialogue Concerning the Two Chief Systems of the World,* in 1632, however, the pope had a change in attitude. It is often suggested that the pope felt mocked by Galileo's Dialogue, rather than intellectually disagreed with its premises (Galileo has a character named Simplicio make the Church's official argument). Despite his ill health and the plague lingering just outside the city's gates, Urban VIII summoned Galileo from

Florence to Rome. In Rome, Galileo was interrogated by the Inquisition, the part of the Catholic Church responsible for investigating possible heresies.

The Papal Court of the Inquisition found Galileo's work went against Church doctrine and thus seemed to question God's omnipotence. Having been found "vehemently suspect of heresy, namely of having held and believed a doctrine that is false and contrary to the divine and Holy Scripture," as the Inquisition wrote, Galileo was condemned by the pope and exiled to Siena, where he lived the rest of his life under house arrest.

Urban VIII rejected all pleas to have Galileo exonerated. Galileo died in 1642. Over 350 years later, the Church issued a pardon for the scientist, diminishing centuries of accusations that the Church was opposed to scientific inquiry.

Extended the Papal Reign

Under Urban VIII, Catholic foreign missions flourished. He provided enormous financial assistance for missionary work, enlarged the bailiwick of the Congregation of Propaganda, and in 1627 created the Collegium Urbanum, whose purpose was to train missionaries for work in foreign countries.

One of the pope's most conspicuous weaknesses was his nepotism. Less than a week after his installation as pope, Urban named his nephew Francesco Barberini cardinal, then Vatican librarian, and in 1632, vice chancellor. Another nephew, Antonio, became cardinal in 1627, then commander-in-chief of the pope's army, and legate at Avignon, Urbino, Bologna, Ferrara, and Romagna. Taddeo Barberini, a third nephew, was created Prince of Palestrina and Prefect of Rome. The pope's brother (also named Antonio) became a cardinal in 1628. Additional members of the family won gifts of land and titles.

Urged by his nephews into a war with the Duke of Parma over a petty incident of protocol, in January 1642 Urban VIII excommunicated the duke and took control of his fiefs. Allied with Modena, Tuscany, and Venice, the duke marched on Rome and ousted the papal troops. Peace was declared, but Urban VIII refused to yield. The following year hostilities erupted once more, and by March 1644 the pope, humiliated, was forced to accept the peace.

Urban VIII spent lavishly on military fortifications, building a munitions factory at Tivoli, creating a military port at Civitavecchia, and erecting numerous forts along Rome's Tiber river. He also built numerous churches, monasteries and papal villas, and enhanced the city with a variety of civic beautification projects. Appreciative of the arts, Urban VIII hired the brilliant Baroque sculptor and architect Gianlorenzo Bernini (1598-1680) to create the baldachin over the high altar at the Basilica of St. Peter, the Triton fountain in the Piazza Barberini in Rome, and his own famous tomb at St. Peter's.

War-Time Pontificate

Despite the raging of the Thirty Years War throughout Europe, a war that would last throughout his pontificate, Urban VIII was strangely remote and loathe to actively, zealously take the side of the Catholic Hapsburgs. Though the war began as a battle between Catholics and Protestants in Germany, it eventually spread throughout central Europe transforming itself into a struggle for dominance, and for Germany, by the powerful Hapsburg family of Austria and Spain.

The battle was critical for the Catholic Church, yet Urban VIII gave little support to the Catholic Hapsburgs. It has been suggested that Urban felt menaced by the powerful Hapsburgs and therefore failed to adequately assist the Holy Roman Emperor Ferdinand II in his war against Sweden's Gustavus Adolphus and the remaining Protestants. When France entered the fray, the pope had the option of excommunicating Louis XIII and his minister Richelieu, yet he refrained from doing so. By the end of his reign as pope, the Catholic Counterreformation had definitely subsided.

Urban VIII died July 29, 1644.

Online

Calvinists and Jansenists, www.geocities.com/Athens/Olympus/2961/jansen1.htm (February 28, 2006).
Catholic Encyclopedia, www.newadvent.org/ (February 28, 2006).
Columbia Encyclopedia, http://aol.bartleby.com/ (February 28, 2006).
Institute and Museum of the History of Science-Florence, http://galileo.imss.firenze.it/ (February 28, 2006).
Papal Library, www.saint-mike.org/ (February 28, 2006).
Rice University Electronic Studios, http://es.rice.edu/ (February 28, 2006).
Web Gallery of Art, http://www.wga.hu/index1.html (February 28, 2006). □

Omara Portuondo

Cuban vocalist Omara Portuondo (born 1930), long a well-loved star in her native country, reached an international audience with the release of the *Buena Vista Social Club* album and film of the late 1990s.

The elegant Portuondo, who was nearly 70 at the time, was the only woman among the Buena Vista Social Club artists who reintroduced classic Cuban music to the world. She stood out from that group in another way as well: in contrast to the Afro-Cuban roots music featured in most of the project, Portuondo specialized in a different kind of Cuban song, one with a thoroughly romantic spirit and with strong influences from American jazz and pop as well as other non-Cuban traditions. She was not a forgotten treasure but a modern figure, less well known in the United States than her compatriot Celia Cruz partly because of the political estrangement between the U.S. and Cuba. "In Cuba we have always had the opportunity to get to know many parts of the world, the music of South America, North

America, Latin America. I take the best from everywhere,'' Portuondo told *San Diego Union-Tribune* writer Andrew Gilbert.

Started Out in Chorus Line

Portuondo was born on October 20, 1930, in the musically fertile Cayo Hueso neighborhood of Havana, Cuba. Her parents were an unusual couple who raised eyebrows: her mother was an upper-class woman of Spanish descent who was expected to marry a man with the same kind of background but instead chose an Afro-Cuban baseball star, Bartolo Portuondo. For many years they could not walk down the street in public, but the marriage endured. Living on a modest income, the family could not afford a record player, and Portuondo's parents liked to sing romantic duets around the house. Though they were not involved in music themselves they had a circle of musician friends. Portuondo's father had attended school with Cuban song composer Ernesto Grenet.

Portuondo was shy as a child, and at first she left the spotlight to her sister Haydee, a member of the chorus line at Havana's Tropicana Club. When Omara was 15, her mother talked her into a filling in for another dancer who was sick that day. She tried to refuse, saying that she was ashamed to show her legs. ''Then my mother said, 'Do it for me. You'll see, one day you'll represent your country all over the world with your art,' '' Portuondo recalled to Rob Adams of Scotland's *Glasgow Herald*. It was not a problem

for Portuondo to learn the chorus line's steps, for she had been watching the dancers closely as they rehearsed.

She and Haydee soon joined forces as a harmony duo, performing in nightclubs for audiences that were heavily sprinkled with American tourists. Portuondo won a lead-vocalist slot with a group called Loquibambla Swing, fronted by a blind pianist named Frank Emilio Flynn. The group contained several American musicians, and they created a new style called ''fillin''—feeling—that was a stew of pan-American sounds including Brazilian bossa nova music. Heard daily on a Cuban radio show called *Mil diez*, Portuondo was dubbed ''La novia del filín,'' or the fiancée of feeling.

In 1952, Portuondo formed the group Cuarteto las d'Aida with her sister Haydee, Elena Burke, and Moraima Secada. The group took its name from pianist and director Aida Diestro, and Cuban jazzman Chico O'Farrill composed many of their vocal arrangements. The quartet was a hit from the start, and Portuondo appeared on stage with such 1950s stars as Nat ''King'' Cole and Sarah Vaughan. Cuarteto las d'Aida toured the U.S. and Europe beginning in 1957, and Portuondo released a solo album, *Magía Negra*. In 1961, Cuarteto las d'Aida was performing in Miami when Cuban-American relations reached a crisis point: after the unsuccessful Bay of Pigs invasion of Cuba, assisted by the United States Central Intelligence Agency, the U.S. and the Soviet Union came to the brink of nuclear war over missiles the U.S.S.R. had installed on the island. Portuondo, who remained a lifelong supporter of Cuban leader Fidel Castro, returned to her homeland. Her sister, along with a host of other Cuban performers, remained in the U.S.

Continued International Touring Despite U.S. Ban

To some degree, Portuondo filled a gap left by the departure of so many other Cuban creative artists, and her career flourished at home, at first with a reformed Cuarteto Las d'Aida and then, from 1967 on, as a soloist. (For a time she sang revolutionary songs and participated in vocal events around the socialist world.) Continuing to entertain in nightclubs, she also appeared in several films and told Adams that she could easily have become an actress instead of a vocalist: ''They're similar artforms anyway. In Cuba, I was taught that singers have to be able to get across what we are singing. ... Technique and the voice are of the first order, but one must know how to transmit, understand, and explain the music to the audience.'' Unlike most of the other musicians featured in the Buena Vista Social Club album and film, Portuondo suffered no real hiatus in her career. She worked with some of Cuba's top musicians, including future Gloria Estefan arranger Juanito Marquez. America was off-limits to Portuondo, but she toured both Western and Eastern Europe with the Orquesta Aragón, a legendary Cuban dance band. ''Omara is a legend in Cuba, and it's safe to say there's no one of my age who didn't grow up under her influence,'' 31-year-old Cuban-born ballet dancer Carlos Acosta told Jenny Gilbert of England's London *Independent*. ''When I was a kid I'd see her all the time on television, singing the kinds of songs my parents liked.''

The music Portuondo made as a solo artist continued to draw on a diverse set of cultural influences, including American ones. Her shows often included a Spanish translation of George and Ira Gershwin's "The Man I Love." "I admired Louis Armstrong, Lena Horne, Tommy Dorsey, and Barbra Streisand," Portuondo told John Soeder of the Cleveland *Plain Dealer*. "In my past repertoire, I included many standards, including 'Summertime' and other pieces from *Porgy and Bess*." Her specialty was the Cuban song genre known as the bolero, a type of romantic ballad emphasizing love, memory, and loneliness. Portuondo could sing the upbeat jazz that became known as salsa, but at heart she was a classic vocal stylist sometimes compared to the melancholy American jazz diva Billie Holiday or the French chanteuse Edith Piaf. Portuondo married and divorced, and her son, Ariel, became her manager.

Omara, a documentary film about her career, won a prize at the Cannes Film Festival in France in 1986, and she visited the United States that year for the first time since the revolution. She did not make her solo performing debut in the U.S., however, until a Carnegie Hall concert of 1997. By the early 1990s, just when Portuondo's career might have begun to slow down, the Buena Vista Social Club projects raised her profile around the world. She became involved with the group after its organizer and producer, American slide guitarist and world music enthusiast Ry Cooder, heard her on a visit to Havana in the mid-1990s. As Cooder assembled his group of aging Cuban musicians at the government-owned Egrem studios in 1996, Portuondo was coincidentally recording a new album of her own in the same building. Bandleader Juan de Marcos Gonzalez, Portuondo recalled to Adams, "looked in on me and said: 'We need a female voice for a duet with [octogenarian] Compay Segundo, why don't you do it?'" The 66-year-old Portuondo thought, "'What, a love duet with that old guy?' I hadn't seen him for years."

Enjoyed Wide Success with Duets

For her duet with Segundo, Portuondo chose a song called "Veinte Años" (20 Years) that she had recorded many times and had originally learned from her parents years before. She thought that little would come of the session, but the album sold upwards of six million copies around the world, and new touring opportunities began to mushroom. On the soundtrack of the *Buena Vista Social Club* film (1999), directed by German filmmaker Wim Wenders, Portuondo was featured in a different duet: in "Silencio," her duet partner Ibrahim Ferrer, a classic vocalist of the 1950s bolero era, was seen using a handkerchief to wipe away a tear from her face. The film's Academy Award nomination for best documentary feature helped make Portuondo better known among U.S. audiences.

The Buena Vista Social Club projects were more than career valedictions; they relaunched Portuondo's career as well as those of many of the other performers involved. Her voice, like that of Ferrer, retained its essential sound, and she still had an unmistakable diva quality in performance. Her *Buena Vista Social Club Presents Omara Portuondo* album of 2000, with full-scale string arrangements, was one

of several successful spin-offs from the original *Buena Vista Social Club* album, and it brought her a Grammy award nomination for best traditional tropical Latin album. "Making a record like this one had always been a dream of mine," Portuondo told Ernesto Lechner of *Interview*. "I finally got some good production values and a whole string section to work with." Also in 2000, Portuondo launched her first U.S. tour since the Cuban missile crisis, and she performed frequently in the U.S., Mexico and Europe over the next five years. Though she was thrilled to be playing 20,000-seat venues, she drew a contrast between entertainment in capitalist countries and her life back home. "People are not rich here," she told Joe Muggs of England's *Daily Telegraph*, "but life is relaxed. When I tour the world, I see your celebrities kept apart from the audience, and I wonder why that is; it seems a little sad." She was backed for the most part not by the Buena Vista Social Club musicians but by a jazz-style big band, and she showed no signs of being ready to retire.

Portuondo saw herself as a musical ambassador, connecting Cuba with the rest of the world. "I've done well in Cuba because I can sing with young pop stars, or with great musical heroes like Ibrahim [Ferrer]; I can be at the front of the stage to sing the big emotional songs, but I can join in with the rhythms of the band, too," she explained to Muggs. "If I can get the world audiences to understand what all these different musical expressions mean to us here, I will be very happy." Creatively restless as she approached her 80th year, Portuondo explored Brazilian sounds on her 2004 album *Flor de Amor.* The album included an old song called "Tabu" that addressed the theme of interracial love. The year 2005 saw her with a full schedule of appearances, including one at the Latin Passion festival in the Chinese enclave of Hong Kong.

Books

Contemporary Musicians, volume 42, Gale, 2003.

Periodicals

Daily Telegraph, April 29, 2004.
Herald (Glasgow, Scotland), May 1, 2004.
Independent (London, England), April 16, 2004; June 6, 2004.
Interview, September 2000.
New York Times, July 2, 2002.
Plain Dealer (Cleveland, OH), April 17, 2002.
San Diego Union-Tribune, March 28, 2002; October 30, 2003.
Sunday Times (London, England), May 2, 2004. □

Alexander Posey

Alexander Lawrence Posey (1873-1908) became known as a Creek poet and essayist, writing humorous works about the very serious issues surrounding Creek politics and the disbandment of tribal government.

osey was the owner and editor of the *Indian Journal,* for which he received national recognition. It was the first Native American-published daily newspaper in the United States. *World Literature Today* wrote, "Of the many American Indian and non-Indian dialect humorists of turn-of-the-century Oklahoma, the Creek journalist Alexander Posey emerged as one of the brightest lights. His satiric letters, written under the persona of Fus Fixico, drew the attention of regional and national newspapers when Posey published them from 1902 until his death in 1908."

Descended from Influential Wind Clan

Posey was born on August 3, 1873, in the Creek Nation near Eufaula (now known as McIntosh County, Oklahoma) to a Creek/Chickasaw mother and white father, although his father called himself Creek as he was raised in the Creek Nation after he was orphaned. Posey's father, Lewis Henderson Posey, was a member of the Broken Arrow tribal town. Posey's mother's English name was Nancy Phillips; she was the daughter of Pahosa Harjo, a member of one of the most prominent and oldest of the Creek families. She eventually bore a total of 13 children. Posey, from his mother's mother (Thlee-sa-ho-he, also called Eliza), inherited, along with his other brothers and sisters, membership in the Upper Creek town of Tuskegee. Tuskegee was known as a peace town, one that was interested in political and social change. Posey and his siblings then were raised among the more liberal of their Native American kin, something that had a great impact on the development of young Posey's thinking. Posey's mother was also a member of the Wind Clan, the most powerful and influential of the Creek clans. Posey's mother did not speak English, but she was a devout Christian, belonging to the Baptist Church, the most significant and quickest expanding denomination in the Creek Nation at the time. Posey, therefore, was exposed to both Creek and Baptist religious ceremonies as a child. He often pointed to his childhood as being a major influence on his later writings.

Posey learned to speak English when he was 14 at his father's insistence. His father resolved that his children should learn the language well enough to communicate with Americans, and so he would punish them if they spoke their native tongue while they were being instructed in English. His father knew that English, as the prominent language of the United States, was important to learn if his son ever wanted to have dealings with anyone off the reservation, and therefore he emphasized its importance. Both of Posey's parents also stressed the importance of education, and Posey entered his studies at an early age. Posey attended the Creek national school at Eufaula before going on to attend Bacone Indian University in Muskogee.

Discovered Love of Writing

While at the University Posey discovered a love of literature that would shine throughout the rest of his life, and he began writing, taking a job with the *Bacone Indian University Instructor,* a newsletter that published some of Posey's first poems and articles, as well as some of the older Creek legends that Posey translated into English. Posey rev-

eled in his studies and found a multiplicity of influences to encourage him in his endeavors. Later, when asked, Posey named some of his most prominent influences as the writings of John Greenleaf Whittier, Henry Wadsworth Longfellow, Rudyard Kipling, and Alfred Tennyson, as well as naturalists like Henry David Thoreau and John Burroughs.

His favorite poet, though, was the Scottish writer Robert Burns, who was famous for writing in the Scottish dialect. It was this influence that would be seen in Posey's own dialectical works later on. Literature written in the form of dialect was extremely popular at the beginning of the twentieth century, although Posey himself could not stand writers who wrote in dialects simply because it was popular. The Houghton Mifflin College Division Web Site quoted Posey as having said, "Those cigar store Indian dialect stories . . . will fool no one who has lived 'six months in the precinct.' Like the wooden aborigine, they are the product of a white man's factory, and bear no resemblance to the real article." Posey was raised listening to and reading stories told in a myriad of dialects, and the sounds rang true to his ears. According to the Houghton Mifflin College Division website, "Posey's father liked to tell stories in black dialect . . . Posey read the dialect literatures of poet James Whitcomb Riley and Paul Laurence Dunbar and dialect humorists such as Josh Billings and Max Adler. But he was doing far more than simply catering to U.S. national taste. He switched from poetry to dialect writing as he became more politically active, and his dialect writings represent Creek life more effectively than does his poetry." The characters in Posey's poems speak Creek-English, and his dialectical writings represent the richness of the Creek oral culture. Posey wanted to write in English, so that they could be read by a wider audience, including his English-speaking classmates, but he was not impressed with the way Creek writings sounded translated into English. Posey felt that English expressed the more Creek-based rhythms that he was trying to create, so he tried to replicate in his English poetry the rhythms and tempos of the more mellifluous Creek language. He found that by using a Creek dialect, he could combine the two languages and their rhythms in a new, interesting, and satisfying way.

Became Involved in Education and Politics

After graduation, Posey published his first few stories under the pseudonym Chinnubbie Harjo. It was at this same time that Posey was given the opportunity to serve as superintendent of the Creek schools at Eufaula and Wetumuka, as well as superintendent of public instruction. He also became superintendent of the Creek Orphan Asylum at Okmulgee. It was while he was there that he met and married Minnie Harris. They were married on May 9, 1896. The couple eventually had two sons: Yohola and Pachina, although Pachina only survived one year. Posey resigned from the superintendent jobs in 1897. After leaving school Posey had also become actively involved in politics. As he had been raised as a radical thinker, he was interested in helping the Creeks make changes in order to survive in the modern world. He was elected to the Creek National

Council at the young age of 22, and he continued on in that capacity until his death. At the same time, Posey worked as a field worker for the Dawes Commission. The Dawes Commission was formed on March 3, 1893 to give Native Americans, who were on tribal land that was being dissolved and sold off to settlers, the opportunity to become citizens of the United States and buy some of the land that they had previously owned by rights. It was a difficult line for Posey to straddle, because if he helped the Commission he would seem like a traitor to his people, but if he did not help, then there would be no Native American voice in the commission to make certain that the Native Americans were treated as fairly as possible. Many misunderstood Posey's purpose for being on the commission.

Posey believed that Native Americans needed to at least partially assimilate with whites if they were going to get along in the world with any success. People called him a progressivist because of this theory. Posey criticized those Native Americans who believed that Native Americans should separate from the white American culture, although he did respect older Native Americans who could remember another, different way of life. He just did not believe it was feasible to live in the past any longer. Because of this line of thinking Posey had been despised among Creeks for his part in the official procedures surrounding the break up of the tribal government and for his efforts in selling part of the Creek lands as real estate ventures. Posey, however, believed he had to work with the outside government because this position allowed him the strongest podium to argue against it. He wrote some of the most well-argued and far-sighted critiques of both the bureaucracy and the voracity outsiders felt to gain land traditionally belonging to Native Americans. It was a difficult time for Posey to live, as the politics involved between the Creek Nation and the United States were exceptionally complicated, but Posey tried to walk a line between his Creek ancestral way of life and his new country, often writing humorous essays to deal with those complexities.

Head of the *Indian Journal*

In 1902 Posey became the owner and editor of the *Indian Journal* at Eufaula. Within the confines of the journal Posey was finally able to state his views on the way his world was changing. He dealt with the horribly complex issues of Native American assimilation and the break up of lands that had belonged to Native Americans for centuries in a funny and often touching manner. He was recognized nationally for his work with the paper, which was the first Native American-published daily newspaper in the United States. It was while he was working for the paper that he began publishing his *Fus Fixico* (Heartless Bird) essays. They took the place of editorials and were written by Posey from the perspective of a full-blooded Creek man writing about his everyday life in the constantly changing Creek world. "Sometimes read as expressions of nostalgia for a vanishing way of life, the *Fus Fixico* letters are also cogent political commentary aimed at influencing Native American Territory, Oklahoma, and United States politics," according to the Houghton Mifflin College Division Web Site. Posey was named Poet Laureate of the Indian Territory Press Associa-

tion in 1903 for his work as a poet and newspaperman. Posey owned the paper, which was very successful in many markets, for six years before he died on May 27, 1908. He drowned while crossing the Oktahutche River while it was flooding. He was only thirty-five years old.

Almost one hundred years after his death, Posey's writings are still circulating. *The Fus Fixico Letters,* edited by Carol Hunter and Daniel F. Littlefield, Jr., were published to give the world a taste of the wit and astuteness that marked Posey during his life. According to *World Literature Today,* "What emerges is a playful, tongue-in-cheek account of Posey's often trenchant criticisms of federal policy, state politics, and the foibles of local Creek leaders as they engaged their new neighbors and supposed protectors." And *Atlantic Monthly* said of the author, "Posey was an intelligent journalist (he correctly predicted the outcome of the Russo-Japanese War) and his humor retains mirth and bite despite time and changes of literary fashion." Other books published of Posey's works are *The Poems of Alexander Lawrence Posey,* and *Poems of Alexander Lawrence Posey, Creek Indian Bard.*

Books

Almanac of Famous People, 8th edition, Gale Group, 2003.
Dictionary of American Biography Base Set, American Council of Learned Societies, 1928-1936.
Notable Native Americans, Gale Research, 1995.

Periodicals

Atlantic Monthly, January 1994.
World Literature Today, Summer 1994.

Online

"Alexander Lawrence Posey, 1873-1908," Native American Authors Project, http://www.ipl.org/div/natam/bin/browse.pl-A86 (January 6, 2006).
"Alexander Lawrence Posey (Creek)," Houghton Mifflin College Division, http://college.hmco.com/english/lauter/heath/43/students/author_pages/late_nineteenth/posey_al.html (January 6, 2006).
Biography Resource Center, http://galenet.galegroup.com/servlet/BioRC (January 6, 2006). □

Florence Beatrice Price

Florence B. Price (1887-1953) was the first African-American woman in history to have a symphony she composed performed by a major orchestra. Price wrote works in genres ranging from orchestral music to radio commercials, and her music, widely heard in its day, has been rediscovered as researchers have delved into the early days of classical music composed by African Americans.

In spite of a difficult life that involved a flight from the violence of Southern segregation and on-and-off periods of sparse financial resources, Price was a prolific composer. She wrote more than 300 works, and her fame extended to many American cities and even to England. Sometimes characterized as a musical conservative, Price wrote crowd-pleasing romantic works that drew on the musical language of the late nineteenth century. She also incorporated specifically African-American traits into her compositions—not, as was sometimes done at the time, by quoting the melodies of African-American spirituals, but by organizing her music in line with the importance of rhythm in African-based musical traditions.

Born to Dentist and Music Teacher

Born Florence Beatrice Smith in Little Rock, Arkansas, on April 9, 1887, Price was the daughter of James Smith, a prominent Little Rock dentist who had been born to free blacks in Delaware. He was also a painter whose work was exhibited at the Columbian Exposition in Chicago in 1893. Her mother, also named Florence, was a music teacher from Indianapolis. Classical music was valued in the household, and all three Smith children took piano lessons from their mother. The standout from the beginning was Price, who gave a recital at age four. Price attended elementary school in Little Rock and had another future American symphonic great, William Grant Still, as a classmate. Both students were influenced and inspired by one of the area's legendary African-American educators, Charlotte Andrews Stephens, who had herself dreamed of becoming a composer but was stymied by financial problems. Price graduated in 1903 from Capitol High School in Little Rock; she was valedictorian of her class.

Price had already published a few compositions by that time, and she was admitted to the New England Conservatory of Music. At her mother's urging, Price tried, apparently successfully, to "pass" as Mexican; she listed her hometown as Puebla, Mexico, and as late as 1906 a conservatory yearbook still gave that city as her family's residence. Segregation in New England was much less severe, however, and Price met other African-American students who were enrolled at the conservatory. Studying piano and organ, Price aimed toward a career as a music teacher. But she also took composition lessons from members of the school's faculty, which included some of the top composers in the United States. One of them, George Whitefield Chadwick, was a follower of nationalist styles and urged Price to incorporate African-American materials into her music; despite the rampant prejudice of the day, many musical observers believed that African-American spirituals could form the basis for a distinctively American school of classical music. Price found time to write several major compositions during her student years, even as she traveled as far as Nantucket Island to make extra money by playing at church services. She graduated in 1906 with teaching certificates in piano and organ, and returned to Arkansas to teach at Shorter College in North Little Rock.

Even in the midst of the South's segregated educational system, Price's music attracted notice; the white Memphis composer and educator Neumon Leighton heard some of her songs and assigned them to voice students. She moved to Atlanta in 1910 to head the music department at Clark University there, returning to Little Rock in 1912 to marry lawyer Thomas J. Price. For several years her musical activities were confined to giving lessons in a private studio. Price's daughter Florence Louise was born in 1917, and another daughter, Edith, followed in 1921. From time to time she mailed off compositions to musical competitions sponsored by magazines, and in 1925 and 1927 she took second prize in an *Opportunity* magazine contest. Most of her pieces at this point were songs; one of them was written in memory of a third child, a son who was stillborn.

Shocked by a terrorist attack—a lynching—in their neighborhood, Price and her family moved to Chicago, Illinois, in 1927. With both her children now in school, Price jumped at the opportunity to broaden her musical education. She took classes at a variety of educational institutions, including the Chicago Musical College, American Conservatory of Music, Chicago Teachers College, Central YMCA College, Lewis Institute, and the University of Chicago. Price financed her musical activities partly by accompanying silent films on the organ. She faced dire financial straits off and on, and at one point she moved in with one of her piano students, Margaret Bonds, who later became a noted composer herself.

Welcomed Broken Foot

In spite of these problems, Price found the musical atmosphere in Chicago stimulating. She met other African Americans interested in classical music, including William Dawson, a composer who later taught at the Tuskegee Institute and became a prolific arranger of spirituals. Price's studies and musical interactions began to bear fruit around 1928, when the G. Schirmer and McKinley publishing companies began to issue her songs, piano music, and especially her instructional pieces for piano. Price also applied her newfound musical knowledge to the composition of works larger than piano pieces and songs. When she could, she worked on a symphony. Early in 1931 she wrote to a friend (as quoted in an article by Barbara Garvey Jackson in *Black Perspective in Music*), "I found it possible to snatch a few precious days in the month of January in which to write undisturbed. But oh, dear me, when shall I ever be so fortunate again as to break a foot?."

The work made possible by the broken foot was Price's Symphony No. 1 in E minor, which she entered in the annual Wanamaker music competition for 1932. It took the top honor, the Wanamaker Prize, bringing Price a much-needed cash award of $500. Price also won several other smaller prizes in the same competition that year, and her student Margaret Bonds also took a prize for her song "The Sea Ghost." As a result of the prize for Price's symphony, the work crossed the desk of Chicago Symphony Orchestra conductor Frederick Stock, who put the work on the program for a concert held at the Century of Progress fair in 1933. That concert marked the first time a major orchestra had performed a symphony by a black, woman composer.

Price experienced another success the following year with her Piano Concerto in One Movement, which she performed as a soloist with the Chicago Woman's Symphony Orchestra. A reviewer in the *Chicago Herald and Examiner* (quoted in *American Music* by Rae Linda Brown) termed it "the most successful effort to date to lift the native folk-song idiom of the Negro to artistic levels." The work used the rhythm of the slave "juba" dance, which involved body percussion, and it became one of Price's most popular pieces.

The rhythmic approach of the piano concerto was typical of Price's attitude toward African-American folk or vernacular musical materials. Jackson quoted Price, who wrote in a set of program notes for her Symphony in E minor, "It is intended to be Negroid in character and expression. In it no attempt, however, has been made to project Negro music solely in the purely traditional manner. None of the themes are adaptations or derivations of folk songs." Instead, Price focused on rhythm. In program notes for a performance of a set of piano pieces, she wrote (quoted by Jackson) that "In all types of Negro music, rhythm is of preeminent importance. In the dance, it is a compelling, onward-sweeping force that tolerates no interruption. . . . All phases of truly Negro activity—whether work or play, singing or praying— are more than apt to take on a rhythmic quality." Some of Price's piano works used syncopation in a classical context in an unusual and distinctive way. A few of her works, such as the *Mississippi River Suite,* did quote spirituals.

Set Langston Hughes Text

Price's compositional reputation continued to spread in the late 1930s. She performed the Piano Concerto in One Movement with the Detroit Symphony, and she wrote other orchestral works that were performed in Chicago. The list of large ensembles that performed Price's works also included the Michigan WPA Symphony, the Brooklyn Symphony, the Bronx Symphony, the Pittsburgh Symphony, the Chicago Chamber Orchestra, the New York City Symphonic Band, and the U.S. Marine Band. Around 1940, pioneering operatic soprano Marian Anderson began singing Price's arrangement of the spiritual "My Soul's Been Anchored in the Lord." She then performed Price's original setting of the Langston Hughes poem cycle "Songs to a Dark Virgin," which a *Chicago Daily News* reviewer (quoted by Jackson) called "one of the greatest immediate successes ever won by an American song." The Hughes song cycle was published in 1941, and other leading black vocalists, among them Leontyne Price and Roland Hayes, began to sing Price's vocal music. Among her other admirers was composer John Alden Carpenter, who sponsored her for membership in the American Society of Composers, Authors, and Performers (ASCAP).

Price continued to write music through the 1940s and early 1950s, penning two concertos for violin and orchestra as well as three more symphonies, one of which has apparently been lost. She gained recognition as far away as England, where conductor John Barbirolli commissioned a Suite for Strings from Price and premiered it with the famed Hallé Orchestra in Manchester. Parts of Price's output were written for specific uses; she wrote music for choruses that performed on radio station WGN, and her organ music was heard in churches around Chicago. This music has been little studied even as other aspects of Price's catalog have been rediscovered. Price died in Chicago after suffering a stroke, on June 3, 1953.

The tuneful and rhythmically lively style of Price's music plainly pleased audiences at the time, but as ultramodern styles gained currency after her death, her music was eclipsed. In the 1970s scholarly investigations into music by African Americans and women brought a new appreciation of her accomplishments. Few recordings of her work appeared at first, but a disc of Price's orchestral works was recorded by the Bay Area Women's Philharmonic, and by 2002 some 20 of her pieces had been issued on CD. Given the positive reactions that audiences had to Price's music during her lifetime, her music now seemed a good bet for an ensemble hoping to make a name by reviving worthwhile but unknown music of the past.

Books

Brown, Rae Linda, *The Heart of a Woman,* University of Illinois Press, forthcoming.
Contemporary Black Biography, vol. 37, Gale, 2003.
Southern, Eileen, *Biographical Dictionary of Afro-American and African Musicians,* Greenwood, 1982.
———, *The Music of Black Americans,* 3rd ed., Norton, 1997.

Periodicals

American Music, Summer 1993.
Black Perspective in Music, Spring 1977.

Online

"Florence Beatrice Price (1887-1953)," AfriClassical.com, http://www.chevalierdesaintgeorges.homestead.com/Price .html (February 16, 2006).
"The Price Is Right," *Ms. Magazine,* August-September 2001, http://www.msmagazine.com.aug01/price.html (February 16, 2006). □

Q

Eve Queler

American conductor Eve Queler (born 1936) founded the Opera Orchestra of New York (OONY) in 1967 as a means of gaining conducting experience at a time when that profession was largely the domain of men. Concentrating on seldom-performed works and yet-undiscovered singers, she built the company into a much-beloved and viable member of New York's sophisticated opera scene. And while some continued to resent Queler's success, few could deny her achievements.

Trained and Frustrated

Queler was born on January 1, 1936, to an Orthodox Jewish family in New York City. Something of a musical prodigy, she began studying the piano at the age of five. She attended the New York City High School of Music and Art, and graduated in 1954. At this point, Queler's musical education became more complicated.

As the young pianist took classes at the City College of New York and the Hebrew Union School of Education and Sacred Music, she started to become interested in conducting, and in 1956 she entered the Mannes College of Music, where she began studying the discipline with Carl Bamberger. Queler then continued her training with such major American and European figures as Igor Markevitch, Herbert Blomstedt, Leonard Slatkin, and Joseph Rosenstock. Despite impressive training and obvious talent, she received

little encouragement to pursue her preferred career. The famed Juilliard School turned her down for its conducting program. Rosenstock, who often conducted both the New York City Opera and the Metropolitan Opera (Met), told her that the best she could hope for was conducting a symphony orchestra somewhere in the hinterlands, and that opera was not even a possibility. Even the female manager of the New York Philharmonic, Helen Thompson, assured Queler that women were simply not suited to conducting the music of certain composers, such as Johannes Brahms and Richard Wagner. Conducting, in short, was a man's world.

In the late 1950s Queler took a job with the New York City Opera as a rehearsal and audition pianist. She progressed to become a performing pianist and, finally, an assistant conductor. Yet even that triumph was short-lived. "But I didn't get to conduct," Queler told Donald Rosenberg of the Cleveland *Plain Dealer.* "The boys got to conduct (in the pit), and the girls got to conduct the backstage bands." It was well into the 1960s by that time, and Queler decided to take matters into her own hands.

Began Opera Orchestra of New York

Queler made her conducting debut with *Cavalleria rusticana* at an outdoor concert in Fairlawn, New Jersey, in 1966. Although this was undoubtedly satisfying to some extent, the aspiring maestro realized she would have to do more to achieve her goals. "I needed experience as a conductor," she explained to Stacey Kors of the *American Record Guide.* "And I didn't expect anybody to offer it to me. So I started getting people together to rehearse and play in a school. It was an amateur symphony with practically no money." The enterprise, begun in 1967 as the New York Opera Workshop, was soon given an assist by a Martha Baird Rockefeller Fund grant. By 1969 it had moved to new digs in Alice Tully Hall, and in 1971 the company became known as the Opera Orchestra of New York (OONY) and began its long residency at Carnegie Hall.

Outside of a brief posting to Fort Wayne, Indiana, as associate conductor of its symphony and musical director of the opera, Queler devoted herself to her fledgling venture. OONY presented opera in a concert setting, as opposed to full-blown stage productions, and Queler quickly recognized that she would have to carve a niche in order to survive. She told Kors, "I realized that I couldn't really do what the opera companies were doing—there wasn't much point to it. After all, their works are staged. They have the full element there; I only have the music." So she set about acquiring long-neglected and little-known operas, many of which had rarely, or never, been heard in the United States. This, coupled with the flexibility that a small company could offer in terms of dates and repertoire, attracted both emerging vocal talent and established performers in search of uncommon vehicles with which to display their voices. Queler also saw an opportunity in the Met's failure to showcase *bel canto* opera. The term, strictly translated as "beautiful singing," refers to a style of Italian singing and also to Italian operas of the early nineteenth century by such composers as Gioachino Rossini, Vincenzo Bellini, and Gaetano Donizetti. In the 1970s there were European opera stars who specialized in the genre, but who rarely appeared in New York because there was no venue. This hole in the New York music scene was yet another opening Queler was quick to seize.

OONY's well-received 1972 season offered a prime example of Queler's willingness to offer artists a chance to perform unusual works. Nicolai Gedda and Richard Tucker were seasoned tenors with a yen to sing something outside the Met's offerings, and Queler obliged them with Rossini's *William Tell* and Meyerbeer's *L'Africaine*, both *bel canto* operas. Although Gedda did not end up singing because of illness, the performance of the two little-known operas caused New York music society to take notice. That same year, an unknown Jose Carreras (later to become renowned as one of "The Three Tenors") demonstrated Queler's eye for spotting new talent when he made his American debut at OONY. Two years later Spanish superstar and Met veteran Placido Domingo got his wish to perform Massenet's *Le Cid,* a work the Met would not stage, in front of a New York audience, thanks to Queler and OONY. The widely-hailed performance was recorded live, and marked the first time a commercially-recorded opera had been conducted by a woman. Queler filled still another gap in New York opera by presenting Czechoslovakian works and artists, such as Gabriela Benackova in Janacek's *Katya Kabanova* in 1978. Over time, OONY performed myriad *bel canto* operas, including Donizetti's *Parisina d'Este, Gemma di Vergy,* and *Dom Sebastien,* and Bellini's *La Sonnambula, Il Pirata,* and *Beatrice di Tenda,* as well as others by Rossini and Meyerbeer. U.S. premiers of works by composers such as Modest Mussorgsky, Mikhail Glinka, and Richard Strauss were also presented. Further, OONY provided a debut venue for dozens of artists, including Aprile Millo, Ghena Dimitrova, Richard Leech, and Jennifer Larmore, who went on to enjoy major American careers. By 2005 Queler's

company had staged more than 90 concert performances and had become a much-loved institution in New York opera. Even Queler seemed a bit nonplussed by such success. She told Rosenberg, "It just took off. I managed to develop an orchestra that is really devoted. They get a big kick out of the concerts. The audience goes bonkers."

Not everyone was a fan, of course. Queler had plenty of critics, especially in the early years, when journalists inexplicably found her physical appearance as compelling as the music they were ostensibly reviewing, and others objected to her husband providing the company's financial support. Her conducting, too, was a point of contention that continued throughout OONY's success. While some saw Queler's style as too lax and accommodating to the singers, others found it refreshingly sensitive and innately musical. Long-time colleague Doug Martin described Queler's relationship to the music to Anne Midgette of *Opera News:* "She doesn't impose her will on it, but lets it grow." Known as a "singer's conductor," she was, naturally, adored by her performers. Larmore, one of Queler's "finds," told Midgette in the *New York Times,* "She's a singer's dream. . . . She wants to support you, to collaborate, and you need a collaborator, not a dictator. She's good at finding the right tempo, breathing with you." But whichever side of the question one espoused, it was difficult to ignore the maestro's accomplishments.

Succeeded and Prospered

As OONY approached its 35th season in 2006, Queler could surely look back on her career with satisfaction. Even in the twenty-first century, she was still one of few professional female conductors in the world. Among several other "firsts," she was the first woman to conduct at Lincoln Center's Philharmonic Hall, and the first female to conduct the Philadelphia, Cleveland, and Montreal Symphony Orchestras, a far cry from Rosenstock's long-ago prediction of obscurity. She received France's insignia of the Chevalier of the Order of Arts and Letters in 2003, in recognition of her many contributions to the arts. Despite such accolades and trailblazing, however, it was perhaps most gratifying to reflect on the continued success of OONY itself. "I never expected Opera Orchestra to last so long," Queler told Kors in 1996. "When I started it, I was not thinking ahead. It never dawned on me that it would flourish. At the end of each season I thought I should stop, because I was sure I couldn't possibly top the season before. . . . And I still feel that way. I feel as if I've exhausted nearly all the possibilities of interesting operas that people haven't done yet." But of course, she had not. Queler continued to come up with ideas, and OONY continued to prosper into the twenty-first century.

It was difficult to pinpoint the exact reasons for OONY's ongoing success. Certainly, Queler's talent for filling in musical spaces in New York's opera experience was vital. And although by the turn of the century even the venerable Met had begun to put more new faces before its audience and had effectively halted Queler's access to Russian works via the installment of Valery Gergiev at its helm, but there were still plenty of uncommon works to be found and produced. Opera stars retained the desire to perform music the Met would not stage, European singing sensations existed who had not been asked to join the cast at the Met, and there would always be lesser-known lights who deserved a shot at fame. Thus, it appeared that OONY still had an important role to fill. Queler's knack for identifying opportunities, her gift for nurturing singers and audiences alike, and her skill with the music itself were unlikely to go out of fashion anytime soon. But perhaps the real key to Queler's achievements lay in her way with people. Longtime OONY volunteer Louis Ruffalo put it succinctly for Midgette in the *New York Times,* saying, "She makes people want to do their best for her. She finds a different way of getting what she wants." That may well be a universal recipe for success.

Books

Baker's Biographical Dictionary of Musicians. Centennial Edition. Nicolas Slonimsky, editor emeritus. Schirmer, 2001.

Periodicals

American Record Guide, March-April 1996.
New York Times, March 2, 2001.
Opera News, October 1999.
Plain Dealer (Cleveland, Ohio), March 13, 2005.
World and I, August 2000.

Online

"Contributions of Jewish Women to Music and Women to Jewish Music," JMWC, http://www.jmwc.org/Women/womenp-q.html (January 14, 2006).
"Eve Rabin Queler," About, http://www.womenshistory.about.com/library/bio/blqueler.htm (January 14, 2006).
"France Honors Eve Queler," French Culture, http://www.frenchculture.org/people/honorees/queler.html (January 14, 2006).
"Queler, Eve," Ask Jeeves, http://www.britannica.com/eb/article-9125944 (January 14, 2006). □

R

Ted Radcliffe

American baseball player Ted "Double Duty" Radcliffe (1902-2005) excelled as a pitcher and catcher for numerous Negro League baseball teams. Radcliffe played ball professionally for 32 years, managing teams as well for 22 of them. He later was a scout for the Cleveland Indians. When he died at age 103 on August 11, 2005, he was the oldest known living professional baseball player in the United States.

Radcliffe was born on July 7, 1902, in Mobile, Alabama. His father was a house builder and he had eight siblings, including a brother, Alex, who also played in the Negro Leagues. Radcliffe took an early interest in baseball and grew up playing with legendary pitcher and sometime teammate Satchel Paige. He learned to control his pitches by tossing a ball into a bucket. Other big names from Mobile include Billy Williams, Willie McCovey, Cleon Jones and home–run king Hank Aaron.

A team in Montgomery, Alabama, tried to recruit Radcliffe when he was 15 or 16, but his father rejected the potential deal, saying his son was too young. When he was 17, Radcliffe and one of his brothers hopped a freight train to Chicago, Illinois, where they joined with a third brother who had relocated to the Midwest after serving in the U.S. Army. The rest of the family joined them there. For a while, Radcliffe made a living laboring at brickyards and other sites throughout the Midwest, and shooting dice on the side. At that time, African–American players were not permitted to play in the major leagues. The Radcliffe family lived just four blocks from the field where the Negro League Ameri-

can Giants played, and Radcliffe also had an aunt who lived next door to the ballpark. He and his brothers snuck into the park regularly to watch games and eventually the team asked him to pitch batting practice, rewarding him with a soft drink or lemonade.

Debuted Professionally

Radcliffe often played baseball at a nearby playground, where one day he pitched against the semi-professional Illinois Giants. He struck out so many pro players, the manager invited him to join the team. "We'd go out every year and make $50 for every fifteen games," Radcliffe recalled in John Holoway's 1975 book, *Voices from the Great Black Baseball Leagues.* "[The manager] would pay all our expenses, which wasn't bad in those days." The team toured throughout the United States and Canada playing semipro white teams. "Traveled in a bus like those school buses," Radcliffe recalled in *Voices.* "You had fourteen ballplayers, all we carried. Seven on that side, seven on this side, luggage in the back. And the owner drove the bus. Sometimes one of us would help him. They taught me how to drive because I didn't need sleep much, and so I had to drive most of the time. He would give me big money—$10 a week—to help him drive. Ten dollars was a lot of money in those days. You could get ham and eggs for a quarter."

Radcliffe stayed with the Giants through 1927 and made his Negro League debut with the Detroit Stars in 1928, serving as both pitcher and catcher. His first year with the team, the Stars played the major league all–stars. He left the team in 1929 after the manager refused his request for a raise and he returned to another Chicago team, the Union Giants. In 1930, the St. Louis Stars traded three players for Radcliffe. He stayed with the team one year, during which they won the pennant. Radcliffe next played for the Homestead Grays in Pittsburgh. In 1931, he hit the longest home run of his career. "I don't know how far the ball went," he recalled in *Voices.* "There was a playground for kids in back of the fence, and the left fielder didn't even bother to go get it. That was the most terrific ball I ever hit in my life."

Radcliffe joined hometown friend, Paige, on the better-paying Pittsburgh Crawfords in 1932, along with Grays teammates Josh Gibson, Oscar Charleston and Ted Page. That year, the team played a doubleheader at Yankee Stadium. While writer Damon Runyon came to see Paige, he left impressed with Radcliffe's ability to pitch and catch—he caught while Paige pitched a shutout in the first game, then pitched his own shutout in the second. "It was worth the price of two admissions to see 'Double Duty' Radcliffe play," Runyon wrote in his newspaper column the next day. The nickname stuck with Radcliffe. In his later years, Radcliffe made no secret of his illegal pitching methods. Although he was never caught, he was known for his "emery ball" in which he scratched one side of the ball with an emery board. Radcliffe' methods behind the plate were unorthodox as well. He had the words "Thou Shalt Not Steal" emblazoned across his chest protector and in the latter part of his career wrapped a steak in a handkerchief inside his mitt for extra padding against Paige's fastballs.

Combined Player and Manager

In 1934, Radcliffe moved to Jamestown, North Dakota, to manage a white team that traveled throughout Canada playing major league all-stars. The tour was canceled after player Jimmy Foxx was hit in the head with a pitch during a game in Winnipeg, Manitoba. The next year, Radcliffe and Paige played for a predominantly white team in Bismarck, North Dakota. The team won a semipro tournament in Wichita, Kansas, with Paige pitching five games and Radcliffe pitching two and catching two. In *Voices,* Radcliffe recalled that when the Bismarck team arrived in Wichita, he and Paige—the only African American players on the team—were barred from the hotel where the team had reservations. Although the team manager threatened to sue the hotel, Radcliffe and Paige settled the matter quietly by staying instead at a rooming house.

In 1936, Radcliffe managed the Claybrook Tigers of Memphis, Tennessee. They drew more fans than the city's white team. Radcliffe then managed the Memphis Red Sox from 1937 to 1942. Beginning in 1941, after the regular season, he and Paige played with a team that challenged the major league all-stars in a series of games. From 1941 to 1945 they did not lose a single game in which Paige pitched. Radcliffe returned to Chicago in 1943 to manage the pennant-winning American Giants. That year, he was named the Most Valuable Player in the Negro American League. Abe Saperstein, owner of the Harlem Globetrotters basketball team and an entrepreneur in the Negro Baseball League, recruited Radcliffe to the pennant-winning Black Barons in Birmingham, Alabama, where he played in 1944 and 1945. Radcliffe also managed the Globetrotters baseball team briefly in 1945. He played for a year in Mexico after that, and was recruited back to the Homestead Grays in 1947. That team also won the pennant.

Radcliffe joined back up with the Globetrotters for a series of "barnstorming" games across the United States against the House of David team, associated with a religious colony based in Benton Harbor, Michigan. The Globetrotters won 105 games and lost 10. Radcliffe returned again to Chicago as manager of the American Giants in 1950, his last year in the Negro Leagues. In 1951 he managed a pennant-winning white team in Winnipeg and, at the end of that season, Radcliffe retired. By the end of his baseball career, he had played in six East-West all-star games, three times as a pitcher and three as a catcher. In the 1944 all-star game at Chicago's Comiskey Park, he hit a game-winning home run. He exited the Negro Leagues with a .282 batting average and a 53-33 pitching record. He batted .407 in eight recorded games against white major league teams.

In a 1992 interview with Shelley Smith for *Sports Illustrated,* Radcliffe recalled his many exhausting but exciting days during his 32 years as a baseball player: "We loved it most when we were playing doubleheaders. One time we played four games in one day. At 9:45 a.m. we played an exhibition against Stan Musial's high school team in Pennsylvania. At 1 p.m. we played the Ethiopian Clowns in a doubleheader. Then at 8:30 p.m. in Wheeling, West Virginia, we played an American Legion team. I went back to the house at 4:30 a.m., and my landlord wanted to know if I was hungry and did I want a steak. I said yes. I woke up later that day with me on the bed still in my wet uniform and the steak still on the dresser."

Retired but Active

After retiring, Radcliffe served as the Globetrotters' secretary for two years. From 1962 to 1966, he worked as a scout for the Cleveland Indians, a job he secured through Saperstein. Later, he ran a bar in Chicago and toward the end of his life was invited to throw out the ceremonial first pitch for the Chicago White Sox each year on his birthday. Radcliffe faced difficulties in later life as well, however. Living in a public housing project overrun by gangs, he and his wife of 58 years, Alberta, who died in 1992, faced violence and fear. "I've been held up twice in front of my house and in my car. They beat on me. You're always living in doubt, like something's going to happen. When you go out your door, you don't know what's going to happen," *Chicago Tribune* columnist Mike Royko quoted Radcliffe as saying in 1989. The couple was even once beaten and robbed. Following Royko's column and outcries from other members of the media, the Chicago mayor's office and the Baseball Assistance Team, which provides aid to needy former baseball players, helped the Radcliffes relocate.

Radcliffe was honored along with 14 other Negro League legends at Washington D.C.'s RFK stadium in May 2005. He threw the ceremonial first pitch from a golf cart behind the mound by handing the ball to Washington Nationals coach Don Buford. At the time, Radcliffe was the oldest living known professional baseball player alive. He died on August 11, 2005, in Chicago. "Double Duty shared such a love for baseball and a passion for life," White Sox owner Jerry Reinsdorf remembered in an obituary posted on ESPN.com. "We all loved to see him at the ballpark, listen to his stories and share in his laughter. He leaves such a great legacy after experiencing so much history and change during his long life."

In *Voices from the Great Black Baseball Leagues,* Radcliffe recounted the joys of playing in the Negro Leagues—and the discrimination he faced over the years. "I've had a good life," he stated. "Of course, we didn't have as much luck as the people got today, 'cause we couldn't stay in the white hotels then. The only place we stayed in a white hotel was up around North Dakota or Canada. We couldn't do it around here (Chicago). But then some people never had the opportunity we had. Some people come along and dig ditches all their lives." In a 2002 interview with Nancy Armour of the *Los Angeles Times,* Radcliffe reflected on his long career. "I could pitch and catch all my life," he said. "I thank God he gave me the strength to make a good name for myself."

Books

Holway, John, *Voices from the Great Black Baseball Leagues,* rev. ed., Da Capo Press, 1992.

Periodicals

Chicago Tribune, November 20, 1989.
Los Angeles Times, June 23, 2002.
Sports Illustrated, July 6, 1992.

Online

" 'Double Duty' Radcliffe Dies at 103," *ESPN online,* http://espn.go.com/classic/obit/s/2005/0811/2131415.html (December 3, 2005). □

Rain in the Face

Rain in the Face (c.1835-1905), also called Itonagaju, was a Hunkpapa Sioux Native American. He was a warrior, often leading the band, in several battles with the United States in the 1860s and 1870s, including the famous Battle of the Little Bighorn in June of 1876—the battle where Sitting Bull led troops against the forces of General Armstrong Custer, where both Custer and his brother were killed.

The warrior was known as Chief Rain in the Face, and as he had no chiefs on either side of his family, it was a title he had to work for. Chief did not mean leader of a tribe; things were decided by council. Chief was an honorary title that was applied to a warrior whose deeds in battle were considered to be great, and Rain in the Face certainly fit the bill.

Acquired His Name

Rain in the Face was born around 1835 in North Dakota at the forks of the Cheyenne River. He was one of five sons, including Bear's Face, Red Thunder, Iron Horn, Little Bear, and Shave Head. There have been many debates about how Rain in the Face got his name—Native Americans put a great emphasis on their acquired names, and therefore how a person got their name was important. One story said that he received his name as a child. Purportedly he was hanging in his cradle from a tree branch when it began to rain. Some of the rain made it through the branches and hit his face, hence the name Rain in the Face. In a famous interview with Charles Eastman, however, he said he got his name from two other happenings in his life. One incident occurred when he was fighting with a Cheyenne youth and blood washed his face paint away. The second one occurred when he was a young man and was battling the Gros Ventre. Eastman quoted Rain in the Face as having said: "I had wished my face to represent the sun when half covered with darkness, so I painted it half black, the other half red. We fought all day in the rain, and my face was partly washed and streaked with red and black: so again I was christened Rain in the Face. We considered it an honorable name." However he came to earn his name, it is certain that Rain in the Face became a powerful and venerable warrior.

Battled Encroaching White Men

Rain in the Face became a warrior very young, and almost from the beginning he was fighting against the whites who were forcing their way onto Sioux land, as well as fighting with neighboring enemy tribes. At the mere age of ten Rain in the Face took part in a war against the Gros

Ventres. One of his first important battles was in December of 1866 when he fought against Captain William Fetterman's troops at Fort Phil Kearny, Wyoming. This was one of the famous battles fought by the Native American warrior Red Cloud who was trying to gain back control of all the land along the Bozeman Trail in Wyoming and Montana. Fetterman was under strict instructions not to fight or engage the Native Americans, but he went against his orders when a small band of Native Americans approached his men. The warriors ran away and the soldiers followed them into a valley where the soldiers were surrounded by a much larger delegation of warriors and were completely massacred. It became known as the Fetterman Massacre. The battle was a victory for Red Cloud and his band of warriors, and Rain in the Face gained great honor for his part in the battle.

At this same time Rain in the Face fought against other Native American tribes, including the Crow, Mandan, Gros Ventre, and Pawnee tribes. It was the custom for Native Americans to join in these battles against opposing tribes in order to gain recognition and honor as strong and mighty warriors. It was seen as just as good and honorable as fighting those white men who were crossing their land uninvited. One such opportunity to battle with opposing tribes came for Rain in the Face when he joined in raids against expeditions of white men crossing Sioux territory on their way to the gold mines in the Black Hills of South Dakota. According to Eastman, Rain in the Face said, "It was when the white men found the yellow metal in our country, and came in great numbers, driving away our game, that we took up arms against them for the last time. . . . We young warriors began to watch the trails of the white men into the Black Hills, and when we saw a wagon coming we would hide at the crossing and kill them all without much trouble. We did this to discourage the whites from coming into our country without our permission. It was the duty of our Great Father at Washington, by the agreement of 1868, to keep his white children away." Rain in the Face was referring to the Treaty of Fort Laramie, which said that the Black Hills belonged to the Sioux. When the pioneers ignored this treaty, the Sioux would feel completely justified in fighting them.

Battled Near Tongue River

In 1873 Rain in the Face was involved in the most controversial of his battles. In the summer of 1873 General George Armstrong Custer led his troops into the Yellowstone River area to serve as protectors and escorts for the people surveying for the Northern Pacific railroad. They were attacked by a band of Native Americans near the mouth of the Tongue River and then again near the mouth of the Big Horn. One soldier and two civilians, Balliran and Honsinger were killed in the first battle. Four men were killed in the second battle. Word was brought to Custer that Rain in the Face was boasting that he had killed the two civilians. Custer sent his brother, Captain Tom Custer, and another officer Captain Yates to go to the Standing Rock Agency to put Rain in the Face under arrest. They took 100 men with them and managed to bring Rain in the Face

back to Fort Abraham Lincoln where General Custer was stationed.

Rain in the Face confessed to the murders and was imprisoned. Not long after, however, a guard who felt badly for the Native American let him escape, and he was never recaptured. The case went to court several years later, and Rain in the Face was tried for murder, but it was decided by the judge that the two men were killed during a battle and therefore the killings were not murder, but the natural happenings of war. Rain in the Face was cleared of all charges. It later came out that Rain in the Face never really understood what he had been imprisoned for, as he did not speak English. He thought he was in prison because of killing a lone soldier, a different man than any from the battle he was arrested for. The battle he had considered himself arrested for was one he fought because he had not yet become noted for any great deed. Another Sioux, Wapaypay, and Rain in the Face seized and killed a soldier who was traveling from his fort to his home back East. It had been an ambush, clear and simple, and it was this murder that Rain in the Face was admitting to. It was supposed then that Rain in the Face was confused by all the events in his case, and never actually learned what he was charged with when he was captured and exonerated. Since he was exonerated, the confusion never mattered.

Fought in the Battle of Little Bighorn

The stories around Rain in the Face are many and varied, and it will probably never be known which ones are true and which ones were made up—to strike fear or revenge in the hearts of his enemies. One of the most pervasive said that Rain in the Face swore to get revenge on Tom Custer for his arrest, threatening to tear out his heart as recompense. Whatever the truth of the matter, not long after Rain in the Face was arrested and released he was one of the leading warriors in the most famous of battles: Sitting Bull's fight against General Custer's troops when those troops were defeated at the Battle of Little Bighorn in southern Montana. The fight was started because Sitting Bull, tired of all the white men intruding onto their lands illegally, had put together a band of warriors, including Rain in the Face, to push back the white soldiers. General Custer, tired of the killing of his men, gathered and led a troop to stop the Native Americans before the situation got worse. The general came upon a small group of the Native Americans and put together a plan to attack them, going against orders. It ended up that there were three times the amount of Native Americans hidden in the area than the General had troops, and the entire fighting delegation was wiped out. It was a move that was not well thought out because the General did not know the terrain very well, and Rain in the Face and his fellow warriors did. Rumors ran throughout the country that Rain in the Face at the battle got his revenge on Tom Custer by taking his heart. Many people wrote about the incident, some writing on the side of Rain in the Face and some on Custer's. Each, however, seemed to write with a particular political design in mind, and therefore it was very difficult to make out the truth of the matter. In any case, Tom Custer's body was found mutilated after the battle, but his chest cavity was intact.

After the battle, when the Sioux Native Americans were displaced from their home, Rain in the Face moved to Canada with a group of warriors, including Sitting Bull. By the winter of 1880 to 1881 Rain in the Face had returned to the United States and surrendered with others at Fort Keogh in Montana. He spent the rest of his life on the Standing Rock reservation in North Dakota. Rain in the Face was quoted in the interview with Eastman as having said, "I have lived peaceably ever since we came upon the reservation. No one can say that Rain in the Face has broken the rules of the Great Father. I fought for my people and my country. When we were conquered I remained silent, as a warrior should. Rain in the Face was killed when he put down his weapons before the Great Father. His spirit was gone then; only his poor body lived on, but now it is almost ready to lie down for the last time. Ho, hechetu! [It is well.]" Rain in the Face died on September 14, 1905, in North Dakota at his home on the Standing Rock reservation. He was buried near Aberdeen, South Dakota.

Books

Almanac of Famous People, 8th edition, Gale Group, 2003.
Notable Native Americans, Gale Research, 1995.

Online

"Excerpt from Interview with Charles A. Eastman," Carved Eggs, http://www.carved-eggs.com/rain_in_the_face's_story.htm (January 6, 2006).
"Rain in the Face," Custer's Last Stand Reenactment, http://www.custerslaststand.org/source/rainface.html (January 6, 2006).
"Rain-in-the-Face/Itonagaju," Indigenous People, http://www.indigenouspeople.net/rainface.htm (January 6, 2006).
"Rain in the Face," Spartacus Educational, http://www.spartacus.schoolnet.co.uk/Wwrain.htm (January 6, 2006).
"Rain-in-the-Face," World Wide School, http://www.worldwideschool.org/library/books/hst/northamerican/IndianHeroesGreatChieftains/chap8.html (January 6, 2006).
"Who Was Rain-in-the-Face," *Canku Ota,* http://www.turtletrack.org/Issues00/Co06172000/CO_06172000_Who.htm (January 6, 2006). □

Fritz Reiner

One of a group of Hungarian-born orchestral conductors who shaped American musical life in the decades on either side of World War II, Fritz Reiner (1888-1963) brought American orchestras in Cincinnati, Ohio, Pittsburgh, Pennsylvania, and Chicago, Illinois, to new levels of competence during his years of autocratic rule.

Reiner was a perfectionist and, some said, a sadist. Notorious for losing his temper in rehearsals, he berated players who he felt did lot live up to his high standards, and he did not fail to back up his words with actions; in a time when the will of orchestral conductors reigned supreme, he fired players without hesitation. A

player in the Pittsburgh Symphony, where Reiner conducted in the 1930s, was quoted (by Michael Anthony of the Minneapolis *Star Tribune*) as saying that "his look was like a stigmata. It could turn a fellow to stone." The results of Reiner's blustery discipline, though, were spectacular; leading the Chicago Symphony on a series of recordings made during the early years of the high-fidelity LP record, he created an orchestral sound so precise, detailed, and lush that many of the recordings were reissued on compact disc and remained in print half a century later.

Heard Hungarian Rhythms

Reiner was born on December 19, 1888, in Budapest, at that time part of the Austro-Hungarian empire. His family was Jewish but was highly assimilated into Hungarian society, and he later converted to Catholicism. Reiner grew up speaking both Hungarian and German, and he used different forms of his name according to his linguistic situation; when he studied at the Budapest Academy of Music between 1898 and 1908, he was Reiner Frigyes, following the Hungarian custom of putting the family name first. He was interested in music from a very early age and was encouraged by his mother, especially after it was discovered that he could play through major orchestral works on the piano from memory. He made his concert debut as a pianist in a performance of Mozart's Piano Concerto No. 26 at age nine, enrolling at the Franz Liszt Academy of Music the following year. The young composer Béla Bartók, who had made pioneering studies of Eastern folk music, was one of Reiner's teachers, and it is possible that Reiner's later skill in conducting rhythmically difficult contemporary works had roots in his early exposure to Hungarian folk rhythms.

Going along with pressure to follow his father into the legal profession, Reiner studied law at the University of Budapest. He turned to music after his father's death. Reiner supported himself partly by teaching music, and one of his students got an early taste of his famous temper: she reported that he threw volumes of music around the studio. He quickly landed conducting jobs after finishing his schooling at the Academy, starting out as a rehearsal coach at the Comic Opera of Budapest and then becoming, at age 22, conductor of the Landestheater (Regional Theater) of Laibach (now Ljubljana, Slovenia). He also led symphony performances there.

Returning to Budapest to take a post of the Volksoper (the People's Opera House), he became enamored with the gigantic operas of German composer Richard Wagner, which at the time could only be performed at the theater Wagner had built in Bayreuth, Germany. Reiner organized a performance of *Parsifal* in Budapest and mounted it the day after the opera's original copyright expired. Gaining more and more attention as a conductor, Reiner moved on to the central German city of Dresden, becoming city music director, conductor of the Saxon State Orchestra, and a much-in-demand opera conductor. He became friends with composer Richard Strauss and would later specialize in Strauss's huge orchestral works. He was also inspired by Hungarian-born conductor Artur Nikisch, whose minimal arm movements he imitated.

Those minimal arm movements became one of Reiner's trademarks; he could control the baton with tiny flicks of his wrist. Orchestral players sometimes complained that they were hard to see, and one musician in the Pittsburgh Symphony invited the ax by bringing a telescope with him to a rehearsal one day. But Reiner maintained that his technique actually compelled close attention to his direction on the part of the musicians. He stressed the importance of using the eyes as well as the arms in conducting, making eye contact with players and giving them cues. Reiner was well-liked in Dresden, remaining there until 1921. He married twice, had two children, and seemed to have been settling into a secure position. But he wrangled with the orchestra's management and resigned his position so that he could pursue other opportunities. Reiner was often restless, and among the top rank of conductors he held an unusually large number of positions over his long career.

Moved to Cincinnati

American orchestras were growing by that time, and Reiner was already receiving attention from agents anxious to lure him across the ocean. Vacationing in Italy with his wife, Reiner was tracked down by two of them and accepted an offer from one, a German-born representative of the Cincinnati Symphony. Reiner took to the podium in Cincinnati in the fall of 1921, and it was not long before he was arguing over pay for recording sessions with the symphony's board. Reiner took a meat ax to the orchestra's established roster and went about building *his* orchestra. By 1926, of the orchestra's 92 players, he had hired all but 26 of them.

Compounding fears about employment security for the players was Reiner's often abusive attitude (with criticism dished out in German, Italian, and English); one local writer quoted by Reiner biographer Philip Hart noted dryly that "Any day on which he failed to lose his temper was a day on which he was actually too sick to conduct."

The changes Reiner made quickly showed results, however. After an initial plan to take the orchestra to perform in New York fizzled, Reiner led the group on several East Coast tours in the late 1920s. The orchestra's concerts in Cincinnati were widely heard on the powerful radio station WLW, building a strong following around the Midwest. Reiner's programming was adventurous. His carefully chiseled interpretations clarified dense symphonic works, and he programmed Bartók's music even as other American orchestras were turning it down on the grounds that it was too difficult. Reiner also showed a commitment to the music of his adopted country, becoming one of the first major symphony conductors to champion the crossover music of George Gershwin. Gershwin performed his *Rhapsody in Blue* and Piano Concerto in F under Reiner's baton in Cincinnati in March of 1928. Reiner became an American citizen that year.

In the spring of 1930 Reiner divorced his second wife, Berta, in order to marry actress Carlotta Irwin. The marriage was a happy one and endured for the rest of Reiner's life, but at the time, in conservative Cincinnati, it caused a scandal. Reiner was forced to resign as conductor after subscriptions plummeted. For much of the 1930s he taught at the Curtis Institute of Music in Philadelphia, making frequent trips to conduct opera performances. In London he conducted the first performance of the legendary Norwegian soprano Kirsten Flagstad as Isolde in Wagner's *Tristan und Isolde*, and at home in Philadelphia he conducted the premiere of Gian-Carlo Menotti's *Amelia Goes to the Ball*. Among Reiner's students was Leonard Bernstein, whose athletic leaps on the podium represented the polar opposite of Reiner's style. Yet Bernstein (according to Hart) felt that "Reiner was responsible for my own very high standards."

After several years of searching for a new symphonic post, Reiner was hired as music director of the Pittsburgh Symphony in 1938. He once again went on a firing spree, replacing 90 percent of the orchestra's personnel over his first three years at the helm. Players joked that at his own funeral, he would fire some of the pallbearers. But some members of Reiner's old Cincinnati Symphony, knowing that a high-quality musical experience was guaranteed despite all the abuse, followed him to Pittsburgh, and Reiner once again helped an only moderately well-known orchestra make its mark. Reiner led the Pittsburgh Symphony to its first recording contract (with the Columbia label) in 1941, and his programming in Pittsburgh testified to both his skill and his variety of interests; over ten years he conducted more than 500 works, at least half of them for the first time. A 1947 ranking of American symphony orchestras put Pittsburgh's in first place in both the amount of new music and the amount of American music programmed, and Reiner could claim credit.

Returned to Opera Pit

It was financial disputes once again that led to Reiner's departure from Pittsburgh, in 1948. He moved to New York and was signed to conduct a series of performances at the Metropolitan Opera, making a splash with his debut in 1949 with a performance of Richard Strauss's *Salome;* the performance featured soprano Ljuba Welitsch in the title role and is considered one of the great moments in Met history. Leading 113 performances over five years, Reiner confirmed his reputation as one of the opera world's conducting luminaries. His talents ran from the lush, decadent *Salome* to Igor Stravinsky's dry *The Rake's Progress,* which Reiner conducted in its first Met performance. Critics split hairs over whether Reiner was superior as an operatic or as a symphonic conductor, but he approached each task with the same rigor and perfectionist spirit.

In 1953 Reiner was hired as conductor of the Chicago Symphony Orchestra, remaining in the post until 1962. The Chicago Symphony was an organization with a long history, already ranked among the country's top ensembles, and Reiner cut less of a swath through the group of established players there than he had in Pittsburgh and Cincinnati. He continued to challenge audiences with new music and also to challenge himself—even in his old age, about one-third of the roughly 500 works he conducted in Chicago were pieces he had not previously known. Reiner liked to shut himself away to study new scores closely, and in the case of a large Wagner opera he might meditate for years on parts of it before announcing that he was ready to perform it.

Feared by musicians, Reiner was respected by his fellow conductors. "To his colleagues he was a conductor's conductor . . .," noted Harold C. Schonberg in *The Great Conductors.* He was "a musician of formidable background and knowledge who could do anything with an orchestra. In certain kinds of contemporary music . . . he had a stupendous ability to clarify the most complicated writing. A score like Bartók's *Miraculous Mandarin* came out with titanic surges of sound and wild (but perfectly controlled) rhythms, and with textures that in their clarity and balances were positively Mozartean." Reiner's recordings in Chicago, released on the RCA label in top-notch recorded sound, remained strong sellers even after a new generation of conductors and sound engineers had come to the fore.

Reiner suffered from heart problems over his last few years in Chicago, and it was probably because of those that he canceled a major tour of Western and Eastern Europe with the Chicago Symphony in 1960—a decision that caused an uproar in Chicago, for the crossing of the Iron Curtain into the Communist world would have marked a major breakthrough for the orchestra. After several years of part-time conducting, Reiner left his post in Chicago in 1962. He was appointed musical advisor at the Metropolitan Opera in New York and signed to conduct a new performance of Wagner's *The Twilight of the Gods,* but he contracted pneumonia and died in New York on November 15, 1963.

Books

Hart, Philip, *Fritz Reiner,* Northwestern University Press, 1994.

International Dictionary of Opera, St. James, 1993.
Morgan, Kenneth, *Fritz Reiner, Maestro and Martinet,* University of Illinois Press, 2004.
Schonberg, Harold C., *The Great Conductors,* Simon and Schuster, 1967.

Periodicals

Pittsburgh Post-Gazette, January 22, 2006.
Sensible Sound, January-February 2005.
Star Tribune (Minneapolis, MN), August 22, 2004.

Online

"Fritz Reiner," Chicago Symphony Orchestra, http://www.cso.org/main.taf?p = 7,3,1,4,6 (January 26, 2006). □

Mikolaj Rej

Known as the Father of Polish Literature, Mikolaj Rej (1505-1569) was the first writer to produce a substantial body of original work in the Polish language. "Let the neighboring nations know that Poles are not geese, but have their own language," he once wrote, according to Czeslaw Milosz's *The History of Polish Literature.*

The comment was characteristic of Rej, whose writings were practical, often humorous, and down-to-earth in a way that recalled such Western European writers as medieval England's Geoffrey Chaucer and François Rabelais of early Renaissance France. Rej's own writings were poised between the Middle Ages and the Renaissance. For the circle of Polish nobles, of which he was a part, he wrote instructional texts, humorous and satirical poems and dialogues, and sermons. Like the medieval writers of the West, he struggled to shape a vernacular, everyday language into a literary instrument. In one critical way, however, Rej's writing was on the cutting edge in its own time: he dealt frequently with the great schism in European Christianity between Catholicism and Protestantism.

Had Spotty Education

Rej (or Rey) was born February 4, 1505, in Zurawno, near Halicz, Poland. Rej's father, a minor nobleman, was illiterate, and Rej spent much of his childhood hunting and fishing, activities for which he never lost the taste. Starting school at the age of nine, he attended primary schools for four years in the cities of Skalmierz and Lwów and spent part of one year at Jagiellonian University in Krakow. Despite the brevity of his formal education, Rej was curious and read widely on a great variety of subjects, studying drama and the history of art, among other fields. In 1525 the 20-year-old Rej was sent to the court of a relative in Sandomierz, a nobleman named Andrzej Teczynski, to acquire the Polish expected of an aristocratic young man.

Rej's father died in 1531, and at that point he moved on to the court of another relative, Herman Mikolaj Sieniawski, near Chelm. Sieniawski was a leading figure of Polish Protestantism, and at some point in the 1540s Rej became a member of the Calvinist faith. Earlier in his life he had been described as anticlerical (an opponent of the clergy). It is possible that he had Protestant sympathies during this time, but hid them; Protestantism was repressed under the reign of Poland's King Sigismundus I (died 1548). Rej admired the German religious reformer Martin Luther, and later wrote a short poem praising him. Well-connected and active in Polish politics, Rej moved at some point to the Naglowice and was appointed administrator of towns in the vicinity.

Rej began his literary career in 1543, using the pen name Mikolaj from Naglowice. (He also sometimes used the pseudonym Ambrozy Korczbok Rozek.) Rej's first book, often still considered his greatest, was a 2,000-line satirical poetic dialogue called *Krótka rozprawa miedzy trzema osobami, Panem, Wójtem a Plebanem* (A Short Discourse Among the Squire, the Bailiff, and the Parson). The three figures in the poem represent the three classes of Polish society, the nobility, the common people, and the clergy, respectively; they are Polish counterparts to the various social types represented in Chaucer's *Canterbury Tales.* They argue, point out each other's failings, and form temporary alliances. The Parson, at one point addressing the Squire, asks (as translated by Michael J. Mikoś), "Is this the bailiff cackling loud? / With what could we fill up his mouth? /If we had a jug of good beer / We could talk down the wise master." Though Rej was himself a member of the noble class, the Squire and the Parson get the worst of it in the debate.

Corruption among the Catholic clergy was an important theme in the *Discourse,* and it frequently recurred in the work of the Protestant Rej. Although his work was often humorous and even obscene at times, Rej felt that his writing had a moral purpose. He was tolerant in spirit, however, and as he grew to a position in which he oversaw large estates, he permitted his subjects to hold Catholic services if they wished, and he had friends among both Protestants and Catholics.

Adapted Works by Foreign Authors

Rej wrote two other poetic dialogues during the 1540s, works that lay closer to the dramatic end of the spectrum between poetry and play than did the *Short Discourse Among the Squire, the Bailiff, and the Parson.* The *Zywot Józefa z pokolenia zydowskiego, syna Jakubowego* (Life of Joseph of a Jewish Tribe, 1545) was a 12-act biblical drama modeled on a play by a Dutch author. The work also incorporated elements of earlier Latin religious dramas. "Even if Joseph is very boring in his Puritan virtue, one cannot say that the siren who tries to seduce him, the wife [Zefira] of the Egyptian lord Potiphar, does not make a lively figure of a woman possessed by her passion," Milosz wrote. These scenes of temptation are comic interludes in the otherwise serious work. Despite its length, the play has been staged by modern theatrical producers. When Rej adapted works by other writers, he always added a great deal of local and characteristically Polish detail. His works are considered valuable sources of information about Polish life in the sixteenth century.

Rej's other verse drama of the 1540s was *Kupiec* (The Merchant, 1549). That morality play, about the final judgment of an immoral merchant, had an explicitly Protestant theme, perhaps made possible by the death of King Sigismundus the previous year. It was based on a play by a German writer, Neogeorgus. The merchant is brought before the scales of justice along with a group of powerful churchmen—princes, bishops, and abbots of monasteries. They throw the records of their churches, monasteries, and good deeds onto the scales, along with letters from the Pope, but the scales do not move. The merchant has no such good works to advance his case, but in the end, consistent with the Protestant doctrine of faith in Christ as the sole path to salvation, he is saved by his faith alone.

Rej also wrote a lot of specifically religious material, beginning with a prose paraphrase of the Psalms of David in 1546. His major religious work was the *Postilla* of 1557, a 7,000-page collection of sermons filled with Rej's particular brand of down-to-earth religious maxims. The *Postilla* was a key work in spreading Rej's reputation around northeastern Europe; it was translated into Lithuanian and Ruthenian, and went through five editions in Polish.

By the time he wrote these works, Rej was a wealthy man, the owner of two castles. He founded two new towns, Rejowiec and Oksza, and was the administrator for 20 others, establishing Protestant churches and schools in many of them. Rej tried to avoid the entanglements of administrative work, however, so that he could devote as much time as possible to writing and to his favorite leisure pursuits. By the mid-1550s he was considered an old man in a society where the average lifespan was about 20-25 years. His last decade of writing, indeed, was as productive as his first.

Wrote Major Work in 1568

In 1558 Rej published *Wizerunek wlasny zywota czlowieka poczciwego* (A Faithful Image of an Honest Man), a 10,000-line poem about a young man who travels the world in search of truth, visiting ancient philosophers and sages such as Aristotle, Diogenes, and Epicurus, and asking them about the secrets of life. The work was modeled on a Latin-language poem called *Zodiacus vitae* by the Italian writer Paligenius, but Rej once again added a wealth of local detail that made it familiar to Polish readers. The Greek sages visited by the young man, in the words of Manfred Kridl (writing in *A Survey of Polish Literature and Culture*), "discuss, with great knowledge, the deficiencies of the Polish gentry and clergy (already known to us from the *Short Discourse*); they are very well acquainted with Polish cuisine, accuse the Poles of dining too elaborately, holding bizarre parties, and characterize Polish officials and landlords." *A Faithful Image of an Honest Man* appeared in several new editions after Rej's death.

Rej's sense of humor also appeared intermittently in his next work, *Zwierzyniec* (The Zoo, or the Bestiary, 1562). The book was a collection of eight-line poems on subjects ranging from historical and mythological figures to current events and human follies. Rej wrote poems about himself, about his contemporary Jan Kochanowski, about Martin Luther, and about the pope. He also aimed gibes at

Catholicism in such poems as "The Old Woman Who Cried During the Passion of Christ." As a priest intones the Passion story in Latin, the woman says (in Mikoś's translation), "I don't cry because of that; But recall my dear little donkey which is dead / It brayed with the voice which sounded just like the priest's / It whimpered from time to time and then was at peace."

The major work of Rej's late years was *Zwierciadlo* (The Mirror, 1568), a work that has parallels among other national literatures in its attempt to define the well-lived life. *The Mirror* is a large work, written partly in verse and partly in prose, and it once again is an invaluable source of information on the life of Poland's upper classes during the period in which Rej lived. Rej begins with a lengthy discourse on the astrological and chemical forces that shape the lives of humans; he believed in the medieval doctrine of the four humors, but he believed that reason could overcome such forces. He proceeds through the proper education of a young man, stressing the importance of horseback riding, shooting, and sports. Rej believed that literacy was important but asserted that such difficult subjects as grammar and logic should be avoided at all costs.

Moving on to adulthood, Rej stresses the importance of choosing a good wife and gives advice to this end; he was perhaps qualified in view of his own happy marriage to one Zofia Kosnowna. He extolled the joys of life on a country estate, delving into cuisine, hunting, and the natural world. Christian themes are introduced, with the warning that moderation is necessary in whatever pleasures a nobleman may seek out. Written as a philosophical meditation on life and virtue, the book was perhaps a portrait and a summing-up of Rej's own long and happy life.

Rej died at Rejowiec between September 8 and October 5 of 1569. For several centuries his name was little known, but he was rediscovered by the nineteenth-century Polish poet and nationalist Adam Mickiewicz. He was the subject of scholarly studies and plays (in Polish) in modern times, and one of his descendants, Nicholas Andrew Rey, served as Poland's ambassador to the United States in the late twentieth century. Not widely read in the West, partly due to the difficulty of translating his colloquial Polish, he remained an appealing figure with high status in his native land. In 2005, on the 500th anniversary of his birth, Poland's parliament proclaimed a "Year of Mikolaj Rej."

Books

Kridl, Manfred, *A Survey of Polish Literature and Culture,* Translated by Olga Scherer-Virski. Mouton & Co. ('s-Gravenhage, Netherlands), 1956.

Mikoś, Michael J, *Polish Literature from the Middle Ages to the End of the Eighteenth Century: A Bilingual Anthology,* Constans (Warsaw), 1999.

Milosz, Czeslaw. *The History of Polish Literature,* 2nd ed. University of California Press, 1983.

Online

"Mikolaj Rej, the Father of Polish Literature, 500th Anniversary of His Birth," http://www.culture.polishsite.us/articles/art343fr .htm (January 20, 2006).

"Prominent Poles: Mikolaj Rej of Naglowice (aka Ambrozy Korczbok Rozek), writer, politician, musician," http://www .angelfire.com/scifi2/rsolecki/mikolaj_rej.html (January 20, 2006). □

John G. Roberts, Jr.

When he was sworn in by Associate Justice John Paul Stevens on September 29, 2005, John Glover Roberts, Jr. (born 1955) became the seventeenth Chief Justice of the United States Supreme Court.

At age 50, Roberts was the youngest chief justice since John Marshall sat on the bench in the early nineteenth century. He had served as a staff attorney in the Republican party administrations of Presidents Ronald Reagan and George H.W. Bush, worked in private practice, and spent a short time as a judge on the U.S. Court of Appeals. But he did not have a long trail of legal opinions, and court watchers waited to learn of the direction in which he would steer the highest court in the United States. Roberts was thought to be conservative by temperament but not necessarily by ideology. Those who looked into Roberts's background, however, agreed on one thing: he had a deep reverence for the law as an institution and as a profession, and his career had been marked by an ambition to advance to its highest levels.

Attended Catholic Boarding School

Born in Buffalo, New York, on January 27, 1955, Roberts was the son of steel mill manager John "Jack" Roberts and his wife Rosemary. He had three sisters. The family soon moved to Long Beach, Indiana, on the southern end of Lake Michigan, where Jack Roberts was sent by his employer, Bethlehem Steel, to help with the opening and administration of the electrical engineering section of a new plant in nearby Burns Harbor. The area was heavily Catholic, and John Roberts attended an elementary school affiliated with Notre Dame Church, where the family worshiped. For high school he was sent to a nearby Catholic academy, all-male La Lumiere School, in La Porte, Indiana. In a high school newspaper opinion piece he argued against making the school coeducational. "I would prefer to discuss Shakespeare's double entendre and the latus rectum of conic sections without a [b]londe giggling and blushing beside me," he wrote (according to Guy Taylor of the *Washington Times*).

Double entendres aside, Roberts was a top-flight student in high school. His expository essays, classmates remembered, were so persuasive that he could argue successfully in favor of even preposterous positions. He blazed through La Lumiere's Latin-language classes, demanded an independent study course in his senior year, and reached a point where he could translate Virgil's *Aeneid* as well as or better than his teacher. "It became very, very clear and evident when he first came here that he was a person who was destined to do big things," La Lumiere

math teacher Lawrence Sullivan told the *International Herald Tribune*. A well-rounded student, Roberts also played football, won 12 out of 13 wrestling matches one year, and even took on the thankless role of Peppermint Patty in an all-male production of the musical *You're a Good Man, Charlie Brown*.

On his high school admissions application, Taylor reported, Roberts wrote, "I won't be content to get a good job by getting a good education, I want to get the best job by getting the best education." The first La Lumiere student to attend Harvard University, Roberts continued to put that philosophy into practice there. Several of his undergraduate papers won coveted Harvard prizes; one of them, "The Utopian Conservative," was about statesman Daniel Webster and his devotion to his deeply held principles. At Harvard, Roberts was thought of as conservative, but he arrived at the school in the relatively apolitical 1970s and never struck classmates as in any way outspoken. He did little that would distract him from his focus on his studies, and he graduated *summa cum laude* in 1976. A devoted alumnus, he remained "romantic about all things Harvard," according to a law clerk quoted in *Newsweek*.

He immediately entered Harvard Law School, and he continued to avoid activist stances. The law school at the time was roiled by controversies over the relationship between the law and politics, but Roberts steered clear. Impressing professors of various political stripes, he was appointed managing editor of the *Harvard Law Review*, a plum post. "From our time in law review, it wasn't like John was a gung-ho conser-

vative," lawyer Stephen Galebach told the *International Herald Tribune*. "He wasn't active. He wasn't a gung-ho liberal on liberal causes." Instead, Galebach said, Roberts focused "on the craftsmanship" of laws. Shortly after receiving his law degree, *magna cum laude,* in 1979, he was hospitalized, suffering from exhaustion.

Won Top Clerkships

With his stellar credentials, Roberts had no trouble lining up top jobs in the next stage of his legal apprenticeship. He became a clerk for Judge Henry J. Friendly of the U.S. Court of Appeals for the Second Circuit in New York City in 1979 and then for Associate Supreme Court Justice (later Chief Justice) William Rehnquist the following year. The demanding Friendly was a strong influence on Roberts, who (according to *Newsweek*) spoke of his mentor with "deep reverence" and "a certain twinkle in his eye," and sometimes quoted him in his own opinions as an appeals court judge. With the election of Ronald Reagan to the presidency in 1980, Roberts went to work for the new Republican administration. He became special assistant to Attorney General William French Smith in 1981 and was elevated to the position of Reagan's associate counsel in 1982, which made him part of the White House staff.

The energetic Roberts had little patience with the argument commonly made by Supreme Court justices that the high court was overburdened, writing in a memo quoted by *Time* that "[s]o long as the court views itself as ultimately responsible for governing all aspects of our society, it will, understandably, be overworked." In 1986 Roberts left government to take a position at the prestigious Washington law firm Hogan & Hartson LLP, rising to the position of head of the firm's appellate practice division. The new administration of President George H.W. Bush, however, brought him back to the White House in 1989 to become principal deputy solicitor general of the United States. In this position he became a frequent visitor to the halls of the Supreme Court as he often argued the government's position. He appeared before the high court more than 30 times.

Roberts's writings during his two periods of service in Republican administrations emerged as sources of controversy during the U.S. Senate confirmation hearings preceding his elevation to the Supreme Court. He favored narrow interpretations of civil-rights and voting-rights statutes, and he argued in favor of attempts to reverse several decades of Supreme Court decisions affirming and extending the concept of separation of church and state. He wrote in support of religious groups seeking the right to assemble on school grounds, and he opined that a court decision striking down an Alabama law providing for a moment of silence in schools was "indefensible." An unsuccessful government argument authored by Roberts contended that a Presbyterian minister should be allowed to address a Rhode Island public high school graduation.

On the hot-button issue of abortion, Roberts wrote in a 1990 Justice Department memo (quoted in *Time*) that the original Supreme Court decision mandating a right to abortion was "wrongly decided," and his opinions on other issues relating to women's rights also appeared strongly conservative. When a group of Republican congresswomen wrote a letter to President Bush arguing in favor of pay-equity legislation, Roberts wrote caustically (again according to *Time*) that "[t]heir slogan may as well be, 'From each according to his ability, to each according to their gender," parodying Karl Marx's famous formulation about worker pay. Roberts would later argue that many of his writings executed in a political context should not be taken as indications of how he would rule in a court of law.

Lent Support to Gay-Rights Group

Roberts was nominated to the Washington, D.C., Court of Appeals in 1991, but his nomination stalled in a struggle between Bush and the Democratic-controlled Senate in the fall of 1992, in the waning days of Bush's term. Roberts was seriously disappointed by this frustration of one of his lifetime ambitions, and he endured another blow when he suffered a serious and still unexplained seizure while golfing in January of 1993. The episode may have been due to stress, but it did not recur. He returned to Hogan & Hartson, at a salary that eventually exceeded $1 million a year. Roberts and his wife Jane married in 1996 and adopted two children, Josephine and John. Jane Roberts was a member of an anti-abortion group called Feminists for Life. But Roberts's reputation as a staunch conservative was muddied considerably when he did consulting work for a group that ultimately succeeded in overturning a Colorado law that struck down local gay-rights measures.

Roberts gained a reputation as one of Washington's top lawyers when it came to shepherding a case through the upper layers of the American court hierarchy. He and his family attended the Catholic Church of the Little Flower in Bethesda, Maryland, and he enjoyed opera, golf, and the comic novels of P.G. Wodehouse. Despite his high-powered position, it was widely reported when he was nominated to the Supreme Court, he could often be seen mowing his own lawn. The return of the Republicans to power in 2000 finally gave Roberts his second chance at the federal court bench; after a second nomination ending in a partisan impasse in 2001, he was finally nominated and confirmed for a seat on the U.S. Court of Appeals for the District of Columbia Circuit in May of 2003.

Almost immediately, speculation began to swirl that Roberts would be in the running to replace one of the aging members of the Supreme Court. According to his own testimony, he grew in the job, telling a friend quoted in *Newsweek* that being a judge was "much harder than I thought it was going to be. The questions are much harder and closer than I thought." He sent a strong signal in favor of states' rights when he dissented in a ruling upholding the application of the Endangered Species act to a California development that threatened an endangered toad species. After Associate Justice Sandra Day O'Connor announced her retirement from the Supreme Court, President Bush nominated Roberts as her replacement on July 19, 2005. After the death of Chief Justice William Rehnquist on September 3 of that year, the Roberts nomination was shifted to that seat. He was confirmed by the U.S. Senate in a 78-22 vote.

The first case to come before the Roberts court in late 2005 involved an Oregon law legalizing assisted suicide, and Roberts had the responsibility of steering the court through cases affecting a host of other controversial issues. Abortion regulations, the application of the death penalty, church-state questions, and states' rights issues were all on the court's docket for the 2005-06 term, and the critical issue of government wartime powers seemed likely to confront the court soon as national divisions deepened over the Iraq war and over government antiterrorist measures that came into conflict with established civil-liberties safeguards. The nature of the consensus Roberts would shape as Chief Justice remained to be seen. But few doubted his commitment to the Supreme Court as an institution—he had said during his Senate confirmation hearings that whenever he ascended the steps of the Court building to argue a case, he had felt a lump in his throat.

Periodicals

Christian Century, August 23, 2005.
International Herald Tribune, July 22, 2005.
Newsweek, August 1, 2005; August 8, 2005; August 15, 2005.
Time, September 5, 2005.
Washington Times, August 16, 2005.

Online

"The Justices of the Supreme Court," http://www.supremecourtus.gov/about/biographiescurrent.pdf (December 29, 2005). □

Luisa Ignacia Roldán

Spanish sculptor Luisa Roldán (c.1650-c.1706) was a member of a family of prominent sculptors and herself the first recognized female sculptor in Spain. Although her life was often marred by deprivation and hardship, she dedicated herself to sculpture and served for several years in the Spanish court, first under Charles II and later Philip V. Roldán is particularly recognized for her terracotta figure groupings, a format she innovated and which are now considered an early version of the Rococo porcelain grouping.

Luisa Ignacia Roldán, also called La Roldána in her native Spain, was born around 1650 in Seville, Spain. Her parents, sculptor Pedro Roldán and his wife, Teresa Ortega y Villavicencio, had relocated to Seville from Granada in 1646. The young Roldán grew up surrounded by artistry; her father, active throughout Spain in the mid-to-late seventeenth century, is recognized as one of Spain's finest Baroque sculptors. According to Grove Art Online, his "achievement was to continue and develop the style of wood sculpture in Seville, and his work anticipates 18th-century styles in its naturalism and emotive power;" in this, his influence on his daughter's work can readily be seen.

Roldán received her early training in the Seville workshop of her father and later collaborated with him. The family workshop included not only Roldán and her father, but also one sister and two brothers who helped with the sculpting and a sister who painted the finished pieces.

As a teenager, Roldán married an artist in her father's workshop, Luis Antonio Navarro de los Arcos. This marriage seems to have been disapproved of by her family, particularly her father, who did not attend either her wedding ceremony or the later wedding blessing. Shortly before her marriage, Roldán left the family studio, presumably because of familial disapproval of her match; she and her husband lived for several years in the home of his family in the San Vicente parish of Seville. During these early years of her marriage spent at her husband's family's home, Roldán gave birth to the majority of her children: Luisa Andrea, Fernando Maximo, Fabiana Sebastiana, and Maria Petronila Gertrudis. Additionally, Roldán had one son and one daughter who did not survive infancy long enough to receive names.

In 1680, having lived with Navarro de los Arcos' family for almost a decade, Roldán, her husband and their children at last moved into their own home. This house, although rented, was located in Seville's most upscale neighborhood indicating the family's confidence in their continued success as sculptors. At this time, Seville—like most of Spain—was in the throes of an economic depression, with many inhabitants suffering from a lack of even the basic necessities for survival. However, Roldán and her family seemed to have escaped the deprivations typical of their day. Despite this relatively elevated status, they were not immune from tragedy; in 1683, two of Roldán's daughters, Luisa Andrea and Fabiana Sebastiana, died within a month of each other at the ages of ten and six, respectively. Although the official causes of death are unknown, the close chronological proximity of the two deaths point to one of the illnesses rampant in the depressed area at the time. A little under a year after the deaths of these two daughters, Roldán gave birth to her final child, another daughter named Rosa Maria Josepha.

Worked with Husband

After their marriage, Roldán and Navarro de los Arcos had left Pedro Roldán's family studio and set up as independent artists, with Roldán acting as a sculptor and her husband serving as a polychromist, or a painter of sculptures, pottery and other three-dimensional pieces. Navarro de los Arcos received his first independent commission in 1674 to construct a float which would support a later sculpture; undoubtedly, Roldán assisted in the creation of this piece. Roldán herself did not receive any independent commissions during this stage of her career; in seventeenth century Spain, respect and demand for women artists was practically non-existent, although female artists did work in the trade. This was exemplified by Roldán and her sisters, who had all served in her father's workshop. Roldán worked closely with her husband, however, and did produce pieces despite the lack of personal commissions. Overall, few pieces from these years in Seville survive, among them four polychrome wooden angels and two thieves made in 1683

and 1684 and a sculpture of Seville's patron saint, the ''Virgen de la Macarena.'' (While this latter piece cannot be definitely attributed to Roldán, it is typically assumed to be her work.)

Commissioned at Cádiz

Sometime around 1684, Roldán and her family moved to Cádiz, on the southwestern coast of Spain, where she at last received her first independent commission for a work called Ecce Homo for the Regina Angelorum Convent. The Roldán family returned briefly to Seville in 1685, but came back to Cádiz a year later to accept a commission from that city's cathedral chapter to execute several wooden sculptures. These sculptures, now located in the crypt of the Catedral Vieja, include depictions of six to eight angels, the seven cardinal and theological Virtues, and several prophets. Upon completion of those, Roldán accepted a 1687 commission from the city to make two polychrome wooden statues of Cádiz's patron saints, St. Servandus and St. Germanus. The two saints lived under Roman rule and were persecuted for their Christian faith, finally being put to death at or near Cádiz around the turn of the fourth century. In the early seventeenth century, they were declared the patron saints of Cádiz. These sculptures were a family effort, with Pedro Roldán designing them, Luisa Roldán sculpting them and her husband painting them.

Took a Court Position

Once her work in Cádiz was complete, Roldán moved to Spain's capital, Madrid, to petition for the position of Escultora de Cáma, or Sculptor of the Chamber, at King Charles II's court. Roldán was acquainted with a courtier, Don Cristóbal de Hontañón, and with his help received this position, essentially that of Court Sculptor, in 1692; however, it did not come with the customary benefits of a court position. The reign of Charles II—known as Carlos Segundo in Spain—was marked by severe economic hardship and deprivation throughout Spain, at least partially due to the monarch's weakness and general unfitness for rule. These hardships were felt as high as the King's court, leaving Roldán, her husband and their children to struggle to survive even in their privileged surroundings. Initially, Roldán seems to have declined the position because it was offered without pay; however, a few months later, the king bestowed a small salary and residency in a house upon the sculptor. These recompenses do not appear to have been bestowed in fact, but merely given in name. Records reflect Roldán's near-continual petitions for the pay promised to her and for a place for her family to live. By 1698, Roldán's personal circumstances were improving even as Madrid's general population suffered from increasing food shortages.

King Charles II died in 1700, leaving no natural heir. He had designated Phillippe de Bourbon, the French Duke of Anjou and relative of his first wife, as his successor; the line was contested, but Phillippe took the Spanish throne in 1701 as Phillip V of Spain. The new king brought his French artistic tastes with him and was less interested in Roldán's clearly Spanish sculptures than had been his predecessor. Roldán nevertheless sought to have her court position maintained and, despite mixed reviews from court officials, was reaffirmed in her position in October 1701. She had by then spent nearly a decade as a member of the court; although many of those years had been unpaid and marked by deprivation, Roldán had been paid fairly regularly during the last few years of Charles II's reign and did not wish to give up her place at court.

Roldán's works after her court appointment can be readily identified, for she typically signed her pieces not only with her name but with the title "Escultora de Cama" for the rest of her career. In 1692, Roldán received a royal commission to produce a wooden statue of St. Michael for the Royal Monastery. Grove Art Online noted that "this is one of her finest works, combining a dynamic composition with the rich sensuality of the flowing cloak and plumed helmet of the saint and the twisted naked body of Satan under his feet." Other noteworthy works of this period include Roldán's polychrome terracotta figure groups, essentially unknown before the Spanish sculptor.

A few years after Phillip V rose to the throne, Roldán began to suffer from failing health. Sources differ on the year of her death, placing it either in 1704 or 1706, but the most likely date seems to be January 10, 1706; Roldán's will was dated only a few days before that date. Although Roldán had been paid during the last few years of her life and her husband seems to have been fairly wealthy by the time of her death, Roldán claimed in her will that she was a pauper and had nothing to leave to her heirs. It seems likely that this stemmed from Spanish women's inability to control their own assets at that time, rather than actual destitution. Whatever the case may have actually been, Roldán was buried in a pauper's grave in Madrid.

Left Influential Legacy

Although she had no protegés to take over her work, Roldán influenced the upcoming eighteenth-century Spanish style. Roldán's style was based in the lush Baroque elements which dominated the arts in seventeenth-century Europe. The Baroque movement started around the turn of the century in Italy and spread north through the continent; Roldán's group sculptures, with their bright colors, use of gold, and religious themes exemplify the Spanish Baroque style. Roldán's figures are noted for their strong, clear profiles; thick, often curling hair; dreamy-looking faces with furrowed brows and parted lips; and flowing garments. Today, her best-known work is a sculpture of St. Catherine.

In *Women Artists,* Nancy G. Heller commented that "Roldán's group sculptures have the intimacy of genre scenes," and she added to their charm by including numerous details. For example, in *The Death of Saint Mary Magdalene,* besides the saint herself, two large angels, and a pair of cherubs, there are the standard still-life elements that identify the subject-Mary's scourge, a skull, and a book-plus a lizard, a snake, an owl, two rabbits nibbling on grass, and some flowers." These stylistic elements are evident in eighteenth-century design aesthetics; the J. Paul Getty Museum's website also argued that "with their bits of still life, flowers, and animals, [Roldán's terracotta groups] prefigured Rococo porcelain groups." As Spain's acknowl-

edged first female sculptor, Roldán laid the groundwork for women to succeed in the arts for years to come.

Books

Hall van den Elsen, Catherine *The Life and Work of the Sevillian Sculptor Luisa Roldán (1652-1706) with a Catalogue Raisonné,* La Trobe University, 1992.
Heller, Nancy G., *Women Artists: An Illustrated History,* Abbeville Press, 1987.
Uglow, Jennifer S., ed., *The Continuum Dictionary of Women's Biography,* Continuum, 1989.
Zilboorg, Caroline, ed., *Women's Firsts,* Gale, 1997.

Online

Grove Art Online, "Luisa Roldán" http://www.groveart.com, January 20, 2006.
J.P. Getty Museum, "Luisa Roldán" http://www.getty.edu/art/gettyguide/artMakerDetails?maker = 3503, January 20, 2006. □

Irma Rombauer

Irma von Starkloff Rombauer (1877-1962), a Missouri homemaker who developed *The Joy of Cooking* at the age of 54, is one of the most influential figures in American home cooking in the twentieth century. *The Joy of Cooking* has been continuously in print since 1936.

A Privileged Upbringing

The youngest child of a well-off St. Louis doctor, Max von Starkloff and his second wife Emma Kuhlmann, Rombauer was born October 30, 1877. The Starkloff family lived in Carondelet, a former suburb of St. Louis, which had been annexed by the city less than a decade before Rombauer's birth. During her early childhood, Rombauer and her elder sister, Elsa, were educated at home and later at local schools. When Rombauer was twelve, her father took a government posting in Bremen, Germany, where the family remained for five years. During these years, she continued her somewhat sporadic formal education, being taught by governesses or at girls' schools in Bremen or, briefly, Lausanne. In late summer 1894, the von Starkloffs returned to Missouri, settling in fashionable South St. Louis.

Upon the family's return, Rombauer began taking art courses at local Washington University—although she did not formally pursue a degree—and spent time visiting family in Indianapolis. In 1897, the still-Irma von Starkloff met young lawyer Edgar Rombauer; the two became engaged in early 1899 and married in a civil ceremony on October 14 of that year. Rombauer's income was limited, and the young couple lived in a small rented apartment with reportedly no domestic help, a state which Anne Mendelson noted in *Stand Facing the Stove* was "outlandish indeed for a bride of

[Rombauer's] social position,'' adding that this story may have been an exaggeration.

Married Life

Short months after the Rombauers' marriage, the couple's first child, Roland, was born on July 27, 1900. However, the baby was not strong and died in March of the following year. Both father and mother were devastated by this loss, and the Rombauers left their apartment to move in with the von Starkloffs. In March 1902, Edgar Rombauer had a nervous breakdown; to help him recover, he and his wife traveled to a resort at Eureka Springs, Arkansas. By the end of April, he was sufficiently recovered to return to St. Louis, where the couple's second child and only daughter, Marion, was born on January 2, 1903. The growing family continued to live with the von Starkloffs until 1906, when Edgar Rombauer became the legal guardian of his fourteen-year-old nephew, Roderick, and the Rombauers took up residence in the home of their new charge's deceased family. (Roderick, who turned out to be a somewhat rebellious and unruly teenager, quickly found himself sent to military school.)

The Rombauer family grew in a more traditional way the following year, when Irma Rombauer gave birth to what would be the last Rombauer child, Edgar Roderick Rombauer Junior, on August 15, 1907. Rombauer was not a traditional mother figure, spending much of her time out of the house; after 1911, she was particularly involved with St. Louis' elite Wednesday Club. Edgar Rombauer was an avid outdoorsman, and the family maintained a vacation cottage in Michigan. Here, Rombauer would later claim, she learned the basics of cooking from her husband. As the Rombauer children progressed through school and their parents through their upper-middle-class lives, nothing portended that Irma Rombauer would, in middle age, write one of America's most enduring cookbooks.

Tragedy Spured *The Joy of Cooking*

By 1929, Irma Rombauer had become prominent in St. Louis' social circles, serving that year, for example, as president of the Women's Committee of the St. Louis Symphony Orchestra Board of Directors. However, her husband had continued to suffer nervous attacks every few years since the initial breakdown in 1902; in the fall of 1929, a particularly severe breakdown struck him. Mendelson comments that ''despite the timing, it is doubtful that the Great Depression . . . was the clue to this collapse.'' Possibly contributing factors included a recent loss in a Board of Education election or a possible recurrence of a bladder cancer Edgar Rombauer had battled years previously. Whatever the cause, the Rombauers spent most of December 1929 and January 1930 in South Carolina in the hopes that the milder climate would ease Rombauer's recovery. When the couple returned to St. Louis at the end of January, Edgar Rombauer seemed improved and ready to return to normal life.

However, on February 3, 1930, while Irma Rombauer was out of the house shopping, Edgar Rombauer committed suicide by shooting himself through the mouth with a shotgun. The act was completely unexpected and the Rombauer family was shocked and devastated. To complicate matters, the Great Depression was taking its toll on Irma Rombauer; she realized quickly that she would need to find another source of income to replace the money her husband had earned. Rombauer moved to a smaller, cheaper apartment in the West End of St. Louis. Unable to fathom the idea of finding regular employment, she determined to write a cookbook to bring in some money.

An Amateur Wrote a Classic

No evidence of Rombauer having any experience or talent as a cook exists. Rather than using her own recipes exclusively, Rombauer spent months collecting recipes from acquaintances, testing them to decide whether or not they would suitable for inclusion in her burgeoning cookbook. Her daughter Marion, then living in New York City, assisted in the testing process and later, illustrated the manuscript. Rombauer did not have a publisher for the cookbook, instead used part of her $6,000 legacy from her husband's death to pay the Clayton Company to print 3,000 copies of *The Joy of Cooking: a Compilation of Reliable Recipes with a Casual Culinary Chat*. Indeed, to fans of the cookbook, much of its charm lies in Rombauer's chatty tone, with anecdotes woven into the recipes. Unlike traditional cookbooks, Rombauer's voice infuses *The Joy of Cooking*, as though she were sitting in the kitchen of each reader, telling them personally how to prepare a certain dish. Rombauer marketed the book herself, selling copies to friends; convincing shops in St. Louis, Michigan, and other areas to carry the cookbook; and generating publicity through contacts with newspapers.

The original release of *The Joy of Cooking* enjoyed modest success. In *Little Acorn*, Irma Rombauer's daughter Marion Rombauer Becker commented that ''Mother's friends made sales lively, but not brisk enough to suit her.'' By 1935, an expanded version was set to be published by Bobbs-Merrill. Rombauer and her publisher had an acrimonious relationship from the start, often arguing over costs and royalties. However, when the cookbook was released nationally in 1936, it enjoyed moderate success and seemed to be on its way to becoming a standard, accepted cookbook like the popular *Fannie Farmer's Boston Cooking-School Cookbook*. The 1936 edition introduced what was then a revolutionary format for the recipes themselves; instead of listing the ingredients directly after the recipe's title and then providing instructions for the creation of the dish, *The Joy of Cooking* presented the directions chronologically, setting the required ingredients in bold type.

Rombauer Chose an Heir

By the mid-1940s, when *The Joy of Cooking* truly became an unmitigated success, Irma Rombauer was approaching her 70th birthday. Her health was starting to fade, perhaps spurred by her stressful working relationship with her publisher and some family disputes. Rombauer's next cookbook, *A Cookbook for Girls and Boys*, was completed with the assistance of her daughter Marion Rombauer Becker, by then living in Cincinnati, Ohio.

Although Rombauer Becker had provided mostly artistic contributions to previous editions, the 1951 revision of *The Joy of Cooking* recognized her as a genuine co-author. She, rather than her mother, took up much of the debate with Bobbs-Merrill over matters related to the publication of the cookbook, only truly taking over as head of the content later.

With the 1951 edition safely handled, Irma Rombauer, indulging a life-long love of travel, set off to Europe with her grandson for an extended tour and later visited Mexico City. However, in 1955, she suffered a mild stroke; although this stroke did not impair her mental process, it did mark the beginning of a continuing series of strokes that struck Rombauer down over the next few years. These strokes gradually robbed Rombauer of her strength, speech, and ability to perform even simple tasks such as writing. She found herself in a situation she had feared: being unable to control her body, while maintaining mental awareness and her sense of self. Marion Rombauer Becker was forced to take control of *The Joy of Cooking* due to her mother's deteriorating health.

Rombauer's health continued to falter and, in 1962, at last failed. Her first stroke had paralyzed the left side of her body; now, her left leg had become infected with gangrene. To complicate the problem, Rombauer had an irregular heartbeat and had recently experienced a bout of seizures triggered by the failure of some brain functions. Her left leg was amputated but did not properly heal. Rombauer was transferred to a nursing home due to the infection from her leg and died there after a steady deterioration on October 17, 1962.

The Later History of *The Joy of Cooking*

After her mother's death, Marion Rombauer Becker became responsible for the updates and revisions to *The Joy of Cooking* until the mid-1970s. The cookbook then remained essentially unchanged for nearly two decades, with her fifth edition acting as the standard text. In 1997, Ethan Becker, Marion Rombauer Becker's son and Irma Rombauer's grandson, headed up a major revision, incorporating more modern recipes and ingredients. The following year, Ethan Becker wrote an introduction for Simon and Schuster's reprint of an exact reproduction of the original 1931 self-published edition with Marion Rombauer Becker's illustrations. *The Joy of Cooking* today remains one of the most respected cookbooks in America, considered by many to be one of the most essential cooking texts available.

Books

Becker, Marion Rombauer, *Little Acorn: Joy of Cooking: the First Fifty Years, 1931-1981,* Bobbs-Merrill, 1966, 1981.

Mendelson, Anne, *Stand Facing the Stove: The Story of the Women who Gave America The Joy of Cooking,* Henry Holt, 1996.

Online

"History of Carondelet," http://stlouis.missouri.org/carondelet/history/incorporation6.html (December 27, 2005).

"American National Biography Online: Irma Rombauer," http://www.anb.org (December 27, 2005). □

Susan Rothenberg

Bringing a sense of personal, narrative imagery to an otherwise abstract style of painting, artist Susan Rothenberg (born 1945) rose to a place of prominence on the New York art scene in the 1970s, and has continued to gain critical acclaim for her work in the decades since.

Rothenberg has forged a long and distinguished career that has seen her hold fiercely to her roots in Abstract Expressionism while exploring a minimalist aesthetic that has led her to varied and surprising places. Working on large canvases with a cool palette and rich, often haunting imagery, Rothenberg has continued to evolve in her art through the decades, but most critics agree that one constant has been the artist's aggressive, kinetic brushwork and stark imagery on fields of muted black, blue, and white. Her early works depicting ghostly images of horses brought her international acclaim, both for their powerful effect and the fact that the artist was bringing a representational image into her otherwise purely abstract paintings. In that sense she became a bridge connecting the new artists of the 1960s with the mid-century giants of American Expressionism.

"Because she has maintained a strict reliance upon imagery throughout her career and wrestled with the lessons of Modernism, she has often been a singular voice in contemporary painting," wrote Cheryl Brutvan of Boston's Museum of Fine Art. "At the same time, her physical approach and gestural application of paint place her in the tradition of an earlier generation of American painters that includes Jackson Pollock and Willem de Kooning."

Rothenberg has been a largely self-made artist who, as a woman, required an uncanny drive and persistence of vision to emerge from the traditionally male-dominated New York art world of the mid-twentieth century, and to carve a place in the art pantheon that has continued to inspire and amaze. In perhaps the truest compliment of all, she has been often imitated. And to her admirers in the world of art criticism, Rothenberg has been able to make her canvases express something deeper about the world and times she has inhabited.

Rothenberg, Mark Stevens stated in an article in *The New Republic,* "is a painting painter. She has attracted attention not only because she has made some good pictures, but because she seems to be struggling to maintain the world of painting. Implicit in her art, I think, is a concern that the world is threatened, fading, even dead. . . . Rothenberg's art is full of remembering that is not quite nostalgic. Her pictures leave the impression of an artist trying to recover painting's secrets, of trying to begin again."

Destined to be an Artist

Born in 1945 in Buffalo, New York, Rothenberg received a comfortable upbringing. Rothenberg actually dreamed of being an artist's wife (a dream fulfilled twice, in fact); little did she know that she would become a great artist herself. After trying sculpture first, she eventually switched to painting and received a fine arts degree from Cornell University before moving to Washington, D.C., to study at George Washington University and the Corcoran Museum. After moving to New York in 1969, Rothenberg did not paint at first, but instead worked briefly in the trendy fields of installation art with Nancy Graves, and as a dancer with the performance artist Joan Jonas.

She married the sculptor George Trakas in 1971 and the following year gave birth to her only child, daughter Maggie. She raised her daughter and painted at night. Like many students, she worked in the style of her times, which was then a kind of flat, abstract painting in the Modernist tradition. It was purely by chance, or—she would later recall—perhaps not by chance at all, that in 1973 an image much like a horse crept into one of her paintings as a dividing element. It was a happy accident that subsequently became the fulcrum of her painting career. With deep roots in both human psychology and artistic tradition (early humans painted horses on cave walls), the horse is a powerful symbolic image often metaphorically linked to the mysterious and primal forces within human sexuality. It was an almost constant thematic element in Rothenberg's work for many years.

"For five years, from 1974 to 1979, Rothenberg painted horses almost exclusively," wrote Thomas Buser of the University of Louisville. "She painted her first horse impulsively, as a 'doodle' that immediately seemed right for her. In her mind she had the vague desire to paint something simple, magical, and universal like the prehistoric cave paintings of animals. Despite the serendipitous beginning, Rothenberg soon realized that her horse was a surrogate for the human figure. But her lifesize, powerful animals represent living spirits without the specifics of age, sex, or personality that accompany nearly every depiction of human beings."

Was at the Forefront of 1980s Art Boom

It was during this period that Rothenberg was swept up by the whirlwind of the New York art world. Critics raved, art dealers lined up to exhibit Rothenberg's work at one-woman shows, and of course the prices of her canvases went up. The attention strained her marriage, there were problems with alcohol, and in 1979 she was divorced from Trakas, an event that fueled her work with an even greater intensity. Soon bones, human heads, and other body parts began creeping into her work, usually depicted in stark black imagery on solid white canvases. "Many of those are divorce images," Rothenberg recalled for Michael Auping in the catalog to her 1992 retrospective at Buffalo's Albright-Knox Gallery. "It was not a happy time. If you want to use modern talk, I would say things were about my energies being blocked and the flow being screwed up. . . . You know, the whole choked-up mess of separating from somebody you care for and a child being involved. That's what those drawings are about."

As things in her personal life became more settled, Rothenberg continued to enjoy critical and commercial success at the top of the New York scene in the 1980s. She worked relatively slowly, spending hours in her studio conjuring images from her subconscious, drawing them, and tacking them to the walls. After settling on an image or group of images, she would then work it out very loosely on canvas, and pause, sometimes for hours or days, to sit in her rocking chair and contemplate the work. Working in brief bouts of intense, kinetic brushwork, pausing again, and so on, Rothenberg would finally finish the piece. Once during the 1980s she created an image that looked startlingly like the famed early-twentieth century Dutch artist Piet Mondrian. Rothenberg had been an admirer of Mondrian's, an early Expressionist who painted for many years in a severe abstract style. Her paintings "Tattoo, Mondrian" and "Mondrian Dancing" grew out of this particular phase.

In 1989 Rothenberg was introduced to the New Mexican sculptor and artist Bruce Nauman and a romance flourished. It was a long-distance relationship for some time—Nauman was as devoted to his quiet life in the rural desert as Rothenberg was to cosmopolitan New York. But when her daughter left home, the artist decided that a break from her surroundings might lead to new revelations in her work, and she joined and later married Nauman in New Mexico. The pair designed and built their own house on a 600-acre ranch, where they now raise horses, rising each morning to do farm chores before parting ways to their separate studios for the day.

Critics have continued to uphold the high quality of Rothenberg's work over the last decade. Though her output has diminished and her work has shown less frequently in New York, a major exhibition of her work at that city's Sperone Westwater gallery in 2002 did show that desert life had introduced subtle but definite changes in Rothenberg's painting. "Her sensibility has always been tactile, but in the dozen years that she has spent living in the Southwest, it has become more so, and more kinetic," wrote Nancy Princenthal in *Art in America*. "Avid, anxious and hyperalert, her habits of vision can be deduced from the way she wields a brush, making it dart across the canvas like the eyes of a hiker hunting for pottery shards, or like fingers probing for bones in the dirt. The field thus painted is dry and brushy as a back pasture. But there is nothing naturalistic about it. Rothenberg's paintings are almost completely devoid of natural light, and have little modeling and barely any perspective."

Additionally, Princenthal found it ironic that Rothenberg's early horse paintings seemed to foretell her life and work far away from the big city and decades in the future. "Among the earliest works in this [the 2002 Sperone Westwater] show (none go back more than a few years) are paintings, presumably from observation, of doglike deer that are fast as horses and stampede like cattle on the range."

Critic Malin Wilson-Powell of the *Albuquerque Journal* was able to survey more than a quarter-century of Rothenberg's development after attending a traveling exhibition of the artist's work in 2002. Organized by Rothenberg's alma mater, Cornell University, and including a lecture from the artist herself, the show featured more than 120 slides of her paintings from the early 1970s to her work from the New Mexico years. Wilson-Powell described how the scenes on canvas, "excerpted from daily life-whether highlighting an untoward event or a moment of remembrance-come to life through Rothenberg's thickly layered and nervous brushwork." He added, "Her works are perpetual mystery and mystification generators." What was surprising for Wilson-Powell in viewing the body of Rothenberg's work, was that so much of the imagery had "taken up residence in my memory over the years."

Rothenberg has received numerous awards and commendations for her art over the years, among them a Guggenheim Fellowship, the Skowhegan Medal for Painting, and a fellowship from the National Endowment for the Arts. She has had one-woman exhibitions at the Museum of Fine Arts, Boston; Dallas Museum of Art; Hirshhorn Museum and Sculpture Garden, Washington, D.C.; Los Angeles County Museum of Art; Museum of Contemporary Art, Chicago; and the Tate Gallery, London, among others.

Books

Contemporary Women Artists, St. James Press, 1999.
Newsmakers, Gale Research, 1995.
Rothenberg, Susan, Michael Auping, *Susan Rothenberg: Paintings and Drawings,* Rizzoli, 1992.

Periodicals

Albuquerque Journal, April 8, 1999.
ArtForum International, October 1993.
Art in America, July 2002.
New Republic, May 17, 1993.
School Arts, October, 2005.
Vanity Fair, December 1992.
W, April 2002.

Online

Museum of Fimes Arts, Boston, http://www.mfa.org/exhibitions/sub.asp?key=15&subkey=619 (March 20, 2006).
University of Louisville Online Catalog, http://www.louisville.edu/a-s/finearts/VRC/buser203/rothenberg.html (March 17, 2006). □

S

Oliver Sacks

Neurologist Oliver Sacks (born 1933) told *Psychology Today,* "It is the remarkable which captures my attention." In a series of bestselling books drawn from his own remarkable life and clinical career, Sacks has been an explorer of unfamiliar territory in the human brain.

Sacks's work has been motivated not by an obsession with the bizarre but by a sense of wonder and respect at how human beings react and adapt to serious illness. A generalist and a humanist in a profession that inclines toward specialization, Sacks has seen his work inspire a hit film, *Awakenings,* a play, and even an opera. He has become one of the most celebrated and respected science writers in the United States.

Sent to Country School During War

Sacks was born in London, England, on July 9, 1933. His parents were both doctors, and they guided him from the start toward the medical profession. They were very different in personality; Sacks's father was fascinated by literature and human behavior, while his mother, who once (when he was a teenager) made him dissect the leg of a corpse of a young woman his own age, was mechanistically and mechanically inclined. "Her love of structure extended in all directions," Sacks wrote in his memoir *Uncle Tungsten.* She enjoyed tinkering with the family's grandfather clock, and "there was nothing she liked more," Sacks wrote, "than mending a leaky faucet or a toilet, and the services of outside plumbers were usually not required." Sacks's childhood was disrupted by Germany's air attacks against Britain during World War II. To get him and his brother Michael out of London during the worst of the bombing, their parents enrolled them in a boarding school, Braefield, in the English Midlands.

The headmaster there, Sacks wrote in *Uncle Tungsten,* "seemed to have become unhinged by his own power." Sacks and his brother were physically and psychologically abused. The food packages their parents sent were stolen, and they were fed vegetables normally meant for cattle. The experience sensitized Sacks to the plight of individuals trapped in situations caused by unfortunate circumstances, but it also did more. Over four years at the school, with only occasional (and bomb-riddled) visits to London, Sacks's brother Michael began to display psychotic symptoms. Yet what affected his brother was not exactly mental illness. "This is something I don't go into [in the new book]," Sacks told *Publishers Weekly* when *Uncle Tungsten* was published, "but when my brother Michael had his breakdown and became psychotic, one of the things he said was, don't call this a disease. It is my struggle, my world, my attempt to find meaning."

After the war, Sacks made his own attempt to find meaning, immersing himself in all kinds of scientific subjects. Chemistry was a special favorite, and the Uncle Tungsten described in his book stimulated his interest. He found company among several like-minded friends. "Life is not all electrostatics," one friend, Jonathan Miller, teased him while he was in a physics phase (as he recalled to Erica E. Goode of *U.S. News & World Report*). But Sacks looked up from his book and said, "Yes it is." Sacks and two of his friends went to visit science writer Julian Huxley in London. "I think the great man was both amused and impressed by such undersized, ink-stained, and sort of grim children," Sacks told Goode.

Finding his way back to the family profession, Sacks graduated from Queen's College, Oxford, in 1954 and went on for a series of medical degrees between 1954 and 1958. In 1960 he moved to the United States after first hitchhiking around Canada and working as a firefighter during the wildfire season in British Columbia, Canada. He told Sandee Brawarsky of *The Lancet* that he had a "hunger for a new world. I felt, probably unfairly, that England was small and crowded and conservative, and that I might be able to make more of a life here in the states, which I imagined to be more spacious, in every way. I first went to California [in 1961] and somehow the physical spaciousness seemed to take on a moral and intellectual spaciousness as well."

Joined Biker Gang

Sacks did an internship at Mount Zion Hospital in San Francisco in 1961 and 1962, moving on to a residency in neurology at the University of California at Los Angeles from 1962 until 1965. The formerly bookish young doctor took to the athletic and outdoorsy aspects of the California lifestyle, winning a weightlifting championship and spending time with the Hell's Angels motorcycle gang. An avid cyclist, he sometimes rode from UCLA to the Grand Canyon on weekends. Even then, before American medicine had begun to take on qualities of an industrial assembly line, Sacks was noted for his one-on-one approach to patient care. He once smuggled a dying multiple sclerosis patient out of the hospital for a ride on the back of his motorcycle.

Sacks's unconventional ways did not always endear him to UCLA's medical faculty. When one teacher said (as he recalled to *Psychology Today*), "Sacks, I'm worried about you. You don't have any position," Sacks retorted, "Oh, yes I do. . . . I have a position in the heart of medicine." The remark was prophetic enough, but Sacks made one last stab at becoming a research scientist. In 1965 he accepted a fellowship at the Albert Einstein College of Medicine at Yeshiva University in the New York City borough of the Bronx, becoming a researcher in neurochemistry and neuropathology. After several incidents of clumsiness that would have fascinated psychopathologists of everyday life, including one in which he dropped some hamburger into an expensive centrifuge, he accepted his medical destiny and became a staff neurologist Beth Abraham Hospital in the Bronx. He remained in the same position four decades later, but he also continued his association with the Albert Einstein College of Medicine, serving as an instructor there from 1966 until 1975, and rising to assistant professor (1975-78), associate professor (1978-85), and clinical professor of neurology (from 1985 forward).

At Beth Abraham, Sacks soon encountered the first of the unusual patients who populated his books. But at first he dealt with sufferers of one of the most common neurological conditions: migraine headaches. He became fascinated by the condition, which has been well documented back to ancient times and seems to show up frequently among unusually creative figures. A reflexive writer and journal keeper since childhood—he estimated that he has written tens of millions of words—Sacks wrote a book about the migraine phenomenon in 1967. A superior warned him that he had nowhere near enough stature to publish a medical book, locked up the manuscript, and threatened his employment, but he persisted. *Migraine* gained positive reviews and went through several editions, remaining in print in the early 2000s.

Sacks was not against the use of drugs to treat neurological conditions, as his next book would show. But he tried to cultivate a holistic approach, evaluating patients individually and determining how their illnesses interacted with their lives in general. "In my early book, *Migraine,* I talk about all sorts of interventions," he pointed out to *Psychology Today*. "But I also say that just to throw down a medication and then continue rushing around may, in a sense, defeat the purpose, because the migraine is partly saying, 'Hey, stop, take it easy.'"

"Awakened" Patients

At Beth Abraham, Sacks encountered a group of 80 patients who had been in a lethargic trance for decades, not moving or speaking, and interacting with the outside world only in very limited ways. They suffered from a form of encephalitis commonly known as sleeping sickness. Sacks hypothesized that they might be helped by L-dopa, a new drug given to patients suffering from Parkinson's disease. The dosages of L-dopa that he administered in 1969 had seemingly miraculous results; the patients came to life and began to speak and move normally. But the treatment was far from a complete success; the drug had numerous side effects that caused one patient to dub it "hell-dopa." Some patients suffered hallucinations; others were disoriented by the new, modern world in which they found themselves. Some did go on to lead what Sacks on his website called "long and relatively rewarding lives."

The compulsive diarist Sacks filled notebooks with observations on his treatment, but he found medical journals uninterested in the articles he wrote about his experiences. So he compiled his observations into a book, *Awakenings,* which was published in 1973 and became a bestseller. *Awakenings* was made into a play, *A Kind of Alaska,* by Harold Pinter, and into the film *Awakenings* (1990), starring Robin Williams as a doctor clearly based on Sacks. The book made Sacks a well-known author, and he found a ready clientele among magazine editors for case studies he wrote about other patients he encountered. Many of these (the *New Yorker* was a common publication forum for Sacks) served as material for his later books.

In Sacks's next book, however, he was the patient, not the doctor. In 1976 he suffered a serious injury to his left leg in a mountain climbing accident in Scandinavia. Surgeons repaired the physical damage, but Sacks found that he still could not move his leg—it did not seem to be part of his own body. *A Leg to Stand On* (1984) recounted his recovery in detail. One form of therapy that helped was swimming. "I do a certain amount of my writing underwater, . . ." Sacks told *The Writer.* While working on *A Leg to Stand On,* he said, "I would swim for half an hour, come out dripping, and scribble. I remember sending my editor a water-stained manuscript. He said, 'No one has sent me a handwritten manuscript for 30 years, let alone a water-stained one." Even away from the pool, the most complicated word-processing technology Sacks has used is a typewriter.

Sacks published another of his most famous books in 1985; *The Man Who Mistook His Wife for a Hat,* this was a compilation of collected case studies of patients with perceptual difficulties arising from a variety of causes. The title study, which was the basis for an opera by composer Michael Nyman, concerned a music instructor who could not grasp objects as wholes and confused his wife's face for his hat, which he had hung on a nearby rack. Sacks became interested in the phenomenon of autism, which causes young people severe difficulties in social interaction but is sometimes accompanied by spectacular mental powers of a specialized nature. In both *The Man Who Mistook His Wife for a Hat* and a similar later book, *An Anthropologist on Mars* (1995), Sacks included sketches of so-called autistic savants.

Continuing to explore unfamiliar issues of human perception and mental functioning as the spirit moved him—he claimed on his website that his writing was "unanticipatable, unplanned, awaiting inspiration, nucleation"—Sacks wrote books about the culture of the deaf (*Seeing Voices: A Journey into the World of the Deaf,* 1989), and about a Pacific Ocean island where colorblindness was common (*The Island of the Colorblind; and Cycad Island,* (1997). His *Oaxaca Journal* (2002) grew from his interest in ferns, describing a naturalists' expedition to that Mexican region. Some scientists considered Sacks a pop neurologist,

but he received a high scientific honor when he was made an honorary fellow of the American Academy of Arts and Letters and of the American Academy of Arts and Sciences. His books have been translated into 22 languages, and the *New York Times,* according to his website, has proclaimed him "the poet laureate of medicine."

Books

Sacks, Oliver, *Uncle Tungsten: Memories of a Chemical Boyhood,* Knopf, 2001.

Periodicals

Book, November-December 2001.
Economist (US), March 15, 1997.
Lancet, October 11, 1997.
Psychology Today, February 1986; May-June 1995.
Publishers Weekly, October 1, 2001.
U.S. News & World Report, January 21, 1991.
Writer, April 2002.

Online

Oliver Sacks: author. neurologist, "Biography," http://www.oliversacks.com (January 11, 2006). ☐

Saint Genèvieve

French religious figure Saint Genèvieve (c. 422-512) lived a life of constant prayer and charity as well as self-imposed austerity. She became known as the "Patron Saint of Paris" after she supposedly helped avert an attack by Attila the Hun and prevented famine by penetrating a military blockade with boatloads of grain. Accounts of her life mix fact with legend.

Much of the information available about Genèvieve—its validity and worth—has been the subject of controversy. Her biography, not written until many centuries after her death, is considered unreliable. Still, the Celtic cult that developed for her began in ancient times—a reference to it can be found as far back as 592 AD in the *Martyrology of Jerome*—and it endured for years. Further, there is no doubt that she actually lived.

For many years, traditional thought held that Genèvieve was a shepherdess born of peasant parents. But evidence suggests this is a myth promulgated by the way Genèvieve was typically portrayed in paintings. She was often depicted as a shepherdess holding a candle, a book, or torch. Such portrayals may have been merely symbolic.

The more likely scenario, scholars indicate, is that Genèvieve came from a wealthy family. Her exact date of birth is not known but is placed around 422. She was born in Nanterre, a small village outside of Paris, France. Her father was Severus, her mother Gerontia, and it is believed that they were wealthy and respectable citizens.

Consecrated by Saint Germain

Genèvieve's biography recounts several key events. The earliest of these events, and the one that appears to have had the biggest impact on her life, took place in the village of her birthplace when she was about seven. In 429, Saint Germain (also known as Germanus), Bishop of Auxerre, ventured from Gaul into Nanterre en route to Great Britain, where he intended to fight Pelagiansim, which was a belief system that was considered heretical at the time, as it denied the concepts of original sin and Christian grace.

In the village, the worshipful Nanterre inhabitants gathered around Saint Germain, who was a much revered religious figure, and he gave them a sermon as well as his blessings. As he was addressing the crowd, a pious child caught his attention. It was Genèvieve, and Germain motioned for her and her parents to approach him. Saint Germain told her parents that she was resolved to serving God and would compel people to follow her example. Her life would be one of sanctity, and she would foster that quality in others, Germain said.

After his sermon, Saint Germain encouraged Genèvieve to remain virtuous. When he asked her if she desired to serve God as a perpetual virgin, and to be espoused only to Jesus Christ, she answered in the affirmative. In response, he reportedly told her, as captured on the Catholic Community Forum website, "Be of good heart, my child, act with earnestness, and struggle to prove by thy works that which thou believest in thy heart, and professest with thy lips; the Lord will sustain thee, and will give thee the strength that is required to carry out thy holy resolution."

Genèvieve then expressed her wish that Saint Germain would bless her. Granting the child's wish, Saint Germain took her to a local church where he performed the consecration. The next day, before he continued on his journey, Saint Germain gave Genèvieve a brass medal engraved with a cross. He instructed her to always wear it around her neck, in remembrance of her consecration to God and devotion to Christ. Further, he told her to be content with only the medal, and to wear it instead of more showy ornaments such as gold and silver bracelets, and necklaces. She kept the medal all her life, never giving it up even when she badly needed money. She lived a life of fervent devotion and penance. As there were no convents near her village, Genèvieve practiced her religious virtue and prayer at home.

Moved to Paris

Eventually, she formally received the religious veil (or the habit of the nun), when she was either 15 or 16 years old; the exact date is not certain. This popular account holds that she and two other young girls received their veils during a ceremony the bishop of Paris conducted. Though Genèvieve was the youngest of the three, the bishop attended to her first, as she had already been sanctified by heaven, due to her consecration from Saint Germain.

The veiling followed the death of Genèvieve's parents and occurred after she had moved to Paris to live with her godmother, Lutetia. During this period, Genèvieve was ad-

mired for her piety, devotion, and charitable works. She liked to go to church alone at night, praying by candlelight. One night, a gust of wind blew out her candle, and she attributed this to the devil trying to frighten her. The story took on a life of its own and, later, in paintings, Genèvieve would often be depicted as holding a candle while an irritated devil lurked in the background.

Her spiritual regimen included severe penances and austerities. She followed a vegetarian diet and would eat merely twice a week (on Sunday and Thursday), and she drank only water. According to accounts, her meals included only a small portion of barley bread and beans. She adhered to this diet until she was 50 years old, when a counsel of bishop finally advised her that it would be best for her to eat more frequently. She obeyed, but only by adding a little milk and some fish to her diet.

Endured Jealousies and Hostility

While living with her godmother, Genèvieve sometimes made trips of charity to French cities including Meaux, Laon, Tours, and Orleans. Legend says she performed miracles, experienced visions and made prophecies that proved accurate. Genèvieve, however, experienced the jealously and even hatred of some neighbors, who accused her of being a hypocrite and a fraud.

At one point, Genèvieve's enemies even plotted to drown her. Saint Germain, however, heard of the conspiracy and intervened. He helped change the hostile attitudes of those around her. During this visit, he also encouraged Genèvieve to lessen the harshness of some of her own penances. Afterward, the bishop of Paris appointed Genèvieve to protect the welfare of the city's virgins who had dedicated their lives to God. She inspired the young women, which seemed to fulfill the forecast Saint Germain made when he met the seven-year-old Genèvieve in Nanterre.

Protected Paris from Attila the Hun

Another significant and often–reported event in Genèvieve's life occurred around 451, when the barbarian Attila and his army of Huns marched across the continent, intending to take control of Gaul away from the ruling Visigoths. After Attila crossed the Rhine and neared Paris, the Parisian citizens were ready to flee the city in terror. Genèvieve, however, advised them against evacuation. She told them that if they kept their faith in God, fasted, prayed and performed penance, the city would be protected by heaven and their lives would be spared.

The citizens were doubtful, however, as they all knew that Attila was a vicious and merciless warlord who left devastation in his wake. His soldiers were an equally cruel band of marauders who raped, looted, killed and destroyed. Still, many of the citizens passed days and nights in prayer with Genèvieve in the baptistery. But when the crisis neared its peak, and Attila seemed to be right outside the city walls, the people became panic-stricken, and they turned against Genèvieve. They accused her of being a false prophet who would bring about their deaths as well as the destruction of their beloved city, and they threatened to stone her.

Again, Saint Germain's intervention helped her. News of the situation reached him as he lay near death in Ravenna, Italy. In response, he sent his archdeacon, Sedulius, to help calm the citizens. Sedulius counseled them to listen to Genèvieve, saying she was not a prophetess of doom but the means of their salvation.

Still, some inhabitants abandoned Paris. Genèvieve then supposedly gathered the women who had remained behind and led them outside the walls of the city. As the sun rose, and with enemy weapons before them, Genèvieve and the women prayed for deliverance. Later that night, Attila turned away from Paris, leaving the city unharmed, and headed south, to Orleans. Genèvieve was proclaimed a savior and heroine.

Childeric and the Siege of Paris

Genèvieve demonstrated her bravery and helped the people of Paris a second time, almost similarly, more than 30 years later. In 486, Childeric, the king of the Salian Franks, a Germanic tribe, blockaded the city. The prolonged siege created a serious food shortage that brought the citizens to the starvation point.

One night, Genèvieve led 11 boats out onto the river, rowing past the enemy's siege lines. Once safely across, she went from village to village, begging for food. Later that night, she returned to Paris, again slipping safely past the blockade, with boatfuls of precious grain.

When he heard about her deed, Childeric was impressed with Genèvieve, even though he was a pagan and she was a Christian. After the siege had ended, he sent for her and, out of admiration, he asked what he could do for her. She said to him, "Release your prisoners. Their only fault was that they so dearly loved their city." He granted her wish, and later performed other merciful acts at her request.

Helped Build a Cathedral

When Childeric died, King Clovis succeeded him and consolidated control of the land from the Rhine to the Loire. He married Childeric's elder daughter, Clothilde, who was a Christian. Clovis, like Childeric, was a pagan, and his wife often tried to convert him, but without success. Still, Clovis chose Genèvieve to be one of his counselors, and she earned his trust. As Childeric once did, Clovis freed many prisoners at Genèvieve's request.

Once, as Clovis prepared to enter what he knew would be fierce battle, he promised his wife that he would be baptized in the Christian rite if he came back alive. True to his word, when his army won, he became a Christian in 496, guided in his conversion by Genèvieve. His people and servants soon became Christians as well.

Genèvieve is credited with developing the plans for a church to honor Saints Peter and Paul, to be built in the middle of Paris. King Clovis started the church, managing only to lay the foundation before he died in 511. The church was completed by Queen Clothilde. After Genèvieve died, her body was interred in the church. The church was later renamed Sainte Genèvieve and it was rebuilt in 1746.

Named the "Patron Saint of Paris"

Genèvieve died January 3, 512, only five weeks after King Clovis's death. She was in her eighth decade of life; at least one account said she was 89 years old. She was buried in a long, flowing gown with a mantle covering her shoulders, similar to the type of garments worn by the Virgin Mary. Genèvieve's burial site within the church would become a place of pilgrimage, as people had heard many stories of miracles and cures attributed to Genèvieve.

Even after her death, miracles were credited to Genèvieve. Perhaps the most famous account involved the great epidemic of ergot poisoning that afflicted France in the twelfth century. After all efforts to find a cure were unsuccessful, in 1129, Bishop Stephen of Paris instructed that Genèvieve's casket be carried through the city streets in procession to the cathedral. According to reports from the time, thousands of sick people were cured when they saw or touched the casket. The following year, Pope Innocent II visited Paris and ordered an annual feast to commemorate the miracle. Parisian churches still celebrate the feast.

In the late eighteenth century, Genèvieve's shrine and most of her relics were destroyed during the tumult of the French Revolution, but her cult carried on. Later, many churches in France were named after her. Genèvieve came to be known as the Patron Saint of Paris and, throughout the years, many miracles that favored Paris were attributed to her intercession. Her name is invoked during natural disasters such as drought, flooding, and widespread fever.

St. Genèvieve also became known as the Patron Saint of Young Girls. Also, in 1962, Pope John XXIII named her the patron saint of French security forces, a gesture that honored her many efforts to secure Paris. Her feast day is January 3, but it is not part of the general Roman Catholic calendar.

Books

McBrien, Richard P., *Lives of the Saints: From Mary and St. Francis of Assisi to John XXIII and Mother Teresa,* HarperCollins, 2001.

Sanderson, Ruth, *Saints Lives and Illuminations,* Eerdmans Publishing Company, 2003.

Sandoval, Annette, *The Directory of Saints: A Concise Guide to Patron Saints,* Signet, 1997.

Online

"Genèvieve of Paris V (RM)," *Saints O' the Day,* http://www.saintpatrickdc.org/ss/0103.htm (January 12, 2006).

"Patron Saints for Girls-The Life of Saint Genèvieve," *Catholic Community Forum,* http://www.catholic-forum.com/saints/ps4g09.htm (January 12, 2006).

"Saint Genèvieve," *Catholic Encyclopedia,,* http://www.newadvent.org/cathen/06413f.htm (January 12, 2006).

"St. Genèvieve," *Catholic Online,* http://www.catholic.org/saints/saint.php?saint_id=120 (January 12, 2006).

"St Genèvieve, or Ge Novefa Virgin, Chief Patroness of The City Of Paris-422-512 A.D.," *Eternal World Television Network,* http://www.ewtn.com/library/MARY/GENEVIEV.htm (January 12, 2006). □

Buffy Sainte-Marie

A major singer-songwriter of the 1960s and the creator of several of that decade's best-known and most incisive protest anthems, Buffy Sainte-Marie (born c. 1941) remains one of just a few Native Americans to have attained international popularity in the field of popular music.

Sainte-Marie's influence on the 1960s music scene has sometimes been underestimated, for several of her best songs became familiar in versions by other artists. Her antiwar song "The Universal Soldier," for example, became a hit for the Scottish folk singer Donovan. Sainte-Marie was an independent, eclectic musician; even if she was generally categorized under the folk label, she ventured into and rock, and in the 1990s she became an early adopter of the personal computer and its potential uses in musical expression. Tying most of Sainte-Marie's activities together has been her ongoing concern with Native American rights and with presenting an accurate picture of Native American culture to the rest of the world.

Adopted by Massachusetts Family

A member of the Cree Indian tribe, Sainte-Marie was born on a reservation in Qu'Appelle Valley, Saskatchewan, Canada. The year of her birth has been variously given as 1941 and 1942. Orphaned as a baby, she was adopted by a Massachusetts family named Sainte-Marie that was partially of Mi'kmaq Native American descent. As a child, though, Sainte-Marie knew little of her own Native background, and her rediscovery of that background later on became an important stimulus for her creative activity. Given the name Beverly Sainte-Marie and nicknamed Buffy, she was later ceremonially adopted by a Cree family related to one of her birth parents. Sainte-Marie lived for much of her life in the United States, becoming a dual U.S. and Canadian citizen, but she told an *Ottawa Citizen* interviewer in 1993 that she would always identify herself as Canadian.

Sainte-Marie had some piano lessons as a child and also enjoyed writing poetry. She learned the guitar in her teens, and during family vacations in Maine she began writing songs. The timing was good, for when Sainte-Marie began attending the University of Massachusetts at Amherst, coffeehouses with live folk music entertainment were beginning to flower across New England. Sainte-Marie was a coffeehouse favorite as a college student, but she did not neglect her studies, either; she graduated in 1962 with a degree in Eastern philosophy and was recognized as one of the top ten students in her class. She later received a fine arts Ph.D. from the same institution.

After she finished college, Sainte-Marie headed for the Greenwich Village neighborhood of Lower Manhattan in New York City, a mecca at the time for aspiring folk singers. With her unique outlook—virtually no other songwriters dealt with Native American life at the time—and her distinctively edgy vocal vibrato, Sainte-Marie won attention from the start in clubs such as the Gaslight Cafe and Gerdes Folk City. She toured and maintained her Canadian ties, writing "The Universal Soldier" during an appearance one night at Toronto's Purple Onion coffeehouse.

Executives at the folk-oriented label Vanguard signed Sainte-Marie to a contract and released her debut album, *It's My Way!* in 1964. William Ruhlmann of the All Music Guide website called it "one of the most scathing topical folk albums ever made;" its subject matter ranged from incest to drug addiction ("Cod'ine," based on Sainte-Marie's own experiences in the aftermath of a serious bout with bronchial pneumonia in 1963, was later covered by several rock bands), and it included "The Universal Soldier" and another of Sainte-Marie's trademark songs, "Now That the Buffalo's Gone." Sainte-Marie's second album, *Many a Mile* (1965) mixed traditional songs with Sainte-Marie originals such as "Until It's Time for You to Go." That song was never well known in Sainte-Marie's own version, but it was covered by a long list of musicians that included Elvis Presley, Cher, Neil Diamond, Barbra Streisand, British icon Vera Lynn, and jazz vocalist Carmen McRae. Presley's version became a major hit in Europe in 1972 and helped put Sainte-Marie on a firm financial footing.

Traveled to Nashville to Record

Sainte-Marie's next two albums, *Little Wheel Spin and Spin* (1966) and *Fire & Fleet & Candlelight* (1967, with orchestral arrangements by classical-music satirist Peter Schickele), continued to draw attention, and she appeared at major venues such as New York's Carnegie Hall. Having always enjoyed country music, Sainte-Marie recorded in Nashville with country studio musicians for her 1968 album *I'm Gonna Be a Country Girl Again*. At the time, bands such as the Byrds had experimented with country-folk and country-rock fusions, but folk icon Bob Dylan's well-publicized Nashville sessions (and *Nashville Skyline* album) were still at least a year in the future. The album included "Soulful Shade of Blue" and "Sometimes When I Get to Thinkin'," two of Sainte-Marie's most characteristic love songs—a category for which she was known just as much as for her protest songs in the 1960s. Country star Bobby Bare enjoyed a hit with Sainte-Marie's country composition "The Piney Wood Hills," originally recorded on *Many a Mile*.

Appearing on such mainstream media outlets as the *Tonight Show* with Johnny Carson, Sainte-Marie was, if not a star, at least one of the best-known folk musicians in the country. Her songs were often heard on the radio up to that point, but they disappeared as her criticism of the Vietnam War sharpened. According to Sainte-Marie's website, she was blacklisted because her name appeared on a White House list of performers "who deserved to be suppressed." Nevertheless, Sainte-Marie continued to record for Vanguard. Her albums from the end of the 1960s and the early 1970s were an adventurous group; *Illuminations* (1969) employed the psychedelic rock styles of the time and gave advance notice of Sainte-Marie's interest in musical electronics. The 1972 album *Moonshot* was mostly a straight-ahead rock effort except for the country-oriented "He's an Indian Cowboy in the Rodeo." That song was one of a group that gained Sainte-Marie a strong fan base among Native Americans, one which persisted even when she fell out of view in the pop mainstream.

Albums such as *She Used to Wanna Be a Ballerina* (1971) and *Native North American Child* (1973) continued to feature unusual new Sainte-Marie compositions; the title track of the former album put Sainte-Marie back on the pop charts, while that of the latter was a satirical piece pointing to the invisibility of Native Americans in the mass media: "Sing about your ebony African queen/Sing about your lily-white Lili Marleen/Beauty by the dozen, but the girl of the hour/Is your Native North American prairie flower." Sainte-Marie moved to the MCA label in 1974 and issued the experimental *Mongrel Pup* the following year, with cryptic lyrics like "Laughter is the grease of growth/Support your local clown."

Sainte-Marie moved to Hawaii in the late 1960s and continued to make her home there despite frequent projects that took her back to the mainland. A marriage to surfing instructor Dewain Bugbee ended in 1972. Sainte-Marie married actor Sheldon Peters Wolfchild in 1975, and they had a son, Dakota Starblanket Wolfchild. In 1976 Sainte-Marie withdrew from the recording scene in order to concentrate on raising a family, but she did not remain outside the creative sphere for long.

Won Academy Award

Appearing with her son, Sainte-Marie joined the cast of the long-running children's television program *Sesame Street*. She appeared on the show between 1976 and 1981. In a way *Sesame Street* launched the second phase of her career, which was increasingly often concerned with Native American issues. She used the show to introduce children to aspects of Native American life that she felt were poorly served by existing educational materials. Sainte-Marie continued to write songs, and "Up Where We Belong," co-written with Will Jennings and veteran producer Jack Nitzsche, was recorded by Joe Cocker and Jennifer Warnes and used in the 1982 film "An Officer and a Gentleman," bringing Sainte-Marie an Academy Award for Best Original Song. Some obituaries of Nitzsche reported that he and Sainte-Marie were briefly married in the early 1980s.

Sainte-Marie's activities in the 1980s were varied. She appeared in several films, including *Broken Rainbow* (1985), about the long-running land dispute between the Hopi and Navajo tribes. She wrote about Native American issues for a variety of publications, and she penned a children's book, *Nokomis and the Magic Hat*, in 1986. The long effort to free imprisoned Native American activist Leonard Peltier listed Sainte-Marie as a stalwart supporter, and she taught courses at several institutions on a wide variety of subjects that included songwriting, musical electronics, and women's studies. She also appeared in a commercial for the Ben & Jerry's ice cream chain.

One of Sainte-Marie's visiting professorships was at the Institute for American Indian Arts in Santa Fe, New Mexico, where she taught a course in digital technology and art. Perhaps unexpectedly for someone whose creative beginnings lay in the low-tech world of folk music, Sainte-Marie became an enthusiastic user of computers in both her visual-artistic and musical endeavors. Her digital art works, some of them as large as nine feet tall when realized in printed form, were exhibited in Canadian and American museums and galleries including the Glenbow Museum in Calgary, Alberta, and the G.O.C.A.I.A. Gallery in Tucson, Arizona.

In 1992 Sainte-Marie returned to the recording arena, working from a home studio in Hawaii controlled by a Macintosh PowerBook computer. The album *Coincidence and Likely Stories*, released on the Chrysalis label, yielded a British hit in "The Big Ones Get Away." Sainte-Marie became an exponent of the idea that online communication could decentralize power in society generally and facilitate the spread of Native American culture specifically. "It does give an image of Stone Age to space age," she conceded to the London *Independent*. But she pointed out that Native Americans had been involved with computer technology almost since its inception. "It's natural for any indigenous community to be online, because of our desire to remain in the local community, yet be part of the global community," she pointed out.

Sainte-Marie released *Up Where We Belong*, an album of remakes of her earlier hits, in 1996. The following year she was awarded the Order of Canada. Her educational efforts continued to expand; her Cradleboard Teaching Project, which included digital material, was a set of resources for educators who wanted to address deficiencies in the ways Native American history was usually taught—

deficiencies that Sainte-Marie had encountered firsthand when she had looked at her own son's schoolbooks. "It was the same old dead text on dead Indians," she told *USA Today*. "It was shallow, inaccurate, and not interesting." Sainte-Marie also set up a foundation that supported Native Americans who wanted to attend law school. She continued to perform about 20 concerts annually, one of which was captured on her *Live at Carnegie Hall* album of 2004, and the sizes of the crowds she drew—a concert in Denmark, was estimated at over 200,000 people—testified to the lasting impact she had made on the musical world.

Periodicals

Albuquerque Journal, March 31, 2001.
Billboard, June 13, 1992.
Independent (London, England), March 8, 1996.
Ottawa Citizen (Canada), June 30, 1993; March 29, 1994; July 5, 1997; August 24, 2002.
People, June 17, 1996.
Times (London, England), February 16, 1996.
USA Today, December 12, 2000.
Wind Speaker, March 1996.

Online

"Biography," Official Buffy Sainte-Marie website, http://www .creative-native.com/biograp.htm (December 20, 2005).
"Buffy Sainte-Marie," All Music Guide, http://www.allmusic .com (December 20, 2005). □

Pablo de Sarasate

Pablo de Sarasate (1844-1908) was one of the most famous violinists of the late nineteenth century. He gave the premieres of several major works for violin and orchestra, and he composed violin music of his own that is still enthusiastically played and recorded.

Sarasate made his home base in Paris, France, and the exotic Spanish tinge he brought to French concert life helped lay the groundwork for a lasting fascination with Mediterranean sounds among composers in France and other more northerly European countries. Sarasate was also famous far beyond France. When fictional detective Sherlock Holmes and his sidekick Dr. Watson had to spend part of a day waiting for one of their plans to come to fruition (in the story "The Red-Headed League"), they decided to go to a concert by Sarasate. The choice of Sarasate's name was logical for author Arthur Conan Doyle, for Sarasate was a frequent presence on London concert bills. A prolific performer, Sarasate toured North and South America twice, and he was acclaimed in Germany in spite of the traditional German-French animosity, which extended into artistic as well as political and military affairs.

Outstripped Father's Skills

Born Martín Melitón Sarasate y Navascuéz (or Navascues) on March 10, 1844, he adopted his simpler stage name when he moved to Paris and began his career. Sarasate was a native of Pamplona in Spain's culturally distinctive and musically rich Basque region. His father, Don Miguel Sarasate, was a military bandmaster and part-time violinist who, according to one story, got a major shock when his five-year-old son picked up a violin and effortlessly played the passage that he, the father, had been struggling with. The truth of the story is hard to determine, but two facts are part of the historical record: Sarasate and his father did not get along well, and Sarasate became an exceptional child prodigy on the violin. He gave his first concert at age eight and won the admiration of the Countess Espoz y Mina, who removed any financial barrier to his studies with an annual allowance of 2,000 Spanish *reales*.

Spain at the time had vibrant regional traditions but was something of a backwater in terms of the main developments in European classical music. Sarasate went to Madrid and became a favorite of Spain's royal family, but even the best teachers at the Spanish court soon found that their pupil had exceeded anything they could teach him. They urged Sarasate's family to send him to Paris for further study. The 11-year-old Sarasate set off for Paris on a train, accompanied by his mother. The trip was disastrous: at the Spanish-French border, Sarasate's mother died of a heart attack, and the doctor who was called determined that Sarasate himself was suffering from cholera. Nursed back to health by a

Spanish nobleman who saw what was happening, he finally arrived in Paris and was taken in by a bureaucrat at the famed Paris Conservatory.

Under the tutelage of a Mr. Alard, violin professor at the Conservatory, Sarasate continued to make rapid progress. Spaniards applauded his renown, and a grant from the Spanish Queen Isabella aided his studies. In 1857 he won the Conservatory's first prize in violin—an honor that placed him already in the top ranks of Spanish violinists. His teachers warned him not to plunge into the whirl of concert life too soon, and he won another prize, in harmony, in 1859.

By that time, Sarasate was ready to launch what would become a lifetime of concert touring. He moved into a Paris apartment, and though he returned to Spain (especially to Pamplona) for visits, he identified himself more and more as French. His home base was Paris, and when he was able to afford a more luxurious home in 1884, he hired one of the most famous artists of the day, the American-born James McNeill Whistler, to decorate it. Whistler painted a portrait of Sarasate in the process; one of the painter's best-known works, it was given the typically Whistleresque title of *Arrangement in Black* but remains the most familiar image of the violinist.

Toured Americas

At the beginning of his career, Sarasate played mostly the established gems of the violin repertory. His interpretations of the concertos for violin and orchestra of Beethoven and Mendelssohn were well known, and observers generally described his tone as sweet and pure, free of any noise or friction caused by the contact of the bow with the strings. His playing was not sentimental, and he employed comparatively little vibrato. Beyond these individual characteristics of style was Sarasate's demeanor: his real trademark as a performer was that he made even very difficult music look effortless. Sarasate's fame spread with his first tour of the Western hemisphere, which began in 1867, took him from New York to Argentina, and lasted until 1871. He made a return trip in 1889 and 1890, and he also traveled to South Africa and to the Far East.

After returning to France from his first American trip, Sarasate began to attain a new level of renown with his original compositions, mostly for violin and piano. As his fame grew, however, it was often arranged for violin and orchestra when circumstances demanded. Sarasate had written music prior to the American trip, but it was the music written from the mid-1870s until the end of his life that became ensconced in repertory of violinists everywhere. Much of it had a Spanish flavor, and in an age when Spanish music was considered exotic—Georges Bizet's opera *Carmen* was at first rejected by the Parisian public—Sarasate's pieces helped create a vogue for Spanish folk influences that would last for decades.

By the mid-1870s, the only gap in Sarasate's international fame was Germany, where he had never performed. France and Germany had fought a war in the early 1870s, and the musical world, too, was polarized into French and German camps, with partisans of heavier, more intricate German operatic and symphonic works facing off against

lovers of the clarity and balance prized by the French. Sarasate's first tour of Germany in 1876, to the temperamental violinist's consternation, received mixed reviews at first; Sarasate was unfavorably compared to Germany's top violinist, Joseph Joachim, and Sarasate was on the point of boarding a train and returning to Paris. He was talked out of leaving by a promoter, however, and when he appeared at the Gewandhaus concert hall in Leipzig, one of the temples of German concert life, a thunderous ovation brought the house down. Any rivalry between Sarasate and Joachim was purely in the minds of their backers; the two artists admired and dedicated compositions to each other.

Many of Sarasate's most famous compositions were originally published in Germany, and a few bore German titles as a result. His *Zigeunerweisen* (Gypsy Tunes) of 1878 was his first major work to draw successfully on his Spanish musical heritage, and he followed that up with four sets of Spanish Dances issued in Berlin between 1878 and 1882. Sarasate also specialized in medley-like arrangements of tunes from famous operas; the best known among them was his *Concert Fantasies on Carmen* of 1883. All of Sarasate's compositions are technically difficult, but that one poses special challenges for the violinist.

Charmed Women but Never Married

Sarasate never married; early in life he was cast off by a young woman who agreed to take part in an arranged marriage, and he never got over the rejection. The charismatic violinist, who was a sharp dresser and always paid close attention to his public image, charmed women by presenting them with Spanish fans but then spurned their romantic advances. Large amounts of mail from women piled up in Sarasate's Paris apartment, and one married woman kept a diary consisting of love letters to Sarasate that stretched over a period of 18 years. In his infrequent periods of relaxation from the rigors of touring, Sarasate liked to spend time at a home he owned in the French seaside resort of Biarritz.

In the 1880s and 1890s, Sarasate was one of the most famous musicians in the world. Top composers competed to have him give the first performances of their works for violin. The list of works premiered by Sarasate includes the Violin Concertos Nos. 1 and 3 by Camille Saint-Saëns and the Violin Concerto No. 2 and *Scottish Fantasy* by Max Bruch. Sometimes Sarasate took an active hand in works written for him, advising the composers about the capabilities and quirks of the violin. Saint-Saëns, quoted by Grange Woolley in a *Music and Letters* article, felt that in the case of one of his concertos "he [Sarasate] gave me valuable advice to which is due, certainly to some extent, the considerable success of this piece."

Unlike many violin stars, Sarasate enjoyed playing what is known as chamber music—classical music for small ensembles. He continued to perform and compose into the twentieth century, and before his death he became one of the first violinists to record; he made nine cylinder recordings in 1904. Those recordings, which have been reissued on compact discs, confirm the observations made by Sarasate's contemporaries about the lightness and seeming effortlessness of his playing, and he had plainly lost none of his power even as he entered his seventh decade. In the words of an *American Record Guide* reviewer, "Sarasate had a style that was emotionally low-key, glib even, and that presented its extreme virtuosity to the listener as though it were nothing remarkable—no drama, no histrionics, but the fleetest fingers and bow arm in the history of recorded sound.

Sarasate was slowed only by chronic breathing problems, to which he succumbed at his home in Biarritz on September 20, 1908. For much of the twentieth century, he was little more than a name in music history books. As composers tried to outdo each other in devising modern innovations, the tuneful and showy music of Sarasate's era fell out of fashion. Violinists studied the *Spanish Dances* but performed them as encores, if at all.

Young violinists, however, began to rediscover Sarasate's music in the 1990s as classical musicians in general sought to rediscover the direct appeal held by the great performers of the past. American violinists Joshua Bell and Leila Josefowicz, both performers with an interest in crossing the boundary between classical and pop music, recorded Sarasate's *Zigeunerweisen,* and Rachel Barton Pine recorded an entire *Homage to Sarasate* CD as well as recording Sarasate's works on other releases. Once again, Sarasate's name has become known beyond the communities of violin students and Sherlock Holmes enthusiasts.

Books

Sadie, Stanley, ed., *The New Grove Dictionary of Music and Musicians,* 2nd ed., Macmillan, 2001.
Slonimsky, Nicolas, editor emeritus, *Baker's Biographical Dictionary of Music and Musicians,* Schirmer, 2001.

Periodicals

American Record Guide, November-December 1994; March-April 2005.
Music & Letters, July 1955.

Online

"Pablo Sarasate, Biography, http://www.pablosarasate.com (January 29, 2006). □

Clara Schumann

One of the most renowned figures among classical musicians of the nineteenth century, Clara Schumann (1819-1896) was sometimes known as Europe's Queen of the Piano. Her life was partly defined by her marriage to German composer Robert Schumann, whose keyboard works she championed as a performer, but her own accomplishments, which include a small but important body of compositions, have been investigated, in increasing detail, as interest in the creative lives of women has grown.

I ndeed, when Schumann's life story is viewed from a perspective that places her rather then her husband at its center, it emerges as an unusually tumultuous one. Her mother left her when she was five, and her father, a dictatorial but musically informed taskmaster, raised her. She fell in love with Robert Schumann while he was living and taking piano lessons at her family's home, and the two had to go to court to obtain the right to marry over her father's objections. In the 1840s and 1850s she composed some of her best music and toured as a pianist while raising eight children and dealing with her husband's resistance to her performing career. She faced the nightmare of seeing her husband decline into untreatable mental illness, and, at the deepest point of her troubles, she was both heartened and unnerved by romantic attentions from a man much younger than she was, a composer who, she realized, was Robert Schumann's equal. It is not surprising that with the resurgence of interest in Clara Schumann in the 1990s and 2000s, came a novel, an opera, and a play drawn from her life.

Raised in Piano-Dominated Household

Schumann was born Clara Wieck into a middle-class family in Leipzig, Germany, on September 13, 1819. Her father Friedrich Wieck was a piano teacher and music dealer and her mother Marianne was a concert pianist who continued with her own career even during a period in which she had five children in seven years. Clara did not learn to speak until she was four, possibly adopting a withdrawn personality because of frequent arguments in the household; her parents were afraid that she was deaf, but realized she was not when she responded with obvious intelligence to melodies her father played for her on the piano. Early in 1825, Marianne and Friedrich Wieck divorced. This event was traumatic for Clara. Mother and daughter, however, continued to write letters to each other, and undoubtedly Clara was influenced musically by both parents.

Clara started taking piano lessons from her father even before the divorce, and as her talents rapidly developed Friedrich Wieck decided to try to make his daughter into a musical prodigy. She studied not only piano but also music theory and composition with the top teachers in Leipzig, a musically rich city, and she benefited from her father's progressive teaching methods, which emphasized quality of practice over quantity. Wieck's personality was domineering. Clara began a lifelong habit of keeping a diary, and for a time he dictated what she should write in it. This habit did have some positive side effects: Wieck's frequent observations of the business of music and the life of a concert pianist helped prepare Clara for an independent career, and today they offer insight into the musical world of the time.

The year 1830 was an important one for Clara in two respects: she gave her first full recital, at age 11, in Leipzig (having performed at the famed Gewandhaus concert hall two years earlier), and she met the love of her life when Robert Schumann began taking piano lessons with Wieck and rented a room in the family home. Her love for Schumann went through several stages, beginning with preteen infatuation, and by the mid-1830s the two were passionately in love. "When you gave me that first kiss, I thought I would faint; everything went blank and I could barely hold the lamp that was lighting your way out," Clara later wrote to Robert (as quoted by her biographer Nancy B. Reich). Their relationship was deepened by their common musical interests; they played the piano together, studied works by other composers together, and, increasingly often as Clara's own creativity flowered, exchanged compositional ideas.

Robert Schumann proposed marriage in 1837, but Friedrich Wieck refused to give his permission for the match and threatened at one point to shoot Schumann if he ever came near his daughter again. His objections were numerous; Schumann had a reputation as a womanizer and a party animal, and he suffered spells of severe depression, perhaps related to the syphilis that eventually killed him. He was very much a struggling young composer at the time, although his reputation was rapidly on the rise in the late 1830s as he spread his own name through his editorship of a music magazine he created. A lack of respect for Schumann's talents was not among Wieck's objections; even when relations between himself and Schumann were at a low point, he assigned Schumann's piano music to Clara during her lessons. The two lovers wrote each other letters in code, made an engagement in secret, and finally took Friedrich Wieck to court to obtain the right to marry. The court proceedings were messy, as Wieck told some true tales and other nasty and exaggerated ones about Schumann's habits, but Robert and Clara won their case and married on September 12, 1840, a day before her 21st birthday.

Traded Diary Entries

In the early years of their marriage, The Schumann's kept a joint diary, writing in the same book by turns. Their love story became famous, and Clara's devotion to Robert Schumann never waned. The marriage was not without strains, however. Robert Schumann's attitude toward his wife's musical career was ambivalent. During the courtship he had always encouraged her to compose, and he arranged for her music to be published and sometimes wove quotations from her pieces into his own works. The two had something of a symbiotic relationship as composers. Clara's music tended to focus sequentially on different genres just as Robert's did, and both passed in turn through phases of writing piano music, songs, and then larger works. After Robert Schumann's death, Clara stopped composing almost completely.

Conservative public opinion of the time favored the idea, however, that women should stay home and raise children, and Schumann had eight of them between 1841 and 1854. All survived to adulthood. Robert Schumann pushed his wife toward domesticity, and she was able to tour as a pianist only when the family's shaky finances required that she do so. There were other practical problems, too; the household had two grand pianos, but there was no such thing as soundproofing at the time, and Robert's needs took precedence.

Despite these difficulties, Schumann's career was slowed only somewhat during the 1840s. Her total published output of 23 works was small by 19th-century standards, but she got positive responses when publishing her own works. New recordings of such Schumann pieces as the *Six Songs* of 1840-43 have revealed a composer whose style was not a clone of her husband's but drew on influences from various contemporaries, including Felix Mendelssohn and Frédéric Chopin, whose music she often played. The ambitious Piano Trio in G minor of 1846, written with four small children in the house, is often considered Schumann's greatest work.

No matter how much Robert Schumann disliked it when his wife went out on the road, he was dependent on her to some extent: she understood and appreciated his music better than anyone else did, and she was widely known as its greatest interpreter. Robert Schumann, almost alone among 19th-century composers, could not play his own very difficult piano music; he had suffered nerve damage in one of his fingers early in the 1830s, possibly from a finger-strengthening splint he wore in hopes of improving his piano skills, but possibly from the effects of syphilis and its treatment at the time, which involved the ingestion of arsenic.

Separated from Husband During Illness

The last years of Robert Schumann's life were difficult ones for both Robert and Clara. She was left to raise eight children alone but also prized her independence and, when she could, turned down offers of financial help from friends. Robert began to complain of a constant tone he heard in one ear, and his condition soon worsened. He became delusional and aggressive, and in 1854, fearing that he might harm his wife and family, he institutionalized himself. The asylum where he spent his last years, though generally humane, did not permit visits by relatives, and Clara resumed touring and composing in order to support the family. Her three *Romances* for violin and piano, published in 1855, have passages of deep sadness. She did not realize how dire her husband's condition was until she visited him shortly before his death, which was due to syphilis, in 1856.

During this difficult period, Schumann often found moral support from the young composer Johannes Brahms. The two went walking through towns in the Rhine River valley, and Clara, as she had with Robert Schumann, correctly pegged Brahms as a great composer. Brahms wrote her letters that contain a strong element of suggested passion, but an affair behind the back of the hospitalized Robert Schumann was unthinkable. After Robert Schumann's death the two would have been free to marry; they met in Switzerland and had a long discussion of which the contents are unknown. They met again in Düsseldorf, where Schumann and her family were living, and after she saw Brahms off at the train station for his return to Vienna, she wrote (as quoted by biographer Monica Steegmann), she felt that she was coming home "as if from a funeral." The two remained close friends, probably platonic, for the rest of their lives, dying within months of each other.

If Robert Schumann's death put an end to Schumann's compositional career, it had the opposite effect on her concertizing. With both freedom and financial motivation, she restarted her performing career and gained international acclaim. She moved to Berlin in 1857 and was considered one of the elite musicians of the German capital, making nearly 20 trips to England, where she was especially popular, and touring as far away as Russia. Her interpretations were noted for their depth, and her programs for their variety; she played many of Beethoven's works, including four of the profound and punishingly difficult last five, and, at a time when very few other pianists did so, she looked back to the Baroque era of keyboard music, performing works by Johann Sebastian Bach and Domenico Scarlatti. She played a large part in establishing the permanent status of both Robert Schumann and Brahms in the piano repertory.

Schumann moved to Frankfurt-am-Main, Germany, in 1878, and in her later years she taught piano at the Hoch Conservatory there. She continued to perform until 1891, and she died in Frankfurt on May 20, 1896. In the stressed, gender-conflicted culture of the late twentieth century, many people found Schumann an extremely compelling figure. Her life became the subject of an opera (*Clara,* by Robert Convery and Kathleen Cahill), a play (*Clara's Visitor,* by Stephanie Wendt), and a widely acclaimed novel, *Clara,* by Scottish writer Janice Galloway.

Books

Reich, Nancy B., *Clara Schumann: The Artist and the Woman,* rev. ed., Cornell University Press, 2001.
Sadie, Stanley, ed., *The New Grove Dictionary of Music and Musicians,* 2nd ed., Macmillan, 2001.
Steegmann, Monica, *Clara Schumann,* Haus Publishing, 2001.

Periodicals

Guardian (London, England), April 26, 2003.
Milwaukee Journal Sentinel, February 20, 2003.
Star Tribune (Minneapolis, MN), September 13, 2004.
Times (London, England), May 22, 1997.
Washington Times, May 3, 2004.

Online

"Clara Schumann," All Music Guide, http://www.allmusic.com (February 1, 2006).
"Clara Schumann," http://www.geocities.com/Vienna/Strasse/1945/WSB/clara.html (February 1, 2006). □

Artie Shaw

American clarinetist and swing bandleader Artie Shaw (1910-2004), at the peak of his career in the years just before World War II, was matched by few other musicians in popularity and technical skill. Almost as compelling as his musical feats was his attitude toward his own success, which ranged from ambivalence to outright distaste. In his autobiography, *The Trouble with Cinderella,* he spelled the word "$ucce$$."

Shaw's legion of fans was international. An often-quoted *Time* magazine article from the war years stated that to ordinary Germans, America meant "Clark Gable, skyscrapers, and Artie Shaw." And when he sought to retreat from the spotlight, that only increased public fascination with his unusual career and a spicy private life that included eight failed marriages, several of them to headline-making Hollywood beauties. After Shaw laid down his clarinet for good in 1955, however, the publicity died away and Shaw's purely musical legacy came into sharper view. Artie Shaw's hit recordings, such as "Begin the Beguine," "Stardust," and "Frenesi," matched musicianship and popular appeal in a marriage very few other musicians of the twentieth century would accomplish.

Suffered from Anti-Semitic Remarks

Shaw was born Arthur Jacob Arshawsky in New York, New York, on May 23, 1910; his parents were Yiddish-speaking Eastern European Jewish immigrants who worked in the dressmaking business. For the first seven years of his life Shaw lived on New York's heavily Jewish Lower East Side, but financial problems forced the family to move to New Haven, Connecticut. There he encountered anti-Semitism for the first time. A classmate, he recalled in his autobiography, threatened him after he said the Lord's Prayer with the rest of his class, saying, "We don't want no goddamn Christ-killers saying the Lord's Prayer around here, see? Go on home and say your lousy kike prayers, and keep your dirty sheeny nose out of other people's prayers, you hear what I'm telling you?" Such experiences, Shaw wrote, "had more to do with shaping the course and direction of my entire life than any other single thing that has happened to me, before or since." As a teenager he changed

his name to Art Shaw; "Artie" was a further modification suggested by a recording executive who thought "Art Shaw" sounded too much like a sneeze.

Although he studied the piano halfheartedly at his mother's behest, Shaw's real introduction to music came when he sneaked into New Haven's Poli's Palace Theatre while skipping school, and heard a saxophonist take a solo during a vaudeville act. Shaw asked his parents for a saxophone and lessons, but encountered strong parental resistance to his idea of becoming a musician; the best he could do was convince them to let him finance his own instrument purchases and lessons by working at a neighborhood delicatessen. He threw himself into practicing for as much as seven hours a day, stopping only when his lips were worn raw. Within a few months he had won five dollars in a talent contest. He was hired as a substitute sax player and then a full-time touring member of the Johnny Cavallaro dance orchestra. On Cavallaro's instructions he switched from saxophone to clarinet.

Shaw was hired by Cleveland, Ohio, bandleader Austin Wylie in 1925 and spent several years in that city, performing with Wylie's bands in theaters and, from time to time, in Chinese restaurants. He volunteered to write arrangements for the band, learning at first by trial and error with help from the other musicians, and he soon became a proficient orchestrator. Shaw tried to emulate the fiery new jazz styles that were coming out of Chicago, Illinois, and made a trip to hear trumpeter Louis Armstrong in person. In 1928 he traveled to Hollywood and joined another dance

band, this one led by Irving Aaronson. That group moved in 1930 to Chicago, where Shaw encountered contemporary classical music, and then on to New York, where he decided to stay on and resume his interrupted education.

Shaw never obtained a high school degree, but he became a voracious reader and sat in on classes at Columbia University. For the rest of his life, Shaw would educate himself on subjects ranging from literature and art to Zen Buddhism. He made a living in the early 1930s as a recording session player, often with the CBS Orchestra, appearing on numerous recordings of the time. But he became frustrated with what he regarded as purely commercial activity. He listened to the music of jazz pianist Willie "the Lion" Smith and sometimes played in jazz groups that backed the young vocalist Billie Holiday, among others. Rehearsals would often find him with a book propped on the music stand beside the score he was supposed to be learning. Around 1933 Shaw dropped out of music and urban life in general, buying a farm in Bucks County, Pennsylvania, and making a living from its products while trying to write a novel about cornetist Bix Beiderbecke, another major influence on his own style.

Surprised Audience with Classical-Jazz Fusion

Back in New York in 1936, Shaw was booked into the Imperial Theatre to play during an interlude, in front of the curtain, while the stage was set up for the headlining Tommy Dorsey and Bob Crosby swing bands. He seized the opportunity to experiment, forming a band with the then unheard-of combination of classical string quartet, rhythm section (with no piano), and his own clarinet, and writing an original Interlude in B flat for the group. When the audience cheered wildly, the players repeated the piece, having no encore planned. Promoters urged Shaw to form a more conventional swing band, and he agreed.

At the time he was unknown to national audiences, but the Artie Shaw Orchestra soon emerged as a rival to clarinetist Benny Goodman's swing band. The two clarinetists (and another major clarinetist-bandleader, Woody Herman) were often characterized as rivals, but Shaw emphasized the importance of forming one's own style rather than competing with other musicians. He hired Holiday as a vocalist, becoming one of the first white bandleaders to employ a full-time black ensemble member, but she departed after a few months of racist abuse from audiences. Signed to the Bluebird label, Shaw and his orchestra recorded an instrumental version of Cole Porter's "Begin the Beguine" in 1938.

The recording featured a sequence of subtle Shaw solos (and inventive little solo fragments) and rapidly became a massive hit. Shaw contended for Goodman's title of King of Swing and, at a point when swing was the dominant form of American popular music, became one of the most famous figures in the American entertainment industry—"a sort of weird, jazz-band-leading, clarinet-tooting, jitterbug-surrounded Symbol of American Youth," as he called himself (according to *Atlantic Monthly* writer Mark Steyn). Shaw made other hit recordings and appeared on national radio broadcasts, but the bookish performer detested the frenzy of fame. On a bandstand in New York in 1939 (according to a jazz historian quoted by Jesse Hamlin in the *San Francisco Chronicle*) he told vocalist Helen Forrest, Holiday's replacement, that "I hate selling myself. I hate the fans. They won't even let me play without interrupting me. They scream when I play. They don't listen. They don't care about the music." Shaw walked off the stage and hid out in a Mexican seaside town.

Publicity hounds caught up with him after he rescued a drowning swimmer, and the episode, if anything, heightened Shaw's mystique. He formed a new band in Los Angeles in 1940, appeared in several films (including *Second Chorus*), and recorded hits that would become jazz standards—a flawless arrangement of the Mexican popular song "Frenesi"; his own "Summit Ridge Drive;" one of the definitive versions of the Hoagy Carmichael song "Stardust"; and a classical-influenced "Concerto for Clarinet." Shaw's personal life stayed in the headlines, as he dumped one pin-up girl movie star, Betty Grable, to marry another, Lana Turner. Shaw himself had matinee-quality good looks to go with his musical abilities, but his marriages, including one to star Ava Gardner, all soured soon after they began.

Sent to Pacific

In 1942 Shaw enlisted in the U.S. Navy. He was instructed to form a band that would perform for the troops, and played a heavy schedule of concerts in the Pacific theater for a period of 18 months, performing under bomb attack on the island of Guadalcanal at one point. He likely suffered from what would now be called post-traumatic stress disorder and spent time under a psychiatrist's care, an experience that gave *The Trouble with Cinderella* (1952) an introspective spirit rare among jazz biographies. A new marriage to Betty Kern (daughter of composer Jerome Kern) dissolved. Back in New York in 1944, Shaw formed a new band that some observers consider his best; it featured rising African-American trumpeter Roy Eldridge and guitarist Barney Kessel.

Shaw also revived a small group, called the Gramercy Five, that he started before the war; the name came from that of a New York City telephone exchange. The Gramercy Five served as a forum for some of Shaw's more experimental ideas, including the introduction of the harpsichord, a then-rarely-heard predecessor of the piano, into a jazz context. In 1947 Shaw again took a break from performing in order to study classical clarinet. He performed with a number of symphony orchestras, including the New York Philharmonic under the conductorship of a young Leonard Bernstein, and released an album called *Modern Music for Clarinet* that featured his arrangements of contemporary classical pieces.

Shaw's classical experiments were not enthusiastically received by his core of jazz fans, and neither did they follow him as he mastered the new angular bebop jazz style—something few other major swing performers succeeded in doing. The music of the large band Shaw formed in 1949, and the recordings he made with the Gramercy Five toward the end of his career, received only moderate levels of

attention at the time but are highly esteemed today. Increasingly restless, Shaw took another break from performing in 1951 and moved to a dairy farm in upstate New York's Dutchess County. In 1955 he stopped performing on the clarinet and was never lured back, although he did emerge to conduct a revived Artie Shaw orchestra in 1983. Shaw felt that he had accomplished all he could on the clarinet and never touched the instrument again. "I sought perfection," he was quoted as saying by Steve Voce of the London *Independent*. "I was constantly miserable. I was seeking a constantly receding horizon. So I quit."

The final decades of Shaw's life were eventful ones, even if they had little to do with music. He built a house on the northeast coast of Spain and lived there with his eighth wife, Evelyn Keyes, for five years. Shaw, who had two sons (one by Kern, one by sixth wife Doris Dowling), moved to northwestern Connecticut in 1960 and to California in 1973. He took up shooting and was at one point ranked as the fourth-best precision rifleman in the United States. Shaw formed a film distribution company and was a fixture on the college lecture circuit; presenters could choose from one of four talks, one of which dealt with serial monogamy and divorce. According to Steyn, he called himself the "ex-husband of love goddesses." The bulk of Shaw's energy was spent on writing fiction; in 1964 he published a trio of novellas under the collective title *I Love You, I Hate You, Drop Dead*. In his final years he worked on a giant novel about a young jazz musician named Albie Snow; it was never finished or published. Shaw died in Newbury Park, California, on December 30, 2004.

Books

Schuller, Gunther, *The Swing Era,* Oxford, 1989.

Shaw, Artie, *The Trouble with Cinderella: An Outline of Identity,* Farrar, Straus, and Young, 1952.

Simosko, Vladimir, *Artie Shaw: A Musical Biography and Discography,* Scarecrow, 2000.

White, John, *Artie Shaw: His Life and Music,* Continuum, 2004.

Periodicals

Atlantic Monthly, March 2005.

Commentary, March 2005.

Daily Telegraph (London, England), January 1, 2005.

Independent (London, England), January 1, 2005.

New York Times, December 31, 2004.

San Francisco Chronicle, December 31, 2004.

Smithsonian, March 2004.

Times (London, England), January 1, 2005.

Online

"Biography," http://www.artieshaw.com (February 13, 2006). □

Alfred Sisley

Alfred Sisley (1839-1899) was a key painter of the early Impressionist period, a friend and associate of Claude Monet and Pierre Renoir who matched their pathbreaking experiments with light, color, and

brushstroke. He put his own stamp on early Impressionist technique and produced a body of work that art historian Richard Shone called "fundamentally representative of our notion of what constitutes 'pure' Impressionism." His output consisted almost entirely of landscapes.

That consistency of subject matter is partly responsible for the comparative obscurity of Sisley's paintings as compared to the work of other great early Impressionists. While Monet, for example, began to incorporate urban scenes into his art, and Renoir began to specialize in a new kind of portrait, Sisley's style changed little as he moved from town to town and painted the new landscapes he encountered. It was only when Sisley's paintings were reassembled into large museum exhibitions that the dimensions of his achievement became apparent; his subtle grasp of detail and effect was almost the equal of Monet's, and his impact on future landscape painters, many of them American, was strong.

Born to English Parents

Alfred Sisley was born in Paris, France, on October 30, 1839, to William and Felicia Sisley, cousins from England. William Sisley was the manager of a company that made artificial flowers. Despite his English name and occasional references to him as "the English Impressionist," Alfred Sisley rarely left France, and for many years had only an imperfect grasp of English. He applied twice for French citizenship but was turned down both times. Both English (SIS-lee) and French (sees-LEI) pronunciations of his name were current during his lifetime. Sisley was brought up in Paris, and in 1857 he was sent to London, England, to live with relatives, improve his English, and prepare for the business career his parents had planned for him.

Instead, Sisley spent his time studying the great English landscape painters of the time, including John Constable and the proto-Impressionist J.M.W. Turner, whose late paintings almost did away with representation in favor of pure patterns of light. Back in Paris in 1860, Sisley began studying art at the studio of Charles Gleyre, a conservative painter whose classes nevertheless attracted several of the future creators of Impressionism. Sisley became acquainted with Monet, Renoir, and Frédéric Bazille. Sisley and other painters sometimes went out in groups to sketch scenes *en plein aire,* or in open air, a characteristic Impressionist technique Sisley would follow for the rest of his life. Sisley's first surviving paintings are rather gloomy landscapes in the style of the dominant Barbizon school, but he soon began to pay attention to Monet's innovations. Sisley made waves with two paintings of a street in the village of Marlotte that were shown in 1866 at the Salon, a space that exhibited paintings juried by the French Academy of Fine Arts.

Sisley's personal life went through an upheaval at around that time. He met Marie Louise Adélaïde Eugénie Lescouezec, an artist's model and florist who was five years older than he. She became pregnant and gave birth to their son, Pierre, in 1867. Sisley, who was not religious, had no

use for a church ceremony, and the two did not marry until 1897, shortly before Sisley's death. A daughter, Jeanne, followed in 1870, and Sisley's father, whose business was destroyed in the Franco-Prussian War, was outraged by Sisley's non-marital liaison and cut him off from family funds. Sisley, however, usually told people that he was married, and few outside the family knew of the unorthodox arrangement; a bit of scandal, then as now, might actually have helped his career. Sisley remained on the edge financially for much of his life and often borrowed money from friends. Things got even worse in 1870 when Prussian troops pillaged the town of Bougival, west of Paris, where he was living at the time; he lost everything he owned.

By that time, however, Sisley had fully immersed himself in the new techniques that would soon become known as Impressionism. Moving his family to the small town of Louveciennes, he began to paint landscapes of the area; these early Impressionist paintings, such as *Early Snow at Louveciennes* (in the collection of the Boston Museum of Fine Arts) are considered some of his best. His paintings, at first so dark, now seemed bathed in light. Richard Cork wrote in the *Times* of London, "By 1872, two years before the First Impressionist Exhibition, he had liberated his imagination with extraordinary panache. Look at the superb *Bridge of Villeneuve-la-Garenne,* where the sky is at last permitted to assume the importance it would enjoy in so much of his work." Sisley attracted the attention of the influential art dealer Paul Durand-Ruel, who had an international clientele.

Exhibited at Impressionist Shows

The event that gave Impressionism its name was the Impressionist Exhibition of 1874, which featured a number of Sisley's works from the preceding few years—careful, subtle landscape scenes that wound up in collections on both sides of the English Channel, and eventually on both sides of the Atlantic. Sisley's painting *Autumn: Banks of the Seine near Bougival* shared the distinction of being criticized, along with Monet's works, as unfinished. Sisley also exhibited his paintings at the second, third, and seventh Impressionist exhibitions, and the prices his paintings could command rose to a point where he could support his family.

Emboldened by his new success, Sisley made a painter's tour of England in 1874, traveling with French opera singer Jean-Baptiste Faure. Sisley returned twice more to England but otherwise did not travel to seek out artistically stimulating locales the way other artists of the day tended to do; the trip to take in the atmosphere of decaying Venice was a common one at the time, but Sisley never made it. The 1874 visit produced an important series of scenes painted along the Thames River, but Sisley avoided the heavily industrial scenes that were beginning to fascinate other contemporary French painters.

Sisley moved his family to Moret-sur-Loing, southeast of Paris, in 1880. The town nears the Fontainebleau forest beloved by various Impressionist painters, and it became for Sisley something comparable to what Giverny, west of Paris, was for Monet: a source of unusual natural scenes that he knew well and could revisit with a canvas, or occasionally a camera, for despite his devotion to painting in the open air, Sisley seems to have worked from photographs at times. Still short of cash, Sisley sometimes paid off local tradespeople and merchants with paintings. One painting at the time could pay for roughly three months' rent on the Sisley family's house at 19 rue Montmartre. The descendants of some of these townspeople reaped a windfall from their inherited Sisley paintings, but others were reluctant to admit ownership of a Sisley lest they be forced to pay several generations' worth of inheritance taxes. Sisley is thought to have painted up to 1,500 canvases, but only 900 have been identified so far.

Staying close to Moret for the rest of his life, Sisley still sought out new surroundings by moving temporarily to other small towns. His fortunes slowly improved as his reputation solidified. Durand-Ruel mounted an all-Sisley exhibition in Paris in 1883 and another at his satellite gallery in New York in 1889—the point of origin for some of the many Sisley scenes that hang today on the walls of large and medium-sized American museums. The French government confirmed Sisley's status by purchasing one of his paintings in 1888, and in 1890 he was chosen as a member of the Société Nationale des Beaux-Arts (National Society of Fine Arts), a group formed by the sculptor Auguste Rodin and several painters to highlight the best in French modern art. Sisley's paintings were often shown at the group's annual exhibitions in the 1890s.

Painted Cathedral Series

In 1893 and 1894, Sisley produced a series of paintings of a Gothic-era church in Moret-sur-Loing, with close-up views of the church, various lighting conditions, and types of weather. The series is comparable to the more famous series of views of Rouen Cathedral painted by Monet around the same time, and Sisley may have done his own series because he heard about Monet's plans and wanted to use the publicity surrounding Monet to his own advantage. The Monet cathedral series was one of the great breakthroughs of modern art, with unearthly colors and indistinct building shapes that seem to point the way toward abstraction. Sisley's works, by comparison, remained more in the main line of classic Impressionism.

Critics have disagreed on the merits of Sisley's church paintings. Cork declared that "even when glistening from a recent downpour or assailed by the full power of the sun, [Sisley's] church never threatens to dissolve in light. Monet's encrusted visions are ethereal; Sisley's remain earthbound." But Joseph C. Skrapits, writing in *American Artist,* found that "Sisley's churches evoke a depth of poetic feeling missing from Monet's cathedrals, which for all their fireworks display of color seem somewhat chilly exercises in virtuoso technique." Whichever reaction the individual viewer may have, it seemed clear that large exhibitions of Sisley's paintings resulted in a new appreciation of his technique. Seen individually, his paintings do not push the envelope as those of the more progressive Impressionists did, but an immersion in his painterly world reveals the depth of his reactions to natural scenes. Like Monet, Sisley also often painted haystacks in the latter part of his career.

Sisley suffered from cancer of the throat for several years in the late 1890s, and he died at age 59 on January 29, 1899, in Moret-sur-Loing. The Georges Petit gallery in Paris mounted a retrospective of his work in 1897, but for many years after that, despite the wide distribution of his work in museums, he was somewhat undervalued in comparison with the major Impressionists. No full-length biography of Sisley exists, partly because, although he was a prolific letter writer, he was reticent about the personal details of his life. Sisley's paintings are often described as sober, in contrast to the crowd-pleasing ebullience of a painter like Renoir with his intensely colorful palette. A major showing of Sisley's work at the Royal Academy in London and a series of events mounted in Moret in 1999, on the 100th anniversary of Sisley's death, resulted in new interest in his classic Impressionist style. Of the Royal Academy show, the *Economist* noted that Sisley "did not do what art historians like painters to do. He did not constantly push, and twist, and extend his range." But "anyone who does not feel a sudden flush of pleasure when confronted with a classic Sisley needs to take his soul in for a service."

Books

International Dictionary of Art and Artists, St. James, 1990.

Shone, Richard, *Sisley,* Phaidon, two editions, 1992, 1994.

Turner, Jane, ed., *Dictionary of Art,* Macmillan, 1996.

Periodicals

American Artist, March 1995.

Economist, July 18, 1992.

Guardian (London, England), June 7, 1999.

Times (London, England), July 3, 1992.

Online

"Alfred Sisley," The Artchive, http://www.artchive.com/artchive/S/sisley.html (February 13, 2006). □

Lydia Skoblikova

Russian speed skater Lydia Skoblikova (born 1939) became the first athlete to win four gold medals in one Olympiad, in the 1964 Winter Games at Innsbruck, Austria. Her six golds overall for the former Soviet Union remain a record in the sport. The "lightning from the Urals" also won numerous medals in the World Championships.

Had Cold Winters in Siberia

Skoblikova was raised in a metallurgical engineer's family in Zlatoust, in Siberia, a sword-making community in the Ural Mountains that was also the home of world chess champion Anatoly Karpov. Thanks to the long winters, outdoor rinks were abundant, and the sports-

minded city built many athletic facilities. Skoblikova began skating at age 10 and racing at 12. An Associated Press article in the *New York Times* wrote, "In an atmosphere where the winters are long and the skating rinks plentiful, she rapidly mastered the techniques of the sport."

Skoblikova worked up to five hours a day fine-tuning her style, and built her endurance through bicycling and skiing. "In the European countries, skiing and skating is started in babyhood," Arthur Daley wrote in the *New York Times*. "In Innsbruck, for example, the kids gulp down their lunch at the noon recess and snatch a couple of runs down a nearby Alp before returning to classes." And in the Netherlands, many Dutch people get from place to place by skating across the country's frozen canals.

Golden Breakthrough at Squaw Valley

At age 19 Skoblikova qualified for the Soviet team in the 1959 World Championships in Siberia and earned a bronze medal for her third-place finish. Ironically, given her international success, she never won a national championship. She captured two distance events at the Worlds the following year, and won the 500-meter sprint at the Worlds in 49.5 seconds; in the latter event, she led a Soviet sweep of the top four finishes.

In 1960 she qualified for her first Olympiad, the Winter Games in Squaw Valley, California. Skating, including all its subcategories, was one of four winter sports at Squaw Valley. Skoblikova, largely unknown internationally at the time, drew headlines with her Olympic victories in the

1,500 and 3,000 meters; she set a world record in the 1,500 meters. She barely missed another medal in the 1,000 meters, finishing fourth.

Squaw Valley would be a mere opening act for Skoblikova, who balanced her sports regimen with a job teaching anatomy and physical education at the Physical Culture Institute in Chelyabinski, Siberia. She and her Soviet teammates continued to excel in the Worlds. After near misses for golds the previous two years, Skoblikova dominated the 1963 Worlds in Karuizawa, Japan. She won all four events—the 500, 1,000, 1,5000, and 3,000 meters—gliding over what the *New York Times* called "one of the finest 400-meter skating layouts in the world."

Won Four Golds in 1964

One month before the 1964 Olympic Winter Games at Innsbruck, Skoblikova, an Iron Curtain athlete who spoke infrequently and measuredly, suddenly predicted the Soviet Union would sweep the women's figure skating events. "We will pick up silver and bronze medals, too," she said at a Moscow press conference held by the Soviet State Committee for Cultural Relations with Foreign Countries, according to Theodore Shabad of the *New York Times*. The Soviet team was strong in speed skating, entering eleven men and six women at the Innsbruck games, but no female solo figure skaters competed there.

The USSR emphasized nationalism in advance of the Games. According to Shabad, Yuri D. Mashin, the country's leading sports official in his role as chairman of the Central Council of Soviet Sports Societies, said that patriotism "may play a decisive role" in Olympic results. He added that 55 of the 74 Soviet athletes belonged to the Communist Party or the Young Communist League. The 1964 Soviet squad was fairly new; only about one-third of the athletes had Olympic experience, Mashin said.

Skoblikova was considered a solid favorite to prevail in the 1,000, 1,500, and 3,000-meter races at Innsbruck, but beatable in the 500-meter sprint. Skoblikova, however, won the 500 in 45 seconds, and led a Soviet sweep in that event. She won her 1,500 meters in 2 minutes, 22.6 seconds and prevailed in the 1,000 in 1:33.2. The skater, meanwhile, remained self-critical. "I know I was somewhat slow," she said in the *New York Times*. "I didn't take all the advantages I could have."

In the 3,000 meters, her biggest competition appeared to be mushy ice; warm weather made the ice puddly throughout the competition and the lack of snow jeopardized such events as the bobsled, forcing the Austrian army to carve snow out of mountains and transport it to the luge and bobsled runs. Still, Skoblikova made Olympic history, finishing the 3,000 in 5:14.9, to become the first athlete of either gender to win four gold medals in one Olympics. Despite a hot sun and sub-par ice, she missed breaking her own world record by merely a fraction of a second.

"Mrs. Skoblikova had her mind on great things today," Fred Tupper wrote in the *New York Times*. Already possessing World (5:04.3) and Olympic (5:14.3) records in this event, she had hoped to finish in less than five minutes. "But the sun was against her," Tupper wrote. "The early skaters found the ice firm and fast, but by noon pools of water dappled the rink." Skoblikova led by half a second midway through the race, "then she really poured it on," Tupper wrote, adding: "In a furious final lap, her head down and her arms swinging, [she] roared across the finish as the crowd waved and screamed."

The four victories brought her worldwide acclaim. "I like to skate around the stadium after a victory. People applaud and that gives me pleasure," she said after winning the 1,000 meters, as quoted by the Associated Press in a *New York Times* article. Eric Heiden of the United States won all five men's speed-skating events in the 1980 Games at Lake Placid, New York, but Skoblikova is still the only woman to capture six Olympic golds in individual events. American speed skater Bonnie Blair also won five golds, but they covered three Olympiads, including her three victories in 1994 at Lillehammer, Norway.

Women's Sports in Limelight

Skoblikova's success drew attention to women's sports. The women accounted for most of the USSR's 11 gold and 25 overall medals at Innsbruck, and the Western media took notice. "If Lidiya Skoblikova—with her blonde hair, blue eyes, and dimpled cheeks—does not match some Westerners' conception of a Siberian woman speed skater, her grim application to training regimen and fierce determination to win typify the Soviet approach to the IX Winter Olympics," the *New York Times* wrote in a "Women in the News" profile. The newspaper added: "Her voice is strangely harsh, coming from a girlish, heart-shaped face." Her husband, Alexander Polozkov, remained in Siberia during the games but sent congratulatory telegrams.

Media coverage of women's sports was outside the mainstream. Writers in that day often called the athletes "ladies," or "girls," and addressed them by the honorifics Miss or Mrs., with Skoblikova interchangeably called both in the *New York Times*. Arthur Daley, writing an Olympic wrapup column in that newspaper, referred to "dames," "feminine intrusion," "dolls," "distaff," and even track and field "Soviet amazons." He also wrote: "Not only have the dames made the old Grecian ideal crumble, they also have twisted the perspective of the entire operation. Women have been known to do things like that, bless their darling little hearts." Daley called Skoblikova "the speed-skating matron."

Never Won National Championship

Skoblikova won all four events in the World Championships one month after the Olympics, but in the Soviet championships, she did not win a single event. Inga Veronina, her principal competition within the USSR and fully recovered from an illness, emerged as the overall champion. Skoblikova, after a two-year hiatus from the sport, set another record in the 3,000 meters in 1967, but failed to win a medal in the 1967 Worlds or the 1968 Olympics in Grenoble, France. She retired one year later.

After retiring competitively, Skoblikova remained active, joining the Soviet National Olympic Committee. In 1983 she received a silver Olympic Order from the International Olympic Committee for having contributed significantly to the Olympic movement. Skoblikova continued her Olympic involvement after the 1991 fall of the Soviet Union. In 2002 she had trouble obtaining a visa to follow the Russian team to the 2002 Winter Games in Salt Lake City in the United States, but obtained one after appealing to the U.S. embassy, along with Vyacheslav Vedenin, who won two golds in Nordic skiing in 1972.

Changed Face of Russian Sports

Skoblikova and other former Soviet athletes witnessed a new generation of Russian stars benefit financially. She attended a 2002 reception in Salt Lake City that honored athletes with old-style honors and new-style cash. "The money was from a grateful state, which in an earlier era showered privileges and riches on its athletic stars—albeit secretly," Serge Schmemann wrote in the *New York Times.* "But in the new Russia, the state works side by side with generous sponsors, whose posters cover the walls of Russia House, and whose support is critical." Figure skater Anton Sikharulidze told Schmemann: "It's not the Soviet Union, but I think we've kept the good traditions, which is a good thing."

The Slava Academy of Outstanding Sports Achievements in 2005 nominated Skoblikova in the Legend category for a Glory national sports prize. The academy consists of well-known coaches, athletes, journalists, and scientists, as well as others in cultural affairs.

The breakup of the USSR, however, separated Russia from the only skating rink the Soviet Union had built with natural ice—in Kazakhstan, which became independent in 1991. "Russia was a speed-skating powerhouse in the 1960s-80s, but many local skaters have been forced to train abroad for the past two decades, for lack of good facilities," said *Russian Life,* published in the United States by the Russian embassy. In 2004, thanks to the efforts of Skoblikova and others, Russia opened a state of the art, multi-purpose indoor ice skating center, one of the world's largest, in Moscow's Krylatskoye neighborhood. The stadium hosted the International Skating Union's World All-Around Speed Skating Championships. "We've been waiting for it for 20 years," said Skoblikova, according to the Associated Press. "Now we have everything and there will [be] no more excuses for bad results."

Periodicals

Associated Press Newswires, September 9, 2004.
Australian, January 30,2002.
New York Times, January 31, 1960;February 22, 1963; January 18, 1964; February 2, 1964; February 3, 1964; February 11,1964; February 17, 1964; March 4, 1964; February 17, 2002.
RIA Novosty, May 13, 2005.
Russian Life, March 1, 2005.

Online

"Lidiya Skoblikova profile," SkateResults.com, http://www .skateresults.com/skater/show/986 (January 13, 2006). □

Belle Starr

Legendary American outlaw Belle Starr (1848-1889) developed a reputation as a "Bandit Queen" of the Old West. Though she was an expert rider who could handle a gun, and who was associated with famous outlaws such as Frank and Jesse James, many accounts of her life contain more legend than fact. She has been credited with a long list of spectacular crimes, but it appears she did little more than steal some horses and harbor some fugitive friends.

Her popular image, generated by unreliable biographies and motion pictures, was that of an attractive, amorous and ruthless female gang leader—a female Jesse James, as she was often called, usually by those who knew little about her life. The reality of the woman, however, is rather different. "Belle's true life was one without glamour," author Richard D. Arnott wrote in *Wild West* magazine in 1997. "The so-called Bandit Queen was actually an unfortunate woman hardened by her times and associates. . . . In her later years, she really was a companion to known thieves and felons, but it is doubtful she ever did more than steal horses and provide a haven for fugitives."

Starr was born as Myra Maybelle Shirley on February 5, 1848, in Jasper County, Missouri, near Carthage. Her parents were John Shirley and Eliza (Pennington) Shirley, who called their daughter Belle. John Shirley, married three times, was the black sheep of an affluent Virginia family. Pennington, his third wife, came from the Hatfield family of the famous Hatfield-McCoy feud. In 1839, Shirley moved his family to southwest Missouri, where he became wealthy raising wheat, corn, horses, and livestock.

In 1856, Shirley sold his land and moved his growing family—now including the eight-year-old Belle—to Carthage. He used the money to buy property in the prospering city and to build a tavern, livery stable and blacksmith shop. Wealthy and well–respected, he sent his only daughter to the Carthage Female Academy. There, Starr, who became an excellent student, studied music and classical languages in addition to the standard academic curriculum.

Starr had four brothers, but she spent much of her time outdoors with her older brother, Bud, who taught her how to ride horses and shoot guns. In town, she enjoyed playing the role of a little rich girl. However, her family's fortunes were about to fall sharply.

Civil War Ruined Family

During events leading to the Civil War, as well as in the actual conflict, John Shirley was a Southern sympathizer, and he especially admired William Clarke Quantrill, the ruthless leader of the marauding guerilla band "Quantrill's Raiders." So he was fiercely proud when Bud joined with Quantrill to serve as a scout. However, the Raiders were

marked men in the eyes of the Federal troops, and tragedy struck the family when, in 1864, Union soldiers killed Bud.

Shirley also saw his town and, in turn, his businesses destroyed. Grief–stricken and desperate, he sold his property, loaded his family and belongings in a wagon, and went south to Scyene, Texas, a move that represented a big step down. At the time, Texas was an open territory that provided a haven for outlaws and a last–chance refuge for the rootless and destitute.

Scyene was a small settlement southeast of Dallas, and Shirley obtained 800 acres through a land grant. At first, his family had to live in a crude makeshift abode while he constructed a modest clapboard house. On the farm, Shirley grew corn, sorghum, oxen, horses, milk cows, and hogs; and he raised money through horse trades and stud fees.

During this period, newspapers published reports of the criminal activities of notable outlaws such as James and the Younger brothers, former Confederates who, like the late Bud Shirley, had ridden with Quantrill. Sometimes, the Shirley's opened their farm to these outlaws, providing them a hiding place. Thus, Starr became close with members of the James-Younger gang. In fact, one of the famed outlaws, Cole Younger, had been one of her childhood friends in Missouri. This later led to rumors and the myth that Cole Younger had once been Starr's lover.

Married Jim Reed

In Texas, however, Starr actually fell in love with James C. "Jim" Reed. She also knew Reed from her Missouri days, as the Reed and Shirley families were friends. Now, Reed was riding with the Youngers, and he and Starr became reacquainted one night when the gang sought refuge on the Shirley farm. That led to a romance, and Starr and Reed were married on November 1, 1866.

According to legend, Starr's parents objected to the relationship, forcing the couple to elope. In a rather colorful account, Starr and Reed supposedly rode off with a gang of outlaws and were married on horseback. But this was just another Starr myth. The truth is, her parents did not object at all to Reed. In fact, Reed moved in with the Shirley family and helped with the farming.

In 1867, the couple went to live with Reed's mother on the Reed homestead in Missouri. Early in September of 1868, Starr gave birth to their first child, Rosie Lee, who was later nicknamed "Pearl." Another widely circulated Starr myth involved the daughter's birth. Pearl was said to be the illegitimate daughter of Cole Younger, but this rumor has been discredited. Belle and Reed also had a son, James Edwin "Ed," born in 1871. This domestic tranquility was short-lived, as Reed would become increasingly involved in criminal activity.

Lived life on the Run

After several years of marriage, Reed began to get restless. He began spending less time at home and more time with notorious horse thief Tom Starr. His own Cherokee tribe spurned Tom Starr because of his viciousness. In avenging his father's murder, he reportedly killed more than 20 people. Together, Reed and Tom Starr sold whiskey and rustled cattle in Cherokee territory, an area that became Oklahoma. Reed also re-established contact with his friends in the James-Younger gang.

In 1869, Reed shot a man who supposedly killed his brother, forcing him to flee with his family to California. In 1871, after Reed was accused of passing counterfeit money, the family had to flee again, this time moving back to Texas. For the next two years, Reed became involved in livestock rustling and murder with his outlaw associates. When warrants were issued for his arrest, Reed hid out in Choctaw territory, taking Belle Starr with him but leaving the children with the Shirley's in Texas.

After Reed and his gang robbed the Grayson family of about $30,000 in gold coins, in an 1873 incident notorious for its cruel details, Reed went back to Texas with Starr, who was identified as an accomplice in the crime (supposedly, she took part while dressed as a man), even though there was little evidence she was involved. Apparently, during the robbery, the outlaws hung Grayson and his wife from a tree until they revealed the location of the gold.

Back in Texas, Starr left Reed to live with her parents. She had enough of the fugitive life and her husband's criminal activities. Further, she found out that Reed had been seeing another woman.

Death and Destitution Followed

After the separation from his wife, Reed continued robbing stagecoaches and stealing cattle. For a while, he

stayed one step ahead of lawmen. Eventually, former friend John Morris, who had been deputized to capture Reed, shot and killed him in Texas.

The next few years seemed quiet and sad for Starr. Her father died in 1876. Her mother sold the family farm and moved to Dallas. But early biographers embellished these quiet years. According to the Belle Starr legend, Starr moved to Dallas with her children and lived off the money from the Grayson robbery, affecting a rather flamboyant lifestyle, dressing in fancy clothes, boots, and hats and wearing twin-holstered pistols. Supposedly, she spent a lot of time gambling and drinking in saloons and often rode through the streets shooting her pistols.

According to other unreliable accounts, she went on a criminal spree that included burning down a store, robbing a bank while dressed as a man, and robbing a poker game at gunpoint. In addition, she was supposed to have led a ring of horse thieves. But the public record, including newspaper accounts and court documents, did not bear out any of these claims.

The reality was much more mundane. Starr had never financially benefited from her husband's crimes, and after he was killed in 1874, she was broke. Starr sold the farm that she and Reed had bought and, for awhile, lived at the Reed homestead in Missouri.

Married Sam Starr

Local gossip had it that Starr, after Reed's death, lived with Bruce Younger for a short time in Kansas. Bruce was related to Cole Younger, and Starr supposedly married him in 1880. Actually, on June 5 of that year, Belle Shirley officially became Belle Starr when she married Sam Starr, the son of her late husband's former partner in crime Tom Starr. Legal records indicated that Sam was twenty-three while Belle was twenty-seven (she was actually thirty-two).

They settled near the Canadian River on land owned by Tom Starr and called Youngers' Bend, in honor of the Younger gang. As it was located in so-called "Indian Territory," it was in the midst of "outlaw country," and many fugitives, including Jesse James, often sought refuge on the property. Starr, however, wanted only to live in peace, but peaceful periods would be fleeting.

Sentenced to Prison

In July of 1882, the Starr's were accused of stealing horses. The charge came after a horse roundup on a neighbor's land. The Starr's received permission to pen the horses in the neighbor's corral until the horses could be sold. But the neighbor noticed that some of the horses actually belonged to other neighbors, and he informed the Starr's. But the Starr's sold the horses, anyway. They were indicted in November of 1882.

Their four-day trial took place in March of 1883, in the court of "Hanging Judge" Isaac C. Parker. Both were found guilty. Parker, however, went easy on the pair, explaining that it was the first conviction for both. Sam Starr received a twelve–month sentence while Belle received two six–month sentences.

The Starr's were sent to the House of Correction in Detroit, Michigan. Belle Starr reportedly was a model prisoner. After they each served nine months, they returned to Youngers' Bend. Belle Starr had put on weight in prison and appeared dowdy. When she was not busy planting, she liked to read and play the piano. Sam Starr, meanwhile, spent more time away from home, engaging in outlaw activities until he became a wanted fugitive. As such, he only returned home infrequently.

Belle Starr stood trial twice more in 1886. The first trial involved what appeared to be a case of mistaken identity. That year, three bandits had robbed some farms in the Youngers' Bend area, and two witnesses claimed Belle Starr was one of them. She stood trial at Fort Smith in June, but evidence was not enough to convict her. Three months later, she returned to Fort Smith to stand trial for horse theft, after she mistakenly sold a stolen horse to a friend. Again, she was found not guilty.

When she returned home after her second trial, she learned that her husband had been critically wounded after an Indian posse ambushed him. Despite his injuries, Sam Starr escaped and fled to his brother's home. Starr treated his wounds and convinced him to turn himself in. Sam Starr surrendered to authorities in October 1886 and was scheduled to stand trial in February 1887. But he never made it to court. In December of 1886, at a Christmas party that the Starr's attended at a friend's house, Sam Starr was killed in a shootout with his cousin, U.S. Deputy Indian Marshall Franklin West.

The death of her husband placed Belle Starr's claim on Youngers' Bend in the hands of Cherokee authorities. In an attempt to retain the land, she married Sam's adopted brother, Billy July, a member of the Creek tribe who was twenty–four years old. The Cherokee leaders told her she could keep the land as long as she remained married and as long as she stopped allowing fugitives to hide out on the property.

Starr Shot and Killed

Farmers were settling the land near Youngers' Bend, and Starr agreed to rent some of her land to Edgar A. Watson. Later, she learned Watson was wanted for murder in Florida. Not wanting to lose her land, she tried to cancel the rental arrangement. Watson, however, wouldn't leave. In response, Starr insinuated that she knew about his fugitive status and hinted that she'd reveal Watson's whereabouts to Florida authorities. The implied threat had the desired effect; Watson moved to another farm. Apparently, that was not her last encounter with Watson.

Starr was shot and killed on Sunday morning, February 3, 1889, and indications were strong that Watson murdered her. Starr had spent Saturday night with friends and was heading home to Youngers' Bend when she stopped at the home of a neighbor. Several other visitors were there, too, including Watson. When Starr entered, Watson left.

Starr ate and chatted for a while, then continued home. The part of the road she now traveled passed very close to Watson's new home. As she turned a bend in the road, she was blown out of her saddle by a shotgun blast. As she tried to get off the ground, she was shot again, in the face and shoulder. She died from her wounds.

Watson was the primary suspect. Investigators found his footprints near the shooting scene. Also, Watson owned a shotgun. There were no witnesses, however. Some neighbors heard shots but had seen nothing. Watson was arrested but acquitted. The evidence was considered too circumstantial.

After the acquittal, no attempt was made to determine just who shot Starr, although suspects included Starr's third husband and her two children. Her son, Ed, had threatened to kill her after she punished him with a bullwhip. Pearl Starr also was angry with her mother after Belle thwarted her wedding plans and helped get Pearl's own daughter placed in an orphanage. It is still widely believed that Watson committed the murder. He eventually moved back to Florida, where he was killed during a shootout with a posse.

Starr was buried near Lake Eufala, which is just a couple of miles from her Youngers' Bend home, in what is now Porum, Oklahoma. The engraving on her tombstone reads: "Shed not for her the bitter tear, Nor give the heart to vain regret, 'Tis but the casket that lies here, The gem that filled it sparkles yet." Starr was buried with her six-shooters, which were stolen when her grave was vandalized. A protective fence now surrounds the site.

Soon after Starr died, her sensational but apocryphal legend began taking shape. The work most responsible for promulgating her myth was *Belle Starr, the Bandit Queen, or the Female Jesse James: A Full and Authentic History of the Dashing Female Highwayman*, an "authentic" biography written by Richard Fox, who wrote dime-novel westerns. The book contained more fiction than fact. But the inaccurate legends persisted until recent years, when scholars finally began piecing together the truth about Starr's life.

Books

Outlaws, Mobsters & Crooks: From the Old West to the Internet, U*X*L, 1998.

Steele, Phillip W., *Outlaws and Gunfighters of the Old West*, Heritage Publishers, 1991.

Walker, Paul Robert, *Great Figures of the Wild West*, Facts on File, 1992.

Periodicals

Wild West, August 1997.

Online

"Belle Starr," *Women in History*,, http://www.lkwdpl.org/wihohio/star-bel.htm (January 12, 2006).

"Starr, Myra Maybelle Shirley," *The Handbook of Texas Online*, http://www.tsha.utexas.edu/handbook/online/articles/SS/fstbl_print.html (January 12, 2006). □

Barbara Strozzi

Barbara Strozzi (1619-1677), a composer, singer, and intellectual activist in Venice, Italy, during its golden age, in the early and middle seventeeth century, was among the most important of the few female composers active during the early eras of European classical music.

Female classical composers were written out of the history books for many decades. When researchers restored women to their proper places, they learned of women composers earlier than Strozzi—a few, like the medieval abbess Hildegard of Bingen (1098-1179), much earlier. But few of those were at the center of a major new musical scene. Strozzi was born into Venetian musical and literary circles, and she created pieces of music in the most vital genres of the day: works for solo voice or for a group of voices with accompaniment, in an expressive style allied to the new genre of opera. Strozzi never wrote an opera, but she was part of a group of Venetian thinkers who helped to advance the genre. Observers of the day praised her vocal abilities. The outlines of her life outside her compositions and musical performances are hazy, but comments that were made about her tell us much about the situation of women in her time.

Adopted or Illegitimate Daughter of Poet

Strozzi was born in Venice in 1619 and was baptized on August 6 of that year. Her mother was Isabella Garzoni, who worked as a servant in the household of Giulio Strozzi, a poet and a member of one of the most powerful families in the Italian city of Florence. He had moved to Venice and become both a patron of the arts and an influential artist in his own right, creating poetry, plays, and texts for musical works. The Strozzi's father was listed as "incerto" or uncertain, but it is thought that Giulio Strozzi was her father. He designated her as a potential heir in a will of 1628 and, as we will see, took an active interest in her musical career. In the 1628 will she was named as Barbara Valle, but at some point not long after that she began to use the last name Strozzi. Giulio Strozzi's final will of 1650 made the name official by stating that he had adopted Barbara, but the adoption story was commonly used at the time to disguise the status of children resulting from the extramarital liaisons of powerful and influential people.

Very little is known of Strozzi's musical education, but in the dedication to one of her published works she mentions Francesco Cavalli (1602-1676) as her teacher. That fact indicates the status that Strozzi's adoptive father brought her in the Venetian musical world; Cavalli was the city's top opera composer and the music director at the famed St. Mark's Cathedral. From Cavalli, Strozzi would have learned the elements of opera, which was a young genre at the time. The first operas had been written just a few decades earlier, between 1600 and 1610, and the idea

for powerful, passionate solo voice music enhanced by difficult ornamentation was still a new and exciting one.

The basic idea of opera had been proposed just before 1600 by a group of aristocratic intellectuals in Florence, Italy, who styled themselves an "academy;" their aim was to try to replicate what ancient Greek singing might have sounded like. Giulio Strozzi set up similar academies in Venice, and it was in this refined, but musically influential atmosphere that Strozzi grew up. She was mentioned in 1634 as a singer at a gathering in the Strozzi family home, and the following year a composer associate of Giulio Strozzi's named Nicolò Fontei wrote a set of songs he called *Bizzarrie poetiche* (Poetic Bizarre Songs) that he said were inspired by Strozzi's singing. These went over well enough that Fontei produced a second book of songs the following year, again apparently intended for Strozzi, and referring to her as "la virtuosissima cantatrice" (the most virtuosic singer).

In 1637 Giulio Strozzi created a new academy, the Accademia degli Unisoni, partly in order to serve as a showplace for Strozzi's singing. The academy was something of a debating society or discussion group, with musical performances provided by Strozzi. She also apparently served as a mistress of ceremonies, specifying the evening's theme and judging the arguments put forth by other members. Strozzi was well known to all the members of the academy; a book describing its proceedings was dedicated to her.

Became Subject of Satirical Writings

The profession of composer was extremely rare among women at the time. Strozzi had a few predecessors, such as Francesca Caccini, but male composers who visited Venice reacted with surprise when they heard of Strozzi's compositional activities. The profession of singer was more common; some female roles in operas would be sung by male countertenors (falsetto singers), but Strozzi and other singers became famous for their musical abilities. Nevertheless, singing was not considered entirely respectable for women. Strozzi's activities at the Academy seem to have inspired observers to link music-making with sexual promiscuity. An anonymous pamphlet writer from a rival academy, as part of a series of attacks on the Unisoni group, cast aspersions on Strozzi's chastity, writing (as quoted by Ellen Rosand in the *Journal of the American Musicological Society*) that "it is a fine thing to distribute the flowers [Strozzi would apparently pass out flowers to attendees] after having already surrendered the fruit." The writer later suggested that the only reason Strozzi had never become pregnant was that she mostly spent time with a castrato—a male singer who had been castrated in order to preserve his high singing voice.

The significance of these remarks has been debated among music historians. According to Rosand, they could have indicated that Strozzi was a courtesan, or high-class prostitute. An existing painting of Strozzi, holding a stringed instrument and seemingly waiting for another musician to come and join her, could support this interpretation. But Rosand also pointed out that the tone of the anonymous writer's comments was typical of the titillating spirit of writings by the academicians of the time, who frequently discussed sexual matters in a joshing way and resisted the influence of the Venetian clergy. According to this line of thought, the pamphlet was a jibe directed by one colleague at another and intended in a familiar spirit.

This viewpoint has gained support from further researches into Strozzi's domestic life. Strozzi never married, but she embarked on a long-term relationship with Giovanni Paolo Vidman, a friend of Giulio Strozzi's. The couple had four children, and Vidman provided for their religious education; Strozzi's two daughters entered convents, and one son became a monk. Prostitutes were registered with the Venetian city government at the time, and lists do not mention Strozzi's name. The fact that Strozzi and Vidman did not marry is of minor significance; well-off Venetians of a non-religious bent did not consider marriage an indispensable sacrament.

The central activity of Strozzi's life, after her father began to approach old age, was composition. She continued to perform, and it is likely that she wrote most of her music for her own use. Strozzi's first published work was a set of madrigals for groups of two to five voices, published in 1644. The texts of these madrigals were by Giulio Strozzi, but after having helped provide a solid launch to her compositional career he faded into the background; just a few texts by her father are included in Strozzi's later publications. Strozzi published eight books of music during her lifetime, designated as Op. 1 through Op. 8 (a numbered "Opus" was a published musical work). Op. 4, like many other works of the seventeenth century, has been lost, but the unusually high survival rate for Strozzi's works suggests that they were held in high regard.

Wrote for Solo Voice

The predominance of instrumentally accompanied works for one or more solo voices was comparatively new in Strozzi's time, and the terminology used to classify them was fluid. Strozzi wrote works called cantatas, arias, ariettas, motets, and madrigals. These words could mean different things at different times, but the madrigals were generally works for more than one voice; the motets (she wrote only one volume, the *Sacri musicali affetti,* Op. 5) were religious works for solo voice; and the cantatas, arias, and ariettas were expressive solo works in the new operatic style. The arias and ariettas were mostly strophic songs, meaning that they essentially repeated the same music for each verse. The cantatas were more elaborate pieces with multiple sections and a variety of ways of setting the text that ranged from speech-like recitative (ress-iss-a-TEEVE) to full-blown melodies to arioso, an intermediate stage between the two. Few cantatas were written before the time of Strozzi's career, and her importance as one of the creators of the genre is a topic of inquiry among musicologists. The texts for her works, apart from those by her father, were by writers working in the so-called Marinist tradition of poet Giambattista Marini; they were romantic lyrics with elaborate, sometimes overcomplicated concepts.

Strozzi was, in any event, a successful composer. She wrote about 125 works, some of them of considerable length, and the continued demand for her compositions over 20 years—her last collection, *Arie a voce sola,* Op. 8, was published in 1664—testified to strong interest in her music. Many of them contained performance directions and expressive markings that were well beyond the norm for the era, suggesting that singers other than Strozzi were performing them and that she wanted to insure the proper effect. Strozzi did not, however, succeed in finding an aristocratic patron who could have made her life as a composer easier; each of her eight books was dedicated to a different potential noble backer. Her compositions probably served as a major source of income as she grew older.

Strozzi's music has become better known as scholars have begun to make editions suitable for performers and concert presenters have organized programs focused on music by women. Some aspects of her style were intended to show off her vocal technique to best advantage; she wrote spectacular, difficult-sounding melodies that nevertheless lay naturally in a singer's voice range, and she avoided passages of dry recitative where she could. Tim Carter of *Early Music,* reviewing a compact disc of music by *la virtuosissima cantatrice,* praised Strozzi's "contribution to a range of styles and genres in the process of formulation as the Baroque got under way." Her sectional cantatas, he wrote, "are particularly intriguing," and her solos, duets, and trios "ravishing." The music of one of Europe's first major female composers seemed likely to yield more riches as compositional and performing techniques of her era generally became better understood.

Books

Sadie, Stanley, ed., *The New Grove Dictionary of Music and Musicians,* 2nd ed., Macmillan, 2001.

Periodicals

Early Music, August 1994.
Journal of the American Musicological Society, Summer 1978.

Online

"Barbara Strozzi," Here of a Sunday Morning (radio program), http://www.hoasm.org/VD/Strozzi.html (February 9, 2006).
"Barbara Strozzi," http://www.gymell.com/doc/strozzi.shtml (February 9, 2006).
"Biography," http://www.barbarastrozzi.com (February 9, 2006). □

George Szell

As conductor of the Cleveland Orchestra for almost a quarter-century, Hungarian-born George Szell (1897-1970) built the ensemble into one of the world's greatest symphony orchestras. For sheer precision and accuracy of interaction, the Cleveland Orchestra under Szell was unmatched.

In many ways, Szell lived up to the image of European conductors that Americans frequently had and enjoyed. He was an absolute authoritarian who drilled his players relentlessly in order to produce the detailed and fully thought-out interpretations of classical works he demanded. An imposing figure who stood six feet tall on the podium, he loomed larger than life for the orchestra's players, who often feared his withering stare and chilly personality. Szell was the kind of figure around whom anecdotes circulate, each more outrageous than the last. It was said that when a member of the orchestra's violin section suffered a serious fall, Szell phoned the dressing room solely to ask whether the man's violin had been damaged. But the end result of Szell's single-mindedness was an orchestra that could match any other in the world and that excelled those in other medium-sized U.S. cities by far.

Showed Prodigal Talent

The son of attorney and businessman Georg Charles Szell and his wife Margarethe, Szell was born in Budapest, then part of the Austro-Hungarian empire, on June 7, 1897. He sometimes used the Hungarian form of his name, György, and Americanized it to George when he settled in the United States. Szell grew up mostly in Vienna, Austria, and he showed tremendous talent on the piano from an early age. He made his debut with the Vienna Tonkünstler Orchestra (Vienna Musical Artists' Orchestra) when he was 11, playing, in addition to established classical piano concertos, a Rondo for piano and orchestra of his own composition. He quickly performed in several other European capitals and was hailed as a child prodigy in the Austrian tradition of Mozart.

Szell's parents, however, realized that child prodigies often burn out, and they insisted that their son get a better-rounded musical education. Szell studied theory and composition with some of the top figures in the German-speaking musical world, including the composer and organist Max Reger and the musicologist Eusebius Mandyczewski. He began to look to the German capital of Berlin as the height of musical art and was quoted as saying in *Opera News* that he had left before picking up "that phony Viennese gemütlichkeit"—the relaxed sociability exemplified in Vienna's great waltz tradition. Szell was serious-minded from an early age.

Szell found his life's work the first time he picked up a conductor's baton, leading the Vienna Konzertvereins-Orchester (Vienna Concert Association Orchestra) in a 1913 performance. The following year he appeared as piano soloist, guest composer, and conductor with the mighty Berlin Philharmonic; as conductor he led the high-spirited orchestral work *Till Eulenspiegel's Merry Pranks,* by Richard Strauss. Strauss was a noted opera conductor as well as a composer, and Szell offered himself up as an intern. He spent two years as Strauss's assistant, never earning a cent but absorbing the intricacies of the European classical tradition, especially opera. The internship paid off when Strauss recommended his young disciple for a conducting post at the opera house in Strassburg. When that city reverted to French control, Szell moved on to a series of opera conducting posts in mostly German cities—Darmstadt, Düsseldorf, and, from 1929 to 1937, the German opera house in Prague, Czechoslovakia. He married Olga Band in 1920, but the couple divorced six years later.

Szell was by now in demand as a guest orchestral conductor as well, and he made his American debut with the St. Louis Symphony in 1930. Of Jewish background, Szell was unnerved by the rise of fascism in Germany in the mid-1930s. He sought out orchestral posts in Western Europe, landing one with the Scottish Orchestra in Glasgow in 1937. He married Helene Schultz Teltsch the following year. Traveling to Australia in 1939, Szell heard that war had broken out in Europe. He started back to Glasgow via Canada and the United States but then learned that the Scottish Orchestra had disbanded and that he thus had no job to return to.

Taught Composition in New York

Staying on in New York, Szell landed a job as a composition instructor at the Mannes College of Music. After two years in Scotland he was a competent English speaker, and during his years in Cleveland, Ohio, he spoke English with a heavy German accent but perfect grammatical correctness. Szell's name was well known among European conductors who had already ventured to the U.S., and it did not take him long to find major conducting engagements. Szell conducted Strauss's *Salome* at the Metropolitan opera in December of 1942 and appeared as guest conductor with various American orchestras, including the Detroit Symphony and the Cleveland Orchestra. Szell became an

American citizen in 1946, and after several appearances in Cleveland he was offered the post of conductor and music director there that year.

"A new leaf will be turned over with a bang," Szell announced (according to the Cleveland *Plain Dealer*.) "People talk about the New York, the Boston, and the Philadelphia [orchestras]. Now they will talk about the New York, the Boston, the Philadelphia, and the Cleveland." The claim seemed rash; Cleveland had a long tradition of classical music dating back to the large population of German immigrants who settled there in the nineteenth century, but the Cleveland Orchestra was not regarded as a major presence in American music. Szell, after making sure he had the backing of the orchestra's board, immediately set about making changes. He enlarged the orchestra, fired a group of well-entrenched players who he felt were not up to snuff, and scoured American orchestras and music schools for the best new talent. His aim, he was quoted as saying by Harold C. Schonberg in *The Great Conductors,* was to create "a combination of the best elements of American and European orchestral playing. I wanted to combine the American purity and beauty of sound and their virtuosity of execution with the European sense of tradition, warmth of expression, and sense of style."

By the early 1950s the Cleveland Orchestra was essentially an ensemble that Szell had created. The large group of string players interacted seamlessly, like a string quartet, and if emotion was not Szell's strong suit, his attention to detail and his absolute control over the orchestra were widely praised. The Cleveland Orchestra was heard all over the country on the radio, and world-class soloists put Cleveland's east-side Severance Hall on their itineraries. Szell and the Cleveland Orchestra began making a long series of recordings for the Columbia label, covering the symphonies of Beethoven and Brahms, and much of the rest of the standard nineteenth-century Germanic repertory. In music close to his central European roots, such as the Symphony No. 8 of Antonín Dvořák, he was regarded as perhaps the finest conductor alive. Szell was not exactly enamored with contemporary music, and often assigned concerts of new works to assistant conductors, although, he did lead numerous world premieres in Cleveland, including that of Paul Hindemith's Piano Concerto (1947).

Szell often returned to Europe to conduct, and in 1957 he felt the Cleveland Orchestra was ready to face the Continent's notoriously tough newspaper critics. The orchestra won rave reviews and returned to Europe in 1965 and 1967. The orchestra also frequently appeared around the U.S., but Szell refused to allow the group to perform for segregated audiences in Southern cities, and the Cleveland Orchestra became the first top American orchestra to hire an African-American musician. In 1970 the orchestra toured Japan in connection with the Expo '70 world's fair there. His love of Mozart found an outlet in guest-conducting appearances at the Salzburg Festival in Austria, and he often returned to his first love, conducting opera.

Compared Mozart's Music to Asparagus

Szell was popular among Clevelanders; if he could not be said to be exactly friendly, he had a dry wit that appealed to classical music lovers. When asked about the charge that his interpretations of Mozart lacked emotion, he replied (according to the All Music Guide) that one does not pour chocolate sauce over asparagus. He encouraged young musicians and orchestra players and audiences alike were proud that he had put Cleveland on the international musical map.

Stories that circulated about Szell among the musicians of the orchestra, however, often had a less positive flavor. Szell's need for total control led him to act coldly, some felt. "He looks at us the way you study a bug," one musician was quoted as saying in *Opera News*. When musicians encountered Szell on the street he would not acknowledge their presence—to do so, he felt, would be to cross a boundary and thus to diminish his authority. Szell's rehearsals were exacting, and players reported that they were as exhausting as actual concerts. His authoritarian streak was only rarely displayed to audiences; one winter night he stopped the orchestra, announced that he would give audience members five minutes to cough and clear their throats, and stalked off.

Some in the musical community felt that Szell was his own worst enemy, but New York Metropolitan Opera general manager Rudolf Bing, hearing that, replied "Not while I'm alive" (according to Schonberg). Szell ordered around renowned soloists, and one, violinist Henryk Szeryng, decided that he would not put up with it. The two disagreed over the proper tempo for a movement in one concerto, and both refused to back down. The orchestra was forced to slow down when Szeryng started playing and to speed up when Szell was once again in control. But that was a rare lapse in a Szell performance, for his iron control, all agreed, resulted in playing of a remarkably high standard for a very long time. Szell made no friends by saying that the Cleveland Orchestra's rehearsals started where those of other ensembles left off, but the statement had a high degree of truth.

Szell was adamant about bringing out fine musical details. Schonberg quoted him as saying that "everything a good composer writes down is expected to be heard, except in obvious cases where a coloristic impression is intended," and the Cleveland Orchestra on a good night, which was almost every night under Szell, achieved an awe-inspiring clarity of texture. His talents extended beyond German music; he conducted the orchestral music of his adopted country enthusiastically, and he excelled in the work of composers, like Finland's Jean Sibelius, who specialized in complicated orchestral textures. His love for the challenges of good orchestration also made him an admired specialist in the oversized operas of Richard Wagner.

Suffering from cancer in his later years, Szell died in Cleveland on July 30, 1970. Subsequent conductors—Lorin Maazel, Christoph von Dohnányi, and Franz Welser-Möst—inherited a precision-tuned instrument, and the Cleveland Orchestra remained among the world's most renowned. The legacy of George Szell loomed large in American musical life.

Books

International Dictionary of Opera, St. James, 1993.

Sadie, Stanley, ed., *The New Grove Dictionary of Music and Musicians,* 2nd ed., Macmillan, 2001.

Schonberg, Harold C., *The Great Conductors,* Simon and Schuster, 1967.

Periodicals

National Review, June 16, 2003.

Opera News, December 5, 1992.

Plain Dealer (Cleveland, OH), December 31, 1999.

Washington Post, February 12, 1978.

Online

''George Szell,'' All Music Guide, http://www.allmusic.com (January 26, 2006).

''George Szell,'' Sony Classical, http://www.sonyclassical.com/artists/szell/bio.html (January 26, 2006). □

T

Toru Takemitsu

Widely considered modern Japan's greatest composer in the classical music tradition, Toru Takemitsu (1930-1996) merged Japanese and Western instruments and techniques in his music. Equally important, perhaps, was the way he humanized some of the intellectual devices used by contemporary classical composers of the West, not diluting their rigor but attaching them to concrete images rooted in nature and in Japanese aesthetics.

Growing up amid the destruction of World War II, Takemitsu learned to despise the culture of his native country. Almost completely self-taught as a composer, he immersed himself in Western techniques, returning to Japanese music only later, at the suggestion of an American associate. Takemitsu's music is sensuous and accessible, and he was an acclaimed and enthusiastic composer of film music, the classical genre most oriented toward mass appeal. The detail and density of his music also drew the admiration of specialists, including many of his fellow composers. Some of his music involved tonal depictions of Japanese gardens, and he often acknowledged the garden as a source of inspiration. "I can imagine a garden superimposed over the image of an orchestra," Takemitsu was quoted as saying on England's Soundintermedia website. "A garden is composed of various different elements and sophisticated details that converge to form a harmonious whole."

Drafted into Labor Gang

Born October 8, 1930, in Tokyo, Japan, Takemitsu spent his early life in China with his family. By the time he was brought back to Japan to attend school in 1938, Japanese militarism was on the rise and Western music and films were mostly forbidden. Takemitsu kept up a secret fascination with the West. After war broke out he saw a newsreel film of a British destroyer, the Prince of Wales, being sunk by a Japanese attack, but felt only awe at the sophistication of the British ship. In 1944, at 14, Takemitsu was drafted and put to work in a labor gang assigned to build a Japanese army camp. While he was working, an officer played a recording of the French popular song "Parlez-moi d'amour" (Speak to Me of Love, 1930). "I did not know there was such beautiful music in the world," Takemitsu later recalled, according to the *Economist.*

After the war Takemitsu tuned into the American Armed Forces Radio, hearing a broad mix of music, including popular songs, Western classical music, and jazz. In the last of these categories, it was bandleader and composer Edward Kennedy "Duke" Ellington, with his range of instrumental effects, whom he especially admired. By the time he was 16, Takemitsu had decided he wanted to be a composer. He studied briefly with composer Yasuji Kiyose beginning in 1948, but mostly he learned musical composition on his own. "My teachers," he was quoted as saying by Soundintermedia, "are Duke Ellington and nature." He also admired the quiet, subtly colored impressionist music of French composer Claude Debussy.

In poor health due to lung ailments, Takemitsu turned for moral support to his girlfriend, Asaka, who later became his wife and the mother of his daughter Maki. "He had holes in his lungs" when the two first met, Asaka told Kevin Jackson of the London *Independent,* "and his father had died early, so his mother had to go out to work, but in spite of their financial difficulties he really wanted to study music. When I met him, he almost forced me into taking care of him; he needed to be taken care of."

Takemitsu quickly absorbed the latest developments in Western music, proceeding from Debussy to the contemporary French music of Olivier Messiaen. His first work to be publicly performed, the *Lento in Two Movements,* was influenced by Messiaen but had Takemitsu's own distinctive style, which would remain recognizable even as he adopted various new Western techniques. His music was often quiet, with small, sudden climaxes rather than a strong feeling of movement toward a goal, and with a strong focus on timbre (the "color" of a sound"), texture, and register (the highness or lowness of a pitch). There was something Japanese about Takemitsu's music, even during the years when he would have been reluctant to admit such a thing.

Wrote Electronic Piece

During the 1950s Takemitsu kept up with new Western styles, mastered them quickly, and gained wider recognition. He studied the serialist music of Austrian composers Arnold Schoenberg and Anton Webern, which rejected the idea of key and instead derived the pitch material of a piece of music from a small cell or sequence of notes announced at the beginning of the work. Electronic music, made on a large computer apparatus prior to the invention of the synthesizer, was on the rise, and Takemitsu's 1956 piece *Vocalism A.I.,* which manipulated recordings of actors speaking those vowel sounds, was one of Japan's first electronic compositions. Takemitsu's reputation grew when Russian-American composer Igor Stravinsky, visiting Japan, heard Takemitsu's *Requiem for strings* (1957) and praised it.

In the early 1960s Takemitsu began to travel to the West for performances of his works. In Hawaii he met experimentalist composer John Cage, whose works often involved leaving portions of his compositions to chance in one way or another, and the two became friends. Takemitsu had already experimented with chance procedures in such works as *Corona* for one or more pianists, 1962, whose score resembled a diagram rather than conventional music notation. Cage, an adherent of Zen Buddhism, encouraged Takemitsu to reconnect with his Japanese roots, and Takemitsu began to think about the power of ritualistic Japanese art forms such as puppet theater. At the same time, he was becoming disillusioned with the hard-core intellectualism of serialist composers and more and more interested in nature as a source of inspiration. Takemitsu's *Coral Island* (1962) won recognition in the West.

His real breakthrough, however, was *November Steps,* commissioned by the New York Philharmonic Orchestra in 1967 and conducted in its premiere by Seiji Ozawa, a close friend of Takemitsu. One of Takemitsu's first works to use Japanese traditional instruments, it was a concerto for solo *biwa* (a scraped and plucked Japanese lute) and *shakuhachi* (a Japanese flute), with Western orchestra. Barry Conyngham and Roger Woodward wrote in the London *Guardian* that "the music has an almost overpowering focus, as if—in trying to make the two musics one, in striving

to accommodate the two rich worlds—the composer draws himself and us into a strange new state." Other major orchestras performed and recorded the work, and by around 1970 Takemitsu was a well-known name in classical music circles, invited to compose music for ensembles and festivals around the world.

Takemitsu's fascination with gardens came to the fore in his music of the 1970s and 1980s, in such works as *Garden Rain* (1974) for brass ensemble. He likened the intended experience of hearing his music to walking through a garden; the scenery changes as the listener moves through time, but there is no clear starting or end point. One of Takemitsu's best-known works remains the orchestral *A Flock Descends into the Pentagonal Garden* (1977). The piece mixes Japanese and Western techniques at a deep level, with a vivid evocation of the title scene (a solo oboe represents the descending birds) concealing a densely mathematical exploitation of permutations of the number five, based on the use of a pentatonic (five-tone) scale, in the shifting orchestral fields representing the shape of the garden.

Takemitsu's *Waterways* for piano and orchestra (1975) was inspired by the garden at Spain's Alhambra fortress. At first he was unmoved. "Since music is for me not symmetrical, I did not like the regularity of the garden at all," he was quoted as saying by Paula Deitz in the *New York Times.* But then a woman walked through the garden, breaking the symmetry of the scene and disturbing the water on a pond. "Only then, the music came," Takemitsu said.

Composed Film Scores

Despite the cutting-edge qualities of his concert music, Takemitsu never lost his appreciation for the popular songs that had originally inspired him. He was said to have an encyclopedic knowledge of Western pop music. Takemitsu found a meeting place between pop and classical music in his 93 scores for Japanese films, which he wrote with enthusiasm over the last three decades of his life and which covered all genres from sophisticated art-house films to thrillers. Takemitsu's film career began with the 1964 art film *Woman in the Dunes* and included scores for such classics as director Akira Kurosawa's *Ran,* a film based on Shakespeare's *King Lear.* His film scores varied according to the nature of the project; the *Woman in the Dunes* score was a sparse, minimal affair that would not have sounded out of place on a program of his concert music, while other scores were overtly emotional in the Western fashion. Takemitsu viewed some 200 films a year, and one of his favorite activities on arriving in a new city during his world travels was to head for a movie theater, whether he spoke the local language or not. In 1993 he wrote the score for the American film *Rising Sun.* Takemitsu's film scores represent an under-investigated aspect of his total output.

Takemitsu's genial personality won him friends as well as admirers. In person he was more boisterous than his calm music might suggest. Pointing to a picture of a spiritual-looking Takemitsu on a printed concert program, his daughter Maki told Jackson that "he certainly wasn't like that. He loved to play the Beatles or jazz on the piano; he loved to dance around and play, he loved socializing and drinking with other people, especially writers and painters and younger musicians. . . . He was really a lot of fun." Takemitsu had many friends at the top levels of Japanese literature and arts, including novelist Kenzaburo Oe and poet Shuntaro Tanikawa. His sense of humor was legendary. In broken English, he once told an interviewer that he thought silence was the mother of music. Then he backed off and corrected himself, saying that perhaps it was only the grandmother.

One of Takemitsu's major compositions of the 1970s, *In an Autumn Garden* (1979), was written entirely for the traditional *gagaku* Japanese court musical ensemble, but in the last two decades of his life he more often wrote for Western instruments. His music was often gentle in spirit, and he continued to refine his instrumental textures in the direction of greater and greater distinctiveness and clarity. Takemitsu's music continued to be frequently performed in the 1990s. His *Fantasma/Cantos* (1991) was awarded the 1994 Grawemeyer Prize, one of the classical music world's most prestigious honors and one that carried a $150,000 stipend. Little of his music to that point had been for voices, and he set to work on an opera, with a libretto by California novelist Barry Gifford. He was suffering from cancer, however, and he died in Tokyo on February 20, 1996.

Books

Contemporary Musicians, vol. 6, Gale, 1991.
Sadie, Stanley, ed., *The New Grove Dictionary of Music and Musicians,* 2nd ed., Macmillan, 2001.

Periodicals

Daily News (Los Angeles), May 8, 2002.
Economist, March 2, 1996.
Guardian (London, England), February 22, 1996; August 29, 1997.
Independent (London, England), October 1, 1998.
New York Times, February 21, 1996; March 3, 1996.
San Francisco Chronicle, February 21, 1996.
Times (London, England), February 22, 1996.

Online

"Who Was Toru Takemitsu?," http://www.soundintermedia.co .uk/treeline-online/biog.html (February 2, 2006). □

Renata Tebaldi

Soprano Renata Tebaldi (1922-2004) is regarded as one of the greatest opera singers of the second half of the twentieth century. For sheer beauty of vocal tone, she was unmatched.

Tebaldi was often defined in the minds of opera enthusiasts by comparison with her polar opposite, the volatile Greek-American soprano Maria Callas. Where Tebaldi was a supremely consistent singer, delivering a breathtaking, creamy sound nearly every time she took the stage, Callas was uneven, but Callas seemed to engage

herself dramatically with operatic roles in a way that Tebaldi did not. Especially popular in the United States, where she proclaimed herself the queen of New York's Metropolitan Opera, Tebaldi took on relatively few roles, never singing in any language other than Italian, and performing the same set of Italian classics over and over. Yet within that minute repertoire she approached vocal perfection, and she enjoyed an unusually long career atop the operatic world.

Suffered Bout with Polio

A native of the seacoast town of Pesaro, Italy, Renata Ersilia Clotilde Tebaldi was born on February 1, 1922. Her father Teobaldo Tebaldi, a cellist and a World War I veteran, was often absent from family life, and he and Tebaldi's mother Giuseppina, who had hoped to become a singer, split up when Tebaldi was three. Mother and daughter moved to Langhirano, near Parma, Italy. Not long after that, the dreaded childhood disease of polio suddenly afflicted Tebaldi. She underwent five years of treatment that helped her survive where others did not. While still weak, she was pushed by her mother toward piano studies.

It was as a singer, though, that Tebaldi impressed faculty at Parma's Arrigo Boito Conservatory. "I started singing when I was a young girl, but my family wanted me to study piano," she was quoted as saying in London's *Guardian* newspaper, but "my overwhelming need to express myself with my voice made me choose the art of singing." Her teacher Ettore Campogalliani agreed that the voice was her strongest instrument and sent her back to Pesaro to study with singer Carmen Melis, one of the leading voice teachers in Italy at the time. Giuseppina Tebaldi remained her daughter's constant companion as she became an opera star and toured the globe, and one of the few real crises in Tebaldi's even-keeled career came after her mother's death in 1957.

By 1944 Tebaldi was ready for her formal operatic debut in the role of Elena in Arrigo Boito's opera *Mefistofele* at an opera house in Rovigo, Italy. Wartime conditions made for difficult logistics; Tebaldi traveled part of the way to Rovigo by horse cart, and her return train trip came under machine-gun fire. Appearing as Mimi in Giacomo Puccini's *La bohème* early in 1945, she arrived at the theater to hear that her costar had been killed by a bomb. Despite this traumatic start, Tebaldi made the role of the fragile, tuberculosis-stricken Mimi her own, performing it dozens of times over the next several decades.

After the end of the war, Tebaldi landed a plum vocal job in 1946: legendary Italian conductor Arturo Toscanini was slated to conduct a concert to mark the reopening of the bomb-damaged La Scala opera house in Milan, Italy, and Tebaldi was one of two young singers he picked to appear. As the performers rehearsed the program, Tebaldi was placed in a choir loft and began to sing one of her solos in a religious work by Giuseppe Verdi. "Ah! La voce d'angelo" (Ah! The voice of an angel), exclaimed Toscanini (according to a widely reported account quoted in the *International Dictionary of Opera*). Some have claimed that the remark meant simply that Tebaldi's voice was floating down from above, but the larger-than-life conductor had also applauded her audition with an enthusiastic "Brava! Brava!" shortly before.

Performed German Opera in Italian

Whatever Toscanini might have meant, the performance catapulted Tebaldi to the top of the intensely competitive Italian operatic world and secured her a place at La Scala, the country's premier opera house. Touring with a La Scala company, she began to extend her fame to foreign countries as well, although she spoke only Italian and even demanded that chefs prepare Italian food when she traveled. Though Richard Wagner's opera *Tannhäuser* was mostly performed in its original German by that time, even in Italy, Tebaldi sang the old Italian translation. In 1950 she made a triumphant debut in England in the role of Desdemona in Verdi's *Otello,* another of her signature roles, and she also made her first American appearance that year, in San Francisco, California. She soon added the Chicago Lyric Opera to her list of American appearances but jousted with New York Metropolitan Opera director Rudolf Bing over the right moment for her New York debut. In the early 1950s she sang in Spain, Portugal, and South America in addition to her numerous Italian appearances.

In 1951, Tebaldi and Maria Callas were jointly booked for a vocal recital in Rio de Janeiro, Brazil. Although the singers agreed that neither would perform encores, Tebaldi took two, and Callas was reportedly incensed. The incident began a much-discussed feud between the two star so-

pranos, although it was never clear how deep the animosity went. Sniping between the two was a matter of public record; a famous incident in which Callas said that comparing her voice to Tebaldi's was like comparing champagne to Coca-Cola drew the retort from Tebaldi that champagne often goes sour. Yet Tebaldi always downplayed the supposed rivalry, and Callas's husband claimed that it was the invention of record-company marketing gurus intent on keeping both singers in the headlines. Indeed Tebaldi, despite her old-world behavior, adapted to American entertainment methods once she began to appear in New York. Like Luciano Pavarotti a generation later she sometimes performed large stadium shows featuring such fare as "If I Loved You" from the musical *Oklahoma.* The rivalry between the two sopranos boiled down partly to the personal preferences of their respective fans.

Tebaldi's New York debut finally came in 1955, as La Scala temporarily became Callas's domain. She played the role of Desdemona at the Metropolitan Opera on January 31, 1955, and over the next few years she rolled out one perfectly mastered role after another. Between 1955 and 1973 she performed at the Met 267 times in 14 different operas, with the title role in Puccini's *Tosca* becoming her most frequent role. She performed that role 45 times, and a few other roles nearly that often. The statistic was revealing of Tebaldi's musical personality: she was not adventurous, but she was near perfect. Audiences at the Met gave her the nickname of "Miss Sold Out," for the Tebaldi name on the marquee guaranteed an operatic experience that could hardly be matched. "Tebaldi's soprano was rich and creamy, totally secure in technique and breath control," noted the *Times* of London in her obituary. "When she was on stage there was no feeling of apprehension. Nothing was going to go wrong."

A striking beauty and a pleasant interview subject, Tebaldi became well-loved by the American operatic public. She was not a classic temperamental diva but she trusted her own artistic instincts; Rudolf Bing, then General Manager of the Met, once famously said that she had "dimples of iron." Only in the early 1960s did her career falter. Tebaldi began to sing in Italy more often as Callas's career declined, and she suffered symptoms of exhaustion. Her personal life was unhappy; she never married despite several high-profile affairs, and, a strict Catholic, she broke off a relationship with the separated but still-married Italian conductor Arturo Basile. Later she told the *New York Times* that she "was in love many times. This is very good for a woman. [But] how could I have been a wife, a mother, and a singer? Who takes care of the *piccolini* when you go around the world. Your children would not call you Mama, but Renata."

Took Time Off from Singing

Things came to a head in 1963, when Tebaldi's voice began to show its first signs of age and she faced negative reviews for the first time in her career. After pulling out of a production of the opera *Adriana Lecouvreur* midway through its run, the world-famous soprano began taking voice lessons again, studying with teacher Ugo de Caro. The break had its desired results; reporting that her voice felt 12 years younger, Tebaldi returned to the Met in March of 1964 in the role of Mimi in *La bohème*. She took on a few roles with a more dramatic quality and a slightly lower range, but her powers seemed undiminished. She was classified as a lirico-spinto soprano, a soprano specializing in roles that lay between the lyric and dramatic poles. She was photographed being warmly embraced by Callas after a 1968 performance. In 1970 she added the role of Minnie in Puccini's *The Girl of the Golden West* to her repertoire.

In 1973 Tebaldi retired from the operatic stage, with a portrayal of Desdemona as her farewell performance at the Met. She gave a series of recitals around the world, including a stint in the Soviet Union. In 1976 she bade farewell to the recital stage as well, scheduling a Carnegie Hall recital in January of that year. She was unable to finish that recital, breaking off after she became overcome with emotion, but she returned to perform the same program a few weeks later successfully. Though her voice was once again shaky with emotion, she received six curtain calls and standing ovations. Her last public appearance was a vocal recital at La Scala on May 23, 1976. Her 32-year career was unusually durable given the high demands that operatic singers place on their voices. Tebaldi moved out of the New York apartment she had maintained for many years and returned to Italy.

Tebaldi did some teaching after she retired, and her influence was apparent in the voices of many of a new generation of stars. Pure singers such as Kathleen Battle and Renée Fleming carried echoes of Tebaldi's technique in their voices, and young singers could study numerous recordings Tebaldi made for the Decca label. Some critics felt, however, that only by seeing Tebaldi live could one appreciate her mixture of technique and stage presence.

Twenty years after she retired, opera lovers still had great affection for Tebaldi—so much so that the appearance of a new Tebaldi biography in 1995 resulted in lines stretching across Lincoln Center's large plaza from the Metropolitan Opera House, and up Broadway, when the star agreed to sign autographs. In failing health in the early 2000s, she moved to the small enclave of San Marino, an independent country within Italy's borders. She died there on December 19, 2004. "Farewell, Renata," said superstar tenor Luciano Pavarotti (according to the Newark *Star-Ledger*). "Your memory and your voice will be etched on my heart forever."

Books

Casanova, Carlamaria, *Renata Tebaldi: The Voice of an Angel*, Baskerville, 1995.
Harris, Kenn, *Renata Tebaldi: An Authorized Biography*, Drake, 1974.
International Dictionary of Opera, St. James, 1993.

Periodicals

Daily Telegraph (London, England), December 20, 2004.
Guardian (London, England), December 20, 2004.
International Herald Tribune, December 21, 2004.
New York Times, December 20, 2004.
Opera News, November 2004; February 2005.
Philadelphia Inquirer, December 21, 2004.
Star-Ledger (Newark, NJ), December 20, 2004.
Times (London, England), December 20, 2004. □

Vesta Tilley

Vesta Tilley (1864-1952) was a star of the English music hall circuit for more than four decades. Tilley's stage persona was that of an upper-crust male fop, and her cross-dressing made her one of the earliest male impersonators to achieve mainstream renown. Tilley later dressed in the khaki uniform of a World War I-era British soldier and delivered patriotic appeals to help the war effort. Tilley's obituary in the *Times* of London noted that "her power of creating a character was such that no one who saw . . . her walk across the stage as the absurd little red-coated recruit with the large cigar, in her song about 'the girl who loves a soldier,' is ever likely to forget the picture."

Tilley was born Matilda Alice Victoria Powles in the city of Worcester, in England's West Midlands, on May 13, 1864. She was the second of 13 children in her family, and was named after her mother, a dressmaker. Her father's occupation was listed on her baptismal certificate from St. Peter the Great church in Worcester as that of a china gilder, but he would eventually become a stage comic and manager of a music hall in Nottingham, another Midlands city. At some point he changed the family surname to Ball.

Wore Mustache to Impersonate Tenor

English music halls were an immensely popular form of entertainment for the working classes in England after 1850 or so. Their nightly shows offered a mix of popular songs, comedy sketches, and specialty acts, and a distinct musical style emerged around it, with chipper, crowd-pleasing numbers that often skewered the rich. Tilley made her first appearance on the music hall stage at age three, and was appearing in male dress by the time she turned six. Her first notable character was that of "Pocket Sims Reeves," a send-up of a popular music hall tenor of the era, J. Sims Reeves.

Tilley made her London stage debut at Canterbury Hall in 1874. At one point, she was appearing in three shows a night at three separate venues in the city, billed as "Vesta Tilley." Her stage name was taken from the Latin word for "virgin," *vesta*, and was probably a nod to a ubiquitous "Swan Vesta" brand of matches that dominated the British market at the time. The "Tilley" part of her name was a common diminutive of Matilda.

Tilley was a child star who easily moved into her teen and young adult years with increasing success. Her most

popular routine was that of the typical English "toff," or upper-class gentleman. She dressed in dandy-ish suits, and sang songs that poked fun at such types. One of her most famous tunes was "Burlington Bertie," in which she sang, "I'm Burlington Bertie, I rise at ten thirty/And saunter along like a toff/I walk down the Strand with my gloves on my hand/Then I walk down again with them off." Other signature songs of hers were "Following in Father's Footsteps" and "The Midnight Son."

"The London Idol"

Though Tilley dressed as a man, even to the point of wearing men's undergarments—since women's lingerie of the era was designed to emphasize the figure—she sang in a clearly female soprano, and the gender-bending act was a crowd favorite. She became the most popular female performer of the 1870s and 1880s, and was particularly adored by her working class fan base. By then she was also earning a small fortune. Her family was not wealthy by any means, but her success enriched them, and her father would manage her career and restrict her personal life for many years.

Tilley's father died in 1888, and two years later, at the age of 26, she wed Walter de Frece, a successful songwriter and astute entrepreneur who owned a chain of music halls across England. De Frece took over management of her career, and wrote her songs as well. By the 1890s she was the undisputed queen of the English music hall stage. Her publicity materials dubbed her "The London Idol," and she made extensive tours of the country, the British colonies,

and even the United States. She also made some of the first recordings in Britain in 1898, along with fellow music hall stars Bert Shepard, Ada Reeve and Dan Leno, which were done for the Gramophone Company.

During her 1894 American tour, Tilley played the vaudeville circuit, which was the corresponding equivalent to the music hall as a form of popular entertainment in the United States. In 1903 she appeared on the New York stage at the Murray Hill Theatre in *Under Cover*. A *New York Times* review of the show noted that at Tilley's appearance on stage, "the house fell—at her sprightly and nimble feet." The critic paid further homage to her as "an artist . . . to the tips of her toes, and to the last delicately nasal tone of her boylike voice."

Was Present at Historic Event

Tilley still dominated the London music hall scene after the turn of the century. A *Times* of London review of one of her shows at the Palace Theatre in January of 1909 asserted that "her beautifully clear voice, her inimitable walk, and, not least, the excellent quality of her songs, all combine to produce a very attractive turn." Three years later, the Palace was the site of a pivotal event in music hall history, the first Royal Variety Performance. The honored guests of the 1912 charity benefit were King George V and Queen Mary, and the Royal Variety show, with its official royal patronage, was seen as the full legitimatization of the music hall genre. Tilley performed a signature tune as Algy, "The Piccadilly Johnny with the Little Glass Eye." Brian Viner, a journalist for London's *Independent* newspaper, wrote many years later that as "Tilley stepped on stage in gentlemen's trousers—as her act rather demanded—Queen Mary thought the spectacle so immodest that she ostentatiously buried her face in her programme. Applause was consequently muted, and the organisers mortified."

When World War I began in 1914, Tilley enthusiastically participated in recruiting efforts. She dressed in the typical khaki uniform of the British army, sang patriotic tunes written by her husband, with the most popular being "Jolly Good Luck to the Girl Who Loves a Soldier," "The Army of Today's All Right," and "Six Days' Leave." Another was "Your King and Country Want You," which she performed at recruitment rallies and is sometimes known by the alternate title "We Don't Want to Lose You but We Think You Ought to Go." Its lyrics were a blatant appeal for bodies. "We've watched you playing cricket and every kind of game/ At football, golf and polo you men have made your name/ But now your country calls you to play your part in war/ And no matter what befalls you/ We shall love you all the more/ So come and join the forces/ As your fathers did before." Young men at the rallies who failed to be swayed by these songs were given white feathers, the symbol of the shirker, by pre-arranged children in the crowd if they tried to walk away without signing up.

For her role, Tilley was often heralded as "England's Greatest Recruiting Sergeant," but the war spelled the end of the music hall era. Popular support for the war fell as casualties mounted, and Britain would lose 900,000 military personnel, with two million injured or permanently maimed. There was a sense of bitter betrayal among the working classes that the popularity of the music hall had been co-opted for patriotic means, and then resulted in such tragic losses.

Final Performance

Tilley and her husband were now quite wealthy. He was knighted in 1919 for his wartime service, which made her Lady de Frece, and she decided to retire from the stage around the same time that he entered politics. This necessitated her retirement from the stage, because such work would have been unsuitable for the wife of a political candidate. Her farewell performance came in June of 1920 at London's Coliseum. She delivered her usual crowd-pleasers, such as "Jolly Good Luck to the Girl Who Loves a Soldier," and at its line, "Girls, if you want to love a soldier/ You can all love me," a male voice cried out from the audience, "We do!" As the *Times* of London reported, "from that point Miss Tilley began to lose some of her self-control." Following her performance, she was feted with bouquets and speeches, and spoke some words herself, but broke down near the end, the same *Times* article reported. She was also presented with a "People's Tribute" memorial book that had been signed by two million fans.

Tilley campaigned for her husband in the 1924 general elections, in which he won a seat from the riding of Ashton-under-Lyne in Lancashire as a Conservative (Tory) party candidate. He stood in the 1929 elections from the riding of Blackpool, and served in the House of Commons until 1931. Tilley's autobiography, *Recollections of Vesta Tilley*, was published in 1934. Her husband died the following January in Monte Carlo. She died on September 16, 1952, at the age of 88, in London. An editorial in the *Times* of London paid tribute to her the next day, noting that the music hall phenomenon was built around performers who were virtuosos in one particular area, and "no form of virtuosity was more exacting or more nicely poised than that of the male impersonators, and in that little group of virtuosos none was mistress of a more delicate art than Vesta Tilley."

Periodicals

Independent (London, England), December 14, 2005.
New York Times, November 6, 1903.
Times (London, England), January 27, 1909; June 1, 1920; June 7, 1920; September 17, 1952.

Online

"Vesta Tilley," PeoplePlayUK, Theatre Museum, http://www.peopleplayuk.org.uk/guided_tours/music_hall_tour/music_hall_stars/tilley.php (January 2, 2006).
"Vesta Tilley," http://www.btinternet.com/~radical/thefolkmag/vesta.htm (January 2, 2006). □

Shania Twain

With her stunning looks and gritty, upbeat lyrics that often touch on a woman's prerogative, Canadian

singer-songwriter Shania Twain (born 1965) has secured a large fan base of both male and female country and pop fans. With more than 65 million albums sold, Twain is the best-selling country artist of all time. Her 1997 album, *Come on Over,* was the best-selling album of all time by a female artist in any genre. Promoter Harvey Goldsmith told *Music Week*'s Ian Nicolson: "She's not country, she's not pop, she's just a huge talent."

Awed Parents with Vocal Abilities

Twain was born Eileen Regina Edwards on August 28, 1965, in Windsor, Ontario, to Clarence and Sharon Edwards, who soon separated. Sharon Edwards then moved Twain and her two sisters to Timmins, Ontario, a mining and logging town on the northern stretches of Canada, where winter temperatures dip to forty degrees below Farenheit. In Timmins, Sharon Edwards met and married Jerry Twain, an Ojibwa Indian. Jerry Twain adopted the girls, making them official members of his native band, the Temagami Anishnawbe Bear Island First Nation. The new marriage produced two boys. Jerry Twain worked as a logger and mining prospector, but the family of seven struggled to make ends meet.

Early on, Twain's parents noticed her remarkable vocal talents. By age three, Twain could sing on key with a light vibrato, as well as harmonize. A self-taught guitarist, Jerry Twain decided to teach his daughter to play and the pint–sized singer quickly learned about frets, chords and tuning. Twain's arms barely fit around the guitar, which was longer than she was tall. By ten, Twain was writing her own songs.

Unleashed Talents on Local Community

Because they were perpetually poor, Twain's parents hoped Twain could parlay her abilities into a solid, money–making career. They pushed Twain early and often. As a youngster, Twain was shy and her dream was to become a backup singer for Stevie Wonder. Twain's parents, however, had bigger visions and her mother arranged gigs at community centers, nursing homes and hospital wards. As a preteen, Twain walked through nightclub doors after 1 a.m. when the bars stopped serving alcohol and allowed minors inside. Dressed in a denim skirt and a buckskin-fringed shirt, Twain belted out tunes to blue-collar crowds of loggers and miners.

Encouraged by their daughter's reception, the Twains invested in voice lessons, though the closest suitable teacher was in Toronto, which was a 20-hour roundtrip drive. At 16, Twain joined the Canadian rock band Longshot, which was popular in the Timmins area. As a member of Longshot, Twain sang hit songs from Pat Benatar, Journey and REO Speedwagon. She also supplemented the family income by working at McDonald's.

The family was so poor that Twain often relied on mustard sandwiches for lunch. "We would go for days with just bread and milk and sugar—heat it up in a pot," she recalled during an interview with Brian D. Johnson of *Maclean's.* "I'd judge other kids' wealth by their lunches. If a kid had baked goods, that was like, oh, they must be rich." Though Twain eventually escaped poverty, the memory of her childhood hunger pains never left her. She has continued to raise money for Second Harvest Food Bank and frequently plugs the charity at concerts and publicity events. As a child, Twain turned to music to escape her circumstances. According to the *Toronto Sun's* Jane Stevenson, Twain prayed a lot as a child. "I just wanted to be swept away. I wanted music to take me away. I wanted music to adopt me and take me away from all that hell."

Endured Loss of Parents

After Twain graduated from Timmins High in the early 1980s, she moved to Toronto to pursue a singing career. There, she found plenty of rock and pop bands to sing with and was invited to record for the Toronto-based Opry North radio show. One of her first recordings included a duet with Tim Denis on his self-titled 1985 album. She also provided backup vocals for Kelita Haverland's 1986 album, *Too Hot to Handle.*

In 1987, Twain's parents were killed in an accident involving a logging truck. Twain, just 21, found herself responsible for her three siblings, who ranged in age from 13 to 18. The responsibility itself was overwhelming and Twain was further crushed to realize she had to give up her

musical life on the road. Twain got a lucky break, however, and landed an entertainment job at the Deerhurst Resort in Huntsville, Ontario. The job provided a steady paycheck with no traveling. It also offered variety. Some nights Twain sang country or pop hits. Other nights she sang Broadway revues. Singing daily, Twain became more comfortable as a performer.

Landed Recording Deal

Twain's siblings grew up and moved out, allowing Twain to proceed with her career. Around 1991 she hooked back up with longtime mentor Mary Bailey, a 1980s Canadian country music star. Bailey had heard Twain sing as a child and was instantly enamored with her talent. Over the years, Bailey had periodically helped out Twain. Working behind the scenes, Bailey used her connections to circulate Twain's tape. Twain eventually landed a recording contract with Mercury Records. Its executives liked Twain's voice, but not her full name, Eileen Twain. She adopted Shania, an Ojibwa name that means "I'm on my way."

Mercury Records assembled a marquee roster of musicians to work with Twain, including a drummer who had played with Elvis Presley and a guitarist who had played alongside Jimmy Buffett. Mercury also gathered songs from the most fashionable songwriters. Soon, Twain realized Mercury had no intention of letting her record the songs she had written. When she objected, studio executives insisted she only had one chance to make it, so they choose traditional country songs. In the end, Twain co-wrote one song, "God Ain't Gonna Getcha for That," for her self-titled 1993 debut album.

The album was a flop. None of the radio singles even made it into the Top 40. Twain's videos, for "What Made You Say That" and "Dance with the One that Brought You," generated a bit more attention, though mostly because Twain bared her belly button, something Nashville disdained.

Drew Attention of Veteran Producer

When music producer Robert John "Mutt" Lange caught a glimpse of a Twain video, the brunette singer's poise captivated him and he felt the urge to contact her. Lange had created several monster hits, including AC/DC's "Back in Black" and "Shook Me All Night Long" and Def Leppard's "Pour Some Sugar on Me." Lange found a kindred spirit in Twain after just one phone call. At the time Lange lived in London and the two began calling each other regularly. Often, Twain would set down the phone and pick up the guitar, singing her songs for Lange, who found them quite refreshing. He was amazed Twain had not recorded any of them on her first album.

In June of 1993, Lange traveled to the United States to meet Twain in person. He also expressed an interest in producing Twain's next album, though he had never worked in country, and eventually hammered out a deal with Mercury. Next, Twain flew to London to work on the album. On December 28, 1993, they married.

Music insiders have said Twain and Lange are a peculiar mix. For starters, Lange is 16 years older than Twain, and whereas Twain spends time putting together her outfits and hair, Lange keeps his hair shaggy and prefers comfortable, slip-on shoes. Twain lives much of her life in the public eye, though Lange works hard to keep a low profile. Lange hates the public eye so much he has bought the rights to nearly every photo taken of him and has refused interviews for decades. The couple also adheres to an Eastern religion called Sant Mat, which includes spiritual practices such as daily meditation and abstinence from alcohol and drugs. They are also vegetarians.

Despite their disparate personalities, their talents meld perfectly. The husband-wife duo worked tirelessly on Twain's second album. Twain provided the spirited lyrics and Lange used his studio talents to add depth to the melodic lines. In some songs Lange interjected accordion flourishes; in others he piled instruments, such as the fiddle, so deep it sounds as though a full orchestra is backing Twain.

Produced Chart-Busting Albums

Released in 1995, *The Woman in Me* reached number one on the country chart, sold 12 million copies and earned a Grammy Award for best country album. There was some controversy, however, in Twain's decision not to tour. With only one decent album to fall back on for songs, Twain did not feel she could compete with such rivals as Reba McEntire or Wynonna Judd. Critics began to question Twain's ability, suggesting Lange held all the talent and she was merely a studio puppet.

Nonetheless, Twain weathered the controversy and promoted herself through public appearances and videos. She followed with *Come on Over* in 1997, which sold 19 million copies and surpassed Garth Brooks's *No Fences* as the top-selling country album of all time. *Come on Over* was a true crossover album and included songs that became hits on different formats, from pop to country—songs such as "That Don't Impress Me Much" and "You're Still the One."

In May of 1998, Twain decided she was ready for a worldwide tour and entertained 2.5 million fans in 18 months, hitting the United States, Europe, Australia and the Far East. Following the tour, Twain and Lange retreated to Tour-de-Peilz, Switzerland, to the couple's seventeenth-century chateau for a physical and mental break. "I needed to leave behind the whole 'Shania' thing and be myself," she told *People*. "I did a lot of hiking and cooking. I skied.

I spent time with my horses. For the first time in my life, I was just resting."

Juggled Demands of Family, Career

Son Eja D'Angelo Lange was born in August of 2001, though that did not keep Twain from working on another album. The new parents spent their days playing with their son and worked on the album at night at their estate's recording studio. "I'd just put Eja to sleep in his stroller and wheel him over to the studio," Twain told *People*. "Mutt would be in the booth, I'd be in the singing room, and the baby would be in his own little spot with a monitor. And every few hours I'd stop and nurse him." In this manner, the husband-wife team produced the 19-song album *Up!*, released in 2002.

Twain's musical success brought other opportunities. She made a cameo appearance in the 2004 motion picture *I Heart Huckabees*. In 2005, she released a fragrance, called Shania by Stetson, and appeared on NBC's *The Apprentice* with Donald Trump in an episode where the contestants worked to develop a campaign strategy for the product. In addition, Twain also recorded a song for the 2005 ABC-TV *Desperate Housewives* soundtrack. Fans, however, need not worry that Twain is branching out and abandoning her musical career. She has said there will be more albums to come.

Books

Brown, Jim, *Shania Twain: Up and Away,* Fox Music Books, 2004.
McCall, Michael, *Shania Twain: An Intimate Portrait of a Country Music Diva,* St. Martin's Griffin, 1999.

Periodicals

Globe and Mail (Toronto), October 30, 2004.
Maclean's, December 18, 1995.
Music Week, January 31, 1998.
People Weekly, December 16, 2002.
Toronto Sun, November 18, 2005.
USA Today, November 9, 2004.

Online

"About: Award and Accolades," Shania: The Official Site, http://www.shaniatwain.com/about-awards.asp (January 16, 2006). □

V

Luther Vandross

Singer Luther Vandross (1951-2005), best known for his soulful love songs, was one of the most respected R&B singers of the late twentieth century. With multiple Grammy Awards, 14 platinum-selling albums, and over 25 million total albums sold, Vandross rode high from 1980 until his death. Having worked with artists as diverse as David Bowie and Beyoncé Knowles, Vandross has an assured place in the pantheon of genuine R&B superstars.

A New York Upbringing

Born on April 20, 1951, in New York City, New York, Vandross was the youngest child of Luther Vandross, Sr., and Mary Ida Vandross. Musical talent ran in the Vandross family; when Vandross was only a child, his oldest sister Patricia joined a singing group called The Crests, who would go on to find success with the release of "Sixteen Candles." Unfortunately for Vandross, not everything from his child was as pleasant. At the age of eight, Vandross lost his father when Vandross Sr. fell into a diabetic coma and did not wake.

Mary Ida Vandross, a practical nurse, became the head of the family, and aside from a brief stint in Philadelphia, Pennsylvania, the Vandross family remained in New York City. When Vandross was 14, he attended a concert in Brooklyn that would influence him for the rest of his life. There, he first saw Dionne Warwick perform the Burt Bacharach song "Anyone Who Had a Heart;" quoted in

Craig Seymour's biography *Luther,* Vandross recalled that "what she did to me just pierced me to the core . . . I decided right then and there that that's what I wanted to do with my life. I wanted to do to somebody what she did to me." Vandross admired other female singers during the 1960s, including The Supremes and Patti LaBelle. Labelle recalled in *Entertainment Weekly* shortly after Vandross's death that "[when I] first met Luther [in the mid-1960s] . . . I knew he was just a kid trying to get backstage so I let him come and meet us. After that, he became our fan club president."

Made First Recording

Vandross became a part of the Apollo Theater's 16-person high school musical theater group, Listen, My Brother, with whom he cut his first record, a fairly unsuccessful 45 single. The group also provided Vandross with the opportunity to perform on some of the first episodes of Sesame Street. After high school Vandross briefly attended Western Michigan University, but dropped out to pursue his musical ambitions. Back in New York, Vandross wrote and sold songs, much to his delight. His big break did not come until 1974, however, when Vandross began working with David Bowie. After helping the singer with the arrangement for "Young Americans," Vandross set out on tour with Bowie as one of his backing singers. Soon, he was opening for the British star, although his performances were often spectacular failures.

When Bowie's American tour ended, Vandross returned to New York, where he continued to work steadily arranging songs for rising stars like Bette Midler and singing backing vocals for artists as diverse as Peabo Bryson and Gary Glitter. Deciding to form his own band, Vandross called up friends from his Listen, My Brother days as well as

more recent acquaintances. Together, this group, called Luther, scored a minor hit with the song "It's Good for the Soul," although their two albums did not fare as well. In 1977, Vandross formed a professional relationship with disco hit makers Chic, appearing as a vocalist on two Chic albums. He was by then increasingly in demand as a session singer, and was also working as a vocalist for commercial jingles. In 1980, an album by dance act Change contained two songs featuring Vandross's vocals: "The Glow of Love" and "Searching." These songs garnered Vandross several offers of a record contract; however, he wanted to have creative control. Encouraged by longtime friend and associate Roberta Flack, he decided to use some of his savings to make an album.

Succeeded as a Solo Performer

Soon after completing his album *Never Too Much,* Vandross signed with Epic Records. Epic provided him with the artistic license he craved, and the professional relationship was a good one. His first single, the album's title track, quickly rose to the top of the R&B charts. He went out on tour, opening for acts like Chaka Khan, Kool and the Gang and even Aretha Franklin. In 1982, Vandross was nominated for, but did not win, the Grammy Award for Best New Artist. That same year, however, he released his second solo album *Forever, For Always, For Love* to great R&B success. By 1983, when Vandross released his third platinum album, *Busy Body,* he had become one of the most successful African-American solo artists of all time.

Vandross's next album *The Night I Fell in Love,* was released in 1985. This album also achieved million-selling, platinum status, although Vandross's success remained confined to the R&B charts; unlike other successful R&B artists like Lionel Richie, Vandross had not had a crossover hit gain recognition with pop audiences. Vandross's 1985 tour featured an opening act performer who would also make that leap into pop, a young singer named Whitney Houston. Much of Vandross's little time away from his solo career in the early 1980s was spent producing comeback albums for such respected soul singers as Aretha Franklin and Dionne Warwick, the very woman who had inspired Vandross to pursue a singing career as a teenager.

Endured Through Controversy

In 1985, Vandross experienced for the first time one of the negative aspects of celebrity: gossip. Always close-mouthed about his personal life Vandross, who never married and had no children, refused to name anyone with whom he had been romantically involved or even their genders. Throughout his life, Vandross battled weight problems, sometimes weighing over 300 pounds on his six-foot, two-inch frame; when he lost a significant amount of weight and rumors began to circulate that he had AIDS, Vandross found it hard to provide a believable denial. In the mid-1980s, AIDS was a mysterious disease associated at the time with a homosexual lifestyle. Fortunately for him, most people accepted his denials and he emerged essentially unscathed from the controversy. However, his personal reticence would fuel potentially harmful rumors regarding his sexuality for the rest of his life.

In January 1986, misfortune struck Vandross again when he caused a serious automobile accident in Los Angeles, California, where he had recently relocated. His convertible crossed the center line and struck two oncoming cars; Vandross suffered broken ribs and minor cuts and bruises, but his two passengers had far more serious injuries. Teenaged singer Jimmy Salvemini, whose debut album Vandross had just finished producing, had a collapsed lung; his older brother and manager, Larry Salvemini, died as the result of his injuries. Due to the tragedy, Salvemini's album was never released.

To distract himself from recent unpleasant events, Vandross returned to work. His fifth album, *Give Me the Reason,* although containing two more singles that reached the top of the R&B charts—"Stop to Love" and "There's Nothing Better than Love"—did not produce any songs that received attention from a pop audience. The year concluded on a dismal note, when Vandross faced civil charges stemming from the automobile accident that January. He pleaded no contest to reckless driving, was placed on probation for a year's time and directed to perform a benefit concert for a scholarship in the deceased passenger's name within the year. Shortly after the trial, Vandross reached an out-of-court settlement with the Salvemini family, avoiding wrongful death charges. In 1987, Vandross garnered two more Grammy nominations, for Best R&B Male Vocal Performance and Best R&B Song for "Give Me the Reason," although he failed to win either award. Death struck close to home again that summer, when Vandross's drummer Yogi Horton committed suicide.

Succeeded in Mainstream "Pop"

By 1988, Vandross had completed his sixth album, *Any Love,* but the events of the past two years had taken their toll on him physically, and he had regained over 100 pounds. Although *Any Love* was predictably successful on the R&B charts, it took a song co-written by Dionne Warwick's son, David Elliott, to finally bring Vandross the pop success that he long desired. Recorded as a new single for Vandross's 1990 greatest hits album, *The Best of Luther Vandross. . . . The Best of Love,* "Here and Now" became his first Top 10 pop success. The song also won Vandross his first Grammy Award, in 1991, for Best Male R&B Vocal Performance.

When Vandross' next album, *Power of Love,* was released, further pop success seemed imminent: MTV placed his video for "Power of Love/Love Power" in rotation and the song climbed to number four on the pop charts. However, it quickly dropped out of the Top 10, and Vandross, disappointed and angry, filed suit to be released from his contract with Sony. The record company ultimately renegotiated with him, promising to promote his albums more aggressively. In 1992, Vandross received his second Grammy, again in the Best Male R&B Vocal Performance category, for "Power of Love/Love Power." His 1993 follow-up album, *Never Let Me Go,* was not critically well-received and not did match the pop success of his previous effort.

By 1994, Vandross had become increasingly upset by his failure to have a number one pop hit. The head of Sony Music, Tommy Mottola, suggested Vandross work with respected pop producer Walter Afansieff on a cover album; Vandross, despite never having had a producer on his solo albums, agreed. The result, *Songs,* managed to produce a number two hit, a duet with Mariah Carey called "Endless Love." However, the top spot continued to elude Vandross and critics hated his newly-produced sound. Trying to reconnect with his original fans, Vandross released a holiday album, *This is Christmas,* in late 1995, and the following year, an album of new material, *Your Secret Love.* The album went platinum and the title track reached the R&B charts, but music was changing rapidly; as Seymour noted in *Luther,* "the cool, never-break-a-sweat vibe of folks like Luther . . . seemed more dated every day."

In 1997, Vandross completed his contract with Sony with the release of a second greatest hits compilation, *One Night With You.* He signed with Virgin Records and began work on a new album, released in 1998 as *I Know.* This album—the first to miss platinum status—was a crushing disappointment. He left Virgin and took a break from recording. In 2000, Vandross signed with new label, J Records, and the following year commenced work on a new album.

Hit High Notes at the End

The self-titled release in 2001 was much more successful than *I Know,* bringing back his streak of platinum records. The following year, he returned to the studio; seeking

to put some contemporary edge on his sound, he invited rappers Busta Rhymes, Queen Latifah and Foxy Brown, as well as pop star Beyoncé Knowles, to appear on the album. With the help of songwriter Richard Marx, Vandross had written the song he believed would define his career, "Dance with my Father." In the midst of album release preparation, Vandross unexpectedly suffered a stroke and spent weeks in the hospital followed by months at a rehabilitation center. The release of his album, *Dance With My Father,* went ahead as scheduled and debuted at number one on the pop charts, at last garnering Vandross the long wished-for accolades. Vandross received five Grammy nominations, winning four including the prestigious Song of the Year. Still at a rehabilitation center from his stroke, Vandross was unable to attend the ceremony.

Vandross never fully recovered from his 2003 stroke. His long-time battle with his weight added stresses of diabetes and high blood pressure to his body. On July 1, 2005, Vandross died from a heart attack. Hundreds of people, including many of the musical luminaries he had worked with, came to pay their respects at his funeral. In September 2005, J Records released a tribute album, *So Amazing,* featuring well-known artists singing many of Vandross's most enduring songs.

Books

Seymour, Craig, *Luther: The Life and Longing of Luther Vandross,* HarperCollins, 2004.

Periodicals

Entertainment Weekly, December 20, 2005; January 6, 2006.
Jet, July 25, 2005.
New York Times, July 2, 2005; July 7, 2005.

Online

"Luther Vandross: Biography," http://www.luthervandross.com, January 8, 2006. □

Dziga Vertov

The foremost avant-garde figure of Soviet Russian cinema in its early days, Dziga Vertov (1896-1954) attempted to create a purely cinematic language, untouched by the narrative principles of literature or theater.

Vertov's best-known film, a staple of film curricula and an inspiration to experiment-minded young filmmakers of subsequent generations in the West, was *The Man with a Movie Camera,* a sort of silent ballet of everyday life and work as it is captured by the roving camera of the film's title. Vertov made other innovative films, however, and he held an important place among the large group of creative Russian intellectuals that turned out several of the most important landmarks of silent cinema. That he is not better known is due in part to the course of political history; a supporter of Communism, Vertov guessed wrong in opposing the liberalization of Soviet culture in the mid-1920s, and his creativity was eventually suppressed by the Soviet Communist government.

Family Fled Poland

Vertov was born Denis Abramovich Kaufman in Bialystok, Poland, on January 2, 1896. His family was Jewish, and his father owned a bookstore. Vertov was interested in the arts from an early age, writing poetry and playing the violin and piano. His family fled Poland, which at the time was controlled by czarist Russia, in order to escape advancing German troops during World War I. They settled in St. Petersburg, and Vertov changed his middle name to the more Russian-sounding Arkadievich. He took the name Dziga Vertov after he became active in cinema; the name evokes the turning of a movie camera's crank handle (Vertov is derived from the Russian word for "spin," and Dziga is an onomatopoetic representation of the grinding of a piece of machinery).

Enrolling at the Psychoneurological Institute in St. Petersburg, Vertov studied human perception of sound and soon created a makeshift "laboratory of hearing" where he could experiment with sound effects. He was influenced by the Italian Futurists, a group of artists and composers, who strove to create an anti-expressive, mechanistic aesthetic. When the Russian Revolution broke out in 1917 and brought the Communists to power, Vertov and his brother Mikhail took to the streets in support of the Bolsheviks. Both of Vertov's brothers became active in cinema as well; Boris Kaufman served as a cameraman for French director Jean Vigo in the 1930s, and Mikhail Kaufman made some films in Russia that have mostly disappeared from view.

Volunteering for the new Bolshevik government's cinema committee in Moscow, Vertov was put to work on newsreels. He became writer and editor of *Kinonedelia* (Film Week), the first Soviet newsreel agency. Vertov captured the chaotic world of the Soviet Union's first years, as foreign troops aided anti-Communist rebels but were eventually vanquished. Several young filmmakers working in the Soviet Union around this time went on to make cinematic history; Vertov met the experimental director and film editor Lev Kuleshov and camera operator Edouard Tissé, who later worked with Sergei Eisenstein. Revolutionary rhetoric was in the air, and Vertov and his friends began to churn out articles and pamphlets announcing their new artistic aims. In 1919 he made his first feature-length film, *Anniversary of the Revolution,* which was a compilation of earlier newsreels.

Vertov met film archivist Elisaveta Svilova while working on newsreels, and the two married. They founded a new group of filmmakers called *kino-oki* (Cinema Eyes) or Kinoks, devoted to documentary-style filmmaking. "I am kino-eye; I am mechanical eye; I, a machine, show you the world as only I can see it," Vertov wrote in a manifesto quoted on the Images website. "My path leads to the creation of a fresh perception of the world. I decipher in a new way a world unknown to you." In the early 1920s Vertov, under the auspices of the state Goskino cinema agency,

launched a new newsreel series called *Kino-Pravda* or Cinema of Truth. The name reflected the influence of the partyline Soviet newspaper *Pravda,* but Vertov's path soon made a left turn away from sheer realism.

Experimented with Newsreel Format

On one hand, the *Kino-Pravda* films fit the requirements of Communist propaganda. They showed Soviet citizens at work, reported on the completion of civil engineering projects, and presented footage of hospitals and streetcars. But Vertov assembled his crews' footage innovatively and artistically, using such techniques as a split screen, superimposed images, and slow or speeded-up motion, in an attempt to create compositions that would reflect what he called Soviet reality or Life as It Is. "We leave the film studio for . . . that whirlpool of colliding visible phenomena, where everything is real, where people, tramways, motorcycles, and trains meet and part, where each bus follows its route, where cars scurry about their business, where smiles, tears, deaths, and taxes do not obey the director's megaphone," Vertov wrote, as quoted in the *New Republic.* His film *Kino-Eye: Life Caught Unawares* won a silver medal at the 1924 World Exhibition in Paris.

A good example of Vertov's work of this period was *One Sixth of the World,* released in 1926. Writings and films glorifying the Soviet Union's ethnic diversity were a staple of the country's culture for its entire existence, and Vertov's film fell under that classification. But his method was unique. The dialogue of the entire film (on title cards, for this was still during the silent film era) consisted of a series of short geographic calls: "You in the small villages . . . You in the tundra . . . You on the ocean . . . You Uzbeks . . . You Kalmiks." These were blended with film imagery and rhythmic sounds to create a sort of visual poem of the Soviet Union. The *International Dictionary of Films and Filmmakers* noted that the technique results in a mood similar to that of Walt Whitman's poetry, which Vertov knew and liked. The *Kino-Pravda* films, and their successors, the 55 episodes of *Goskino Kalendar,* were closer in general to modern music videos than to the usual run of silent films.

Vertov and his associates continued to buttress their aesthetic experiments with vigorous written justifications of their works. Clearly Vertov benefited from the relatively free atmosphere of the Soviet Union in the mid-1920s, prior to Josef Stalin's ascent to power. Imports of Western films were permitted at this time, and they became popular. But Vertov, anxious to claim the mantle of Communist legitimacy for his experiments, condemned them. "We declare the old films, the romantic, the theatricalised, etc., to be leprous," he wrote, as quoted in a Vertov biography on the University of Glasgow, Scotland, website. "Don't come near! Don't look! Mortally dangerous! Contagious!" According to the Senses of Cinema website, he declared, "The film drama is the Opium of the people . . . down with Bourgeois fairy-tale scenarios . . . long live life as it is!"

Vertov's polemics paid off in government support for several more of his unique films, including *Stride, Soviet!* (1926). But he was playing a dangerous game, for his own work was as artistic and individualistic as that which he fulminated against. In the late 1920s, as the Soviet Union spun toward totalitarian rule, he began to fall out of favor in official circles. In order to make his masterpiece, *The Man with a Movie Camera,* he was forced to leave the Goskino studio and the city of Moscow itself, accepting support from the VUFKU studio in Ukraine, then under Soviet rule but temporarily still somewhat independent-minded.

Incorporated Cameraman into Film

The Man with a Movie Camera (1929) summed up everything Vertov had done thus far, in a large-scale, abstract, self-referential composition. It had no dialogue, and was set in a nameless city that conflated images of Moscow, Kiev, and Odessa. The film, according to *New Republic* writer J. Hoberman, "matches the rhythms of the workday to the cycle of life, and the mechanisms of moviemaking to the processes of industrial production." The film showed Soviet citizens at work and en route to their places of employment. But it added several new elements. Vertov used a full range of cinematic techniques, including special effects and variable-speed filming, to try and demonstrate that cinema could stand on its own as a completely new art form. And he incorporated the camera itself as a participant in his cinematic composition: the camera, operated by Vertov's brother Mikhail, is seen in action as it moves around the city and is superimposed on other images in a dazzling sequence near the film's conclusion.

The Man with a Movie Camera was one of a group of films known to cinema buffs as city symphonies. It remained part of numerous film school curricula three-quarters of a century later, and was performed with a live improvised score by the Alloy Orchestra, a group of experimental silent film accompanists. But at the time of its creation it was condemned in the Soviet Union. Sergei Eisenstein, as quoted on the Silents Are Golden website, said that it was filled with "formalist jackstraws and unmotivated camera mischief."

Vertov was able to make just one more film that reflected his experimental outlook: *Enthusiasm: Donbass Symphony* (1931), his first sound film, used sound as an abstract element, not always synchronized with the action on screen. The film brought Vertov recognition abroad and was hailed as a masterwork by Charlie Chaplin, among others. But Vertov's situation at home deteriorated still further. In 1934 he wrote (according to Hoberman) that he felt "anxiety day and night. I used to think I'd always be tireless. Not so. They've exhausted me. My brain's so tired that a breeze knocks me over." According to Hoberman, Vertov wrote a little satirical sketch of his cultural overlords: "You wish to continue working on the ponetic documentary?," he imagined them saying. "Go right ahead. You have our general permission. . . . You can sit in your damp hole beneath the water tank and above the sobering station for drunks. You can stand in line for the toilet, for the kitchen burner, the sink, the streetcar, and the bath. With no elevator, you can climb up to the sixth floor ten times a day."

The disillusioned Vertov attempted to regain the Party's good graces with *Three Songs of Lenin* (1934), a tribute to the Soviet Union's founder, but even this did not help his

position. The film's release was delayed, perhaps because it did not include any appropriate homage to Stalin. Despite his declining status, Vertov did not end up in a prison camp like so many of his progressive contemporaries. He returned to making propaganda documentaries like *For You at the Front: the Kazakhstan Front* (1942) for the Soviet state, and he survived Stalinist purges and the horrors of the Second World War. Beginning in 1944 he came full circle and worked on Soviet newsreels. He died of cancer on February 12, 1954, in Moscow.

Books

International Dictionary of Films and Filmmakers, vol. 2: Directors, 4th ed., St. James, 2000.

Periodicals

New Republic, December 9, 1985.
Variety, March 15, 2004.

Online

"Dziga Vertov," Senses of Cinema, http://www.sensesofcinema .com/contents/directors/03/vertov.html (February 1, 2006).
"Man with a Movie Camera," Images, http://www.images journal.com/issue05/reviews/vertov.html (February 1, 2006).
"Man with a Movie Camera," Silents Are Golden, http://www .silentsaregolden.com (February 1, 2006).
"No Fiction Films Allowed," University of Glasgow, http://www .hatii.arts.gla.ac.uk (February 1, 2006). □

Victorio

Victorio (c. 1820-1880) was an Apache warrior known as an intelligent and feared fighter. He proved his military cunning by leading small groups of warriors—often consisting of no more than 35 to 50 fighters—in triumphant resistance to American and Mexican troops. In October of 1880 he was eventually captured by Mexican soldiers at Tres Castillos in the state of Chihuahua in Mexico. Killing himself, rather than letting his enemies take him alive, Victorio left behind the legacy of his resistance to the forced movement of Native Americans onto reservations.

Rose to Tribal Leader

Victorio was born around 1820 in the Black Range of New Mexico. It was a rugged region of mountain and desert that might have seemed rather stark and barren to outsiders, but the Native American group that Victorio belonged to thrived upon the landscape. Victorio was a member of the Eastern Chiricahua Apaches, otherwise known as the Warm Springs or Mimbreno Apaches. The Apaches that Victorio belonged to were first united in

1837 by Mangas Coloradas near the Gila River in south-western New Mexico. Little is known about Victorio's early life, but it can be assumed that he spent some of his life learning to be a warrior, fighting against the encroaching white people and other enemy tribes who all fought to keep the best land and supplies. Young Native Americans, at the time, had to prove their worthiness to be called warriors by fighting against such people and demonstrating their military prowess in battle, something that Victorio must have done well.

In the 1850s Victorio engaged in raids in northern Mexico alongside the more famous Native Americans Nana and Geronimo. In 1862 he joined Chief Mangas Coloradas, serving under him in the successful war to expel the Santa Rita del Cobre copper miners from Apache land. It was after Mangas died that Victorio rose to become a tribal leader, as he was next in line to lead. Victorio was the last hereditary chief whose raiding bands roamed over the lands they inhabited without any obstacles to stand in their way. This territory included present-day southwest Texas, New Mexico, southern Arizona, and the northern Mexican states of Sonora and Chihuahua.

Forced to Move to San Carlos Reservation

Victorio gathered together a band of about 300 Eastern Chiricahuas and Mescaleros Native Americans whom he took care of. He was thought, by the United States troops who fought against him, to be a man of sound judgment, tactical expert, and a great leader of men. His band of Native Americans settled near Fort Craig, New Mexico, in 1869, to await the completion of a new reservation near Ojo Caliente (Warm Springs), New Mexico that they had been promised by United States leaders. They were happy with their new home and did little raiding until April 20, 1877, when it was decided by the United States government that they wanted the land they had given the tribe, and that the Native Americans were to move to the San Carlos Reservation in Arizona instead. The move would crowd Victorio's band of Native Americans onto the San Carlos Reservation amidst their traditional enemies. They were given no choice, but had to leave while their crops were only half ripe. Victorio, on behalf of his people, protested the move loudly. Victorio had heard that the conditions at the San Carlos Reservation were horrible, and he had also heard of other Native Americans successfully raiding the nearby lands, rather than submitting to the move. Victorio considered putting together a band of warriors to begin raiding in Mexico, Texas, and New Mexico; however, he first attempted to reason with the men in charge of forcing his people to move.

When Victorio was told that Warm Springs would be taken away from his people and offered to white settlers, it has been passed down that Victorio heatedly pleaded for his fellow men, women, and children to be allowed to keep their land. He passionately argued that if they were left alone at their homes, there would be no trouble. When little heed was paid to his statement, Victorio was quoted as having added, "This is our home, our country. We were born here and we love it." The officers in charge of moving Victorio and his men paid no attention to Victorio's pleadings. So Victorio said that he could not and would not stop them from taking the women and children to the new settlement, but he would not go himself and he would not allow his warriors to go either.

Victorio Forced to Raiding Throughout the Southwest

To deal with the situation the officers threatened to charge Victorio with murder and horse-stealing unless he complied with their wishes. Victorio knew that the white officers could be merciless. Not too long before this Geronimo had been jailed and Mangas Coloradas had been killed for going against the white man's wishes. Victorio feared the same things would happen to him, so he allowed himself and his people to be moved to the San Carlos reservation. He remained there for a very short time, however, choosing instead to run away from the reservation, never to return. He told the white men who he had befriended that he was sorry, but from then on it would have to be war, there would and could be no other way. He put through his earlier plans of raiding rather than submitting to a degrading life on the reservation.

When Victorio left the San Carlos reservation, he took with him a group of approximately 40 warriors. Even though his band was small, Victorio managed to carry out attacks over an amazingly wide area of land, including New Mexico, Texas, and Mexico; he fought more battles over a wider area than any other Native Americans fighting at the time. He was a genius at planning and going through with an attack, and his warriors fought valiantly and loyally at his side. It has been told that there were almost 500 Americans and Mexicans who died during the attacks, which came to be known as Victorio's War.

Fought With Americans Near Rattlesnake Springs

In the summer of 1880 Victorio and his band stayed at many locations, always on the move. These locations included Quitman, Carrizo, and the Guadalupe mountains of far western Texas. Their tactics were those of guerilla warfare, and it made them cunning enemies. Always difficult to catch an enemy who has no base from which to work, the Americans and Mexicans knew that if they were going to catch Victorio and his band they were going to have to pay attention to every whisper of knowledge they received about the warriors' whereabouts. American officers heard just such a whisper in 1880; the rumblings were that Victorio and his band would be moving from the Rio Grande north to the Guadalupe mountains.

Proceeding without verifying the rumor of Victorio's location, they quickly moved their troops into position to intercept the group. Their hope was that they would be able to ensnare the band of Native Americans in the vicinity of a place called Rattlesnake Springs, which they assumed the Native Americans would have to stop at, as it was a sort of oasis in the relatively barren landscape. Their risk paid off, as they did indeed come upon Victorio moving north to the mountains. The two groups met and clashed in the Sierra Diablo Mountains and at Rattlesnake Springs. The battle went on for three hours, each side striking deeply at the other until Victorio and his warriors finally fled into the Carrizo Mountains in the west and on into Mexico. The American officers spent much of that summer and fall looking for Victorio, but were unable to track him and his men down. They eventually returned to their base at Fort Concho empty-handed.

Band Trapped and Caught in Tres Castillas, Mexico

Back at Fort Concho, the American officers enlisted the help of Texas Rangers to track the Apaches down. One such man sent to find Victorio was ranger James B. Gillett, who purportedly rode with a Lt. George W. Baylor, 12 other rangers, and almost 100 civilians into Mexico in September of 1880 looking for the band of Native Americans. According to Gillett, he and the men he rode with were close to tracking down Victorio and his band when they were suddenly forced out of Mexico by the Mexican military soldier Colonel Joaqu'n Terrazas, who himself was a famous Native American fighter and leader of the Chihuahua militia. Terrazas was also looking for Victorio and his men and did not want anyone else to find them. The Americans went home empty–handed again, cursing the Mexican's deportation of them.

Continuing on the trail that the Americans were following, Terrazas proved to be successful. In October of 1880 Terrazas and his men tracked the Apaches down to a range of mountains approximately 60 miles inside the Mexican border, called Tres Castillas. It was a location that Victorio and his warriors often stayed at when they were in Mexico looking for a place to hide out, and unfortunately Victorio heard nothing of the Mexican army's approach until it was too late to escape.

On October 15, 1880, Terrazas and Juan Mata Ortiz, the man who was his second in command, managed to encircle Victorio and his men. The Apaches fought bravely, but in the end Terrazas, Ortiz and their men slaughtered the band of Apaches, leaving only those few women and children who had been traveling with the band alive. Victorio himself, refusing to die an ignoble death, at the hands of his enemies, killed himself. The survivors were made prisoners and were taken to Chihuahua City where they were kept in custody for the next few years.

So ended the great warrior who had been forced off the land of his ancestors. Victorio died on October 15, 1880, in a battle against the Mexicans, but his memory remained vivid in the minds of people and especially his family. Although polygamy had been a status symbol in his tribe, he had only one wife, with whom he had had five children. Three of his sons died in battle before him.

Books

Notable Native Americans, Gale Research, 1995.

Online

"Chief Victorio," King Snake, http://www.kingsnake.com/ hudspeth/victorio.htm (January 6, 2006).

"Victorio," The Handbook of Texas Online, http://www.tsha .utexas.edu/handbook/online/articles/W/fvi3.html (January 6, 2006).

"Victorio's War: A Closer Look," Buffalo Soldier Web Site, http://www.buffalosoldier.net/BuffaloSoldiers&ChiefVictorio .htm (January 6, 2006). ☐

Dominique De Villepin

Dominique de Villepin (born 1953) became prime minister of France during a cabinet reshuffle by French president Jacques Chirac in the spring of 2005.

Villepin was a somewhat surprising choice for the job, partly because he had never held any elected office, but his political career had been closely linked with that of Chirac's during the preceding decade. Villepin achieved a measure of international renown during a stint as France's foreign minister in early 2003, when he challenged U.S. plans to invade Iraq at a United Nations forum. He is also the author of several volumes of poetry and a biography of Napoleon Bonaparte. "It is very rare to meet someone like him," said Chirac of his protégé, according to *Times* of London correspondent Charles Bremner, "who is at one and the same time a poet and a very good commando leader."

Villepin hails from a well-connected family whose roots are in the département, or province, of Yonne. He was born Dominique Marie François René Galouzeau de Villepin on November 14, 1953, in Rabat, the capital of Morocco. His father, Xavier, was a diplomat with France's foreign service, and was posted to the North African country at the time. The family later lived in Venezuela during Villepin's formative years, and some years later his father was elected to the French Senate.

Trained for the Civil Service

As a young man, Villepin studied at one of his country's *grandes écoles,* the prestigious colleges that train the political, cultural, and economic elite of France. His college was the *Institut d'Etudes Politiques de Paris,* or Paris Institute of Political Studies, and he went on to the *École nationale d'administration,* a near-obligatory stop for any future government bureaucrat. But Villepin also earned degrees in law and literature before beginning his first job with the French foreign affairs department in 1980, as a member of an advising committee on Franco-African relations. Four years later he was posted to the French embassy in Washington, D.C., where he served as a media spokesperson for five years. Between 1989 and 1992 he lived in India as an officer with the French embassy in New Delhi, and he then returned to Paris, becoming head adviser at the Foreign Ministry on

Led Opposition to Iraq Invasion

Villepin soon had a more threatening crisis to manage at the Foreign Ministry. The United States, determined to oust Iraqi leader Saddam Hussein, was claiming that weapons inspection teams sent to the Middle Eastern nation under the auspices of the United Nations were being prevented from carrying out their duties. U.S. President George W. Bush was attempting to gather international support for a U.S.-led invasion of Iraq, but three of the four other permanent members of the United Nations (UN) Security Council—France, China, and Russia—were opposed to the plan. The Security Council's resolutions are designed to maintain peace and stability between all member nations of the UN, and all signees to the UN Charter must abide by these decisions.

In January of 2003 Villepin warned that Europe would unite and oppose any unnecessary aggression toward Iraq. A month later he delivered an impassioned speech before the Security Council, reiterating the Chirac government's opposition to the use of force against Iraq. Germany also sided with France, while Russia and China were similarly wary of aggressive military action to oust an unfriendly ruler. "In this temple of the United Nations, we are the guardians of an ideal, the guardians of conscience," Villepin said that day, according to Bremner. "This onerous responsibility and immense honour we have must lead us to give priority to disarmament through peace." His words were greeted by a round of applause, a rare event inside in Security Council chambers.

Villepin was the target of harsh words from the Bush White House, but he reminded interviewers that the goal of civilized nations should be to promote peace and stability in the more troubled regions of the world, not provoke hostility. He responded to claims that he and France both harbored an anti-American bias by asserting that he had lived in the United States for five years, and enjoyed the experience immensely. In an interview with *New York Times* writer Elaine Sciolino, he maintained that he was quite pro-American. "To act like I do, you have to know how much I love America," he told the newspaper.

Critics of Villepin pointed to his 2001 biography about the last hundred days of Napoleon, *Les Cent-jours, ou L'esprit de sacrifice* (The Hundred Days, or the Spirit of Sacrifice), and warned that the foreign minister seemed to be making a bid to reassert French power on the world's stage. "Villepin may pose in the United Nations as the great defender of reason, prudence, and international law against an arrogant, foolhardy, and unreasonable America," noted one scholar of French history, David A. Bell, in the *New Republic,* who went on to assert that the book "suggests that, in fact, he is a man lacking firm political principles, romantically besotted with raw political power, and ready to overlook misdeeds committed in its name—but only when the power in question is French."

Became Interior Minister

By this point, Villepin's RPR had merged with two other parties to become the *Union pour un Mouvement Populaire* (Union for a Popular Movement, or UPM). His main rival

African Affairs. In 1993 the French foreign minister, Alain Juppé, appointed him to serve as his chief of staff.

Juppé became a leading figure in the *Rassemblement pour la République* (Rally for the Republic, or RPR), the right-wing political party founded by Jacques Chirac in 1976. Villepin was tapped to run Chirac's 1995 presidential campaign, which resulted in a victory for Chirac and the party. As thanks, Villepin was appointed secretary-general of the Élysée Palace, the official residence and office of the French president. Two years later, the RPR lost a general election that Villepin had urged Chirac to hold somewhat ahead of schedule. The RPR lost some of its seats in the French National Assembly to the Socialists, and Villepin was widely blamed for the setback. When he tried to submit his letter of resignation, Chirac refused to accept it.

Villepin remained secretary-general of the Élysée Palace until 2002, when Chirac was re-elected to a second term. A new prime minister, Jean-Pierre Raffarin, appointed Villepin as the country's foreign minister. It was a job with immense prestige, but some of Villepin's political foes claimed that he was far too inexperienced for the post. Nevertheless, he survived his first major challenge in the role, when a crisis in Ivory Coast, the West African nation, erupted soon afterward. Religious-fueled unrest led to an attack on French troops stationed in the country, and Villepin ordered a swift military response that decimated the rebels' air-strike capabilities. He also negotiated a tenuous truce to avoid further skirmishes.

within the party ranks was the equally young and charismatic French politician Nicolas Sarkozy, whose flair for a memorable media quip had made him France's most popular conservative politician, according to polls. In a cabinet reshuffle in March of 2004, Sarkozy switched jobs from Interior Minister to Finance Minister, and Villepin was made the new Interior Minister. His year-plus tenure in this post was a controversial one, highlighted by his stance against radical Muslim clerics who headed mosques or organizations among France's five-million-strong Muslim community. Villepin claimed some of these sites or groups served as part of a secretive support network for international Islamic terrorism. As Interior Minister he issued a controversial law that required all Muslim clerics in France to take mandatory courses—offered only in the French language, though only a third of them spoke it fluently—in moderate Muslim theology and French secularism.

On May 29, 2005, France held a referendum on adopting the European Constitution, the next step in a fully integrated European Union. French voters rejected it, which was widely considered a no-confidence vote for the Chirac government. A stagnant economy, high unemployment, and worries about pan-European rules forever ending some of the historic job protections that French workers still enjoyed were all factors that appeared to make voters uneasy. Raffarin resigned as prime minister, and Chirac appointed Villepin in his stead. Again, his critics said that he was not experienced enough to hold the post, let alone shepherd the nation through a particularly difficult identity crisis. Newspapers in London, a country that had long made a sport of mocking French pretensions and political ambitions, immediately published a passage from Villepin's latest book, *Le Cri de la Gargouille* (The Cry of the Gargoyle): "France is a large old oak tree, full of an everlasting sap," Villepin expounded, according to the *Guardian* excerpt. "It is a tree that has thrived and spread for thousands of years in a unique soil, that has been both hospitable and open to all kinds of invasions, whose population is both diverse and yet homogeneous, whose spirit tends to be both rigorous and aesthetically inclined."

Though Sarkozy was considered Villepin's top rival for power, the new prime minister took the unusual step of appointing Sarkozy to a key cabinet post equal to that of a minister of state; in effect, it made Sarkozy the number-three person in France, after Chirac and Villepin. The political futures of all three would be affected by the days of civil unrest that took place in October and November of 2005. The trouble began in a Paris suburb after the deaths by electrocution of two teenagers of North African descent, who were running from a standard police identification check. Long-simmering resentments over racial discrimination erupted, and took the form of car torchings. The unrest quickly spread to other French cities and even across the border into neighboring European Union countries. Nearly 9,000 cars were burned, and Sarkozy was widely condemned for claiming the violence was the work of organized gangs, and that the outer-ring suburbs where immigrants lived needed to be "Karcherised," which refers to a high-pressure industrial cleaning product. His words were said to have further inflamed tensions in the region.

Compared to de Gaulle

Chirac waited nearly ten days before declaring martial law in an attempt to curb the unrest, and the crisis was viewed as the final nail in the coffin of his political career. Villepin's equally cautious response was also mocked, with one writer for London's *Times* imagining the journal entries the prime minister might have written during the crisis. "They burn the cars; yet ultimately, could it not be said that the cars burn them?" wrote Hugo Rifkind in imitation of Villepin's elaborate literary style in both his written works and public speeches. "They fight us and we fight them. Yet are we fighting? Or are we dancing, as France has always danced since gates were breached in 1789?"

Villepin's supporters claimed that his reaction was at least less distasteful than that of Sarkozy's, and a few even compared Villepin to Charles de Gaulle, the most significant French leader of the twentieth century. Others felt the comparison failed to reflect a changing France of the twenty-first century. Rather than seeing him as a new de Gaulle, wrote Bremner, "for many French . . . the image of the dashing, intellectual and aristocratic M. de Villepin really spoke for the continuing failure of the elite to connect with the masses beyond Paris."

Both Villepin and Sarkozy will likely vie for the UPM ballot in the French presidential elections scheduled for 2007. Married to Marie-Lauer Le Gay, Villepin is the father of three and claims to thrive best on less than five hours of sleep a night. In addition to his government duties and literary output, he also runs marathons.

Periodicals

Guardian (London, England), June 1, 2005; November 9, 2005.
Independent (London, England), January 22, 2003.
New Republic, April 14, 2003.
New York Times, March 8, 2003.
Times (London, England), June 1, 2005; November 9, 2005; November 12, 2005. □

Isaac Watts

English writer Isaac Watts (1674-1748) was the creator of the English hymn; he was perhaps second only to Martin Luther in importance among the creative figures who forged a devotional musical language in European Protestantism. In the words of an essay on Watts, appearing on the website of the United Reformed Church of the United Kingdom, "Isaac Watts was the man who, virtually single-handed, introduced, developed, invented the hymn as we know it today."

Hymnals might seem to have been fixtures in churches since time immemorial, but before Watts it was psalm singing, not hymns, that formed the main musical component of church services in the English-speaking world. Watts's influence on American religious music was immense. His hymns are still sung today, and several of them, including "When I survey the wond'rous Cross" and "O, God, our help in ages past," are among the best known of all hymns in English. The hymns of "Dr. Watts," as he was known in the American vernacular, were passionate, devotional, intense, and vivid, sometimes to the point of being graphic. They influenced African-American as well as European-American sacred song, and the very name of the chief religious music of African-American Christianity under slavery, the spiritual, was likely taken from the title of one of his printed works.

Nursed Outside Prison

Isaac Watts was born in Southampton, England, on July 17, 1674. His parents were Dissenters—that is, they were not members of the Church of England. They adhered to the Congregational faith. That was a serious matter at the time; Dissenters, depending on the tolerance of the monarch on the English throne, might be allowed to worship freely but were always denied some measure of civil rights and suffered frequent harassment. Watts, the oldest of nine children, was born while his father, also named Isaac, was in prison. His mother nursed him while sitting on a large stone outside the prison gate, carrying on a silent protest against the unjust treatment meted out to her husband.

Watts showed obvious verbal ability as a child. He was often in poor health and would continue to be troubled by frequent illness throughout his life. In spite of this handicap, he began learning Latin when he was four years old and mastered that language along with ancient Greek, French, and Hebrew by the time he was 13. At seven he was writing poetry, improvising clever rhymed retorts to his family when they scolded him for laughing during prayers, and even writing an elaborate ten-line religious acrostic poem, the first letters of each line combining to spell out his own name. His education began with his father and continued at the Free School of Southampton.

By the time he was 16, Watts had impressed a local physician enough to be offered financial support should he decide to attend Oxford University, one of two universities in England at the time. But both Oxford and its counterpart Cambridge were affiliated with the Church of England, and attending would have meant converting to that church—to "conform," in the language of the day. Watts remained true to his religion and turned the doctor down, choosing instead to attend the Newington Green Academy, a Dissenting institution in London operated by the learned Thomas Rowe. Watts wrote poetry and theological texts at the Academy. His course of study prepared him to become a

minister, but he did not immediately feel ready to begin preaching after finishing his studies at age 20. He moved back home to his family and continued to read, write, and reflect. His first hymn, "Behold the Glories of the Lamb," is said to have been written after he complained to his father about the dull psalm singing at the family's church in Southampton, and his father encouraged him to see what he could do to solve the problem.

For several years Watts worked as a tutor to the Hartopp family of Stoke Newington. Watts was quoted as saying, in a nineteenth-century biography reproduced on the Christian Biography Resources website, "I cannot but reckon it among the blessings of Heaven, when I review those five years of pleasure and improvement which I spent in his [Sir John Hartopp's] family in my younger part of life. And I found much instruction myself, where I was called to be an instructor." Indeed, Watts penned a great variety of educational writings and was well known for these during his lifetime. The Hartopps were Dissenters as well, and Watts's convictions deepened. On his 24th birthday he gave his first sermon, and in 1698 he became an assistant pastor at the Mark Lane Meeting in London, an Independent (or Congregational) church.

Emphasized Role of Music in Worship

Watts became the congregation's pastor in 1702. Just five feet tall, he was an unprepossessing figure in the pulpit. Health problems continued to plague him, and an assistant had to be appointed to fill in for him after a severe bout with

illness in 1703. Despite these problems, Watts was a powerful preacher. The Mark Lane congregation outgrew its quarters and twice had to move to larger facilities, and Watts's sermons began to be collected and printed. Part of his success was due to his emphasis on the role of music in worship. A minister, he felt, should not only write sermons but should seek to involve his congregation in worship through music.

Watts backed up his contention with action. After a volume of his poetry, *Horae Lyricae: Poems, Chiefly of the Lyric Kind, in Two Books,* was published in 1706, he issued the three-volume *Hymns and Spiritual Songs* the following year. In 1709 it was reissued in an enlarged edition, and it went on to become one of the most influential publications in the history of Protestantism. The original American edition of *Hymns and Spiritual Songs* was issued in 1741 by Benjamin Franklin in Philadelphia, and Watts's texts were as widely disseminated in the United States as in England. Watts did not write music. Psalms and hymns at the time were sung to tunes that would be known to most members of a congregation or choir (the tune might have the name of a town where it was thought to have come from), and that fit the rhythm and meter of the words. Even so, he created a musical revolution.

A hymn in the most general sense is a song of praise to God, but it is distinguished from a psalm, a lyrical expression of devotion drawn from the Book of Psalms in the Bible. Psalm singing, or psalmody, was the main form of congregational musical involvement in services when Watts came on the scene. Watts's hymns were often based on psalms, but he put them into a moving new language of personal worship that anyone could understand. "In effect," stated the website of the United Reformed Church, "Watts campaigned to evangelize the Hebrew psalms." Watts wrote for average churchgoers. In the preface to *Hymns and Spiritual Songs* he wrote (as quoted on the same website) that "I have aimed at ease of numbers and smoothness of sound, and endeavored to make the sense plain and obvious; if the verse appears so gentle and flowing as to incur the Censure of Feebleness, I may honestly affirm that sometimes it has cost me labor to make it so."

The most immediate impact of Watts's new hymnody was felt among the Dissenting sects, whose members felt new tensions every time the British monarchy changed hands. A Watts hymn such as "O, God, our help in ages past" was heard by Dissenters in literal terms after the death of Queen Anne, who had championed harsher restrictions on them; Watts's image of "shelter from a stormy blast" was a direct way of expressing the emotions they felt at the time, and it continued to serve that purpose in times of crisis for many Britons. It was played on British Broadcasting Corporation radio as World War II broke out.

Hymns Admired by Slaves

The resonances of *Hymns and Spiritual Songs* and of Watts's later hymns—he wrote about 700 in all—were amplified in the United States, where the passionate emotions of his hymnody fit the temperament of a country founded on dissent. Three hundred years after their composition, Watts's hymns, with music by a host of later composers, still crowd the hymnals of many Christian denominations. Their strongest impact was felt perhaps in the religious life of African-American slaves, to whom the title of Watts's book is thought to have come down in the form of the noun "spiritual" to describe a religious song.

The simple structure of some of Watts's hymns was suited to the call-and-response language of African-American hymnody, and some of them were performed in black churches and congregations in their original form or something close to it. A Watts text such as "When I can read my title clear to mansions in the skies / I bid farewell to every fear, and wipe my weeping eyes / And wipe my weeping eyes, and wipe my weeping eyes / I bid farewell to every fear, and wipe my weeping eyes" had strong connotations for a group of people striving toward literacy, and served as a springboard for African-rooted religious musical performance. More often, the mostly anonymous creators of the spirituals worked Watts's imagery into their own original compositions.

For both black and white Americans, the ideas of personal devotion to Jesus Christ and belief in personal salvation through Christ's suffering were given vivid expression in Watts's texts. "See from His head, His hands, His feet, Sorrow and love flow mingled down!," Watts wrote in "When I survey the wond'rous Cross." And another verse, "His dying crimson, like a robe / Spreads o'er His body on the tree / Then I am dead to all the globe / And all the globe is dead to me." Charles Wesley, the founder of Methodism and a prolific hymn composer himself, is reported to have said that he would have traded away his own entire output if he could have written that one hymn, and there were other Watts hymns that became equally famous: "Am I a soldier of the cross," "There is a land of pure delight," and the text of the Christmas carol "Joy to the world" being just a few of several dozen Watts texts still in common use.

"Joy to the world" was originally published not in *Hymns and Spiritual Songs* but in a later Watts volume, *The Psalms of David Imitated in the Language of the New Testament* (1719). Watts continued to write prolifically for the rest of his life. He cut back on his preaching after suffering a serious illness in 1712. Invited to convalesce at the estate of Sir Thomas Abney, the former mayor of London, he ended up staying on with the Abney family for 36 years, until his death in 1748. He devoted himself mostly to writing. His *Divine Songs Attempted in Easy Language for the Use of Children* (1715) remained in print for over a century and was still well enough known in Victorian England that readers understood and appreciated Lewis Carroll's parody, in *Alice in Wonderland*, of Watts's couplet "How doth the little busy bee / Improve each shining hour?," which became "How doth the little crocodile / Improve his shining tail?." Watts, sometimes directing his efforts toward the Abneys' children, wrote a grammar textbook (*The Art of Reading and Writing English*, 1721) and one on logic; he was well known in his own time for these works and for his poetry, in addition to his hymns. He died at the Abney estate in Stoke Newington on November 25, 1748.

Books

Davis, Arthur Paul, *Isaac Watts: His Life and Works,* Dryden, 1943.
Dictionary of Literary Biography: Vol. 95: Eighteenth-Century British Poets, First Series, Gale, 1990.
Escott, Harry, *Isaac Watts: Hymnographer,* Independent, 1962.
Southern, Eileen, *The Music of Black Americans,* Norton, 1997.

Periodicals

History Today, November 1998.

Online

"Isaac Watts, by Robert Southey, abridged by Stephen Ross," Christian Biography Resources, http://www.wholesome words.org/biography/bwatts2.html (February 7, 2006).
"Perspective: The Importance of Isaac Watts," The United Reformed Church, http://www.urc.org.uk/documents/isaac_watts/watts_index.htm (February 7, 2006). □

Lois Weber

Despite being one of the first women directors in motion picture history, American filmmaker Lois Weber (1881-1939) is not very well remembered today, as her films have not measured well against the test of time.

In the early part of the twentieth century, Weber directed films dealing with social themes and often strived to make moral points in her work. As such, her films tended to be preachy and didactic. But in her prime, she was one of the most popular and highest paid directors in the film industry. Weber was a prolific filmmaker; in the early silent film era, when the art and business of motion pictures was still in its infancy, she made significant contributions to the emerging medium as a director, producer and writer. However, today her work is of interest only to scholars, as it provides historical and social perspective. For modern audiences, her films offer little, if any, entertainment value.

Working in an industry that would eventually become a male-dominated province, Weber thrived during a time when gender was not a major concern. In the period in which Weber toiled, before film became a big business, many other women found ongoing employment as directors, writers, producers, and actors. Weber proved so successful that she eventually started her own production company.

Weber, like her contemporary female colleagues, realized that film provided an opportunity to advance personal attitudes and agendas. She instinctively understood film's unique power to reach out to and influence a large audience. As such, she took advantage of her role to make personal films about social issues close to her heart. She tackled controversial topics such as birth control and abortion in *Where are My Children?* (1916), capital punishment in *The People vs. John Doe* (1916), Christian Science with

Jewel (1915) and *A Chapter in Her Life* (1923). Favorite themes included women's role in society, marriage, social disparity, hypocrisy and the corruption that infests business, politics and religion.

In her cinematic indictments, she challenged her audience's own attitudes. As such her films were lauded as well as reviled, condemned and attacked as being sensational. Further, her work had been criticized as being preachy, as Weber's approach was more evangelical than that of a social reformer. She was not an advocate of women's rights and never became involved in the then-popular women's suffrage movement. Rather, she championed marriage and viewed women's role as that of house keepers.

Weber was born on June 13, 1881, in Allegheny City, Pennsylvania, close to Pittsburgh. While growing up, Weber displayed musical talent. When she was 16, she did a brief tour as a concert pianist and she sang with the missionary Church Army. When she expressed a desire to study voice in New York City, her parents objected, causing her to run away. On her own in New York, she lived in poverty, a circumstance that would later influence her films.

In the 1890s, possessing a missionary zeal to convert people, she worked as a street-corner evangelist and sang hymns in poverty-stricken sections of New York City. She also worked in the Church Home Missionary in Pittsburgh. When she sought to reach more people, she followed her uncle's advice and began a career on the stage.

Weber achieved a degree of success as an actress at the Hippodrome in New York. In 1905, she married fellow actor Phillips Smalley, who she met while touring as a cast member in the period melodrama *Why Girls Leave Home*. On stage, she performed with Smalley, who was also the touring company's manager. Catering to her husband's wishes, however, she temporarily left the stage to become a housewife.

Began Her Film Career

Weber left her role as a homemaker in 1908 when she met Alice Guy Blaché and Herbert Blaché and took a job at Herbert Blache's Gaumont Film Studio, an early film production company located in Fort Lee, New Jersey, where she worked as a writer, director and actress. At the time, all major film studios were located on the East Coast. While at Gaumont, she learned the craft of film direction by working with director Herbert Blaché. The experience was an important turning point in her career. Film, she believed, provided the perfect vehicle for her evangelism, as it would provide her with the broader audience that she sought.

In 1912, she teamed up with her husband to find work in the new film business. In the early part of their shared career, they worked at small film production companies, starting with Gaumont and then moving to Reliance, Rex, and Bosworth. At Rex, they worked for Edwin S. Porter, the film pioneer who made *The Great Train Robbery* (1902). When Porter left the company, Weber and Smalley took over.

At Rex, Weber and Smalley made a large number of shorts and feature films. Weber wrote scripts and screen subtitles. She also acted, directed, designed sets and costumes, edited film, and developed negatives. Throughout her career, Weber liked to be involved in many elements of film production. In a 1916 interview with *The Moving Picture Weekly,* she commented that a director should have sole authority in the ''arrangement, cutting, titling or anything else'' necessary to compete a film. ''What other artist has his work interfered with by someone else?'' she said. At this time, Weber and Smalley also experimented with an early form of sound films, with technology that involved actors' dialogue recorded on phonographs and synchronized to images on the screen.

Films Provoked Controversy

In 1913, Weber began directing regularly, and her films often generated controversy due to the frank nature of the subject matter. One of her most controversial films was *Hypocrites,* released in 1914. It was an indictment of public and religious hypocrisy. In the film, the lead actor, assuming a dual role, plays a monk troubled by the world's rampant hypocrisy and a priest who is stoned to death by his congregation for displaying a statue of a naked woman called ''The Naked Truth''. The priest had hoped the statue would awaken his congregation to their own hypocrisies, but they instead regarded him as immoral.

The depicted statue also generated real public outrage. Censors instructed Weber to cover the image, frame by frame. As often happens with films of this nature, the moviegoers went to see the film for its more sensational elements, rather than its moralistic message. But Weber was undeterred in her perceived purpose, and filmgoers would have to endure a sermon with their titillation. As taken from *The Projector: Film and Media Journal* website, the year of the film's release, she said, "In moving pictures I have found my life work. I find at once an outlet for my emotions and my ideals. I can preach to my heart's content."

Weber would encounter controversy and censorship often throughout her career. On occasion, police shut down showings of her films. In 1918, *Theatre Magazine* ran an article that criticized Weber for the indecency and suggestiveness present in her work. But Weber remained undaunted and continued producing her "missionary pictures" while defending her films against charges of exploitation.

Became Highest-Paid Female Director

In 1915, Universal financed a private film studio for Weber on Sunset Boulevard in Hollywood, California. By 1916, she was the film company's highest paid director, earning five thousand dollars a week, which was a considerable salary at that time. Moreover, she became one of the entire film industry's most compensated directors. Universal paid Weber top dollar and gave her a broad range of artistic freedom because her films were among the studio's biggest hits and, as a filmmaker, she was respected by critics.

Weber's output would be quite prolific. In all, she would make more than 400 films. Today, that amount sounds incredible. However, in the early years of film, most movies were short one- and two-real productions. That, of course, would change, when D.W. Griffith, the pioneering motion picture director and producer, made *The Birth of a Nation* in 1915 and *Intolerance* in 1916, two film spectaculars that stretched the parameters of film production, including screen running time.

Weber herself directed a long, five-reel film in 1916 called *Where are My Children?*, which was anti-abortion yet pro-birth control. The film's sensational subject matter caused it to be banned by the Philadelphia Board of Censors. In the wake of that condemnation, censorship trials involving the film's exhibition took place throughout the country. But the controversy only attracted more people to see the film, which would eventually take in three million dollars.

In 1916, *Where are My Children?* was followed by *Shoes,* which attacked child labor, *Discontent,* which depicted clashes between generations, and *The People vs. John Doe,* which addressed the injustices of capital punishment. In 1917, Weber made *The Hand that Rocks the Cradle* as a tribute to Margaret Sanger, an early advocate of birth control.

Deemed a "Great" Director

At this point in her career, Weber was in her prime productive years, which ran from 1913 to around 1922, a period that saw the release of her most important films. An article in *Moving Picture Stories* called her "the greatest woman director." In 1917, she formed her own production company, Lois Weber Productions, and released her films through Universal.

In 1920, she signed a contract with Famous Players-Lasky for $50,000 per picture and a percentage of profits.

But the arrangement did not work out. She made five films for the company, but she was dropped a year later after she made three films that lost money. Critics were beginning to find her films dull, and she was beginning to lose her audience.

Still, two of the five films she made for Famous Players-Lasky (which would eventually evolve into Paramount Pictures), were regarded as being among her best work. One of the films, *Too Wise Wives* (1921) contrasted two marriages, focusing on the wives. One wife is selfless and devoted to home and family; the other is materialistic and self-absorbed. The film's message stressed the importance of the marriage arrangement. The film met with moderate success. More successful was *The Blot,* also released in 1921. The film focused on a proud-but-poor family loathing to accept charity, and the plot provided Weber with a vehicle that allowed her to condemn a society that places capitalistic pursuits above the intellectual and moral. The most remarkable thing about the film was its ambiguous ending, where the audience was left to ponder the main characters' future. Such a conclusion was unheard of at the time. Perhaps because of this innovative ambiguity, *The Blot* is the best known of all Weber films. After *The Blot,* however, she would only make five more films.

Career Declined

In Weber's independent productions, her husband worked with her as an assistant director. But the couple's fortunes began to fall as her films became less and less successful at the box office. Works like Weber's, which had a heavy moralistic tone, once ruled the day in the early twentieth century, when Victorian attitudes prevailed. However, after World War I, the country's character was undergoing a significant change. Post-war disenchantment was helping to usher in the "Jazz age" and the "Roaring '20s." Weber's style was becoming increasingly unpopular with audiences.

By the middle of the 1920s, she had lost her independent company and she divorced her husband, who had become an alcoholic. The breakup, coupled with her career decline, led to Weber suffering a nervous breakdown. After the release of *A Chapter in Her Life,* in 1923, Weber would not direct another film for three years.

She finally returned to directing with *The Marriage Clause* in 1926, after she remarried. Weber followed that with *Sensation Seekers,* a film critical of then-current "Jazz Age" morality. That same year, she made her last silent film, *The Angel of Broadway,* which involved a cabaret dancer and a Salvation Army girl. The film was not well received. In the era of the "flapper," the plots of both films suggest that Weber was out of touch with the times and audiences.

Weber's last silent film, *Topsy and Eva,* was released in 1927. She made her next film seven years later; *White Heat* (1934), which was Weber's first and only sound motion picture. The independently produced film underscored just how out of touch with the public Weber had become. The rather tastelessly titled film involved miscegenation and racism on a Hawaii sugar plantation. Despite the potentially provocative elements, the film was dull and Weber had a hard time finding distributors.

Following that failure, the remainder of her career was vastly different from its peak. During the last five years of her life, Weber worked as a script doctor for Universal, the company where she once rose to the top of her profession as a director. After several years of illness, Weber died on November 13, 1939, in Hollywood, California. She was penniless and ignored by a once-fledgling industry that she helped nurture to maturity.

In later years, however, she was remembered by other film artists, as well as film historians. Weber was described as having a powerful personality, and she was a great influence on other contemporary woman directors including Frances Marion, Cleo Madison and Ruth Stonehouse. In addition, she helped male directors Frank Lloyd and Henry Hathaway at the start of their long and successful Hollywood careers. Hathaway would later praise Weber for the influence she had on his own work.

Books

International Dictionary of Films and Filmmakers, Volume 2: Directors, Fourth Edition, St. James Press, 2000.

Online

"If She Were Alive Today: Lois Weber," *CineWomenNY,* http://www.cinewomenny.org/cinenews/feb03/ifshewerealive.html (December 20, 2005).

"Lois Weber," *Reelwomen.com,* http://www.reelwomen.com/weberbio.html (December 26, 2005).

"Lois Weber: Woman Filmmaker," *The Projector Film and Media Journal,* http://www.bgsu.edu/departments/theatre/current/projector/vol3issue2folder/vol3issue2art3.htm (December 20, 2005). □

Wim Wenders

Among the directors who emerged during the new wave of German cinema in the 1970s, Wim Wenders (born 1945) has been paradoxically the most complex and, at times, the most commercially successful. His films *Paris, Texas* (1983) and *Wings of Desire* (1987) were among the most widely distributed art films of the 1980s.

Wenders, like many other European filmmakers, was fascinated and influenced by Hollywood cinema. His films, at times, have been difficult to follow, with multiple stories that might or might not be resolved, but they often used the forms of classic American film genres. Wenders used well-known American actors in fresh ways in his films, and beginning early in his career he wove rock music into his cinematic language. His fascination with music led to a new phase in his career later in

life, as he helped launch a worldwide interest in classic forms of Cuban music with his documentary *Buena Vista Social Club* (1999).

Raised in Postwar Germany

Wenders was born in Düsseldorf, Germany, on August 14, 1945, the day World War II ended in the Pacific. Germany had surrendered several months earlier and lay in ruins. "Growing up in postwar Germany wasn't exactly fun," he was quoted as saying in a New Zealand *Dominion Post* interview reproduced on the Asia Africa Intelligence Wire. "It was all about rebuilding the country. Very materialistic, and joyless, not that humor was ever an elaborate German quality." Wenders was the son of a doctor at a Catholic hospital. He was given the name Wim (pronounced Veem) Wenders, but a government official clinging to the last remains of German nationalism insisted that Wim was not a German name. So he was, in officialdom only, named Ernst Wilhelm Wenders.

The materialism of German life did not appeal to Wenders, who made his first film at age 12, pointing a movie camera out a window to record the movement of people and cars on the street below. For the rest of his career, his style would be characterized by long, reflective shots of pure background that provided a canvas on which the action of the film developed. Wenders at first wanted to become a watercolor painter, and his films, like watercolors, had muted, gentle color schemes. He made several stabs at a more practical career, dropping out of medical, philosophy and sociology programs at universities in Munich, Freiberg, and Düsseldorf, respectively. In Düsseldorf he met the young Austrian playwright Peter Handle, who would eventually write scripts for several of his films, and he began to think about a filmmaking career.

Wenders moved to Paris around 1966. He applied to art and film schools there and, with no track record or schooling in either field, was turned down by both. Finally he apprenticed himself to an engraver. But Wenders managed to give himself a film education in cinema-crazy Paris; he went to the Henri Langlois Cinémathèque, a well-known private film archive, nearly every night and, according to his own estimate, saw more than 1,000 films. When he returned to Germany in 1967 he was accepted at the Hochschule für Film und Fernsehen (Film and Television Institute). Before enrolling he completed a three-month internship at a German office of the American United Artists studio. That was enough to convince Wenders that a commercial film career was not what he wanted.

During his student career Wenders made short experimental films such as *Silver City* (1968), a three-minute montage of shots of a Munich street that recalled the film he had made at age 12. His graduation project was a full-length feature called *Summer in the City.*

Adopted Road Movie Genre

The titles of that and some other Wenders film were in English, as was the name of his film production company, Road Movies. As a youth, Wenders loved American culture, which, he told the *Dominion Post,* "offered the great alternatives: comic strips, movies, Tom Sawyer and Huckleberry Finn, chewing gum, rock 'n' roll. America seemed to offer one joyful adventure after another, and already as a little boy I collected pictures of skyscrapers and big cars and beautiful women with beautiful houses behind them and children that had the greatest toys." But Wenders was ambivalent about the effect of American commercialism on German film, and his film *Der amerikanische Freund* (The American Friend, 1977) depicted the negative effects of American culture. Wenders lived in New York in the early 1970s and spent five years in Los Angeles, California, in the late 1970s and early 1980s.

Wenders would adopt the road movie, an American genre filtered through various European influences, including that of German Romanticism, as his favored medium. His breakthrough film in art cinema circles was *Die Angst des Tormanns beim Elfmeter* (The Anxiety of the Goalie at the Penalty Kick, 1971), based on a play by Handke, which followed the often meaningless travels of a loner soccer goalie through Germany and Austria. The WDR (West German Radio) studio, impressed with that debut, signed Wenders to direct a conventional film adaptation of Nathaniel Hawthorne's novel *The Scarlet Letter* in 1972, a project Wenders completed but did not enjoy. He was quoted as saying in a Senses of Cinema essay that he would never make another film in which "no car, service station, television, or jukebox" was allowed to appear.

The American landscapes that figured in many Wenders films made an appearance in *Alice in den Städten* (Alice in the Cities, 1972), which featured the Chuck Berry song "Memphis" at an important juncture in the plot. For *Falsche Bewegung* (The Wrong Move, 1974), Wenders and Handke re-teamed to transplant a novel by Goethe, *Wilhelm Meisters Lehrjahre* (The Education of William Meister), into a distinctly alienated modern setting. *Im Lauf der Zeit* (Kings of the Road, 1975) was a road movie set in Germany but influenced in its look by the work of famed American photographer Walker Evans.

It was *Der Amerikanische Freund* that brought Wenders to international prominence. A thriller about a shady American art dealer who tricks a German picture framer into becoming an organized crime hit man, the film starred American actor Dennis Hopper, along with Germany's leading male actor, Swiss-born Bruno Ganz. The chemistry between the two on the set was explosive, but after they came to blows several times, the two became friends. The intensity of the relationship showed in the film, which was widely exhibited by American art film houses and university film societies. It attracted the eye of American director Francis Ford Coppola, who invited Wenders to make a film in Hollywood.

Married Ronee Blakely

The resulting film, *Hammett,* was a film biography of mystery writer Dashiell Hammett. Coppola was dissatisfied with the results of filming, and re-shot large parts of the film himself, so the final version was more Coppola than Wenders. The film gained little public notice, but Wenders used his extended sojourn in the United States to make new friends and gather new material. He married country-rock backup vocalist Ronee Blakely, but the marriage dissolved when he returned to Germany in the early 1980s. A lasting relationship was forged when Wenders met playwright and actor Sam Shepard on a soundstage next to the one where he was shooting *Hammett.* Shepard wrote the screenplay for *Paris, Texas,* which was released in 1983 and earned Wenders the Palme d'Or (Golden Palm) award, for Best Film, at the Cannes Film Festival in France the following year. The film was moderately successful commercially, beyond the usual art film circles.

Paris, Texas (1983), was a drama that featured actor Harry Dean Stanton as an amnesiac who wanders through the American Southwest and the rather futuristic cities of Los Angeles, California, and Houston, Texas. Wenders's treatment of American landscapes was widely praised; in the words of one commentator it seemed almost as though the landscape was a character in the film. The intense, almost surreal landscapes were reminiscent of those in the desert film *Zabriskie Point* (1971) by Italian director Michelangelo Antonioni, a filmmaker Wenders admired. The film's evocative score was by slide guitarist Ry Cooder, who would later inaugurate another important phase of Wenders's career.

Wenders would return to the United States several more times, but he said that *Paris, Texas* marked the end of the American phase of his career. He made the film *Tokyo-ga* (1985) in Japan, and then returned to Germany for the haunting *Der Himmel über Berlin* (The Skies over Berlin or

The Heavens over Berlin, 1987), usually known by its English title, *Wings of Desire*. Peter Handke wrote the screenplay of the film, which put a unique Wenders spin on the sentimental idea of angels watching over the inhabitants of a city. The film starred Bruno Ganz as an angel—with a long black coat and a ponytail in place of wings—who observes the lives of Berliners but wants to experience human feelings and sensations. Anticipating a technique used in several later American films, Wenders shot scenes pertaining to angels in black and white, but used color for the sphere of human existence. *Wings of Desire* featured American actor Peter Falk, best-known as TV's detective Columbo, playing himself, in a delightfully off-beat treatment of a familiar face. Wenders's fluid camera work, gliding through the streets and alleys of Berlin like the angels depicted in the story, won rapturous praise from critics, and international audiences flocked to the film. *Wings of Desire* was remade in the United States as *City of Angels* in 1998.

Wenders's films of the 1990s, including the *Wings of Desire* sequel *In weiter Ferne, so nah!* (Far Away, So Close, 1993), were not as well received as his earlier works, even though Wenders continued to attract famous guest stars—Soviet leader Mikhail Gorbachev had a small role in *Far Away, So Close,* and Mel Gibson appeared in *The Million Dollar Hotel,* one of two Wenders films made in Los Angeles. Wenders scored a major triumph, however, with *Buena Vista Social Club,* a 1999 documentary he made about a community of aging Cuban musicians discovered by Ry Cooder. Wenders's film earned an Academy Award nomination for best documentary feature, and, in conjunction with several Cooder-produced albums, touched off a renewal of popularity for Cuban music around the world.

In the early 2000s Wenders continued to explore musical themes with a contribution to Martin Scorese's *The Blues,* an anthology that compiled segments by various directors who addressed aspects of the blues tradition. His 2005 film *Don't Come Knocking* reunited him with Sam Shepard, who played a washed-up cowboy film actor who seeks out his family in Montana. Top stars, including Jessica Lange and Eva Marie Saint, continued to jump at the chance to work with Wenders, and his German Romantic perspective on America continued to yield unique results.

Books

International Dictionary of Films and Filmmakers, Volume 2: Directors, 4th ed., St. James, 2000.

Kolker, Robert Philip, *The Films of Wim Wenders,* Cambridge, 1993.

Periodicals

Asia Africa Intelligence Wire, October 31, 2003.
New Statesman, January 2, 1998.
New Yorker, September 29, 2003.
Time, May 9, 1988.
Variety, May 30, 2005.

Online

''Wim Wenders,'' *All Movie Guide,* http://www.allmovie.com (February 24, 2006).

''Wim Wenders Biography,'' Images Journal, http://www .imagesjournal.com/issue01/features/wenders.htm (February 24, 2006).

''Wim Wenders,'' Senses of Cinema, http://www.senses ofcinema.com/contents/directors/03/wenders.html (February 24, 2006). □

Lucy Wheelock

American educator Lucy Wheelock (1857-1946) was one of the leading advocates in the kindergarten movement in the United States. A firm believer in the benefits of early childhood education, Wheelock established a school in Boston, Massachusetts, that trained the first generation of kindergarten teachers in the late nineteenth–and early twentieth–century America.

Wheelock came from an old New England family. She was born on February 1, 1857, in Cambridge, Vermont, the second of six children in her family. Her father Edwin was a graduate of the University of Vermont, and his parents had been among the first settlers of the Vermont town of Eden. Edwin Wheelock was a minister in the Congregationalist church, the same denomination that played an important role in early New England life in its Puritan era, and he was a leading figure in local and state politics. Wheelock's father was also Cambridge's superintendent of schools, and was elected to both the Vermont house and state senate.

Was Eager to Learn

Wheelock's parents valued education for all their children, including their daughters, which was a rather progressive idea at the time. Wheelock's mother, Laura Pierce Wheelock, was a teacher and ran a school in their home for a time, where Wheelock received her first lessons in reading, writing and math. At age 12, she entered the Underhill Academy in the Vermont town by that name, and a year later went on to Reading High School near Boston. She also traveled into the city for French lessons. After she graduated in 1874, she taught school in her hometown for a year, and then decided she would like to enter a nascent women's school, Wellesley College, which was offering four-year degrees.

Wheelock was not yet ready for college work, despite her high school diploma, and in 1876 headed to the Chauncy-Hall School in Boston, an elite private academy that had just begun to admit female students. Her family was not wealthy, but her father knew the Chauncy-Hall headmaster, and Wheelock's tuition fees were waived in return for office work. She never made it into Wellesley, for at Chauncy-Hall she became enthralled with its new kindergarten laboratory school. In her unpublished autobiography, Wheelock wrote that ''the one thing that makes life worth living is to serve a cause, and the greatest cause that can be served is Childhood Education," she said, according to an article by Catherine C. DuCharme in *Childhood Education*. "From the first day of my kindergarten experience I dedicated my life to such service."

The kindergarten concept was barely forty years old in the United States at the time. It had originated in Germany, the term coined by noted educator Friedrich Fröbel (1782-1852). He had endured a sad childhood. In 1837, Fröbel started a "Play and Activity Institute" in Bad Blankenburg, a spa town in the state of Thuringia. He renamed it a *kindergarten,* or "garden for children," around 1840. Though it was somewhat regimented, Fröbel's classroom offered young children an opportunity for learning via interaction with other children, songs and games, and independent playtime. He also devised a set of geometric blocks known as Fröbel's Gifts, which could be assembled in various combinations to form three-dimensional structures. Architect Frank Lloyd Wright (1867-1959) owned a set of them as a child, and later wrote that they greatly later influenced his ideas for buildings.

Found Well-Connected Mentor

Fröbel's ideas caught on in Germany, especially after well-born and even royal women took them up. At the castle of one benefactor, he ran a school that granted its women graduates the *Kindergaertnerin* or "kindergarten teacher" title, which was the first professional degree for women in Europe. His ideas came to the United States via a wave of German immigration, and one of his former students founded the first American kindergarten in 1838 in Columbus, Ohio, which had many German-Americans. Another German-born woman, Margarethe (Margaretta) Meyer Schurz, founded a similar school in Dodge County, Wisconsin in the 1850s.

These first kindergartens were German–language schools that served local immigrants. The first English-language kindergarten was founded in Boston in 1860 by Elizabeth Peabody, a pioneer in early childhood education and follower of Fröbel who soon became a mentor to Wheelock. After her visit to the Chauncy-Hall kindergarten, Wheelock sought out Peabody, who suggested she enroll in a kindergarten–teacher training school that Ella Snelling Hatch ran in Boston. It was a one-year course, and Wheelock and another woman were its only students. She returned to Chauncy-Hall in 1879, fully trained in Fröbel's theories, and became an assistant in the kindergarten school and eventually oversaw it.

Wheelock varied from Fröbel's model and drew some criticism from the more conservative adherents of the kindergarten movement. As a kindergarten teacher, she installed a sandbox in her classroom, and wrote her own songs and stories for the children. Her reputation spread, and she was often asked to lecture in communities that were considering starting their own early-childhood classes in their public school systems. In 1888, when the Boston city council voted to launch a kindergarten program, Wheelock was invited to train the necessary teachers. Chauncy-Hall would play host to this program, which had few qualified teachers for the age group. There were just six students in

Wheelock's first class of teacher-hopefuls, but her program quickly caught on and became an appealing profession for middle-class women. Two years later, in 1890, "Miss Wheelock's Kindergarten Training School" was founded as an independent institution.

Promoted "The Ideal Republic"

Wheelock believed strongly in the notion that early-childhood education provided the foundation for a stable society. In 1891, she reminded educators at a convention of the American Institute of Instruction about the value of kindergartens. "The ideal kindergarten is the ideal republic," she said, according to DuCharme's *Childhood Education* article. "Its little citizens are trained to self-activity, self-control, and the 'due freedom' which comes from a regard for the rights and happiness of others."

Wheelock used one of Fröbel's books, *Mother Play,* as her main textbook, and adhered to his two main ideas: that children needed self-activity for intellectual growth, which involved seeing, thinking and acting for his or herself, and she also supported the idea of continuity—that there should be no break or gap between kindergarten and the primary grades. She also advocated involving mothers in early education, and they could reinforce in the home the benefits of the kindergarten curriculum. She became well-known nationally. A founding member of the International Kindergarten Union (IKU) in 1893 and its president from 1895 to 1899, she also served as chair of the 1908 National Congress of Mothers, the forerunner of the Parent Teacher Association.

The usefulness of kindergarten was still an open debate. In 1912, Wheelock told an audience at the National Education Association in Washington that "the advocates of the theory that the young child is a 'little animal,' and should be left free to carry out his animal impulses in some convenient back yard, forget the scarcity of back yards in a congested city district," she said, according to DuCharme's *Childhood Education* profile. "They also ignore the worldwide proof of the claim that those who guide the first seven years of a child's life may make of him what they will. The state may later have to pay $255 a year to protect itself from the neglected child," likely referring to the cost of prison, noting that a kindergarten year cost the state about one-tenth that figure.

Grew into Four-Year College

Despite skeptics, the kindergarten movement expanded rapidly, as did Wheelock's school over the years. In 1914, it opened in a new home on Boston's Riverway, and by 1929 was offering a three-year course that required graduates to spend time as student teachers. Wheelock remained head of the school until she retired in 1940. Before she departed, she arranged for its incorporation as a nonprofit institution, Wheelock College, which began granting standard, four-year bachelor of science degrees in 1941. She died of coronary thrombosis at her Boston home on October 2, 1946.

Wheelock left behind an impressive body of written work on early education. She authored dozens of articles for the *Journal of Education* and other professional publications, and co-wrote *Talks to Mothers* in 1920. She also translated children's stories from German, most notably two volumes by Johanna Spyri, the author of *Heidi*, a story that was the basis for a much-loved 1937 movie starring Shirley Temple. Wheelock did not translate that title, but brought Spyri's *Red-Letter Stories* and *Swiss Stories for Children* to an English-speaking readership. She also translated some of Fröbel's writings.

In 1937, she commemorated the hundredth anniversary of Fröbel's first kindergarten in a *New York Times* article. "In the modern school for 4 and 5 year olds," she wrote, "where children cover the floor with construction projects, with blocks as big as bricks, there is little external reminder of the old-time kindergarten where youngsters sat in a stiff circle or waited at their little tables with folded hands for a signal to open boxes of tiny blocks or geometric toys." She added that early-childhood ideas had become somewhat less structured, but "the daily program still shows, however, the kindergartners' agreement with Fröbel that 'play is a child's serious business' and is his introduction to the business of life."

Books

Dictionary of American Biography, Supplement 4: *1946-1950.* American Council of Learned Societies, 1974.

Periodicals

Childhood Education, Spring 2000.
New York Times, July 8, 1891; April 18, 1937.

Online

"Biography of Lucy Wheelock," http://www.wheelock genealogy.com/wheelockweb/pages/lucywbio.htm (January 2, 2006).
"Lucy Wheelock's Vision," Wheelock College, http://www .wheelock.edu/lucy/lucyhome.htm (January 2, 2006). □

Reggie White

For a decade and a half, Reggie White (1961-2004) dominated the National Football League as one of its most ferocious defensive players. White habitually struck terror into opposing offenses with his great strength, but he also possessed speed, stamina, and the ability to size up situations for maximum impact.

Former Philadelphia Eagles head coach Buddy Ryan once called White the "perfect defensive lineman . . . probably the most gifted defensive athlete I've ever been around." After eight seasons with the Eagles, in 1993 White signed a four-year, $17-million contract with the Green Bay Packers; it was an unprecedented amount for a defensive player. Upon his retirement from the NFL in 2001, White was credited with a record 198 career sacks; he had been named to the Pro Bowl an impressive 13 times in succession (although he failed to play in 1994 due to injury).

In 1999, the Green Bay Packers retired White's jersey number (92) after his retirement from that team.

Loved His Tennessee Home

White was born on December 19, 1961, and raised in Tennessee. He went to college there—at the University of Tennessee—and he called that state home his entire life. As a child he lived in Chattanooga, where he was raised by his mother and his grandparents. The family was deeply religious; they attended the local Baptist church regularly, and as a youngster White was inspired by the ministers and teachers he met there. He did not undergo a single, charismatic experience of faith, but rather found his ties to Christianity growing stronger over the entire period of his youth. His mother, Thelma Collier, told *Sports Illustrated* that when he was 12 years old he announced that he wanted to be two things: a football player and a minister.

Football was a welcome outlet for a young Christian who was teased and goaded by bullies. "When I was a child, I was always bigger than the other kids," White told *Sports Illustrated.* "Kids used to call me Bigfoot or Land of the Giant. They'd tease me and run away. Around seventh grade, I found something I was good at. I could play football, and I could use my size and achieve success by playing within the rules. I remember telling my mother that someday I would be a professional football player and I'd take care of her for the rest of my life."

White's strength and size indeed seemed to be God-given. He never lifted weights or conditioned himself rigorously, but he was always in shape. At Howard High School in Chattanooga, he played both football and basketball, earning All-America honors in football and all-state honors in basketball. Numerous colleges recruited him, but he chose to stay near home and enrolled at the University of Tennessee, whose team, the Volunteers, were glad to have him. He was a talented and determined athlete who spent his Sundays preaching sermons in churches all over the state. As a senior in 1983, he was a consensus All-American and one of four finalists for the Lombardi Award given annually to the outstanding college lineman. (He did not win.) During his years with the Volunteers, White earned the nickname "minister of defense." The named followed him into his professional career, which began in 1984.

For a while it appeared that White might never leave Tennessee. After graduating from college he signed a five-year, $4 million contract with the Memphis Showboats, one of the teams in the fledgling United States Football League (USFL). The USFL began as an alternative league for cities starved for professional football action. From the outset it was dwarfed by the better-known, better-staffed National Football League, and soon the upstart teams foundered financially. White viewed this financial instability with concern. He also wanted to prove himself against the best players in the game. He began the 1985 season with the USFL but defected to the Philadelphia Eagles. With his wife, Sara—whom he had met in church—he ventured north to join the NFL.

Jumped from USFL to NFL

White took a salary cut in Philadelphia. The Eagles signed him to a four-year, $1.85 million deal after buying out the remaining three years on his Memphis contract. At the time White was still an unproven entity, but his anonymity did not last long. He joined the Eagles after the 1985 season had begun, missing the first few games. When he finally did start, he made ten tackles and two-and-a-half sacks in his very first game. By season's end he had turned in 13 sacks in as many games, and he was named NFC defensive rookie of the year.

Curiously enough, White's singular gift for mayhem began and ended on the gridiron during his 15-year career with the NFL. The rest of his time was always been spent in pursuing humanitarian work inspired by his deep Christian faith. The citizens of Philadelphia soon discovered that they had won the services of more than just a star athlete. "I believe that I've been blessed with physical ability in order to gain a platform to preach the gospel," White told *Sports Illustrated.* "A lot of people look at athletes as role models, and to be successful as an athlete, I've got to do what I do, hard but fair. . . . I try to live a certain way, and maybe that'll have some kind of effect. I think God has allowed me to have an impact on a few people's lives." White spent hours and hours of his spare time preaching on street corners in Philadelphia's troubled inner-city neighborhoods. He gave money to dozens of Christian outreach organizations and spoke as a member of the Fellowship of Christian Athletes. And he led by example. In the rough-and-tumble world of

professional football, none of his opponents or teammates could ever recall hearing him curse or seeing him fight.

White blossomed in 1986 with the arrival of Buddy Ryan as the Eagles' head coach. Ryan had made a name for himself as a defensive coordinator and had worked with some great lines, including the Chicago Bears and the Minnesota Vikings. Quickly Ryan assessed White's potential and built the defense around him. Opponents tried to double- and triple-team White, but still he achieved more than 11 quarterback sacks each season. In his first season under Ryan, he made 18 sacks in 16 games. He was also named Most Valuable Player at the annual Pro Bowl after sacking the opposing quarterback four times in that game. In 1987 he led the league with an NFC-record 21 sacks, and most certainly would have broken the all-time record had the season not been shortened by a players' strike.

Emerged as Team Leader

That players' strike—a particularly bitter one—saw White emerge as a team leader. As one of the team-voted union representatives, White worked hard to keep his fellow Eagles united in the face of "replacement" teams and fan apathy. Didinger wrote in the *Philadelphia Daily News:* "One of the more memorable images of that 1987 season was White wearing a picket sign and blocking a bus loaded with replacement players as it attempted to pull into a South Jersey hotel. . . . [White] spoke loudly and passionately about the need for the veterans to stick together. Other teams broke ranks: the Eagles never did."

The hard feelings between White and the Eagles' front office probably began to develop during this strike season, intensifying as the years passed, but White's continued dominance on the field allayed any talk of trade or release. In 1988 he led the NFL in sacks for the second straight year. Between 1989 and 1991 he was joined on the defensive line by several equally ferocious teammates, including Clyde Simmons, Seth Joyner, and Jerome Brown. This potent defense—with White still as anchor—was widely considered the best in pro football by 1991.

Observers marveled at the way White roared into every play of every game without ever seeming tired or distracted. White told *Sports Illustrated:* "In high school and college you're taught to hit the ground on a double team. Here you're expected to take it on. I get double-teamed on every play, so I expect it. Sacks are great, and they get you elected to the Pro Bowl. But I've always felt that a great defensive lineman has to play the run and the pass equally well. . . . The so-called men of the game pride themselves on being complete players."

In 1989 White signed a four-year, $6.1 million contract that made him the highest-paid defensive player in the NFL at the time. The deal came at the tail end of considerable acrimony between White and the Eagles' ownership and management. Didinger described the relationship between White and the Eagles' brass, headed by owner Norman Braman: "They split on so many issues—the 1987 players' strike, the 1990 firing of head coach Buddy Ryan, the 1992 loss of free agent Keith Jackson—that in the end they had nothing to build on. There was no trust, no goodwill to serve as the foundation for constructive talks." Although he continued to play at the top of his game under new Eagles coach Rich Kotite, White became privately convinced that owner Braman was not pursuing a championship with any great vigor.

As the end of his 1989 contract approached, White grew more and more critical of Braman and his decisions. In the press White suggested that the Eagles' training facilities were inadequate. White spoke of the growing chasm between Braman and the Eagles players, using his own chilly relations with the owner as an example. Not surprisingly, White became one of the plaintiffs in a 1992 lawsuit against the NFL ownership to enlarge the powers of free agency.

Joined the Packers

Unrestricted free agency descended upon the NFL officially on March 1, 1993. Reggie White quickly became the most visible—and sought-after—unrestricted free agent after the 1992-93 football season. His contract with the Eagles had expired, and although he claimed that he would not mind staying in Philadelphia, he was not tendered another offer there. As it happened, Green Bay was one of a half dozen teams that bid quite openly for White's services at that time. He flew to Atlanta, Cleveland, Detroit, Green Bay, New York City, and Washington, D.C., as an all-out war erupted to sign the powerful defensive end. Everywhere he went he was courted not only by team owners, management, and player personnel, but also by ordinary citizens who had heard about his community work and his Christian ethics. In the end, White signed with Wisconsin's Green Bay Packers. The Packers' offer was the most generous financially, with guaranteed earnings of $17 million over four years. Under the contract White became the most highly paid defender in the NFL and a pioneer in the heady new world of unrestricted free agent contracts.

Joining the Packers for the 1993 season, White left behind good will in Philadelphia, where he played for the Eagles through eight seasons. *Philadelphia Daily News* correspondent Ray Didinger called White "a man who made a giant impact . . . a symbol of hope, for the Eagles and for the city in general." Didinger added: "White is more than just a superb football player. He is an ordained Baptist minister whose tireless work in the community touched thousands of lives. He is a man who always wore his heart on his extra-long sleeve."

During his years with the Eagles, White had was named annually to play in the Pro Bowl beginning in 1986; he continued the tradition during his years with Green Bay through 1998, to realize the longest consecutive run of Pro Bowl participation on record. When the Packers won the world championship at the Super Bowl in 1997, White set a Super Bowl game record with three quarterback sacks. The Associated Press named White the defensive player of the year for the second time in his career after the 1998 season, and he announced his retirement soon afterward in 1999. Green Bay honored White's retirement by retiring his jersey number, which was 92, and he spent one year out of football and involved in his ministry.

White returned for one final season in the NFL, lured from retirement for the 2000 season by the Carolina Pan-

thers who paid him one million dollars for the effort. He retired for the second time at the end of that season, leaving behind an NFL record of 198 career sacks after 15 seasons of play. White was voted by the NFL Hall of Fame to the NFL All-time Team in 2000.

Retired to Ministry

White's other career—carrying the gospel of Christ to those in need—lasted his entire life. He and his wife built Hope Place, a shelter for unwed mothers, on property near their home in rural Tennessee; they also founded the Alpha & Omega Ministry to sponsor a community development bank in Knoxville. "I'm trying to build up black people's morale, self-confidence and self-reliance to show them that the Jesus I'm talking about is real," White explained in *Ebony*.

One of the most trying moments in White's career in the ministry came in 1996, when his church was burnt to the ground, one of dozens of black churches torched throughout the South in a string of hate crimes. Throughout the off-season that year, White badgered investigators to discover the arsonist, lobbied lawmakers—including then vice president Al Gore of Tennessee—to speak out against racial violence, and raised money to help his and other black churches throughout the nation. In addition to this work, White pursued missionary work among teenaged gang members, abused children, and young women seeking an alternative to abortion. He also tithed a good portion of his NFL income to several Baptist churches. Reflecting on his work in the *Philadelphia Daily News*, the "minister of defense" concluded: "The Bible says, 'Faith without works is dead.' That is just another way of saying: 'Put your money where your mouth is.'"

White's life work came to an untimely end on December 26, 2004, when he was rushed to the hospital for what was termed a respiratory illness and soon pronounced dead. According to *Jet*, family spokesman Keith Johnson stated that White's death "was not only unexpected, but it was also a complete surprise. Reggie wasn't a sick man . . . he was vibrant. He had lots and lots of energy, lots of passion." In his local church and across the NFL, friends, former players, and fans of White spoke of their sadness at his passing. NFL commissioner Paul Tagliabue issued a statement which read in part: "Reggie White was a gentle warrior who will be remembered as one of the greatest defensive players in NFL history. Equally as impressive as his achievements on the field was the positive impact he made off the field and the way he served as a positive influence on so many young people."

Periodicals

Atlanta Journal and Constitution, August 29, 1993.
Ebony, December 1993.
Jet, September 15, 1986; April 26, 1993; January 29, 1996; November 1, 1999; August 21, 2000; March 19, 2001; January 17, 2005.
Los Angeles Times, October 21, 1989.
New York Times, April 7, 1993.
Philadelphia Daily News, June 7, 1991; April 7, 1993; April 8, 1993.

Sporting News, July 12, 1993; September 13, 1993; July 8, 1996; January 14, 2005.

Sports Illustrated, September 3, 1986; November 27, 1989; March 15, 1993; May 3, 1993; September 2, 1996; January 10, 2005.

USA Today, February 11, 1991; August 4, 1993.

Wall Street Journal, August 20, 1993.

Washington Post, March 14, 1993; March 18, 1993. □

Robert Wise

Best known as the director of the musical smash hits ***West Side Story*** **and** ***The Sound of Music,*** **in the 1960s, director Robert Wise (1914-2005) had a long list of credits that included several other important films as well. Early in his career, he also served as editor on the landmark film** ***Citizen Kane.***

Wise's contributions have sometimes been over-looked by film students and historians, for he did not have one of the distinctive directorial styles that inspire passion in cinema devotees. Instead, he made films in many genres, from war dramas to horror and science fiction genre pieces, from three-handkerchief weepers to serious social tales. And, having avoided musicals for most of his career, he made two of the most famous musicals of all as his career hit its peak. If Wise was under-rated by students of film, his craft was recognized by his fellow directors and industry figures, who honored him richly toward the end of his long life.

Saw Several Movies a Week

Wise was born September 10, 1914, in Winchester, Indiana, and grew up in Connersville in the east-central part of the state. His father was a meatpacker. As a youth Wise went to the movies as often as four times a week, but his first dream was to become a sportswriter. After graduating from high school in 1929 he enrolled at Indiana's Franklin College to study journalism, but the family funds ran out during the Great Depression of the early 1930s. Unable to find a job at home, he took advantage of a family connection in one of the few industries that was hiring: his brother was an accountant at the RKO film studio in Hollywood, so he went to work there in 1933 as a porter, carrying cans of film from one part of the building to another.

Spending plenty of time in RKO's cutting rooms, Wise got a practical course in film editing, and he found a place in the growing industry for his talents. His first film credit was as assistant editor on the film *Stage Door* in 1937, and by 1939 he was serving as editor on such major productions as a remake of *The Hunchback of Notre Dame,* starring Charles Laughton as the unfortunate Quasimodo. He was still considered a fresh face, however, when he met Orson Welles in 1941, as Welles was laying plans for *Citizen Kane,* his ambitious, lightly fictionalized biography of muckraking newspaper publisher William Randolph Hearst.

That was what attracted Welles; he wanted someone "young and uninfluenced by tradition," according to the *Independent.* Wise was hired as editor, and the relationship was mutually beneficial. The clarity and intensity of *Citizen Kane* shaped Wise's approach to filmmaking. "There are a few things I'm sure I learned from him," Wise was quoted as saying in the *Independent.* "One was to try and keep the energy level high, the movement forward in the telling of the story. Another was the use of deep-focus photography. I've shot many of my films, particularly in black-and-white, with wide-angle lenses, so we could have somebody close in the foreground and still have things in the background in focus." As for Welles, although he later tried to claim credit for much of the editing himself, he benefited from a superb job by Wise; others on the set confirmed Wise's key role. Wise earned a 1941 Academy Award nomination for best editing.

Wise and Welles reunited for Welles's next film, *The Magnificent Ambersons,* but this time the collaboration ended less happily. Set in Indianapolis, the film was a complex family drama with an unsympathetic central character, and it tested badly among preview audiences. Executives at the financially troubled RKO panicked, demanded that the original 148-minute film be cut by about an hour, and brought in Wise to direct several new scenes that clarified the action; Welles was in South America, working on a documentary that was never finished; he felt that Wise had butchered the film, but Wise maintained that he had done the best he could under the circumstances. He was partially vindicated by the later reputation of *The Magnificent*

Ambersons as one of the greatest of all American films, even in its shortened state. In the midst of this drama in 1942, Wise married actress Patricia Doyle. They had one son.

Directed Critically Praised Boxing Film

Although Welles may have been dismayed by Wise's actions, the new director was rewarded by RKO. He was asked to step in as director on another behind-schedule film, *The Curse of the Cat People,* in 1944, and when he wrapped that film in ten days he was put behind the camera for several more films. *Mademoiselle Fifi* (1944) was a film of a Guy de Maupassant short story, *Boule de Suif,* about a prostitute who saves a carriage-load of aristocrats during the Franco-Prussian War, and *The Body Snatcher,* starring Boris Karloff, inaugurated Wise's involvement with the horror genre. Wise was behind the camera regularly in the late 1940s, but most of his films were "B-movies," low-budget productions designed for quick consumption at neighborhood cinemas in the days before television. The young director scored his first high-profile success in 1949 with *The Set-Up;* based on a blank-verse poem about a boxer who refuses to throw a fight at the behest of an organized-crime syndicate, it was filmed in "real time," with the elapsed time of the action matching that of the film itself.

The film won raves from attendees at France's famed Cannes Film Festival, but RKO dropped Wise after being acquired by millionaire Howard Hughes in 1950. Undeterred, Wise moved to 20th Century Fox and made the melodrama *Three Secrets.* The following year he directed one of his most highly regarded films, the science-fiction thriller *The Day the Earth Stood Still,* in 1951. The film's story of an alien visitor who warns humans of the dangers of war has been taken as everything from a commentary on the Cold War to a religious allegory. Wise himself was ambiguous about the significance of the alien Klaatu (Michael Rennie). "Put a beard on him and you could have the Christ figure," he is said to have remarked, according to the *Daily Telegraph,* but the *Independent* quoted him as saying that he had missed the potential significance of the fact that Klaatu takes the name Carpenter after being brought back from the dead. "Maybe I was just dumb enough that I didn't catch it," Wise said; the self-effacement was typical. Wise personally selected the composers of soundtracks for his films; he turned in this and several other cases to Bernard Herrmann, whose score was one of the first to use electronic instruments.

Wise became one of Hollywood's most versatile directors over the course of the 1950s, directing the comedy *Something for the Birds* (1952), several war films including *The Desert Rats* (1953) and *Until They Sail* (1957), the big-business drama *Executive Suite* (1954), and the unsuccessful costume epic *Helen of Troy* (1955). *Somebody Up There Likes Me,* a biography of boxer Rocky Graziano, put Wise back in the boxing ring; Graziano was slated to be played by James Dean, whose death resulted in the launch of Paul Newman's career. Wise scored another major critical success with *I Want to Live!* in 1958, a film that brought Susan Hayward the Academy Award for best actress and a best director nomination for Wise himself. The film concerned

an unjust application of capital punishment, and Wise visited the Death Row area of a prison prior to filming in order to familiarize himself with the atmosphere.

These successes led to Wise being selected, along with choreographer Jerome Robbins, to direct the big-budget film adaptation of the Broadway musical *West Side Story* in 1961. The two directors worked through the kinks of the difficult dual-helm arrangement, with Wise supervising the dramatic scenes and Robbins directing the musical numbers. When the film fell behind schedule, though, Robbins was removed in what Wise, according to the *Independent,* called "a very uncomfortable, emotional, and difficult time for everybody." Wise, working with Robbins's assistants, succeeded in bringing the film together, and it became a major commercial success.

Diminished *Sound of Music*'s Sentimental Aspects

In between his two major musicals, Wise made several well-regarded films including *The Haunting* (1963), considered a small classic of the horror genre. He was a logical choice to film *The Sound of Music,* a Broadway show by Rodgers and Hammerstein, in 1965, although he at first refused the assignment and had to be talked into taking on the film by screenwriter Ernest Lehman. Wise intervened to minimize some of the more treacly passages in the original, moving the song "My Favorite Things" to a scene in which lead actress Julie Andrews comforts a group of children during a thunderstorm, among other changes. Some critics found the film's juxtaposition of nuns and Nazis overly sweet anyway, but *The Sound of Music* became one of the most financially successful films of all time. Wise won Academy Awards for Best Director for both *West Side Story* and *The Sound of Music.*

Wise's films of the late 1960s were made on a grand scale and were not uniformly successful; the 1966 epic *The Sand Pebbles* did well at the box office, but *Star!* (1968), a sharp-edged musical film biography of stage comedienne Gertrude Lawrence, bombed despite its reuniting of Wise with Andrews. Wise always felt that the film had been underrated, and Andrews returned to satirical comedy later in her career with *Victor/Victoria.* Wise did somewhat better with *The Andromeda Strain,* a 1971 film about an alien virus running rampant on Earth.

Two more big-budget films were entrusted to Wise in the 1970s. *The Hindenburg* (1975), one of a series of disaster epics that absorbed moviegoers of the day, and Wise's last major film, *Star Trek: The Motion Picture,* released in 1979. Though fans of the original television series on which it was based felt that Wise had not successfully transferred the feel of the series to film, the movie did well at the box office and launched a durable series of *Star Trek* films.

After the death of his wife Patricia, Wise continued to live in Hollywood; he married Millicent Franklin in 1977. He often encouraged younger filmmakers in his positions as president of the Academy of Motion Picture Arts and Sciences and the Directors Guild of America, and he reaped lifetime-achievement honors from those organizations. Among his admirers was director Martin Scorsese. Wise remained active, directing a musical about homeless children, *Rooftops,* in 1989 and making a television film, *A Storm in Summer,* in 2000—well into his ninth decade. Wise died in Los Angeles, California, on September 14, 2005. "Bob's devotion to the craft of filmmaking and his wealth of head-and-heart knowledge about what we do and how we do it was a special gift to his fellow directors," Directors' Guild of America president Michael Apted told *Variety.* "We will deeply miss him."

Books

Carr, Charmian, *Forever Lies!: A Memoir of The Sound of Music,* Penguin, 2001.

Periodicals

Chicago Tribune, September 16, 2005.
Daily Telegraph (London, England); September 16, 2005.
Daily Variety, September 16, 2005.
Entertainment Weekly, September 30, 2005.
Herald (Glasgow, Scotland), September 17, 2005.
Independent (London, England), September 16, 2005.
New York Times, September 16, 2005.
Time, September 26, 2005.
Times (London, England), September 16, 2005.

Online

"Robert Wise," All Movie Guide, http://www.allmovie.com (January 1, 2006). □

Mary Wollstonecraft

English writer Mary Wollstonecraft (1759-1797) and her most famous work, *A Vindication of the Rights of Woman,* both achieved immense notoriety in Georgian England of the 1790s. The book is considered the first written document of the modern feminist movement, and in it Wollstonecraft argued in favor of full legal, social, and economic rights for women. Her achievements and renown, however, could not save her from the most dangerous of all social ills for women in her day—that of childbirth and its attendant medical risks. She died several days after giving birth to her daughter, the novelist Mary Wollstonecraft Shelley, author of *Frankenstein.*

Wollstonecraft was born on April 27, 1759, in Hoxton, near London, England, as the second of seven children in the family. Her grandfather had made a fortune as a master weaver in London and through profitable real estate investments as well, but Wollstonecraft's father, Edward, squandered much of that inheritance. He attempted to establish himself as a gentleman farmer, but nearly all of his ventures failed. Because of this, the family moved several times when Wollstonecraft was a child, and kept growing in size despite their economic hardships. The pressures led Wollstonecraft's father into alcoholism, and the related abuse he inflicted upon his wife, Elizabeth, had a profound impact on their daughter and her attitudes toward marriage.

Disliked Tedium of "Women's Work"

The Wollstonecrafts lived in Yorkshire from 1768 to 1774, on a farm called Walkington in the Wolds. This would be the longest time that Wollstonecraft ever lived in one place in her life. She was sent to a local country school for girls, where the courses were skewed toward housekeeping arts like sewing and gardening. The idea was to prepare adolescent girls for their future roles as wives, mothers, and proper middle-class ladies. After the Walkington farm failed, the Wollstonecrafts lived in Hoxton once again, and then spent a year in Wales before moving back to London. During this period of her life, Wollstonecraft met Frances (Fanny) Blood, who would become her closest friend. She also supplemented her rudimentary education by reading extensively from religious, historical, and philosophical books she managed to buy or borrow, and kept up with current events through newspapers and journals.

Tired of living under her father's tyranny, the 19-year-old Wollstonecraft disobeyed her parents by taking a job as a paid companion to a wealthy widow in Bath, a resort town that was a popular destination for England's newly moneyed classes. After two years, she returned home to care for her mother, whose health was declining. After her mother died, Wollstonecraft lived with Blood's family, and in 1784 the two women, along with two of Wollstonecraft's sisters, founded a boarding school for young women in the north London neighborhood of Islington.

A year later, Blood married and moved to Portugal, but died due to complications from childbirth. Wollstonecraft had already sailed to visit her, and in her absence the school was mismanaged by the Wollstonecraft sisters, who had little financial know-how. It closed in 1786. Wollstonecraft then spent ten months as a governess for the children of Lord and Lady Kingsborough in County Cork, Ireland. As with her paid companionship in Bath, she found the experience degrading, though the children liked her. She reportedly had some memorable battles with Lady Kingsborough.

Found Her Calling as a Writer

The Islington school experience had one positive outcome: it was near the community parkland of Newington Green, and Wollstonecraft fell in with a group of liberal-minded intellectuals known as the Newington Green circle. The group was headed by a Unitarian minister, Richard Price, and they welcomed the spirited, well-read young woman to their discussion groups. The circle served to introduce Wollstonecraft to several influential figures, including the publisher Joseph Johnson, who in 1787 hired her to serve as an editorial assistant for his *New Analytical Review*. Johnson also published Wollstonecraft's first book, *Thoughts on the Education of Daughters*, that same year. The work is a collection of essays for parents concerning schooling and self-esteem issues for girls and young women.

The following year, Wollstonecraft's first novel, *Mary: A Fiction*, was published. The semi-autobiographical work, written in the third person, follows the story of an unhappy wife inside an arranged marriage, who is left alone for long periods of time by her husband. Her close friend dies in Portugal, she finds herself drawn to a male acquaintance, who also dies, and finds little purpose in her life except for charity work.

Wollstonecraft was by then living a life that was drastically opposite to the one she imagined as a married woman's plight. She was independent and had her own income, which was no small feat for a woman of her era and class. At the time, women did not attend university or work outside the home unless they were part of the working classes and took part in menial or farm labor. But Wollstonecraft had her own flat in London, and was able to help her sisters out financially as well. Another book of hers that was published in 1788, *Original Stories, from Real Life*, was the first of her titles to sell well, and part of its appeal seemed to be in the unlikable main characters, two sisters who are the daughters of an affluent family but have little education. Some of the aspects of this book were thought to have been modeled on the Kingsborough family in County Cork.

Challenged Major Political Figure

A rush of new books were printed in the wake of the French Revolution of 1789, a pivotal event in European history that was a beacon of hope for the oppressed while giving a corresponding sense of unease to the rich. Wollstonecraft wrote for the *New Analytical Review*, and also taught herself German, French and Dutch, so that she might translate titles published abroad on philosophy for extra income. Wollstonecraft became part of a well known group of London liberals known as the Johnson circle, and they were collectively outraged at the response from Edmund Burke, a well known member of the House of Commons who had formerly supported the revolt of the American colonies against the British crown. In his *Reflections on the Revolution in France*, Burke argued in support of a hereditary monarchy and an aristocratic class, and warned that events in France would end badly.

Burke's treatise caused a stir in England, and prompted Wollstonecraft to quickly write *A Vindication of the Rights of Man*, which was published anonymously by Johnson in December of 1790, just a month following Burke's book. A second edition issued shortly afterward appeared with Wollstonecraft's name on it. She rebutted Burke's arguments one by one, and the ensuing political debate made her famous in London and throughout England. It was extremely rare for a woman to take part in such public or published discussions of current events, but it was her goal to prove that women were the equals of men on all levels except perhaps the physical.

Wollstonecraft's next book set forth those arguments and affirmed her place in feminist history. *A Vindication of the Rights of Woman* was published in 1792 by Johnson, and again caused a great stir. The author argued that all human beings, no matter their gender, are spiritually equal, and therefore women should be given the same educational opportunities as men. They should also enjoy equality in their marriages, and other legal and social rights. In one particular chapter, Wollstonecraft claimed that a lack of education leaves even well-married women unhappy and prone to torment their servants. "Domestics are deprived of innocent indulgences," she wrote, "and made to work beyond their strength, in order to enable the notable woman to keep a better table, and outshine her neighbours in finery and parade."

Wollstonecraft, meanwhile, continued to pursue her own unconventional lifestyle. She had for some time been platonically involved with Henry Fuseli, the Swiss painter and writer, but he was married. At one point she wrote to his wife, Sophia, and proposed they live in a non-sexual marital threesome, which Madame Fuseli rebuffed. Eager for a new adventure, Wollstonecraft went to Paris, France, so that she might write about the French Revolution firsthand. But the egalitarian spirit of the original event had been hijacked by reactionary forces in France, and a period of human rights abuses known as the "Terror" had arrived. Wollstonecraft was duly disillusioned, which was evident in her 1794 book, *An Historical and Moral View of the French Revolution, and the Effect it Has Produced in Europe*.

Became Single Parent

In Paris Wollstonecraft fell in love with an American explorer, writer and entrepreneur, Gilbert Imlay. He had been a soldier in the Revolutionary army, but was now a trader in alum and soap. The political climate of the Terror descended into such chaos that it became dangerous for British citizens in the city, and at one point Wollstonecraft went with Imlay to the U.S. Embassy, where she officially registered as his wife. They had not wed, but she was expecting her first child, and they set up housekeeping in Neuilly, outside Paris. As predictably as the husband in her novel *Mary*, Imlay left her alone for long periods of time, and dallied with other women. She followed him to Le Havre, where her daughter Fanny was born in May of 1794. He left her again, and she followed him to London, where she discovered he was living with another woman. Her response was a suicide attempt, perhaps by ingesting laudanum, an opium derivative, in May of 1795.

Imlay suggested she take on a business role for him, and arranged for her to travel to Scandinavia to serve as the agent for a new shipping venture of his. She took along the infant Fanny and a maid, and sailed for Goteborg, Sweden. She spent the months of June through October of 1795 traveling trough Sweden, Norway, and Denmark, much of it trying to track down a missing cargo of silver from one of Imlay's ships. It was a dangerous time to travel, with much of Europe at war, and Wollstonecraft was not able to resolve the question of the stolen silver. She did write many letters to Imlay, which were published after her death as *Letters Written during a Short Residence in Sweden, Norway, and Denmark*. Literary critics consider them the best examples of Wollstonecraft's writing, containing her eloquently worded observations of the countryside, cities, and people of Scandinavia, mixed with declarations of her passion for Imlay.

Back in London, however, Wollstonecraft found Imlay living with a stage actress. Distraught, she walked out of her house in an October rainstorm to a bridge over the Thames River, where she tried to commit suicide once again but was saved by fishermen. Her romantic life improved three months later, when she became reacquainted with William Godwin, whom she had known from Johnson's circle. They fell in love, and by the end of the 1796 Wollstonecraft was pregnant again. Though Godwin was, like her, morally opposed to the institution of marriage, he did agree to a formal union to protect the legal rights of their child, and the wedding took place at St. Pancras Church in London on March 29, 1797. They lived in separate but adjoining quarters, which suited both their temperaments.

Grandmother of *Frankenstein*

Wollstonecraft went into labor on August 30, 1797, and gave birth to a daughter named Mary. But the delivery went badly, and the placenta remained inside the mother's body. It became toxic, and led to blood poisoning, which killed Wollstonecraft on September 10, 1797. She left an unfinished novel, *Maria, or the Wrongs of Woman*, which was published a year after her death by Godwin in his *Memoirs of the Author of the Vindication of the Rights of Woman*. His biography once again stirred controversy, for Wollstonecraft's friends were horrified about the revelations concerning Fuseli and Imlay, while her enemies seized upon its tawdrier aspects with glee. Though Wollstonecraft argued so convincingly on women's rights in her writings, her own personal choices made feminists wary of giving her full due. For the generation of activists and theorists who followed, she was judged to be a woman forever at the mercy of her own passions.

Godwin continued his career as political thinker, writer, and liberal maverick, and raised their daughter Mary in a progressive and education-focused environment. At age 16 she eloped with the poet Percy Bysshe Shelley. A few years later she produced one of the classics of Western literature, *Frankenstein*.

Books

Concise Dictionary of British Literary Biography, Volume 3: *Writers of the Romantic Period, 1789-1832*. Farmington Hills, Mich.: Gale, 1992.
Feminist Writers, St. James Press, 1996.

Periodicals

Guardian (London, England), April 12, 2003. □

Y

Rosebud Yellow Robe

Lakota Sioux educator Rosebud Yellow Robe (1907-1992) used storytelling and performance to provide numerous generations of children with an enthusiastic inside look at the folklore and culture of Native Americans. She spent her life fighting prejudice and ignorance with patience, talent and pride—leaving a lasting impression on everyone she met.

Early Life

Yellow Robe was born on February 26, 1907, in Rapid City, South Dakota. The first of three daughters, Yellow Robe's father named her in honor of the Lakota (Teton Sioux) Rosebud Reservation in South Dakota where her extended family was enrolled as members of the Sioux Nation. Her father was educator Chief Chauncey Yellow Robe, and her mother, Lillian Belle Springer—of Swiss-German ancestry—was a volunteer nurse at the Rapid City Indian School. Their loving, interracial marriage was both a foundation and an inspiration for Yellow Robe's highly-developed tolerance and temperance. Her father's mother, Tahcawin (Fawn), was a niece of Sitting Bull—considered to be one of the Sioux's most celebrated leaders.

Yellow Robe's elementary education took place in a one-room school close to her home. She attended the high school in Rapid City, South Dakota and, in the late 1920s, was one of the first female Native American students at the University of South Dakota. Beyond her formal education,

however, Yellow Robe embarked on a more traditionally Native American apprenticeship with the help of her father. She recalled in Marjorie Weinberg's biography entitled *The Real Rosebud* how her father taught her and her sisters "as many Lakota traditions as he could . . . [there were] occasions when elderly Indians would visit the grounds of the Indian School and tell stories in the Lakota language. Chief Chauncey Yellow Robe would have Rosebud listen, even though she could not understand a word, and later he would retell the stories in English." Yellow Robe's mother died in 1922, which prompted her to take over the care of her two younger sisters.

Yellow Robe attracted attention and admiration while enrolled at the University of South Dakota, thanks to her participation in the annual "Strollers" productions. These student presentations included many traditional Native American dances—such as the rabbit dance, the hoop dance and the war dance—performed by Rosebud Yellow Robe in full costume and with a palpable reverence that the audiences found contagious. While at the University, she also rushed a sorority and was accepted, only to be dropped later when the members learned that their charter required members to be Caucasian. U.S. President Calvin Coolidge and his wife visited the South Dakota Black Hills area on August 4, 1927, and attended a ceremony—presided over by Chief Chauncy Yellow Robe—in which President Coolidge was made an honorary member of the Sioux tribe. Rosebud Yellow Robe helped conduct the heartfelt ceremony and personally placed the stunning, handmade Sioux warbonnet on the President's head. The entry in *Notable Native Americans* (1995) describes how "Rosebud's grace and beauty were not lost on the press reporters, who commented on the 'beautiful Indian maiden'."

Was a Native in the City

Yellow Robe moved to New York City in 1927 as a young woman of 20—eager to renovate the population's misconceptions about Native American culture through education and the aesthetic appeal of her traditional performances. At the time, the only exposure the common person had to "Indians" was through the stereotypical, inaccurate portrayals offered by radio shows and silent films. In her 2004 biography *The Real Rosebud: The Triumph of a Lakota Woman,* family friend and author Weinberg explained that Indians were seen "as savages—either noble or cutthroat." In an excerpt from his 2005 review of Weinberg's biography in *American Indian Literatures,* Harvey Markowitz clarified: "Among the many unintended consequences of nineteenth-century assimilationist Indian policy was its tendency to split native communities into . . . opposed factions. . . . [There] were individuals whom federal officials labeled 'blanket Indians' because of their staunch resistance to all government efforts at 'civilization and Christianization.' . . . [and] so–called 'progressivist' Indians who repudiated their native cultures and values for those of Euroamerican society. Falling between these two camps were tribal members who . . . attempted to construct bridges that would allow Indians to operate in both worlds." This last group is the one that both Chauncy and Yellow Robe would have identified with.

Yellow Robe began formally educating children about Native American culture and traditions in the early 1930s. Years later, in a 1975 interview for the *Rapid City Journal* she remembered the experience: "When I first lectured to public school classes in New York, many of the smaller children hid under their desks, for they knew from the movies what a blood-thirsty scalping Indian might do to them." In 1929, Yellow Robe married newspaper reporter Arthur (de Cinq Mars) Seymour, who had met her for the first time while covering the President's 1927 visit. They had a daughter that same year whom they named Tahcawin de Cinq-Mars Moy (referred to as "Buddy") after Rosebud Yellow Robe's paternal grandmother. Seymour supported Yellow Robe both as her spouse, and as her manager. He helped book her at events that would assist her in her desire to expose the general population to the true nature of Indian culture.

In the mid-1930s, Yellow Robe spent two years at CBS radio writing and performing her own scripts on the air. She worked at the same time, and in the same studio as Orson Welles—prompting the widespread belief that the "Rosebud" uttered in the dying breath of the protagonist of his 1941 masterwork *Citizen Kane* was inspired by Yellow Robe. She was sought after by photographers and film directors alike for her unusual, refined Sioux beauty. She even declined to take the title role in Cecil B. De Mille's Indian film, *Ramona.* Yellow Robe's first husband died in 1949, and in 1951 she married photographer Alfred A. Frantz—years after meeting him when he, too, covered the 1927 ceremony for President Coolidge.

Indian Village

In 1930, Yellow Robe became the director of the ever-evolving Jones Beach Indian Village on Long Island in New York. She remained there as director for the next 20 years, as described by Barnett and Klein's 2005 *American National Biography* supplement: "She wore the clothing of her culture, working mostly with children, teaching them about Native Americans through handicraft, games, songs, and stories. Through [her] work, tens of thousands of children were provided with a new and realistic depiction of American Indians." Weinberg—who attended the Village as a child—described how Yellow Robe "dressed in a nineteenth-century Lakota Indian costume: a deerskin dress, leggings, and moccasins, plus a feathered warbonnet (not customarily worn by women) . . ." Children who attended the Village with Yellow Robe staged turtle races, listened to expertly told stories, made handicrafts including carving, pottery, metalwork, weaving, leatherwork, musical instruments and painting. Yellow Robe spent from 1930 to 1950 alternating seasonally between the Indian Village project in the summer months, and speaking and performing in schools all winter long. Each year ended with the Annual American Indian Art Exhibit where the projects the children had been working on were showcased and judged. Winners were awarded with authentic Indian artifacts which were then displayed in participating local schools.

A woman of diverse talents, Yellow Robe also appeared repeatedly throughout the 1950s on NBC children's programs, as well as doing spots for *Bob Montgomery Presents.* She was also a respected author. Her first book, *Album of the American Indian* was published in 1969 and painted a vivid and detailed picture of how seven different Indian tribes lived from day to day before the appearance of the Europeans—as well as mourning the bloodshed and isolation that followed. In 1979 she published her second book, a collection of Native American folk tales for children titled *Tonweya and the Eagles.* The stories featured a young boy named Chano, (short for Canowicakte or "Kill in the Woods", her father's tribal name that was changed to Chauncy when he attended the Carlisle Indian School), who learned how to hunt, ride bareback, wrestle, swim and footrace as well as becoming familiar with the characteristics and lifestyles of the native creatures. This book garnered critical acclaim for its authentic chronicling of traditional tales in a format and style that was engaging for both child and adult readers. The compilation—stories passed down from her father and woven together with a fictional biographical storyline based on her father as a young man—was a great success, appearing in translation and frequently excerpted in academic texts.

Left Lakota Legacy

In 1984 the W.H. Over Museum in Vermillion, South Dakota, commissioned a life-sized portrait of Yellow Robe done in oils and she was the focus of a three-day celebration in May of 1989 that included the observation of "Rosebud Yellow Robe Day" and the presentation of an honorary doctorate in Humane Letters from the University of South Dakota. The reason for the accolade, quoted in *Notable*

Native Americans (1995) read, "paying tribute to Yellow Robe as a gifted communicator 'who, through her talents and native background, promote[d] an authentic view of Indian life and character and who [was] able through her techniques of cultural exchange to pass her scholarly knowledge on to mixed audiences of young and old which numbered many thousands throughout the years.' "

Although Yellow Robe died of cancer on October 5, 1992, her spirit clearly continued to inspire people. *Write Idea*—a textbook published by the MacMillan/McGraw–Hill School Publishing Company in 1993—honored the beloved storyteller by attempting to continue the dissemination of a better understanding of Native American culture. In 1994, the National Dance Institute and folk artist Judy Collins joined a chorus of a thousand children from all over the globe to perform a tribute titled "Rosebud's Song" at Madison Square Garden in New York City. Liz Sonneborn's *A to Z of Native American Women* noted that the program "was dedicated to Rosebud Yellow Robe for devot[ing] her life to children and to preserving and passing on Native American stories and culture." In 1993 and 1994, the University of South Dakota also created the Rosebud Yellow Robe Society for philanthropists as well as a Native American student scholarship established in her name.

Many biographical excerpts focusing on Rosebud Yellow Robe actually spend a surprising amount of space and time covering the biographical details of her father's life. While she always attributed her education and motivation to her father, it was her unique and boundless personal energy, enthusiasm and patience that planted her permanently in the hearts and minds of so many young people. As her grandson Luke Yellow Robe stated in his Foreward to Weinberg's biography, Yellow Robe "set in motion for her people and family a lifetime pursuit of achievement and learning, a pursuit to be duplicated so that we can see the importance of rising above circumstance. Her example has served as an internal compass that has inspired [many] to navigate through the obstacles and barriers of life in order to be an inspiration." Weinberg, in her biography's introduction, said it best when she pointed out that Yellow Robe's unique gifts "had much more to do with encouraging human relationships than with 'Indianness'. Her acceptance of people as they are, her responsiveness to the needs of others, and her ability to encourage their differences while rejoicing in their achievements." Yellow Robe's infectious optimism, tireless generosity and solemn appreciation for her heritage have assured her place in history as a champion of tolerance and compassion in an uncertain age.

Books

A to Z of Native American Women, edited by Liz Sonneborn, Facts On File, Inc., 1998.

Barnett, Karen Bachman and Catherine Dyer Klein, *American National Biography: Supplement 2,* edited by Mark C. Carnes, Oxford University Press, 2005.

Notable Native Americans, edited by Sharon Malinowski, Gale Research, Inc., 1995.

Weinberg, Marjorie, *The Real Rosebud: The Triumph of a Lakota Woman,* University of Nebraska Press, 2004.

Yellow Robe Frantz, Rosebud, *Tonweya and the Eagles and Other Lakota Tales,* Dial Books for Young Readers, 1979.

Online

Markowitz, Harvey, "The Real Rosebud: The Triumph of a Lakota Woman (review)," *Studies in American Indian Literatures, Project Muse,* http://muse.jhu.edu/cgi-bin/access.cgi?uri=/journals/studies_in_american_indian_literatures/v017/17.1markowitz.html (January 5, 2006). □

Maud Younger

American suffragist Maud Younger (1870-1936) was a leading figure in the women's rights movement in the early part of the twentieth century. Rich and colorful, she brought passion and a high degree of enthusiasm into organizations such as the National Women's Party. In the city where she was born, San Francisco, she established the first waitresses' union. Later in her life, she was an early advocate for the Equal Rights Amendment.

Born into Wealth

E xuberant, aggressive, charismatic, and even a bit flamboyant, Younger possessed the kind of character and set of personality traits typically exhibited by the most successful social activists. Driven yet compassionate, Younger generated the respect and affection of colleagues who worked with her in the labor and suffrage movements in the early part of the twentieth century. Almost through sheer force of will, she helped affect societal change. She certainly demonstrated the appropriate skills and talent: She knew how to work the political system, she was a powerful writer, and she could be a compelling public speaker, delivering a message with both force and humor.

Moreover, she had the personal empathy and financial resources to support the causes she embraced. Indeed, Younger, like other important figures in influential organizations like the National Women's Party, was born into a privileged, upper-class existence; but she was still able to easily identify with those who had to work for a living. To be sure, identification resulted from Younger's willingness to roll up her sleeves and work side-by-side with those she endeavored to help. Colorful she was; overly proud, she was not. Younger's wealth never hindered her credibility. Instead it helped build bridges between women of diverse backgrounds with common concerns and goals.

Younger was born in San Francisco, California, on January 10, 1870, into a wealthy family that included five children (four girls and a boy). She was the daughter of William John Younger and his first wife, Annie Maria (Lane) Younger.

Her father, who settled in San Francisco with his Scottish parents in 1848, was a prosperous and well-known

dental surgeon. Through his success, the family had achieved high social standing, both in San Francisco and in Paris, France, where William Younger relocated his dental practice in 1900. Two of his daughters even married Austrian barons. As for Maud Younger, she enjoyed the advantages that wealth brought: She was educated in the best private schools in San Francisco and New York City, New York, and she frequently traveled to Europe and throughout the United States.

Became Advocate for Social Reform

Despite her family's prosperity and prominence, Younger could hardly be considered a spoiled socialite. Rather, she developed a strong social conscience. By the early 1900s, when Younger was around 30 years old, she had visited New York on several occasions, and she became exposed to the efforts of social reformers who worked in the worst parts of the city, where destitute immigrants faced a daily struggle to survive. This had a profound impact on her life course.

During one visit, Younger stayed at a New York settlement house (the College Settlement), intending to observe the kind of poverty suffered by some of New York's inhabitants. The concept behind settlement houses, which were established in the late nineteenth and early twentieth century, was to provide quarters in poverty-stricken areas for wealthy people and students. Once settled, these individuals could then evaluate the surroundings, help provide services to improve quality of life for local residents, and

develop long-range solutions for improved existence. Settlement houses also provided adult education and English classes for immigrants as well as public health services.

Originally, Younger had planned on staying at the settlement house for a week (she had stopped there on her way to Europe). As it turned out, she remained for five years. During this period, she experienced a blooming of social consciousness and became a passionate believer in social reform at the grassroots level. She not only wanted to alleviate the suffering of the poor; she also became a supporter of trade labor unions and an advocate for the protective legislation for working women. Further, she dedicated herself to the woman suffrage movement. (Women suffrage involved the legal right of women to vote in national and local elections.) Later, commenting on her experience, she said that the New York's East Side had transformed her into a woman suffragist.

The "Million Dollar" Waitress

While living in New York, Younger wanted to gain some personal working experience, particularly in the service sector, which employed many women, so she took a job as a waitress. This led her to join the city's Waitresses' Union. Eventually, she wrote about her experiences in the March/April issue of *McClure's* magazine, a leading reform-oriented publication, in an article titled "Diary of an Amateur Waitress: An Industrial Problem from the Worker's Point of View."

When she returned to California, she took on another waitressing job and intended to join the labor union. However, she discovered that no such union existed in San Francisco, so she decided to organize one. By this time, she was nicknamed the "Million Dollar Waitress," and she became president of the union local she helped establish. Not only did she create San Francisco's first waitress union in 1908, she also helped facilitate the passage of several labor laws, including California's eight-hour workday law for women, which was passed in 1911. In these efforts, Younger proved to be an effective lobbyist, and she helped organize the testimony from affected workers that was so instrumental in getting the laws passed.

Championed Women's Rights

When the suffrage movement began gaining momentum in California, Younger encouraged her working colleagues and fellow union members to join in the cause. By this time, working and voting rights were closely related in Younger's mind—she considered suffrage for women as a means to fix other social problems—and she helped establish the Wage Earners' Equal Suffrage League for Working Women. She spread the message in speeches made at union halls and through her writing. She even targeted male members of the working class through pamphlets that she wrote such as "Why Wage-Earning Women Should Vote."

Also, demonstrating her flamboyant side in a 1911 Labor Day parade in San Francisco, she publicized the suffrage case by helping create a float that publicized the Wage Earner's Equal Suffrage League. The float was a wagon pulled by six white horses, and Younger assumed the reins. Younger became the first woman to ever drive a float in the parade, and the high-profile stunt attracted a great deal of attention in the press.

That same year, she lobbied for passage of the 19th amendment, a woman suffrage amendment to the California constitution. For that effort, Alice Paul, one of the leading figures in the women's suffrage movement, had recruited her. After the amendment was adopted by popular vote in October, she lent a hand to similar campaigns in other states.

Also in 1911, Younger returned to New York City, where she worked with the International Ladies Garment Workers Union in their fight against the practice of subcontracting. The following year, she became involved in the "White Goods Strike," initiated by the city's female white goods workers, assisting the effort both in the courts and on the streets, where she joined the strikers on the picket lines.

Became a National Figure

In 1913, encouraged by Paul, Younger moved her activities beyond California and New York and onto the national stage. By this time, Paul wanted to fight for woman suffrage at a national, rather than state, level. To that end, Paul had established the Congressional Union of Woman Suffrage, a more militant wing of the suffrage movement and the forerunner of the National Woman's Party. Its agenda included a campaign for a federal suffrage amendment. Paul enlisted Younger as her "lieutenant" in this effort and suggested that she move to Washington, D.C. In the nation's capital, Younger applied her unique style and effective organizational skills to the federal initiative and, in the process, became a very active and highly visible member of the Congressional Union.

Younger worked with Paul for the next seven years. As a result, she later became one of the National Women's Party's most effective speakers, achieving a celebrity status within the organization. She made for a very distinctive figure, driving in a new convertible automobile accompanied by her dog, embodying the style of the emerging and trendy "flapper" era.

In 1915, Younger became the first lobby chairman of the Congressional Union, and remained at the post until the organization evolved into the National Woman's Party.

Became a Well-known Orator

The National Women's Party came into existence in 1916, with the purpose of mobilizing the votes of recently franchised women in the upcoming presidential election. At the Party's first convention, held in June in Chicago, Younger gave the keynote address. In late November, she gave the memorial oration at the funeral of Inez Milholland Boissevain, a lawyer and leading figure in the suffrage movement. In a gesture that Younger no doubt appreciated, on March 3, 1913, Boissevain had led a suffrage parade in Washington, D.C., riding on a white horse. Unfortunately, Boissevain suffered from pernicious anemia and collapsed while giving a speech in Los Angeles on October 22. She was taken to a hospital, where physicians administered blood transfusions, but she succumbed on November 25.

When not making appearances and giving speeches, Younger continued lobbying and organizing protests and demonstrations. For her lobbying efforts, she developed a very detailed index card system that included information about congressmen and senators and suggested the most effective ways to approach these politicians. Such efforts helped generate public support for the suffrage cause.

She chaired the National Women's Party's lobbying committee from 1917 to 1919 and its legislative committee in 1919. In 1917, she made speeches throughout the country about the party's picketing of the White House and she spoke out about the arrest and imprisonment of demonstrators. The suffragists had developed a strategy of "perpetual picketing," each day sending delegations of women to picket in front of the White House. But delegates were arrested. In their confinement they endured mistreatment and were subjected to injustice in the courts. Younger publicized these developments, generating outrage and sympathy that eventually helped with the final passage of the 19th Amendment by Congress in 1919.

Though great strides were being made, gains never came easy, as the suffrage movement met with considerable obstacles throughout the country. For instance, in Dallas, Texas, just as the United States was ready to enter World War I, National Women's Party organizers were prevented from hiring halls and hotel rooms for Younger and her colleagues. The mayor of the city refused to allow Younger to hold a street meeting. City officials even refused when Younger offered to submit her speech for review and possible censorship. The party met with similar obstacles in Tennessee. Reportedly, members of the War Association and Home Defense League went to every hotel and meeting place in the state and requested that Younger be refused rooms and halls. They also went to city mayors and asked that they refuse to grant permits for street meetings. In 1919, Younger wrote about her experiences in an article for *McCall's* magazine entitled "Revelations of a Woman Lobbyist."

Continued the Struggle

In 1920, Younger had to go to Paris, where her father was dying, and then return to San Francisco to settle his business affairs. She then traveled back to the East Coast in a solo automobile trip that was well publicized. Now that the suffrage amendment had become law, Younger sought other ways to help advance the cause of working women. She served on the advisory committee for the new Women's Bureau when it was set up in the Department of Labor in 1920. She also worked with the Women's Trade Union League and the National Consumers' League.

Younger also became very active in the National Women's Party campaign for the Equal Rights Amendment. This proposed amendment, to the federal constitution, was designed to eliminate any remaining legal restrictions for women. In 1923, as the party's congressional chair (a post she assumed in 1921), Younger helped get the amendment presented to Congress. She campaigned for the amendment until she died.

Younger died of carcinoma on June 25, 1936, at her ranch in Los Gatos, California. She was cremated and her ashes were scattered.

She remained active in women's rights until the end. She continued serving as the National Women's Party congressional chair until her death. In 1928, she was an integral figure in the founding of the Inter-American Commission of Women. The Equal Rights Amendment, Younger's final cause, is still not part of the U.S. Constitution.

Books

Dictionary of American Biography, Supplements 1-2: To 1940, Thomson Gale. 2005.

Online

"Maud Younger," *womenshistory.about.com, http://womens history.about.com/library/bio/blbio_younger_maud.htm (December 24, 2005).*

"Maude Younger (1870-1936), *Library of Congress American Memory,* http://memory.loc.gov/ammem/collections/ suffrage/nwp/profiles5.html (December 24, 2005).

"Western Women's Suffrage-California," *Women of the West Museum,* http://www.autry-museum.org/explore/exhibits/ suffrage/maudyounger_full.html (December 24, 2005).

"Women's Suffrage," *shapethefuture.org,* http://www.shapethe future.org/links/suffragettes.asp (December 24, 2005). □

Z

Rostislav Zakharov

Choreographer Rostislav Zakharov (1907-1975) was one of the foremost figures in Russian ballet during the era of the Soviet Union. Active at Moscow's famed Bolshoi from 1936 to 1956, he created two of the best-known modern ballets in the Russian classical tradition: the elaborate *Fountain of Bakhchisarai* of 1934 and *Cinderella* (1945), set to one of composer Sergei Prokofiev's great works for the ballet theater.

Zakharov is less well known in the West than George Balanchine and the other Russian choreographers who emigrated to Western Europe or the United States and who had a significant impact on the development of dance in those countries. His choreography was shaped by the fundamentally political nature of the arts under Soviet Communism. When Russian dancers began to bring Zakharov's works to the West after the fall of the Soviet Union, however, the same qualities of realism and clarity that had endeared his best ballets to Soviet culture commissars ensured his appreciation by new Western audiences that heretofore had hardly known his name.

Studied both Drama and Dance

Zakharov was born on September 7, 1907, in Astrakhan in Russia's southern Caspian Sea region. He settled early on a career as a choreographer, and attended the Leningrad Choreographic School, graduating in 1926. He had a short career as a dancer at the Kiev Theatre for Opera and Ballet, but choreography was his main interest. At first

he tried to break into the centralized world of ballet by creating dances for amateur productions. These had little to add to the classical ballet tradition and gained only scattered attention. As Zakharov pondered his next move, deep changes were underway in the Soviet cultural scene; Josef Stalin had triumphed over his rivals and emerged in full control of the Communist Party apparatus, and had begun the collectivization of most aspects of Soviet life.

The status of ballet under full-blown Communism was ambivalent. At first it was considered a remnant of the culture of the old czarist regime, but it was also something of a national symbol, an activity at which Russians exceeded the accomplishments of the rest of the world. By 1927 a compromise solution had emerged: the principle of so-called socialist realism had become entrenched in Soviet ballet. Many Soviet dances were developed around realistic stories aimed at promoting the glory of the Soviet state (such as *Gayane,* the source of the famous "Saber Dance" by composer Aram Khachaturian, that dealt with a plot by spies to steal state agricultural secrets from a collective farm). Zakharov sensed the way things were moving, and enrolled in a stage direction course at the Leningrad Theatre Institute, hoping to learn how to add conventional dramatic elements to his choreography.

The plan bore fruit. Zakharov studied under director Vladimir Soloviev, keeping his hand in choreography by creating stage routines for productions mounted at a school for circus clowns. He met Leningrad Theatre Institute instructor Sergei Radlov, a leading director who specialized in the plays of Shakespeare, and was a close friend (and chess-playing partner) of composer Sergei Prokofiev. As artistic director of the Leningrad Opera and Ballet Theatre, Radlov invited Zakharov to choreograph dance scenes in operas. His reputation grew, and in 1932 he contributed dances to a production of Cherubini's opera *Les deux journées* (The Two Journeys, also known as *The Water Carrier*) at Moscow's Bolshoi Theatre, one of the glories of Russian fine arts.

In 1934 Radlov was overseeing a new production at the Leningrad Opera and Ballet Theatre, a ballet based on a long poem by Alexander Pushkin called "The Fountain of Bakhchisarai," with music by Boris Asafiev. Radlov selected Zakharov as choreographer, and Zakharov prepared well for the assignment. He visited libraries to learn more about costumes that would be authentic to the ballet's exotic setting (the swashbuckling story concerns a Polish princess kidnapped by a Tatar tribal chief and killed by her Tatar rival), and spent time with individual dancers discussing the motivations of the characters. One of those dancers was a young Galina Ulanova, considered among the greatest Russian ballerinas of the twentieth century. As *New York Times* dance critic Anna Kisselgoff noted, the ballet fulfilled all the conditions of socialist artistic doctrine: "Its story was drawn from Russia's greatest poet, [and it featured] a use of national literature to project 'real' feelings' and an uplifting theme," as the Tatar chief Girei is changed by love into a heroic figure.

Moved to Bolshoi Ballet

The Fountain of Bakhchisarai was Zakharov's first major independent work as a choreographer, and it became one of his most famous accomplishments. The ballet was a success from the start, and it landed Zakharov a position as choreographer at the State Academic Theater for Opera and Ballet, later renamed the Kirov Ballet, in Leningrad. When the work was mounted in a production at the Bolshoi Ballet in Moscow, it had the same effect: in 1936 Zakharov moved to the Soviet capital to become a Bolshoi choreographer, remaining there until 1956. He continued to create works for the Kirov Ballet as well. *The Fountain of Bakhchisarai* was an influential work in the Soviet Union; choreographers began to follow Zakharov's method of emphasizing mime acting for dancers. He later named this method "dancing through the personality" (tanets v obraze), and the wider style of ballet represented by *The Fountain of Bakhchisarai*, with a clear story and action elevated above abstraction in the choreography, became known among dance lovers as "dram-ballet." It remained in the repertory of the Bolshoi Ballet for decades.

In the late 1930s and early 1940s Zakharov tried to replicate the success of *The Fountain of Bakhchisarai,* often working with composer Asafiev and story adapter Nikolai Volkov. He created ambitious ballets from Russian and foreign literary works, including the Honoré de Balzac novel *Lost Illusions* (1936), two more Pushkin stories, and the epic novel *Taras Bulba* by Nikolai Gogol (1941). These works did not have the mix of strong personality and pageantry that had characterized *The Fountain of Bakhchisarai,* however, and they were less successful. Zakharov's 1947 ballet *The Bronze Horseman,* from a Pushkin story, was a technical tour de force, with a giant flood scene that featured boats, barrels, and even a doghouse that had been washed away by a storm.

More successful than these works, however, was *Cinderella,* which Zakharov choreographed in 1945 to music by Prokofiev. Its success was partly due to the fact that the Prokofiev score was one of the twentieth century's orchestral masterpieces. But Zakharov's choreography also made a strong contribution. Critic Paul Parish, reviewing a contemporary Russian production of *Cinderella* on the Danceviewwest website, wrote that "it maintains that consistency of tone which keeps disbelief suspended and sustains the atmosphere of a fairy tale." Zakharov understood, according to Parish, "what parts of the story can be simply indicated—since everybody knows the story of Cinderella—and what parts should be dwelt on."

The ballet, once again featuring Galina Ulanova in the original production, marked another major success for Zakharov and came at a time when the Soviet people were in a celebratory mood: the German invasion had been beaten back, though at the cost of millions of Russian lives. Composer Dmitri Shostakovich, writing in the Communist Party newspaper *Pravda* (as quoted on the Russian Musical Highlights of the 20th Century website), called the ballet "a veritable landmark bringing out the overall feeling of jubilation felt by our people who know full well the price of Good's victory over the dark forces of Evil." Zakharov became artistic director of the Moscow Choreographic School in 1945, and the following year he was named head of the choreography department at the State Institute of Theatrical Art in Moscow, an influential position that effectively made him one of the nation's cultural overseers.

Attacked Ballet Experimenters

Cinderella proved to be the high point of Zakharov's career. He continued to teach until his death, but his style did not evolve fundamentally. He set himself up as a guardian of Communist values, attacking "decadent" Western arts and modern "formalist" experiments. As Stalinism faded and the Soviet arts scene opened up, Zakharov's own works came under criticism from younger choreographers. Zakharov responded with articles and books, including *The Art of the Choreographer* (1954), which condemned his detractors as political troublemakers and reasserted his own aesthetic principles.

Zakharov's reputation was on the decline, however. He retained his teaching post, but his chances to choreograph major productions became less frequent, and his activities with the Bolshoi Ballet came to an end after he directed and created dances for a production of the opera *Carmen* in 1953. Tours of Western ballet companies in the United Soviet Socialist Republics (U.S.S.R.) met with an unfriendly reception from Zakharov, but he was unsuccessful in turning the tide, and an attempt at a revival of his own career, the ballet *Into the Port Came "Russia,"* failed to make much of an impact after its premiere at the Kirov Ballet in 1964. Zakharov died in Moscow on January 15, 1975, little known in the West and no longer influential at home.

As Communism declined and it was possible to sort out the artifacts of Soviet Russian culture in a dispassionate way, *The Fountain of Bakhchisarai* and *Cinderella* were revived by Russian companies. (Dances are transmitted by means of a writing system called Labanotation.) Ballet director Sergei Radchenko's touring production of *Cinderella,* which visited 88 cities in the United States in 2004, was a success, and the Kirov added *The Fountain of Bakhchisarai* to its repertoire once again.

Brought to the United States and the United Kingdom, *The Fountain of Bakhchisarai* received mixed reviews. Kisselgoff wrote that "like the so-called masses, the audience at the Met[ropolitan Opera House] . . . could respond easily to an accessible message through accessible choreography." Debra Craine of the *Times* of London felt that "Zakharov's choreography had plenty of gusto: Polish ladies swooning into savage Tatar arms; fierce whip-cracking war dances in the courtyard of the Palace of Bakhchisarai; serpentine sensuality in the harem." *Dance Magazine* writer Roslyn Sulcas, however, was less impressed, arguing that "Zakharov sets an interminable series of ensemble dances for the court against solos and pas de deux for the young lovers in the first act, then an interminable series of harem-girl dances between Zarema's [the Khan's mistress] solos in the second act—few of which seem to emerge from any dramatic necessity." *Cinderella,* however, was recommended by several critics as a ballet that could appeal to all ages. Zakharov's reputation, after several ups and downs, was finding a level place in the historical pantheon of dance.

Books

International Dictionary of Ballet, St. James, 1993.

Periodicals

Albuquerque Journal, February 17, 2004.
Dance Magazine, March 1995.
New York Times, July 8, 1999; August 22, 1999.
Times (London, England), July 31, 1995.

Online

"Cinderella: Moscow Festival Ballet," Danceviewwest, http://www.danceviewtimes.com/dvw/reviews/2004/winter.suburban.htm (February 5, 2006).
"Russian Musical Highlights of the 20th Century: 1945," http://www.vor.ru/century/1945m.html (February 5, 2006). □

Yevgeny Zamyatin

Russian writer Yevgeny Zamyatin (1884-1937) was the creator of the novel *We* (1920), a science fiction satire on totalitarianism that was both notable and extremely influential. He also wrote shorter fiction, mostly satirical, that remains less well known but has much to offer students of the early Soviet period of Russian literature.

The first book banned in the young Soviet Union, *We* was not published in Russian in a complete version until 1952, and was not officially approved until the

perestroika era of cultural openness that preceded the fall of Communism. It circulated in manuscript, however, and was well known to a variety of Russian writers. The novel's greatest influence was visible abroad; it was admired by English novelist George Orwell and was a key predecessor to *1984.* The extent of its influence on another major work of futurism, Aldous Huxley's *Brave New World,* has been debated; Huxley denied that he had read the book, but Orwell and others identified strong similarities between Huxley's and Zamyatin's novels, and the central plot device of a romance that arises in the midst of a completely centralized and mechanized society is common to the two books.

Born in Small Town

Zamyatin was a native of Lebedian, Russia, a small town about two hundred miles south of Moscow. He was born early in 1884; the conflicting dates of January 20 and February 1 that appear in literary sources may result from the conflicting calendrical systems in force in Russia at the time. Zamyatin's father was a Russian Orthodox priest and a school principal, but the atmosphere of the small town, despite his mother's love for literature and classical music, was not intellectual. Zamyatin retreated into a world of books; he loved Dostoyevsky and later wrote of being "initiated into this mysterious thing, letters" (as quoted on the website *Yevgeny Ivenovitch Zamyatin: The Russian Revolutionary Romantic Distopian Writer*). Attending high school in the city of Voronezh, Zamyatin excelled in English but did poorly in math classes. With typical perversity, he decided to become an engineer. Honored with a gold medal at his high school graduation, he pawned the medal shortly afterward.

Zamyatin studied naval engineering at the St. Petersburg Polytechnic Institute from 1902 to 1908, and he made a living until the time of the Russian Revolution mostly in that field. He had begun to write when he was very young, however, and continued to do so despite the warnings of teachers who tried to alert him to the dangers of antagonizing the czarist secret police. Not heeding these warnings, Zamyatin joined the revolutionary Communist Bolshevik party. He took advantage of a summer job on a ship to make his way to Odessa, where he joined city residents in backing the mutiny of the crew of the battleship *Potemkin* in rebellion against being given maggot-infested food to eat. Zamyatin participated in the abortive leftist rebellion of 1905, and was arrested, beaten and held for several months in solitary confinement. That experience was reflected in Zamyatin's first published story, *Odin* (Alone), which appeared in 1908.

Although Zamyatin was officially told to stay clear of St. Petersburg, the secret police made a clerical error that allowed him to slip back into engineering classes, stay under the radar, graduate from the Polytechnic Institute and even teach there for several years. He continued writing fiction and published several technical articles. In 1911 the police realized their error, arrested him again, and sentenced him to internal exile in the provincial city of Lakhta. Zamyatin made good use of the time by writing a set of short stories, *Uezdnoye* (District Tales), that satirized small-town

Russian life. Two years later, having served his time, he was officially rehabilitated. He promptly antagonized authorities once again with *Na kulichkakh* (A Godforsaken Hole), a story that depicted a group of drunk, intolerant Russian soldiers in Vladivostok. The journal that published the story was seized by police.

In 1916 Zamyatin traveled to England on a long-term engineering assignment: he was to oversee the construction of Russian icebreakers that had been commissioned from a Newcastle shipyard. Zamyatin, who spoke only broken English, did not feel at ease in Britain and filled his notebooks with jaundiced observations. His satirical eye was busily at work, however, and while he was there he wrote two short comic novellas about life in England, *Ostrovitiane* (The Islanders) and *Lovets cheloveka* (The Fisher of Men). These books (later published together in English under the title *The Islanders*) delved only superficially into English life but showed Zamyatin's fantastic humor developing to a new level. In *The Islanders* he imagines a bill introduced in the English Parliament that would make all noses the same length. Zamyatin took to wearing tweed suits, and England made enough of an impact on him that his Russian friends dubbed him "the Englishman" after he returned home.

Celebrated Revolution

When Zamyatin heard that a revolt against czarist rule had broken out in Russia in 1917, he hastened back home, traveling in a small British ship that was vulnerable to attack by German submarines. He was overjoyed by the Communist takeover and thought that it heralded a bright new future. Zamyatin wrote numerous newspaper articles, sometimes using the pseudonym M. Platonov, and edited several literary magazines. He also supervised Russian translations of foreign novels by, among others, Jack London, O. Henry, and H.G. Wells, the latter a science fiction writer and fellow engineer whom he greatly admired. Zamyatin's reputation was riding high in the early days of the Soviet regime, and he inspired a group of younger followers in St. Petersburg to form a writers' association called the Serapion Brothers.

Beginning in 1919 Zamyatin worked on drafts of *We*, whose Russian title was *My*. It was his only full-length novel. As state repression descended over Russia, Zamyatin vigorously protested the deteriorating civil rights situation. When he finished *We* in 1920 it was branded a slander against socialism and was left unpublished. The book appeared for the first time in English translation, in 1924. Russian writers passed copies of it from hand to hand, and a group of Russian expatriates in what is now the Czech Republic published a version in Czech in 1927, further angering Soviet authorities. The book was also issued in French and, thanks to high-profile reviews by George Orwell and other writers, became well known in the West.

The immediate inspiration for *We* was probably H.G. Wells's *The Time Machine*. Both books are set in a distant future depicted as an extreme development of contemporary trends. *We* is said to take place in the twenty-sixth century. It was not just an early science fiction novel but also among the very first examples of the dystopic, or

nightmare future, an offshoot of the genre. The citizens represented in the novel, who have had their imaginations surgically removed, live within a glass dome under the rule of the One State and its leader, the Benefactor. The planet outside the dome had been made uninhabitable by a war that lasted for two centuries. Buildings are all made of glass, and a police force called the Guardians watches all citizens for any trace of unapproved behavior. Culture is entirely government-controlled; music comes from a Music Factory that prefigures the emergence of Muzak and other industrial uses of music over the next several decades. Citizens can obtain time alone only for sexual intercourse, for which a stamped pink coupon is required.

The novel's title refers to the elimination of first-person pronouns in the world Zamyatin imagines; "we" is the only acceptable first-person pronoun. Individuals are known by numbers (actually addresses) rather than names, and the novel's central figure is D-503, an engineer like Zamyatin (actually a spaceship builder) and at first a supporter of the regime. He begins to see through the regimentation of his life after he is seduced by a woman, I-330, who stands for the human spirit of irrationality and chaos. *We* is not a heavy symbolic political tract but, like Orwell's *1984*, a highly readable and often funny satire on totalitarianism. That its significance extended beyond Soviet Communism was immediately grasped by Orwell, who wrote, as quoted by Alan Myers in his article "Zamyatin in Newcastle," that "what Zamyatin seems to be aiming at is not any particular country but the implied aims of industrial civilization."

Headed Russian Writers' Union

Even in the face of his lack of success in getting *We* published, and even though he was detained by police on several occasions, Zamyatin continued to write. His essay "I Am Afraid" questioned government censorship, and an experimental long story, *Peshchere* (The Cave), was published in 1922. The story was set amid the privations of wartime in St. Petersburg, with an extended metaphor likening the cold and darkness of the city to life in a cave. The story inspired a 1927 film, *House in the Snow Drifts,* by Soviet director Friedrich Ermler. Despite (or perhaps because of) his problems with the authorities, Zamyatin was admired by other Russian writers and was chosen as president of the All-Russian Writers' Union.

Zamyatin wrote several plays in the middle and late 1920s; *Atilla* (1925) was based on the figure of Attila the Hun, and *Blokha* (The Flea) was based on a folk-style story. *Blokha* was staged with sets by a top designer, Boris Kustodiyev, and was enthusiastically received by the public in its opening performances, but by this time the comparative liberalism of the early 1920s had disappeared and Zamyatin was under constant attack in the government-controlled press. He was singled out for criticism by Leon Trotsky himself, then in the midst of a power struggle with future dictator Josef Stalin, but he did not back down from his view that a writer ought to be, as he often put it, a heretic. *Blokha* was closed down by government censors, and Zamyatin was forced into near-total obscurity. He may have contributed to the text of the Dmitri Shostakovich comic opera *The Nose,* which was based on a novel by Nikolai Gogol, a comic novelist whose outlook bore some similarities to Zamyatin's own.

Finally Zamyatin's situation in the Soviet Union became untenable, and he wrote a letter to Stalin personally, asking that he be allowed to leave the country. Possibly due to support from writer Maxim Gorky, permission was granted, and he left for Paris. In his last years he dreamed of returning to the Soviet Union and refrained from contributing writings to the anti-Communist press in the West. This earned him the enmity of Russian emigrés. In his last years he worked on a novel about Attila the Hun, but it was never finished. Zamyatin died in Paris on March 10, 1937. *We* continued to be widely read in the West, and collections of Zamyatin's stories and essays appeared in English translation from the 1960s through the 1980s. Zamyatin was officially rehabilitated in the Soviet Union in 1988, and today *We* is frequently assigned in literature classes in Russian schools.

Books

Ginsburg, Mirra, edited and translated, *A Soviet Heretic: Essays,* University of Chicago Press, 1970.

Shane, Alex M., *The Life and Times of Evgenij Zamjatin,* University of California Press, 1968.

Online

Contemporary Authors Online, Gale, 2006. Reproduced in *Biography Resource Center,* Thomson Gale, 2006, http://www.galenet.galegroup.com/servlet/BioRC (February 7, 2006).

Stifled Heresy, "Yevgeny Ivenovitch Zamyatin: the russian revolutionary romantic distopian writer," http://www.geocities.com/Athens/Delphi/1634/Zamyatin.html (February 7, 2006).

"Yevgeny Ivanovich Zamyatin (1884-1937)," Books and Writers, http://www.kirjasto sci.fi/zamyatin.htm (February 7, 2006).

"Yevgeny Zamyatin, *We,*" Green Man Review, http://www.greenmanreview.com/book/book_zamyatin_we/html (February 7, 2006).

"Zamyatin, Evgeny Ivanovich," Encyclopedia of Soviet Writers, http://www.sovlit.com/bios/zamyatin.html (February 7, 2006).

"Zamyatin, Evgeny Ivanovich," http://www.orwell.ru/people/zamyatin/zei_en (February 7, 2006).

"Zamyatin in Newcastle," The Myers Project, http://www.pages.britishlibrary.net/alan.mysers/zamyatin.html (February 7, 2006). □

Fred Zinnemann

Director Fred Zinnemann (1907-1977) was one of the central European-born filmmakers who shaped the classic era of Hollywood film. He directed films whose images are etched deeply into the imaginations of filmgoers everywhere, especially the 1951 Western *High Noon* and the wartime drama *From Here to Eternity,* in 1953.

A true craftsman of cinema, Zinnemann worked slowly. He made only about 20 feature films over his long career, but many of them were high-minded, detailed films only slightly less significant than his two great classics. Schooled in documentary techniques when he was young, Zinnemann did much to give mainstream American film a straightforward, realistic look. His handling of actors was superb, and a long list of future stars began their careers facing the lens of his camera. The most distinctive characteristic of Zinnemann's films, however, was their consistent focus on integrity as a theme. That integrity carried over into Zinnemann's approach to filmmaking; although he was not of a revolutionary temperament, he often faced down Hollywood money men and insisted on making films as he thought best.

Distracted from Law Studies

Zinnemann was born in Rzeszów, Poland, on April 29, 1907, and grew up in Vienna, Austria. He was of Jewish background, and his father, a doctor, expected him to pursue a professional career. After going to a college-preparatory high school, the Franz-Josef Gymnasium, Zinnemann dutifully enrolled in law classes at the University of Vienna. But he was bored with the law and discouraged about his prospects. "As a Jew, one was a second-class citizen," Zinnemann told David Robinson of London's *Guardian* newspaper. "I would probably have become a doctor like my father, but there were too many doctors after the first world war, so I was made to study law. To avoid the boredom of the lectures, I went to the movies."

That was during the classic era of European silent film, and Zinnemann saw one directorial masterpiece after another: Sergei Eisenstein's *The Battleship Potemkin* from Russia, Erich von Stroheim's *Greed* from Germany, and King Vidor's war drama *The Big Parade* from the United States. Zinnemann's parents resisted his desire to study film, but eventually gave in and allowed him to attend the Ecole Technique de Photographie et Cinématographie in Paris, France, one of just two film schools in Europe at the time. He had trouble getting a permit to work in France and so moved to Berlin, where he served as an assistant cameraman on several films and met a group of young directors who were thinking of seeking their fortunes in the growing American film industry. Zinnemann sailed for America himself in 1929, arrived in New York on the day the stock market crashed, and took a Greyhound bus to California.

If Zinnemann had stayed in Germanic Europe, he was quoted as saying in the *Times* of London, "I'd be dead by now. Probably not even buried." Zinnemann's parents, indeed, died in the Holocaust. But Zinnemann prospered in Hollywood. He landed a job as an extra in the antiwar classic *All Quiet on the Western Front* and was hired as an assistant by the pioneering documentary filmmaker Robert Flaherty, the director of *Nanook of the North*. Zinnemann accompanied Flaherty back to Europe to work on a documentary set in Central Asia. The film fell through, but Zinnemann benefited from long discussions with Flaherty. "He influenced me in every possible way, not only technically, but also in what I learned from him by being his assistant, his whole spirit of being his own man, of being independent of the general spirit of Hollywood, to the point where he didn't worry about working there," Zinnemann told Brian Neve of *Cineaste*.

Back in the Western hemisphere, Zinnemann directed a documentary, *Los redes* (The Waves), that was funded by the Mexican government and dealt with the lives of fishermen in the Veracruz area. Armed with a letter of introduction from Flaherty, he got a job at the MGM studio. Zinnemann worked his way up the studio hierarchy in the late 1930s, starting out as a film cutter and later being allowed to direct short subjects. He married English-born Renée Bartlett, a costume assistant, in 1936; they had a son, Tim, who went into the film industry. The following year, Zinnemann became an American citizen. One of his short subjects, *That Mothers Might Live* (about deaths in childbirth), won an Academy Award in 1938.

Directed Film About German War Resister

It was during World War II that Zinnemann was elevated to the roster of feature-film directors at MGM. After the crime potboiler *Kid Glove Killer* in 1942 he made his first serious film two years later: *The Seventh Cross,* with an all-star cast that included Spencer Tracy, Jessica Tandy and Hume Cronyn, dealt with a group of German concentration camp escapees. The subject matter of moral individuals surrounded by corrupt organizations or societies would attract Zinnemann throughout his career.

Zinnemann's realistic style proved invaluable in bringing to life the war's aftermath; some dubbed his style neorealist by analogy with the gritty style of contemporary Italian films, but Zinnemann credited his training with Flaherty as a more important influence. *The Search* (1948), starring a then-unknown Montgomery Clift, marked Zinnemann's emergence as a distinctive talent; its story of European war orphans mixed documentary-style footage with scripted narrative. Clift was cast at Zinnemann's insistence, and he became the first of a long list of actors whose careers the director launched or furthered in their early stages. The list included Marlon Brando who starred in *The Men*, Zinnemann's 1950 film about disabled veterans, Ava Gardner, Grace Kelly, Rod Steiger, Paul Scofield, Meryl Streep and John Hurt. Another important early Zinnemann film, highly esteemed by film buffs, was *Act of Violence* (1949), a dark-hued drama about survivor's guilt. Zinnemann left MGM after that film and worked mostly with independent producer Stanley Kramer over the next several years. In 1951 he picked up his first Academy Award, a best director nod for the short subject *Benjy*.

The spare style Zinnemann favored was applied with brilliant effect to the Western genre in *High Noon* (1952), which brought star Gary Cooper an Academy Award for best actor and a best director nomination for Zinnemann himself. Zinnemann and cinematographer Floyd Crosby set out to duplicate the plain style of a newsreel, and the film was shot in real time, over 85 minutes approaching a showdown between a marshal and a murderous gang. Abandoned by deputies, townspeople and even his wife, Cooper's marshal was both a classic lone hero and, in the view of some observers, an indictment of a corrupt society spiraling into the repressive years of the Red Scare.

The theme of an individual with a conscience recurred in *From Here to Eternity,* released in 1953 and considered perhaps his greatest film. Zinnemann won the Academy Award for best director, and the film won a host of other awards including one for Frank Sinatra in the role of Angelo Maggio, a soldier friend to Montgomery Clift's Private Prewitt. The film's most famous scene was a beach rendezvous between adulterous lovers Burt Lancaster and Deborah Kerr, complete with water splashing over the embracing pair, but much of the rest of the story, set in the days surrounding the bombing of Pearl Harbor, brought a new level of realism to Hollywood film. Zinnemann used newsreel footage of the bombing.

Attracted by Big Screen Format

Zinnemann's next film was atypical within his overall output; *Oklahoma!* (1955) was a musical comedy, the only one he directed. He was offered the helm of the big-budget production because of the success of his last two films, and he agreed to direct it because, as he told Neve, "I found it fascinating to try a new medium, this huge screen." The film was a hugely popular success although one critic joked that Zinnemann's rather dry style had in effect removed the exclamation point from the film's title. Zinnemann returned to more serious fare *A Hatful of Rain* (1957), a drama about drug addiction, and *The Nun's Story,* a 1959 film starring

Audrey Hepburn as a Belgian missionary nurse serving in the Congo.

The Nun's Story earned eight Academy Award nominations, including one for Zinnemann as best director. He added to his nomination tally with *The Sundowners* (1960), a family drama set on the Australian frontier, but his next film, the Spanish Civil War tale *Behold a Pale Horse,* was less successful despite the presence of Gregory Peck in the lead role. Zinnemann moved to London, England, in the early 1960s. He had several motivations: England was his wife's homeland, and he had often worked in Europe and thought about returning there. He was also still troubled by the blacklisting and loyalty oaths that had plagued Hollywood in the anti-Communist atmosphere of the 1950s.

Zinnemann's career got a second wind in London with the historical drama *A Man for All Seasons* (1966), which starred unknown Paul Scofield as St. Thomas More, another of Zinnemann's maverick heroes. The film took Academy Awards for best director and best picture among others. Despite this success, Zinnemann's next film, *Man's Fate,* was cancelled by the MGM studio just before Zinnemann was set to begin shooting. Zinnemann rebounded in the 1970s, however, with the taut thriller *The Day of the Jackal* (1973), in which he returned to his classic detached style. *Julia* (1977) introduced Meryl Streep in a small role. Based on the memoirs of playwright Lillian Hellman and starring liberal icons Jane Fonda and Vanessa Redgrave, the film brought Zinnemann his final best director Academy Award nomination.

Zinnemann made one more film, the gentle romance *Five Days One Summer* (1982); it featured Sean Connery as its star and a generous portion of mountain scenery in the Swiss Alps. Zinnemann himself was an avid mountaineer. He was frequently honored in the late 1980s for his lifetime of achievements and remained active in film circles, working for directors' rights to resist colorization of their black-and-white films. Ambulatory only with the aid of a walking stick, he nevertheless served as president of the Britain's Directors Guild. In the last year of his life, Zinnemann successfully resisted filmmakers' attempts to give a remake of *The Day of the Jackal* the same title, arguing that it had been altered too much from the original story (it was eventually released as *The Jackal*). Asked by Neve shortly before his death about his view of the future of cinema, he replied, ''I would like to be optimistic, because we have brilliant directors and writers and actors, but I tend to be pessimistic. We have enormous powers of persuasion, and we are role models for the rest of the world, but we no longer have a positive attitude towards life. Until that is changed, I think it is not going to be good.'' Zinnemann died in London on March 14, 1997.

Books

International Dictionary of Films and Filmmakers, 4th ed., St. James, 2000.
Zinnemann, Fred, *An Autobiography: A Life in the Movies,* Scribner's, 1990.

Periodicals

Australian, March 24, 1997.
Chicago Sun-Times, March 15, 1997.
Cineaste, Winter 1997.
Entertainment Weekly, March 28, 1997.
Guardian (London, England), March 17, 1997.
Mail on Sunday (London, England), March 16, 1997.
New York Times, March 15, 1997.
Times (London, England), March 17, 1997.
Variety, March 17, 1997.
Washington Times, March 23, 1997.

Online

''Fred Zinnemann,'' All Movie Guide, http://www.allmovie.com (January 30, 2006). □

HOW TO USE THE *SUPPLEMENT* INDEX

The *Encyclopedia of World Biography Supplement (EWB)* Index is designed to serve several purposes. First, it is a cumulative listing of biographies included in the entire second edition of *EWB* and its supplements (volumes 1-26). Second, it locates information on specific topics mentioned in volume 26 of the encyclopedia—persons, places, events, organizations, institutions, ideas, titles of works, inventions, as well as artistic schools, styles, and movements. Third, it classifies the subjects of *Supplement* articles according to shared characteristics. Vocational categories are the most numerous—for example, artists, authors, military leaders, philosophers, scientists, statesmen. Other groupings bring together disparate people who share a common characteristic.

The structure of the *Supplement* Index is quite simple. The biographical entries are cumulative and often provide enough information to meet immediate reference needs. Thus, people mentioned in the *Supplement* Index are identified and their life dates, when known, are given. Because this is an index to a *biographical* encyclopedia, every reference includes the *name* of the article to which the reader is directed as well as the volume and page numbers. Below are a few points that will make the *Supplement* Index easy to use.

Typography. All main entries are set in boldface type. Entries that are also the titles of articles in *EWB* are set entirely in capitals; other main entries are set in initial capitals and lowercase letters. Where a main entry is followed by a great many references, these are organized by subentries in alphabetical sequence. In certain cases—for example, the names of countries for which there are many references—a special class of subentries, set in small capitals and preceded by boldface dots, is used to mark significant divisions.

Alphabetization. The Index is alphabetized word by word. For example, all entries beginning with *New* as a separate word (*New Jersey, New York*) come before

Newark. Commas in inverted entries are treated as full stops (*Berlin; Berlin, Congress of; Berlin, University of; Berlin Academy of Sciences*). Other commas are ignored in filing. When words are identical, persons come first and subsequent entries are alphabetized by their parenthetical qualifiers (such as *book, city, painting*).

Titled persons may be alphabetized by family name or by title. The more familiar form is used—for example, *Disraeli, Benjamin* rather than *Beaconsfield, Earl of.* Cross-references are provided from alternative forms and spellings of names. Identical names of the same nationality are filed chronologically.

Titles of books, plays, poems, paintings, and other works of art beginning with an article are filed on the following word (*Bard, The*). Titles beginning with a preposition are filed on the preposition (*In Autumn*). In subentries, however, prepositions are ignored; thus *influenced by* would precede the subentry *in* literature.

Literary characters are filed on the last name. Acronyms, such as UNESCO, are treated as single words. Abbreviations, such as *Mr., Mrs.,* and *St.,* are alphabetized as though they were spelled out.

Occupational categories are alphabetical by national qualifier. Thus, *Authors, Scottish* comes before *Authors, Spanish,* and the reader interested in Spanish poets will find the subentry *poets* under *Authors, Spanish.*

Cross-references. The term *see* is used in references throughout the *Supplement* Index. The *see* references appear both as main entries and as subentries. They most often direct the reader from an alternative name spelling or form to the main entry listing.

This introduction to the *Supplement* Index is necessarily brief. The reader will soon find, however, that the *Supplement* Index provides ready reference to both highly specific subjects and broad areas of information contained in volume 26 and a cumulative listing of those included in the entire set.

INDEX

A

AALTO, HUGO ALVAR HENRIK (born 1898), Finnish architect, designer, and town planner **1** 1-2

AARON, HENRY LOUIS (Hank; born 1934), American baseball player **1** 2-3

ABAKANOWICZ, MAGDALENA (Marta Abakanowicz-Kosmowski; born 1930), Polish sculptor **25** 1-3

ABBA ARIKA (circa 175-circa 247), Babylonian rabbi **1** 3-4

ABBAS I (1571-1629), Safavid shah of Persia 1588-1629 **1** 4-6

ABBAS, FERHAT (born 1899), Algerian statesman **1** 6-7

ABBOTT, BERENICE (1898-1991), American artist and photographer **1** 7-9

ABBOTT, DIANE JULIE (born 1953), British politician and journalist **26** 1-3

ABBOTT, EDITH (1876-1957), American social reformer, educator, and author **26** 3-5

ABBOTT, GRACE (1878-1939), American social worker and agency administrator **1** 9-10
Abbott, Edith **26** 3-5

ABBOTT, LYMAN (1835-1922), American Congregationalist clergyman, author, and editor **1** 10-11

ABBOUD, EL FERIK IBRAHIM (1900-1983), Sudanese general, prime minister, 1958-1964 **1** 11-12

ABD AL-MALIK (646-705), Umayyad caliph 685-705 **1** 12-13

ABD AL-MUMIN (circa 1094-1163), Almohad caliph 1133-63 **1** 13

ABD AL-RAHMAN I (731-788), Umayyad emir in Spain 756-88 **1** 13-14

ABD AL-RAHMAN III (891-961), Umayyad caliph of Spain **1** 14

ABD EL-KADIR (1807-1883), Algerian political and religious leader **1** 15

ABD EL-KRIM EL-KHATABI, MOHAMED BEN (circa 1882-1963), Moroccan Berber leader **1** 15-16

ABDELLAH, FAYE GLENN (born 1919), American nurse **24** 1-3

ABDUH IBN HASAN KHAYR ALLAH, MUHAMMAD (1849-1905), Egyptian nationalist and theologian **1** 16-17

ABDUL RAHMAN, TUNKU (1903-1990), Former prime minister of Malaysia **18** 340-341

ABDUL-BAHA (Abbas Effendi; 1844-1921), Persian leader of the Baha'i Muslim sect **22** 3-5

ABDUL-HAMID II (1842-1918), Ottoman sultan 1876-1909 **1** 17-18

ABDULLAH II (Abdullah bin al Hussein II; born 1962), king of Jordan **22** 5-7

'ABDULLAH AL-SALIM AL-SABAH, SHAYKH (1895-1965), Amir of Kuwait (1950-1965) **1** 18-19

ABDULLAH IBN HUSEIN (1882-1951), king of Jordan 1949-1951, of Transjordan 1946-49 **1** 19-20

ABDULLAH IBN YASIN (died 1059), North African founder of the Almoravid movement **1** 20

ABDULLAH, MOHAMMAD (Lion of Kashmir; 1905-1982), Indian political leader who worked for an independent Kashmir **22** 7-9

ABE, KOBO (born Kimifusa Abe; also transliterated as Abe Kobo; 1924-1993), Japanese writer, theater director, photographer **1** 20-22

ABEL, IORWITH WILBER (1908-1987), United States labor organizer **1** 22-23

ABEL, NIELS (1802-1829), Norwegian mathematician **20** 1-2

ABELARD, PETER (1079-1142), French philosopher and theologian **1** 23-25

ABERCROMBY, RALPH (1734-1801), British military leader **20** 2-4

ABERDEEN, 4TH EARL OF (George Hamilton Gordon; 1784-1860), British statesman, prime minister 1852-55 **1** 25-26

ABERHART, WILLIAM (1878-1943), Canadian statesman and educator **1** 26-27

ABERNATHY, RALPH DAVID (born 1926), United States minister and civil rights leader **1** 27-28

ABIOLA, MOSHOOD (1937-1998), Nigerian politician, philanthropist, and businessman **19** 1-3

Abolitionists, American
African Americans
Hall, Prince **26** 136-138
colonizationists
Hall, Prince **26** 136-138

ABRAHAM (Abraham of the Chaldrrs; Father Abraham; c. 1996 BCE - c. 1821 BCE), considered the "father of the world's three largest monotheistic religions **23** 1-3

ABRAHAMS, ISRAEL (1858-1925), British scholar **1** 29

ABRAMOVITZ, MAX (1908-2004), American architect **18** 1-3

ABRAMS, CREIGHTON W. (1914-1974), United States Army commander in World War II and Vietnam **1** 29-31

ABRAVANEL, ISAAC BEN JUDAH (1437-1508), Jewish philosopher and statesman **1** 31

Abstract expressionism (art)
Rothenberg, Susan **26** 326-328

405

BACON, PEGGY (Margaret Francis Bacon; 1895-1987), American artist and author **25** 29-31

BACON, ROGER (circa 1214-1294), English philosopher **1** 425-427

BAD HEART BULL, AMOS (1869-1913), Oglala Lakota Sioux tribal historian and artist **1** 427-428

BADEN-POWELL, ROBERT (1857-1941), English military officer and founder of the Boy Scout Association **21** 16-18

BADINGS, HENK (Hendrik Herman Badings; 1907-1987), Dutch composer **23** 26-28

BADOGLIO, PIETRO (1871-1956), Italian general and statesman **1** 428-429

BAECK, LEO (1873-1956), rabbi, teacher, hero of the concentration camps, and Jewish leader **1** 429-430

BAEKELAND, LEO HENDRIK (1863-1944), American chemist **1** 430-431

BAER, GEORGE FREDERICK (1842-1914), American businessman **22** 39-41

BAER, KARL ERNST VON (1792-1876), Estonian anatomist and embryologist **1** 431-432

BAEZ, BUENAVENTURA (1812-1884), Dominican statesman, five time president **1** 432-433

BAEZ, JOAN (born 1941), American folk singer and human rights activist **1** 433-435

BAFFIN, WILLIAM (circa 1584-1622), English navigator and explorer **1** 435-436

BAGEHOT, WALTER (1826-1877), English economist **1** 436-437

BAGLEY, WILLIAM CHANDLER (1874-1946), educator and theorist of educational "essentialism" **1** 437-438

BAHR, EGON (born 1922), West German politician **1** 438-440

BAIKIE, WILLIAM BALFOUR (1825-1864), Scottish explorer and scientist **1** 440

BAILEY, F. LEE (born 1933), American defense attorney and author **1** 441-443

BAILEY, FLORENCE MERRIAM (1863-1948), American ornithologist and author **1** 443-444

BAILEY, GAMALIEL (1807-1859), American editor and politician **1** 444-445

BAILEY, MILDRED (Mildred Rinker, 1907-1951), American jazz singer **23** 28-30

BAILLIE, D(ONALD) M(ACPHERSON) (1887-1954), Scottish theologian **1** 445

BAILLIE, ISOBEL (Isabella Baillie; 1895-1983), British singer **26** 27-29

BAILLIE, JOHN (1886-1960), Scottish theologian and ecumenical churchman **1** 445-447

BAKER, ELLA JOSEPHINE (1903-1986), African American human and civil rights activist **18** 26-28

BAKER, HOWARD HENRY, JR. (born 1925), U.S. senator and White House chief of staff **18** 28-30

BAKER, JAMES ADDISON III (born 1930), Republican party campaign leader **1** 447-448

BAKER, JOSEPHINE (1906-1975) Parisian dancer and singer from America **1** 448-451

BAKER, NEWTON DIEHL (1871-1937), American statesman **1** 451

BAKER, RAY STANNARD (1870-1946), American author **1** 451-452

BAKER, RUSSELL (born 1925), American writer of personal-political essays **1** 452-454

BAKER, SIR SAMUEL WHITE (1821-1893), English explorer and administrator **1** 454-455

BAKER, SARA JOSEPHINE (1873-1945), American physician **1** 455-456

BAKHTIN, MIKHAIL MIKHAILOVICH (1895-1975), Russian philosopher and literary critic **1** 456-458

BAKUNIN, MIKHAIL ALEKSANDROVICH (1814-1876), Russian anarchist **1** 458-460

BALAGUER Y RICARDO, JOAQUÍN (1907-2002), Dominican statesman **1** 460-461

BALANCHINE, GEORGE (1904-1983), Russian-born American choreographer **1** 461-462

BALBOA, VASCO NÚÑEZ DE (circa 1475-1519), Spanish explorer **1** 462-463

BALBULUS, NOTKER (circa 840-912), Swiss poet-musician and monk **11** 434-435

BALCH, EMILY GREENE (1867-1961), American pacifist and social reformer **1** 463-464

BALDWIN I (1058-1118), Norman king of Jerusalem 1100-1118 **1** 464-465

BALDWIN, JAMES ARTHUR (1924-1987), African American author, poet, and dramatist **1** 465-466

BALDWIN, ROBERT (1804-1858), Canadian politician **1** 466-468

BALDWIN, ROGER NASH (1884-1981), American civil libertarian and social worker **25** 31-33

BALDWIN, STANLEY (1st Earl Baldwin of Bewdley; 1867-1947), English statesman, three times prime minister **1** 468-469

BALFOUR, ARTHUR JAMES (1st Earl of Balfour; 1848-1930), British statesman and philosopher **1** 469-470

BALL, GEORGE (1909-1994), American politician and supporter of an economically united Europe **1** 470-471

BALL, LUCILLE (Lucille Desiree Hunt; 1911-1989), American comedienne **1** 472-473

BALLA, GIACOMO (1871-1958), Italian painter **1** 473-474

BALLADUR, EDOUARD (born 1929), premier of the French Government **1** 474-475

BALLARD, LOUIS WAYNE (born 1913), Native American musician **26** 29-31

BALLARD, ROBERT (born 1942), American oceanographer **19** 10-12

Ballet (dance)
Ashton, Frederick **26** 22-24
Fokine, Michel **26** 112-115
Hightower, Rosella **26** 154-156
Zakharov, Rostislav Vladimirovich **26** 396-398

Ballets Russes de Sergei Diaghilev (dance company)
Fokine, Michel **26** 112-115

BALLIVIÁN, JOSÉ (1805-1852), Bolivian president 1841-1847 **1** 475

BALMACEDA FERNÁNDEZ, JOSÉ MANUEL (1840-1891), Chilean president 1886-1891 **1** 475-476

BALTHUS (Balthasar Klossowski; born 1908), European painter and stage designer **1** 476-477

BALTIMORE, DAVID (born 1938), American virologist **1** 477-478

BALZAC, HONORÉ DE (1799-1850), French novelist **1** 478-480

BAMBA, AMADOU (1850-1927), Senegalese religious leader **1** 481-482

BAMBARA, TONI CADE (1939-1995), African American writer and editor **1** 482-483

BAN ZHAO (Pan Chao, Ban Hui-ji, Cao Dagu; c. 45-51-c. 114-120), Chinese author and historian **24** 38-40

BANCROFT, ANNE (nee Anna Maria Louisa Italino; 1931-2005), American actress **26** 31-33

BANCROFT, GEORGE (1800-1891), American historian and statesman **1** 483-484

BANCROFT, HUBERT HOWE (1832-1918), American historian **1** 484-485

BANDA, HASTINGS KAMUZU (1905-1997), Malawi statesman **1** 485-486

BANDARANAIKE, SIRIMAVO (also Sirima) RATWATTE DIAS (born 1916), first woman prime minister in the world as head of the Sri Lankan Freedom party government (1960-1965, 1970-1976) **1** 486-488

BANERJEE, SURENDRANATH (1848-1925), Indian nationalist **1** 488

BANKS, DENNIS J. (born 1932), Native American leader, teacher, activist, and author **1** 488-489

BANKS, SIR JOSEPH (1743-1820), English naturalist **1** 489-490

BANNEKER, BENJAMIN (1731-1806), African American mathematician **1** 490-491

BANNISTER, EDWARD MITCHELL (1828-1901), African American landscape painter **1** 491-493

BANNISTER, ROGER (born 1929), English runner **21** 18-20

BANTING, FREDERICK GRANT (1891-1941), Canadian physiolgist **1** 493-494

BAÑUELOS, ROMANA ACOSTA (born 1925), Mexican businesswoman and American government official **24** 40-42

BANZER SUÁREZ, HUGO (1926-2002), Bolivian president (1971-1979) **1** 494-496

BAO DAI (born 1913), emperor of Vietnam 1932-1945 and 1949-1955 **1** 496-497

BAR KOCHBA, SIMEON (died 135), Jewish commander of revolt against Romans **2** 5

BARAK, EHUD (born 1942), Israeli prime minister **1** 497-498

BARAKA, IMAMU AMIRI (Everett LeRoi Jones; born 1934), African American poet and playwright **1** 498-499

BARANOV, ALEKSANDR ANDREIEVICH (1747-1819), Russian explorer **1** 499-500

BARBEAU, MARIUS (1883-1969), Canadian ethnographer, anthropologist, and author **24** 42-44

BARBER, SAMUEL (1910-1981), American composer **1** 500-501

BARBIE, KLAUS (Klaus Altmann; 1913-1991), Nazi leader in Vichy France **1** 501-503

BARBIROLLI, JOHN (Giovanni Battista Barbirolli; 1899-1970), British conductor **24** 44-46

BARBONCITO (1820-1871), Native American leader of the Navajos **20** 25-27

BARBOSA, RUY (1849-1923), Brazilian journalist and politician **1** 503-504

BARDEEN, JOHN (1908-1991), American Nobel physicist **2** 1-3

BARENBOIM, DANIEL (born 1942), Israeli pianist and conductor **2** 3-4

BARENTS, WILLEM (died 1597), Dutch navigator and explorer **2** 4-5

BARING, FRANCIS (1740-1810), English banker **21** 20-22

BARLACH, ERNST (1870-1938), German sculptor **2** 5-6

BARLOW, JOEL (1754-1812), American poet **2** 6-7

BARNARD, CHRISTIAAN N. (1922-2001), South African heart transplant surgeon **2** 7-8

BARNARD, EDWARD EMERSON (1857-1923), American astronomer **2** 8-9

BARNARD, FREDERICK AUGUSTUS PORTER (1809-1889), American educator and mathematician **2** 9-10

BARNARD, HENRY (1811-1900), American educator **2** 10

BARNES, DJUNA (a.k.a. Lydia Steptoe; 1892-1982), American author **2** 11-13

BARNETT, ETTA MOTEN (1901-2004), African American actress and singer **25** 34-36

BARNETT, MARGUERITE ROSS (1942-1992), American educator **21** 22-24

BARNUM, PHINEAS TAYLOR (1810-1891), American showman **2** 13-15
Lind, Jenny **26** 233-235

BAROJA Y NESSI, PÍO (1872-1956), Spanish novelist **2** 15-16

BARON, SALO WITTMAYER (1895-1989), Austrian-American educator and Jewish historian **2** 16-17

Baroque music (German and Austrian) instrumental
Landowska, Wanda **26** 215-218

Baroque music (Italian) instrumental
Geminiani, Francesco Saverio **26** 123-125

BARRAGÁN, LUIS (1902-1988), Mexican architect and landscape architect **2** 17-19

BARRAS, VICOMTE DE (Paul François Jean Nicolas; 1755-1829), French statesman and revolutionist **2** 19

BARRE, RAYMOND (1924-1981), prime minister of France (1976-1981) **2** 19-20

BARRÈS, AUGUSTE MAURICE (1862-1923), French writer and politician **2** 20-21

BARRIE, SIR JAMES MATTHEW (1860-1937), British dramatist and novelist **2** 21-22

BARRIENTOS ORTUÑO, RENÉ (1919-1969), populist Bolivian president (1966-1969) **2** 22-23

BARRIOS, JUSTO RUFINO (1835-1885), Guatemalan general, president 1873-1885 **2** 23-24

BARRY, JOHN (1745-1803), American naval officer **2** 24-25

BARRY, MARION SHEPILOV, JR. (born 1936), African American mayor and civil rights activist **2** 25-28

BARRYMORES, American theatrical dynasty **2** 28-30

BARTH, HEINRICH (1821-1865), German explorer **2** 30-31

BARTH, KARL (1886-1968), Swiss Protestant theologian **2** 31-32

BARTHÉ, RICHMOND (1901-1989), African American sculptor **2** 33-34

BARTHOLOMAEUS ANGLICUS (Bartholomew the Englishman; Bartholomew de Glanville; flourished 1220-1240), English theologian and encyclopedist **21** 24-25

BARTLETT, SIR FREDERIC CHARLES (1886-1969), British psychologist **2** 34-35

BARTÓK, BÉLA (1881-1945), Hungarian composer and pianist **2** 35-36

BARTON, BRUCE (1886-1967), American advertising business executive and congressman **2** 36-37

BARTON, CLARA (1821-1912), American humanitarian **2** 37-39

BARTON, SIR EDMUND (1849-1920), Australian statesman and jurist **2** 39-40

BARTRAM, JOHN (1699-1777), American botanist **2** 40-41

BLANC, MEL (1908-1989), American creator of and voice of cartoon characters **2** 319-320

BLANCHARD, FELIX ("Doc" Blanchard; born 1924), American football player and military pilot **21** 43-45

BLANCHE OF CASTILE (1188-1252), French queen **21** 45-47

BLANCO, ANTONIO GUZMÁN (1829-1899), Venezuelan politician, three-times president **2** 320-321

BLANDIANA, ANA (born Otilia-Valeria Coman, 1942), Romanian poet **2** 321-322

BLANDING, SARAH GIBSON (1898-1985), American educator **2** 322-323

BLANKERS-KOEN, FANNY (Francina Elsja Blankers-Koen; born 1918), Dutch track and field athlete **20** 50-52

BLANQUI, LOUIS AUGUSTE (1805-1881), French revolutionary **2** 323-324

BLAVATSKY, HELENA PETROVNA (Helena Hahn; 1831-1891), Russian theosophist **22** 67-69

BLEDSOE, ALBERT TAYLOR (1809-1877), American lawyer, educator, and Confederate apologist **2** 324-325

BLEULER, EUGEN (1857-1939), Swiss psychiatrist **2** 325

BLEY, CARLA (nee Carla Borg; born 1938), American composer and pianist **26** 40-42

BLIGH, WILLIAM (1754-1817), English naval officer and colonial governor **2** 325-326

BLOCH, ERNEST (1880-1959), Swiss-born American composer and teacher **2** 326-327

BLOCH, ERNST (1885-1977), German humanistic interpreter of Marxist thought **2** 327-328

BLOCH, FELIX (1905-1983), Swiss/American physicist **2** 328-330

BLOCH, KONRAD (born 1912), American biochemist **2** 330-332

BLOCH, MARC (1886-1944), French historian **2** 332-333

BLOCK, HERBERT (Herblock; 1909-2001), American newspaper cartoonist **2** 333-334

BLODGETT, KATHARINE BURR (1898-1979), American physicist **24** 54-56

BLOK, ALEKSANDR ALEKSANDROVICH (1880-1921), Russian poet **2** 335

BLOOM, ALLAN DAVID (1930-1992), American political philosopher, professor, and author **2** 335-337

BLOOMER, AMELIA JENKS (1818-1894), American reformer and suffrage advocate **2** 337

BLOOMFIELD, LEONARD (1887-1949), American linguist **2** 338

BLOOR, ELLA REEVE ("Mother Bloor"; 1862-1951), American labor organizer and social activist **2** 338-340

BLÜCHER, GEBHARD LEBERECHT VON (Prince of Wahlstatt; 1742-1819), Prussian field marshal **2** 340-341

Blues (music)
Gaye, Marvin **26** 119-123
Joplin, Janis **26** 183-187
Little Milton **26** 236-237
Vandross, Luther **26** 364-366

BLUFORD, GUION STEWART, JR. (born 1942), African American aerospace engineer, pilot, and astronaut **2** 341-343

BLUM, LÉON (1872-1950), French statesman **2** 343-344

BLUME, JUDY (born Judy Sussman; b. 1938), American fiction author **2** 344-345

BLUMENTHAL, WERNER MICHAEL (born 1926), American businessman and treasury secretary **2** 345-346

BLY, NELLIE (born Elizabeth Cochrane Seaman; 1864-1922), American journalist and reformer **2** 346-348

BLYDEN, EDWARD WILMOT (1832-1912), Liberian statesman **2** 348-349

BOAS, FRANZ (1858-1942), German-born American anthropologist **2** 349-351

BOCCACCIO, GIOVANNI (1313-1375), Italian author **2** 351-353

BOCCIONI, UMBERTO (1882-1916), Italian artist **2** 353-354

BÖCKLIN, ARNOLD (1827-1901), Swiss painter **2** 354-355

BODE, BOYD HENRY (1873-1953), American philosopher and educator **2** 355-356

BODIN, JEAN (1529/30-1596), French political philosopher **2** 356-357

BOEHME, JACOB (1575-1624), German mystic **2** 357

BOEING, WILLIAM EDWARD (1881-1956), American businessman **2** 357-358

BOERHAAVE, HERMANN (1668-1738), Dutch physician and chemist **2** 358-359

BOESAK, ALLAN AUBREY (born 1945), opponent of apartheid in South Africa

and founder of the United Democratic Front **2** 359-360

BOETHIUS, ANICIUS MANLIUS SEVERINUS (480?-524/525), Roman logician and theologian **2** 360-361

BOFF, LEONARDO (Leonardo Genezio Darci Boff; born 1938), Brazilian priest **22** 69-71

BOFFRAND, GABRIEL GERMAIN (1667-1754), French architect and decorator **2** 361

BOFILL, RICARDO (born 1939), post-modern Spanish architect **2** 362-363

BOGART, HUMPHREY (1899-1957), American stage and screen actor **2** 363-364

BOHEMUND I (of Tarantò; circa 1055-1111), Norman Crusader **2** 364

BOHLEN, CHARLES (CHIP) EUSTIS (1904-1973), United States ambassador to the Soviet Union, interpreter, and presidential adviser **2** 364-366

BÖHM-BAWERK, EUGEN VON (1851-1914), Austrian economist **2** 366

BOHR, AAGE NIELS (born 1922), Danish physicist **25** 53-55

BOHR, NIELS HENRIK DAVID (1885-1962), Danish physicist **2** 366-368

BOIARDO, MATTEO MARIA (Conte di Scandiano; 1440/41-1494), Italian poet **2** 369

BOILEAU-DESPRÉAUX, NICHOLAS (1636?-1711), French critic and writer **2** 369-371

BOIVIN, MARIE GILLAIN (née Marie Anne Victorine Gillain; 1773-1841), French midwife and author **25** 55-56

BOK, DEREK CURTIS (born 1930), dean of the Harvard Law School and president of Harvard University **2** 371-372

BOK, EDWARD WILLIAM (1863-1930), American editor and publisher **22** 71-73

BOK, SISSELA ANN (born 1934), American moral philosopher **2** 372-374

BOLEYN, ANNE (1504?-1536), second wife of Henry VIII **18** 47-49

BOLINGBROKE, VISCOUNT (Henry St. John; 1678-1751), English statesman **2** 374-375

BOLÍVAR, SIMÓN (1783-1830), South American general and statesman **2** 375-377

BROOKE, ALAN FRANCIS (Viscount Alanbrooke; 1883-1963), Irish military leader **20** 59-61

BROOKE, SIR JAMES (1803-1868), British governor in Borneo **3** 21-22

BROOKE, RUPERT (1887-1915), English poet **3** 22-23

BROOKNER, ANITA (born 1928), British art historian and novelist **3** 23-24

BROOKS, GWENDOLYN (born 1917), first African American author to receive the Pulitzer Prize for Literature **3** 24-26

BROOKS, MEL (Melvin Kaminsky; born 1926), American actor, playwright, and film and theatre producer/director **23** 48-50

BROOKS, PHILLIPS (1835-1893), American Episcopalian bishop **3** 26

BROTHERS, JOYCE (Joyce Diane Bauer; born 1927), American psychologist who pioneered radio phone-in questions for professional psychological advice **3** 26-28

BROUDY, HARRY SAMUEL (born 1905), American philosopher, teacher, and author **3** 28-29

BROUGHAM, HENRY PETER (Baron Brougham and Vaux; 1778-1868), Scottish jurist **22** 83-85

BROUWER, ADRIAEN (1605/06-1638), Flemish painter **3** 29-30

BROWDER, EARL RUSSELL (1891-1973), American Communist leader **3** 30-31

BROWN, ALEXANDER (1764-1834), American merchant and banker **3** 31-32

BROWN, BENJAMIN GRATZ (1826-1885), American politician **3** 32-33

BROWN, CHARLES BROCKDEN (1771-1810), American novelist **3** 33

BROWN, CHARLOTTE EUGENIA HAWKINS (born Lottie Hawkins; 1882-1961), African American educator and humanitarian **3** 34

BROWN, GEORGE (1818-1880), Canadian politician **3** 35-36

BROWN, HELEN GURLEY (born 1922), American author and editor **3** 36-37

BROWN, JAMES (born 1928), African American singer **3** 37-39

BROWN, JOHN (1800-1859), American abolitionist **3** 39-41

BROWN, JOSEPH EMERSON (1821-1894), American lawyer and politician **3** 41-42

BROWN, LES (Leslie Calvin Brown; born 1945), American motivational speaker, author, and television host **19** 36-39

BROWN, MOSES (1738-1836), American manufacturer and merchant **3** 42-43

BROWN, RACHEL FULLER (1898-1980), American biochemist **3** 43-44

BROWN, ROBERT (1773-1858), Scottish botanist **20** 61-63

BROWN, RONALD H. (1941-1996), African American politician, cabinet official **3** 44-47

BROWN, TINA (Christina Hambly Brown; born 1953), British editor who transformed the English magazine *Tatler*, then the United States magazines *Vanity Fair* and the *New Yorker* **3** 47-48

BROWN, TONY (William Anthony Brown; born 1933), African American radio personality **24** 68-70

BROWN, WILLIAM WELLS (1815/16-1884), African American author and abolitionist **3** 48-49

BROWNE, SIR THOMAS (1605-1682), English author **3** 49-50

BROWNE, THOMAS ALEXANDER (Rolf Bolderwood; 1826-1915), Australian author **22** 85-87

BROWNER, CAROL M. (born 1955), U.S. Environmental Protection Agency administrator **3** 50-52

BROWNING, ELIZABETH BARRETT (1806-1861), English poet **3** 52-53

BROWNING, ROBERT (1812-1889), English poet **3** 53-55

BROWNLOW, WILLIAM GANNAWAY (1805-1877), American journalist and politician **3** 55-56

BROWNMILLER, SUSAN (born 1935), American activist, journalist, and novelist **3** 56-57

BROWNSON, ORESTES AUGUSTUS (1803-1876), American clergyman and transcendentalist **3** 57-58

BRUBACHER, JOHN SEILER (1898-1988), American historian and educator **3** 58-59

BRUBECK, DAVE (born 1920), American pianist, composer, and bandleader **3** 59-61

BRUCE, BLANCHE KELSO (1841-1898), African American politician **3** 62-63

BRUCE, DAVID (1855-1931), Australian parasitologist **3** 63

BRUCE, JAMES (1730-1794), Scottish explorer **3** 63-64

BRUCE, LENNY (Leonard Alfred Schneider; 1925-1966), American comedian **19** 39-41

BRUCE OF MELBOURNE, 1ST VISCOUNT (Stanley Melbourne Bruce; 1883-1967), Australian statesman **3** 61-62

BRUCKNER, JOSEPH ANTON (1824-1896), Austrian composer **3** 64-65

BRUEGEL, PIETER, THE ELDER (1525/30-1569), Netherlandish painter **3** 65-67

BRÛLÉ, ÉTIENNE (circa 1592-1633), French explorer in North America **3** 67-68

BRUNDTLAND, GRO HARLEM (1939-1989), Norwegian prime minister and chair of the United Nations World Commission for Environment and Development **3** 68-69

BRUNEL, ISAMBARD KINGDOM (1806-1859), English civil engineer **3** 69-70

BRUNELLESCHI, FILIPPO (1377-1446), Italian architect and sculptor **3** 70-72

BRUNER, JEROME SEYMOUR (born 1915), American psychologist **3** 72-73

BRUNHOFF, JEAN de (1899-1937), French author and illustrator **19** 41-42

BRUNNER, ALOIS (born 1912), Nazi German officer who helped engineer the destruction of European Jews **3** 73-74

BRUNNER, EMIL (1889-1966), Swiss Reformed theologian **3** 74-75

BRUNO, GIORDANO (1548-1600), Italian philosopher and poet **3** 75-76

BRUTON, JOHN GERARD (born 1947), prime minister of Ireland **3** 76-77

BRUTUS, DENNIS (born 1924), exiled South African poet and political activist opposed to apartheid **3** 77-78

BRUTUS, MARCUS JUNIUS (circa 85-42 B.C.), Roman statesman **3** 79-80

BRYAN, WILLIAM JENNINGS (1860-1925), American lawyer and politician **3** 80-82

BRYANT, PAUL ("Bear;" 1919-1983), American college football coach **3** 82-83

BRYANT, WILLIAM CULLEN (1794-1878), American poet and editor **3** 83-85

BRYCE, JAMES (1838-1922), British historian, jurist, and statesman **3** 85

BRZEZINSKI, ZBIGNIEW (1928-1980), assistant to President Carter for national security affairs (1977-1980) **3** 85-87

CANNON, JOSEPH GURNEY (1836-1926), American politican **3** 261-262

CANOT, THEODORE (1804-1860), French-Italian adventurer and slave trader **3** 262-263

CANOVA, ANTONIO (1757-1822), Italian sculptor **3** 263-264

CANTINFLAS (Mario Moreno Reyes; 1911-1993), Mexican comedian **26** 53-55

CANTOR, EDDIE (Isador Iskowitz; 1892-1964), American singer and comedian **3** 264-265

CANTOR, GEORG FERDINAND LUDWIG PHILIPP (1845-1918), German mathematician **3** 265-266

CANUTE I THE GREAT (c. 995-1035), Viking king of England and Denmark **3** 266-269

CANUTT, YAKIMA (Enos Edward Canutt; 1896-1986), American rodeo performer, actor, stuntman, and film director **21** 71-72

CAO YU (Wan Jibao; Tsao Yu; Xiaoshi; 1910-1996), Chinese playwright **26** 55-57

CAPA, ROBERT (Endre Friedmann; 1913-1954), Hungarian-American war photographer and photojournalist **3** 269-271

ČAPEK, KAREL (1890-1938), Czech novelist, playwright, and essayist **3** 271-272

CAPETILLO, LUISA (1879-1922), Puerto Rican labor leader and activist **20** 73-74

CAPONE, AL (Alphonso Caponi, a.k.a. "Scarface;" 1899-1947), American gangster **3** 272-273

CAPOTE, TRUMAN (born Truman Streckfus Persons; 1924-1984), American author **3** 273-275

CAPP, AL (Alfred Gerald Capp; 1909-1979), American cartoonist and satirist **3** 275-276

CAPRA, FRANK (1897-1991), American film director **3** 276-278

CAPRIATI, JENNIFER (born 1976), American tennis player **3** 278-281

CAPTAIN JACK (Kientpoos; circa 1837-1873), American tribal leader **21** 72-74

CARACALLA (188-217), Roman emperor **3** 281-282

CARAGIALE, ION LUCA (1852-1912), Romanian author **23** 62-64

CARAVAGGIO (1573-1610), Italian painter **3** 282-284

CARAWAY, HATTIE WYATT (1878-1950), first woman elected to the United States Senate in her own right **3** 284-285

CARDANO, GERONIMO (1501-1576), Italian mathematician, astronomer, and physician **3** 285-286

CARDENAL, ERNESTO (born 1925), Nicaraguan priest, poet, and revolutionary **19** 57-59

CÁRDENAS, LÁZARO (1895-1970), Mexican revolutionary president 1934-1940 **3** 286-287

CÁRDENAS SOLORZANO, CUAUHTÉMOC (born 1934), Mexican politician **3** 287-288

CARDIN, PIERRE (born 1922), French fashion designer **18** 79-81

CARDOSO, FERNANDO HENRIQUE (born 1931), sociologist and president of Brazil **18** 81-83

CARDOZO, BENJAMIN NATHAN (1870-1938), American jurist and legal philosopher **3** 288-290

CARDUCCI, GIOSUÈ (1835-1907), Italian poet **3** 290-291

CAREW, ROD (born 1945), Panamanian baseball player **3** 291-292

CAREY, GEORGE LEONARD (born 1935), archbishop of Canterbury **3** 293-294

CAREY, HENRY CHARLES (1793-1879), American writer on economics **3** 294-295

CAREY, PETER (born 1943), Australian author **3** 295-297

CAREY, WILLIAM (1761-1834), English Baptist missionary **3** 297

CAREY THOMAS, MARTHA (1857-1935), American educator **3** 297-298

CARÍAS ANDINO, TIBURCIO (1876-1969), Honduran dictator (1932-1949) **3** 298-299

CARISSIMI, GIACOMO (1605-1674), Italian composer **3** 299-300

CARLETON, GUY (1st Baron Dorchester; 1724-1808), British general and statesman **3** 300-301

CARLIN, GEORGE (born 1937), American comedian **3** 301-303

CARLSON, CHESTER F. (1906-1968), American inventor of the process of xerography **3** 303-304

CARLYLE, THOMAS (1795-1881), Scottish essayist and historian **3** 304-305

CARMICHAEL, HOAGY (Hoagland Howard Carmichael; 1899-1981), American songwriter **26** 57-60

CARMICHAEL, STOKELY (1941-1998), African American civil rights activist **3** 305-308

Carmina Burana (set of songs) Orff, Carl **26** 276-278

CARNAP, RUDOLF (1891-1970), German-American philosopher **3** 308-309

CARNÉ, MARCEL ALBERT (1909-1996), French film director and screenwriter **26** 60-62

CARNEADES (circa 213-circa 128 B.C.), Greek philosopher **3** 309

CARNEGIE, ANDREW (1835-1919), American industrialist and philanthropist **3** 309-312

CARNEGIE, HATTIE (born Henrietta Kanengeiser; 1889-1956), American fashion designer **3** 313

CARNOT, LAZARE NICOLAS MARGUERITE (1753-1823), French engineer, general, and statesman **3** 313-314

CARNOT, NICHOLAS LÉONARD SADI (1796-1832), French physicist **3** 315

CARO, ANTHONY (born 1924), English sculptor **3** 316

CARO, JOSEPH BEN EPHRAIM (1488-1575), Jewish Talmudic scholar **3** 316-317

CAROTHERS, WALLACE HUME (1896-1937), American chemist **3** 317-318

CARPEAUX, JEAN BAPTISTE (1827-1875), French sculptor and painter **3** 318-319

CARR, EMILY (1871-1945), Canadian painter and writer **3** 319

CARR, EMMA PERRY (1880-1972), American chemist and educator **22** 89-91

CARR-SAUNDERS, SIR ALEXANDER MORRIS (1886-1966), English demographer and sociologist **3** 333-334

CARRANZA, VENUSTIANO (1859-1920), Mexican revolutionary, president 1914-1920 **3** 321-322

CARREL, ALEXIS (1873-1944), French-American surgeon **3** 322-323

CARRERA, JOSÉ MIGUEL (1785-1821), Chilean revolutionary **3** 323-324

CARRERA, JOSÉ RAFAEL (1814-1865), Guatemalan statesman, president 1851-1865 **3** 324-325

CUNNINGHAM, GLENN (1909-1988), American track and field athlete **21** 96-99

CUNNINGHAM, IMOGEN (1883-1976), American photographer **19** 84-86

CUNNINGHAM, MERCE (born 1919), American dancer and choreographer **4** 337-338

CUOMO, MARIO MATTHEW (born 1932), Democratic New York state governor **4** 338-339

CURIE, ÈVE (Eve Curie Labouisse; born 1904), French musician, author and diplomat **18** 109-111

CURIE, MARIE SKLODOWSKA (1867-1934), Polish-born French physicist **4** 339-341

CURIE, PIERRE (1859-1906), French physicist **4** 341-344

CURLEY, JAMES MICHAEL (1874-1958), American politician **4** 344-345

CURRIE, SIR ARTHUR WILLIAM (1875-1933), Canadian general **4** 345

CURRIER AND IVES (1857-1907), American lithographic firm **4** 345-346

CURRY, JABEZ LAMAR MONROE (1815-1903), American politician **4** 346-347

CURTIN, ANDREW GREGG (1815-1894), American politician **4** 347-348

CURTIN, JOHN JOSEPH (1885-1945), Australian statesman, prime minister **4** 348-349

CURTIS, BENJAMIN ROBBINS (1809-1874), American jurist, United States Supreme Court justice **4** 349

CURTIS, CHARLES BRENT (1860-1936), American vice president (1929-1932) and legislator **21** 99-100

CURTIS, GEORGE WILLIAM (1824-1892), American writer and reformer **4** 349-350

CURTISS, GLENN HAMMOND (1878-1930), American aviation pioneer **4** 350-351

CURZON, GEORGE NATHANIEL (1st Marquess Curzon of Kedleston; 1859-1925), English statesman **4** 351-352

CUSA, NICHOLAS OF (1401-1464), German prelate and humanist **4** 352-353

CUSHING, HARVEY WILLIAMS (1869-1939), American neurosurgeon **4** 353-354

CUSHMAN, CHARLOTTE (1816-1876), American actress **4** 354-355

CUSTER, GEORGE ARMSTRONG (1839-1876), American general **4** 355-356 Rain in the Face **26** 314-316

CUTLER, MANASSEH (1742-1823), American clergyman, scientist, and politician **4** 356-357

CUVIER, BARON GEORGES LÉOPOLD (1769-1832), French zoologist and biologist **4** 357-359

CUVILLIÉS, FRANÇOIS (1695-1768), Flemish architect and designer **4** 359-360

CUYP, AELBERT (1620-1691), Dutch painter **4** 360-361

CYNEWULF (8th or 9th century), Anglo-Saxon poet **20** 103-104

CYPRIANUS, THASCIUS CAECILIANUS (died 258), Roman bishop of Carthage **4** 361-362

Cyrenaica (province, Ottoman Empire) Arete of Cyrene **26** 18-20

CYRIL (OF ALEXANDRIA), ST. (died 444), Egyptian bishop, Doctor of the Church **4** 362

CYRIL, ST. (827-869), Apostle to the Slavs **4** 362

CYRUS THE GREAT (ruled 550-530 B.C.), founder of the Persian Empire **4** 363-364

D

DA PONTE, LORENZO (Emanuele Conegliano; 1749-1838), Italian librettist and poet **20** 105-106

DAGUERRE, LOUIS JACQUES MANDÉ (1787-1851), French painter and stage designer **4** 365-366

DAHL, ROALD (1916-1990), Welsh-born English author **4** 366-367

DAIGO II (1288-1339), Japanese emperor **4** 367-368

DAIMLER, GOTTLIEB (1834-1900), German mechanical engineer **4** 368

DALADIER, ÉDOUARD (1884-1970), French statesman **4** 369

DALAI LAMA (Lhamo Thondup; born 1935), 14th in a line of Buddhist spiritual and temporal leaders of Tibet **4** 369-371

DALE, SIR HENRY HALLETT (1875-1968), English pharmacologist and neurophysiologist **4** 371-373

DALEN, NILS GUSTAF (1869-1937), Swedish engineer and inventor **25** 99-101

DALEY, RICHARD M. (born 1942), mayor of Chicago **24** 102-104

DALEY, RICHARD J. (1902-1976), Democratic mayor of Chicago (1955-1976) **4** 373-375

DALHOUSIE, 1ST MARQUESS OF (James Andrew Broun Ramsay; 1812-1860), British statesman **4** 375-376

DALI, SALVADOR (1904-1989), Spanish painter **4** 376-377

DALLAPICCOLA, LUIGI (1904-1975), Italian composer **4** 377-378

DALTON, JOHN (1766-1844), English chemist **4** 378-379

DALY, MARCUS (1841-1900), American miner and politician **4** 379-380

DALY, MARY (born 1928), American feminist theoretician and philosopher **4** 380-381

DALZEL, ARCHIBALD (or Dalziel; 1740-1811), Scottish slave trader **4** 381-382

DAM, CARL PETER HENRIK (1895-1976), Danish biochemist **4** 382-383

DAMIEN, FATHER (1840-1889), Belgian missionary **4** 383

DAMPIER, WILLIAM (1652-1715), English privateer, author, and explorer **4** 384

DANA, CHARLES ANDERSON (1819-1897), American journalist **4** 384-385

DANA, RICHARD HENRY, JR. (1815-1882), American author and lawyer **4** 385-386

Dance with My Father (song) Vandross, Luther **26** 364-366

DANDOLO, ENRICO (circa 1107-1205), Venetian doge 1192-1205 **4** 386-387

DANDRIDGE, DOROTHY (1922-1965), African American actress and singer **18** 112-114

DANIELS, JOSEPHUS (1862-1948), American journalist and statesman **4** 387

D'ANNUNZIO, GABRIELE (1863-1938), Italian poet and patriot **4** 388

DANQUAH, JOSEPH B. (1895-1965), Ghanaian nationalist and politician **4** 388-389

DANTE ALIGHIERI (1265-1321), Italian poet **4** 389-391

DANTON, GEORGES JACQUES (1759-1794), French revolutionary leader **4** 391-393

DANTZIG, GEORGE BERNARD (1914-2005), American mathematician **26** 81-83

DARBY, ABRAHAM (1677-1717), English iron manufacturer **20** 106-107

DARÍO, RUBÉN (1867-1916), Nicaraguan poet **4** 393-394

DARIUS I (the Great; ruled 522-486 B.C.), king of Persia **4** 394-395

DARROW, CLARENCE SEWARD (1857-1938), American lawyer **4** 396-397

DARWIN, CHARLES ROBERT (1809-1882), English naturalist **4** 397-399

DARWIN, ERASMUS (1731-1802), English physician, author, botanist and inventor **18** 114-116

DARWISH, MAHMUD (born 1942), Palestinian poet **4** 399-401

DAS, CHITTA RANJAN (1870-1925), Indian lawyer, poet, and nationalist **4** 401-402

DATSOLALEE (Dabuda; Wide Hips; 1835-1925), Native American weaver **22** 130-131

DAUBIGNY, CHARLES FRANÇOIS (1817-1878), French painter and etcher **4** 402

DAUDET, ALPHONSE (1840-1897), French novelist and dramatist **4** 402-403

DAUMIER, HONORÉ VICTORIN (1808-1879), French lithographer, painter, and sculptor **4** 403-405

DAVENPORT, JOHN (1597-1670), English Puritan clergyman **4** 405-406

DAVID (ruled circa 1010-circa 970 B.C.), Israelite king **4** 406-407

DAVID, JACQUES LOUIS (1748-1825), French painter **4** 407-409

DAVID, SAINT (Dewi; 520-601), Welsh monk and evangelist **23** 83-85

DAVID I (1084-1153), king of Scotland **4** 407

DAVIES, ARTHUR BOWEN (1862-1928), American painter **4** 409-410

DAVIES, RUPERT (1917-1976), British actor **18** 116-117

DAVIES, WILLIAM ROBERTSON (1913-1995), Canadian author **18** 117-119

DAVIGNON, VISCOUNT (ETIENNE) (born 1932), an architect of European integration and unity through the Commission of the European Communities **4** 410-411

DAVIS, ALEXANDER JACKSON (1803-1892), American architect **4** 411

DAVIS, ANGELA (Angela Yvonne Davis; born 1944), African American scholar and activist **4** 412-413

DAVIS, ARTHUR VINING (1867-1962), general manager of the Aluminum Company of America (ALCOA) **4** 413-414

DAVIS, BENJAMIN O., SR. (1877-1970), first African American general in the regular United States Armed Services **4** 414-415

DAVIS, BETTE (1908-1989), American actress **18** 119-121

DAVIS, COLIN REX (born 1927), British conductor **22** 131-133

DAVIS, ELMER HOLMES (1890-1958), American journalist and radio commentator **22** 133-136

DAVIS, GLENN (1925-2005), American football player **21** 101-103

DAVIS, HENRY WINTER (1817-1865), American lawyer and politician **4** 415-416

DAVIS, JEFFERSON (1808-1889), American statesman, president of the Confederacy 1862-1865 **4** 416-418

DAVIS, JOHN (circa 1550-1605), English navigator **4** 419

DAVIS, MILES (1926-1991), jazz trumpeter, composer, and small-band leader **4** 419-421

DAVIS, OSSIE (1917-2005), African American playwright, actor, and director **4** 421-422

DAVIS, RICHARD HARDING (1864-1916), American journalist, novelist, and dramatist **4** 422-423

DAVIS, SAMMY, JR. (1925-1990), African American singer, dancer, and actor **4** 423-424

DAVIS, STUART (1894-1964), American cubist painter **4** 424-425

DAVIS, WILLIAM MORRIS (1850-1934), American geographer and geologist **4** 425-426

DAVY, SIR HUMPHRY (1778-1829), English chemist and natural philosopher **4** 426-427

DAWES, HENRY LAURENS (1816-1903), American politician **4** 427

DAWSON, WILLIAM LEVI (1899-1990), African American composer, performer, and music educator **4** 427-428

DAY, DOROTHY (1897-1980), a founder of the Catholic Worker Movement **4** 428-429

DAYAN, MOSHE (1915-1981), Israeli general and statesman **4** 429-431

DAYANANDA SARASWATI (1824-1883), Indian religious leader **4** 431

DE ANDRADE, MARIO (Mario Coelho Pinto Andrade; born 1928), Angolan poet, critic, and political activist **4** 434-435

DE BEAUVOIR, SIMONE (1908-1986), French writer and leader of the modern feminist movement **4** 440-441

DE BOW, JAMES DUNWOODY BROWNSON (1820-1867), American editor and statistician **4** 441-442

DE BROGLIE, LOUIS VICTOR PIERRE RAYMOND (1892-1987), French physicist **4** 442-444

DE FOREST, LEE (1873-1961), American inventor **4** 459-460

DE GASPERI, ALCIDE (1881-1954), Italian statesman, premier 1945-1953 **4** 462-463

DE GAULLE, CHARLES ANDRÉ JOSEPH MARIE (1890-1970), French general, president 1958-1969 **4** 463-465

DE GOUGES, MARIE OLYMPE (born Marie Gouzes; 1748-1793), French author **23** 85-88

DE GOURNAY, MARIE LE JARS (1565-1645), French author **23** 88-90

DE HAVILLAND, SIR GEOFFREY (1882-1965), British aviator and aeronautical engineer **25** 101-103

DE HIRSCH, MAURICE (Baron de Hirsch; 1831-1896), Austro-Hungarian financier and philanthropist **24** 104-106

DE KLERK, FREDRIK WILLEM (born 1936), state president of South Africa (1989-) **4** 466-468

DE KOONING, WILLEM (1904-1997), Dutch-born American painter **4** 468-469

DE LA MADRID HURTADO, MIGUEL (born 1934), president of Mexico (1982-1988) **4** 471-472

DE LA ROCHE, MAZO LOUISE (1879-1961), Canadian author **4** 474-475

DE LEMPICKA, TAMARA (Maria Gorska; Tamara Kuffner; 1898-1980), Polish American artist **24** 106-109

DE LEON, DANIEL (1852-1914), American Socialist theoretician and politician **4** 479-480

DE L'ORME, PHILIBERT (1510-1570), French architect **9** 519

DE MILLE, AGNES (1905-1993), American dancer, choreographer, and author **4** 486-488

DE NIRO, ROBERT (born 1943), American actor and film producer **21** 103-106

DE PISAN, CHRISTINE (1363-1431), French poet and philosopher **24** 109-111

DE SANCTIS, FRANCESCO (1817-1883), Italian critic, educator, and legislator **4** 505

DE SAUSSURE, FERDINAND (1857-1913), Swiss linguist and author **24** 111-113

DE SICA, VITTORIO (1902-1974), Italian filmmaker **21** 106-108

DE SMET, PIERRE JEAN (1801-1873), Belgian Jesuit missionary **4** 509-510

DE SOTO, HERNANDO (1500-1542), Spanish conqueror and explorer **4** 510-511

DE VALERA, EAMON (1882-1975), American-born Irish revolutionary leader and statesman **4** 514-515

DE VALOIS, NINETTE (Edris Stannus; 1898-2001), English choreographer and ballet dancer **25** 103-105

DE VERE, EDWARD (Earl of Oxford; 1550-1604), English author **25** 105-107

DE VRIES, HUGO (1848-1935), Belgian botanist in the fields of heredity and the origin of species **4** 516-518

DE WOLFE, ELSIE (1865-1950), American interior decorator **20** 107-108

DEÁK, FRANCIS (1803-1876), Hungarian statesman **4** 431-432

DEAKIN, ALFRED (1856-1919), Australian statesman **4** 432-433

DEAN, JAMES (James Byron Dean; 1931-1955), American actor and cult figure **4** 433-434

DEANE, SILAS (1737-1789), American merchant lawyer and diplomat **4** 435-437

DEB, RADHAKANT (1783-1867), Bengali reformer and cultural nationalist **4** 437

DEBAKEY, MICHAEL ELLIS (born 1908), American surgeon **4** 437-438

DEBARTOLO, EDWARD JOHN, SR. and JR., real estate developers who specialized in large regional malls **4** 438-440

DEBS, EUGENE VICTOR (1855-1926), American union organizer **4** 444-445

DEBUSSY, (ACHILLE) CLAUDE (1862-1918), French composer **4** 445-447

DEBYE, PETER JOSEPH WILLIAM (1884-1966), Dutch-born American physical chemist **4** 447-448

DECATUR, STEPHEN (1779-1820), American naval officer **4** 448-449

DEE, JOHN (1527-1608), British mathematician and astronomer **25** 107-110

DEE, RUBY (born Ruby Ann Wallace; born 1924), African American actor **4** 449-452

DEER, ADA E. (born 1935), Native American social worker, activist, and director of Bureau of Indian Affairs **4** 452-454

DEERE, JOHN (1804-1886), American inventor and manufacturer **4** 455

DEERING, WILLIAM (1826-1913), American manufacturer **4** 455-456

DEES, MORRIS S., JR. (born 1936), American civil rights attorney **4** 456-457

DEFOE, DANIEL (1660-1731), English novelist, journalist, and poet **4** 457-459

DEGANAWIDA (also DeKanahwidah; c. 1550-c. 1600), Native American prophet, leader, and statesman **4** 460-461

DEGAS, (HILAIRE GERMAIN) EDGAR (1834-1917), French painter and sculptor **4** 461-462

DEISENHOFER, JOHANN (born 1943), German biochemist and biophysicist **23** 90-93

DEKKER, THOMAS (circa 1572-circa 1632), English playwright and pamphleteer **4** 465-466

DELACROIX, (FERDINAND VICTOR) EUGÈNE (1798-1863), French painter **4** 469-471

DELANCEY, STEPHEN (1663-1741), American merchant and politician **4** 473

DELANY, MARTIN ROBINSON (1812-1885), African American army officer, politician, and judge **4** 473-474

DELAUNAY, ROBERT (1885-1941), French abstract painter **4** 475-476

DELBRÜCK, MAX (1906-1981), German-born American molecular biologist **4** 476-478

DELCASSÉ, THÉOPHILE (1852-1923), French statesman **4** 478-479

DELEDDA, GRAZIA (Grazia Maria Cosima Damiana Deledda; 1871-1936), Italian author **24** 113-115

DELGADO, JOSÉ MATIAS (1768-1832), Salvadoran political leader **24** 115-117

DELL, MICHAEL SAUL (born 1965), American businessman **23** 93-95

DELLINGER, DAVID (born 1915), American pacifist **4** 480-481

DELORIA, ELLA CLARA (1889-1971), Native American ethnologist, linguist, and author **22** 136-138

DELORIA, VINE, JR. (1933-2005), Native American author, poet, and activist **4** 481-484

DELORS, JACQUES (born 1925), French president of the European Commission and chief architect of Western Europe's drive toward market unity by 1992 **4** 484-486

DEL PILAR, MARCELO H. (1850-1896), Philippine revolutionary propagandist and satirist **4** 486

DELAY, TOM (Thomas Dale Delay; born 1947), American politician **26** 83-85

DEMILLE, CECIL BLOUNT (1881-1959), American film director and producer **4** 488-490

DEMIREL, SÜLEYMAN (born 1924), Turkish politician, prime minister, and leader of the Justice party **4** 490-493

DEMOCRITUS (circa 494-circa 404 B.C.), Greek natural philosopher **4** 493-494

DEMOIVRE, ABRAHAM (1667-1754), Franco-English mathematician **4** 494-495

DEMOSTHENES (384-322 B.C.), Greek orator **4** 495-496

DEMPSEY, JACK (William Harrison Dempsey; 1895-1983), American boxer **4** 496-497

DEMUTH, CHARLES (1883-1935), American painter **4** 497-498

DENG XIAOPING (Teng Hsiao-p'ing; 1904-1997), leader in the People's Republic of China (PRC) in the 1970s **4** 498-500

DENIKIN, ANTON (1872-1947), Russian soldier **20** 108-111

DENKTASH, RAUF (born 1924), president of the Turkish Republic of Northern Cyprus (1985-) **4** 500-502

DENNING, ALFRED THOMPSON (Tom Denning' 1899-1999), British judge and author **22** 138-140

Dentistry (medical science)
Fauchard, Pierre **26** 103-105

DISRAELI, BENJAMIN (1st Earl of Beaconsfield; 1804-1881), English statesman, prime minister 1868 and 1874-1880 **5** 27-29

DITTERSDORF, KARL DITTERS VON (Karl Ditters; 1739-1799), Austrian musician and composer **25** 117-119

DIVINE, FATHER (born George Baker?; c. 1877-1965), African American religious leader **5** 29-32

DIX, DOROTHEA LYNDE (1802-1887), American reformer **5** 32-33

DIX, OTTO (1891-1969), German painter and graphic artist **5** 33-34

DJILAS, MILOVAN (1911-1995), Yugoslavian writer **5** 34

DO MUOI (born 1917), prime minister of the Socialist Republic of Vietnam (1988-) **5** 53-55

DOBELL, SIR WILLIAM (1899-1970), Australian artist **5** 34-35

DOBZHANSKY, THEODOSIUS (1900-1975), Russian-American biologist who studied natural selection **5** 35-37

DOCTOROW, EDGAR LAURENCE (born 1931), American author **19** 89-91

Doctors of the Church
see Religious leaders, Christian—Doctors

DODGE, GRACE HOADLEY (1856-1914), American feminist, philanthropist, and social worker **5** 37-38

DODGE, GRENVILLE MELLEN (1831-1916), American army officer and civil engineer **22** 142-145

DODGE, HENRY CHEE (circa 1857-1947), Navajo Tribal leader **26** 89-92

DODGE, JOHN FRANCIS (1864-1920) AND HORACE ELGIN (1868-1920), American automobile manufacturers **18** 121-123

DOE, SAMUEL KANYON (1951-1990), Liberian statesman **5** 38-39

DOENITZ, KARL (1891-1980), German naval officer **20** 116-117

DOI TAKAKO (born 1928), chairperson of the Japan Socialist party **5** 39-41

DOLE, ELIZABETH HANFORD (born 1936), American lawyer, politician, and first female United States secretary of transportation **5** 41-43

DOLE, ROBERT J. (born 1923), Republican Senator **5** 43-46

DOLE, SANFORD BALLARD (1844-1926), American statesman **5** 46

DOLLFUSS, ENGELBERT (1892-1934), Austrian statesman **5** 47

DÖLLINGER, JOSEF IGNAZ VON (1799-1890), German historian and theologian **5** 47-48

DOMAGK, GERHARD JOHANNES PAUL (1895-1964), German bacteriologist **5** 48-50

DOMINGO, PLACIDO (born 1941), Spanish-born lyric-dramatic tenor **5** 50-51

DOMINIC, ST. (circa 1170-1221), Spanish Dominican founder **5** 51-52

DOMINO, FATS (Antoine Domino, Jr.; born 1928), African American singer, pianist, and composer **22** 145-147

DOMITIAN (Titus Flavius Domitianus Augustus; 51-96), Roman emperor 81-96 **5** 52-53

DONATELLO (Donato di Niccolò Bardi; 1386-1466), Italian sculptor **5** 55-56

DONATUS (died circa 355), schismatic bishop of Carthage **5** 56-57

DONG, PHAM VAN (born 1906), premier first of the Democratic Republic of Vietnam (DRV) and after 1976 of the Socialist Republic of Vietnam (SRV) **5** 57-59

DONIZETTI, GAETANA (1797-1848), Italian opera composer **5** 59-60

DONLEAVY, JAMES PATRICK (born 1926), Irish author and playwright **19** 91-93

DONNE, JOHN (1572-1631), English metaphysical poet **5** 60-61

DONNELLY, IGNATIUS (1831-1901), American politician and author **5** 62

DONNER, GEORG RAPHAEL (1693-1741), Austrian sculptor **5** 63

DONOSO, JOSÉ (1924-1996), Chilean writer **5** 63-65

DONOVAN, WILLIAM JOSEPH (1883-1959), American lawyer and public servant **22** 147-149

DOOLITTLE, HILDA (1886-1961), American poet and novelist **5** 65-66

DOOLITTLE, JAMES HAROLD (1896-1993), American transcontinental pilot **5** 66-68

DORIA, ANDREA (1466-1560), Italian admiral and politician **18** 123-125

DORR, RHETA CHILDE (1868-1948), American journalist **5** 68-69

DORSEY, JIMMY (James Dorsey; 1904-1957), American musician and bandleader **19** 93-95

DORSEY, THOMAS ANDREW (1900-1993), African American gospel singer and composer **22** 149-151

DOS PASSOS, RODERIGO (1896-1970), American novelist **5** 69-71

DOS SANTOS, JOSÉ EDUARDO (born 1942), leader of the Popular Movement for the Liberation of Angola and president of Angola **5** 71-72

DOS SANTOS, MARCELINO (born 1929), Mozambican nationalist insurgent, statesman, and intellectual **5** 72-74

DOSTOEVSKY, FYODOR (1821-1881), Russian novelist **5** 74-77

DOUGLAS, DONALD WILLS (1892-1981), American aeronautical engineer **5** 77

DOUGLAS, GAVIN (circa 1475-1522), Scottish poet, prelate, and courtier **5** 77-78

DOUGLAS, SIR JAMES (1286?-1330), Scottish patriot **5** 80-82

DOUGLAS, MARY TEW (born 1921), British anthropologist and social thinker **5** 79-80

DOUGLAS, STEPHEN ARNOLD (1813-1861), American politician **5** 80-82

DOUGLAS, THOMAS CLEMENT (1904-1986), Canadian clergyman and politician, premier of Saskatchewan (1944-1961), and member of Parliament (1962-1979) **5** 82-83

DOUGLAS, WILLIAM ORVILLE (1898-1980), American jurist **5** 83-85

DOUGLAS-HOME, ALEC (Alexander Frederick Home; 1903-1995), Scottish politician **20** 117-119

DOUGLASS, FREDERICK (circa 1817-1895), African American leader and abolitionist **5** 85-86

DOUHET, GIULIO (1869-1930), Italian military leader **22** 151-152

DOVE, ARTHUR GARFIELD (1880-1946), American painter **5** 86-87

DOVE, RITA FRANCES (born 1952), United States poet laureate **5** 87-89

DOVZHENKO, ALEXANDER (Oleksandr Dovzhenko; 1894-1956), Ukrainian film director and screenwriter **25** 120-122

DOW, CHARLES (1851-1902), American journalist **19** 95-97

DOW, NEAL (1804-1897), American temperance reformer **5** 89-90

DOWLAND, JOHN (1562-1626), British composer and lutenist **5** 90

DOWNING, ANDREW JACKSON (1815-1852), American horticulturist and landscape architect **5** 90-91

DOYLE, SIR ARTHUR CONAN (1859-1930), British author **5** 91-92

DRAGO, LUIS MARÍA (1859-1921), Argentine international jurist and diplomat **5** 92-93

DRAKE, DANIEL (1785-1852), American physician **5** 93-94

DRAKE, EDWIN (1819-1880), American oil well driller and speculator **21** 108-110

DRAKE, SIR FRANCIS (circa 1541-1596), English navigator **5** 94-96

DRAPER, JOHN WILLIAM (1811-1882), Anglo-American scientist and historian **5** 96-97

DRAYTON, MICHAEL (1563-1631), English poet **5** 97-98

DREISER, (HERMAN) THEODORE (1871-1945), American novelist **5** 98-100

DREW, CHARLES RICHARD (1904-1950), African American surgeon **5** 100-101

DREW, DANIEL (1797-1879), American stock manipulator **5** 101-102

DREXEL, KATHERINE (1858-1955), founded a Catholic order, the Sisters of the Blessed Sacrament **5** 102-103

DREXLER, KIM ERIC (born 1955), American scientist and author **20** 119-121

DREYER, CARL THEODOR (1889-1968), Danish film director **22** 152-155

DREYFUS, ALFRED (1859-1935), French army officer **5** 103-105

DRIESCH, HANS ADOLF EDUARD (1867-1941), German biologist and philosopher **5** 105

DRUCKER, PETER (1909-2005), American author and business consultant **21** 110-112

DRUSUS, MARCUS LIVIUS (circa 124-91 B.C.), Roman statesman **5** 105-106

DRYDEN, JOHN (1631-1700), English poet, critic, and dramatist **5** 106-107

DRYSDALE, SIR GEORGE RUSSELL (1912-1981), Australian painter **5** 107-109

DUANE, WILLIAM (1760-1835), American journalist **5** 109

DUARTE, JOSÉ NAPOLEÓN (1926-1990), civilian reformer elected president of El Salvador in 1984 **5** 109-111

DUBČEK, ALEXANDER (1921-1992), Czechoslovak politician **5** 112-113

DUBE, JOHN LANGALIBALELE (1870-1949), South African writer and Zulu propagandist **5** 113

DU BELLAY, JOACHIM (circa 1522-1560), French poet **5** 113-114

DUBINSKY, DAVID (1892-1982), American trade union official **5** 114-115

DUBNOV, SIMON (1860-1941), Jewish historian, journalist, and political activist **5** 115-116

DU BOIS, WILLIAM EDWARD BURGHARDT (1868-1963), African American educator, pan-Africanist, and protest leader **5** 116-118

DU BOIS-REYMOND, EMIL (1818-1896), German physiologist **5** 118-119

DUBOS, RENÉ JULES (1901-1982), French-born American microbiologist **5** 119

DUBUFFET, JEAN PHILLIPE ARTHUR (born 1901), French painter **5** 119-120

DUCCIO DI BUONINSEGNA (1255/60-1318/19), Italian painter **5** 121-122

DUCHAMP, MARCEL (1887-1968), French painter **5** 122-123
Guggenheim, Peggy **26** 131-133

DUCHAMP-VILLON, RAYMOND (1876-1918), French sculptor **5** 123

DUDLEY, BARBARA (born 1947), American director of Greenpeace **5** 123-124

DUDLEY, THOMAS (1576-1653), American colonial governor and Puritan leader **5** 124-125

DUFAY, GUILLAUME (circa 1400-1474), Netherlandish composer **5** 125-126

DUFF, ALEXANDER (1806-1878), Scottish Presbyterian missionary **5** 126-127

DUGAN, ALAN (born 1923), American poet **5** 127-128

DUGDALE, RICHARD LOUIS (1841-1883), English-born American sociologist **5** 128-129

DUHEM, PIERRE MAURICE MARIE (1861-1916), French physicist, chemist, and historian of science **5** 129

DUKAKIS, MICHAEL (born 1933), American governor of Massachusetts **5** 130-133

DUKE, DORIS (1912-1993), American philanthropist **24** 118-121

DUKE, JAMES BUCHANAN (1856-1925), American industrialist and philanthropist **5** 133-134

DULL KNIFE (born Morning Star; c. 1810-1883), Northern Cheyenne tribal leader **5** 135-136

DULLES, JOHN FOSTER (1888-1959), American statesman and diplomat **5** 134-135

DUMAS, ALEXANDRE (1803-1870), French playwright and novelist **5** 136-138

DUMAS, JEAN BAPTISTE ANDRÉ (1800-1884), French Chemist **5** 138-139

DU MAURIER, DAPHNE (Lady Browning; 1907-1989), English author **18** 125-127

DUN, TAN (born 1951), Chinese American musician **24** 121-123

DUNANT, JEAN HENRI (1828-1910), Swiss philanthropist **5** 139-141

DUNBAR, PAUL LAURENCE (1872-1906), African American poet and novelist **5** 141-142

DUNBAR, WILLIAM (circa 1460-circa 1520), Scottish poet and courtier **5** 142-143

DUNBAR, WILLIAM (1749-1810), Scottish-born American scientist and planter **5** 143-144

DUNCAN, ISADORA (1878-1927), American dancer **5** 144-145

DUNHAM, KATHERINE (born 1910), African American dancer, choreographer, and anthropologist **5** 145-146

DUNMORE, 4TH EARL OF (John Murray; 1732-1809), British colonial governor **5** 147

DUNNE, FINLEY PETER (1867-1936), American journalist **5** 147-148

DUNNIGAN, ALICE ALLISON (1906-1983), African American journalist **25** 122-123

DUNNING, WILLIAM ARCHIBALD (1857-1922), American historian **5** 148-149

DUNS SCOTUS, JOHN (1265/66-1308), Scottish philosopher and theologian **5** 149-150

DUNSTABLE, JOHN (circa 1390-1453), English composer **5** 150-151

DUNSTAN, ST. (circa 909-988), English monk and archbishop **5** 151-152

DUNSTER, HENRY (circa 1609-1659), English-born American clergyman **5** 152-153

FARMER, MOSES GERRISH (1820-1893), American inventor and manufacturer **5** 385

FARNESE, ALESSANDRO (Duke of Parma; 1545-1592), Italian general and diplomat **20** 132-135

FARNSWORTH, PHILO T. (1906-1971), American inventor of the television **5** 386-387

FAROUK I (1920-1965), king of Egypt 1937-1952 **5** 387-388

FARRAGUT, DAVID GLASGOW (1801-1870), American naval officer **5** 388-389

FARRAKHAN, LOUIS (Louis Eugene Walcott, born 1933), a leader of one branch of the Nation of Islam popularly known as Black Muslims and militant spokesman for Black Nationalism **5** 389-390

FARRAR, GERALDINE (1882-1967), American opera singer **23** 106-108

FARRELL, JAMES THOMAS (1904-1979), American novelist and social and literary critic **5** 390-391

FARRELL, SUZANNE (née Roberta Sue Ficker; born 1945), American classical ballerina **5** 391-393

FASSBINDER, RAINER WERNER (1946-1982), German filmmaker **26** 101-103

"Father of . . ."
see Nicknames

Fathers of the Church
see Religious leaders, Christian—Fathers

FAUCHARD, PIERRE (1678-1761), French dentist **26** 103-105

FAULKNER, BRIAN (1921-1977), prime minister of Northern Ireland (1971-1972) **5** 393-395

FAULKNER, WILLIAM (1897-1962), American novelist **5** 395-397

FAURÉ, GABRIEL URBAIN (1845-1924), French composer **5** 397-398

FAUSET, JESSIE REDMON (1882-1961), African American writer and editor **20** 135-138

FAVALORO, RENE GERONIMO (1923-2000), Argentine physician **24** 131-133

FAWCETT, MILLICENT GARRETT (1847-1929), British feminist **5** 398-400

FAYE, SAFI (born 1943), Senegalese filmmaker and ethnologist **5** 400-401

FECHNER, GUSTAV THEODOR (1801-1887), German experimental psychologist **5** 401-402

FEE, JOHN GREGG (1816-1901), American abolitionist and clergyman **5** 402-403

FEIFFER, JULES RALPH (born 1929), American satirical cartoonist and playwright and novelist **5** 403-404

FEIGENBAUM, MITCHELL JAY (born 1944), American physicist **5** 404-405

FEIGL, HERBERT (born 1902), American philosopher **18** 135-137

FEIJÓ, DIOGO ANTÔNIO (1784-1843), Brazilian priest and statesman **5** 405-406

FEININGER, LYONEL (1871-1956), American painter **5** 406-407

FEINSTEIN, DIANNE (Goldman; born 1933), politician, public official, and San Francisco's first female mayor **5** 407-408

FELA (Fela Anikulapo Kuti; 1938-1997), Nigerian musician and activist **21** 127-129

FELICIANO, JOSÉ (born 1945), Hispanic American singer and guitarist **19** 109-110

Felix V (1383-1451), antipope 1439-49 Nicholas V **26** 299-300

FELLER, BOB (Robert William Andrew Feller; born 1918), American baseball player **21** 129-131

FELLINI, FEDERICO (1920-1993), Italian film director **5** 408-409

FELTRE, VITTORINO DA (1378-1446), Italian humanist and teacher **5** 409-410

Feminist movement
see Women's rights

Feminists
English
Wollstonecraft, Mary **26** 387-389
Norwegian
Collett, Camilla **26** 73-75
Swedish
Bremer, Fredrika **26** 46-48

FÉNELON, FRANÇOIS DE SALIGNAC DE LA MOTHE (1651-1715), French archbishop and theologian **5** 410-411

FENG KUEI-FEN (1809-1874), Chinese scholar and official **5** 411-412

FENG YÜ-HSIANG (1882-1948), Chinese warlord **5** 412-413

FERBER, EDNA (1887-1968), American author **5** 413

FERDINAND (1865-1927), king of Romania 1914-1927 **5** 413-414

FERDINAND I (1503-1564), Holy Roman emperor 1555-1564, king of Hungary

and Bohemia 1526-64 and of Germany 1531-1564 **5** 414-415

FERDINAND II (1578-1637), Holy Roman emperor 1619-1637, king of Bohemia 1617-1637 and of Hungary 1618-1637 **5** 415

FERDINAND II (1810-1859), king of the Two Sicilies 1830-1859 **5** 415-416

FERDINAND III (1608-1657), Holy Roman emperor 1637-1657, king of Hungary 1626-1657 and of Bohemia 1627-1657 **5** 416-417

FERDINAND V (1452-1516), king of Castile 1474-1504, of Sicily 1468-1516, and of Aragon 1479-1516 **5** 417-418

FERDINAND VII (1784-1833), king of Spain 1808 and 1814-1833 **5** 418-420

FERGUSON, ADAM (1723-1816), Scottish philosopher, moralist, and historian **5** 420-421

FERGUSON, HOWARD (1908-1999), Irish musician and composer **18** 137-138

FERMAT, PIERRE DE (1601-1665), French mathematician **5** 421-422

FERMI, ENRICO (1901-1954), Italian-American physicist **5** 422-424

FERNÁNDEZ DE LIZARDI, JOSÉ JOAQUIN (1776-1827), Mexican journalist and novelist **5** 424-425

FERNEL, JEAN FRANÇOIS (circa 1497-1558), French physician **5** 425-426

FERRARO, GERALDINE (born 1935), first woman candidate for the vice presidency of a major U.S. political party **5** 426-428

FERRER, GABRIEL MIRÓ (1879-1930), Spanish author **5** 428

FERRER, IBRAHIM (1927-2005), Cuban musician **26** 105-107

FERRER, JOSÉ FIGUÉRES (born 1906), Costa Rican politician **5** 428-429

FERRERO, GUGLIELMO (1871-1942), Italian journalist and historian **5** 429-430

FERRY, JULES FRANÇOIS CAMILLE (1832-1893), French statesman **5** 430

Fertilization (biology)
Jones, Georgeanna Seegar **26** 181-183

FEUCHTWANGER, LION (1884-1958), post-World War I German literary figure **5** 430-432

FEUERBACH, LUDWIG ANDREAS (1804-1872), German philosopher **5** 432

GILBRETH, FRANK (1868-1924), American engineer and management expert **21** 162-163

GILBRETH, LILLIAN (born Lillian Evelyn Moller; 1878-1972), American psychologist and industrial management consultant **6** 315-317

GILBERTO, JOAO (Joao Gilberto do Prado Pereira de Olivera; born 1931), Brazilian musician **25** 154-156

GILES, ERNEST (1835-1897), Australian explorer **6** 317-318

GILKEY, LANGDON BROWN (1919-2004), American ecumenical Protestant theologian **6** 318-319

GILLARS, MILDRED ELIZABETH (nee Mildred Elizabeth Sisk; 1900-1988), American broadcaster and traitor **26** 125-127

GILLESPIE, DIZZY (born John Birks Gillespie; 1917-1993), African American jazz trumpeter, composer, and band leader **6** 320-322

GILLETTE, KING CAMP (1855-1932), American businessman and inventor **21** 163-166

GILLIAM, SAM (born 1933), American artist **6** 322-323

GILMAN, CHARLOTTE ANNA PERKINS (1860-1935), American writer and lecturer **6** 323-325

GILMAN, DANIEL COIT (1831-1908), educator and pioneer in the American university movement **6** 325-326

GILPIN, LAURA (1891-1979), American photographer **6** 326-327

GILSON, ÉTIENNE HENRY (1884-1978), French Catholic philosopher **6** 327-328

GINASTERA, ALBERTO EVARISTO (1916-1983), Argentine composer **6** 328-329

GINGRICH, NEWT (born 1943), Republican congressman from Georgia **6** 329-332

GINSBERG, ALLEN (1926-1997), American poet **6** 332-333

GINSBURG, RUTH BADER (born 1933), second woman appointed to the United States Supreme Court **6** 333-336

GINZBERG, ASHER (Ahad Ha-Am; means "one of the people;" 1856-1927), Jewish intellectual leader **6** 336-337

GINZBERG, LOUIS (1873-1953), Lithuanian-American Talmudic scholar **6** 337-338

GINZBURG, NATALIA LEVI (1916-1991), Italian novelist, essayist, playwright, and translator **6** 338-339

GIOLITTI, GIOVANNI (1842-1928), Italian statesman **6** 339-340

GIORGIONE (1477-1510), Italian painter **6** 340-341

GIOTTO (circa 1267-1337), Italian painter, architect, and sculptor **6** 342-345

GIOVANNI, YOLANDE CORNELIA, JR. (born 1943), African American poet **6** 346-347

GIOVANNI DA BOLOGNA (1529-1608), Italian sculptor **6** 345-346

GIPP, GEORGE (1895-1920), American football player **19** 124-126

GIRARD, STEPHEN (1750-1831), American merchant and philanthropist **6** 347-348

GIRARDON, FRANÇOIS (1628-1715), French sculptor **6** 348-349

GIRAUDOUX, JEAN (1882-1944), French novelist, playwright, and diplomat **6** 349-350

Girl from Ipanema, The (song) Moraes, Vinicius de **26** 268-269

GIRTY, SIMON (1741-1818), American frontiersman **6** 350

GISCARD D'ESTAING, VALÉRY (born 1926), third president of the French Fifth Republic **6** 350-352

GISH, LILLIAN (1896-1993), American actress **20** 155-158

GIST, CHRISTOPHER (circa 1706-1759), American frontiersman **6** 352-353

GIULIANI, RUDOLPH WILLIAM (born 1944), mayor of New York City **6** 353-355

GIULIANI, MAURO (Mauro Giuseppe Sergio Pantaleo Giuliani; 1781-1829), Italian guitarist and composer **25** 156-157

GJELLERUP, KARL ADOLPH (1857-1919), Danish author **25** 157-159

GLACKENS, WILLIAM (1870-1938), American painter **6** 355-356

GLADDEN, WASHINGTON (1836-1918), American clergyman **6** 356-357

GLADSTONE, WILLIAM EWART (1809-1898), English statesman **6** 357-360

GLASGOW, ELLEN (1873-1945), American novelist **6** 360-361

GLASHOW, SHELDON LEE (born 1932), American Nobel Prize winner in physics **6** 361-362

GLASS, PHILIP (born 1937), American composer of minimalist music **6** 362-364

GLASSE, HANNAH (Hannah Allgood; 1708-1770), English cookbook author **21** 166-167

GLEDITSCH, ELLEN (1879-1968), Norwegian chemist **23** 124-126

GLENDOWER, OWEN (1359?-1415?), Welsh national leader **6** 364-365

GLENN, JOHN HERSCHEL, JR. (born 1921), military test pilot, astronaut, businessman, and United States senator from Ohio **6** 365-367

GLIDDEN, JOSEPH (1813-1906), American businessman and inventor **21** 167-170

GLIGOROV, KIRO (born 1917), first president of the Republic of Macedonia **6** 367-369

GLINKA, MIKHAIL IVANOVICH (1804-1857), Russian composer **6** 369-370

GLOUCESTER, DUKE OF (1391-1447), English statesman **6** 370-371

GLUBB, SIR JOHN BAGOT (1897-1986), British commander of the Arab Legion 1939-56 **6** 371-372

GLUCK, CHRISTOPH WILLIBALD (1714-1787), Austrian composer and opera reformer **6** 372-374

GLUCKMAN, MAX (1911-1975), British anthropologist **6** 374-375

GLYN, ELINOR (born Elinor Sutherland; 1864-1943), British author and filmmaker **23** 126-128

GOBINEAU, COMTE DE (Joseph Arthur Gobineau; 1816-1882), French diplomat **6** 375-376

GODARD, JEAN-LUC (born 1930), French actor, film director, and screenwriter **19** 126-128

GODDARD, ROBERT HUTCHINGS (1882-1945), American pioneer in rocketry **6** 376-377

GÖDEL, KURT (1906-1978), Austrian-American mathematician **6** 377-379

GODKIN, EDWIN LAWRENCE (1831-1902), British-born American journalist **6** 380

GODOLPHIN, SIDNEY (1st Earl of Godolphin; 1645-1712), English statesman **6** 380-381

GODOY Y ÁLVAREZ DE FARIA, MANUEL DE (1767-1851), Spanish statesman **6** 381-382

GROVE, FREDERICK PHILIP (circa 1871-1948), Canadian novelist and essayist 7 20-21

GROVES, LESLIE (1896-1970), military director of the Manhattan Project (atom bomb) during World War II 7 21-22

GRÜNEWALD, MATTHIAS (circa 1475-1528), German painter 7 23-24

GUARDI, FRANCESCO (1712-1793), Italian painter 7 24-25

GUARINI, GUARINO (1624-1683), Italian architect, priest, and philosopher 7 25-26

GUASTAVINO, RAFAEL (Rafael Guastavino Morano; 1842-1908), Spanish-American architect 23 132-134

GUBAIDULINA, SOFIA (Sofia Asgatovna Gubaydulina; born 1931), Russian composer 26 127-129

GUCCIONE, BOB, JR. (born ca. 1956), American publisher 7 26

GUDERIAN, HEINZ (1888-1953), German military leader 20 163-165

GUDJÓNSSON, HALLDÓR KILJAN (Halldór Laxness; 1902-1998), Icelandic author 25 169-171

GÜEMES, MARTÍN (1785-1821), Argentine independence fighter 7 26-27

GUERCINO (Giovanni Francesco Barbieri; 1591-1666), Italian painter 7 27

GUERICKE, OTTO VON (1602-1686), German physicist 7 27-28

GUERIN, VERONICA (1959-1996), Irish investigative reporter and journalist 18 174-176

GUERRERO, LALO (Eduardo Guerrero, Jr.; 1916-2005), Mexican American singer and songwriter 26 129-131

GUERRERO, VICENTE (1783-1831), Mexican independence fighter, president 1829 7 28-30

GUEVARA, ERNESTO ("Che"; 1924-1967) Argentine revolutionary and guerrilla theoretician 7 30-31

GUEYE, LAMINE (1891-1968), Senegalese statesman 7 31

GUGGENHEIM, DANIEL (1856-1930), American industrialist and philanthropist 21 185-187

GUGGENHEIM, MEYER (1828-1905), Swiss-born American industrialist 7 31-32
Guggenheim, Peggy 26 131-133

GUGGENHEIM, PEGGY (nee Marguerite Guggenheim; 1898-1979), American art collector and dealer 26 131-133

GUICCIARDINI, FRANCESCO (1483-1540), Italian historian and statesman 7 32-33

GUIDO D'AREZZO (circa 995-circa 1050), Italian music theorist 7 33

GUILLAUME, CHARLES-EDOUARD (1861-1938), Swiss Scientist 25 171-173

GUILLAUME DE LORRIS (circa 1210-1237), French poet 7 33-34

GUILLÉN, NICOLÁS (born 1902), Cuban author 7 34-35

GUILLÉN Y ALVAREZ, JORGE (1893-1984), Spanish poet 7 35-36

GUINIZZELLI, GUIDO (1230/40-1276), Italian poet 7 36-37

GUINNESS, ALEC (born 1914), British actor of the stage, films, and television 7 37-38

GÜIRÁLDEZ, RICARDO (1886-1927), Argentine poet and novelist 7 38-39

GUISCARD, ROBERT (1016-1085), Norman adventurer 7 39-40

GUISEWITE, CATHY (born 1950), American cartoonist and author 18 176-177

Guitar (music)
Little Milton 26 236-237

GUIZOT, FRANÇOIS PIERRE GUILLAUME (1787-1874), French statesman and historian 7 40-41

GUMPLOWICZ, LUDWIG (1838-1909), Polish-Austrian sociologist and political theorist 7 41

GUNN, THOM (born 1929), English poet 18 177-178

GÜNTHER, IGNAZ (1725-1775), German sculptor 7 41-42

GUSTAVUS I (Gustavus Eriksson; 1496-1560), king of Sweden 1523-1560 7 42-43

GUSTAVUS II (Gustavus Adolphus; 1594-1632), king of Sweden 1611-1632 7 43-45

GUSTAVUS III (1746-1792), king of Sweden 1771-1792 7 45-46

GUSTON, PHILIP (1913-1980), American painter and a key member of the New York School 7 47-48

GUTENBERG, JOHANN (circa 1398-1468), German inventor and printer 7 48-49

GUTHRIE, EDWIN RAY (1886-1959), American psychologist 7 49-50

GUTHRIE, TYRONE (1900-1971), English theater director 7 50-51

GUTHRIE, WOODROW WILSON ("Woody"; 1912-1967), writer and performer of folk songs 7 51-52

GUTIÉRRÉZ, GUSTAVO (born 1928), Peruvian who was the father of liberation theology 7 52-53

GUY-BLACHÉ, ALICE (Alice Blaché; 1873-1968), French filmmaker 26 133-135

GUY DE CHAULIAC (circa 1295-1368), French surgeon 7 54

GUZY, CAROL (Born 1956), American photographer 25 173-175

Gymnastics (sport)
Latynina, Larisa 26 222-224

Gynecology (science)
Jones, Georgeanna Seegar 26 181-183

Gypsy music
see Folk music—Hungarian

H

HABASH, GEORGE (born 1926), founder of the Arab Nationalists' Movement (1952) and of the Popular Front for the Liberation of Palestine (PFLP; 1967) 7 55-56

HABER, FRITZ (1868-1934), German chemist 7 56-58

HABERMAS, JÜRGEN (born 1929), German philosopher and sociologist 7 58-60

HABIBIE, BACHARUDDIN JUSUF (born 1936), president of Indonesia 19 134-136

HADRIAN (76-138), Roman emperor 117-138 7 60-61

HAECKEL, ERNST HEINRICH PHILIPP AUGUST (1834-1919), German biologist and natural philosopher 7 61-62

HAFIZ, SHAMS AL-DIN (circa 1320-1390), Persian mystical poet and Koranic exegete 7 63

HAGEN, UTA THYRA (born 1919), American actress 18 179-180

HAGEN, WALTER (1892-1969), American golfer 21 188-190

HAGUE, FRANK (1876-1956), American politician 7 63-64

HAHN, OTTO (1879-1968), German chemist 7 64-65

HOFFA, JAMES R. ("Jimmy"; 1913-1975) American union leader 7 436-437

HOFFMAN, ABBIE (1936-1989), American writer, activist, and leader of the Youth International Party 7 437-439

HOFFMANN, ERNST THEODOR AMADEUS (1776-1822), German author, composer, and artist 7 439-440

HOFFMANN, JOSEF (1870-1956), Austrian architect and decorator 7 440-441

HOFFMAN, MALVINA CORNELL (1885-1966), American sculptor 23 148-150

HOFHAIMER, PAUL (1459-1537), Austrian composer, and organist 7 441

HOFMANN, AUGUST WILHELM VON (1818-1892), German organic chemist 7 441-442

HOFMANN, HANS (1880-1966), German-American painter 7 442-443

HOFMANNSTHAL, HUGO VON (1874-1929), Austrian poet and dramatist 7 443-444

HOFSTADTER, RICHARD (1916-1970), American historian 7 444-445

HOFSTADTER, ROBERT (1915-1990), American physicist 25 199-202

HOGAN, BEN (1912-1997), American golfer 19 148-150

HOGARTH, WILLIAM (1697-1764), English painter and engraver 7 446-447

HOGG, HELEN BATTLES SAWYER (1905-1993), Canadian astronomer 22 244-247

HOKINSON, HELEN ELNA (1893-1949), American cartoonist 23 150-152

HOKUSAI, KATSUSHIKA (1760-1849), Japanese painter and printmaker 7 447-448

HOLBACH, BARON D' (Paul Henri Thiry; 1723-1789), German-born French encyclopedist and philosopher 7 448-449

HOLBEIN, HANS, THE YOUNGER (1497/98-1543), German painter and graphic artist 7 449-450

HOLBERG, LUDVIG (Hans Mikkelsen; 1684-1754), Scandinavian author 23 152-155

HOLBROOK, JOSIAH (1788-1854), American educator 7 450-451

HÖLDERLIN, JOHANN CHRISTIAN FRIEDRICH (1770-1843), German poet 7 451-452

HOLIDAY, BILLIE (1915-1959), American jazz vocalist 7 452-453

HOLLAND, JOHN PHILIP (1840-1914), Irish-American inventor 7 453-454

HOLLERITH, HERMAN (1860-1929), American inventor and businessman 19 151-152

HOLLY, BUDDY (Charles Hardin Holley; 1936-1959), American singer, songwriter, and bandleader 22 247-249

HOLM, HANYA (née Johanna Eckert; born 1893), German-American dancer and teacher 7 454-455

HOLMES, ARTHUR (1890-1965), English geologist and petrologist 7 455-456

HOLMES, JOHN HAYNES (1879-1964), American Unitarian clergyman 7 456-457

HOLMES, OLIVER WENDELL (1809-1894), American physician and author 7 457-458

HOLMES, OLIVER WENDELL, JR. (1841-1935), American jurist 7 458-459

HOLST, GUSTAV (1874-1934), English composer 7 459-460

HOLYOAKE, KEITH JACKA (1904-1983), New Zealand prime minister and leader of the National Party 7 460-462

HOLZER, JENNY (born 1950), American Neo-Conceptualist artist 7 462-463

HOMANS, GEORGE CASPAR (1910-1989), American sociologist 7 463-465

HOMER (ancient Greek epic poet) 7 468-469

HOMER, WINSLOW (1836-1910), American painter 7 468-469

HONDA, ISHIRO (Inoshiro Honda; 1911-1993), Japanese filmmaker 26 158-160

HONDA, SOICHIRO (1906-1991), Japanese automaker 7 469-470

HONECKER, ERICH (1912-1994), German Communist Party leader and head of the German Democratic Republic (1971-80s) 7 471-472

HONEGGER, ARTHUR (1892-1955), Swiss composer identified with France 7 472-473

HONEN (1133-1212), Japanese Buddhist monk 7 473

HOOCH, PIETER DE (1629-after 1684), Dutch artist 7 473-474

HOOK, SIDNEY (1902-1989), American philosopher and exponent of classical American pragmatism 7 474-475

HOOKE, ROBERT (1635-1703), English physicist 7 475

HOOKER, JOHN LEE (1917-2001), African American musician 23 155-157

HOOKER, RICHARD (1554-1600), English theologian and Church of England clergyman 7 475-476

HOOKER, THOMAS (1586-1647), English Puritan theologian, founder of Connecticut Colony 7 476-477

HOOKS, BELL (born Gloria Jean Watkins, born 1952) African American social activist, feminist, and author 7 477-481

HOOKS, BENJAMIN LAWSON (born 1925), executive director of the NAACP and first African American commissioner of the FCC 7 481-483

HOOVER, HERBERT CLARK (1874-1964), American statesman, president 1929-1933 7 483-485

HOOVER, JOHN EDGAR (1895-1972), American lawyer, criminologist, and FBI director 7 485-487

HOPE, BOB (born Leslie Townes Hope; born 1903), entertainer in vaudeville, radio, television, and movies 7 487-489

HOPE, JOHN (1868-1936), African American educator and religious leader 7 489-490

HOPKINS, ANTHONY (Philip Anthony Hopkins; born 1937), Welsh actor 18 196-198

HOPKINS, ESEK (1718-1802), American Revolutionary patriot 7 490-491

HOPKINS, SIR FREDERICK GOWLAND (1861-1947), English biochemist 7 496

HOPKINS, GERARD MANLEY (1844-1889), English Jesuit poet 7 492-494

HOPKINS, HARRY LLOYD (1890-1946), American statesman 7 494-495

HOPKINS, JOHNS (1795-1873), American financier and philanthropist 24 178-180

HOPKINS, MARK (1802-1887), American educator 7 495-496

HOPKINS, SAMUEL (1721-1803), American clergyman and theologian 7 496

HOPKINSON, FRANCIS (1737-1791), American politician, writer, and composer 7 496-497

HOPPER, EDWARD (1882-1967), American realist painter 7 497-498

K

KAPITSA, PYOTR LEONIDOVICH (born 1894), Soviet physicist **8** 433-435

KAPLAN, MORDECAI MENAHEM (1881-1983), American Jewish theologian and educator **8** 435-436

KAPP, WOLFGANG (1858-1922), German nationalist politician **8** 436

KAPTEYN, JACOBUS CORNELIS (1851-1922), Dutch astronomer **8** 436-437

KARADZIC, RADOVAN (born 1945), leader of the Serbian Republic **8** 437-440

KARAJAN, HERBERT VON (1908-1989), Austrian conductor **26** 190-192

KARAMANLIS, CONSTANTINE (1907-1998), Greek member of parliament, prime minister (1955-1963; 1974-1980), and president (1980-1985) **8** 440-441

KARAMZIN, NIKOLAI MIKHAILOVICH (1766-1826), Russian historian and author **8** 441-442

KARAN, DONNA (born 1948), American fashion designer and businesswoman **8** 442-444

KARENGA, MAULANA (born Ronald McKinley Everett; born 1941), African American author, educator, and proponent of black culturalism **8** 444-447

KARIM KHAN ZAND (died 1779), Iranian ruler, founder of Zand dynasty **8** 447

KARLE, ISABELLA (born 1921), American chemist and physicist **8** 447-449

KARLOFF, BORIS (William Henry Pratt; 1887-1969), British actor **26** 192-194

KARLSTADT, ANDREAS BODENHEIM VON (circa 1480-1541), German Protestant reformer **8** 449

KARMAL, BABRAK (born 1929), Afghan Marxist and Soviet puppet ruler of the Democratic Republic of Afghanistan (1979-1986) **8** 449-451

KÁRMÁN, THEODORE VON (1881-1963), Hungarian-born American physicist **8** 451-452

KARSH, YOUSUF (1908-2002), Canadian photographer **23** 184-187

KARTINI, RADEN AJENG (1879-1904), Indonesian activist **24** 201-203

KARUME, SHEIKH ABEID AMANI (1905-1972), Tanzanian political leader **8** 452-453

KASAVUBU, JOSEPH (circa 1913-1969), Congolese statesman **8** 453-455

KASSEBAUM, NANCY (born 1932), Republican senator from Kansas **8** 455-457

KASTRIOTI-SKANDERBEG, GJERGJ (1405-1468), Albanian military leader **23** 187-189

KATAYAMA, SEN (1860-1933), Japanese labor and Socialist leader **8** 457

KAUFFMAN, ANGELICA (Maria Anna Angelica Catherina Kauffman; 1741-1807), Swedish artist **25** 229-231

KAUFMAN, GEORGE S. (1889-1961), American playwright **8** 457-458

KAUFMAN, GERALD BERNARD (born 1930), foreign policy spokesman of the British Labour Party **8** 458-460

KAUFMANN, EZEKIEL (1889-1963), Jewish philosopher and scholar **8** 460

KAUNDA, KENNETH DAVID (born 1924), Zambian statesman **8** 460-461

KAUTILYA (4th century B.C.), Indian statesman and author **8** 462

KAUTSKY, KARL JOHANN (1854-1938), German Austrian Socialist **8** 462-463

KAWABATA, YASUNARI (1899-1972), Japanese novelist **8** 463-464

KAWAWA, RASHIDI MFAUME (born 1929), Tanzanian political leader **8** 464-465

KAYE, DANNY (David Daniel Kaminsky; 1913-1987), American film and stage actor **25** 231-234

KAZAN, ELIA (born 1909), American film and stage director **8** 465-466

KAZANTZAKIS, NIKOS (1883-1957), Greek author, journalist, and statesman **8** 466-468

KEAN, EDMUND (1789-1833), English actor **21** 237-239

KEARNEY, DENIS (1847-1907), Irish-born American labor agitator **8** 468

KEARNY, STEPHEN WATTS (1794-1848), American general **8** 468-469

KEATING, PAUL JOHN (born 1944), federal treasurer of Australia (1983-1991) **8** 469-470

KEATON, BUSTER (Joseph Frank Keaton; 1895-1966), American comedian **20** 199-201

KEATS, JOHN (1795-1821), English poet **8** 470-472

KEFAUVER, CAREY ESTES (1903-1963), U.S. senator and influential Tennessee Democrat **8** 472-474

KEILLOR, GARRISON (Gary Edward Keillor, born 1942), American

humorist, radio host, and author **22** 271-273

KEITA, MODIBO (1915-1977), Malian statesman **8** 474-475

KEITEL, WILHELM (1882-1946), German general **18** 224-226

KEITH, SIR ARTHUR (1866-1955), British anatomist and physical anthropologist **8** 475-476

KEITH, MINOR COOPER (1848-1929), American entrepreneur **8** 476-477

KEKKONEN, URHO KALEVA (1900-1986), Finnish athlete and politician **23** 189-191

KEKULÉ, FRIEDRICH AUGUST (1829-1896), German chemist **8** 477-478

KELLER, ELIZABETH BEACH (Elizabeth Waterbury Beach; 1918-1997), American biochemist **25** 234-235

KELLER, GOTTFRIED (1819-1890), Swiss short-story writer, novelist, and poet **8** 478-479

KELLER, HELEN ADAMS (1880-1968), American lecturer and author **8** 479-480

KELLEY, FLORENCE (1859-1932), American social worker and reformer **8** 483-484

KELLEY, HALL JACKSON (1790-1874), American promoter **8** 480

KELLEY, OLIVER HUDSON (1826-1913), American agriculturalist **8** 480-481

KELLOGG, FRANK BILLINGS (1856-1937), American statesman **8** 481

KELLOGG, JOHN HARVEY (1852-1943), American health propagandist and cereal manufacturer **21** 239-242

KELLOR, FRANCES (1873-1952), American activist and politician **8** 481-482

KELLY, ELLSWORTH (born 1923), American artist **8** 482-483

KELLY, GENE (born Eugene Curran Kelly; 1912-1996), American actor, dancer, and choreographer **8** 484-486

KELLY, GRACE (Grace, Princess; 1929-1982), princess of Monaco **19** 174-176

KELLY, PATRICK (1954-1990), African American fashion designer **22** 273-275

KELLY, PETRA (born 1947), West German pacifist and politician **8** 486-487

KELLY, WALT (Walter Crawford Kelly; 1913-1973), American Cartoonist **22** 275-278

MARCOS, FERDINAND (1917-1989), president of the Republic of the Philippines (1965-1986) 10 240-242

MARCOS, IMELDA ROMUALDEZ (born 1930), wife of Philippine President Ferdinand Marcos and governor of Metro Manila 10 242-243

MARCOS DE NIZA, FRIAR (circa 1500-1558), Franciscan missionary in Spanish America 10 240

MARCUS AURELIUS ANTONINUS (121-180), Roman emperor 161-180 10 243-245

MARCUS, STANLEY (1905-2002), American businessman 19 222-224

MARCUSE, HERBERT (1898-1979), German-American philosopher 10 245-247

MARCY, WILLIAM LEARNED (1786-1857), American statesman 10 247-248

MARENZIO, LUCA (1553/54-1599), Italian composer 10 248

MARGAI, SIR MILTON AUGUSTUS STRIERY (1895-1964), Sierra Leonean physician and statesman 10 248-249

MARGARET OF ANJOU (1430-1482), queen consort of Henry VI of England 10 249-250

MARGARET OF DENMARK (born Margaret Valdemarsdottir; 1353-1412), queen of Denmark 10 250-252

MARGARET OF SCOTLAND, SAINT (1045-1093), wife of Malcolm III of Scotland 10 252-253

MARGGRAF, ANDREAS (1709-1782), German chemist 21 273-275

MARGULIS, LYNN (born 1938), American biologist 10 253-254

MARIA THERESA (1717-1780), Holy Roman empress 1740-1780 10 256-258

MARIANA, JUAN DE (1536-1624), Spanish Jesuit historian 10 254-255

MARIÁTEGUI, JOSÉ CARLOS (1895-1930), Peruvian writer 10 255-256

MARIE ANTOINETTE (1755-1793), queen of France 1774-1793 10 258-259

MARIE DE FRANCE (flourished late 12th century), French poet 10 259

MARIN, JOHN, III (1870-1953), American painter 10 259-260

MARINI, MARINO (1901-1980), Italian sculptor 10 260-262

MARINO, DAN (Daniel Constantine Marino, Jr.; born 1961), American athlete 26 243-245

MARION, FRANCIS (1732-1795), American Revolutionary War leader 10 262-263

MARITAIN, JACQUES (1882-1973), French Catholic philosopher 10 263

MARIUS GAIUS (circa 157-86 B.C.), Roman general and politician 10 264-265

MARIVAUX, PIERRE CARLET DE CHAMBLAIN DE (1688-1763), French novelist and dramatist 10 265-266

MARK, SAINT (flourished 1st century), Apostle of Jesus 10 266-267

MARKHAM, BERYL (1902-1986), British aviator, author, and horse trainer 20 241-243

MARKHAM, EDWIN (1852-1940), American poet 10 267

MARKIEVICZ, CONSTANCE (1868-1927), Irish nationalist, labor activist, and feminist 10 267-271

MARLBOROUGH, 1ST DUKE OF (John Churchill; 1650-1722), English general and statesman 10 271-272

MARLEY, BOB (Robert Nesta Marley; 1945-1981), Jamaican musician 24 239-241

MARLOWE, CHRISTOPHER (1564-1593), English dramatist 10 272-274

MÁRMOL, JOSÉ (1817-1871), Argentine writer and intellectual 10 274

MARQUETTE, JACQUES (1637-1675), French Jesuit, missionary and explorer 10 274-275

Marriage of Maria Braun (film) Fassbinder, Rainer Werner 26 101-103

MARSALIS, WYNTON (born 1961), American trumpeter and bandleader 19 224-226

MARSH, GEORGE PERKINS (1801-1882), American diplomat, philologist, and conservationist 21 275-277

MARSH, NGAIO (Edith Ngaio Marsh; 1899-1982), New Zealander author and playwright 19 226-228

MARSH, OTHNIEL CHARLES (1831-1899), American paleontologist 10 275-276

MARSH, REGINALD (1898-1954), American painter and printmaker 10 276-277

MARSHALL, ALFRED (1842-1924), English economist 10 277-278

MARSHALL, GEORGE CATLETT (1880-1959), American soldier and statesman 10 278-279

MARSHALL, JOHN (1755-1835), American jurist, chief justice of United States. Supreme Court 1801-1835 10 279-281

MARSHALL, PAULE BURKE (born 1929), American author 10 281-282

MARSHALL, THURGOOD (1908-1993), African American jurist 10 282-284

MARSILIUS OF PADUA (1275/80-1342), Italian political philosopher 10 284

MARTEL, CHARLES (circa 690-741), Frankish ruler 10 285

MARTÍ, JOSÉ (1853-1895), Cuban revolutionary, poet, and journalist 10 285-286

MARTIAL (Marcus Valerias Martialis; circa 38/41-circa 104), Roman epigrammatist 10 286-287

MARTIN V (Oddone Colonna; 1368-1431), pope 1417-1431 10 287-288

MARTIN, AGNES (1912-2004), American painter 10 288-289

MARTIN, DEAN (Dino Paul Crocetti; 1917-1995), American entertainer 26 245-247

MARTIN, GREGORY (circa 1540-1582), British Bible translator and scholar 21 277-279

MARTIN, LUTHER (1748-1826), American lawyer and Revolutionary patriot 10 289-290

MARTIN, LYNN MORLEY (born 1939), Republican representative from Illinois and secretary of labor under George Bush 10 290-292

MARTIN, MARY (1913-1990), popular stage actress, singer, and dancer and a television and film star 10 292-293

MARTIN, WILLIAM MCCHESNEY, JR. (1906-1998), American business executive and federal government official 10 293-295

MARTIN DU GARD, ROGER (1881-1958), French author 10 295-296

MARTINEAU, HARRIET (1802-1876), English writer and philosopher 10 296-297

MARTINEZ, MARIA MONTOYA (Maria Antonia Montoya; Marie Poveka; Pond Lily; 1881?-1980), Pueblo potter 24 241-243

MARTÍNEZ, MAXIMILIANO HERNÁNDEZ (1882-1966), president of El Salvador (1931-1944) 10 297-298

MARTINEZ, VILMA SOCORRO (born 1943), Hispanic American attorney and activist **18** 276-279

MARTINI, SIMONE (flourished 1315-1344), Italian painter **10** 298-299

MARTINU, BOHUSLAV (1890-1959), Czech composer **10** 299-300

MARTY, MARTIN E. (born 1928), Lutheran pastor, historian of American religion, and commentator **10** 300-301

MARVELL, ANDREW (1621-1678), English poet and politician **10** 301-303

MARX, KARL (1818-1883), German political philosopher **10** 304-308

MARX BROTHERS, 20th-century American stage and film comedians **10** 303-304

MARY, QUEEN OF SCOTS (1542-1587), queen of France and Scotland **10** 308-309

MARY, SAINT (Blessed Virgin Mary; late 1st century B.C.-1st century A.D.), New Testament figure, mother of Jesus **10** 308-309

MARY I (1516-1558), queen of England 1553-1558 **10** 308-309

MARY II (1662-1694), queen of England, Scotland, and Ireland 1689-1694 **10** 309-310

MARY MAGDALENE (Mary of Magdala), Catholic saint and biblical figure **24** 243-246

MASACCIO (1401-1428), Italian painter **10** 312-313

MASARYK, JAN (1886-1948), Czech foreign minister **20** 243-246

MASARYK, TOMÁŠ GARRIGUE (1850-1937), Czech philosopher and statesman, president 1919-1935 **10** 314-315

MASINISSA, KING OF NUMIDIA (240 B.C. - 148 B.C.), prince of the Massylians who consolidated the Numidian tribes to form a North African kingdom **10** 315-317

MASIRE, QUETT KETUMILE (born 1925), a leader of the fight for independence and president of Botswana **10** 318-319

MASON, BRIDGET (Biddy Mason; 1818-1891), African American nurse, midwife, and entrepreneur **22** 312-314

MASON, GEORGE (1725-1792), American statesman **10** 319-320

MASON, JAMES MURRAY (1796-1871), American politician and Confederate diplomat **10** 320-321

MASON, LOWELL (1792-1872), American composer and music educator **10** 321-322

Masonic Fraternity
 see Freemasonry

MASSASOIT (1580-1661), Native American tribal chief **10** 322-324

MASSEY, VINCENT (Charles Vincent Massey, 1887-1967), Canadian governor-general **24** 246-248

MASSEY, WILLIAM FERGUSON (1856-1925), New Zealand prime minister 1912-1925 **10** 324

MASSINGER, PHILIP (1583-1640), English playwright **10** 324-325

MASSYS, QUENTIN (1465/66-1530), Flemish painter **10** 325-326

MASTERS, EDGAR LEE (1869-1950), American author and lawyer **10** 326-327

MASTERS, WILLIAM HOWELL (born 1915), American psychologist and sex therapist **10** 327-328

MASUDI, ALI IBN AL- HUSAYN AL- (died 956), Arab historian **10** 328-329

MASUR, KURT (born 1927), German conductor and humanist **20** 246-248

MATA HARI (Margaretha Geertruida Zelle; 1876-1917), Dutch spy **21** 279-282

MATAMOROS, MARINO (1770-1814), Mexican priest and independence hero **10** 329-330

Mathematics
 and astronomy
  Al-Kashi **26** 12-13
  Brahmagupta **26** 44-46
 applied
  Dantzig, George Bernard **26** 81-83
 pi
  Al-Kashi **26** 12-13
 simplex method
  Dantzig, George Bernard **26** 81-83

MATHER, COTTON (1663-1728), American Puritan clergyman and historian **10** 330-332

MATHER, INCREASE (1639-1723), American Puritan clergymen, educator, and author **10** 332-333

MATHEWSON, CHRISTY (Christopher Mathewson; 1880-1925), American baseball player **21** 282-284

MATHIAS, BOB (Robert Bruce Mathias; born 1930), American track and field star **21** 284-286

MATHIEZ, ALBERT (1874-1932), French historian **10** 333-334

MATILDA OF TUSCANY (ca. 1046-1115), Italian countess **10** 334-336

MATISSE, HENRI (1869-1954), French painter and sculptor **10** 336-337

MATLIN, MARLEE (born 1965), American actress **19** 228-230

MATLOVICH, LEONARD (1943-1988), American gay rights activist **20** 248-250

MATSUNAGA, SPARK MASAYUKI (1916-1990), Asian American U.S. senator **18** 279-281

MATSUSHITA, KONOSUKE (1918-1989), Japanese inventor and businessman **19** 230-232

MATTA ECHAURREN, ROBERTO SEBASTIAN ANTONIO (Matta, 1911-2002), Chilean artist **24** 248-250

MATTEI, ENRICO (1906-1962), Italian entrepreneur **10** 337-339

MATTEOTTI, GIACOMO (1885-1924), Italian political leader **10** 339-340

MATTHAU, WALTER (Walter Matthow; Walter Matuschanskayasky; 1920-2000), American actor **22** 314-316

MATTHEW, SAINT (flourished Ist century), Apostle and Evangelist **10** 340-341

MATTHEW PARIS (circa 1200-1259), English Benedictine chronicler **10** 341-342

MATTINGLY, GARRETT (1900-1962), American historian, professor, and author of novel-like histories **10** 342-344

MATZELIGER, JAN (1852-1889), American inventor and shoemaker **19** 232-234

MAUCHLY, JOHN (1907-1980), American computer entrepreneur **20** 250-252

MAUDSLAY, HENRY (1771-1831), British engineer and inventor **21** 286-288

MAUGHAM, WILLIAM SOMERSET (1874-1965), English author **10** 344-345

MAULBERTSCH, FRANZ ANTON (1724-1796), Austrian painter **10** 345

MAULDIN, BILL (1921-2003), cartoon biographer of the ordinary GI in World War II **10** 345-346

MAUPASSANT, HENRI RENÉ ALBERT GUY DE (1850-1893), French author **10** 347

MAURIAC, FRANÇOIS (1885-1970), French author **10** 347-348

MUSIL, ROBERT EDLER VON (1880-1942), Austrian novelist, dramatist, and short story writer **11** 268-269

MUSKIE, EDMUND SIXTUS (1914-1996), United States senator and Democratic vice-presidential nominee **11** 269-271

MUSSET, LOUIS CHARLES ALFRED DE (1810-1857), French poet, dramatist, and fiction writer **11** 271-272

MUSSOLINI, BENITO (1883-1945), Italian Fascist dictator 1922-1943 **11** 272-274

MUSSORGSKY, MODEST PETROVICH (1839-1881), Russian composer **11** 274-276

MUSTE, ABRAHAM JOHANNES (1885-1967), American pacifist and labor leader **11** 276-277

MUTESA I (circa 1838-1884), African monarch of Buganda **11** 277

MUTESA II (1924-1969), Monarch of Buganda **11** 277-278

MUTIS, JOSÉ CELESTINO (1732-1808), Spanish-Colombian naturalist **11** 278-279

MUTSUHITO (a.k.a. Meiji; 1852-1912), Japanese emperor **11** 279-282

MUYBRIDGE, EADWEARD (1830-1904), English photographer **21** 305-308

MWANGA (circa 1866-1901), Monarch of Buganda **11** 282-283

MYDANS, CARL (1907-2004), American photojournalist **11** 283-284

MYRDAL, ALVA (1902-1986), Swedish social reformer and diplomat **24** 274-276

MYRDAL, KARL GUNNAR (1898-1987), Swedish economist and sociologist **11** 284

MYRON (flourished circa 470-450 B.C.), Greek sculptor **11** 285

Mysticism (religion)
Hindu
Kabir **26** 188-190
in literature
Kabir **26** 188-190
Islamic
Kabir **26** 188-190

MZILIKAZI (circa 1795-1868), South African warrior leader **11** 285-286

N

NABOKOV, VLADIMIR (1899-1977), Russian-born American writer, critic, and lepidopterist **11** 287-288

NABUCO DE ARAUJO, JOAQUIM AURELIO (1849-1910), Brazilian abolitionist, statesman, and author **11** 288-289

NADELMAN, ELIE (1882-1946), Polish-American sculptor and graphic artist **11** 289-290

NADER, RALPH (born 1934), American lawyer and social crusader **11** 290-291

NADIR SHAH (born Nadir Kouli; 1685-1747), Emperor of Persia **20** 278-281

NAGEL, ERNEST (1901-1985), American philosopher of science **11** 291-292

NAGUMO, CHUICHI (1887-1944), Japanese admiral **19** 263-266

NAGURSKI, BRONKO (Bronislaw Nagurski; 1908-1990), Canadian football player **21** 309-311

NAGY, IMRE (1896-1958), prime minister of Hungary (1953-55, 1956) **11** 292-293

NAHMANIDES (1194-1270), Spanish Talmudist **11** 293-294

NAIDU, SAROJINI (1879-1949), Indian poet and nationalist **11** 294-295

NAIPAUL, V. S. (born 1932), Trinidadian author of English-language prose **11** 295-296

NAISMITH, JAMES (1861-1939), Canadian inventor of basketball **21** 311-313

NAJIBULLAH, MOHAMMAD (born 1947), Soviet-selected ruler of the Republic of Afghanistan **11** 296-298

NAKASONE, YASUHIRO (born 1918), prime minister of Japan (1982-1987) **11** 298-300

NESTORIUS (died circa 453), Syrian patriarch of Constantinople and heresiarch **11** 349-350

NETANYAHU, BINYAMIN (born 1949), Israeli ambassador to the United Nations (1984-1988), head of the Likud Party, and prime minister **11** 350-351

NETO, ANTÓNIO AGOSTINHO (1922-1979), Angolan intellectual and nationalist and first president of the People's Republic of Angola **11** 351-352

NEUFELD, ELIZABETH F. (born 1928), American biochemist **11** 352-353

NEUMANN, BALTHASAR (1687-1753), German architect **11** 354-355

Neurology
Sacks, Oliver Wolf **26** 329-331

NEUTRA, RICHARD JOSEPH (1892-1970), Austrian-born American architect **11** 355-356

Neutron (physics)
Libby, Leona Marshall **26** 231-233

NEVELSON, LOUISE (1900-1988), American abstract sculptor **11** 356-357

NEVERS, ERNIE (Ernest Alonzo Nevers; 1903-1976), American athlete **20** 281-283

NEVIN, JOHN WILLIAMSON (1803-1886), American Protestant theologian **11** 357

NEVINS, ALLAN (1890-1971), American historian **11** 357-359

NEVSKY, ALEXANDER (ca. 1220-1262), Russian grand duke and prince **11** 359

New Amsterdam
see New York City

New York City (New York State)
• MODERN PERIOD
architecture
Huxtable, Ada Louise **26** 162-165

New York Times (newspaper)
Adler, Renata **26** 8-9
Huxtable, Ada Louise **26** 162-165

New Yorker (magazine)
contributors
Adler, Renata **26** 8-9

NEWBERY, JOHN (1713-1767), English publisher **11** 360-361

NEWCOMB, SIMON (1835-1909), American astronomer **11** 361-362

NEWCOMEN, THOMAS (1663-1729), English inventor and engineer **11** 362

NEWHOUSE, SAMUEL IRVING (1895-1979), American media tycoon **11** 362-364

NEWMAN, BARNETT (1905-1970), American painter **11** 365

NEWMAN, JOHN HENRY (1801-1890), English cardinal and theologian **11** 365-367

NEWMAN, PAUL LEONARD (born 1925), American actor and humanitarian **18** 306-308

NEWTON, HUEY P. (born 1942), co-founder of the Black Panther Party **11** 367-369

NEWTON, SIR ISAAC (1642-1727), English scientist and mathematician **11** 369-372

NEXØ, MARTIN ANDERSON (1869-1954), Danish author **11** 372

NEY, MICHEL (1769-1815), French marshal **11** 372-373

NEYMAN, JERZY (1894-1981), American statistician **21** 316-318

NGALA, RONALD GIDEON (1923-1972), Kenyan politician **11** 373-374

NGATA, SIR APIRANA TURUPA (1874-1950), Maori leader, politician, and scholar **11** 374-375

NGOR, HAING S. (circa 1947-1996), Cambodian American actor and human rights activist **25** 310-312

NGOYI, LILLIAN (1911-1980), South African civil rights activist **20** 283-284

NGUGI WA THIONG'O (James Ngugi; born 1938), Kenyan writer **11** 375-376

NI TSAN (1301-1374), Chinese painter **11** 400

NICHIREN (1222-1282), Japanese Buddhist monk **11** 376-377

NICHOLAS I (1796-1855), czar of Russia 1825-1855 **11** 377-378

NICHOLAS II (1868-1918), czar of Russia 1894-1917 **11** 378-380

NICHOLAS V (Tommaso Parentucelli; 1397-1455), Italian pope 1447-1455 **26** 299-300

NICHOLAS OF ORESME (circa 1320-1382), French bishop, writer and translator **11** 380

NICHOLAS, SAINT (Santa Claus; died 345), Lycian bishop **20** 284-285

NICHOLSON, BEN (1894-1982), English painter **11** 380-381

NICHOLSON, SIR FRANCIS (1655-1728), English colonial governor **11** 381-382

Nickelodeon (cable TV network)
Laybourne, Geraldine **26** 224-226

NICKLAUS, JACK (born 1940), American golfer **11** 382-383

Nicknames
Axis Sally
Gillars, Mildred Elizabeth **26** 125-127
father of Chicano music
Guerrero, Lalo **26** 129-131
father of Polish literature
Rej, Mikolaj **26** 318-320
father of 20th-century ballet
Fokine, Michel **26** 112-115
father of zero
Brahmagupta **26** 44-46
founder of modern dentistry
Fauchard, Pierre **26** 103-105
founder of Russian national drama
Ostrovsky, Alexander **26** 280-283
lightning from the Urals
Skoblikova, Lydia Pavlovna **26** 344-346
patron saint of Paris
Saint Genèvieve **26** 331-333
peasant poet of Northamptonshire
Clare, John **26** 69-71
poet laureate of medicine
Sacks, Oliver Wolf **26** 329-331

NICHOLS, MIKE (Michael Igor Peschkowsky; born 1931), American film and theater director and producer **20** 285-288

NICOLSON, HAROLD GEORGE (1886-1968), British diplomat, historian, biographer, critic and journalist, and diarist **11** 383-384

NICOLSON, MARJORIE HOPE (1894-1981), American educator **11** 384-385

NICOMACHUS OF GERASA (circa 60-circa 100), Greek mathematician, philosopher, and musical theorist **25** 312-314

NIDETCH, JEAN (born 1927), founder of Weight Watchers **21** 318-320

NIEBUHR, BARTHOLD GEORG (1776-1831), German historian and statesman **11** 385-386

NIEBUHR, HELMUT RICHARD (1894-1962), American Protestant theologian **11** 386-387

NIEBUHR, REINHOLD (1892-1971), American Protestant theologian **11** 387-388

NIELSEN, CARL AUGUST (1865-1931), Danish composer **11** 388-389

NIEMEYER SOARES FILHO, OSCAR (born 1907), Brazilian architect **11** 389-390

NIETZSCHE, FRIEDRICH (1844-1900), German philosopher and poet **11** 390-392

Nigeria, Federal Republic of (nation; West Africa)
religion

PAUL V (Camillo Borghese; 1550-1621), Italian pope 23 297-299

PAUL VI (Giovanni Battista Montini; 1897-1978), pope 12 146-148

PAUL, ALICE (1885-1977), American feminist and women's rights activist 19 277-280
Younger, Maud 26 392-395

PAUL, SAINT (died 66/67), Christian theologian and Apostle 12 141-143

PAULI, WOLFGANG ERNST (1900-1958), Austrian theoretical physicist 12 149

PAULING, LINUS CARL (born 1901), American chemist 12 150-152

PAUSANIAS (flourished circa 150), Greek traveler and geographer 25 326-327

PAVAROTTI, LUCIANO (born 1935), Italian tenor 12 152-154

PAVESE, CESARE (1908-1950), Italian novelist, poet, and critic 12 154-155

PAVLOV, IVAN PETROVICH (1849-1936), Russian physiologist 12 155-157

PAVLOVA, ANNA (1881-1931), Russian ballet dancer 12 157-159

PAYNE, JOHN HOWARD (1791-1852), American actor, playwright, and songwriter 12 159

PAYNE-GAPOSCHKIN, CECILIA (1900-1979), American astronomer 12 159-161

PAYTON, WALTER (1954-1999), American football player 20 294-296

PAZ, OCTAVIO (1914-1998), Mexican diplomat, critic, editor, translator, poet, and essayist 12 161-162

PAZ ESTENSSORO, VICTOR (1907-2001), Bolivian statesman and reformer 12 163-164

PAZ ZAMORA, JAIME (born 1939), president of Bolivia (1989-) 12 165-167

PÁZMÁNY, PÉTER (1570-1637), Hungarian archbishop 12 164-165

PEABODY, ELIZABETH PALMER (1804-1894), American educator and author 12 167-168
Wheelock, Lucy 26 380-382

PEABODY, GEORGE (1795-1869), American merchant, financier, and philanthropist 12 168

PEACOCK, THOMAS LOVE (1785-1866), English novelist and satirist 12 169

PEALE, CHARLES WILLSON (1741-1827), American painter and scientist 12 169-171

PEALE, NORMAN VINCENT (1898-1993), American religious leader who blended psychotherapy and religion 12 171-172

PEALE, REMBRANDT (1778-1860), American painter 12 172-173

PEARSE, PATRICK HENRY (1879-1916), Irish poet, educator, and revolutionary 12 173-174

PEARSON, LESTER BOWLES (1897-1972), Canadian statesman and diplomat, prime minister 12 174-175

PEARY, ROBERT EDWIN (1856-1920), American explorer 12 175-176

PECHSTEIN, HERMANN MAX (1881-1955), German Expressionist painter and graphic artist 12 176-177

PECK, ANNIE SMITH (1850-1935), American mountain climber 24 304-306

PECK, MORGAN SCOTT (1936-2005), American author and psychologist 26 288-291

PECK, ROBERT NEWTON (born 1928), American author of children's literature 12 177-178

PECKINPAH, SAM (1925-1984), American film director 21 338-340

PEDRARIAS (Pedro Arias de Ávila; circa 1440-1531), Spanish conqueror and colonial governor 12 179

PEDRO I (1798-1834), emperor of Brazil and king of Portugal 12 179-180

PEDRO II (1825-1891), emperor of Brazil 1831-89 12 180-181

PEEL, SIR ROBERT (1788-1850), English statesman, prime minister 1834-35 and 1841-46 12 181-183

PÉGUY, CHARLES PIERRE (1873-1914), French poet 12 183-184

PEI, I. M. (Ieoh Ming Pei; born 1917), Chinese-American architect 12 184-187

PEIRCE, BENJAMIN (1809-1880), American mathematician 21 340-342

PEIRCE, CHARLES SANDERS (1839-1914), American scientist and philosopher 12 187-188

PEIXOTO, FLORIANO (1839-1895), Brazilian marshal, president 1891-94 12 188-189

PELAGIUS (died circa 430), British theologian 12 189-190

PELE (Edson Arantes Do Nascimento Pele; born 1940), Brazilian soccer player 12 190-191

PELLI, CESAR (born 1926), Hispanic American architect and educator 12 191-192

PELOSI, NANCY (Nancy D'Alesandro; born 1940), American politician 25 328-330

PELTIER, LEONARD (born 1944), Native American activist 12 193-195

PEÑA, PACO (Francisco Peña Pérez; born 1942), Spanish guitarist and composer 23 299-301

PENDERECKI, KRZYSZTOF (born 1933), Polish composer 12 195-197

PENDLETON, EDMUND (1721-1803), American political leader 12 197-198

PENDLETON, GEORGE HUNT (1825-1889), American politician 12 198

PENFIELD, WILDER GRAVES (1891-1976), Canadian neurosurgeon 12 198-200

PENN, WILLIAM (1644-1718), English Quaker, founder of Pennsylvania 12 200-202

PENNEY, J. C. (James Cash Penney; 1875-1971), American chain store executive and philanthropist 12 202-203

PENNINGTON, MARY ENGLE (1872-1952), American chemist 22 352-355

PENROSE, BOIES (1860-1921), American senator and political boss 12 203-204

PENROSE, ROGER (born 1931), British mathematician and physicist 12 204-205

PENSKE, ROGER (born 1937), American businessman and race car team owner 19 280-282

PENZIAS, ARNO ALLEN (born 1932), German American physicist 23 301-304

PEP, WILLIE (William Guiglermo Papaleo; born 1922), American boxer 21 342-344

PEPPER, CLAUDE DENSON (1900-1989), Florida attorney, state representative, U.S. senator, and U.S. representative 12 205-206

PEPPERELL, SIR WILLIAM (1696-1759), American merchant and soldier 12 206-207

PEPYS, SAMUEL (1633-1703), English diarist 12 207-208

PERCY, WALKER (1916-1990), American author 19 282-284

PEREGRINUS, PETRUS (flourished 1261-69), French scholastic and scientist **12** 208

PEREIRA, ARISTIDES MARIA (born 1923), Cape Verdean president **24** 306-308

PERELMAN, S. J. (Sidney Jerome Perelman; 1904-1979), American cartoonist, satirist, and parodist **12** 209-210

PERES, SHIMON (born 1923), head of the Israel Labour Party and Israeli prime minister (1984-1986) **12** 210-211

PERETZ, ISAAC LOEB (1851-1915), Jewish poet, novelist, and playwright **12** 212

PÉREZ, CARLOS ANDRÉS (born 1922), president of Venezuela (1989-1993) **12** 212-214

PÉREZ DE CUELLAR, JAVIER (born 1920), Peruvian foreign service officer and secretary general of the United Nations (1982-) **12** 214-215

PÉREZ ESQUIVEL, ADOLFO (born 1931), Argentine artist and human rights activist **12** 215-217

PÉREZ JIMENEZ, MARCOS (1914-2001), Venezuelan dictator **12** 217-218

PERGOLESI, GIOVANNI BATTISTA (1710-1736), Italian composer **12** 218-219

PERICLES (circa 495-429 B.C.), Athenian statesman **12** 219-221

PERKIN, WILLIAM H. (1838-1907), British chemist **25** 330-332

PERKINS, FRANCES (1882-1965), American statesman and social worker **12** 221-222

PERKINS, GEORGE WALBRIDGE (1862-1920), American businessman and banker **21** 344-347

PERKINS, WILLIAM MAXWELL EVARTS (1884-1947), American editor of fiction who discovered and developed brilliant authors **12** 222-223

PERLASCA, GIORGIO (Jorge Perlas; 1910-1992), Italian activist **25** 332-334

PERLE, GEORGE (born 1915), American musician **12** 223-224

PERLMAN, ITZHAK (born 1945), American musician **18** 318-320

PERÓN, EVA (MARÍA) DUARTE DE (1919-1952), the second wife and political partner of President Juan Perón of Argentina **12** 225-226

PERÓN, ISABEL MARTINEZ DE (born 1931), first woman president of Argentina (1974-1976) **12** 226-228

PERÓN, JUAN DOMINGO (1895-1974), Argentine statesman, president 1946-55 **12** 228-230

PEROT, HENRY ROSS (born 1930), American businessman and activist **12** 230-231

PÉROTIN (Perotinus; flourished circa 1185-1205), French composer and musician **12** 231-232

PERRAULT, CLAUDE (1613-1688), French scientist and architect **12** 232-233

PERRET, AUGUSTE (1874-1954), French architect **12** 233

PERRIN, JEAN BAPTISTE (1870-1942), French physicist **12** 233-236

PERRY, HAROLD ROBERT (1916-1991), African American Roman Catholic bishop **12** 236-237

PERRY, MATTHEW CALBRAITH (1794-1858), American naval officer **12** 237-239

PERRY, OLIVER HAZARD (1785-1819), American naval officer **12** 239

PERRY, RALPH BARTON (1876-1957), American philosopher **12** 239-240

PERRY, WILLIAM JAMES (born 1927), President Clinton's secretary of defense (1994-) **12** 240-242

PERSE, SAINT-JOHN (Alexis Saint-Léger Léger; 1887-1975), French poet and diplomat **12** 242-243

PERSHING, JOHN JOSEPH (1860-1948), American general **12** 243-244

PERTH, 16TH EARL OF (James Eric Drummond; 1876-1951), English statesman **12** 244-245

PERUGINO (circa 1450-1523), Italian painter **12** 245-246

PERUTZ, MAX (1914-2002), English crystallographer and biochemist **12** 246-248

PESOTTA, ROSE (1896-1965), American union organizer **12** 248-249

PESTALOZZI, JOHANN HEINRICH (1746-1827), Swiss educator **12** 249-250

PÉTAIN, HENRI PHILIPPE (1856-1951), French general and statesman **12** 250-252

PETER I (Peter the Great; 1672-1725), czar of Russia 1682-1725 **12** 253-256

PETER I (1844-1921), king of Serbia 1903-18, and of the Serbs, Croats, and Slovenes 1918-21 **12** 256

PETER III (Pedro; circa 1239-85), king of Aragon 1276-85 **12** 256-257

PETER, SAINT (died circa 65), apostle and bishop of Rome **12** 252-253

PETERS, CARL (1856-1918), German explorer and colonizer **12** 257-258

PETERSON, EDITH R. (born Edith Elizabeth Runne; 1914-1992), American medical researcher **12** 258-259

PETERSON, OSCAR (born 1925), Canadian pianist **23** 304-306

PETO, JOHN FREDERICK (1854-1907), American painter **12** 259

PETÖFI, SÁNDOR (1823-1849), Hungarian poet and revolutionary leader **23** 306-308

PETRARCH (Francesco Petrarca; 1304-74), Italian poet **12** 259-261

PETRIE, SIR WILLIAM MATTHEW FLINDERS (1853-1942), English archeologist **12** 261-262

PETRONIUS ARBITER (died circa 66), Roman author **12** 262-263

PEVSNER, ANTOINE (1886-1962), Russian sculptor and painter **12** 263-264

PHAEDRUS (c. 15 BC-c. 50), Greek/Roman fabulists **20** 296-297

PHIBUN SONGKHRAM, LUANG (1897-1964), Thai statesman, prime minister 1938-44 and 1948-57 **12** 264-265

PHIDIAS (flourished circa 475-425 B.C.), Greek sculptor **12** 265-267

Philadelphia Inquirer (newspaper)
Annenberg, Walter Hubert **26** 16-18

Philanthropists, American
20th century
Annenberg, Walter Hubert **26** 16-18

PHILIDOR, FRANÇOIS-ANDRÉ (François-André Danican-Philidor; 1726-1795), French composer and chess player **21** 347-349

PHILIP (died 1676), American Wampanoag Indian chief 1662-76 **12** 267-268

PHILIP (Prince Philip; Philip Mountbatten; born 1921), Duke of Edinburgh and husband of Queen Elizabeth II of the United Kingdom **24** 308-310

PHILIP II (382-336 B.C.), king of Macedon 359-336 **12** 269-271

POMBAL, MARQUÊS DE (Sebastião José de Carvalho e Mello; 1699-1782), Portuguese statesman 12 386-387

POMPEY (106-48 B.C.), Roman general and statesman 12 387-389

POMPIDOU, GEORGES (1911-1974), second president of the French Fifth Republic (1969-1974) 12 389-390

POMPONAZZI, PIETRO (1462-1525), Italian Aristotelian philosopher 12 390-391

PONCE DE LEÓN, JUAN (1460?-1521), Spanish conqueror and explorer 12 391-392

PONIATOWSKA, ELENA (born 1933), Mexican journalist, novelist, essayist, and short-story writer 12 392-393

PONTIAC (circa 1720-69), Ottawa Indian chief 12 393-394

PONTOPPIDAN, HENRIK (Rusticus; 1857-1943), Danish author 25 336-338

PONTORMO (1494-1556), Italian painter 12 394-395

POOL, JUDITH GRAHAM (1919-1975), American physiologist 23 315-316

POPE, ALEXANDER (1688-1744), English poet and satirist 12 395-397

POPE, JOHN RUSSELL (1874-1937), American architect in the classical tradition 12 397-399

POPHAM, WILLIAM JAMES (born 1930), American educator active in educational test development 12 399-401

POPOVA, LIUBOV SERGEEVNA (1889-1924), Russian and Soviet avant-garde artist 12 401-402

POPPER, SIR KARL RAIMUND (1902-1994), Austrian philosopher 12 402

PORSCHE, FERDINAND SR. (1875-1951), Austrian German automobile designer and engineer 19 293-295

PORTA, GIACOMO DELLA (circa 1537-1602), Italian architect 12 402-403

PORTA, GIAMBATTISTA DELLA (1535-1615), Italian scientist and dramatist 12 403-404

PORTALES PLAZAZUELOS, DIEGO JOSÉ VÍCTOR (1793-1837), Chilean statesman 12 404

PORTER, COLE ALBERT (1891-1964), American composer 12 405-406

PORTER, EDWIN STRATTON (1870-1941), American filmmaker 20 299-301

PORTER, KATHERINE ANNE (1890-1980), American writer 12 406-407

PORTINARI, CÂNDIDO (1903-1962), Brazilian painter 12 407-408

PORTOLÁ, GASPAR DE (circa 1723-1784), Spanish explorer and colonial governor 12 408

PORTUONDO, OMARA (born 1930), Cuban singer 26 302-304

PORTZAMPARC, CHRISTIAN DE (born 1944), French architect 18 324-326

POSEY, ALEXANDER LAWRENCE (1873-1908), Native American author and politician 26 304-306

POST, CHARLES WILLIAM (1854-1914), American pioneer in the manufacture and mass-marketing of breakfast cereals 12 408-409

POST, EMILY PRICE (1873-1960), American authority on etiquette 12 409-410

Postmasters general
see Statesmen, American

POTEMKIN, GRIGORI ALEKSANDROVICH (1739-1791), Russian administrator and field marshal 12 411-412

POTOK, CHAIM (Herman Harold Potok; Chaim Tzvi; 1929-2002), American author 25 338-341

POTTER, BEATRIX (Helen Beatrix Potter; 1866-1943), English author and illustrator 18 326-328

POTTER, DAVID M. (1910-1971), American historian 12 412

POTTER, DENNIS (1935-1994), British essayist, playwright, screenwriter, and novelist 12 412-414

POULENC, FRANCIS (1899-1963), French composer 12 414-415

POUND, EZRA LOOMIS (1885-1972), American poet, editor, and critic 12 415-417

POUND, ROSCOE (1870-1964), American jurist and botanist 12 417-418

POUSSAINT, ALVIN FRANCIS (born 1934), African American psychiatrist 24 313-316

POUSSIN, NICOLAS (1594-1665), French painter 12 418-420

POWDERLY, TERENCE VINCENT (1849-1924), American labor leader 12 420-421

POWELL, ADAM CLAYTON, JR. (1908-1972), African American political leader and Baptist minister 12 421-422

POWELL, ANTHONY (1905-2000), English novelist 12 422-423

POWELL, COLIN LUTHER (born 1937), African American chairman of the Joint Chiefs of Staff 12 424-425

POWELL, JOHN WESLEY (1834-1902), American geologist, anthropologist, and explorer 12 425-426

POWELL, LEWIS F., JR. (1907-1998), U.S. Supreme Court justice (1972-1987) 12 426-428

POWERS, HIRAM (1805-1873), American sculptor 12 428-429

POWHATAN (circa 1550-1618), Native American tribal chief 12 429-430

POZZO, BROTHER ANDREA, S.J. (1642-1709), Italian artist and architect 25 341-342

PRADO UGARTECHE, MANUEL (1889-1967), Peruvian statesman 12 430-431

PRAETORIUS, MICHAEL (circa 1571-1621), German composer and theorist 12 431-432

PRAN, DITH (born 1942), Cambodian American journalist and activist 18 328-331

PRANDTAUER, JAKOB (1660-1726), Austrian baroque architect 12 432

PRASAD, RAJENDRA (1884-1963), Indian nationalist, first president of the Republic 12 433

PRAXITELES (flourished circa 370-330 B.C.), Greek sculptor 12 433-434

PREBISCH, RAÚL (1901-1986), Argentine economist active in the United Nations 12 434-436

PREGL, FRITZ (1869-1930), Austrian physiologist and medical chemist 12 436-437

PREM TINSULANONDA (born 1920), military leader and prime minister of Thailand (1979-1988) 12 437

PREMADASA, RANASINGHE (born 1924), president of Sri Lanka (1988-) 12 437-439

PREMCHAND (1880-1936), Indian novelist and short-story writer 12 439

PREMINGER, OTTO (1895-1986), Austrian filmmaker and theater producer/director 18 331-332

PRENDERGAST, MAURICE BRAZIL (1859-1924), American painter 12 440

PRESCOTT, WILLIAM HICKLING (1796-1859), American historian 12 440-441

PRESLEY, ELVIS ARON (1935-1977), American singer and actor 12 441-442

REYES, RAFAEL (1850-1920), Colombian military leader, president 1904-09 **13** 113

REYMONT, WLADYSLAW STANISLAW (Wladyslaw Rejment; 1868-1925), Polish author **25** 352-353

REYNOLDS, ALBERT (born 1932), prime minister of Ireland **13** 113-115

REYNOLDS, SIR JOSHUA (1723-1792), English portrait painter **13** 115-116

REYNOLDS, RICHARD JOSHUA JR. (R.J. Reynolds; 1906-1964), American businessman and philanthropist **19** 308-310

REZA SHAH PAHLAVI (Reza Khan; 1878-1944), Shah of Iran 1925-41 **13** 116-117

RHEE, SYNGMAN (1875-1965), Korean independence leader, South Korean president 1948-60 **13** 117-120

RHETT, ROBERT BARNWELL (1800-1876) American statesman **13** 120

RHODES, CECIL JOHN (1853-1902), English imperialist and financier **13** 120-122

RHODES, JAMES FORD (1848-1927), American historian **13** 122

RHYS, JEAN (Ella Gwendolen Rees Williams; 1890-1979), English author **19** 310-312

RIBERA, JUSEPE DE (1591-1652), Spanish painter **13** 122-123

RICARDO, DAVID (1772-1823), English economist **13** 123-124

RICCI, MATTEO (1552-1610), Italian Jesuit missionary **13** 124-125

RICE, ANNE (born 1941), American author **13** 125-126

RICE, CONDOLEEZZA (born 1954), African American national security advisor **23** 335-338

RICE, ELMER (1892-1967), American playwright and novelist **13** 126-127

RICE, JOSEPH MAYER (1857-1934), American education reformer **13** 127-128

RICH, ADRIENNE (born 1929), American poet **13** 128-130

RICHARD I (1157-1199), king of England 1189-99 **13** 130

RICHARD II (1367-1400), king of England 1377-99 **13** 130-131

RICHARD III (1452-1485), king of England 1483-85 **13** 132-133

RICHARD, MAURICE ("Rocket" Richard; born 1921), Canadian hockey player **19** 312-313

RICHARDS, ANN WILLIS (born 1933), Democratic governor of Texas **13** 133-134

RICHARDS, ELLEN H. (born Ellen Henrietta Swallow; 1842-1911), American chemist and educator **13** 134-136

RICHARDS, IVOR ARMSTRONG (1893-1979), English-born American semanticist and literary critic **13** 137

RICHARDS, THEODORE WILLIAM (1868-1928), American chemist **13** 137-138

RICHARDSON, HENRY HANDEL (pen name of Ethel Florence Lindesay Richardson; 1870-1946), expatriate Australian novelist **13** 139

RICHARDSON, HENRY HOBSON (1838-1886), American architect **13** 139-141

RICHARDSON, RALPH DAVID (1902-1983), British actor **24** 332-334

RICHARDSON, SAMUEL (1689-1761), English novelist **13** 141-142

RICHELIEU, ARMAND JEAN DU PLESSIS DE (1585-1642), French statesman and cardinal **13** 142-144

RICHET, CHARLES ROBERT (1850-1935), French physiologist **13** 144-145

RICHIER, GERMAINE (1904-1959), French sculptor **13** 145-146

RICHLER, MORDECAI (1931-2001), Canadian author **22** 371-373

RICHTER, BURTON (born 1931), American physicist **25** 354-356

RICHTER, CHARLES F. (1900-1985), American seismologist **13** 146-148

RICHTER, CONRAD MICHAEL (1890-1968), American novelist and short-story writer **13** 148-149

RICHTER, GERHARD (born 1932), German artist **23** 338-340

RICHTER, HANS (Johann Siegried Richter; 1888-1976), German-born film director **13** 149-150

RICHTER, JOHANN PAUL FRIEDRICH (1763-1825), German humorist and prose writer **13** 150-151

RICIMER, FLAVIUS (died 472), Germanic Roman political chief **13** 151-152

RICKENBACKER, EDWARD VERNON (1890-1973), World War I fighter pilot and airline president **13** 152-153

RICKEY, WESLEY BRANCH (1881-1965), innovative baseball executive **13** 153-155

RICKOVER, HYMAN GEORGE (1900-1986), U.S. Navy officer **13** 155-157

RICOEUR, PAUL (born 1913), French exponent of hermeneutical philosophy **13** 157-158

RIDE, SALLY (born 1951), American astronaut and physicist **13** 158-160

RIDGE, JOHN ROLLIN (Yellow Bird; 1827-1867), Native American author **22** 373-375

RIDGE, THOMAS JOSEPH (born 1946), American governor of Pennsylvania and first secretary of the Department of Homeland Security **24** 334-337

RIDGWAY, MATTHEW BUNKER (1895-1993), American general **13** 160-161

RIDGWAY, ROZANNE LEJEANNE (born 1935), American diplomat **24** 337-338

RIEFENSTAHL, LENI (born 1902), German film director **13** 161-163

RIEL, LOUIS (1844-1885), Canadian rebel **13** 163-164

RIEMANN, GEORG FRIEDRICH BERNARD (1826-1866), German mathematician **13** 164-165

RIEMENSCHNEIDER, TILMAN (1468-1531), German sculptor **13** 166

RIENZI, COLA DI (or Rienzo; 1313/14-1354), Italian patriot, tribune of Rome **13** 166-167

RIESMAN, DAVID (1909-2002), American sociologist, writer, and social critic **13** 167-168

RIETVELD, GERRIT THOMAS (1888-1964), Dutch architect and furniture designer **13** 169

RIIS, JACOB AUGUST (1849-1914), Danish-born American journalist and reformer **13** 169-170

RILEY, JAMES WHITCOMB (1849-1916), American poet **13** 170-171

RILKE, RAINER MARIA (1875-1926), German lyric poet **13** 171-172

RILLIEUX, NORBERT (1806-1894), American inventor **20** 309-311

RIMBAUD, (JEAN NICOLAS) ARTHUR (1854-1891), French poet **13** 172-174

RIMMER, WILLIAM (1816-1879), American sculptor, painter, and physician **13** 174

RIMSKY-KORSAKOV, NIKOLAI ANDREEVICH (1844-1908), Russian composer and conductor **13** 174-175

S

SAGAN, CARL E. (born 1934), American astronomer and popularizer of science **13** 424-425

SAGER, RUTH (1918-1997), American biologist and geneticist **13** 425-426

SAICHO (767-822), Japanese Buddhist monk **13** 426-428

SAID, SEYYID (1790-1856), Omani sultan **13** 428-429

SAIGO, TAKAMORI (1827-1877), Japanese rebel and statesman **13** 429

St. Charles Borromeo, Church of
see Karlskirche, The (church, Vienna)

ST. CLAIR, ARTHUR (1736-1818), Scottish-born American soldier and politician **13** 429-430

ST. DENIS, RUTH (1878?-1968), American dancer and choreographer **13** 430-431

SAINT GENÈVIEVE (Genovefa; circa 422-512), French religious figure **26** 331-333

ST. LAURENT, LOUIS STEPHEN (born 1882), Canadian statesman **13** 434

St. Peter's (new; Rome)
rebuilding
Urban VIII **26** 301-302

SAINTE-BEUVE, CHARLES AUGUSTIN (1804-1869), French literary critic **13** 438

SAINTE-MARIE, BUFFY (Beverly Sainte-Marie; born 1941), Native American singer and songwriter **26** 334-336

SAINT-EXUPÉRY, ANTOINE DE (1900-1944), French novelist, essayist, and pilot **13** 431-432

SAINT-GAUDENS, AUGUSTUS (1848-1907), American sculptor **13** 432

SAINT-JUST, LOUIS ANTOINE LÉON DE (1767-1794), French radical political leader **13** 433

ST. LAURENT, YVES (born 1936), French fashion designer **20** 327-329

SAINT-PIERRE, ABBÉ DE (Charles Irénée Castel; 1658-1743), French political and economic theorist **13** 434-435

SAINT-SAËNS, CHARLES CAMILLE (1835-1921), French composer **13** 435-436

SAINT-SIMON, COMTE DE (Claude Henri de Rouvroy; 1760-1825), French social philosopher and reformer **13** 436-437

SAINT-SIMON, DUC DE (Louis de Rouvroy; 1675-1755), French writer **13** 436

SAIONJI, KIMMOCHI (1849-1940), Japanese elder statesman **13** 438-439

SAKHAROV, ANDREI (1921-1989), Russian theoretical physicist and "father of the Soviet atomic bomb" **13** 439-441

SALADIN (Salah-ad-Din Yusuf ibn Aiyub; 1138-93), Kurdish ruler of Egypt and Syria **13** 441-442

SALAM, ABDUS (1926-1996), Pakistani physicist **24** 344-346

SALAZAR, ANTÓNIO DE OLIVEIRA (1889-1970), Portuguese statesman **13** 442-443

SALIH, ALI'ABDALLAH (born 1942), president of the Yemeni Arab Republic (North Yemen) and first president of the United Republic of Yemen **13** 443-445

SALINAS DE GORTARI, CARLOS (born 1948), president of Mexico (1988-) **13** 445-447

SALINGER, J. D. (born 1919), American author **13** 447-448

SALISBURY, HARRISON EVANS (born 1908), American journalist **13** 449-451

SALISBURY, 3D MARQUESS OF (Robert Arthur Talbot Gascoyne-Cecil; 1830-1903), English statesman and diplomat **13** 448-449

SALK, JONAS EDWARD (1914-1995), American physician, virologist, and immunologist **13** 451-452

SALLE, DAVID (born 1952), American artist **13** 452-453

SALLINEN, AULIS (born 1935), Finnish composer **25** 368-370

SALLUST (Gaius Sallustius Crispus; 86-circa 35 B.C.), Roman statesman and historian **13** 454

SALOMON, CHARLOTTE (1917-1943), German artist **13** 454-455

SALOMON, HAYM (c. 1740-1785), American financier **20** 329-331

SALVEMINI, GAETANO (1873-1957), Italian historian **13** 455-456

SAMAR, SIMA (born 1957), Afghan physician ans human rights activist **25** 370-372

Samarkand, University of
Al-Kashi **26** 12-13

SAMPSON, EDITH (nee Edith Spurlock; 1901-1979), African American social worker, judge, and promoter of the United States **23** 356-358

SAMUEL (circa 1056-1004 B.C.), Hebrew prophet, last judge of Israel **13** 457-458

SAMUELSON, PAUL ANTHONY (born 1915), American economist **13** 458-459

San Carlos reservation (Arizona)
Victorio **26** 368-370

SAN MARTÍN, JOSÉ DE (1778-1850), Argentine soldier and statesman **13** 468-469

SANA'I, HAKIM (Adam al-Ghaznawi; Abu al-Majd Majdud ibn Adam; c. 1050-c. 1131), Persian mystic poet **24** 346-347

SANAPIA (Mary Poafpybitty; 1895-1979), Comanche medicine woman **23** 350-360

SANCHEZ, SONIA (Wilsonia Benita Driver; born 1934), African American author and educator **24** 347-350

SANCTORIUS (1561-1636), Italian physician and physiologist **13** 459

SAND, GEORGE (1804-1876), French novelist **13** 459-461

SANDAGE, ALLAN REX (born 1926), American astronomer **21**

SANDBURG, CARL (1878-1967), American poet, anthologist, and biographer **13** 461-462

SANDERS, BARRY (born 1968), African American football player **25** 372-374

SANDERS, COLONEL (Harland David Sanders; 1890-1980), American businessman **19** 323-325

SANDINO, AUGUSTO C. (1894-1934), Nicaraguan guerrilla leader **13** 462-463

SANDYS, SIR EDWIN (1561-1629), English statesman and colonizer in America **13** 463-464

SANGALLO FAMILY (flourished late 15th-mid-16th century), Italian artists and architects **13** 464-466

SANGER, FREDERICK (born 1918), English biochemist **13** 466-467

SANGER, MARGARET HIGGINS (1884-1966), American leader of birth control movement **13** 467-468

SANMICHELI, MICHELE (circa 1484-1559), Italian architect and military engineer **13** 469-470

SANSOVINO, JACOPO (1486-1570), Italian sculptor and architect **13** 470-471

SANTA ANA, ANTONIO LÓPEZ DE (1794-1876), Mexican general and statesman, six times president **13** 471-472

TRUONG CHINH (1909-1988), Vietnamese Communist leader **15** 319-320

TRUTH, SOJOURNER (circa 1797-1883), African American freedom fighter and orator **15** 320-321

TRYON, WILLIAM (1729-1788), English colonial governor in America **15** 321

TS'AI YÜAN-P'EI (1867-1940), Chinese educator **15** 322

TS'AO TS'AO (155-220), Chinese general, statesman, and folk hero **15** 322-323

TSCHERNICHOWSKY, SAUL (1875-1943), Hebrew poet, translator, and physician **15** 323

TSENG KUO-FAN (1811-1872), Chinese statesman, general and scholar **15** 324-325

TSHOMBE, MOÏSE KAPENDA (1919-1969), Congolese political leader **15** 325-326

TSIOLKOVSKY, KONSTANTIN EDUARDOVICH (1857-1935), Russian scientist **15** 326-328

TSO TSUNG-T'ANG (1812-1885), Chinese general and statesman **15** 328-329

TSOU YEN (flourished late 4th century B.C.), Chinese philosopher **15** 329-330

TU FU (712-770), Chinese poet **15** 335-336

TUBMAN, HARRIET ROSS (circa 1820-1913), African American Underground Railroad agent **15** 330-331

TUBMAN, WILLIAM VACANARAT SHADRACH (1895-1971), Liberian statesman, president 1943-71 **15** 331

TUCHMAN, BARBARA (born 1912), American Pulitzer Prize-winning historian and journalist **15** 331-332

TUCKER, C. DELORES (Cynthia DeLores Nottage; 1927-2005), African American civil rights activist **18** 395-397

TUCKER, GEORGE (1775-1861), American historian **15** 332-333

TUCKER, PRESTON (1903-1956), American businessman and automobile designer **18** 397-399

TUDJMAN, FRANJO (1922-1999), Croatian president **15** 333-335

TUGWELL, REXFORD GUY (1891-1979), American politician, educator, and public servant **15** 336-339

TULL, JETHRO (1674-1741), English agriculturist and inventor **21** 411-413

TUNG CH'I-CH'ANG (1555-1636), Chinese calligrapher, painter, and historian **15** 339-340

TÚPAC AMARU, JOSÉ GABRIEL (1742-1781), Peruvian revolutionist, last of the Incas **15** 341

TUPOLEV, ANDREI NIKOLAEVICH (1888-1972), Soviet aeronautical engineer and army officer **15** 341-342

TUPPER, SIR CHARLES (1821-1915),Canadian statesman, prime minister 1896 **15** 342-343

TURA, COSIMO (1430-1495), Italian painter **15** 343-344

TURABI, HASSAN ABDULLAH AL- (born 1932), major leader of the Sudan's Islamic fundamentalist movement **15** 344-345

TURENNE, VICOMTE DE (Henri de la Tour d'Auvergne; 1611-1675), French military commander **20** 381-383

TURGENEV, IVAN SERGEYEVICH (1818-1883), Russian novelist, dramatist, and short-story writer **15** 345-348

TURGOT, ANNE ROBERT JACQUES (Baron de l'Aulne; 1721-81), French economist **15** 348-349

TURING, ALAN MATHISON (1912-1954), British mathematician **15** 349-350

TURNER, FREDERICK JACKSON (1861-1932), American historian **15** 350-351

TURNER, HENRY MCNEAL (1834-1915), African American racial leader **15** 351-352

TURNER, JOSEPH MALLORD WILLIAM (1775-1851), English painter **15** 352-354

TURNER, LANA (Julia Jean Mildred Frances Turner; 1920-1995), American actress **19** 388-390

TURNER, NATHANIEL (1800-1831), African American slave leader **15** 354

TURNER, TED (Robert Edward Turner; born 1938), American television entrepreneur **15** 355-357

TURNER, TINA (Anna Mae Bullock; born 1939), African American singer, dancer, and actress **15** 357-359

TUTANKHAMEN (reigned 1361-1352 B.C.), twelfth king of the Eighteenth Egyptian Dynasty **15** 359-360

TUTU, ARCHBISHOP DESMOND (born 1931), South African Anglican archbishop and opponent of apartheid **15** 360-361

TUTUOLA, AMOS (born 1920), Nigerian writer **15** 361-362

TV Guide (magazine) Annenberg, Walter Hubert **26** 16-18

TWACHTMAN, JOHN HENRY (1853-1902), American painter **15** 362-363

TWAIN, MARK (Samuel Langhorne Clemens; 1835-1910), American humorist and novelist **15** 363-366

TWAIN, SHANIA (Eileen Regina Edwards; born 1965), Canadian singer-songwriter **26** 361-363

TWEED, WILLIAM MARCY (1823-1878), American politician and leader of Tammany Hall **15** 366-367

TYLER, ANNE (born 1941), American author **15** 367-368

TYLER, JOHN (1790-1862), American statesman, president 1841-45 **15** 368-369

TYLER, MOSES COIT (1835-1900), American historian **15** 369-370

TYLER, RALPH W. (born 1902), American educator/scholar **15** 370-371

TYLER, ROYALL (1757-1826), American playwright, novelist, and jurist **15** 371-372

TYLOR, SIR EDWARD BURNETT (1832-1917), English anthropologist **15** 372-373

TYNDALE, WILLIAM (circa 1495-1536), English biblical scholar **15** 373-374

TYNDALL, JOHN (1820-1893), Irish physicist **15** 374

Typhoid Mary see Mallon, Mary

TYRRELL, GEORGE (1861-1909), Irish-English Jesuit priest and theologian **15** 374-375

TYRRELL, JOSEPH BURR (J.B. Tyrrell; 1858-1957), Canadian geologist and explorer **23** 410-412

TZ'U-HSI (1835-1908), empress dowager of China 1860-1908 **15** 375-376

U

UBICO Y CASTAÑEDA, GENERAL JORGE (1878-1946), president of Guatemala (1931-1944) **15** 377-378

UCCELLO, PAOLO (1397-1475), Italian painter **15** 378-379

UCHIDA, MITSUKO (born 1948), Japanese pianist **23** 413-415

UEBERROTH, PETER VICTOR (born 1937), Former baseball commissioner **15** 379-381

YAMAGATA, ARITOMO (1838-1922), Japanese general **16** 428-429

YAMAMOTO, HISAYE (born 1921), Japanese American author **25** 446-448

YAMAMOTO, ISOROKU (born Takano Isoroku; 1884-1943), Japanese admiral **16** 429-433

YAMANI, AHMED ZAKI (born 1930), Saudi Arabian lawyer and minister of petroleum and mineral resources (1962-1986) **16** 433-435

YAMASHITA, TOMOYUKI (1885-1946), Japanese general **16** 435-436

Yamato-e school
see Japanese art—Yamato-e school

YANCEY, WILLIAM LOWNDES (1814-1863), American politician **16** 436-437

YANG, CHEN NING (born 1922), Chinese-born American physicist **16** 437-438

YARD, MARY ALEXANDER ("Molly"; 1912-2005), American feminist, political organizer, and social activist **16** 438-439

YASUI, MINORU (1917-1987), Asian American attorney **16** 440-444

YEAGER, CHUCK (born 1923), American pilot **16** 444-445

YEAGER, JEANA (born 1952), American pilot **23** 449-451

YEATS, WILLIAM BUTLER (1865-1939), Irish poet and dramatist **16** 445-447

YEH-LÜ CH'U-TS'AI (1189-1243), Mongol administrator **16** 447-449

YEKUNO AMLAK (ruled circa 1268-1283), Ethiopian king **16** 449

YELLOW ROBE, ROSEBUD (Rosebud Yellow Robe-Frantz; 1907-1992), Native American author and educator **26** 390-392

YELTSIN, BORIS NIKOLAEVICH (born 1931), president of the Russian Republic (1990-) **16** 449-452

YEN FU (1853-1921), Chinese translator and scholar **16** 452

YEN HSI-SHAN (1883-1960), Chinese warlord **16** 452-453

YEN LI-PEN (died 673), Chinese painter **16** 453-454

YERBY, FRANK (Frank Garvin Yerby; 1916-1991), American Author **25** 448-450

YERKES, ROBERT MEARNS (1876-1956), American psychologist **16** 454-455

Yeshiva University (New York City) Sacks, Oliver Wolf **26** 329-331

YEVTUSHENKO, YEVGENY ALEXANDROVICH (born 1933), Soviet poet **16** 455-456

YI HWANG (1501-1570), Korean philosopher, poet, scholar, and educator **16** 457

YI SNG-GYE (1335-1408), Korean military leader, founder of the Yi dynasty **16** 458-459

YI SUNSIN (1545-1598), Korean military strategist and naval hero **16** 459-461

YO FEI (Yo P'eng-chü; 1103-41), Chinese general **16** 462

YOGANANDA (Mukunda Lal Ghose; 1893-1952), Indian yogi **16** 462-463

YÔNGJO (1694-1776), king of Korea 1724-76 **16** 461-462

YORITOMO, MINAMOTO (1147-1199), Japanese warrior chieftain **16** 463-464

YOSHIDA, SHIGERU (1878-1967), Japanese diplomat and prime minister **16** 464-465

YOSHIMUNE, TOKUGAWA (1684-1751), Japanese shogun **16** 465-466

YOULOU, FULBERT (1917-1972), Congolese president **16** 466-467

YOUNG, ANDREW JACKSON JR. (born 1932), African American preacher, civil rights activist, and politician **16** 467-469

YOUNG, BRIGHAM (1801-1877), American Mormon leader and colonizer **16** 469-470

YOUNG, COLEMAN ALEXANDER (1918-1997), first African American mayor of Detroit **16** 470-471

YOUNG, CY (Denton True Young; 1867-1955), American baseball player **24** 447-449

YOUNG, LESTER WILLIS ("Prez";1909-59), American jazz musician **16** 471-473

YOUNG, LORETTA (Gretchen Michaela Young; 1913-2000), American actress **22** 427-430

YOUNG, OWEN D. (1874-1962), American industrialist and monetary authority **16** 473-474

YOUNG, STARK (1881-1963), drama critic, editor, translator, painter, playwright, and novelist **16** 474-475

YOUNG, THOMAS (1773-1829), English physicist **16** 475-476

YOUNG, WHITNEY MOORE, JR. (1921-1971), African American civil rights leader and social work administrator **16** 476-477

YOUNGER, MAUD (1870-1936), American suffragist and trade unionist **26** 392-395

YOUNGHUSBAND, SIR FRANCIS EDWARD (1863-1942), English soldier and explorer **16** 477

YOURCENAR, MARGUERITE (Marguerite Antoinette Ghislaine; 1903-87), French novelist, poet, essayist, dramatist, world traveller, and translator **16** 477-479

YÜAN, MA (flourished circa 1190-circa 1229), Chinese painter **10** 379

YÜAN MEI (1716-1798), Chinese author **16** 479-480

YÜAN SHIH-K'AI (1859-1916), Chinese military leader **16** 480-481

YUKAWA, HIDEKI (1907-1981), Japanese physicist **16** 481-482

YUN SONDO (1587-1671), Korean sijo poet **16** 483

YUNG-LO (1360-1424), Chinese emperor **16** 482-483

YZAGUIRRE, RAUL (Raul Humberto Yzaguirre; born 1939), Hispanic American civil rights leader **24** 449-452

YZERMAN, STEVE (born 1965), Canadian hockey player **23** 451-453

Z

ZACH, NATHAN (Natan Sach; born 1930), Israeli poet **24** 453-455

ZADKINE, OSSIP JOSELYN (1890-1967), Russian sculptor **16** 484

ZAGHLUL PASHA, SAAD (1859-1927), Egyptian political leader **16** 485-486

ZAH, PETERSON (born 1937), Native American leader and activist **16** 486-487

ZAHARIAS, MILDRED DIDRIKSON ("Babe"; 1913-56), Olympic athlete and golfer **16** 487-488

ZAHIR SHAH, MUHAMMAD (born 1914); Afghani King **22** 431-433

ZAKHAROV, ROSTISLAV VLADIMIROVICH (1907-1975), Russian choreographer **26** 396-398

ZAMYATIN, EVGENY IVANOVICH (Yevgeny Zamyatin; 1884-1937), Russian author **26** 398-400

ZANGWILL, ISRAEL (1864-1926), Jewish author and philosopher **16** 488-489

ZANUCK, DARRYL F. (1902-1979), American film producer and executive **19** 435-437